Foreword

Over the past 10 years, those of us who have been involved with databases and database applications have seen a remarkable transformation occur in the functionality databases have been required to provide. In addition to payables records, order and customer information, and inventory counts, databases may now need to store more complex pieces of data such as video or time-series calculations. The focus of the database environment has also expanded (and grown in size) to include being an analytical tool to find weaknesses in your own organization or in the performance of your competitors. With this shift and growth of responsibilities, the database engine and related technologies must now support an enterprise-wide, mission-critical computing environment.

Deciding which database product to use has a significant impact on the ability of your company to execute its strategies, to provide the appropriate level of service to your customers, and, ultimately, to survive in this highly competitive business environment.

Informix Software and its products have undergone a similar transformation during this same 10 year period. My experience with Informix products began back when all they had was the INFORMIX-4GL programming language and a C-ISAM–based flat-file–oriented database engine. Through the years, other products were launched. Wingz and the Turbo engine stand out in my memory, along with INFORMIX-4GL/GX, the precursor to NewEra.

Finally, the INFORMIX-OnLine Dynamic Scalable Architecture engine was born. With this engine product, what was once a little-known, second-level database vendor could legitimately compete—and win—against all other database vendors on almost any scale you would care to use. Informix's market share began to grow at a tremendous rate as the engine began to prove itself in real-world applications as the best product on the market. Informix increased its technological lead when it purchased and integrated Illustra's object-oriented server product into OnLine DSA to create INFORMIX-Universal Server. Where that product will go and what it will be able to do is limited only by the imagination of the people using it.

Informix now stands as the number-two database vendor in the world in terms of total revenue, yet it does not compete in as many markets as its competitors. This is an indication of how powerful the Informix products are, and how well received they have been. Almost without exception, analysts and objective reviewers have been highly complimentary of the changes Informix has made to its most important products. Those of us who have toiled in the shadows of other (now defunct or almost defunct) vendors are beginning to feel a little bit vindicated in placing our trust in Informix and its overall product strategies laid out over the past several years.

The fact that a general technical publisher like Sams would produce the book you are holding in your hands is another example of the respect Informix products—and those who use them—have in the marketplace. Written to provide a broadbrush, general overview of Informix's products, this book contains a lot of valuable information that you can use whether you are new to Informix's products or have been using them for awhile. The authors who contributed to this volume live in England, Australia, New Zealand, Latin America, and the United States. They write about more than just the dry technical details; they share their experiences and expertise developed, in part, because of their diverse backgrounds. Being a published author myself, I know how hard this is to do. I recognize and commend them for their work.

Included at the back of this book is a CD-ROM that contains a number of tools, utilities, and scripts you will find helpful. Use them to automate tasks and increase your productivity. Study them as well to increase your understanding of how to work with Informix's products.

With the Informix database technology, and market share, continuing to expand, *Informix Unleashed* will help get you up to speed with the knowledge and information you need to use Informix products successfully in your particular environment. Good luck and have fun!

Carlton Doe

President, International Informix Users Group

`http://www.iiug.org`

Informix®

John McNally, Glenn Miller,
Jim Prajesh, José Fortuny, et al.

SAMS PUBLISHING

201 West 103rd Street
Indianapolis, IN 46290

UNLEASHED

Copyright © 1997 by Sams Publishing

FIRST EDITION

International Standard Book Number: 0-672-30650-6

Library of Congress Catalog Card Number: 95-72925

2000 99 98 97 4 3 2 1

Interpretation of the printing code: the rightmost double-digit number is the year of the book's printing; the rightmost single-digit, the number of the book's printing. For example, a printing code of 97-1 shows that the first printing of the book occurred in 1997.

Composed in AGaramond and MCPdigital by Macmillan Computer Publishing

Printed in the United States of America

Trademarks

Publisher and President *Richard K. Swadley*
Publishing Manager *Rosemarie Graham*
Director of Editorial Services *Cindy Morrow*
Managing Editor *Mary Inderstrodt*
Director of Marketing *Kelli S. Spencer*
Product Marketing Manager *Wendy Gilbride*
Assistant Marketing Manager *Rachel Wolfe*

Acquisitions Editors
Elaine Brush
Steve Straiger

Development Editor
Todd Bumbalough

Software Development Specialist
John Warriner

Production Editor
Ryan Rader

Copy Editors
Kris Simmons
Fran Blauw
Charles A. Hutchinson
Anne Owen

Indexers
Bruce Clingaman
Johnna VanHoose

Technical Reviewer
Karen Clere

Editorial Coordinator
Katie Wise

Technical Edit Coordinator
Lorraine Schaffer

Resource Coordinator
Deborah Frisby

Editorial Assistants
Carol Ackerman
Andi Richter
Rhonda Tinch-Mize

Cover Designer
Tim Amrhein

Book Designer
Gary Adair

Copy Writer
David Reichwein

Production Team Supervisors
Brad Chinn
Charlotte Clapp

Production
Michael Dietsch
Michael Henry
Brad Lenser
Carl Pierce

Overview

Contents

Part VI Data Modeling

Part VII Appendixes

Acknowledgments

Writing anything of this size is no easy task. A book that encompasses this much information cannot be written alone, which I tried to do at first. Even after other authors were brought on, I still relied on friends, family, and co-workers for help. My biggest thanks goes to Barbara Marie Vassallo, whom I also love very much. Without her proofing my chapters, redrawing my drawings (so that the artists at Sams could read them), and having plenty of caffeinated soda on hand, this would not have been possible. The support Barbara provided helped me complete this book without losing my mind. Her help and support really meant a lot to me. I'd also like to thank my mother, Mary Gillespie, whose example in her many projects and endeavors gave me the drive to take on this project. But even in my adult age, she can still make me feel guilty for not getting the book done so that I could visit her more often. I must also thank Lisa Manno at AT&T, whose help with creating the chapters was undeniably a big asset. Finally, I must thank the folks at Sams Publishing—especially Rosemarie Graham and Steve Straiger. The patience and support that they and everyone else gave made an impossible task become possible.

—John McNally

Crafting even part of a work like this is a team effort. I was a meager fountainhead, providing grist for the team of Sams editors. Riding herd on them and me, Acquisitions Editor Elaine Brush corralled our efforts into a work I'm proud to be associated with. Her good humor and irreverent homilies made the work seem a little more like play. Thanks especially to my technical conscience and pool nemesis, Bob Davis, who was gracious enough to tell me that my words were complete and accurate, while simultaneously enhancing and correcting them. You the man, Bob.

Oh, and "Thanks, Mom."

—Glenn Miller

I want to acknowledge the contributions of Dr. Robert Mantha, Dr. Daniel Pascot, and Dr. Dzenan Ridjanovic for their contributions to the field of modeling for Information Systems, to techniques used in implementation of models, and of course, to my knowledge in this area. I also want to thank my many clients who forced me to come up with ways to deliver a lot with the least amount of work and time possible. That is, of course, the goal of modeling.

—Jim Prajesh

I would like to thank James Hartwright for his invaluable assistance in reviewing my work as I wrote this chapter, and Nicola for her support throughout this endeavour.

—Rick Ward

Sams Publishing would like to thank Sandy Emerson of Informix Press for her enthusiasm, input, and dedication to this project. Other individuals who were a tremendous help with *Informix Unleashed* are Carlton Doe, President of the Informix International User Group; Scham Myfor of Informix Technical Support; and Bill Maderas of Computer Systems Advisers, Inc.

—*Sams Publishing*

About the Authors

Matt Bentley is a database analyst at American Stores Company in Salt Lake City, Utah. He has seven years of experience in software development and database administration in the medical/insurance, manufacturing, and retail industries. In his spare time, he enjoys hiking, biking, fishing, and camping with his wife and two sons in Utah's great outdoors.

Robert Donat is a Technical Consultant for CNA Financial Corporation in Chicago, IL, and he lives near the Cubs' Wrigley Field. Previously, at the Signature Group in Schaumburg, IL, he administered more than 50 Informix, Sybase, and Oracle database servers, which comprised over a terabyte of storage. Robert is working on his Masters Degree in Computer Science at DePaul University, holds a B.S. in Finance from the University of Illinois, and has served as an Army Artillery Officer. He enjoys skydiving, scuba diving, and maintaining several saltwater aquariums in his spare time. Robert can be reached by e-mail at `donat@wwa.com` or on his Web page at `http://sashimi.wwa.com/~donat`.

Sandy Emerson is an independent consultant and the Program Manager of Informix Press and Informix publishing programs. Sandy, who previously managed Sybase Press, is a co-author of *The Practical SQL Handbook* and three other computer trade books. A current resident of Half Moon Bay, California, Sandy can be reached via e-mail at `semerson@informix.com`.

Ron Flannery has a diverse background in Informix. He has worked for eight years in various aspects of design, coding, implementation, and database and systems administration. He is a certified Informix Data Specialist and Data Administrator. He co-founded the Michigan Informix User Group in 1992 and is now its president. He currently works as a consultant—mostly in DBA, Internet, and data warehouse roles. He can be reached at `rflanner@speedlink.net` or through his Web site at `www.speedlink.net/~rflanner`.

Ron is an employee of ZenaComp in Livonia, Michigan. ZenaComp specializes in customized database architecture and integration services across a wide range of industries. As one of a select number of certified Informix Consulting Partners, ZenaComp is recognized as a nationwide expert for the entire suite of Informix products. They provide project-oriented solutions for client/server, Internet/intranet, and data warehousing. ZenaComp is an Informix Authorized Education Center.

José Fortuny (`jfortuny@compuserve.com`) is a systems consultant specializing in the design, development, and integration of customized business databases and applications. Many of the projects he works on involve a mixture of production, manufacturing, and accounting components.

Fortuny Software Systems, Inc.—a corporation that he started in the early 90s—is a development partner of Informix, offering consulting services and software development services in character-based, GUI, and browser interfaces on networked environments.

José holds a Ph.D. in Industrial Engineering/Operations Research from Purdue University and also teaches Production Management for the Continuing Education Division of Drury College, in Springfield, Missouri.

Gordon Gielis is a Director of Select Software Solutions Pty Ltd, an Informix software company based in Sydney, Australia. Gordon is a Certified Informix Professional with more than 12 years of experience developing software for a wide variety of industries.

Kevin Kempter is a consultant for Informix Software with the Informix data-warehouse group. He has been working with Informix products for a variety of companies for more than seven years. He has experience in UNIX/C and ESQL/C application development, Database Design, Data Architecture, Database Administration, System Administration, and other generally cool stuff. Kevin can be contacted at `kkempter@informix.com`.

John Patrick McNally is an information systems specialist with AT&T. Over the last eight years, John has worked on many projects such as developing C applications that access Informix servers, being the primary DBA for a very large OLTP Informix system, working on a document and image management system as the technical lead, and developing a two-terabyte OLTP database system as the lead technical and operational architect. John is also involved in multimedia, information systems, and artificial intelligence consulting with his own company, Windward Solutions. John earned his B.S. in Computer Science from Salisbury State University and his M.S. in Multimedia and Artificial Intelligence from The George Washington University. You can reach John on the Internet at `jpmcnally@attmail.com` or `McNallyJP@aol.com`.

Glenn Miller is president and co-founder of tsunami consulting group, a Denver-based information services provider. tsunami, an Informix Solutions Alliance Partner, excels in developing client/server and Web-based applications built on sophisticated relational database models.

One of the first Informix Certified Professionals, Glenn has been a hands-on developer and administrator of Informix products for more than 13 years. He currently oversees a large data warehouse for MCI, using Informix Extended Parallel Server. He also plays a mean game of chess. Glenn can be reached at `glenn@tsunami.com`.

Mary Mudie is a Consulting Engineer with Informix Software. She has specialized in database management systems for 20 years with IBM, Illustra, and Informix. She has co-authored several IBM "red books" on IMS and DB2, and she has developed and taught classes on database implementation, performance, and recovery. More recently, she has been working with the Illustra and INFORMIX-Universal Server database products and is now fulfilling her secret desire to be a WebMistress. Mary (and her dog) can be reached at `MaryMudie@compuserve.com`.

Gavin Nour is a Director of Select Software Solutions Pty Ltd, an Informix software company based in Sydney, Australia. Gavin is also the Secretary of the Informix Users Group in NSW and is on the Board of Directors of the International Informix Users Group. He has more than 12 years of experience developing and tuning Informix applications covering a wide variety of industries.

Select Software Solutions (www.selectsoftware.com.au) was formed in 1994 and provides the following services: customized software development (for example, INFORMIX-NewEra, INFORMIX-4GL, Visual Basic, or Web database applications for the Internet and intranets); application tuning/optimization or application migration projects (for example, migration of INFORMIX-4GL to a client/server-based application such as Windows, NT, intranet, or Internet); database tuning or database migration projects (for example, Informix database upgrades such as OnLine DSA to Universal Server); general Informix consulting; project management; Informix training; database administration; and database design. Gavin can be contacted at Select Software Solutions by telephone at 0419-803-113 (mobile); by fax at 02-9-314-6310; or by e-mail at nourg@selectsoftware.com.au.

Jim Prajesh is manager of Information Technology Services for Computer Systems Advisers, Inc. He provides training and consulting services to a wide variety of leading international organizations, often managing multimillion dollar projects. He also trains people in methodologies and other techniques in model-driven development of large systems. He has spoken at many major IT conferences in the U.S. and abroad. Mr. Prajesh holds a Master of Science degree in Computer Science and a Master of Business Administration. He can be reached via e-mail at prajesh@ix.netcom.com.

Jan Richardson is currently enjoying the position of Systems and Operations Manager for the city of Aurora, Colorado. She has been working with Informix database products since 1985. Jan started her career with Southwestern Bell Telephone Company in St. Louis, Missouri. She held the position of Coordinator of Computer Services for two years at East Central College in Union, Missouri. Just prior to moving to Colorado, she spent 11 years as a senior applications and database consultant for major corporations in the Midwest.

Kerry Sainsbury has been professionally developing applications software since 1985, and he is still loving every minute of it. His current project, for Quanta Systems' new Financial and Distribution package, includes the formidable combination of Borland's Delphi (his first OO language), Business Logic coded in INFORMIX-4GL (his second tongue), and an Informix 7.*x* database on a UNIX server. Kerry is a current board member of the International Informix User Group, and he created and maintains the Informix FAQ. Kerry lives in Auckland, New Zealand with his fantastic wife, Fidelma, and their spectacular children, Ryan and Erin. He can be contacted via e-mail at kerry@kcbbs.gen.nz.

Mark D. Stock started his IT career in 1983 by developing bespoke software for a small software house. Mark was introduced to the INFORMIX-SQL and INFORMIX-4GL products in 1987 and began working with SE, OnLine, 4GL, 4GL-RDS, and ESQL/C for a varied selection of application developments in 1988. In 1991, Mark emigrated to South Africa and joined the then Informix distributor, InfoWare.

In 1994 Mark joined his business partner and set up the West Solutions Group, a group of companies supplying IT services primarily based on Informix products. These include consulting, development, training, recruitment, hardware solutions, and cabling. Mark is the Managing Director of two companies in the group and concentrates on the consulting and training aspects of the business. The West Solutions Group keeps a close alliance with Informix SA and, as such, provides most of the training services for Informix in Southern Africa. Mark gives a number of Informix courses both at the Informix training center and at client sites.

Mark has been in the IT industry for 14 years, using most flavors of UNIX throughout that time. He has been using and supporting the Informix products for the last 10 years.

Rick Ward has been employed at Great Universal Stores Home Shopping, the UK's largest mail order retailer, since 1991. He worked as an IBM Mainframe assembler and CICS, COBOL, and DB2 programmer, before joining a newly formed Database Administration team in 1993. Since that time, Rick has been responsible for implementing Informix SE, OnLine V5, and OnLine DSA V7 on a wide range of Sun UNIX platforms, working within development teams promoting good database and program design for both DB2 and Informix projects.

Tell Us What You Think!

As a reader, you are the most important critic and commentator of our books. We value your opinion and want to know what we're doing right, what we could do better, what areas you'd like to see us publish in, and any other words of wisdom you're willing to pass our way. You can help us make strong books that meet your needs and give you the computer guidance you require.

Do you have access to CompuServe or the World Wide Web? Then check out our CompuServe forum by typing `GO SAMS` at any prompt. If you prefer the World Wide Web, check out our site at `http://www.mcp.com`.

NOTE

If you have a technical question about this book, call the technical support line at 317-581-3833.

As the publishing manager of the group that created this book, I welcome your comments. You can fax, e-mail, or write me directly to let me know what you did or didn't like about this book—as well as what we can do to make our books stronger. Here's the information:

Fax: 317-581-4669
E-mail: `enterprise_mgr@sams.mcp.com`
Mail: Rosemarie Graham
Sams Publishing
201 W. 103rd Street
Indianapolis, IN 46290

Introduction

This book focuses on all aspects of data processing, involving every available Informix relational database management system and other Informix products. Information is provided on all the different Informix products and how to use them to solve business problems—whether the business's size is very small or as large as most corporations. Designed for the beginner-to-advanced reader, this book covers the basic and advanced concepts required of database administrators, system administrators, and application developers that use Informix products. This book specializes in providing and explaining issues beyond system manuals and training classes.

Informix Unleashed will fulfill the following needs of readers (such as database administrators, system administrators, application developers, and general users of Informix-based applications and products):

- It introduces and explains all of the current Informix Server environments and the services and functionality differences between each of them. It also explains how each server performs these services and functions.
- It prepares the reader to set up, configure, and administer an Informix server. This includes hardware and operating system configurations. Further information is given on tuning, monitoring, backing up, planning for future growth, and handling an outage.
- It provides a complete section that is dedicated to creating databases and using structured query language, or *SQL*, to access these databases. Detail is provided on all SQL-related issues, including creating efficient and relationally correct databases while enforcing business and referential rules, security, and data integrity. Many SQL examples using Informix SQL extensions are provided.
- It explains all the current ways to build applications that access an Informix database system. Great detail is given on how to use embedded SQL to build applications in programming languages such as COBOL and C. A section of this book is dedicated to all the aspects of building applications using INFORMIX-4GL. A similar section is dedicated to building applications using another Informix tool called NewEra.
- It also covers other Informix-related issues: for example, storing and managing other forms of data such as images and other multimedia data types. In addition, a section is included on using Informix products to build, run, and provide database stored content to a Web site.

Informix Unleashed uses step-by-step procedures interspersed with figures and examples to further explain each issue.

Part I

Introduction

IN THIS PART

CHAPTER 1

Informix Company Overview

by Sandra L. Emerson

IN THIS CHAPTER

NOTE

This chapter is based on information from the quarterly customer newsletter *Informix Times* (formerly *Spectrum*) and from Informix Annual Reports 1987–1996. Thanks to Michael Pooley, Marketing Communications Manager, for making these archives available.

Informix Software, Inc.

Informix Software, Inc.—with a 48 percent database revenue growth rate for 1996, annual revenues of close to a billion dollars, and over 4,500 employees worldwide—has successfully built its business on two strengths: innovative technology and strong worldwide partnerships.

Market Share from Technological Innovation

Informix based its relational database management products on open systems and standards such as industry-standard Structured Query Language (SQL) and the UNIX operating system. Two notable innovations have propelled Informix to an industry-leading position in database management technology: the parallel processing capabilities of Informix Dynamic Scalable Architecture (DSA) and the ability to extend relational database management to new, complex data types using the object-relational powers of INFORMIX-Universal Server.

Dynamic Scalable Architecture

Dynamic Scalable Architecture is multithreaded, supporting many users and many tasks with a single operating system process rather than requiring one process per user. This multithreading layer opens the way for concurrent tasks to be performed in parallel, which can significantly enhance throughput and performance. The fact that Informix built its own multithreading layer instead of relying on operating system thread support gives servers based on the Dynamic Scalable Architecture the ability to make maximally efficient use of a wide variety of hardware and software environments.

Object-Relational Database Management

Object-relational database management is embodied by INFORMIX-Universal Server, which combines the functionality of INFORMIX-OnLine Dynamic Server with the object-relational Illustra Server. Because the designers of these servers (both influenced by Dr. Michael Stonebraker's Postgres project at the University of California at Berkeley) shared certain design goals and made similar decisions on aspects of architecture and modularization, the two technologies comfortably merged. The result is an extensible database management system, or DBMS, that can manage all the structured and unstructured data in an enterprise, and can adapt to new data management challenges as they arise.

INFORMIX-Universal Server is extended with DataBlade modules, which are plug-in components that add functionality for new data types and applications. One or more DataBlade modules can be installed in INFORMIX-Universal Server, as desired, to facilitate tasks ranging from audio library management to cyberpublishing to geographic information systems.

Mind Share from Strong Partnerships

Informix has always valued its partnerships with key application vendors, hardware manufacturers, systems integrators, and value-added resellers. More than 4,500 software application partners, software tools partners, service partners, and hardware and operating system partners participate in the Informix Solutions Alliance. Partners are supported with early access to software, Internet and intranet resources, training, conferences, and preferential access to the Informix Certified Professional program.

Long-standing alliances with partners worldwide provide Informix with a solid reputation in the developer and user communities. In addition, partners connect Informix to new lines of business and industry sectors. Rather than lose focus on its core competency of databases, Informix has created profitable joint ventures in the industry areas of retail, telecommunications, World Wide Web, workflow, document management, imaging, multimedia, and financial services.

Informix as a Global Enterprise

Informix has more than 118 sales offices in 42 countries, with significant development and support activity in England, Ireland, Western and Eastern Europe, India, and Asia Pacific. In most years since Informix became a public company in 1986, more than half of annual net revenues have come from Informix's international operations.

With the formation of development and localization centers beginning with Singapore and Europe in 1993, and continuing with major investments such as the India Development Center, Informix has continually strengthened its commitment to international customers. Product features such as Informix Global Language Support (GLS) let developers localize applications for language, alphabet, and cultural features such as date, time, and currency. In recent years, Informix has made key acquisitions and business alliances with dozens of additional international distributors and partners.

Initiatives in Service and Support

In keeping with Informix's broad market and platform coverage, the company provides customers, prospects, developers, and end users with many avenues for obtaining technical and market information. As might be expected from a company that supplies key technology for the Internet and the World Wide Web, the external Web site at `www.informix.com` is increasingly seen as the main vehicle for distributing information of all types. The Informix Web site, driven by the Informix Web DataBlade module and INFORMIX-Universal Server, contains links to the following:

- Corporate information and events (conferences, white papers, user groups)
- Partners and industries
- Business solutions
- Products and technology
- Services and support (tech pubs, training, and tech support)
- News room (press releases)
- Cyber store (downloadable software)

A random browse through the Informix Web pages could lead to features such as a video on Informix's technical sponsorship of the MILIA 97 International Publishing and New Media Market property licensing conference, to the monthly Cyber Planet online magazine, to a technical brief on INFORMIX-OnLine Dynamic Server 7.22, or to an online registration form for an upcoming event. Informix has had a presence on the Web since January 1995, and the company is using this medium with considerable commitment and enthusiasm.

The Early Years: 1980–1988

In 1980, Roger Sippl and Laura King founded Relational Database Systems (RDS) in Sunnyvale, California. In February 1988, RDS merged with Innovative Software of Overland Park, Kansas, which had been founded by Mike Brown and Mark Callegari in 1979. The 1988 merger, which was the first major acquisition by Informix, was an effort to broaden platform coverage for the Informix DBMS and add needed end-user tools. The tools (initially Macintosh-based) never did exactly meet the executives' expectations, but the acquisition could be interpreted as a welcome gesture of support for the end user.

A User-Friendly Database System

Roger Sippl and Laura King founded Relational Database Systems at a time when both relational database management and the UNIX operating system were just beginning to be encountered on mini- and micro-computers. From the beginning, the company sought a broad market: Rather than tailoring the DBMS for mainframe hardware and proprietary operating systems, RDS built a product that used an open operating system, ran on small, general-purpose hardware, used a standard programming interface (SQL), and supplied a number of end-user tools and utilities. RDS was among the first companies to bring enterprise-level database management out of the computer room and onto the desktop.

The corporate culture that RDS fostered during its first decade—as it grew to a size of several hundred employees and $150 million in revenues—formed the basis for Informix Software, Inc., which still promotes open systems and standards, aims at a very broad market, and widely distributes information, tools, programs, and enabling technologies.

Informix Phase Two: New Leadership

The year 1990 marked the end of the first decade of Informix's growth. Phil White, who joined Informix as chief executive officer in January 1989, had a remarkable first year at the helm. Revenues for 1989 grew by no less than 40 percent compared to 1988, accompanied by a 338 percent increase in earnings and a 300 percent increase in earnings per share for stockholders.

White redefined corporate strategy and made the hard decisions that ultimately resulted in the financial turnaround of the company. (Early in 1991, Informix voluntarily changed its revenue recognition policy, which resulted in a huge restatement of revenue for fiscal 1990; this painful but necessary change in accounting practices provided a sound basis for the unbroken string of profitable years that followed.) For several years in a row, Phil White has been ranked among the nation's top executives by a number of industry publications: he was named CEO of the Year by *Financial World* magazine from 1993–1995.

Technology Objectives

In 1990, early in his tenure as CEO, Phil White and his executives forged the corporate mission statement that is still in force in 1997: "The mission of Informix is to provide, through partnerships worldwide, the best technology and services for developing enterprise-wide data management applications for open systems."

White and his team also set forth a number of specific product and corporate objectives. Informix pledged to provide the following:

- A robust server running on an open operating system such as UNIX
- Clients running on all popular desktop platforms
- Support for easy-to-use information retrieval tools
- Interoperability of SQL among major database vendors
- A global presence enabled by strong relationships with distributors and partners
- Entry into a broad spectrum of industries through partners and channels

Entering New Markets with INFORMIX-OnLine

In 1990, the original INFORMIX-SE (Standard Engine) database server was joined by INFORMIX-OnLine, which added features such as fault-tolerant online transaction processing, logging, and recovery, in addition to support for multimedia database applications. The (loosely defined) multimedia support was provided by new BLOB (Binary Large OBject) data types such as BYTE and TEXT. Binary large object types permit users to store up to two gigabytes of unstructured data such as text or image data. Like other vendors, Informix stores only the pointer to a BLOB in the primary table and puts the BLOB data in a storage space of its own. Informix was one of the first vendors to implement BLOB types for relational database management.

Although the INFORMIX-OnLine multimedia database was definitely not the same as an object-oriented database, in which a variety of complex relationships are supported among objects having attributes and behavior, the BLOB did provide a general-purpose method of incorporating more complex data into the core database management system.

Championing Open Systems and Standards

Informix persistently championed open systems such as UNIX and industry-standard SQL. The 1990s marked the decade when UNIX finally became a popular commercial operating system, nearly 20 years after its inception. UNIX ran on a wide variety of general-purpose hardware; a UNIX multiprocessor could provide the power of mainframe-level processing at a fraction of the cost.

Led by founder and chairman Roger Sippl, Informix drove the effort to make SQL-based DBMSs interoperable. The SQL Access group, founded in 1989, included among its members Hewlett-Packard, Informix, Ingres, Microsoft, Oracle, Sun, Sybase, and X/Open (itself an open standards advocacy group). Roger Sippl resigned from Informix in December 1992 and soon thereafter founded Visigenic, an object request broker (ORB) technology company.

Reaching Out to Partners and to the Public

The InformixLink information system was the first of several information services for partners and support customers. InformixLink is now available through the Web, on CD-ROM, or as "InformixLink Classic" (the original dial-up electronic bulletin board version). In addition to InformixLink, Informix provides technical publications on CD-ROM and on the Web, support publications such as *CS Times* and *Tech Notes*, and many other information dissemination projects.

Informix, intent on getting its technology message out, even equipped a 72-foot tractor-trailer truck as a rolling demo station! In the early 1990s, the Informix truck would reliably appear at conferences and events, bearing a variety of personal computers and workstations running Informix-based applications.

Since 1992, the Informix Worldwide User Conference has been a major arena for reaching the user, developer, and partner communities. At the first Informix Worldwide User Conference in 1992, Informix expected 1,000 attendees and had 1,500; there were 3,000 in 1993; and at the 1997 conference, Informix expects 6,000 attendees from all over the world.

The Informix Certified Professional Program was launched in 1995 to certify Informix application developers and database administrators. In 1997, Informix created the Informix Developers Network as a Web-enabled community for sharing information and getting early access to software.

Growing Into Distributed Client/Server

The server and connectivity products that made up INFORMIX-OnLine 5.0 supported client/server computing and distributed transaction processing, with improved performance, bandwidth, and scalability. New features in OnLine 5.0 included two-phase commit, stored procedures, the DB-Access utility, and Level 1 FIPS compliance (certification of standard SQL). To complement its server products, Informix increasingly sought solutions from outside vendors in the areas of CASE modeling, transaction monitoring, and database gateways (DRDA support between Informix and IBM mainframes running DB2).

Late in 1992, Informix added trigger support to the 5.01 release of INFORMIX-OnLine and INFORMIX-SE, adding a valuable tool for enforcing consistent application of business rules and conditions, and supplementing the ANSI-compliant declarative integrity constraints that had previously been implemented in 5.0.

The Right Tools for the Job

In 1992, the Informix product family included client tools such as INFORMIX-SQL, INFORMIX-ESQL/C, and INFORMIX-4GL; connectivity products such as INFORMIX-NET; INFORMIX-NET PC; and servers including INFORMIX-OnLine for UNIX and INFORMIX-SE for DOS, UNIX, and NetWare. In fact, the single-threaded INFORMIX-SE engine is still supported in 1997 as a bulletproof, load-and-go database engine that can run on practically anything.

The search for a breakthrough client tools product continued in the early 1990s. Although Informix had delivered successful SQL tools products such as INFORMIX-SQL and INFORMIX-4GL, the company hoped to develop a next-generation client tool that could capture a larger market share of the tools business.

The Wingz and HyperScript tools that Informix had acquired in 1988, and which had been through several incarnations, were sold to Investment Intelligence Systems Corporation (IISC) of London, UK, in 1995.

The Money Will Follow

The tools-side disappointments did little to affect the world's good opinion of INFORMIX-OnLine and other innovative Informix technologies. In 1992, Informix and Kmart were awarded the prestigious Computerworld Smithsonian Award for the development and implementation of the Kmart Information Network (KIN II). KIN II allowed store employees to scan a product code using a hand-held scanning device and access up-to-the-minute information about the product from the INFORMIX-OnLine database via radio waves. This early application of wireless technology was on the leading edge at the time. Other 1992 awards included Reader's Choice Awards (Best 4GL) from *DBMS Magazine* and *Datamation* (INFORMIX-OnLine 5.0). Informix continues to win industry awards: In 1997, Informix was named "Most Influential Database Vendor" by *Database Programming and Design* (Illustra won the same award in 1996).

The Multithreaded Revolution: OnLine Dynamic Server

The earthshaking events of 1993–1994 were the advent of the multithreaded INFORMIX-OnLine Dynamic Server (planned for a series of releases) and the integration of the server family under the rubric Dynamic Scalable Architecture (DSA). The DSA architecture creates a database system that can scale up to increased demands, accommodating more users, more data, and more processors. With DSA, Informix servers could suddenly handle hundreds of concurrent users, online transaction processing (OLTP) volumes in the tens-of-gigabytes range, and decision support in the hundreds-of-gigabytes range, across the full spectrum of uniprocessor and multiprocessor hardware.

The secret of this scalability is performing tasks in parallel—for example, parallel queries, parallel index creation, parallel joins—and taking advantage of multiprocessing hardware to break each individual task into subtasks. DSA can partition tables across disks and tasks across multiple CPUs, resulting in a near-linear improvement in processing times as disk drives are added.

In addition to parallel processing, the INFORMIX-OnLine Dynamic Server of 1994 supported data replication and other facilities for enterprise-wide client/server computing. According to an Informix advertisement of the time, the following database management activities could be done in parallel (on more than 25 platforms): OLTP, queries, indexing, load, backup, recovery, parallel resource management and control, parallel hash joins, and static database partitioning.

Customers and partners experienced substantial performance gains with the new and improved parallel processing. AT&T Network Systems Group developed an enhanced 911 emergency information system using INFORMIX-OnLine Dynamic Server and reported that their database build time was reduced from two weeks to 30 minutes. An AT&T subsidiary reported that database load time decreased from 4 hours to 10 minutes.

Aggressive Growth in Sales and Marketing

With the OnLine Dynamic Server product in its arsenal, Informix increased its investment in its sales and marketing organizations. The company created the position of Vice President of Marketing to champion the aggressive marketing efforts that could take Informix to the next level.

Informix was the first database company to offer user-based pricing: a pricing structure that is supposed to be easy to understand and administer, removing confusing options and tiers. The user-based pricing scheme bundles the core server and connectivity functionality, and charges customers according to the number of users they want to support, at a fixed price per user.

The Beginnings of the Benchmark Wars

If you're going to do battle in the database market, you have to keep posting performance wins with the industry-standard benchmarks administered by the Transaction Processing Council. Informix published its first benchmarks in 1991, with scores from TPC-A and TPC-B for measuring response time and throughput of transactions. (TPC-A simulates a single-user environment; TPC-B simulates a batch environment; TPC-C simulates a multi-user environment doing real work.) By 1994, INFORMIX-OnLine had already been used in 15 TPC-C benchmarks. Recent ads proudly display its top-of-the-charts TPC-C results; TPC-D results are also available.

Targeted Industries and Markets

The major market sectors for Informix include finance, manufacturing, retail, telecommunications, hospitality, health care, oil and gas, media, transportation, and government. Because of its early emphasis on partnering and broad support of lower-end platforms, Informix counts such household names as Wal-Mart, Kmart, Good Guys, and Home Depot among its customers in the retail sector.

Moving Toward the Microsoft Demographic

Although Informix server technology began on the UNIX operating system, the company displayed early support for Microsoft operating environments. Beginning with INFORMIX-SE for DOS, Informix ported INFORMIX-SE and INFORMIX-OnLine to Windows NT; it supports knowledge base products such as InformixLink on Windows and Windows NT; and it supports client tools such as INFORMIX-4GL for Microsoft Windows. In a creative foray into the Microsoft server market, INFORMIX-SE (the old reliable) was shipped bundled with Windows NT. CEO Phil White said in a recent interview that Informix intends to port the entire product line to Windows NT.

The DSA server family is now routinely ported to Windows NT, where applicable. INFORMIX-OnLine Workgroup Server and Workstation Server can be downloaded from the Informix Web site. The effort of developing products for the NT market has resulted in some useful features such as improved installation and administration tools.

A New Era in Tools

Informix introduced the INFORMIX-NewEra client tool in the third quarter of 1994. INFORMIX-NewEra is an open, graphical, object-oriented application development environment for creating and deploying production-level applications. NewEra includes its own compiled language and an application repository for class libraries (new and existing C and C++ class libraries). NewEra lets application developers partition their application processing among server, middleware, and client. With NewEra, you can create specialized application servers that act as an intermediary between client and server tasks.

NewEra application layers can handle the interface with the database server, permitting developers to use their choice of client tools such as Java, ActiveX, or Visual Basic. The Informix tools strategy is evolving into a mix-and-match component approach, which should fit well with Internet and intranet application development approaches. In 1997, Informix acquired CenterView software, a developer of Visual Basic tools.

Interoperability Goals: Gateways and Connectivity

Middleware support by Informix and other vendors' products lets an Informix database environment interoperate with databases from other vendors, including mainframe, legacy, and proprietary systems. A database company's connectivity strategy is the plumbing—a collection of pipes and fittings—a developer uses to connect all the desired pieces of a distributed database management system. Informix's latest efforts in connectivity products have been to integrate more of the products into a single bundle, for ease of use. INFORMIX-Enterprise Gateway provides transparent access to multiple enterprise data sources such as ODBC, DRDA, NT, Macintosh, Motif, OS/2, and UNIX.

OnLine Dynamic Server Today

INFORMIX-OnLine Dynamic Server 7.x stepped up from the Release 6 foundation with full-blown Parallel Data Query (PDQ), improved support for local table partitioning, dynamic memory allocation and management, and high-availability data replication. The product suite also supplied more comprehensive database administration and monitoring tools. Wherever possible, the 7.x release sought to enhance the scalable performance enabled by its parallel processing architecture.

The appearance of 7.x so soon after Release 6.0 confirmed another key OnLine Dynamic Server design decision—namely, incremental releases. The dramatically shorter six-month development cycle, resulting in releases every nine months, allowed Informix to put a huge amount of new product into the market.

Modular Subsystems

The INFORMIX-OnLine Dynamic Server architecture isolated the abstract type manager into its own subsystem so that adding data types would affect only a small portion of the code. This modularization made it possible to merge with the Illustra extensible-data type system without massive disruption to OnLine Dynamic Server.

Industry analysts have pointed out that both the Illustra Server and OnLine Dynamic Server were influenced by Dr. Michael Stonebraker's Postgres project at UC Berkeley. Dr. Stonebraker, the founder of Illustra, became Chief Technical Officer of Informix after its merger with Illustra in 1996.

Data Warehousing and Decision Support

Data warehouses and data marts are supported both by INFORMIX-OnLine Dynamic Server and by the INFORMIX-OnLine Extended Parallel Server (XPS). XPS supports specialized hardware and operating environments: loosely coupled clusters and massively parallel processing, and shared-nothing computing environments, including clusters of SMP systems and MPP systems. The DSA parallel processing architecture is well suited to handling a data warehouse's extensive data queries, index scans, loading, indexing, updates, inserts, deletes, and backup and recovery.

XPS-caliber database management is demanded by customers who need to process and manage very large amounts of data in OLTP, decision-support systems, data warehousing, batch processing, and other applications. Data warehousing—deriving market intelligence from enterprise-wide collections of current and historical data—is an activity being keenly pursued by the Fortune 2000.

Data Analysis with ROLAP

Making market sense out of a data warehouse usually involves extracting a snapshot of the data for use with an OnLine Analytical Processing (OLAP) tool. To handle this part of the data warehousing effort, Informix acquired the Stanford Technology Group in 1996 and created the MetaCube ROLAP (Relational OLAP) engine, which is multidimensional OLAP software integrated with OnLine Dynamic Server.

ROLAP begins with the premise that data does not need to be stored multidimensionally to be viewed multidimensionally. While resting firmly on the relational model, ROLAP presents users with a multidimensional view that makes logical sense in the context of their complex queries. The INFORMIX-MetaCube family (based on the Stanford Research Group technology) is a collection of tools including an analysis engine and an ad hoc decision support tool, a tool that exports data warehouse data to the Excel spreadsheet program, and a graphical management and administration tool.

Informix and the Internet

Informix opened for business on the World Wide Web early in 1995 and later that year announced the prospective merger with Illustra. Essentially, when Informix turned toward the Internet, it never looked back. Most of the Informix product line today is aimed at Internet application development in one form or another.

Partnering with Netscape

An early partnership with Netscape spurred Informix Internet product development efforts. Marc Andreessen, Netscape's founder and chief technology officer, gave the 1995 Informix

Worldwide User Conference keynote address; Andreessen continues to make frequent appearances at Informix conferences and events.

Informix and Netscape have created several bundled products. For example, INFORMIX-SE formed the foundation technology for Netscape's I-Store product. As an easy-to-use-and-administer, load-and-go database server, I-Store targeted the individual business owner and provided the integrated data management, online credit card authorization, and billing and order-processing capabilities required for an electronic storefront.

Netscape LiveWirePro is a bundle integrated with INFORMIX-OnLine Workgroup Server. The Netscape Internet Applications (AppFoundry) family of turnkey software solutions also incorporates Informix database technology.

Other Informix Web efforts include Web Interface Kits for 4GL and NewEra (downloadable from the Cyber Store on the Informix Web site) and the announced Jworks tools for integrating Java-based applications with Informix database technology.

In addition to the Netscape alliance and Web-enabling technologies, the acquisition of Illustra is the most significant step that Informix has taken toward creating a family of products for the Internet, intranets, and the World Wide Web. The INFORMIX-Universal Server supports the Informix Web DataBlade module as a complete package for developing INFORMIX-Universal Server Web applications.

Acquiring Illustra: The Web Is Wide

For Informix, 1996 was The Year of the Web: With the acquisition of Illustra, Informix's potential on the World Wide Web exploded. Suddenly, Informix was the database management system best suited to the Web. Whenever a new type of data or new access method is required, a developer can meet the challenge by creating another DataBlade extension for INFORMIX-Universal Server, the hybrid object-relational DBMS that in fact represents the latest incarnation of INFORMIX-OnLine Dynamic Server.

The Need for INFORMIX-Universal Server

Up to 85 percent of all data that could be managed is unstructured, complex, and probably not yet digitized. INFORMIX-Universal Server provides scalable high-performance support for new and increasingly complex types of data in a way that can be extended by Informix, third parties, or customers. INFORMIX-Universal Server's greatest value lies in enabling users to store all desired corporate and personal data in the same system as their corporate data. INFORMIX-Universal Server goes beyond storage of BLOBs, supporting information retrieval functions on the content of these large objects. With INFORMIX-Universal Server, the user can search an image file to find "all images that look like [this sample] that were created by a graphic artist living in Canton, Ohio" and other queries possible only in an object-relational system.

The Edge of Extensibility: DataBlade Modules

Despite skeptics who claimed that Informix would never be able to integrate Illustra with OnLine Dynamic Server, INFORMIX-Universal Server shipped on schedule in December 1996, to great fanfare. DataBlade partners provided DataBlade modules ranging from 2D/3D spatial DataBlade modules, to text and image DataBlade modules, to time series modules, to modules for geographic information systems.

In its campaign to proselytize DataBlade module development, Informix was vastly more successful than in its attempt to foster class library development for NewEra. DataBlade modules are practical, possible, and desirable, and Informix is standing behind them with a full DataBlade Developers Program including software, training, support, and joint marketing opportunities.

Currently, 29 DataBlade modules have been released as full-fledged products, and dozens more are under development.

Cyberpublishing and Event Support

INFORMIX-Universal Server is also spawning a new Web enterprise: live, real-time coverage of events anywhere in the world. The concept of *cyberpublishing* was pioneered by photographer Rick Smolan, who used the Illustra-Server for his February 1996 Web event "24 Hours in Cyberspace." At the July 1996 Informix Worldwide User Conference, "24 Hours in Cyberspace" became "72 Hours in Chicago." Everything from conference keynote addresses to instant quotes from conference attendees went into the cyberpublishing mix. This live project showed how Informix technology on the Web makes it possible to manage and publish digital content from anywhere in the world and to update that content in real time. As an Informix promotional tag line puts it, "If you can imagine it, we can manage it."

Overview of Current Products

The following overview of Informix Current Products is derived directly from the "Informix At A Glance" article on the Informix Web site and from the latest Informix Technology Overview.

Database Servers

The following sections cover the Informix Dynamic Scalable Architecture family of servers.

INFORMIX-Universal Server

INFORMIX-Universal Server is the industry's only fully extensible *object-relational database management system* that is designed explicitly to handle rich, complex data types. INFORMIX-Universal Server combines the power and scalability of Informix's Dynamic Scalable Architecture with the extensibility of DataBlade technology—enabling the intelligent management of complex data while preserving the superior performance and manageability that's required for OLTP-intensive and data warehousing applications.

DataBlade Modules

DataBlade Modules are plug-in object extensions that expand the general-purpose capabilities of INFORMIX-Universal Server to manage complex data types such as video, audio, image, spatial, time-series, and Web (HTML). DataBlade modules provide data storage and management functionality attuned to the needs of a specific application and can be used independently or in conjunction with one another. Customers can choose from a wide selection of Informix and third-party DataBlade modules, or they can design their own to meet their unique data management requirements. Currently, 29 DataBlade modules are available, and dozens more are under development. In addition, through the DataBlade Developers Program, Informix provides DataBlade partners with a DataBlade Developers Kit that assists them with building DataBlade modules and ensures that all DataBlade code meets Informix's quality assurance standards.

INFORMIX-OnLine Extended Parallel Server (OnLine XPS)

INFORMIX-OnLine Extended Parallel Server (OnLine XPS) is Informix's powerful, multithreaded database server that is designed to exploit the capabilities of loosely coupled or shared-nothing computing architectures, including clusters of symmetric multiprocessors and massively parallel processors. OnLine XPS is designed to support large database environments for OLTP, data warehousing, imaging, document management, and workflow database applications. In addition, OnLine XPS delivers new features, including enhanced parallel SQL operations, high availability capabilities, enterprise replication, and a suite of systems management tools.

INFORMIX-OnLine Dynamic Server

INFORMIX-OnLine Dynamic Server is Informix's powerful, multithreaded database server that is designed to exploit the capabilities of both symmetric multiprocessor and uniprocessor architectures to deliver breakthrough database scalability, manageability, and performance. OnLine Dynamic Server provides superior transaction processing and optimal decision support through parallel data query (PDQ) technology, high availability, data integrity, mainframe-caliber administration, enterprise replication facilities, graphical monitoring tools, client/server and Web connectivity, and multimedia capabilities—all within a single package.

INFORMIX-OnLine Workgroup Server

INFORMIX-OnLine Workgroup Server is the industry's first complete database solution for developing and deploying client/server and Web/intranet applications across an organization (that is, distributed workgroups and cross-functional departments). It combines a high-performance, scalable, multithreaded database server; complete connectivity for client/server and desktop applications; and Web/intranet services—all within a single package featuring easy-to-use administration and configuration tools.

INFORMIX-OnLine Workstation

INFORMIX-OnLine Workstation is a single-user, cost-effective platform for the development and deployment of workgroup applications. Like INFORMIX-OnLine Workgroup Server, OnLine Workstation combines a database server, complete connectivity for client/server and desktop applications, and a Web/intranet server and browser into a single package with easy-to-use administration and configuration tools. OnLine Workstation allows for development on lower-cost platforms and can serve as an entry point to the full OnLine Dynamic Server family.

INFORMIX-OnLine/Secure Dynamic Server

INFORMIX-OnLine/Secure Dynamic Server offers all the capabilities of OnLine Dynamic Server, with added features for multilevel secure applications.

INFORMIX-SE

INFORMIX-SE is an easy-to-use, low-maintenance, "load-and-go" database server that provides excellent performance, data consistency, client/server capabilities, and SQL compliance with minimal database administration.

C-ISAM

C-ISAM is Informix's indexed sequential access method library of C functions for creating and using indexed sequential files.

Enabling Technology: Connectivity Products

Informix's array of enabling technology and connectivity products includes the products covered in the following sections.

INFORMIX-Universal Web Connect

INFORMIX-Universal Web Connect is an open platform that provides high-performance connectivity between Web servers and databases. Universal Web Connect enables Web developers to create intelligent Web applications that dynamically deliver multimedia-rich, tailored Web pages to a corporation's Internet, intranet, and extranet users. Features include an Application Page Builder API, state and connection management capabilities, subscription and notification features, Java connectivity, and a security interface.

INFORMIX-Enterprise Gateway Manager

INFORMIX-Enterprise Gateway Manager is a member of the INFORMIX-Enterprise Gateway family, a complete set of standards-based gateways. Enterprise Gateway Manager is a high-performance gateway solution that allows Informix application users and developers to transparently access Oracle, Sybase, DB2, and other non-Informix databases.

INFORMIX-Enterprise Gateway for EDA/SQL

INFORMIX-Enterprise Gateway for EDA/SQL allows tools and applications running on UNIX and Microsoft Windows to access data located anywhere in your enterprise. It provides both SQL and remote procedure call access to over 60 relational and nonrelational data sources on 35 different hardware platforms and operating systems.

INFORMIX-Enterprise Gateway with DRDA

INFORMIX-Enterprise Gateway with DRDA integrates IBM relational databases (that is, DB2, DB2/400, and DB2/VM) with Informix applications on open systems without the need for host-resident software.

INFORMIX-ESQL for C and COBOL

INFORMIX-ESQL for C and COBOL embeds SQL statements directly into the code of your favorite third-generation languages.

INFORMIX-CLI

INFORMIX-CLI is a call-level interface that enables application developers to access Informix database servers dynamically, eliminating the need for an SQL preprocessor and for the recompilation of source code for each independent data source. Based on Microsoft's Open Database Connectivity (ODBC) architecture, INFORMIX-CLI provides an industry-standard means of connecting to Informix data.

INFORMIX-Connect

INFORMIX-Connect provides the runtime libraries required for INFORMIX-ESQL for C and COBOL and INFORMIX-CLI.

INFORMIX-DCE/NET

INFORMIX-DCE/NET is a Distributed Computing Environment (DCE)–based connectivity product that allows users to access Informix databases transparently and other relational databases via ODBC, while taking advantage of DCE features such as security and naming services.

Relational OnLine Analytical Processing Technology

Informix ROLAP strategy is founded on the MetaCube product line, as outlined in the following sections.

INFORMIX-MetaCube Product Suite

INFORMIX-MetaCube Product Suite is a family of decision-support software designed specifically for large-scale data warehouses. The product suite is based on an open, extensible architecture that integrates tightly with Informix DSA technology. The MetaCube family includes the following products:

- INFORMIX-MetaCube Analysis Engine is a sophisticated ROLAP engine that provides the backbone for high-performance data warehouse applications. The MetaCube engine takes advantage of the relational power of your Informix database, eliminating the need to manage and maintain a separate proprietary multidimensional database.
- INFORMIX-MetaCube Explorer is an ad hoc decision-support tool for end user access and analysis. MetaCube Explorer provides data warehouse access, reporting, charting, and desktop productivity application integration through a sophisticated, yet easy-to-use, drag-and-drop interface.
- INFORMIX-MetaCube for Excel brings MetaCube-based multidimensional analysis of very large data warehouses to the Excel environment, allowing you to take advantage of the Excel tools that your organization understands.
- INFORMIX-MetaCube Warehouse Manager offers a point-and-click graphical tool for managing metadata—information that describes your data warehouse—in a logical, user-friendly manner.
- INFORMIX-MetaCube Warehouse Optimizer analyzes and recommends a data warehouse aggregation strategy to improve query performance and overall usability of the data warehouse.
- INFORMIX-MetaCube Scheduler is an easy-to-administer batch processor that manages any server-based task, such as a query or data load.
- INFORMIX-MetaCube QueryBack executes long-running user queries in the background while managing recurring jobs with intelligence about relative time.
- INFORMIX-MetaCube Aggregator creates and maintains aggregates in the data warehouse, providing for incremental as well as full aggregation through summarization, resulting in better performance.
- INFORMIX-MetaCube for the Web brings the MetaCube analysis capabilities to your intranet via integration with popular Web servers and Web browsers.

Application Development Tools

Informix's current application development products, such as INFORMIX-NewEra and INFORMIX-4GL, have been incorporated into the Universal Tools Strategy announced in March of 1997. The Universal Tools Strategy gives application developers a wide choice of application development tools for Informix database servers, permitting developers to take a modular, component-based, open tools approach. The INFORMIX-Data Director family of plug-in modules lets developers extend, manage, and deploy applications for INFORMIX-Universal Server using their choice of Informix and other industry-standard tools.

The following products are included under the Universal Tools Strategy:

- INFORMIX-Data Director for Visual Basic
- INFORMIX-Data Director for Java (formerly Jworks)
- INFORMIX-NewEra
- INFORMIX-4GL
- INFORMIX-Java Object Interface (JOI) (formerly Java API)
- INFORMIX-JDBC
- INFORMIX-C++ Object Interface (COI)
- INFORMIX-CLI
- INFORMIX-ESQL/C
- INFORMIX-Developer SDK

The following sections describe currently available Informix tools.

INFORMIX-NewEra

INFORMIX-NewEra builds client/server, Web-enabled, and dynamic content management applications. NewEra features a component-based, object-oriented architecture with an impressive set of next-generation features including a powerful and flexible database application language; facilities for distributed, partitioned applications, and team-oriented development; OLE and ActiveX support and Java code generation; and a comprehensive suite of productive visual programming tools.

INFORMIX-NewEra ViewPoint Pro

INFORMIX-NewEra ViewPoint Pro is a suite of graphical development and database administration tools designed to simplify the creation of small- to mid-range database applications. It features a graphical forms painter, report writer, and application builder (for creating user menu systems), as well as a database schema builder, SQL editor, and *SuperView* builder (for creating highly specialized views to the database that simplify the access, retrieval, and analysis of corporate data). SuperViews are used in NewEra, NewEra ViewPoint Pro, and NewEra ViewPoint.

INFORMIX-Mobile

INFORMIX-Mobile turns an INFORMIX-NewEra application into a powerful message-based system for remote access to standard LAN-based applications such as e-mail and fax as well as more specialized applications such as sales force automation—all through a single wireless communication connection.

INFORMIX-4GL Product Family

INFORMIX-4GL Product Family includes INFORMIX-4GL Rapid Development System (RDS), INFORMIX-4GL Interactive Debugger, and INFORMIX-4GL Compiled. Together they form a comprehensive fourth-generation application development and production environment that provides abundant power and flexibility for all your application development needs.

INFORMIX-SQL

INFORMIX-SQL is a complete database application development tool suite that includes a schema editor, menu builder, SQL editor, forms builder, and report writer.

INFORMIX-Ada/SAME

INFORMIX-Ada/SAME is an SQL module language compiler extended to support Ada's advanced features.

INFORMIX-Data Director for Visual Basic

INFORMIX-Data Director for Visual Basic is a versatile product that enables Visual Basic developers to prototype, build, and extend workgroup and enterprise applications rapidly. Data Director accelerates the entire development process and simplifies working with different data types—while leveraging the performance and extensibility of INFORMIX-Universal Server. Data Director vastly reduces the amount of application code that programmers need to write for client/server solutions by automating all the data access operations of the client application. This automation allows programmers to incorporate sophisticated functionality easily without having to be SQL experts and enables project teams to deliver timely, scalable applications that solve real business problems.

INFORMIX-Data Director for Java

INFORMIX-Data Director for Java is a drag-and-drop Java development component that allows developers to build database-aware Java applets for Informix's family of database servers—including INFORMIX-Universal Server. Unlike other Java development components, Data Director for Java supports the new SQL3 standard, so organizations can use worldwide Internet or corporate intranet applications to provide access to corporate data. Data Director for Java can be used in conjunction with any Java-based Web development environment to generate Java automatically so that developers can build Web-enabled applications—without writing any code.

Informix Client SDK for C/C++ and Java

Informix Client SDK for C/C++ and Java is a collection of Informix APIs that provide native access to Informix servers, focusing on C/C++ and Java applications. It includes ESQL/C, LibC++, and CLI developer components. It also contains the Java API, including both JDBC and RIM support.

Third-Party Products

Many third-party products are available in the following categories:

Analysis and Design
Connectivity and APIs
Database Administration Tools
Data Access Tools
Data Modeling
Data Mining Tools
Data Warehouse Management Tools
DataBlade Modules
Development Languages
Form Painters and Code Generators
Imaging Tools
INFORMIX-NewEra Class Libraries
Life Cycle Management
Office Automation
Publishing
Report Writers and Query Tools
Specialty Tools
Statistical Analysis
Windows End-User Tools
Windows Application Development Tools

Summary

Decentralized, distributed computing environments are becoming the norm in the corporate landscape as organizations expand geographically and strive for greater agility in competitive markets. However, developing and maintaining IT solutions that support the information management needs of today's distributed enterprise present a host of new challenges in terms of complexity, connectivity options, and application development requirements.

Informix's database technology is designed with distributed enterprise requirements in mind—and delivered through an integrated, extensible database architecture that combines the mainframe-caliber performance and scalability of DSA server technology with off-the-shelf configuration, connectivity, replication, and administration facilities. The Informix database management products support multi-tier client/server development, support Internet and intranet applications, and set the standard for next-generation application support.

CHAPTER 2

Informix's Future Direction

by Ron M. Flannery

IN THIS CHAPTER

You'll learn a lot about Informix in this book. You'll be exposed to the many tools that are used with Informix, including 4GL, NewEra, and DataBlade modules. You'll understand Dynamic Scalable Architecture (DSA), which is the core of all Informix database servers. You'll have a good understanding of how to set up and administer databases and instances. You'll be exposed to Informix and Web database applications.

But now it's time to talk about the future of Informix.

Informix: Always on the Leading Edge

Informix has always stayed on top of technology. Informix was originally created as a UNIX-only database. At that time, UNIX was just beginning to be recognized as an enterprise-wide server for Information Systems. Through the years, Informix continued to adapt to the ever-improving world of UNIX and database computing. Then came the Web, object-relational databases, and workgroup computing. Informix was always willing to adapt to current and future technologies. Some specific examples include the following:

- **Dynamic Scalable Architecture (DSA).** When Informix created DSA in 1993, it effectively rewrote the product's entire core technology. Although this was a major undertaking, it built a solid foundation upon which DSA could grow. The fact that Informix was able to combine object-relational technologies (that is, Illustra) into DSA in less than a year is an excellent example of the power of the code base. It is compact, well-written, and will change with technology.
- **Object-Relational DBMS (ORDBMS).** The acquisition of Illustra brought Informix into the forefront of database technology. Illustra was combined into Informix's DSA-based OnLine Dynamic Server to create Universal Server. The object technologies inherent in Universal Server enable users to combine nonstandard data types (for example, pictures, movies, and text) with relational data. This is considered to be the future of relational database technology. Again, Informix had its eye on the future.
- **Massively Parallel Processing.** Informix created Extended Parallel Server (XPS), which is designed to support large to very large databases. XPS utilizes Massively Parallel Processing (MPP) and clustered Symmetrical Multiprocessing (SMP). MPP enables databases to span a number of computers and/or processors, making the most of their resources (such as CPU and memory). SMP can exploit the power of CPUs that share the same memory, disk, and I/O systems. XPS allows the creation of very large databases (VLDB), including OLTP systems, imaging applications, and data warehouses. We all know how important these environments are in today's world.
- **World Wide Web.** Recently, Informix took the wraps off the Informix Universal Web Architecture (IUWA), Universal Tools, and Data Director. These tools help create powerful Web-enabled applications. As companies move toward open, Web-oriented database applications, Informix moves with them. Informix's Web tools and Universal Server embrace these technologies.

- **Workgroup Computing**. When NT began to be accepted as a viable and popular solution, Informix created workgroup database servers, including OnLine Workgroup Server and OnLine Workstation. Workgroup Server and Workstation are, of course, based on DSA. Informix also enabled OnLine Dynamic Server for NT platforms. Workgroup computing is considered a major area of growth in the computing world.
- **Open Standards.** Through its Informix Universal Web Architecture, Universal Tools Strategy, and Data Director, Informix is keeping on top of industry standards. The computing world of the future will provide many interoperable computing platforms that Informix is including in its current product offerings.
- **Smart Cards.** Hewlett-Packard, GEM, and Informix partnered to create Smart Card technology with their Imagine Cards. Imagine Cards are about the size of a credit card. They store information about the current user and his or her needs. They will be very important in the future of electronic check paying, credit card processing, and many other things. They will be vital to computer security. The market for these is also expected to explode.

As you can see, Informix has never watched technology go by; the company always embraces it and changes with it. Why should the future be any different?

High-Level Direction

As evidenced by its past accomplishments, Informix will always continue to move with the needs of the market. The following provides a high-level ("executive summary") list of Informix's future goals. It is from focusing on these goals that the specific technologies will continue to evolve.

1. **Extensibility of data.** This is the ability to create applications that can adapt to the needs of their environment. Many current and future Informix products include object-oriented technologies, allowing the products to handle the data needs of any application. It is predicted that a great majority of the database market will be using nonstandard data in the very near future. To handle this, the database must be able to extend into various data types, including those defined by users.
2. **Enterprise computing.** Applications across a company must be able to communicate. Regardless of whether the applications are mainframe, PC, Macintosh, or anything, it is important that they share their data. Today's computing world provides many evolving standards. Informix will stay on top of these standards and combine them into its products. Informix designs its products to be highly scalable and interchangeable, allowing the products to be enabled across entire corporations.
3. **Ease of use**. The components in an open computing environment must be easy to use. Through the aid of different vendors and products, Informix will continue to simplify the use of applications. This includes not only application development, but user access as well.

4. **High-end OLTP and data warehouse.** Major corporations need to be able to efficiently process large amounts of data. The database server must be able to exploit the ever-increasing power of hardware and software platforms. Informix scales well and will continue to use the power of DSA to increase its leadership in this area.
5. **Web-enabled applications.** Certainly, the power of Web-enabled applications can't be ignored. The advent of the Web and its browser front ends allows a very open and powerful computing world.
6. **Workgroup computing.** Windows NT has opened up the workgroup computing portion of the applications market. The workgroup market includes offices varying in size from small to medium. Informix acknowledges this and includes the workgroup market as a major part of its direction.
7. **Open standards.** It is very exciting to see the advent of standards in the computing world. Standards allow various computer applications to "talk" to each other, based on some well-defined protocols. The advantages are incredible. Informix conforms to all the important standards of the computing world.
8. **Partnerships.** Informix has always been very focused on its core products: database servers and enabling technologies. Many companies tend to try to do too many things. Because Informix remains focused, it can deliver higher quality in its products. The company can then leverage its quality partnerships to provide "best of breed" solutions.

Soon, I'll show you how Informix is incorporating these high-level goals into its future product direction. For now, let's try to gauge the direction of the market in general.

Where Is Technology Going?

Where is technology going? How can anyone predict? We can only take our best guess based on current products and trends. Before getting into specific Informix products, let's examine some of the currently evolving trends in computing, many of which are a common thread throughout this chapter. It is very likely that the following trends will be a major part of database application development, at least in the near term.

Object-Relational Databases

An object-relational database management system (ORDBMS) combines many types of data, including standard relational, text, pictures, movies, Web pages, and Java programs. All the major database vendors—Informix, Oracle, Sybase, IBM, and CA—are heavily embracing ORDBMS.

Each vendor implements ORDBMS somewhat differently. In fact, many of the vendors' plans seem to be in flux. Oracle is planning to separate its nonrelational data processing from the database engine. Sybase intends to use a middleware-based approach. Informix and IBM store the data and the methods to operate on it in the database. CA will have an entirely separate object-oriented database for nonrelational data.

> **TIP**
>
> For an *excellent* overview of ORDBMSs and how they relate to data processing needs, take a look at Mike Stonebraker's whitepaper at
>
> `http://www.informix.com/informix/corpinfo/zines/whitpprs/illuswp/wave.htm`
>
> He also wrote a book called *Object-Relational DBMSs—The Next Great Wave*, which clearly describes ORDBMS. Mr. Stonebraker was very involved with the development of the Illustra database and is currently the Chief Technology Officer at Informix.

There have been a lot of predictions about what percentage of corporate data will be stored in object-relational databases. Some estimates say that 85 percent of all "loose" data (which means anything on paper) will eventually be stored in databases. In fact, because this technology is so new and these types of objects can be very large, this might not be too far from reality.

The power of ORDBMS is incredible. It can greatly simplify the storage and retrieval of information in a company. One good example is in the advertising industry: An ORDBMS can store various pictures and videos. Because of this, a future database vendor must implement a strong ORDBMS.

Web-Enabled Technologies

Certainly, Web-enabled technologies are a part of the future. This can't be denied. Basically, Web-enabled database technologies allow deploying the browser as a front end to database applications. The application does not *have* to be on the World Wide Web: It can be on the user's hard drive, the local network, or the Web. The important part is that the browser is the front end to the application.

There are *many* different ways to create Web-enabled applications. Chapter 42, "Serving Data on the WWW," provides an in-depth discussion of this. The future of data processing will certainly have these technologies as a core. Databases must be able to adapt to these technologies.

Workgroup Computing

Workgroup computing was more or less started with the introduction of Windows NT. Microsoft provided a flexible database server that was less expensive and easier to use than UNIX. The sales of NT have skyrocketed. Some estimates say that it is currently outselling UNIX, and if not, it is certainly headed in that direction.

The workgroup market—not only NT but new UNIX solutions—must certainly be addressed by the database vendors. And all the major vendors do in fact have NT solutions now.

Open Standards

There has been a large drive toward open standards in the computer industry. And that makes good sense: With all the computing platforms out there, standards must exist. Standards simplify communication between various computers and networks, and they make programming and communication much easier.

A lot of attention has been focused on Common Object Request Broker Architecture (CORBA) and Distributed Component Object Model (DCOM). CORBA is an open standard that provides a complete model of how objects should communicate across a network or the Internet. CORBA is a product of the Object Management Group (OMG), a consortium of hundreds of hardware and software vendors. DCOM has many of the characteristics of CORBA, but it was created by Microsoft and tends to lean more toward Microsoft platforms. The future suggests a CORBA/DCOM interoperability and a more open DCOM.

It is very likely that CORBA and DCOM will greatly influence the way applications are developed in the future. They provide excellent models of how to enable communications.

High-End Database Servers

With the incredible increase in processing power of UNIX and NT computers, higher-end databases are now possible. Some of the increased performance includes processing speed, amount of memory, and hard disk size and speed. Databases that were unimaginable just five years ago are now very much a reality.

To keep up with technology, database vendors need to take full advantage of these products. Technologies such as massively parallel processing (MPP) and symmetrical multiprocessing (SMP) can do this. These concepts will lead to more powerful products that will process large amounts of data at an incredible speed.

Creating the Future: Informix Products

This book provides details on how to use the many products provided by Informix. These include products that are "legacy"—those that are older but still very functional—products using the current best technologies, and the real leading edge products. Most Informix products are leading edge. The following sections describe Informix's plans to leverage the current products and how they will all be merged into the future technology direction.

INFORMIX-4GL

The INFORMIX-4GL language is a server-based fourth-generation language. It provides a wide range of functionality, including user input screens, reports, data loading, database updates, and database administration functions. Although some consider it obsolete, it certainly provides a great deal of functionality that can be used in the future.

Informix has Webkits that allow linking of 4GL, NewEra, and ESQL/C programs into CGI Web applications.

Languages such as Java can work well with the distributed world of the future, but 4GL still will have its place. 4GL is easy to use and deploy on the server side of things and can be much quicker to develop in many cases; also, you can find a large number of existing 4GL applications. Sometimes it's not practical to jump on the technology bandwagon.

INFORMIX-NewEra

NewEra is one of Informix's object-oriented development tools. It provides many powerful client/server and distributed-processing capabilities. It includes support for many object-oriented concepts and is generally a very strong language. Informix will incorporate NewEra into its overall architectures. NewEra has function calls that allow it to directly interface to Universal Server databases. NewEra also has a Webkit that allows CGI deployment.

ESQL/C

The ESQL/C product provides APIs that allow C programs to interact with Informix databases. C is a very powerful, albeit cryptic, language. It will have a continuing role in the direction of Informix, perhaps more so than NewEra and 4GL. It is important to note, though, that C functions can be called from within NewEra and 4GL programs.

The C language is very widely used. Vendors support many different APIs for it. Informix readily provides the C APIs for its database server and Web products. Also, C can be used to communicate directly with Web servers and is used by many third-party vendors. So it will indeed be an important part of the future.

Java

What more can be said about Java? It has taken the Web world by storm and now can be deployed in many non-Web applications. Java is a new language, created with object-orientation and open interoperability in mind. It has excellent functionality for creating applications on a large number of computing platforms—which is perhaps the biggest part of its power. It ties well into CORBA and DCOM. Numerous vendors provide high levels of Java support. It is hard to imagine going wrong by choosing Java as a direction.

Informix is heavily embracing Java. Java is supported in the Informix Universal Web Architecture, Data Director, and Universal Tools Strategy. In addition, JDBC drivers, which connect to databases, have strong Informix support.

The Informix Universal Web Architecture (IUWA)

The IUWA is a complete set of products and technologies that enables the interoperability of applications using Web technologies. It is covered in some detail in Chapter 42. The IUWA is a framework that really enables intelligent Web applications. It provides for applications to work in synch with open standards and Web technologies. The IUWA—as much as anything—truly demonstrates Informix's commitment to the future of computing. It can be used in conjunction with any DSA-enabled database to provide browser-enabled applications.

Standard Engine

The INFORMIX-Standard Engine is the current name for the original Informix database. It runs on UNIX platforms and is very easy to use and administer. It provides good performance, though it can't really scale to the levels of the DSA databases. It should continue to be supported, but it is probably advisable to consider moving into the DSA line of databases, considering the power they provide.

OnLine Server

The INFORMIX-OnLine Server (version 5.*x*) family of databases works well in many environments. It runs on UNIX platforms and provides more functionality than Standard Engine, including administrative utilities and the ability to use "raw disk space" to store data. It is a good database that will be around for awhile. It is not built on the DSA, though, so it might not plug in as well to the newer environments.

Dynamic Scalable Architecture (DSA)

As discussed previously, the DSA is the core architecture for most of the Informix database servers. This is important because it allows each of the servers to have the same powerful functionality based on a parallel processing model. The DSA will continue to be used as the enabling technology in Informix server products. The databases currently using DSA include the following:

- OnLine Dynamic Server
- XPS
- Workgroup Server and Workstation
- Universal Server

It is easy to see why one architecture across all servers is so important. This advantage will be demonstrated more in the "Universal Server" section that follows.

OnLine Dynamic Server (ODS)

ODS is the original DSA database. It is very powerful and easy to administer on many UNIX and NT platforms. It provides a well-balanced set of administration tools, as well as parallel-processing capabilities. ODS will continue to work well in environments that scale from small to very large databases. (XPS is more appropriate in some situations.)

Informix Extended Parallel Server (XPS)

XPS is Informix's massively parallel database platform. It provides a *shared-nothing* model, which allows multiple computers and processors in a network to share large databases. This is obviously an important part of the future, considering the availability of the hardware and software to support such databases.

Workgroup Server and Workstation

These are the two newest products in the Informix database family. As stated previously, they generally were created to compete in the lower-end market (small- to medium-sized applications). They run on both UNIX and NT. One of the major selling points of these products is their ease of use: They are very easy to install and administer. This is very consistent with the goals of a workgroup environment. These products blend well into the IUWA. They are easy to use as Web database servers and should be considered for particular Web and workgroup applications.

Universal Server

The INFORMIX-Universal Server (IUS) implements the best of both worlds: object and relational. In the near future, Informix plans to have the full line of DSA-enabled products migrated to Universal Server. Universal Server provides full object-oriented functionality within the database. The database can be extended using DataBlades, which allows operating on many nonstandard data types. Data types that can be handled in Universal Server include the following:

- Standard relational data
- Pictures
- Movies
- Graphics
- Web pages
- Audio

The object-oriented functionality of DataBlades allows easy operation on all these types of data. This goes back to the extensibility aspect. For example, a user can search for different pictures, based on some of their characteristics. Movies can be stored in the database and processed in a similar manner.

Many analysts throughout the industry predict that object-relational databases will take over the market. Now that the technology is available, people can start using it. This has been affirmed with the amount of attention these servers have received.

By combining the best of both worlds—high-performance relational DSA and object-relational—Informix has created a great product that manages all of a company's database needs. The market certainly will explode in the very near future and Informix is well positioned.

Informix Unleashed...Into the Future

Informix has seen its revenues grow 33-fold since it was created in 1986. The incredible growth rate doesn't seem to be slowing down, despite heavy competition from Oracle and Sybase. Informix continues to be the fastest-growing of the three companies. Phil White, CEO of Informix, predicted that Informix would pass Oracle in database revenues in 1999. It certainly isn't out of the question. Either way, the future certainly seems bright for Informix.

By moving with the needs of technology, Informix has firmly established itself as a leader in the industry. There certainly is no sign of that changing. Informix is an exciting, leading-edge company that will continue well into the future.

Summary

This chapter helped prepare you for what you are about to learn in this book. You saw historical examples of how Informix has remained on the leading edge of technology. I summarized Informix's high-level direction and the direction of technology. Finally, I described the products that Informix is using to continue positioning itself for the future.

Informix is a database vendor that has prepared itself to continue growing for many years to come. The rest of this book describes how to use Informix now and in the future.

CHAPTER

Database Concepts

by John McNally

IN THIS CHAPTER

This chapter provides

- A description of a database management system, commonly referred to as a DBMS
- A list and explanation of the benefits of a DBMS
- A description of the different types of DBMSs
- An explanation of the types of DBMSs built by Informix and the relational database management system, commonly referred to as an RDBMS
- A brief description of types of RDBMS users
- An explanation of client/server processing
- A description of the different types of applications, batch and OLTP, that access the Informix RDBMS
- A description of the types of tasks that are requested by the applications
- An explanation of data warehousing

Data Management Concepts

A database management system, or DBMS, is considered a basic component of data processing. A DBMS is a collection of programs that are constantly running processes. They are used to control the activities required to store, retrieve, and manage data in a database or databases. Most DBMSs available today, such as Informix, can manage not only multiple data columns, rows, and tables within a database but multiple databases as well.

The DBMS software product came about in the early 1960s when software developing scientists realized that every time they built an application, they duplicated code to handle the data functions of store, retrieve, and maintain. Over time, the programs that perform these same functions became a separate, generic system. This new separate, generic data management system could be used for multiple applications. Moreover, these different applications needed only to contain calls to access the data management system to perform specific data operations.

This data management system evolved into the DBMSs of today. Besides reducing the need for duplicating code, DBMSs provide many other benefits:

- Scalability
- Better developer productivity
- Shared data
- Security
- Data integrity management, redundancy, and consistency
- Data independence

The first benefit is that a DBMS is scalable. This means the DBMS is able to grow and expand so that it can run across many machines or stay on a single machine. A DBMS is a single software system that runs many individual processes, like an operating system. The DBMS can share a machine's resources, such as CPUs and disk, or it can use them all itself. Because the DBMS can run in many different configurations, it is considered scalable. Most DBMSs start on a single machine, sharing that machine's resources with other applications and processes. As the DBMS increases in the amount of data it stores and the number of applications it services, it needs more resources. The database administrator, or DBA, then starts to scale the DBMS to a different configuration that satisfies the growing processing needs.

Because the DBMS is a stand-alone software system that can grow to meet the application and data storage needs, the developers building the applications can spend more time concentrating on their applications. Developing time and costs are lower because the DBMS already has the data processing functions built in. In addition, the developer does not have to rebuild those functions into the application software. Whenever developers need their application to deal with the database, a call to the DBMS is placed within the application code that tells that DBMS which data to find and what to do with it.

The DBMS also allows for data sharing because the DBMS is a single, scalable system that is easy to access by an application or multiple, different applications. All Informix and most other DBMSs allow for many users through multiple applications that can access the same data. This access is available as long as the users have the proper permissions.

The next benefit of a DBMS is security. A DBMS allows or disallows any user from accessing specific data columns, rows, tables, or databases.

Rules involving security, however, are not the only rules a DBMS can enforce. Data integrity, consistency, and redundancy types of rules can also be enforced. For example, a DBMS can be given the responsibility to ensure the data types are correct, multiple data items are not stored, and the data meets a specific criteria such as true or false, or a specific state such as MD, VA, or CA.

The final benefit of a DBMS is that it maintains different views of the data and the databases it manages. These DBMS-provided views, usually referred to as schemas, are broken down into three different types: physical (or internal), conceptual, and user (or external). The physical schema is the actual layout of the data and databases in their physical locations on the disk or tape. The conceptual view is how the data and the databases look in column, row, and table layout. The user view is also in column, row, and table layout, but it is tailored to each user's security access levels. With these views, the DBMS provides data independence. Data independence occurs when the applications and users are separate and have no impact on the representations of the actual data they use. For example, if a physical location is changed for an entire database within the DBMS, the conceptual and user views do not change, which means the applications don't need to change or be recompiled. For example, if an application changes a column's name from Soc_Sec_Numb to SSN, the conceptual and physical views do not have to change. Data independence saves a lot of time and effort for the application developers and DBAs.

The first type of DBMS to receive standard use throughout the data processing community in the 1960s was file processing. The actual data was kept within flat files, which are basic text-based files. As these files became larger, the speed and efficiency of data access degraded. By the early 1970s, file processing was replaced by the hierarchy and network-style DBMSs. The hierarchy DBMS used structured trees to store data. On the other hand, the network DBMS used records to store each data entity. Both of these DBMSs allowed for larger, more robust databases with faster and more efficient access. Because they didn't provide the best data independence, they were replaced by the current type of DBMS—relational.

Relational databases are the result of Dr. E.F. Codd's frustrations with the standard database management systems available at the time. A researcher at IBM in 1969, Dr. Codd discovered that algebraic concepts can be applied to the database world, where data can be organized into tables that contain columns and rows. Each column, row, and table must adhere to specific relationships.

Relational database management systems, or RDBMSs, gained popularity in the late 1970s and became the standard by the mid-1980s. About the same time, Informix introduced its first RDBMSs—INFORMIX-Standard Engine and INFORMIX-OnLine.

Many chapters in this book are dedicated to setting up a relational database, applying the relational rules, and accessing the data using the latest Informix RDBMS products.

There are four major types of Informix RDBMS product users. These users include the database administrator or DBA, the system administrator or SA, the application developer, and the application user. The DBA is the person generally responsible for keeping the Informix RDBMS running. The SA is responsible for the operating system and the machine on which the RDBMS is running. An application developer builds the applications that access the Informix RDBMS. Finally, the application user is the person who runs the application to access the data in the Informix RDBMS and performs specific tasks on that data.

All user applications that access the Informix RDBMS are considered clients, and the actual Informix RDBMS is considered the server. The client/server process is natural in the RDBMS world because the RDBMS is its own software process, running throughout the day and waiting for tasks to perform. These tasks are specified by the accessing client applications, which run for the duration of the task. There are many types of clients. Some are provided by Informix to perform tasks such as database backups and system checks. Other clients are user-built applications that perform tasks such as collecting data to store or creating and printing reports on the information stored in the database.

A client can have the Informix RDBMS server perform one of four basic tasks. These tasks are select, insert, update, or delete. A select is considered a query because it looks at a specific set of data. An insert actually adds new information, usually an entire row, into the database. An update task changes existing data. A delete actually removes an entire row of data; consider it the opposite of an insert.

The two different types of clients that perform these tasks are batch or online. A batch client performs many tasks for a long period of time, usually without involving a user. For example, a batch process can read thousands of addresses from a file and store them, or insert them, into the database. Each set of tasks performed by the batch client is considered a transaction. A single transaction can contain many long tasks or a few short tasks.

An online client is an example of a process that uses transactions containing a few short, quick, single-minded tasks. In contrast to a batch client, which runs a single transaction containing hundreds of tasks that might run for minutes or hours until completed, an online transaction contains a few tasks and should complete within seconds. Known as OLTP, or online transaction processing, this client is usually run by a user sitting at a keyboard, performing his own tasks. When that user needs to retrieve or store data, his application makes a quick access to the DBMS.

The databases used by these clients are sometimes considered the most important part of day-to-day business. A database is usually set up to represent a specific view of a company's business world. For example, a company that sells auto parts could have three major areas of its business world represented in databases: parts inventory, customers, and orders. All a company needs to know about its day-to-day activities resides in the company's databases, and the applications it builds are the way to access that data.

Most databases are under a gigabyte in size, but some can grow to be quite large. They utilize the most popular application client—OLTP. Batch processing was very popular in the 1970s and 1980s, but with the decrease in desktop equipment prices, companies can afford to have more online users. Most of this book is dedicated to building these business world databases in an Informix RDBMS, tuning these databases for efficient access, and building application clients to access those databases.

Sometimes companies build extremely large databases called data warehouses. Although most databases contain a company's world of information, a data warehouse contains the universe of an entire corporation. Data warehouses are not generally used to perform daily OLTP activities. A data warehouse is used to perform intense data analysis, called data mining. These databases can be expected to grow into a terabyte or larger in size.

Summary

No matter what type of RDBMS user you are—DBA, SA, application developer, or application user—database management encompasses a lot of different technology and information systems concepts. Many of the concepts touched on in this chapter are covered in greater detail throughout this book. All these concepts are explained while using the Informix RDBMS products. No one is expected to know it all, but with an Informix RDBMS, it is easy to start learning.

PART

IN THIS PART

Informix Environments

CHAPTER 4

Informix Environment Introduction

by John McNally

IN THIS CHAPTER

This chapter provides a description of the different types of open systems, including hardware and operating systems, that run Informix RDBMS products.

Range of Environments

The following chapters in this part describe in detail all the different Informix RDBMSs. It starts with INFORMIX-Standard Engine and ends with INFORMIX-Parallel Server. All the Informix RDBMSs described in the following chapters are available to run in many different computer environments. Which environment will meet the database processing needs of a business?

The first thing needed to run an Informix RDBMS is a computer system. To run Informix products, this machine must be able to run as an open system. An open system consists of two key components—the hardware and the operating system. An open system is loosely defined as a multiple-processing, resource-sharing system that allows the operating system or other processes to determine how things are processed. Almost all computer systems available today are considered open systems. Computer systems using UNIX or Windows NT as their operating systems are the most widely known open systems. Even though computer systems using DOS or Windows 95 are not open systems, they are still very popular.

As previously mentioned, hardware is a key component to making a system open. A standard desktop PC is very powerful but is usually unable to gain the true power of being an open system. To truly be open, the computer hardware must have multiple central processing units, or CPUs. The CPU is the brain of the computer. With multiple CPUs, an open system can spread the workload between each CPU or split a single process between multiple CPUs to perform parallel processing. Commonly referred to as server machines or just servers, these computer systems usually have multiple CPUs, large amounts of internal memory, and even larger amounts of disk space.

Having all this hardware, CPUs, memory, and disk space without being able to manage it is a waste. That is where an open systems operating system comes in handy. An operating system, or OS, is the master control program that manages and allows access to all the hardware's resources—that is, memory, disk, and CPUs. Only specific OSs such as UNIX, Windows NT, and OS/2 are capable of handling true multiprocessing or multiple CPUs. Other OSs, such as Windows 95, simulate multiprocessing by swapping processes within one CPU very quickly. This swapping of processes within a single CPU is called multitasking.

All Informix RDBMS products are available for UNIX systems. UNIX was created in the early 1970s by Bell Laboratories. A very portable OS, UNIX is used on a wide variety of computers, from mainframes to personal computers, that support multitasking and are ideally suited to multiuser applications. UNIX is a very flexible operating system, well-suited to the needs of advanced computer users.

Bell Labs gave UNIX away after it was created. Because of that, every hardware vendor has tailored UNIX to work differently on its own machines. For example, HP/UX, HP's version of UNIX, does not run on an IBM RS6000. An IBM RS6000 uses AIX, IBM's version of UNIX. There are dozens of different computer hardware server manufacturers, and there are dozens of different UNIX OSs. Because of all the multiple hardware and OS combinations, there are many different versions of the same Informix product. For example, there are versions of INFORMIX-OnLine Dynamic Server for HP/UX, Sun OS, AIX, and many others. There is even a version of INFORMIX-OnLine Dynamic Server for a totally different type of OS—Windows NT.

A Microsoft product, Windows NT is a 32-bit operating system that can run on high-end Pentium systems with or without multiple CPUs. Windows NT provides the performance of a medium to low-end UNIX workstation but at a lower cost. For companies already running with Windows 95 products on their desktops, the same products are available on Windows NT.

Which hardware and OS system does a company need? That all depends on three major factors: system requirements, existing equipment, and available capital. The first and most important factor is the entire system's requirements. Some of these requirements include the number of users, the amount of processing to be done, the time needed to perform the processing, the amount of data to store, how long to keep the data, the importance of the data, and most importantly, how much money this system makes or saves in the long run.

After a clear-cut set of system requirements is created, see whether any existing hardware and software can be reused or upgraded. Look at placing the new RDBMS on an existing machine that is not processing at 100 percent. Possibly take a machine that is running at 100 percent capacity and upgrade it by adding more memory, CPUs, and disk space.

If an existing machine is not a feasible solution, then see what is available for purchase that fits the company's budget. You can almost always find an appropriate machine because there are so many options when purchasing a new system. The more time you spend investigating a solution to meet the system requirements, the better the system will be.

In cases when you need a solution immediately but the company does not contain the expertise to make a proper selection, it is time to bring in a consultant. Informix, all hardware vendors, and other companies can provide consultants to help create the best solution to meet the company's database, hardware, and OS needs.

Summary

Many different types of open systems are available today, and Informix has versions of its products for most of them. When reading the next few chapters, keep in mind the type of hardware and OS that a business needs. Also keep in mind the overall system requirements, including software, applications, OS, hardware, and RDBMS. Learn as much as possible when creating a new system. If internal sources are not available, use other resources to gain this information, such as the Web, consultants, and other companies. Throwing away money and resources to build a system that doesn't meet the requirements is a very expensive way to learn.

CHAPTER

INFORMIX-Standard Engine

by John McNally

IN THIS CHAPTER

This chapter provides

- A description of how INFORMIX-Standard Engine works
- Advantages of INFORMIX-Standard Engine
- Uses for INFORMIX-Standard Engine
- Limitations of INFORMIX-Standard Engine
- A description of Standard Engine's client/server architecture

What Is INFORMIX-Standard Engine?

In the early 1980s, Informix released its first relational database product for small- to medium-sized data storage requirements. This product was one of the first professionally supported database systems to run on the UNIX operating system. INFORMIX-Standard Engine, also known as INFORMIX-SE, was designed to provide a dependable relational database solution for small- to medium-sized businesses without placing extra demands on the business's human and machine resources.

A client/server database system is where the application programs, known as clients, must run as processes separate from the programs that maintain and store the data, called servers. A client process does not necessarily have to be running on a different machine from the server. It simply must be a different process. An example of a non-client/server database system, where the program maintaining the database also controls the user's access to that data, is Microsoft Access. The client/server relationship is only possible because the clients must communicate with the server to access the data.

INFORMIX-SE is a relational database server that allows many different types of clients to access the stored data using the Structured Query Language, or SQL. For more information about SQL, refer to Chapter 28, "INFORMIX-SQL." The relational database system is one where data is stored and accessed by its relationship to important data items, known as *keys.* SQL is the language used by relational databases to work with the data using these keys. INFORMIX-SE is a complete relational database management system, also known as RDBMS, that comes with not only the previous mentioned server, but also its own front-end client—DBaccess. By using DBaccess, users and administrators can use SQL and menu-driven commands to create and maintain databases on every type of UNIX platform.

To automate database processing, you can run SQL statements by referencing DBaccess within a UNIX *shell program.* A UNIX shell program is where UNIX commands can be combined with standard programming conditional structures, such as `if-then-else` and `case` statements, to perform a task. Administrators can place commonly used SQL commands in time-managed processes, such as `cron` and `at`, to run at regular cycles. Two examples of queries or job updates that a database administrator (DBA) might run on a daily basis are row counts and table reindexing. Rather than run these jobs during normal working hours, when users also access the database, the administrator can have cron run them in the middle of the night. Other users can also automate their queries and updates by creating UNIX shell programs to perform their tasks. Because these shell programs have the capability to pass data through variables, these programs can perform some complicated tasks.

Sometimes the user's task becomes too complicated for DBaccess and shell programs. These complicated tasks include interactive screens and data migrations (importing and exporting between databases). In these situations, the SE server permits database access from other types of user-built client applications. You can create C, C++, and COBOL applications with an additional product called *INFORMIX-ESQL*. INFORMIX-ESQL provides the capability to compile programs that contain SQL statements embedded within the program code. Informix also sells a fourth generation language (4GL), called INFORMIX-4GL, that allows users to build applications to access SE databases. For more information on 4GL, see Chapter 35, "Introduction to 4GL." The general idea behind a 4GL tool is to assist users in building screens for data input, deciding what form the output will take, and processing this data. When the user completes these screens, the 4GL tool generates the necessary code and compiles it into a new application. Part V, "Application Development," deals with creating client applications.

Performance

Because INFORMIX-SE's server deals with the client and the server as separate entities, it is able to provide better performance. Because the client applications are responsible for creating, processing, and displaying the data, the server can concentrate on storing and retrieving the data faster and more safely.

SE's server is able to retrieve and store data quickly by using a *cost-based optimizer* and various indexing strategies. A cost-based optimizer is a program that decides the best possible way to do something before it actually does it. For example, if you need to go from one town to another, you don't jump in a car and go. You consult a map, a friend, or a road sign to figure out the best route to take. The cost-based optimizer does the same thing. Before storing data in a table, the optimizer decides where and how it should be stored, keeping in mind how often it will be retrieved or changed. Less-used data and tables have a lower priority than frequently used data and tables.

INFORMIX-SE uses a *B+ tree algorithm* to build its indexes from table data. A B+ tree is a dynamic structure built on specific data keys. Only the outside nodes, or leaves, of the B+ tree contain the pointers to each data row. Inserting or deleting from the index is easier because only the ends and edges of the tree must be changed, and not an entire branch.

SE uses two types of B+ tree indexing strategies: *unique* and *clustered*. A unique indexing strategy is one in which each key in the index is different. A unique index prevents duplicate entries in a table and automatically maintains data integrity. The least amount of storage time is used with a unique index because SE knows that only one key exists for each row. For better retrieval times, use clustering, the other indexing strategy available to SE. A clustered index achieves this improvement by physically organizing the layout of the table to match the index. Therefore, a clustered index can retrieve data faster, but storage time is increased due to its reorganizing during writes to the table.

Data Protection

Data in the database can become corrupt in two ways. The first is when a failure occurs with the hardware, operating system, or database server. To make sure that the data is safe and sound after such an event, SE uses transaction logging, auditing, and backups. Every activity performed by the SE server is considered a transaction, whether it's a query, an insertion, or a deletion. As SE performs the activity, it also writes what it did in a log file. When a failure occurs, SE uses an auditing process to compare what is in the log file to what is actually in the database. If they don't match, the audit process applies the activities from the log against the database.

With major data corruption in the database, it may be best to restore the entire database from a backup. After the backup is restored, applying the log files from the last backup to the time of the failure restores the database to the state it was in before the corruption.

Databases can also become corrupt from overzealous client applications. Many client applications access the database at the same time throughout the processing day, usually trying to access the same data and tables. For data to maintain its integrity and consistency, SE uses *integrity constraints*, *data locking*, and *process isolation levels*.

Integrity Constraints

Sometimes referred to as business rules, integrity constraints are divided into two types:

- Entity integrity
- Referential integrity

Entity Integrity

The first type of integrity constraint at the data level is called *entity integrity*. Entity integrity includes any constraints placed on a specific entity's data range. For example, a data item called discount can have a constraint of 0 to 50. This implies that any percentage between 0 and 50 is permitted for the entry stored in the discount field in the database. A client application that tries to store 75 percent is rejected by the SE server. Another example is a different database field called `marital_status` that allows only M, S, D, or W for married, single, divorced, or widowed. All other entries fail when the client tries to update or insert the data.

Referential Integrity

The other integrity constraint, *referential integrity*, deals with the relationships between data. Referential integrity prevents client applications from breaking any predetermined rules when dealing with a data item that has a relationship with other data items. Some examples follow:

A client application can add an address, but referential integrity can require that a zip code also be present; an employee's salary can be updated but not without changing the tax bracket; or a customer can be deleted but not if the customer has a balance past due.

Data Locking

SE uses data locking to stop a client from changing a data item while another client is working with the same item. Locking does not prevent other clients from querying data that is currently being updated; it only restricts concurrent updates on the same data. The three levels of data locking are

- Table row
- Entire table
- Database

Table Row Level

The lowest level, the table row level, locks only the current row being updated.

When a clustered index is present on the table containing the row, to maintain index integrity, SE actually locks three rows: the current row, the row above, and the row below. Row locking is recommended for database systems where many clients access the same data to perform small updates. Row locking requires the least wait time for other clients waiting to update the same data, but it also requires the most processing from SE. An adjustable lock limit parameter for SE is used to keep track of the number of locks currently held. Because row-level locking is the smallest lock level, there is the potential to have more locks at one time than for any other level. SE must keep track of all these locks, which causes greater processing overhead. Row locking is set as the default when a table is created.

Long transactions that change many rows may cause problems when clients access the database. A single transaction that updates hundreds of rows locks each row as it makes the change, but it does not release the lock until all the rows are changed. Any other clients trying to update rows locked by the long transaction must wait until the long transaction is complete.

Entire Table Level

The next locking level covers an entire table. This forces more clients to wait to perform updates and inserts on the same table but uses fewer locks and less overhead. Table locking is better for long transactions that update many rows all in the same transaction. An example of a mass update is the following: All the customers with a standard purchase plan get a discount of 10 percent. This data is stored in a database where both the customer and payment tables have thousands of rows. The single transaction SQL statement looks like this:

```
UPDATE customers
SET (discount=10)
WHERE purchase_plan='s';
```

Database Level

The final locking level covers a database. This level is not recommended for systems with more than a couple concurrent users. Locking the entire database improves performance of batch jobs that update or insert many rows in different tables within the same transaction. An example of this type of mass update is one in which all the standard purchase plan customers without balances due in the payment table get a discount of 25 percent. This information is in a database where both the customer and payment tables have thousands of rows each. The SQL statement for this single transaction with multiple tables looks like this:

```
UPDATE customers
SET (discount=25)
WHERE purchase_plan='s'
AND customer_id =
   (SELECT customer FROM payments
     WHERE balance=0);
```

Isolation Levels

When client applications are querying the database, another client process can change the data being accessed. To prevent data change during a read, SE has built-in process isolation levels. A process isolation level is the stage at which a data update can or cannot occur while a select (or read) query is being performed. The standard level is the basic `SELECT` statement. By using this basic `SELECT` statement, the client is letting any other client process change the data while the original client is still viewing the data. When the data is in the process of being updated, the `SELECT` statement retrieves the most current data.

The next level is the `SELECT FOR UPDATE` statement. This statement locks the data at the current locking level, preventing other clients from changing the data until the original client completes its query. A `SELECT FOR UPDATE` query fails if the data is already locked by another client.

The prevention of data corruption through logging and locking is important when system failures and clients stress the server, but it is also necessary to prevent clients from accessing certain data all together. Database security is managed by SE at the database and table levels. A database-level security restriction prevents specific users from creating and deleting tables and indexes. This ensures that a user without the proper security level running a specific report application doesn't delete an entire table just to see whether he can.

The next restriction is placed at the table level. Privileges at this level let specific users access data that others may not have permission to see. A restriction placed on the employee payroll data field may be a good idea unless a company benefit permits your employees to give themselves raises. You can leave open (unlocked) the fields that contain information on addresses and dependents so employees can update these fields when they change residence or add a new family member.

Keeping a current backup and transaction log reduces the time and effort required after a failure. Even maintaining proper locking and security helps SE run more smoothly and efficiently. SE has an extra feature to improve performance and security called stored procedures. A stored procedure is a single SQL statement or a group of SQL statements kept within the SE servers' own tables. Rather than send the SQL command to the SE server to be optimized and processed, the client can just send a request to execute the stored procedure that contains the already processed and optimized SQL commands. Any commonly used, non-changing commands can and should be stored procedures, independent of their size or complexity.

A stored procedure can be quite elaborate, accepting variable input and performing multitask insert, delete, and update operations. Stored procedures reduce server optimization and the communication between the client and server. A stored procedure `EXECUTE` command is four words long, `EXECUTE STORED PROCEDURE PROCEDURE_1`, plus any input data.

In an office that receives hundreds of payments a day, rather than send the same SQL to post the payment and adjust the balance for each customer, a stored procedure can be created to perform the post, update the balance, and return the new balance. You can also build security into stored procedures. Clients can be restricted from accessing specific database tables through normal SQL commands but can be allowed to use a stored procedure that works with the table. In this way, employees can look at their own personal information but not at the information of other employees. Stored procedures can also restrict some users from performing operations while allowing others. For example, branch managers of sales offices can be the only clients allowed to apply a discount or refund to a customer's account, preventing the sales personnel from adjusting the same data.

Stored procedures can also be activated by a particular event occurring on a data field. This event is called a *trigger*. SE allows you to activate triggers whenever an insert, update, or delete is performed by a client on a specific field. A trigger can start a stored procedure to check whether a customer's current balance is past due before inserting a new order into the database. Triggers are also useful for logging events. When companies need their own auditing information, rather than build the tracking into each client application, you can set up a trigger at the database level.

Uses

The most common use of INFORMIX-SE is the standard business-related database. These databases contain information used on a daily basis for the non-corporate sized company. You can store information concerning the location of a specific part in a warehouse and mailing lists of interested customers in SE's database. With Informix's development tools, these businesses can create elaborate front-end programs to customize the storage and retrieval of their companies' important information.

Here are some possible uses for INFORMIX-SE:

- Controlling a department's inventory
- Managing employee personal records
- Storing ordering data for a small telemarketing company
- Maintaining address lists for a catalog distribution company

Although SE is recommended for small- to medium-sized databases, this recommendation does not mean SE can't handle large amounts of data. SE can manage multiple databases, each with hundreds of tables containing up to a million rows per table. Of course, the limitations depend on the machine on which SE is running, the amount of memory, and the disk space. Most companies find that SE is perfect in situations where personal computer database systems are too small for the company's data and don't provide future growth possibilities. In addition, companies looking to take advantage of UNIX-based systems' capability to handle client/server applications find SE a good starting database system.

Whether these companies' needs include a hundred users accessing the database all day long or just 10 users accessing it occasionally, SE can meet most database processing needs without much hassle. Setting up the database, deciding the type of client, and determining whether to build or buy a client takes more effort than maintaining the database. Running on a UNIX-based minicomputer, SE offers the storage and processing power of the big mainframe systems with the tools, ease of use, and low maintenance of the personal computer systems.

Limitations

The largest of SE's limitations is that it is not an online transaction processing (OLTP), client/server-type of system. An OLTP system has multiple users connected to a database system at the same time, accessing the database constantly during the day. Each access is considered a transaction, a specific task that is performed on the database, such as a query, an insert, or a delete. A client/server system is where the database is managed by a continuously running program called the server. Clients are separate programs that contact the server for access to the needed data within the database. When the client is finished, it disconnects from the server. In an OLTP, client/server system, many client processes connect to a database server for extended periods of time. SE is a client/server system, but due to its limited processing capability, SE is unable to provide standard OLTP performance to hundreds of users at the same time.

As mentioned at the beginning of this chapter, SE permits client connection with DBaccess, SQL in shell programs, compiled code with INFORMIX-ESQL, and applications created with INFORMIX-4GL. SE can handle any or all of these client-types accessing the database at the same time, but the more clients, the slower the response. A standard OLTP system must be able to handle hundreds of client transactions at the same time, returning the transactions' results from the server within a few seconds. National airline reservation systems and bank automated teller systems are examples of OLTP, client/server database systems. SE does not have the processing power to filter that many transactions that quickly. If an OLTP system is needed or an SE system is not performing well, using INFORMIX-OnLine might be the answer. INFORMIX-OnLine is designed for OLTP database processing, using the same clients and development tools used for SE.

Although SE is not intended for OLTP processing, it can perform all other types of database processing. SE can handle batch client processes that make hundreds of accesses to the database without any problem. SE can also have a small number of users, under 25, making many daily short transactions with one or two database updates per client connection without performance degradation. SE cannot handle hundreds of these connections at the same time, needing 24 hours of database availability a day.

Availability is another limitation of SE. A transaction log is maintained by SE, recording all changes made to the database. This log is cleared and restarted fresh after you make a backup on the database. If a crash occurs and some recent data is lost, you must restore the last backup and then apply the last transaction log. If it's been seven days since the last backup when a crash occurs, you must apply seven days worth of work from the transaction log. Of course, higher activity databases should get backups on a more regular basis than once a week—usually once a night so that the maximum restore is one day of activity from the transaction log.

Unfortunately, backups, restores, and transaction log application can take a few hours to perform, which restricts all activity on the database from the client processes. Systems that can allow only a bare minimum of down time should use more enhanced database servers with built-in safety measures. INFORMIX-OnLine is just such a system; it uses transaction logging to track changes applied to the data since a checkpoint created a clean version of the database. Checkpoints usually perform this cleaning every five to 10 minutes within OnLine. This means that an OnLine database has only five to 10 minutes of database to rebuild, but an SE must rebuild from the last backup.

System Architecture

INFORMIX-SE relies heavily on the UNIX operating system to provide a backbone architecture. UNIX has its own set of programs that provide interprocess communications (IPCs) and file system operations. Because SE is UNIX-based, an administrator actually needs more UNIX knowledge than database knowledge.

Interprocess communications is one running program sending or receiving data from other running programs. As shown in Figure 5.1, these UNIX IPCs cause the SE client/server relationship to occur. When a client process starts, so does the IPC connection to the server. As the client sends an SQL statement to the server, it happens over that IPC. Results from the server are then sent back over that IPC to the client. The IPC connection is held until the client process ends—

not when the individual transactions are completed, but when the entire client process is completed. The client process shown in Figure 5.1 allows users to enter information through an entry screen and hold its IPC connection until the user ends the entry screen program.

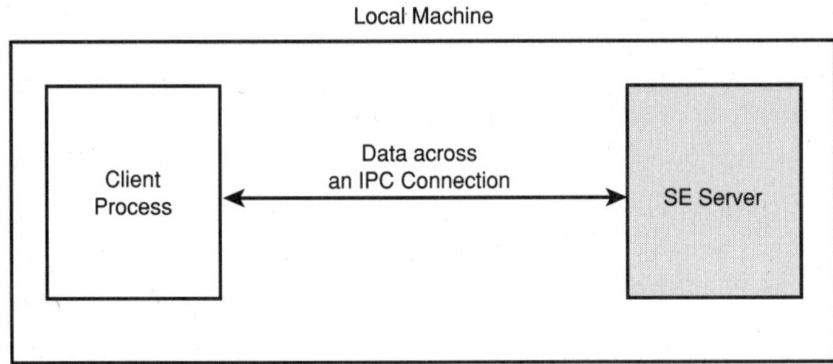

FIGURE 5.1.
A client process connected to an SE server by UNIX IPCs.

When multiple clients are connected to the server, there are also multiple IPC connections. As shown in Figure 5.2, SE's server must be able to handle many different client applications at the same time. To reduce the amount of processing required by the server, users can build a mid-process for client connections.

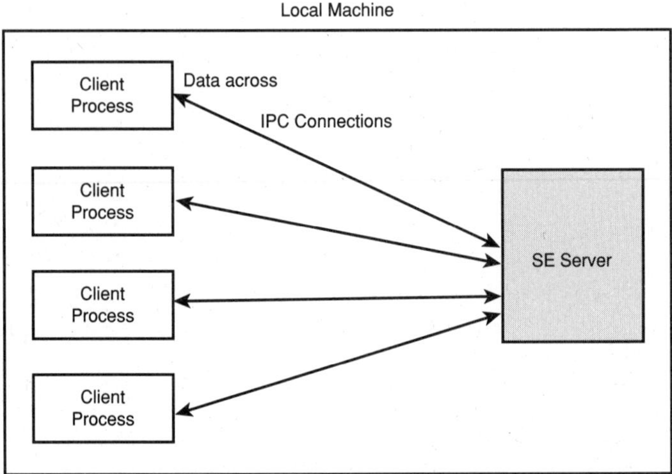

FIGURE 5.2.
Multiple client processes connected to an SE server by UNIX IPCs.

Called a *two-tier client/server system,* clients connect and disconnect from processes that perform specific tasks. If multiple users are running the same client program, when database activity is needed, the client programs connect to a specific middle process that has an IPC connection with SE already established. That middle process sends the SQL to and receives the results from the SE server. The middle process then sends the results back to the client and drops the communication with the client but maintains its connection to the server. Figure 5.3 shows multiple clients connected to specific task middle processes that are connected to the SE server. Communication between the middle process and the client is usually achieved through transaction processing software.

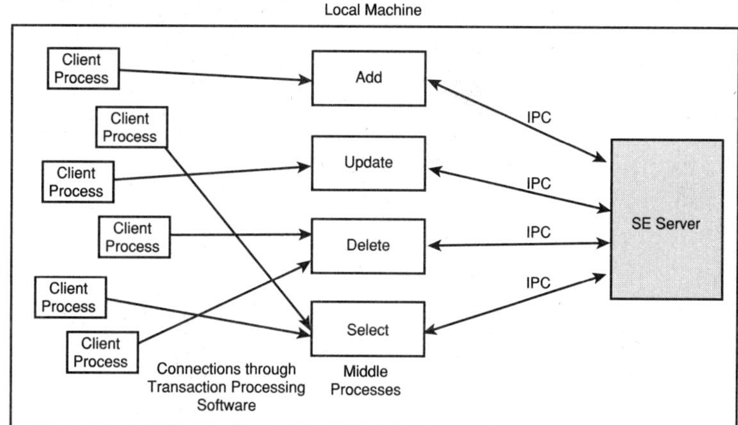

FIGURE 5.3.
Clients accessing an SE server through task-specific middle processes.

The file system access performed by SE is also achieved through UNIX. Each table is stored as a UNIX file. When data in that table is needed, SE makes a call to native UNIX file utilities to perform the work. Backup and restores are also done through INFORMIX-SE programs using UNIX file system utilities.

The table file is possibly three separate UNIX files for each table in the database. A `.DAT` file contains the actual row-by-row data contained in the table. An `.IDX` file contains the index on the table by data key and index configuration. A third file is an `.LOK` file, used to keep track of locks; this file exists only when locks are held.

Summary

Most small- to medium-sized companies don't need database systems that are extremely large, but they do have enough data to exceed the storage limitations of personal desktop computers. Moreover, these companies might have enough concurrent users to exceed a network of desktop computers. INFORMIX-SE provides a UNIX, minicomputer, multiuser solution to handle these database needs.

Requiring little maintenance while providing high reliability, INFORMIX-SE furnishes a powerful relational database management system. With its natural client/server architecture, SE provides processing beyond batch and single-user access. Many different types of client access are provided by SE, all using Structured Query Language (SQL).

Because SE is UNIX-based, the amount of database administration is minimal. A system administrator who manages the hardware and operating system can also manage INFORMIX-SE.

All the functionality found in INFORMIX-SE is also found in Informix's later server products—INFORMIX-OnLine, INFORMIX-OnLine Dynamic Server, and INFORMIX-OnLine Universal Server. This enables companies to start out with small database systems and then grow, gaining a more powerful system with new features without losing functionality originally found in SE. Chapters 6, "INFORMIX-OnLine," 7, "INFORMIX-OnLine Dynamic Server," and 8, "INFORMIX-Universal Server," contain more information about these more powerful database servers and the functionality that they contain beyond the basics found in INFORMIX-SE.

CHAPTER

INFORMIX-OnLine

by John McNally

IN THIS CHAPTER

This chapter provides

- A description of INFORMIX-OnLine and its advantages
- Uses for INFORMIX-OnLine
- Limitations of INFORMIX-OnLine
- Differences between Standard Engine and OnLine
- A detailed description of OnLine's two-process system architecture
- An explanation of how INFORMIX-STAR and INFORMIX-NET open network and data distribution options for OnLine systems

What Is INFORMIX-OnLine?

INFORMIX-OnLine is the follow-up and enhancement to the Standard Engine product. Originally a UNIX product, OnLine has been ported to almost all current UNIX system machines, and it is even available for the Windows NT platform. Released in the late 1980s, OnLine is Informix's answer to the business world's need to use online transaction processing (OLTP) technology to add more users without retrieval time increases and allow for a growth in data storage with a minimal amount of down time and data loss.

When most people think of online, they think of a person connected via a local computer, through a network or phone line, to a central main computer, as shown in Figure 6.1. This main computer is usually larger than the user's computer, with a lot of processing power. The location of this main computer can be a local site in the same city or a remote site across the country.

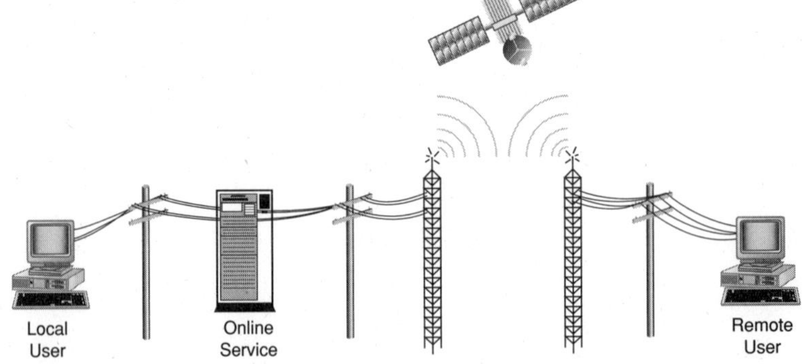

FIGURE 6.1.
Local and remote users connected to an online service.

INFORMIX-OnLine is based on this same concept; it acts as the online service on the main computer. OnLine is actually a continuously running program on a main computer; this program is known as a *database server* or an *engine*. This engine controls how the data is stored, retrieved, physically maintained on the computer, and presented logically to users—all done within the rules of the relational database model. Therefore, Informix's database server engine is actually a relational database management system (RDBMS). Refer to Chapter 3, "Database Concepts," for more information on database management systems and relational models.

The server engine, shown in Figure 6.2, also provides a way that the outside users can connect to the server's relational database and request tasks to be performed on the data. This user task is called a *client process.* Multiple users can connect to the engine at the same time. Users can also connect from the same computer or from a remote computer via a network or a modem, as shown in Figure 6.3.

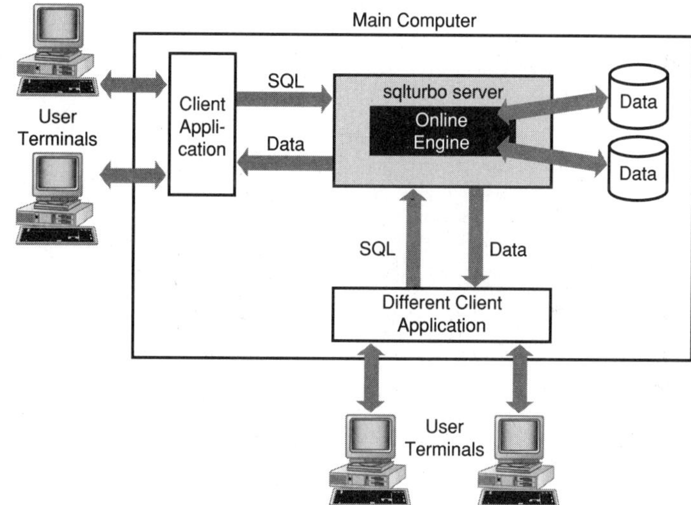

FIGURE 6.2.
A main computer running the INFORMIX-OnLine server engine.

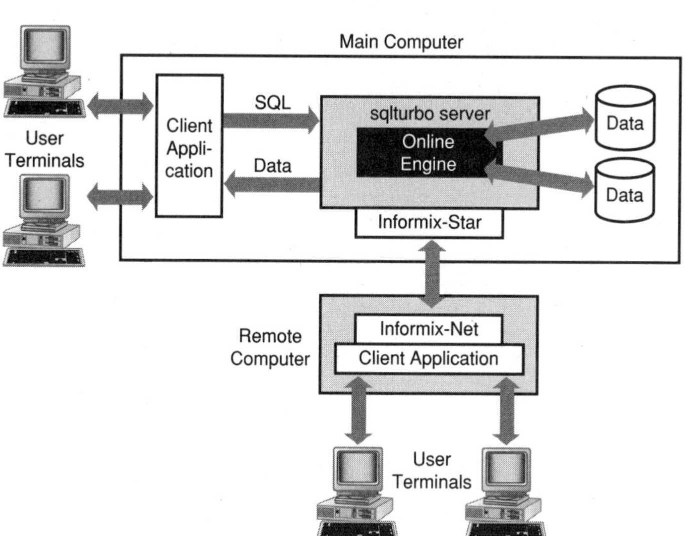

FIGURE 6.3.
Local and remote users connected to the main computer running INFORMIX-OnLine.

The complete client/server relationship is what makes INFORMIX-OnLine an online transaction processing server, where each transaction is related to a single client's tasks. For example, a client requests Informix to change 10 phone numbers in 10 different database accounts. The update to these 10 accounts is considered one transaction. The transaction is not complete until all 10 accounts change. Other client processes are unable to access these 10 accounts until the first client's transaction is complete. This type of built-in logic allows many clients to access the database at the same time without causing data confusion.

With all the processing power of the OLTP server, Informix can provide a higher-performance database system while controlling data reliability and consistency. INFORMIX-OnLine achieves better performance by building its own I/O and multiprocessor routines. Rather than use the UNIX operating system routines, Informix takes control of disk and CPU management to achieve faster, more efficient results.

The I/O routines, called *direct memory access* (DMA), allow Informix to write from memory directly to disk, and vice versa for reading. Built-in UNIX buffering is skipped entirely.

DMA works with raw disk devices only. A raw disk device is one that was not configured or formatted to represent a UNIX file system. Informix uses raw disk devices to control how data is stored on the disks. UNIX does not always allocate space contiguously, which causes a problem when working with sequential indexes. OnLine solves that problem by creating its own storage system to work on the raw disk devices.

OnLine also performs CPU management to take advantage of multiprocessor machines. More efficient than UNIX 's or NT's CPU management, Informix is capable of setting specific CPUs to work on single processes or subprocesses only. The CPU does not share its time between multiple processes, which is the default for the UNIX and NT CPU managers. In those managers, each CPU is given multiple processes to work on, each a little bit at a time, pausing on one process to work a little on the next. With OnLine's manager, most processes are handled in the same way, a little bit at a time; however, in some cases, OnLine will tell the CPU to work exclusively on a specific process or processes. This management allows for some subprocesses, such as sorting and resource access, to be performed at the same time on different CPUs, even though both of these subprocess tasks are part of the same process. The CPU manager can also assign specific client processes directly to specific CPUs rather than assign all processing to one CPU. Spreading out processes across multiple CPUs prevents more than one process from being swapped in and out of a single CPU—instead of giving each process a part of the single CPU's time slice.

Keeping databases available all the time and maintaining safe data are two important priorities of Informix. Therefore, the capability to mirror all vital information is standard with OnLine. When one drive is unavailable, OnLine automatically uses its mirror. The switch to the mirrored drive is transparent to the user. In the event that OnLine does go down because of a system or hardware crash, OnLine has built-in logging and archiving to help get the database back up as quickly as possible.

Uses

Here are some possible uses for INFORMIX-OnLine:

- Manage accounts receivable
- Catalog scans of baseball cards
- Act as an ordering system
- Catalog satellite images
- Store legal documents

The most common use of INFORMIX-OnLine is a standard business-related database. These databases contain information about mundane employee data as well as vital money-making information such as sales lead lists. INFORMIX-OnLine's flexibility makes it able to fulfill most of the needs of a business's information systems departments.

To grow with technology, INFORMIX-OnLine offers a wide array of uses beyond the standard accounts-receivable or ordering types of database systems. OnLine can store special data types such as date and time, in addition to character, numeric, or combination types. INFORMIX-OnLine also can store multimedia files such as images and sound, and it can store entire documents and large text files without reformatting.

These special data types that store files, images, and sounds are called *blobs* in INFORMIX-OnLine. Blob is an acronym for *binary large object*. It's not an object in the object-oriented paradigm, but it's a single entity. TIFF, GIF, or JPG image files or MPEG, AVI, or QuickTime movie files are quite large and in a non-ASCII format. These file types are considered binary objects. INFORMIX-OnLine can catalog these types of files in a database. The same can be said of a database that stores the print files of bills sent to customers. If you need a reprint, the client application retrieves the bill from INFORMIX-OnLine and then reprints it. No conversion from one format to another is necessary.

Limitations

Although INFORMIX-OnLine is a powerful database system, it does have some limitations. One limitation that was solved in the next family of Informix products, Dynamic Server, is the lack of a built-in wait queue in OnLine. This decreases throughput because too many clients attach to the server at one time. OnLine tries to process each client at the same time, which causes the machine's CPUs to constantly switch between client processes, trying to perform the requested task within a CPU time slice. The maximum number of clients depends on what type of machine OnLine is running. Instead of upgrading to Dynamic Server, you can build a midpoint process using transaction processing middleware such as INFORMIX-TP/XA or third-party software such as Tuxedo between the client and server. This midpoint process then filters clients' requests into a queue to limit the connections to the server. See the section "OLTP

Applications" in Chapter 34, "Application Development Introduction," for more information on OLTP alternatives.

OnLine is limited in how it handles bad sectors in a disk platter. Disk checks and management are performed by the UNIX operating system, but all other disk I/O is done by OnLine. When a disk contains bad sectors due to a hardware or software problem, rather than avoid the bad sectors, OnLine stops using the entire logical partition of the disk that contains the problem. OnLine is also unable to provide any information to the administrator about where the problem resides beyond the logical partition. OnLine actually shuts itself down if the logical partition contains system tables or logs. One alternative is to mirror all important system and database disks. Disk mirroring allows OnLine to continue processing as long as one of the twin partitions does not contain bad sectors.

Another limitation of OnLine is how it handles the multimedia blobs. There are no built-in processes to scan and insert binary objects into a file. All multimedia files must be created or scanned through an outside application such as a draw program or digital cameras and scanners. There is also no way for OnLine to automatically compress and uncompress blobs or save and retrieve requests. Compression, if needed, must be built into the client application before the object is inserted into the database, and similarly, an uncompress must be done after the compressed object is retrieved from the database.

Differences Between INFORMIX-Standard Engine and INFORMIX-OnLine

Because OnLine is meant for larger databases on larger machines, the differences between it and Standard Engine (SE) are important. SE was designed for small companies to store their internal databases, whereas OnLine was created for the corporate-level type of database. Although SE is a relational database management system with the capability for client/server processing just like OnLine, SE is not an OLTP system. OnLine does continue to provide the functionality such as logging, security, locking, triggers, and stored procedures that were originally provided by SE. Major differences between the two database systems are a result of the size and OLTP options available in OnLine, as shown in Table 6.1.

Table 6.1. Differences between SE and OnLine.

INFORMIX-SE	*INFORMIX-OnLine*
Small databases	Large databases
Manual recovery	Automatic recovery
Requires little administration	Requires full-time administration
Does not use shared memory	Uses shared memory

INFORMIX-SE	INFORMIX-OnLine
	Automatic data consistency
	Quick performance
	Crucial availability
	Supports distributed databases
	Stores multimedia data types

Important data with high availability needs should be placed on an OnLine system. OnLine has a better data safety mechanism built in than SE. OnLine also automatically fixes and rebuilds the data after a hardware crash.

Due to SE's small size, the computer administrator can also act as the database administrator when needed. OnLine's complexity and size require more of a DBA's time for daily and weekly monitoring.

Database tables on an SE system shouldn't exceed 10,000 rows. OnLine can have much larger tables, and it also can have more of them. Multiple databases and tables can be on a local machine or distributed on different machines. OnLine also offers the capability to store multimedia data.

Two-Process System Architecture

Understanding that INFORMIX-OnLine is an OLTP client/server relational database management system is one thing; understanding how it works is another. INFORMIX-OnLine uses the two-process architecture to create a natural client/server system. Users or users' processes, also known as *clients*, can connect to a database by going through standard UNIX pipes, called *interprocess communications*, or *IPCs*. Each client/server connection uses two one-way pipes, one for sending and the other for receiving, as shown in Figure 6.4. Because UNIX is such an open environment, it doesn't make a difference to Informix whether this user connection is from a machine far away or from a machine in the same room.

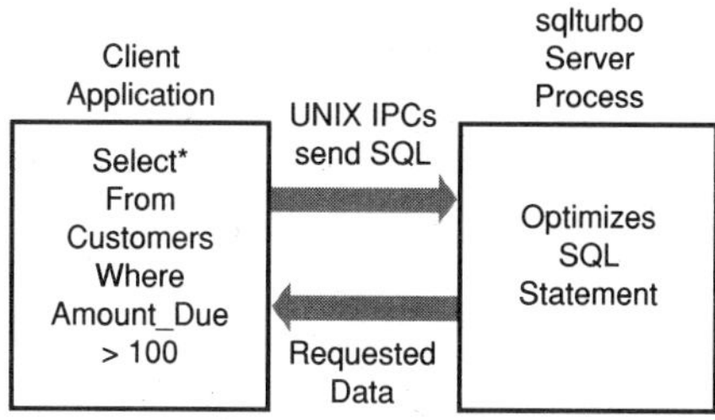

FIGURE 6.4.
A user client application sending SQL to a `sqlturbo` *server process.*

All client connections contain SQL statements to perform some kind of task on the database. Refer to Chapter 28, "INFORMIX-SQL," for more information on SQL and its relationship to databases. The SQL statements are received from the client by the server process, which is called a `sqlturbo`. Each client process has its own `sqlturbo` link into the OnLine database.

Each `sqlturbo` server process is actually four subprocesses running as one, as shown in Figure 6.5. The first subprocess handles the communication to and from the client. It also communicates with the next subsystem, the SQL parser.

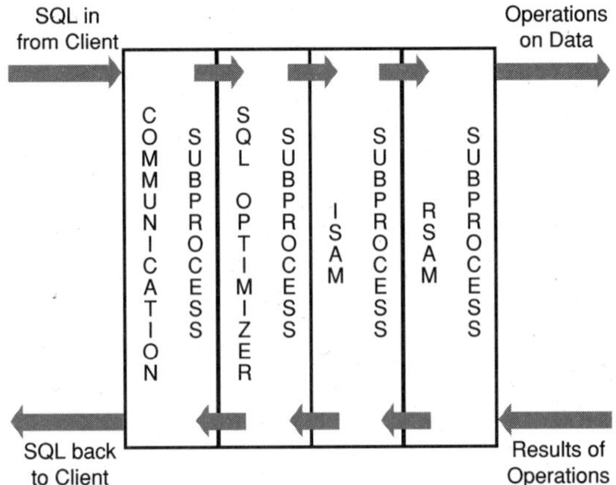

FIGURE 6.5.
A `sqlturbo` *server process and its four subprocesses interacting with each other.*

Because the client sent its request in the form of SQL, the SQL Optimizer must parse these SQL statements into individual tasks. After they are optimized and converted to more machine-like tasks, the statements are placed into a query plan and passed to the next subprocess, the Indexed Sequential Access Method (ISAM) library. The ISAM library contains the basic I/O functions to perform reads, writes, verifies, commits, and so on.

These functions are performed on the actual physical storage devices by the last subprocess, the Random Sequential Access Method library, or RSAM library. The ISAM functions know what to perform, but the RSAM functions know how. The RSAM functions are what interact with the *OnLine System.*

The OnLine System controls and manages the data. Up and running at all times, the OnLine System fulfills the client's requests while maintaining the integrity and order of the stored data.

Figure 6.6 shows the three major parts to the OnLine System. The first is the UNIX daemons (pronounced "demons"). OnLine has three different types of daemons running in the background. These daemons keep the data in order, making sure everything is cleaned up after a client makes changes. This ensures that even after a crash, the data is complete. These daemons usually perform cleaning tasks at certain intervals, called checkpoints, or when the data changes extensively. OnLine uses a *checkpoint* as a clean starting point to apply changes to the database after a system crash.

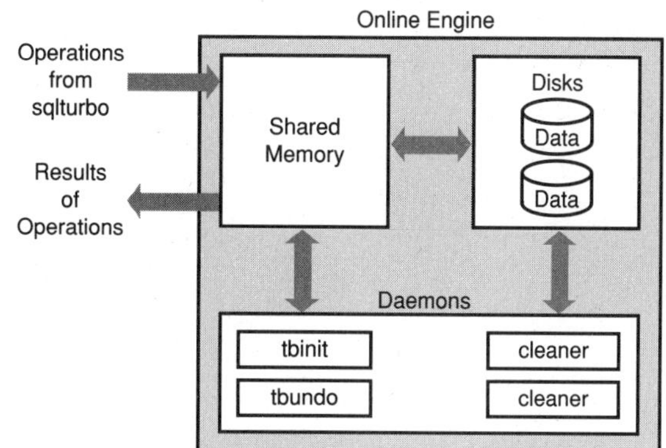

FIGURE 6.6.
The OnLine System and its three parts.

The main daemon, the `TBINIT` process, is created when OnLine is started. The `TBINIT` process is responsible for managing shared-memory and disk space. Another responsibility of the `TBINIT` process is to manage the other two daemons—`TBUNDO` and `TBPGCL`. The `TBUNDO` daemon process cleans up or continues the task of a `sqlturbo` server process after it dies or loses the connection to OnLine. The last daemon process, `TBPGCL`, is commonly called the page cleaner. Its task is to periodically check shared memory for a major amount of data change. Unlike `TBINIT` and `TBUNDO`, there can be multiple `TBPGCL`s running within OnLine. It's recommended that one page cleaner runs for every disk used by OnLine. When needed, the page cleaner updates disk storage to represent the changes in shared memory. This updating of the disk from shared memory is known as *flushing*. Page cleaner daemons also flush data at DBA-set increments called checkpoints. For more information on page cleaners and checkpoints, see Chapter 23, "Tuning Your Informix Environment."

The second part of the OnLine System is shared memory. This is where all the changes to the data are made and retrieved. When INFORMIX-OnLine is installed and set up, the shared memory size is one of the most important configuration components. Not designating enough shared memory requires a lot of I/O to and from physical storage. Designating too much shared memory requires major cleaning at each checkpoint by the daemon processes. Refer to Chapter 11, "Configuring the Informix Environment," for more information on the amount of shared memory needed.

A copy of the data pages, usually the most active and recently used pages, resides in shared memory. When a client process requests that an action be performed on a specific data item, it is performed within shared memory.

The last part of the OnLine System is physical storage. Dedicated for OnLine's use only are disks where a clean untouched copy of the database resides. The daemon cleaners update the copy on disk when the daemon cleaners feel that the active copy of the data in shared memory differs from what's on disk.

The entire process, shown in Figure 6.7, consists of a client process creating SQL to perform a task on the database. The client uses an IPC to send the SQL to a `sqlturbo` server process. That server optimizes the SQL statement and performs the individual SQL tasks on the copy of the data in shared memory of the OnLine System. If the data is not in shared memory, the OnLine System retrieves the information needed from disk and places it in shared memory. After the tasks are performed, the `sqlturbo` server sends the results back to the client. During a routine checkpoint or special cleaning, the daemons of the OnLine System make sure the data in shared memory is updated to disk.

As described in the last paragraph, shared memory is an important part of the OnLine System. Shared memory is a concept created in the UNIX environment to allow different processes to share the same data at the same time. This gives OnLine the capability to have each incoming client/server process look in the same area for data, rather than having each process manage its own resources to access data on disk and to maintain its own memory area in which to store that data.

Not only does this give the `sqlturbo` server less to do, but it also makes it easier for the OnLine System to maintain data integrity. The only versions of the data are the original on disk and the working copy in shared memory. Disk I/O is also reduced because the most popular data pages are already in shared memory and new server processes won't require the OnLine System to swap new pages in from disk into shared memory and vice versa.

Understanding how each component of the OnLine client/server relationship works and how data is passed along to the next component is necessary when investigating problems. Tracking a client's SQL statements from end to end helps determine system bottlenecks. Each client's SQL or group of SQL statements is considered a single database transaction.

These are the steps in a standard database transaction:

1. The client sends a request for a task to be performed.

   The task is in the form of SQL.
2. UNIX IPCs start an `sqlturbo` process.
3. The communication subsystem of the `sqlturbo` acknowledges that the client's task is received.
4. The communication subsystem then sends the received information to the SQL subsystem.
5. The SQL subsystem parses the SQL statement into individual tasks, placing these tasks into the most optimal order for processing.
6. The SQL subsystem then passes this optimal order list to the ISAM library subsection.
7. The ISAM library processes each task in the list one at a time.
8. When a task is required to interact with the database, the ISAM library calls the appropriate low-level function residing in the RSAM library subsection.

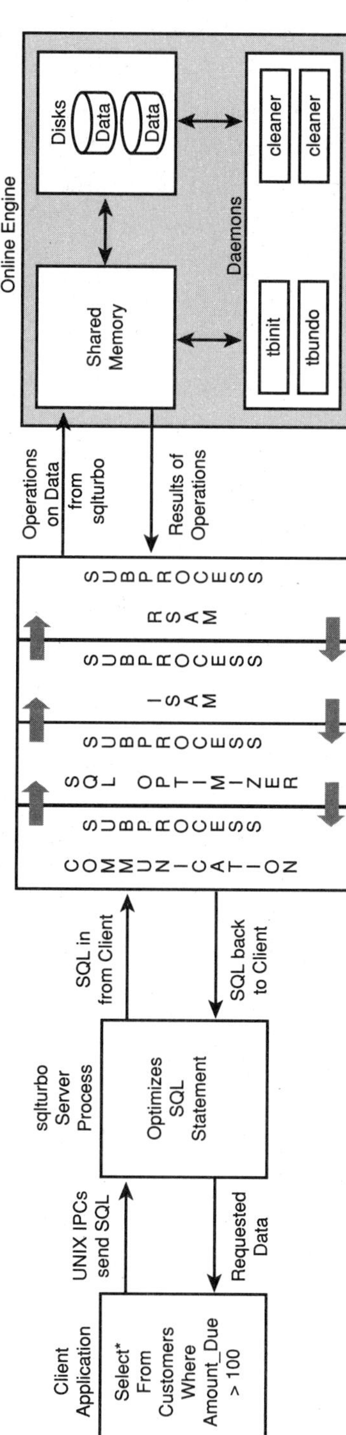

FIGURE 6.7.
A client process connected to the `sqlturbo` *server, which is connected to the OnLine System.*

9. The RSAM library's functions connect with the OnLine System's shared memory area.
10. If the data requested is not in shared memory, the OnLine System daemon swaps data pages between shared memory and disk.
11. When the RSAM function has performed its task within the OnLine System, the next ISAM function is performed.
12. After all the ISAM/RSAM tasks are performed, the SQL subsection receives the results of the tasks and puts them in an order that the client can understand.
13. The SQL subsection sends the formatted results to the communication subsection.
14. The communication subsection sends these results back to the client.
15. Daemons in the OnLine System clean and maintain the shared memory and disk areas while the client/`sqlturbo` processes also access the OnLine System.

Networking with INFORMIX-NET and INFORMIX-STAR

The capability to network remote users in an OnLine database or distributed data is not included within the standard OnLine software. The two additional software systems you need are INFORMIX-STAR to provide distributed database support and INFORMIX-NET to provide support for remote users to access INFORMIX-OnLine servers across a network. Remember that local servers need INFORMIX-STAR only if they share data with other servers or act as a remote server for a client over a network that is running INFORMIX-NET.

INFORMIX-STAR

INFORMIX-STAR enables OnLine servers to share data with other servers that are also using INFORMIX-STAR. This data sharing is a concept known as *distributed database technology*. Many companies have different databases on different machines that are maintained by different divisions within the company. Distributed database technology allows information from these individual machines to be available to each other, without maintaining multiple copies of each database.

Within one SQL statement, client processes can query and update data on any of the databases within the INFORMIX-STAR network, as long as they have read and write privileges on the remote databases. The client processes don't communicate directly with the other database; it's the local server that does. The local server knows that specific data is stored on remote servers. When activity to be performed on one of these remote databases is requested by a client application, the client's local server connects to the proper remote server and requests that the task be performed.

The connection between the two servers, as shown in Figure 6.8, is done through a `sqlexecd` daemon process. This `sqlexecd` process is essential to the INFORMIX-STAR network. Every INFORMIX-STAR server must have a `sqlexecd` process available for every other INFORMIX-STAR server it needs to communicate with. Not only does the `sqlexecd` process make sure that all incoming and outgoing requests are processed, but it also makes sure that OnLine's standard of automatic recovery is maintained. If one of the INFORMIX-STAR servers crashes, not only does OnLine's recovery apply the local changes since the last checkpoint, but when INFORMIX-STAR reconnects to the other servers, it also applies any changes needed on the remote databases.

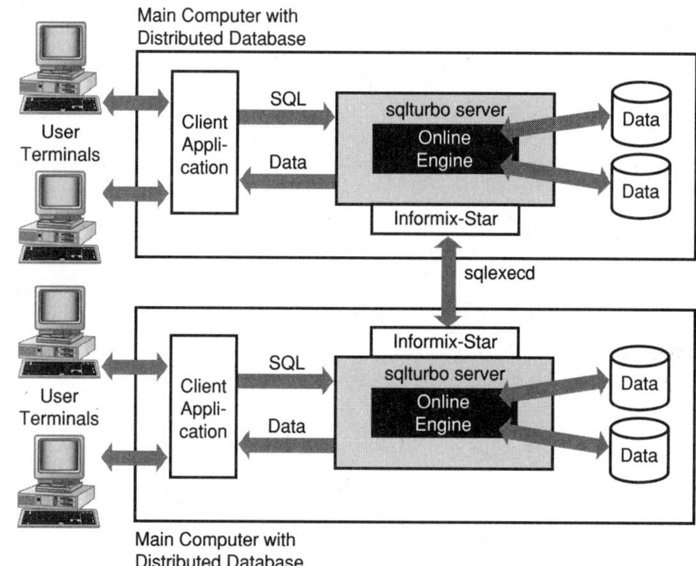

FIGURE 6.8.
Local clients connected to an INFORMIX-STAR server that is connected to another INFORMIX-STAR server.

INFORMIX-NET

The other Informix network product is INFORMIX-NET. As shown in Figure 6.9, INFORMIX-NET is needed on the client applications that want to access remote database servers across a network. INFORMIX-NET client applications can access only remote OnLine servers that have INFORMIX-STAR running. This differs in an SE environment; INFORMIX-STAR is not necessary, but INFORMIX-NET is used at both ends of the client-to-SE-server connection. Remember that client applications that run on the same system as the OnLine server do not need INFORMIX-NET.

There are many advantages in using INFORMIX-NET. First, the client application can act as a single entity, thus reducing the OnLine server's processing requirements and network traffic. All the data processing is done on the client machine, not on the server. In most cases, the client applications and OnLine run on the same machine, causing the CPUs of that machine to constantly work. With INFORMIX-NET clients, the server machine can concentrate on just being a database server. Refer to Chapter 13, "Advanced Configurations," for ways to achieve machine task independence by using other network software or two-tier client/server configurations.

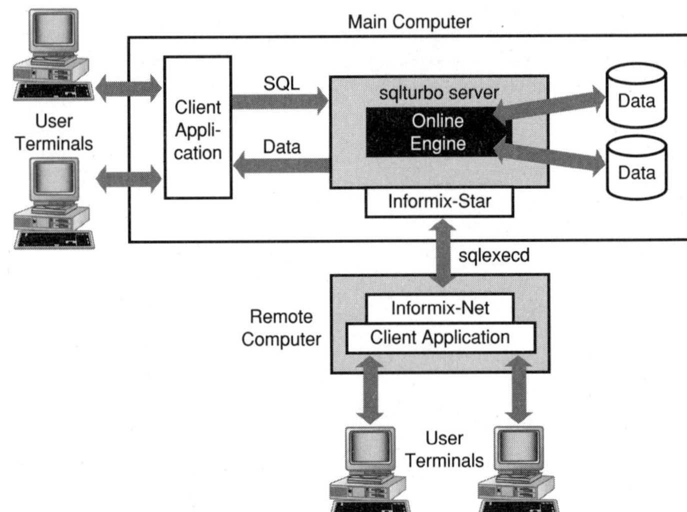

FIGURE 6.9.
Local and remote clients connected to an INFORMIX-STAR server.

Not only does the client application use its CPU to process the data, but it also performs some of the optimizing usually done by the `sqlturbo` process. Before sending the SQL statement to the OnLine server across the `sqlexecd` connection, INFORMIX-NET organizes and optimizes just like the `sqlturbo` does. In this way, only the bare machine-like tasks are sent across the network, rather than the entire SQL statement in user-readable form. This reduces both network activity and processing activity by the OnLine server.

The second advantage is that INFORMIX-NET runs on many different platforms over many different transfer protocols. Currently, INFORMIX-NET is available on every known UNIX platform, and it is also available for PC DOS and Windows. The OnLine/INFORMIX-STAR server still resides on a UNIX machine, but it does not care what the client runs on as long as the network protocol is the same.

INFORMIX-NET supports the standard network communication protocol, which is Transmission Control Protocol/Internet Protocol (TCP/IP). Therefore, any client machine with TCP/IP or socket calls can communicate with any remote OnLine/INFORMIX-STAR servers and their distributed data on other connected remote OnLine/INFORMIX-STAR servers.

Using INFORMIX-STAR and INFORMIX-NET Together

Businesses can set up client applications in many different sites on different platforms that all require the same database information. With only the delay of communication connections as an impact on the user, through INFORMIX-STAR and INFORMIX-NET connections to the remote database server are made without any extra effort by the user or by the client application providing access for the user. When the remote database is also distributed, the client's request might travel even further across a network to obtain the needed data. By combining INFORMIX-STAR and INFORMIX-NET with OnLine as shown in Figure 6.10, you can create an endless number of solutions for any business's needs with minimal impact to the user.

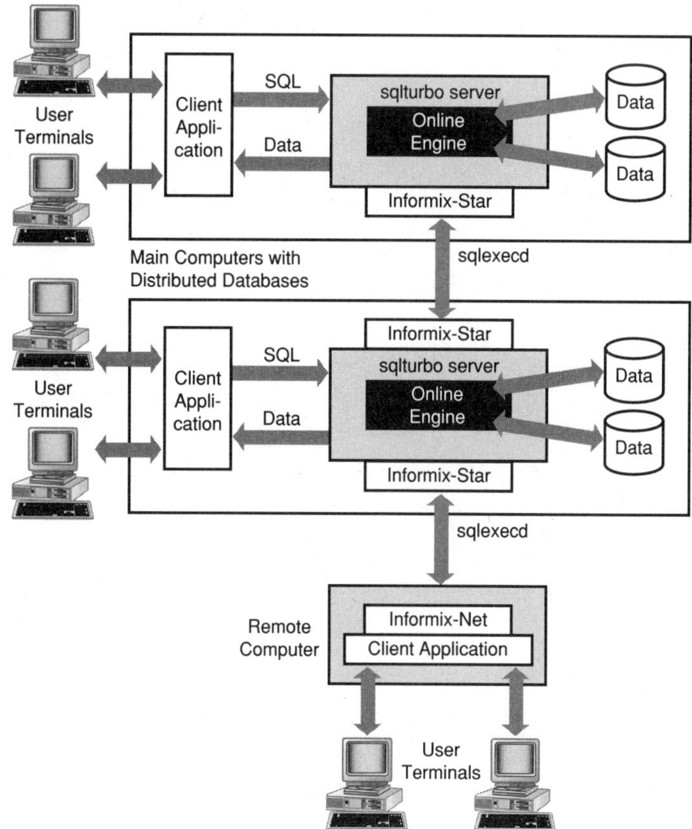

FIGURE 6.10.
A combination of INFORMIX-NET clients, INFORMIX-STAR servers, and INFORMIX-STAR servers connected to other INFORMIX-STAR servers, with and without local clients.

Many companies have needs that go beyond the scope of a standard client/server database management system. Here are possible scenarios where you use INFORMIX-NET and INFORMIX-STAR with INFORMIX-OnLine:

- A remote client (INFORMIX-NET) accesses OnLine database (INFORMIX-STAR) with or without local clients.
- Local clients have access to a local OnLine server and a remote server through the local server (INFORMIX-STAR to INFORMIX-STAR).
- Combinations of the preceding scenarios.

Summary

INFORMIX-OnLine is a powerful OLTP client/server database management system for medium to large businesses. Building on the functionality started with INFORMIX-SE, OnLine adds more security and safety to data handling. OnLine uses its own I/O file system to increase the speed and efficiency of data access. Shared memory provides an area for OnLine to work on data while maintaining a safe copy on disk.

OnLine can store data beyond the normal character and number. With its ability to store blobs, OnLine can store multimedia objects such as images and sounds.

Networking and distributing data with INFORMIX-NET and INFORMIX-STAR increases the usability of OnLine. With these products, OnLine is able to handle more users from farther distances and allow access to data on different OnLine systems.

CHAPTER 7

INFORMIX-OnLine Dynamic Server

by John McNally

IN THIS CHAPTER

This chapter provides

- A description of INFORMIX-OnLine Dynamic Server and its advantages
- An explanation of the new Dynamic Scalable Architecture
- Uses for INFORMIX-OnLine Dynamic Server
- Limitations of INFORMIX-OnLine Dynamic Server
- Differences between Dynamic Server and the previous version of OnLine
- A detailed listing of standard and new functionality provided by INFORMIX-OnLine Dynamic Server
- A detailed description of Dynamic Server's multithreaded architecture
- A complete listing of each virtual processor and its uses
- An explanation of how Dynamic Server replaces the way it performs client/server connections locally and remotely over a network

What Is OnLine Dynamic Server?

As with INFORMIX-SE and INFORMIX-OnLine, INFORMIX-OnLine Dynamic Server is a relational database management system (RDBMS) that provides client/server processing. Where INFORMIX-OnLine stops in functionality is where Dynamic Server continues. Version 5 was the last release of OnLine. Version 6 was a transitional release of OnLine that included some new dynamic features. The current version, 7, contains the complete OnLine Dynamic Server. The additional functionality is what the term *dynamic* refers to. It is Dynamic Server's capability to change its configuration through its Dynamic Server Architecture, when needed, without affecting the clients or taking the system offline. Dynamic Server also increases processing while lowering overhead with its virtual processors to achieve a multithreaded architecture and parallel data queries.

Throughout the processing day, which is becoming a complete 24 hours by necessity, the activity levels fluctuate for clients accessing the database. The need for 24-hour, 7-days-a-week availability makes it hard to fit batch processing in an online transaction processing (OLTP) system running an INFORMIX-OnLine system. You cannot run batch jobs that perform mass updates, inserts, or deletes during the peak online hours. Sometimes these jobs are so large that they don't finish for hours or days.

To make the batch jobs faster or to handle the high points of OLTP users during the day, you need to make configuration changes in OnLine. The changes make the batch jobs faster, but OLTP processes might run slower and inefficiently. These configuration changes also require that OnLine be brought offline before they take effect, inconveniencing any OLTP users who are working on the system. With Dynamic Server comes a new feature to change configuration parameters without taking the database offline. Dynamic Scalable Architecture (DSA) provides the capability to add and decrease available shared memory and server processes without bouncing the database system. With Dynamic Server's DSA, batch jobs and a high amount of OLTP users do not slow the system. When these new activities start, Dynamic Server adjusts to meet the need for extra processing. When the processing level lowers, Dynamic Server relinquishes the extra resources and shared memory it grabbed to handle the strain.

Shared memory is the area in which all data activity is performed. This data is kept in shared memory by OnLine and Dynamic Server in order to keep frequently accessed and common data pages available, without performing disk I/O each time the data is needed. OnLine shared memory is restricted to a predetermined size that is allocated when OnLine is started. Dynamic Server is also started with a predetermined shared memory size but is able to increase or decrease the size, depending on memory availability and hardware limitations. This resizing can be automatically changed by Dynamic Server or by an administrator. These changes can occur at any time while the system is in use without affecting the current client processes actively using the database.

There is a lot of processing overhead involved with keeping shared memory and disk versions of the database clean, up to date, and available. Long transactions are sometimes required to swap large amounts of data off disks and into shared memory. If shared memory is not large enough to hold all the data, early data within the transaction is swapped to a temporary disk area and then more data is retrieved from disk. When the transaction is complete and committed, the changed data is then transferred back to the original disk from the temporary disk through shared memory. All this I/O can be avoided by Dynamic Server's server process's capability to make shared memory large enough to hold the entire transaction's data.

The server processes are individual jobs, known as *daemons* in OnLine, that run concurrently within the server. Dynamic Server calls these daemons *virtual processors*, and each virtual processor performs a specific task within the server. OnLine has three types of daemons: a single main process, TBINIT; a single backout process, TBUNDO; and multiple page-cleaner processes, TBPGCLs. As shown in Table 7.1, Dynamic Server has 11 classes of virtual processors to perform specific tasks, and each class can have multiple versions of itself running concurrently.

Table 7.1. Classes of virtual processors.

VP Class	*Function*
ADM	Performs administrative operations
ADT	Performs auditing operations
AIO	Performs disk-related I/O, not associated with logging
CPU	Performs main processing and starts and manages other virtual processors
LIO	Writes activity information into the logical-log file
MSC	Performs miscellaneous system calls

continues

Table 7.1. continued

VP Class	*Function*
PIO	Writes activity information into the physical-log file
OPT	Performs optical disk-related I/O, not associated with logging
SOC	Performs socket-related network communications
SHM	Communicates with shared memory
TLI	Performs TLI-related network communications

Just as shared memory can be increased or decreased by the administrator or automatically by Dynamic Server, so can the number of virtual processors. When peak processing increases beyond the normal configuration, or large batch jobs monopolize resources, Dynamic Server can change to meet these needs without hindering any other client processing.

Besides the benefit gained by dynamically changing the amount of shared memory and number of virtual processors, Dynamic Server benefits from having many individually tasked virtual processors. Using a "divide-and-conquer" technique to break down processing, Dynamic Server first separates into the individual virtual processors. Second, each virtual processor has its own processes to perform subtasks, called *threads*. Threads are very specialized, small tasks to be performed. A virtual processor is considered a multithreaded process, because it manages many threads at the same time that all require the same type of processing.

Threads are actually pieces of client or system task instructions. A system task is a client process that performs a job required by OnLine but is not started by a user's client process, such as a checkpoint-initiated page cleaning. In OnLine, each client and system task has its own daemon called a `sqlturbo`. Each `sqlturbo` represented a one-to-one connection between the client and the server that had to be managed by the CPU and processed in shared memory. The virtual processors of Dynamic Server can handle many threads from many client and system tasks at the same time, reducing the amount of CPU and shared memory management needed.

When a virtual processor cannot handle any more threads, another virtual processor in the same class automatically runs to manage the extra threads. This prevents threads from waiting for the first virtual processor to become free. When the system load decreases, the extra virtual processors end.

On a multi-CPU computer system, Dynamic Server allows for a specific virtual processor to be associated with a specific CPU. Referred to as processor affinity, it allows a specific process to run only on a designated CPU and on no others. A CPU class virtual processor has the capability to be bound to a specific CPU, which prevents other CPU class virtual processors from using the CPU. The bound virtual processor's performance is greatly improved because it does not have to fight for a CPU time slice and it does not have to swap its information in and out when other CPU class virtual processors need the CPU.

CPU class virtual processors can break a thread's subtask into even smaller parts. Thread tasks that require activity such as sequential queries, loads and unloads, indexing, joins, and sorting can be done with multiple threads working in parallel. Known as the parallel database query (PDQ) feature, it provides an efficient way to use more resources for a short period, rather than use one resource for a longer period of time.

Dynamic Server's memory grant manager (MGM) is what allows the degree of parallelism. The MGM works with the cost-based optimizer to ensure that parallelism is used whenever possible without utilizing all available resources. The cost-based optimizer is a feature, originally from OnLine, that determines the best possible way to retrieve and store data.

Partitioning table data increases the opportunities to use PDQ. With this fragmentation, Dynamic Server allows tables to be physically spread across multiple disks. Rather than start a table in one disk and sequentially spread it in that disk's space, Dynamic Server can store the table by specific key values, where each key value or range of values has its row stored on a specific disk. If a table contains customer information and it is fragmented between two disks, the fragmentation strategy could be to have one disk hold all the rows for customers added before a specific date and the other disk contain the customer's rows on or after that specific date. When working with fragment tables, Dynamic Server processes the intelligence to realize where to get the data it needs. With the customers separated by date, Dynamic Server skips over the partition that does not contain the correct date range and proceeds right to the other partition. When looking for a date range that spans both partitions, Dynamic Server searches both partitions in parallel.

Uses

Dynamic Server has the same use that OnLine has, to store business-related data, but it can do it faster, safer, and on larger amounts of data. Business databases have become large and sophisticated as technology makes advances in tools used to build client applications. Many companies use UNIX-based minicomputers and networks to replace the old mainframes. Not only does this migration from mainframes require new client applications, but new databases are needed to store the vast amounts of data once contained in these older systems. Companies are now realizing that having their data more accessible allows them to create all types of applications to use it, which were impossible to build when the data was stored in the old MVS system. This makes the data more valuable. The following examples of high-availability databases illustrate some possible uses for INFORMIX-OnLine Dynamic Server:

- Manage a hospital's patient care system.
- Act as a 24-hour ordering system.
- Serve data on the World Wide Web.
- Store and provide data for an airline reservation system.
- Track information and pictures of criminals nationwide.

Dynamic Server is a more powerful database system than the ones that run on the old mainframes. It can handle OLTP system requirements while maintaining millions of data items. Dynamic Server can actually maintain more than four billion rows per table fragment and more than two thousand fragments per table. Of course, achieving these numbers is possible as long as hardware is available to store all this data. The lack of hardware shouldn't be an issue because memory and storage come at a lower cost than some software products.

On the old mainframe systems, access to the data was not quick enough to merit elaborate client applications. Many large banks, airlines, and telecommunication companies still have examples of these old systems. As these companies create graphical user interface (GUI) applications to replace and combine the old systems, the need for data is greater and the hours it's needed are longer. Many databases must be available 24 hours a day, 7 days a week. When databases are down, millions of dollars are lost due to customers waiting and employees staring at blank screens.

Dynamic Server maintains the functionality created with OnLine to provide fast recovery after an unexpected system failure. However, OnLine requires expected down times to do backups and configuration changes. With Dynamic Server, there is less need for scheduled down times. You can do backups and configuration changes while the database is online and clients access the data.

Limitations

As described in Chapter 6, "INFORMIX-OnLine," there are three limitations found in OnLine. Two of these limitations are also contained in Dynamic Server. The first limitation is the capability to handle bad sectors and the second is the lack of blob management. The third limitation found in OnLine, the lack of a built-in wait queue, was satisfied by Dynamic Server's multitasking parallel virtual processors.

Disk errors are still managed by the UNIX operating system. Like OnLine, Dynamic Server stops using an entire logical partition of a disk where a bad-sector error occurs. If the disk partition contains system tables, Dynamic Server shuts itself down. The only way to avoid data loss or shutdown is to mirror the partitions. Mirroring is the process of writing the same information to two different disks. When a bad-sector error occurs, Dynamic Server automatically uses the mirrored partition. Mirroring is a configurable option within Dynamic Server. It is highly recommended that you mirror the system information. Mirroring requires two disks rather than one, so mirroring all the data-related disks can be a great hardware expense. Data in high-availability systems should be mirrored.

Although there are many ways to load and retrieve multimedia blobs into Dynamic Server's databases, there are still no tools to create, collect, view, and compress them. A blob is a binary large object, which can be an executable file or a photographic image. Dynamic Server can manage this data with indexes and keys. To do anything with these objects, such as view or edit, Dynamic Server requires client applications to incorporate their own tools.

As the World Wide Web becomes a popular environment to distribute and display data, the need to manage blob data is increasing. Informix is currently working on tools to incorporate multimedia blobs within WWW pages and use Dynamic Server as the database server. It's only a matter of time before Informix solves this limitation.

Differences Between OnLine and OnLine Dynamic Server

The main reason for the differences between Dynamic Server and OnLine is all the new functionality added to Dynamic Server. They both are client/server, OLTP, relational database management systems, but Dynamic Server has more functionality and performs at a much higher level than OnLine.

Major functionality available in INFORMIX-OnLine is continued in INFORMIX-OnLine Dynamic Server. Any OnLine database can easily be switched over to Dynamic Server without requiring the upgraded system to use the new functionality. Dynamic Server can run and act just like an OnLine system and still show performance improvements because Dynamic Server uses its improved architecture to perform all its tasks.

The following list outlines the original INFORMIX-OnLine functionality continued in Dynamic Server:

- Client/server architecture: Informix naturally allows connection to the server using the Informix-built clients INFORMIX-ISQL and DBaccess, through SQL commands placed within UNIX shell programs, and through self-built clients using INFORMIX-ESQL/C, INFORMIX-ESQL/COBOL, INFORMIX-NewEra, and INFORMIX-4GL.
- High-performance OLTP: Informix allows many concurrent clients to attach to the server to perform quick transactions many times a day.
- Automatic quick recovery: Informix uses physical and logical logs to rebuild the database after a system crash and applies these logs to the database bringing it to the state it was at the last checkpoint. A checkpoint is a timed event to make sure that the database and shared memory contain the same data. Checkpoints usually occur every 10 minutes, so recovery could take 10 minutes. Archive and restore utilities were improved in Dynamic Server to take advantage of its built-in parallel capabilities.
- Raw disk management: Rather than use UNIX's disk management and the processing overhead associated with it, Informix uses its own disk management routines that minimize disk I/O and provide better organization than UNIX provides.
- Mirroring: Support to mirror the raw disks used by the server is built in. When configuring the original raw disk partition, a mirror version of that disk's data can be assigned. Dynamic Server improves mirroring by performing writes to the original and mirrored disk at the same time rather than serially, as done in OnLine.

- Structured Query Language: An enhanced version of ANSI SQL is used to tell the database server what task to perform on the data.
- Multimedia/blob support: Any binary object can be stored within the database with associated keys to index, store, and update the data.
- OnLine backup: You can perform backups of the database while the database is in use by clients. A shutdown of the server is not necessary. OnLine required that the entire database be backed up at the same time. Dynamic Server has the capability to back up and restore at the `dbspace` (disk partitions) and `blobspace` (blob disk partitions).
- Data security: You can apply many different levels of security to the data within the database, allowing specific users privileges from read, write, and delete to read-only.
- Integrity constraints: Business rules and how data relates to other data items are enforced through integrity constraints.
- Cost-based optimizer: Informix has the capability to find the best possible way to perform a database task before actually doing the task.
- Cursors: Informix provides a way to dynamically allocate SQL to create a pointer at a data item within a group of data items. The pointer can move up and down the group to perform its work.
- Deadlock management: Informix allows one update transaction to complete its work on a data item before other transactions can start their work on that same data item, which provides the capability to keep separate database transactions on the same data item from getting mixed up. It also stops the working transaction from locking out other transactions for a long time. Dynamic Server uses a new level of locking, called key value locking, to provide an increase in concurrent data access by different client processes.
- Isolations levels: Informix has the capability to allow or restrict specific client processes from reading data that other clients are currently working with.
- Networking: Informix has a built-in capability to spread client processes across a network rather than tie them directly to the machine that runs the database server. Dynamic Server does not require INFORMIX-NET and INFORMIX-STAR as did OnLine and SE.
- Distributed databases: This built-in capability gives clients access to remote databases through one local database server. Dynamic Server does not require INFORMIX-STAR as does OnLine.
- Optical disk storage: Informix has the capability to store blob data on optical disk storage devices rather than just disk and tape.
- Stored procedures: Informix provides the capability to build reusable, generic database transactions that are maintained by the database server rather than the client. It skips the transmission and optimizing steps that client SQL must go through before being processed by the server.

- Triggers: Informix lets specific events start processes within the database server.
- System Monitoring Interface (SMI) : Informix has the capability to track database administration information using SQL, `onstat`, and `oncheck`. `onstat` and `oncheck` are referred to as `tbstat` and `tbcheck` in releases prior to INFORMIX-OnLine Version 6. Extra tables and flags were added to the SMI tables and utilities to track the extra features of Dynamic Server.

New functionality in Dynamic Server improves how all other functionality performs. OnLine-created functionality is improved because of Dynamic Server's capability to dynamically allocate resources and perform tasks in parallel.

The following list outlines the new INFORMIX-OnLine Dynamic Server functionality:

- Dynamic resource allocation: Dynamic Server provides the capability to adjust resources at high and low processing points. During peak periods, administrators or Dynamic Server can automatically add more virtual processor and thread resources, if more are available, to process the extra load. At lower periods, these resources can be suspended until needed.
- Shared memory management: Dynamic Server has the capability to automatically add and increase the amount of shared memory segments needed to perform its database tasks.
- Parallelization: Dynamic Server features the capability to improve performance by processing scans, joins, and sorts on data in parallel using Parallel Database Queries (PDQ).
- Fragmentation: Dynamic Server provides the capability to spread table data and indexes across multiple disk partitions with some form of algorithm. Fragmentation increases the capability to perform PDQ tasks on the data.
- Event alarms: Just like triggers, event alarms start processes when administrative actions occur. When table space is nearly full, Dynamic Server starts an alarm or process before a problem occurs.
- Asynchronous I/O: Dynamic Server speeds up I/O processing by creating its own I/O utilities, separated into four classes— logical log, physical log, asynchronous, and kernel asynchronous I/O.
- Read ahead: Dynamic Server provides the capability to read several pages of data ahead during sequential table and index scans.
- DB/Cockpit: Dynamic Server has a graphical user interface utility that aids administrators in monitoring the database server environment. It provides a user-friendly way to set alarms and measure system resources.
- OnPerf: Dynamic Server provides a graphical user interface utility that provides information usually retrieved by the `onstat` utility.

- Cascading deletes: Dynamic Server has the capability to delete all rows related to one specific main row. With this parent/child relationship, you can set up Dynamic Server to delete all children rows when a parent is deleted.
- Communication: Although database distribution and networking is functionality that originally started with OnLine, other Informix products were required to provide the functionality completely. Dynamic Server has the functionality built in, so these products are no longer required.
- High-availability data replication: The capability to create a remote hot backup is available in Dynamic Server. You can create a second database server to maintain the same database as the original. As changes are made to the original, they are also made on the backup. When problems occur on the primary site, Dynamic Server can automatically switch all clients to use the remote backup before the primary system fails.

Dynamic Server's new functionality offers many benefits for new database systems or for upgrading database systems from previous versions of OnLine. Regardless of whether you use all the new features, Dynamic Server provides a safer, faster system than could be achieved with OnLine.

Multithreaded Architecture

As mentioned previously in this chapter, Dynamic Server can provide better performance through the new functionality designed with its Dynamic Scalable Architecture (DSA). DSA allows administrators and Dynamic Server to reduce OS overhead, memory requirements, and resource contention by changing its configuration without taking the system offline.

DSA is made possible by Dynamic Server's multithreaded architecture. Multithreading is the method of running many copies of the same process for different users without replicating the entire operating system. To the UNIX operating system, the multithreaded process is a single process.

Consider multithreading at another level: Most UNIX machines have multiple CPUs. Each of these CPUs runs multiple UNIX processes to keep track of the multiple users logged onto the machine. As shown in Figure 7.1, one CPU might be processing three users' processes—`ls`, `cat`, and `ls`—at the same time, while another CPU is handling other users and their processes. The CPU processing the `ls`, `cat`, and the other `ls` command can be considered a multithread process because it's one CPU handling three tasks. These three tasks—`ls`, `cat`, and `ls`—can be considered threads.

A thread is a piece of work being performed, a sequence of instructions executed within a program. Multiple threads can be the same, such as two `ls` commands, or different, such as `ls` and `cat`. But if they run within the same process or CPU, it is considered multithreading.

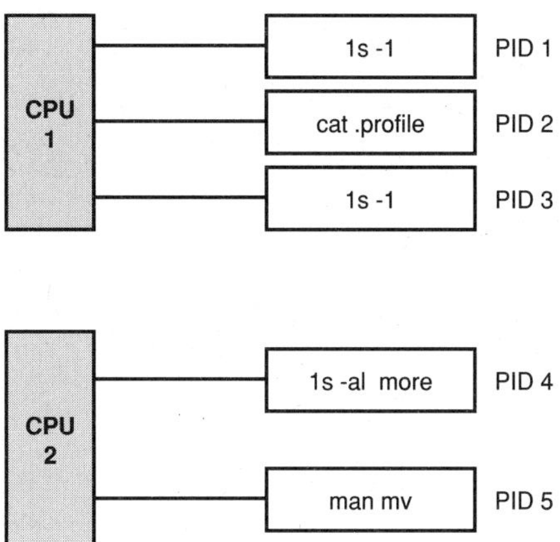

FIGURE 7.1.
Individual processes accessing a single CPU.

The CPU processes the first `ls` command until it is complete or until the amount of time a process is allowed with the CPU expires. Suppose that the `ls` completes before its time is up. Then, the CPU processes the `cat` command. It runs longer than the allocated CPU time slice, so the CPU saves information on where it stopped with the `cat` command and starts processing the second `ls` command. The `ls` command also uses up the allocated time slice. The CPU saves where it stopped on the `ls` command and returns to the `cat` command. Starting where it previously stopped, the CPU is still unable to complete the `cat` command. Once again, it saves the `cat` command's information at the new stopping point and starts the `ls` command at its last stopping point. The `ls` command is able to complete, so the CPU starts the `cat` command from its last stopping point. The CPU continues to process the `cat` command until it is complete or until new processes wait for the next time slice.

This swapping processes in and out of the CPU is called context switching. The information on each process contains the program counter value where the process's next or first instruction resides, a stack pointer to any local variables needed by the process, and a pointer to registers that contain data needed by the process. This information is commonly referred to as the process context. A context switch occurs when the CPU time slice expires, the process completes, or an interrupt occurs. The context of the current process is saved and the next process's context is given to the CPU.

Dynamic Server takes this concept one level lower, into individual processes, as shown in Figure 7.2. A running process has multiple threads waiting to be operated on. This one process performs a context switch on each thread in and out until all threads are complete. As mentioned earlier in this chapter, many different types of these single multithread processes make up the database server. These processes are called virtual processors (VP). As shown in Figure 7.3, each virtual processor has many threads attached to it, and each CPU can have many virtual processors attached to it. Each VP swaps threads around to be processes just as each CPU swaps VPs for processing.

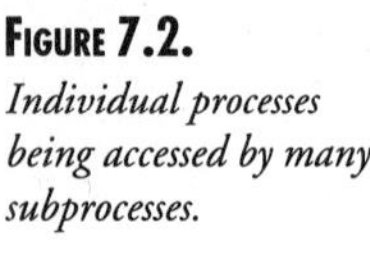

FIGURE 7.2.
Individual processes being accessed by many subprocesses.

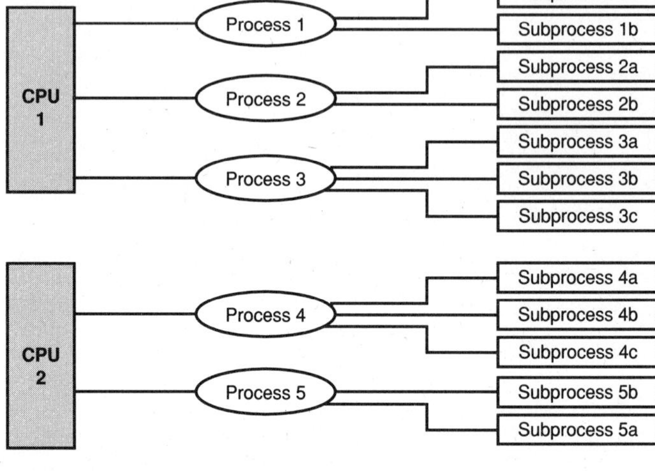

FIGURE 7.3.
Individual CPUs accessed by many virtual processors, which are accessed by multiple threads.

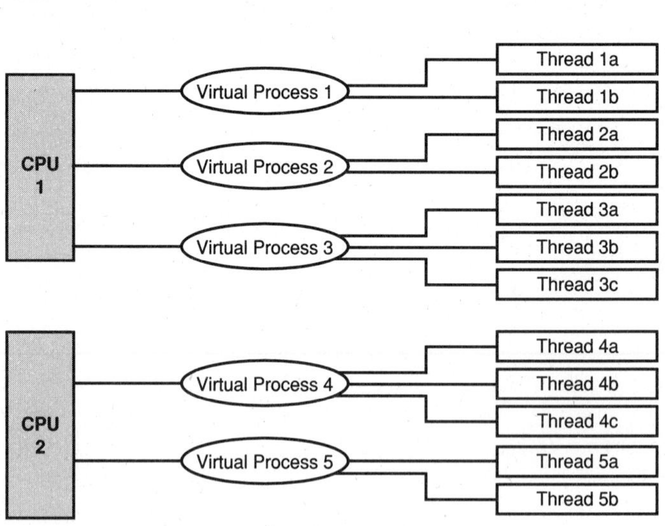

Many different types of virtual processors perform specific groups of tasks. Table 7.2 provides detailed descriptions of Dynamic Server's 11 classes of virtual processors.

Table 7.2. Classes of virtual processors.

VP Class	*Function*
ADM	Performs administrative operations related to start and stop time-related threads. A time-related thread runs in specific increments and sleeps in between these increments. An ADM thread is responsible for starting and stopping page cleaners. One ADM VP is always running.

VP Class	*Function*
ADT	Performs secure auditing operations to track all database activity server-wide. One VP runs when auditing is required. When no auditing is needed, there is no ADT VP running.
AIO	Performs disk-related I/O, which includes SQL-related reads and writes, checkpoints, and any other non-logging associated I/O. There can be as many AIO VPs as needed by the system to handle the I/O load.
CPU	Performs main processing and starts and manages other virtual processors. Responsible for running all threads required to process a client's task. Also responsible for some internal threads needed to maintain the server environment. There can be as many CPU VPs as needed by the system.
LIO	Performs internal threads to write activity information into the logical-log file. One LIO VP is started with Dynamic Server. Two LIO VPs are started when the logical log disk partition is mirrored.
MSC	Performs threads to process miscellaneous system calls to check user licensing and UNIX authentication. One MSC VP is started with the database server.
PIO	Performs internal threads to write activity information into the physical-log file. One PIO VP is started with Dynamic Server. Two PIO VPs are started when the logical log disk partition is mirrored.
OPT	Performs threads to place blob information into a staging area before performing optical disk I/O. When INFORMIX-OnLine/Optical software is not installed, there is no OPT VP running.
SOC	Runs threads to perform socket-related network communications to watch and wait (known as *polling*) for incoming TCP/IP client requests. The number of SOC VPs is configurable to the amount of network traffic. When no network traffic is expected, you can configure zero SOC VPs.
SHM	Runs threads that poll for connections into shared memory. There can be as many SHM VPs as needed by the system.
TLI	Runs threads that poll for TLI-related network communications. The number of TLI VPs is configurable to the amount of network traffic. When no network traffic is expected, you can configure zero TLI VPs.

These virtual processors run two types of threads—session and internal. A session thread is a process to complete a task requested by a client's SQL statement. In multiple CPU systems, multiple session threads can run for a specific client to achieve parallel processing. An internal thread is used to handle the server, maintaining tasks such as logging and page cleaning.

Another label attached to threads is called user threads, which encompasses all external task-driven threads. All session threads are considered user threads because they come into the server from the external client processes. Other external tasks that use user threads but are not driven by a client program are recovery and page-cleaner processes.

As you see in Figure 7.4, many threads are processed by a few VPs. These VPs are in turn processed by a few CPUs. This fan-in is much different from the previous OnLine processing done with `sqlturbos`. Every client had its own `sqlturbo` connected with the server that connected to CPUs. This used a lot of overhead just to keep track of all the context switching that occurred at the CPU. With Dynamic Server, UNIX requires less overhead to swap processes in and out. The VPs use less overhead to swap the threads around. Because the VPs handle the switching, they don't get swapped out of the CPU. Dynamic Server purposely keeps a VP running on a CPU as long as it can.

FIGURE 7.4.
Many threads connected to fewer virtual processors.

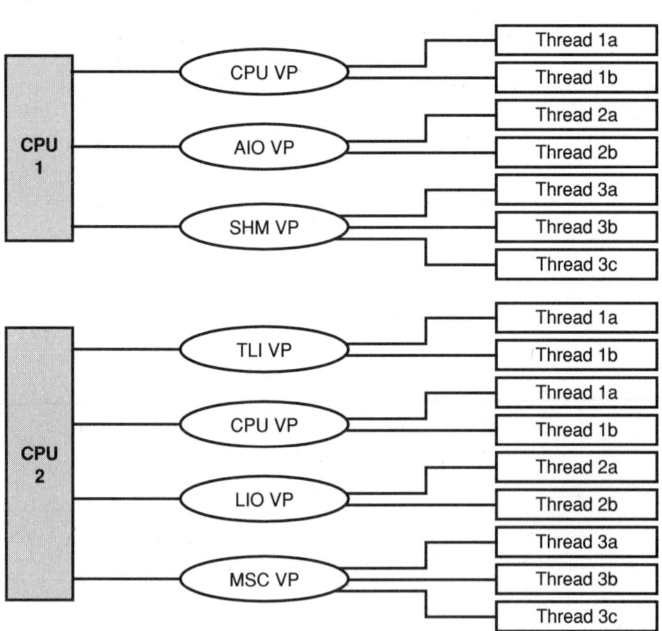

Some multiprocessor systems allow specific processes to be directly tied to one CPU. This processor affinity sets a process to run exclusively on a specific CPU. Dynamic Server has the capability to tie CPU VPs directly to CPUs. This reduces overhead even further by preventing UNIX from managing any context switches at the CPU level.

Much of the UNIX operating system overhead required to switch processes in and out of the CPU is reduced because context switching of threads is performed within each VP. Just like processes running on a CPU, each thread has its own context information. It stores the same type of information that is stored during a CPU context switch, but not as much. VPs can perform context switches much faster because there is not as much information to swap. This context information is stored by the VP in a thread-control block (TCB). Figure 7.5 shows the layout of a thread-control block.

FIGURE 7.5.
Thread-control block layout.

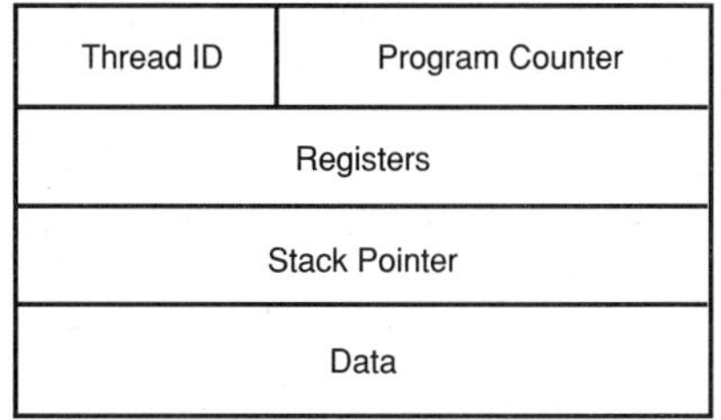

The VP holds the same responsibilities that the UNIX operating system has, managing time slices and the priority levels of the jobs allowed to run on the CPU. The VP manages the priority and scheduling of the threads connected to it. VPs are also responsible for switching threads when needed. Figure 7.6 shows a VP switching the context of two threads.

FIGURE 7.6.
Context switching performed on two threads by a virtual processor.

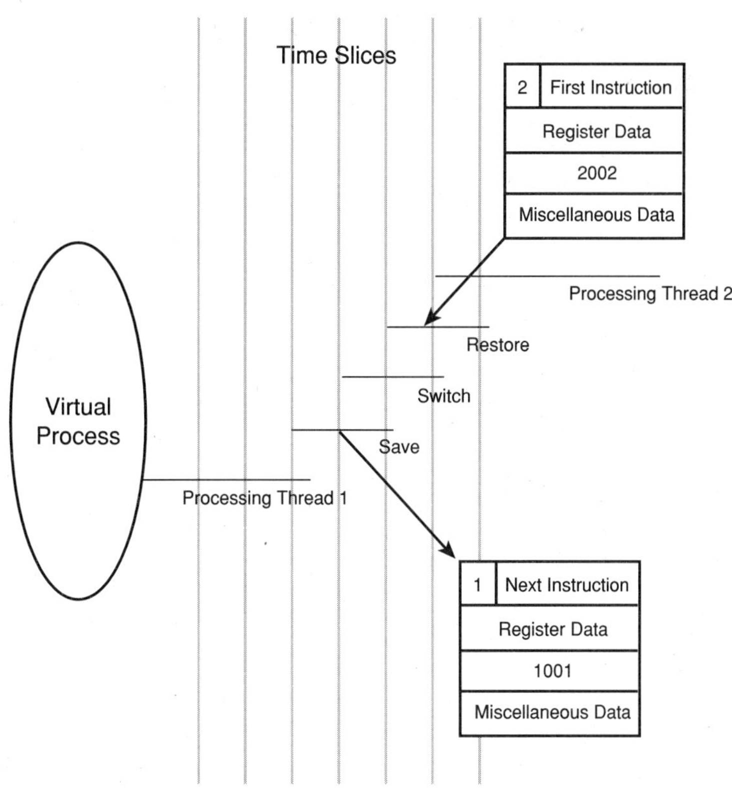

Threads are not restricted to work under a specific time slice as CPU processes are. A thread continues processing in the VP until it completes its task or until it must wait for something else to occur before it can continue. These waits are built into the thread's instructions, usually to take care of reads or writes or to free up locks. The VP sometimes learns from the running thread which thread should run next. This learning occurs when the thread realizes that it needs more information; it allows itself to be switched out so that another thread can be started to satisfy the need of the original thread.

Three types of queues hold the threads not running for each VP class. The *ready queue* is where all threads that are ready to run reside; that is, they have all the data needed to perform their task. The *sleep queue* is where threads that have no work to perform reside until there is work for them to do. The *wait queue* is where threads are placed when they need something else to complete before they can continue. Threads in sleep and wait queues are placed in the ready queue when they are needed to run again.

When there is more than one VP of the same class running, there is still only one set of queues. A thread waiting in the class queue is run on the first VP available. This provides a balance in the workload of each VP and provides faster work throughput of ready threads.

Multiprocessor systems also provide the capability to perform some tasks in parallel. Usually a client process has one session thread associated with it at one time. Tasks that require index building, sorting, sequential scanning, and joining can have more than one session thread. Figure 7.7 shows a client process with more than one session thread attached to various VPs. An example is when a client process reads through table data sequentially. If this table is fragmented over different disk partitions, a thread to read each partition's data can run at the same time. After all the partition reads are complete, the data is placed together by one thread and returned to the client. This process is also known as *fan-out*, where the single starting point of the fan is at the client. The fan becomes wider as multiple threads are created and connect to multiple VPs. Each of these VPs then connects to multiple CPUs.

FIGURE 7.7.
Fan-out thread processing.

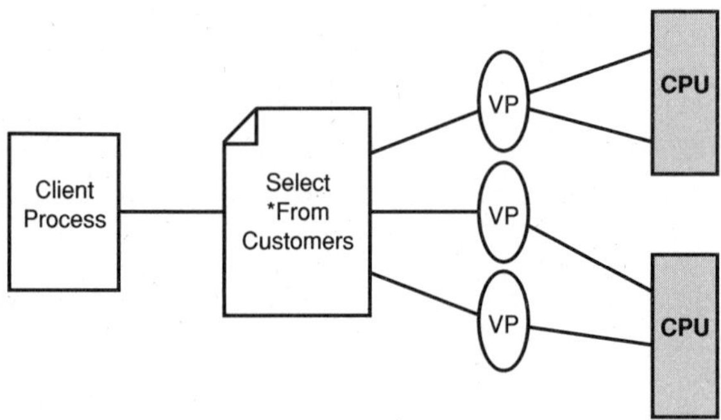

Dynamic Server's multithreaded architecture provides a valuable backbone to the database servers' processing capability. Using virtual processors and threads reduces the UNIX operating system overhead needed to service client processes. On multiprocessor systems, it provides the means to perform parallel processing.

Dynamic Server's Client/Server Configuration

Dynamic Server continues to maintain its built-in capability to perform client/server database processing. Client/server processing occurs when the client processes and the database are separate running programs. A client process can run locally on the same machine as the database server, or it can access the database remotely through a network.

Version 5 of OnLine requires INFORMIX-NET and INFORMIX-STAR to perform remote client/server and distributed database connections. UNIX pipes are used to make the connection between each client and the server. With the release of Dynamic Server, remote connection functionality is built-in through network interfaces using popular UNIX network protocols.

A network protocol is a standard format for transmitting data between applications. One of the reasons UNIX is considered an open system is that the code for network protocols was ported on every system running UNIX. An HP machine can talk to a Sun machine because they use the same network protocols. These protocols were expanded to run on PCs, Macs, and MVS mainframes.

Dynamic Server supports the two most popular network protocols: TCP/IP and IPX/SPX. TCP/IP, or Transmission Control Protocol/Internet Protocol, is a network protocol that originally was built to exchange information between UNIX machines across a simple generic network. TCP/IP is now standard as a network protocol on all operating systems. IPX/SPX or Internet packet exchange/sequenced packet exchange was originally built to exchange information across Novell networks, but it is also now available for most networks. Both client and server systems must support the same protocol. Clients running on a system using TCP/IP cannot connect to a database server running on a system using IPX/SPX. Dynamic Server can receive connections from clients of both types, but it is recommended that you use only one.

Shown in Figure 7.8, Dynamic Server's database server and clients use a network interface to invoke the protocol communications. A network interface is a piece of program code that sends and receives calls to perform a program function. Referred to as an application programming interface (API), these programs contain routines that communicate with other running applications.

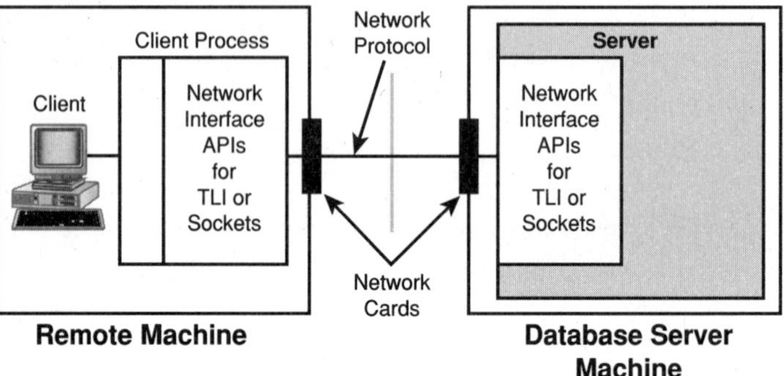

FIGURE 7.8.
Using network interfaces at each end of the client/server connection.

Dynamic Server supports two types of network interfaces—TLI and sockets. Transport layer interface (TLI) uses a continuous stream of data when exchanging data across a network. Think of it like water through a hose; as the data comes across it is read bit by bit. Sockets, on the other hand, send information in a single file, and usually are not processed until the entire file is across.

Although you must use the same network protocol on both ends of the client/server connection, the network interfaces do not need to be the same on both ends. IPX/SPX is required to use TLI, but TCP/IP can use both TLI and sockets. Figure 7.9 illustrates how clients running with TLI and sockets can connect to the same database server when all three machines rely on TCP/IP as their protocol.

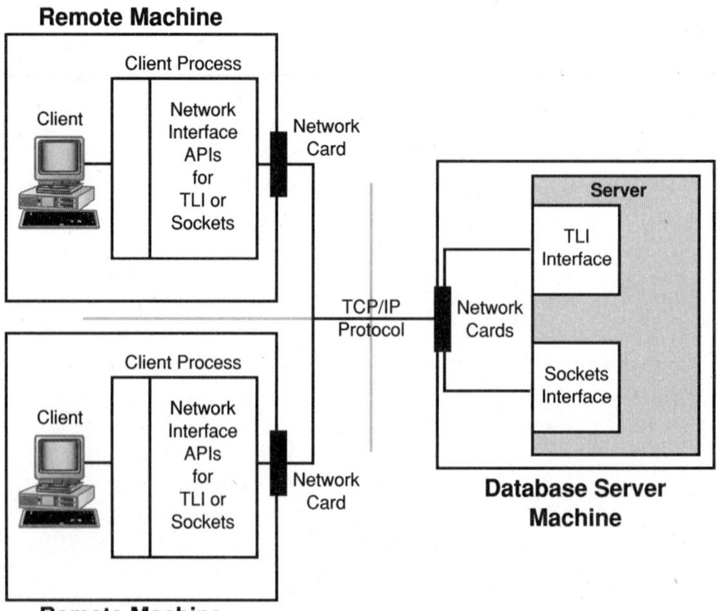

FIGURE 7.9.
TCP/IP connection to the server using both TLI and sockets at the client processes.

Both of these protocols and interfaces are popular and available on most operating systems for most platforms. Check with your network and hardware administrators about which are used internally at your company.

When client applications run on the same system as the database server, there is no need for network protocols and interfaces between the two. Figure 7.10 shows how Dynamic Server allows local clients to connect directly to a shared memory area on the local machine. Do not confuse this area with the shared memory used by the database server to make changes to the database. This area is shared between clients and Dynamic Server.

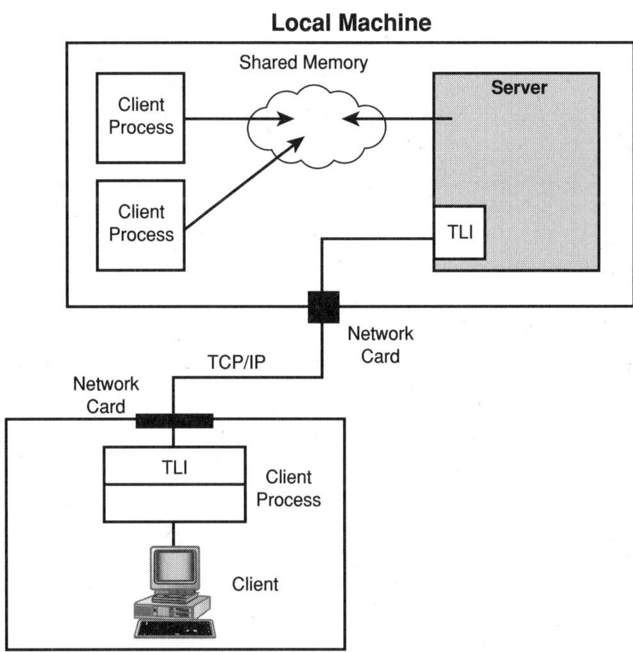

FIGURE 7.10.
Client/server connections by using shared memory.

Shared memory connections are very fast but have less protection from problem clients. Shared memory connections are really a back door into the database server. The UNIX operating system is very open with its internal buffers and registers. Most client applications developed internally by companies are written in C or C++, a language that takes advantage of access to UNIX's lower levels. When client processes with logic and memory allocation errors get in that back door, all types of havoc can occur.

Using a network connection locally provides a safer, but slightly slower, way for clients to communicate with the database server. You can set up the client and server to use network protocols and interfaces for local communications as you do for remote communications. With this local loopback, a transaction from a network interface is bounced back to itself. A ping on your own IP address results in a local loopback, as shown in Figure 7.11. This occurs when the network interface of the sender and receiver is the same, residing on the same machine. Because the client and server are two separate processing entities, they each think they're using a different network interface. As shown in Figure 7.11, when a transaction leaves the client or the server, it is bounced to the other.

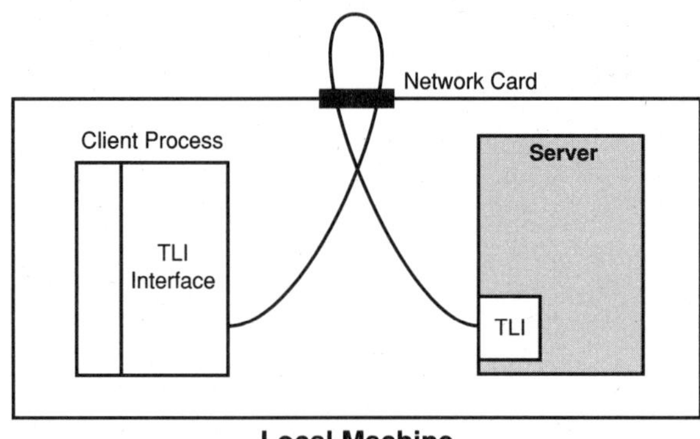

FIGURE 7.11.
Local client/server connections using loopback.

When the connection between the client and the server is made, the server waits for a transaction. A special thread, `poll`, waits and watches a port associated with the chosen network protocol and interface. The `poll` thread is part of the network virtual processors. There is a SOC VP for sockets and a TLI VP for TLI communications. On single processor systems, the CPU VP takes over the responsibility of running the polling thread so that less switching occurs. On multiprocessor systems, it's good to have one network VP for every 150 to 200 clients.

After receiving a connection, the `poll` thread sends the connection request to a `listen` thread. One `listen` thread is assigned to each network port. Its task is to verify the users, establish the connection, create the session and thread control blocks, and start an `sqlexec` thread. After the connection is verified as valid, control returns to the poll thread, which places the request and data into the control blocks and wakes the `sqlexec` thread created by the `listen` thread. When shared memory is used as a communication connection, there is no port to be established by the `listen` thread, so the `sqlexec` thread starts rather than waits after it's created by the `listen` thread.

All processing is performed by the `sqlexec` thread. After processing starts, all further communication with the client is performed by the `sqlexec` through the port established by the `listen` thread. Figure 7.12 shows the `poll`, `listen`, and `sqlexec` threads connecting and processing a client's request.

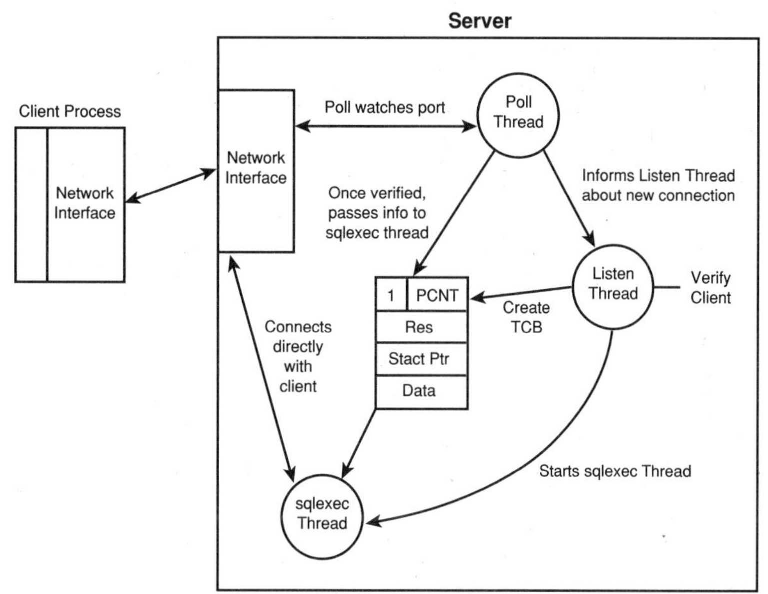

FIGURE 7.12.
Client connections processed by `poll`, `listen`, *and* `sqlexec` *threads.*

Compared to OnLine's one `sqlexecd` connect per client, Dynamic Server can process many client requests faster and more efficiently. Not requiring extra communication software for the client and server to connect remotely allows the workload to be removed from the server machine and spread out on other processors. Client applications using the old communication add-on INFORMIX-NET are still able to run without any changes or recompiles. These clients using INFORMIX-NET actually use TCP/IP to connect to a server running with INFORMIX-STAR. Dynamic Server's polling thread works just like INFORMIX-STAR does.

Summary

Dynamic Server is an excellent client/server relational database management system. Its multithreaded architecture provides superior functionality and processing speeds with its DSA, PDQ, virtual processors, and built-in networking. All these features make Dynamic Server the right choice for new systems or migrations from earlier versions of INFORMIX-OnLine.

The capability to add or decrease resources while the server is running comes from Dynamic Server's DSA functionality. No longer will spikes in client usage cause the system to slow or force administrators to take the system offline to add more resources.

The multithreaded architecture benefits both single- and multiple-processor systems by efficiently using the CPU and other resources. On multiprocessor systems, Dynamic Server has the capability to use PDQ to perform some database operations in parallel.

Processing in a client/server application is what Dynamic Server is meant to do. Using virtual processors and threads to manage the workload, Dynamic Server can handle hundreds of clients simultaneously. Connecting to Dynamic Server is easier than with earlier versions of OnLine. Remote and local connections look and act the same, using standard network protocols such as TCP/IP and IPX/SPX. INFORMIX-STAR and INFORMIX-NET are no longer required to perform remote client connections.

CHAPTER 8

INFORMIX-Universal Server

by Mary Mudie

IN THIS CHAPTER

INFORMIX-Universal Server is an object-relational database management system that allows developers to extend the range of available data types, add routines that operate on those data types, and access methods to ensure good performance. It is based on the Informix Dynamic Scalable Architecture (DSA) and, thus, inherits the performance, scalability, and reliability characteristics of previous products based upon that architecture, such as INFORMIX-OnLine Dynamic Server 7.2. This chapter focuses on the object-oriented enhancements supplied with INFORMIX-Universal Server and assumes an understanding of DSA, such as is provided elsewhere in this book.

Overview

Traditional relational database systems restrict the user to character string and numeric data types. Some systems support the storage of binary large objects (blobs) but cannot manipulate the contents of these objects or perform searches based upon their content. INFORMIX-Universal Server allows the developer to define new types of data and build routines to allow user access to the data via SQL statements. This extensibility supports the development of applications that use rich data types like multidimensional and time-series data and multimedia data types like audio, video, image, and text objects. INFORMIX-Universal Server developers can either design and build their own sets of data types and associated routines or can purchase *DataBlade* modules, which are packages of predefined types and routines that address a specific domain, such as text storage and retrieval. DataBlade modules are generally developed by domain experts and can be "mixed and matched" with DataBlade modules from other vendors that address other business requirements.

Architecture

The underlying architecture of INFORMIX-Universal Server is based upon that of INFORMIX-OnLine Dynamic Server 7.2. The major difference is the capability to "plug in" DataBlade modules that extend server functionality.

In INFORMIX-Universal Server, information about data types, functions, and access methods is stored in catalog tables, rather than being hard-coded in the server. This means that all types, functions, and access methods, when registered, are treated in the same way whether they are user-defined or built-in objects provided with the server.

Figure 8.1 shows the various components of the server engine that are involved in the execution of an SQL query.

FIGURE 8.1.
INFORMIX-Universal Server architecture.

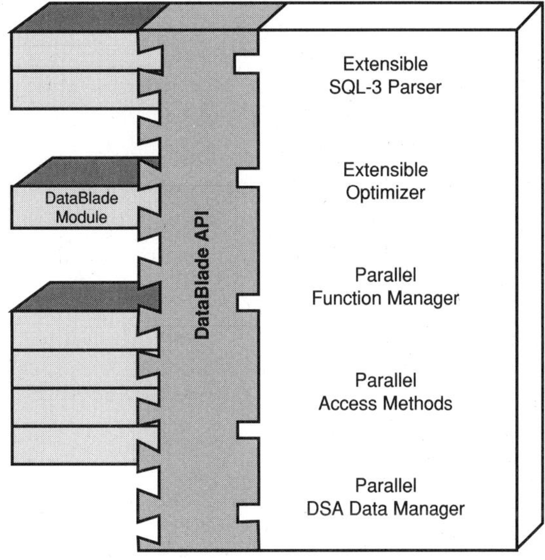

The following list shows the components of the server engine and their functions:

- The *parser* reads and verifies the syntax. User-defined functions and data types are recorded in the catalog tables and, therefore, will be recognized by the parser.
- The *optimizer* chooses the best path to access the data needed to satisfy the query. The query plan chosen by the optimizer will depend on the relative costs of different paths to the data. Information about the cost of user-defined functions is provided by the DataBlade developer to assist the optimizer in making its choice.
- The *function manager* finds and executes the user-defined functions because they are recorded in the catalog tables.
- The appropriate *access method* is chosen for the data being retrieved. The access method may be provided with INFORMIX-Universal Server or supplied by the DataBlade developer.
- The *data manager* physically moves the data on and off the disk.

To summarize, DataBlade modules (for example, user-defined types, routines, and access methods) appear to be built into the engine. They execute in the same address space, are callable in the same way as existing built-in functions, are correctly optimized, and can interact with other DataBlade modules and applications.

New Data Types

New data types provided by INFORMIX-Universal Server include row types, collections, and user-defined data types that can be distinct or opaque, as well as the new built-in types `lvarchar`, `boolean`, `blob`, and `clob`.

Row types provide the capability of grouping multiple columns together for ease of access and processing. For example, an address row type could include elements for street address, apartment number, city, state, and zip code. If the whole address is required, a simple SQL statement such as

```
select name, address from employee;
```

will retrieve all the fields. If only one element is required, dot notation is used, as in

```
select name, address from employee where address.state = 'CA';
```

Collections allow for the definition of repeating elements within one column, addressing a common "normalization" dilemma. Using a combination of collections and row types, you could store the various phone numbers for a customer contact in one row by creating a table like this:

```
create table customer_contact (name char(20),
                               phone set (row (phonetype varchar(10),
                                               phoneno char(10))
                                          not null)
                               );
```

Collections can be extended and updated in much the same way as tables.

Developers can define new data types to suit their particular needs. These can either be *distinct data types*, which are based on some existing type, or *opaque types*, which are encapsulated data types that can be defined to store data of any format.

Distinct data types allow the developer to differentiate between different types of business data, even when the underlying storage mechanism is the same. INFORMIX-Universal Server supports *strong typing*, which means that data of different types cannot inadvertently be compared or operated upon without the appropriate conversion being performed. For example, by defining types for different currencies (dollar, franc, yen, and so on), you can ensure that a column defined as type `dollar` cannot be added to a column defined as `franc` without some conversion (or *casting*) being performed.

Opaque types, also known as *abstract data types*, are generally used to represent complex internal structures for storing rich data, such as text, audio, or video objects. Developers with domain expertise in some particular area can construct opaque types to hold data and define functions, operators, and access methods to operate on them. Opaque types support the object-oriented notion of *private data*, which means that users can access the contents only via associated functions.

Inheritance

INFORMIX-Universal Server supports inheritance for row types and tables. A typed table inherits the behaviors (functions and routines) and the structural characteristics (storage options, indices, constraints, and triggers) from its supertable, thus facilitating the reuse of code. A search against the supertable will automatically search all tables below it in the hierarchy, unless the query is specifically restricted with the keyword `only`.

User-Defined Routines

User-defined routines can be used to encapsulate complex business logic and extend SQL to meet unique processing needs. For example, you can define a routine that will crop an image to meet specific requirements and invoke it in an SQL statement by coding

```
select crop(image_name, crop_specifications) from myimages;
```

User-defined routines can be *overloaded*, which allows the same routine name to be used for different routines that perform the same function but against different data types. A user wanting to crop an image will always invoke the crop function, but a different version of the function will be used depending on the data type of the image that is being passed.

Access Methods and Indices

INFORMIX-Universal Server includes two secondary access methods (or indices): generic B-tree and R-Tree. The latter is particularly appropriate for indexing multidimensional data, such as spatial data. Developers can also write their own secondary access methods to improve performance in accessing a user-defined data type. Indices can also be defined on the output of a function operating upon some data, rather than on the data itself.

Access methods can be developed by using the *Virtual Table Interface* to access data stored externally to the server. User-defined routines are needed to map the data so that it can be retrieved using standard SQL statements. This interface can be used to provide access to data that may be better stored in a specialized server, such as a video server, or to build a gateway to heterogeneous database servers. After the data is defined as a virtual table, the user can select, join, and process the data as if it were stored in the INFORMIX-Universal Server database.

Smart Large Objects

Along with support for the traditional large objects (BYTE and TEXT), INFORMIX-Universal Server introduces *smart large objects* that provide the capability for developers to seek, read from, and write to segments within the object. Smart large objects are recoverable, although logging can be disabled if required. The following are the two types:

- Character large objects (clobs) used for storing ASCII text objects
- Binary large objects (blobs) generally used for storing user-defined data types, such as video and audio clips, images, pictures, drawings, and maps

DataBlade Modules

DataBlade modules are software packages that take advantage of the extensibility options to provide new capabilities. DataBlades are generally developed by domain experts to meet a specific business need, such as image processing, text retrieval, or spatial systems. A DataBlade typically consists of a set of user-defined types, routines and casts, table and index definitions, and appropriate documentation. It may also include access methods and indices, and a client interface if appropriate.

The Spatial DataBlade module, for example, adds definitions for data types that contain the representation of such objects as circles, polygons, rectangles, and points defined by x and y coordinates. Functions are provided that allow the user to search and manipulate these spatial objects. The server's R-tree index access method is used to accelerate performance when searching on spatial data types.

For example, assume that a table has been created that contains restaurant names, addresses, and locations specified as (x,y) coordinates with the `pnt` data type, which is defined in the Spatial DataBlade:

```
create table restaurant(
             name char(5),
            address char(50),
             category char(10),
             location pnt);
```

You could then find all restaurants within a certain distance of some specific point that serve Italian food by using the `distance` function.

```
select name, address from restaurant
             where distance(location, startpoint) < 5
             and category = 'Italian';
```

Some basic DataBlade modules are developed by Informix, but most are developed by third-party vendors who have considerable expertise in their fields. Examples of currently announced DataBlade modules include the following

- The Informix TimeSeries DataBlade module adds support for the management of time-series and temporal data. It can be used, for example, to store and query a time-based series of stock prices, including open, high, low, and close values. Calendaring functions are provided so that calculations take into account weekends and holidays.
- The MapInfo Geocoding DataBlade module performs all the calculations necessary to geocode addresses. It can create a geographic point (Latitude and Longitude) from any address and allow applications to locate the nearest product or service relative to a particular point.
- The Excalibur Face Recognition DataBlade module searches and retrieves facial images based on feature vector comparison (for example, eyes, nose, and mouth). It can be used in security applications with other verification techniques to control access to secure areas.

- The MuscleFish AIR DataBlade module provides content-based retrieval of digital audio and enables users to search for audio clips that "sound like" some target sound.
- The NEC TigerMark DataBlade module enables content owners to embed imperceptible watermarks in images of all sorts and to extract and verify watermarks from retrieved images. TigerMarks help protect images displayed or sold on the Internet or other digital medium.
- The Virage VIR DataBlade module enables users to search for images by the intrinsic properties of the images themselves: the color, texture, structure, and composition.
- The Verity Text DataBlade module enables full-text search of data, which is especially useful for applications that need fuzzy-search capability.
- The Informix Web DataBlade module is a toolkit for developing complex dynamic HTML pages without the use of scripting languages such as Perl or TCL.

Purchasing a DataBlade module allows a developer to build applications using new types of data, without needing to develop in-house expertise in the manipulation, storage, and retrieval of that data. For example, a text DataBlade can provide fuzzy searches of large text documents without the application developer needing to understand the mechanisms behind such a search. This capability to plug in new technology can lead to dramatic improvements in application development times.

Multiple DataBlade modules can be used in one application to meet business requirements. In the previous example, the restaurant menu could be included in the table, and text DataBlade functions could be used in the search criteria to enable a traveler to locate a restaurant that served Bombay curry within walking distance of her hotel.

Informix provides a DataBlade Developer's Kit to assist developers with expertise in some particular domain in designing DataBlade objects and in building a package that can be easily deployed to customers. There is also a certification process used to evaluate quality, documentation, compatibility, and conformance to development guidelines.

Configuration Changes

Configuration changes have been made to support the extensibility options provided with INFORMIX-Universal Server. These changes include the addition of a new virtual processor class, new storage spaces, and changes to the system catalog tables.

User-Defined Virtual Processor Classes

INFORMIX-Universal Server is a multithreaded server, based on the Informix Dynamic Scalable Architecture (DSA). It supports the same virtual processor (VP) classes as INFORMIX-OnLine Dynamic Server 7.2 (CPU, PIO, LIO, AIO, SHM, TLI, SOC, OPT, ADM, ADT, and MSC) and has a new VP class for running user-defined routines. It is designed to be used by user-defined routines not suitable for running in the CPU class because they make blocking calls, do not yield control to other threads, or modify the global VP state. Typically, these classes would be used for DataBlade routines that need to issue direct file system calls (which are blocking calls).

A new parameter, VPCLASS, has been added to the ONCONFIG file to specify the number and classes of virtual processors to start. You can also disable priority aging, if this is permitted by your operating system, and assign VPs to specific CPUs when running in a multiprocessor environment that supports processor affinity. The VPCLASS is an alternative to the parameters AFF_SPROC, AFF_NPROCS, NOAGE, NUMBERCPUVPs, NUMAIOVPS, and SINGLE_CPU_VP.

To create a user-defined class of VPs to run DataBlade or user-defined routines, you must include a VPCLASS parameter that specifies the name of the class and the number of VPs to start. Here is an example:

```
VPCLASS my_udrs,num=3
```

This will cause the server to start three virtual processors that will be used for any user-defined routines that have been assigned to the class my_udrs. Assigning classes is done with the CLASS parameter on the CREATE FUNCTION statement.

Sbspaces

An *sbspace* is composed of one or more chunks that store clobs (character large objects) and blobs (binary large objects), which can contain up to 4 terabytes of data. Like a dbspace, an sbspace is a collection of chunks and is created by the onspaces or the OnMonitor utilities. It also includes a metadata partition that contains descriptive information about the smart large objects stored in the sbspace to enable the server to manipulate and recover the objects. Information about smart large objects is also stored in the system catalog. Smart large objects are recoverable, but logging can be turned off if desired—for example, when loading large numbers of objects. Metadata is always logged. The structure of an sbspace is shown in Figure 8.2.

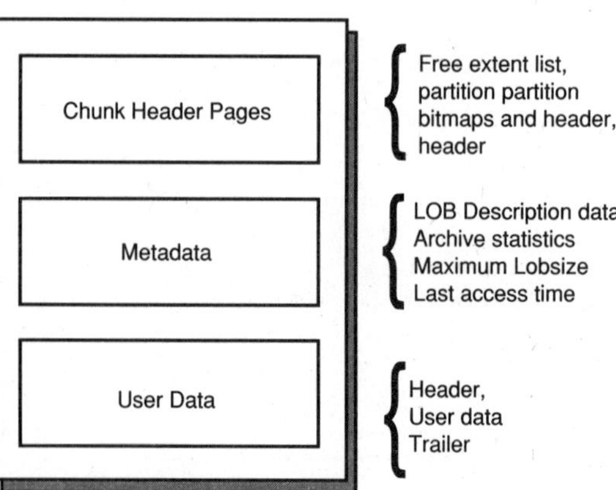

FIGURE 8.2.
Layout of an sbspace.

SBSPACENAME is a new ONCONFIG parameter that specifies the name of the system default sbspace. INFORMIX-Universal Server will store smart lobs in the default sbspace unless you specify otherwise.

Extspaces

An extspace is a logical name associated with a pointer to any kind of file on any kind of device. A user-defined access method must be supplied to provide access to the contents of the file. Application developers can then use SQL statements to access the data. More information on user-defined access methods is provided later in this chapter.

System Catalog Changes

New system catalog tables have been added to store information about the extensibility features of INFORMIX-Universal Server. The new tables are shown in Table 8.1.

Table 8.1. New systems catalog tables.

Table	*Contents*
sysams	Access methods.
sysattrtypes	Members of a complex type.
syscasts	Casts.
sysdomains	Domains.
sysindices	Replacement for sysindexes. (There is a view that provides access as sysindexes for backward compatibility.)
sysinherit	Table and type inheritance.
syslangauth	Authorization on languages.
syslogmap	Changes to table or row ids after new table creation or row movement.
sysopclasses	Operator classes.
sysroutinelangs	Languages for writing routines.
systabamdata	Options selected after table creation.
sysxtddesc	Domain and user-defined type descriptions.
sysxtdtypeauth	Domain and user-defined types.

Systems Monitoring Interface

A new table has been added to the sysmaster database for use by the Systems Monitoring Interface (SMI). The sysextspaces table provides information on external spaces.

Application Programming Interfaces

New APIs include C++, Java, and the DataBlade API. ESQL/C, ESQL/COBOL, the INFORMIX-CLI, and the GLS API are still supported.

DataBlade Application Programming Interface

This C-based API is used for the development of applications or routines that access data stored in an INFORMIX-Universal Server database. The DBAPI interface sends SQL command strings to the server for execution and processes results returned by the server to the application. It should always be used for developing external routines that run in the server (user-defined routines, operator class functions for access methods, support functions for user-defined types, implicit casts and triggers) because it includes functions and routines that promote the development of thread safe code. For example, there are memory management routines that allocate space from shared memory rather than from process-private memory.

New Object-Oriented Application Programming Interfaces

In addition to the existing INFORMIX-CLI, INFORMIX-Universal Server provides the Java API and C++ APIs for object-oriented programmers. These APIs offer dynamic type extensibility in the client, encapsulating server features into an object library that allows client programs to adapt as the server schema changes. Both APIs support the following classes:

- *Operation classes* provide access to common database methods for issuing queries and retrieving results. Operation classes encapsulate database objects such as connections, cursors, and queries.
- *Value interfaces* are abstract classes that encapsulate database objects such as object types. They support a COM-style capability-based paradigm where objects are accessed or known only through interfaces and where each capability is represented by an interface. Database objects accessed through this interface are implementation-independent. Value objects can also be used to manage display behavior and GUI components.

Both the C++ and Java APIs are designed to support component-based architectures. The C++ interface is compatible with the Microsoft Common Object Model (COM) value object model for native ActiveX support. The Java API has been modeled to support Java Beans and when used with Remote Method Invocation (RMI), provides a fully "remoted" client, allowing workstations to run Java database applications without preloaded client connectivity software. Java Database Connectivity (JDBC) can also be used for SQL92 standards-based access to INFORMIX-Universal Server.

User-Defined Routines

A user-defined routine is a piece of code written either in SPL (Stored Procedure Language) or in C that performs some application logic or other function on data stored in INFORMIX-Universal Server. Java will be supported for user-defined routines in a future release. Typically, user-defined routines perform operations on user-defined data types, but they can also be used to encapsulate some frequently used application logic against built-in data types. User-defined routines can also be coded in C++ and are then executed within a C wrapper.

User-defined routines can be functions, or they can be procedures similar to those currently available with INFORMIX-OnLine Dynamic Server 7.2. Both functions and procedures accept arguments, but only functions return values, while procedures do not. However, for backward compatibility, the current version of INFORMIX-Universal Server allows procedures to return values as well.

User-defined routines are frequently used to provide support for new data types. For example, if you have defined a data type to hold temperatures recorded in Celsius and another data type to hold temperatures recorded in Fahrenheit, you can write a user-defined routine to perform the conversion between the two. User-defined routines can also be used to perform complex calculations that are frequently required, thus reducing application development time as well as enhancing code quality.

Creating a User-Defined Routine

The `CREATE FUNCTION` and `CREATE PROCEDURE` statements are used to register functions in the server. If the routine is written in SPL, the SPL code is included in the `CREATE` statement and is stored internally in the server; if the routine is written in C, it must be stored externally in a shared library.

Typically, C code is required for more complex operations; for example, if you need to execute routines that are external to the server, such as sending e-mail, you will need to code in C and use the DataBlade API. If you plan to develop user-defined routines, you should consider acquiring the DataBlade Developer's Kit. This provides guidance on good coding practices and development techniques, as well as tools for facilitating development of such routines.

Assume that you have a product table containing price and discount information:

```
create table product (
        product_id integer,
        description char(20),
        price money,
        discount decimal(4,2));
```

You could create a function, `calc_cost`, which would calculate the cost of the product as being the price multiplied by the quantity ordered:

```
create function calc_cost(price money,
                          quantity integer)
                          returning money;
    return (price*quantity);
end function;
```

Then you could use that function to determine the cost if a particular quantity, let's say 12, was ordered. You do not need to know whether a user-defined routine was written in SPL or in C in order to use it. It is invoked in the same way as built-in functions like MAX or MIN; however, you do need to know the arguments that need to be passed and what, if anything, will be returned.

If you insert a row into the table, like

```
insert into product values (111,'Spanner',10.99,2.25);
```

and then you execute the statement

```
select product_id, description, calc_cost(price,12) cost from product;
```

the following result will be returned:

```
product_id description                           cost
       111 Spanner                            $131.88
```

Routine Overloading

Often, you might need to develop routines that have the same objective but execute different logic depending on the arguments that are passed to them. The calculation of the cost of an order might depend on whether a discount percentage was to be applied. You could create another routine, also called `calc_cost`, to perform this calculation:

```
create function calc_cost(price money,
                          quantity integer,
                          discount decimal(4,2))
                          returning money;
    return (price*quantity - price*quantity*discount/100);
end function;
```

These routines are said to be *overloaded.* While they have the same name, they have different *signatures*, which uniquely identify them. The signature of a routine includes the following items:

- Routine type (procedure or function)
- Routine name
- Number of parameters
- Data types of parameters
- Order of parameters

When you invoke a routine, the server searches for a routine whose signature matches what you have specified. Issue this statement against the same data that you inserted previously:

```
select product_id, description, calc_cost(price,12,discount) cost
        from product;
```

This returns the following result:

```
product_id description                        cost
       111 Spanner                         $128.91
```

Data Types

INFORMIX-Universal Server allows you to manage many different types of data, ranging from traditional numbers and character strings to complex constructs such as spatial data, video, image, audio, and encoded documents. Certain built-in and extended data types are provided with the server, and, in addition, you can define your own types to suit your requirements. You can also write routines and functions to manipulate existing or user-defined types and provide new access methods for them.

When you create a table, you specify the data types associated with each column. The data type associated with a column provides information to the server on how the data is to be stored, what operations can be performed on it, what access methods can be used to locate it, and how it should be converted to or from a different data type.

Figure 8.3 shows the different kinds of data types supported by INFORMIX-Universal Server. Some are provided with the server; others are defined by the user.

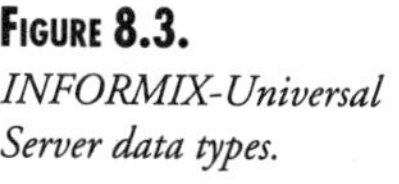

FIGURE 8.3.
INFORMIX-Universal Server data types.

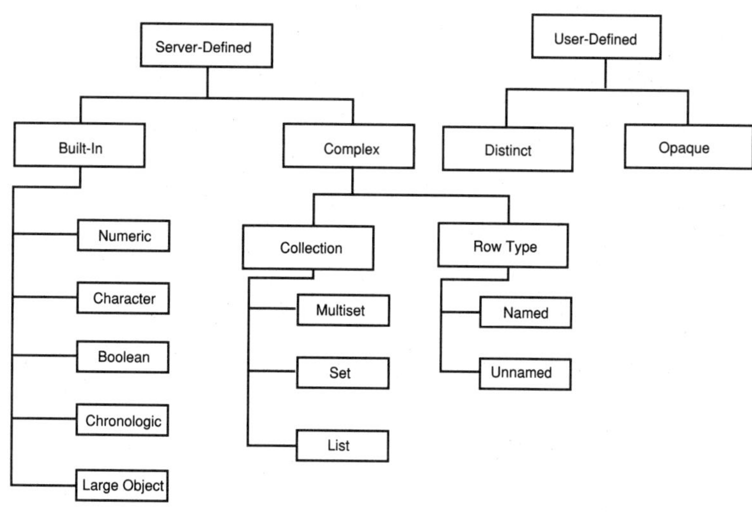

Built-In Data Types

Built-in data types are provided by the server and include the traditional data types such as integer, date, decimal, character, and float. Built-in types new with INFORMIX-Universal Server are listed in Table 8.2.

Table 8.2. New built-in data types.

Data Type	*Description*
`boolean`	Provides a one byte true/false indicator.
`serial8`	Similar in function to serial but stores a large sequential integer.
`integer8`	Stores a whole number ranging from -2,147,483,647 to +2,147,483,647.
`byte`	Stores any kind of binary data and is generally used for upward compatibility with existing applications. `blob` should be used for new applications.
`text`	Stores any kind of text data and is generally used for upward compatibility for existing applications. `varchar` or `clob` should be used for new applications.
`blob`	Stores any kind of binary data, including images.
`clob`	Stores large text items.
`lvarchar`	Stores varying length data up to 32KB.

Complex Data Types

Complex data types are extended data types built from a combination of other data types. Unlike a built-in type, you can manipulate the individual components of a complex data type through SQL. Complex types can be collections or row types.

Collection Types

A collection is a complex type made up of individual elements, each of which is the same data type. But these elements could themselves be complex types, or built-in or user-defined types. There are three kinds of collections: `SET`, `MULTISET`, and `LIST`.

A `SET` collection is a set of unique elements (that is, no duplicate values) in no implied order. Like a `SET`, a `MULTISET` collection has no implied ordering, but duplicate values are allowed.

The following example shows how you could create a table that would contain the list of available colors for an item.

```
create table items (
                    item_number integer,
                    description varchar(40),
                    colors multiset (char(10) not null));
```

You insert rows into the set using the following syntax:

```
insert into item values (1234,
                         'gardening clogs',
                         "multiset{'red','blue','green'}");
insert into item values (3456,
                         'short-handled rake',
                         "multiset{'green'}");
```

When you retrieve rows, you can search on the value of a particular item of the set. Searching on the color green returns two rows:

```
select item_number, description from item
            where 'green' in (colors);
item_number description
       1234 gardening clogs
       3456 short-handled rake
```

Searching on the color red, on the other hand, returns only one:

```
select item_number, description from item
          where 'red' in (colors);
item_number description
       1234 gardening clogs
```

Unlike a SET or MULTISET, a LIST collection is an ordered set of elements, and duplicate values are allowed. The following table could be used to hold the average temperatures for each month during the year:

```
create table city_temps (city_name char(30),
                         avg_temps LIST(integer not null));
```


Row Types

Whereas collections are groups of elements of the same type, row types are groups of elements of different types and form the template for a record. You can set up a row type to define a frequently used set of closely related fields and thus ensure consistency across different tables, as well as saving time in coding table definitions. A common example would be to set up the row type for an address, such as

```
create row type address_t (street char(30),
                           city   char(20),
                           state  char(2),
                           zip    char(5));
```

Now you could create different tables using this row type and ensure that everybody uses the same names and field lengths for the different elements, as in the following example:

```
create table customer (customer_no integer,
                       name char(30),
                       address address_t,
                       balance money);
```

Here's another example:

```
create table vendor (vendor_no integer,
                     company_name char(30),
                     address address_t,
                     contact_name char(30));
```

To insert data into a table containing a row type, you need to use the cast (::) function, described in the "Casting" section, later in this chapter:

```
insert into customer
        values (12345,
                'John Smith',
                row('355 27th Street','San Jose','CA','12355')::address_t,
                1000.00);
insert into customer
        values (22222,
                'Fred Brown',
                row('355 Oak Street','Fairoaks','CA','92355')::address_t,
                2000.00);
```

Dot notation is used to manipulate the individual fields of a row type. The statement

```
select customer_no, name from customer
          where address.state='CA'
```

will retrieve

```
customer_no name
      12345 John Smith
      22222 Fred Brown
```

When you update a row type, you must specify all the fields; however, you can update an individual field by using the following technique:

```
update customer
   set address=row(address.street, address.city,'AZ',address.zip)::address_t
                    where customer_no=22222;
```

The select statement shown in the preceding example will now retrieve only one row:

```
customer_no name
      12345 John Smith
```

You can use row types within row types. For example, if you wanted to use an extended zip code, you could define a row type

```
create row type zip_t (code char(5),
                       suffix char(4));
```

and use it in the definition of the `address_t` row type, like this:

```
create row type address_t (street char(30),
                           city   char(20),
                           state  char(2),
                           zip    zip_t);
```

Creating the types and table would now look like this:

```
create row type zip_t (code char(5),
                       plus4 char(4));
create row type address_t (street char(30),
                           city   char(20),
                           state  char(2),
                           zip    zip_t);
create table customer (customer_no integer,
                       name char(30),
                       address address_t,
                       balance money);
```

To insert data, you would need to cast the zip code fields, as well as the address fields:

```
insert into customer
        values (12345,
                'John Smith',
                row ('355 27th Street', 'San Jose','CA',
                        row('94131','2011')::zip_t)::address_t,
                1000.00);
insert into customer
        values (22222,
                'Fred Brown',
                row('355 Oak Street','Fairoaks','CA',
                        row('92355','3245')::zip_t)::address_t,
                2000.00);
```

The preceding are all examples of named row types, and the convention of naming a row type is to append _t to the end of a descriptive name, as in address_t or zip_t. You can also define unnamed row types, as shown here:

```
create table customer (customer_no integer,
                       name char(30),
                       address row(street char(30),
                                   city char(20),
                                   state char(2),
                                   zip char(5)),
                       balance money);
```

In this example, you cannot reuse the definition of the row type describing address because it does not have a name. But, like a named row type, a user can either retrieve all the fields by selecting the column name or use dot notation to access an individual field.

You can create a typed table by assigning a named row type to the table. You can assign the same named row type to different tables, thus creating multiple tables with the same structure:

```
create row type city_t (city_name varchar(30),
                        population integer);
create table city of type city_t;
```

Inheritance

Inheritance allows an object to acquire the properties of another object. For example, if a table is defined as a subtable of another one, it will inherit behaviors of the supertable, such as constraints, triggers, indices, and storage options. So, if the supertable is specified as having a referential constraint, the subtable will inherit that same constraint. Similarly, a named row type that is defined as a subtype of another row type will inherit the data fields and the behavior of the supertype, including routines, aggregates, and operators. If a user-defined routine had been created that operated on the supertype, the same routine could be used against the subtype.

In INFORMIX-Universal Server, inheritance is supported for named row types and typed tables. This means that you must define the row types before you can define the tables.

Here you are creating an employee row type, which contains basic information about each employee: name, department, and base salary. Then you create two row types for employees of different categories: salesmen who are paid on a commission basis and manage various accounts, and engineers who receive a bonus and possess various skills:

```
create row type employee_t (name char(20),
                            dept integer,
                            salary money);
create row type salesman_t (quota money,
                            attainment decimal(4,2),
                            commission decimal(4,2),
                            accounts set(varchar(30) not null))
          under employee_t;
create row type engineer_t (MBO_bonus money,
                            skills set(varchar(30) not null))
          under employee_t;
```

Because `salesman_t` and `engineer_t` are defined under `employee_t`, they will inherit the data fields `name`, `dept`, and `salary`, as well as any behaviors, such as user-defined routines, that may have been defined on `employee_t`. Both `salesman_t` and `engineer_t` are said to be subtypes of `employee_t`. `employee_t` is a supertype of `salesman_t` and `engineer_t`.

Now you can create tables based on these row types:

```
create table employee of type employee_t;
create table salesman of type salesman_t under employee;
create table engineer of type engineer_t under employee;
```

`employee` is a supertable, and `salesman` and `engineer` are subtables. When you define a table hierarchy, you must ensure that the relationships between the tables in the hierarchy match the relationships between the types in the type hierarchy, as shown in Figure 8.4.

The subtables `salesman` and `engineer` inherit all the properties of the supertable `employee`. This includes all the columns, indices, triggers, storage options, and any constraints, such as referential integrity constraints.

FIGURE 8.4.
Table and type hierarchies.

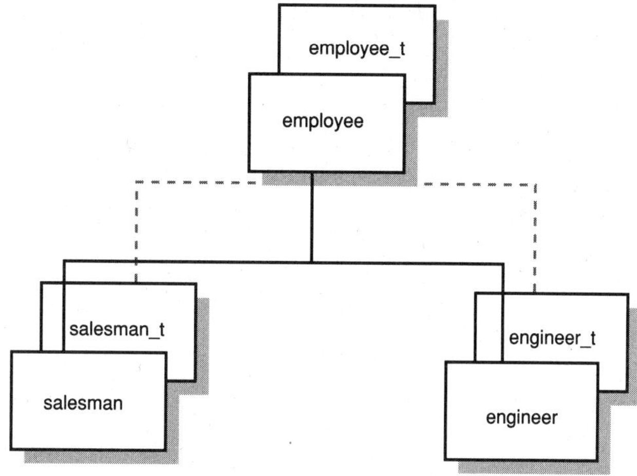

When you insert a row into one of the subtables, you must insert data for the columns inherited from the supertable:

```
insert into employee
            values('Fred Smith',
                   111,
                   1000.00);
insert into salesman
           values ('Tom Jones',
                   222,
                   2000.00,
                   50000.00,
                   80.00,
                   5.00,
                   "set{'ABC Shoes','Leiner Boots'}");
insert into engineer
           values ('Janet Brown',
                   333,
                   3000.00,
                   1000.00,
                   "set{'Cobol','Java'}");
```

When you have a table hierarchy, you can build an SQL statement whose scope is a supertable and its subtables. A `SELECT` statement against a supertable will return data for all the columns defined in that supertable, as well as for the inherited columns in the subtable:

```
select name, dept from employee;
```

returns

```
name                        dept
Fred Smith                   111
Tom Jones                    222
Janet Brown                  333
```

So if you have several different employee categories and define a separate subtable for each category, you do not need to query each table individually if what you want to retrieve is common data that is stored in the supertable. And if you add another subtable, you do not need to recode your query.

If you want to restrict the query to the supertable, you must use the ONLY keyword:

```
select name, dept from only (employee);
```

This returns

```
name                         dept
Fred Smith                    111
```

You can also retrieve all the columns in all the tables with one SELECT statement. This results in rows of varying length, known as *jagged rows*:

```
select employee from employee;
```

This returns

```
employee  ROW('Fred Smith           ',111          ,'$1000.00')
employee  ROW('Tom Jones            ',222          ,'$2000.00','$50000.00',80     ,
          5      ,SET{'ABC Shoes','Leiner Boots'})
employee  ROW('Janet Brown          ',333          ,'$3000.00','$1000.00',
          SET{'Cobol','Java'})
```

Notice that the columns in the rows are returned in row type format.

You can develop user-defined routines against row types defined in a type hierarchy. In the example, the total compensation for different categories of employees is calculated in a different way. An administrative employee simply receives a base salary; a salesman receives a base salary plus a commission based on quota attainment, and an engineer receives a base salary plus a bonus.

If you initially define only one compensation function against the employee type that simply returns the base salary, it will be used for all types in the hierarchy:

```
create function compensation(emp employee_t)
                             returning money;
    return emp.salary;
end function;
select name, salary, compensation(e) compensation
                              from employee e;
```

This returns

```
name                             salary     compensation
Fred Smith                     $1000.00         $1000.00
Tom Jones                      $2000.00         $2000.00
Janet Brown                    $3000.00         $3000.00
3 row(s) retrieved.
```

You could also create functions against the different types that perform different calculations:

```
create function compensation (sales salesman_t)
                              returning money;
       return (sales.salary
               +sales.commission/100
               *sales.attainment/100*sales.quota);
end function;
create function compensation(eng engineer_t)
                              returning money;
       return (eng.salary+eng.MBO_bonus);
end function;
```

Now using the same SQL statement as in the first example, different results are returned because different routines are invoked, depending on the row type passed to the function:

```
select name, salary, compensation(e) compensation
                from employee e;
```

This now returns

```
name                               salary     compensation
Fred Smith                       $1000.00         $1000.00
Tom Jones                        $2000.00         $4000.00
Janet Brown                      $3000.00         $4000.00
```

What is happening in these examples is *function overloading.* When routines are defined for types in a type hierarchy, the function manager will look for a routine with a signature of the row type that is being passed. If there is no routine with that signature, it can use an inherited routine from the supertype. The specific routine is selected only when the data is passed; this is known as *late binding.*

User-Defined Data Types

In addition to the data types you have already reviewed, you can extend the functionality of INFORMIX-Universal Server by defining your own data types to meet the needs of your application. For example, if you have an application dealing with weather information from different countries, where temperatures are recorded in Celsius or Fahrenheit, you can define data types to hold the readings and develop user-defined routines to convert from one scale to the other. The strong typing characteristic of INFORMIX-Universal Server ensures that a user cannot inadvertently compare readings on different scales without doing the appropriate conversion.

Distinct Data Types

A distinct data type is based on an existing type, such as a built-in type or a complex type, and has the same internal structure as the type on which it is based. Because it is based on a type that is already defined, the server knows how to store it, access it, and operate on it.

Assume you have a table that contains average summer and winter temperatures for different cities. You will use a user-defined data type, `fahrenheit`, based on an integer data type, to hold temperature values for cities in the United States, and another one, `celsius`, to hold temperature values for cities in the Republic of South Africa:

```
create distinct type fahrenheit as integer;
create distinct type celsius as integer;
create table rsa_city (city_name char(20),
                      population integer,
                      avg_summer_temp celsius,
                      avg_winter_temp celsius);
create table usa_city (city_name char(20),
                      population integer,
                      avg_summer_temp fahrenheit,
                      avg_winter_temp fahrenheit);
```

You can define functions for the type that allow you to *cast* it to and from another data type, as well as functions to perform different operations on the type. Because distinct types are strongly typed, you cannot, for example, do a direct compare between a column of a distinct type and a column defined as the base type without casting one type to the other.

Casting

Casting functions perform the operations necessary to convert data from one type to another. For example, casting from decimal to integer would include truncating the digits after the decimal point. Implicit cast functions are defined in the server for converting character types to other character types, numeric to numeric, time to or from date time, and character to or from any other built-in type. Implicit casts are automatically invoked by the server when required.

When you define a distinct type, INFORMIX-Universal Server automatically creates explicit casts between the new type and its source type. Because these casts are explicit, you must use the cast operator to invoke them, as shown in the following `INSERT` statements:

```
insert into rsa_city values ('CapeTown',
                             3200000,
                             21::celsius,
                             14::celsius);
insert into rsa_city values ('Johannesburg',
                             1900000,
                             19::celsius,
                             9::celsius);
insert into usa_city values ('Anchorage',
                             250000,
                             45::fahrenheit,
                             20::fahrenheit);
insert into usa_city values ('Miami',

                             2100000,
                             82::fahrenheit,
                             67::fahrenheit);
```

You can also create casting functions to perform the conversions between the `celsius` and `fahrenheit` data types:

```
create function c_to_f (temp celsius)
                        returning fahrenheit;
    return (9*temp::integer/5 +32)::fahrenheit;
end function;
create explicit cast (celsius as fahrenheit with c_to_f);
```

This would allow a user to perform comparisons between temperatures in different cities. The SQL statement

```
select city_name, avg_summer_temp::fahrenheit avg_summer
               from rsa_city
   union
select city_name, avg_summer_temp avg_summer
               from usa_city
order by 2 desc;
```

will produce

```
city_name   Miami
avg_summer  82
city_name   CapeTown
avg_summer  69
city_name   Johannesburg
avg_summer  66
city_name   Anchorage
avg_summer  45
```

You could create a function that would calculate whether a temperature was above or below freezing. Because the calculation is different depending on whether the temperature was recorded in Celsius or Fahrenheit, you could overload the function name, as shown here:

```
create function above_freezing(temp celsius)
        returning boolean;
if ( temp::integer > 0 ) then
        return 't'::boolean;
else
        return 'f'::boolean;
end if
end function;
create function above_freezing(temp fahrenheit)
        returning boolean;
if ( temp::integer > 32 ) then
        return 't'::boolean;
else
        return 'f'::boolean;
end if
end function;
```

Then you could use that function to determine which cities had temperate winter climates. For example, for the U.S. cities, the average winter temperature in Anchorage is recognized as being below freezing:

```
select city_name, 'Warmish' Comfort_Level, avg_winter_temp
          from usa_city
          where above_freezing(avg_winter_temp)
```

```
union
select city_name, 'Coldish' Comfort_Level, avg_winter_temp
         from usa_city
         where not above_freezing(avg_winter_temp)
order by 2 desc;
```

This returns

```
city_name        Miami
comfort_level    Warmish
avg_winter_temp  67
city_name        Anchorage
comfort_level    Coldish
avg_winter_temp  20
```

For the South African cities, temperatures below 20 are recognized as being above freezing because they are on the Celsius scale:

```
select city_name, 'Warmish' Comfort_Level, avg_winter_temp
         from rsa_city
         where above_freezing(avg_winter_temp)
union
select city_name, 'Coldish' Comfort_Level, avg_winter_temp
         from rsa_city
         where not above_freezing(avg_winter_temp)
order by 2 desc;
```

This returns

```
city_name        CapeTown
comfort_level    Warmish
avg_winter_temp  14
city_name        Johannesburg
comfort_level    Warmish
avg_winter_temp  9
```

Opaque Data Types

Opaque types are named as such because INFORMIX-Universal Server does not know anything about the internal representation of the data. Distinct types are not opaque because they are based on other types that are known to the server. Similarly, row types and collections are based on other defined types. And if distinct row types or collections are based on opaque types, those opaque types must already have been defined to the server. An opaque type is similar to a built-in type in that it cannot be broken into smaller pieces; you cannot use SQL statements to access its components. The only way a user can access or manipulate an opaque type is via user-defined functions. Opaque types are typically used to store complex data structures—such as image, audio, or video objects—or to represent complex relationships such as networks or geometric shapes. An opaque type can store data within its internal structure or, for very large amounts of data, can embed a smart large object.

Creating an opaque type is not a trivial task. Opaque types are generally created by DataBlade developers. When you create an opaque type, you must provide the following information:

- A C structure to describe the data so that it can be stored correctly. This structure can be of fixed or variable length.
- Support functions that allow the server to interact with the data. Examples of support functions include functions to convert the opaque data from its internal representation to its external representation, or to compare two data items of this opaque type during a sort. If the data type includes embedded smart large objects, additional support functions are required to allow INFORMIX-Universal Server to search for references to these objects.
- Additional routines to support user requirements for interacting with the data. For example, if the opaque data type is used for storing text, you would probably want to create search routines. You might also want to overload existing built-in functions such as `length()`.

If you plan to make extensive use of opaque types and their associated routines, you should consider acquiring the DataBlade Developer's Kit. This provides guidance on recommended coding practices and development techniques.

Large Object Support

INFORMIX-Universal Server supports both simple large objects (BYTE and TEXT) and smart large objects (BLOB and CLOB) to handle large amounts of data (greater than 255 bytes). The main difference between simple large objects (which were available with INFORMIX-OnLine Dynamic Server 7.2) and smart large objects is that programs can randomly access data within a smart large object and can update portions of the data. Simple large objects, on the other hand, can only be inserted or deleted; they cannot be updated. The BYTE and TEXT data types are provided for backward compatibility, and for new applications you should generally use the BLOB and CLOB data types.

Smart large objects are generally used for storing user-defined data types that contain images, audio or video clips, large documents, or spatial objects like drawings or maps. The random access capability allows you to manipulate portions of a large object, thus giving you the ability to access data within the object without retrieving the entire object.

Creating a Table with a Smart Large Object

When you create a table containing a smart lob, you can specify the sbspace where the lob is to be placed, as well as other options, such as whether lob actions are to be logged and what kind of integrity checks are to be performed when the lob is updated. This example shows that the `picture` large object is to be placed in the sbspace called sbspace3:

```
create table cars (make char(20),
                   model char(20),
                   picture blob)
      put picture in (sbspace3);
```

Inserting and Deleting Smart Large Objects

Four functions are provided to move data into and out of smart lobs. The `FiletoBLOB` and `FiletoCLOB` functions copy an external flat file into an sbspace while the `LOtoFile` function copies a blob or a clob from the sbspace to an external file. For all three of these functions, you can specify whether the external file resides on the server or the client:

```
insert into cars values ('Toyota',
                         'Celica',
                         filetoBLOB('celica.gif','client'));
```

The `LOCopy` function allows you to copy a lob from one table to another. For example, if you have defined a table "assets" as

```
create table assets (asset_id char(5),
                     asset_type char(15),
                     picture blob)
                     put picture in (sbspace3);
```

you could copy a picture from the cars table with this statement:

```
update assets set
        picture=LOCopy(picture,'cars','picture')
        where asset_id='12345';
```

Manipulating Data Within a Smart Large Object

If you select a column containing a smart large object from a tool like DBaccess, you will not actually see the object because DBaccess does not know how to present it. (It could be an image, a video stream, a spreadsheet, or anything else that you have chosen to store there.) Instead, you will receive a message indicating that smart lob data is present.

```
select * from cars;
make     Toyota
model    Celica
picture  <SBlob Data>
```

If you want to manipulate data within a smart lob, you will need to use the ESQL/C or DataBlade APIs. These allow you to seek to a given position within the lob and read or write a user-specified number of bytes from that position. DataBlade developers often use smart lobs to store their user-defined data types and will provide you with user-defined functions or end-user tools to perform these manipulations, so that you do not need to code to these APIs.

Access Methods

A primary access method is a set of routines used to access data directly. INFORMIX-Universal Server provides a built-in primary access method that performs table operations such as scan, insert, update, and delete. In addition, the *virtual table interface* allows you to develop primary access methods for accessing data stored external to the server—for example, data stored in other vendor databases or in flat files. You can then define a table and specify that it is stored in an *extspace*, which is a storage space not managed directly by the server. You must also specify the access method to be used to access that table.

Secondary access methods, often called indices, provide alternate access paths to data managed by the server. The primary access method supplied with INFORMIX-Universal Server supports two secondary access methods: generic B-tree and an R-tree.

B-Tree Indexes

The generic B-tree access method can be used to index user-defined types as well as built-in data types. When indexing on user-defined types, you may need to define additional functions to enable the server to index and retrieve the data correctly.

If you are indexing on a distinct type whose logical sequence is the same as the sequence of the underlying base type, you need not define additional functions. For example, the distinct type CELSIUS could be indexed using a generic B-tree index without coding any additional routines because a temperature of 100° is greater than a temperature of 80°, just as the integer 100 is greater than 80. On the other hand, if you want to use a generic B-tree on an opaque type, you must code functions that the server can use to compare different values.

R-Tree Indexes

The R-tree index is used for columns that contain spatial data such as maps. It is a dynamic balanced multiway tree structure that uses a concept called bounding boxes, which are sets of coordinates that enclose one or more objects. Non-leaf pages contain bounding boxes that contain all the lower-level children. If a WHERE clause contained an EQUAL, GREATERTHAN, or LESSTHAN function, the optimizer would evaluate using a B-tree index; if it contained an OVERLAP, EQUAL, CONTAINS, or WITHIN function, an R-tree index would be considered.

Functional Indexes

You can create an index on the values of a function performed against one or more columns. For example, if you have defined a function TOTAL_PAY() that computes the total compensation of an employee as the sum of a base salary and a bonus, you could define an index as

```
create index pay_index on employee
          (total_pay(salary,bonus));
```

In this case, the server will build the index using the computed values and will update the index if the underlying data changes.

DataBlade Indices

DataBlade developers can create their own access methods in order to improve performance by providing indices on opaque types they have defined. To do this, they need to extend the operator class that includes the set of functions that supports a secondary access method. These functions include

- Strategy functions that tell the optimizer which predicates in the query are indexable. Examples of strategy functions for a B-tree index are the operator functions less than (<), equals (=), and so on.
- Support functions that the optimizer uses to evaluate the strategy functions. The support function for a B-tree index is a `compare()` function.

To build an index on an opaque type they have defined, DataBlade developers must overload the existing strategy and support functions by defining new functions with the same name that take their data type as an argument.

A similar process can be used to extend the operator class for R-tree indexes.

Developing DataBlades

The first step in building a DataBlade is to decide on the requirements you want to address. The typical DataBlade has a fairly narrow focus on some specific domain in which the developer has significant expertise. DataBlades may address horizontal markets, such as text, audio, or image processing, or vertical industry markets, such as insurance, manufacturing, or medical applications. Multiple DataBlades may be appropriate even within one domain. For example, in the audio arena, you could develop a DataBlade to perform voice recognition (that is, identify a person by his speech patterns), another one to find all sounds similar to a particular sound, and a third to implement a voice-to-text system.

Developing a DataBlade includes building some or all of the following components:

- User-defined data types
- C functions using the DataBlade API or stored procedures to support the data types
- Casts for converting values between data types
- Secondary access methods
- Interfaces that register dependencies on any other DataBlades
- Tables, views, and indices to support client applications
- Test cases
- Documentation
- Help files
- Client applications
- Installation and maintenance scripts

DataBlade Developer's Kit

To facilitate the development of DataBlade modules by third-party vendors, Informix offers a DataBlade Developer's Program that offers tools, training, and joint-marketing opportunities. The DataBlade Developer's Kit (DBDK) provides a graphical development environment for creating new data types and functions, and for managing the packaging, registration, and installation of the resulting DataBlade modules. Using this tool ensures that DataBlade users have a consistent interface for the installation of DataBlades they purchase.

DataBlade API

The DataBlade API is a call-level interface that provides access to database objects from client applications written in C, C++, and Visual Basic, and from user-defined functions and support routines written in C. DataBlade code executes in the INFORMIX-Universal Server threaded environment and shares memory with other server processes. Guidelines are provided with the DBDK documentation to assist you in developing safe, efficient modules. They include recommendations for using the DataBlade API memory allocation routines—`mi_alloc()` and `mi_free()`—rather than the C library `malloc()` and `free()`, and other methods for writing thread-safe code. You can also create a private installation of the server that can be used for debugging DataBlade modules.

BladeSmith

BladeSmith, shown in Figure 8.5, assists with DataBlade development projects by providing a visual representation of the objects in a DataBlade module and by allowing you to add new objects and modify object properties. It is designed for a team development environment and includes facilities for copying components between projects.

When you define a new data type, you can specify the various operators and support functions that are needed. BladeSmith will generate the SQL statements needed to define the data type and, if it is based on a C structure, will also generate a starter set of C code for the operators and functions necessary to support a B-tree or R-tree index, as well as many of the other operators and support functions.

After the objects have been defined, BladeSmith will generate source code files, SQL scripts, and the installation packaging files.

BladePack

BladePack, shown in Figure 8.6, packages the various components of the DataBlade and prepares a distribution file for delivery to a customer. It takes SQL scripts, shared object files, and other components and generates diskette images or a directory tree that can be packaged using a program such as `tar` or `pkzip` for final distribution.

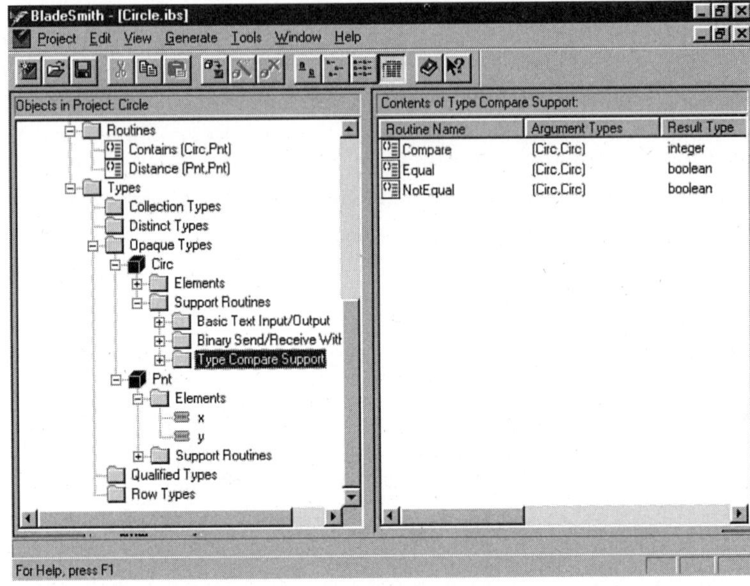

FIGURE 8.5.
The BladeSmith tool.

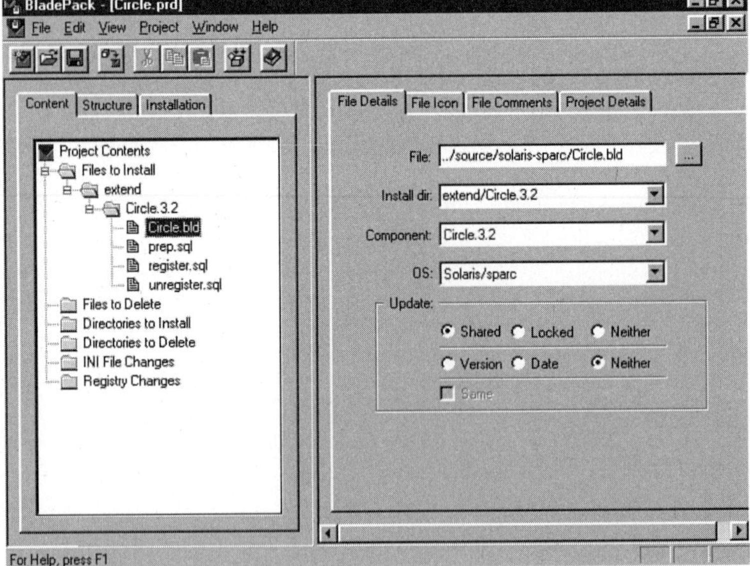

FIGURE 8.6.
The BladePack tool.

Tools and Utilities

The onspaces, oncheck, and onstat utilities have been enhanced to support the new objects. Onspaces is used to create, drop, or extend sbspaces that are used for storing smart large objects. New parameters with the onspaces utility include specification of metadata storage size and options relating to logging, access time tracking, and expected object sizes.

Existing tools previously available with INFORMIX-OnLine Dynamic Server 7.2 are supported under INFORMIX-Universal Server and have been extended to support the new objects as appropriate. These include dbload, dbexport/dbimport, dbschema, and dbaccess. Three new DBA tools are provided: BladeManager, Schema Knowledge, and the SQL Editor.

BladeManager

BladeManager allows you to register and unregister DataBlades in a particular database. The registration process involves reading a script that contains SQL statements to register each function, data type, aggregation, and cast into the database catalog. BladeManager runs as a GUI interface on Windows clients or as a text interface on UNIX systems.

Options are available to list the DataBlade modules that are installed on the system but are not registered in a database, to list the modules that are registered, and to install client files to support a DataBlade module. Figure 8.7 shows the screen you would use to register a DataBlade.

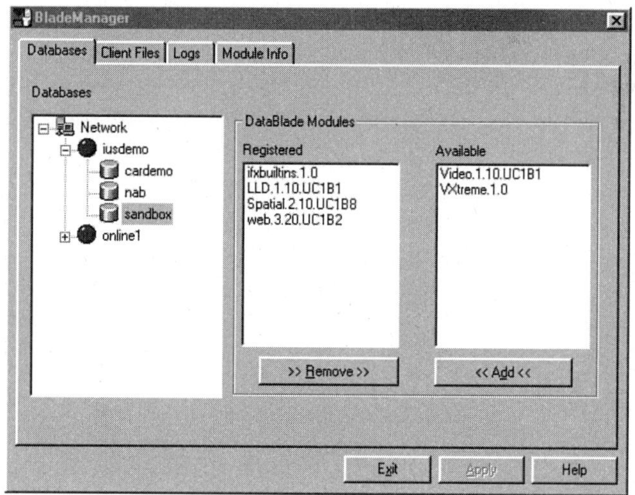

FIGURE 8.7.
Using BladeManager to register a DataBlade.

Schema Knowledge

Schema Knowledge is a Windows-based tool that allows you to see the metadata about objects in your database. For example, you can see what tables have been defined, what columns are in a particular table, and what the definitions of those columns are. Schema Knowledge can be particularly valuable in determining what casts have been defined, what inheritance hierarchies exist, and what arguments are needed by different functions.

After you have connected to a database, Schema Knowledge presents a window divided into two main views: a Database view that contains a list of objects and an Item view that contains details of the object that has been selected in the Database view. Figure 8.8 shows the objects in the database "sandbox" and a list of all the tables.

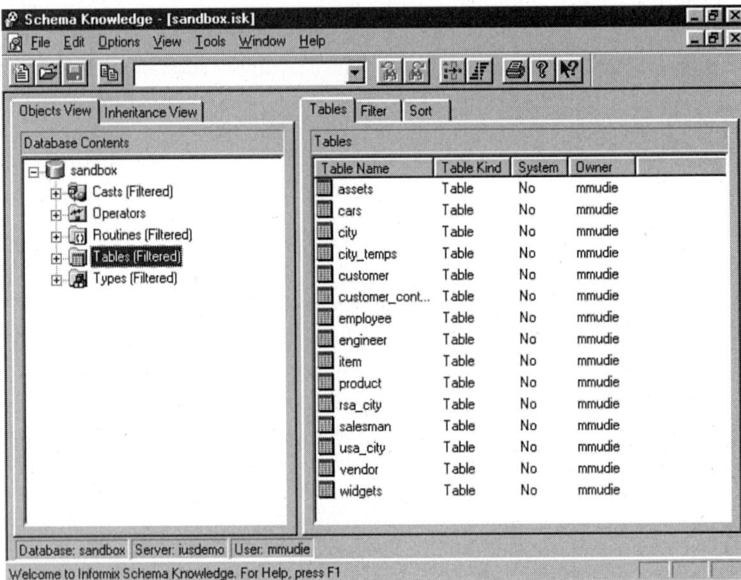

FIGURE 8.8.
Schema Knowledge.

You can set a filter to restrict the objects displayed; you can filter by owner name or other object attributes. Navigation is similar to Windows 95 Explorer; clicking on an object in the Database view will cause a list of the contents to be displayed in the Items view; double-clicking will expand the hierarchy in the Database view. If the object selected is at the lowest level in the hierarchy, details about that object will be displayed in the Items view.

Figure 8.9 shows an example of the information provided for a user-defined routine. The SPL code is displayed; if the routine had been developed in C, the path to the binary object would have been displayed instead.

Interrelationships between objects can be explored using the Hyperlink facility. For example, if you are displaying column details in the Item view, as shown in Figure 8.10, clicking on the arrow next to the column type will take you to information about the definition of that column type. The Jump History toolbar allows you to traverse back and forth across the path you have followed.

Schema Knowledge can be very useful in providing a view of the hierarchical relationship between tables or types. The Database view shows the Inheritance view for the whole database when the Inheritance tab is selected. The Items view shows the immediate supertable and subtable for the table selected in the Database view. Hyperlinks are provided so that you can jump to view information about any of these objects.

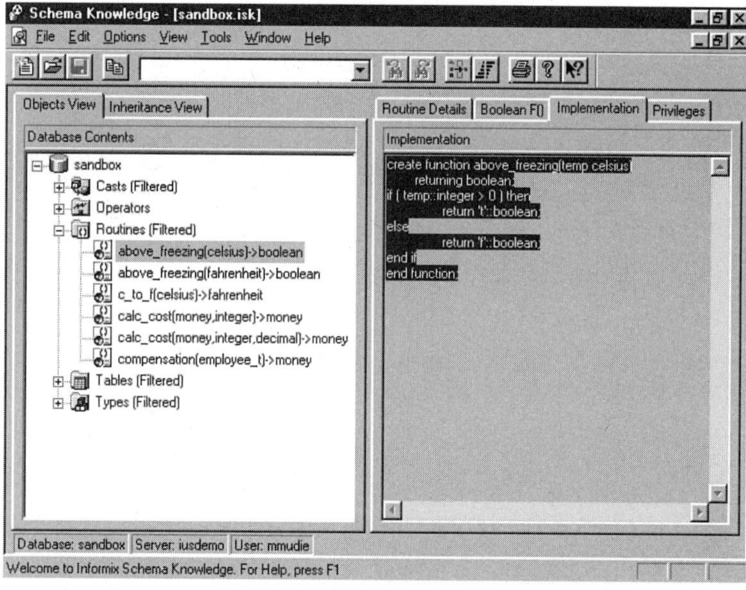

FIGURE 8.9.
User-defined functions.

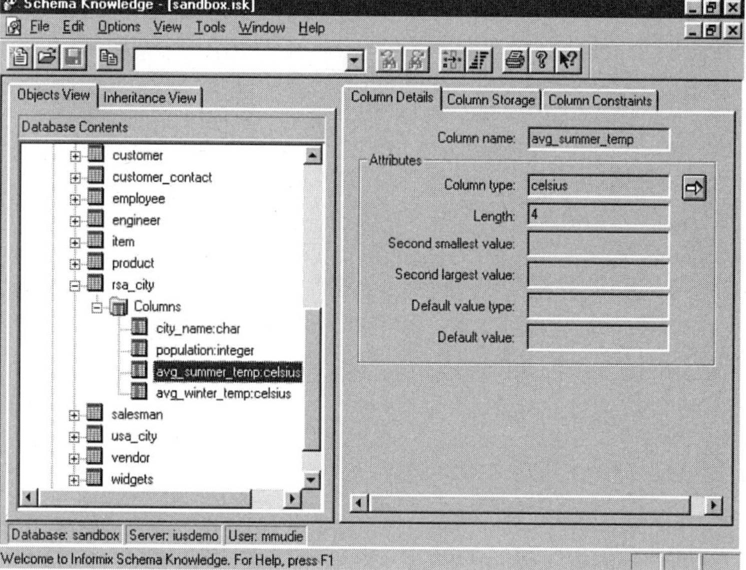

FIGURE 8.10.
Column details in Schema Knowledge.

SQL Editor

The SQL Editor, shown in Figure 8.11, is a Windows-based tool that allows you to test SQL statements and view their results. You can enter SQL statements on the screen or use statements that have been stored in a text file.

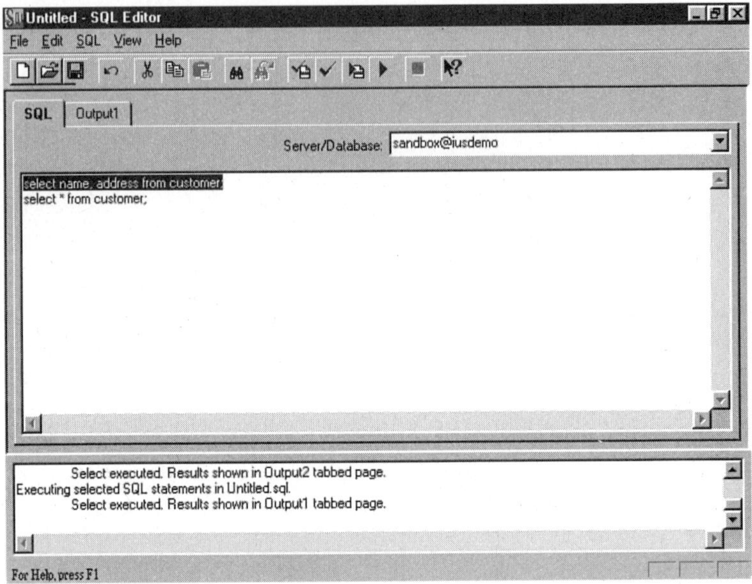

FIGURE 8.11.
Using SQL Editor to enter SQL statements.

As you can see in Figure 8.11, the SQL Editor window contains a text box in which you can enter SQL statements. You can use icons on the tool bar to request a syntax check on all statements in the text box or only statements you have highlighted. Similarly, you can request that all statements be executed or only selected ones. When a statement is executed, the returned results can be seen by selecting the Output tab. Status messages are displayed in the Result History text box.

The SQL statement used to produce the return results is shown at the top of the Output folder. In the example in Figure 8.12, one of the columns, Address, was in fact a row type, and you can see the primary heading Address with secondary headings below it for the individual fields, street, city, state, and zip. You can select some or all of the columns and copy and paste them to some other application, such as a spreadsheet.

If the data returned cannot be displayed in the Returned Rows grid, the Cell Viewer can be used to display the contents of a particular cell. Figure 8.13 shows how the Cell Viewer can be used to see the individual elements of a `MULTISET` collection data type.

FIGURE 8.12.
Looking at results in SQL editor.

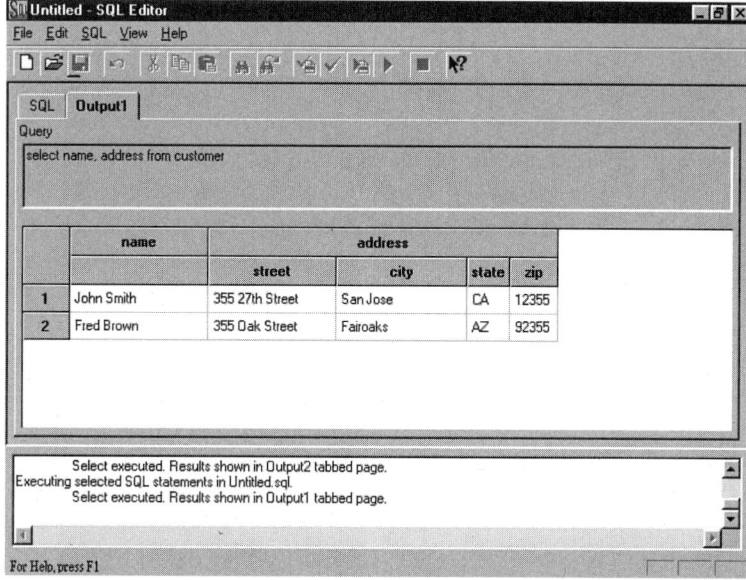

FIGURE 8.13.
Using the Cell Viewer.

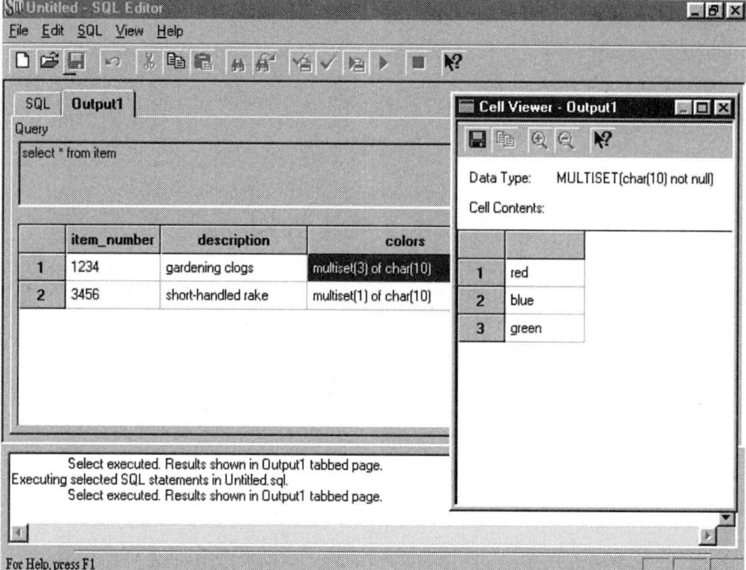

The Informix Web DataBlade

The Web DataBlade is a set of tools that enables you to build dynamic Web applications without having to write CGI scripts in Perl, TCL, or C. Instead, it provides a database-resident scripting metaphor, which includes the capability to publish any database content on the Web.

HTML documents that include these scripting tags are called AppPages. The database-resident parser (which scans HTML documents for specific tags) works in conjunction with a general-purpose middle-tier component—Webdriver. This middle tier, which is implemented for both `cgi` and `nsapi/isapi` environments, can retrieve HTML documents (with embedded tags) and large objects with their associated mime types from the database. This enables you to store your entire Web site (HTML, images, documents, and application data) in the database. Object and page caching functions are included. Figure 8.14 illustrates the architecture.

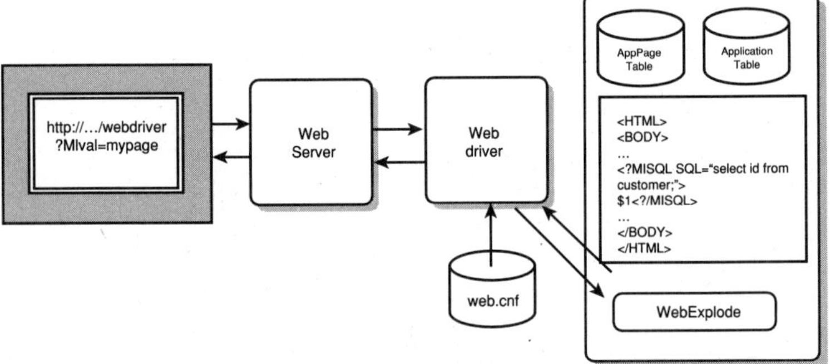

FIGURE 8.14.
Web DataBlade architecture.

If the browser requests a URL that specifies Webdriver (for example, `http://server.domain.com/cgi-bin/webdriver?Mival=apppage`), the server will invoke the Webdriver CGI interface. Using a configuration file called `web.cnf` as well as the parameters passed from the browser, Webdriver executes a WebExplode function (provided with the Web Blade) that retrieves the AppPage from the database and executes any SQL contained within the AppPage. The results are formatted and returned as HTML via Webdriver to the Web server, which, in turn, sends it to the client browser.

The power of the WebExplode function is that the SQL it executes can retrieve not just application data from database tables, but also further HTML definitions, so that the structure, appearance, and components of the final HTML page can be dynamically generated. The final appearance of the page can be based on requests passed by the browser, parameters stored in the configuration file, and/or data retrieved from the database during page generation. You can also access variables from the Web Server environment and work with cookies to track users or develop a transaction mode of operation. The Web DataBlade can be used in conjunction with other DataBlades such as a text or spatial DataBlade, so that you can search across different data types and/or display them on your Web site.

The Web DataBlade includes the following SGML-compliant tags:

- `<?MISQL>` contains SQL statements and formatting specifications for the data that is retrieved.
- `<?MIVAR>` is used to create, assign, and display user variables.

- <?MIBLOCK> delimits logical blocks of HTML that can be executed based on user-defined conditions.
- <?MIERROR> is used to manage error processing.

In addition, you can define your own tags. This feature allows you to reuse HTML and can help ensure consistency across a Web site as well as cut down on development time. SQL-proficient developers can code tags that allow HTML coders to retrieve application data from the database without understanding the intricacies of SQL.

The `web.cnf` configuration file contains environment variables used by Webdriver, as well as user application variables. Environment variables include

`WEB_HOME`: The URL-mapped path to the Webdriver binary.

`MIval`: The name of the AppPage to be retrieved.

`MItab`: The name of the table containing the AppPages.

Other variables are used to specify the table that contains images, the names of the columns that contain the AppPage or image, and so on.

Application Page Builder (APB)

The Web DataBlade module also includes a sample application that allows you to create and maintain AppPages. Figure 8.15 shows the initial page.

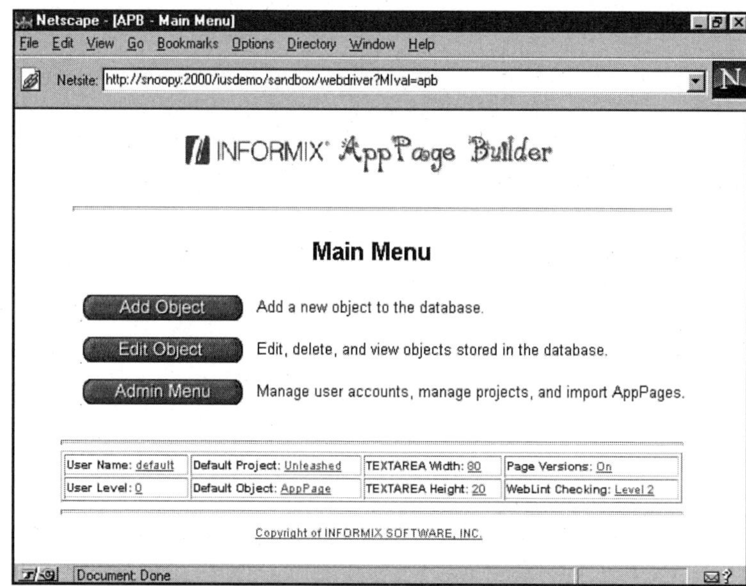

FIGURE 8.15.
The application page builder menu.

APB also provides good examples of how to code AppPages and user-defined tags. During the APB installation process, a set of tables is created for storing AppPages, images, audio clips, videos, and documents, as well as other administrative pages. You can use these for storing objects you plan to use on your Web site, such as buttons, logos, or background images.

Building a Sample Web Page

Let's assume that you want to build a Web page that displays the contents of a widgets table. You would like to use a standard header and footer layout to ensure consistency across all the pages on your site. But you would like to be able to vary the color or background image to be used, depending on which part of the site you are in.

To achieve these objectives, you would need to do the following:

1. Construct the overall page definition and store it in the webPages table.

```
<?web_header TITLE="Wilhelmina Widget Factory" BGIMG=jazzbkgd>
<CENTER>
<TABLE border=2 width=400>
<?MiSQL SQL="select picture, id, name, price from widgets;">
<TR ALIGN=CENTER>
    <TD><IMG SRC=$WEB_HOME?LO=$1&MItypeObj=image/gif></TD>
    <TD>$2</TD>
    <TD ALIGN=LEFT>$3</TD>
    <TD>$4</TD>
</TR>
<?/MISQL>
</TABLE>
</CENTER>
<?web_footer>
```

   The first thing you should do is invoke a tag to set up the header. As you'll see later on, this tag will provide the `<HTML>`, `<HEAD>`, and `<BODY>` tags. You pass two parameters—the phrase you want to display as the title, and the name of a gif that is to be used as the background.

   Then you set up a table to display the output of the SQL call that follows. The MISQL tag contains a `SELECT` statement that retrieves four columns from the widgets table. The results from the `SELECT` statement are returned as numbered column variables ($1, $2, and so on). The first column retrieved is a picture of the widget. The "handle" of the picture (which is stored in a blob column) is passed to the `IMG` tag as column variable `$1`. The `IMG SRC` parameter specifies the `$WEB_HOME` variable that will expand to the URL-mapped path to the Webdriver module as defined in the `web.cnf` configuration file. Webdriver will then retrieve the actual picture from the database. The remaining column variables—`$2`, `$3`, and `$4`—will be placed in the other table columns. A new table row will be generated for each row of data returned by the SQL statement.

Finally, you invoke the `web_footer` tag to display the footer. As you'll see later on, this tag will provide the `</BODY>` and `</HTML>` tags.

2. Define the header tag that would be stored in the webTags table.

```
<?MIVAR NAME=bgcolor>@BGCOLOR@<?/MIVAR>
<?MIVAR NAME=bgimg>@BGIMG@<?/MIVAR>
<HTML>
<HEAD>
<TITLE>Informix Universal Server - @TITLE@</TITLE>
</HEAD>
<?MIVAR>
<BODY BGCOLOR=$bgcolor
      BACKGROUND=$WEB_HOME?MIvalObj=$bgimg>
<?/MIVAR>
<CENTER>
<TABLE WIDTH=400>
<TR ALIGN=CENTER>
<TD WIDTH=80>
   <IMG SRC=<?MIVAR>$WEB_HOME<?/MIVAR>?MIvalObj=mylogo ALIGN=middle>
</TD>
<TD ALIGN=CENTER>
   <FONT SIZE=+2>@TITLE@</FONT>
</TD>
</TR></TABLE>
</CENTER>
<BR>
<HR>
```

The `MIVAR` tags define two variables: `bgcolor` and `bgimg`. These variables are set to the values passed when this tag is invoked. The title is set to the title phrase that is passed.

The `BODY` tag illustrates another way of loading images. Here you pass the name of the image to be retrieved (which was supplied in the `bgimg` variable) to Webdriver to retrieve from the database. You use the same technique to retrieve the company logo.

3. Define the footer tag, which would be stored in the webTags table.

```
<HR>
<P ALIGN=RIGHT>Powered by
<?MIVAR>
<A HREF=$WEB_HOME?MIval=web_info>Informix Universal Server</A>
<?/MIVAR>
</BODY>
</HTML>
```

Here you see an example of setting up a reference to another AppPage. Again, the `$WEB_HOME` variable will be expanded to the URL of the Webdriver module.

The page produced is shown in Figure 8.16.

The generated HTML for this page, as displayed at the browser, is shown in Listing 8.1. (The LO handles have been abbreviated for clarity.)

FIGURE 8.16.
A sample Web page.

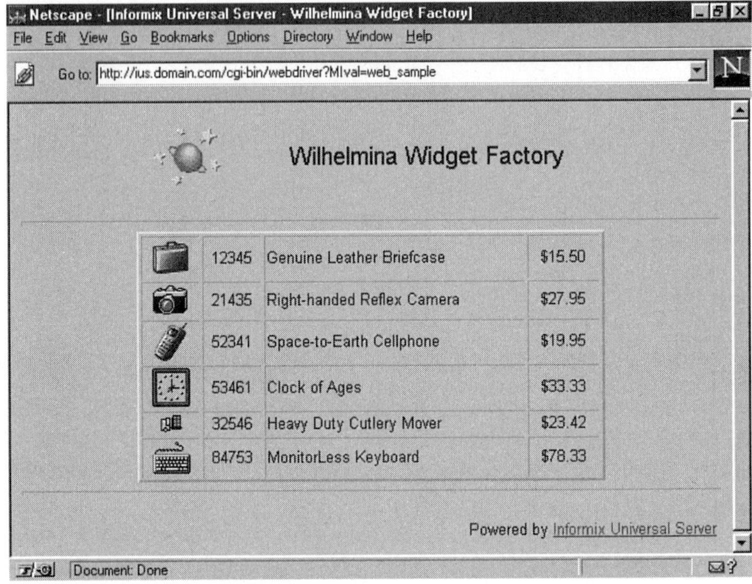

Listing 8.1. Generated HTML.

```
<HTML>
<HEAD>
<TITLE>Informix Universal Server - Wilhelmina Widget Factory</TITLE>
</HEAD>

<BODY BGCOLOR=#B0C4DE
      BACKGROUND=http://ius.domain.com/cgi-bin/webdriver?MIvalObj=>

<CENTER>
<TABLE WIDTH=400>
<TR ALIGN=CENTER>
<TD WIDTH=80>
   <IMG SRC=http://ius.domain.com/cgi-bin/webdriver?MIvalObj=mylogo ALIGN=middle>
</TD>
<TD ALIGN=CENTER>
   <FONT SIZE=+2>Wilhelmina Widget Factory</FONT>
</TD>
</TR></TABLE>
</CENTER>
<BR>
<HR>
<CENTER>
<TABLE border=2 width=400>

<TR ALIGN=CENTER>
    <TD><IMG SRC=http://ius.domain.com/cgi-bin/
    ➥webdriver?LO=000…00&MItypeObj=image/gif></TD>
    <TD>12345</TD>
    <TD ALIGN=LEFT>Genuine Leather Briefcase</TD>
    <TD>$15.50</TD>
</TR>
```

```
<TR ALIGN=CENTER>
    <TD><IMG SRC=http://ius.domain.com/cgi-bin/
    ➥webdriver?LO=006…00&MItypeObj=image/gif></TD>
    <TD>21435</TD>
    <TD ALIGN=LEFT>Right-handed Reflex Camera</TD>
    <TD>$27.95</TD>
</TR>

<TR ALIGN=CENTER>
    <TD><IMG SRC=http://ius.domain.com/cgi-bin/
    ➥webdriver?LO=006…00&MItypeObj=image/gif></TD>
    <TD>52341</TD>
    <TD ALIGN=LEFT>Space-to-Earth Cellphone</TD>
    <TD>$19.95</TD>
</TR>
<TR ALIGN=CENTER>
    <TD><IMG SRC=http://ius.domain.com/cgi-bin/
    ➥webdriver?LO=006…00&MItypeObj=image/gif></TD>
    <TD>53461</TD>
    <TD ALIGN=LEFT>Clock of Ages</TD>
    <TD>$33.33</TD>
</TR>

<TR ALIGN=CENTER>
    <TD><IMG SRC=http://ius.domain.com/cgi-bin/
    ➥webdriver?LO=006…00&MItypeObj=image/gif></TD>
    <TD>32546</TD>
    <TD ALIGN=LEFT>Heavy Duty Cutlery Mover</TD>
    <TD>$23.42</TD>
</TR>

<TR ALIGN=CENTER>
    <TD><IMG SRC=http://ius.domain.com/cgi-bin/
    ➥webdriver?LO=006…00&MItypeObj=image/gif></TD>
    <TD>84753</TD>
    <TD ALIGN=LEFT>MonitorLess Keyboard</TD>
    <TD>$78.33</TD>
</TR>

</TABLE>
</CENTER>
<HR>
<P ALIGN=RIGHT>Powered by

<A HREF=http://ius.domain.com/cgi-bin/
➥webdriver?MIval=web_info>Informix Universal Server</A>

</BODY>
</HTML>
```

Summary

INFORMIX-Universal Server extends traditional relational database technology to support more complex data types with associated user-defined functions and access methods. You can define your own extensions to support the data types needed by your applications, or you can purchase DataBlade modules from third-party vendors with domain expertise. The underlying Dynamic Scalable Architecture provides a multithreaded, parallelized, and high-performance fault-tolerant environment suitable for building industrial-strength business applications, and it allows you to leverage skills gained with earlier Informix database products.

III PART

IN THIS PART

Informix Administration

CHAPTER 9

Administration Introduction

by John McNally

IN THIS CHAPTER

This chapter provides

- A description of the different types of database administrators (DBAs)
- A breakdown of tasks performed by DBAs
- A description of batch and online transaction processing and how they affect a DBA's tasks
- An analysis of the interaction between DBAs and developers
- An analysis of the interaction between DBAs and users

Being a DBA

Of all the jobs in the data-processing world, being a DBA can be the most precarious. The DBA is always in the middle when a problem occurs. If the system is not running very well, the DBA is usually the first person blamed, even when a hardware or application software situation is causing the problem. It seems natural for the rest of the data-processing community to blame the database or the database administrator, because the database is the one area users see as a "black box." Programmers, application managers, and users do not understand what the DBMS is doing to manage their data. It is this lack of understanding—combined with the need for their data to be easily accessed—that makes non-DBAs look toward the database first when a problem occurs. But if the DBA is a calm person, able to explain the DBMS process to others, and able to handle stress well, then being a DBA is a technically challenging and rewarding job.

Not all DBA positions are as stressful as the ones just mentioned, but it's true that the DBA is in the middle of things. The data that the DBA is responsible for is important to certain people, or they would not need the data stored at all. The DBA must make sure that the data is available and safe, and that the system is providing that data as quickly and efficiently as possible. How "mission-critical" this data is and how well the system is running determines the amount of stress in the DBA's job.

Most of the DBA's stress comes from unexpected system problems. All DBMSs have problems with bugs and operating system compatibility. These problems are usually solved with system patches, with small fixes from the vendor, or by complete software upgrades. But this is a never-ending cycle; every time a bug is fixed, a new one is created somewhere else. And with every new software version installed, a new set of problems is found. Informix products suffer from these situations, like every other software product sold, for the multitude of different operating systems. Fortunately, being a DBA on an Informix database system has its benefits over other database management systems.

One benefit is that Informix provides a DBMS that is very easy to administer. As explained in the previous chapters on each of the Informix DBMS products, all the Informix database management systems have many built-in functions to monitor and manage themselves. A well-tuned and trimmed, standard-sized Informix database requires very little DBA interaction on a daily basis. This allows the DBA to concentrate on other issues, such as data layouts and the application's performance.

Another benefit of Informix is that the time required to become an Informix DBA is short when compared to other DBMSs. Because of this, many computer professionals are not full-time Informix DBAs. Usually, people are dedicated Informix DBAs for companies with extremely large databases or for companies with many smaller separate database systems. This explains why there are many different types of Informix DBAs.

Types of DBAs

As you know, there are many types of Informix DBAs. The size of the company or the size of the database determines the type of DBA that is needed.

Here are the two main types of DBAs:

- Operational
- Combination

Combination DBAs can be further broken down into these categories:

- Developer
- System Administrator

The operational DBA performs only the tasks required to maintain and tune an Informix DBMS. Usually a dedicated operational DBA is needed only for very large, mission-critical, or multiple-database systems. This person (or persons) spends every day watching the database and taking care of problems and tuning.

The combination DBA is the standard and most popular type of Informix DBA. This person spends only a portion of the time performing the tasks that an operational DBA does all day. Again, this is because most Informix systems are not large enough to require the full-time daily attention of one or more people. The Informix DBMS was built to require less administrative attention when dealing with standard business-size databases.

In some situations, one or two people involved with the development of applications that require access to an Informix database are the same people who administer the database. These people have an intimate knowledge of the data and how it is stored within the database. This knowledge makes administering any DBMS easier, especially when tuning. The knowledge of how the data is accessed will help these people adjust Informix to provide efficient performance.

In systems where the development of applications is a large effort, or where the application is purchased, the person who administers the system (the *SA*) usually also administers Informix. An SA is responsible for hardware and operating system issues as well as memory and disk space.

The SA installs, configures, and monitors the Informix DBMS as well as all the products running on the hardware systems under his or her responsibility.

An Informix DBA can hold many responsibilities beyond the ones required by the database. In smaller companies, one or two people could fill the positions of application developer, SA, DBA, and possibly user of the very same system. This is possible because the basic tasks of a standard-sized database's administrator are quick and easy.

Tasks of DBAs

The DBA must perform many tasks to create, maintain, and manage an Informix DBMS. The amount of overlap among the roles of application developer, system administrator, and DBA dictates who performs each task. Throughout the rest of this section, it is assumed that the DBA is a combination of all three roles and is able to perform all tasks required by an Informix DBMS. These tasks include the following:

- Installing an Informix DBMS environment
- Upgrading the Informix DBMS environment
- Configuring that environment
- Creating or incorporating a database
- Tuning
- Daily Monitoring
- Migrations
- Backups and recovery
- Problem investigations

Installing and upgrading the Informix environment is the physical act of loading the Informix software onto the system that will be used to run that software. Similar to when you install any software, Informix requires specific amounts of disk and memory in order to be able to run properly. For more information on how to plan, install, or upgrade an Informix DBMS, refer to Chapter 10, "Installing an Informix Environment."

After the Informix DBMS is installed, it should be configured to manage your planned database. Disk space must be divided to hold tables, and communications must be set up for clients to access the database. Chapter 11, "Configuring the Informix Environment," provides information on how to set up Informix.

The act of creating a database or incorporating an existing database into the Informix DBMS is the most important task of a DBA. The amount of time and effort put into making sure that the database is properly created, that tables are laid out correctly, and that indexes are based on the application's needs helps to reduce the need for changes in the future. The more the DBA knows about the applications that require the database and about the data stored in the database, the better the DBA can create the database to serve the application more usefully. Many of the chapters within this book will help DBAs create a database. Start with Chapter 12, "Incorporating a Database in Your Informix Environment," and Chapter 29, "Creating a Database Using SQL."

After the database is created, the DBA tunes and monitors it by adjusting the data layout, adding more memory, and changing tables and rows. As the database grows, the DBA makes changes here and there to improve performance. Depending on the amount of data and users, tuning and monitoring can be a minor or major effort. Many chapters of this book are also dedicated to tuning and monitoring the Informix DBMS. Start with Chapter 21, "Monitoring Your Informix Environment," and Chapter 23, "Tuning Your Informix Environment."

As the database grows, new data might become important and old data might become useless. New data fields and tables will be required, whereas existing tables contain information that is no longer needed. To handle these changes, and to keep the database at a manageable size, the DBA needs to perform migrations. A *migration* is the act of moving data from one area to another, usually changing the layout of that data in the process. When a new field is added to a table, Informix automatically migrates the data that exists in the table into the new layout. The same applies when fields are removed.

Another form of migration is a *data purge*, which occurs when data that is no longer needed (which is decided by some factor, such as date) is removed from the database. For example, a database that keeps track of orders might need to keep only three years worth of orders in the database. A purge could be done on a regular basis to remove orders older than three years from the database and put them onto tape. When you do this, the database will stay at a relatively consistent size. Chapter 24, "Anticipating Future Growth," discusses migration and database layout change situations and how to handle them.

Another primary task of the DBA is to make sure that data within the database is properly backed up and able to be used for recovery at all times. It's an unavoidable situation when the system crashes due to a hardware problem; but if the data is lost as a result of this crash, the DBA could be out of a job (depending on the importance of the lost data). It is the DBA's responsibility to create a backup strategy that corresponds to the importance of the data within the database. If the data is easily replicated, backups might not be needed. But if the data is worth hundreds, thousands, or millions of dollars, the database must be backed up on a regular basis. Chapter 18, "Managing Data Backups," deals with these issues and explains the many ways Informix can keep data backed up.

When things go wrong or the DBMS is not running correctly, it's the DBA's job to find the problem and fix it. Sometimes, the problems have nothing to do with Informix and the way the database is designed. Problems that look like they occur within the DBMS might actually be caused by the application accessing the database or by the hardware that is running the DBMS.

That is why the DBA should have knowledge beyond the Informix DBMS. The more the DBA knows about the entire system, the more successful he or she will be at finding the problems or bottlenecks. Chapter 26, "Problem Handling," explains how to locate the source of problems and what to do about them.

Not every DBA has to perform all of these tasks, and the importance of each task is determined by the importance of the database and how it is configured. Three basic configurations of an Informix DBMS determine where the DBA's work will be concentrated. These DBMS configurations are as follows:

- Online transaction processing (OLTP)
- Batch processing
- A combination of both OLTP and batch processing

An OLTP system is a system in which actions on the database are performed in a client-server situation. User applications send transactions to the database to do something with the data within that database. The client is the user's application, and the server is the Informix DBMS. These transactions between the client and the server are usually small and happen multiple times each day. This configuration allows for multiple clients to use the database without having to run on the same machine as the DBMS. Clients run on their own machines, using their own resources, although it is not necessary to have a client and the server on separate machines to achieve an OLTP configuration. A system is considered OLTP when multiple, separate, small transactions interact with the DBMS at the same time all day long. Each transaction takes less than a second to process. For example, a library's electronic card catalog system would check books in and out all day, and also perform checks to see whether books are available.

A batch configuration occurs when the DBMS processes a single long transaction from one distinct process. A batch process can work with hundreds of data items within a database during the life of the single batch process. Batch processes are expected to run minutes to hours, depending on the size of the database. An example of a batch process is a mailing process that creates a letter for every customer stored within the database.

In most Informix DBMSs, the DBA has to manage both OLTP and batch processes. This requires the DBA to perform specific monitoring and adjustments to meet both OLTP and batch needs.

The following tasks are required by an OLTP system:

- Thread multiprocessing monitoring
- Logging
- Managing multiple access paths
- Client communication connections

The following tasks are required by a batch system:

- Specific indexing for batch processes
- Stop/restart processing
- Locking limitations

The following tasks are required in a system that performs both OLTP and batch processing:

- All OLTP tasks
- All Batch tasks
- Manage performance to find an efficient processing mix

Several chapters throughout this section deal with all of these issues. When setting up an Informix DBMS, remember to keep in mind the type of processing that will be performed. An incorrect configuration will drag the performance down on any DBMS. Better performance from the DBMS leads to a better relationship between the DBA and the people needing the database.

Interaction Between the DBA and the Developer

The DBA is in the middle of everything, because the data managed by the DBA is important to everyone. On one side of the DBMS are the developers—the people that build or buy the applications that access the database. If the database fails or is designed poorly, that will make the application look bad. A partnership must be formed between the DBA and developer teams. Without the application, the database would not be needed. Without the database, the application would not be able to process. In order to ensure the best database design, when a new application is being created or bought, the DBA must be involved from the beginning.

It would be ideal for the project to be small enough that the DBA is also a developer or evaluator of the software to be purchased. If a DBA is not part of the development or evaluation team, a DBA should be brought in to oversee all predesign efforts and the gathering of data requirements.

The DBA should be involved at this early stage to avoid data view misconceptions. The view of the database to the application or the developer could be very different from the database view. A *view* is how the data is perceived to be stored within tables and rows. The view of the database does not always match physically and logically. So, letting the application determine the layout could create a database that is not very efficient.

The DBA should be involved to ensure that the relational rules are followed. That is, the DBA should ensure that all primary and foreign keys are correctly established. The DBA should spread tables and data apart to take advantage of multiprocessing. Most developers and application salespeople will not have these concerns.

Make sure that a DBA is represented when choosing a new application. A good relationship between the DBA and the development teams will help lay the groundwork for a stable and efficient database system.

Interaction Between the DBA and the User

Because of the relationship between the developer and the DBA, the DBA might consider the developer to be a specific kind of user of the DBMS because developers need to access the database to add new data elements and to perform testing. However, the actual user—the people who access the database through the developer's application—is another relationship that the DBA must maintain. The user usually does not distinguish between the application and the database. Because the data is important, the user thinks of the application as a tool to use the data. That data must be safe, secure, and correct. If it is not, the user community will be forming a lynch mob to find the DBA.

The DBA must make adjustments for the users—usually more than is required of the developers. The more the DBA can do to maintain data integrity, security, and efficient access, the happier the users will be.

Summary

This chapter laid the groundwork for a DBA to start with when administering an Informix DBMS. It is important to remember that a DBA might need knowledge in many different areas of the information system beyond the database. The DBA might have to wear the hat of a DBA, a developer, a system administrator, or a combination of all three roles.

The DBA also needs to perform many tasks to maintain a stable and secure Informix DBMS. Fortunately, learning how to be an administrator of Informix is quick and easy, and some of these tasks are performed automatically by Informix.

Different systems process data in different modes. Some systems use OLTP, and others use batch only. Most Informix systems need to be set up to do a combination of both OLTP and batch processing. The DBA must be able to adjust and administer either situation.

The relationships between developers, users, and the DBA are important. The better the communication, the better the system. The DBA should be involved in all aspects of a new system in order to create a database that meets all of the company's needs.

The job of a DBA can become hectic and stressful if it is not properly managed. The more upfront work a DBA can perform on a database, the better it will perform when it is in production.

CHAPTER 10

Installing an Informix Environment

by Robert Donat

IN THIS CHAPTER

This chapter details the steps required to install, start, and test an Informix database instance. The installation of OnLine Dynamic Server for UNIX involves much more instruction than the installation of both the Informix Standard Engine and INFORMIX-OnLine for Windows NT. For this reason, the details in this chapter relate mostly to OnLine Dynamic Server because many are unnecessary for the other two types of installation. This chapter applies to the installation of application development tools, SQL Application Programming Interfaces (APIs), the OnLine server itself, and additional Informix products.

Preparing to Install the INFORMIX-OnLine Product Family

A few small but critical steps need to take place prior to beginning your Informix installation. They include setting up UNIX configuration parameters, creating appropriate users, and determining the proper placement of the INFORMIX-OnLine products on your system. In the case of Windows NT installations, the necessary registry entries and users are created automatically as part of the setup. To complete installation, run the `d:\setup.exe` program that comes on the Informix for NT CD-ROM.

Setting Up UNIX Configuration Parameters and Environmental Variables

Before you attempt to install INFORMIX-OnLine on your server, a few entries and changes must be made on your UNIX server. Environmental variables must be declared, `/etc/system` shared memory parameters must be set, and `/etc/services` entries must be made.

Environmental Variables

A few Informix environmental variables must be set for the installation and for all users of that installation in the future. These environmental variables are as follows:

- `INFORMIXSERVER`
- `INFORMIXDIR`
- `PATH`
- `ONCONFIG`
- `INFORMIXTERM`

`INFORMIXSERVER` is set to the name of the INFORMIX-OnLine instance that you are installing. You can call it anything you like, but be sure to make it descriptive and concise. Examples would be `finance`, `ol_prod`, or `mozart`, to indicate the purpose, scope, or server name for the Informix server. You might want to distinguish the platform of your INFORMIX-OnLine instance in the `INFORMIXSERVER` variable as well. This could help you distinguish NT instances from UNIX instances, for example.

`INFORMIXDIR` is the base directory of the Informix installation. Set this to the area of the disk you will use for your installation or the symbolic link that points to it. For this example, `INFORMIXDIR` is set to `/usr/informix`, which is a symbolic link to `/home/informix`.

`PATH` is the set of directories in which the server searches for executable files when you do not specify their fully qualified pathname. `PATH` must include `${INFORMIXDIR}/bin` in order to install and run Informix properly.

`ONCONFIG` is optional, and it is set only if you want to use a different configuration file than `${INFORMIXDIR}/etc/onconfig`. The file used during startup is `${INFORMIXDIR}/etc/${ONCONFIG}`.

`INFORMIXTERM` is set to `termcap` or `terminfo` in order to allow character-based Informix clients (`dbaccess`, `onmonitor`, 4GL programs, and so on) to function properly with the terminal type and preferences you use in your UNIX environment.

NOTE

Usually, setting `INFORMIXTERM` to `termcap` will work in your environment. However, Informix supplies its own `termcap` file in `${INFORMIXDIR}/etc` if you experience difficulty with your UNIX terminals. In addition, `termcap` files for specific hardware configurations are available in the International Informix Users' Group Web site, at `http://www.iiug.org`.

The way to set these environmental variables depends on the shell you use. Here are some examples:

Bourne or Korn shells:

```
INFORMIXDIR=/usr/informix; export INFORMIXDIR
PATH=${PATH}:${INFORMIXDIR}/bin; export PATH
```

C shell:

```
setenv INFORMIXDIR /usr/informix
setenv PATH ${PATH}:${INFORMIXDIR}/bin
```

TIP

Place these entries in a file such as `/etc/profile` or `/etc/.login` (depending on the default shell), which is executed for each user when that user logs on.

You can verify that these variables are set by typing `echo $PATH` or `echo $INFORMIXDIR`.

Ensure that all appropriate environmental variables are set for your environment before you continue. They should look like those in Listing 10.1.

Listing 10.1. Obtaining Informix environmental variables.

```
root@sams> env¦egrep '(INF¦^PATH)'
PATH=/usr/sbin:/usr/bin:/usr/local/bin:/usr/informix/bin
INFORMIXBIN=/usr/informix/bin
INFORMIXTERM=terminfo
INFORMIXDIR=/usr/informix
INFORMIXSERVER=sams
```

Shared Memory

Shared memory is a facility provided by the operating system that allows Informix to use a reserved area of memory. This allows Informix to communicate faster between processes and threads than if independent areas of memory were used for each process or if disk I/O were required.

Several platform-specific shared memory parameters need to be set prior to rebooting the UNIX server and beginning the installation process. If they are not configured properly, OnLine will not initialize. Because these parameters differ between specific UNIX vendors' platforms, they are not detailed here.

The directory `${INFORMIXDIR}/release` has a subdirectory structure based on your platform, Informix version, and default language. The file named `ONLINE_7.2` (or something similar) has sample configuration parameters for your version of OnLine. Your platform documentation will help you determine the best way to tune shared memory based on your platform memory resources and the applications that share the server with Informix. Listing 10.2 shows a typical `ONLINE_7.2` file.

Listing 10.2. The beginning of the ONLINE_7.2 file.

```
=================================
                         MACHINE SPECIFIC NOTES
                                  FOR
           INFORMIX-OnLine Dynamic Server 7.22.UC1 PRODUCT RELEASE
                            DATE: 26 Dec 1996
                      =================================


PORT NUMBER: 042949, 042974
IRIS JOB NUMBER: 9462

INFORMIX-OnLine Dynamic Server Shared Memory Parameters and Kernel Parameters:
==============================================================================

The following entries were put in /etc/system while doing the port.

set enable_sm_wa = 1
set shmsys:shminfo_shmmax=268435456
set semsys:seminfo_semmap=64
set semsys:seminfo_semmni=4096
set semsys:seminfo_semmns=4096
```

```
set semsys:seminfo_semmnu=4096
set semsys:seminfo_semume=64
set semsys:seminfo_semmsl=100
```

Services Entries

You need to enter a few /etc/services entries, based on your configuration. These identify TCP/IP or network ports that are used for specific purposes. They can be customized based on your network needs, but they must remain consistent across the network for servers and clients that will use them. These entries consist of the following elements:

- nettcp 1400/tcp: nettcp is used for network communication for INFORMIX-OnLine 6 and 7.
- sqlexec 1399/tcp: sqlexec is used for network communication for Informix 5.
- oncockpit 1401/tcp: oncockpit is optional and is used with onprobe and the oncockpit graphical performance monitor.
- egm 1402/tcp: If the Enterprise Gateway Manager will be installed, it will need its own port and service name.
- secondserver 1402/tcp: Each of a machine's distinct servers will need its own port if they are to run simultaneously.

For a simple installation, however, only nettcp is necessary, and it can be named and numbered any way you choose, as long as it is consistent and referenced in the ${INFORMIXDIR}/etc/sqlhosts Informix communications parameters file. These examples are shown in an actual /etc/services file in Listing 10.3.

Listing 10.3. Informix entries in /etc/services.

```
sqlexec      1399/tcp      #Informix 5
nettcp       1400/tcp      #Informix 7
oncockpit    1401/tcp      #Informix GUI monitor
egm          1402/tcp      #Enterprise Gateway Manager
secondsrvr   1403/tcp      #Informix 7, server 2
```

Creating the Informix User and Group

A user and group, each with the name informix (in lowercase) must exist before you install the server. They need to be placed in the /etc/passwd and /etc/group files, respectively. Placing the user and group in NIS (Network Information Service) instead, or in /etc/shadow, might be necessary, depending on the UNIX security scheme you use. Be sure to make the informix user's home directory the same directory where you want to install the server. Typical user and group entries can be seen in Listing 10.4.

Listing 10.4. Informix user and group entries.

```
root@sams> grep informix /etc/passwd /etc/group
/etc/passwd:informix:x:201:200:Informix DBA:/usr/informix:/bin/ksh
/etc/group:informix::200:
```

NOTE

If you want to use Informix role separation to facilitate auditing, create the groups `ix_aao` and `ix_dbsso` for the audit analysis officer and system security officer roles. You must also create at least one user for each role. (They can be `ix_aao` and `ix_dbsso` as well.) These users and groups will be granted ownership of certain directories when installing OnLine, and you will be prompted for them during the install. Role separation allows different users to administer the online instance, set up auditing, and review auditing independent of each other. In order to enable this functionality during the installation, the environmental variable `INF_ROLE_SEP` must be set to any value prior to installing the online engine.

Creating the Appropriate Devices and Directories

Before installing Informix, you must decide where you want to place your installation files, as well as how much space to give the database and where that space will reside. These decisions must be based on several factors:

- Your current server configuration
- Initial and anticipated database sizes
- Database usage type and criticality

A typical Informix installation with 4GL and ESQL products included could take between 60MB and 90MB of free disk space. Your database or databases might take up only 50MB of space, or they might take up 100GB or more of space. In addition, some types of applications might require huge amounts of temporary storage space because of their processing requirements, and others might require very little space. Storage considerations must be appropriate for your specific installation, server usage, and resource limitations.

Create a directory in the most appropriate file system on your machine, and symbolically link that file to `/usr/informix` or an appropriate site-specific convention. Change the ownership of both the directory and the link to user and group `informix`. An example of how these look when done can be seen in Listing 10.5.

Listing 10.5. A typical file system and creating the Informix directory structure.

```
root@sams> df -k
Filesystem            kbytes    used   avail capacity  Mounted on
/dev/md/dsk/d0        144799   91454   38875    71%    /
/dev/md/dsk/d30       336863  105905  197278    35%    /usr
/proc                      0       0       0     0%    /proc
fd                         0       0       0     0%    /dev/fd
/dev/md/dsk/d50      1170638  622555  431023    60%    /home
/dev/md/dsk/d60      1074590  605587  361553    63%    /home2
/dev/md/dsk/d40       288855   65145  194830    26%    /opt
/dev/md/dsk/d70       288855  106438  153537    41%    /usr/openwin
swap                  835312      28  835284     1%   /tmp
root@sams > mkdir /home/informix_7
root@sams > ln -s /home/informix_7 /usr/informix
root@sams > chown informix:informix /home/informix_7
root@sams > chown -h informix:informix /usr/informix
root@sams > ls -ld /home/informix_7
drwxr-xr-x  17 informix informix    1536 Apr  1 23:56 home/informix_7
root@sams > ls -l /usr/informix
lrwxrwxrwx   1 root     other          17 Mar 25 12:56 /usr/informix ->
➥/home/informix_7
```

You can use *raw* disk partitions or *cooked* files in an existing file system for your database storage space. Raw disk space is the recommended approach, because the database manages it directly. This speeds up activity because the system-level file processing does not need to occur. It also ensures recoverability because the database knows exactly what has been written to disk. This is not the case with cooked files, which buffer disk input and output and might report to the database that an activity has occurred on disk that has actually been cached in memory instead. If the system fails at a time like this, information will be unrecoverable, and the database could become corrupt. It is recommended that you symbolically link your raw partitions to easy-to-manage filenames, such as the ones shown in Listing 10.6.

Listing 10.6. Samples of Informix raw devices and links.

```
root@sams > ls -l /dev/vx/rdsk/db_chunk00?
crw-rw----   1 informix informix 112,  5 Mar 23 08:43 /dev/vx/rdsk/db_chunk001
crw-rw----   1 informix informix 112,  6 Mar 22 17:57 /dev/vx/rdsk/db_chunk002
crw-rw----   1 informix informix 112,  7 Mar 22 17:57 /dev/vx/rdsk/db_chunk003
crw-rw----   1 informix informix 112,  8 Mar 22 17:57 /dev/vx/rdsk/db_chunk004
crw-rw----   1 informix informix 112,  9 Mar 22 17:57 /dev/vx/rdsk/db_chunk005
crw-rw----   1 informix informix 112, 10 Mar 22 17:57 /dev/vx/rdsk/db_chunk006
crw-rw----   1 informix informix 112, 11 Mar 22 17:57 /dev/vx/rdsk/db_chunk007
crw-rw----   1 informix informix 112, 12 Mar 22 17:57 /dev/vx/rdsk/db_chunk008
crw-rw----   1 informix informix 112, 13 Mar 22 17:57 /dev/vx/rdsk/db_chunk009
root@sams > ls -l /dev/online_space001
lrwxrwxrwx   1 root     other          24 Mar 22 17:57 /dev/online_space001 ->
➥/dev/vx/rdsk/db_chunk001
```

If you require your database to continue to run even if a disk error occurs, you might want to `mirror` your database chunks. In this case, the raw partitions are duplicated across two similarly sized areas of disk. Although this allows uninterrupted activity to occur in case of hardware failure, it also demands twice the normal amount of available disk space and only helps if the mirrors are on separate physical disk drives.

The largest chunk of raw disk space that can be allocated to Informix is usually 2GB. You can check your machine notes in the `${INFORMIXDIR}/release` directory for more specific limitations.

After you decide which areas of disk you will dedicate to the Informix installation and which raw partitions you will dedicate to the database itself, you are ready to install the pieces of the database, one product at a time.

Installing Informix Products

There are a few easy steps to follow to install the Informix products after setting up the UNIX environment. The products must be installed in the appropriate order. The tape or CD-ROM that contains each product must be unloaded to `${INFORMIXDIR}`, and the installation can then be run on each product in succession by the user root.

Informix Product Installation Order

When you install an Informix instance, you usually need to install several different products. Here are some examples:

- Application Development Tools
  - INFORMIX-4GL
  - INFORMIX-4GL Rapid Development Package
  - INFORMIX-4GL Interactive Debugger
- SQL Application Programming Interfaces (APIs)
  - INFORMIX-SQL
  - INFORMIX-ESQL/C
  - INFORMIX-ESQL/COBOL
  - INFORMIX-Connect
  - INFORMIX-CLI
- Database Servers
  - INFORMIX-OnLine Dynamic Server
  - INFORMIX-OnLine Dynamic Server Runtime Facility
- Additional Products
  - C-ISAM
  - C-ISAM Runtime Facility

- Informix Messages and Corrections
    - INFORMIX-OnLine/Optical
    - INFORMIX-Enterprise Gateway for DRDA
    - INFORMIX-Enterprise Gateway Manager

This list gives examples of the types of products that belong in each of the four "stages" of installation. The products all have a similar installation procedure, but they must be installed in this order, with the most recent versions of each subproduct installed last. For example, if you have a more recent version of INFORMIX-4GL than the INFORMIX-4GL Interactive Debugger, install the Debugger first so that the most recent shared files will not be overwritten by the older debugger files. When upgrading to a new version of one of these products, you need to reinstall all remaining products in order.

Retrieving the Informix Product Files from Tape or CD

Retrieving the product files is very simple. Informix ships its products on tape or on CD-ROM. In either case, the retrieval instructions are similar. Mount the tape or CD so that it is available to the server on which you want to install. Change to the correct directory with `cd ${INFORMIXDIR}`. Depending on the media and the instructions on the tape or CD, you need to execute a `tar` or `cpio` command. They would look like this:

- `cpio -ivdBum < devicename [e.g. cpio -ivdBum</dev/rmt/1]`
- `tar xvf devicename [e.g. tar xvf /cdrom/unnamed_cdrom/online.tar]`

You will see a list of files that are taken from the media and placed in your `${INFORMIXDIR}`. When the files have all been retrieved, you then need to run (as root) the `installxxxxxx` script that is particular to the product you have just retrieved.

NOTE

It is advisable to read the machine-specific notes at this time in the `${INFORMIXDIR}/release` directory for helpful information relating to your specific platform.

TIP

If you want to install on more than one machine, you might want to archive and compress the CD or tape files before installation or modification, so that you do not need to load them again from media, which can take some time.

Running the Install Script

Each product comes with its own install script, which will modify the files you just retrieved, as well as their ownership, permissions, and application licensing information. The following are some install scripts:

Product	*Installation Command*
INFORMIX-CLI	`/installcli`
INFORMIX-ESQL/C	`/installesql`
INFORMIX-ESQL/COBOL	`/installesqlcob`
INFORMIX-OnLine Dynamic Server	`/installonline`
INFORMIX-Messages and Corrections	`/installpsmsg`

You will be able to tell which script is appropriate for the product you just retrieved by looking at the install scripts that exist in the `${INFORMIXDIR}` directory and comparing them with the ones you have already used.

You need to run the install script as root from the `${INFORMIXDIR}` directory. It verifies that you are running it as root, and then it prompts you for licensing information, which might have come with your media or you might have received it separately. After you successfully enter a valid Serial Number and Key, the script installs the product and lets you know when it is done. You then see something similar to what is shown in Listing 10.7. The script should, but might not, link all shared objects to `/usr/lib` for you. When convenient, find all shared objects under `${INFORMIXDIR}` and verify that they have been linked to `/usr/lib`. You might use a UNIX command such as `find ${INFORMIXDIR} -name "*.so" -print` to list all shared objects and then link them, if they are not already, with `ln -s ${INFORMIXDIR}/lib/libesql.so /usr/lib/libesql.so` or a similar command for each unlinked object.

Listing 10.7. Running an Informix install script.

```
root@sams# cd $INFORMIXDIR
root@sams# pwd
/usr/informix
root@sams# ls -l installonline
-rwxr-xr-x   1 informix informix   10008 Dec 26 17:26 installonline
root@sams# ./installonline

INFORMIX-OnLine Dynamic Server Version 7.22.UC1
Copyright (C) 1986-1996 Informix Software, Inc.


Installation and Configuration Script

This installation procedure must be run by a privileged user (Super User)
It will change the owner, group, mode, (and other file attributes on
Secure systems) of all files of this package in this directory.
```

```
There must be a user "informix" and a group "informix" known to the system.

Press RETURN to continue,
or the interrupt key (usually CTRL-C or DEL) to abort.

Enter your serial number (for example, INF#X999999) >
INF#X999999
Enter your serial number KEY (uppercase letters only) >
ABCDEF

WARNING!
         This software, and its authorized use and number of users, are
subject to the applicable license agreement with Informix Software, Inc.
If the number of users exceeds the licensed number, the excess users may
be prevented from using the software. UNAUTHORIZED USE OR COPYING MAY
SUBJECT YOU AND YOUR COMPANY TO SEVERE CIVIL AND CRIMINAL LIABILITIES.

Press RETURN to continue,
or the interrupt key (usually CTRL-C or DEL) to abort.
...
Installing directory gls/lc11/os
Installing directory gls/lc11/pl_pl
Installing directory gls/lc11/ru_ru
Installing directory gls/lc11/sv_se
Installing directory bitmaps

Installing Shared Libraries in System Directories ...

Linking /usr/lib/ismdd07b.so from lib/ismdd07b.so
Previous version of /usr/lib/ismdd07b.so saved as /usr/lib/ismdd07b.so.970208

Linking /usr/lib/ismdd07a.so from lib/ismdd07a.so
Previous version of /usr/lib/ismdd07a.so saved as /usr/lib/ismdd07a.so.970208

Installation of INFORMIX-OnLine Dynamic Server complete.
root@sams >
```

When you have installed all the Informix products you have purchased or need to install, you are ready to configure your instance and bring the Informix engine online for the first time.

TIP

If you intend to configure several identical instances of Informix on identical machines, and you are licensed to do so, you might want to make a *snapshot* of this installation before modifying it. You can do this like so:

```
cd ${INFORMIXDIR}
tar cvf informixinstall.tar .
compress informixinstall.tar
mv informixinstall.tar.Z /archivedir
```

continues

continued

When you need to reinstall Informix on a new machine (or reinstall from scratch on this one), you then need only to move the `informixinstall.tar.Z` file to the new server and install like this:

```
cd ${INFORMIXDIR}
zcat /tmp/informixinstall.tar.Z¦tar xvf -
cd lib [and each subdirectory with shared objects ]
[in ksh syntax]
for i in *.so
do
ln -s 'pwd'/$i /usr/lib/$i
done
```

Now you have a complete install without all of the individual installations.

Bringing the Informix Database Server OnLine

You need to perform a few small steps before you can use the INFORMIX-OnLine Server for actual development or production. The two configuration files that need to be changed are `${INFORMIXDIR}/etc/sqlhosts` and `${INFORMIXDIR}/etc/onconfig`. The sample files `sqlhosts.std` and `onconfig.demo`, which are shown in Listing 10.8, should be copied into `sqlhosts` and `onconfig` to be used as templates. You need to edit `sqlhosts`, and you can either edit `onconfig` directly or use the Informix utility `onmonitor` to edit it through a convenient interface. Then the database can be initialized for the first time.

Listing 10.8. Copying and editing sample `onconfig` and `sqlhosts` files.

```
root@sams# su - informix
Sun Microsystems Inc.   SunOS 5.5       Generic November 1995
informix@sams> cd etc
informix@sams> ls -l sqlhosts* onconfig*
-rw-r--r--   1 informix informix    7171 Dec 26 17:29 onconfig.std
-rw-r--r--   1 informix informix     978 Dec 26 17:27 sqlhosts.demo
informix@sams> cp onconfig.std onconfig
informix@sams> cp sqlhosts.demo sqlhosts
informix@sams> vi sqlhosts
```

The `sqlhosts` File

`sqlhosts` contains information about the local and networked INFORMIX-OnLine instances. It contains one entry for each connection to an Informix engine, either through a network or through shared memory. The four or five columns for each entry are as follows:

- The name of the database server that is listed
- The connection mechanism or net type
- The network name of the machine that hosts the server
- The port name from /etc/services, which is used for a network connection
- The options, if any

The name of the database server should match the DBSERVERNAME or DBSERVERALIASES in the onconfig file for that server.

The connection mechanism or net type is an eight-character field that represents three different instance specifics. The first two characters (on) indicate that it is an online net type. The next three letters indicate the connection type—either shared memory (ipc) or network (tli for transport-level interface, or soc for sockets). The last three letters indicate the protocol type. Examples are shm for shared memory, tcp for TCP/IP, or spx for IPX/SPX.

The network name of the server's host is simply the hostname, which is reachable and resolvable to a valid IP address on the network.

Options allow you to specify different parameters for security, connection keep-alive configuration, and TCP/IP communication buffer size. These are advanced configuration settings and are not necessary for the initial configuration. They can be changed at any time in the future. The sqlhosts entries for this example can be seen in Listing 10.9.

Listing 10.9. A sample sqlhosts file.

```
#    Title:        sqlhosts.demo
#    Sccsid:       @(#)sqlhosts.demo       9.2      7/15/93  15:20:45
#    Description:
#                  Default sqlhosts file for running demos.
#
#**************************************************************************

#demo_on onipcshm       on_hostname     on_servername
sams     onipcshm       sams            anything
sams_net ontlitcp       sams            nettcp
```

The onconfig File

The onconfig file is the master configuration file for all Informix parameters. It contains roughly 90 parameters that can be tuned to obtain optimum performance for your particular resources and needs. It can be edited directly, in which case changes might not take place until the next time OnLine is initialized, or it can be changed from within onmonitor, which often allows changes to take place immediately while the engine is online. There are two ways to initialize the Informix instance for the first time.

Initializing from the Command Line

If you want to edit the onconfig file directly, a few changes should be made within your editor before the database can be initialized. The changes are as follows:

- ROOTNAME: The name you want to give to your root database space.
- ROOTPATH: The pathname to the raw or cooked file for your rootdbs.
- ROOTOFFSET: The number of kilobytes to be skipped from the beginning of ROOTPATH.
- ROOTSIZE: The size allocated in the ROOTPATH for ROOTNAME. Note that this does not need to be the entire free space on the device.
- DBSERVERNAME: The name of the Informix instance you entered in sqlhosts.
- NETTYPE: The type of network and number of threads to poll for that network.
- MULTIPROCESSOR: Whether or not the machine is multiprocessor.
- NUMCPUVPS: The number of CPU virtual processors.
- SINGLE_CPU_VP: Whether or not the number of CPU VPs is limited to one.
- NUMAIOVPS: The number of I/O VPs.

The entries for these variables can be seen in Listing 10.10.

Listing 10.10. A partial onconfig file with Root Dbspace and system configuration changes made.

```
#**************************************************************************
#
#                           INFORMIX SOFTWARE, INC.
#
#  Title:       onconfig
#  Description: INFORMIX-OnLine Configuration Parameters
#
#**************************************************************************

# Root Dbspace Configuration

ROOTNAME        rootdbs         # Root dbspace name
ROOTPATH        /dev/online_space001 # Path for device containing root dbspace
ROOTOFFSET      2               # Offset of root dbspace into device (Kbytes)
ROOTSIZE        1023998         # Size of root dbspace (Kbytes)

# Disk Mirroring Configuration Parameters

MIRROR          0               # Mirroring flag (Yes = 1, No = 0)
MIRRORPATH                      # Path for device containing mirrored root
MIRROROFFSET    0               # Offset into mirrored device (Kbytes)

...
LTAPEDEV        /dev/tapedev    # Log tape device path
LTAPEBLK        16              # Log tape block size (Kbytes)
LTAPESIZE       10240           # Max amount of data to put on log tape (Kbytes)

# Optical
```

```
STAGEBLOB                          # INFORMIX-OnLine/Optical staging area

# System Configuration

SERVERNUM        0                 # Unique id corresponding to a OnLine instance
DBSERVERNAME     sams              # Name of default database server
DBSERVERALIASES  sams_net          # List of alternate dbservernames
NETTYPE          tlitcp,5,250,NET        # Configure poll thread(s) for nettype
NETTYPE          ipcshm,2,250,CPU        # Configure poll thread(s) for nettype
DEADLOCK_TIMEOUT        60         # Max time to wait of lock in distributed env.
RESIDENT         0                 # Forced residency flag (Yes = 1, No = 0)

MULTIPROCESSOR   0                 # 0 for single-processor, 1 for multi-processor
NUMCPUVPS        1                 # Number of user (cpu) vps
SINGLE_CPU_VP    0                 # If non-zero, limit number of cpu vps to one

NOAGE            0                 # Process aging
```

The specifics of all of the `onconfig` variables and their usages are fully documented in the *Informix Administrator's Guide.* These are the minimum variables that must be set manually if you want to initialize the Informix engine from the command line.

After you have edited the appropriate areas of the `onconfig` file, you can simply use the command `oninit -i` to initialize the disk space allocated for your Informix instance. The `oninit` program will ask for verification before initializing and destroying any information on the disk space that has been allocated. After it completes, you can verify that the engine is online by typing `onstat -`. This is shown with the code in Listing 10.11.

Listing 10.11. Steps to initialize the database instance and confirm its OnLine status.

```
informix@sams> oninit -i

This action will initialize INFORMIX-OnLine;
any existing INFORMIX-OnLine databases will NOT be accessible -
Do you wish to continue (y/n)? y
informix@sams> onstat -
INFORMIX-OnLine Version 7.22.UC1    -- On-Line -- Up 00:00:27 -- 8944 Kbytes
```

Working with `vi` and the command line is quicker for experienced administrators, but it is much easier for first-time installations if you use the `onmonitor` utility to initialize your database.

Initializing from Within `onmonitor`

If you choose to use the Informix administration utility `onmonitor` to initialize your new database server, the utility prompts you to change the appropriate variables. In addition, it provides descriptions of each variable to aid you in the installation process. You can begin by typing `onmonitor` as `informix`. You will see a screen like that shown in Figure 10.1.

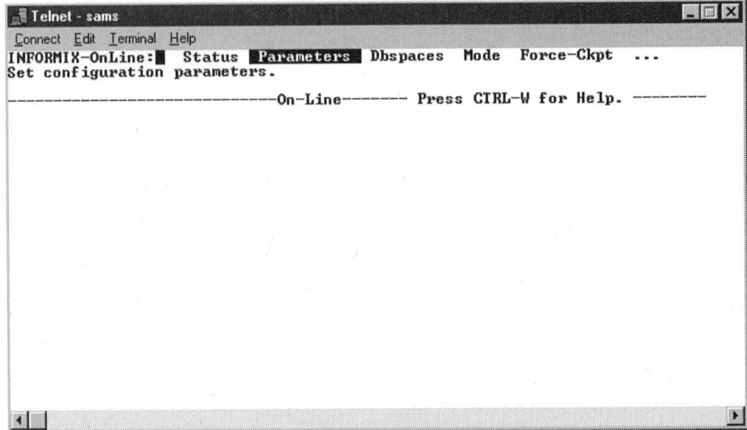

FIGURE 10.1.
The onconfig *main menu.*

> **TIP**
>
> If your onconfig screen becomes unreadable and lines display themselves improperly, make sure your TERM and LINES environmental variables are set properly. Usually TERM=vt100 and LINES=24 correct these problems.

After bringing up the onconfig main menu, you need to choose the Parameters option by arrowing to it and pressing Return, or by pressing the key that is in a capital letter (P) as a shortcut to that menu.

> **TIP**
>
> Sometimes the arrow keys do not function properly within the onmonitor and dbaccess Informix utilities. In this case, using the capitalized shortcut keys is recommended. If you must navigate using arrow keys, you can use the Control key and the standard up, down, left, and right keys for the UNIX editor vi. They are, respectively, Ctrl+k, Ctrl+j, Ctrl+h, and Ctrl+l.

Choose Initialize from the Parameters menu, and you will be placed in your first initialization screen, shown in Figure 10.2. You can edit the fields and blank them out with spaces, but certain fields do not allow you to exit unless valid parameters are specified. Ctrl+C or the Delete key exits you from the screen without saving, and the Escape key accepts all changes and moves you to the next screen.

A few additional parameters need to be specified when using onmonitor to initialize the engine, but the majority of necessary changes consists of the variables mentioned in the prior section.

The first necessary changes are the two tape device names. You need to provide valid tape devices or `/dev/null` in order to continue past these parameters. Root Size, Primary Path, and Root Offset (a minimum of 2 is recommended) need to be modified before continuing.

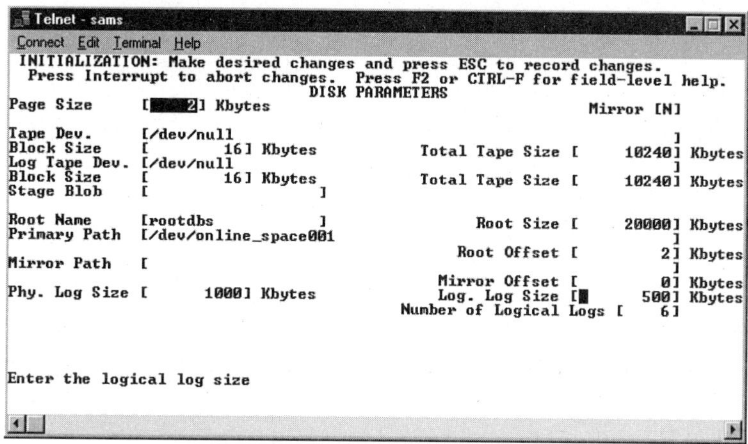

FIGURE 10.2.
The `INITIALIZATION` `onconfig` *screen.*

The next two pages contain the only other fields necessary to be changed. They can be seen in Figures 10.3 and 10.4. The Server Name and Server Aliases need to be specified and accepted using the Escape key. Then the CPU-specific fields must be customized to your particular configuration on the next form. The `NETTYPE` settings must be set in the same way as detailed before, and they must reflect your particular resources and needs.

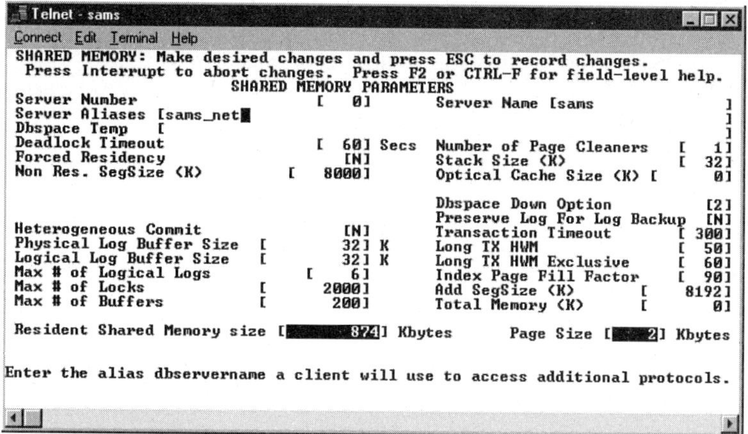

FIGURE 10.3.
The `SHARED MEMORY` `onconfig` *screen.*

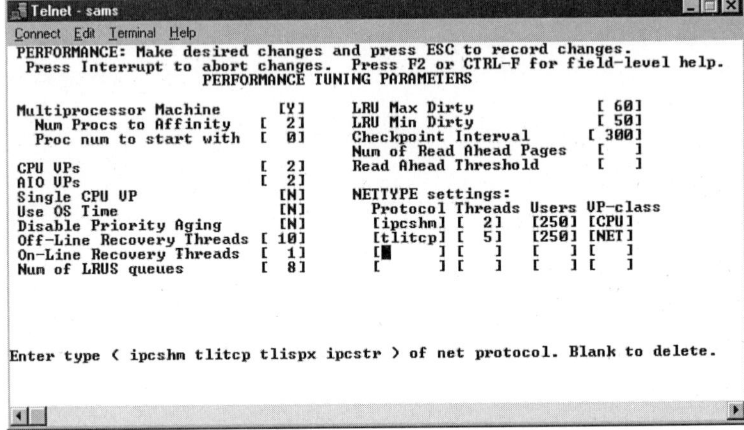

FIGURE 10.4.
The PERFORMANCE onconfig *screen.*

The remaining screens might be interesting for you to look through and read the field level help for, but they do not need to be changed. Escape through them until you are asked `Do you really want to continue?`. Press Y and your database will be initialized, as shown in Figure 10.5.

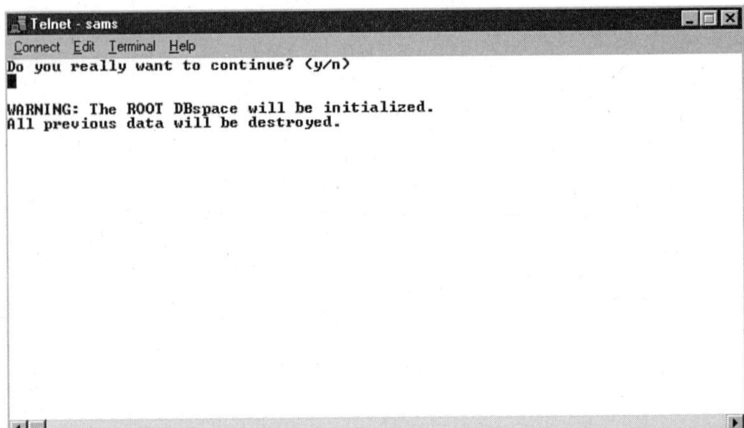

FIGURE 10.5.
The onconfig *initialization warning message.*

The screen then shows the database state as *quiescent.* This means it is active but in single-user mode, which allows no actual database connections. You can bring it online by exiting to the main menu and then choosing Mode|On-Line. The status bar then shows On-Line, and you are ready to continue.

Verifying Your Installation

When your installation has finished with no errors and the database is in On-Line mode, you can install the sample database to verify that everything is functioning properly. You can do this by typing dbaccessdemo7 stores. You can replace the word stores with whatever you would like the database to be named. Do this from a directory other than $INFORMIXDIR, because the installation asks to copy some sample files to your current directory. When this is done, you can start dbaccess by typing dbaccess stores, which places you in the correct database. This screen looks like the one in Figure 10.6.

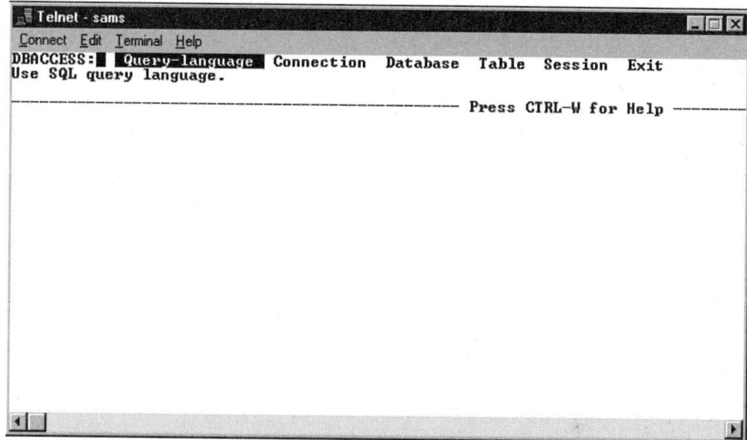

FIGURE 10.6.
The main dbaccess *menu.*

When you start dbaccess, the INFORMIX-SQL client, you get a menu structure the same way you do in onmonitor. Choose Query Language|New, and type select * from state;. Then press the escape key to go to the prior menu, and run the SQL. You then see the list of states that exist in the state table of the stores database. Congratulations! You have just executed the first query on your new Informix database server.

Customizing Your Informix Environment

Now that your Informix environment has been properly installed, you need to make some tuning and configuration changes. Tuning is covered in detail in Chapter 23, "Tuning Your Informix Environment," but a few quick additions to your installation are appropriate at this time. Based on your database size, system resources, and needs, you probably need to add temporary database spaces, change the location and size of your physical log, and add database spaces for your application needs.

Adding Temporary Database Spaces

In order to add a temporary database space, you need another raw partition or cooked file available. The advantage of a raw partition dedicated to Informix for temporary space is that instead of using file system space in /tmp, the default temporary dbspace, Informix will have a dedicated and faster area of disk to perform temporary activity.

Additional database spaces can be added through the `onmonitor` utility, under the Dbspaces|Create menu. The dbspace name is first specified (`tmpdbs`, for instance). `"N"` is entered in the `mirror` field because temporary dbspaces are never mirrored. `"Y"` is entered in the `temporary` field to indicate the temporary nature of this new database space to the Informix engine. The full pathname (or a symbolic link), offset, and size then need to be specified. Additional chunks can be added in the Dbspaces|Add_chunk menu of `onmonitor`.

When you finish configuring your temporary dbspace, you need to change the value of `DBSPACETEMP` in your `${INFORMIX}/etc/onconfig` file to reflect the name or names you chose for your temporary database space or spaces.

Changing the Size and Placement of the Physical Log

The physical log is a system area that takes a snapshot of the disk pages changed during database activity. It aids in recovery in case of failure, as well as with transaction processing. If you expect to have a very busy database, you definitely need to expand your physical log. First create an appropriately sized dbspace—for example, `phydbs`—and then bring the database into `quiescent` mode with `onmode -s` or from the `onmonitor` Mode menu. Then, from the `onmonitor` menu Parameters|Physical-log, modify the size and placement parameters, as shown in Figure 10.7. The physical log takes some time to format and recover.

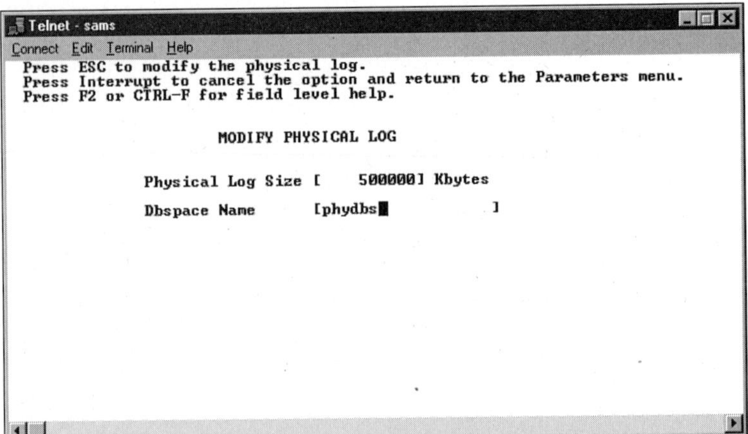

FIGURE 10.7.
The physical log modification screen.

Adding Application Database Spaces and Chunks

You should segment certain databases into specific database spaces, depending on your particular needs. Otherwise, disk contention and the time necessary for recovery will hamper your important applications if less critical or development database activity takes place in the same dbspace. The dbspaces are added in the same manner as with the tempdbs, but the `temporary` status flag will be `"N"` this time. You can add chunks from the Dbspaces|Add_chunk menu again if necessary.

When you have finished adding all the dbspaces and chunks, you can verify their existence and sizes with the `onstat -d` command. Note that the `phydbs` will show that the area allocated to the physical log is used. You can check in the Status|Logs menu to see how full the physical log actually is.

Upgrading the Informix Version

You might need only to upgrade your database server rather than create a brand new instance. Upgrading from a 6.0, 5.0, or 4.1 version must be done after carefully verifying pre-upgrade database consistency, and archiving both the database and the Informix file system components.

Depending on the version you are upgrading from, you need to make certain environmental variables, shared memory, and disk modifications. These details are very nicely detailed in the Informix Migration Guide, and there are version- and platform-specific notes under the `release` directory in the file `MIGRATEDOC_7.2`. After the necessary changes have been made, you should place the new executables in a separate directory to ensure recoverability. When the engine is brought online, it does the necessary conversions. This is also the case for upgrades to new versions of Informix 7.*x*.

CAUTION

Do not initialize the database the same way you would for a new install. This destroys your current database. Instead, make sure that the configuration files (`onconfig` and `sqlhosts`) match the settings for the previous version—especially the root dbspace location, size, and so on. When you bring up the engine with `oninit` or the `onmonitor` Mode menu, the conversion takes place for you. *Never use `oninit -i` or the `onmonitor` Initialize menu with an upgrade!*

The most convenient way to do any upgrade is to place the new executables in a new directory and relink `/usr/informix` to the new directory. That way, the `INFORMIXDIR` environmental variable doesn't need to be changed. If you are doing an incremental upgrade, you might want to do only a backup of both your database and your `${INFORMIXDIR}`, and then overwrite the executables with the new version. Always make sure that the OnLine engine is in Off-Line mode when doing an upgrade.

Problems You Might Encounter

You might encounter a few problems when attempting to install Informix for the first time. The problems usually occur either during the installation or during the first initialization.

Installation Failed

If you receive errors when you run an Informix install script, it means that the distribution might be corrupt, or your Serial Number and Key are invalid or have been improperly entered. Check with Informix if you still have problems after re-entering the codes.

OnLine Will Not Initialize

If your installation will not initialize, the problem is very likely with either your shared memory parameters or your disk allocation.

Make sure that the shared memory parameters from the `ONLINE_7.2` file have been placed into `/etc/system`, and make sure that the machine has been rebooted and the kernel has been reconfigured. Often, having `touch /reconfigure` as root will help to ensure that a reboot re-builds the kernel.

Make sure that your disk parameters are set properly and the sizes, ownership, permissions, and locations of the disk partitions or files you have allocated for the root dbspace are correct. Remember that the owner and group need to be `informix`, and the permissions must be set to read/write for the owner and group (`660`). Also make sure you have not allocated more than 2GB for any chunk. If Informix generates an error during installation, you can look at the description by typing `finderr ???`, where `???` is the error code number returned.

Summary

This chapter has shown what is necessary for a typical Informix installation. Although a few UNIX parameters, Informix modifications, and installation-specific decisions must be made, it is very easy to install an instance of the INFORMIX-OnLine Dynamic Server, as well as all of the Informix application interfaces.

Configuring the Informix Environment

by Kevin Kempter

IN THIS CHAPTER

The INFORMIX-OnLine environment consists of several components, including a configuration file, connectivity files, log files, disk layout, and UNIX environment variables. This section describes the basics for initially setting up and configuring an INFORMIX-OnLine environment.

Message and Log Files

The INFORMIX-OnLine engine uses two important files to communicate what is happening within the engine and its processes: the message log file and the console message file. Each file contains a specific type of information for the Informix DBA. The INFORMIX-OnLine log and console files are both UNIX flat files, which are specified in the Informix `onconfig` file, via the `CONSOLE` and `MSGPATH` `onconfig` parameters. The message log file contains routine informational messages, assertion failure messages, messages requiring administrative action to be taken, and fatal error messages. The default path is `/usr/informix/OnLine.log`. The alarm program specified by the `ALARMPROGRAM` `onconfig` file parameter can be set to the pathname of a script or program to be run whenever certain events take place within the message log file.

The console message file is used to display routine status messages and diagnostic messages. The default path is `/dev/console`.

Connectivity Files

The INFORMIX-OnLine engine uses a number of files to define its communications protocol and network interface. This allows the OnLine engine to communicate and transfer data to and from various client connections. This communication requires the proper entries in the following UNIX environment variables and key files:

- `INFORMIXSERVER`
- `/etc/hosts`
- `/etc/services`
- `$INFORMIXDIR/etc/sqlhosts`

The `INFORMIXSERVER` UNIX environment variable indicates which database server (`DBSERVERNAME` in the `sqlhosts` file, which is the same as `DBSERVERNAME` in the `onconfig` file) to connect to by default.

The `/etc/hosts` file contains an entry for every machine on the network that will connect to the INFORMIX-OnLine engine. The `/etc/hosts` entries contain the following information:

- IP/Internet address
- Host name
- Host alias names (optional), such as

```
/etc/hosts entry:
     MeanMachine
```

The /etc/services file contains an entry for each service that will use TCP/IP as a connection protocol. Each entry in the /etc/services file contains the following information:

- The service name
- The port number/the protocol
- Any alias names (optional), such as

```
/etc/services entry:
            dbservice           1525/tcp
```

The $INFORMIXDIR/etc/sqlhosts file contains information that allows an INFORMIX-OnLine database client/server connection to occur from any client on the network. Each type of connection to each separate instance of the OnLine engine (database server) requires an entry in the sqlhosts file.

The following fields are required for each entry into the sqlhosts file:

- dbservername
- nettype
- hostname
- service name

The dbservername corresponds to the DBSERVERNAME entry in the OnLine configuration file associated with an instance of the OnLine engine. This name is used to look up all the other connection information for a particular database instance.

The nettype field describes three attributes about the connection:

- The database server type
- The network interface
- The communications protocol

The database server type indicates which Informix database server product is being used:

- on represents a connection to INFORMIX-OnLine engine.
- ol provides another way to represent a connection to INFORMIX-OnLine.
- se represents a connection to the INFORMIX-SE engine.
- dr represents a connection to INFORMIX-Gateway with DRDA.

The network interface describes what type of communication interface will occur:

- ipc: PC (UNIX interprocess communication)
- soc: NIX sockets
- tli: LI (transport-level interface)

The communications protocol determines the specific type of connection mechanism:

- shm is a shared memory connection.
- tcp is a TCP/IP network connection.
- spx is a PX/SPX network connection.

The hostname field serves as a way for the INFORMIX-OnLine engine to look up the hostname entry in the /etc/hosts file, indicating which machine is the server.

NOTE

When defining a shared memory connection (shm), the hostname and service name fields are not used. The names can be arbitrary, although entering the actual hostname and an actual service name makes maintenance easier.

The service name field, when using a shared memory connection, allows OnLine to look up shared memory information on the host machine, based on whatever arbitrary name is provided as long as it is unique to the host machine environment. When using a TCP/IP network connection, the service name allows the OnLine engine to look up the service name entry in the /etc/services file in order to establish the client/server connection. When using an IPX/SPX network, the service name field can be arbitrary as long as it is a unique name across the IPX/SPX network environment. If you are using INFORMIX-OnLine for NetWare v4.1, the service name must be the same as the dbservername.

Here are some examples of sqlhosts entries:

```
dbservername        nettype         hostname        service name
grndkahuna          onsoctcp        MeanMachine     dbservice
mstrdba             ontlitcp        MeanDBA         dbservice2
```

The Root dbspace

The root dbspace is a special dbspace that the INFORMIX-OnLine engine creates during disk initialization. The root dbspace contains several pages of key information:

- OnLine reserved pages
- The first chunk free list
- The tblspace table
- The database table
- Physical and logical logs (which can be moved after disk initialization)

The INFORMIX-OnLine reserved pages are the first 12 sequential pages of space in the root dbspace. These 12 pages are reserved for use internally by the OnLine engine. The Informix reserved pages contain the information listed in Table 11.1.

Table 11.1. Information contained in the Informix reserved pages.

Reserved Page(s)	*Information Stored*
1	Internal engine/system information
2	The current `onconfig` file
3–4	OnLine checkpoint information
5–6	`dbspace` information/status
7–8	Chunk information
9–10	Mirror information
11–12	Archive and data-replication information

The first chunk free list page is a standard free list page (a page on disk that contains a list of free space within a chunk).

Each `tblspace` table in the root `dbspace` describes a `tblspace`. As tables are created, as fragments are added, and so on, additional `tblspace` pages in the root `dbspace` are added.

Each database page in the root `dbspace` contains information about a database within the OnLine engine instance.

The physical log is a series of pages where "before" images of buffer pages are stored before they are modified. When OnLine changes a page in the shared memory buffer pool, it first stores a copy of the page in the physical log buffer in shared memory. The physical log buffer retains all "before" image pages until they are flushed to disk via the OnLine page cleaners.

INFORMIX-OnLine stores all changes to the database data in the logical logs. The logical logs can be used to roll-forward any recorded changes or transactions in the event of a restore, or to roll-back any failed or otherwise canceled (such as with a `rollback` statement) transactions.

Estimating the Size of the Root dbspace

The following calculations and information should be considered when attempting to estimate the necessary size for the root `dbspace`.

The Physical Log

The initial physical log size can be estimated by using the following calculation:

> (*The number of anticipated users*)×(*The max number of OnLine pages per critical section*)×4

The number of anticipated `userthreads` should be set in the `NETTYPE` parameter in the INFORMIX-OnLine configuration file (the `onconfig` file).

The maximum pages per critical section, according to the INFORMIX-OnLine documentation, is five. This is the maximum number of pages per section that absolutely must be completed as a single unit or transaction. When OnLine modifies data, the maximum number of pages is five, so no more than five should be used for this value.

The Logical Log

To determine the initial number and size of the logical logs, use the following calculation, which is a starting point only. The only way to configure the size and number of the logical logs correctly is through examination of the system design and use, as well as tuning. Here is the calculation:

(*Number of log files*)×(*Number of userthreads*)×(*2 log pages*)×(*The system page size*)

Additional logical logs can always be added to increase the size allowed for your logical logs. When the INFORMIX-OnLine engine is initialized for the first time, the minimum number of logs is three.

TIP

Whenever possible, move the logical logs out of the root dbspace after the engine is initialized for the first time, and mirror the dbspace that contains them. Additional logs can be added at any time to provide more space, based on the monitoring of the engine.

Temp Space

The default for INFORMIX-OnLine temp space is to use the root dbspace. There are several advantages to using separate temp dbspaces (which are discussed in the "Informix Temp Space" section of this chapter). Like sizing the logical logs, determining the optimal amount of space for temp space requires monitoring and research to be optimized. An initial size for temp space can be estimated by evaluating the following guidelines.

Table Join Space

Attempt to estimate which tables will be joined often, and estimate the size of the largest join that could take place. You should size for the worst-case scenario (using the formula *table A total size* + *table B total size*). If a fairly accurate estimate is impossible, use the following calculation:

(*Projected size of the largest table*)×1.5

Logical Log Size

Consider the size of your logical logs. In the event of a warm restore, the OnLine engine needs to create a temp file as large as your logical log, which requires the following formula:

(*The* `LOGSIZE onconfig` *parameter*)×(*The number of logs*)

> **TIP**
>
> The INFORMIX-OnLine performance can be greatly enhanced by creating separate `dbspaces` for temp processing. See the "Informix Temp Space" section, later in this chapter, for more information.

Data Space

If you allow databases and tables to be stored in the root `dbspace`, you need to estimate the size of the space they will occupy in the root `dbspace`.

> **TIP**
>
> Most DBAs would never allow any developers to create tables in the root `dbspace`. In fact, many DBAs would become violent at the suggestion.
>
> The majority of systems I have worked on create databases only in the root `dbspace` and create all tables in other `dbspaces`, or they create both the databases and the tables in other `dbspaces`.

If you allow databases to be created in the root `dbspace`, the growth of the system catalogs and reserved pages needs to be estimated. (See the *INFORMIX-OnLine Dynamic Server Administrators Guide* for what happens when a database is created.)

If you allow tables to be created in the root `dbspace`, you also need to estimate the size of the `tblspace` pages and the data for the tables.

On-Archive Catalogs

Although this chapter does not cover the On-Archive product, if you decide to use On-Archive to perform your archives, you will also need to account for the size of the On-Archive catalog data. Refer to the *INFORMIX-OnLine Dynamic Server Performance Guide* for guidelines on sizing each of the On-Archive catalog tables.

Reserved Pages

The recommendation according to the INFORMIX-OnLine documentation is to allow an additional 3 percent of the size of the root dbspace, plus the size of 14 pages, following this formula:

(*current root* dbspace *size*×.03)+(*system page size*×14)

Table 11.2 contains an example sizing of an INFORMIX-OnLine root dbspace. The following configuration describes the system being sized:

- 20 processor MPP box
- 2GB main memory
- 100GB disk space for the database (partitioned as eight 500MB partitions per disk across 25 4.5GB disks)
- System page size of 4KB (4,096 bytes)
- Largest table estimated at a size of 10GB
- Estimate of 150 as the maximum number of users
- 20 logical logs of 10MB each and LOGSIZE set to 10MB (10,240,000 bytes)

Table 11.2. A sample root dbspace sizing.

Step	*Calculation*	*Size*
Size for physical log	150×5×4	3,000
Size for logical logs (sized for 3 logs because logs will be moved)	3×150×2×4,096	3,686,400
Size for temp space (separate dbspaces will be created as temp dbspaces)		0
Data space (no databases/tables will live in the root dbspace)		0
On-Archive (On-Archive will not be used)		0
Reserved pages	(3,689,400×.03)+(4,096×14)	168,026
Total root dbspace size		3,857,426 (3.8MB)

onconfig Parameters

This section covers the basic Informix `onconfig` configuration file parameters needed in order to initialize an instance of the INFORMIX-OnLine Dynamic server. Information on additional parameters can be found in the *INFORMIX-OnLine Dynamic Server Administrators Guide.* The `onconfig` configuration file is identified to Informix via the UNIX environment variable `ONCONFIG`. The default file name for the Informix `onconfig` file is `onconfig.std`. The `onconfig` file is always found in the `etc` directory in the Informix base directory specified by the UNIX environment variable `INFORMIXDIR`.

ALARMPROGRAM

The ALARMPROGRAM parameter allows the path to a shell script or executable program to be specified. If set, this program is run when an alarm condition occurs, such as the logical logs being full or a logical recovery failure. If an alarm program is put in place, the INFORMIX-OnLine engine passes the following parameters when calling it:

- Event severity level
- Event class ID
- Event class message string
- Event specific message
- Event "see also" file

The shell script shown in Listing 11.1 is an example of a script to mail the database administrator when the logical logs are full.

Listing 11.1. The `log_full_alarm.sh` script.

```
#!/bin/ksh
#
# log_full_alarm.sh
# Shell to alert the DBA if the logs are full.
# Written by:    The DBA (Master of Technology)
#
# Syntax: log_full_alarm.sh
#           <event severity> <class id> <class msg>
#           <event specific msg> <see also file>

# check for logical logs full class id
if [ $2 = "20" ]
then
     # mail a message to the informix login
     mailx informix < "HEY THE LOGS ARE FULL"
fi
exit 0
```

BUFFERS

The `BUFFERS` parameter specifies the maximum size (in pages) of the INFORMIX-OnLine shared memory buffer pool. This parameter determines how much memory the OnLine engine can utilize to cache disk I/O. The default value is `200`. Informix recommends a starting value of approximately 20 percent to 25 percent of the physical memory on the machine. Informix also recommends that you set this parameter first, and base all other related parameters on the size of the `BUFFERS` parameter. After the OnLine engine is initialized, the buffer cache should be monitored with the `onstat -p` command. If the cache read rate is less that 90 to 99 percent, more buffer pages should be added.

TIP

When you reach a 98 to 99 percent cache read rate, start to back off on the number of buffer pages configured. This enables you to configure the minimum number of pages needed to attain an optimized buffer cache size. If this is not done, you could end up with too many buffer pages when increasing the size to get a 90 to 99 percent read cache rate. If this happens, you could hurt system performance by causing the system to start paging due to having insufficient memory resources left for other applications.

CHUNKS

The `CHUNKS` parameter defines the maximum number of chunks that the OnLine engine can use. Informix recommends that the `CHUNKS` parameter be set as close as possible to the maximum number of files that the operating system can have open simultaneously. The maximum number of simultaneously open files is a tunable UNIX kernel parameter. The maximum number that the `CHUNKS` parameter can be set to is `2047`.

CKPTINTVL

The `CKPTINTVL` parameter specifies, in seconds, how often the OnLine engine checks to see whether a checkpoint is needed. When a checkpoint is performed, all the *dirty* pages (which are buffer pages that have been modified in memory, but not yet updated on disk) in the buffer cache are flushed to disk. To optimize this parameter, you need to find a balance between how long you are willing to wait while the checkpoint is performed, and the amount of time you are willing to allow to pass before your disks are updated. Obviously, the longer you wait between checkpoints, the longer the checkpoint will take to perform, depending on the amount of activity in the database.

CLEANERS

The CLEANERS parameter determines how many threads will be allocated to flush the dirty buffer pages to disk. Informix recommends that you specify one page cleaner per disk drive. If your system contains more than 20 disks dedicated to the database, the recommendation is one page cleaner for every two disks. For systems that contain more than 100 database disks, Informix recommends one page cleaner to be configured for every four database disks on the system.

CONSOLE

This parameter determines where OnLine will write system console messages. The default is `/dev/console`. You can specify the path to any valid filename for which Informix has read and write permissions.

DBSERVERNAME

The DBSERVERNAME parameter contains the name you decide to give to this particular instance of the OnLine engine. The default is the hostname of the machine. The DBSERVERNAME parameter is used in the `sqlhosts` file to allow connectivity between the database server and clients submitting requests to the database. The DBSERVERNAME parameter must meet the following criteria to be valid:

- All lowercase letters
- No spaces, tabs, newlines, or comment characters

DBSPACES

The DBSPACES parameter indicates the maximum number of `dbspaces` that the OnLine engine can utilize. This parameter should be close to the number of chunks specified, because each `dbspace` must contain at least one chunk. However, `dbspaces` can contain multiple chunks. The default value for DBSPACES is `8`.

DBSPACETEMP

The DBSPACETEMP parameter specifies which `dbspaces` will be utilized when temp space is needed. Informix uses temp space for operations such as creating temp tables, sorting data, performing joins, and performing recovery processing. The DBSPACETEMP parameter can list as many `dbspaces` as you want, separated by a comma (,) or a colon(:), as long as the entire list is less than 254 characters. If 254 characters is not enough space to list all of your temp `dbspaces`, you can also use the DBSPACETEMP UNIX environment variable. (See the *Informix Guide to SQL: Reference* for more information.)

LOGBUFF

The LOGBUFF parameter defines the size of the logical log buffers. INFORMIX-OnLine allocates three buffers of size LOGBUFF at the time of the shared memory initialization. See the section "Estimating the Size of the Root dbspace" for more information.

LOGFILES

The LOGFILES parameter simply specifies the initial number of logical logs at initialization time.

LRUS

The LRUS parameter specifies the number of LRU (least recently used) queues. Informix utilizes LRUs to determine which buffer cache pages will be flushed to disk when a new page from disk is needed and no free pages are in the buffer cache. Informix recommends that you set this parameter equal to the number of CPU VPs (Virtual Processors of the CPU class) configured on the system (covered in greater detail under the NUMCPUVPS parameter), or at least to 4 in the case of a system with fewer than four CPU VPs. The LRUs help control how often the buffer pool dirty pages are flushed to disk. After the INFORMIX-OnLine engine is initialized, you should monitor the LRUs with the onstat -R command. If the number of dirty pages is consistently greater than the LRU_MAX_DIRTY parameter, you need to add more LRUs or CLEANERS. (See the INFORMIX-OnLine Dynamic Server Performance Guide for more information.)

LRU_MAX_DIRTY

The LRU_MAX_DIRTY parameter is a high-water mark for the percentage of pages allowed to be dirty at any given point. When the number of dirty pages exceeds this threshold, the OnLine engine page cleaner threads start flushing dirty pages to the disk.

LRU_MIN_DIRTY

The LRU_MIN_DIRTY parameter is the low-water mark for the dirty pages. Page cleaners flush dirty pages to disk from the buffer pool until the LRU_MIN_DIRTY percentage of dirty pages is reached.

LTXHWM

This value specifies the long transaction high-water mark. If the value is set to 80 and the logical logs become 80 percent full, OnLine checks for a long transaction. A long transaction is a single transaction that requires more space than is available across all the logical logs. The logs cannot be backed up until the transaction is completed. If OnLine detects a long transaction in progress, it rolls the transaction back and frees the logs.

LTXEHWM

This parameter specifies the exclusive transaction high-water mark. If OnLine detects a long transaction in progress and the percentage of the logical logs that are full via this transaction exceeds the exclusive high-water mark, the threads attempting to roll back the transaction are given exclusive access to the logical logs.

MSGPATH

The `MSGPATH` parameter indicates where the INFORMIX-OnLine engine will write log messages. The message log contains OnLine processing information. This file is usually set to a file in an `$INFORMIXDIR/logs` directory. The default is `/usr/informix/OnLine.log`.

MULTIPROCESSOR

The `MULTIPROCESSOR` parameter indicates to the OnLine engine whether or not the machine is a multiprocessor box. The values are as follows:

- `0` = Single processor
- `1` = Multiprocessor

NETTYPE

The `NETTYPE` parameter is a field that specifies several values separated by commas. The first value indicates the connection protocol. The `onconfig` file can contain multiple `NETTYPE` settings—one for each type of connection. The valid values for the connection are the same as the `nettype` field in the `sqlhosts` file (discussed in the "Connectivity Files" section of this chapter), minus the server product information (which is the first two letters).

The next value indicates the number of poll threads for that connection type. If the number is unspecified, the default is one poll thread. As a general rule, each poll thread can effectively handle 200 to 250 users.

Next is the maximum number of concurrent users. (This is not needed for a shared memory connection.)

The last piece is the VP (Virtual Processor) class entry. This entry defines which CPU class the connection uses—either `CPU` or `NET`. The OnLine engine attempts to use the best type, if unspecified, based on the connection type.

The CPU class is generally more efficient.

NUMAIOVPS

The `NUMAIOVPS` parameter specifies the number of AIO virtual processors to launch at initialization. If kernel asynchronous I/O (KAIO) is implemented, set this parameter to the number of cooked files (UNIX files used for database data rather than UNIX raw space) that you have configured and add 1. If KAIO is not implemented, Informix recommends that you use one AIOVP per disk that contains database data.

NUMCPUVPS

The NUMCPUVPS parameter indicates to the OnLine engine how many CPU virtual processor threads to use when the engine is initialized. If you are running on a multiple CPU box, Informix recommends that you configure NUMCPUVPS to the number that is one less than the number of CPUs your machine has. If you have a single processor box, configure NUMCPUVPS to 1.

PHYSBUFF

OnLine uses two buffers in shared memory in which to store "before" images before writing them to the physical log. The PHYSBUFF parameter defines how much memory OnLine can allocate to these buffers. Each write to the physical log buffers is one page, so make the size evenly divisible by your system page size. The size of this parameter determines how often the physical log buffer will be flushed. The default is 32.

PHYSFILE

The PHYSFILE parameter determines the size of the physical log. The more update-intensive your application will be, the bigger your physical log should be. The following is the calculation recommended by Informix to determine the maximum size:

$$(\textit{number of concurrent connections} \times 20 \times \textit{system page size}) \div 1024$$

RESIDENT

If your system supports forced residency, this parameter can force the resident portion of the OnLine shared memory to never be swapped. Be careful with this parameter. If you force residency while the system needs to swap, and not enough memory is left to perform the system processes, you will have serious performance problems. The default is 0 (no forced residency). To force residency, set this parameter to 1.

ROOTNAME

This is the name of the root dbspace. It is an arbitrary name, although it must be unique among the dbspaces for this instance of OnLine. The default is rootdbs.

ROOTOFFSET

The ROOTOFFSET parameter specifies how many kilobytes to offset the start of the root dbspace into the partition defined in ROOTPATH. The default is 0.

ROOTPATH

This is the full pathname (including the device/file name) to the device file or cooked file that will be used as the root dbspace.

> **TIP**
>
> You can use links to the raw devices named for the use of the dbspace to help manage your raw devices. In this case, you would specify the link to the root dbspace. If your root device is /dev/informix/vg0037R, you could create a link of /informix/root and specify /informix/root in your ROOTPATH parameter.

ROOTSIZE

The ROOTSIZE parameter specifies the size of the root dbspace in kilobytes. See the section "Estimating the Size of the Root dbspace" in this chapter for more information.

SINGLE_CPU_VP

Set this parameter to 1 if you are running on a single-processor system. This allows the OnLine engine to optimize for a single processor. For multiprocessor boxes, set SINGLE_CPU_VP to 0.

Initializing the OnLine Engine

There are two types of initialization for the INFORMIX-OnLine engine. One initializes the disk for initial use. This completely wipes out any information that was previously on the disk where the dbspaces are initialized, making the data absolutely unrecoverable. The second type of initialization is simply to start the engine and bring it to an online (currently running) state.

The command used for initialization is the oninit command. If you run oninit without any parameters, it attempts to bring online or up an existing instance of INFORMIX-OnLine. There are a number of UNIX environment variables that tell oninit which instance to initialize.

The other type of initialization used to initialize a new instance is run when you provide a -i parameter to the oninit command. The oninit command prompts you to verify that this is what you want to do and indicates that it will destroy all existing data. You can use oninit -iy if you want to bypass the verify prompt.

The following UNIX environment variables need to be set in order to run oninit, for initialization, or to bring an existing instance online:

- DBSERVERNAME: The name of the database server instance.
- onconfig: The name of the configuration file.

- `INFORMIXDIR`: The base directory of the Informix installation.
- `INFORMIXSERVER`: The same as the `DBSERVERNAME` if you want the sysmaster database to be built during disk initialization.
- `PATH`: The `PATH` needs to include `$INFORMIXDIR/bin`.

Creating Additional dbspaces

After you have initialized the INFORMIX-OnLine system, you will probably want to configure additional `dbspaces`. Informix `dbspaces` can be a raw device (UNIX space set aside for a process to access the space directly without the overhead of the UNIX kernel handling the I/O) or a cooked UNIX file (a UNIX file accessed via the UNIX kernel I/O processes). There are valid reasons why you would want to use both cooked and raw `dbspaces`.

Cooked Files

An Informix cooked file is a UNIX file, so UNIX manages all of the I/O to the `dbspace`. Although Informix manages the data structure within the cooked files, allowing UNIX to manage the I/O poses additional overhead that affects performance.

In some instances, you will want to use cooked files instead of raw devices. The following sections outline some of the benefits of using cooked files as `dbspaces`.

Cooked File Setup

Cooked files are very easy to set up. Simply create a UNIX file and verify the correct permissions as follows:

- Log in as user `informix`.
- `cd` to the directory where the cooked `dbspaces` will live (that is, `cd /informix/cooked_files`)
- Create an empty file by using the `touch` command or the following command:

  ```
  > roasted_chunk
  ```
- Change the permissions on the new file using the following command:

  ```
  chmod 660 roasted_chunk
  ```
- Change ownership of the new file with the following commands:

  ```
  chown informix roasted_chunk
  chgrp informix roasted_chunk
  ```

NOTE

There are several ways to create a UNIX file, and all of the methods are equally good. Here are a few methods:

- `> file` creates a file named `file`, which is shorthand for the command `cat /dev/null > file`
- `touch file`

Generally, cooked files are a good choice when setting up a training environment or when performance is not a factor. When performance is an issue, cooked files are rarely an acceptable method.

Raw Devices

A raw device is a "character-special" file that can be accessed using direct memory access (DMA). This type of access allows Informix to bypass the UNIX file management and manage the I/O to the device via a direct transfer to and from shared memory. This type of access is dramatically faster than using cooked files. The process to set up a raw device is more involved than setting up a cooked file, but the performance increase is well worth the effort. When raw devices are used, the INFORMIX-OnLine engine can guarantee that the committed data is stored on the disk; when cooked files are used, the UNIX kernel can buffer the data, thus creating a risk of lost data in the event of a system crash.

Raw Device Setup

Every version of UNIX has a method of creating raw devices, and all of the methods are fairly similar. Usually, the creation of raw devices involves some setup within the UNIX system administrators tools.

After the raw devices have been created, the steps are pretty similar to the cooked file setup:

1. Change the permissions on the raw device with the following command:

   ```
   chmod 660 /dev/raw_chunk
   ```

2. Change ownership of the raw device with the following commands:

   ```
   chown informix /dev/raw_chunk
   chgrp informix /dev/raw_chunk
   ```

Create dbspaces

After the raw devices or the cooked files have been created, you can create the dbspaces. Informix dbspaces can be created via the ON-Monitor tool or via command-line utilities. The ON-Monitor tool is discussed later in this chapter. The onspaces command can be used to create dbspaces. The following command creates a 100MB dbspace called big_boy, starting at an offset of 8KB into the raw device:

```
onspaces -c -d big_boy -p /dev/raw_chunk -o 8 -s 100000
```

Mirroring Strategy

This section discusses what mirroring is and how it is implemented. Whether to mirror or not and an approach to mirroring will be examined as well.

What Is Mirroring?

Mirroring is the process of replicating a dbspace for the purpose of reducing the risk of data loss in the event of a hardware failure. When mirroring is in place, both the primary and the mirror chunks are written to automatically. If a hardware failure causes the primary chunk to be inaccessible, Informix automatically reads from the mirror chunk.

Why Mirror?

Mirroring provides a method of real-time recovery from media failure, without having to bring down the OnLine engine. Any database that contains business-critical data should be mirrored. The root dbspace, the physical log, and logical logs should always be mirrored.

TIP

Mirroring can also be handled at the UNIX level. For many types of UNIX, the presence of a mirror raw space automatically causes reads from the mirror chunk when the primary chunk is in use. This can improve performance immensely.

Mirroring Costs

The biggest cost associated with mirroring is the disk space. Mirroring consumes twice as much disk space for your database. This is why you should carefully weigh which dbspaces to mirror. Certainly temp dbspaces would be the lowest priority, and root and the logs are probably the highest priority. The data chunks must be evaluated as to how critical they are to the business. If one of the critical chunks (such as root dbspace, logical logs, or physical log) is not mirrored and the media fails, OnLine will go offline immediately.

Recovering a Failed Mirror

If a mirrored disk fails, after the disk has been replaced the following onspaces command recovers and resyncs the primary and the mirror chunks:

```
onspaces -s  big_dbspace  -p /dev/chunk_to_recover  -o 8   -O
```

Managing the Logs

The Informix logical logs are critical to the welfare of the INFORMIX-OnLine instance. The DBA needs to ensure that every effort has been taken to manage the logs properly and limit the risk of losing the logs. The previous section on mirroring covers why and how you would attempt to minimize the risk of losing the logs. The management of the logs generally includes moving the logs to a separate dbspace.

Moving the Logs

Placing the logs in separate dbspaces can boost performance because they are written to so often. In order to do this, the following steps need to be taken:

1. Free the logical logs. (Normally, an intake archive to /dev/null frees all logs except the current log.)
2. Add new logical logs to the new dbspace using the onparams command, like this:

   ```
   onparams  -a -d new_dbspace -s 50000
   ```

3. Create a level 0 archive so that the new logs can be used with ontape.
4. Use onmode -l to switch the current log to one of the new logs.
5. Create an archive again to free the original logs.
6. Drop the original logs from the root dbspace using the onparams command:

   ```
   onparams -d -l 2 (where 2 is the log number from an onstat -l output)
   ```

Informix Temp Space

The INFORMIX-OnLine engine uses temp space to perform tasks such as sorts, joins, the creation of tables and indexes, and various other operations. If unspecified, the root dbspace will be used as the temp dbspace. By creating temp dbspaces, you can improve performance and reduce the size needed for the root dbspace. The value of creating additional dbspaces exclusively for the use of the OnLine engine's temporary operations should not be underestimated. The impacts on performance, as well as on general administration of the database, can be dramatic.

Temporary dbspaces can be created for the exclusive use of temp tables. Temp dbspaces can be created like other dbspaces, using the onspaces command. The following command creates a 500MB temp dbspace named temp1, with an offset of 8KB. The -t flag indicates to the OnLine engine that this will be a dbspace used exclusively for temporary operations.

```
onspaces  -d temp1  -t  -p /dev/tmp_chunk01   -o 8   -s 500000
```

A Sample onconfig File

The following onconfig file contains *only* the parameters discussed in this chapter. The system represented is as follows:

- 20 processor MPP box
- 2GB main memory
- 50GB disk space for the database (partitioned as four 1GB partitions per disk across 13 4.5GB disks)
- System page size of 4KB (4,096 bytes)
- Estimated 150 as the maximum number of users

The following onconfig file would serve as a good starting point in the creation of an OnLine instance. Further tuning is always an ongoing task. Comments can be placed in the onconfig file by using the pound sign.

```
BUFFERS    80000     # 327MB
CHUNKS          120
CKPTINTVL         60
CLEANERS         27
CONSOLE         /informix/logs/console.log
DBSERVERNAME     enterprise
DBSPACES         60
DBSPACETEMP     dbs_t1,dbs_t2,dbs_t3,dbs_t4,dbs_t5
LOGBUFF         65536    #informix recommended value (16 pages)
LOGFILES         3
LRUS             19
LRU_MAX_DIRTY      60
LRU_MIN_DIRTY      50
LTXHWM          80
LTXEHWM          90
MSGPATH          /informix/logs/online.log
MULTIPROCESSOR     1
NETTYPE          soctcp,1,150,NET
NUMAIOVPS          2    # using KAIO
NUMCPUVPS         19
PHYSBUFF         65536    #informix recommended value (16 pages)
PHYSFILE         12000
RESIDENT         0
ROOTNAME           rootdbs
ROOTOFFSET          0
```

```
ROOTPATH        /dev/rootvg
ROOTSIZE        3857426
SINGLE_CPU_VP    0
```

Starting and Stopping the OnLine Engine

The INFORMIX-OnLine engine can be started and stopped from the ON-Monitor tool (which is discussed in the next section of this chapter), as well as from the command line. To start and stop the INFORMIX-OnLine engine from the command line, use the `oninit` and `onmode` commands. Table 11.3 describes the OnLine commands to start up and shut down the engine.

Table 11.3. OnLine startup and shutdown commands.

Command	*Flags*	*Description*
`oninit`		Brings an offline instance online, leaving disk/data intact.
`oninit`	`-i` (initialize disk)	Initializes OnLine (disk initialization, OnLine asks whether you are sure you want to do this because any existing data will be lost).
`oninit`	`-iy` (answer yes to prompts)	Initializes OnLine (disk initialization without asking whether you are sure).
`onmode`	`-k` (shut down the engine)	Brings OnLine offline (prompts you to confirm).
`onmode`	`-ky`	Brings OnLine offline without any confirmation.

Using Informix ON-Monitor

Informix ON-Monitor is an easy-to-use monitoring and tuning tool. The ON-Monitor tool allows a variety of operations and status listings to be performed. When you are in the ON-Monitor menus, you can select options by using the Spacebar to highlight the option and pressing Return, or by pressing the first letter of the option that you want to run.

The following lists provide a brief summary of the options available in the Informix ON-Monitor tool. The options are self-explanatory for the most part, so I didn't go into great detail for any of them. For more information, see the *INFORMIX-OnLine Dynamic Server Administrators Guide.*

ON-Monitor Main Menu

Status	Status options
Parameters	Set/modify OnLine parameters
Dbspaces	Create, monitor, and modify dbspaces and related parameters
Mode	Alter modes such as online, offline/shutdown options, and so on
Force-Ckpt	Force a checkpoint to occur
Archive	Set tape device parameters
Logical-Logs	Modify logging status and set logical log tape device parameters
Exit	Exit the ON-Monitor menu

ON-Monitor Status Menu

Profile	Display performance statistics
Userthreads	Display status of active user threads
Spaces	Display status information about dbspaces, chunks, and so on
Databases	Display information about the OnLine databases
Logs	Display status info about the logs
Archive	Display ontape archive information
data-Replication	Display data replication status information
Output	Store any of the status displays in a file
Configuration	Create a copy of the current config file
Exit	Get out

ON-Monitor Parameters Menu

Initialize	Initialize disk space
Shared-Memory	Set shared memory parameters
perFormance	Specify virtual processors
data-Replication	Set data replication parameters
diaGnostics	Set diagnostic parameters
pdQ	Modify the PDQ priority (parallel data query) parameter
Add-Log	Add a logical log
Drop-Log	Drop a logical log
Physical-Log	Modify size/location of the physical log
Exit	Previous menu

ON-Monitor Dbspaces Menu

Create	Create a `dbspace`
BLOBSpace	Create a `blobspace`
Mirror	Add or end mirroring
Drop	Drop a `dbspace` or `blobspace`
Info	Usage info and space used for `dbspaces`
Add_chunk	Add a chunk to a `dbspace`
datasKip	Modify the `DATASKIP` parameter to enable/disable dataskip for `dbspaces`
Status	Modify the status of a mirrored chunk
Exit	Previous menu

ON-Monitor Mode Menu

Startup	Bring the engine up to quiescent mode
On-Line	Bring the engine from quiescent mode to On-Line mode
Graceful-Shutdown	Take the engine to quiescent mode, allowing users to complete their work
Immediate-Shutdown	Take the engine to quiescent mode in 10 seconds
Take-Offline	Take the engine from quiescent to Offline mode
Add-Proc	Add virtual processors
Drop-Proc	Drop virtual processors
deCision-support	Set DSS (decision-support system) parameters
Exit	Previous menu

ON-Monitor Force-Ckpt Menu

Forces a checkpoint

ON-Monitor Archive Menu

Tape-Parameters	Set archive tape parameters
Exit	Previous menu

ON-Monitor Logical-Logs Menu

Databases	Change database logging status
Tape-Parameters	Set logical-log tape parameters
Exit	Previous menu

Summary

As you can see, configuring an INFORMIX-OnLine environment can be a complex task, and tuning that environment can be even more complex. This chapter provided you with a methodical way to set up the INFORMIX-OnLine environment, and it gave you some realistic guidelines for assigning initial values to the various settings and parameters involved.

12

Incorporating a Database in Your Informix Environment

by Matt Bentley

IN THIS CHAPTER

A properly designed database can enhance the performance and simplify development of the application. Before the first table is created, there must be detailed planning of the database and how it will be used. When you understand the trade-offs of the different features in Informix, the database can be implemented for best performance and still satisfy its purpose.

Designing the Database

Designing a physical database should follow a thorough investigation of the requirements, data needs, and development of a solid logical data model. Considering the developers' point of view will add significantly to the progress of the project.

Normalization Versus Denormalization

Some of the benefits of normalizing your database include the ability to

- Identify dependencies
- Identify which attributes belong in which tables
- Reduce redundant data
- Create a flexible design

A fully normalized database offers flexibility to the data but can cause complexities when accessing and maintaining it. The physical implementation of a database generally involves some level of denormalizing, mostly to increase performance and simplify development.

Denormalizing the database involves splitting tables if there is a logical separation of how the columns are selected or maintained. In some cases, it means combining tables where columns from those tables are always selected together. In addition to splitting and combining tables, duplicating columns can also be done for performance reasons.

Online Transaction Processing and Decision Support

The purpose of a database is to store information. Frequently the data is very dynamic and it is changed often. Databases in which the data is constantly changing are called *online transaction processing (OLTP)* databases.

Information is valuable when used correctly. When you analyze data, intelligent decisions can be made by finding patterns and trends in the data. When the purpose of the database is primarily decision support, it is called a *Decision Support System (DSS)* or an *OnLine Analytical Processing (OLAP)* database. These types of databases are also known as *data warehouses.*

When the database serves both purposes, it is important to understand the trade-offs in performance when designing the database and tuning the database engine. Identifying those trade-offs is difficult, and in many cases it cannot be done until development has begun or the database is fully populated with many users accessing it.

Size or potential size of the database will drive a lot of decisions about the design and implementation. If the database is small and will not grow, many performance considerations can be set aside; however, if the database will be large, decisions such as the data type of a column can impact the maintenance and performance of the database.

Table Placement and Fragmentation

Tables that will be accessed or updated frequently should be placed on separate disks to limit disk head movement and contention. Consider fragmenting large tables across multiple disks and even isolating them on their own disks. This will allow the data in that table to be accessed in parallel.

Performance comes from some combination of fragment elimination and parallel queries. If the optimizer identifies that any of the fragments of a table can be eliminated, it will do so. Fragment elimination will not occur when the table is fragmented by round-robin methods. However, round-robin ensures evenly distributed data across all fragments. If the table will be fully scanned or the majority of the data in the table is being accessed, round-robin might be an appropriate fragmentation strategy.

Indexes

Indexes provide a shortcut to the data. When the optimizer determines that an index is available and will be used to access the data, the index pages are read into the buffers. The `btree` index is then traversed until the key or keys in the index match the criteria supplied. When the matching key is found, the data page that contains the specific row is retrieved into the buffers and the specific row is returned to the application that requested the data. Columns that are used to qualify which row or rows are selected should be included in an index to make accessing the data more efficient. Understanding how the data will be accessed by users will help when trying to identify which columns need to be indexed. When you create multiple indexes on a table, many different qualifiers can be used to more effectively implement the request for data. An example is changing Mr. Jones's address in the address table because he has moved. The update can be qualified on his name, account number, phone number, or even his old address. When individual indexes are on each of these columns, the optimizer chooses one of them to use. When implementing indexes, also remember that having too many indexes on a table degrades the performance of changes to the data and that each index consumes disk space.

Informix stores the keys of an index on separate pages from the data. The smaller the index key, the more keys will fit on each index page. Having more keys on an index page means fewer disk reads.

When indexes are created on tables with a high volume of inserts, they become inefficient quickly and should be re-created. By specifying a `FILLFACTOR` when the index is created, you can reduce the frequency of re-creating them.

Indexes can dramatically help improve the performance of an application, but they can also hinder the performance of the application that is primarily inserting rows. This is also the case when the application frequently summarizes or scans the majority of the data in the table and chooses an index path rather than a sequential scan of the table.

If the data that is being selected is contained in the index key, only the index pages will be read into buffers. For example, if the date an account is opened is part of the key with the account number, and you want to know the date that account 123456 was opened, no data pages will be read into the buffers because all information being requested is stored in the index pages.

TIP

The optimizer chooses to use a composite index even though not all columns are used to qualify the request. In these cases, the optimizer uses the composite index only if the leading columns are used to qualify data. To benefit from this, create the index with the leading columns being the ones most likely to be qualified on.

Although accessing data is more efficient with indexes, the overhead of adding keys in the index is costly for inserting rows. This is true because every time a row is written, both a data page and an index page are affected. This is also the case if columns in an index key are updated.

A feature of OnLine Dynamic Server Architecture (DSA) is the capability to detach and fragment indexes. Detaching indexes separates the index pages from the data pages on separate disks. Parallel reads and writes can happen when the data being accessed is on separate disks. You must provide a dbspace name for the index to be created in if you want the index to be detached. The following `CREATE INDEX` statement shows a detached index being created in the dbspace `cust_dbsp`:

```
CREATE INDEX customer_x ON customer (cust_id) IN cust_dbsp;
```

Fragmenting an index can speed access by spreading it across multiple disks. An index can be explicitly fragmented only by expression. If an index is created on a fragmented table but is not explicitly detached or fragmented, it will be fragmented the same as the table. The following `CREATE INDEX` statement shows it being fragmented by expression across three different dbspaces in a separate table space from the data:

```
CREATE INDEX customer_x ON customer (cust_id)
   FRAGMENT BY EXPRESSION
   cust_id <=1500                          IN cust_dbsp1,
   cust_id <= 5000 AND cust_id > 1500 IN cust_dbsp2,
   cust_id > 5000                          IN cust_dbsp3;
```

Tables are accessed more efficiently if the rows are sorted the same as the index. When you create a `CLUSTER` index, the table will be physically sorted the same as the index. You must have adequate disk space because the table is copied while it is being sorted. The order in the table is not maintained, so you might need to run this periodically to re-sort the table.

SET EXPLAIN

`SET EXPLAIN` is an SQL statement that is very useful in revealing how the database engine will access the data for a given query. By using `SET EXPLAIN` you can identify that you have correct indexes and which columns should be indexed. When you run `SET EXPLAIN ON`, the output is written to the file `sqexplain.out` in the current directory. Output from each query continues to be appended to `sqexplain.out` for the entire session unless you issue a `SET EXPLAIN OFF`.

`SET EXPLAIN` shows the query plan, estimated number of rows that will be returned, and an estimated cost of the query. The estimated cost is strictly an estimate used by the optimizer when comparing access paths.

The query plan shows the access path to each table and the order in which each table is read. For each table, you are shown the following:

- Whether the table was sequentially scanned or read by an index
- Which index was used
- Whether the database engine satisfied the query by doing an index-only read
- Which columns were being joined between tables
- The remote table when distributed queries are run and where the filter occurs
- Fragment elimination or parallel access for fragmented tables
- If `PDQPRIORITY` is not set, `SET EXPLAIN` shows that the fragments were accessed serially

TIP

When a query is executed, it is first checked for syntax and then optimized. After the query is optimized, the query path is written to `sqexplain.out`, and then the data is retrieved. At this point, the query can be aborted. This is especially useful when analyzing long-running queries.

Because the query plan is influenced by the statistics of the underlying tables, the plan might be different in a production database from the development or test databases. Because the data in the database will change over time, it is necessary to run `SET EXPLAIN` periodically against the production database.

TIP

Because of changing data in the database, an application might begin to run slowly for no apparent reason. By implementing SET EXPLAIN in the application, you can identify problems in the query plan for the SQL statements in the application. By passing an argument to the application, you can change to SET EXPLAIN ON when you want.

Business Rules and Referential Integrity

Business rules are implemented at the database through referential integrity, which is an important aspect of the database. Maintaining that integrity in the database rather than in the application ensures that data relationships are not compromised. With all the tools available to access a database, making sure all users keep referential integrity in the database would be difficult. Many features are available to enforce integrity at the database level. This puts the logic on the database server rather than in the applications. These features include constraints, triggers, stored procedures, and defaults.

Constraints

Constraints are implemented at the table or column level. When there is an update to a row in the table, the table-level constraints are evaluated. When a column with a constraint is updated, the constraint for the column is evaluated. If the constraint check fails, an error is returned to the application. PRIMARY KEY and FOREIGN KEY constraints are a good way to enforce the relationship between parent and child tables. If you try to insert a child row without a related row in the parent table, the insert will fail. Similarly, a constraint error will occur if you attempt to delete a row in the parent table and there are still related rows in the child table. You can specify in Data Definition Language (DDL) that when the parent row is deleted from a table with a PRIMARY KEY constraint, cascading deletes can occur. The database engine will automatically delete the child rows if there is a FOREIGN KEY constraint defined in the child tables. The cascade delete is performed as a transaction, so logging is required on the database.

A UNIQUE constraint ensures that rows do not have duplicate key values. NOT NULL constraints force columns to contain data where the data is required.

Triggers

Triggers can also be used to implement referential integrity. There are three types of triggers: insert, update, and delete. For each trigger, you can do many things, including calling a stored procedure, which really gives you a lot of flexibility. A triggered event can execute triggered actions BEFORE, AFTER, or FOR EACH ROW. Separate update triggers can be created for each column, but each column can be included in only one update trigger event.

An example of using triggers would be an invoice header table that has the total of all invoice line items. Each time a line item is added, updated, or deleted, it is necessary to change the total in the invoice header table. Do this by implementing an insert trigger on the invoice line item table to add the new amount to the total in the invoice header table. Similar triggers would also be created for deleting and updating line items.

Stored Procedures

Stored procedures can be used in many different ways. As mentioned earlier, they can be called from triggers to extend the ability of the trigger. They can be embedded in SQL statements such as the SELECT statement. They can be called with the EXECUTE PROCEDURE statement. Stored procedures can have arguments passed to them, making them dynamic. It is also possible using the SYSTEM command to execute OS commands and programs to further extend the functionality of the stored procedure. Stored procedures can also be implemented to further secure a database from unauthorized access.

Views

Views are used for many different purposes. A view can be defined to allow access to only certain columns from a table or to summarize and derive data columns. A view can be defined to restrict users from accessing certain groups of rows by limiting the view's SELECT statement in the WHERE clause. Views can be defined to summarize and derive data columns.

When defining a view, an SQL SELECT statement is the underlying structure of the view. The statement need not be limited to a single table, but it can include several tables with complex joins and filter criteria. Each time the view is accessed, the SQL SELECT statement is executed.

Views are updateable if the definition is based on a single table and there are no GROUP BY clauses, no DISTINCT or UNIQUE clauses, and no aggregated or derived columns. Updates can be restricted, ensuring that the updated row still qualifies for the view by using the WITH CHECK OPTION. The following view definition is an updateable view using WITH CHECK OPTION:

```
CREATE VIEW utah_customers
   (cust_id, f_name, l_name, city, state) AS
   SELECT cust_id, f_name, l_name, city, state
   FROM customers
   WHERE state = "UT"
   WITH CHECK OPTION ;
```

Synonyms

A synonym creates an alias to a table or view. Synonyms are a convenient way of making a remote table look local. Any data manipulation statements can be executed against a synonym, provided the user has the appropriate privileges on the underlying table.

Synonyms are PUBLIC by default. PRIVATE synonyms can be created but are accessible only by the owner of the synonym. If you create a PRIVATE synonym of the same name as a PUBLIC synonym and you use the synonym in a select statement, the PRIVATE synonym is used, unless the synonym name is qualified by the owner's ID of the PUBLIC synonym. Here is an example of a PUBLIC synonym created by user informix and a PRIVATE synonym with the same name created by tjones. tjones wants to select from the PUBLIC synonym, so he must qualify the synonym name:

```
CREATE SYNONYM informix.corp_sales FOR sales;
CREATE SYNONYM tjones.corp_sales FOR div_sales;
SELECT * FROM informix.corp_sales;
```

Replication

Business-critical databases that cannot go down for any period of time can be replicated to ensure availability. Replication requires twice the hardware. One machine is the primary server, which is where updates to the data occur. As the data is updated on the primary server, changes are sent to the secondary server through the logical logs. The logs are then processed on the secondary server, in turn updating the data there. If the secondary server detects that the primary server has failed, all uncommitted transactions are rolled back and the secondary server switches to normal database server mode. The two servers can be synchronized after the primary server is up again.

Though replication requires redundant hardware, the secondary server can be used to reduce the system load of the primary server by having other applications access the database on the secondary server for read-only purposes.

Mirroring

To minimize downtime, consider mirroring some or all of your dbspaces. If a dbspace is mirrored and the disk crashes the mirror, dbspace takes over until the disk of the primary dbspace is recovered and brought back online. Critical dbspaces should be mirrored to avoid a full instance restore in the event of a disk failure. The critical dbspaces include rootdbs and those dbspaces where the logical and physical logs are placed.

The database engine will perform parallel reads from the mirrored dbspaces by reading data that is on one half of the primary disk and data placed on the other half of the mirrored disk. Any writes to the dbspace must occur to both the primary and mirror dbspaces.

NOTE

If the table does not span both halves of the dbspace, only a single scan thread will be used to get the data from disk.

Mirroring can be achieved outside the database server by implementing it in a disk subsystem or a logical volume manager. Many believe this is a more efficient and reliable method of mirroring.

Security

Security levels for the database are CONNECT, RESOURCE, and DBA. CONNECT allows the user to access database objects for the database in which the privilege is granted. RESOURCE has the same privileges as CONNECT, plus it allows the user to create database objects. After creating objects, the user can ALTER or DROP only those objects created by that user. DBA privilege allows the user unlimited capabilities in that database.

Table security can be granted to allow the user to SELECT, INSERT, DELETE, UPDATE, INDEX, and ALTER that table. SELECT and UPDATE can be granted at the column level, also allowing an even finer granularity of data access. Any or all of the privileges can be granted or revoked.

Restricting access to groups of rows can be accomplished in three ways. The user with DBA privileges can create a view that selects specific columns, filters the data in the WHERE clause, and then grants access to the view to individuals or roles and revokes privileges from public on the table. The second is by granting access to specific dbspaces of a fragmented table. Of course, this applies only to fragmented tables. The third option is to REVOKE all access to tables and allow access to data only through stored procedures. This eliminates the need to know and understand the underlying table structures.

To execute a stored procedure, the user must have the EXECUTE privilege for the specific stored procedure. A stored procedure can be created as a DBA procedure. When the DBA procedure is executed, the user inherits the DBA privilege for all commands in the stored procedure.

Roles ease the administration of table security. Roles are similar to UNIX groups; by adding users to roles, privileges can be maintained for the ROLE rather than individual users.

Database Design Considerations

In addition to the database structures, other factors influence the physical implementation of the database.

Users and Transactions

Resources allocated to the database server are limited. These resources must be shared by all users and processes that connect to the database server. As the number of users and transactions increases, the likelihood is greater for contention of these limited resources. This is where it is important to balance and share the resources so that the processes will have the resources they need when they need them.

Database Size

When designing large databases, give extra attention so that you reduce major administrative activities later. Most maintenance tasks will take longer and consume more resources because of the sheer volume of the data.

Access Tools and Development Tools

Many tools are available to access and manipulate the data in the database, such as DBaccess, which comes with Informix. Query and reporting tools such as Viewpoint and Crystal Reports simplify SQL for the user who doesn't know SQL. Development tools include INFORMIX-4GL, NewEra, PowerBuilder, and Delphi. Decision Support tools include MetaCube and Microstrategy. Designing the database should take into account the tools that will be used to access the database. These tools are very powerful; however, a database design that complicates the access path to the data will result in complex applications and limit the ability of users and developers to use these tools. The design of the database must accommodate how the tools expect to see the data or what types of database models they work best with.

Database Logging

When you log your database, many updates can be treated as a single logical unit of work. If any statement from that unit fails, the data that was changed is returned to its original state. Logging a database maintains a *before* and an *after* copy of every row that changes. Maintaining a *before* and an *after* copy of each row that changes has a considerable amount of overhead associated with it. Use `BEGIN WORK` to start a transaction and `COMMIT WORK` to end the transaction. `ROLLBACK WORK` undoes any changes during a transaction. If `BEGIN WORK` and `COMMIT WORK` are not coded in the application and the database has logging, each SQL statement will be treated as a single transaction. The database implicitly does a `BEGIN WORK` and `COMMIT WORK` for each statement. Log the database only if it is necessary.

CAUTION

After an application is coded for transactions, database logging must remain on when the application is trying to access the database or the application will receive an error.

Multiple Instances

Databases with different purposes require different tuning parameters. If resources are available, consider putting the databases in separate instances. Additional instances will create more administration and coordination than the single instance. Each instance can be tuned to perform better for the expected activity of the database. For example, in an OLTP database, the engine should be tuned for quick updates and response time of transactions.

Populating the Database

Little benefit is gained from an empty database. Populating the database can be done in many ways. The source of the data can come from many different places and formats. How to deal with the different formats can be the biggest challenge.

When building a new database, the formats you might have to deal with can only be paper forms or lists. Occasionally, the data does not fit the relationships built in the database. When this happens, the database might need to be changed to accommodate the data. At other times, the data is made to fit by manipulating the data or by creating business rules to ensure that the data fits.

Migrating from Legacy Mainframe Systems

A lot of companies thought downsizing was the answer to their high cost of maintaining mainframe hardware and applications. Other companies realized that their mainframe could not go away, but they could save CPU cycles by moving users to smaller systems. Many data warehouses that are implemented on midrange systems are sourced from legacy systems. Nightly, weekly, or monthly data is extracted from a database on the mainframe and loaded into the midrange database system.

Moving data from the legacy system can be done with a gateway product that often has tools to take data in one format and put it into another for a specific database. Some of the tools Informix has will reformat data as it loads into the database. Converting data from one format to another will have overhead associated with it. If you plan ahead, the data can be converted on the legacy system to a format that will be easier to deal with and requires less processing when trying to load into the database.

Migrating from Desktop Databases

Nearly all desktop databases can be unloaded in a format that can be read by the Informix load utilities. Knowing the utilities and the formats they support will simplify moving data from the desktop database to an Informix database.

Open database connectivity (ODBC) is a convenient way of connecting to multiple RDBMSs at the same time, using the same application. An ODBC driver is probably available for all desktop databases. When you use the ODBC driver for Informix and the driver for the desktop database, you might be able to use a desktop utility to move the data into an Informix database.

Migrating from Prior Versions of Informix

With each new release of the Informix database, you get several options for migrating the existing database to the new version. In most cases, it is as simple as bringing the database engine offline, installing the new version, and bringing the database engine online. The old structures are automatically converted to the new structures.

It is not uncommon for companies to require thorough testing of new versions of software to ensure that there are no incompatibilities. In these cases, a copy of the database from the old version needs to be taken and put into the new version. It is not difficult to have two different versions of Informix running on the same machine, given adequate resources to do so.

Load Utilities

Informix provides a wide range of utilities for loading and unloading data. The granularity, ease of use, and performance vary significantly across those utilities.

INSERT

The standard SQL `INSERT` statement is very easy to use and can be used in a 4GL language or embedded SQL (ESQL) language such as ESQL/C. Using an embedded language gives you the flexibility of that language, and you have access to the data in the database for validating or crosswalking as you insert. Sometimes it is necessary to manipulate the data as it is loaded. That manipulation could be more complex than the load utilities can handle and must be done in an application.

Each row is inserted one row at a time using the `INSERT` statement. Using an insert cursor speeds the application by buffering the inserts, flushing them to the database when the buffer is full. Preparing the `INSERT` statements avoids the need to check the syntax of the `INSERT` statement each time it is executed.

LOAD and UNLOAD

`LOAD` is another SQL statement that will load data from a file and insert it into a table. The file must be delimited. You can specify the delimiter using the `DELIMITER` clause; the default is the vertical bar (`|`).

Dbload

`Dbload` is a command-line utility for loading and formatting data. It can read delimited and fixed-length records. `Dbload` is always accompanied by a command file that defines the format rules. You can specify the row in the load file to begin with when loading, as well as how many rows to read before quitting. A threshold can be set for the number of bad rows that can be rejected before aborting the load. For logged databases, a commit interval can be set to avoid long transactions.

In the command file, you identify the filename of the datafile, the delimiter character, the field beginning and ending positions in the datafile, and the `INSERT` statement.

dbimport and dbexport

The simplest way to migrate data between Informix instances, regardless of the version, is to use `dbimport` and `dbexport`. The `dbexport` command unloads the data from every table in the database and generates a schema of that database. The unloads can be written to tape or file. Using the `-ss` switch, the server-specific configurations of the database, such as extent size, lock mode, and dbspace placement, are retained. The `dbexport` command tries to get an exclusive lock on the entire database that is being exported. If an exclusive lock cannot be obtained, the command fails. Because `dbexport` locks the database, no users can be connected to the database. This guarantees the referential integrity of the database when it is imported using `dbimport`.

`dbimport` takes the schema file generated from the `dbexport` command and creates the database loading the data from the unload files. You can specify the dbspace in which to create the database by using the `-d` option. Using the `-l` option, you can create the database with logging.

TIP

`dbimport` loads data into the table immediately after the table is created and then creates any indexes. This ensures that the entire table is in contiguous disk space. If you find that many of your tables have multiple extents and are unintentionally fragmented, use `dbexport` and `dbimport` to reorganize the database.

Onload and Onunload

`Onunload` dumps a table to a file or tape. A copy of all pages allocated to the table, including index and free pages, is dumped. Because every page is dumped with no regard to the contents, this utility runs very fast.

When you `Onload` a table, you must specify the table name. The table cannot already exist in the database or you will receive an error. Indexes are preserved when using `Onunload`; however, privileges, views, synonyms, and constraints are lost. Use `dbschema` to get the DDL for privileges, views, synonyms, and constraints related to the table you are `Onloading` so that you can re-create these objects.

High-Performance Loader

High-performance loader (HPL) is the latest utility Informix has developed for loading large amounts of data. HPL maximizes performance by running each step of the load process in parallel. This includes parallel reads from the data files or tape devices, formatting the data, converting the data, and inserting the data into the table. To take advantage of the parallelism, the load data must be split into multiple files or multiple tape drives and the table must be fragmented.

HPL has two modes of running—express and deluxe. Express mode writes directly to a new extent. After it completes, that extent is appended to the existing extent of the table. If the table has indexes, they are re-created after the express mode HPL is run. If the database is logged, the inserts are not logged. Constraints and triggers are also not maintained during express load, but they are checked after the load completes. After using HPL in express mode, the table is read-only until a level-0 archive has been taken. Running HPL in deluxe mode maintains the indexes, constraints, and triggers during the load.

HPL job definitions are stored in the onpload database. The interface for creating jobs is an X Window interface. You can also populate the tables manually, but this is not recommended because of the complexity of the onpload database.

Improved Processing

Turn off logging on a logged database while loading or updating large amounts of data. Dropping indexes, constraints, and triggers or disabling them also improves performance. If you do this, remember that indexes are re-created when enabling them, and triggers and constraints are validated or executed when they are enabled or re-created. Locking the database or table in exclusive mode reduces the overhead of lock management.

TIP

On a multiprocessor machine, running multiple loads in parallel might gain some performance if the load utility or program is serially reading data from files and serially inserting rows. If the application is doing a lot of processing such as calculations or conversions of data before the actual insert occurs, it might benefit from multiple instances of the application. Be careful to watch the CPU utilization so that not all processes are contending for the same CPU cycles. Also watch how busy the CPUVPs are.

If the initial extent of a table was not defined, you can potentially have multiple extents. When you have multiple extents scattered across the disk, the head must do more work to get the data. To avoid this, be sure to specify the size of the initial extent when creating the table and the size of the next extent. After the table is created, the initial extent size cannot be changed without re-creating the table, but the `NEXT SIZE` can. Also, if an extent fills and another extent is created, and if the next extent immediately follows, the two extents will be concatenated forming a single extent. This happens as long as the space being used by each additional extent is contiguous.

Monitoring, Tuning, and Configuring

Tuning the database engine is an iterative process. You must first monitor the system to identify potential problems, and then change configuration parameters and monitor the system again.

Incrementally change configuration parameters to recognize the impact of each parameter that has changed.

> **NOTE**
>
> The `onstat` command is very useful when monitoring the performance of the database engine.
>
> The statistics reported by the `onstat` command are accumulated since the database engine was brought online. The statistics can be reset using `onstat -z`. When comparing these statistics, keep in mind the period of time since the statistics were reset.

ONCONFIG Parameters

The INFORMIX-OnLine DSA configuration file is where the database engine tuning takes place. Changing the parameters in the `ONCONFIG` file might significantly increase performance and eliminate bottlenecks. The usage of the database will help identify which parameters should be changed. Some parameters will impact the database, depending on its purpose, and other parameters will not impact performance at all.

Buffers

Before the engine can process data and index pages, the pages must be read into buffers. After they are read into the buffers, the pages will stay there if they are accessed frequently. Having more buffers increases the likelihood that a requested row will be in memory. There is a point at which adding more buffers does not produce a benefit. `Onstat -p` shows buffer reads (`bufreads`) and writes (`bufwrits`). It is not uncommon to achieve greater than 95 percent buffer reads and greater than 90 percent buffer writes.

The way to tune the buffers is to watch the read/write buffer hit ratio. If the values are less than 95/90 reads/writes, add buffers and monitor during normal activity for a period of time. Keep adding buffers until no advantage is gained by adding more. Do not allocate too much memory to the database, or the operating system and other applications will suffer.

> **CAUTION**
>
> Adding buffers might increase the checkpoint duration, because there are more buffers to write to disk each time a checkpoint occurs. Because the pages are sorted, writes are more efficient when done during a checkpoint; however, all processing is stopped during the checkpoint. `LRU_MIN_DIRTY` and `LRU_MAX_DIRTY` can be tuned to reduce this duration.

Checkpoint Duration

Long checkpoints can cause bad response time for interactive applications. But overall runtime of batch programs might benefit from long checkpoints if a lot of data is changing or being inserted.

Long checkpoint duration can be decreased by reducing LRU_MIN_DIRTY and LRU_MAX_DIRTY to 5 and 10 respectively (or even lower). This forces the engine to write modified data pages between checkpoints, so there is less work to do when a checkpoint is required. Keep in mind that writes are more efficient during a checkpoint because the pages are sorted.

Parallel Data Query (PDQ)

To take advantage of parallel queries, you must have multiple CPUVPs, have PDQPRIORITY set, and fragment the tables you want to access. Several configuration parameters manage the resources allocated to parallel queries.

PDQPRIORITY can be set to a number between 0 and 100, or it can be set to OFF(0), LOW(1), or HIGH(100). This specifies the percentage of resources that a query will use. PDQPRIORITY can be set three ways. The first is in the ONCONFIG file. All queries will run with this value when set in the ONCONFIG file, unless the application overrides it.

Using the SQL statement, SET PDQPRIORITY overrides the value in the ONCONFIG file. When you set the environment variable, PDQPRIORITY overrides both. If the PDQPRIORITY is set to a value higher than MAX_PDQPRIORITY, the priority is set to MAX_PDQPRIORITY.

Other configuration parameters that manage and control parallel queries are as follows:

- DS_MAX_QUERIES
- DS_MAX_SCANS
- DS_TOTAL_MEMORY

DS_MAX_QUERIES is the total number of parallel queries that can run at the same time.

Pages are read from disk by the scan threads. DS_MAX_SCANS sets the number of parallel scan threads to be used by parallel queries.

DS_TOTAL_MEMORY is the amount of memory that is shared by parallel queries.

CAUTION

If a query has PDQPRIORITY set to 50 and half the resources are unavailable, that query must wait until enough resources are available before it can run.

onstat -g mgm shows the number of parallel queries, scan threads, and memory usage, and it shows whether any queries are waiting on resources.

RA_PAGES and RA_THRESHOLD

RA_PAGES specifies how many pages should be read into buffers when a query is doing a sequential scan of a table or an index. RA_THRESHOLD specifies when another read ahead should take place. When the number of pages (RA_THRESHOLD) has been processed, another read ahead occurs. onstat -p shows whether read ahead pages are being used efficiently.

CPUVPs

The CPUVPs are the virtual processors that do most of the work in the database engine. If there are multiple physical processors and the machine is primarily an Informix database server, NUMCPUVPs should be set to the number of physical CPUs minus one. If there are multiple instances, the physical CPUs will be shared between instances.

Ongoing Maintenance

After implementing the database, several things should be done and checked on a regular basis.

Update Statistics

Information about a table and the data in it is gathered and stored by the UPDATE STATISTICS command. The optimizer uses the statistics gathered to determine the best access path of all queries. These are especially important when joining multiple tables in a query. Statistics should be regenerated any time there is significant activity in the database or a table.

UPDATE STATISTICS can be run for a specific table or all tables in the database. Stored procedures are reoptimized when UPDATE STATISTICS is run for them.

Statistics can be generated at three levels for tables: LOW, MEDIUM, and HIGH. At each level, a certain amount of information is gathered. LOW gathers and stores as little information as necessary, such as row and page counts. MEDIUM gathers distribution information about the data in the table by taking samples. HIGH gathers exact distributions. HIGH might have to scan a table several times to gather information for each column.

If statistics are out of date, queries could actually run slower because of inaccurate information about tables.

oncheck

oncheck verifies the consistency of the database. This includes checking, displaying, and repairing the database structures. The -pe option shows the physical location of database objects on each disk. This report is useful in identifying tables with multiple extents.

Backups

Backups must be considered when designing and implementing a database. Two utilities are provided for online backups—`ontape` and `onarchive`. These utilities back up the data while there is activity against the database. They both require log backups in addition to the archives that are taken, even if the database is not logged. You can restore the entire instance back to the time of the archive you are restoring from. Then apply the logs to roll forward any transactions since that archive.

Archives are necessary to recover from a disaster, but to restore specific rows or a table because of an accidental delete or drop of a table could be very difficult. It is a good idea to periodically unload the data from the tables. Unloading the tables requires additional disk space, but certain utilities, such as compressing the files or writing them to tape, can minimize that disk space. It might not be necessary to unload all tables.

Summary

Creating a database is much more than deciding which columns belong to which tables and creating them. When you understand the purpose of the database and the features available, your database and application will be a success.

CHAPTER 13

Advanced Configurations

by Kevin Kempter

IN THIS CHAPTER

Introduction

Now that you have an instance of INFORMIX-OnLine up, as you learned in Chapter 11, "Configuring the Informix Environment," this chapter can cover advanced configuration topics.

The Informix ONCONFIG File

The Informix `ONCONFIG` file is the method by which the OnLine engine determines what tunable values to use. The `ONCONFIG` file is always located in the `$INFORMIXDIR/etc` directory, where `$INFORMIXDIR` is the UNIX environment variable that contains the full path to the Informix root installation directory.

This chapter discusses all the IINFORMIX-OnLine engine `ONCONFIG` file parameters, outlines their uses, and recommends efficient values.

DSS Versus OLTP Configurations

There are two main approaches to setting up the `ONCONFIG` file, geared toward DSS (Decision Support System) queries, or toward OLTP (online transaction processing) queries.

DSS queries are generally very large queries, often containing many joins and returning hundreds or thousands of rows. OLTP queries are transaction-based, returning only a few rows at a time (often only one), generally for some sort of modification.

DSS Overview

DSS or data-warehousing is becoming increasingly popular in today's information technology market. Most DSS systems have the same basic characteristics, although there are often exceptions, such as these:

- The database is read-only.
- The data is time-sensitive (that is, representative of snapshots in time across several months or years).
- The physical model is a star or a snowflake schema. A star schema is one or more large fact tables linked to tables that represent categories or dimensions that help define a snapshot in time of the fact table records—thus the term dimensional modeling. One example of a very basic star schema would be a fact table that represents sales, which would include sales figures such as cost, margin, profit, units sold, and so on. This table by itself is pretty meaningless. But add the dimension tables that represent time, geography, and products, and now you can ask questions such as, "What were the gross profits for brand X in the northwest region for the past three quarters?," or "Show it to me by city and by week, and summarize the quarterly net profits." A

snowflake schema is a star with each dimension broken out into more normalized tables. (For example, the geography dimension could contain city, state, county, and region tables.)

Figure 13.1 depicts a very basic star schema.

FIGURE 13.1.
A basic retail star schema.

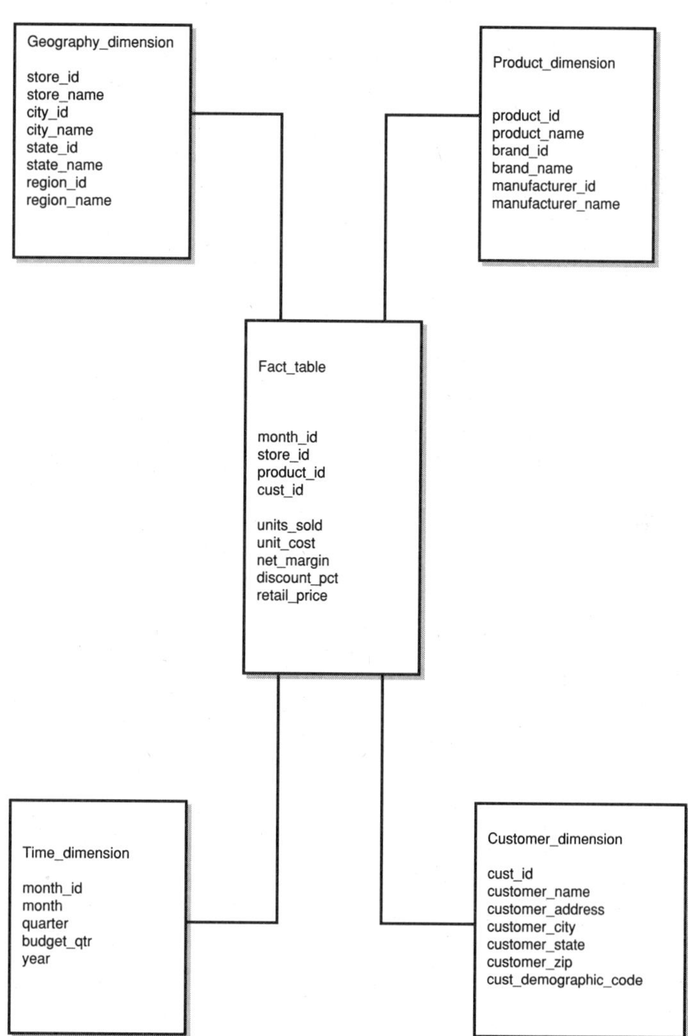

DSS ONCONFIG Parameters

The Informix `ONCONFIG` file contains several parameters that are associated with DSS environments. These parameters allow the OnLine engine to be optimized for a data warehouse environment.

PDQPRIORITY

The Informix PDQPRIORITY ONCONFIG parameter determines what percentage of resources OnLine allocated to PDQ (Parallel Data Queries). The INFORMIX-OnLine engine weighs the request against other requests and determines whether the amount requested or some lesser, more proportional amount is allocated to the query.

NOTE

In version 7.2 of INFORMIX-OnLine, the PDQPRIORITY parameter is no longer set in the ONCONFIG file. The new method is to set the PDQPRIORITY as a UNIX environment variable, or to set PDQPRIORITY in the informix.rc file in the $INFORMIXDIR/etc directory.

TIP

The only way you will ever get any degree of parallel processing of a query is by setting the PDQPRIORITY value to a value greater than zero. This is the only method OnLine uses to determine whether a query is a parallel or a DSS query.

You can set the PDQPRIORITY parameter to several recognized values:

- 0 or OFF
- 1 or LOW
- HIGH
- A specified value (up to 100)

DS_MAX_QUERIES

The DS_MAX_QUERIES parameter determines how many concurrent DSS queries can be active.

INFORMIX-OnLine considers a DSS query to be any query with a PDQ priority set to a nonzero value.

Although this parameter is difficult to generalize, a good guideline to set it by would be the Informix default value, which is the value of NUMCPUVPS * 2 * 128.

DS_MAX_SCANS

The DS_MAX_SCANS parameter regulates how many scan threads can be launched in order to process any one query. This parameter is very helpful in disallowing any single user from hogging all possible threads, thus forcing the DBA to go berserk and choke that particular user. (So it's sort of a DBA blood pressure regulator.)

As in the case of DS_MAX_QUERIES, this parameter is difficult to generalize. It varies based on your use of DSS. Again, the default value—1,048,576 (1024*1024)—is probably a good starting point.

DS_TOTAL_MEMORY

The DS_TOTAL_MEMORY parameter sets a maximum amount of shared memory that can be allocated concurrently to DSS (or PDQ) queries. This value obviously should never be greater than, or even equal to, the SHMTOTAL (total max shared memory) parameter.

OLTP Overview

OLTP (online transaction processing) is just about the exact opposite of DSS. Whereas DSS queries are large read-only queries, returning large datasets, OLTP queries generally attempt to modify a small dataset or even a single record at a time.

OLTP ONCONFIG Parameters

There really aren't any ONCONFIG parameters dedicated specifically to OLTP. Like some of the DSS parameters, the standard ONCONFIG parameters are associated with the OnLine engine in general.

Memory Utilization

The INFORMIX-OnLine Dynamic Server utilizes shared memory extensively in order to perform database functions as quickly as possible. This makes the OnLine engine very dependent on how the operating system handles memory. Knowing how your particular operating system handles memory can provide useful insight when performance-tuning.

Because there is a finite amount of memory on any given machine, and the DBAs are generally restricted to some portion for the database engine (most DBAs push for 90–95 percent), at some point the machine needs to allocate more memory than it has for a running process. At this point, the CPU searches the physical memory looking for any free memory pages. When no free memory pages are found, the CPU then looks for any pages that are unlikely to be needed immediately. Most operating systems utilize LRU (least-recently used) algorithms within their memory management systems. An LRU algorithm determines which pages are unlikely to be used immediately, by selecting the oldest or least-recently used pages in memory. The CPU then begins to copy these pages to a swap area on disk. This is referred to as *paging*.

At some point, these pages are needed by their respective processes, so they are copied back into memory. If there are not enough free pages to copy the needed pages into, more pages are paged out to make room. Under extremely heavy processing and memory usage, this paging can become so bad that the CPU spends more time paging than processing jobs. This is known as *thrashing*, or by the less-technical term *hosed*.

Some operating systems employ a threshold algorithm that forces the CPU to copy all pages associated with a process into the swap area after a certain threshold of paging is reached. This is called *swapping*. Swapping is a desperate attempt to recover from too much paging. If your system is swapping consistently, it is generally performing poorly, and a few long nights of performance-tuning are in order (or at least kick all those pesky users off the system).

Most operating systems provide some method of monitoring paging activity. When monitoring paging activity, look for page-out activity, because this is done only when there are no free pages in memory. If you see a high rate of page scans (the CPU scanning for free pages), this might be an early warning that your system memory is beginning to bottleneck and your system could soon be in an undesirable state.

INFORMIX-OnLine Dynamic Server also uses an LRU algorithm to page database data pages between the memory buffer pool and the disk.

The use of shared memory allows INFORMIX-OnLine virtual processors (a set of process threads that service processes similar to how CPUs service processes) and other OnLine processes, tools, utilities, and so on, to share data without having to store the data in multiple places. Shared memory also allows extremely fast communications and transferring of data.

Overview

The INFORMIX-OnLine shared memory is divided into three basic components:

- The resident portion
- The message portion
- The virtual portion

The resident portion of shared memory is the section of memory that contains the buffer pool, log files, locks, reserved pages, and so on. The following `ONCONFIG` parameters are directly tied to the resident portion of Informix shared memory:

- `BUFFERS`
- `LOGBUFF`
- `PHYSBUFF`
- `LOCKS`

BUFFERS

This parameter determines how many pages will be allocated to the buffer pool, thus seriously affecting how often your database can read from memory and how often the pages in memory must be written to the disk. The `BUFFERS` `ONCONFIG` parameter and recommended sizing guidelines are discussed in Chapter 11 in the "`ONCONFIG` Parameters" section.

LOGBUFF

The LOGBUFF parameter specifies how big the buffer in memory for the current logical log is. INFORMIX-OnLine holds three logical logs in shared memory at all times. OnLine uses only one logical log at a time; any changes taking place in the database are written to the logical log buffer. If OnLine needs another log, the next log is marked as the current log so that transactions can begin writing to the new log while the previous log is flushed to disk. The logical log buffer is used for both buffered and unbuffered logging. For unbuffered logging, the logical log buffer is flushed to disk every time a transaction is committed. For buffered logging, the transactions are held in the log buffer as long as possible, until one of the following events occurs:

- The buffer becomes full
- A checkpoint is executed
- The connection to the database is closed
- A commit is performed on a database with unbuffered logging

PHYSBUFF

OnLine contains two physical log buffers in memory. The PHYSBUFF parameter specifies the size for each of the physical log buffers. The physical log buffers work similar to the logical buffers for the before-image pages. When a before image is written to the physical buffer, it always writes a full page. When one of the physical log buffers becomes full, the next buffer becomes the current buffer while the full buffer is flushed to disk. The size of this parameter will dictate how often the physical log buffer needs to be flushed to disk. Informix recommends a value equal to 16 pages for the PHYSBUFF parameter.

TIP

Always make the size of the physical log buffers divisible by the system page size. If this value is not divisible by a page, OnLine rounds down to the next value that is divisible by a page. In this case, the extra space is simply unusable.

LOCKS

The INFORMIX-OnLine engine uses shared memory locks to maintain a balance between sharing data in the fastest possible way and keeping any threads from using stale data (changed and uncommitted data, deleted data, and so on). To accomplish this, Informix uses two types of shared memory locks—a shared lock and an exclusive lock.

The shared lock allows an INFORMIX-OnLine thread to lock a data buffer, while other OnLine threads still have access to the data buffer in read-only mode. The exclusive lock completely disallows all access to the data buffer until the lock is freed.

The LOCKS ONCONFIG parameter specifies the maximum number of LOCKS that can be used concurrently. Each lock OnLine uses 44 bytes of memory in the resident portion of shared memory. Although 44 bytes is not much of a concern, if you allocate 500,000 locks, for example, you would use 20MB of resident memory space. The maximum number of locks that any instance of OnLine can use is 8 million. The LOCKS parameter should be set to the maximum number of locks that any one user query could use, multiplied by the number of concurrent users expected. See the *Informix OnLine Dynamic Server Performance Tuning Guide* for more information pertaining to how many locks a query will use.

DSS Versus OLTP Memory Usage

OLTP applications generally access small sets of data, often one row at a time, and often for the purpose of modification. An OLTP application typically supports a high number of concurrent users and provides sub-second response time.

DSS applications provide methods for strategic planning, forecasting, and summarization of a company's data. DSS queries are typically very large, complex, and often take several minutes to several hours to run. DSS systems generally support very few concurrent users.

Due to the extreme differences in OLTP versus DSS application traits, the memory usage for OLTP queries is often detrimental to DSS queries and vice versa. When both DSS and OLTP are to be utilized on the same system, which is rare (because it really irritates DBAs), the PDQPRIORITY ONCONFIG parameter discussed in the "PDQ" section later in this chapter becomes an extremely important tool for maintaining an acceptable level of performance.

Informix ONCONFIG Parameters That Affect Memory

The resident portion of Informix shared memory was discussed earlier in this chapter in the section titled "Memory Utilization." The remaining two portions of INFORMIX-OnLine shared memory are as follows:

- The virtual portion
- The message portion

The Virtual Portion of Informix Shared Memory

The virtual portion of shared memory is dynamic. OnLine will allocate more segments as needed. The virtual portion of shared memory contains the components covered in the following sections.

Big Buffers

OnLine uses big buffers to manage any instances of multiple contiguous pages of data that need to be written to or retrieved from disk. A big buffer is a buffer that is large enough to contain 32 pages of data.

The Dictionary Cache

OnLine maintains a set of structures in memory that allow the system catalog table data to be accessed in an efficient manner. When OnLine receives a request to access a system catalog table, the table is read and stored in the memory structures. These memory structures constitute the dictionary cache.

The Global Pool

OnLine stores all structures that are global to OnLine in this section of shared memory. The message queues, where poll threads place messages from clients, are in the global pool.

Session Data

When OnLine begins a session with a client application, a data structure in memory is populated. This is the SCB (session control block). In addition to several status flags, the SCB contains the following information:

- Session ID
- User ID
- Client Process ID
- Hostname

The Sorting Pool

The INFORMIX-OnLine engine allocates memory for sorts. The size of this sorting pool depends on the number of concurrent sorts taking place. The maximum amount of memory that OnLine will allocate for sorts is 5MB.

The Stored Procedures Cache

The stored procedure cache is a nonconfigurable section of memory that stores any called stored procedures in an executable format the first time each stored procedure is called. This cache can then be accessed by any subsequent calls to the same stored procedures.

Thread Data

When connections are made to OnLine, or when internal threads are needed, OnLine launches both a thread and a TCB (thread control block). When OnLine performs a context switch (switches one thread out and begins running another), the TCB retains all the needed information to run the thread when it is switched back. INFORMIX-OnLine adds more memory for TCBs as it is needed.

The Message Portion of Informix Shared Memory

The message communications portion of INFORMIX-OnLine shared memory is simply the memory allocated at initialization time to allow connections to communicate with the OnLine engine. The amount of memory is based on the number of users specified in the `NETTYPE` parameter, or the `USERTHREADS` `ONCONFIG` parameter, whichever is less.

Shared Memory ONCONFIG Parameters

The following Informix `ONCONFIG` parameters specifically affect the use of shared memory.

RESIDENT

The `RESIDENT` `ONCONFIG` parameter indicates whether or not OnLine should enforce residency for the resident portion of Informix shared memory. If your system supports forced residency, and you specify OnLine to force residency, the LRU queues will never be swapped or paged out of physical memory. This can greatly increase performance of the OnLine engine. This increase in performance in the OnLine engine can come at a cost to other applications.

SHMBASE

The `SHMBASE` `ONCONFIG` parameter specifies the base address of the OnLine shared memory, where any additional virtual segments will be attached.

SHMVIRTSIZE

`SHMVIRTSIZE` specifies the initial size for the virtual portion of shared memory. You should attempt to size this segment large enough that most day-to-day processing requires no additional memory segments, but small enough that spikes in workload will require additional segments to be added. This balance between having enough memory to support 90 percent of all requests and not having so much memory that memory is needlessly being wasted is the optimal configuration. Use the `onstat -g seg` command (described later in this chapter in the section titled "Monitoring") to determine whether too few or too many memory segments are being allocated. Informix recommends that you use as an initial value the item in the following list that produces the largest setting:

- 8000KB
- 350 × (*the number of connections specified in one or more* `NETTYPE` *parameters*)

SHMADD

`SHMADD` indicates how big each additional memory segment added to the virtual portion of shared memory will be. As in the case of the `SHMVIRTSIZE` parameter, `SHMADD` is also optimally configured based on finding a balance between allocating too many small segments and too few large segments. Too many small segments will waste CPU cycles because the CPU will need to add segments more often. Allocating too few large segments will hog too much memory, depriving memory available for other processes, and possibly leading to performance problems. (Refer to the "Memory Utilization" section earlier in this chapter.) Table 13.1 indicates the Informix recommended initial settings for the `SHMADD` parameter. The recommended values are based on the amount of physical memory on the machine.

Table 13.1. Informix recommended initial values for SHMADD.

Physical Memory Size	*Initial* `SHMADD` *Setting*
(greater than 512MB)	32,768KB
(less than 256MB and less than or equal to 512MB)	16,384KB
(less than or equal to 256MB)	8,192KB

SHMTOTAL

The `SHMTOTAL` parameter places a ceiling on the total amount of shared memory that an instance of INFORMIX-OnLine can use. If you set `SHMTOTAL` to `0`, OnLine will continue to allocate more memory until no virtual memory is left to allocate on the machine. Setting `SHMTOTAL` is generally the best method.

STACKSIZE

`STACKSIZE` indicates the initial stack size per thread. This amount of memory is initially allocated to each thread. You can reduce the size of the virtual portion of shared memory by attempting to estimate what this total size should be and sizing the virtual portion of shared memory appropriately. You can then modify the `SHMVIRTSIZE` parameter accordingly. The `STACKSIZE` is a portion of the thread data in the virtual portion of shared memory. The following calculation is the Informix recommended calculation to estimate the total `STACKSIZE` needed:

(*total virtual memory for threads*) = `STACKSIZE` × (*avg. no. of concurrent threads*)

PDQ

PDQ (Parallel Data Query) is the method Informix uses to control parallelism in the tasks performed by the engine when querying the database.

PDQ Overview

PDQ allows OnLine to greatly improve the performance of a DSS query by utilizing parallelism. OLTP queries should run at peak performance with the default OnLine setting, which is `0` for no parallelism. DSS queries are typically large, long-running queries, sometimes involving very large table scans. PDQ can allow a large table scan to run faster, and more efficiently, by launching multiple threads to read through the table in parallel. OLTP queries, on the other hand, would probably not benefit from parallelism because a typical OLTP query attempts to fetch a very small set of rows or a single row. PDQ allows INFORMIX-OnLine DSA to handle both types of queries. Consider the following example:

- The number of concurrent active queries (`DS_MAX_QUERIES`) is set to `5`.
- Five large DSS queries, each using PDQ, are currently running, with an expected finish time of 45 minutes.
- A user wants to find out whether the Northridge store has the coolbreeze cordless mouse in stock (an OLTP query).

If the user launches the preceding query using PDQ, the query will be queued up for about 45 minutes, until one of the current PDQ queries is finished. However, if this query is launched with no PDQ, the number of concurrent active queries (`DS_MAX_QUERIES`) limitation no longer applies. Because this is an OLTP query, combined with the fact that the database was designed by an incredible DBA, the user receives the answer in sub-second response time.

Informix ONCONFIG Parameters That Affect PDQ

The following `ONCONFIG` parameters (described in the "DSS `ONCONFIG` Parameters" section in this chapter) all affect PDQ resources:

- `DS_MAX_QUERIES`
- `DS_MAX_SCANS`
- `DS_TOTAL_MEMORY`
- `PDQPRIORITY`

OnLine considers any query with a `PDQPRIORITY` value greater than `0` to be a PDQ or a DSS query. When OnLine receives a DSS query, the query request is placed in a priority queue (the priority based on the value of `PDQPRIORITY`). MGM (the Memory Grant Manager) performs the following five checks (referred to as gates) for each DSS query to determine when the queries are granted resources and to determine the amount of resources as the query is processed:

- If initialization is in progress, all queries wait for initialization to complete.
- If the number of running DSS queries is equal to the value specified by DS_MAX_QUERIES, all queued queries wait until one or more DSS queries finish.
- If a DSS query with a higher PDQPRIORITY than the one being checked (passed through the gates) is found, the DSS query (the one currently being checked) returns to the queue.
- If no more DSS memory (or any memory) is available, the queries wait until some memory is freed up.
- If the number of threads allocated to the query is equal to the value set for DS_MAX_SCANS, the query waits until one or more threads complete.

CPU Utilization

This section describes the various factors and parameters that affect the system CPU.

Overview

In order to maximize how efficiently INFORMIX-OnLine utilizes CPU processing, you need to look at both UNIX kernel parameters and Informix ONCONFIG parameters. The UNIX parameters allow system functions related to the database operations to be efficient. The ONCONFIG parameters allow the OnLine engine to operate efficiently.

UNIX Parameters That Affect CPU Utilization

The UNIX level parameters that affect OnLine are the UNIX semaphore and file-descriptor–related parameters.

There are two semaphore-related kernel parameters that you should tune:

- The parameter for your particular flavor of UNIX that controls the number of semaphore sets allocated
- The parameter that sets the maximum number of semaphores

Semaphore Sets

Informix recommends that at least the following three semaphore sets be allocated, in addition to any required by other software on the system:

- One set for each 100 (or fraction of) VPs (virtual processors) that are configured in the ONCONFIG file.
- One set for each additional VP that you feel you might add dynamically after the engine is online.

- One set for each 100 (or fraction of) users that will connect concurrently via a shared memory connection type.

Informix recommends that you double the value for the shared memory connections and set the poll threads value in the `NETTYPE` `ONCONFIG` parameter as if the number of expected users were doubled.

Number of Semaphores

The value of the kernel parameter that sets the maximum number of semaphores for the system should be set to a minimum of 100. INFORMIX-OnLine uses at least two semaphores for each instance of the engine.

TIP

A single instance managing several databases will almost always outperform multiple Informix instances on the same box.

One UNIX kernel parameter related to file descriptors affects INFORMIX-OnLine performance. That is the kernel parameter that sets the number of files that can be open at any one time.

This parameter directly controls the number of chunks your instance of OnLine can have. The following calculation is what Informix recommends as a starting point for this parameter:

> (*number of chunks* × `NUMAIOVPS`) + `NUMCPUVPS` + (*number of non-shared memory connections*)

Informix ONCONFIG Parameters That Affect CPU Utilization

Several `ONCONFIG` parameters affect CPU utilization. This section explains their usage and recommended values.

AFF_NPROCS

If your operating system supports processor affinity, you can direct OnLine to automatically affinitize or bind CPU VPs to processors. The `AFF_NPROCS` parameter specifies the number of CPUs that OnLine will use to bind CPU VPs. The OnLine CPU VPs are assigned to the specified number of CPUs serially. When a CPU VP is bound to a CPU, the CPU VP will run exclusively on that CPU. Binding CPU VPs to CPUs does not prevent other processes (database or not) from running on that CPU.

AFF_SPROC

The AFF_SPROC parameter specifies which processor to start binding CPU VPs. If your system has 20 processors and you set AFF_NPROCS to 10, which forces OnLine to bind CPU VPs to 10 processors and AFF_SPROC to 11, then OnLine will bind CPU VPs to processors 11–20.

MULTIPROCESSOR

The MULTIPROCESSOR ONCONFIG parameter specifies whether you are running on a multiprocessor box. If you specify 0, indicating that you are on a single CPU box, the AFF_NPROCS and AFF_SPROC parameters are ignored, and locking is done in a manner suitable for a single CPU machine. If you specify 1, indicating that you are on a multiprocessor box, OnLine performs locking in a way that is suitable for a multiprocessor box.

NOAGE

Some breeds of the UNIX operating system will continually lower the priority of a process the longer the process has been running. This is referred to as priority aging (although DBAs tend to use other less flattering terms for it). Obviously, this can be a bad thing for the database, especially in the case of a large DSS query. NOAGE allows this feature to be disabled. If your OS supports priority aging, Informix recommends that you set NOAGE to 1, which disables aging. Setting NOAGE to 0 (the default) allows the system to perform priority aging.

NUMAIOVPS

The NUMAIOVPS parameter specifies the number of AIO VPs (AIO class virtual processors). Each chunk is assigned a queue by OnLine, in which all I/O requests are placed. OnLine prioritizes the order of the requests in order to minimize disk head movement. The I/O requests are then serviced in a round-robin sequence. Informix recommends that you set NUMAIOVPS to the number of disks that contain database chunks on your system.

Some systems support KAIO (Kernel Asynchronous I/O). KAIO is extremely efficient. Your OS machine notes describe how to enable KAIO. If you enable KAIO, OnLine makes raw I/O requests directly to the kernel. If you use KAIO, Informix recommends that you configure NUMAIOVPS to 1, plus 1 for each cooked file you have. I generally configure no less than three NUMAIOVPS on a system utilizing KAIO.

NUMCPUVPS

NUMCPUVPS specifies the number of CPU VPs (CPU class virtual processors) to launch when OnLine is initialized. The CPU VPs are a set of virtual processors that launch threads to process all SQL requests. To maximize your use of the CPU VPs, you want the CPU threads to be busy as often as possible (no sleeping CPU threads), but not so busy that you have a bottleneck. Informix recommends that you set NUMCPUVPS to one less than the number of CPUs on your system, or to 1 for a single CPU system. There is some question as to whether setting NUMCPUVPS to 2 on a two processor box will increase performance or create more overhead than it is worth. You will need to run some tests if this is your situation (or scream for more CPUs).

OPTCOMPIND

OPTCOMPIND helps guide the OnLine engine in decisions of how to process joins. The two basic types of joins are hash joins and nested loop joins. Hash joins are definitely superior in performance. However, a drawback to using hash joins is that during a large hash join, the conditions could exist (if isolation is set to repeatable read) that would lock all records in a table for a short amount of time. For some people, this is a problem. The alternative is to perform nested loop joins, which create less contention by using fewer locks but perform with a less than superior rating. So, depending on your situation and priorities, you can choose from the following settings for OPTCOMPIND:

- 0 forces a nested loop join whenever an index can be used, regardless of the cost (default setting).
- 1 is used for an isolation setting of anything except repeatable read. The optimizer uses the setting below for 2. If isolation is set to repeatable read, the above 0 setting is used.
- 2 makes the optimizer always weigh the cost of the execution path. There is no preference given to either type of join. The cost factor is the only consideration.

SINGLE_CPU_VP

The SINGLE_CPU_VP allows OnLine to utilize code that has been specifically optimized for little single-processor machines. You should watch the following things carefully when you set this parameter to 1, indicating that you are on a single-processor box:

- If you set SINGLE_CPU_VP to 1 and NUMCPUVPS to >1, initialization will bomb.
- If you attempt to add a CPU VP dynamically while OnLine is up, the attempt will fail.

Disk and I/O Utilization

This section describes the various database configuration issues that affect system I/O utilization.

Overview

Disk and I/O utilization allows a DBA to optimize the performance of OnLine I/O processes. In order to do this, you must consider several factors, including disk layout, fragmentation, indexes, and extents.

Managing Disk Layout

Managing the layouts of your disks starts with proper planning. In order to effectively plan a layout that will perform well, you need to optimize the way you initially set up your database. This section discusses some of the key components you need to consider when planning your database.

Table Placement

There are two major factors in creating your tables on disk: where the table is created (dbspace/chunk) and where the dbspace/chunk actually resides on the disk. Most DBAs utilize a logical volume tool, provided by the OS. Using a logical volume manager allows the creation of disk slices called logical volumes, and it allows the DBA to know where the LV (logical volume) lives on the disk. The cylinders in the center of a hard drive are considered to be the highest performance areas of a disk, because the read/write heads have less distance to move. After the LVs are created, dbspaces/chunks can be created in those areas of the disk.

High-Use Tables

The tables that will be accessed the most should be isolated, preferably from all other tables, but at least from other high-use tables. When you place high-use tables on separate disks, obviously the performance will be increased because now the I/O for those tables can occur concurrently without creating contention due to threads wanting to read both dbspaces at the same time from the same disk.

Multiple Disks

A table can be created across multiple dbspaces, and if those dbspaces are on separate drives, the dbspaces can be read in parallel.

Creating Tables

There are two basic ways to control where a table lives:

- `CREATE TABLE`: The create table statement, by default, creates any tables in the dbspace where the database was created. If no dbspace was specified for the create database statement, the default is the rootdbs.

- `CREATE TABLE IN DBSPACE`: The syntax for the create table statement allows you to specify a dbspace or several dbspaces in which the table will live. If a table has five dbspaces, the engine under certain conditions will read all five dbspaces in parallel.

Fragmentation

Fragmentation is the term for creating several dbspaces across disks and creating tables that span some or all of those dbspaces. There are several key benefits to fragmentation:

- Parallel scans: The OnLine engine can launch multiple threads in parallel, each reading from a separate disk. The benefits from this are obviously dramatic, especially if those same disks are isolated across SCSI channels, and even more so if they are isolated across I/O controllers.
- Balanced data: I/O bottlenecks can be greatly reduced because, via fragmentation, you can easily ensure that the data is evenly distributed across all its dbspaces.
- High availability: If you lose a disk that contains part of a fragmented table, and the data in that table is non-critical for continued operation, you can set a flag (`DATASKIP`) to `ON` for that dbspace, and until you repair and restore the dbspace it will simply be skipped in queries. This would allow the business to continue to be online, and if you know exactly what data is on that disk, you could perform other business functions until it is fixed.
- Archiving: Fragmentation allows you to back up specific dbspaces, which makes your job of managing your data much easier.

Fragmentation is set up one of two ways—fragmentation by round-robin or fragmentation by expression. Round-robin fragmentation places rows sequentially across the fragment dbspaces in round-robin fashion. This is absolutely the fastest method of loading large amounts of data, and it guarantees an even distribution of data. Expression-based fragmentation can offer other benefits such as not even searching certain dbspaces (fragmentation elimination). Fragmentation elimination can occur in an expression-based fragmentation scheme because OnLine knows what values of data live in which dbspaces. When a query is running and specific values have been specified, fragments that do not contain those values will not be searched.

Here are some fragmentation strategy guidelines:

- Avoid expressions that require conversion (that is, dates).
- Define the fragmentation expression list with the most restrictive expressions first. The order of the expression list is the order in which OnLine will perform the checks.
- For expression-based fragmentation, try to evenly distribute the keys or datasets that will be hit the most often across disks, even if this forces you to have an overall uneven data distribution.
- Per your fragmentation expressions: *Keep it simple.*

OLTP Versus DSS Considerations

When you lay out your fragmentation strategy, you need to consider whether you are setting up a DSS or an OLTP system. The type of system you have can significantly impact your layout. The following list describes some basic guidelines recommended by Informix:

- Don't fragment every table; pick your fragmented tables intentionally.
- For DSS systems, fragment your large, high-use tables but not the indexes. Create detached indexes in a separate dbspace.
- For large DSS tables that will generally be sequentially scanned, use round-robin fragmentation. This guarantees an even distribution, and because most DSS queries scan the entire table anyway, fragmentation elimination is less of a concern.
- Fragment the indexes for OLTP systems. This allows multiple users to be scanning/searching different index fragments concurrently.
- Don't fragment small tables. The overhead to fragment them might not be worth the benefit.

Temp Tables and Sorting

Temp tables can be extremely useful when processing large or very complex queries. INFORMIX-OnLine stores both tables specified as temp tables, and it stores internal work space tables in defined temp space. INFORMIX-OnLine dbspaces can be tagged as temp-only dbspaces. To create a temp dbspace, use the `-t` flag in the `onspaces` command. The following command is a sample `onspaces` command that creates a 1GB temp space in a dbspace called `temp_dbs01`, with an offset of 8KB in the UNIX raw device `/dev/informix/rvgc1d2s3`:

```
onspaces  -c  -d  temp_dbs01  -p  /dev/informix/vgc1d2s3  -o 8  -s  1024000000
```

The `DBSPACETEMP` parameter helps you manage temp space.

DBSPACETEMP

The `DBSPACETEMP` `ONCONFIG` parameter specifies a list of dbspaces for OnLine to use as temp table and sorting space. If multiple dbspaces are specified, OnLine fragments the temp tables across the temp dbspaces and uses parallel scans to process them. The list of dbspaces for `DBSPACETEMP` must be a colon- or comma-separated list of dbspace names. The maximum size of the list is 254 characters. If you need more room to list temp dbspaces, you can use the `DBSPACETEMP` UNIX environment variable to add more dbspace names in the same fashion.

Multiple Instances

INFORMIX-OnLine DSA supports the creation of multiple instances of the OnLine engine on a single machine, referred to as *multiple residency.* Here are a couple of benefits to using multiple residency:

- Isolation of databases for security, separation of development for contention reasons, and so on
- The testing of a distributed environment

In order to set up multiple instances, you would go through the same steps you did to initialize your first instance. Several key differences would be made, as demonstrated in the following sections.

SERVERNUM

The `SERVERNUM` `ONCONFIG` parameter would need to be changed. This value must be unique across all instances of OnLine on the machine.

ROOTPATH and ROOTOFFSET

The `ROOTPATH` and `ROOTOFFSET` `ONCONFIG` parameters must also be unique. Multiple instances of OnLine cannot share the same root dbspace. The same applies to the root `MIRRORPATH` and `MIRROROFFSET` parameters.

DBSERVERNAME

The `DBSERVERNAME` again must be unique; without this unique identifier, no clients could connect to the new instance.

MSGPATH

The `MSGPATH` is where the INFORMIX-OnLine log file is written to. Without this as a unique value, debugging and maintenance would be impossible.

Connections

You need to set up new connections, as you learned in Chapter 11. This might require an entry into the `/etc/services` file and the `$INFORMIXDIR/etc/sqlhosts` file.

Connect

After the preceding steps are done, you can change the users' `$DBSERVERNAME` environment variable to be the new `ONCONFIG` setting, which also is the first entry in the new line in the `sqlhosts` file. A connection to the new OnLine instance can now be completed.

Multiple Database Servers

In the same way you can define multiple instances of OnLine on a single machine and connect to them, you can also define instances of OnLine on several different machines and connect to any one of them. Many of the parameters in the preceding section can be the same in this case; however, the following parameters should be unique:

- DBSERVERNAME
- Entries in the `/etc/services` file
- Entries in the `$INFORMIXDIR/etc/sqlhosts` file

As in the multiple residency section, changing the `$DBSERVERNAME` parameter should allow connections, assuming that the clients either have the same `/etc/services` and `$INFORMIXDIR/etc/sqlhosts` files, or the files are NFS mounts.

Client-Server Architecture

Chapter 11 described the connectivity files and their use concerning INFORMIX-OnLine's client-server architecture. This section discusses more on some of the more common types of client-server configurations.

Shared Memory Connections

Shared memory connections are the fastest type of connection you can use. If your OnLine server and the client are both residing on the same machine, you can use a shared memory connection.

The following list describes how a shared memory connection would be set up:

```
DBSERVERNAME      grnd_kahuna_shm
```

```
$INFORMIXDIR/etc/sqlhosts File
```

```
dbservername        nettype         hostname          servicename
grnd_kahuna_shm    onipcshm    bogus_entry        another_bogus_entry
```

Network Connection

A network connection is a connection via the network, when the database server resides on one machine and the client lives on another machine. The following section shows what the configuration for a network connection looks like:

```
DBSERVERNAME     grnd_kahuna
$INFORMIXDIR/etc/sqlhosts entry for host big_kahuna
dbservername        nettype        hostname        servicename
grnd_kahuna        onsoctcp        big_kahuna        grnd_kahuna_soc
$INFORMIXDIR/etc/sqlhosts entry for host little_kahuna
dbservername        nettype        hostname        servicename
grnd_kahuna        onsoctcp        big_kahuna        grnd_kahuna_soc
```

NOTE

If the `little_kahuna` host used a different network interface, the `nettype` could be different—perhaps `ontlitcp` for a `tli` connection. The `nettype` field must always reflect the network interface on the host where the `sqlhosts` file lives.

Mirroring and Replication

Mirroring and replication can help create a more fault-tolerant system. This section describes why and how to set up both mirroring and data replication.

Mirroring

Mirroring is a method in which a primary and secondary chunk of the database can be logically connected, or *paired*. Every write to that chunk or dbspace is then written to both chunks. If one disk is lost, INFORMIX-OnLine automatically starts using the mirror.

Adding Mirror Chunks

You can use two methods to start mirroring—`onmonitor` and `onspaces`. You can start mirroring for an existing dbspace, or you can start mirroring when you create the dbspace.

The following `onspaces` command creates a new dbspace called `dbs1` in `/dev/rvg01`, and it automatically starts mirroring to `/dev/mirror/rvg01`:

```
onspaces  -c  -d  dbs1  -p /dev/rvg01  -o 0  -s 500000  -m /dev/mirror/rvg01 0
```

The next `onspaces` command shows how you would start mirroring for an existing dbspace to an existing dbspace. This command would start mirroring for dbspace `dbs2` in `/dev/rvg02`, and mirror it to `dbmirror_01` in `/dev/mirror/rvg02`:

```
onspaces  -m dbs2  -p /dev/rvg02  -o 0  -m dbmirror_01  -p /dev/mirror/rvg02  0
```

Monitoring

There are several ways to monitor your mirror chunks—`onstat`, `onmonitor`, and querying the SMI tables. My preference is to use `onstat`. The `onstat -d` command lists all the dbspaces you have and their respective chunks. The `onstat` flags indicate whether a chunk is mirrored, whether it is a primary or mirror, and whether it is down. See the `onstat` command for more information.

Recovery

When you perform a recovery, OnLine performs basically the same steps as when you started mirroring. OnLine marks the chunk as in recovery mode, copies all data from the mirror chunk, and then sets the status of the chunk to online.

The following `onspaces` command would initiate recovery for a down dbspace named `dbs04` in `/dev/rvg04`:

```
onspaces  -s dbs04  -p /dev/rvg04  -o 0  -O
```

Data Replication

This section describes how data replication works and how to set up data replication for INFORMIX-OnLine.

Overview

Data replication in simple terms is basically mirroring an instance of OnLine on a different machine, possibly at a different site. Data replication provides clients the ability to read from both the primary and secondary servers, so some contention can be eliminated by pointing specific processes to the secondary server. Only the primary server can be modified; the secondary server is read-only. High availability is achieved via data replication; if the primary server is lost, clients can access the secondary server.

NOTE

Any blobs stored in dbspaces will be replicated; however, blobspaces will not be replicated.

How Replication Works

Informix uses a level-0 archive and the logical log records to initially replicate the server. After it is replicated, OnLine keeps the servers in sync by continuously sending all the logical logs from the primary server to the secondary server.

If a server fails, you have several options for handling redirection of the connections to the secondary server.

DBPATH Redirection

Upon the failure of a connection attempt, the client application will use the `DBPATH` UNIX environment variable to try to find the dbserver (specified by the `INFORMIXSERVER` environment variable) to which it wants to connect.

Administrator Controlled Redirection

The database administrator can handle redirection by performing any one of the following tasks:

- Modify the `sqlhosts` file to force the connection to connect to the secondary server.
- Change the setting for all users' `$INFORMIXSERVER` environment variables.

Replication Setup

The first step in data replication is to set up the system to be the replication secondary server.

The following steps need to be taken in order to configure the secondary server:

1. The hardware servers must be identical.
2. The software versions must be identical.
3. The amount of dbspace/disk space must be equal.
4. Transaction logging must be turned `ON`.
5. `ROOTNAME`, `ROOTPATH`, `ROOTOFFSET`, and `ROOTSIZE` must be identical on both servers.
6. If the primary server has root mirroring turned on, the secondary server must mirror root as well. The mirror paths, however, can be different.
7. The `PHYSDBS` and `PHYSFILE` `ONCONFIG` parameters must be identical.
8. The `TAPEBLK`, `TAPESIZE`, `LTAPEBLK`, and `LTAPESIZE` `ONCONFIG` parameters must be identical. The tape devices can be different.
9. `LOGFILES` and `LOGSIZE` must match; also any additional log files you have configured on the primary server must be set up on the secondary server.
10. All shared memory parameters must match.
11. The data replication `ONCONFIG` parameters—`DRINTERVAL`, `DRLOSTFOUND`, `DRTIMEOUT`, and `DRAUTO`—must be identical on both servers.
12. Both servers must have one entry for each of the servers (both primary and secondary) in their respective `$INFORMIXDIR/etc/sqlhosts` files.
13. Each server must have entries in `/etc/hosts` and `/etc/services` for the other server.

After you have the preceding requirements set up, you can start data replication by performing the following steps:

1. Create a level-0 archive on the primary server.
2. Use `onmode -d primary_name secondary_name` on the primary server, providing the names of the primary and secondary servers to set the primary and secondary server names. The connection attempt will fail at this point, which is expected.
3. Restore onto the secondary server the level-0 archive you just created. (Use `ontape -p` if using ontape; `ontape -r` will not work.)
4. Run `onmode -d _secondary_name primary_name` on the secondary server. At this point, the attempted connection will be successful (as shown in the OnLine log files). The secondary server now automatically performs a logical-log recovery. If you have backed up and freed logs on the primary server since the level-0 archive, you will be prompted for the log tapes.

Data replication is now complete.

Replication Failures

Several types of data replication failures can occur. A data replication failure is the loss of the connection between the servers.

In the event of a data replication failure that causes a loss of your primary server, the following steps should recover your primary server and restore data replication:

- If `DRAUTO` was set to `0` or `1`, run `onmode -s` and then `onmode -d secondary_name primary_name` on the secondary server.
- Run `ontape -p` on the primary server.
- Run `onmode -d primary_name secondary_name` on the primary server.
- Run `ontape -l` on the primary server.

Data replication should now be restored.

Monitoring

This section discusses the various tasks involved in monitoring an instance of INFORMIX-OnLine. Included are detailed descriptions of commands and some sample UNIX shell scripts.

Overview

Monitoring is a big portion of a DBA's job. The system should be continually monitored and tuned in order to keep the system performing at its peak, even amidst continually changing workloads, user types, and so on. This section highlights some of the more common methods for monitoring what is going on in the OnLine engine.

onstat

The `onstat` command is a DBA's best friend. I use the `onstat` command probably more than any other. The `onstat` command allows the DBA to look at activity in the OnLine engine and make decisions about changes that might boost performance. Table 13.2 provides a high-level look at `onstat` and its parameters.

Table 13.2. The `onstat` utility.

Command	*Purpose*
`onstat -`	Indicates whether the engine is online.
`onstat --`	Displays a list of all `onstat` options.
`onstat -a`	Displays everything.
`onstat -b`	Displays information about all buffers currently in use, including the buffer address, most recent user thread address, page number, memory address, number of slot-table entries, lock info, owner of the lock, and so on.
`onstat -c`	Displays the current `ONCONFIG` file.
`onstat -d`	Information about dbspaces and chunks.
`onstat -f`	Displays dataskip status.
`onstat -k`	Displays lock info.
`onstat -l`	Displays logging info.
`onstat -m`	Displays message log info.
`onstat -p`	Displays profile.
`onstat -s`	Displays general latch info.
`onstat -t`	Displays TBLspaces.
`onstat -u`	Displays user threads.
`onstat -x`	Prints transactions.
`onstat -z`	Zeroes all stats.
`onstat -B`	Same as `-b`, but for all buffers.
`onstat -C`	B+ tree cleaner information.
`onstat -D`	Displays page read and write info for the first 50 chunks of each dbspace.

Command	*Purpose*
`onstat -F`	A counter of the following types of writes: foreground writes, LRU writes, chunk writes, the address of the structure assigned to this page cleaner thread, the page cleaner number, the current state of the page cleaner, and additional data.
`onstat -R`	Displays LRU queues.
`onstat -X`	Displays entire list of sharers and waiters for buffers.
`onstat -r`	Repeats options every *n* seconds (default: 5).
`onstat -o`	Puts shared memory into specified file (default: `onstat.out`) `infile`. Use `infile` to obtain shared memory information.
`onstat -g all`	All multithreading information.
`onstat -g ath`	Displays all threads.
`onstat -g wai`	Displays waiting threads.
`onstat -g act`	Prints all active threads.
`onstat -g rea`	Displays ready threads.
`onstat -g sle`	Displays all sleeping threads.
`onstat -g spi`	Prints spin locks with long spins.
`onstat -g sch`	Prints VP scheduler statistics.
`onstat -g lmx`	Displays all locked mutexes.
`onstat -g wmx`	Displays all mutexes with waiters.
`onstat -g con`	Conditions and waits.
`onstat -g stk <tid>`	Dumps the stack of a specified thread.
`onstat -g glo`	Global multithreading info, including CPU use information about VPs.
`onstat -g seg`	Displays memory segment statistics.
`onstat -g rbm`	Prints block map for resident segment.
`onstat -g mem <pool name>` or `<session id>`	Memory stats for a pool.
`onstat -g nbm`	Blocks bitmap for all nonresident memory segments.
`onstat -g afr <pool name>` or `<session id>`	Allocated memory fragments for a shared memory pool or a session.

continues

Table 13.2. continued

Command	*Purpose*
`onstat -g ffr` <pool name> or <session id>	Prints free fragments for a shared memory pool.
`onstat -g ufr` <pool name> or <session id>	Displays allocated fragments listed by use.
`onstat -g iov`	Displays disk I/O statistics by VP.
`onstat -g iof`	I/O stats, by chunk.
`onstat -g ioq`	I/O queuing information.
`onstat -g iog`	I/O global information.
`onstat -g iob`	Big-buffer usage listed by I/O VP class.
`onstat -g ppf` <partition no> or <0>	Displays partition profile data for the partition number provided. Number `0` provides data for all partitions.
`onstat -g tpf` <tid> or <0>	Displays thread profile info for the provided thread id (`tid`); `tid 0` provides info for all threads.
`onstat -g ntu`	Displays net user thread profile information.
`onstat -g ntt`	Displays net user thread access times.
`onstat -g ntm`	Displays net message information.
`onstat -g ntd`	Prints net dispatch information.
`onstat -g nss`	Network shared memory stats.
`onstat -g nss` <session id>	Network shared memory stats by session id.
`onstat -g nsc` <client id>	Prints net shared memory status.
`onstat -g nsd`	Network shared memory stats for poll threads.
`onstat -g sts`	Displays max and current stack sizes.
`onstat -g dic`	One line for each table cached in the shared memory dictionary.
`onstat -g dic` <tablename>	Internal SQL information for the specified table.
`onstat -g dsc`	Data distribution cache info.
`onstat -g opn` <tid>	Displays open tables.
`onstat -g qst`	Prints queue statistics.
`onstat -g wst`	Prints thread wait statistics.
`onstat -g ses`	Prints session summary info for all sessions.
`onstat -g ses` <session id>	Prints session information for the specified session id.

Command	Purpose
`onstat -g sql`	Prints sql summary information for all sql statements.
`onstat -g sql <session id>`	Prints sql information for the specified sql statement.
`onstat -g stq <session id>`	Prints stream queue information.
`onstat -g dri`	Data replication information.
`onstat -g pos`	Displays `/INFORMIXDIR/etc/.infos.DBSERVERNAME` file.
`onstat -g mgm`	Memory grant manager information, including the mgm gates.
`onstat -g lap`	Displays light append information.
`onstat -g ddr`	Displays DDR log post processing information.
`onstat -g dmp <address>` and `<length>`	Dumps shared memory.
`onstat -g src <pattern>` and `<mask>`	Searches memory for `(mem&mask)==pattern`.

The oncheck Utility

The `oncheck` utility is a tool that allows the validation, display, and repair of the internal INFORMIX-OnLine disk structures. The `oncheck` utility checks catalog tables, reserved pages, free list pages, index information, and several other areas. The Informix `oncheck` tool has numerous options for check, display, and repair processing. See the *INFORMIX-OnLine Dynamic Server Administrators Guide* for more information on `oncheck`.

The onlog Utility

The `onlog` utility displays the contents of the logical log files. The `onlog` tool is generally used in cases where a specific transaction may help debug an application. For more information on the `onlog` utility, see the *INFORMIX-OnLine Dynamic Server Administrators Guide.*

Sample Scripts

As a DBA, you will use a wide variety of shell scripts to do everything from creating dbspaces and tables, to unloading data and running backups. Listings 13.1, 13.2, and 13.3 show a few sample shell scripts that perform some of the day-to-day DBA tasks you might run into.

Listing 13.1. The grant_perms.sh shell script.

```
#!/bin/ksh
#
# grant_perms.sh
#
# Author -The MasterDBA
#
#  shell to grant permissions to a list of users
#  shell grants resource to all users at the dbase level
#   as well as specified table level perms if any.
#
# Syntax: grant_perms.sh <dbase_name> <owner> <users_list> {-s -u -d -i}
#         dbase_name: the name of the database to use
#         owner:      grant perms for all tables owned by <owner>
#         users_list: file containing comma seperated list of users(NO spaces)
#         -s:         grant select on all tables
#         -u:         grant update on all tables
#         -d:         grant delete on all tables
#         -i:         grant insert on all tables
# get the params
# see if user needs help
if [ -z "$1" ]
then
    echo
    echo "Syntax: "
    echo "Syntax: grant_perms.sh <dbase_name> <owner> <users_list> {-s -u -d -i}"
    echo "  dbase_name: the name of the database to use"
    echo "  owner:      grant perms for all tables owned by <owner>"
    echo "  users_list: file containing comma seperated list of users(NO spaces)"
    echo "  -s:         grant select on all tables
    echo "  -u:         grant update on all tables
    echo "  -d:         grant delete on all tables
    echo "  -i:         grant insert on all tables
    echo
    echo "Get it Right!"
    exit 1
else
    db=$1
    own=$2
   usrs="$3"
    shift
    shift
    shift
fi
echo "set params"
for param in $*
do
    case $param
    in
        -s)
            select="1"
            tab_perms="1"
            ;;
        -u)
            update="1"
            tab_perms="1"
            ;;
```

```
        -d)
            delete="1"
            tab_perms="1"
            ;;
        -i)
            insert="1"
            tab_perms="1"
            ;;
        *)
            echo "Invalid parameter [$param]"
            echo
            exit 1
            ;;
    esac
done
echo "Building grant resource/connect file"
echo "[$usrs]"
for usr_name in 'cat $usrs'
do
    # grant resource
    echo "dbase stmt"
    echo "database $db;" > grant.sql
    echo "chmod"
    chmod 777 grant.sql
    echo "resource"
    echo "grant resource to $usr_name;" >> grant.sql
    echo "clean log file"
    >grant_perms.log
    echo "perms"
    chmod 777 grant_perms.log
    dbaccess -e  - grant.sql > grant_perms.log 2>&1
    if [ $? -ne 0 ]
    then
        echo
        echo "Error granting resource to $usr_name"
        echo "Exiting.."
        echo
        exit 1
    fi
    #table level stuff
    echo "Building list of tables"
    # build list of tables
    echo "database $db;" > get_tbls.sql
    echo " select tabname from systables" >> get_tbls.sql
    echo " where tabid > 99 and owner = '$own'"  >> get_tbls.sql
    echo " and tabtype  = 'T';"  >> get_tbls.sql
    chmod 777 get_tbls.sql
    > tbls.lst
    chmod 777 tbls.lst
     dbaccess - get_tbls.sql ¦ grep -v tabname \
     ¦ grep -v '^$' >tbls.lst 2>> grant_perms.log
    rm -f get_tbls.sql
    if [ $? -ne 0 ]
    then
        echo
        echo "Error building list of table names"
        echo "Exiting.."
```

continues

Listing 13.1. continued

```
    echo
    exit 1
else
    echo "Table list created " >> grant_perms.log
fi
for tab in 'cat tbls.lst'
do
    echo "Table: $tab" >> grant_perms.log
    # select
    echo "database $db;" > grant.sql
    if [ "$select" = "1" ]
    then
        echo " grant select on $tab to $usr_name;" >> grant.sql
    fi
    dbaccess -e  - grant.sql >> grant_perms.log 2>&1
    if [ $? -ne 0 ]
    then
        echo
        echo "Error granting select to $usr_name"
        echo "Exiting.."
        echo
        exit 1
    else
        echo "Select" >>grant_perms.log
    fi
    # update
    echo "database $db;" > grant.sql
    if [ "$update" = "1" ]
    then
        echo " grant update on $tab to $usr_name;" >> grant.sql
    fi
    dbaccess -e  - grant.sql >> grant_perms.log 2>&1
    if [ $? -ne 0 ]
    then
        echo
        echo "Error granting update to $usr_name"
        echo "Exiting.."
        echo
        exit 1
    else
        echo "Update" >>grant_perms.log
    fi
    # delete
    echo "database $db;" > grant.sql
    if [ "$delete" = "1" ]
    then
        echo " grant delete on $tab to $usr_name;" >> grant.sql
    fi
    dbaccess -e  - grant.sql >> grant_perms.log 2>&1
    if [ $? -ne 0 ]
    then
        echo
        echo "Error granting delete to $usr_name"
        echo "Exiting.."
        echo
        exit 1
```

```
        else
            echo "Delete" >>grant_perms.log
        fi
        # insert
        echo "database $db;" > grant.sql
        if [ "$insert" = "1" ]
        then
            echo " grant insert on $tab to $usr_name;" >> grant.sql
        fi
        dbaccess -e  - grant.sql >> grant_perms.log 2>&1
        if [ $? -ne 0 ]
        then
            echo
            echo "Error granting insert to $usr_name"
            echo "Exiting.."
            echo
            exit 1
        else
            echo "Insert" >>grant_perms.log
        fi
    done
done
rm -f grant.sql
rm -f tbls.lst
```


Listing 13.2. The `mk_table_list.sh` shell script.

```
#!/bin/ksh
#  mk_tbl_list builds a list of dbase table names
#   Author -The MasterDBA
#
# syntax: mk_tbl_list [dbase_name] [output_filename]
if [ -z "$1" ]
then
    echo "Syntax :"
    echo "   mk_tbl_list [dbase_name] [output_filename]"
    echo "                 dbase_name: name of the informix dbase to "
    echo "                             build list for"
    echo
            echo "Get it Right!"
    exit
fi
if [ -z "$2" ]
then
    echo "Syntax :"
    echo "   mk_tbl_list [dbase_name] [output_filename]"
    echo "                 dbase_name: name of the informix dbase to "
    echo "                             build list for"
    echo
    exit
fi
echo "select tabname from systables" > tbl_sel.sql
echo "where tabid > 99" >> tbl_sel.sql
dbaccess "$1" tbl_sel.sql ¦ grep -v tabname ¦ grep -v '^$' > $2
rm -f tbl_sel.sql
```

Listing 13.3. The dbase_dump.sh shell script.

```
#!/bin/ksh
# dbase_dump.sh
# dumps a dbase to flat files
#
# Author -The MasterDBA
#
# syntax  dbase_dump.sh [dbase] [target_dir]
# check syntax
if [ $# -lt 2 ]
then
    echo "syntax  dbase_dump.sh [dbase] [target_dir_list] "
    echo "        dbase:           name of the database to unload"
    echo "        target_dir_list: name of file holding a list of target dir's"
    echo "        The data will span the filesystems in the target list as "
    echo "          the filesystems fill up"
    echo
    echo "Get it Right!"
    exit
else
    dbase="$1"
    target_lst="$2"
fi
# make_restore function call
make_restore() {
#     set - 'isql db_admin <<!
#         select dbspace from disk_layout
#         where dbase = '${dbase}'
#         and tabname = '${table}'
#!'
#dbspace="$2"
echo
    echo "load from ${target}/${dbase}/${table}.unl " >> ${restore_file}
    echo "   insert into ${table};\n" >> ${restore_file}
}
# next_target function call
next_target() {
    old_target="$target"
    curr_tgt_found="0"
    for new_target in 'cat $target_lst'
    do
        if [ "$curr_tgt_found" = "1" ]
        then
            target="$new_target"
            break
        fi
        if [ "$target" = "$new_target" ]
        then
            curr_tgt_found="1"
        else
            curr_tgt_found="0"
        fi
    done
    if [ "$old_target" = "$new_target" ]
    then
        echo "Error, no more targets left to hold data"
        echo "Get some more disks and try again"
        exit
```

```
    else
        echo "rm -fr ${target}/${dbase}"
        rm -fr ${target}/${dbase}
        wait
        mkdir ${target}/${dbase}
        chmod 777 ${target}/${dbase}
        echo "rm -fr ${old_target}/${dbase}/${table}.unl"
        rm -fr ${old_target}/${dbase}/${table}.unl
        >${target}/${dbase}/${table}.unl
        chmod 666 ${target}/${dbase}/${table}.unl
        echo "${target}/${dbase}/${table}.unl"
        isql ${dbase} <<!
            unload to  ${target}/${dbase}/${table}.unl
            select * from ${table};
!
        make_restore
    fi
}
# echo start time
clear
date
# get first target
for new_target in 'cat $target_lst'
do
    target=$new_target
    break
done
# create a list of all dbase tables
mk_tbl_list ${dbase} ${dbase}.list
# setup the target directory
echo "rm -fr ${target}/${dbase}"
rm -fr ${target}/${dbase}
mkdir ${target}/${dbase}
chmod 777 ${target}/${dbase}
# clear out the restore file
restore_file=${target}/${dbase}/${dbase}_restore.sql
> ${restore_file}
# put a dbschema in the target dir
if [ -z ${INFORMIXDIR} ]
then
    echo
    echo "The env var \$INFORMIXDIR is not set "
    echo "  run the script again when you "
    echo"   have a clue of what you're doing"
    echo
    exit 1
fi
$INFORMIXDIR/bin/dbschema -d ${dbase} -ss  ${target}/${dbase}/schema.sql
# loop thru tables & do the backup thing
for table in 'cat ${dbase}.list'
do
    >${target}/${dbase}/${table}.unl
    chmod 666 ${target}/${dbase}/${table}.unl
    echo "${target}/${dbase}/${table}.unl"
    isql ${dbase} <<!
        unload to  ${target}/${dbase}/${table}.unl
        select * from ${table};
```

continues

Listing 13.3. continued

```
!
    set - 'df ${target}'
    if [ "${13}" = "99%" -o "${13}" = "100%" ]
    then
        next_target
    else
        make_restore
    fi
done
rm -f ${dbase}.list
chmod 666  ${restore_file}
# echo done time
date
echo "Done.."
```

Summary

As you can see, configuring a properly tuned Informix database is not a trivial task. A good DBA must know how to tune the various aspects of the server pertaining to memory, CPU, and I/O utilization. The DBA must also know when to use different types of connections to the database, when and why to mirror or use data replication, and how to monitor the database efficiently through the use of various commands and shell scripts.

CHAPTER 14

Managing Data with Stored Procedures and Triggers

by John McNally

IN THIS CHAPTER

This chapter provides

- A description of stored procedures and their advantages
- How to create stored procedures
- How to use the Stored Procedure Language to provide functionality found in other programming languages
- How to store, maintain, and remove stored procedures
- A description of triggers and their advantages
- How to create a trigger
- How to store, maintain, and remove triggers

Stored Procedures

A stored procedure is a small program written in a limited language containing embedded SQL statements. This limited language is called *SPL*, or *Stored Procedure Language*. The small program is stored internally in the database server system tables waiting to be run at a later time. Introduced in the OnLine release, stored procedures are available in the SE, OnLine, and Dynamic Server products.

There are two major advantages to using stored procedures. The first advantage is that time and processing overhead is reduced by putting large, complicated, and common SQL tasks in stored procedures. All SQL sent to the server from clients goes through a parsing and optimizing step before actually performing its task. With stored procedures, parsing and optimizing is part of the storage process. Placing the SQL in a stored procedure requires some internal overhead to retrieve, but no conversion or optimization is needed. Figure 14.1 shows the difference between a normal SQL task and a stored procedure task processed by the database server.

The second advantage of stored procedur es is that they can reduce network usage considerably. Large, complicated SQL statements performed numerous times during the processing day can slow down networks. Placing these statements into stored procedures drastically reduces network traffic because you send only the command to run the stored procedure and related input data across the network to the server.

TIP

Stored procedures are a waste of server memory and overhead when used for infrequently run, small tasks. It is best to use stored procedures when the task is larger than three SQL statements and is used many times a day.

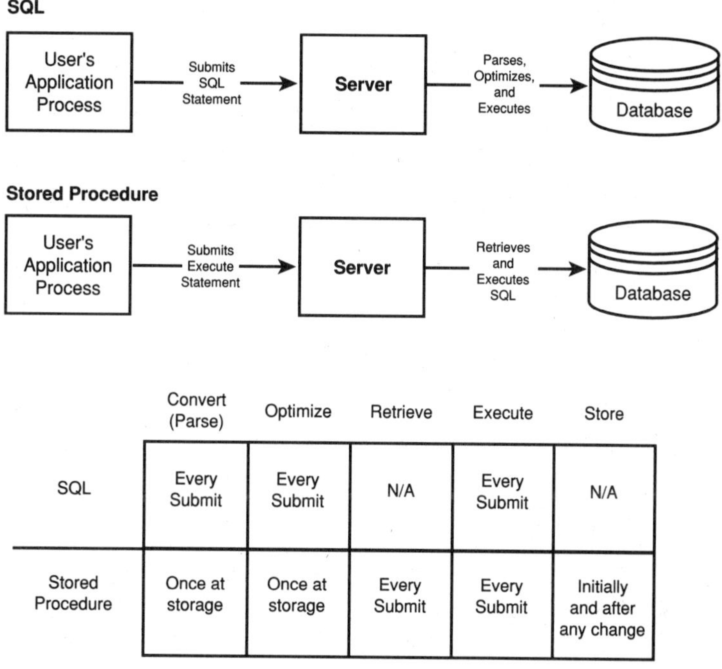

	Convert (Parse)	Optimize	Retrieve	Execute	Store
SQL	Every Submit	Every Submit	N/A	Every Submit	N/A
Stored Procedure	Once at storage	Once at storage	Every Submit	Every Submit	Initially and after any change

FIGURE 14.1.
Side-by-side processing of a task through SQL and a stored procedure.

Stored procedures also offer two smaller benefits. The first is that stored procedures can act as a central library for reusable SQL commands so that you don't use the same statement in different client applications. Design the stored procedures to be generic enough to handle different forms of data and different tables and rows. Client applications need to know how to call the stored procedures and what type of data to send in order to achieve the client applications' desired results from the stored procedure.

The other small benefit is that stored procedures also offer a means to limit some client applications from performing certain tasks by using privilege levels. You can give access to only certain users and applications to run specific stored procedures. Privileges on stored procedures help to enforce business rules by not only stopping client processes from accessing data, but also limiting them to what actions can be performed on the data.

Another benefit is possible through Dynamic Server. Although the SQL commands related to creating and executing stored procedures are not processed in parallel, the SQL statements within the procedure are. The advantage of performing some tasks in parallel is not lost when called from within a stored procedure.

It's not a good idea to place most SQL tasks in stored procedures. *Overhead* results from retrieving and processing a stored procedure. When retrieved, the stored procedure is placed into a cache in shared memory. Every time a stored procedure is placed into this cache from disk, it must be compiled from text into an executable format. The server allows only 16 stored procedures to reside in cache at the same time. As a result, frequently used stored procedures reside in cache, whereas others are swapped out. Every time a stored procedure is swapped out of cache and must be retrieved, a compile is performed. Unless the stored procedure is used consistently, it does not fully take advantage of the stored procedure benefits.

On the older server systems, SE and OnLine, the stored procedures residing in cache can be reused only by the client process that caused them to be retrieved. If a different client wants to use the same stored procedure, another version of the procedure is placed in cache. Dynamic server uses a stored procedure memory pool to cache the retrieved stored procedures. This memory pool allows all client processes to share access to one version of the same stored procedure.

Changing tables, rows, and indexes used by the stored procedure requires it to be re-optimized. As a result, it's better to have different stored procedures for each data area, even if the task being performed is the same. The only time you might want a "data-generic" stored procedure is when you use stored procedures for a central library of reusable tasks.

Updating database statistics at the table level also requires the stored procedure to be re-optimized the next time it is used. Running update statistics against the entire database performs the re-optimization at the same time. When updating statistics only for tables, it is wise to update statistics on the procedures that use that table.

Creating and Storing Stored Procedures

To develop a stored procedure, you must make a connection to the server as you do with any other database transaction. The SQL command `create` performs the parsing, optimizing, and storage of the procedure. DBaccess is the easiest way to create the procedure and run the `create procedure` command, but you can also do it through any other client, such as a UNIX shell or a C program with embedded SQL.

The `create procedure` command has six separate parts:

- Procedure name
- Parameters area
- Returning section
- Statement block
- Document section
- With listing

The procedure name is the name that is used in calling and running the stored procedure. It can be 18 characters or fewer in size.

The parameters area is where data values passed by the calling client are tied to variable names. These names can be associated with individual data types such as date, integer, or string, as well as complete columns and rows. Clients that execute the procedure do not have to send data to the procedure when a default value is included for each variable.

The returning section is optional for the `create procedure` statement. If you do not need to return results to the calling client, you can omit the returning section. When you do return results, the returning statement must have a listing for each data item by its data type, separated by a comma and ending with a semicolon. The variable name that holds the value for this data type is referenced by the SPL `return` command in the statement block.

The statement block is where the actual procedure is created. The statement block is what is saved in the data server by the `create procedure` command. This area is where the SPL/SQL program is placed or referenced. The procedure listing concludes with the line `end procedure`.

The document section is optional and is used for comments and descriptions of the stored procedure. The information in the document section is stored in a system table that contains all the document descriptions of created stored procedures.

The last section, the with listing, is also optional. It is used to specify a filename where compile messages and errors are placed. Every time the stored procedure is retrieved from disk and placed in cache to be used, it is compiled. If the table or row layout has changes but the stored procedure does not, this file is where Informix places the error messages. The first time the procedure is compiled, which occurs when you submit the `create procedure` command, compile messages are displayed back to you. The with listing file is only for compiles performed after it is stored.

After the `create procedure` statement is complete, submit the statement as if it is any other SQL command. The procedure from the statement block is parsed, optimized, and converted to ASCII before it is actually stored in server-owned tables. The process of placing stored procedures within the servers' system tables has six steps:

1. The `create procedure` statement is received.
2. Parse and optimize SQL producing query tree and dependency list.
3. Store query tree and dependency list in ASCII format.
4. Parse SPL code, producing `pcode`.
5. Store `pcode` in ASCII format.
6. Store owner information.

The `sysprocedures` table is where all the procedure's characteristics are stored. Information such as owner and size are placed in the row associated with the procedure being created.

The SQL is parsed and optimized the same way all SQL statements are compiled, and a query tree and a dependency list are created. A query tree is a structure that places SQL in a layout that the server can store and execute easier than line-by-line SQL commands. A dependency list contains all the tables, indexes, rows, and columns involved in the stored procedure. Before every execution of the stored procedure, items in this list are checked to see whether they still exist. Generic stored procedures need to be optimized each time they are run because the data items used at execution do not reside in the dependency list. The query tree and dependency list are stored in the `sysprocplan` system table.

The SPL statements are also parsed into pseudocode called `pcode`. `pcode` serves the same purpose that the query tree does. They both have a format that is easy to store and execute. The `pcode` for the stored procedure is placed in the `sysprocbody` system table. If the document section of the `create procedure` statement is provided, the comments and descriptions of the stored procedure from this section are also stored in the `sysprocbody` table.

The `sysprocauth` table is another important system table for stored procedures. It holds permission information for accessing each stored procedure. When the procedure is created, permission defaults to the creator only. To provide other users with the ability to execute the procedure, you must use a `grant execute on` *`procedure_name`* `to` *`user_list`* statement, where the *`procedure_name`* can be an asterisk for all procedures and the *`user_list`* can be one or more user IDs. You can use the keyword `PUBLIC` to indicate that all users have access. You can use the `revoke execute on` *`procedure_name`* `from` *`user_list`* to prevent specific users from executing a specific stored procedure.

There are two ways to access the system tables to see what stored procedures are available and what they do. The first method is to issue `dbschema -d` *`database_name`* `-f` *`procedure_name`*. To list all available procedures, use `all` as the procedure name. The other method is to write a SQL query against the previously mentioned system tables.

Developing SPL/SQL Procedures

Replacing code that currently resides in client applications is the main purpose of stored procedures. Standard SQL statements might not have enough functionality to perform the original task. As mentioned earlier in this chapter, the limited programming language that is used with SQL to create stored procedures is called Stored Procedure Language (SPL). SPL allows users to develop their stored procedures with some of the same programming structures found in standard programming languages. With SPL and SQL, you can perform almost all database tasks with stored procedures.

Some SQL commands are not allowed in stored procedures. The following statements have a direct impact on data and tasks beyond the scope of a stored procedure:

```
CHECK TABLE                 CLOSE
CLOSE DATABASE              CONNECT
CREATE DATABASE             CREATE PROCEDURE
CREATE PROCEDURE FROM       DATABASE
DECLARE                     DESCRIBE
EXECUTE                     EXECUTE IMMEDIATE
```

FETCH	FLUSH
FREE	GET DESCRIPTOR
INFO	LOAD
OPEN	OUTPUT
PREPARE	PUT
REPAIR	ROLLFORWARD DATABASE
SET DESCRIPTOR	START DATABASE
UNLOAD	WHENEVER

Some SQL statements have limitations in stored procedures. For example, you can use the `DROP` procedure in a stored procedure as long as it's not trying to drop itself. You cannot use statements such as `alter`, `create`, `delete`, `drop`, `insert`, and `update` in a procedure that is called by a client process performing an `insert`, `delete`, or `select`. An example is a `select` statement that searches for all customers' names that have `total_purchases` meeting the results of the stored procedure `premiere_customer`. The `premiere_customer` stored procedure cannot alter data in tables in any way. If the `premiere_customer` procedure has an `update` within it, the original `select` fails.

SPL provides extra functionality to the SQL commands to perform logic usually found in standard programs. Branching and variable substitution are the main features of the SPL commands.

CALL

The `CALL` statement is used to execute another stored procedure. It works just like the `execute procedure` SQL statement that is sent to the database server to start a stored procedure. The `CALL` statement is able to send and receive data.

Here are some examples of the `CALL` statement:

- A stored procedure `update_balance` processes a task using the `customer_id` and `payment`:

  ```
  CALL update_balance(customer_id, payment);
  ```

- A stored procedure `get_balance_due` processes a task using the `customer_id` and places its results in a variable called `balance`:

  ```
  CALL get_balance_due(customer_id) RETURNING balance;
  ```

Comments

To place comments within the procedure code, use the double hyphen (`--`), which separates the rest of the line as a comment.

Here are some examples of comments:

- Add a comment to an entire line:

```
-- Stored Procedure: Send_Mail
-- Sends e-mail to customers
```

- Add a comment to a statement line:

```
CALL getmid(cust_id) RETURNING mail_id; -- finds email id
```

- Comment out a statement line so that it is not processed when run:

```
-- CALL getmid(cust_id) RETURNING mail_id;
```

CONTINUE

The `CONTINUE` statement is used to jump to the next loop value without processing any more of the statements in the current iteration of a `FOR`, `WHILE`, or `FOREACH` loop. When a `CONTINUE` statement is run, processing returns to the top of the loop.

The following procedure sets the discount of products with IDs 1 through 100 to 10 percent. Every product except 50 is added to the `sale_table`:

```
FOR count IN (1 to 100)
    UPDATE inventory_table
        SET discount = 10
        WHERE product_id = count;
    IF count = 50
        CONTINUE FOR;
    INSERT (count, "ON SALE") into sale_table;
END FOR;
```

DEFINE

The `DEFINE` statement is used to create local variables for use within the stored procedures. You can assign any SQL data type from `INT` for integer through blobs to specific variable names with the `DEFINE` statement. Refer to Chapter 28, "INFORMIX-SQL," for a complete list of SQL data types. The `DEFINE` keyword is followed by a unique variable name up to 18 characters long, a data type description, and a semicolon. You can use as many `DEFINE` statements as you need in the procedure. All `DEFINE` statements must come directly after the `CREATE PROCEDURE` and `RETURNING` statements and before any other statements.

Using the `DEFINE GLOBAL` keyword declares the variable usable beyond the scope of the defining procedures. All other procedures running at the same time can access the global variable. When the defining procedure ends, the global variable no longer exists. Global variables are not shared between different databases but only between different procedures in the same database.

When you place the `DEFAULT` keyword and a specific value after the data type, the specified value is used when no other value is assigned to the variable. You can use only six default values with the `DEFAULT` keyword:

`NULL`	Any data type with no value.
`SITENAME`	A character string containing the name of the machine site.
`DBSERVERNAME`	A character string containing the name of the data server.
`USER`	A character string containing the name of the user that the procedure is running for.
`CURRENT`	A `DATETIME` data type that holds the specified date and time values when running, such as `SECOND` or `YEAR`.
`TODAY`	A `DATE` data type that holds the current date when running.

The `DEFAULT` keyword is available only with the `DEFINE GLOBAL` label. Local variables cannot have default values.

Use the `LIKE` keyword instead of a data type to assume the data type of a specific database column. When the procedure runs, it resolves the variable's data type by checking the data type of the column.

To override SQL commands that are considered reserved words, use the `PROCEDURE` keyword in place of a data type. This indicates that a variable is a user-defined procedure rather than a predefined SQL or SPL command.

To work with blob data types, use `BYTE` and `TEXT` as the data type labels but precede them with the `REFERENCES` keyword. Blob data items are much too large to be sorted in a register assigned to manage each variable. The `REFERENCES` label creates a pointer to the data type. Pointers are addresses to where the blobs exist. A pointer is a numeric value small enough to be managed by registers.

The following paragraphs present some examples using the `DEFINE` statement.

Declare `count` to be an integer data type. When the `RETURNING` statement is present, all `DEFINE`s go after it:

```
CREATE PROCEDURE test_define()
    RETURNING INT;
    DEFINE count INT;
```

Declare `balance` as a shared integer variable during the life of the procedure. There is no `RETURNING` statement, so `DEFINE`s start after the `CREATE PROCEDURE` statement:

```
CREATE PROCEDURE test_define2()
    DEFINE GLOBAL balance INT;
```

The next `DEFINE` declares `payment` as a global integer with a default value of `NULL`:

```
DEFINE GLOBAL payment INT DEFAULT NULL;
```

The next `DEFINE` declares a character string of eight characters for a global variable called `operator`, which defaults to the user's UNIX ID:

```
DEFINE GLOBAL operator CHAR(8) DEFAULT USER;
```

The next example declares a global character string of five characters with the word "SALE" as the default:

```
DEFINE GLOBAL topic CHAR(5) DEFAULT 'SALE';
```

The next example uses the LIKE keyword to assign the email_address data type from the customer table to the local variable mail_id:

```
DEFINE mail_id LIKE customer.email_address;
```

Using the PROCEDURE keyword redefines the SQL function of date to a user-defined procedure called date. The redefine lasts for the life of the defining procedure:

```
DEFINE date PROCEDURE;
```

The next statement declares the variable sale_flyer as a pointer to blob data item:

```
DEFINE sale_flyer REFERENCES BYTE;
```

EXIT

The EXIT statement is used to stop a loop before the looping condition is met. This occurs where EXIT is followed by a FOR, WHILE, or FOREACH keyword, ending with a semicolon. The keywords FOR, WHILE, and FOREACH represent the three types of loops in SPL.

In the following example, each looping statement has an EXIT associated with it. The for loop exits halfway. The while loop starts at 50, due to the exit from the for loop, and exits after 20 iterations.

The FOREACH loop starts at the first customer ID and continues looping until all 100 customers are processed. The exit occurs when the hundredth customer is reached.

```
CREATE PROCEDURE exit_loops()
    DEFINE count INT;
    FOR count = 1 TO 100
        IF count = 50 THEN
            EXIT FOR;
        END IF
    END FOR
    WHILE count < 75
        LET count = count + 1;
        IF count = 70 THEN
            EXIT WHILE;
        END IF
    END WHILE
    FOREACH SELECT customer_id INTO count from customers
        IF count = 100 THEN
            EXIT FOREACH;
        END IF
    END FOREACH
END PROCEDURE
```

FOR

The FOR statement is used to perform definite loops, whereas the WHILE statement is used for indefinite loops. The FOR statement is followed by a variable name, and then the expression range is specified.

An expression range is started one of two ways: with the keyword IN or with the equal sign, =. IN specifies that the variable is in the expression range. For example, if the expression range is all the letters of the alphabet, A through Z, a variable of eight causes the loop to stop. A loop continues until the variable is no longer in the range. The equal sign assigns the current expression iteration to the variable. If the range is from 1 to 100, the variable is the value of 1, 2, 3, … until 100.

Ranges can be generalized by the TO keyword. For the range of 1, 2, 3, … 100, rather than list each value, use 1 TO 100. The loop automatically cycles through each number, one at a time.

To cycle through a list at different rates other than one at a time, use the STEP keyword. Specifying STEP after the range allows different jump iterations. With a STEP 2, the 1 TO 100 range actually hits every odd-valued number.

You can use SQL statements as part of the expression range. A SELECT statement is very useful in creating ranges of values from tables that can be used for looping while a variable labeled as IN is found within the SELECT statement's output.

You can use two or more ranges to specify the loop conditions, separating each range with a comma when listing in the expression. The ranges are performed in the order in which they are listed in the expression.

In the first example, the for loop starts at 1 and continues until 100, stepping one number at a time:

```
FOR count = 1 TO 100
    SELECT balance FROM customer
        WHERE customer_id = count;
```

The next for loop also goes from 1 to 100, but at every 5 value: 1, 5, 10, 15 … 100:

```
FOR count = 1 TO 100 STEP 5
SELECT balance FROM customer
        WHERE customer_id = count;
```

The next loop continues while the input_value is one of the four listed character strings:

```
FOR input_value IN ('YES', 'Y', 'NO', 'N')
```

The next loop continues while the input_value is in the list of survey result's values:

```
FOR input_value IN (SELECT value_1 from survey_results)
```

FOREACH

The FOREACH statement loops until a specific task is complete. Each step of the task is considered an iteration of the loop.

Three types of tasks are used in the FOREACH statement: SELECT INTO, a cursor select, or another procedure.

The SELECT INTO loops until the select has performed its search. Each data item found by the search is placed into the loop variable.

The cursor select is similar to the SELECT INTO. The same process happens in each situation because cursors are processes that naturally stop at each find during a search.

You can also use another procedure to provide individual data items for processing. The procedure you call must contain a RETURN *value* WITH RESUME statement, so the next iteration starts where the last left off.

The first example loops at each customer ID found in the customer table. The current customer ID is placed in the procedure variable cid:

```
FOREACH SELECT cust_id INTO cid FROM customer
```

The next example loops again for each customer ID found in the customer table. The cursorpoint variable is the cursor or point where the search has progressed:

```
FOREACH cursorpoint FOR SELECT cust_id INTO cid FROM customer
```

The next example loops for each returned value from the get_cust_id procedure. Each returned value is placed in cid and processed by the loop. Then, the procedure is called again, and the next value is returned.

```
FOREACH EXECUTE PROCEDURE get_cust_id INTO cid
```

IF

The IF statement provides the capability to branch as specific conditions are met. You can embed almost any other SQL or SPL statement within the IF statement. Conditions are evaluated as true or false.

You build conditional statements using any SQL conditional comparison operator, such as BETWEEN, IN, IS NULL, LIKE, or MATCHES. You can also use relational operators, such as =, !=, >, <, >=, and <=.

You can evaluate more than one conditional statement within the IF statement. Using the keyword AND requires all conditional statements to be true for the entire IF to be true. Using the keyword OR allows only one of the conditional statements to be true for the entire IF to be true.

When the IF statement is evaluated as true, the statements directly under the IF are performed. When the IF is evaluated as false, an ELIF, ELSE, or statement following the END IF statement is performed.

An ELIF statement is used to perform another evaluation when the IF is considered false. When the ELIF is true, the statements directly beneath it are executed. When the ELIF is false, the next ELIF, ELSE, or statement following the END IF statement is performed.

The ELSE statement is used to handle processing of statements when an IF or an ELIF are evaluated as false.

The END IF statement ends the scope of the IF statement and sequential processing resumes.

The IF example processes one set of statements if count is over 50. The ELIF processes another set when count is between 25 and 50, and the ELSE processes another set if count is under 25.

```
IF count > 50 THEN
    ...
ELIF count > 25 THEN
    ...
ELSE
    ...
```

LET

The LET statement is used to assign values to variables. LET is followed by a variable name, an equal sign, and any other expression that provides a value. The other expressions can be simple assigns or calls to other procedures.

The first example assigns the value of 100 to the integer variable count:

```
LET count = 100;
```

The next example assigns count the value of itself plus 1:

```
LET count = count + 1;
```

The next example assigns count the value of a SELECT statement that determines the number of customers in the customers_table:

```
LET count = (SELECT count(*) from customers_table);
```

The last example assigns count the value returned by another shared procedure:

```
LET count = get_tot_customers();
```

ON EXCEPTION

The ON EXCEPTION statement is used to specify what action to take when an error occurs. If there is no matching ON EXCEPTION statement for an error, it stops processing the procedure. When you provide an ON EXCEPTION statement for an error code, special processing can be done before the procedure is stopped. When you provide an ON EXCEPTION statement with the keyword WITH RESUME, the procedure is able to continue rather than fail.

The first procedure automatically raises an exception with the error code value of -206, table name not in the database, which is handled by the ON EXCEPTION statement:

```
CREATE PROCEDURE test_error
    ON EXCEPTION IN (-206)
        TRACE 'table not found';
    END EXCEPTION
    SELECT * FROM test_table;
TRACE 'This message should never happen';
```

The next stored procedure continues even after the exception is raised because ON EXCEPTION uses WITH RESUME:

```
CREATE PROCEDURE test_error_with_resume
    ON EXCEPTION IN (-206)
        TRACE 'table not found, will create it';
        CREATE TABLE test_table;
        TRACE 'run procedure again to use new table'
    END EXCEPTION WITH RESUME
    SELECT * FROM test_table;
TRACE 'This message should happen';
```

RAISE EXCEPTION

The RAISE EXCEPTION statement is used to create an error situation determined within the stored procedure. RAISE EXCEPTION works with the ON EXCEPTION statement. You must create an ON EXCEPTION statement to handle the RAISE EXCEPTION statement. RAISE EXCEPTION is followed by an SQL error number, an ISAM error number, and a message surrounded by quotes.

The first procedure automatically raises an exception with the error code value of -999, which is handled by the ON EXCEPTION statement:

```
CREATE PROCEDURE test_error
    ON EXCEPTION IN (-999)
        TRACE 'hit my error';
    END EXCEPTION
    TRACE 'In procedure test_error';
    RAISE EXCEPTION -999, 0, 'My own error message';
    TRACE 'This message should never happen';
```

The next stored procedure continues even after the exception is raised because ON EXCEPTION uses WITH RESUME:

```
CREATE PROCEDURE test_error_with_resume
    ON EXCEPTION IN (-999)
        TRACE 'hit my error';
    END EXCEPTION WITH RESUME
    TRACE 'In procedure test_error';
    RAISE EXCEPTION -999, 0, 'My own error message';
    TRACE 'This message should happen';
```

RETURN

The RETURN statement is used to send results back to the process that started the stored procedure. The starting process can be another stored procedure or a client program. The RETURN statement is followed by whatever statement is needed to provide a value. The type and number of data values listed with the RETURN statement should match what was declared in the create procedure statement's RETURNING clause. If the RETURN statement does not return values to match the RETURNING clause, the waiting variables are populated with NULL.

Adding the WITH RESUME keyword after the return value returns the value after each loop iteration.

The first example returns a NULL value:

```
RETURN;
```

The next example returns the value contained in the variable some_value:

```
RETURN some_value;
```

The next example returns the values contained in variables some_value1 and some_value2:

```
RETURN some_value1, some_value2;
```

The next example returns the value contained in some_value at each iteration of the loop. This process continues until the loop condition is met. The return value of some_value is 3, 5, 7, 9 … until 100 is reached:

```
FOR some_value IN (1 TO 100)
    LET some_value = some_value + 2;
RETURN some_value WITH RESUME;
```

SYSTEM

The SYSTEM statement provides a way to run an operating system–owned process. These processes can range from UNIX commands to executable programs. The SYSTEM statement is followed by the command and the data needed for the command. Anything related to the operating system and the command must be surrounded by single quotes. Any value from the stored procedure must be referenced by the variable name that is not in quotes. Use the double pipe symbol, ||, to append local variables. If a variable name is within the single quotes, it is used as is and not as its value.

In the example, the section of stored procedures loops through the customer table and retrieves each customer's e-mail ID. A SYSTEM statement then starts a UNIX program file called send_sale_notice to each customer's mail ID with the system date. To UNIX, the command looks like

```
send_sale_notice bigbuyer@money.com 1/1/97
   WHILE count <> last_customer_id
       SELECT mail_id from customer_table
```

```
        WHERE count = customer_id
        INTO send_id;
    SYSTEM 'send_sale_notice ' || send_id || ' date'
    LET count = count + 1;
```

TRACE

The TRACE statement allows you to capture debugging information while the stored procedures run. The debugging information includes specialized messages, variable values, procedure arguments, return values, SQL error codes, and ISAM error codes.

The following list outlines the different formats and uses of TRACE:

- TRACE ON traces every statement and variable until a TRACE OFF statement is encountered.
- TRACE OFF stops the tracing started by TRACE ON.
- TRACE PROCEDURE traces only calls and return values of other procedures used in the top-level procedure.
- You can single out special messages and values by placing the message in quotes after the keyword TRACE.

This example shows how you can use the TRACE statement within a procedure:

```
CREATE PROCEDURE test ()
    DEFINE count INT;
BEGIN
    TRACE 'starting test procedure';
    TRACE ON;
    WHILE count < 100
        LET count = count + 1;
    END WHILE
    TRACE OFF;
    TRACE 'Finished test procedure';
    TRACE 'Last count value is ' || count;
```

WHILE

The WHILE statement is used to loop indefinitely and is formed by following the WHILE statement with the condition to be met. The END WHILE statement designates the end of statements that are repeated until the condition is met.

In the example, this section of a stored procedure loops until the balance of all payments in the database matches the total_payments variable:

```
    WHILE balance <> total_payments
        CALL get_next_payment(customer_id)
RETURNING payment;
        LET balance = balance + payment;
    END WHILE;
```

Executing Stored Procedures

There are two main ways to execute a stored procedure. The most common method is from a client process using SQL. These processes can range from DBaccess to UNIX to C/C++ programs with embedded SQL. The other way is from another stored procedure.

The SQL statement to run the stored procedure is `EXECUTE PROCEDURE`, which is followed by the procedure name and a list of data to pass to the procedure within parentheses, `()`. You can use the keyword `INTO` and a list of variable names separated by commas to trap returned values. When using DBaccess or UNIX shells, you can send the return values to the screen by not including the `INTO` keyword.

To submit the `EXECUTE PROCEDURE` command, the user must have permission. The `GRANT EXECUTE ON` *`procedure name`* `TO` statement followed by the user name is the SQL command that gives users permission to run stored procedures.

The database server receives an `EXECUTE PROCEDURE` statement or an SPL `CALL` statement to start a procedure. First, the `pcode` is retrieved from the `sysprocbody` system table, and the query tree and dependency list are retrieved from the `sysprocplan` system table. They are then converted from ASCII to binary format so that the server can read them.

The server checks the dependency list to make sure that all the dependencies were updated. If dependencies still exist, the procedure is re-optimized. When an item on the dependency list no longer exists, an error occurs.

After the dependencies are checked and any necessary optimizing is performed, the data passed in by the calling process is parsed and evaluated to resolve data names into actual data values.

Finally, the binary procedure, possibly re-optimized, and the passed-in data are presented to the interpreter to be executed.

After a procedure is retrieved and converted to binary, it resides in cache to be used again. The least recently used procedures are bumped out of the cache when new procedures are retrieved. Frequently used procedures usually stay in the cache after they are initially retrieved.

Procedures that reside in the cache do not have to be retrieved when executed again, nor do they usually need to be re-optimized.

Maintenance on Stored Procedures

When a change is needed within a stored procedure, you must redo the creation process. Rather than retype the entire procedure, however, you can edit and store the latest version in the system tables. When a current copy is not available for editing, you can perform a query on the system tables to retrieve the procedure.

The system tables are very helpful in maintaining stored procedures. It is wise to keep a copy of the procedure in the database, rather than keep copies of the procedure on many individual accounts. One person's changes may be overwritten by another version of the same procedure.

TIP

Always retrieve the current version of a stored procedure to make changes. In that way, you'll ensure that you have the latest and best version.

To see a list of all the stored procedures within the database, use DBaccess to query the `sysprocedures` table.

The statement `SELECT procname from sysprocedures;` displays all procedure names. Figure 14.2 shows the layout of all the columns in the `sysprocedures` table.

FIGURE 14.2.
The column layout of the `sysprocedures` *system table.*

Column Name	Type	Description
procname	18 characters	Name of the procedure
owner	8 characters	Name of the owner
procid	serial number	Procedure identifier
mode	1 character	Procedure's mode type (either Owner or DBA)
retsize	integer	Compiled size of values (number of bytes)
symsize	integer	Compiled size of symbol table (number of bytes)
datasize	integer	Compiled size of constant data (number of bytes)
codesize	integer	Compiled size of Pcode (number of bytes)
numargs	integer	Number of procedure arguments

The `sysprocplan` table contains the query plan and dependency list for each procedure. Figure 14.3 shows the layout of its columns. To view the query plan of procedures, use the query `SELECT * FROM sysprocplan WHERE datakey='Q';` or `SELECT * FROM sysprocplan WHERE datakey='D';` for the dependency list.

FIGURE 14.3.
The column layout of the `sysprocplan` *system table.*

Column Name	Type	Description
procid	integer	Procedure identifier
planid	integer	Plan identifier
datakey	1 character	Identifier
seqno	integer	Plan's line number
created	date	Date plan was created
datasize	integer	Size of the list or plan (number of bytes)
data	256 characters	Compiled list or plan

The `sysprocbody` table contains the actual procedure and its `DOCUMENT` description. Figure 14.4 shows the layout of its columns. To view each procedure's description created from the `DOCUMENT` statement during the `CREATE PROCEDURE`, use `SELECT data FROM sysprocbody WHERE datakey='D';`. To view the actual procedure code, use `SELECT data FROM sysprocbody WHERE datakey='T';`.

FIGURE 14.4.
The column layout of the sysprocbody *system table.*

Column Name	Type	Description
procid	integer	Procedure identifier
datakey	1 character	Identifier
seqno	integer	Procedure's line number
data	256 characters	Procedure's code (as text)

The best way to retrieve the stored procedure for editing is to use the dbschema program at a UNIX prompt. dbschema is a utility that looks at the current database and builds an SQL script to build a database exactly like the current one. You should run dbschema after you make layout changes to the database because it is useful if a rebuild is required or a duplicate copy of the database is needed.

The command dbschema -d *database name* -f *procedure name* builds the CREATE PROCEDURE statement with the SPL and SQL procedure. Pipe the dbschema output to a file, and you have an editable copy of the latest version of the procedure.

After you make the changes to the procedure, it's a good idea to remove the version in the database. Do this before running the CREATE PROCEDURE to place the edited version in the database. You can remove a procedure from the database by running the SQL statement DROP PROCEDURE *procedure_name*;.

After the version of the stored procedure has been dropped from the database, run the edited dbschema version of the CREATE PROCEDURE statement. This places the newest, just edited, version of the procedure back in the database.

You can use DROP PROCEDURE to remove any old, no longer used procedures from the database as long as the user submitting the DROP has permission to do so.

Stored Procedure Conclusion

Stored procedures offer a viable means to reduce processing and network traffic. This is achieved by moving task-related code away from the client processes and into the database server as stored procedures. Functionality in the client programs is not lost. All programming structure and functionality can be replicated through the Stored Procedure Language (SPL) with embedded SQL commands.

Triggers

A trigger is a process that is set off when a specific event occurs. With Informix database servers, you can assign triggers to inserts, updates, and deletes on specific tables and columns. The action performed by the trigger can also be one or more insert, update, and delete statements. Triggers can also start stored procedures, which is the reason triggers and stored procedures are usually presented together.

Because triggers occur when an action is performed on columns and tables, there is no way to circumvent it. If a trigger is designed to activate when a delete occurs on the customer table, it occurs no matter what, even if the permissions are different for the users accessing the table. Whether a DBA deletes a customer or a standard user does the delete, a trigger occurs. Triggers also don't care what type of client application is used. Whether the delete was performed through DBaccess or a C program, the trigger occurs. Because triggers are consistent to their tasks, setting them up to enforce rules and perform audit tracking is a great benefit.

A business rule is considered a rule used to match the needs of the business and how the business handles its activities. An example of a business rule is to not let an account's ATM card withdraw money if the ATM card is reported stolen. Another example is that a customer's request to stop service alerts a salesperson to contact the customer and keep him from switching services.

An audit trail is used to track specific data changes in some reports. You can use an audit trail to track how many new customers are added per day. Another audit trail can track how many customers are lost each day.

You can also use triggers to perform data manipulations and authorizations. During data manipulations, you can record an automatic copy of the data before the data is changed or deleted. You can do this in cases when data changes might need to be backed out, such as when a customer places an order and then calls back an hour later to change part of it. Some data manipulations can cause other data to be changed or new data to be created. For instance, when a payment is received, the posting of that payment can trigger the balance to be updated by subtracting the payment from the balance to create a current balance. Security authorizations can be done prior to data changes by a trigger that verifies that user has the permission to do a specific task. For example, regular sales agents might not be able to provide a customer a discount, but a sales manager can. You can set up a trigger to determine whether the client process is done by a sales agent or manager.

Triggers provide a simple way of placing these needs into an automated system with little impact on the client or the server.

Creating and Storing Triggers

You use the SQL statement `CREATE TRIGGER` to place information on what is performed when an action occurs.

The `CREATE TRIGGER` statement has three main parts: the trigger name, the triggering action definition, and the action to perform.

The Trigger Name

The trigger name can be any combination of characters, no longer than 18 characters. The trigger name is used to reference that trigger after it is created. The trigger name should follow directly after the `CREATE TRIGGER` keywords, like this:

```
CREATE TRIGGER test1 ...
```

The Triggering Action Definition

The three types of action definitions are `INSERT ON`, `DELETE ON`, and `UPDATE ON`.

The `INSERT ON` keyword, combined with a table name, designates that the table makes a trigger occur whenever an insert is performed on the table:

```
CREATE TRIGGER test1 INSERT ON customer_table ...
```

The `DELETE ON` keyword, combined with a table name, works just like the `INSERT ON`. Whenever a delete occurs on the table, a trigger is performed:

```
CREATE TRIGGER test1 DELETE ON customer_table ...
```

You can place a trigger with an update for the entire table or on a specific column contained in the table. This way, you can assign different triggers to different data changes.

To place a trigger to handle an update for an entire table, use the `UPDATE ON` keyword:

```
CREATE TRIGGER test1 UPDATE ON customer_table ...
```

To place a trigger to handle an update to a specific data column, use the `UPDATE OF` keyword with the column name, followed by the `ON` and table name:

```
CREATE TRIGGER test1 UPDATE OF balance_due ON customer_table ...
```


The Action to Perform

After you define the action to trigger on, you must set up the action to be performed. You also define the time that the trigger is performed. The three keywords used to indicate when an action is performed are `AFTER`, `BEFORE`, and `FOR EACH ROW`.

The `AFTER` keyword makes sure that the action to be performed is done after the triggering event completes. For example, when a trigger is set up for a delete and `AFTER` is used, the delete completes before the action is performed. `AFTER` is good to build triggers for audit functions. After a data item is changed, the trigger can log information on what and when it was changed.

The following example uses the `AFTER` keyword:

```
CREATE TRIGGER test1 INSERT ON customer_table AFTER ...
```

The BEFORE keyword makes sure that the action to be performed is done before the triggering event starts. For example, when a trigger is set up to kick off for a delete and BEFORE is used, the delete must wait until the trigger action completes. BEFORE is useful for setting up triggers to verify or copy data before something is done.

The following example uses the BEFORE keyword:

```
CREATE TRIGGER test1 INSERT ON customer_table BEFORE ...
```

The FOR EACH ROW keyword is used to make sure that the trigger action is performed for every row affected by the triggering event. For example, a trigger is set to occur when a delete occurs from a table. When a delete is performed on the table, the trigger is started. On multirow deletes, such as DELETE FROM customers WHERE balance=0, all the customers with no balance are deleted. Without FOR EACH ROW, only one triggered event occurs. With it, a trigger occurs for each row deleted:

```
CREATE TRIGGER test1 INSERT ON customer_table FOR EACH ROW ...
```

Combinations of BEFORE, AFTER, and FOR EACH ROW are allowed in a specific order. Combinations are useful for situations when one action must perform before the data change and a different action is needed after. BEFORE must precede any other keywords in the syntax, and AFTER must come last.

TIP

BEFORE and AFTER keywords perform a trigger action only once per table access. In cases where multiple changes occur from one triggering event, only one trigger action is performed. Use FOR EACH ROW to trigger an action for every change in an event.

The following list outlines allowable combinations and the order they must follow:

```
BEFORE action
AFTER action
FOR EACH ROW action
BEFORE action FOR EACH ROW action
AFTER action FOR EACH ROW action
BEFORE action AFTER action
BEFORE action FOR EACH ROW action AFTER action
```

When you use the FOR EACH ROW keyword, you can save any data value being changed, inserted, or deleted by the SQL statement that is causing the trigger. Therefore, when the trigger performs its actions, it will have a copy of the original data value to work with. For example, when deleting rows from the customer table where the balance is zero, you can save the entire row for the trigger to use, even though the row was deleted. This situation might occur when deleting customers to kick off a trigger for each row deleted. The trigger's action might be to place the customer ID in a report, or the trigger might check to see whether the customer purchases a lot but keeps a zero balance.

Three keyword statements are used to hold data to be used in the trigger action: `REFERENCING NEW AS`, `REFERENCING OLD AS`, and `REFERENCING OLD AS NEW AS`. All three are required with the `FOR EACH ROW` keyword, but the `FOR EACH ROW` keyword does not require any of the three hold data keywords when no data is needed for the trigger to perform its action.

The name specified to hold the data in the `REFERENCING` statements is a pointer to the entire row of data. With an insert, the specified variable contains all the data of the row in the exact layout as it was stored in the database. With delete, the entire row is available through the specified variable. With updates, just the data being changed is available.

For inserts, `REFERENCING NEW AS` allows a variable to hold the information being inserted into the new row.

In the first example, the customer table has a row layout of `customer_id`, `phone`, and `balance`:

```
CREATE TRIGGER test1
INSERT ON customer_table
REFERENCING NEW AS original
FOR EACH ROW ...
```

To reference each data item being inserted, use the referenced name separated by a period and then the column name:

```
original.customer_id
```

For deletes, `REFERENCING OLD AS` allows a variable to hold the information being deleted from the table.

In the next example, the customer table has a row layout of `customer_id`, `phone`, and `balance`:

```
CREATE TRIGGER test1
DELETE ON customer_table
REFERENCING OLD AS original
FOR EACH ROW ...
```

To reference each data item being deleted, use the referenced name separated by a period and then the column name:

```
original.customer_id
```

For updates, `REFERENCING OLD AS NEW AS` allows two variables to hold how the row looks before and after the information is changed in the row.

In this example, the customer table has a row layout of

```
customer_id, phone, balance.
```

The update statement causing the trigger is

```
UPDATE customer SET balance=0 WHERE balance < 10.
CREATE TRIGGER test1
UPDATE OF balance ON customer_table
REFERENCING OLD AS original NEW AS newversion
FOR EACH ROW ...
```

To reference each data item being inserted, use the referenced name separated by a period and then the column name:

```
original.customer_id
newversion.customer_id
original.balance
newversion.balance
```

You can perform a conditional test to further qualify whether a trigger action should be performed. You can use the `WHEN` keyword with a condition to evaluate whether a trigger should be performed. Execution of the trigger action occurs when a true evaluation results; the trigger action is not performed with a false result. The conditions used within the `WHEN` are the same ones used for the `IF` statement of SPL:

```
CREATE TRIGGER test1
UPDATE OF balance ON customer_table
REFERENCING OLD AS original NEW AS newversion
FOR EACH ROW WHEN (original.balance=0)
```

After the trigger is named, the causing event is defined, the time the action should be performed is specified, any necessary data is saved, and any special qualifications are met, then you can determine the action to be performed. A trigger can perform `INSERT`, `DELETE`, `UPDATE`, and `EXECUTE PROCEDURE`. You can put any combination of these tasks in the action area:

```
CREATE TRIGGER test1
DELETE ON customer_table
REFERENCING OLD AS original
FOR EACH ROW WHEN (original.balance>0)
(INSERT INTO notpaid
    VALUES(original.customer_id, original.balance));
CREATE TRIGGER test1
UPDATE OF balance ON customer_table
REFERENCING OLD AS original NEW AS newversion
BEFORE WHEN (original.balance=0)
    (EXECUTE PROCEDURE track_balance (original.balance))
AFTER (EXECUTE PROCEDURE adust_worth (newversion.balance));
```

When the trigger is created, its information is stored in two system tables. The `systrigger` table shown in Figure 14.5 contains the information on the owner, type of trigger, and the data or table that starts the trigger. The `systrigbody` table shown in Figure 14.6 contains the information on what actions to take when the trigger occurs.

FIGURE 14.5.
The column layout of the `systrigger` *system table.*

Column Name	Type	Description
trigid	serial number	Trigger identifier
trigname	18 characters	Trigger name
owner	8 characters	Trigger owner
tabid	integer	Identifier of triggering table
event	1 character	Triggering event
old	18 characters	Value's name before update
new	18 characters	Value's name after update
mode	1 character	Currently not used

FIGURE 14.6.
The column layout of the `systrigbody` *system table.*

Column Name	Type	Description
trigid	integer	Trigger identifier
datakey	1 character	Identifier
seqno	integer	Sequence number
data	256 characters	Trigger's code (as text)

To query the system tables for information on currently stored triggers, use the following SQL statement:

```
SELECT trigname, data FROM systrigbody, systriggers
    WHERE systrigbody.trigid = systriggers.trigid
    AND (systrigbody.datakey = "D"
         OR systrigbody.datakey = "A")
```

Triggers are retrieved for execution in the same way stored procedures are. The first time a trigger is executed, it is retrieved from the two system tables and optimized. After optimization, the trigger is stored in a shared cache. The popular triggers are maintained in cache throughout the processing day.

To remove a trigger from the database system tables so that it is no longer used, you use the `DROP TRIGGER` SQL statement. This statement totally removes the trigger from the database server, and events that once caused the trigger no longer have that effect:

```
DROP TRIGGER test1
```

WARNING

Dropping tables and columns from the database that invokes triggers also deletes the triggers associated with them.

Triggers Conclusion

Triggers offer a valuable functionality to automatically start processes at the database server rather than at the client. Triggers provide a single point to track and manage data activity and perform specialized tasks, so you don't need to use many different client applications.

Summary

Stored procedures and triggers are two essential features that make a successful database server and also a successful database management system. Not only do stored procedures offer a viable means to reduce processing and network traffic, they also help remove general and repetitive functionality from the different client applications and put them into a central server. Triggers provide the means to automatically process when other events occur in the database. By combining triggers with stored procedures, you can build a library of processes to manage repetitive or special processing, without forcing the client applications to deal with building the logic into their code to handle the special situations.

CHAPTER

Managing Data with Locking

by John McNally

IN THIS CHAPTER

This chapter provides

- A description of what locking is and how it works within Informix database servers
- A description of the two major types of locks: shared and exclusive
- A description of the different levels of locks and how to create and use them
- How to use isolation levels to view data even if it's locked or how to restrict other processes from viewing
- How to use lock modes to wait for a lock to be released from a lock placed by another process
- A description of situations in which you can use locks, isolation levels, and lock modes to create efficient but safe concurrent database servers
- How to use system utilities to track locking

Introduction to Locking

In a multiuser database management system, locking is very important. Locking allows one user to work with a data item without another user changing the data item's value. Locking is necessary for maintaining data integrity while concurrent users access database information. Figure 15.1 shows the scenario in which locking is not present on a multiuser system. The value of a payment is lost when the process (user process 1) crediting the balance finishes before the process (user process 2) that increases the balance is finished. The correct end value of the balance should be $125, but the $50 payment was lost.

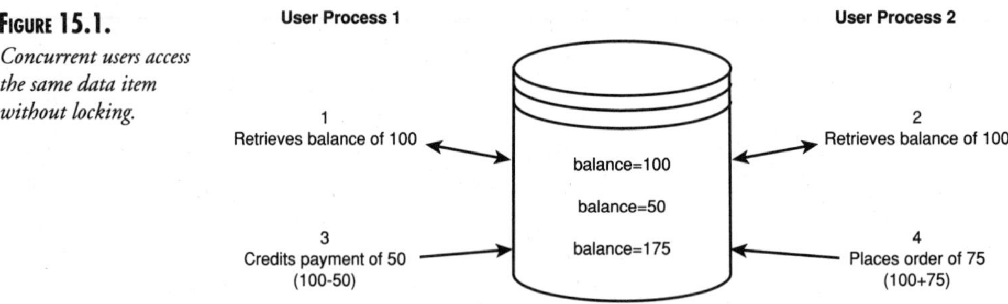

FIGURE 15.1.
Concurrent users access the same data item without locking.

Relational databases should have the capability to use locking to prevent the situation shown in Figure 15.1. All Informix database servers—INFORMIX-SE, INFORMIX-OnLine, and INFORMIX-OnLine Dynamic Server—have locking as a standard feature. Through SQL, you can specify locks on rows of tables and entire databases. Figure 15.2 shows the same scenario used in Figure 15.1 but with locking. Now the second process is unable to access the balance until the first process is complete.

FIGURE 15.2.
Concurrent users access the same data item with locking.

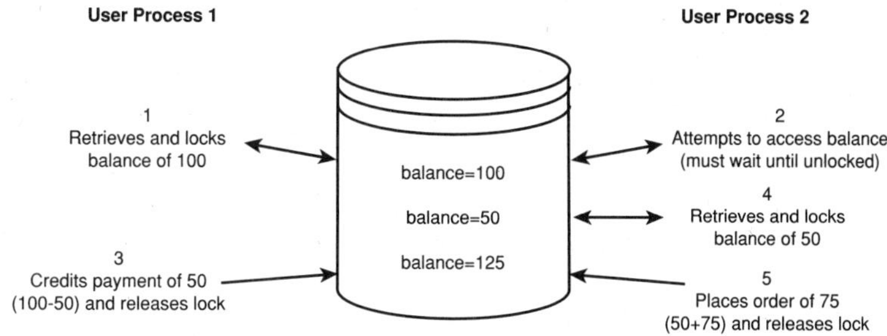

Locks not only maintain data integrity, but they also keep things moving. Without locking, the only other way to prevent the situation shown in Figure 15.1 is to allow one user access to the entire database at a time, which results in a very slow database management system. Every user would have to wait his turn regardless of whether he accessed the same data item. Using different degrees of locking allows users access to the same database, even the same table, without causing one to wait until a lock is freed.

Lock Types

You can place two major types of locks on data items. The first is a shared lock. When a process places a shared lock on a data item, the process declares that it is just viewing the data and it allows others to look, but no other processes can change the data item. Figure 15.3 shows a shared lock in action. Process 1 places the shared lock, which keeps process 3 from changing the value but doesn't stop process 2 from reading the value. Other processes can place shared locks on the same data item already locked by a shared lock. Shared locks are used by processes that are reading data that should not be changed while the process is reading it.

FIGURE 15.3.
Concurrent users access the same data item with a shared lock placed by the first user process.

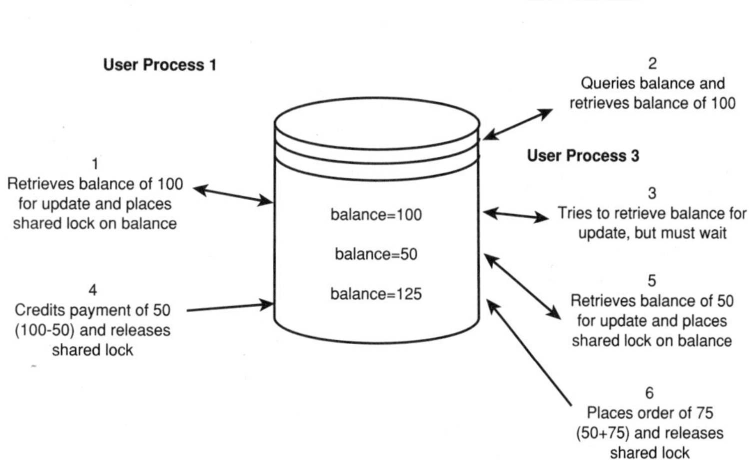

The second lock type is called an exclusive lock. When a process places an exclusive lock on a data item, the process declares that it will probably change that data item. This prevents other processes from slipping in and changing the data item before the first process finishes. This type of lock also warns processes that are "just looking" that they can continue to look, but the data may change. Figure 15.4 shows an exclusive lock preventing other processes from accessing the data. Now process 3 and process 2 must wait until process 1 releases the lock.

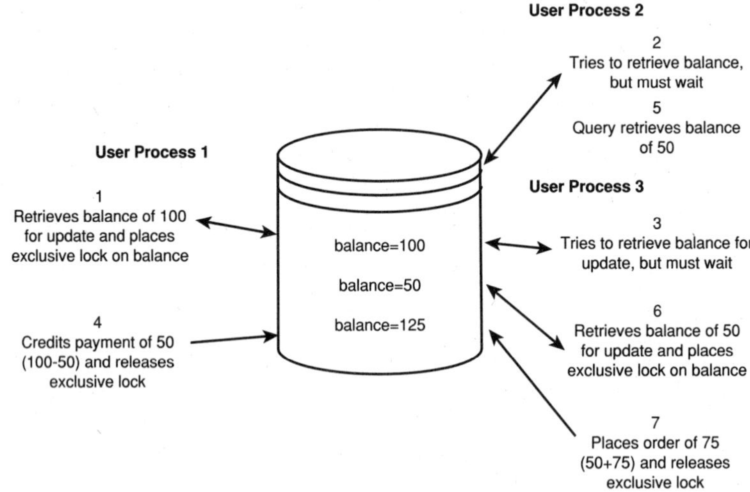

FIGURE 15.4.
Concurrent users access the same data item with an exclusive lock placed by the first user process.

An exclusive lock is used automatically during `DELETE`, `INSERT`, and `UPDATE` processes. You cannot place an exclusive lock on a data item already locked by a shared or another exclusive lock. You cannot place a shared lock on a data item held by an exclusive lock, but `select` type processes can view the data. Table 15.1 shows a grid of when locks can overlap.

Table 15.1. Locking overlap.

	Exclusive	*Shared*
Exclusive	Not allowed	Not allowed
Shared	Not allowed	Allowed

A third type of lock is the promotable lock, which allows processes to lay claim to a data item that is currently under a shared lock. A promotable lock tells Informix that the process placing that lock plans to update the item being locked very soon. A promotable lock can be thought of as a shared lock that automatically becomes exclusive. Until the promotable lock holder is ready to make the update, other processes can place shared locks on that item. When the promotable lock holder is ready to perform the update, the lock is "promoted" to an exclusive lock. All the other processes must have also finished their work and dropped their shared locks before the promotion can occur.

Lock Levels

The four levels on data item locks are page, row, table, and database.

Page

A page is a physical amount of data that Informix works with at one time. When Informix retrieves data from disk to place in shared memory, it gets the entire data page rather than one row or data field. When placing the data back to disk, Informix writes the entire page. Working at the page level makes Informix's reading and writing of data more efficient.

Because pages are what Informix uses to access data, page level locking is the default. Whenever a process updates, inserts, or deletes rows from a table, the entire page where the row resides is locked exclusively. Whenever a process performs a select on data, it places a shared lock on the page or pages where the data resides.

Locking at page level is very efficient for OLTP processing environments because users can access different data items residing on different pages. OLTP transactions are usually short in duration because they change only a specific data item. Page locking is not recommended for batch processes because it uses large transactions that lock many pages, which requires a lot of overhead. Also, long transactions hold locks until all the work is complete, even if it finishes its work on most of the pages.

When a process performs an update, insert, or delete on a page with an index, a lock is also placed on the index page. This prevents one process from changing an index while another process changes the data. The index and data pages must remain in sync.

To create a table that uses page locking, the SQL statement looks like this:

```
CREATE TABLE table_name
    {
    ... data field declarations ...
    )
LOCK MODE PAGE
```

Because page is the default locking level, `LOCK MODE PAGE` is optional. All processes use page locking unless they override to a different locking level or alter the table to use a different level.

To change a table's locking mode, you must alter the default:

```
ALTER TABLE table_name LOCK MODE (PAGE)
```

After they are altered, all processes use the new locking level unless they override to a different locking level or the table is altered again.

A page lock is released when the locking process completes its work, but page locking is used by all processes that access the table.

Row

Locking at the row level is perfect in very heavy OLTP processing systems. When page-level locking is not low enough to handle many concurrent users, row locking is. Like page locking, row locking is specified at table creation and used whenever a process performs activity on data in a table.

An exclusive lock is created whenever a process inserts, deletes, or updates data in a row. A shared lock is created whenever a process performs a select on data residing in a row.

Row locking requires the most overhead of all the lock levels because each row used in a transaction requires a specific lock. For an index, three more locks are necessary—one lock for the accessed row, one for the row before the accessed row, and one for the row after the accessed row. These three locks maintain the accessed row's position in the index. When a table has multiple indexes, add three locks for each index.

If you use row locking in a batch transaction that accesses millions of rows, you might have millions of locks for every row and three times more for each index containing these rows. It isn't a good idea to use row locking in non-OLTP systems.

Row locking is great for very busy OLTP systems. Because only the row is locked, many users can access different data items that reside only a few rows apart without causing either process to wait.

To create a table that uses row locking, the SQL statement looks like this:

```
CREATE TABLE table_name
    (
   ... data field declarations ...
    )
LOCK MODE ROW
```

Because page is the default locking level, the `LOCK MODE ROW` clause is required to achieve row locking. All processes use row locking unless they override to a different level temporarily or the table is altered to page locking.

To change a table's locking mode, you must alter the table:

```
ALTER TABLE table_name LOCK MODE (ROW)
```

A row lock is released when the locking process finishes its work.

Row locking is the only level supported by INFORMIX-SE. For more information on the limitations of SE compared to the rest of the Informix server products, refer to Chapter 5, "INFORMIX-Standard Engine."

Table

Systems that fall between OLTP and batch processing should use table locking. Locking at the table level uses more resources than a database lock and less than a row or page lock. Table locking temporarily overrides row or page locking. Whereas row and page locking are used by all processes, a table lock is used only by the one process that specifies the lock for the duration of the process. It is best to use a table lock when running batch processes against the database. A single process that accesses specific tables works best with table locking. When you lock only those specific tables, your process will run more efficiently and other processes can work in other areas of the database. OLTP should be careful with table locks if most of the processing is performed on the same table. Shared and exclusive locking are also available at the table level.

A shared lock placed on a table allows other users to view the data, but no processes can change the data. To place a shared lock on an entire table, use this syntax:

```
LOCK TABLE table_name IN SHARED MODE
```

An exclusive lock allows a process to change data without letting other processes change the data at the same time. The data is available for viewing, but another shared or exclusive lock is prevented. To place an exclusive lock on an entire table, use this syntax:

```
LOCK TABLE table_name IN EXCLUSIVE MODE
```

To release a lock held on a table, the locking process must use this syntax:

```
UNLOCK TABLE table_name
```

After the lock is released, locking returns to the page or row locking specified in the `create` or `alter` statement.

Database

A database-level lock allows only other user processes to view the data within the entire database. This lock is perfect for batch processing that performs multiple updates, deletes, or inserts. It is not recommended that you use a database lock in OLTP systems where hundreds of users access the database at the same time. There is no shared lock at the database level. A database-level lock is best when running a single, very large database that is performing a lot of activity batch processes. For example, when reloading or refreshing the database, purging the database, or running database-wide reports, you might want to lock the entire database.

To override page or row locking and lock the entire database, use the following SQL statement:

```
DATABASE database_name EXCLUSIVE
```

To release the lock, you must perform a close:

```
CLOSE DATABASE
```

To access a database without locking out other processes and use the created lock level of row or page, drop the exclusive tag:

```
DATABASE database_name
```

Usually, it is better to lock at a lower level—such as table, row, or page—than to lock an entire database.

Isolation Levels

Selecting data from the database usually creates a shared lock. There are different degrees of locks and how locks are handled by `select` statements. These degrees, called *isolation levels*, are what determines the amount of concurrency achieved by processes accessing the data. The four isolation levels used by Informix database servers are dirty read, committed read, cursor stability, and repeatable read.

Dirty Read

A dirty read provides no isolation from locks, which means that all locks are ignored by the `select` statement. Regardless of whether an exclusive or shared lock is placed on an item, a select process can view the data. This is handy for processes that don't care whether the data being viewed is up-to-date. Processes that need the most current data value should not run at the dirty read isolation level because they might get a value that is in the process of changing.

Running at dirty read level also prevents the `select` statement from placing a shared lock on a data item. Another process could put an exclusive lock on the data item while the first process is still working on the data item.

The fastest and most efficient isolation level, dirty read, is perfect for systems that don't care about how up-to-date the data is and do not want updates, inserts, and deletes to wait for a select to finish. For example, a system that is used during the day for mostly read-only activity, where most of the updates and inserts occur at night, would be a good system to set for a dirty read. Database systems without logging automatically have dirty read as their default isolation level.

Committed Read

An isolation level of committed read makes sure that the select returns only values that are committed to the database. All exclusive locks held by other processes cause the select to fail or wait. A select running at the committed read isolation level does not place shared locks on the data it's viewing. Other processes can place exclusive locks on data being used by the select without causing the select to fail.

Databases with logging that are not ANSI-compliant, which is the default Informix database type, keep committed read as their default isolation level.

Cursor Stability

When using cursors to select multiple rows from the database, cursor stability isolation level places a shared lock on the current row to make sure that the current row is not changed by other processes. When the shared lock is placed on the current row, cursor stability prevents other processes from placing an exclusive lock on that row. When the cursor moves to the next row in the select, it releases the shared lock on the previous row.

Repeatable Read

Repeatable read performs similarly to cursor stability, but it places a shared lock on all items selected, whereas cursor stability places the lock on only one row at a time. The lock is held until the entire transaction is complete. For ANSI-compliant databases, repeatable read is the default.

Isolation Level Defaults

As indicated in the previous descriptions, some isolation levels are defaults for specific database types. Table 15.2 shows the different database types and their associated isolation level defaults. The defaults are determined by how a database is created.

Table 15.2. Database type isolation level defaults.

Database Type	*Isolation Level*
No logging and not ANSI-compliant	Dirty Read
Logging and not ANSI-compliant	Committed Read
ANSI-compliant	Repeatable Read

To create a dirty read default database, use this syntax:

```
CREATE DATABASE database_name
```

To create a committed read default database, use this syntax:

```
CREATE DATABASE database_name
    WITH LOG
```

To create a repeatable read default database, use this syntax:

```
CREATE DATABASE database_name
    WITH LOG MODE ANSI
```

Setting Isolation Levels

Sometimes it is necessary to override the default isolation level, such as when you use a cursor with cursor stability or run a single process that doesn't care whether the data is committed so that it can use dirty read to speed up its processing.

To change or initially set the isolation level for an individual process, that process should use any one of these statements:

```
SET ISOLATION TO DIRTY READ SET
SET ISOLATION TO COMMITTED READ
SET ISOLATION TO CURSOR STABILITY
SET ISOLATION TO REPEATABLE READ
```

The isolation level continues to override the default until the process ends or it performs a different `SET ISOLATION` statement. A database that does not use logging can use only dirty read, but a logged database can use any of the four isolation levels.

Lock Modes

Usually when an exclusive lock is placed on a data item, a different process trying to place an exclusive lock on the same data will fail. This also happens when a shared lock is placed on a data item and another process tries to place an exclusive lock on the same data item. Rather than fail, the second process can wait for a specified amount of time or until the lock is released by the first process.

To allow a process to wait for a specified amount of time, the process should declare

```
SET LOCK MODE TO WAIT time_amount_in_seconds
```

To set the wait to 10 seconds, use

```
SET LOCK MODE TO WAIT 10
```

For an entire minute, use

```
SET LOCK MODE TO WAIT 60
```

To let the process wait until the locking process releases its lock, use

```
SET LOCK MODE TO WAIT
```

To return to the default, use

```
SET LOCK MODE TO NOT WAIT
```

The lock mode continues until the process completes or it issues a different `SET LOCK MODE` command.

Locking Efficiency

A lock at a specific level should be determined by the activity and throughput of client processes. High-level locks, such as database and table, use less overhead and provide faster performance for a single process. High-level locks are perfect for batch processing systems or systems where few users concurrently update the same data within a database. Lower-level locks, such as page and row, require more overhead to manage the locks, but they also allow concurrent users to access the same data without much wait.

You should also use isolation levels with throughput in mind. Repeatable read creates a lot of shared locks, especially when the lock level is set to page and the select spans thousands of pages. It might be better to use committed or dirty read levels for all select processes and use repeatable read when it's absolutely necessary.

It's also wise not to use a lock mode of wait but use wait with a time limit that recycles the request a few times when the time limit expires. This prevents a deadlock situation. Informix checks each lock request to see whether it creates a deadlock, and it fails the request when a deadlock situation may occur no matter what lock mode is set. Sometimes Informix is unable to determine whether a deadlock will occur. When you use wait with a time limit, a deadlock will not happen for very long.

The reason for this minimum overhead, maximum throughput discussion is a direct result of how Informix tracks each lock.

Lock Tracking

A configuration parameter called `LOCKS` determines the maximum number of locks that can be held by a process at one time. INFORMIX-OnLine has a limit of 256,000 locks per user process. INFORMIX-OnLine Dynamic Server allows up to 8,000,000. Both servers default to 2,000 locks per user process. When a process exceeds the lock limit set in the configuration file, Informix fails the process and rolls back the changes. This can cause the entire system to slow down because the entire system is consumed by tracking all the locks—44 bytes of shared memory per lock, which is 44MB for 1,000,000 locks. When the lock limit is exceeded, the system must concentrate on rolling back all the data. Procedures must determine a safe number of locks to set without using all the shared memory.

The database administrator should monitor locks to determine how many locks to allow and what type of locking to use.

Use `onstat -p` (`tbstat -p` for versions earlier than OnLine Dynamic Server) to display profile counts, as shown in Figure 15.5. The column labeled `lokwaits` displays the number of times that processes had to wait for locks to be released since the online started. If this number is high, over a hundred per one online day, you might want to adjust to a different locking type. Use page locking rather than table or row locking.

FIGURE 15.5.
Output of the `onstat -p` *command.*

```
RSAM Version 7.10.UC2  -- On-Line -- Up 4 days 11:33:10 -- 9840 Kbytes

Profile
dskreads pagreads bufreads %cached dskwrits pagwrits bufwrits %cached
3212     56794    18463    82.60   1154     2535     3596     67.91

isamtot open  start read  write rewrite delete commit rollbk
10107   1958  1467  4024  0     0       14     44     0

ovtbls ovlock ovuserthread ovbuff usercpu syscpu numckpts flushes
0      0      0            0      124.31  329.79 11       2584

bufwaits lokwaits lockreqs deadlks dltouts ckpwaits compress seqscans
59       0        23646    0       0       6        15       258

ixda-RA idx-RA da-RA RA-pgsused lchreqs lchwaits
99      0      40    139        2699715 483
```

There are also labels for deadlocks prevented (`deadlks`) and deadlock time-outs that were not prevented (`dltouts`). If either of these numbers is high, 10 or more per day, it might be wise to change the way processes wait for locks and use dirty read isolation levels when possible.

To view a list of current locks, use the `onstat -k` command. This can be a very large list, so you can pipe the output to the UNIX command `more` or into a file. As shown in Figure 15.6, the output contains information on every lock held by all users on the system.

FIGURE 15.6.
Output of the `onstat -k` *command.*

```
RSAM Version 7.10.UC2  -- On-Line -- Up 4 days 15:50:29 -- 9840 Kbytes

Locks
address  wtlist owner    lklist type  tblsnum rowid key#/bsiz
c11fd3c8 0      c11bf1d8 0      HDR+S 100002  109   0
 1 active, 6000 total, 512 hash buckets
```

Information contained in the output is labeled as in the following table:

`address`	The address of the lock in the lock table.
`wtlist`	The address of any user threads that are waiting for this lock to become free. Use the `onstat -u` to match this address to an actual user.
`owner`	The address of the thread that is holding the lock. Use the `onstat -u` to match this address to an actual user.

`lklist`	The address of the next lock held by the same owner. It should be listed in the same output.
`type`	The type of lock held:
	`S` for shared.
	`X` for exclusive.
	`IX` for intent exclusive (exclusive in progress).
	`IS` for intent shared (shared in progress).
`tblsnum`	The hex number representing a specific table. Do a query on `systable` to see the actual table name.
`rowid`	Contains the level of the lock:
	`0` for a table lock.
	Ends in `00` for a page lock.
	Six digits or less not ending in `0` for a row lock; the value represents the actual row address.
	Larger than six digits for a lock on the index related to a specific row.
`key#/bsiz`	The index key address or the number of bytes for a `VARCHAR` data type that is locked.

At the very bottom of the list is a number of active locks on the system and a number of total locks since the online started. If the active number is close to the `LOCK` parameter, it is wise to increase the `LOCK` value or check to see whether some of the processes are using a lower level of locking than they should. When a batch process that updates every row of a thousand-row table uses row-level locking, you should change it to use a table-level lock instead to reduce the number of locks from 1000 to 1.

To periodically check the total number of active locks, use

```
onstat -k ¦ grep active
```

This shows only the list of all the locks currently held.

Summary

Locking is a necessary evil of database management. Done correctly, locking can protect the database and keep the data integrity intact while allowing the maximum amount of concurrent accesses. Informix provides many different locking schemes to run an efficient batch, OLTP, or batch/OLTP-combination database system.

It is also important to monitor locking and locks during the online day. Not only does under- or over-locking cause efficiency problems with the server, but it causes processes to display errors and roll back their changes.

CHAPTER

Privileges and Security Issues

by John McNally

IN THIS CHAPTER

This chapter provides

- A description of privileges and security issues that affect database management
- How to set and revoke privileges at the database, table, and column levels
- How stored procedures and triggers can aid in enforcing and tracking security
- How to use views to force specific users to access distinct subsets of the data contained within tables and columns
- How you can use operating system procedures to prevent unauthorized users from accessing the database data areas and client applications

Introduction to Privileges

The data stored within the database is very important to running a business. Not only should the data be protected from loss with backups and logging, but it should also be protected from overzealous and unscrupulous users by enforcing security access through privileges. A company shouldn't maintain a totally separate database system of employee information that is only accessible to payroll personnel. The payroll data should reside on the same system where the ordering database resides. You should not need two machines and two database server software packages. Even though two separate databases are managed by one server, access to each database or even specific tables or data fields should be restricted to certain users.

You can protect data and provide security with four different features:

- Privileges that restrict or authorize access to databases, tables, and data items
- Stored procedures and triggers that can watch and audit processes as they access the data
- Views to limit what specific processes see as the database
- Operating system protection to restrict or authorize access to database-related programs and tools

Privileges

Three levels of data-related security keep database users (users who must have some type of access to data in the database) from accessing specific data items. These levels are database, table, and column.

Database-Level Privileges

All users must have access to a database to use data within a server. The three database-level privileges are connect, resource, and DBA. Table 16.1 shows the different authority levels associated with each privilege.

Table 16.1. Database-level privileges.

Privileges	*Connect*	*Resource*	*DBA*
Select, insert, update, delete, use temporary tables, and use views.	Yes	Yes	Yes
Create, alter, drop, and index own tables.	No	Yes	Yes
Grant, revoke, drop other owned tables, and start and stop server.	No	No	Yes

Connect

The minimum database-level privilege is the connect level. Users with connect can perform select, insert, update, and delete statements, run stored procedures against tables, create views on tables, and create temporary tables with or without indexes.

Resource

Users with resource privileges have all the privileges of connect users. They also have the added ability to create, alter, and drop their own tables and place indexes on these tables.

DBA

The creator and owner of a database is automatically given DBA privileges. A DBA has the same privileges as the connect and resource users with added abilities. The added abilities include granting and revoking connect, resource, and DBA privileges to and from other users, and dropping and altering other users' tables and views. Users with DBA privilege can also drop, start, stop, and recover the database.

Granting and Revoking Database-Level Privileges

The user who creates the database is automatically given DBA privileges, which is the only level that can perform grants and revokes. The first DBA can create other DBAs with a `grant` statement in SQL. A grant gives authority to specific users at whatever level you choose. The DBA can also use a revoke to remove or lower the authority.

Informix has a keyword called `PUBLIC` that represents all users who access the database server. To specify users, use their UNIX IDs. You can specify a list of users by separating each UNIX ID with a comma.

The database to which users get access is the database to which the DBA is connected when running the SQL to perform the grant. If the database server has multiple databases, the DBA must perform a grant for each database to provide access to them all. If the user is allowed access to only one of the available databases, you perform the grant within only that specific database when it is open.

To grant connect privileges, use this syntax:

```
GRANT CONNECT TO PUBLIC;
GRANT CONNECT TO user1;
GRANT CONNECT TO usera,userb,userc;
```

To revoke connect privileges, use this syntax:

```
REVOKE CONNECT FROM PUBLIC;
        REVOKE CONNECT FROM user1;
        REVOKE CONNECT FROM usera,userb,userc;
```

To grant resource privileges, use this syntax:

```
GRANT RESOURCE TO PUBLIC;
GRANT RESOURCE TO user1;
GRANT RESOURCE TO usera,userb,userc;
```

To revoke resource privileges, use this syntax:

```
REVOKE RESOURCE FROM PUBLIC;
        REVOKE RESOURCE FROM user1;
        REVOKE RESOURCE FROM usera,userb,userc;
```

To grant DBA privileges, use this syntax:

```
GRANT DBA TO user1;
GRANT DBA TO usera,userb,userc;
```

To revoke DBA privileges, use this syntax:

```
REVOKE DBA FROM user1;
REVOKE DBA FROM usera,userb,userc;
```

It is not a good idea to grant DBA privileges to `PUBLIC`. Imagine giving hundreds of users the ability to drop the database! When initially granting privileges, remember to grant only connect or resource levels to `PUBLIC`.

Table-Level and Column-Level Privileges

When a user has access to a database, the DBA can limit access to specific tables and columns within tables. The creator of the table or any resource-level or DBA-level user can create tables. That owner or any DBA can grant table-level privileges to other users for that table. A total of eight keywords provide different table-level privileges: insert, delete, select, update, references, index, alter, and all.

Insert

Granting insert privileges allows users to add new data to the table. Revoking that privilege stops users from adding data to the table.

```
GRANT INSERT ON customer_table TO user1;
REVOKE INSERT ON customer_table FROM PUBLIC;
```

Delete

Granting delete privileges allows users to remove data from a table. Revoking that privilege stops users from removing data from the table.

```
GRANT DELETE ON customer_table TO user1;
    REVOKE DELETE ON customer_table FROM PUBLIC;
```

Select

Select privileges can be granted at the table level or at specific column levels. Users can have the ability to query an entire row in the table or just specific fields. In the first example, *user1* can look at any column or any row of the `customer_table`. The second grant only allows `PUBLIC` to query only the `customer_id` and `balance` columns of the `customer_table`. You can revoke privileges in the same way.

```
GRANT SELECT ON customer_table TO user1;
GRANT SELECT (customer_id, balance)
ON customer_table TO PUBLIC;
REVOKE SELECT ON customer_table FROM user3;
REVOKE SELECT (customer_id, balance)
ON customer_table FROM user4;
```

Update

You can grant update privileges at the table level or specific column levels. Users can have the ability to change an entire row in the table or just specific fields. In the first example, *user1* can update any column or any row of the `customer_table`. The second grant allows `PUBLIC` to update only the `customer_id` and `balance` columns of the `customer_table`. You can revoke privileges in the same way.

```
GRANT UPDATE ON customer_table TO user1;
GRANT UPDATE (customer_id, balance)
ON customer_table TO PUBLIC;
REVOKE UPDATE ON customer_table FROM user3;
REVOKE UPDATE (customer_id, balance)
ON customer_table FROM user4;
```

References

You can grant users the ability to force referential constraints on the entire row or specific columns of a table. The user must be a resource database-level user before the references privilege works. Referential constraints perform tasks such as cascading deletes or any other task that relies on how columns relate to other columns.

```
GRANT REFERENCES ON customer_table TO user1;
GRANT REFERENCES (customer_id, balance)
ON customer_table TO PUBLIC;
REVOKE REFERENCES ON customer_table FROM user3;
REVOKE REFERENCES (customer_id, balance)
ON customer_table FROM user4;
```

Index

The index privilege grants users the ability to create and drop indexes related to a table. Users must have the resource privilege in combination with the index privilege. Users with connect cannot create an index, even if they have the index privilege. There is no column-level privilege because indexes are built on all table rows.

```
GRANT INDEX ON customer_table TO user1;
REVOKE INDEX ON customer_table FROM user3;
```

Alter

The alter privilege allows users to change the layout of the columns within the table. Users with alter can add, delete, and change columns and the column data types. Only users with knowledge of the database system and how to protect it should have this privilege. This privilege is almost as high-level as DBA. Alter applies only to the table level.

```
GRANT ALTER ON customer_table TO user1;
REVOKE ALTER ON customer_table FROM user3;
```

All

The keyword `all` provides all table and column privileges to users. Using the `all` keyword grants or revokes any table privileges that the user might have.

```
GRANT ALL ON customer_table TO user1;
REVOKE ALL ON customer_table FROM user2;
```

Combinations

You can grant or revoke different combinations of table and column privileges in one command. Place the privileges in any sequence, separated by a comma, after the `grant` or `revoke` keyword.

```
    GRANT INSERT, DELETE, UPDATE
ON customer_table TO PUBLIC;
    GRANT SELECT, UPDATE (customer_id, balance)
        ON customer_table TO user2;
    REVOKE INDEX, ALTER ON customer_table FROM user1;
```

You can also combine table-level and column-level privileges in one statement. Column-level privileges use the specified columns, and table-level privileges use the specified table.

```
    GRANT INSERT, DELETE, SELECT, UPDATE
(customer_id, balance)
        ON customer_table TO user2;
REVOKE INDEX, SELECT, ALTER (customer_id, balance)
        ON customer_table FROM user3;
```

Other Keywords

You can use two other keywords in conjunction with the GRANT command. The first is the WITH GRANT OPTION keyword. When combined with the GRANT command, the user receiving the privileges can also grant the same privileges to other users.

In the following example, *user1* not only has insert, delete, select and update privileges on customer_table, but he or she can also grant any or all of these privileges to other users.

```
    GRANT INSERT, DELETE, SELECT, UPDATE
ON customer_table TO user1
WITH GRANT OPTION;
```

If *user1* has one or all of the privileges revoked, all the users that *user1* granted privileges to will also have the same privileges revoked.

The other keyword used with grant is the AS keyword. The AS keyword allows you to perform a grant as if another user performs the grant. This sets up the situation described previously; if the grantor is revoked, all the users granted by that user are also revoked.

Continuing with the preceding example, *user1* was given insert, delete, select, and update privileges on customer_table and the right to grant these privileges. A DBA, the owner of the table, or the user that granted *user1* the privileges could then grant as *user1* to other users:

```
    GRANT INSERT, DELETE, SELECT, UPDATE
ON customer_table TO user2, user3, user4, user5
AS user1;
```

Now *user1* through *user5* have the same privileges. To revoke the privileges on all five users, just revoke *user1*:

```
REVOKE ALL ON customer_table FROM user1;
```

Stored Procedures and Triggers

Stored procedures and triggers are two essential functions that make a successful database server and also a successful database management system. Not only do stored procedures offer a viable means to reduce processing and network traffic, but they also help remove general and repetitive functionality from the different client applications.

Stored procedures are considered separate database entities, and because they are separate, users must have the appropriate privileges to create, edit, and execute them. What is nice about stored procedures is that they can have access to specific areas of the database that users are not able to see. However, these same users might have the ability to run the stored procedure, which in turn performs specific functions in restricted areas. Therefore, the stored procedure enables users to go into restricted areas, but does not let them have full access to run wild. For example, a table contains all employees' salary and bonus information. A stored procedure is executed when a user enters information about a sale that earned commission. The stored procedure checks to see whether it's a valid commission, and then adds that amount to the appropriate person's salary. The user has no access to the table that contains the salary information, and if he or she tried to add the commission to the table without using the stored procedure, or perform any other activity on the table, it would fail.

Triggers provide the means to automatically process a task when other events occur in the database, such as specific data access or creation. By combining triggers with stored procedures, you can build a library of processes to manage data security and auditing. Chapter 14, "Managing Data with Stored Procedures and Triggers," describes in detail how to use stored procedures and triggers to manage security.

Views

A view is a logical representation of physical columns from one or multiple tables. A view looks and acts like a table, but it really isn't a physical table that resides on disk. Referred to by Informix as a virtual table, a view is a great way to present specific information to specific users, without placing an entire table's data in the open or keeping multiple versions of the data for different groups of users. Figure 16.1 shows how users view data from single or multiple tables through a view.

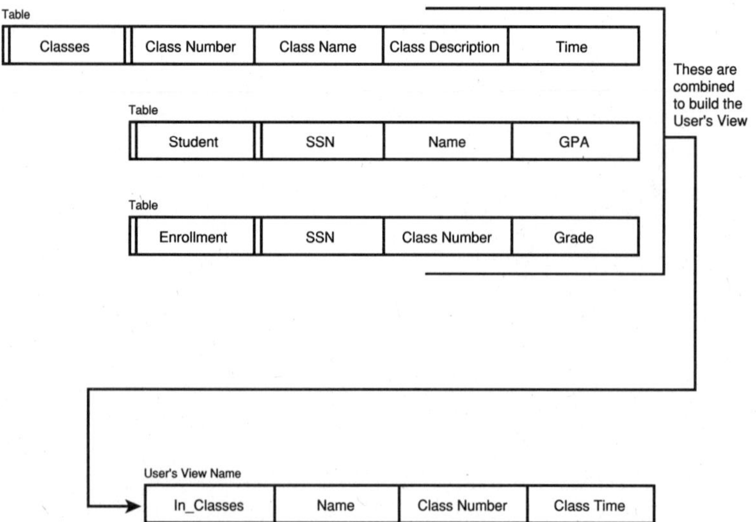

FIGURE 16.1.
A user's view of data compared to the actual database layout.

Views provide a means to restrict certain columns from users. Sometimes tables contain tons of information that is useful to only a small segment of users. Most of the time, only one or two columns are actually accessed. A view can show and allow access to those few columns. This method makes the tables seem less overwhelming to users who don't fully understand all the data columns.

Some data contained in a table may be sensitive to specific users for legal or moral reasons. You can use a view to allow users access to some of the data contained in sensitive tables while restricting access to other columns. For example, an employee table might contain information on each employee's address, phone number, who to notify in case of an emergency, and salary. Obviously, employees should not have access to other employees' salaries, but contact information could be important.

Views can represent derived values as easily as they can show stored column data. Any computations allowed by SQL can be represented in a view with a virtual column. For example, you can create a current balance column in a view to represent the sum of all current orders, subtracting any payments received. Every time the database makes an order or payment, the balance column in the view is updated.

You can represent derived data values within a view. By using the columns from one or more tables, the data placed in a view can be a derived value by using additions, subtraction, or any other mathematical function. For example, you can create a view showing the items, quantity, and value of orders placed by the customer Joe's Pizza, where the value is equal to the quantity multiplied against the price.

Creating a View

To create a view, the user attempting the create must have at least select privileges on all the tables with columns that are represented in the view. The two parts to the view creation statement are view naming and column selection.

A view's name must be a unique name of up to 18 characters. This name is used to access the view after it is created:

```
CREATE VIEW view_name AS
```

To assign columns to a view, use a standard SQL `SELECT` statement. The keywords `ORDER BY` and `UNION` are not allowed within a view's `select` statement, but all other select keywords are allowed.

Data type values are automatically inherited from the original columns to the new view columns. The names of the columns can also be inherited to the view unless specified as something different. When creating a virtual column, you must specify a name for the new column. When a column name is specified, the `CREATE VIEW` statement requires that all column names be specified, regardless of whether the names are different:

```
CREATE VIEW view_name (column list) AS
SELECT columns FROM tables
```

The first example sets up a standard view for the addresses of all employees who are currently employed full-time. No columns are renamed, so no column list is required.

```
CREATE VIEW empl_address    AS
    SELECT name, street, city, zip
    FROM employee_info
    WHERE current = Y AND
         work_status = F
```

The next create sets up a view for all customers' ordering and payment activity. A virtual column is also created. You must list all columns because the virtual column needs a name. This view also joins two tables to retrieve the information:

```
CREATE VIEW customer_bal
(cust_id, last_order, last_payment, current_balance) AS
    SELECT cust_id, total_order, total_payment,
  total_order - total_payment
    FROM order_table, payment_table
    WHERE order_table.cust_id = payment_table.cust_id
```

You can use other views' columns to build other views. The next create example determines the total outstanding balance owed to the company from the `customer_view` view. You can also use aggregate SQL commands to create virtual columns. Aggregate commands include `SUM`, `MIN`, `MAX`, `AVG`, and `COUNT`. The `SUM` command is used to add all the balances together:

```
CREATE VIEW total_balance (balance) AS
    SELECT SUM(current_balance)
    FROM customer_view
```

The next create example sets up a view on all the column data related to specific rows. All sales made by salesperson 12, Joe, are listed in the view:

```
CREATE VIEW joes_sales AS
    SELECT *
    FROM sales
    WHERE sales_person = 12
```

Accessing and Using Views

The creator of a view is considered the owner; owners and DBA-level users can grant and revoke access to the view to other users. You can restrict access to an entire table but give users access to the table's data through a view. This forces the users to use the view to access the data.

To restrict standard users from accessing the entire employee table but still allow them to access their addresses, you use the following example:

```
REVOKE ALL ON employee_info;
CREATE VIEW empl_address    AS
    SELECT name, street, city, zip
    FROM employee_info;
GRANT SELECT, UPDATE ON empl_address TO PUBLIC;
```

Working with a view is just like accessing a table. Use the view name instead of the table name in all SQL commands. Some restrictions related to views are not found with individual tables. First, no indexes can be created on a view. Any table-related indexes are used when accessing the indexed data through a view. Any columns or tables used in a view must be present. If a table or view is dropped, any views that use the table or column are also dropped. Views that contain joins or aggregates can be accessed only with SELECT statements because a join or aggregate view takes different data items from different places and makes it look like it's all from one place. Informix cannot determine how a change to data in a view relates back to the original tables. Almost the same situation applies to virtual columns; because virtual columns are derived from multiple data sources, it is impossible to insert or update that value in a view. It is possible to delete the row from a view that contains a virtual column because Informix can trace back to the original column and keys.

Check Option

As mentioned in the previous discussion on creating views, you can create a view with information related to a specific data value or row. As in the joes_sales example, a view can contain a subset of a table or table's data.

The joes_sales example showed the following code:

```
CREATE VIEW joes_sales
(sales_person, customer, sub_length, price) AS
    SELECT *
    FROM sales
    WHERE sales_person = 12;
```

If this view is available for Joe to use, he might want to insert his new sales directly through this view rather than use the entire sales table. If Joe sells newspaper subscriptions and he makes a sale of a one month subscription to Mary Jones at $9.99, this information is placed in the sales table through the joes_sales view:

```
INSERT INTO joes_sales
    VALUES (12, "Mary Jones", 1, 9.99);
```

If Joe makes a mistake and uses the wrong sales_person number, his sale is credited to someone else:

```
INSERT INTO joes_sales
    VALUES (11, "Mary Jones", 1, 9.99);
```

Although he uses joes_sales, the insert for sales_person 11, Jake, succeeds back to the sales table. Joe can check his view:

```
SELECT * FROM joes_sales;
```

The entry for 11 does not show up because the view is limited to sales_person 12. Jake can see the entry if he has his own view:

```
SELECT * FROM jakes_sales;
```

Users with direct access to the sales table can also see the entry:

```
SELECT * FROM sales;
```

To prevent this problem, use the keyword WITH CHECK OPTION when creating the view. The WITH CHECK OPTION allows inserts, updates, and deletes to occur only when they meet the view select criteria:

```
CREATE VIEW joes_sales
(sales_person, customer, sub_length, price) AS
    SELECT *
    FROM sales
    WHERE sales_person = 12
WITH CHECK OPTION;
```

When Joe tries to insert his sales with the wrong sales_person number, he receives an error message.

Dropping a View

An owner of the view or a DBA can drop an existing view. When you drop a view, you do not lose the data, columns, and tables; only the view to that data is gone. The data still resides in the underlying tables and columns of the database. On the other hand, if the actual tables and columns are dropped, any views that use those tables and columns are automatically dropped. In views such as joes_sales, if Joe has no sales in the sales table, the view continues to exist, but it contains zero rows.

To drop a view, use the DROP VIEW command:

```
DROP VIEW view_name;
```

The following example uses DROP VIEW:

```
DROP VIEW joes_sales;
```

Changing a View

You cannot use an ALTER to change the layout of a view. If you need to change a view layout, you must drop and re-create the view with the new layout.

To verify the current view layouts, use the sysviews and sysdepends system tables. The sysviews system table contains the actual CREATE VIEW statement originally entered.

To see all the views currently in the database server, use

```
SELECT * FROM sysviews;
```

The sysdepends system table contains information on each view and the tables or other views that provide the data that makes up the original view.

To see all the dependencies each view contains, use

```
SELECT * FROM sysdepends;
```

When a view is dropped, its information no longer resides in the `sysviews` or `sysdepends` tables. It is a good idea to save a copy of the preceding queries as a backup listing of all the views to use as a reference when creating or re-creating a view.

Operating System

As mentioned in Chapter 4, "Informix Environment Introduction," the Informix database servers run on a multitude of UNIX-based systems and a few Windows NT environments. Using the operation system's security and permission is another level of allowing some users access to the database while preventing others. The following list outlines various ways to use the operating system to limit database access:

- The logon can prevent unauthorized users from accessing the entire system.
- You can limit specific groups of users with the right to execute client software to access the database.
- Build client applications that also require specific logon security.
- You can set directory permission to prevent unauthorized users from accessing the actual files and data on disk that make up the database server.
- Create backups often and use mirrors just in case a user accidentally crashes the machine, which can corrupt the database.

Summary

Security is an important issue with database creators, owners, providers, and users. Not only does security provide a means of keeping the data safe and intact from loss, but it also goes another level by keeping the content of the data safe and secure from misuse or abuse.

You can achieve both levels of database security by using `GRANT` and `REVOKE` statements to set privileges at the database, table, and column levels. Setting different types of users also separates users responsible for managing the database, DBAs, and normal users.

You can use stored procedures and triggers to audit how and when data is used or changed and also restrict access to data. You can set up a stored procedure to perform a task on data, and only privileged users can access that stored procedure to perform the task.

Another way of restricting how users access data is through views. You can use a view to force users to perform tasks on a subset of the actual data, rather than access the entire database.

Finally, you can use the operating system procedures to lock users out of the database and the entire system. Client applications should build in specific logon processes to allow only privileged users into the database server.

CHAPTER 17

Managing Data Integrity with Constraints

by John McNally

IN THIS CHAPTER

This chapter provides descriptions of

- Data integrity and constraints
- How to create and use semantic integrity constraints such as data type, default value, and column-level and table-level check constraints
- How to create and use entity integrity coinsurance
- How to create and use referential integrity constraints to enforce parent-child data relationships
- How to change the way Informix checks constraints before, during, or after a database task occurs by using constraint modes

Introduction to Data Integrity and Constraints

Previous chapters discussed how to keep users from accessing specific data items and how to protect the data from harm or loss. What helps make sure the data is correct and accurate? For example, is there a way to ensure that a field holding a person's gender is populated with only M for male or F for female? Can a database automatically verify that an item is in stock before an order is placed for that item?

These questions all deal with the data's integrity, or whether the data stored in the database is complete and sound. Data integrity constraints help keep the data sound and complete. Integrity constraint functionality is built into all Informix database servers to handle these situations.

Data integrity constraints can prevent data from becoming incorrect but cannot guarantee its accuracy. There is still plenty of room for human error. Integrity constraints can prevent a gender data item from straying beyond M or F or verify that items are in stock, but they cannot prevent a person from accidentally entering F for a male or M for a female, or miscounting the stock during inventory.

Referred to as *business rules,* integrity constraints help keep the data in line with how its values relate to the real world. Whereas security can prevent actions for specific users during insert, update, delete, and select operations, integrity constraints look at the data that is updated, inserted, or deleted—and don't look at the user.

The three types of integrity constraints that can be enforced by all Informix database servers are semantic, entity, and referential. Semantic integrity constraints deal with how a column handles specific data types and the value that is stored in that column. Entity constraints enforce rows within a table to maintain proper primary keys. Referential integrity constraints deal with how rows within tables correspond with other rows within other tables. You should use a combination of all three types of integrity at the server and client applications to make sure the data is correct.

Semantic Integrity

Semantic integrity is the most basic of all integrity constraints. Also known as *domain constraints*, semantic constraints work directly with the data type and its initial value. The three types of semantic constraints used by Informix database servers are data type, default value, and check constraint.

Data Type

A data type is assigned to the column when the table is originally created or altered later. For example, a column labeled `balance` can be created as a small integer, an integer, or possibly a float data type because a balance value is numeric. An insert or update trying to place a character in that column fails due to type mismatch. Informix never allows a value in a column with a different data type. Table 17.1 shows the different data types allowed by Informix and the values limited to each.

Table 17.1. Informix data types.

Data Type	*Data Value*
`BYTE`	Blob data
`CHAR` or `CHARACTER`	Determined size string
`DATE`	Configurable date layouts
`DATETIME`	Configurable date and time layouts
`DEC`, `DECIMAL`, or `NUMERIC`	Numbers configured to a specific precision
`FLOAT` or `DOUBLE PRECISION`	Numbers preset to double-precision
`INT` or `INTEGER`	Whole numbers from –2,147,483,647 to 2,147,483,647
`INTERVAL`	Configurable time span layout
`MONEY`	Configurable currency layout
`NCHAR`	Mixed mode (letters, numbers, and symbols), determined size string
`NVARCHAR`	Mixed mode (letters, numbers, and symbols), varying size string
`REAL` or `SMALLFLOAT`	Single-precision numbers
`SERIAL`	Sequential integers
`SMALLINT`	Whole numbers from –32,767 to 32,767
`TEXT`	Varying size text streams
`VARCHAR` or `CHARACTER VARYING`	Varying size string

Data types are assigned when the table is created. The standard SQL CREATE TABLE statement is used to assign the data types within Informix:

```
CREATE TABLE customer
    (
        customer_name        CHAR(20),
        customer_id          SERIAL,
        street               VARCHAR(30,20),
        city                 CHAR(20),
        state                CHAR(2),
        zip                  CHAR(10),
        last_update          DATE,
        balance              MONEY(5,2),
        total_orders         INT
    );
```

To change a data type, use the SQL ALTER TABLE statement. During an ALTER, Informix copies the data out of the table, changes the data type, attempts to convert the data value, and then places the database back in the table. Make sure that the data type is not going to cause a failure, such as when changing an INT to a CHAR. The data type change must be able to handle the copied back data, such as changing a SMALLFLOAT to a FLOAT or a CHAR to a VARCHAR.

To alter an existing table's columns, use the MODIFY keyword within the ALTER statement. You can change more than one column within parentheses, separated by a comma:

```
ALTER TABLE customer MODIFY
city VARCHAR(20,10);

ALTER TABLE customer MODIFY
(
city VARCHAR(20,10),
total_orders SMALLINT
);
```

You can also use the ALTER statement to add new columns to an existing table. Rather than use MODIFY, use the ADD keyword. You can use the BEFORE keyword to specify where the new columns sit in the row. Not using BEFORE places the new column at the end of the row:

```
ALTER TABLE customer ADD
    phone CHAR (10) BEFORE last_update;

ALTER TABLE customer ADD
(
    area_code CHAR (3),
    line        CHAR (7)
);
```

Default Value

Setting a default value is another semantic constraint. If no data is provided for specific columns during an insert, a predetermined default value is used instead. Data used for the default can be a constant defined by a literal, such as 1 or Y. You can use functions as defaults for special data types, such as today's date for a DATE data type. Table 17.2 shows which data types can have specific literal default values, and Table 17.3 shows which data types can have specific functions as defaults.

Table 17.2. Data type default literals.

Data Type	*Literal*	*Examples*
INT, SMALLINT, DEC, MONEY	Integer	1, 258, 999
FLOAT, SMALLFLOAT, DEC, MONEY	Decimal	1.1, 2.58, .999
FLOAT, SMALLFLOAT, CHAR, NCHAR, NVCHAR, VARCHAR, DATE	Character	"Y", "Joe", "1-1-90"
INTERVAL	Interval	(2 11) DAY TO DAY
DATETIME	Date and time	96-04-19 11:30

Table 17.3. Data type default functions.

Data Type	*Function*	*Purpose*
CHAR, NCHAR, NVARCHAR, VARCHAR	DBSERVERNAME or SITENAME	Provides database server name.
CHAR, VARCHAR	USER	Provides the user ID.
DATE	TODAY	Provides the current calendar date in *mm-dd-yy* format.
DATETIME	CURRENT	Provides the current calendar date and current time in *mm-dd-yy hh:mm:ss* format.

Use the SQL keyword DEFAULT within the CREATE TABLE and ALTER TABLE statements to assign a default value within Informix. The ALTER statement uses the MODIFY keyword, as shown in the previous data type section, to specify the default for existing columns:

```
CREATE TABLE customer
(
    customer_name        CHAR(20) NOT NULL,
    customer_id         SERIAL,
    street             VARCHAR(30,20),
    city                 CHAR(20),
    state             CHAR(2) DEFAULT "VA",
    zip                 CHAR(10),
    last_update         DATE DEFAULT TODAY,
```

```
    balance              MONEY(5,2) DEFAULT 0,
    total_orders          INT DEFAULT 0
);

ALTER TABLE customers MODIFY
(
    city DEFAULT "Sterling",
    zip DEFAULT "20164"
);
INSERT INTO customer (customer_name) VALUES ("Joes Pizza");
```

The previous insert places a row into customer that looks like the following (assuming the current date is 4/19/96):

Column	*Value*
customer_name	Joes Pizza
customer_id	1
street	NULL
city	Sterling
state	VA
zip	20164
last_update	4-19-96
balance	0.00
total_orders	0

When no default is specified and no value is provided, a NULL value is placed in the column. Using the keyword NOT NULL forces a value to be inserted for each column containing the NOT NULL keyword. In the preceding example, customer_name specified NOT NULL, so an insert without a customer_name value would fail. Specifying DEFAULT NULL is allowed even though not specifying any default implies the same thing. A combination of DEFAULT NULL and NOT NULL is not allowed, but any other default and NOT NULL is allowed.

Check Constraints

When data must be within a specific range of values—a subset of a specific data type, such as an integer between 5 and 10 or a character equal to M or F—you can achieve data integrity through value bounding by the check constraint. A check constraint provides the means to specify data items that must fall within predetermined limits. Within Informix, the check constraint is available at the column and table levels. Any row updated or inserted in the table must pass the check constraints before the values are allowed in the columns or rows.

Column-Level Check Constraints

To place a check constraint on a column, use the SQL keyword CHECK with the CREATE TABLE or ALTER TABLE with MODIFY statements. The CHECK keyword must be followed by some form of condition. The condition cannot contain subqueries or functions. The following example uses the CHECK keyword:

```
CREATE TABLE customer
    (
        customer_name     CHAR(20) NOT NULL,
        customer_id     SERIAL,
        street         VARCHAR(30,20),
        city             CHAR(20),
        state          CHAR(2) DEFAULT "VA"
CHECK (state IN ("VA","MD","DC")),
        zip                CHAR(10),
        last_update     DATE DEFAULT TODAY,
        balance          MONEY(5,2) DEFAULT 0
                      CHECK (balance BETWEEN 0 and 999),
        total_orders      INT DEFAULT 0
                      CHECK (total_orders >= 0)
    );
```

Any values inserted or updated within these columns must meet the check criteria. Using a value outside the criteria, such as a State code of "PA", causes an error.

When altering a table to add or change a check constraint, all the data currently in the table must pass the new condition. Data values that do not meet the new constraint cause the alter to fail:

```
ALTER TABLE customer MODIFY
total_orders CHECK (total_orders >= 1);
```

This alter statement is valid as far as formatting, but the original create statement had total_orders default to 0 when no data was entered. Any rows that still exist with a total_orders value of 0 cause the alter to fail.

Table-Level Check Constraints

Placing a check at the table level means that an entire row must pass these checks to be added to the table. With column-level checks, an entire insert for adding a new row fails when a column-level check fails. With individual inserts for each column, only the insert for the failed column-level check does not succeed; the other columns are populated by the other inserts. Table-level constraints allow for an entire row check every time new data is entered into the row.

Table-level checks allow access to all the columns within the row, whereas column-level checks allow access only to the current column. To create a table with a table-level check, use the CHECK keyword on an independent line within the CREATE TABLE statement. Because the CHECK keyword is on its own line, Informix knows that it is not associated with a specific column. The following example uses this technique:

```
CREATE TABLE customer
(
    customer_name    CHAR(20) NOT NULL,
    customer_id    SERIAL,
```

```
    street         VARCHAR(30,20),
    city             CHAR(20),
    state          CHAR(2) DEFAULT "VA"
CHECK (state IN ("VA","MD","DC")),
    zip             CHAR(10),
    last_update     DATE DEFAULT TODAY,
    cur_balance     MONEY(5,2) DEFAULT 0
                CHECK (cur_balance BETWEEN 0 and 999),
prev_balance    MONEY(5,2) DEFAULT 0
                CHECK (prev_balance BETWEEN 0 and 999),
last_payment    MONEY(5,2) DEFAULT 0
                CHECK (last_payment BETWEEN 0 and 999),
    total_orders     INT DEFAULT 0
                CHECK (total_orders >= 0),
    CHECK (prev_balance - last_payment = cur_balance)
);
```

Any time a row is changed or inserted into the customer table, the previous balance minus the last payment must always equal the current balance. All the column-level checks are also checked.

To add a table-level constraint to an existing table, use the ALTER command with the ADD CONSTRAINT keywords rather than MODIFY:

```
ALTER TABLE customer ADD CONSTRAINT
    CHECK (prev_balance - last_payment = cur_balance);
```

Entity Integrity

An *entity* is like a noun in the English language; it is a person, place, or thing. An entity is usually the main column used to reference the other columns in that row. Because this column is important to finding the row, it is considered a primary key. To be a primary key, the data in that column must be unique. In the relational database model, the requirement for having a unique primary key that identifies each row in a table is referred to as the entity integrity constraint. Informix has a built-in process to ensure that every table has rows with unique primary keys.

Informix actually has two ways to ensure that a column used to identify each row is unique. The first way is by using the UNIQUE keyword in a CREATE or ALTER TABLE statement.

A table containing information about advisors for a college uses the individual advisor's Social Security number to uniquely identify each person:

```
CREATE TABLE advisors
(    ssn CHAR (9) UNIQUE,
    name CHAR (20)
);
```

To make the column unique after the table exists, use the ALTER TABLE statement with the MODIFY keyword. Remember that altering a column to be unique will fail if it already contains duplicate data:

```
ALTER TABLE advisors MODIFY
    ssn UNIQUE;
```

The other way to ensure that the main entity is unique is to specify it as the primary key. Primary keys are mainly used to enforce referential integrity, as discussed in the next section. By default, a primary key enforces entity uniqueness because it is a basic requirement of a primary key to be unique. To specify a column as a primary key, use the `PRIMARY KEY` keyword in the `CREATE` or `ALTER TABLE` statement:

```
CREATE TABLE advisors
(     ssn CHAR (9),
    name CHAR (20),
    PRIMARY KEY (ssn)
);
```

The `ALTER TABLE` uses the `ADD CONSTRAINT` keyword with the `PRIMARY KEY` label. When you change a table's primary key from one column to another, the previous primary key's column is labeled `UNIQUE`:

```
ALTER TABLE advisors ADD CONSTRAINT
    PRIMARY KEY (name);
```


When you need multiple columns to make a row unique, the `UNIQUE` keyword does not work. You must use the `PRIMARY KEY` keyword instead. You can combine multiple columns to make the primary key; referred to as a composite key, it's two or more semi-unique columns that become unique when combined. For example, a table containing class information on courses in a college might have a column that identifies the course number of each topic being taught, but some classes are taught on the same topic at different times and days. A primary key is a combination of the course number and the day and time it is taught.

The following example uses a composite key:

```
CREATE TABLE classes
(     course_number INT (5),
    daytaught     CHAR,
    timetaught DATETIME (HOUR),
teacher CHAR (9),
    PRIMARY KEY (course_number, daytaught, timetaught)
);
```

If all classes start at the same time, regardless of the day, then the primary key must contain only a combination of the `course_number` and `daytaught`. Use the `ALTER TABLE` statement with the `ADD CONSTRAINT` keyword to change the primary key. Any existing primary key is dropped automatically:

```
ALTER TABLE classes ADD CONSTRAINT
    PRIMARY KEY (course_number, daytaught);
```

In all three examples—unique, primary key, and multicolumn primary key—any insert or update of an entity that already exists will fail. Not only does an entity integrity constraint provide a database layout that meets relational database model requirements, but it also provides a faster means for indexing. An index built on unique keys provides processing improvement over a non-unique entity table.

Referential Integrity

The integrity used to bind primary and foreign keys together is called *referential integrity.* This binding of the relationship between primary and foreign keys is commonly referred to as the *parent-child relationship,* where the child is a foreign key and the parent is the primary key. Figure 17.1 shows parent and child and their relationship to each other. Throughout this section, you can assume that the term *parent* is synonymous with *primary* and *child* is synonymous with *foreign.*

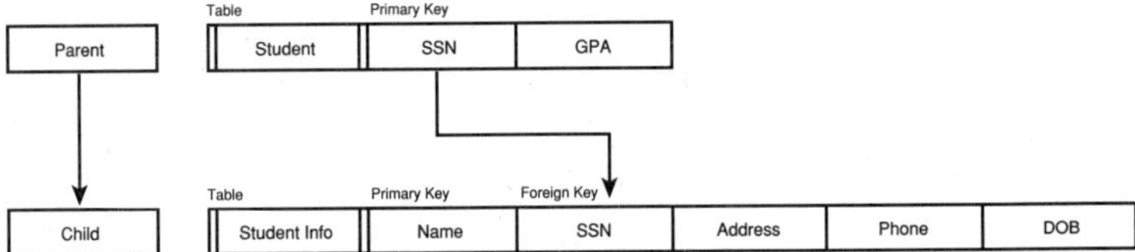

FIGURE 17.1.
Parent and child table relationships.

The primary key is a unique column that represents the entire row in a table. For example, a Social Security number is a unique key, which means that everyone has a different one. A table containing information on students attending a college can use Social Security numbers as the primary key of the table. A primary key is required in the relational database model for every table within a database. To the database user, it's a must because an index is usually built from a primary key. With an index, the user's retrieval rate is dramatically increased over the retrieval rate on the same tables without an index. Without a primary key and an index, you use a sequential search to find the requested row. On large tables, this sequential search can take a long time.

When no single column in the row uniquely identifies that row within a table, you can combine multiple columns to make the primary key. Referred to as a composite key, it's two or more semi-unique columns that become unique when combined. For example, a table containing information on college courses can have a column that identifies the course number of each topic being taught, but some classes teach the same topic at different times and days. A primary key is a combination of the course number and the day and time it is taught.

A foreign key is a column, usually in another table, that matches the primary key of another table. This match can include multiple columns when you have composite primary keys. The relationship between primary and foreign keys is considered a join. An example is a table containing students enrolled in a specific class. This table has its own primary key, a combination of the current semester, a course, a date-time column, and a student's Social Security number. The table can also contain extra information, such as the final grade of that student, but this information is not part of the key.

Figure 17.2 shows the first two sample tables and how their primary keys become foreign keys in the third table example. This join also demonstrates a basic parent-child relationship.

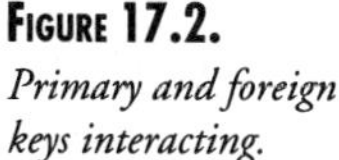

FIGURE 17.2.
Primary and foreign keys interacting.

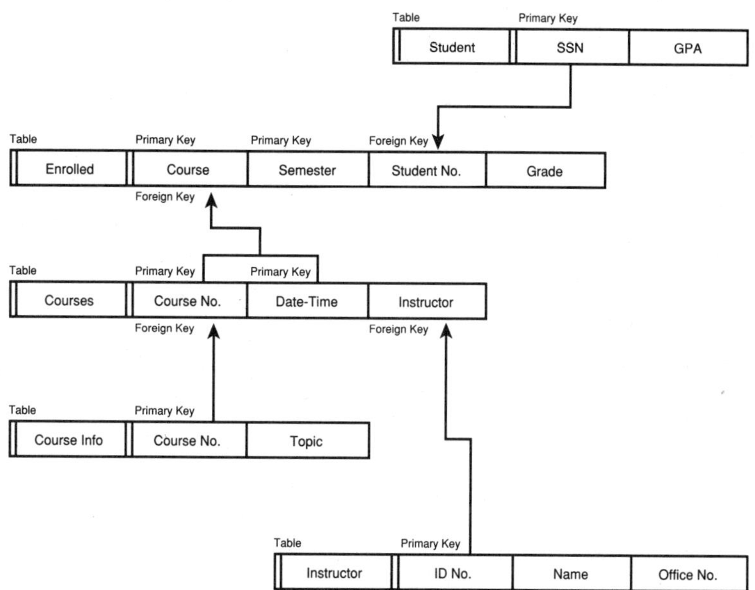

The basic parent-child relationship rule states that every parent must be unique and every child must have a parent. Informix has the capability to enforce this rule and all the situations that arise while trying to maintain it. The following are some of these situations:

Inserts	A primary key must exist when you insert a child. You cannot create a primary key if it already exists.
Updates	Changing a foreign key cannot separate it from an existing primary key, but it can change it to a different primary key. Changing a primary key cannot separate it from its children foreign keys. The children must be moved to a different primary key first.
Deletes	A primary key with children cannot be removed until its children are removed or moved to a different parent.

Even though Informix is set up to enforce parent-child relationships, it must be configured for a specific type of parent-child relationship.

Types of Parent-Child Relationships

Three types of parent-child relationships exist in the relational database model. All three can be represented in Informix databases. Each of these types is different in the way its keys are positioned within the database tables. When the parent and child reside in the same table, it is called *self-referencing*. When parent and child reside in different tables, the relationship is considered *cyclic*. When a cyclic relationship is defined between a parent in one table and children in different tables, it is considered *multiple path*. Figure 17.3 diagrams the three types of relationships between parent and child.

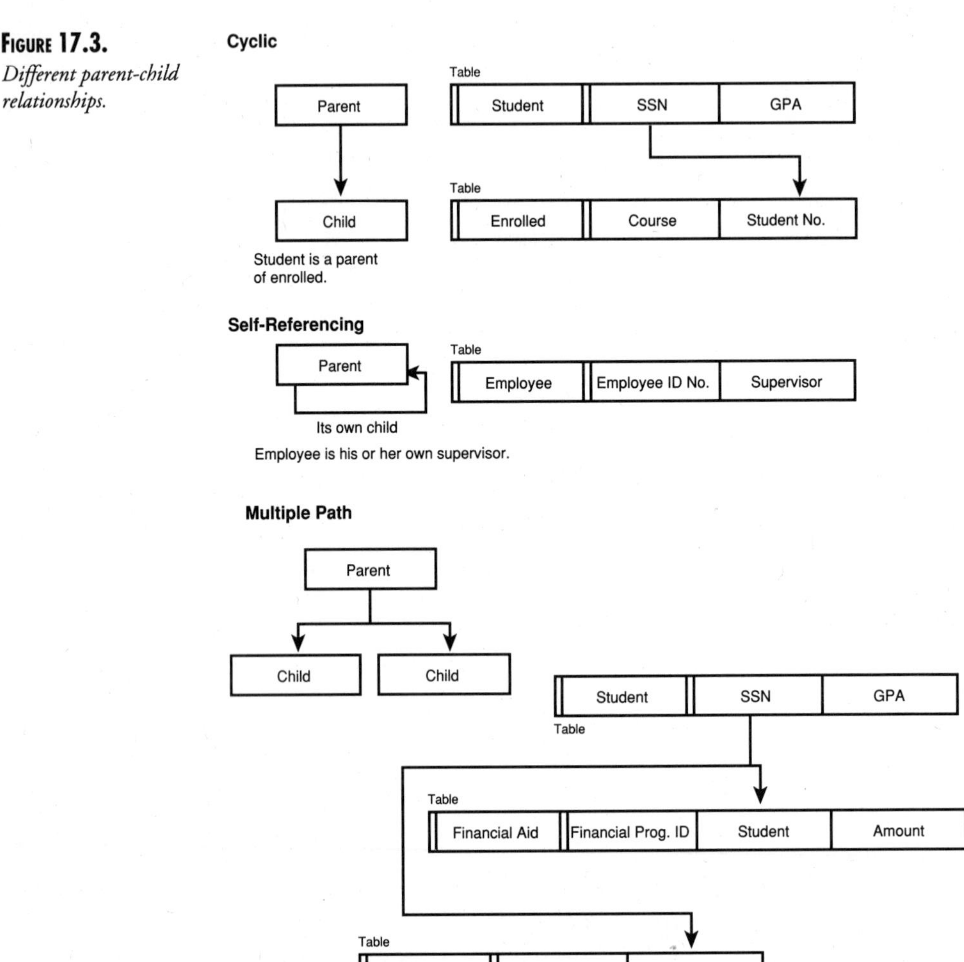

FIGURE 17.3.
Different parent-child relationships.

Informix's Referential Constraints

Informix provides the capability to enforce referential integrity in all three parent-child relationships. Informix applies referential constraints to specific columns to ensure that the update, delete, and insert rules are enforced. Informix uses four pieces within the `CREATE` or `ALTER TABLE` statement, in different combinations, to enforce the different parent-child relationships. These four pieces are the keywords `PRIMARY KEY`, `FOREIGN KEY`, `REFERENCES`, and `CONSTRAINT`.

You must specify a parent or primary key with the `PRIMARY KEY` keyword:

```
CREATE TABLE mutual_funds
(    fund_id     INT,
    fund_name CHAR(12),
```

```
    numofowners INT,
    value    INT,
    PRIMARY KEY (fund_id)
);
```

To produce the same result, the keyword can follow the column definition:

```
CREATE TABLE mutual_funds
(    fund_id    INT PRIMARY KEY,
    fund_name CHAR(12),
    numofowners INT,
    value    INT
)
```

To add or change the primary key of an existing table, use the ALTER TABLE statement with the MODIFY keyword:

```
ALTER TABLE mutual_funds
fund_id PRIMARY KEY;
```

You use the next two keywords to create the child or foreign key. Use the FOREIGN KEY keyword in the CREATE or ALTER statements. Unlike the PRIMARY KEY keyword, the foreign key definition also requires the REFERENCES keyword. The REFERENCES keyword specifies in what table the child's parent resides:

```
CREATE TABLE fund_owners
(    owner_id    INT,
    owner_name CHAR(15),
    fund_id    INT,
numofshares INT,
    FOREIGN KEY (fund_id)
        REFERENCES mutual_funds
);
```

To produce the same result, the keyword can follow the column definition:

```
CREATE TABLE fund_owners
(    owner_id    INT,
    owner_name CHAR(15),
    fund_id    INT FOREIGN KEY
        REFERENCES mutual_funds,
numofshares INT
);
```

To add or change the foreign key of a table, use the ALTER TABLE statement with the MODIFY keyword. Use the FOREIGN KEY and REFERENCES labels as you do in CREATE, but you do not need to reassign the data type INT:

```
ALTER TABLE fund_owners MODIFY
    fund_id FOREIGN KEY
        REFERENCES mutual_funds;
```

The final piece is the CONSTRAINT keyword, which you use to name each piece of the parent-child constraint. It works as an alias for each parent and child.

For example, place a constraint name on the primary key example:

```
CREATE TABLE mutual_funds
(    fund_id     INT PRIMARY KEY
CONSTRAINT pk_fund_id,
    fund_name CHAR(12),
    numofowners INT,
    value     INT
);
```

All interaction with this table's primary key constraint is referred to as `pk_fund_id`. If you attempt to insert a duplicate primary key, Informix refers to `pk_fund_id` in the duplicate key error message.

Place a constraint name on the foreign key example:

```
CREATE TABLE fund_owners
(    owner_id     INT,
    owner_name CHAR(15),
    fund_id     INT,
numofshares INT,
    FOREIGN KEY (fund_id)
        REFERENCES mutual_funds
        CONSTRAINT fk_fund_id
);
```

All interaction with a table's child constraint is referenced by foreign key's constraint name. One example is adding a row with a `fund_id` that does not exist in the `mutual_funds` table. The error specifying that the parent does not exist contains a reference to the constraint name `fk_funk_id`.

You don't need to specify constraint names; Informix creates a default name automatically, but it is rather cryptic. To find the Informix default constraint name, query the `sysconstraints` system table, which contains all constraint names and their tables.

To remove a constraint that is holding a parent-child relationship together, use the `ALTER TABLE` statement with the `DROP CONSTRAINT` keyword. This breaks the ties between tables so that you no longer require a unique parent or a parent for every child. Dropping the primary or foreign key columns gets the same results, except that both columns are physically dropped from each table. It is better to drop the constraint, rather than delete the columns:

```
ALTER TABLE mutual_funds
DROP CONSTRAINT pk_fund_id;
```

After you decide the table's primary and foreign keys, you should decide how they relate to each other in the database layout. Different types of parent-child relationships cause different table layouts.

Self-Referencing Referential Constraints

A parent and its children residing in the same table have a self-referencing parent-child relationship. Informix provides a means to enforce this relationship by using its built-in referential constraints.

For example, you can create a table to track college students and their advisors. Assume that advisors can advise many students and these student advisees can also be advisors to other students. The primary key is `advisor` and the foreign key is `student`, and both keys are the person's Social Security number. This first insert creates a main advisor—probably not a student because he advises himself:

```
CREATE TABLE advising
(    advisee CHAR (9),
advisor CHAR (9),
    PRIMARY KEY (advisee)
        CONSTRAINT pk_advisee,
    FOREIGN KEY (advisor)
        REFERENCES advising (student)
        CONSTRAINT fk_advisee
);
INSERT INTO advising VALUES ('215909999', '215909999');
```

These inserts create a few students who are advised by the main advisor:

```
INSERT INTO advising VALUES ('215908888', '215909999');
INSERT INTO advising VALUES ('215907777', '215909999');
INSERT INTO advising VALUES ('215906666', '215909999');
```

The next insert creates a student who is advised by another student:

```
INSERT INTO advising VALUES ('215905555', '215907777');
```

The next insert fails because the advisor `215904444` does not exist as a student or a main advisor in the table:

```
INSERT INTO advising VALUES ('215903333', '215904444');
```

The sample table enforces that an advisee (student) must have an existing advisor. Even an advisor must be advised by another advisor. Those two rules and all the other insert, update, and delete rules specified are automatically enforced between the parent and its children in the single table.

Cyclic-Referential Constraints

Cyclical parent-child relationships occur when the primary key is in one table and the foreign key is in a different table. Unlike the self-referencing example that required that an advisor have advisors, in the next example all advisors are college staff who do not need advisors. The following code sets up the parent table:

```
CREATE TABLE advisors
(    advisor CHAR (9),
    PRIMARY KEY (advisor)
        CONSTRAINT pk_advisor
);
```

This is the child table:

```
CREATE TABLE advising
(    advisee CHAR (9),
advisor CHAR (9),
```

```
    FOREIGN KEY (advisor)
        REFERENCES advisors (advisor)
        CONSTRAINT fk_advisor
);
```

With this parent-child example, every advisor must be unique in the advisors table and every advisee must have an existing advisor. That rule and all the other insert, update, and delete rules specified are automatically enforced between the parent and its child table. There is no built-in logic, as in the self-referencing example, to require that even advisors have advisors.

Multiple-Path Referential Constraints

When a cyclical relationship occurs between one parent and many different child tables, it is considered to have multiple paths. For example, if the advisors also taught classes, their primary keys are linked to two child tables—the existing advisors table and a new course table.

For this example, change the name of the advisors table to staff. The new parent table looks like this:

```
CREATE TABLE staff
(    staff_member CHAR (9),
    PRIMARY KEY (staff_member)
        CONSTRAINT pk_staff_member
);
```

The advising child is the same but now references the staff table and the `staff_member` primary key:

```
CREATE TABLE advising
(    advisee CHAR (9),
advisor CHAR (9),
    FOREIGN KEY (advisor)
        REFERENCES staff (staff_member)
        CONSTRAINT fk_advisor
);
```

The advising child table is changed to use the new staff parent table. Notice that the foreign key advisor does not have to be named the same as the primary key it relates to because the `REFERENCES` keyword ties them together. The following code shows the new teaching child:

```
CREATE TABLE classes
(    course_number INT (5),
teacher CHAR (9),
    FOREIGN KEY (teacher)
        REFERENCES staff (staff_member)
        CONSTRAINT fk_teacher
);
```

Not only is every student required to have an advisor that exists on staff, but also every course must have a teacher that exists on staff. Those rules and all the other insert, update, and delete rules specified are automatically enforced between the parent and its children.

Constraint Modes

With the three constraints discussed previously, it was implied that the check for these constraints occurred as the task (insert, update, or delete) occurred on the row or column. For semantic constraints, this is true. An incorrect data type fails as soon as you attempt to place an incorrect value in the column. This is also the case for default and check constraints but not for entity and referential constraints. You can indicate when entity and referential constraints should be checked.

Informix can set three time frames to check an entity or referential constraint. These times are referred to as constraint modes, and the three are immediate, deferred, and detached.

The default mode is immediate, which is what was assumed during the constraint descriptions. Immediate mode checks for a failure at the end of each individual task. For an update that impacts 40 rows in a table, immediate checking occurs as each update is completed 40 times.

Deferred mode waits until all the tasks of a statement are complete. Using the same example, deferred mode waits until all 40 updates are complete and the statement is about to commit before the check occurs.

The last mode, detached, checks as the task is occurring. Like immediate, detached checks 40 times, but it doesn't wait for the single task to complete; as soon as a violation occurs, the task stops. Detached mode is possible only when you turn off logging. Logging and detached mode are incompatible because logging must place a copy of every task performed in the transaction log, but detached mode causes a task to stop before it can write a copy in the log.

To change the constraint mode within Informix, use the `SET CONSTRAINTS` statement with the `IMMEDIATE` or `DEFERRED` keywords. You can set every existing constraint to a specific mode by using the `ALL` keyword, or you can set individual constraints or groups of constraints with their names:

```
SET CONSTRAINTS ALL DEFERRED;
SET CONSTRAINTS pk_table1 IMMEDIATE;
SET CONSTRAINTS pk_table1, pk_table2 IMMEDIATE;
```

Constraints are named during the `CREATE` or `ALTER TABLE` statements by the `REFERENCES` keyword. If a constraint is not named, Informix generates a name for it. You can find all constraint names in the `sysconstraints` system table.

To achieve detached mode, use immediate mode without logging. Detached mode is the only mode available to INFORMIX-SE servers. All modes are available in INFORMIX-OnLine and INFORMIX-OnLine Dynamic Server.

Summary

Data integrity is a very important part of any database system. By adding constraints to the database, you keep the data's value clean and correct. Any business rules that associate the data with the real world can be enforced through data integrity constraints.

Semantic constraints are the most basic forms of data constraints. You can use semantic constraints to make sure the data placed in the database meets three levels of standards. The first standard is met with data type constraints. Data type constraints make sure that values going into a column match the data type of the column. The next level enforces that a default value is used when no data is present. This is done with default value constraints. The final semantic constraint level makes sure that data in a column or table falls into a predetermined range. Called check constraints, they perform user or administrator checks on the actual value of the data entered into the database.

Entity constraints enforce the basic rules of the relational database model; every row must be uniquely identified. The column or columns used to uniquely identify a row is referred to as the primary key. You can place entity constraints on tables to make sure that primary keys are unique and present.

Referential constraints enforce the relationship and dependencies held between tables and rows. Known as the parent-child relationship, referential constraints make sure that primary keys (as parents) and foreign keys (as children) are correctly connected.

You can check entity and referential constraints at specified times by using constraint modes. You can set constraint modes to check during or after a specific database task. Constraint modes can also wait until a group of tasks are completed before performing constraint checks. Semantic constraints are restricted to check only during each database task.

With the three types of constraints—semantic, entity, and referential—it is very simple to configure a database system to enforce any data-related rules that arise. With constraint modes, you can also configure when the database should enforce these rules.

CHAPTER 18

Managing Data Backups

by Mario Estrada

IN THIS CHAPTER

This chapter explains how to implement a backup and recovery strategy for Informix Database Servers, which is one of the most important activities in any database environment. The system administrator is in charge of such activity, but the database administrator is still responsible for the data in the Informix Database Server.

Why Make Backups?

Information is a vital component in a company. A hardware failure, a disaster, a human error, or a software error can put your company's operation in jeopardy. This problem can be solved if you are ready with a recovery strategy. Usually, the better strategy is the one that takes less time to bring your company online again. As a guideline, the system administrator should automate the backup procedures and have the more appropriate recovery strategy on hand. Informix has backup and recovery systems as well as utilities to accomplish this guideline. But remember that many third-party products are specialized in enterprise backup management. This chapter emphasizes the tools available in Informix Database Servers only.

Data Availability

For mission-critical applications, the information must be available 24 hours a day. It will be your responsibility as a system administrator to provide this availability, and your goal will be to reduce the downtime required to bring your database system online again.

Data Reliability

You can ensure data reliability by implementing hardware and software that is optimal for the type of operation your company performs. For example, the reliability of jukeboxes is jeopardized when a lot of dust is present in the room where the equipment is stored. Therefore, the environment is a factor that you must be aware of when you are concerned about the reliability of your storage devices, such as jukeboxes.

When your data becomes available after a recovery procedure, you have to corroborate the consistency of the information. Usually, you work with the DBA, who is responsible for the accuracy of the data. Checking the database server integrity involves checking indexes, system catalogs, reserved pages, and data integrity as well as referential integrity.

Terminology

When Informix describes backup and restore activities, you will see that the terminology might differ from that used by other database systems. Although the activities are described differently, the end result is usually the same. You need to understand the terms and the database activity involved with them. The following sections explain these activities as two major operations—backup and restore.

Backup Operations

The first major component operation is backup. Informix provides you with complex backup systems, as well as utilities to perform this task. This chapter discusses the use of the `onbar` backup system and the `ontape` utility. There are two types of backups—physical and logical. Usually, you need to implement a strategy to perform both backup types. Most sites do not take advantage of logical backups, but I will explain further why it is important to consider logical backups when planning the best strategy for your backup activity.

Before attempting to perform a backup operation, keep in mind the data consistency verification, using the `oncheck` utility as follows:

- `oncheck -cD` or `-cd` performs data checks.
- `oncheck -cI` or `-ci` performs index checks.
- `oncheck -cr` performs reserved pages checks.
- `oncheck -cc` performs system catalog checks.

Backup Levels

Informix implements three levels of backup operation—level 0, level 1, and level 2. Figure 18.1 shows an example of the proportions of data backed up for each level; this is useful when your system manages large databases and you can't afford the time it takes to perform a whole system backup. The level 0 backup copies all the pages that contain data in the specified dbspaces, the level 1 backup copies only the pages that have changed since the last level 0 backup, and the level 2 backup copies all the pages that have changed since the last level 1 backup.

You can take advantage of these three backup levels by using the schedule specified in Table 18.1.

Table 18.1. A simple schedule you can follow to take advantage of backup levels included in Informix Database Servers.

Day	*Backup Level*
Monday	0
Tuesday	1
Wednesday	2
Thursday	1
Friday	0
Saturday	1
Sunday	2

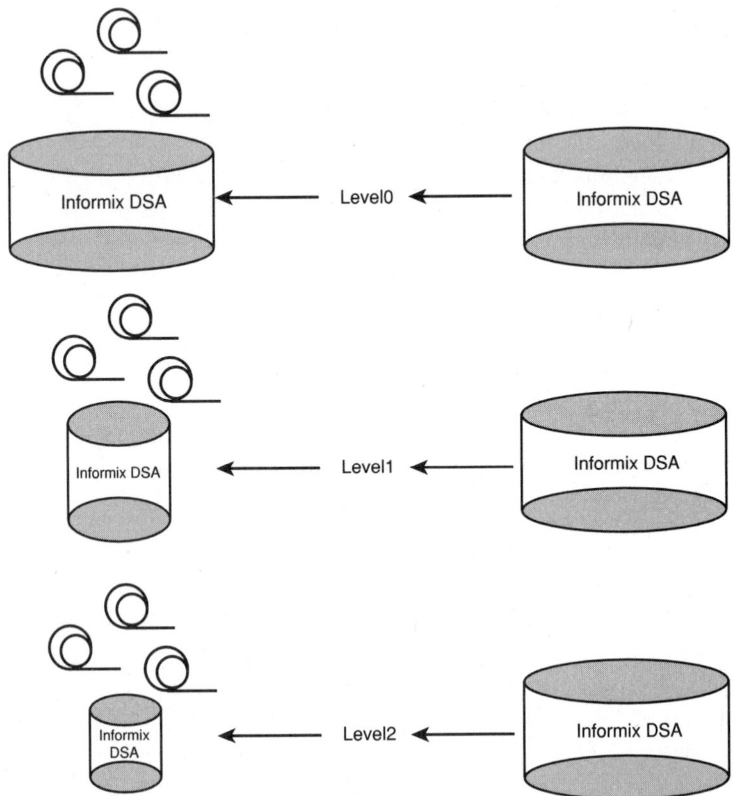

FIGURE 18.1.
The three backup level operations.

What Is a Physical Backup?

This operation involves all or selected database spaces (dbspaces). You can instruct Informix to perform a backup while Informix is in online mode or in quiescent mode. These two options are related to the operation mode of your Informix Database Server. Remember that the `rootdbs` keeps information about your whole system, so it will be important for you to back up that dbspace to restore the entire system.

Informix does not back up the pages that are available for a dbspace but still are not assigned to an `extent` of a table space (`tblspace`). Also none of the blobspaces located in any optical subsystem are backed up. Figure 18.2 shows you the physical backup diagram.

Informix does not perform a physical backup for the following conditions:

- A temporary dbspace (created with the flag `"t"`)
- Dbspaces or blobspaces marked as down are skipped

- Mirror chunks when the primary chunks are accessible
- Blobs in blobspaces managed by INFORMIX-OnLine/Optical and stored in optical platters
- Dbspace pages allocated to Informix DSA but still not allocated to an extent in a tblspace

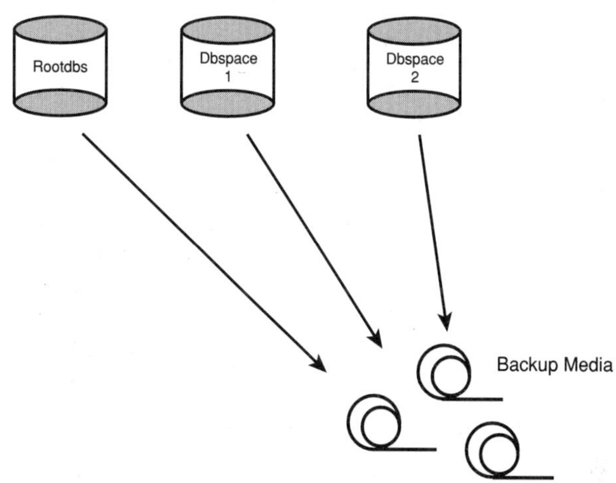

FIGURE 18.2.
A diagram of the physical backup.

> **NOTE**
>
> None of these tools backs up your `onconfig` or `sqlhosts` files or any other configuration file. You can accomplish this by using UNIX commands such as `cpio` or `tar`.

OnLine Mode Backup

When your Informix Database Server is in online mode, the backup operation increases the duration of a checkpoint, thus reducing the performance, but it is compensated by the availability of the data to users. During the online mode backup operation, Informix creates a temporary table for those pages residing in the `physical log`. Usually pages residing in this log are called *before-image pages.* During this operation, the allocation of any disk page to a tblspace or dbspace could remain temporarily unresolved until the operation is over. The online mode backup operation is shown in Figure 18.3.

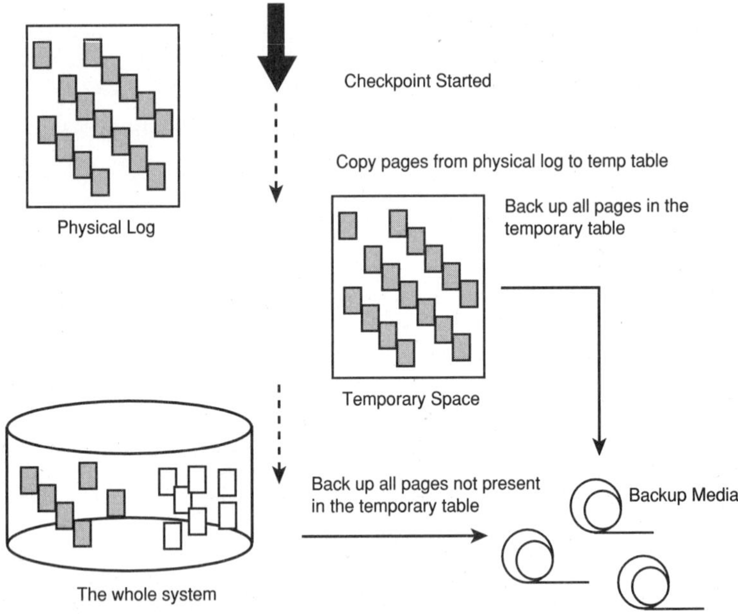

FIGURE 18.3.
The online mode backup operation.

Quiescent Mode Backup

The quiescent mode backup operation can be an impractical solution when data availability is a concern; however, this can be useful when you want to eliminate from your archive all those transactions that can be partial or incomplete. In other words, this is useful when you want to be sure that the data you are backing up represents an exact copy of the data you have on disk, and no transactions will be occurring during your backup operation to violate this consistency.

What Is a Logical Backup?

In an OLTP environment, transactions play an important part of the game. All databases with log mode or ANSI mode need to insert transaction information in the logical log files. Suppose that you performed an archive yesterday at 8:00 PM. Your data might have changed by 10:00 AM today. Every operation that caused a change to the data is in the logical-log files. If your system suffers a severe system crash at 11:00 AM, you can restore your last night backup and restore your logical-log files to roll forward the transactions and leave your Informix Database Server in a consistent state. Figure 18.4 shows the logical backup operation.

> **NOTE**
>
> Informix uses the logical logs when an administrative task such as checkpoint activities is performed. Thus, you will still look at activity in the logical logs, even if you don't have a database created with `log` or defined as ANSI mode.

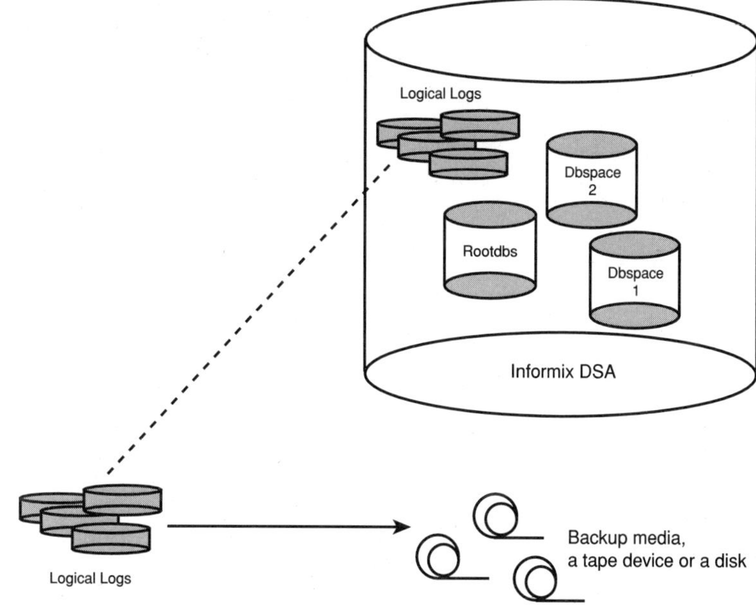

FIGURE 18.4.
The logical backup operation.

Full Logical Log Backup

This operation backs up all the logical log files that are currently full. Usually, you perform this type of backup when only one tape device is available in your system. A schedule for this type of backup will be needed in order to avoid collision with other administrative tasks.

TIP

You can use the alarm program, the new feature of Informix Database Servers, to automatically back up a log. An event is fired when a log becomes full; thus, you can monitor it and perform the backup of the log. The advantage over a continuous backup mode is that whenever the tape is unavailable, you can bypass the current log backup until the event is fired again.

Continuous Logical Log Backup

Normally, if you have two tape devices available on your system, you will dedicate the one with less capacity for backing up the logical log files in a continuous manner. In most systems, it is not necessary to attend this type of operation because the transaction activity will not require the full tape capacity for one normal day of operation.

NOTE

Some system administrators also back up the logical log files to disk. Assuming that the disk is in another physical area, the recovery strategy can be implemented without involving a tape device for logical log recovery.

Restore Operations

After you have implemented a backup strategy, you need to know how data can be restored from those backup tapes in case of a system failure. Remember that Informix has a fast recovery facility that can fail for any number of reasons. If that happens, you will have only the choices of performing a restore operation or calling Informix support so that they can log into your machine and put your instance online again.

There are two types of restore operations:

- A physical restore operation
- A logical restore operation

What Is a Physical Restore?

Whenever you restore a dbspace, you are performing a physical restore. Suppose a chunk that was part of the dbspace `foo` is marked as down, probably for hardware failure. In that case, you will be able to restore that dbspace from your backup tapes. The physical restore operation is illustrated in Figure 18.5.

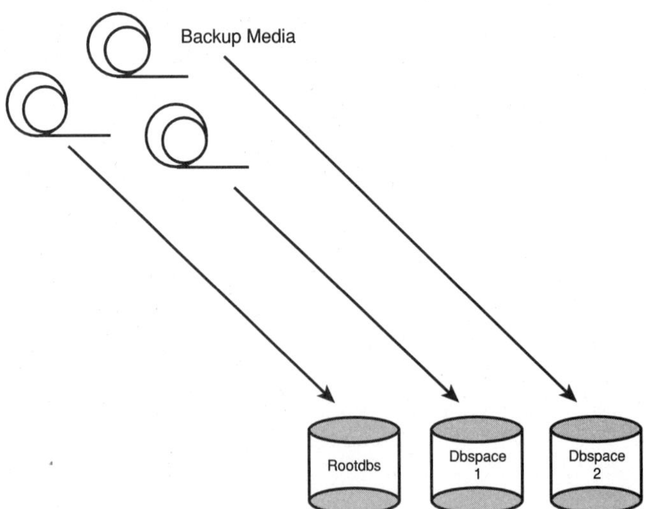

FIGURE 18.5.
The physical restore operation.

What Is a Logical Log Salvage?

The logical log salvage is executed automatically by Informix before the restore operation takes place, but you can accomplish it in a manual fashion. The goal is to back up the logical logs that were not backed up normally before the system crash. This feature is very convenient when you want to return your Informix Database Server to the state it was in at a specific time—in this case, the specific time when the system failed.

NOTE

All databases not created with logging mode will not be restored to a specific point in time, but to the state they were in at the time of the last backup containing such databases.

What Is Logical Restore?

After you have performed a physical restore, you need to restore the logical logs that were backed up before the failure to roll them forward. Whether the logical logs reside on disk or on tape, you will be performing a logical restore operation, as shown in Figure 18.6.

FIGURE 18.6.
The logical restore operation.

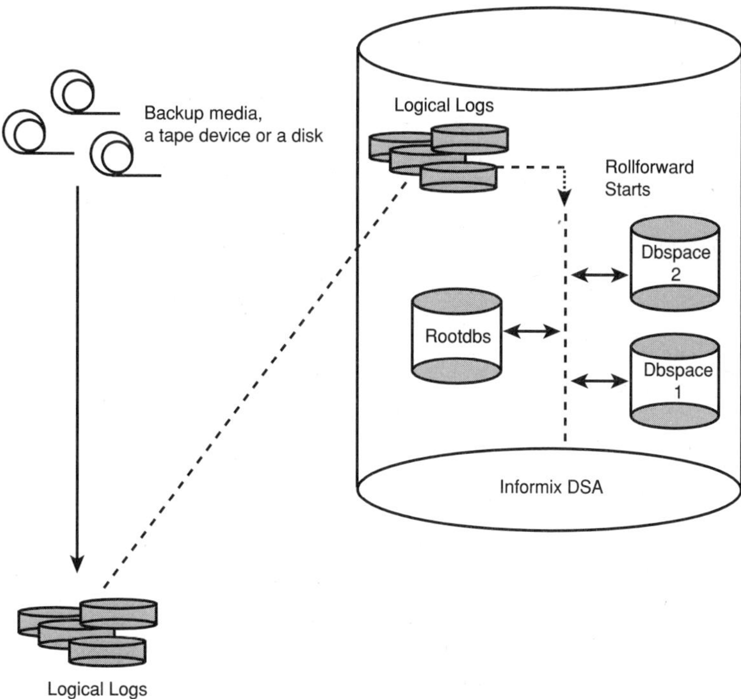

The information stored in the logical log files is read and sorted by table space (tblspace). You can speed up the restore operation by increasing the number of threads that will perform this operation. This can be achieved by modifying the default configuration for the `onconfig` parameters `ON_RECVRY_THREADS` and `OFF_RECVRY_THREADS`. Depending on the state of your Informix Database Server (`online` or `offline`), by the time of the logical restore, one of these two parameters will be read to start the specified number of recovery threads. For example, if your Informix Database Server is in `online` mode, the number specified in the `ON_RECVRY_THREADS` will be used to start the recovery threads.

Informix needs to replay the transactions specified in the log files for certain dbspaces. Informix creates the logs that will be used to replay those transactions in temporary dbspaces to avoid overwriting the original logical log files. Therefore, it is important to check your environment variable or your configuration parameter `DBSPACETEMP` so that it points to specific dbspaces with enough space to hold those logical logs (normally, the size of the total number of logs currently configured).

NOTE

Informix automatically rolls back any unresolved transaction when the logical restore operation is complete.

Restore Types

Informix helps you restore your data in three ways:

- Performing a cold restore
- Performing a warm restore
- Performing a mixed restore

The method you choose depends directly on the information you are restoring and the mode the Informix Database Server instance is in by the time you need to perform the restore operation.

Remember that Informix divides the dbspaces into two groups—the critical dbspaces and the noncritical dbspaces. The `rootdbs` is a critical dbspace, because it contains the information Informix needs in order to work. Also, a critical dbspace is any other dbspace containing the physical log and logical log files. The rest of the dbspaces are known as noncritical because they are not important to help recover your Informix Database Server after a system crash. However, they are a vital component for your application because they contain your data.

What Is a Cold Restore?

Whenever serious damage is done to one of the critical dbspaces, Informix goes offline, and sometimes it does not come up again. This is the situation in which you will have to perform a cold restore. A cold restore restores the whole system while Informix is in offline mode. After it has restored the reserved pages from the `rootdbs`, it goes into a recovery mode until the logical restore operation is complete. An illustration of the cold restore operation is shown in Figure 18.7.

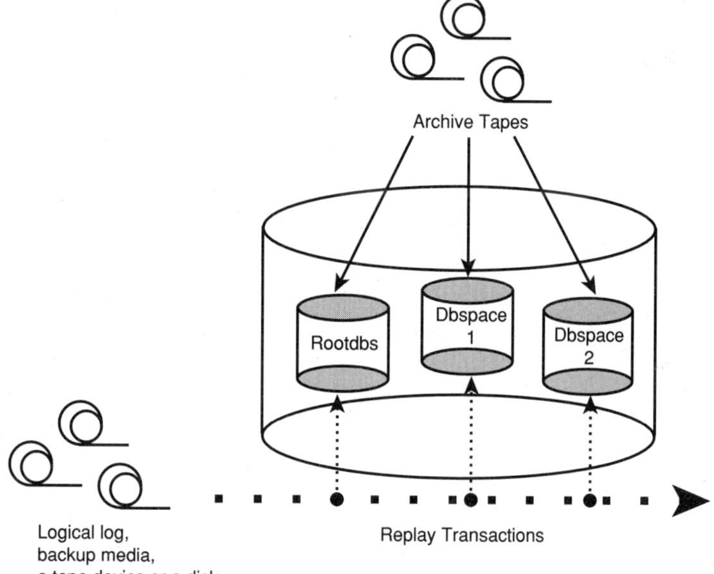

FIGURE 18.7.
The cold restore operation.

A cold restore consists of the following operations:

1. A physical restore of one or more database objects
2. A logical log salvage
3. A logical restore

After the logical restore operation, Informix is in quiescent mode until you manually change its mode using the `onmode` command line or the `onmonitor` utility.

NOTE

After a cold restore is performed, the next backup operation must always be a level 0 backup to maintain the backup information in the reserved pages accurately and ensure backup reliability.

What Is a Warm Restore?

When one of your chunks fails due to disk damage or any other circumstance, but your Informix Database Server instance remains in online mode (which is basically whenever a noncritical dbspace fails), you have to perform a warm restore operation.

A warm restore can be performed whether Informix is in online mode or in quiescent mode. Users might still be generating transactions by the time you are executing the restore of your dbspaces. Informix has to replay the transactions in the logical logs for the dbspaces that are being restored. To avoid overwriting the transaction information in the current logical log, Informix writes the logical log files to temporary space specified in the `DBSPACETEMP` environment variable and configuration parameter.

A warm restore consists of the following activities:

1. One or more physical restore operations
2. A logical log backup of the current logs on disk to tape
3. A logical restore

The warm restore operation is shown in Figure 18.8.

FIGURE 18.8.
The warm restore operation.

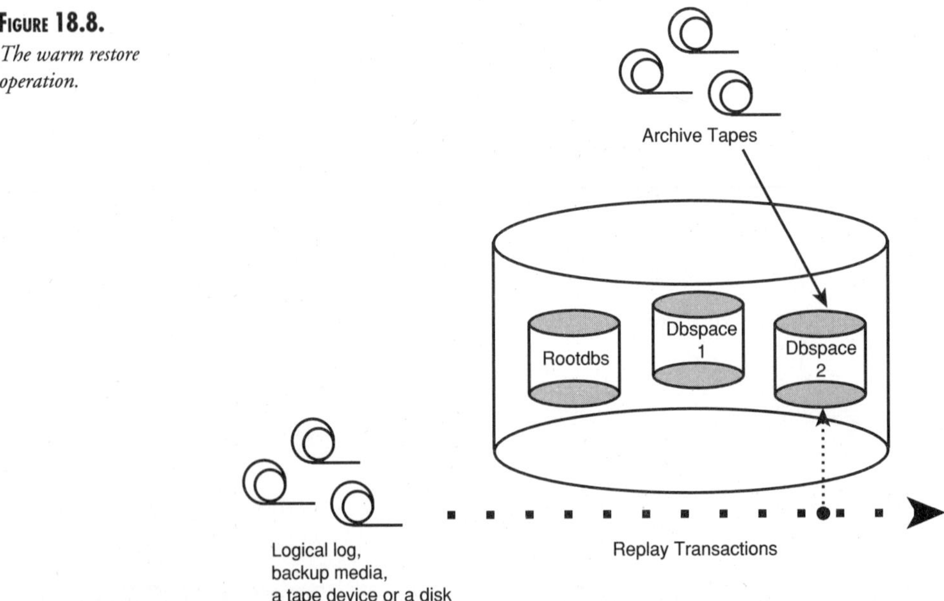

What Is a Mixed Restore?

This operation requires a cold restore of the critical dbspaces while your Informix Database Server is in offline mode, and a warm restore for the rest of the dbspaces to ensure data availability. If you need to restore your whole Informix Database Server system, but you want some users to have access to some information before the whole operation is completed, you should take advantage of this type of restore operation. The mixed restore operation takes more time and temporary space than the cold restore because the first one has to perform two logical restore operations—one for the cold portion (shown in Figure 18.9) and the other for the warm portion (shown in Figure 18.10). But data availability is achieved for those dbspaces restored during the cold restore phase.

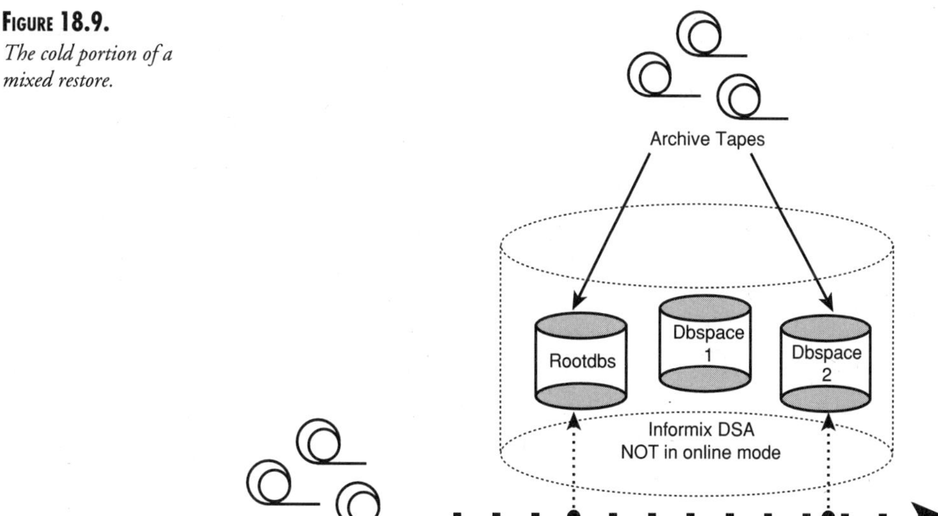

FIGURE 18.9.
The cold portion of a mixed restore.

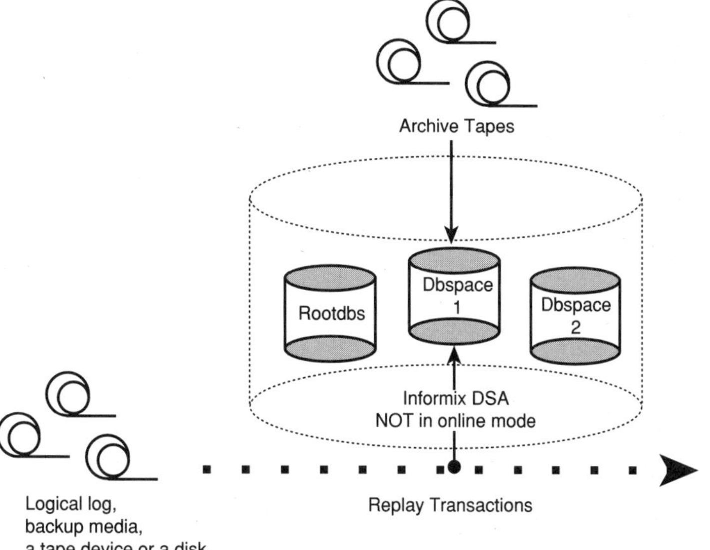

FIGURE 18.10.
The warm portion of a mixed restore.

OnBar Backup and Restore System

Informix introduced OnBar in engine 7.21. It is equipped with a storage management API, which allows you to interface it with many sophisticated third-party storage management vendor subsystems on the market today. OnBar allows you to back up and restore single or multiple `dbobjects` (such as dbspaces, blobspaces, and logical log files). Although OnBar performs some tasks similar to On-Archive, it is a whole new product. It is much easier to use and is available on all UNIX platforms such as Sun Solaris, Digital Equipment Corp., Hewlett-Packard, IBM, Intel SCO, Intel Solaris, Pyramid, Sequent, SGI, SNI, Data General, Tandem, Unisys, NCR, NEC, and Windows NT from Microsoft Corporation.

TIP

OnBar can back up and restore anything at the dbspace level. If you want a higher availability of your information, consider table fragmentation so that you can back up and restore at the partition level, or try to put tables such as customer information in a single dbspace so that you can back up and restore at the table level.

What Is the onbar Utility?

The `onbar` utility is a program that can accept an action from a command line or from a storage manager through the X/Open Backup Services Application programmer's interface (XBSA). This utility is the communication facility between Informix Database Servers and any XBSA-conforming storage management application (such as Legato and ADSM). When a backup operation is requested by the storage manager, the `onbar` utility asks Informix questions about the `dbobjects` and translates the information to the storage manager. When a restore operation is required, the process is reversed.

The `onbar` utility doesn't create an intermediate file while it is performing a backup or restore operation. It supports database and dbspace backup granularity, and it also supports incremental backups. The administration of the storage manager server is out of the scope of this chapter.

OnBar Architecture Overview

The `onbar` utility is just one component of the whole OnBar system. For every backup and restore operation, the following components are involved in the operation:

- The `onbar` utility
- The XBSA interface
- The storage manager client/storage manager server

- The emergency boot file
- The Message File, which is different from the Informix Database Server message log

These components of the OnBar architecture are shown in Figure 18.11.

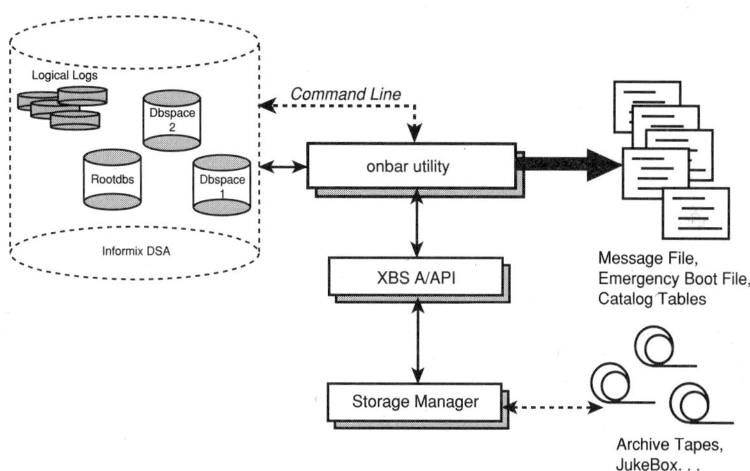

FIGURE 18.11.
The OnBar architecture.

What Is a Storage Manager?

A storage manager is a third-party application program that controls all the storage devices in your system. Usually, those storage devices are tape storage devices, jukeboxes, and stackers. When you use OnBar, you direct orders to the storage manager, using the X/Open API, which in turn directs orders to the storage manager server. The way a storage manager controls storage devices is transparent to Informix and the `onbar` utility.

For large systems, using a storage manager can be very advantageous because it supports networked and distributed backup and restore operations, as well as data compression, encryption, and automation of all backup tasks.

NOTE

If you are using the Windows NT version of the Informix OWS Database Server, you can take advantage of the storage manager bundled with Informix. Sun Microsystems private-labels the Legato NetWorker for Solaris product line under the name Solstice Backup, which is a single server edition of the Legato NetWorker. Check the following address to see whether your UNIX operating system appears in the OEM's list software:

`http://www.legato.com/documents/NetWorker/compat.html`

What Kind of Storage Managers Are Compatible with OnBar?

Informix is planning to provide a simple storage manager of its own by mid-1997, so it would be helpful for you to check out your release notes. At the time I wrote this chapter, the bundled storage manager was available only for Windows NT. If you are using a UNIX platform, you can evaluate the Legato Networker (`http://www.legato.com`) and the ADSTAR Distributed Storage Manager (ADSM) from IBM (`http://www.storage.ibm.com/storage/software/adsm/adsmhome.htm`). ADSM server works with HP UX, Solaris, AIX, and Windows NT. The Omniback II from Hewlett-Packard (`http://www.hp.com`) should also be considered. Keep in mind that this chapter does not discuss any of these products; only the administration of the Informix backup and restore tools are covered. You should refer to your storage manager manuals to see how to configure and administer your storage manager.

In the case of the Windows NT platform, Informix ships bundled with its database servers a DLL library called the Informix Storage Manager. It is easy to administer. You must specify in the `Onconfig` file what devices will be available to the storage manager. For more information, refer to your *Informix Backup and Restore Manual.*

The ADSM X/Open API, ADSM backup/archive command-line client component, and ADSM common files module (for AIX or Solaris) must be installed on the machine where OnBar is installed. These three pieces are available via the AIX or Solaris client code packages on the IBM ftp server at `index.storsys.ibm.com`.

What Is the XBSA Interface?

The X/Open Backup Services Application Programmer's Interface (XBSA) is a collection of functions that makes possible the communication of the `onbar` utility with any storage manager that can talk to the XBSA interface. OnBar uses the XBSA interface to exchange information about dbspaces, blobspaces, and logical log files (dbobjects) with the storage manager. It is also used to exchange control data information such as backup history of dbobjects and XBSA/`onbar` compatibility verification.

NOTE

The X/OPEN API is available for the C language, so you can write a user program that interacts with many of the storage managers available today.

Making OnBar Communicate with the Storage Manager

If you are using Legato NetWorker or any Legato OEMs such as Solstice Backup, you need to download the Informix BusinesSuite Module from `http://www.legato.com`. It is usually a 30-day free evaluation copy. The Informix BusinesSuite Module provides preconfigured media pools. A media pool is a collection of backup media (tapes or optical media). Each media pool contains backup data that fits a specific profile. For example, a media pool called "FullOnly" might contain only data from a full backup. This is useful to separate devices dedicated to logical log backups from the normal backup operations. If you are using the Network Edition of NetWorker for UNIX release 4.2, you also need the TurboPak option to use BusinesSuite Module.

NOTE

The Informix BusinesSuite Module preconfigured media pools are DBMIData and DBMILogs for Data and Log backup, respectively.

If you are using ADSM, the ADSM X/Open API, ADSM backup/archive command-line client component, and ADSM common files module (for AIX or Solaris) must be installed on the machine where OnBar is installed. These three pieces are available via the AIX or Solaris client code packages on the IBM ftp server at `index.storsys.ibm.com`.

Configuring OnBar

Configuring OnBar requires changes only to some configuration parameters located in the `onconfig` file. The major task is to configure the storage manager itself. In the case of Legato and ADSM, depending on the platform, both include GUI and command-line interfaces for the following tasks:

- Administrative tasks
- Backup/restore operations
- Scheduling

During the administrative task, a hierarchy of storage media can be used to define the media pools. The media pools can contain disk storage, optical devices, and tape devices. If you want to perform scheduled backups using the storage manager, you need to create backup groups with descriptive names, and assign them *save sets.* The save sets must include the Informix Database Server name and a list of dbobjects. For example, if you want to back up the dbspace `data01` from the Informix Database Server `mcp`, the save set list would be `INFORMIX:/mcp/data01`. If you don't specify a list of dbobjects, all the dbobjects available in your Informix Database Server will be included in the backup list automatically.

If you are using Legato NetWorker and a backup or restore is required from the storage manager and not from the `onbar` utility, enter `nsrdbmi` as the entry for "Backup command." This is a script located in the `/usr/sbin/nsrdbmi` directory for SOLARIS and in the `/usr/bin/nsrdbmi` directory for AIX.

NOTE

The onbar utility and the BusinesSuite Module from Legato rely on a shared XBSA library to perform storage management tasks for OnLine Dynamic Server. Before using onbar with the BusinesSuite Module, you must tell onbar where the NetWorker XBSA portion of the library exists. Use the root name on the system running onbar, and create a symbolic link using the following commands for each system:

SOLARIS

```
ln -s /usr/lib/libbsa.so \ /usr/lib/ibsad001.so
```

AIX

```
ln -s /usr/lib/libbsa.a \ /usr/lib/ibsad001.a
```

HP-UX

```
ln -s /usr/lib/libbsa.sl \ /usr/lib/ibsad001.sl
```

WARNING

If you are using the Business Module from Legato and you do not run the dbmi_config script to create media pools and label templates for your database data, NetWorker sends the data to the Default pool. Refer to the "Using Volumes Pools" section in Chapter 3, "Database Concepts," of the *BusinesSuite Module for Informix Administrator's Guide* for more information.

NOTE

Unfortunately, it isn't possible to include in this chapter every configuration for all the storage managers on the market. You should carefully read the documentation included with your storage manager and the Informix interface modules.

The Configuration Parameters

In the onconfig file, located in the $INFORMIXDIR/etc/ directory, you find four parameters dedicated to the exclusive use of the OnBar Backup and Restore System. You don't have to specify the location of any storage media you want to use with the onbar utility, because it is configured as media pools in the storage manager configuration. These parameters only affect the performance of the OnBar system. The parameters and their explanations are listed in Table 18.2.

Table 18.2. OnBar configuration parameters.

ONCONFIG *Parameter*	*Function*
BAR_ACT_LOG	OnBar writes information about its activity to a log file, which is different from the message log of Informix DSA. You specify in this parameter the full pathname of this log file and its location; the default value is bar_act.log.
BAR_MAX_BACKUP	This parameter limits the number of processes that can be started by each onbar command; the default value is 1.
BAR_XPORT_COUNT	OnBar exchanges information with the Informix Database Server using data buffers. The number of buffers that can be started by one onbar process is specified in this parameter; the default value is 10, and it can range from 1 to an unlimited number. You should be careful when tuning this and the BAR_XFER_BUFSIZE values, because they can affect the performance in the communication with the Informix Database Server. Also keep in mind that, in the same way, you will have to tune some similar parameters in the storage manager configuration file.
BAR_XFER_BUFSIZE	OnBar receives information from the Informix Database Server in buffers. You will have to set a similar configuration parameter in your storage manager. Suppose that onbar receives 10KB buffers. It wouldn't make sense to have onbar send 5KB buffers to the SMCL, because that would require two transfers to send the entire 10KB buffer but would depend on the type of connection you are using to communicate with the Storage Manager Server. The default value depends on the OS page size. If the operative system page size is 4KB, the default value will be 15. For a 2KB page size, the default value is 31. To calculate the actual size of a transfer data buffer, use the formula (BAR_XFER_BUFSIZE * os_page_size + 500 bytes). The result will be in byte units.
BAR_RETRY	If for any reason onbar fails to perform a backup or restore operation of certain dbobjects, you must set what onbar should do next. You can direct onbar to wait *n* number of times to see whether the dbobject becomes available (BAR_RETRY = *n*), to skip to the next dbobject (BAR_RETRY = BAR_CONT), or to abort the operation whenever it happens (BAR_RETRY = BAR_ABORT). The default value is BAR_CONT.

WARNING

The onbar utility communicates to the Storage Manager Command Line (SMCL) through the XBSA interface. It puts the pages that it reads from the database server in buffers. Depending on the size of these buffers, you might saturate the stream communication between onbar and the SMCL, affecting performance.

The OnBar Emergency Boot File

The emergency boot file contains the necessary information to perform a cold restore. It is used by onbar to direct the storage manager to what information needs to be restored in case of a system failure. The file is located in the $INFORMIXDIR/etc directory. The name is ixbar.*servernum*, where *servernum* is the value of the SERVERNUM configuration parameter in the $ONCONFIG file.

Performing a Backup

You can perform a backup of 0, 1, or 2 level. You can also specify whether you want to back up the whole system or a specific number of dbspaces. Remember that the X/OPEN API handles information about your instance. That information is kept in the storage manager database, which is administered by the storage manager itself and is different from the sysutil database used by OnBar.

The client indexes and the server's bootstrap file are vital for restoring data to the Informix Database Server in the event of a disaster. Occasionally, you might need to perform an on-demand backup of the Informix Database Server dbobjects by using the onbar utility. After performing an on-demand backup, back up the NetWorker server's client index and bootstrap manually by invoking the savegrp command line from the NetWorker server using the savegrp -O -l full -c *client-name* -c \ *networker-servername* command, where *client-name* is the value of the INFORMIXSERVER environment variable. All storage managers include this capability to back up the client indexes. Refer to your storage manager documentation.

Backing Up the Whole System

There are two ways to back up the whole system. You can specify the -w option, or you can choose not to specify the -w or the -f option, without any dbspace listed.

The following operation directs onbar to execute a whole system backup. The default level is 0. Notice the -b option, which tells onbar to perform a backup operation.

```
%onbar -b -w
```

NOTE

If you specify an incremental backup with the -L option, the previous level will be performed if OnBar doesn't find it. If you specify -L 1 but you haven't performed the level 0, the level 0 will be performed.

Backing Up Specified Database Objects

You can also specify a list of dbspaces that you want to archive. Usually, you list those dbspaces separated by a space, or you can use a file that contains a list of dbspaces, which in turn has the same functionality.

If you want to make a level 1 backup of the `rootdbs` and the `physdbs`, you must type the following command:

```
% onbar -b -L 1 rootdbs physdbs
```

Now assume that you have created a file named `foo`, containing the two dbspaces (one dbspace per line) that you want to archive at level 0. You should execute the following command line:

```
% onbar -b -L 0 -f foo
```

NOTE

If you are using your storage manager instead of the `onbar` utility to perform backups, remember to configure backup groups and save sets to back up specified dbobjects.

Administrative Tasks Requiring a Backup

Some administrative tasks, such as changing the logging mode of a database and adding a mirror chunk, require you to make a level 0 backup. Sometimes it is necessary for you to synchronize those administrative tasks with your next backup activity, but if you want to make them now, you can perform a simulated backup operation by using the `-F` option of the `onbar` utility. Keep in mind that you will not restore any information from a simulated backup because it is not actually a backup, just an internal procedure. There are some exceptions such as adding a new dbspace for a simulated backup, even if it is allowed. Refer to the *Informix Backup and Restore Manual* for more information about the administrative tasks that require a backup operation.

Suppose that you changed the logging mode of the database `sams`, which is located in the dbspace `edbspace`. Then you can perform a simulated backup for that dbspace, as follows:

```
% onbar -b -L 0 -F edbspace
```

Backing Up the Logical Logs

The log files contain records of transactions and other administrative tasks performed by the Informix Database Server. For instance, when a new reserved page is allocated, the RSVXTEND record is written to the logical log. The size of each logical log is specified by the DBA. When the log becomes full, it will have the flag "U", depending on the number of logical logs configured. You will have to back them up to free the logical log space so that Informix can reuse it. After a logical log is backed up, you can use it in the logical-restore event, such as a warm restore.

WARNING

If LTAPEDEV is undefined or set to /dev/null in the ONCONFIG file, an OnBar logical log backup returns the error code 131, and a message is sent to BAR_ACT_LOG. The error occurs when the Informix Database Server switches to the next log before OnBar has a chance to send the logical log data to the storage manager server. Keep in mind that OnBar does not use the LTAPEDEV configuration parameter. To avoid this situation, configure LTAPEDEV to a valid tape device or a UNIX file.

NOTE

To monitor the state of each logical log, you should use the onstat -l command line.

On-Demand Logical Log Backup

You can back up all the logical logs that are full (100 percent used). This is known as the on-demand logical log backup. The following command line accomplishes the on-demand logical log backup:

```
% onbar -l
```

It is useful when you want to schedule the backup of your logical logs—assuming that you have enough logical log space (the sum of all your logical log files)—to support your operations between each logical backup event.

Backing Up the Current Logical Log

Sometimes you need to back up the current logical log, which is the one with the "C" flag from the onstat -l output, no matter how full the logical log is. The following instruction backs up the current logical log, and the pointer is switched to the next logical log:

```
% onbar -l -c
```

Continuous Logical Log Backup

The continuous backup of your logical logs limits your loss to only a percentage of the last logical log file in use. Most sites implement the strategy of many small log files, thus reducing the percentage of the transactions that are lost in a system crash. Informix tries to salvage the logical log when you perform a cold restore, but serious damage in the media containing the logical log will restrict Informix from succeeding in the salvage operation. In such situations, Informix skips the salvage of the logical log and continues the restore operation.

Informix provides a shell script called `log_full.sh`, located in the `$INFORMIXDIR/etc` directory. This script contains a sample set of instructions you should use to direct `onbar` to perform continuous backup of your logical logs. This script works with the event alarm program feature of Informix, which triggers the event class number 20 when a logical log becomes full. If you already have a main shell script that is fired by the alarm event, you should modify your main script to call the `log_full.sh` when the event class is the number 20.

NOTE

A continuous backup of the logical logs requires a permanent backup medium—which means that a tape or any other device must always be available.

For more information about the `ALARMPROGRAM` configuration parameter, refer to the *Informix Database Server's Administrator's Manual*. Refer to your storage manager documentation for information about how to back up the logical log in a continuous manner from your storage manager server.

Salvaging the Logical Logs

Informix automatically performs a log salvage during a cold restore; however, it will be necessary for you to salvage the logical logs that haven't been backed up yet before you replace a damaged medium. This is the only case in which you need to salvage the logical log manually.

The following instruction accomplishes this task:

```
% onbar -l -s
```

Performing a Restore

As explained before, there are three types of restores. If you are performing a cold restore—that is, one or more of your critical dbspaces became corrupted and Informix DSA doesn't come up—you must use the emergency boot file located in the `$INFORMIXDIR/etc/ixbar.`*`server_num`* directory. This file contains information that OnBar needs in order to perform the cold restore. If you are performing a warm restore, OnBar reads the `sysutil` database to perform the restore.

Restoring the Whole System

If you are restoring the whole system, you are performing a whole system cold restore. In this case, OnBar restores all the dbspaces, even those not marked as down. The critical dbspaces will be restored first, as indicated in the emergency boot file.

The following example performs a whole system cold restore. Keep in mind that Informix will try to salvage the logical logs on disk.

```
% onbar -r -w
```

Restoring Down Dbspaces

If one or more of your dbspaces are marked as down, you can restore those dbspaces as follows:

```
% onbar -r -p
```

Then you can inform OnBar to restore the appropriate logical logs for the dbspaces that have been restored, as follows:

```
% onbar -r -l
```

> **NOTE**
>
> When restoring down dbspaces, it is not necessary to list those dbspaces. OnBar checks the state of every dbspace and performs the restore.

Restoring a Particular Dbspace

To perform a restore of a particular dbspace, you can specify a list of dbspaces separated by a space; or if the list is large, you can create an ASCII file containing one dbspace per line.

Suppose that you have the table `sameditor`, which is fragmented in three dbspaces (`compbks`, `scienbks`, and `electbks`), and you want to restore the `compbks` and `electbks` fragments. If you use the `-p` option, a logical restore will be required. If you don't want to restore the logical logs, you must execute the following command:

```
% onbar -r compbks elctbks
```

If you have a large list of dbspaces, you must create a file containing the dbspaces, one per line. If you name the file `samdbspaces`, the following command will restore all the dbspaces listed in the file `samdbspaces`:

```
% onbar -r -f samdbspaces
```

As you can see, a restore without specifying the `-p` option does not require a logical log restore.

NOTE

The -f option also works with the physical restore specified with the -p option.

A Point-in-Time Recover

OnBar supports the point-in-time recovery feature. It is based on a simple and highly valuable concept that makes OnBar stop rolling forward the logical logs until a specified time has been reached. The time is specified by the -t option of the restore process.

Let's assume you have a table, sams_delivery, that is fragmented by expression in three dbspaces (onehour, twohour, and morehour). Yesterday you performed a level 0 backup of those dbspaces. Today at 8:00 AM a batch process started, which finished at 8:30 AM. At 8:35 AM another process changed the information from the twohour dbspace, and you cannot reverse the change. In this case, you should perform a point-in-time recover for the twohour dbspace. Assuming that you want the dbspace returned to the state it was in at 8:30 AM, you should perform the following commands.

First perform a physical restore of the twohour dbspace:

```
% onbar -r -p twohour
```

The physical restore requires a logical restore in order to leave the twohour dbspace available to the users, as follows:

```
% onbar -r -t8:30 -l
```

NOTE

You can also restore at a specified number of logical logs, using the -n option instead of the -t option.

Monitoring the OnBar Activity

Your storage manager provides you with information about the backup and restore activity, using its own database. You can use the graphical interface provided by your storage manager server to view the backup history and the future backup activities. OnBar uses the database sysutil to keep information about its backup and restore activity. The database sysutil is created when the Informix Database Server is initialized the first time. Informix executes the bldutil.sh script to accomplish this task.

The Catalog Tables

The tables created in the sysutil database are used by OnBar to store useful information about the backup and restore activity. Table 18.3 lists those tables with a short description of each.

Table 18.3. An overview of the sysutil database tables.

Table	Purpose
Bar_action	Lists the backup and restore activities performed for a database object. Even if the action was not successful, it will be listed here.
Bar_instance	Lists the successful actions attempted to a database object.
Bar_version	Lists the compatible version of OnBar, XBSA interface, and the storage manager for every successful action registered in the bar_instance table.
Bar_object	Keeps track of all the database objects that have been involved with the OnBar system.
Bar_server	Keeps track of all the Informix DSA instances.

If you installed Legato NetWorker, OnBar does not automatically insert the required version values for the shared NetWorker XBSA library into the bar_version table. To accomplish this manually, follow these steps:

1. Create or append the file sm_versions located in the $INFORMIXDIR/etc/ directory.
2. Execute the following command line. Enter the string in quotes exactly as shown, without blank spaces:

```
echo "1¦1.0.1¦nwbsa¦1">> \$INFORMIXDIR/etc/sm_versions
```

3. If you don't intend to reinitialize your Informix Database Server using the oninit -i command, connect to the sysutil database using DBaccess and run the following SQL command:

```
insert into bar_version values ('1','1.0.1','nwbsa','1');
```

4. If you want to reinitialize your Informix Database Server, the bldutil.sh script will load the contents of the sm_versions file into the bar_version table.

The ontape Utility

This utility is easy to use and configure. If your site doesn't manage large complex databases, ontape will do the job of archiving and restoring your information in a simple and efficient way. ontape doesn't have a menu-driven interface; it has only a command line. It cannot make archives at the dbspace level, only at the system level; but the restore operation can be done at the dbspace level. ontape supports the incremental archives 0, 1, and 2 and provides on-demand and automatic backup of your logical logs.

NOTE

The ontape utility will not retry an operation. Therefore, if a tape or a database object is not available at the time of the backup operation, ontape aborts the process.

WARNING

The ontape utility must be executed by the Informix user. If you execute it as root, an su -informix command is issued, and the operation will be executed as informix. Any other user will receive an error.

NOTE

The Legato NetWorker 4.1 storage manager server can work with the ontape utility using the Informix Database Toolkit ASM available at

http://www.legato.com

The download form is available at

http://www.legato.com/forms/ev-form.html

It works only with Informix Database Servers 7.1 and up.

Configuring the ontape Parameters

Six parameters from the onconfig file are used by the Ontape utility, as explained in Table 18.4.

Table 18.4. The ontape configuration parameters.

Parameter	Purpose
TAPEDEV	The tape device used for archiving
TAPEBLK	The block size of the tape device used for archiving in kilobytes
TAPESIZE	The size of the tapes used for archiving in kilobytes
LTAPEDEV	The tape device used for backup and restore of logical logs
LTAPEBLK	The block size of the logical log tape device in kilobytes
LTAPESIZE	The size of the logical log tapes in kilobytes

These parameters can be changed while Informix is in online mode, using the `onmonitor` utility or by editing the `$INFORMIXDIR/etc/$ONCONFIG` file. If you change the `onconfig` file, the changes will be available the next time you bring Informix DSA online.

As you can see, the logical log tape device is specified in a different configuration parameter. It would be better for you to have an available tape device for archiving and restoring your logical logs, usually the tape device with less capacity. Most system administrators back up the logical logs to disk. This can be very useful and convenient when you don't have a tape device available for the logical logs.

It is also recommended that you use symbolic links when specifying the path of the tape devices. This can be useful when you want to change the tape device path while Informix is in online mode. A good example of its usefulness can be seen whenever you perform an administrative task that requires a level 0 backup, such as changing the logging mode to a database. This can be simulated by changing the tape device to `/dev/null`; thus, you have to change only the symbolic link without changing any configuration parameter from the `onconfig` file.

For example, you can create a symbolic link for the `/dev/rmt/0` device, as follows:

```
% ln -s /dev/rmt/0 /ifx/logtape
```

And then in the `onconfig` file, the `TAPEDEV` configuration parameter could be set to `/ifx/logtape`. When you want to change the tape device path, you have to change only the symbolic link.

Remote Tape Configuration

You can even perform a backup operation using a tape device located in another machine. If the other machine's hostname is `samsnet2`, the `TAPEDEV` or `LTAPEDEV` configuration parameters can contain the value `samsnet2:/dev/rmt/0`. Assuming that the tape device is the `/dev/rmt/0` in the other machine, you can even specify a symbolic link in the other machine.

Tape Size and Block Size Considerations

When you specify a tape size for your tapes, it is necessary that this value be a multiple of the block size specified. Check your hardware's manual to see what would be the most optimal block size for the tape you are using. For example, in the AIX manual, it says that the 8mm tape devices, should be specified as a 1024 block size, and the 4mm tape devices should be of 512 block size. Sometimes, depending on your operating system, it is necessary to synchronize the configuration of the tape device and block size between your OS and Informix. This is the case for the AIX OS, on which you must use SMIT to configure the tape devices. You should set it to zero—that is, of variable length—so that you don't experience any problems with Informix and other OS administrative tasks when both of them use the tape device.

Performing a Backup

Informix performs some internal steps before performing a backup. You should have enough logical log space available, because if the total logical log free space is less than one half of a logical log file, the process will be aborted. In this case, you should back up the logical logs.

Informix requires temporary disk space, usually from those dbspaces specified in the DBSPACETEMP configuration parameter or environment variable. This is necessary because Informix has to create a list of pages from the physical log file for every dbspace to be archived.

The following information is stored in a tape containing an archive. This information is presented in the order in which it is stored:

- A control page, containing a list of database objects archived.
- The system reserved pages.
- If the archive is level 0, information about logical logs containing open transactions at the time of the archive is stored.
- Blobspaces, if your system contains them.
- The dbspaces are archived in no particular order.
- The before-image from the temporary files is appended for every dbspace.
- A Trailer page is written when the last page of the last chunk is stored, marking the end of the archive.

NOTE

If a dbspace or blobspace is marked as down, `ontape` aborts the operation. This is not the case when using the `OnBar` utility.

Performing a Whole System Backup

`ontape` prompts you to mount the tape, and if you don't specify the backup level, you are prompted to specify it, also. The following command makes and archives level 0 of your whole system:

```
% ontape -s -L0
```

As you can see, it is not necessary to specify a tape device. `ontape` will read it from the reserved page that contains a copy of the `onconfig` file in memory.

Scheduling Backups

Whenever ontape asks for a tape to be mounted, you must press the Enter key in order to continue. Most system administrators implement a simple routine to accomplish this task, which is useful when you use the cron utility of UNIX to run a script at a specified time. The following example should resolve the please-mount-the-tape problem. (Thanks to our friends at c.d.i., comp.databases.informix.)

```
% ontape -s -L 0<<hit
  \n
  \n
  hit
```

Or if you're editing your script using vi, for example, you just need to press the Enter key in the here-document between the two hit words, as follows:

```
ontape -s -L 0 <<hit
 press_enter_here
  hit
```

Label Your Tapes

It is important to label your tapes so that, in the unlikely event of a system crash when you need to perform a restore, you can easily identify the tapes that are needed. The tapes must contain at least the following information, some of which is provided by the ontape utility:

- The archive level 0, 1, 2, or logical log backup
- The date and time of the archive
- The tape number
- The logical log numbers contained on the tape

TIP

The logical log numbers contained on the tape should be backed up to restore your system to the state it was in at the moment of the archive date and time.

Backing Up Your Logical Logs

This process can be accomplished in two ways:

- A continuous logical log backup
- On-demand logical log backup

Continuous Logical Log Backup

You can use the -c option of the ontape utility to perform a continuous backup of your logical logs. Therefore, whenever a logical log becomes full, it will be backed up immediately. You need a dedicated terminal, a window from your graphic environment to be dedicated to this task, which in turn can be canceled by pressing the interrupt key (usually the Ctrl+C key combination).

For example, if you execute the command

```
% ontape -c
```

your terminal or active window will become busy, exclusively using the ontape utility. When you press the interrupt key, the utility quits; it terminates the next time it goes to the loop or simply quits if it was already in the loop.

NOTE

Whenever ontape is run with the -c option, it will remain in a loop until a logical log becomes full.

On-Demand Logical Log Backup

To perform an on-demand logical log backup, you can use the -a option of the ontape utility. This is useful when you want to schedule your logical log backup. You must make sure that the tape is available. The following command line accomplishes this task:

```
% ontape -a
```

The following is a sample output of the ontape -a command line:

```
Performing automatic backup of logical logs.
Please mount tape 1 on /dev/rmt/0 and press Return to continue
. . .
Do you want to backup the current logical log? (y/n) Y
Please label this tape as number 1 in the log tape sequence.
This tape contains the following logical logs:
1 - 5
```

WARNING

The ontape utility overwrites the tape whenever a new operation is performed on it. Think of it like the tar command in UNIX.

Performing a Restore

The `ontape` utility can restore the information at the dbspace level or at the system level; the cold restore, warm restore, and mixed restore are also supported. You need to have the tapes to be restored on-hand. Also remember that it is a good idea to label them.

Performing a Whole System Restore

A whole system restore is also known as a whole system cold restore. In general, you use this level of restore because of a serious system crash, or you use it when Informix becomes looped in the fast recovery mode. In these cases, if you cannot afford to attempt a whole system restore, call Informix Technical Support. They have special utilities to clean some part of the log file, causing Informix to become looped when attempting the fast recovery procedure.

The following is a sample session of the whole system restore:

```
% ontape -r
```

The information about your archive is on the tape in the control list page. The sample output session is as follows:

```
Please mount tape 1 on /dev/rmt/0 and press Return to continue
Archive Tape Information
Tape type: Archive Backup Tape
Online version: INFORMIX-OnLine Version 7.21.UC2
Archive date: Tue Mar 15 10:34:02 1997
User id: informix
Terminal id: /dev/pts2
Archive level: 0
Tape device: /dev/rmt/0
Tape blocksize (in k): 1024
Tape number in series: 1
Spaces to restore: rootdbs samdbs1
Continue restore?(y/n) y
```

After reading the chunk information, a similar output should be displayed:

```
Archive Information
INFORMIX-OnLine Copyright© 1986,1987 Informix Software, Inc.
Initialization Time 03/16/97 11:30:33
System Page Size 2048
Version 2
Archive Checkpoint Time 03/15/97 10:34:02
Dbspaces
number flags fchunk nchunks flags owner     name
1         1      1       1      N   informix rootdbs
2         1      2       1      N   informix samdbs1
Chunks
chk/dbs  offset   size  free  bpages  flags   pathname
 1  1    5000     5000  3201          PO-    /dev/rchk1
 1  1    10000    5000  4747          PO-    /dev/rchk2
Continue restore? (y/n) Y
```

At this point, you are asked whether you want to perform a logical log salvage, like so:

```
Do you want to backup the logs? (y/n) y
Please mount tape 1 on /dev/rmt/0 and press Return to continue
```

You are also asked whether you want to restore any other level of archive:

```
Restore a level 1 or 2 archive (y/n) n
```

Next, you are asked whether you have a log tape device that you want Informix to use to replay the transactions specified in those log files:

```
Do you want to restore log tapes? (y/n) y
Roll forward should start with log number 3
Please mount tape 1 on /dev/logtape and press Return to continue
Do you want to restore another log tape? (y/n) n
Program over.
```

Performing a Warm Restore

A warm restore is used when Informix DSA is in online mode, a noncritical dbspace is marked as down, and you want to restore it. Suppose that the dbspace `samsdb1` has been marked as down, and you want to perform a restore. You should accomplish it by executing the following command line:

```
% ontape -r -D samsdb1
```


> **NOTE**
>
> Note that the `-r` option physically and logically restores a dbspace or a list of space-separated dbspaces.

Summary

The availability and reliability of your information is becoming a serious subject for companies dedicated exclusively improving the backup and restore operations in software and hardware. Informix provides a communication mechanism so that you can take advantage of those specialized software and hardware vendors. The release of the OnBar system makes the Informix database backup and restore operations easy, with a higher level of availability and granularity.

CHAPTER

Parallel Database Query

by Mario Estrada

IN THIS CHAPTER

This chapter explains, in detail, how to take advantage of the Informix Dynamic Scalable Architecture (*DSA*), included in the Informix ODS, XPS, and OWS database servers, for PDQ processing. It helps you to understand how PDQ works and how to implement OLTP and DSS systems environments within the same instance of the OnLine database server. From this chapter, you also learn the tools necessary to monitor, use, and improve your PDQ performance.

NOTE

Informix Universal Server is also based on the Informix Dynamic Scalable Architecture. The concepts you learn in this chapter will also apply to this state-of-the-art database server.

What Is PDQ?

PDQ stands for *Parallel Database Query*, which is a new implementation of Informix updated since the release of the 7.*x* engines. It accomplishes complex SQL operations in parallel across several processors, thus reducing the execution time. PDQ breaks down large query operations into small tasks, so that multiple threads can execute their portion of the large task in parallel. The tasks that can be executed in parallel are scan queries, joins, sorts, aggregates, groups, delete, insert, and index creation operations. The PDQ architecture is best suited for Decision Support Systems that require a lot of reads with complex query operations against the database engine. However, if your environment requires you to take advantage of both OLTP and DSS systems in the same instance of Informix DSA, you need to configure and monitor the resources allocated for PDQ so that it does not decrease the performance for OLTP operations. An illustration of parallel computing is shown in Figure 19.1.

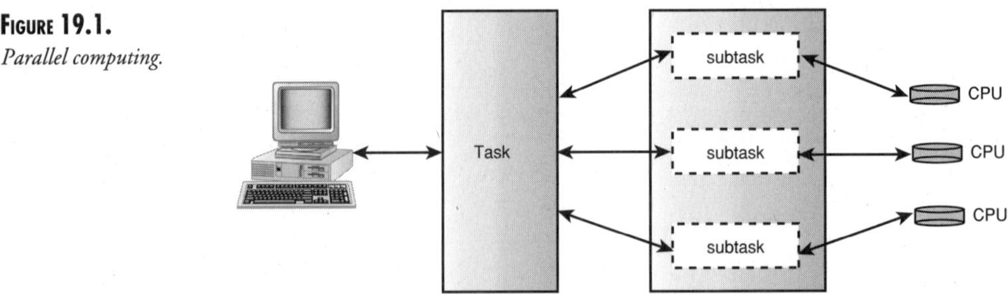

FIGURE 19.1.
Parallel computing.

Overview of PDQ Architecture

Informix implementation of parallel database queries consists of five principal components. Occasionally, Informix DSA makes use of these components in parallel. Every component can be attended by multiple threads; this is known as *intra-query parallelism.* These threads do the job assigned to a component, running on different virtual processors of the class CPU, which in turn can run across multiple processors to achieve a true parallelism. (See Figure 19.2.) The degree of parallelism is specified by the user and limited by the administrator and the resources available in the system.

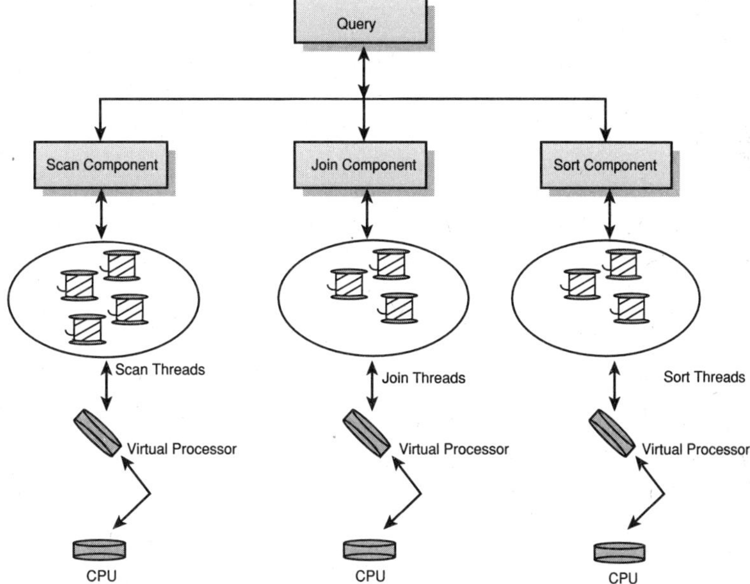

FIGURE 19.2.
Informix's PDQ architecture.

PDQ Components

PDQ consists of seven parallel components, which are well known as SQL operations that usually involve large amounts of data and consume a lot of system resources such as memory, CPU, and disk I/O bandwidth. The parallel database query components in Informix DSA are as follows:

- Parallel Scan
- Parallel Join
- Parallel Sort
- Parallel Aggregation
- Parallel Grouping
- Parallel Insert
- Parallel Index Builds

NOTE

Whenever the query is a parent of a correlated subquery, or you declare a cursor with the clause "for update," Informix will not treat the query as a PDQ query.

A PDQ query can have one or more parallel components. Sometimes these components can be run in parallel, which is known as *inter-operator parallelism.* Suppose that you have a complex query with a join clause. First, Informix must scan the data in parallel. As soon as it has sufficient information, it starts the join, and while the join runs, Informix sorts the information. The parallelism will indicate how many threads will be started to attend a component, and how many components will be executed in parallel, thus improving the execution time, as shown in Figure 19.3.

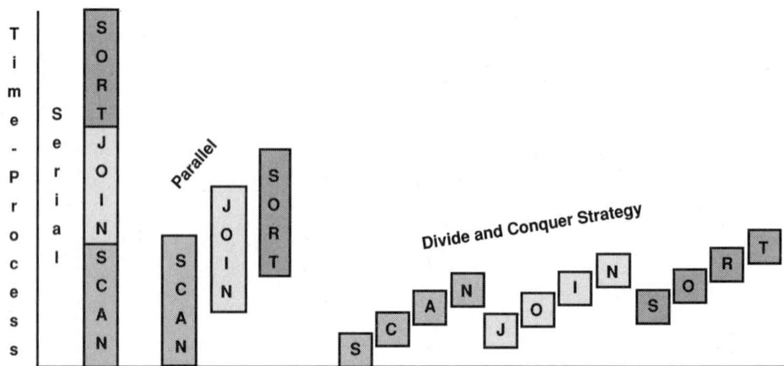

FIGURE 19.3.
The response time for scan, join, and sort operations is significantly improved in PDQ technology.

The primary thread component is the scan thread; the join, sort, aggregate, and group threads are secondary threads. These thread components communicate to each other with an internal mechanism called *exchange.* One thread can be a producer or a consumer. Suppose that a scan thread feeds information to a join thread, which in turn processes the information and feeds the group thread. Thus, the join thread is known as a *consumer* and a *producer* thread. The information about these threads is located in an internal table called the *thread control block* or simply `tcb`, which is coordinated by the `sqlexec` session-thread. An example of the internal communication mechanism is shown in Figure 19.4.

Parallel Scan

Scanning a table is a basic activity for many database operations. The time needed to complete the whole operation may be significantly affected by the time required to complete a scan operation. The parallel scan component reduces scan times dramatically by taking advantage of table fragmentation (as shown in Figure 19.5), because the whole operation could be carried out by multiple threads reading the fragments in parallel. Usually, if a fragment strategy is implemented, Informix starts one scan thread for every fragment. Whether it scans the table or scans the index, Informix can be configured to asynchronously read several pages ahead while the current page is being processed. With this read-ahead capability, applications spend less time waiting for disk access to complete. You configure the read-ahead capability by setting the configuration parameters RA_PAGES and RA_THRESHOLD.

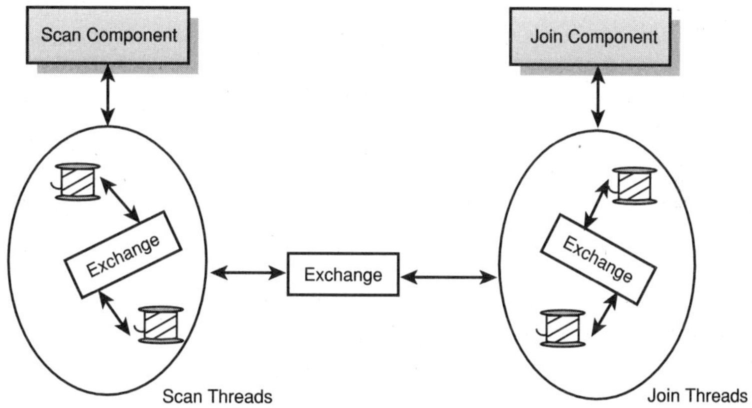

FIGURE 19.4.
An example of the exchange mechanism.

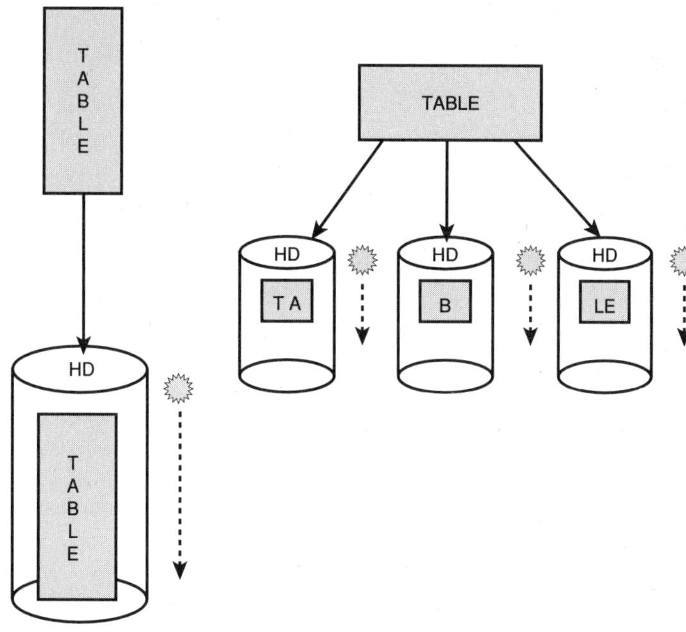

FIGURE 19.5.
The table fragmentation strategy.

The following SQL statement directs the engine to scan the entire table:

```
SELECT * FROM customers;
```

Imagine that the table is across 10 fragments. If PDQ is not used to execute this query, all the fragments are read serially. Using PDQ, those fragments could be read in parallel by 10 scan threads, thus reducing the execution time by 90 percent, depending on many other factors that you will learn about in this chapter.

Parallel Join

The parallel join component sometimes works in parallel with the parallel scan component. As the results are being set in the temporary buffers or in the temporary tables, a join activity is started to form a `tuple`. Informix supports the following join strategies, depending on the value of the configuration parameter `OPTCOMPIND`:

- A *nested loop join* scans the table chosen by the optimizer in any order and then matches the corresponding columns in the second table. As rows are read and matched, a `tuple` is created.
- A *sort merge join* orders every table involved in the join by the join column, merging the results to form a `tuple`.
- *Hash joins* are faster than the other two methods. A hash table is typically created on the smaller table. Informix executes a hash function on every row in the table, determining the hash `bucket` that will hold the row. The rows in the `buckets` are not sorted. The hash table is created in the virtual portion of the shared memory. When no space is available in the virtual portion, it is partitioned out to the dbspaces specified in the `DBSPACETEMP` environment variable or configuration parameter.

TIP

Informix recommends the following calculation to estimate the size of memory in bytes required by a hash join:

(32 bytes * *row_size*) * *#rows_in_the_smallest_table*

An example of a SQL statement that would take advantage of the parallel join component is the following:

```
SELECT * FROM customers,orders
WHERE customers.cust_id = orders.cust_id;
```

WARNING

Using *repeatable read* isolation level with hash joins can temporarily lock all records in the join, because it reads all the records in the table to determine their qualification.

Parallel Sort

Informix implements the philosophy of divide and conquer by breaking each list to be sorted into sections, which in turn are directed to a separate processor for action. Every processor will cooperate to assemble the final result. The `Group by` clause in SQL statements, sort-merge joins, the `update statistics` statement, and the creation of an index will benefit from this component. An overview of the parallel sort package is shown in Figure 19.6.

FIGURE 19.6.
The parallel sort package overview.

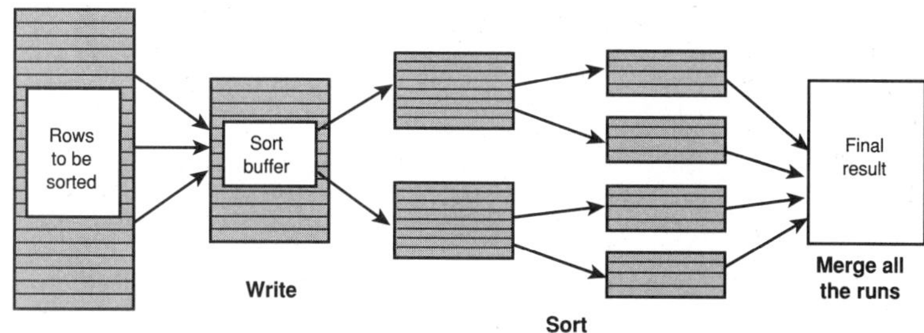

The following SQL statement would benefit from the parallel sort component:

```
SELECT * FROM customers
WHERE customer_id BETWEEN 1000 AND 1050
ORDER BY f_name;
```

> **NOTE**
>
> The `update statistics` SQL statement is not processed in parallel, but it is affected by the values of the PDQ parameters because it must allocate memory for sorting.

Parallel Aggregation

Sometimes a query operation includes other types of operations, such as `SUM`, `COUNT`, `AVG`, `MAX`, and `MIN`. These operations do not return rows from the database server. Instead, they give you information about those rows; and, to obtain that information, they usually have to read rows from the database. You can think of parallel scan, join, and sort working in cooperation with any of these aggregate functions.

The following example shows SQL statements using aggregate functions, which take advantage of PDQ:

```
SELECT SUM(total) FROM orders
WHERE order_date BETWEEN '01/01/1995' AND '01/01/1996';
SELECT COUNT(*) FROM orders
WHERE order_num BETWEEN '1020' AND '20050'
  AND order_status = 'S';
```

Parallel Grouping

The parallel grouping component is invoked when the SQL statement includes the `GROUP BY` clause, and it will work in parallel with the parallel aggregation component. It feeds information to the threads in charge of the aggregate functions, so that they can work on the data sets supplied by this component.

The following SQL statements would benefit from the parallel grouping component:

```
SELECT user_id FROM activity_log
GROUP BY user_id;
SELECT order_num,COUNT(*) number ,SUM(total_price) price
FROM items
GROUP BY order_num;
```

Parallel Insert

The key for this type of parallel operation is `FRAGMENTATION`. Informix recognizes the following two types of insert operations that take advantage of PDQ:

- Insert operations using explicit temporary tables
- Insert operations using implicit temporary tables

NOTE

When inserting a large number of records using the `INSERT INTO` statement, the parallel insert component will dramatically speed up the transaction by inserting the records in parallel.

Insert Operations Using Explicit Temporary Tables

This operation is of the type `SELECT...INTOTEMP`, provided that you have set PDQ priority greater than 0 and you have listed two or more temporary dbspaces in the `DBSPACETEMP` environment variable or in the configuration file. Informix writes to the temporary dbspaces in a round-robin fashion. Remember that true parallelism is achieved if you specify two or more temporary dbspaces. Figure 19.7 shows you this concept.

TIP

Increase the number of temporary dbspaces available to your system if you want to improve performance for this operation, because every temporary dbspace becomes a fragment for the temporary table, and Informix writes to them in parallel.

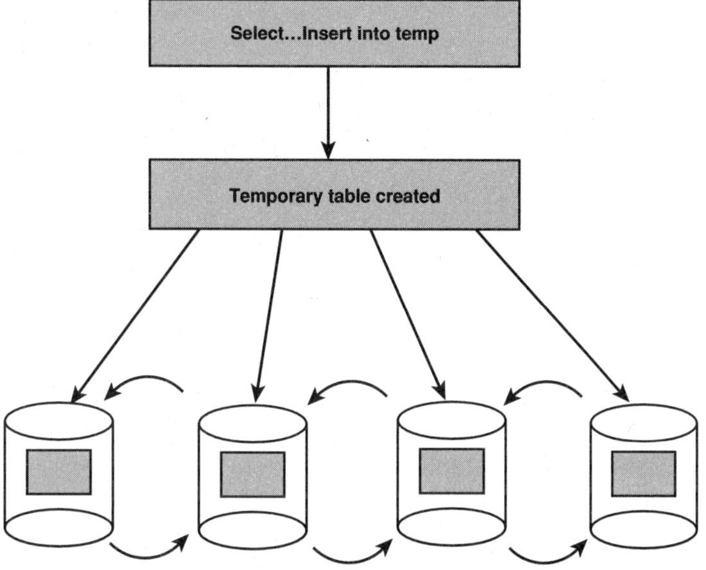

FIGURE 19.7.
The concept of inserting operations using explicit temporary tables.

Insert Operations Using Implicit Temporary Tables

Informix also uses the parallelism for implicit tables that it creates or tables that already exist. For implicit temporary tables, the list of temporary dbspaces discussed earlier still applies, and for normal tables, the parallelism depends directly on how fragmented the table is. Note that not only fragmentation, but also many other parameters that are covered later in this chapter, impose a limit on the number of threads started to achieve this parallel operation. These SQL statements are of the form `INSERT...INTO...SELECT`, where the target table can be either a permanent table or a temporary table.

To take advantage of PDQ in these types of SQL statements, PDQ priority must be greater than 0 and the target table must meet the following criteria:

- If it is a permanent table, it must be fragmented into two or more dbspaces.
- If it is a temporary table, you must specify a list of two or more temporary dbspaces in the `DBSPACETEMP` environment variable or configuration file.
- The table must not reside in another database, whether the database is in the same instance or in another instance.
- The table has no referential constraints enabled or triggers defined.
- The table does not contain fields of the type `TEXT` or `BYTE`.
- If the database has logging enabled, the table must not contain defined filtering constraints.

As mentioned, the key is fragmentation, because the threads insert the information to temporary tables or normal tables in a round-robin fashion.

TIP

When you list a dbspace in the DBSPACETEMP environment variable, this dbspace should be declared as a temporary dbspace when created, so that no log activity is started for it.

NOTE

Informix does not process the operation in parallel if a stored procedure is used to generate the information for the select statement.

Parallel Index Builds

The Informix XPS server builds an index in parallel. When you issue a CREATE INDEX statement, Informix XPS samples the data and determines how many scan threads will be required in order to scan the table. The scan threads read the table in parallel and put the results in shared memory buffers called *bins.* The bins are then sorted in parallel, generating a subtree. The subtrees generated are merged into the final index. As you can see, the Informix XPS does not implement a serial-based architecture when building an index.

The following SQL statement would benefit from the parallel index builds component:

```
CREATE INDEX idx01 ON customer(customer_id,customer_category);
```

How Memory Is Granted

Every PDQ query must register with the Memory Grant Manager (MGM), which coordinates the resources for PDQ. The MGM is explained further later in this chapter. However, keep in mind that PDQ takes more memory and resources from the virtual portion of the shared memory, and that there are approximately 50 pools configured to work in the virtual portion. Among the pools that PDQ queries use most are the sort pools and the pools required by hash joins.

Every PDQ query registered with the MGM is assigned a unit of memory, which is called *quantum* and is the result of dividing the total memory available for PDQ by the maximum number of queries that can be executed concurrently (DS_TOTAL_MEMORY/DS_MAX_QUERIES). The quantum is the smallest unit of memory that can be granted to a query.

Depending on the value of PDQPRIORITY assigned to a query, MGM assigns a percentage of the total memory available for PDQ to the query, according to the formula DS_TOTAL_MEMORY * (PDQPRIORITY/100) * (MAX_PDQPRIORITY/100) rounded to the nearest quantum. MGM reserves a percentage of the resources available for PDQ to each query; it's up to the query to use all or part of it.

Asking More Than a User Is Allowed

If a user asks for more priority than he or she is allowed, the MGM grants a percentage of what the user is asking. For example, suppose the `MAX_PDQPRIORITY` parameter is set to `50` by the administrator, and an end user is trying to obtain 80 percent. If `PDQPRIORITY` is set to `80`, MGM gives the query 40 percent of the resources. You can see that, as an administrator, you will be able to limit the resources for PDQ queries, even if a user asks for a higher priority.

WARNING

If you set `PDQPRIORITY` greater than 0, a query will be treated as a PDQ query, even if it doesn't use any parallel processing at all, thus consuming memory for PDQ. If `PDQPRIORITY` is set to `0`, all PDQ queries will be executed without taking advantage of the resources available for PDQ.

What Resources Are Allocated by Informix?

PDQ processing requires a lot of system resources, including the following:

- CPU
- Memory
- Disk usage (usually involving I/O operations for temporary table spaces and fragmented tables)
- Scan threads (parallel scan operations)
- Secondary threads (dedicated to join, sort, group, and aggregate parallel operations)

You can administer what percentage of these resources will be available for PDQ processing. It is up to you how to balance the resources between DSS, OLTP applications, and non-Informix operations in your system.

You can accomplish the task of balancing by setting some parameters dedicated exclusively for PDQ administration, as explained further later in this chapter. But, generally, you have to do it in the following way:

1. Limit the priority for PDQ queries.
2. Limit the amount of memory allocated for PDQ processing.
3. Limit the number of scan threads.
4. Limit the number of PDQ queries that can run concurrently.

Applications Supported in Informix DSA

Applications supported by Informix can be divided into two major groups:

- OnLine Transaction Processing (OLTP) applications
- Decision Support System (DSS) applications

The division is made because OLTP and DSS perform different types of queries and require different resources from the system and different proportion from the resources that are commonly used for each one. For example, a PDQ query requires more memory from the virtual portion than does an OLTP query, as you can see in Figure 19.8.

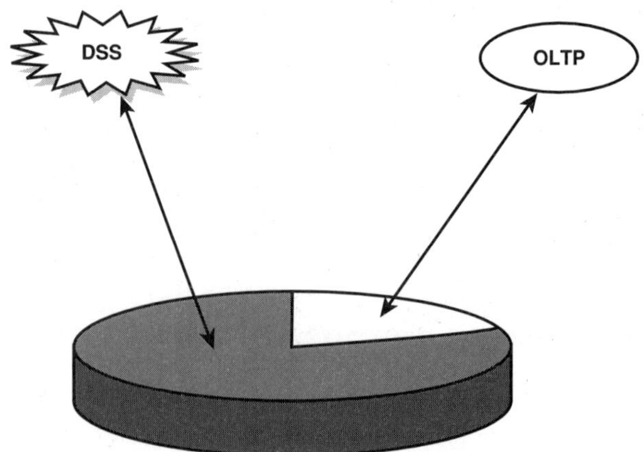

FIGURE 19.8.
A comparison of virtual memory portion usage for OLTP and DSS.

DSS Applications

This type of application usually involves large complex query operations, requiring disk space for temporary table creation, memory for a session, sorting, threads, and CPU utilization.

Informix implements PDQ technology to manage PDQ queries. Usually this type of query requires a lot of memory from the virtual portion of the shared memory allocated by Informix. Remember that approximately 50 pools are designed to work in the virtual portion. PDQ queries require space from the shared structures in the form of AIO vector and sort memory, and also from the thread pool.

DSS applications usually meet the following criteria:

- Many rows are read, usually sequentially.
- The transaction output is extremely low, and sometimes no transaction activity is involved.
- Large temporary tables are created.

- Complex SQL statements are executed, involving the join of large tables.
- The response time of a single operation is usually measured in hours and minutes.
- They are usually involved in batch processes, such as report creation.

OLTP Applications

The OLTP applications usually involve simple writes and reads, require less memory from the virtual portion, and require more memory from the resident portion of the shared memory in the form of buffer pools. An example of this type of application is an Order Entry application, which requires simple lookup queries using an index. The response time for this application is fast, assuming that you have tuned your instance well.

OLTP applications usually meet the following criteria:

- They have high transaction activity.
- Few rows are read, and usually an index read is involved.
- The SQL operations are simple, usually in the form of lookup queries.
- The response times are measured in seconds to fractions of seconds, depending on how well-tuned your instance is.

NOTE

Usually, as an OnLine Administrator, you must balance the resources for both types of applications. A good start is limiting the percentage of the virtual portion of shared memory that a PDQ query can gain (`DS_TOTAL_MEMORY`); then you adjust it, depending on how the rest of it has been used by OLTP queries, so that a higher percentage can be supplied for the PDQ queries.

PDQ Administration

So far, you have learned about the two types of applications supported by Informix DSA and what resources are required for PDQ queries. Now you will learn how to administer the resources available on your system, even if you run both types of applications or only DSS applications.

How to Configure Informix DSA for PDQ

Before running a query, if `PDQPRIORITY` is set to a value greater than 0, you are telling Informix to treat the query as a PDQ query, which must be registered with the Memory Grant Manager. Configuration is that easy. However, you need to limit the resources available for a query, such as memory usage, the number of scan threads available for the query, the number of secondary threads, and the number of queries that can run concurrently. No well-defined rule exists for setting these parameters. It is your responsibility to monitor your system and set adequate parameters for your needs.

An overview of the parameters from the configuration file involved in PDQ administration is shown in Table 19.1 and Table 19.2.

Table 19.1. Parameters involved in PDQ administration from the `onconfig` file.

`onconfig` *Parameter*	*Effect*
`DS_MAX_QUERIES`	Maximum number of concurrent PDQ queries in your system
`DS_TOTAL_MEMORY`	Maximum memory for PDQ queries, in kilobytes
`MAX_PDQPRIORITY`	Maximum priority system-wide that a query can claim
`OPTCOMPIND`	Used with the optimizer
`DBSPACETEMP`	One or more temporary dbspaces
`DATASKIP`	Indicates whether a dbspace should be skipped whenever it is down

Table 19.2. Parameters in the form of environment variables and SQL statements.

Parameter/SQL Statement	*Effect*
`PDQPRIORITY/SET PDQPRIORITY`	What priority a user is requesting for a query
`DBSPACETEMP/`	One or more temporary dbspaces

WARNING

If `MAX_PDQPRIORITY` is not set, a default value of 100 percent is assigned by Informix, so be careful to limit the priority for all the PDQ queries using this configuration parameter.

How to Determine the Degree of Parallelism for a PDQ Query

When using `PDQPRIORITY`—regardless of whether it is defined from an environment variable or from an SQL statement—you are telling Informix what priority you need for the next query to be run in your session. This also determines how many secondary threads (Sorts, Joins, Groups, and Aggregates) will be available to attend the query, using the following formula:

```
secondary_threads = (PDQPRIORITY/100)* number_of_virtual_processors
```

In earlier versions of Informix DSA, the `PDQPRIORITY` parameter was in the `onconfig` file. But having it there didn't make sense, because every query should set its priority; therefore, the parameter has been removed from the `onconfig` file. Thus, you have only two choices for setting this parameter (unless your system still supports it). The choices are as follows:

- You can use the environment variable `PDQPRIORITY`, which supersedes the configuration parameter if your system still has it in the `onconfig` file.
- You can use the SQL statement `SET PDQPRIORITY`, which supersedes both the environment variable and the configuration parameter (if applicable).

Table 19.3 shows the possible values for the `PDQPRIORITY` environment variable or the `SET PDQPRIORITY` SQL statement.

Table 19.3. Values for the PDQPRIORITY parameter allowed by Informix.

Value	*Meaning*
`0`	(OFF) No parallel processing; even if the query is a PDQ query.
`1`	(Scan Only) Only scan parallelism is achieved. The other components are executed serially.
`2-100`	Specifies the degree of parallelism a query is claiming, which is the number of secondary threads (not scan threads) available for PDQ queries, and the percentage of the resources available for PDQ processing.

For scan threads, the degree of parallelism depends greatly upon the number of fragments for a table, the PDQ priority claimed by the user or the application, and of course, the limit specified in the `DS_MAX_SCANS` configuration parameter. Suppose you have a table consisting of 50 fragments, and `DS_MAX_SCANS` is set to `25`. Twenty-five scan threads will be available to scan the entire table, and one scan thread will read two fragments serially. Therefore, the response time might be affected for that single query operation.

You can use the following formula to determine how many scan threads will be available to your PDQ queries:

```
#scan_threads = MINimum value of(#_of_fragments for the table to be scanned or
(DS_MAX_SCANS * PDQPRIORITY/100 * MAX_PDQPRIORITY/100))
```

NOTE

If you want to achieve only scan parallelism, you should specify it by setting the `PDQPRIORITY` parameter to `1`. This directs Informix to activate the scan threads for the query to be run, and the other components are executed serially.

How to Limit the Degree of Parallelism for All PDQ Queries

You must limit the degree of parallelism in your system, because it consumes a lot of memory when threads have to be started to complete a PDQ query task. (Remember that a thread is an instance of the same program, and it must be allocated in memory in order to run.) The degree of parallelism refers to the number of threads allocated to a single query operation. Because you have scan threads and secondary threads, the limitation should exist for both types of threads, and the limitation is accomplished in different ways.

> **NOTE**
>
> Informix reduces the PDQ priority to 1 (Low) during the duration of a query, whenever a query asks for a priority of more than 1 and contains `OUTER` index joins. In the case of subqueries, the reduction is made to the subqueries and not for the parent queries.

Limiting the Degree of Parallelism for Scan Operations

The following three configuration parameters and a fragmentation strategy affect the parallelism for scan operations:

- The `DS_MAX_SCAN` configuration parameter (located in the `onconfig` file)
- The `MAX_PDQPRIORITY` configuration parameter (located in the `onconfig` file)
- The `PDQPRIORITY` parameter (environment variable or SQL statement)
- The maximum number of fragments for a given table

The formula mentioned earlier gives you an idea of how Informix determines the number of scan threads available for scan operations. But consider the following situation:

- `PDQPRIORITY` is set to 50 percent
- `MAX_PDQPRIORITY` is set to 40 percent
- `DS_MAX_SCAN` is set to 20
- 24 is the maximum number of fragments for a given table in your system

Informix starts eight scan threads (which is the minimum value from the formula) for a PDQ query with scan parallelism (`PDQPRIORITY >=1`) activated. It is up to you as an administrator to set the optimal value for your system. In this scenario, eight threads will have to work on 24 fragments, which means that three fragments are executed serially by a single thread and the whole operation will be executed in parallel. For batch processing executing large report operations, you can configure these parameters dynamically using the `onmode` command line, which is covered later in this chapter in the "Changing the Parameters Dynamically" section.

Even if the optimal performance can be obtained by having one scan thread per fragment, the rest of the activities would be affected because more memory and CPU utilization would be required.

Using the configuration parameter DS_MAX_SCAN, you tell Informix the maximum number of scan threads that can be allocated system-wide to run concurrently. Assume that you have set this parameter to 100. If two queries requiring 30 scan threads are executed and a query that requires 50 scan threads registers with the MGM, the last query is held in the ready queue until one of the first two queries releases the scan threads.

NOTE

Keep in mind that if the value of the configuration parameter DS_MAX_SCAN is too short, some users will be waiting for long periods of time.

Improving Performance for Scan Operations

The I/O wait time for sequential reads is significantly affected by the amount of time Informix takes to locate where to start reading the next group of pages, because Informix first has to locate the starting page. This situation can't be avoided, but your process can avoid the waiting time by configuring how many pages Informix will read ahead of the first set of pages. Thus, whenever a scan thread requires the next set of pages, they will already be in shared memory.

Even when the DATASKIP configuration parameter indicates whether a dbspace should be skipped by a query whenever it is down—affecting the result of sequential scans—the only two parameters affecting read ahead operations are RA_PAGES and RA_THRESHOLD.

The RA_PAGES parameter indicates how many pages will be read ahead, and RA_THRESHOLD places a limit on the number of pages that must remain in shared memory before the next set of pages are read.

The three forms of read ahead are as follows:

- Sequential scans
- Searches using an index key only
- Sequential scans using an index key

The concepts of these three forms of read-ahead operations are illustrated in Figure 19.9.

Sequential scans are performed for queries not having a WHERE clause or whenever there is not a usable index in the table for that query.

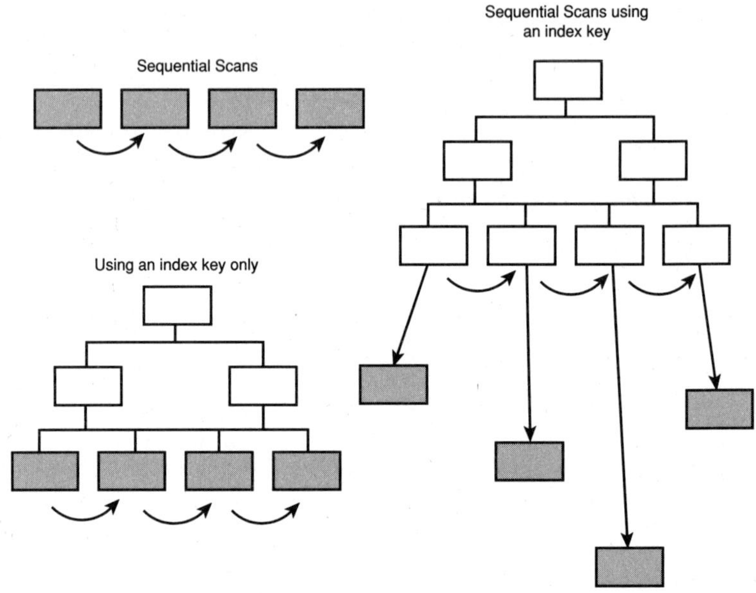

FIGURE 19.9.
The three types of read-ahead operations.

When all the columns specified in the `SELECT` clause are part of an index, instead of reading the table, the index will be read, and as long as the columns are present in the index, no additional read will have to be performed. This type of operation is well-known as a "search using an index key only." Here's an example:

```
SELECT customer_id,customer_rank
FROM customer
WHERE customer_id BETWEEN 1000 and 25000
  AND customer_rank BETWEEN 1 AND 3;
```

If you use the preceding SQL statement, and an index exists on columns customer_id and customer_rank, Informix will read the index to extract the information on the two columns, and no additional read will have to be performed; that is, it will not be necessary to read the table to extract the customer_id and customer_rank information.

The sequential scans using an index key are not appropriate for PDQ queries. Scan threads must read the index leaf nodes sequentially, but then they must read the key's associated data page, which is probably not sequential. That's why it is sometimes better to remove the index to improve a PDQ query's performance.

If you don't set the `RA_PAGES` configuration parameter, Informix uses as a default value the maximum value of the following two expressions:

```
(number of buffers / number of sessions)
```

```
(total number of buffers * 75/100)
```

As a starting point, you should consider the following formulas for both configuration parameters:

```
RA_PAGES = (BUFFERS * %of_the_buffers) / (2* concurrent_PDQ_queries) + 2
RA_THRESHOLD = (BUFFERS * %of_the_buffers) / (2* concurrent_PDQ_queries) - 2
```

In this formula, `%of_the_buffers` is the percentage of the total number of buffers that you want to assign for large scan operations, and `concurrent_PDQ_queries` is the maximum number of concurrent PDQ queries performing large scan operations. For more information refer to the *INFORMIX-OnLine Dynamic Server Performance Guide.*

You should monitor the read ahead parameter using `onstat -p`, which can give you information about the read ahead activity. In general, check the output of `%cached` (for reads), `bufwaits`, `ixda-RA`, `idx-RA`, `da-RA`, and `RA-pgsused`.

If the output of `%cached`—which is the percentage of the read cache—is decreasing, your RA_PAGES parameter is set too high, meaning that too many pages are being read for a single user. This causes a flush activity for other pages needed by other users.

If a query requires more pages but the read ahead activity is still being performed, the output of `bufwaits` will be increased. To avoid this situation, make sure that you haven't configured RA_PAGES too high or RA_THRESHOLD too low.

If all the pages read ahead are being used by the session, the output of `RA-pgsused` would be equal or close to the sum of (`ixda-RA + idx-RA + da-RA`).

WARNING

If you configure RA_PAGES too large and RA_THRESHOLD too high, you will have a lot of page cleaning activity because Informix has to make room for the subsequent set of pages that are being read but are not yet used.

TIP

The size of the light scan buffer used by read ahead operations can be obtained from `RA_PAGES / 8`.

Limiting the Degree of Parallelism for Secondary Operations

The secondary threads in charge of activities such as joining, sorting, grouping, and aggregating information are directly related to the number of CPUs available in your OnLine system (configured in the NUMCPUVPS configuration parameter) and the priority claimed by the query before its execution.

It is well known that parallel processing requires a multiprocessor machine for best performance. Informix PDQ is no exception, because its secondary threads are started and limited by the number of virtual processors of the class CPU, which in turn are linked to a physical processor.

The formula `secondary_threads = (PDQPRIORITY/100)* NUMCPUVPS` is used by Informix to determine the number of these threads to be started by your OnLine system. Given this formula, you should see that four secondary threads will be started if your PDQ priority is set to `100` and you have four `cpu_vps` configured in your OnLine system. Therefore, having more processors available helps you achieve a higher degree of parallelism for joining, sorting, grouping, and aggregating operations.

Special Discussion About Sort Threads

Sort threads require a special mention because the environment variable `PSORT_NPROCS` specifies a maximum number of threads (working directly in a physical processor) for sorting operations that can be started by a session.

Parallel sorting can be achieved even if `PDQPRIORITY` is set to `0`. But when specifying a PDQ priority greater than `0`, you obtain benefits from PDQ because operations such as scan and join are executed in parallel. Informix grants a specific size of memory for sorting, and this memory is represented as a number of sort pools in the virtual portion of shared memory. Figure 19.10 shows you four threads working in parallel, sorting the information in the sort pools from the virtual portion of shared memory, and then concatenating the results.

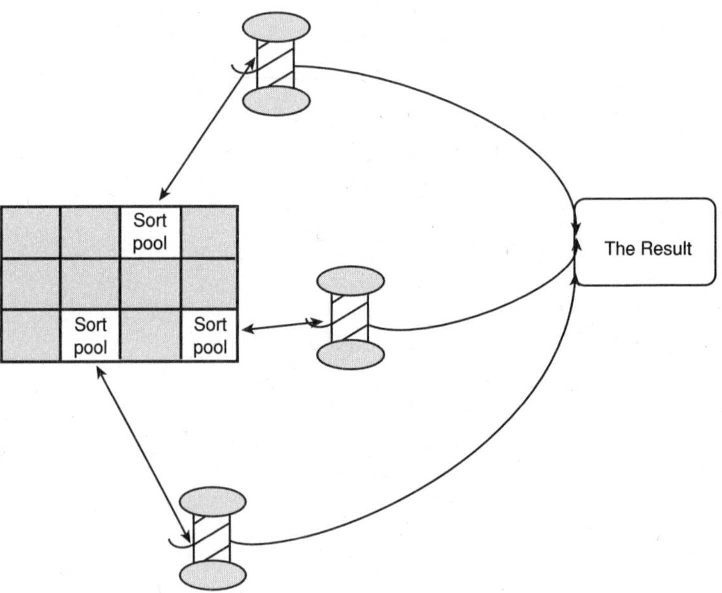

FIGURE 19.10.
A parallel sorting package.

You can also specify where the sort files or temporary tables will be stored. Although the environment variable PSORT_DBTEMP can be used to specify one or more file systems for sort files, the configuration parameter or environment variable DBSPACETEMP gives you better performance because you can define temporary dbspaces configured as raw devices. Remember that a raw device is more efficient for I/O than are cooked files.

NOTE

Because the PSORT_NPROCS environment variable is not set in Version 7 of Informix DSA, a default value of 2 is placed by the server. When a parallel index build is required, two threads are started for every thread that is in charge of building the index subtrees. These threads are called btappender threads.

Limiting the Maximum Number of PDQ Queries Running Concurrently

Many factors affect the concurrence of PDQ queries, including the following:

- Virtual portion size of shared memory
- DS_TOTAL_MEMORY configuration parameter
- DS_MAX_QUERY configuration parameter
- PDQPRIORITY environment variable or SET PDQPRIORITY SQL statement

The virtual portion size of shared memory and the DS_TOTAL_MEMORY configuration parameter limit the memory used by a PDQ query. It is up to the query to ask for all the memory or just a percentage of it, by using the PDQPRIORITY environment variable or simply executing the SET PDQPRIORITY SQL statement. The percentage of that memory required for a PDQ query will limit the number of queries that can be executed concurrently.

An Example of PDQ Query Concurrence and Sorting Memory Required

The following example will give you a better idea of how memory resource for sorting operations are calculated for PDQ processing and how PDQ parameters can affect the number of PDQ queries that can run at the same time.

Assume that the following query will be executed in your system:

```
SELECT * FROM item
order by order_num,order_date;
```

I won't concentrate on the parallelism, because all the memory required by the query will be distributed evenly among the threads required to perform the operation. Instead, this example focuses on the sorting memory required and the parameters that may change the PDQ concurrence, assuming you have the following parameters configured:

- The average number of rows in the item table is 2,000.
- PDQPRIORITY is set to 25 for all users.
- DS_TOTAL_MEMORY is set to 2MB (2,048KB in the configuration file).
- MAX_PDQPRIORITY is set to 100.
- DS_MAX_QUERIES is set to 8.
- OnLine virtual segment size is 8MB (8,192KB in the configuration file).
- The average row size is 300 bytes for the table item.

The memory required from the virtual portion for a single sort is

```
(average_rowsize*average_number_of_rows)
```

In our example, this value is approximately 600KB.

Based on the values of PDQPRIORITY and DS_TOTAL_MEMORY, the maximum concurrent queries for this operation are four PDQ queries. Any other query should be received by the MGM and remain in the ready queue until resources are available—that is, until at least one of the queries finishes its job and releases its resources.

If you change the PDQPRIORITY to 50 for all users, the first query makes a claim for the 50 percent of the resources available, reserving 1,024KB from the virtual portion of shared memory. Thus, only two queries can run concurrently. If a query asks for a priority, MGM allocates what the query asks; it is up to the query to use all of it or just part of it. In this case, if the query requires just 600KB, but claims for 1,024KB, MGM reserves 1,024KB for it.

Now change the MAX_PDQPRIORITY to 50, and set PDQPRIORITY to 50 for all users. Fifty percent of the MAX_PDQPRIORITY configuration parameter is 25 percent. Therefore, every query receives 25 percent of the DS_TOTAL_MEMORY configuration parameter, and four queries could be executed concurrently again, as in the first example.

As you can see, everything depends on your system resources, the volume, and the type of information in the database. In the end, how you configure all these parameters is up to you, based on your own needs.

Limiting the Memory Used by PDQ

Limiting the memory available for your PDQ queries is important because some degradation can occur for OLTP queries and other non-Informix activities. The limit size is specified in the DS_TOTAL_MEMORY configuration parameter. Remember that your PDQ queries consume a lot of memory, especially the memory allocated for PDQ from the virtual portion of the shared memory. Because OLTP queries require less memory from the virtual portion and more memory from the resident portion, which is not related to the DS_TOTAL_MEMORY configuration parameter, the balancing of the resources is applied only to the virtual portion.

If you are going to run a DSS system only, you should set the value of DS_TOTAL_MEMORY to 60 or 90 percent of the total shared memory virtual size. You can check this size using the command onstat -g seg. If you must balance the resources between OLTP and DSS applications, start by applying 20 percent of the total shared memory virtual size, and monitor the use of the virtual segment for OLTP queries. If OLTP queries are not using a lot of memory from the virtual portion, try to increase DS_TOTAL_MEMORY gradually.

If DS_TOTAL_MEMORY and DS_MAX_QUERIES are not set and the SHMTOTAL configuration parameter is set to 0, Informix allocates a default value of (NUMCPUVPS*2*128). Remember that the 128KB value comes from the default value that Informix sets for sort operations.

If DS_TOTAL_MEMORY is not set, DS_MAX_QUERIES is greater than 0, and SHMTOTAL is set to 0, then Informix computes DS_MAX_QUERIES*128, and the result is DS_TOTAL_MEMORY. As you can see, Informix at least needs space for sorts, which in turn make room for other operations.

If DS_TOTAL_MEMORY is not set but SHMTOTAL is greater than 0, Informix computes the following formula:

```
DS_TOTAL_MEMORY = (total_physical_memory_available -
 memory_occuppied_by_the_OS - size_of_the_resident_portion_of_informix -
(128 * number_of_users) - other_non_informix_process_memory)
```

Then Informix assigns you the result as a default value for DS_TOTAL_MEMORY. You can use this formula for yourself as a starting value for DS_TOTAL_MEMORY. Remember to monitor your OnLine activity.

WARNING

If you set DS_TOTAL_MEMORY too high, your operating system starts paging. Use your OS monitor tools to monitor paging and swapping. If paging is increasing, you should consider decreasing the value of DS_TOTAL_MEMORY.

In any of the aforementioned cases, Informix informs you about the result by writing to the OnLine message log file. When you use a default value, if there is no physical space in your computer, Informix assigns the maximum possible value. The maximum value to assign is 1024 * 1024. A good starting point is dividing SHMVIRTSIZE by 4 and assigning the result to DS_TOTAL_MEMORY (which is 25 percent of the total virtual portion of shared memory).

Using Environment Variables and SQL Statements to Configure PDQ

An application can claim a PDQ priority by executing the SET PDQPRIORITY SQL statement, which supersedes the environment variable. Pre-7.0 versions of Informix DSA used the PDQPRIORITY configuration parameter. This was helpful when you wanted a global behavior of the PDQ priority parameter in your system. You can have the same functionality with the most recent versions of Informix DSA by setting the environment variable in a common resource file such as `informix.rc` or even in the system profile.

The main reason for this change is that every different query deserves special attention and different priority, depending on the time, user, and system activity at the time the query is being executed.

The other environment variable affecting PDQ is `DBSPACETEMP`. As mentioned earlier in this chapter, when you specify two or more temporary dbspaces in this environment variable or in the configuration file, the insert operation that creates implicit or explicit temporary tables is executed in parallel.

An Overview of Environment Variables Affecting PDQ Operations

In summary, the following environment variables affect PDQ operation:

- `PDQPRIORITY`
- `PSORT_DBTEMP`
- `DBSPACETEMP`
- `PSORT_NPROCS`

Changing PDQ Parameters

Usually, you have to change the PDQ configuration parameters in order for your Informix DSA instance to work properly. The adjustment of these parameters can be made before Informix is brought online, and some adjustments can be made dynamically while Informix is online using the `onmode` utility.

Changing the Configuration File

The configuration file specified by the `$ONCONFIG` environment variable, located in `$INFORMIXDIR/etc`, contains the following parameters:

- `PDQPRIORITY` (in earlier versions of Informix DSA)
- `MAX_PDQPRIORITY`
- `DS_MAX_QUERIES`
- `DS_TOTAL_MEMORY`
- `DS_MAX_SCANS`

Other configurations related to PDQ, located in the configuration file, are as follows:

- `RA_PAGES`
- `RA_THRESHOLD`

- DBSPACETEMP
- DATASKIP, for which three possible values can be assigned: OFF (no dbspaces will be skipped), ALL (all dbspaces will be skipped), and ON with a list of dbspaces to be skipped
- OPTCOMPIND (the value of 2 is best suited for PDQ operations)

These parameters can be changed using the onmonitor utility or simply by editing the configuration file. The changes take effect when the engine is online again.

Changing the Parameters Dynamically

Informix provides the onmode utility to change some parameters dynamically while the engine is up and running. The onmode utility itself provides a great number of options, but this section focuses on those available to change PDQ parameters.

You receive benefits from this feature whenever you want to perform batch processing at night, and you want your script to change the configuration dynamically. Table 19.4 shows you the options available using the onmode utility and the PDQ parameters affected.

Table 19.4. An overview of the onmode utility for PDQ dynamic configuration.

Command Line	*Configuration Parameter Affected*
onmode -M	DS_TOTAL_MEMORY
onmode -Q	DS_MAX_QUERIES
onmode -D	MAX_PDQPRIORITY
onmode -S	DS_MAX_SCANS

The onmode utility does not make any changes to the configuration file; instead, it directs the engine to change the new value in the engine's internal structures.

NOTE

If you change the parameters dynamically, the queries already running or in the ready queue will not be affected by the new values of the DS_TOTAL_MEMORY and DS_MAX_SCANS configuration parameters.

The Memory Grant Manager

Imagine that you have a set of queries running concurrently in your system and taking from your host computer as many resources as they want, with no program available to control what they take. This could be a disaster. It would be similar to entering a supermarket that has no employees and many customers who want service. Informix implements a memory manager, which is a set of functions capable of administering the resources available for PDQ processing and coordinating the execution of every query with a `PDQPRIORITY` greater than `0`.

What Is MGM?

The Memory Grant Manager is implemented by Informix to manage the resources available for PDQ and to check every query with a PDQ priority greater than `0`, so that it can reserve the memory and other resources available in a given time. The following activities are performed by the Informix MGM:

1. Control the number of concurrent PDQ queries.
2. Supervise the maximum number of scan threads that can be started.
3. Control the degree of parallelism for a query—which is basically the number of PDQ threads that can be started by a single query.
4. Reserve the amount of memory and CPU utilization for a PDQ query.

You can influence the MGM by modifying the parameters available for PDQ processing.

Analyzing the Output of `onstat -g mgm`

Using `onstat -g mgm` at the command line, you get a picture of what is happening at the instant when PDQ processing is taking place. I'll describe every single output from an example so that you can understand what is happening and why some users might still be having low response times.

The following example shows the output of the command `onstat -g mgm`:

```
Memory Grant Manager (MGM)
--------------------------
MAX_PDQ_PRIORITY: 100
DS_MAX_QUERIES: 3
DS_MAX_SCANS: 10
DS_TOTAL_MEMORY: 3000 KB
Queries:     Active    Ready    Maximum
               1         3        3
Memory:      Total     Free     Quantum
(KB)         3000       0        1000
Scans:       Total     Free     Quantum
              10        8         3
Load Control:(Memory) (Scans) (Priority) (Max Queries) (Reinit)
               Gate 1   Gate 2  Gate 3      Gate 4         Gate 5
(Queue Length)  1        0        2           0              0
Active Queries:
--------------
Session    Query    Priority    Thread    Memory    Scans    Gate
 11        cca79c     100       be62d8   375/375     0/2       -
Ready Queries:
--------------
```

```
Session    Query    Priority   Thread   Memory   Scans   Gate
 12        ccd079c    100      bee908    0/375    0/2     1
 13        cd679c     100      bfa508    0/375    0/2     3
 14        cdc79c     100      c06718    0/375    0/2     3
Free Resource    Average #    Minimum #
-------------    ---------    ---------
Memory          0.0 +- 0.0        0
Scans           2.0 +- 0.0        2
Queries          Average #   Maximum #    Total#
-------------    ---------   ---------    ------
Active           1.0 +- 0.0     1            1
Ready            3.0 +- 0.0     3            3
```

To make it more simple, let's divide the output into seven parts.

Part 1: PDQ Parameters

This shows you the values of the `MAX_PDQPRIORITY`, `DS_MAX_QUERIES`, `DS_MAX_SCANS`, and `DS_TOTAL_MEMORY` configuration parameters that Informix took from the configuration file or from the last dynamic change using the `onmode` utility.

Part 2: Queries

This shows you how many PDQ queries are being executed, how many are ready to run but are hindered by something (which is usually reflected in the fourth part, called load control), and how many threads will be allowed to be active or how many threads could be running concurrently (shown in the last field). In this example, only one query is running. Three queries in the ready queue, and a maximum of three, can be executed concurrently, which is the value of `DS_MAX_QUERIES`.

Part 3: Memory

The field `Total` reflects the value of the `DS_TOTAL_MEMORY` configuration parameter. The next field shows the memory available or the memory that is free. The last field shows the value of the quantum, which is derived from the formula `(DS_TOTAL_MEMORY/DS_MAX_QUERIES)`. In this case, `Quantum` is `1000`, and no free memory is available for other queries.

Part 4: Scans

This line shows you information about scan threads. The field `Total` reflects the value of the `DS_MAX_SCANS` configuration parameter. The `Free` field shows how many scan threads are available for other queries. The `Quantum` field shows the smallest unit of scan threads that can be started. Remember that usually one scan thread is started for every fragment of a table, and it is constrained by the `DS_MAX_SCANS` configuration parameter. In this case, two scan threads are working and eight are free.

Part 5: Load Control

Every query registered in the MGM has to pass the load control line. This is implemented as a series of gates, and every gate has some functionality. Every gate shows you the number of queries waiting for the resource controlled by the gate, and every query has to pass from gate 5 to gate 1.

The gates control resources for memory, scan threads, priority, and maximum queries that can be executed at a time. The gate 5 controls the queries affected by the changes made to the PDQ parameters using the `onmode` utility.

In the sample output, one query is waiting for memory, and two queries are waiting for other queries with a higher priority to be executed. The Load Control components are explained in detail as follows:

- **Waiting for Memory (Gate 1).** If you see an increment in the number of queries in this gate, this means you've reached the amount of memory constrained by the `DS_TOTAL_MEMORY` configuration parameter, and the query must wait for some memory to be released. You could probably increment the `SHMVIRTSIZE` (or `onmode -a` dynamically) of the configuration parameter, and then add more memory for PDQ processing (incrementing `DS_TOTAL_MEMORY`), or you can simply monitor what OLTP queries are running and what portion of the shared memory they are using (`onstat -u`, `onstat -g ath`, and `onstat -g ses #`), so that you can increment the total memory for PDQ.
- **Waiting for Scan threads (Gate 2).** If the query requires more scan threads than are available (`Free from Scans:`), it has to wait in this gate until the scan threads needed to start running the query are available. If you see an increment in this gate, your `DS_MAX_SCANS` might be too low or too high, depending on the fragments contained by the table to be scanned. (For more information, refer to the "Limiting the Degree of Parallelism for Scan Threads" section in this chapter.)
- **Waiting for Priority (Gate 3).** This gate keeps all the queries waiting for other queries with higher priority to complete their tasks. It is really up to you and up to the application to control what priority a query should claim. If you see an increment in this gate, you should reconfigure the priority for your queries, or constrain them by modifying the value of the `MAX_PDQ_PRIORITY` configuration parameter.
- **Waiting for a Slot Available (Gate 4).** If a query enters this gate, the limit imposed by `DS_MAX_QUERIES` has been reached; that is, no slot is available for the query, so it needs to wait until at least one of the queries actually running terminates its job.
- **Waiting for Reinitialization (Gate 5).** Whenever you use the `onmode` utility to change PDQ parameters dynamically, Informix has to modify its internal tables, usually located in the reserved pages of the rootdbs. Any new query registering with MGM will be placed in this gate until the reinitialization of these parameters is complete.

Part 6: Active Queries

This part shows you information about the active (or actually running) queries and the ready queries, which are not running because of a resource constraint, explained in the load control line (the gates 1 to 5).

The information given for every query is the session identification (`Session`), the hexadecimal address of internal control block associated with the query (`Query`), the priority claimed by the query (`Priority`), and the hexadecimal address of the thread that registered the query with MGM (`Thread`). The `Memory` field contains two numbers: The first number indicates the number of memory internal get calls and the amount of memory reserved for the query. These numbers represent blocks of 8KB each. The `Scans` field shows the number of scan threads allocated for the query and the number of scan threads currently in use. Finally, if the query is in a ready state, the field `Gate` shows you what kind of resources the query is awaiting.

In the sample output, only one query is running because it has a priority of 100 percent and `MAX_PDQ_PRIORITY` is set to 100 percent. The other three queries are in the ready queue. As you can see, the first query in the ready queue is in gate 1 waiting for memory. It is claiming 375 units of memory, but no memory has been granted because the query that is running has reserved all the memory available.

The other two queries are in gate 3, which means that they are both waiting for the thread in gate 1 to be executed. After the query in gate 1 goes to the active queue, one of the two queries in gate 3 goes to gate 1.

Part 7: Statistics

This part of the output shows you statistics about free resources and queries. These statistics are reset whenever the system is initialized or an `onmode -Q`, `-M`, or `-S` is issued.

The free resource section lists the averages, the minimum amount of memory for PDQ in units of 8KB, and scan threads. The standard deviation from that average is also presented for both memory and scan threads.

The query section lists information about the active ready queue. The first column gives information about the average length for every queue. The second column shows the maximum size the queues have been. The last column (`Total#`) increments every time a query is in every queue, so it tells you how many threads have been in the ready queue and in the active queue respectively. You can use these statistics to tell how your PDQ queries are being executed, how often they are running concurrently, and whether the average time they are waiting for other queries to be executed is making more users wait for a large query to be completed.

Tuning PDQ

As you can see, no fixed rule exists for configuring PDQ. You need to start with some default values. After some monitoring activities, you should write down your expectations, so that you can find a balance in the resources available in your system. Informix PDQ is very flexible, and how it performs really depends on the resources available and how you configure it.

An Overview of the Factors to Consider When Tuning PDQ

Here are some questions you need to answer before implementing PDQ in your system:

- How many users will be executing PDQ queries concurrently?
- What queries will enjoy a high priority, and what kind of reports should work in the background (lower priority)?
- Should all the PDQ queries run at the same time? The best thing you can do is to implement a little benchmark in your system, and test everything before deciding which queries should run at the same time.
- Are OLTP queries running in the same instance? If so, determine the amount of memory that should be allocated for PDQ queries, and remember that PDQ queries use a great deal of memory.
- What kind of table fragmentation are you using? Is it the best in the world? Does it take advantage of different physical hard disks? Remember that having a lot of fragments does not mean a good fragmentation strategy is being used.
- Are you using the temporary dbspaces? If so, how are they configured?

In fact, the best thing you can do before implementing values in your production system is to make some tests with the parameters you have in mind for PDQ.

OLTP and DSS Applications in the Same Instance

By now, you have learned how you can control the resources available for PDQ. When you have control of PDQ, you can have both types of applications in the same instance. A balance of resources must exist, and it is your responsibility to balance those resources (memory, disk I/O bandwidth, and CPU utilization).

Conserving the Resources of Your System

If only some of your applications make use of join, sort, group, and aggregate parallel components, you should set the `PDQPRIORITY` to `1` and `DS_MAXPQPRIORITY` to `25` or `40`. This should conserve PDQ resources for some applications, while others receive the benefits of a higher parallelism using the `SET PDQPRIORITY` SQL statement inside the application or a stored procedure.

This should balance the resources between your normal DSS applications, your large DSS applications, and your OLTP applications.

Factors to Consider for OLTP Queries

The first factor is memory. Even if OLTP applications don't require a great deal of memory from the virtual portion, they require memory from the resident portion for transaction operations. And you should remember that other processes are involved in OLTP.

The second factor is disk usage. OLTP queries usually require a disk read for every operation. To avoid this, the buffers that hold data pages from disk must be tuned for optimal performance.

You might experience some degradation when large reads are executed by PDQ queries, which could reduce some read response times for query lookups (OLTP queries). But remember that when you have more users concurrently running the same DSS application, performance can be improved because some data pages are already in memory.

You have the tools to constrain the resources available in your system for PDQ, and also the tools to monitor the PDQ activity.

Maximizing OLTP Throughput

If you want to maximize OLTP throughput for a query at the cost of some DSS activities, you should set `MAX_PDQ_PRIORITY` to `0`. This forces any query claiming a PDQ priority greater than 0 to be granted `0`, which means that the query is executed without parallelism.

Improving OLTP Queries

OLTP queries usually decrease in performance whenever they have to make sequential scans over large tables or whenever they have to order the rows from tables. Even the join method really impacts OLTP operations. Here are some guidelines you can use as a starting point to optimize your OLTP queries:

1. Avoid sequential scans on large tables.
2. Have an index in the columns in the `ORDER BY` statement that directs Informix DSA to read the index and avoids the sort operation.
3. Set `OPTCOMPIND` to `0`, which avoids the hash and sort merge joins.
4. Influence the query path for the optimizer by using indexes and reading data distributions.
5. Use the `SET OPTIMIZATION` statement to reduce the time the optimizer takes when choosing the best query path.

Improving PDQ Queries

Not having an index improves performance for your PDQ queries, just as it does when you configure the read-ahead capability. If your queries join large tables, it is better to use the hash join method, which is the faster method. As you've already learned, this is done by setting the `OPTCOMPIND` configuration parameter to `2`. Also, for large table scans, it is necessary to have the table fragmented, so that multiple scan threads can work in parallel. If a certain number of users will be working simultaneously in PDQ queries, you should consider setting your PDQ parameters so that those queries can be executed concurrently and the response time can be improved. A recent benchmark for Informix XPS proved that this is true. In general, you should adhere to the following guidelines to improve your PDQ query's response time:

1. If the optimizer is using an index to read a large table, first check your `OPTCOMPIND` parameter, which should be set to `2`. If the parameter is set to `2`, try to remove the index from that table. Remember that scanning a table based on an index read operation decreases your performance.
2. Set `OPTCOMPIND` to `2`. This option tells the optimizer to consider all possible query paths. It also tells the optimizer to choose the lowest costing method between index join, hash join, or sort merge join.
3. Of course, turning on PDQ is necessary. Otherwise, the query will be executed serially and will not take advantage of the resources available for PDQ queries.
4. Try to fragment your large tables so that parallel scans can be invoked.

PDQ and Stored Procedures

A stored procedure is considered to be an object that should contain many SQL statements. The benefit of using PDQ inside a procedure is usually known as *intraquery parallelism*, because it can start with a global priority and change the value after it has been started. Also, intraquery parallelism exists for complex queries that sometimes change the priority for subqueries.

What to Do When Stored Procedures Are Implemented Using PDQ

The recommendation is to set PDQ priority to `0` as the first executable line inside the procedure (`SET PDQPRIORITY 0`), because Informix freezes the PDQ priority available in the environment whenever a stored procedure is created or a manual compilation is taking effect using `UPDATE STATISTICS`.

NOTE

None of the operations that make use of stored procedures will be executed in parallel. The SQL statements inside a stored procedure are the ones that really can take advantage of PDQ.

Who Controls PDQ Resources?

As an administrator, you have to allocate resources for PDQ activity, and you have to exert control over the configuration parameters. Your users will also be responsible for the PDQ behavior in some way. The application itself can change some PDQ priority inside, and it could cause some other queries to start complaining about resources. It is your responsibility to talk with the application engineers and with the end users about the pros and cons of PDQ processing in your system.

How a User Can Control PDQ Resources

An end user can simply specify the environment variable `PDQPRIORITY` to a value of `0` to `100`. This is the end user's only weapon. But even if the end user specifies a high or a low priority, the application can ask for more or less. Remember that the `SET PDQPRIORITY` SQL statement supersedes the environment variable, so the end user basically depends on the application, unless the application doesn't make use of the `SET PDQPRIORITY` SQL statement.

How an Administrator Can Control PDQ Resources

The administrator is the king in this context, because he controls everything by using the configuration parameter file, using the `onmonitor` utility, or simply changing dynamically the PDQ parameters using the `onmode` utility.

The Optimizer Compare Index Parameter

The `OPTCOMPIND` configuration parameter and environment variable is used to tell the optimizer the intended use of the application. It can have only the following three values:

- `0` means that nested-loop joins will be the preferred method chosen by the optimizer. This is a behavior of the optimizer in past releases of Informix.
- `1` means that the optimizer will base the join strategy on costs if the isolation level of a query is not a repeatable read.
- `2` means that the optimizer will base join strategy on costs, regardless of the isolation level of a query.

Usually, the nested-loop join locks fewer rows than hash and sort-merge joins, but it performs more slowly when large tables are involved.

For DSS systems, `1` and `2` are the best choice. If you do not set the isolation level to repeatable read, use the `2` value, which gives the optimizer more query paths to choose from. The query path is a method that the optimizer chooses to form the `tuples`. (It contains rows from a join.)

If a good query path is chosen, the amount of data to be examined will be minimized, and extra sorting for `ORDER BY` and `GROUP BY` statements will be avoided, thus improving performance.

TIP

You should always run `update statistics`. This is the basic principle for tuning your engine, because the information provided helps the optimizer to choose the better query path.

Understanding the SET EXPLAIN Functionality

Sometimes you can monitor your individual queries by using the `SET EXPLAIN ON` SQL statement. Using `SET EXPLAIN ON` generates the file `sqexplain.out`, which contains the query plans for all SQL statements executed until Informix finds the `SET EXPLAIN OFF` statement or the client application ends. This can help you determine which query path the optimizer chose for a given query. If the file `sqexplain.out` already exists, it will be appended, which is useful when you want to collect a log of selected queries.

Each query plan in the `sqexplain.out` file contains some information. Depending on the query, some information will not be present. The general information is as follows:

NOTE

Only the query path chosen is listed by `SET EXPLAIN ON`. You can't find the alternates paths that were considered by the optimizer.

- **The query.** The chosen query will be printed out before any documentation.
- **Estimated cost in units.** The units are not very important; they are used only to compare the cost with other query paths, and they are not used to determine how long the query will take.
- **Estimated number of rows returned.** This is only an estimate. Sometimes it is most accurate when the statistics for the tables are up to date and all filter and join conditions are associated with indexes.
- **Temporary files required.** If the query requires you to create temporary tables, you are shown which clause of the SQL statement was involved when the optimizer decided to create that temporary table.

- **The type of access.** The type of access can be `SEQUENTIAL SCAN` when all rows will be read sequentially, `INDEX PATH` when one or more indexes will be used to read the rows, and `AUTOINDEX PATH` when Informix will create a temporary index. Sometimes the creation of the index is faster than the sequential scan. `REMOTE PATH` is used when a remote server will decide the type of access.
- **The type of join.** Informix uses this type of join to join two tables. The nested-loop join, sort-merge join, and hash join are the only valid join methods supported by Informix. The hash join is available only in engines later than 7.*x*.
- **The `SORT SCAN`.** The `SORT SCAN` keyword tells you that Informix executes a sort in preparation for a sort-merge join. It displays the columns that will form the sort key.
- **The `MERGE JOIN`.** This tells you that Informix will execute a sort-merge join on the tables and columns specified below this keyword.
- **`DYNAMIC HASH JOIN`.** This keyword indicates that a hash join method will be used to join the tables listed below the keyword `DYNAMIC HASH JOIN`. It also prints the columns to be used for the join operation. This is the best join method for DSS systems.
- **`Parallel, fragments: #`.** This keyword was introduced in engines later than Version 7. It tells you whether a table will be read in parallel and how many fragments will be used to accomplish the scan operation. If all the fragments will be used, the keyword `ALL` is present after the word `fragments:`.
- **`# of Secondary Threads:`** This shows you the number of threads started for operations such as join, sort, group, and aggregate.

Suppose that you have the following `sqlexplain.out` file:

```
Query:
SELECT sales_cd, prod_cd, manufact, company
FROM product, sales
WHERE sales_cd IN ('new') AND product.prod_cd = sales.prod_cd
GROUP BY 2,3,1;
Estimated cost: 1088090
Estimated # Rows Returned: 20
1) informix.product: SEQUENTIAL SCAN (Parallel, fragments: ALL)
2) informix.sales: SEQUENTIAL SCAN
filters: informix.sales.sales_cd IN ('new')
DYNAMIC HASH JOIN
Dynamic hash Filters:
               informix.product.prod_cd = informix.sales.prod_cd
# of Secondary Threads: 11
```

From the information contained in the `sqexplain.out` file, you can tell that the scan join will be executed in parallel for the table `product`, the sequential scan for the table `sales` contains a filter condition, a dynamic hash join will be performed, the table `product` will be used by the hash function, and 11 threads will be started to perform the `join` and `group` parallel components. For the scan operation, you limit the number of scan threads, as explained in this chapter, and you can look at more information using the Memory Grant Manager if the query is a PDQ query.

Summary

The PDQ technology implemented by Informix is a result of new computer market trends. After the evolution of data-warehouse implementations, it was necessary to create a new database server and new hardware that could give similar or better performance for parallel query operation than those implemented by proprietary mechanisms in mainframes. Because the Dynamic Server of Informix offers great flexibility in the configuration and monitoring of the database parallel processing, it can fit in any computer environment. The DBA must make it work according to his or her own special needs.

CHAPTER 20

Data and Index Fragmentation

by Glenn Miller

IN THIS CHAPTER

Fragmentation is the deliberate placement of data and indexes on disk according to predefined rules. The term is also commonly used to describe the state of physical files that have become dispersed across a disk, effectively slowing sequential access to them. This disparity is unfortunate. However, because Informix chose to use the term *fragmentation* for its data distribution terminology, the same is done here, and *scattering* is used to characterize noncontiguous files. Reducing scattering as a means of improving database performance is discussed in Chapter 23, "Tuning Your Informix Environment."

Beginning with version 7 of the INFORMIX-OnLine Dynamic Server Architecture (DSA), you can intelligently fragment tables and indexes among several disks as a means of balancing I/O. Systems that can parallelize disk operations can take advantage of this intelligent fragmentation and reduce dramatically the time needed for massive reads or writes. This chapter describes how and when to employ data and index fragmentation.

Reasons to Fragment

Databases are disk hogs. Those few that are not, and that do not tax system I/O, are exceptions. Should you be endowed with such a gift, move on. This chapter is not for you.

The main goal in fragmentation is to balance I/O across multiple disks. Maximizing throughput in this way is especially critical in very large databases, such as those seen in Decision Support Systems (DSS) and Data Warehouses. As opposed to OnLine Transaction Processing (OLTP) environments, DSS systems are characterized by sequential scans of the data, with concomitant slow response times. OLTP applications, conversely, usually perform indexed reads and have sub-second response times. DSS systems usually find themselves disk-bound, so it is crucial that such environments employ the most effective means of scanning data rapidly. Fragmentation is such a means.

The gain for OLTP systems is in reduced contention. When indexes and data are fragmented evenly across multiple disks, simultaneous requests can be served more efficiently. Less contention for single disks results in more concurrency and faster overall system performance.

Parallel Disk Operations

When a table's data is fragmented across multiple disks, a DSS query under OnLine-DSA spawns multiple scan threads in parallel to read the data. This crucial component of PDQ (covered in Chapter 19, "Parallel Database Query") accounts for significant performance gains.

NOTE

When using INFORMIX-DSA for DSS applications, the biggest benefit of fragmentation—even more important than balancing I/O—is using parallel scans.

The ability to invoke parallel scans is one of the reasons that database-level fragmentation can be more effective than hardware striping. Disk striping at the hardware level can help balance I/O for reads and writes but cannot notify OnLine to create parallel scan threads.

Informix's Extended Parallel Server (XPS), an extension of DSA designed for parallel architectures, can take even greater advantage of parallel disk operations. OnLine-XPS can also perform inserts across coservers in parallel, using its Pload/XPS utility. Such inserts are considerably faster than standard loads when inserting into a fragmented table. In addition to inserts and scans, XPS also performs the following functions in parallel:

- Aggregation
- Deletes
- Index builds
- Joins
- Logging
- Sorts
- Unloads
- Updates

This broad range of parallelized functions underscores the importance of implementing an effective fragmentation scheme for an XPS platform.

Fragment Elimination

In certain circumstances, Informix can eliminate fragments from a search. When this occurs, system resources such as CPU cycles, cache buffers, and LRU queues are freed for other operations. Whether fragment elimination can occur depends on the form of the query and the distribution scheme of the table being searched. In brief, this can happen when the query is equality-based and uses filters on the same columns as those that define the fragmentation scheme. Fragment elimination is described further in the section "DSA Data Fragmentation," later in this chapter.

Dataskip

When increased availability of data during disk failures is paramount, fragmentation can mitigate the effects of failed devices. If an application does not need access to all fragments of a table, such as when retrieving data where OnLine has invoked fragment elimination, a query can succeed even when some of the table's data is unavailable.

Additionally, some applications may be designed to tolerate the unavailability of some data. In such cases, if the administrator has marked a fragment unavailable by setting `DATASKIP ON`, the query will still complete. The application may even anticipate such failures and, by executing the SET DATASKIP ON statement internally, specify which fragments may be safely ignored if they are unavailable.

Dbspace Management

Another benefit of fragmentation is finer control over disk usage. The following examples suggest just some of the ways to manage custom dbspaces effectively.

Reliability

OnLine performs backups and restores at the dbspace level. A *dbspace* is a collection of disk regions specifically allocated by the OnLine administrator. Because fragments are assigned to dbspaces, you can implement fine granularity for recovery planning with a judicious fragmentation scheme. Especially critical data can be assigned to its own dbspace for rapid recovery in the event of a disk failure. Index-only dbspaces can be eliminated from the backup plan. Index-only dbspaces can always be reconstructed from the base data, so it is often reasonable not to archive them and to speed up the archive process instead.

Flexibility

The fragmentation scheme for a table can be fluid. That is, fragments can be attached to, and detached from, a table over time. With the ATTACH FRAGMENT statement, you can maintain a "rolling" fragmentation mechanism. This is often useful in a data warehouse application. Usually with such applications, summary data is added to the warehouse periodically—monthly, for example. This load need not disturb the warehouse proper. You can load new data into tables that match the format of the warehouse. When loaded, these tables can be attached to the warehouse's existing tables as fragments, as long as the warehouse's tables are fragmented by expression on, in this case, month. Because attaching fragments is quicker than loading, the warehouse stays more available to its users. Conversely, when warehouse data becomes stale, you can use DETACH FRAGMENT to delete old data or move it to slower disks.

Security

With the GRANT FRAGMENT and REVOKE FRAGMENT statements, you can give individual users custom permissions on specific fragments. In the preceding example, perhaps one set of users is granted permission to alter current data, but permissions on older fragments are more restrictive. The GRANT FRAGMENT statement, while only valid for tables fragmented according to an expression-based distribution scheme, can still be a useful complement to your security planning.

Reasons Not to Fragment

The primary reason to avoid fragmentation is that it is often not needed. Too often, through over-fragmentation, schemas become overcomplicated, dbspaces become difficult to manage, and administrators' jobs become arduous. Fragmentation should be driven by need, not caprice. Small tables should not be fragmented. Infrequently accessed tables should not be fragmented. Most indexes should not be fragmented. Rather, given the option, choosing a fragmentation scheme ought to be done after a system is in operation. Usually, just a few tables or indexes reveal themselves as candidates for fragmentation. By using `onstat -g iof` and other monitoring tools, described later in the section "Monitoring Fragment Usage," you can identify eligible hot spots and construct custom fragmentation schemes for them.

Physical Storage of Informix Databases

Before you can design effective fragmentation schemes, you need to understand how Informix stores its database objects. This section reviews the fundamentals of these basic but crucial concepts.

Standard Engine

SE databases reside entirely in a single directory, `*databasename*.dbs`. Within that directory, each table, including each system table, is stored as a set of files with the same (full or partial) name as the table, a unique number starting at 100, and an extension. For a table such as `stores`, the files might be `stores100.dat` for data, `stores100.idx` for indexes and, on certain platforms, `stores100.lok` for locks.

OnLine, Including DSA

OnLine differentiates between two distinct types of storage: physical units and logical units. Physical units are those sections of disk available for the database to exploit; logical units are internal groupings Informix uses to manage the database. Logical units overlay and generally span physical units.

Physical Units

Informix uses the following units of physical storage:

- Chunk
- Page
- Blobpage
- Extent

The largest physical unit is the chunk. It is a contiguous region of disk, and on most platforms, it has a maximum size of 2GB. It is the only unit allocated to the database directly by the OnLine administrator. Within a chunk, the most atomic unit of physical disk storage is a page. A page is typically 2KB or 4KB, but it is system-dependent and unchangeable. As shown in Figure

20.1, chunks are composed end-to-end of contiguous pages, and because pages are the building blocks of chunks, pages can never cross chunk boundaries.

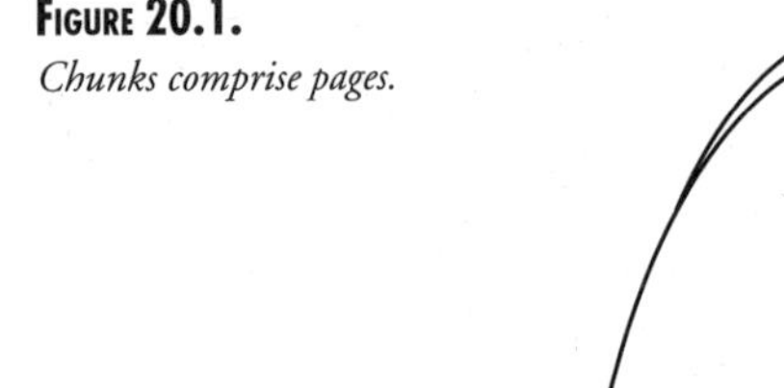

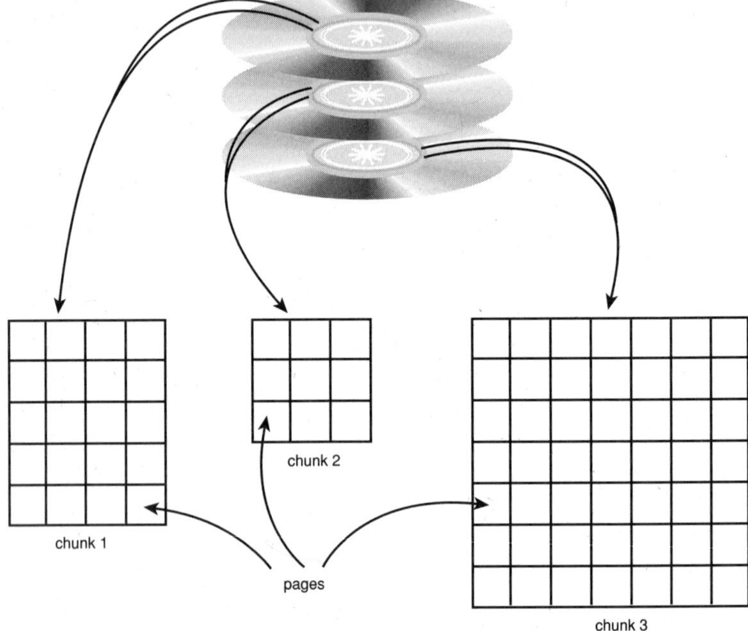

FIGURE 20.1.
Chunks comprise pages.

A blobpage is the unit of disk space that Informix uses to store blobs, or binary large objects. Byte and text are the two blob data types currently supported. Blobpages are specified as multiples of the page size. As with standard chunks, chunks in a blobspace consist entirely of adjacent, whole blobpages. It is possible to store blobs in a standard dbspace, with standard pages; however, when blobs span multiple pages, using custom blobpages is more efficient.

Extents are contiguous groupings of pages within a chunk that store data for a given table. When a table is defined, you can specify its initial extent size and next extent size. The default size for each is eight pages. Upon the creation of a table, the system finds an area of disk large enough to allocate the first extent. Over time, as a table grows beyond its first or any subsequent extents, additional extents of the current next size for that table are allocated. Succeeding data rows are stored in this next extent. As with pages, extents must exist entirely within a chunk. This does not mean that tables cannot span multiple chunks; different extents for the same table can be in different chunks. In fact, this flexibility is what allows for the myriad fragmentation schemes available to an administrator.

Logical Units

Informix uses the following units of logical storage:

- Dbspace
- Blobspace
- Database
- Table
- Tblspace

A dbspace is a collection of one or more chunks in which databases and other Informix objects are stored. The root dbspace is one dbspace that must exist on every instance. It is where Informix stores housekeeping data and is the default dbspace for all other operations. Overriding the root dbspace defaults with deliberate dbspaces is usually the first step toward effective data distribution. At the least, moving the physical and logical logs to separate devices, as described in the section "OnLine Data Distribution," is almost always worthwhile.

Besides standard dbspaces, OnLine version 6.0 and OnLine-DSA also support the use of temporary dbspaces. Temporary dbspaces are those reserved exclusively for the storage of temporary tables and are temporary only insofar as their contents are not preserved in the case of a shutdown. Temporary dbspaces also escape logical and physical logging. Because of this reduced overhead, temporary dbspaces are ideal for transitory database operations.

A blobspace is a logical storage unit consisting of chunks that contain only blobpages. Blobs from several tables can be stored in the same blobspace. Because blob data is so voluminous, Informix has chosen to write blob data directly to the blobspaces, rather than shunting writes through resident shared memory, as it does with all other data types. Likewise, blob updates are never written to the logical or physical logs. Instead, the blobspaces are written directly from disk to the logical log backup tapes when the logical logs are backed up.

As a logical storage unit containing related tables and indexes, a database is initially created within a single dbspace. Also in that dbspace are the system tables Informix uses to store information about that database's structure and internal relationships. If no dbspace is named when a database is created, it is created in the root dbspace. By default, tables are created in the same dbspace as their database. Much of the remainder of this chapter describes how and when to override those defaults to recognize the advantages of data and index fragmentation.

Informix uses the tblspace as a logical grouping to indicate all the pages that are allocated for a table. In addition to data and index pages, tblspaces contain pages used to store blob data (when stored in a dbspace), remainder pages, and bitmap pages that track page usage within the table extents. When a table is fragmented, it consists of several tblspaces because each fragment is considered to be its own tblspace.

Figure 20.2 depicts how tblspaces can exist on more than one disk and how tables within that tblspace can span disks.

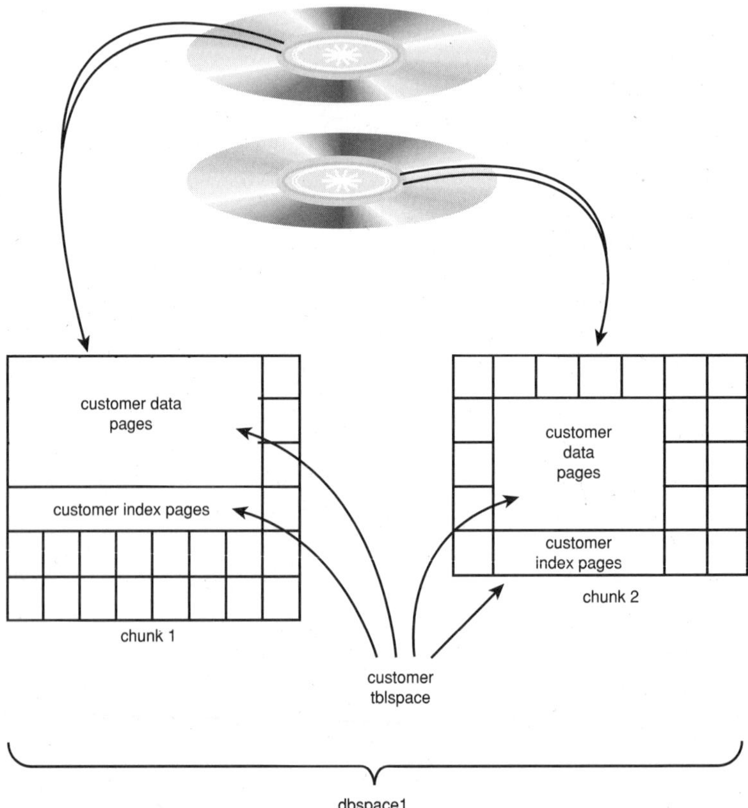

FIGURE 20.2.
Tblspaces can span disks.

Extended Parallel Server

Informix recently introduced an extension of its DSA engine suitable for loosely coupled cluster and massively parallel processor architectures. The Extended Parallel Server (XPS) shares many features of DSA but adds functionality designed specifically to exploit the parallelism of these new architectures. Because of its efficiency at performing parallel operations, XPS is especially suitable for very large (more than 50GB) DSS and data warehouse applications.

An XPS system is designed around a multiple coserver model. On each coserver, or node, is a separate Informix instance that communicates with the other coservers through a high-speed internal switch. Coservers have their own CPUs, memory, and disk. It is this segregation of functions that allows database operations to be performed in parallel. The performance improvements achievable for simple parallel operations such as loading are dramatic: Speeds increase nearly linearly as additional nodes are added. The challenge for the administrator is to marshal the independent resources of the coservers into an effective team.

OnLine-XPS adds the following units of storage to those described earlier:

- Dbslice
- Logslice
- `ROOTSLICE`
- `PHYSSLICE`

One construct available to help deploy coservers effectively is the dbslice. A dbslice is a collection of automatically generated dbspaces, usually identical, and usually on multiple coservers, which can be administered concurrently. As with dbspaces, dbslices may be standard or temporary. The derived dbspaces contain all the traditional OnLine storage units but allow you to apply a single reference to the dbslice to each dbspace simultaneously. Without such a consistent means of managing the numerous dbspaces usually required for an XPS system, OnLine administration quickly becomes unwieldy.

Figure 20.3 shows a series of derived dbspaces, named `cust_slice.1` through `cust_slice.6`, which are the components of the `cust_slice` dbslice. In this example, each of the three coservers uses two disks for this dbslice.

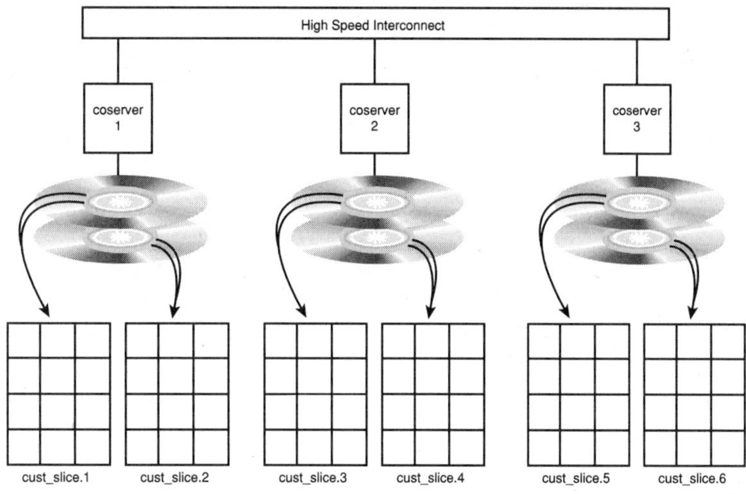

FIGURE 20.3.
Dbslices simplify XPS administration.

A logslice is a type of dbslice used only for managing logical logs. Logslices simplify the creation and management of logical logs across coservers by treating sets of logs as a single entity.

`ROOTSLICE` is an optional configuration parameter that specifies a root dbspace on each defined coserver. If used, it supersedes the `ROOTNAME` parameter. It takes effect only when the disk is initialized and creates one derived dbspace per coserver. The dbspaces that are created are named *`rootslicename.n`*, where *`n`* is the coserver number. You cannot change the `ROOTSLICE` parameter once the instance is initialized.

When used, PHYSSLICE, another optional global configuration parameter, dictates where the physical log resides. As with ROOTSLICE, it is used to specify a range of derived dbspaces and takes effect when the Informix instance is initialized. You can use the coserver-specific parameter PHYSDBS after initialization to migrate the physical log if needed.

Standard Engine Data Distribution

There is no fragmentation *per se* with the Standard Engine. SE is used primarily where reliability is more important than performance and when the sacrifice of flexibility in tuning is acceptable. Moreover, SE databases are generally small and, on the whole, less complex than OnLine databases. Often, there is only one disk; fragmentation then is unreasonable. Nonetheless, when multiple disks are available, especially if they are on different disk controllers, you should place the database on its own disk. The best option is to separate the database's disk from other disk-intensive areas, such as system swap space, or drives where the operating system is mounted.

Table Placement

You can use tools available within the operating system to distribute heavy-use or large tables to dedicated disks if needed. If you can predict that a table or set of tables would benefit from being placed on its own drive, you can define this with a statement like the following:

```
CREATE TABLE stores (
store_no     INTEGER,
store_mgr    CHAR(20))
IN "/disk2/store";
```

After an SE database is created, it is trickier to move an existing table. Re-creating the table with a designated directory and reloading the data are preferred. Another option is to move the table to another disk and then create a symbolic link at its original location. The following syntax shows one way to accomplish this:

```
mv /busy_disk/retail_db.dbs/stores100.dat /quiet_disk/stores100.dat
ln -s /quiet_disk/stores100.dat  /busy_disk/retail_db.dbs/stores100.dat
```

If you decide to move files in this way, be sure to keep the index file (.idx) and data file (.dat) in the same location.

CAUTION

Exercise care when moving existing data and index files in this manner. This method of distributing data is *not* supported by Informix.

Logical Volume Manager

Some operating systems provide a Logical Volume Manager (LVM). With an LVM, you can create a custom pool of available space, called a logical volume, which can span disk drives. Directories can be allocated to a logical volume, instead of to a fixed partition. These logical volumes can therefore be arranged to balance I/O by partitioning a database directory, or a heavily used table, across several drives.

OnLine Data Distribution

Informix's OnLine Engine is characterized by its internal management of dbspaces. Even though fragmentation proper is not available with INFORMIX-OnLine version 5, many tools do exist with which to allocate and distribute data effectively.

Logs

In an OLTP environment, gaining maximum advantage from "prime real estate," the center of the disks, is critical. Because a dbspace may be composed solely of one chunk and a chunk's location is determined exactly by the administrator, you can precisely define the location of a dbspace on disk. Therefore, you can place the most active dbspaces on the most efficient disk drives. For OLTP systems, the disk hot spot is usually the logical log.

TIP

In an OLTP environment, migrate the logical logs to the fastest dedicated drive available. Because writes to the logical logs are sequential, the disk head is always positioned correctly.

For systems with rapidly changing data, the physical log can also create a performance bottleneck, especially when it resides on the same disk as the root dbspace. After migrating the logical logs, consider moving the physical log next.

Custom Dbspaces

At the extreme, you can place each table in its own dedicated dbspace. With such a strategy, you can achieve exact partitioning of the disk. This is almost never worthwhile. Instead, after migrating databases and logs out of the root dbspace, only spend the time to distribute high usage or very large tables. In addition, if certain tables are always being joined, consider placing them on separate disks.

When a critical table requires the use of several disks to balance I/O, you can mimic disk striping with the tactic pictured in Figure 20.4.

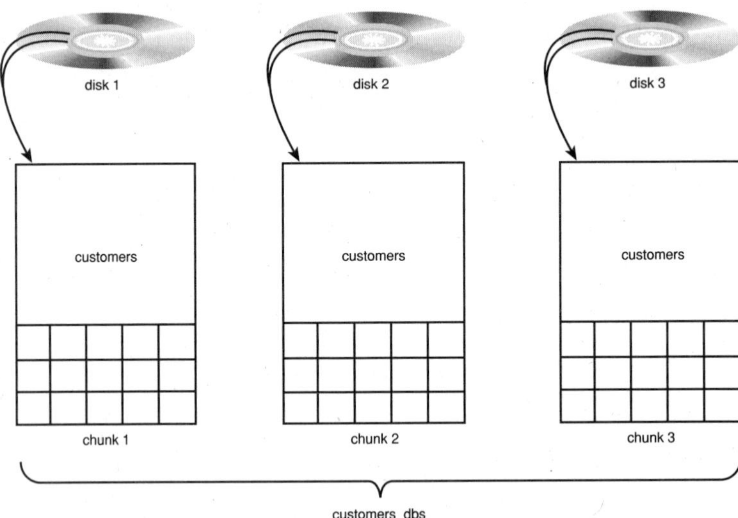

FIGURE 20.4.
How to mimic disk striping.

In this case, the `customers_dbs` dbspace comprises three chunks, one per disk. Each chunk is 100MB. The customer table's first and next extents are defined to be 60MB. The first extent is placed in `chunk1` on `disk1`. Informix allocates extents with contiguous pages, if possible. After 60MB of data are loaded, OnLine allocates the next extent, another 60MB. Because there is insufficient space in `chunk1` to allocate the entire next extent, it is created in `chunk2`. 40MB of `chunk1` remain unused. An extent is created in `chunk3` in a similar fashion. You can place other tables, or even indexes from this table, in the unused space; alternatively, the space can remain available to accommodate further growth.

Temporary Spaces

Even though OnLine version 5 does not support temporary dbspaces *per se*, you can still create a dbspace for the exclusive use of explicit temporary tables. By default, explicit temp tables are placed in the dbspace of the current database, but this may be superseded:

```
CREATE TEMP TABLE work_area (
cust_no     INTEGER,
cust_totals INTEGER)
IN temp_dbs;
```

You can place this `temp_dbs` dbspace on a high-speed disk if one is available. Such a dedicated dbspace can help ensure that space is always available for those operations that use explicit temporary tables.

You can create two other kinds of temp tables: sort and implicit. Sort temp tables are created with the following kind of SQL statement when no index on last_name exists:

```
  SELECT *
    FROM customer
ORDER BY last_name;
```

Sort temp tables are created in the /tmp directory, unless other directories are specified with the environmental variable DBTEMP. You can name several directories, separated by colons.

If a multiprocessor machine is used and the environmental variable PSORT_NPROCS is set, then OnLine can invoke parallel processing for sorts. Candidates for parallel sorting include not only ORDER BY statements but also SELECT UNIQUE commands and sort/merge joins. When this happens, Informix writes these temporary sort files to the directories listed in PSORT_DBTEMP. When this variable is set to multiple directories, those writes are spread across multiple file systems. For instance, by setting PSORT_DBTEMP=/tmp:/tmp2, you place sort files alternately in /tmp and /tmp2. Naturally, these directories should be on different disks. If a parallel sort is invoked and PSORT_DBTEMP is not set, OnLine uses the value of DBTEMP. If DBTEMP is not set, it uses /tmp.

Finally, implicit tables are those generated internally in the process of executing a statement such as a SCROLL CURSOR.

For Informix versions prior to 6.0, implicit temp tables are created in the root dbspace. With OnLine version 6.0, you can use true temporary dbspaces. When available, Informix uses these for implicit and sort temp tables. A temporary dbspace can—and should—also be used for explicit temp tables.

DSA Data Fragmentation

The general goal of fragmentation is to distribute data evenly. Any fragmentation scheme selected ought to have this idea paramount. When an improper fragmentation strategy distributes data unevenly, such that one dbspace has an inordinate quantity of data, the result is known as *data skew.* The choice of which fragmentation scheme to use depends largely on which can properly avoid data skew. An additional benefit afforded by expression-based and hash-based fragmentation is that certain fragments can be eliminated from a search. Fragment elimination can substantially reduce contention and increase search speed.

NOTE

When a table is fragmented, the extent size specified in the CREATE TABLE statement is applied to each fragment. Thus, extent sizes calculated for a table as a whole need to be divided by the number of fragments to be appropriate for a fragmented table.

Round-Robin Fragmentation

The round-robin fragmentation scheme is the easiest to use. It places rows of data alternately into each dbspace specified in the `CREATE TABLE` statement. This is best used when all fragments must be scanned, as is often true with DSS applications:

```
CREATE TABLE tablename (column list)
FRAGMENT BY ROUND ROBIN
IN (list of dbspaces);
```

The primary advantage of a round-robin fragmentation scheme, besides simplicity, is that it is guaranteed to avoid data skew. However, because the scheme is not expression-based, the OnLine engine is never able to eliminate fragments from a query that accesses a table fragmented by round robin.

Expression-Based Fragmentation

The expression-based fragmentation strategy places related rows in the same dbspace. An SQL expression that identifies a set of rows is specified for each fragment. Rows that match the criteria in an expression are placed in the corresponding dbspace:

```
CREATE TABLE tablename (column list)
FRAGMENT BY EXPRESSION
SQL expression IN dbspace,
SQL expression IN dbspace,
REMAINDER IN dbspace;
```

The SQL expression can refer only to columns in the table and cannot contain subqueries, stored procedures, or references to external tables. The `REMAINDER IN` clause is optional and indicates where rows that do not match any of the SQL expressions should be placed.

TIP

Be cautious with the `REMAINDER IN` clause of the `FRAGMENT BY EXPRESSION` statement. Remainder fragments often become overloaded with data, creating data skew. Additionally, OnLine is not always able to eliminate a remainder fragment from a search.

Fragmenting by expression is especially beneficial when it allows OnLine to eliminate fragments to be scanned. This occurs when the query expression can unequivocally identify the fragment to be scanned based solely on the fragmentation expressions. Generally, this means that the query contains an equality or range expression, and the fragmentation rule creates non-overlapping fragments. In such situations, when the data is accessed with a high degree of selectivity, fragmenting by expression is most advantageous.

Choosing the Proper Strategy

The first step in choosing the proper fragmentation strategy is understanding your application. Primarily, is it a DSS application, where improved single user response time is important, or is it an OLTP application, where reducing contention matters most? For a review of the differences, refer to the section "Reasons to Fragment," earlier in this chapter.

If you have a DSS application, maximum data throughput is generally your primary concern. Often, all data fragments have to be scanned. When this is true, you should fragment your data to increase parallelism but not fragment your indexes. You may have few indexes; those you do have should be detached and placed in separate dbspaces.

If there is a reasonable set of expressions that can be established to distribute your data evenly (see "Avoiding Data Skew," later in this chapter), then you should use a `FRAGMENT BY EXPRESSION` scheme. Otherwise, as long as the application will not delete many rows, use `FRAGMENT BY ROUND ROBIN`. DSS queries primarily demand balanced I/O and permit no fragment elimination. Round-robin fragmentation provides this.

The exigencies of OLTP applications demand a different strategy. Fragment elimination is usually your chief interest. When you eliminate fragments—usually index fragments—individual queries run faster, simultaneous sessions contend less for disk, and concurrency is generally increased.

The goal is to design an effective *rule*, or set of expressions, by which to fragment. In most cases, the same rule is applied both to the data and to the index. When designing the fragmentation rule, try to create non-overlapping expressions based on a single column with no remainder clause. OnLine is best able to eliminate fragment when these conditions are true. For a clear example of how fragment elimination occurs with such a rule, refer to the section "Monitoring Fragment Usage," later in this chapter.

Tuning the Expressions

The following tips will help you create more efficient SQL expressions when you use an expression-based fragmentation scheme:

- Order the expressions by their likelihood of being true. The expressions are evaluated in order, with a row's destination determined as soon as an expression evaluates to true.
- Keep expressions simple, so as not to confuse the optimizer and to make it more likely that fragmentation elimination will occur.
- Do not fragment on a data type that needs conversion, such as date. Type conversions increase the time needed to evaluate the expression.

CAUTION

Some Informix manuals recommend using the MOD operator in a FRAGMENT BY EXPRESSION to simulate a hash scheme. Don't do this. The supposed advantage is to create an even distribution of data; instead, use round robin. The overhead required to parse the MOD value makes it unacceptable as a fragment key.

Avoiding Data Skew

Starting with OnLine version 6.0, Informix has the capability to generate and report on data distributions for a column. By examining these distributions, you can create a FRAGMENT BY EXPRESSION strategy that avoids data skew. In the following example, imagine that you want to fragment the orders table among five disk drives. You decided that you will construct range-based expressions on cust_no, but you want to be sure to create balanced fragments. With the following SQL statement, you instruct OnLine to sample the orders table and apportion the values it finds for cust_no into 10 bins:

```
UPDATE STATISTICS HIGH FOR TABLE orders(cust_no)
RESOLUTION 10 DISTRIBUTIONS ONLY;
```

TIP

When you invoke UPDATE STATISTICS to generate distributions for refining your fragmentation expression, add the DISTRIBUTIONS ONLY clause. This keeps OnLine from reconstructing index information. The time savings can be considerable.

After the statistics are calculated, you can examine the results with the following Informix utility:

```
dbschema -d retail_db -hd orders
```

The following code shows a portion of the output:

```
Distribution for informix.orders.cust_no
High Mode, 10.000000 Resolution
--- DISTRIBUTION ---
     (                        1)
 1: (  1257,    965,     967)
 2: (  1257,   1065,    2032)
 3: (  1257,   1149,    3182)
 4: (  1257,    715,    3900)
 5: (  1257,   1213,    5113)
 6: (  1257,    899,    6012)
 7: (  1257,   1205,    7317)
 8: (  1257,   1244,    8642)
 9: (  1257,    619,    9261)
10: (  1218,   1166,   10427)
```

Each bin's statistics are shown on one line. The first value is the number of rows in the bin; the second value is the number of unique values for `cust_no` in the bin; the last column shows the high value for that bin.

With these values, you can build the following accurate fragmentation strategy:

```
FRAGMENT BY EXPRESSION
cust_no                          < 2032 IN dbspace1,
cust_no >= 2032 AND cust_no < 3900 IN dbspace2,
cust_no >= 3900 AND cust_no < 6012 IN dbspace3,
cust_no >= 6012 AND cust_no < 8642 IN dbspace4,
cust_no >= 8642                         IN dbspace5;
```

Because each bin represents 10 percent of the data, by adopting the high value for every second bin as the barrier between fragments, you ensure an equal distribution of data among the five disks. If this distribution becomes inefficient over time, you can change it when the need arises. For details on how to do this, refer to the section "Modifying Fragmentation Strategies," later in this chapter.

Creating Data Skew

In some situations, it might actually be beneficial to create an intelligent data skew. Suppose that in the previous example, the older data (lower `cust_no` values) is seldom accessed. The need then is to balance I/O requests across disks, rather than data. You can separate a smaller amount of heavily accessed data from larger amounts of lightly accessed data. To accommodate spreading active portions of the data across disks might call for a scheme like this one:

```
FRAGMENT BY EXPRESSION
cust_no                          <  5000 IN dbspace1,
cust_no >=  5000 AND cust_no <  7500 IN dbspace2,
cust_no >=  7500 AND cust_no <  9000 IN dbspace3,
cust_no >=  9000 AND cust_no < 10000 IN dbspace4,
cust_no >= 10000                         IN dbspace5;
```

The net performance for accessing the table with this strategy might improve, even though there is an uneven distribution of data rows.

Minimizing Overhead

Do not fragment capriciously. There is some overhead in creating and maintaining a table's fragments, so do not create very small fragments. Also, do not fragment seldom used tables or indexes; the complexity is unnecessary.

Over-fragmenting can lead to thread saturation, when too many scan threads are generated and overwhelm the CPU VPs. Although it is true with individual queries that parallel I/O performance increases nearly linearly with the number of fragments added, this increase has a limit. With very small fragments, the limits of the bus bandwidth and the number of CPUs defeat any gains from parallel scans. Any benefits of fragmentation are offset by the need to coordinate multiple scan operations.

Another way to avoid unnecessary overhead is to choose stable columns in the fragmentation expression. If a column that is updated is part of a fragment-by-expression rule, the database engine needs to reevaluate the row to see if its distribution should change. The evaluation is slow; actually moving a row is even slower.

Monitoring Fragment Usage

You have a number of tools for monitoring fragment usage. A few of them are described in the following sections. For more information about monitoring in general, see Chapter 21, "Monitoring Your Informix Environment," and Chapter 22, "Advanced Monitoring Tools."

SET EXPLAIN

The SQL statement `SET EXPLAIN ON` displays the path Informix uses to process a query. As a general monitoring tool to optimize your applications, it is invaluable. You can find an extensive discussion of this tool in Chapter 23. A subset of its output reveals which fragments of a table Informix needs to use to satisfy a query. This is especially useful to recognize whether Informix can eliminate fragments from a query.

The following examples show fragment elimination occurring for a table when it is fragmented by expression but not when it is fragmented by round robin. Consider the following two fragmentation schemes:

```
CREATE TABLE customers (
cust_no    INTEGER,
last_name  CHAR(20))
FRAGMENT BY EXPRESSION
cust_no >      0 AND cust_no <  5000 IN dbspace1,
cust_no >= 5000 AND cust_no < 10000 IN dbspace2,
cust_no > 10000                     IN dbspace3;
```

```
CREATE TABLE customers (
cust_no    INTEGER,
last_name  CHAR(20))
FRAGMENT BY ROUND ROBIN IN dbspace1, dbspace2, dbspace3;
```

When a query that filters only on `cust_no` is run, Informix may be able to eliminate fragments when the table is fragmented by expression:

```
SELECT *
  FROM customers
 WHERE cust_no < 6212;
```

The database engine needs to examine only fragments 0 and 1 (`dbspace1` and `dbspace2`). The relevant lines from the `SET EXPLAIN` output reveal this:

```
Estimated Cost: 342
Estimated # of Rows Returned: 6155
1) informix.customers: SEQUENTIAL SCAN  (Parallel, fragments: 0, 1)
    Filters: informix.customers.cust_no < 6212
```

As Table 20.1 shows, certain equality and range operators allow fragment elimination for expression-based fragmentation, but Informix can never use round-robin fragmentation to eliminate fragments.

Table 20.1. SET EXPLAIN reveals fragment elimination. These fragments must be scanned to satisfy the query.

Filter	*Expression-Based Fragmentation*	*Round-Robin Fragmentation*
`cust_no = 432`	0	All
`cust_no < 6212`	0, 1	All
`cust_no > 5200 and cust_no < 7219`	1	All
`cust_no in (502, 11312)`	0, 2	All
`cust_no between 10342 and 12335`	2	All
`cust_no > 0`	All	All
`cust_no < 0`	None	All

The last row in the table is of special interest. Informix recognizes, solely from the fragmentation expression, that no rows can satisfy this query.

The Sysfragments Table

Informix stores information about the structure of its databases and storage units in a set of internal tables called system tables. One of these tables, `sysfragments`, keeps a row for each fragment managed by OnLine. Table 20.2 shows some of the useful columns in this table.

Table 20.2. Useful Sysfragments components.

Column Name	*Description*
`fragtype`	Type of fragment: (I)ndex or (T)able
`tabid`	The table ID that corresponds to this table's entry in `systables`
`indexname`	The name of the index, if this entry describes index fragmentation
`partn`	Unique number that identifies the physical location of the fragment

continues

Table 20.2. continued

Column Name	*Description*
`strategy`	(R)ound robin, (H)ash, (E)xpression, (I)ndex, detached from table, (T)able-based, or attached index
`exprtext`	Fragmenting expression
`dbspace`	The dbspace where this fragment is located
`levels`	The number of levels for the B+ tree index, if this is an index
`npused`	Number of pages used (for table: data pages; for index: leaf node pages)
`nrows`	Number of rows in the fragment (for table: data rows; for index: unique values)

One way to use this table is to examine the amount of data in each fragment to see whether data and indexes are distributed evenly. The following SQL query shows all user-defined fragments:

```
  SELECT t.tabname, f.partn, f.dbspace, f.npused, f.nrows
    FROM sysfragments f, systables t
   WHERE f.tabid > 99
     AND f.tabid = t.tabid
ORDER BY 1, 2;
```

With this query, you can tell at a glance whether a distribution is even. A sample output, which shows effective fragmentation of the customer table, might look like

```
tabname       partn   dbspace    npused     nrows
customers   2752556    dbspace1      316     24678
customers   3473452    dbspace2      319     24879
customers   4128812    dbspace3      317     24733
```

The values in this table are refreshed only when you run `UPDATE STATISTICS`. Therefore, be sure to run `UPDATE STATISTICS` after loading data into fragments.

onstat

Several options of the OnLine utility `onstat` are effective for monitoring fragment usage. The following option displays page reads and page writes by chunk:

```
onstat -D
```

One especially useful form of this command is to isolate which disks are the most active. It zeroes the read and write counts between each interval you specify—in this case, 10 seconds:

```
onstat -D -z -r 10 ¦ grep /
```

It runs until you interrupt it. Adding the repeat flag (`-r 10`) and resetting the counts (`-z`) can be combined with any of these `onstat` commands.

The following option displays asynchronous I/O frequency by chunk for each dbspace:

```
onstat -g iof
```

It also displays statistics for temporary files and sort-work files. The `ppf` (partition profile) option shows statistics about each fragment that is currently open:

```
onstat -g ppf
```

Although actual disk reads and writes are not listed, the `isrd` (ISAM reads) and `iswrt` (ISAM writes) columns indicate which fragments are used heavily. The output shows I/O activity by `partnum`, so you might have to translate that value to find the table being referenced. One way is with the following query:

```
SELECT t.tabname
  FROM sysfragments f, systables t
 WHERE f.partn = partnum
   AND f.tabid = t.tabid;
```

The next option displays the dataskip status for each dbspace:

```
onstat -f
```

When you execute this statement, you see one of the following three results:

```
dataskip is OFF for all dbspaces
dataskip is ON for all dbspaces
dataskip is ON for dbspaces:
     dbspace1     dbspace2
```

Exploiting Temporary Spaces

With OnLine-DSA, all temporary tables—explicit, temp, and sort—are created in the temporary spaces defined by the environmental variable `DBSPACETEMP`, if set. If this variable is not set, these tables are created in the same space as the database. Because decision support queries typically use temporary dbspaces extensively, especially for large joins and sorts, setting `DBSPACETEMP` properly is crucial. In your OnLine configuration, you should set `DBSPACETEMP` to a list of temporary dbspaces on different disks. OnLine then alternates the use of these spaces as it creates temporary tables. Although this does not imply actual fragmentation of the temporary tables, it does afford some degree of load balancing.

You can fragment explicit temporary tables if you choose. The syntax is the same as for regular tables.

TIP

Fragment large, explicit temporary tables by round robin across temporary dbspaces.

Avoiding ROWIDS

With the onset of fragmentation, Informix eliminated the virtual column ROWID, which had previously been available in every table. Some applications exploited ROWID as a handy alternate key—that is, as a handle with which to select a known row quickly. This was effective because ROWID stored the physical location of a data row and allowed for immediate data access. In versions 7.0 and higher, this pseudocolumn is no longer created by default for fragmented tables.

If you must have ROWIDS available for a fragmented table, you can force OnLine to generate them explicitly with

```
CREATE TABLE tablename (column list)
FRAGMENT BY (fragmentation scheme)
WITH ROWIDS;
```

When you do this, OnLine assigns a unique, invariant value for every row. It also creates an index that it uses to find the physical location of each row. In addition, it adds four bytes to each row. Finally, it inserts a sysfragments row to indicate the existence and attributes of the ROWID column. Consequently, creating ROWIDS for a fragmented table adds significant overhead and will impair performance.

TIP

Avoid using ROWIDS for access to fragmented tables. Use primary keys instead.

XPS Data Fragmentation

Fragmentation with XPS is fundamentally similar to fragmentation with OnLine-DSA. Two innovations are most noteworthy: dbslices and hash fragmentation. Dbslices, groups of related dbspaces, greatly simplify dbspace administration. Hash fragmentation is an alternative fragmentation strategy that can both minimize data skew and offer fragment elimination.

Dbslices

For the examples in this section, consider that cust_slice is a dbslice that defines six identical derived dbspaces, cust_slice.1 through cust_slice.6. Refer to Figure 20.3 for a diagram of this construct.

When a dbslice exists, it can be used in a fragmentation expression wherever a list of dbspaces is legal in OnLine-DSA. For example, the statement

```
CREATE TABLE stores (column definitions)
FRAGMENT BY ROUND ROBIN IN cust_slice;
```

is identical to and easier to administer than

```
CREATE TABLE stores (column definitions)
FRAGMENT BY ROUND ROBIN IN cust_slice.1, cust_slice.2, cust_slice.3,
                           cust_slice.4, cust_slice.5, cust_slice.6;
```

To best distribute the workload, when establishing a dbslice, you should have the number of dbspaces equal a multiple of the number of coservers.

System-Defined Hash Fragmentation

Available only with XPS, fragmentation by a system-defined hash key combines ease of distribution with some opportunity for fragment elimination. A column or set of columns is defined as the hash key, and a list of destination dbspaces—or a dbslice—is named:

```
CREATE TABLE tablename (column list)
FRAGMENT BY HASH (hash key columns)
IN list of dbspaces OR dbslice;
```

Using an internal algorithm, XPS determines the dbspace in which to place each row. Generally, if the data for the hash key is evenly distributed, then the data should be evenly spread over the fragments. A serial key that is used as a table's primary key, and often used for joins, is an ideal candidate for a hash key. If such a choice is not available, consider using a composite hash key to ensure an even distribution of the data. Because data skew is still a concern, the size of each fragment should be checked after a table is loaded to verify that a reasonable hash key was selected.

A sample hash fragmentation scheme for the `customer` table follows:

```
CREATE TABLE customers (
cust_no    SERIAL,
last_name  CHAR(20))
FRAGMENT BY HASH (cust_no) IN cust_slice;
```

In this case, given that `cust_no` is serial, the distribution of rows among the six dbspaces comprising `cust_dbslice` ought to be even. If no naturally variant key existed, it might be necessary to use a composite hash key to avoid data skew.

Fragment elimination can occur with a system-defined hash scheme but only when the query has an equality operator (=, IN) on the entire hash key. A statement such as

```
SELECT last_name
  FROM customers
 WHERE cust_no IN (325, 6642);
```

will eliminate fragments from the search.

Monitoring Fragment Usage

OnLine-XPS includes a new utility, onutil, to help create and monitor storage units. With it, you can observe the allocation status of a fragment. First, you must determine the tblspace number (partn) for a fragment, perhaps with an SQL statement such as

```
database sysmaster;
SELECT *
  FROM systabnames
 WHERE tabname = "customers";
```

This statement returns the partn for each fragment of the specified table. You can then examine the space usage information for any of these table fragments. For example, if the preceding query identified partn 3473452 as a fragment of customers, then from within onutil, you could execute

```
CHECK TABLE INFO IN TABLESPACE 3473452;
```

Data returned includes the number of extents, the extent sizes, the number of pages allocated and used, and the number of rows. Finally, it lists each extent that was allocated for the fragment. At a glance, you can recognize whether space is used efficiently and whether significant scattering of the table occurred. The CHECK TABLE INFO statement is functionally equivalent to oncheck -pt, available in earlier OnLine versions.

Enabling Co-Located Joins

When tables that span coservers are joined, XPS must merge the data from each table before executing the join. Passing the raw data between coservers can be slow. You can mitigate this traffic if you can create a co-located join. This occurs when data from rows to be joined are found on the same coserver. For XPS to recognize this, you must create the hash key equal to the join key.

TIP

When possible, create your hash key equal to your join key to enable co-located joins. A co-located join allows the join for the tables to occur locally per coserver so that data does not need to be shipped to other coservers until after the join is completed.

Using Flex Temporary Tables

OnLine-XPS adds a useful mechanism for the internal management of certain explicit temporary tables. Those eligible have the following format:

```
   SELECT *
     FROM customers
INTO TEMP temp_cust;
```

For this kind of statement, XPS create a *flex temporary table*, one in which OnLine determines a fragmentation strategy automatically. As long as DBSPACETEMP is defined, OnLine fragments such a table across temporary dbspaces in a round-robin fashion. The details of this parallelized operation follow:

- If the query produces no rows, OnLine creates an empty, nonfragmented table in a single dbspace.
- If the data returned requires less than 8KB to store, the temporary table resides in a single dbspace.
- If the data returned exceeds 8KB, OnLine creates multiple fragments and distributes the data using a round-robin scheme.

Index Fragmentation

If you create an *attached* index on a fragmented table—that is, without specifying an explicit scheme for the index—OnLine fragments the index with the same distribution scheme as the table. Alternatively, you can dictate an independent fragmentation strategy for an index, thus creating it *detached*. A detached index need not be fragmented; with a statement such as

```
CREATE INDEX ix_cust ON customers (cust_no) IN dbspace2;
```

it can merely be placed in a separate dbspace.

For a nonfragmented table, index pages and data pages are intermingled in the same extent. This is not true for a fragmented table with an attached index. Instead, although the data fragment and index fragment are still stored in the same dbspace, they are kept in separate tblspaces.

User Indexes

User indexes are those defined explicitly with the SQL statement CREATE INDEX. Of these, any statements that include an IN clause to specify location are detached. The following SQL statement shows one method of creating a detached, and, in this case, fragmented index:

```
CREATE INDEX ix_cust ON customers (cust_no)
FRAGMENT BY EXPRESSION
cust_no <  1000 IN dbspace1,
cust_no >= 1000 IN dbspace2;
```

In OLTP environments, fragmenting an index is an important way to reduce contention. The principles of fragment elimination apply to indexes as well as to tables, so different users can read different fragments of the same index at the same time. However, this does not demand that you should fragment an index differently from its table. In fact, if the table is fragmented by expression, you should generally create the indexes attached.

TIP

If a table is fragmented by expression, fragment the indexes the same way.

An additional benefit of fragmenting indexes is that each fragment that holds an index maintains its own complete B+ tree. The B+ tree is Informix's internal method of storing an index and, for a large index, can become excessively complex. By fragmenting an index, you keep each individual B+ tree simpler. Simpler B+ tree structures are cached more readily and traversed more quickly than complex ones.

It is not always true that a fragmented index is beneficial. When OnLine uses a fragmented index, it must scan each fragment and then combine the results. Because of this overhead, explicitly fragmenting an index by round robin is not allowed. However, when you fragment a table by round robin, any attached indexes adopt the same fragmentation scheme by default and create the very kind of index Informix disallows explicitly. Performance suffers if you allow this.

TIP

If a table is fragmented by round robin, do not create attached indexes. Place them in separate dbspaces.

System Indexes

System indexes—those used to enforce unique constraints and referential constraints—are not fragmented. They instead are created as detached indexes in the dbspace where the database was created. Nonetheless, it is possible to fragment a system index if needed. When a system index is created, it adopts a user index if one exists. Therefore, to fragment a system index, first create a user index on the same columns used for the constraint and then rebuild the constraint with the proper `ALTER TABLE` statement. For instance, if a primary key constraint is constructed this way, and the underlying index is subsequently dropped, the system index that enforces the primary key constraint retains the fragmentation scheme of the old index.

Modifying Fragmentation Strategies

A table's fragmentation scheme can be modified or created even after the table already exists. The various forms of the `ALTER FRAGMENT` statement shown in this section are used for this purpose. It is often sensible to create your tables initially without any fragmentation and, only through monitoring a live system, decide which tables merit being fragmented.

The examples in this section assume you have used monitoring tools such as those outlined in the section "Monitoring Fragment Usage" earlier in this chapter. With them, you determined that a change in a specific fragmentation scheme is necessary. The remainder of this section details the various forms of the `ALTER FRAGMENT` statement that you might employ.

CAUTION

For databases with logging, the entire `ALTER FRAGMENT` statement is executed as a single transaction. Each row is thus written to the logical logs, and may, in the case of large tables, risk creating a long transaction. Consider turning off logging before performing such operations.

The examples in this section also assume that the following two tables already exist and have the fragmentation schemes shown:

```
CREATE TABLE stores (column definitions)
FRAGMENT BY ROUND ROBIN IN dbspace1, dbspace2, dbspace3;
CREATE TABLE customers (column definitions)
FRAGMENT BY EXPRESSION
cust_no <  5000                      IN dbspace1,
cust_no >= 5000 AND cust_no < 10000 IN dbspace2,
REMAINDER                            IN dbspace3;
CREATE INDEX ix_cust ON customer (cust_no);
```

Creating a New Fragmentation Strategy

You use the `INIT` clause to create a new fragmentation scheme for a table or index, regardless of whether it is currently fragmented. Any current storage option is discarded.

Creating New Table Fragmentation

With the `INIT` clause, you completely rewrite the fragmentation scheme for a table. For example, use the following code to initiate round-robin fragmentation on the `customers` table:

```
ALTER FRAGMENT ON TABLE customers
INIT FRAGMENT BY ROUND ROBIN IN dbspace1, dbspace2, dbspace3;
```

You can also use `INIT` to convert a fragmented table to a nonfragmented one. You might decide that the round-robin fragmentation defined previously for the `stores` table is no longer needed. To rebuild the table in a single dbspace, use

```
ALTER FRAGMENT ON TABLE stores
INIT IN dbspace1;
```

When you convert a fragmented table in this way, you must explicitly name a dbspace for the table.

Creating New Index Fragmentation

Although all the `ALTER FRAGMENT` statements apply to indexes as well as tables, they are used much less often for indexes. Generally, rebuilding the index is sufficient and obviates needing to master the several `ALTER FRAGMENT` options. Still, there are times when using the `ALTER FRAGMENT` statement is sensible. One such occasion is to use the `INIT` clause to detach an index from a table's fragmentation strategy:

```
ALTER FRAGMENT ON INDEX ix_cust
INIT IN dbspace4;
```

Not all index changes are initiated so explicitly. Changing a table's fragmentation strategy causes a concomitant change in any attached indexes, although certain system indexes create exceptions to this rule:

- When you convert a nonfragmented table to fragmented, an existing system index generated by creating a primary key is not fragmented in the same fashion. Rather, the index remains in the dbspace where the database was created.
- Regardless of the current status of an index generated from a primary key constraint (attached, fragmented by expression, or fragmented in one dbspace), when a fragmented table is converted to nonfragmented, the index reverts to an attached index.
- Any system indexes that rely on detached user indexes are not affected by the `INIT` operation.

Changing a Fragmentation Strategy

You use the `MODIFY` clause to alter an existing expression-based fragmentation scheme. With it, you can change the dbspace for a fragment, the expression that dictates which rows are placed in a fragment, or both. For example, you may determine that you prefer the data currently in `dbspace3` for the `customers` table to be moved to `dbspace4` instead. To accomplish the migration, use

```
ALTER FRAGMENT ON TABLE customer
MODIFY dbspace3 TO REMAINDER IN dbspace4;
```

CAUTION

OnLine maintains space for the original fragment until the ALTER FRAGMENT statement completes. Make sure that you have enough disk space to simultaneously accommodate the fragment being deleted and the fragment being added.

Alternatively, through monitoring your fragmentation usage, you may find that dbspace2 has a disproportionate amount of data. To move some of those rows to the remainder space, you can restrict the expression on dbspace2:

```
ALTER FRAGMENT ON TABLE customer
MODIFY dbspace2 TO cust_no >= 5000 AND cust_no < 7500 IN dbspace2;
```

With MODIFY, you cannot change the number of fragments in your distribution scheme. For that, use the ADD, DROP, or INIT clause.

Adding a Fragment

Adding a fragment is especially useful when a new disk is added to a system. With the following ADD clause, you can add another fragment to the stores table:

```
ALTER FRAGMENT ON TABLE stores
ADD dbspace4;
```

You can also add additional fragment expressions to an existing expression-based distribution scheme. This can be useful when one fragment becomes too large or too active:

```
ALTER FRAGMENT ON TABLE customers
ADD cust_no >= 10000 AND cust_no < 15000 IN dbspace4
AFTER dbspace2;
```

All rows that were in the remainder fragment are reevaluated. Those that match the new range are moved to dbspace4. For an expression-based strategy, the ADD clause includes the optional BEFORE and AFTER statements so that you can customize the order in which the expressions are evaluated.

Dropping a Fragment

With the DROP clause, you can eliminate a fragment from a fragmentation list. Note that the data from the dropped fragment is not lost: It moves to another appropriate fragment. With an expression-based scheme, you must be sure that a destination exists for data in a dropped fragment. If the data cannot be moved to another fragment, the operation fails. To drop one of the fragments from the stores fragmentation scheme, use

```
ALTER FRAGMENT ON TABLE stores
DROP dbspace2;
```

> **NOTE**
>
> You cannot drop a fragment when the table contains only two fragments. Instead, to make a fragmented table nonfragmented, use either the INIT or DETACH clause.

Combining Fragments into One Table

The attach and detach flavors of the ALTER FRAGMENT statement are especially useful to implement the kind of rolling table described in the section "Dbspace Management" earlier in this chapter. These statements combine tables with the same structure into a single fragmented table or isolate a fragment of a table into a separate table.

Two or more tables on different dbspaces can be combined with the ATTACH clause into a single fragmented table. The fragmentation scheme for the resultant table can be any mechanism allowed by your version of OnLine. Consider a table that tracks sales by month, fragmented by expression on month:

```
CREATE TABLE sales (
store_no     INTEGER,
sales_month  SMALLINT,
sales_totals MONEY(12,2))
FRAGMENT BY EXPRESSION
sales_month = 1 IN dbspace1,
sales_month = 2 IN dbspace2,
sales_month = 3 IN dbspace3;
```

Furthermore, suppose that current sales are stored in the following nonfragmented table:

```
CREATE TABLE current_sales (
store_no     INTEGER,
sales_month  SMALLINT,
sales_totals MONEY(12,2))
IN dbspace4;
```

The following expression consolidates the current_sales table with the sales table:

```
ALTER FRAGMENT ON TABLE sales
ATTACH dbspace4 AS sales_month = 4;
```

In the process, the current_sales table is consumed and no longer exists. All the rows that were in current_sales are now in dbspace4 of sales.

You can also use ATTACH to combine several nonfragmented tables, which have identical structures and are on separate dbspaces, into a single fragmented table. Suppose that sales1, sales2, and sales3 are such nonfragmented tables. With the following statement, you can combine them into a single table, fragmented by round robin, with three fragments:

```
ALTER FRAGMENT ON TABLE sales1
ATTACH sales1, sales2, sales3;
```

When this statement completes, sales2 and sales3 are dropped. With this construct, you must name the surviving table—in this case, sales1—as the first element in the attach list.

Splitting a Table into Component Fragments

The DETACH clause is used to segregate a fragment of a table into a separate nonfragmented table. In the sales example, to detach old sales data to its own table, use

```
ALTER FRAGMENT ON TABLE sales
DETACH dbspace1 AS old_sales;
```

This creates the independent, nonfragmented table old_sales in dbspace1.

NOTE

The new table created by the DETACH statement does not inherit indexes or constraints from the original table. Only data is preserved.

Summary

The judicious use of fragmentation, especially when using DSA for DSS and data warehouse applications, can produce dramatic performance improvements. Even in OLTP environments, fragmentation can significantly decrease contention and thus increase concurrency.

This chapter described the benefits and methods of implementing data and index fragmentation for an Informix environment. Developing a mastery of these concepts is essential to becoming an effective OnLine administrator.

CHAPTER 21

Monitoring Your Informix Environment

by Rick Ward

IN THIS CHAPTER

This chapter discusses the components that constitute performance and database monitoring and the tools available to perform monitoring. Performance monitoring can occur for two reasons: where there is an immediate problem with the system that needs rectification and to show resource usage over a time period, with a view to using these figures to "capacity plan" for the future. This chapter has been structured to allow quick access to the information you require when you are most likely to need it and is split into two main sections:

- Performance Monitoring
- Database Monitoring

The first section explains how to monitor the running performance of the Informix database and covers the following:

- The physical components of performance monitoring
- The tools available for monitoring the components in Standard Engine, OnLine 5.0, and OnLine DSA 7.1 environments
- How to apply the tools for high-level system overview monitoring for each environment
- How to apply the more detailed options within the tools to more specific problems

The second section explains how to monitor the physical data structures that constitute the Informix database and covers the following:

- The physical components of database monitoring
- The tools available for monitoring the components in Standard Engine, OnLine 5.0, and OnLine DSA 7.1 environments
- How to apply the tools for monitoring for each environment

This layout has been designed to give the reader a more practical approach to monitoring an Informix database system. Much can be written about what to monitor, how to monitor, and when to monitor. What this chapter does is enable you to select the correct tools for the type of monitoring being performed, without deluging you with extraneous information.

NOTE

This chapter has been written with the following products in mind:

- Sun Solaris 2.4 and 2.5 Operating System
- INFORMIX-Standard Engine V5.0
- INFORMIX-OnLine V5.0
- INFORMIX-OnLine Dynamic Server Architecture V7.1

Please refer to your own product's manuals for further information regarding any differences from the commands described here.

This chapter addresses the basics of monitoring an Informix database system, but in order to keep the chapter concise, it does not address the following:

- Universal Server
- Database monitoring issues surrounding blobs, PDQ, network traffic for client-sever applications, and read ahead techniques under OnLine DSA 7.1
- Use of the onlog utility for transaction log analysis
- Informix tools released with OnLine DSA, such as onprobe or db/cockpit

An Introduction to Monitoring

Monitoring a system is fundamental to understanding how it is currently operating, and this is vital for solving problems and ensuring there is capacity for future growth and developments. By adopting a monitoring strategy, the Database Administrator should be able to provide a system that will never suffer downtime due to preventable problems.

It is important to understand that monitoring in its basic form is just the collection of statistics about various elements. It is only when those statistics are placed in context that they have any worth. Two similar systems might have wildly differing statistics for the same components—for example, I/O—but that does not mean that one system is necessarily slower or less efficient than the other. It is true to say that the I/O is slower, but if this system has only 10 percent of the number of users had by the other system, the user response time might still be satisfactory.

It is important, therefore, when monitoring any system not to take any statistic in isolation. You do not want to start adding faster hardware to your system just because the I/O rate isn't as fast as you think it should be. If the end users' response times are within the Service Level Agreement (SLA), the system is performing adequately. However, when changes are in the pipeline that might increase demand for I/O and might therefore break the SLA, if the Database Administrator is aware of these I/O rates, he or she can request the required hardware changes prior to the new changes being implemented.

Timing is critical when taking measurements of a system. It is important that you understand as much as possible about the demands being made of the database system at all periods of the day and night. There is little point monitoring a system, finding the I/O queues growing, and investigating this if the system is extremely busy processing a large batch run as normal. Consider also the transience of the data in the tables because this will affect any sizing reports that are run.

Performance Monitoring

A variety of statistics are available to monitor the performance of any of the Informix database servers, and a number of tools are available with which to measure and display these statistics.

These are provided by both the UNIX operating system and Informix themselves. Knowing the appropriate tool to use for measuring each statistic is key to quickly building a complete picture of current system performance.

Given the usual scenario where users are complaining of slow response, or batch jobs taking too long to complete, knowing where to start looking for the cause of the problem and being able to investigate further is important in improving the situation. The section on performance monitoring explains the following:

- The components that, when combined, give the users their response time
- The tools available to monitor these components and, therefore, your environment
- Which tools to use to begin identifying the cause of any poor response times
- Which tools to use to further investigate specific performance components

Performance monitoring can be broken into two levels:

- Overview monitoring, which can be used to determine the area in which the cause of a problem can be found
- Low-level monitoring to drill down further into the specifics of that area

In this section, I will describe the tools and techniques to use to quickly identify where a problem lies and, after the problem area has been identified, how to obtain as much detailed information as possible for that area. The level of detail does depend, however, on the version of Informix being monitored. Standard Engine has few tools to monitor at detail and relies heavily on UNIX system–provided tools to offer any information. OnLine 5.0 and OnLine DSA 7.1 both provide much better facilities for investigating problems, with OnLine DSA 7.1 giving extremely low-level information for the threads running within the system.

This section discusses monitoring components of the Informix database system, but no firm guidelines can be made about what values should be observed for a smooth running system. A multitude of UNIX servers are available, each with different hardware configurations, operating systems, and applications. The only way you are going to get any guideline figures for your particular server and application is to monitor it while it is running, collate the data taken with the times the system is reported as underperforming, and work out what values are significantly different and why.

Performance Components

Several components define how the Informix system performs; these can be categorized broadly as

- Disk
- Memory
- CPU

The performance of these components (or lack of performance) determines the response time of your SQL. In order to monitor these components, it is important to understand the basic operations performed by each.

Disk Operations

In order for Informix to satisfy your SQL, the required data must be read from and written to disk. Disk operations are physical operations requiring the movement of physical devices and, therefore, are the slowest component of any database access. The total access time taken for a disk I/O is made up of seek time, latency time, and transfer time. These times vary depending on the

- Type of disk
- Speed of the disk
- Access profile the application has to the data
- Data placement strategy
- Other system and application I/O requests

As you can see, disk I/O can be affected by numerous factors, many of which cannot be measured easily. For Informix monitoring, the total access time is sufficient to determine whether a disk I/O bottleneck is occurring.

Memory

Physical memory is used by Informix to hold system and application data. In Standard Engine (SE), the memory used is the process memory of the sqlexec thread and UNIX disk I/O cache. In OnLine, memory is much more extensively used by Informix for the sharing of application and system data, all to prevent disk I/O operations, thus improving data access times.

A memory bottleneck occurs when not enough memory is available to the system to allow processes to meet their memory requirements. This manifests itself at a system level as disk I/O for paging and swapping operations, or at database level as increased disk I/O to access data.

Virtual memory is the concept of using disk space to extend the physical memory of a machine. When all physical memory pages have been used, the least recently used (LRU) pages can be paged out to an area of disk allowing requests for new memory pages to be satisfied. This paging activity can be monitored and gives a guide to the use of physical memory.

CPU

The physical CPUs execute the instructions for the processes running under UNIX. The speed at which these processors can execute the instructions for the many processes running determines how quickly your Informix processes will be serviced. A CPU bottleneck occurs when a constant queue of processes is ready and waiting to run on the CPUs and leads to slow performance of the system overall.

Monitoring Tools

The monitoring tools provided as standard with UNIX and Informix vary depending on the versions of both being run. I will list the commonly available UNIX tools, but you should check the documentation of your version of UNIX for further details.

UNIX Tools

UNIX tools can be used to measure the activity occurring on the system as a whole. These tools are not detailed or specific enough when considering measuring Informix in depth but give a rough guide to the level of activity of each performance component. For Standard Engine implementations, these tools are the only ones available.

The `sar` command can be used to give overall system utilization figures, `iostat` gives disk I/O statistics, and `vmstat` shows memory utilization.

INFORMIX-OnLine 5 Monitoring Tools

The introduction of INFORMIX-OnLine brought two major changes that affect the monitoring of Informix:

- Shared memory, providing the sharing of data read from disk by several user processes
- Raw disk usage, removing the UNIX File System calls for disk I/O to provide faster disk access

Informix UNIX processes running as database server processes now execute on the machine to enable the use of shared memory, with user processes connecting to the database server processes to access the data required. The data no longer resides as a single UNIX file for each table in the database as with Standard Engine, but as either a UNIX (cooked) file containing a dbspace or as raw disk space containing one or many dbspaces. Each dbspace can now contain one or more tables, as well as other Informix system structures, such as the logical logs and the physical log.

In order to examine the utilization being made of the shared memory and dbspaces, a new command, `tbstat`, was introduced by Informix. `tbstat` has several options that allow you to take a snapshot of the disk, memory, and CPU utilization at that point in time. Table 21.1 shows the options available from `tbstat` and their meanings.

Table 21.1. The `tbstat` options for OnLine 5.0.

Option	*Meaning*
`-a`	Print options `bcdklmpstu` (as described below)
`-b`	Print shared memory buffers
`-c`	Print current configuration file for this database server
`-d`	Print defined dbspaces and chunks
`-k`	Print locks currently active
`-l`	Print logical and physical details
`-m`	Print message log
`-p`	Print profile
`-s`	Print latches currently held
`-t`	Print tblspaces currently in use
`-u`	Print users connected to server
`-z`	Zero all `tbstat` counts
`-B`	Print all buffers
`-D`	Print dbspaces and detailed chunk I/O statistics
`-F`	Print page flushing activity
`-P`	Print profile, including BIGreads
`-R`	Print LRU queues
`-X`	Print entire list of sharers and waiters for buffers
`-r`	Repeat options every *n* seconds; default is 5

TIP

Brief status information is provided on all the `tbstat` command outputs. The first line shows the version of INFORMIX-OnLine that is running, its current operating mode, the up-time (time since the INFORMIX-OnLine server was restarted), and the size of the current shared memory allocation. The current operating mode can be online (normal operation), quiescent (administration only), shutdown (shutting down), and recovery (fast recovery in progress). An example of this is shown in Figure 21.1, which shows a database server in quiescent mode.

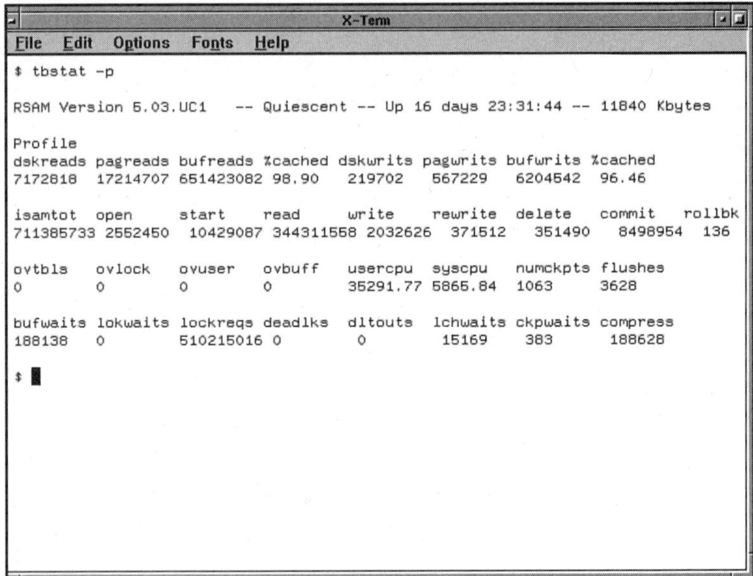
X-Term
File Edit Options Fonts Help
$ tbstat -p
RSAM Version 5.03.UC1 -- Quiescent -- Up 16 days 23:31:44 -- 11840 Kbytes
Profile
dskreads pagreads bufreads %cached dskwrits pagwrits bufwrits %cached
7172818 17214707 651423082 98.90 219702 567229 6204542 96.46
isamtot open start read write rewrite delete commit rollbk
711385733 2552450 10429087 344311558 2032626 371512 351490 8498954 136
ovtbls ovlock ovuser ovbuff usercpu syscpu numckpts flushes
0 0 0 0 35291.77 5865.84 1063 3628
bufwaits lokwaits lockreqs deadlks dltouts lchwaits ckpwaits compress
188138 0 510215016 0 0 15169 383 188628
$

FIGURE 21.1.
Output from the `tbstat -p` *command.*

INFORMIX-OnLine DSA 7.1 Monitoring Tools

Informix moved from OnLine 5 to OnLine 6 Dynamic Server Architecture (DSA) and quickly to OnLine DSA 7.1. These new releases changed the architecture of OnLine 5, essentially taking much of the UNIX process scheduling "under the covers" to allow the Informix server to best decide which processing user threads were serviced in what order. This is known as the multithreaded architecture of OnLine DSA 7.1. To enable monitoring of these threads and how OnLine DSA 7.1 is scheduling them, Informix built upon the existing `tbstat` command to produce `onstat` with extra options for thread monitoring. Table 21.2 shows the extra options available under `onstat -g`.

Table 21.2. The `onstat -g` options.

Option	*Meaning*
`all`	Print all MT information
`ath`	Print all threads
`wai`	Print waiting threads
`act`	Print active threads
`rea`	Print ready threads
`sle`	Print all sleeping threads
`spi`	Print spin locks with long spins

Option	*Meaning*
sch	Print VP scheduler statistics
lmx	Print all locked mutexes
wmx	Print all mutexes with waiters
con	Print conditions with waiters
stk	Dump the stack of a specified thread
glo	Print MT global information
mem	Print pool statistics
seg	Print memory segment statistics
rbm	Print block map for resident segment
nbm	Print block map for nonresident segments
afr	Print allocated pool fragments
ffr	Print free pool fragments
ufr	Print pool usage breakdown
iov	Print disk IO statistics by vp
iof	Print disk IO statistics by chunk/file
ioq	Print disk IO statistics by queue
iog	Print AIO global information
iob	Print big buffer usage by IO VP class
ppf	Print partition profiles
tpf	Print thread profiles
ntu	Print net user thread profile information
ntt	Print net user thread access times
ntm	Print net message information
ntd	Print net dispatch information
nss	Print net shared memory status, using session id
nsc	Print net shared memory status, using client id
nsd	Print net shared memory data
sts	Print max and current stack sizes
dic	Print dictionary cache information
opn	Print open tables
qst	Print queue statistics
wst	Print thread wait statistics

continues

Table 21.2. continued

Option	*Meaning*
`ses`	Print session information
`sql`	Print sql information
`dri`	Print data replication information
`pos`	Print `/INFORMIXDIR/etc/.infos.DBSERVERNAME` file
`mgm`	Print mgm resource manager information
`ddr`	Print DDR log post processing information
`dmp`	Dump shared memory
`src`	Search memory for `(mem&mask)==pattern`

There are many parameters to the `onstat -g` command; however, it is beyond the scope of this chapter to discuss in detail all of the options available and their uses. I will concentrate on the more useful commands required to monitor an Informix database server.

TIP

Brief status information is provided on all the `onstat` command outputs. The first line shows the version of INFORMIX-OnLine that is running, its current operating mode, the up-time (time since the INFORMIX-OnLine server was restarted), and the size of the current shared memory allocation. The current operating mode can be online (normal operation), quiescent (administration only), shutdown (shutting down), and recovery (fast recovery in progress). In addition, later versions of OnLine DSA 7.1 include a block reason line that shows if and why the OnLine server is blocked: for example, LBU (last logical log used) and CKPT (checkpoint in progress). Figure 21.2 shows an example of a database server blocked by a checkpoint.

In addition to the new functionality provided by `onstat -g`, a new database called sysmaster is automatically created with OnLine DSA 7.1. This contains a series of pseudo-tables that represent snapshots of Informix shared memory. Standard SQL queries can be executed against these tables to obtain information such as users waiting to execute in Informix, the number of full logical logs, and the number of ISAM (I/O request) calls a particular session has made. These tables, called the System Monitoring Interface (SMI) tables, can be used as the data source for any system monitoring script or 4GL you want to code to enable system activity to be investigated.

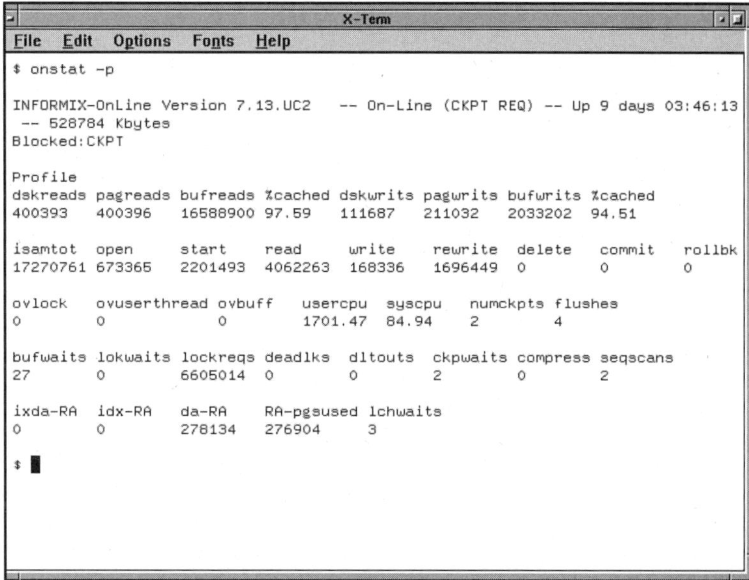

X-Term
File Edit Options Fonts Help
$ onstat -p
INFORMIX-OnLine Version 7.13.UC2 -- On-Line (CKPT REQ) -- Up 9 days 03:46:13
-- 528784 Kbytes
Blocked:CKPT
Profile
dskreads pagreads bufreads %cached dskwrits pagwrits bufwrits %cached
400393 400396 16588900 97.59 111687 211032 2033202 94.51
isamtot open start read write rewrite delete commit rollbk
17270761 673365 2201493 4062263 168336 1696449 0 0 0
ovlock ovuserthread ovbuff usercpu syscpu numckpts flushes
0 0 0 1701.47 84.94 2 4
bufwaits lokwaits lockreqs deadlks dltouts ckpwaits compress seqscans
27 0 6605014 0 0 2 0 2
ixda-RA idx-RA da-RA RA-pgsused lchwaits
0 0 278134 276904 3
$

FIGURE 21.2.
Output from the `onstat -p` *command.*

WARNING

The SMI tables provide the capability to interrogate diagnostic information in a large variety of ways. You can design SQL to join the pseudo-tables in the sysmaster database with tables in a user-created database—for example, systables. Be aware that the sysmaster database is created as an unbuffered logged database, and, therefore, joins of this type must be to databases that are also logged. You cannot remove the logged status of the sysmaster database (although you can change it to buffered if required). Refer to Chapter 12, "Incorporating a Database in Your Informix Environment," for a discussion of database logging.

Overview Monitoring

This section describes how to apply the tools mentioned previously in the chapter to monitor each performance component for Standard Engine, OnLine 5.0, and OnLine DSA 7.1. It details how to provide an overview of your system performance in those component areas and how to further identify whether or not the components are causing a problem. If further investigation of a component is required, the next section explains how to break down the component to identify its present utilization.

UNIX Tools

The UNIX tools available can be used to monitor Standard Engine, OnLine 5, and OnLine DSA 7.1. For Standard Engine, UNIX tools are the only tools available for performance monitoring. For the OnLine engines, these tools can provide a monitoring start point.

The UNIX command `sar` can be used to show an overview of system resource utilization, as shown in Figure 21.3.

FIGURE 21.3.
Output from the `sar` *command.*

```
X-Term
File  Edit  Options  Fonts  Help
$ sar 5 15

SunOS gpsdv003 5.4 Generic_101945-37 sun4d      02/26/97

13:10:17    %usr    %sys    %wio   %idle
13:10:23      27      17       2      53
13:10:28      19      10       2      69
13:10:33      14      11       2      74
13:10:38      15      16      21      48
13:10:43      16      13       2      69
13:10:48      33      17       6      44
13:10:53      19      10       3      68
13:10:58      21      27       1      51
13:11:03      15      12       4      69
13:11:08      12       7       5      76
13:11:13      11      13      19      57
13:11:18      17      27       5      51
13:11:23      24      30       3      43
13:11:28      17       9       4      71
13:11:33      32       9       5      54

Average       19      15       6      60
$
```

Four columns relate to system activity:

- `usr` shows the percentage of user-assigned CPU activity.
- `sys` shows the percentage of system-assigned CPU activity.
- `wio` shows the percentage of time idle waiting for I/O operations to complete.
- `idle` shows the percentage of time the system is available to process work.

`sar` can be used with two parameters. The first is the number of seconds delay between snapshots, and the second is the number of iterations. At the end of the iterations, an average figure is given for the time period measured. This allows for the smoothing of any peaks and troughs in system activity.

It is also important to know how many processes are accessing the database data. For Standard Engine, this is possible only using `ps -fe ¦ grep sqlexec`. This shows the number of processes that are executing the binaries that access the database.

Disk Monitoring

To monitor disk utilization generally, the UNIX command `iostat` can be used, as shown in Figure 21.4.

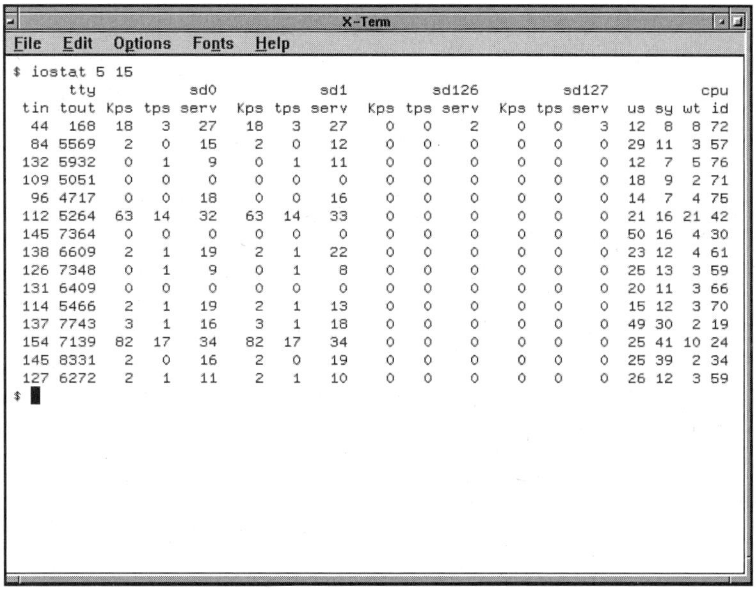

FIGURE 21.4.
Output from the `iostat` *command for UNIX I/O monitoring.*

```
X-Term
File  Edit  Options  Fonts  Help
$ iostat 5 15
      tty          sd0            sd1            sd126          sd127          cpu
 tin tout Kps tps serv  Kps tps serv  Kps tps serv  Kps tps serv  us sy wt id
  44  168  18   3   27   18   3   27    0   0    2    0   0    3  12  8  8 72
  84 5569   2   0   15    2   0   12    0   0    0    0   0    0  29 11  3 57
 132 5932   0   1    9    0   1   11    0   0    0    0   0    0  12  7  5 76
 109 5051   0   0    0    0   0    0    0   0    0    0   0    0  18  9  2 71
  96 4717   0   0   18    0   0   16    0   0    0    0   0    0  14  7  4 75
 112 5264  63  14   32   63  14   33    0   0    0    0   0    0  21 16 21 42
 145 7364   0   0    0    0   0    0    0   0    0    0   0    0  50 16  4 30
 138 6609   2   1   19    2   1   22    0   0    0    0   0    0  23 12  4 61
 126 7348   0   1    9    0   1    8    0   0    0    0   0    0  25 13  3 59
 131 6409   0   0    0    0   0    0    0   0    0    0   0    0  20 11  3 66
 114 5466   2   1   19    2   1   13    0   0    0    0   0    0  15 12  3 70
 137 7743   3   1   16    3   1   18    0   0    0    0   0    0  49 30  2 19
 154 7139  82  17   34   82  17   34    0   0    0    0   0    0  25 41 10 24
 145 8331   2   0   16    2   0   19    0   0    0    0   0    0  25 39  2 34
 127 6272   2   1   11    2   1   10    0   0    0    0   0    0  26 12  3 59
$
```

The `iostat` command reports the utilization for all I/O devices, including screens and keyboards. The disk I/O statistics are represented showing kilobytes per second data transfer rates (Kbps). `sar -d` can also be used to monitor disk I/O rates.

Memory Monitoring

To monitor memory utilization generally, the UNIX command `sar -p` can be used, as shown in Figure 21.5, along with the command `vmstat`, as shown in Figure 21.6.

The `sar -p` command reports the paging activity occurring on the system. The columns `pgin/s` and `ppgin/s` show the average number of paging operations per second and, therefore, indicate how well utilized the physical memory is. If pages are being written to the disk, the physical memory is at its limit, and the least recently used pages are being written to disk in order to satisfy memory requests from processes running on the system. Paging is an acceptable method of removing the restriction on the physical memory limit, but too much paging delays the speed at which processing can take place with processes waiting for their pages to be transferred from disk to physical memory.

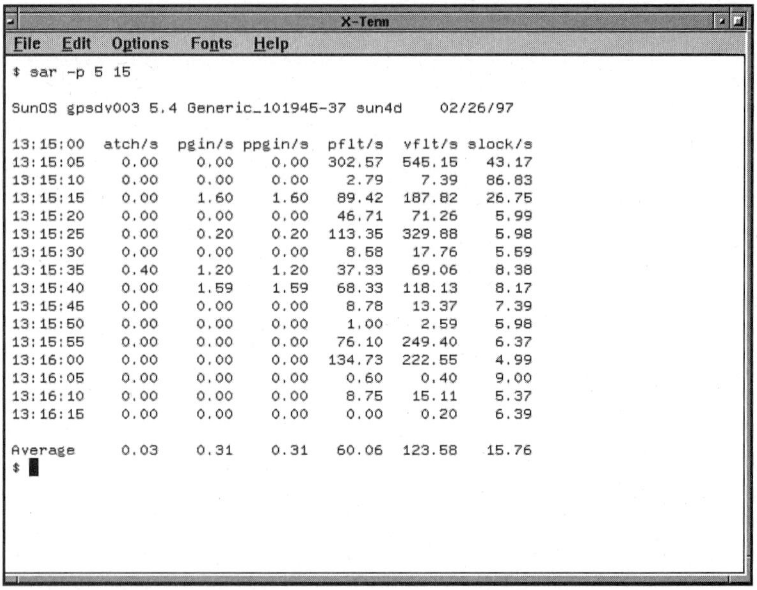

FIGURE 21.5.
Output from the `sar -p` *command for memory monitoring.*

```
X-Term
File  Edit  Options  Fonts  Help
$ sar -p 5 15

SunOS gpsdv003 5.4 Generic_101945-37 sun4d    02/26/97

13:15:00  atch/s  pgin/s ppgin/s  pflt/s  vflt/s slock/s
13:15:05    0.00    0.00    0.00  302.57  545.15   43.17
13:15:10    0.00    0.00    0.00    2.79    7.39   86.83
13:15:15    0.00    1.60    1.60   89.42  187.82   26.75
13:15:20    0.00    0.00    0.00   46.71   71.26    5.99
13:15:25    0.00    0.20    0.20  113.35  329.88    5.98
13:15:30    0.00    0.00    0.00    8.58   17.76    5.59
13:15:35    0.40    1.20    1.20   37.33   69.06    8.38
13:15:40    0.00    1.59    1.59   68.33  118.13    8.17
13:15:45    0.00    0.00    0.00    8.78   13.37    7.39
13:15:50    0.00    0.00    0.00    1.00    2.59    5.98
13:15:55    0.00    0.00    0.00   76.10  249.40    6.37
13:16:00    0.00    0.00    0.00  134.73  222.55    4.99
13:16:05    0.00    0.00    0.00    0.60    0.40    9.00
13:16:10    0.00    0.00    0.00    8.75   15.11    5.37
13:16:15    0.00    0.00    0.00    0.00    0.20    6.39

Average     0.03    0.31    0.31   60.06  123.58   15.76
$
```

FIGURE 21.6.
Output from the `vmstat` *command for memory monitoring.*

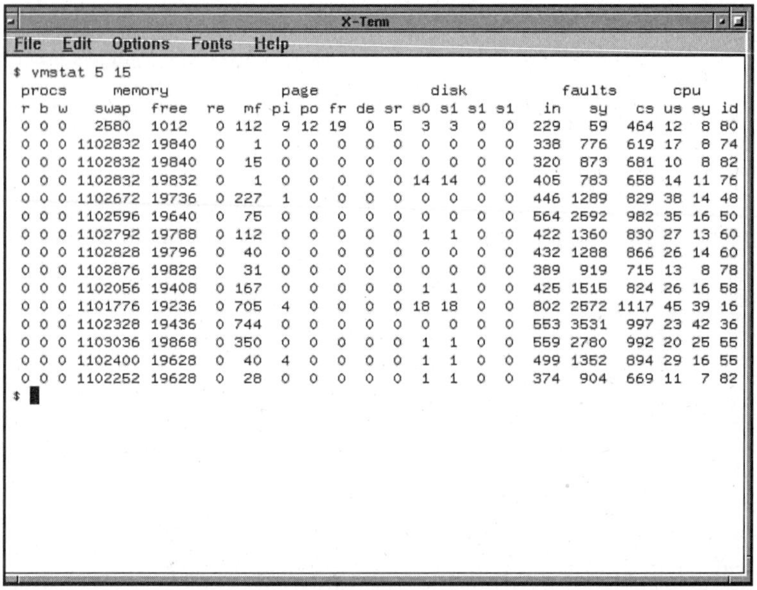

```
X-Term
File  Edit  Options  Fonts  Help
$ vmstat 5 15
 procs     memory            page            disk          faults      cpu
 r b w   swap  free  re  mf pi po fr de sr s0 s1 s1 s1   in   sy   cs us sy id
 0 0 0   2580  1012   0 112  9 12 19  0  5  3  3  0  0  229   59  464 12  8 80
 0 0 0 1102832 19840  0   1  0  0  0  0  0  0  0  0  0  338  776  619 17  8 74
 0 0 0 1102832 19840  0  15  0  0  0  0  0  0  0  0  0  320  873  681 10  8 82
 0 0 0 1102832 19832  0   1  0  0  0  0  0 14 14  0  0  405  783  658 14 11 76
 0 0 0 1102672 19736  0 227  1  0  0  0  0  0  0  0  0  446 1289  829 38 14 48
 0 0 0 1102596 19640  0  75  0  0  0  0  0  0  0  0  0  564 2592  982 35 16 50
 0 0 0 1102792 19788  0 112  0  0  0  0  0  1  1  0  0  422 1360  830 27 13 60
 0 0 0 1102828 19796  0  40  0  0  0  0  0  0  0  0  0  432 1288  866 26 14 60
 0 0 0 1102876 19828  0  31  0  0  0  0  0  0  0  0  0  389  919  715 13  8 78
 0 0 0 1102056 19408  0 167  0  0  0  0  0  1  1  0  0  425 1515  824 26 16 58
 0 0 0 1101776 19236  0 705  4  0  0  0  0 18 18  0  0  802 2572 1117 45 39 16
 0 0 0 1102328 19436  0 744  0  0  0  0  0  0  0  0  0  553 3531  997 23 42 36
 0 0 0 1103036 19868  0 350  0  0  0  0  0  1  1  0  0  559 2780  992 20 25 55
 0 0 0 1102400 19628  0  40  4  0  0  0  0  1  1  0  0  499 1352  894 29 16 55
 0 0 0 1102252 19628  0  28  0  0  0  0  0  1  1  0  0  374  904  669 11  7 82
$
```

The `vmstat` command also shows paging rates in the columns `pi` and `po` (pages in and pages out). The columns `swap` and `free` indicate the amount of swap space left for process swapping and free memory available, respectively.

CPU Monitoring

To monitor CPU utilization generally, the UNIX command sar can be used, as shown in Figure 21.7.

FIGURE 21.7.
Output from the sar *command for CPU monitoring.*

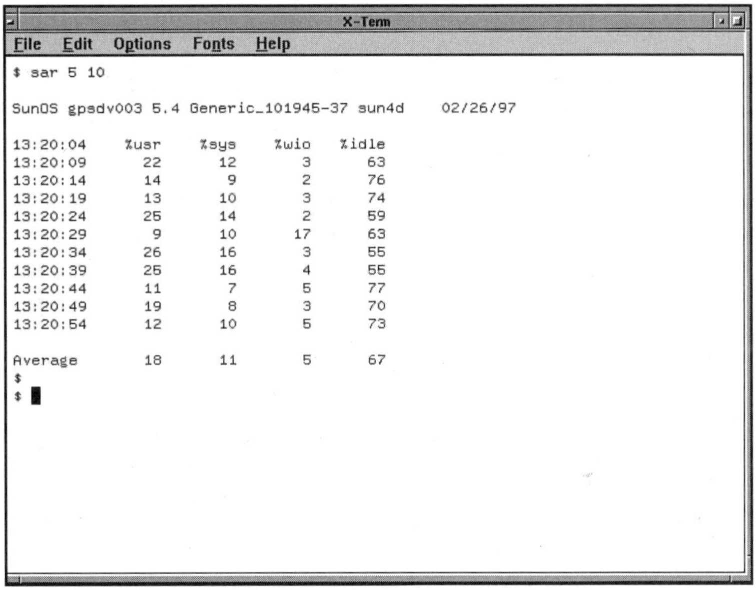

```
$ sar 5 10

SunOS gpsdv003 5.4 Generic_101945-37 sun4d     02/26/97

13:20:04    %usr    %sys    %wio   %idle
13:20:09      22      12       3      63
13:20:14      14       9       2      76
13:20:19      13      10       3      74
13:20:24      25      14       2      59
13:20:29       9      10      17      63
13:20:34      26      16       3      55
13:20:39      25      16       4      55
13:20:44      11       7       5      77
13:20:49      19       8       3      70
13:20:54      12      10       5      73

Average       18      11       5      67
$
$
```

usr combined with sys shows the total CPU utilization of the system, and, therefore, this shows if there is a CPU bottleneck. wio indicates the level of I/O occurring on the system and, therefore, whether or not it is a bottleneck. idle indicates how heavily utilized your system is as a whole.

INFORMIX-OnLine 5.0 Monitoring Tools

In addition to using the UNIX tools described in the preceding sections, to get general system activity, OnLine 5.0 has tbstat available for specific OnLine 5 monitoring. The tbstat command interrogates the shared memory allocated to the Informix server and reports back different information, depending on the option used.

TIP

A good practice to adopt is to check configuration parameters using tbstat -c. This will show you all of the parameters for the Informix server you are investigating as it is running, not as detailed in the tbconfig file. Changes might have been made to the file on disk, but the Informix server has not been restarted to incorporate the changes yet. tbstat -c will give you the correct values for the various configuration parameters.

In order to get an overview of the INFORMIX-OnLine 5.0 server's current performance, I recommend the following procedure:

1. Check the OnLine message log.
2. Check the OnLine system profile.

It is important to know how many users are accessing the OnLine server at the time of taking the measurements. This can be achieved by using `tbstat -u`, which will show a total number of users active on the system.

Check the OnLine Message Log

The first piece of vital information might come from the message log. This log is written to by the INFORMIX-OnLine server and records events the OnLine server considers worth noting. This can be the fact that a checkpoint has taken place, a logical log file has been backed up, or the OnLine server has crashed. `tbstat -m` displays the last 20 lines of the message log, as shown in Figure 21.8.

FIGURE 21.8.
Output from the `tbstat -m` *command.*

```
X-Term
File  Edit  Options  Fonts  Help
$ tbstat -m

RSAM Version 5.03.UC1    -- On-Line -- Up 14 days 13:25:50 -- 11840 Kbytes

Message Log File: /usr/informix/online.log

17:52:17  Checkpoint Completed
17:57:37  Checkpoint Completed
18:02:57  Checkpoint Completed
18:08:17  Checkpoint Completed
18:13:37  Checkpoint Completed
18:18:57  Checkpoint Completed
18:24:17  Logical Log Files are Full -- Backup is Needed

18:24:18  Logical Log Files are Full -- Backup is Needed

18:24:19  Logical Log Files are Full -- Backup is Needed

18:24:20  Logical Log Files are Full -- Backup is Needed

18:24:21  Logical Log Files are Full -- Backup is Needed

18:24:22  Logical Log Files are Full -- Backup is Needed

18:24:23  Logical Log Files are Full -- Backup is Needed

$
```

The example in Figure 21.8 shows the OnLine server has stopped because the logical logs for the OnLine server have filled and need backing up, causing the OnLine server to suspend processing until at least one logical log is freed. This example shows a relatively easy problem to diagnose, but, unfortunately, examining the message log tends to resolve only critical "show-stopping" errors. However, you can save time by checking it just in case.

Sometimes it is necessary to look further back than the last 20 lines shown in the `tbstat -m` output. Listed at the top of the `tbstat -m` display is the location of the message log file. You can use `tail` and `more` on this file to examine the contents further back than 20 lines; for example, `tail -100 /usr/informix/online.log | more` will show the last 100 lines.

TIP

The message log file is appended one line at a time by the INFORMIX-OnLine server. To prevent this file from becoming too large, the file can be copied elsewhere for long-term storage if required and the existing file cleared down by issuing the UNIX command `cat /dev/null > online.log`.

If the message log does not show anything unfavorable, the OnLine system profile should be examined.

Check the OnLine System Profile

The OnLine system profile presents you with an overview of the OnLine server's activity, giving some idea as to any serious system exceptions, such as resource shortages and general performance statistics. By checking the overall profile of the system, it might be possible to determine a performance component that is causing a problem. When you determine which component is performing poorly, you can then examine that component further in a lower-level investigation. Figure 21.9 shows the output of the `tbstat -p` command.

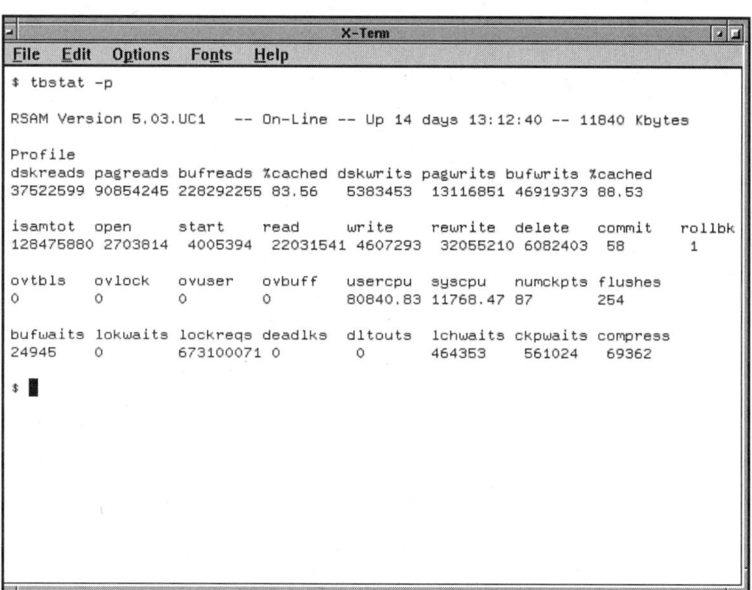
X-Term
File Edit Options Fonts Help
$ tbstat -p
RSAM Version 5.03.UC1 -- On-Line -- Up 14 days 13:12:40 -- 11840 Kbytes
Profile
dskreads pagreads bufreads %cached dskwrits pagwrits bufwrits %cached
37522599 90854245 228292255 83.56 5383453 13116851 46919373 88.53
isamtot open start read write rewrite delete commit rollbk
128475880 2703814 4005394 22031541 4607293 32055210 6082403 58 1
ovtbls ovlock ovuser ovbuff usercpu syscpu numckpts flushes
0 0 0 0 80840.83 11768.47 87 254
bufwaits lokwaits lockreqs deadlks dltouts lchwaits ckpwaits compress
24945 0 673100071 0 0 464353 561024 69362
$

FIGURE 21.9.
Output of the `tbstat -p` *command.*

NOTE

Within this section, I refer to statistical values as a *rate per second* (r.p.s.). This is because the values shown in the `tbstat -p` output are a snapshot of the system at that time and do not represent the rate at which any statistic is changed. A value of 1,000 dskreads (physical disk reads) does not indicate whether the 1,000 reads from disk have occurred over 24 hours or in the last 10 seconds. Knowing the rate at which disk reads are occurring obviously determines whether the read rate should be investigated further. Whenever checking `tbstat -p`, it is important to take a couple of readings over a fixed time period, such as one minute. From this, a rate per second value can be calculated for each of the statistics output and will give a far better picture of the current system activity. An alternative is to reset the statistics using `tbstat -z` and to check the values from that point onward. This will work fine as long as you do not have any background monitoring of statistics occurring that can be damaged by resetting the figures.

The statistics output from `tbstat -p` can be grouped into four areas:

- Read and write activity
- ISAM calls
- Resource shortage counts
- Miscellaneous counts

WARNING

All statistics shown in the `tbstat` command output are cumulative since either the OnLine server was started or the last execution of `tbstat -z`, which resets all statistics to zero. Unfortunately, the Informix server does not record when these statistics were last reset.

Read and Write Activity

These statistics show the request rates for the INFORMIX-OnLine disk and memory components. From these, it can be determined how well utilized the disks and memory are and whether or not a problem might be caused by their overuse. The top portion of statistics is headed with the read and write activity for the system, the values of which are described in Table 21.3.

Table 21.3. `tbstat -p` read and write activity statistics.

Statistic	*Meaning*
`dskreads`	The number of read requests that have had to be satisfied from physical disk
`pagreads`	The number of actual pages read from physical disk

Statistic	*Meaning*
`bufreads`	The number of read requests satisfied from the shared memory buffers
`%cached`	The read cache percentage, calculated as `100 * (bufreads - dskreads)/bufreads`
`dskwrits`	The number of physical writes to disk, including physical and logical log writes
`pagwrits`	The number of actual pages written to physical disk
`bufwrits`	The number of writes to the shared memory buffers
`%cached`	The write cache percentage, calculated as `100 * (bufwrits - dskwrits)/bufwrits`

The two most important statistics to observe are the `%cached` statistics for reads and writes. This shows how well the shared memory buffers are being utilized to satisfy data transfer requests. The higher the `%cache` rate, the less physical I/O will be taking place. It is recommended that the read cache percentage should be 95 percent or greater, and the write cache percentage should be 87 percent or greater; however, this depends on the applications running on your system. Certainly for an OLTP system this is a good guideline, but for a batch or Decision Support System these values might be too high. This is because most pages will not be in the shared memory buffer pool because of the large data processing nature of the SQL. If this is the case, physical I/O performance is much more critical. Be aware that a high-percentage cache rate does not necessarily mean no problems exist with data requests. If your application is repeatedly requesting too much data from the buffers, this will manifest itself as a CPU bottleneck.

WARNING

As mentioned earlier, it is important to obtain the rate of change of these statistics as a guide to the current system activity. The `%cache` values might be very high if, for example, 10,000 disk reads (`dskreads`) are occurring per second, which could be a serious problem. Remember to reset the statistics using `tbstat -z` when it is necessary, or take two snapshots and calculate a current percent cache value.

ISAM Calls

The ISAM calls statistics are detailed on the second portion of the `tbstat -p` output. ISAM calls are the calls made at the lowest level of the OnLine server. One SQL statement can result in any number of ISAM calls, so this command cannot be used to monitor the performance of individual SQL statements in a typical production application. The statistics are grouped into

ISAM call types and record the number of times that particular call type was made. They can be used to monitor the type of activity across the OnLine server, such as mainly read-only or mainly insert activity. Table 21.4 details the ISAM statistics and what they denote.

Table 21.4. `tbstat -p` ISAM call activity statistics.

Statistic	*Meaning*
`isamtot`	Total number of calls made to ISAM.
`open`	Number of open tablespace calls made.
`start`	Number of index position calls made.
`read`	Number of read function calls made.
`write`	Number of write function calls made.
`rewrite`	Number of rewrite function calls made when an update is requested.
`delete`	Number of delete function calls.
`commit`	Number of `iscommit()` calls made. This does not match the `commit work` statements.
`rollbk`	Number of transactions rolled back.

Resource Shortage Counts

The third portion of the `tbstat -p` output details the number of times a resource was requested by the OnLine server and none was available. These resources are defined at the configuration time of the OnLine server, and any shortage can cause the OnLine server to perform extremely poorly. The statistics should be checked frequently to detect any memory over-utilization occurring on the system. Table 21.5 shows the typical statistics output when there is a resource shortage.

Table 21.5. `tbstat -p` resource request overflows.

Statistic	*Meaning*
`ovtbls`	The number of times the OnLine server could not open a tablespace because it would exceed the limit set by `tblspaces` in the configuration file
`ovlock`	The number of times the OnLine server could not take a lock because it would exceed the limit set by `locks` in the configuration file

Statistic	Meaning
ovuser	The number of times a user was refused connection to the OnLine server because it would exceed the limit set by user in the configuration file
ovbuff	The number of times the OnLine server attempted to exceed the maximum number of shared memory buffers

Also within the third portion of the tbstat -p display are the unrelated statistics listed in Table 21.6.

Table 21.6. tbstat -p CPU statistics.

Statistic	Meaning
usercpu	Total user CPU time used by processes, in seconds
syscpu	Total system CPU time used by processes, in seconds
numckpts	Number of checkpoints that have occurred since restart or tbstat -z
flushes	Number of times the shared memory buffer pool has been flushed to disk

Taking the usercpu and syscpu r.p.s. values shows how busy the OnLine server is on this system. If the total r.p.s. of these two figures is close to the percentage of CPU utilization shown in sar, the OnLine server is using most of the CPU, and, if not, some other application is. As an example, consider the following statistics:

- sar shows the percentage idle is 60% and, therefore, is 40% active.
- tbstat -p has been taken twice, 60 seconds apart.
- The first tbstat -p shows usercpu at 100.00 seconds and syscpu at 30.00 seconds.
- The second tbstat -p shows usercpu at 115.08 seconds and syscpu at 36.5 seconds.
- Therefore, the total r.p.s. is (15.08+6.5)/60, which equals 0.35 seconds.
- This gives 35% CPU utilization, meaning that most CPU consumption is being made by Informix.

Miscellaneous Counts

The fourth portion of the tbstat -p display shows miscellaneous counts that do not fall inside any other grouping but mainly show the number of times a process had to wait for a resource to be made available. High values in these statistics might explain the reasons for slow response times from the OnLine server. If a process must wait for resources to be released from another process before it can execute, then processes will be delayed, increasing the execution time. Table 21.7 shows the statistics output.

Table 21.7. `tbstat -u` miscellaneous counts.

Statistic	*Meaning*
`bufwaits`	Number of times a process has been made to wait for a buffer becoming available from the shared memory buffer pool
`lockwaits`	Number of times a process has been made to wait to obtain a lock
`lockreqs`	Number of lock requests that have been made
`deadlks`	Number of times a potential deadlock has been detected
`dltouts`	Number of times a process waiting for a lock waited for longer than the distributed deadlock time-out value was set to
`lchwaits`	Number of times a process has been made to wait for a shared memory resource to become available
`ckpwaits`	Number of times a process waited while a checkpoint completed
`compress`	Number of data page compressions that have occurred

It is quite normal to observe low values in the preceding statistics, but if the rate at which those values increase is too rapid, it might point to a deficiency in resource allocation. For example, if the `ckpwaits` value is climbing by 100 at every checkpoint and 200 users are connected to the OnLine server, 50 percent of users are experiencing a delay when a checkpoint occurs. It is unlikely that 100 users will all be blocked by the checkpoint at exactly the same point in time, so it is highly likely that the checkpoint is taking too long, and steps should be taken to reduce the checkpoint time.

As a guide to lock usage, `lockwaits/lockreqs * 100` should be less than `1%`. If it is not, processes are waiting for locks to become available to gain access to the data they require. Under these circumstances, it might be necessary to review the lock mode set for the tables. If it is page level, consider changing it to row level to allow greater concurrency.

The `tbstat -p` command output combined with UNIX system tools output can determine if any area needs further investigation—such as disk, memory, or CPU—and should give the likely cause of the problem. These could be

- Disk I/O rate too high and causing bottleneck
- Shared memory buffer pool over-utilized
- System CPU far higher than user CPU

- Requests for resource being made when none is available
- Requests for resource being made, and user process needs to wait for it to become available

INFORMIX-OnLine DSA 7.1 Monitoring Tools

OnLine DSA 7.1 contains the same tools as OnLine 5.0, but the utility for monitoring is `onstat` instead of `tbstat`. Extra functionality is contained within the `onstat` commands to support new features in the OnLine DSA 7.1 server architecture.

In order to get an overview of the INFORMIX-OnLine DSA 7.1 server's current performance, I recommend the following procedure:

1. Check the OnLine message log.
2. Check the OnLine system profile for memory, disk, and I/O usage.
3. Check for I/O queue activity.
4. Check for CPU queue activity.

It is important to know how many users' threads are on the OnLine database. `onstat -u` will show the number of users' threads running in the database, where one user could have several threads active on his behalf. `onstat -g ses` shows the number of active users connected to the database and the number of threads each user has running, while `onstat -g sql` *`session id`* can be used to display the SQL a user is executing. This can be very useful in identifying poorly written SQL executing within the OnLine server.

Check the OnLine Message Log

The OnLine message log can be displayed using the `onstat -m` command. The use and output of this command is the same as I have described for the `tbstat -m` command previously in the "INFORMIX-OnLine 5.0 Monitoring Tools" section, with the following additional information being available:

- Checkpoint messages contain the duration time of the checkpoint. This is useful for confirming whether user threads are being delayed due to long checkpoints.
- Details of the dbspaces archived.
- Assertion Failure messages for reporting internal inconsistencies.

Check the OnLine System Profile for Memory, Disk, and I/O Usage

The OnLine system profile can be displayed using the `onstat -p` command. Again, the use and output of this command is the same as described for the `tbstat -p` command in the

"INFORMIX-OnLine 5.0 Monitoring Tools" section of this chapter and has the following additional information available:

> Extra statistics on the use being made of the read ahead facility, `ixda-RA`, `idx-RA`, and `da-RA`.

The system profile statistics can also be read from the sysmaster database. The table sysprofile contains two columns. The first contains the value description, and the second contains the value itself. Listing 21.1 shows how to select all the values stored using SQL while connected to the sysmaster database.

Listing 21.1. Using SQL to select profile information.

```
select   name, value
from     sysprofile ;
```

The output from the sysprofile table contains more statistics than those available via the `onstat -p` command. These are detailed in the *INFORMIX-OnLine Dynamic Server 7.1 Administrator's Guide, Vol. 2*, Chapter 39, but this provides information at basically an overview level.

Check for I/O Queue Activity

If I/O queuing is occurring on your system, you have an I/O bottleneck. I/O queuing occurs when the data transfers to and from the physical disks cannot achieve the rate required to satisfy the workload. In OnLine DSA 7.1, these queues can be monitored for each Virtual Processor (VP) using `onstat -g ioq`. Figure 21.10 shows the output from the `onstat -g ioq` command. The output shows the I/O request queue statistics for each VP capable of asynchronous I/O, the two important columns being `len` and `maxlen`; `len` shows the current length of the queue, and `maxlen` shows the maximum length the queue has been since the OnLine server was started or the last `onstat -z` was performed. If `maxlen` is into double figures, I/O requests are being queued, and this could cause a performance problem.

Check for CPU Queue Activity

If user threads can be seen queuing and ready for a CPU VP to become available, you have a CPU bottleneck. CPU queuing occurs when a thread is ready to run, but all the CPU VPs are busy executing other threads. This queuing can be monitored using `onstat -g rea`, which shows the user's threads ready to run, but having to wait for a CPU VP to become available so they can be executed. Figure 21.11 shows the output from the `onstat -g rea` command. In this example, you see that five of the threads are waiting, ready to run. This shows a considerable number of threads are not getting any service, and, therefore, the response time for each thread might be very poor. It is, however, quite normal to see a few threads in the ready queue for any given snapshot. It is only when the queue becomes longer than the number of CPU VPs defined on the system and the same threads are in the queue repeatedly that the CPU can be considered a bottleneck.

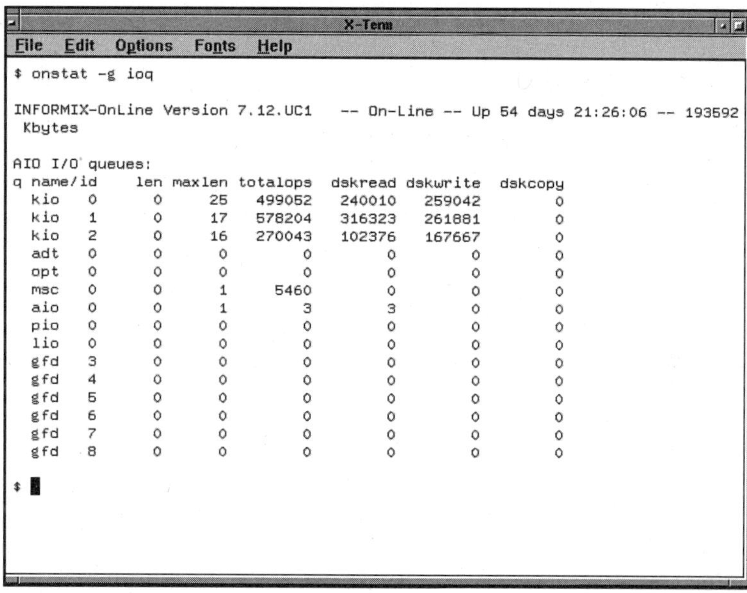

```
$ onstat -g ioq

INFORMIX-OnLine Version 7.12.UC1    -- On-Line -- Up 54 days 21:26:06 -- 193592
 Kbytes

AIO I/O queues:
q name/id    len maxlen totalops  dskread dskwrite  dskcopy
  kio   0      0     25   499052   240010   259042        0
  kio   1      0     17   578204   316323   261881        0
  kio   2      0     16   270043   102376   167667        0
  adt   0      0      0        0        0        0        0
  opt   0      0      0        0        0        0        0
  msc   0      0      1     5460        0        0        0
  aio   0      0      1        3        3        0        0
  pio   0      0      0        0        0        0        0
  lio   0      0      0        0        0        0        0
  gfd   3      0      0        0        0        0        0
  gfd   4      0      0        0        0        0        0
  gfd   5      0      0        0        0        0        0
  gfd   6      0      0        0        0        0        0
  gfd   7      0      0        0        0        0        0
  gfd   8      0      0        0        0        0        0

$
```

FIGURE 21.10.
Output from the `onstat -g ioq` *command.*

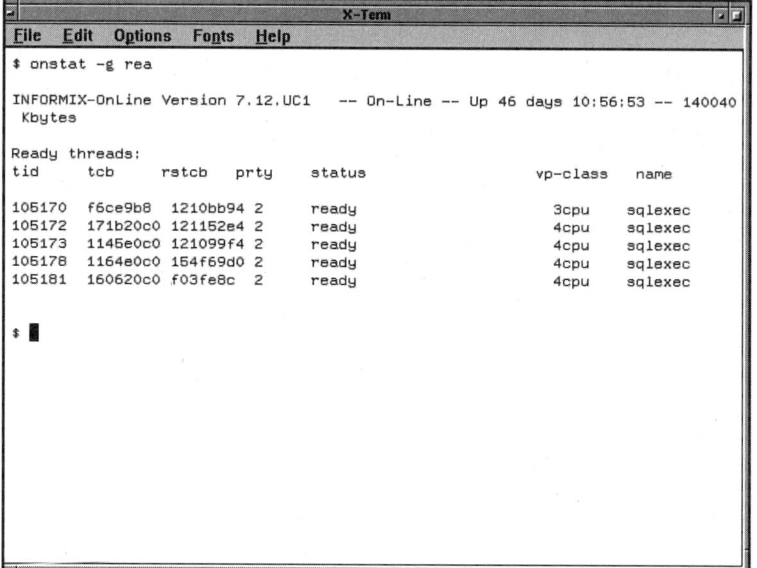

```
$ onstat -g rea

INFORMIX-OnLine Version 7.12.UC1    -- On-Line -- Up 46 days 10:56:53 -- 140040
 Kbytes

Ready threads:
tid      tcb      rstcb    prty    status                  vp-class   name

105170   f6ce9b8  1210bb94 2       ready                     3cpu     sqlexec
105172   171b20c0 121152e4 2       ready                     4cpu     sqlexec
105173   1145e0c0 121099f4 2       ready                     4cpu     sqlexec
105178   1164e0c0 154f69d0 2       ready                     4cpu     sqlexec
105181   160620c0 f03fe8c  2       ready                     4cpu     sqlexec

$
```

FIGURE 21.11.
Output from the `onstat -g rea` *command.*

Detailed Monitoring

This section describes how to investigate any one of the performance components more deeply, possibly to identify the cause of any over-utilization. Only OnLine 5.0 and OnLine 7.1 are discussed in this section, because they have extended tools available provided by Informix that allow for more detailed statistics to be obtained and analyzed. Standard Engine users must rely on UNIX tools and any tools provided as part of the disk subsystem they are using, such as a Logical Volume Manager (LVM).

> **NOTE**
>
> Much of the low-level information provided by the SMI tables in OnLine DSA 7.1 really can be interpreted only by Informix Engineers who understand the inner working of the database server. I will, therefore, not discuss most of the SMI tables listed in the Informix published manuals, because the data provided by those tables can easily be misinterpreted and lead to an incorrect problem diagnosis.

Disk I/O Monitoring

If you want to investigate further the disk I/O performance your system is achieving, OnLine 5.0 and OnLine DSA 7.1 have tools available to measure this. The tools available in OnLine 5.0 can be used in OnLine DSA 7.1 (using `onstat` instead of `tbstat`), but OnLine DSA 7.1 is able to provide more information than OnLine 5.0 tools because of its extended multithreading options.

By using `tbstat -D`, it is possible to examine the page read and write information for the first 50 chunks in each dbspace. Figure 21.12 shows an example of this, with the columns in the second section showing the number of pages read from and written to the chunk (`page Rd` and `page Wr`, respectively). This will show which chunks have the highest I/O activity and, if monitored over a period of a minute, will show which are the most active.

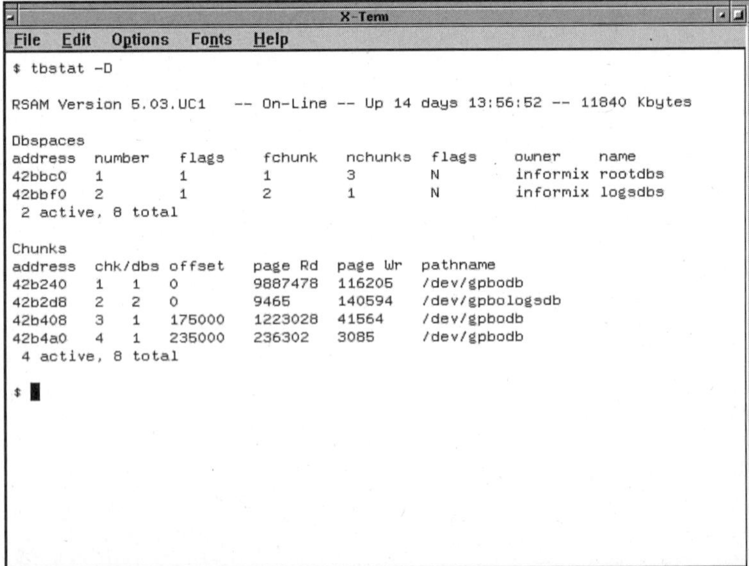


```
$ tbstat -D

RSAM Version 5.03.UC1    -- On-Line -- Up 14 days 13:56:52 -- 11840 Kbytes

Dbspaces
address  number   flags    fchunk   nchunks  flags    owner    name
42bbc0   1        1        1        3        N        informix rootdbs
42bbf0   2        1        2        1        N        informix logsdbs
 2 active, 8 total

Chunks
address  chk/dbs offset   page Rd  page Wr  pathname
42b240   1   1   0        9887478  116205   /dev/gpbodb
42b2d8   2   2   0        9465     140594   /dev/gpbologsdb
42b408   3   1   175000   1223028  41564    /dev/gpbodb
42b4a0   4   1   235000   236302   3085     /dev/gpbodb
 4 active, 8 total

$
```

Figure 21.12.

Output from the `tbstat -D` *command.*

The aim of configuring the I/O usage of a database is to balance the I/O across all of the disks as evenly as possible, thereby getting the most use from your disks. The output from the `tbstat -D` command can help in determining if the load is balanced across the disks.

If the chunk is a data chunk (that is, not a chunk containing the physical logs, logical logs, or temporary dbspace), you can find out which tables are in that chunk by running the `tbcheck -pe` utility. The output from this is a listing of the allocation of extents within all of the chunks defined to the OnLine server. By finding the chunk listing you are interested in, you can find a list of tables in that chunk. An example of the output from the `tbcheck -pe` command is shown in the "Database Monitoring" section of this chapter, in Figure 21.21.

OnLine DSA 7.1 can provide more accurate information regarding table access statistics. The utility `onstat -g ppf` can provide ISAM call and buffer read and write details for each partition. Unfortunately, no table name is printed, only the partnum, which is a hexadecimal number representing the partition number. A more useful way to get the same information is by executing SQL against the sysmaster database as in Listing 21.2.

Listing 21.2. SQL to select table access information.

```
select dbsname,  tabname,
  isreads, iswrites,
  isrewrites, isdeletes,
  bufreads,   bufwrites
from   sysptprof
where bufreads > 0 or bufwrites > 0
order  by dbsname, tabname ;
```

The `where` clause ensures that only partitions with access statistics are selected. This SQL can be tailored to your environment, for example, to select only those tables in a particular database by adding `and dbsname = "`*`dbspacename`*`"` to the `where` clause.

WARNING

The output from the SQL in Listing 21.2 is at partition level. A table partition can be spread over more than one chunk, and, therefore, the statistics from `onstat -D` might not correspond to those output from this SQL.

At this point, you might want to know which user threads are accessing your shortlist of tables. This is not easy to find, but a rough guide is given by the SQL in Listing 21.3, again executing against the sysmaster database. This SQL is for OnLine DSA 7.1 only and will only show users who have taken locks either because they are modifying the data, or because they have an isolation level of cursor stability or repeatable read and share locks are taken.

Listing 21.3. SQL to find users modifying a table.

```
select     s.username, l.type
from      syssessions s, syslocks l
where    s.sid          = l.owner
and        l.tabname = "tablename"
and        l.dbsname = "database name" ;
```

If the chunks you are interested in are the physical or logical logs, more information regarding their activity can be gained from `tbstat -l` or `onstat -l`. This display has two portions: the upper being the physical log information and the lower the logical log information. Figure 21.13 shows the output from `tbstat -l`. If the `%used` figure changes for either the physical log or the current logical log (denoted by a `C` in the fifth position of the flag column), pages are being written to the physical disk. This can be measured to determine if it requires tuning.

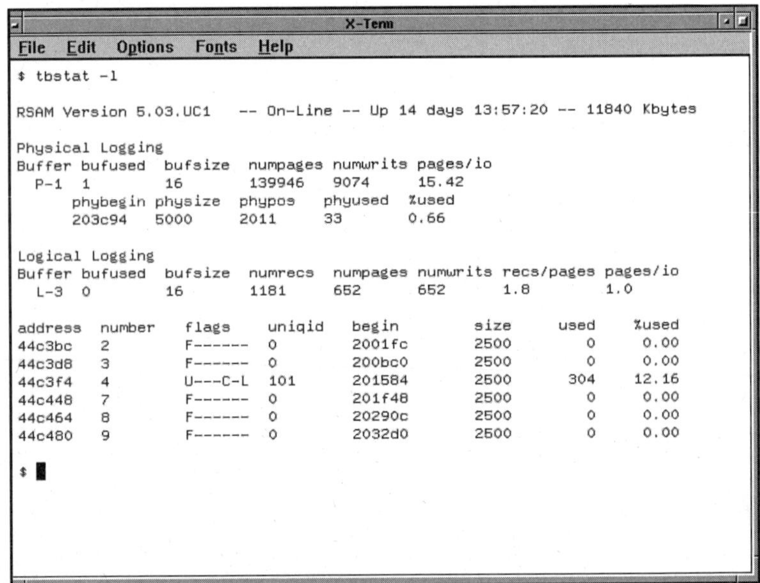

FIGURE 21.13.
Output from the `tbstat -l` *command.*

The writes to the logical logs and physical log are cached in buffers, which are flushed to disk only when full. In order to monitor the effectiveness of this buffering, the two statistics for logical log `pages/io` and physical `pages/io` should be examined in conjunction with the `bufsize` value for each. The closer the value of `pages/io` to `bufsize`, the better the buffering and, therefore, the better the I/O rate. The exception to this is for databases with unbuffered logging, where the logical log buffer is guaranteed to be written to the disk on every commit. In this case, the logical log `pages/io` is likely to be 1.0, which is normal.

Memory Monitoring

To monitor buffer memory usage, the `bufwaits` value of `tbstat -p` shows if enough buffer pages have been configured in the buffer pool. If this value is constantly increasing, user threads are having to wait for a buffer to become available, and increasing the number of buffers will help resolve this if it is possible to increase them.

In OnLine DSA 7.1, session memory details can be accessed using `onstat -g ses`. Figure 21.14 shows the output of the `onstat -g ses` command detailing each user thread's total memory allocated and total memory currently used. This shows which threads are using the most memory and which hold the most memory but are not presently using it.

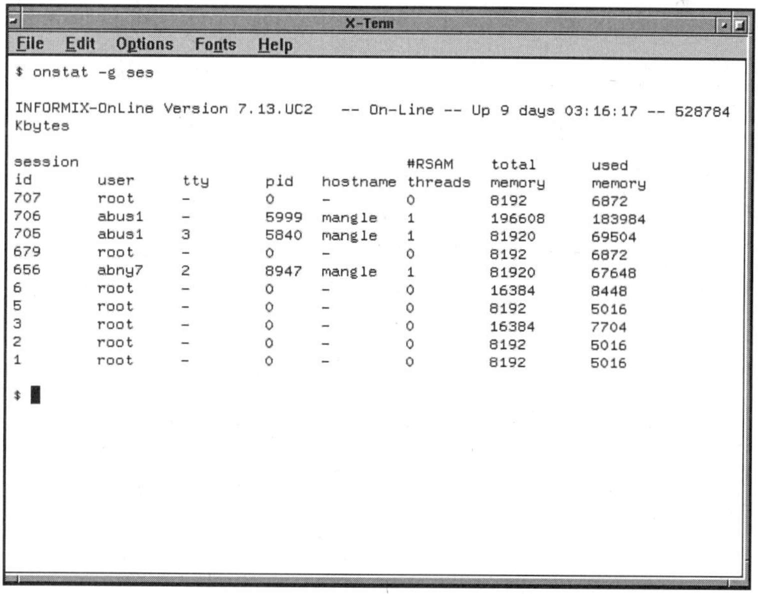

FIGURE 21.14.
Output from the `onstat -g ses` *command.*

```
X-Term
File  Edit  Options  Fonts  Help
$ onstat -g ses

INFORMIX-OnLine Version 7.13.UC2    -- On-Line -- Up 9 days 03:16:17 -- 528784
Kbytes

session                                        #RSAM    total      used
id        user     tty     pid    hostname   threads   memory     memory
707       root     -       0      -          0         8192       6872
706       abus1    -       5999   mangle     1         196608     183984
705       abus1    3       5840   mangle     1         81920      69504
679       root     -       0      -          0         8192       6872
656       abny7    2       8947   mangle     1         81920      67648
6         root     -       0      -          0         16384      8448
5         root     -       0      -          0         8192       5016
3         root     -       0      -          0         16384      7704
2         root     -       0      -          0         8192       5016
1         root     -       0      -          0         8192       5016

$
```

In OnLine DSA 7.1, this memory can be dynamically allocated from the UNIX server's available memory and can be an explanation of increased system paging.

CPU Monitoring

OnLine 5.0 does not provide any facilities for further investigating the usage being made by the user processes. These can be monitored only by UNIX commands such as `ps`, which can show the CPU time for each sqlexec thread.

To further investigate CPU usage under OnLine DSA 7.1, the `onstat -g glo` command shows a breakdown of CPU usage for each VP class, such as CPU and AIO. Figure 21.15 shows the output of `onstat -g glo`, which provides information about which VP class, if any, is currently receiving CPU service from the physical CPUs.

FIGURE 21.15.
Output of the `onstat -g glo` *command.*

```
X-Term
File  Edit  Options  Fonts  Help
$ onstat -g glo

INFORMIX-OnLine Version 7.13.UC2    -- On-Line -- Up 9 days 08:05:48 -- 8976 Kb
ytes

MT global info:
sessions threads  vps      lngspins
0        19       12       0

          sched calls     thread switches yield 0   yield n   yield forever
total:    6274730         3028398         3248919   2034448   12784
per sec:  7               3               4         2         0

Virtual processor summary:
class      vps      usercpu          syscpu          total
 cpu        1        85.26            74.84          160.10
 aio        6        19.44            77.91           97.35
 pio        1         2.66            12.51           15.17
 lio        1         2.61            11.80           14.41
 tli        1         7.42            25.67           33.09
 str        0         0.00             0.00            0.00
 shm        0         0.00             0.00            0.00
 adm        1         5.36            13.75           19.11
 opt        0         0.00             0.00            0.00
 msc        1         0.23             0.51            0.74
 adt        0         0.00             0.00            0.00
 total     12       122.98           216.99          339.97
$
```

A second section to the `onstat -g glo` display shows the CPU times for each VP in each VP class.

It is possible to examine which user threads are running on the CPU VPs and, therefore, whether it is just one thread constantly running or a large number of threads actively attempting to get CPU service. The `onstat -g act` command will show the active threads running on all CPU VPs at that moment. Figure 21.16 shows a sample output from this command. If the same thread ID appears constantly, one thread is swamping the CPU VPs with requests for service. If many thread IDs are appearing, the workload of the OnLine server is such that a CPU bottleneck is occurring and must be addressed to improve response times.

The output of the example in Figure 21.16 shows one active user thread on the CPU VPs.

Serious Event Monitoring

Under OnLine 5.0 and OnLine DSA 7.1, it is important to monitor the various database structures to ensure smooth running of the system. Some of the problems that can occur with these can be preempted, given the correct monitoring; others can merely be reported when observed.

Logical Logs Filling

In OnLine 5.0 and OnLine DSA 7.1, if the logical logs are not backed up, the OnLine server will suspend processing of user threads if all logical logs become full. Sometimes this can happen if an unexpectedly high volume of transactions is passed through the system. In order to detect the logs filling, the `tbstat -l` command should be used. Figure 21.17 shows the output from `tbstat -l` where the logical logs are about to fill. The `flags` column shows the status of each logical log. If a log has the status of `F` in the first position (signifying it as free), or `U` in the first position and `B` in the third position (signifying the log has been used, but backed up), then it is available for use. If it has any other status, it is not available. When all logs have a status of not available, the system will suspend processes awaiting a logical log backup process to complete.

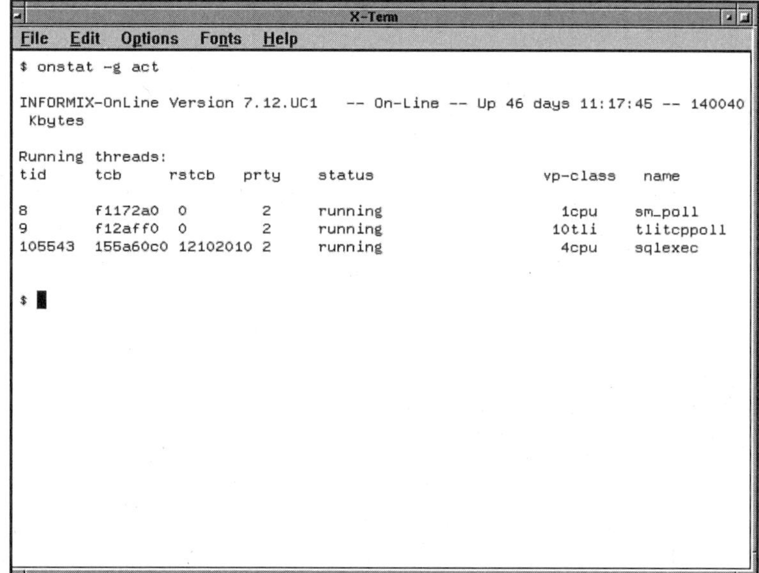

X-Term
File Edit Options Fonts Help
$ onstat -g act
INFORMIX-OnLine Version 7.12.UC1 -- On-Line -- Up 46 days 11:17:45 -- 140040 Kbytes
Running threads:
tid tcb rstcb prty status vp-class name
8 f1172a0 0 2 running 1cpu sm_poll
9 f12aff0 0 2 running 10tli tlitcppoll
105543 155a60c0 12102010 2 running 4cpu sqlexec
$

FIGURE 21.16.
Output from the `onstat -g act` *command.*

In OnLine DSA 7.1, a table in the sysmaster database called syslogs also tracks the status of each logical log, and from this, you can see how many logs are available.

Chunk Media Failure

If a chunk fails with an I/O error, it is flagged as down, signifying it is no longer usable. Later in this chapter, in the section "OnLine 5.0 Table and Index Size," Figure 21.20 shows the output from this command. Position 2 of the `flags` column for the chunk shows the status of the chunk:

`O` for online

`D` for down

`R` for in recovery

The normal status is `O`, with `D` indicating the chunk is unusable due to an error. `R` indicates the chunk needs to be logically recovered before it can be used.

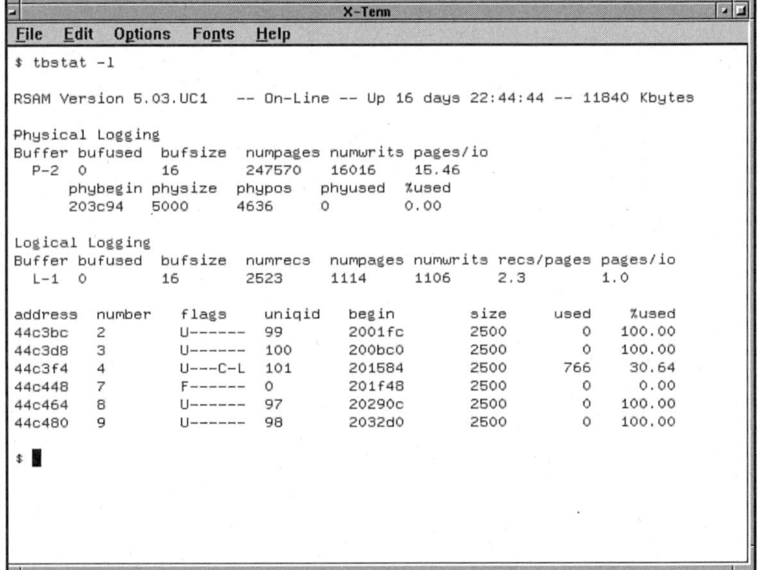
```
X-Term
File  Edit  Options  Fonts  Help
$ tbstat -l

RSAM Version 5.03.UC1   -- On-Line -- Up 16 days 22:44:44 -- 11840 Kbytes

Physical Logging
Buffer bufused  bufsize  numpages numwrits pages/io
  P-2  0        16       247570   16016    15.46
      phybegin physize  phypos   phyused  %used
      203c94   5000     4636     0        0.00

Logical Logging
Buffer bufused  bufsize  numrecs  numpages numwrits recs/pages pages/io
  L-1  0        16       2523     1114     1106     2.3        1.0

address  number   flags    uniqid   begin      size    used    %used
44c3bc   2        U------  99       2001fc     2500       0   100.00
44c3d8   3        U------  100      200bc0     2500       0   100.00
44c3f4   4        U---C-L  101      201584     2500     766    30.64
44c448   7        F------  0        201f48     2500       0     0.00
44c464   8        U------  97       20290c     2500       0   100.00
44c480   9        U------  98       2032d0     2500       0   100.00

$
```

FIGURE 21.17.
Output from the `tbstat -l` *command showing nearly full logical logs.*

Database Monitoring

This section is concerned with the monitoring of the physical database—the actual physical disk space being used by the Informix database system. Several data structures for both system and user data reside on disk to enable the Informix database environment to operate. This section will not cover the Informix programs and their maintenance.

This section discusses which physical database components require monitoring, which tools are available to monitor them, and how to apply those tools to monitor.

Physical Database Components

There are several physical components that support the Informix database, with different structures existing across the versions:

- Tables containing data
- Indexes referencing table data for fast access
- Physical log, in OnLine servers only, recording data page images before amendment
- Logical logs, in OnLine servers only, recording any transactions in logged databases

These are the core elements to monitor for the Informix database environment, but depending on your implementation environment, there could be more, such as temporary dbspaces and blobspaces. I won't discuss more than these because these are the critical components.

It is possible to use a spreadsheet package to build a spreadsheet to calculate the size of a database table and its indexes based on formulae provided in the Informix manuals. These spreadsheets can be used to determine the amount of disk space required for a system and what table layout strategy to adopt. When the system is live, these spreadsheets can be referenced to measure the table sizes to ensure they are within the expected limits and can be amended as table alterations are proposed to assess system impact.

Physical Database Monitoring

Standard Engine databases have different monitoring tools than OnLine server databases because Standard Engine stores its tables as UNIX files.

Standard Engine—Table and Index Size

Standard Engine tables and indexes reside in UNIX files managed by the UNIX File System. In order to monitor their size, the UNIX command `ls -l` *`tablename`*`.dat` will display the size of the table in bytes. The `ls -l` *`tablename`*`.idx` command will display the size of the indexes for the tables in bytes. These commands must be issued in the database directory in which the table and index files are located. The *`tablename`* used in the `ls` command is not the one referenced in any SQL except the UNIX filename. Listing 21.4 gives SQL code to select the UNIX filename from the database system catalog for any given table.

Standard Engine—Index Integrity

Index integrity can be compromised, leaving the index pointers within the index structures incorrectly referencing table data rows. This occurs because Standard Engine relies on UNIX I/O for its disk writes. The UNIX operating system uses cache to improve disk I/O times, but the trade-off is that there is no guarantee that the writes to disk have been made.

Indexes can be checked for consistency using the `bcheck` utility, the options of which are shown in Figure 21.18.

> **NOTE**
>
> The table name supplied for the `bcheck` utility is not the table name as known in the system catalog and used in SQL. Instead, the UNIX filename is used without the .dat extension, and your current working directory must contain the database files you are checking.

In order to determine the filename for a particular table, use the SQL in Listing 21.4.

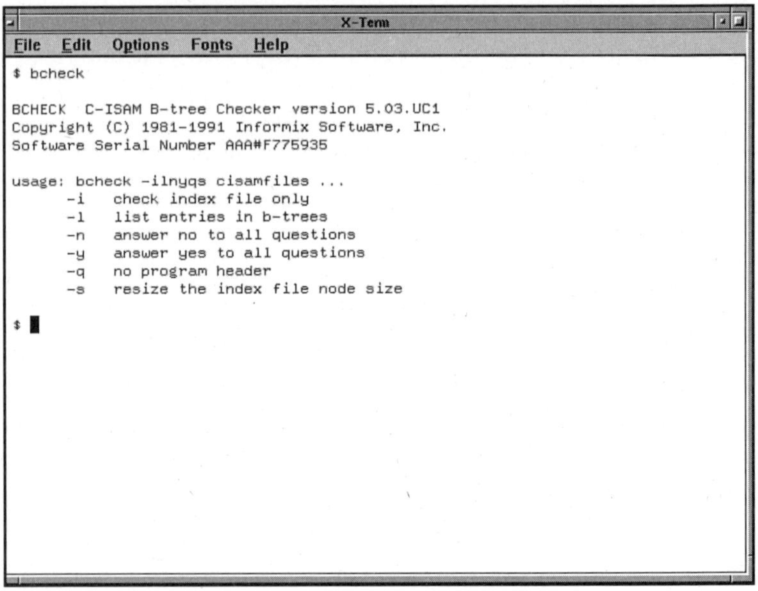

FIGURE 21.18.
bcheck *options.*

```
X-Term
File  Edit  Options  Fonts  Help
$ bcheck

BCHECK  C-ISAM B-tree Checker version 5.03.UC1
Copyright (C) 1981-1991 Informix Software, Inc.
Software Serial Number AAA#F775935

usage: bcheck -ilnyqs cisamfiles ...
        -i    check index file only
        -l    list entries in b-trees
        -n    answer no to all questions
        -y    answer yes to all questions
        -q    no program header
        -s    resize the index file node size

$ █
```

Listing 21.4. The SQL to retrieve a Standard Engine filename for a table.

```
select dirpath
from   systables
where tabname = "table name" ;
```

The bcheck utility will show whether there are any integrity errors and allow you the option of deleting and rebuilding the index, as shown in Figure 21.19.

The SQL command `check table` *`table name`* can also be used to check table and index integrity with the SQL command `repair table` *`table name`* available to repair any errors. Both of these SQL commands are executed while connected to the database containing the table, and both run the `bcheck` utility.

I recommend checking the integrity of your table data and index structures on a regular basis. This could be daily, weekly, or monthly, depending on the activity on your system and any available maintenance windows.

OnLine 5.0 Table and Index Size

OnLine 5.0 server databases can be monitored using Informix utilities such as `tbstat` and `tbcheck`. `tbstat` can be used to display the dbspaces that have been allocated. `tbcheck` shows the allocation of table extents within those dbspaces. This applies for both cooked and raw file systems.

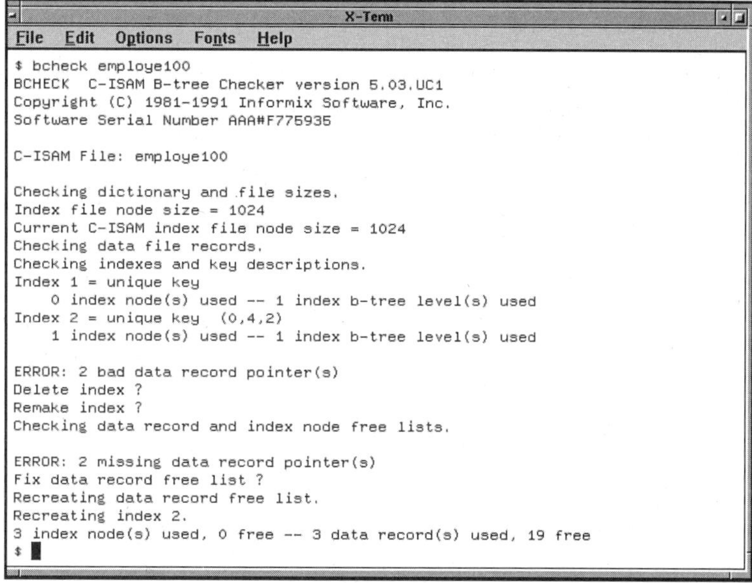

```
$ bcheck employe100
BCHECK  C-ISAM B-tree Checker version 5.03.UC1
Copyright (C) 1981-1991 Informix Software, Inc.
Software Serial Number AAA#F775935

C-ISAM File: employe100

Checking dictionary and file sizes.
Index file node size = 1024
Current C-ISAM index file node size = 1024
Checking data file records.
Checking indexes and key descriptions.
Index 1 = unique key
    0 index node(s) used -- 1 index b-tree level(s) used
Index 2 = unique key  (0,4,2)
    1 index node(s) used -- 1 index b-tree level(s) used

ERROR: 2 bad data record pointer(s)
Delete index ?
Remake index ?
Checking data record and index node free lists.

ERROR: 2 missing data record pointer(s)
Fix data record free list ?
Recreating data record free list.
Recreating index 2.
3 index node(s) used, 0 free -- 3 data record(s) used, 19 free
$
```

FIGURE 21.19.
`bcheck` *output showing corrupt index.*

There are three levels at which OnLine server space utilization can be monitored:

- Allocated chunks within dbspaces
- Allocated table extents within allocated chunks
- Used pages within allocated table extents

`tbstat -d` provides a map of the dbspaces that have been defined and the chunks that have been allocated to them. Figure 21.20 shows a sample output from `tbstat -d`. The upper portion of the display lists the dbspace `number` against the dbspace `name`. The lower portion shows the chunks that have been allocated to that dbspace, where the number in the `dbs` column is the number of the dbspace to which the chunk is allocated. The `size` column of the chunks display shows the number of pages allocated to the chunk, with the `free` column showing the number of pages not yet allocated to tables and indexes.

NOTE

The `tbstat -d` display shows values in pages, not kilobytes, for the `offset`, `size`, and `free` columns. Make sure that you know the page size of your system in order to calculate the actual size in kilobytes.

FIGURE 21.20.
Output from the `tbstat -d` *command showing defined dbspaces and allocated chunks.*

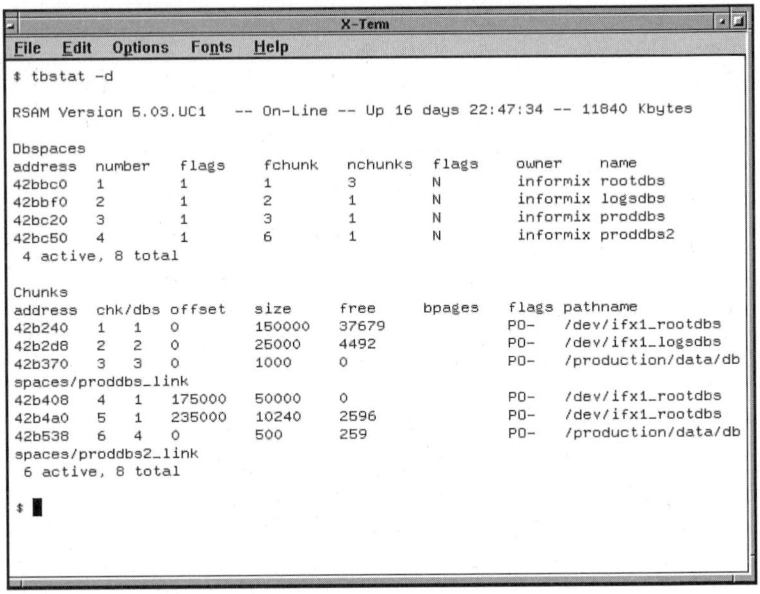

```
X-Term
File  Edit  Options  Fonts  Help
$ tbstat -d

RSAM Version 5.03.UC1   -- On-Line -- Up 16 days 22:47:34 -- 11840 Kbytes

Dbspaces
address  number   flags    fchunk   nchunks  flags    owner    name
42bbc0   1        1        1        3        N        informix rootdbs
42bbf0   2        1        2        1        N        informix logsdbs
42bc20   3        1        3        1        N        informix proddbs
42bc50   4        1        6        1        N        informix proddbs2
 4 active, 8 total

Chunks
address  chk/dbs offset   size     free     bpages   flags pathname
42b240   1   1   0        150000   37679             PO-   /dev/ifx1_rootdbs
42b2d8   2   2   0        25000    4492              PO-   /dev/ifx1_logsdbs
42b370   3   3   0        1000     0                 PO-   /production/data/db
spaces/proddbs_link
42b408   4   1   175000   50000    0                 PO-   /dev/ifx1_rootdbs
42b4a0   5   1   235000   10240    2596              PO-   /dev/ifx1_rootdbs
42b538   6   4   0        500      259               PO-   /production/data/db
spaces/proddbs2_link
 6 active, 8 total

$
```

Given that a chunk has been allocated a number of pages and that a number of those pages have been used, it is important to understand to what database structure these pages have been allocated. `tbcheck -pe` is the utility for displaying the chunk and extent information and will display information about which tables and indexes have extents allocated to them within a chunk. Figure 21.21 shows an example of a chunk that has several tables allocated within it.

FIGURE 21.21.
A page from the `tbcheck -pe` *output.*

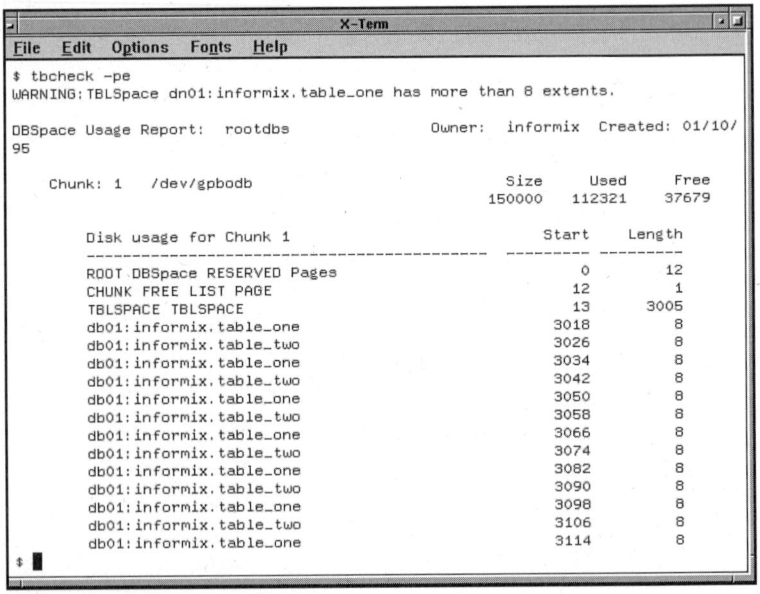

```
X-Term
File  Edit  Options  Fonts  Help
$ tbcheck -pe
WARNING: TBLSpace dn01:informix.table_one has more than 8 extents.

DBSpace Usage Report:  rootdbs              Owner:  informix  Created: 01/10/
95

    Chunk: 1   /dev/gpbodb                          Size      Used      Free
                                                  150000    112321     37679

        Disk usage for Chunk 1                          Start     Length
        ----------------------------------------     ---------  ---------
        ROOT DBSpace RESERVED Pages                          0         12
        CHUNK FREE LIST PAGE                                12          1
        TBLSPACE TBLSPACE                                   13       3005
        db01:informix.table_one                           3018          8
        db01:informix.table_two                           3026          8
        db01:informix.table_one                           3034          8
        db01:informix.table_two                           3042          8
        db01:informix.table_one                           3050          8
        db01:informix.table_two                           3058          8
        db01:informix.table_one                           3066          8
        db01:informix.table_two                           3074          8
        db01:informix.table_one                           3082          8
        db01:informix.table_two                           3090          8
        db01:informix.table_one                           3098          8
        db01:informix.table_two                           3106          8
        db01:informix.table_one                           3114          8
$
```

This example shows that table_one and table_two have interleaved extents (contiguously allocated pages), which could lead to a performance problem because the disk heads need to move further in order to locate all the data within the table.

TIP

The `tbcheck -pe` utility contains a series of warning messages at the start of the output listing if any table has eight or more separate extents allocated to it, as shown in the example in Figure 21.22. This includes extents within one chunk or table extents that spread across several chunks. This is a handy method for finding which tables might need unloading and reloading to "shuffle" the data together again within one extent, or to have the first extent size increased to accommodate the data in one extent.

FIGURE 21.22.
`tbcheck -pe` *reporting tables with more than eight extents.*

```
X-Term
File  Edit  Options  Fonts  Help
$ tbcheck -pe
WARNING:TBLSpace db1:usab1.syscolumns has more than 8 extents.
WARNING:TBLSpace db1:usab1.table_one has more than 8 extents.
WARNING:TBLSpace db1:usab1.log_report has more than 8 extents.

DBSpace Usage Report:  rootdbs              Owner:  informix  Created: 01/10/
95

    Chunk: 1   /dev/gpbodb                          Size     Used     Free
                                                  150000   112321    37679

        Disk usage for Chunk 1                           Start    Length
        ---------------------------------------------   -------- ---------
        ROOT DBSpace RESERVED Pages                            0        12
        CHUNK FREE LIST PAGE                                  12         1
        TBLSPACE TBLSPACE                                     13      3005
        kab1:usab1.systables                                3018         8
        kab1:usab1.syscolumns                               3026         8
        kab1:usab1.sysindexes                               3034         8
        kab1:usab1.systabauth                               3042         8
        kab1:usab1.syscolauth                               3050         8
        kab1:usab1.sysviews                                 3058         8
        kab1:usab1.sysusers                                 3066         8
        kab1:usab1.sysdepend                                3074         8
$
```

Although a table has pages allocated to it as extents within a chunk, all of those pages might not be used, and not all of them might be used by the table alone; there could be indexes included, also. To determine this information, the `tbcheck -pT` ***`databasename:tablename`*** command will examine the table and its indexes and display the number of pages used. Figure 21.23 shows typical output from this command.

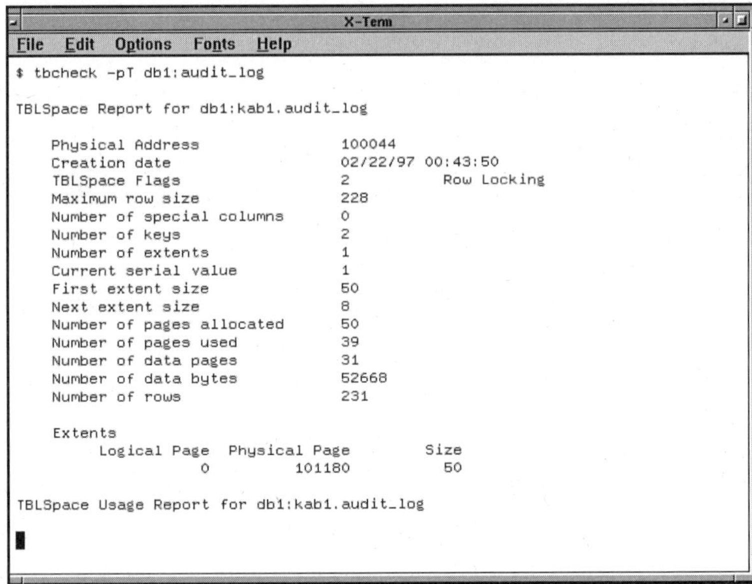

```
X-Term
File  Edit  Options  Fonts  Help
$ tbcheck -pT db1:audit_log

TBLSpace Report for db1:kab1.audit_log

    Physical Address                100044
    Creation date                   02/22/97 00:43:50
    TBLSpace Flags                  2          Row Locking
    Maximum row size                228
    Number of special columns       0
    Number of keys                  2
    Number of extents               1
    Current serial value            1
    First extent size               50
    Next extent size                8
    Number of pages allocated       50
    Number of pages used            39
    Number of data pages            31
    Number of data bytes            52668
    Number of rows                  231

    Extents
         Logical Page  Physical Page        Size
                    0         101180          50

TBLSpace Usage Report for db1:kab1.audit_log
```

FIGURE 21.23.
Sample output from the `tbcheck -pT` *command (part one).*

In the first section of the display, various table statistics are displayed. The column `number of pages allocated` shows the total number of pages allocated to the table and any indexes defined as part of this table. The column `number of pages used` shows the maximum number of pages used within this tablespace's allocation at any time; it is not necessarily the number of pages currently used. The column `number of data pages` represents the maximum number of data pages used within this tablespace's allocation at any time.

The second portion of the output, shown in Figure 21.24, shows the tablespace details for the table and indexes at the current time. This shows how many pages are free, how many pages have been allocated to the indexes, and how many pages have been allocated to the data pages. If any indexes are defined on the table, their details are displayed in the third section, as shown in Figure 21.25.

By using these figures, you can check that the table has the number of rows you anticipated and that the expected amount of space is being used. If not, the table might need to be reloaded to remove any unwanted holes in the data and index pages.

The portion of the `tbcheck -pT` output detailing index statistics is useful for determining whether or not to rebuild an index. The average bytes free figure indicates the average number of free bytes on a page for that level of the index. If there are not many bytes available on each page and you expect insert activity to occur on that index, you might want to rebuild it to improve access times for the index.

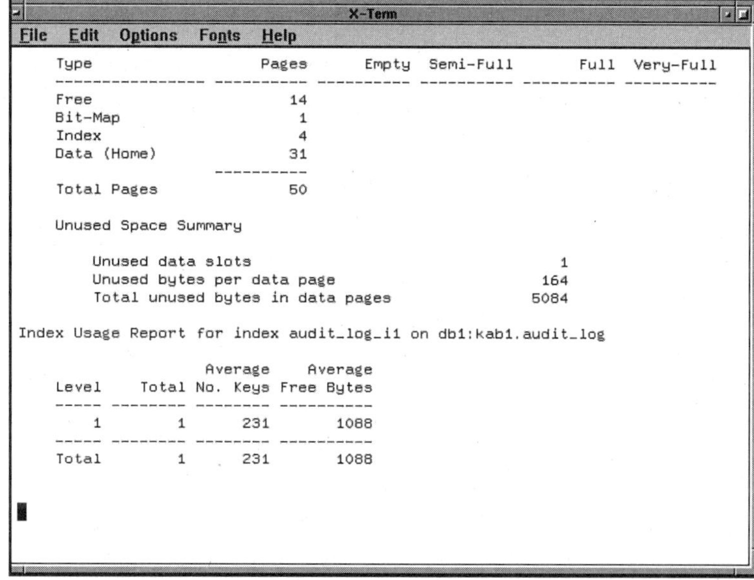

X-Term
File Edit Options Fonts Help
Type Pages Empty Semi-Full Full Very-Full
Free 14
Bit-Map 1
Index 4
Data (Home) 31
Total Pages 50
Unused Space Summary
Unused data slots 1
Unused bytes per data page 164
Total unused bytes in data pages 5084
Index Usage Report for index audit_log_i1 on db1:kab1.audit_log
Level Total Average No. Keys Average Free Bytes
1 1 231 1088
Total 1 231 1088

FIGURE 21.24.
Sample output from the `tbcheck -pT` *command (part two).*

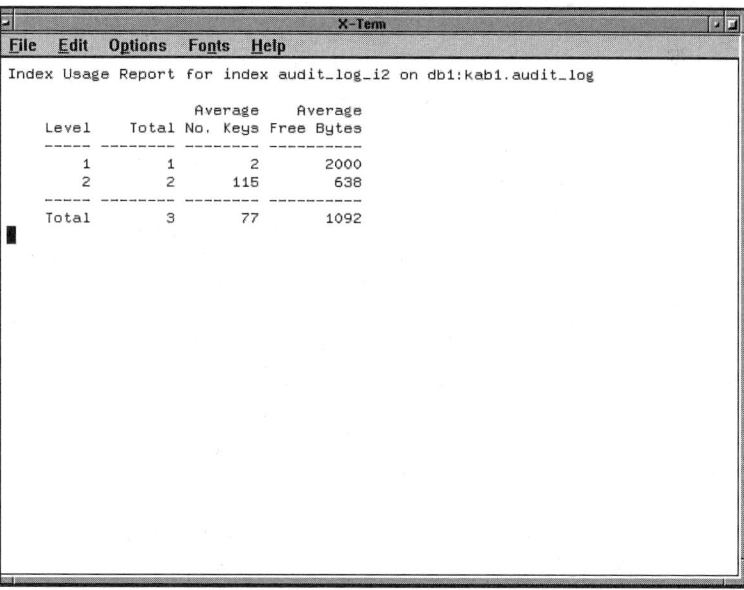

X-Term
File Edit Options Fonts Help
Index Usage Report for index audit_log_i2 on db1:kab1.audit_log
Level Total Average No. Keys Average Free Bytes
1 1 2 2000
2 2 115 638
Total 3 77 1092

FIGURE 21.25.
Sample output from the `tbcheck -pT` *command (part three).*

OnLine 5.0 Consistency Checking

To comprehensively monitor the consistency of the data and system structures within an OnLine 5 server, you should run the following:

- `tbcheck -cD` *`databasename:tablename`* to check the consistency of the data pages (non-blob)
- `tbcheck -cI` *`databasename:tablename`* to check and repair the consistency of the index pages
- `tbcheck -cr` to check the consistency of the reserved pages in the root dbspace
- `tbcheck -cc` *`databasename`* to check the consistency of the database system catalog pages

WARNING

`tbcheck -cD` and `tbcheck -cI` both lock the table being checked in exclusive mode. `tbcheck -cc` locks the system catalog tables in share mode, preventing any modifications occurring, such as creating or dropping tables, databases, or indexes. Caution must be exercised when using these utilities.

These utilities can be used to ensure that no internal inconsistency within the OnLine server is allowed to prevail once detected. It is recommended to run these consistency checks, if time allows, before any archive to ensure the archive is of good enough quality to be recovered if required.

OnLine DSA 7.1 Table and Index Size

Like OnLine 5.0, OnLine 7.1 server databases can be monitored using Informix utilities such as `onstat` and `oncheck`. The monitoring is the same as that detailed in the previous section, "OnLine 5.0 Table and Index Size"; however, the System Monitoring Interface tables can also be used to gather monitoring data. In this section, I describe only how to use SQL to access the SMI tables in the sysmaster database in order to obtain monitoring data. Please refer to the section "OnLine 5.0 Table and Index Size" for details of how to obtain this information by using the `onstat` and `oncheck` utilities.

There are three levels at which OnLine server space utilization can be monitored:

- Allocated chunks within dbspaces
- Allocated table extents within chunks
- Used pages within table extents

Listing 21.5 shows SQL that will display a summary of the space allocated to a dbspace and how much of it has been used. This SQL shows the amount allocated and the percentage of free space available, but only if the percentage of free space available falls below 10 percent of the allocated space, which is useful for proactive space monitoring.

Listing 21.5. The SQL reporting dbspaces with less than 10 percent free space.

```
select       d.name,     (sum(c.nfree)/sum(c.chksize))*100 pctfree
from        sysdbspaces d,     syschunks c
where      d.dbsnum = c.dbsnum
group by  d.name
having     (sum(c.nfree)/sum(c.chksize))*100 < 10;
```

If you want to examine the usage of the individual chunks allocated to the dbspaces, Listing 21.6 shows SQL that will display the dbspaces that have been defined, the chunks associated with them, and the space allocated and used.

Listing 21.6. The SQL to obtain dbspace and chunk usage information.

```
select d.name,          c.chknum,
          c.chksize,        c.nfree
from   sysdbspaces d, syschunks, c
where d.dbsnum = c.dbsnum
order by d.name;
```

> **NOTE**
>
> This SQL does not show the chunks in the allocated order, only the details of their space allocation. Columns exist on the syschunks table that will allow you to follow the allocated order chain, but a more complicated program will need to be written in order to process the linked-list data rows.

Given that a chunk has been allocated a number of pages and that a number of those pages have been used, it is important to understand the database structure that is using those pages. The `oncheck -pe` utility can be used to display the chunk and extent information and will display information about which tables and indexes have extents allocated to them within the chunk.

This information can also be gathered from the SMI tables in the sysmaster database, although the `oncheck -pe` might be more accurate because it looks at the physical disk in order to get its information. Listing 21.7 shows how to use SQL to obtain the table allocations for a dbspace and the chunks within it.

Listing 21.7. Reporting on page usage within chunks for a dbspace.

```
select     e.tabname,        hex(e.start) startaddr,
              e.size
from       sysextents e,    syschunks c,
              sysdbspaces d
where     d.name = "dbspace name"
and          d.dbsnum = c.dbsnum
and          c.chknum = round(e.start/1048576,0)
order by 2;
```

TIP

The oncheck -pe utility contains a series of warning messages at the start of the output listing if any table has eight or more separate extents allocated to it. The SMI tables can be used much more efficiently to access this information, as shown in Listing 21.8, and have the added benefit of your controlling what is displayed on the report.

Listing 21.8. The SQL to report tables with eight extents or more.

```
select    dbsname, tabname, count(*)
from     sysextents
group  by dbsname, tabname
having  count(*) > 7 ;
```

Although a table has pages allocated to it as extents within a chunk, not all of those pages may be used, and not all of them may be used by the table alone; indexes could be included also. To determine this information, the `oncheck -pT` *`databasename:tablename`* command will examine the table and its indexes and display the number of pages used, as shown and described in Figure 21.23, earlier in this chapter in the section "OnLine 5.0 Table and Index Size."

OnLine DSA 7.1 Consistency Checking

To comprehensively monitor the consistency of the data and system structures within an OnLine DSA 7.1 server, you should run the following:

- `oncheck -cD` *`databasename:tablename`* to check the consistency of the data pages (non-blob)
- `oncheck -cI` *`databasename:tablename`* to check and repair the consistency of the index pages
- `oncheck -cr` to check the consistency of the reserved pages in the root dbspace
- `oncheck -cc` *`databasename`* to check the consistency of the database system catalog pages

WARNING

`oncheck -cD` and `oncheck -cI` both lock the table being checked in exclusive mode. `oncheck -cc` locks the system catalog tables in share mode, preventing any modifications from occurring, such as creating or dropping tables, databases, or indexes. Caution must be exercised when using these utilities.

These utilities can be used to ensure that no internal inconsistency within the OnLine server is allowed to prevail once detected. It is recommended to run these consistency checks, if time allows, before any archive to ensure the archive will be of good enough quality to be recovered if required.

Long-Term Monitoring Strategy

It is extremely beneficial to understand how to obtain statistics on system performance if the system is performing poorly. Could the poor performance have been anticipated? If it has been caused because an index has been filling its leaf pages until the inserts have little space left on a page, maybe it could have been anticipated.

At the beginning of this chapter, I described the statistics as being useful only if they were taken in the context of other statistics to provide useful system performance information. Trying to gather all of that information at a time of crisis is extremely difficult, unless it is automated in some way.

To provide a comprehensive monitoring strategy, I recommend building a database to contain the various statistics you would like to collect and building an application to interrogate that data to provide a true picture of the system by bringing together statistics, such as I/O rates, memory usage, CPU usage, and number of users on the system. The data held in this database could be summarized at regular intervals, such as daily, weekly, and monthly, to provide the information for any system reviews you might want to perform later. This sort of information could also be used to assess the impact of any application implementations or volume growth and enable future changes to be assessed and maybe even modeled.

Such a system will take some of the guesswork out of planning new database systems and monitoring current ones, which can only help the database administrators do their jobs better and enable them to concentrate on other activities. At the time of writing this chapter, I have not yet seen a good, comprehensive, off-the-shelf package that will allow this type of functionality for complex distributed database systems.

Summary

This chapter has explained some of the tools that can be used to monitor the Informix database systems from various aspects. There are no hard and fast rules regarding what are the correct and incorrect statistics to observe being reported by these systems, because each implementation is different. The only sure-fire method of understanding what measurements your systems should be reporting is by monitoring them over a period of time and in different situations.

CHAPTER 22

Advanced Monitoring Tools

by Matt Bentley

IN THIS CHAPTER

Having adequate tools makes the job of monitoring OnLine much easier. When administering a system, you can be proactive or reactive. INFORMIX-OnLine provides the tools for both types of administration. Not every problem is foreseeable, so you will always have to react to problems.

What to Watch

Operating systems, relational database management systems, and applications are all very complex. Understanding the components of each and how they relate is difficult and comes from experience. It is important when you begin monitoring to identify the elements you will watch and to understand what the statistics for those elements are.

When monitoring relational database management systems, you should watch four major areas:

- User activity
- Database design
- Operating system
- INFORMIX-OnLine

All of these areas must be watched regularly. Looking at just one area, you are apt to miss a real problem. The relationship among these areas and how one can influence the other is critical to understanding what is happening with the system.

User Activity

User activity comprises the types of queries, the volume of data, the volume of transactions, the types of transactions, and the times of most heavy usage. These all impact performance and cannot be regarded lightly when monitoring resources.

Database Design

It is important to monitor the database and its objects, identifying heavily used tables, proper indexing, table placement, frequency of updates to tables, and contention against tables. Some of these statistics are difficult to gather and can be gathered only by regular and consistent monitoring.

Operating System

Because of the integration of OnLine with the operating system, it is important to understand and monitor the various aspects of the operating system upon which OnLine depends.

OnLine can report how it uses the resources that have been allocated to it. These resources might be only a small percentage of a very large system. The only way to monitor the utilization of the allocated resources is by using the operating system utilities. Checking each component that has been allocated for usage is necessary, especially when the resources are shared or divided. Consider disk activity, for example. OnLine can report how much disk space is used and how many read and write operations have been made to those disks. Only by using the operating system tools can you know the wait time for each read and write operation, how busy a specific disk is, and how busy the disk is while servicing each operation.

INFORMIX-OnLine

Understanding the complex architecture of the OnLine environment helps you understand the relationships of the different utilities and reports used to monitor OnLine.

Available Tools

Informix has recognized the importance of monitoring tools and has done a good job of adding to the toolbox with each major release of OnLine. This provides access to the statistics for the same components through multiple interfaces.

Sysmaster Database

The sysmaster database is an interface into the OnLine engine through standard SQL. This is a read-only relational database with dynamic pseudo-tables. These tables are updated by OnLine.

These pseudo-tables do not reside on disk, but they are structures located and maintained dynamically in memory. Consecutive queries against the tables will probably return different results because the tables contain only snapshot data and are always changing.

Of the 19 supported sysmaster tables, 15 are addressed here. If you list all of the tables in the sysmaster database, you will see there are more than 19 tables. Several tables are included that are used by the onarchive utility and several that are not supported.

WARNING

You can still access the unsupported tables, but do not rely on those tables to always be in the database or retain the same structure for future versions of OnLine.

The following is the type of information that is available from the sysmaster database. The tables are shown in parentheses:

- Dbspace information and statistics (`sysdbspaces`)
- Database information (`sysdatabases`)

- Chunk information and statistics (`syschunks`, `syschkio`)
- Table information (`systabnames`, `sysptprof`)
- Extent allocation (`sysextents`)
- Configuration information (`sysconfig`)
- System profile (`sysprofile`)
- CPU utilization for each virtual processor (`sysvpprof`)
- Logical log information (`syslogs`)
- Lock information (`syslocks`)
- User session information (`syssessions`, `sysseswts`, `sysessprof`)

You can add to the monitoring tools provided by Informix by creating your own scripts and programs. Any development tool that can be used to create applications that access Informix databases and tables can also access the sysmaster database.

Here are some examples of extending the monitoring tools using SQL:

- Display user locks, table locks, and who is waiting for those locks to be released.
- Display table size and the number of extents.
- Display dbspace statistics.
- Display session information.

Listing 22.1 shows a set of SQL statements that first display the database, table, and lock type for each lock a user has. Then the users waiting for the locks are shown.

Listing 22.1. SQL statements that list all locks and waiters.

```
-- First get a list of owners.
select l.dbsname, l.tabname, l.type, s.username,
       l.owner sid, l.waiter
   from syslocks l, syssessions s
     where s.sid = l.owner into temp owners;
-- Display all owners of locks
select * from owners;
-- Display all waiters.
select o.dbsname, o.tabname, o.type, o.username,
       s.username, s.sid
   from owners o, syssessions s
   where o.waiter = s.sid;
```

Knowing the size of tables and how many extents tables have enables you to identify inefficient tables so that you can reorganize them. Listing 22.2 shows the SQL statement to display the number of extents and the number of pages allocated for each table in each database.

Listing 22.2. An SQL statement displaying table size and the number of extents for each table in each database.

```
select dbsname, tabname, sum(size), count(*)
      from sysextents
      group by dbsname, tabname
```

Listing 22.3 is an SQL statement that shows how many pages are allocated for each dbspace, how much of that is free, the free space as a percentage, the number of reads, the number of writes, and the physical device name. This is the `onstat -d` and `onstat -D` reports combined into a single report.

Listing 22.3. Dbspace statistics.

```
select dbs.name, chk.chksize, chk.nfree,
      (chk.nfree/chk.chksize)*100, io.reads,
      io.writes, fname
   from sysdbspaces dbs, syschunks chk, syschkio io
      where dbs.dbsnum=chk.dbsnum and
            chk.chknum = io.chunknum
```

Listing 22.4 shows lock requests, ISAM reads, and ISAM writes for each session attached to OnLine. Additional columns in both the `syssessions` and `syssesprof` tables can be added to this statement to show other statistics you might be interested in.

Listing 22.4. User session information.

```
sid, a.username, b.lockreqs, b.isreads, b.iswrites
   from syssessions a, syssesprof b
      where a.sid = b.sid
```

Event Alarms

Another useful source of information is in the OnLine message log file. While OnLine is running, it reports warnings and statuses to the message log file.

Incorporated into the OnLine engine is the facility to trigger actions based on the messages written to the log file. The majority of the messages written are informational, but some messages identify fatal events within OnLine that need immediate attention.

A sample script to monitor the message log file is provided with INFORMIX-OnLine. This is a good start to developing your own event monitor application. You should review the types of messages that will be written and decide which messages you want to respond to.

Each time a message is written to the log file, the program specified by the ONCONFIG parameter ALARMPROGRAM is executed. Each time the program is executed, up to four arguments are passed to it. These are the event severity; the event class ID and class message; specific messages; and in some cases, additional messages that relate to the specific event. Possible event severity values are listed in Table 22.1.

Table 22.1. Possible severity codes.

Severity	*Description*
1	Not noteworthy. Messages with this severity will not be reported to the alarm program.
2	Information. There were no errors. This is a routine message.
3	Attention. This event needs attention, but no data is lost.
4	Emergency. An unexpected event occurred, and action must be taken immediately.
5	Fatal. The database server failed because of an unexpected event.

Onperf

Onperf is a tool for monitoring OnLine through a graphical interface (as shown in Figure 22.1). You can show the data points in different graph formats. Line, vertical bar, horizontal bar, and pie charts show the trends of the data points visually. You pick the data points to be displayed at configurable intervals.

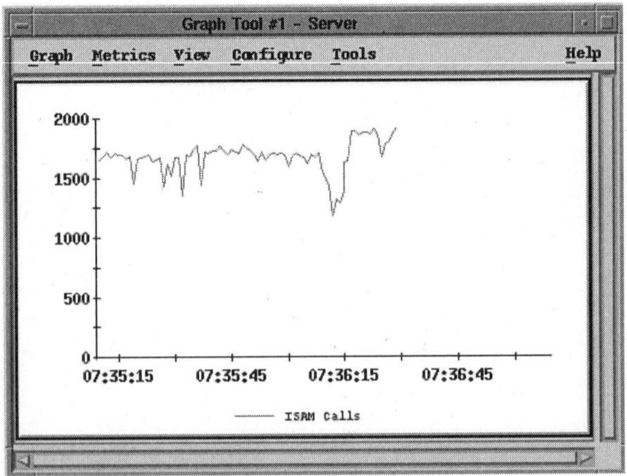

FIGURE 22.1. *The onperf main screen.*

Onperf consists of a data collector, a graphical display, and a query tree tool. The data collector and graphical display work together to gather and display the information. The query tree tool gathers data directly from shared memory about a specific session.

You specify the metrics that you want the data collector to retrieve and display. These metrics are stored to a buffer and displayed in the graphical format you choose. The different metrics categories are chunks, disks, fragments, physical processors, servers, sessions, tblspaces, and virtual processors. There are many metrics per category that can be chosen for monitoring.

Data gathered by the collector can be saved to a file and replayed at a later time. The data is stored in binary or ASCII format.

NOTE

With the ASCII format, the file can be moved to another system and accessed there. Binary format is platform-specific but can be written and accessed very quickly.

Within onperf, several tools are available that simplify monitoring some groups of resources. The available tools on the Tools menu of onperf are predefined views of specific metrics. Each tool has a useful purpose when monitoring OnLine. The tools are status, query tree, disk activity, disk capacity, session activity, physical processor activity, and virtual processor activity.

Status

The status tool is rather simple; it shows the current status of OnLine, such as whether it is in fast recovery, quiescent mode, offline, or online. Also, some statistics on the size of shared memory and data collector information are displayed with this tool.

Query Tool

The query tool shows the progress of a long-running query for a selected session. Figure 22.2 shows how the query tool breaks down the query to show each step of the query and how many rows have been processed in each step. If multiple tables are being joined, each table is shown with the join step also visible. Analyze long running queries with this tool to identify the section of the query that is taking the longest to perform. For example, a sequential scan of a large table would be shown in one box, and the count of processed rows would increase until all rows were processed in the table. This tool could also be analyzed with the output of `SET EXPLAIN`.

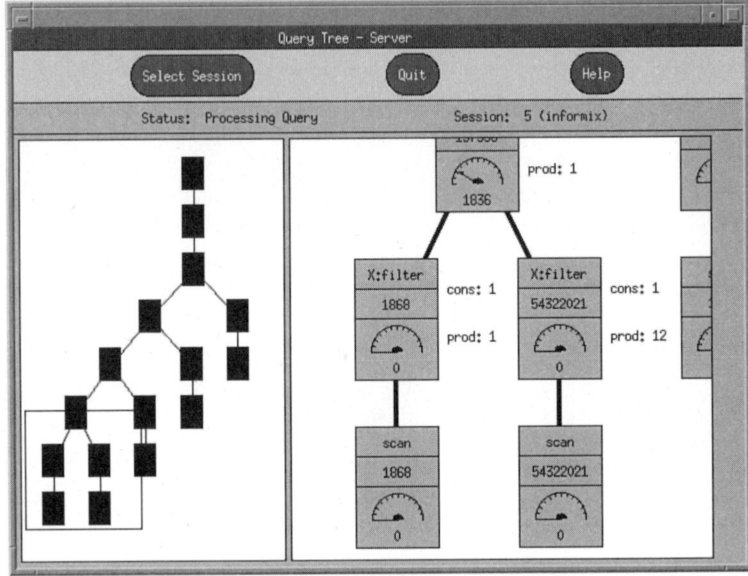

FIGURE 22.2.
The query tool.

Disk Activity

Each chunk is listed with the number of disk reads and writes per second using the disk activity tool. Use this tool to identify high-activity chunks. Perhaps a table should be fragmented or isolated on a separate disk to distribute some of that activity.

Disk Capacity

You can monitor available space by using the disk capacity tool. Used space and free space are displayed for each chunk defined to OnLine.

Session Activity

Each session that is connected to OnLine is displayed with the session activity tool. The statistics that are displayed are reads and writes per session. Monitoring this will help you identify active user sessions.

Physical Processor Activity

The physical processor activity tool shows how busy the CPUs are at the hardware level. Figure 22.3 shows the activity on each of the 12 processors for a 12-processor machine. Each bar changes at frequent intervals, showing user time and system time as a percentage of total processor activity. By watching the activity of the physical processors, you can determine whether additional CPU VPs can be added or whether additional physical processors are needed.

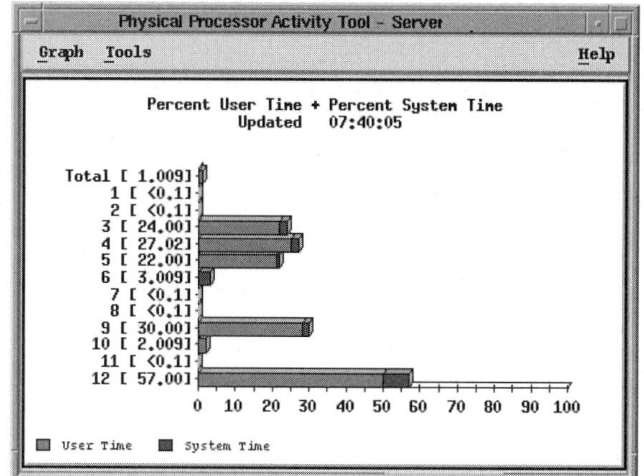

FIGURE 22.3.
The physical processor activity tool.

Figure 22.4 shows the virtual processor activity tool. The VPs are listed only by their numeric identifier. You can watch as the VPs become active to monitor how busy OnLine is when processing database activities. If the CPU VPs are always at a high percentage, you might need to add another one. Virtual processor activity is also reported as user time and system time as a percentage.

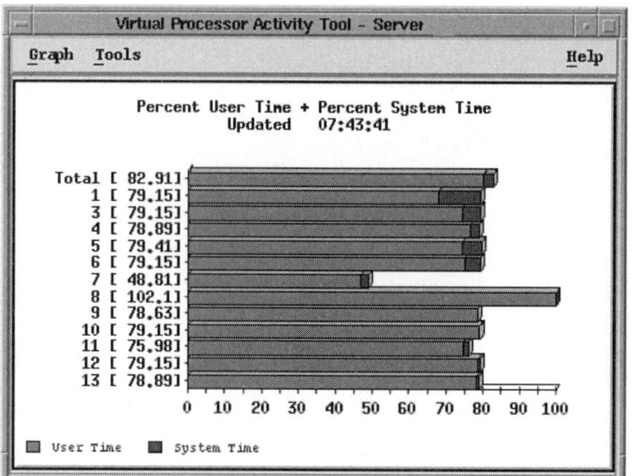

FIGURE 22.4.
The virtual processor activity tool.

Summary

You should periodically reevaluate the goals and objectives that you are trying to accomplish from monitoring, in order to be sure that the correct information is being monitored. Because of the variety of monitoring tools available, nearly every aspect of the database server can be monitored.

CHAPTER 23

Tuning Your Informix Environment

by Glenn Miller

IN THIS CHAPTER

Databases can always be made faster—at a cost. The goal in tuning an Informix environment effectively is to know what improvements will have the biggest effects and what trade-offs are required to implement them. This effort demands that you be comfortable with an unfinished task because you will never be done. This chapter will help you decide where to start and when to stop.

The first requirement is to know your system. You can find information about ways to take your system's pulse in Chapter 21, "Monitoring Your Informix Environment," and Chapter 22, "Advanced Monitoring Tools." Monitoring must be done not only when troubles arise, but also when no performance issues are pressing. You need to recognize your system's baseline activity and fundamental limitations.

In an ideal world, the topic of tuning might arise when a system is being designed: How best should the disks be arranged, what data model is most efficient, what coding standards enhance performance? More commonly, however, tuning becomes necessary when an already operational system is unacceptably slow. This more frequent scenario is not a bad thing. Rather, with a live system you have much more data regarding system load, background processes, and disk activity. The problems are tangible, not theoretical. This concreteness helps you focus your effort where it is needed the most.

Tuning Your Efforts

Be sure you are examining the real problem. Not all slow processes indicate that Informix should be tuned. The elapsed time of an activity is a combination of network communication time, CPU time handling the user process, CPU time handling system activities such as paging, and I/O time. Use tools such as `vmstat` to find out which component is the limiting factor. Use `ps -ef` to see which other activities are running simultaneously. Discover whether other elements have changed recently. Was there an operating system upgrade? Did the network configuration change? Look around.

Narrow your efforts by examining what is out of the ordinary. At any given time, something is always slowest. Find that "hot spot," and address it individually. When disk I/O is the limiting factor, look for ways to reduce or balance I/O. If the CPU is *pegged*—fully utilized—but is never waiting for I/O, then tuning disk access is pointless. If the database engine is overburdened, use `onstat -g ses` to inspect the active SQL operations. Address slow SQLs one at a time. The principle is to maintain as close to a controlled environment as you can so that you can see the effect of individual changes. Tune one thing. Examine the results. Verify that you have not slowed anything else unduly. Verify that you have not broken anything. Repeat this process until the diminishing returns you achieve are no longer worth your effort.

Taking the First Steps

The relevancy of most tips depends on your specific system configuration. These first two, however, do not.

TIP

Run `UPDATE STATISTICS`. The optimizer needs the information about your database's contents that only this statement can supply. Refer to the section "Tuning Your Informix Operations" for complete details about this crucial command.

TIP

Read the release notes. Upon installation, Informix stores the release notes in the `$INFORMIXDIR/release` directory. You will find valuable information there on new features, known problems, workarounds, new optimization schemes, optimal Informix parameters, compatibility issues, operating system requirements, and much more. Because its products are constantly evolving, Informix uses the release notes as the most direct, and often the only, means of communicating essential system-specific and version-specific information.

Recognizing Your Application

The primary distinction here is between OLTP and DSS. OnLine Transaction Processing (OLTP) systems are characterized by multiple users with simultaneous access. Generally, they select few rows, and they perform inserts and updates. OLTP applications usually use indexed reads and have sub-second response times. Fast query speed is paramount. As opposed to OLTP environments, Decision Support Systems (DSS) are characterized by sequential scans of the data, with concomitant slow response times. Data warehouses are prime examples of DSS applications. Maximizing throughput is especially critical for these very large databases. They usually find themselves disk-bound, so it is crucial that such environments employ the most effective means of scanning data rapidly.

If your environment is OLTP, and an SQL process is slow, fix it with an index.

TIP

Add an index. In most OLTP environments, for most databases, for most applications, adding a well-considered index will provide the greatest performance improvement at the least cost. Hundredfold decreases in query execution time are not uncommon. Really. Look to indexes first. Refer to the section "Tuning Your Informix Database" later in this chapter for a thorough (perhaps excruciating) explanation of indexing mechanics and guidelines.

In a DSS environment, the primary concern is reading huge amounts of data, usually for aggregation, or to summarize for trends. Disk I/O and specifically disk reads are most important. In such environments, fragmenting tables and indexes intelligently will generally produce the most significant improvements. *Fragmenting* is partitioning data or indexes horizontally across separate disks for parallel access. For more information on distributing data in this way, refer to Chapter 20, "Data and Index Fragmentation."

TIP

Fragment your critical tables and indexes. Fragmentation allows parallel scans and, for query execution, elimination of those fragments that cannot satisfy the query. These two advantages can dramatically improve your overall performance. If invoking fragmentation means that you need to upgrade to Informix-DSA, you should consider doing so.

Tuning Your Informix Instance

An *instance* is a single installation of an Informix database engine, such as OnLine or Standard Engine. For the most part, the topics in this section refer only to OnLine. Administration of SE is intentionally simple and mostly not tunable.

Optimizing Shared Memory

A crucial feature of OnLine is its management of shared memory segments, those reserved sections of RAM isolated for OnLine's private use. By adjusting the values in `onconfig`, you can tune the way in which OnLine allocates resources within its shared memory pool for greatest efficiency. Refer to Chapter 13, "Advanced Configurations," for more information about these important settings.

Installing more than one instance of OnLine on a system is possible. Having multiple database servers coexisting on the same computer is called *multiple residency*. On occasion, creating such a residency is done to segregate production environments from development environments or to test different server versions, but, for performance, it is a bad idea.

CAUTION

Avoid multiple residency. Informix is unable to manage the separate segments of shared memory efficiently.

In addition, maintaining separate environments is tricky and prone to error.

Optimizing Disk Usage

For most databases, disk I/O presents the chief bottleneck. Finding ways to avoid, balance, defer, minimize, or predict I/O should all be components of your disk tuning toolkit. It is also true that disks are the most likely component of a database environment to fail. If your disks are inaccessible because of a disk failure, and you do not have a proper archiving scheme, tuning cannot fix it. Before you implement any of these changes, ensure that your archiving procedure is sturdy and that your root dbspace is mirrored. For more information about developing a complete archiving strategy, refer to Chapter 18, "Managing Data Backups."

Increasing Cached Reads

Informix can process only data that is in memory, and it stores only whole pages there. First, these pages must be read from the disk, a process that is generally the slowest part of most applications. At any given time, the disk or its controller might be busy handling other requests. When the disk does become available, the access arm might have to spend up to hundreds of milliseconds seeking the proper sector. The *latency*, or rotational time until the page is under the access arm, could be a few milliseconds more. Disks are slow.

Conversely, reads from shared memory buffers take only microseconds. In these buffers, Informix caches pages it has read from disk, where they remain until more urgent pages replace them. For OLTP systems, you should allocate as many shared memory buffers as you can afford. When your system is operational, use `onstat -p` to examine the percentage of cached reads and writes. It is common for a tuned OLTP system to read from the buffer cache well over 99 percent of the time. Although no absolute tuning rule applies here, you should continue allocating buffers until the percentage of cached reads stops increasing.

Some DSS applications can invoke *light scans*, described later in this chapter. These types of reads place pages of data in the virtual segment of shared memory and bypass the buffer cache. In such cases, your cached read percentage could be extremely low, even zero. See the "Light Scans" section for ways to encourage this efficient behavior.

Balancing I/O

With a multidisk system, a primary way to ease an I/O bottleneck is to ensure that the distribution of work among the disks is well balanced. To do so, you need to recognize which disks are busiest and then attempt to reorganize their contents to alleviate the burden. On a production system, you can use any number of disk monitoring utilities, especially `iostat` and `onstat -g iof`, to recognize where activity is highest. For a development environment or for a system being designed, you have to rely instead on broad guidelines. The following general priorities indicate a reasonable starting point in identifying which areas ought to receive the highest disk priority—that is, which dbspaces you will place on the "prime real estate," the centers of each disk, and which items are good candidates for fragmentation. For an OLTP system, in descending order of importance, try the following:

1. Logs
2. High Use Tables
3. Low Use Tables
4. DBSPACETEMP

For DSS applications, a reasonable order is as follows:

1. High Use Tables
2. DBSPACETEMP
3. Low Use Tables
4. Logs

Additionally, prudent disk management should also include the use of raw, rather than cooked, disks. Among the numerous reasons for using these disks, performance is foremost. Not only do raw disks bypass UNIX buffering, but if the operating system allows, raw disk access might use kernel-asynchronous I/O (KAIO). KAIO threads make system calls directly to the operating system and are faster than the standard asynchronous I/O virtual processor threads. You cannot implement KAIO specifically; it is enabled if your platform supports it. Read the release notes to determine whether KAIO is available for your system.

Many hardware platforms also offer some version of striping, commonly via a logical volume manager. Employing this hardware feature as a means of distributing disk I/O for high-use areas is generally advantageous. However, if you're using Informix-specific fragmentation, you should avoid striping those dbspaces that contain table and index fragments.

CAUTION

Hardware striping and database-level fragmentation are generally not complementary.

Finally, set DBSPACETEMP to a series of temporary dbspaces that reside on separate disks. When OnLine must perform operations on temporary tables, such as the large ORDER BY and GROUP BY operations typically called for in DSS applications, it uses the dbspaces listed in DBSPACETEMP in a round-robin fashion.

Consolidating Scattered Tables

Disk access for a table is generally reduced when all the data for a table is contiguous. Sequential table scans will not incur additional seek time, as the disk head continues to be positioned correctly for the next access. One goal of physical database design is preventing pieces of a table from becoming scattered across a disk. To prevent this scattering, you can designate the size of the first and subsequent extents for each table when it is created. Unfortunately, if the extents are set too large, disk space can be wasted. For a review of table space allocation, refer to Chapter 20. In practice, unanticipated growth often interleaves multiple tables and indexes across a dbspace. When this scattering becomes excessive—more than eight non-contiguous extents for the same table in one dbspace—"repacking" the data is often worthwhile. With the Informix utility `oncheck -pe`, you can examine the physical layout of each dbspace and recognize those tables that occupy too many extents.

You can employ several straightforward methods to reconsolidate the data. Informix allows the `ALTER TABLE NEXT EXTENT` *`extentsize`*, but this command alone does not physically move data; it only changes the size of the next extent allocated when the table grows. If a table is small, with few constraints, rebuilding the table entirely is often easiest:

1. Generate a complete schema.
2. Unload the data.
3. Rebuild the table with larger extents.
4. Reload the data.
5. Rebuild any indexes.
6. Rebuild any constraints.
7. Rebuild any triggers.
8. Rebuild any views dependent on the data.
9. Rebuild any local synonyms.

Note that whenever a table is dropped, all indexes, constraints, triggers, views, and local synonyms dependent on it are also dropped. You can see that this process can become complicated and often impractical if many database interdependencies exist. The simplest alternative when many tables are scattered is to perform an `onunload/onload` of the entire database. This operation reorganizes data pages into new extents of the size currently specified for each table. Just before unloading the data, you can set the next extent size larger for those tables that have become excessively scattered. Upon the reload, the new value will be used for all extents beyond the first that are allocated.

An alternative for an individual table is to create a *clustered index*, described more fully later in this chapter. When a clustered index is built, the data rows are physically rewritten in newly allocated extents in index order. If you have just set the next extent size to accommodate the entire table, the rebuilt table will now be in, at most, two extents. When you use a clustered index for this purpose, any other benefits are merely a bonus.

Light Scans

Light scans are efficient methods of reading data that OnLine-DSA uses when it is able. These types of reads bypass the buffer pool in the resident portion of shared memory and use the virtual segment instead. Data read by light scans to the virtual buffer cache is private; therefore, no overhead is incurred for concurrency issues such as locking. When the goal is to read massive amounts of data from disk quickly, these scans are ideal. Unfortunately, DSA does not always choose to always employ them. In general, the following conditions must be true for light scans to be invoked:

- PDQ is on.
- Data is fragmented.
- Data pages, not index pages, are being scanned.
- The optimizer determines that the amount of data to be scanned would swamp the resident buffer cache.
- The Cursor Stability isolation level is not being used.
- The selectivity of the filters is low, and the optimizer determines that at least 15 to 20 percent of the data pages will need to be scanned.
- Update statistics has been run, to provide an accurate value for `systables.npused`.

TIP

Design your DSS application to exploit light scans.

You can examine whether light scans are active with `onstat -g lsc`. You can employ a few tricks to encourage light scans if you think they would be beneficial for your application:

- Reduce the size of the buffer cache by reducing `BUFFERS` in `onconfig`.
- Increase the size of the virtual portion of shared memory by increasing `SHMVIRTSIZE` in `onconfig`.
- Drop secondary indexes on the table being scanned. They include foreign key constraints and all other non-primary key indexes.
- Manually increase the `systables.npused` value.

Enabling light scans is worth the effort. Performance increases can be in the 100 to 300 percent range.

LRU Queues

As a means of efficiently managing its resident shared memory buffers, OnLine organizes them into LRU (Least Recently Used) queues. As buffer pages become modified, they get out of synch with the disk images, or *dirty*. At some point, OnLine determines that dirty pages that have not been recently accessed should be written to disk. This disk write is performed by a *page cleaner* thread whenever an individual LRU queue reaches its maximum number of dirty pages, as dictated by LRU_MAX_DIRTY. After a page cleaner thread begins writing dirty pages to disk, it continues cleaning until it reaches the LRU_MIN_DIRTY threshold.

These writes can occur as other processes are active, and they have a minimal but persistent background cost. You can monitor these writes with onstat -f. Here is a sample output:

```
Fg Writes      LRU Writes   Chunk Writes
0              144537       62561
```

The LRU Writes column indicates writes by the page cleaners on behalf of dirty LRU queues. Earlier versions of OnLine included Idle Writes, which are now consolidated with LRU Writes. Foreground writes (Fg Writes) are those caused by the server when no clean pages can be found. They preempt other operations, suspend the database temporarily, and are generally a signal that the various page cleaner parameters need to be tuned to clean pages more frequently. Chunk writes are those performed by checkpoints, and they also suspend user activity. They are described in the "Checkpoints" section later in this chapter. You should consider tuning the LRU queue parameters or number of page cleaners if the temporary suspensions of activity from checkpoints become troublesome.

Generally, the LRU_MAX_DIRTY and LRU_MIN_DIRTY are the most significant tuning parameters. To increase the ratio of LRU writes, decrease these values and monitor the performance with onstat -f. Values as low as 3 and 5 might be reasonable for your system.

You can use onstat -R to monitor the percentage of dirty pages in your LRU queues. If the ratio of dirty pages consistently exceeds LRU_MAX_DIRTY, you have too few LRU queues or too few page cleaners. First, try increasing the LRUS parameter in onconfig to create more LRU queues. If that is insufficient, increment CLEANERS to add more page cleaners. For most applications, set CLEANERS to the number of disks, but not less than one per LRU so that one is always available when an LRU queue reaches its threshold. If your system has more than 20 disks, try setting CLEANERS to 1 per 2 disks, but not less than 20.

Checkpoints

One of the background processes that can affect performance is the writing of checkpoints. Checkpoints are occasions during which the database server, in order to maintain internal consistency, synchronizes the pages on disk with the contents of the resident shared memory buffer pool. In the event of a database failure, physical recovery begins as of the last checkpoint. Thus, frequent checkpoints are an aid to speedy recovery. However, user activity ceases during a checkpoint, and if the checkpoint takes an appreciable amount of time, user frustration can result. Furthermore, writing checkpoints too frequently incurs unnecessary overhead. The goal is to balance the concerns of recovery, user perceptions, and total throughput.

Checkpoints are initiated when any of the following occurs:

- The checkpoint interval is reached, and database modifications have occurred since the last checkpoint.

- The physical log becomes 75 percent full.
- The administrator forces a checkpoint.
- OnLine detects that the next logical log contains the last checkpoint.
- Certain dbspace administration activities occur.

Each time a checkpoint occurs, a record is written in the message log. With `onstat -m`, you can monitor this activity. You can adjust the checkpoint interval directly by setting the `onconfig` parameter `CKPTINTVL`. If quick recovery is not crucial, try increasing the 5-minute default to 10, 15, or 30 minutes. Additionally, consider driving initiation of checkpoints by decreasing the physical log size.

TIP

Set the checkpoint frequency by adjusting the size of the physical log. Using the trigger of having a checkpoint forced when the physical log is 75-percent full ensures that checkpoints are used only when needed.

There is one additional performance consideration for large batch processes. Note that page cleaner threads write pages from memory to disk both when LRU queues are dirty and when a checkpoint is performed. However, the write via a checkpoint is more efficient. It uses *chunk writes*, which are performed as sorted writes, the most efficient writes available to OnLine. Also, because other user activity is suspended, the page cleaner threads are not forced to switch contexts during checkpoint writes. Finally, checkpoint writes use OnLine's big buffers, 32-page buffers reserved for large contiguous reads and writes. These advantages make chunk writes preferable to LRU writes. Large batch processes can be made more efficient by increasing the ratio of chunk writes to LRU writes. To do so, increase the `LRU_MAX_DIRTY` and `LRU_MIN_DIRTY` values, perhaps as high as 95 percent and 98 percent. Then decrease the `CKPTINTVL` or physical log size until the bulk of the writes are chunk writes.

Read Aheads

When OnLine performs sequential table or index scans, it presupposes that adjacent pages on disk will be the next ones requested by the application. To minimize the time an application has to wait for a disk read, the server performs a *read ahead* while the current pages are being processed. It caches those pages in the shared memory buffer pool. When the number of those pages remaining to be read reaches the read ahead threshold (`RA_THRESHOLD`), OnLine fetches another set of pages equal to the `RA_PAGES` parameter. In this way, it can stay slightly ahead of the user process.

Although the default parameters are usually adequate, you can adjust both `RA_PAGES` and `RA_THRESHOLD`. If you expect a large number of sequential scans of data or index pages, consider increasing RA_PAGES. You should keep RA_PAGES a multiple of 8, the size of the light scan buffers in virtual memory. For most OLTP systems, 32 pages is generous. Very large DSS applications could make effective use of RA_PAGES as high as 128 or 256 pages. The danger in setting this value too high is that unnecessary page cleaning could have to occur to make room for pages that might never be used.

Optimizing Network Traffic

In a client/server environment, application programs communicate with the database server across a network. The traffic from this operation can be a bottleneck. When the server sends data to an application, it does not send all the requested data at once. Rather, it sends only the amount that fits into the *fetch buffer*, whose size is defined by the application program. The fetch buffer resides in the application process; in a client/server environment, this means the client side of the application.

When only one row is being returned, the default fetch buffer size is the size of a row. When more than one row is returned, the buffer size depends on the size of three rows:

- If they fit into a 1,024-byte buffer, the fetch buffer size is 1,024 bytes.
- If not, but instead they fit into a 2,048-byte buffer, the fetch buffer size is 2,048 bytes.
- Otherwise, the fetch buffer size is the size of a row.

If your application has very large rows or passes voluminous data from the server to the application, you might benefit from increasing the fetch buffer size. With a larger size, the application would not need to wait so often while the server fetches and supplies the next buffer-full of data. The FET_BUF_SIZE environmental variable dictates the fetch buffer size, in bytes, for an ESQL/C application. Its minimum is the default; its maximum is generally the size of a SMALLINT: 32,767 bytes. For example, with the following korn shell command, you could set the fetch buffer size to 20,000 bytes for the duration of your current shell:

```
export FET_BUF_SIZE=20000
```

You can also override the FET_BUF_SIZE from within an ESQL/C application. The global variable FetBufSize, defined in sqlhdr.h, can be reset at compile time. For example, the following C code excerpt sets FetBufSize to 20000:

```
EXEC SQL include sqlhdr;
...
FetBufSize = 20000;
```

Tuning Your Informix Database

Database tuning generally occurs in two distinct phases. The first, at initial design, includes the fundamental and broad issue of table design, incorporating normalization and the choices of data types. Extent sizing and referential constraints are often included here. A primary reason that these choices are made at this stage is that changing them later is difficult. For example, choosing to denormalize a table by storing a derived value is best done early in the application development cycle. Later justification for changing a schema must be very convincing. The second phase of tuning involves those structures that are more dynamic: indexes, views, fragmentation schemes, and isolation levels. A key feature of these structures is their capability to be generated on-the-fly.

Indexing Mechanics

Much of this chapter describes when to use indexes. As an efficient mechanism for pointing to data, indexes are invaluable. However, they have costs, not only in disk space, but also in maintenance overhead. For you to exercise effective judgment in their creation, you need a thorough understanding of Informix's indexing mechanics and the overhead involved in index maintenance.

The remainder of this section describes how Informix builds and maintains indexes through the use of B+ tree data structures. *B+ trees* are hierarchical search mechanisms that have the trait of always being balanced—that is, of having the same number of levels between the root node and any leaf node.

B+ Tree Index Pages

Indexes comprise specially structured pages of three types: root nodes, branch nodes, and leaf nodes. Each node, including the singular root node, holds sets of associated sorted keys and pointers. The keys are the concatenated data values of the indexed columns. The pointers are addresses of data pages or, for root and branch nodes, addresses of index pages. Figure 23.1 shows a fully developed index B+ tree, with three levels. In this diagram, finding the address of a data element from its key value requires reading three index pages. Given a key value, the root node determines which branch to examine. The branch node points to a specific leaf node. The leaf node reveals the address of the data page.

Leaf nodes also include an additional element, a delete flag for each key value. Furthermore, non-root nodes have lateral pointers to adjacent index nodes on that level. These pointers are used for horizontal index traversal, described later in this section.

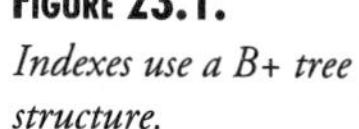

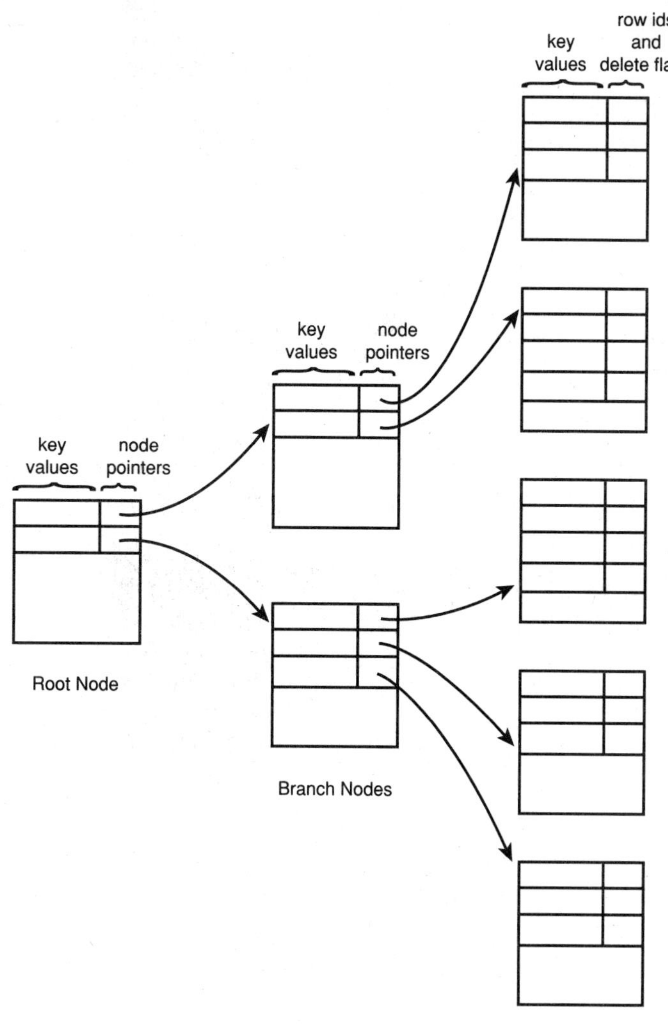

FIGURE 23.1.
Indexes use a B+ tree structure.

Index Node Splits

Indexes are not fully formed when they are created. Instead, they start out as a single page: a root node that functions also as a leaf node. They evolve over time. When enough index entries are added to fill a node, it splits. To split, it creates another node at its level and moves half its index entries to that page. It then elevates the middle key value, the one dividing the two nodes, to the parent node. There, new index entries that point to these two nodes are created. If no parent node exists, one is created. When the root node splits, its new parent page becomes the root node. Figure 23.2 shows this process of splitting an index node to create a new level in the B+ tree index.

FIGURE 23.2.
Index node split creates a new root node.

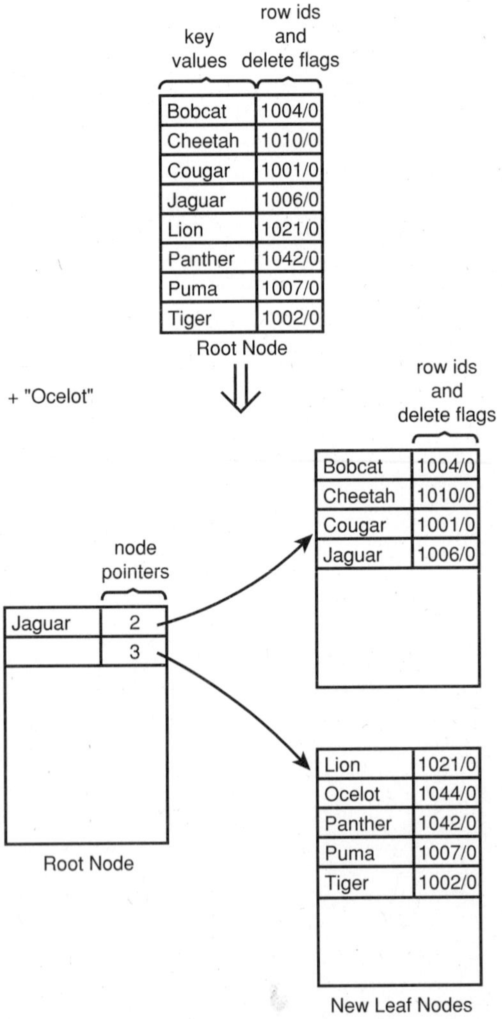

> **NOTE**
>
> If a table has multiple indexes, inserting a data row forces the index creation step for each index. The performance and space overhead can be significant.

Delete Flagging

For OnLine versions after 6.0, when a data row is deleted, its index rows are not immediately removed. Instead, the index row is marked with a delete flag, indicating that this row is available for deletion. Marking deleted index entries with a delete flag avoids some locking and concurrency problems that could surface with the adjacent key locking mechanism used in older Informix versions. The rows are actually deleted by a page cleaner thread. The page cleaner examines the pages in its list—whose entries were placed there by the delete process—every minute, or whenever it has more than 100 entries.

When the page cleaner thread deletes a row, it checks to see whether two or fewer index entries remain on the page. If so, OnLine tries to merge the entries on the page with an adjacent node. If it can, it then frees the current page for other purposes. If no space is available on an adjacent node, OnLine instead shuffles data from the adjacent node into the current page to try to balance the index entries. The merging and shuffling caused by massive deletes not only invoke considerable processing overhead, but also can leave many semi-empty index pages.

Update Costs

When an indexed value is updated, Informix maintains the index by first deleting the old index entry and then inserting a new entry, thus invoking the overhead of both operations. You will find that bulk updates on indexed columns can consume considerable resources.

Optimal Structure

Index pages, like any pages, are read most efficiently when cached in the shared memory buffers. Because only whole pages are read from disk, only whole pages can be cached. Non-full index nodes therefore take more space to store, thus reducing the number of keys that can be stored at once. It is usual for the root node of an index to remain cached, and common for the first branch nodes as well. Subsequent levels are usually read from disk. Therefore, compact, balanced indexes are more efficient.

Checking the status of indexes occasionally, especially after numerous database operations, is therefore prudent. `Oncheck` is designed for this purpose. Here is a sample `oncheck` command, followed by the relevant part of its output:

```
oncheck -pT retail:customers
```

```
                    Average    Average
Level     Total No. Keys Free Bytes
----- -------- -------- ----------
    1        1        2       4043
    2        2      246       1542
    3      492      535       1359
----- -------- -------- ----------
Total      495      533       1365
```

Note that this index B+ tree has three levels and that the leaf nodes (level 3) average about one-third empty. An index with a high percentage of unused space, for which you do not anticipate many inserts soon, is a good candidate for rebuilding. When you rebuild an index, consider setting the `FILLFACTOR` variable, described in the next section.

The preceding index was rebuilt with a `FILLFACTOR` of `100`. Notice how much less free space remains in each page and, therefore, how many more key values each leaf node contains. Additionally, an entire level was removed from the B+ tree.

```
                    Average    Average
Level     Total No. Keys Free Bytes
----- -------- -------- ----------
    1        1      366        636
    2      366      719        428
----- -------- -------- ----------
Total      367      718        429
```

FILLFACTOR

When OnLine builds an index, it leaves 10 percent of each index page free to allow for eventual insertions. The percent filled is dictated by the `onconfig` parameter `FILLFACTOR`, which defaults to `90`. For most indexes, this value is adequate. However, the more compact an index is, the more efficient it is. When you're creating an index on a static read-only table, you should consider setting `FILLFACTOR` to `100`. You can override the default with an explicit declaration, as in the following example:

```
CREATE INDEX ix_hist ON order_history (cust_no) FILLFACTOR 100;
```

Likewise, when you know that an index will undergo extensive modifications soon, you can set the `FILLFACTOR` lower, perhaps to `50`.

`FILLFACTOR` applies only to the initial index creation and is not maintained over time. In addition, it takes effect only when at least one of the following conditions is true:

- The table has over 5,000 rows and over 100 data pages.
- The table is fragmented.
- The index is fragmented, but the table is not.

Indexing Guidelines

Crafting proper indexes is part experience and part formula. In general, you should index columns that are frequently used for the following:

- Joins
- Filters that can usually discriminate less than 10 percent of the data values
- `UNIQUE` constraints, including `PRIMARY KEY` constraints
- `FOREIGN KEY` constraints
- `GROUP BY` operations
- `ORDER BY` clauses

In addition, try to avoid indexes on the following:

- Columns with few values
- Columns that already head a composite index
- `VARCHARS`, for which the entire maximum length of the column is stored for each index key value

Beyond these general guidelines, index what needs to be indexed. The optimizer can help you determine what should be indexed. Check the query plans, and let the optimizer guide you. In the section called "Tuning Your Informix Application" later in this chapter, you learn how to use the `SET EXPLAIN ON` directive to examine Informix's use of specific indexes.

Unique Indexes

Create a unique index on the primary key, at least. One is generated automatically for unique constraints, but the names of system-generated constraints start with a space. Naming your `PRIMARY KEY` indexes yourself is best. Explicit names are clearer and allow for easier modification later. For example, altering an index to cluster, or changing its fragmentation scheme, is simpler for a named index.

Cluster Indexes

Clustering physically reorders the data rows to match the index order. It is especially useful when groups of rows related by the index value are usually read together. For example, all rows of an invoice line item table that share an invoice number might usually be read together. If such rows are clustered, they will often be stored on the same or adjacent pages so that a single read will fetch every line item. You create a clustered index with a statement like this:

```
CREATE CLUSTER INDEX ix_line_item on invoice_lines (invoice_no);
```

When it creates the index, Informix first allocates new extents for the table and then copies the data to the new extents. In the process, room must be available for two complete copies of the table; otherwise, the operation will fail.

CAUTION

Before you create a cluster index, verify that two copies of the table can coexist in the available space.

Because clustering allocates new extents, it can be used to consolidate the remnants of a scattered table.

The clustering on a table is not maintained over time. If frequent inserts or deletes occur, the benefits of clustering will diminish. However, you can recluster a table as needed, like this:

```
ALTER INDEX ix_line_item TO CLUSTER;
```

This statement instructs the database engine to reorder the rows, regardless of whether the index named was previously a cluster index.

Composite Indexes

Composite indexes are those formed from more than one column, such as

```
CREATE INDEX ix_cust_name ON customer (last_name, first_name, middle_name);
```

You can use this index to accomplish searching or ordering on all three values, on `last_name` and `first_name`, or on `last_name` alone. Because the index keys are created from concatenated key values, any subset of the columns, left to right, can be used to satisfy queries. Therefore, any independent indexes on these columns would be redundant and a waste of space.

Because the column order in a composite index is so significant, you should put the most frequently used column first. Doing so will help ensure that the index has greater utility. That is, its component parts can also be used often to fulfill index criteria.

One other use for composite indexes is to store the data for key-only reads, described in the next section. By doing so, you can, in effect, create a subset of the table's data that can be used very effectively in certain queries. Of course, there is a cost. You must balance the overhead of index maintenance and extra disk usage with the benefits of quicker performance when the key-only reads occur.

TIP

Consider creating an artificial composite index whose only purpose is to allow a key-only read.

Key-Only Reads

Key-only reads are those that can satisfy the query entirely with values found in the index pages alone. Naturally, the avoidance of invoking the I/O required to access the data pages affords a considerable performance improvement. You can generally predict a key-only read by examining the indexes available to the optimizer. For example, consider the following query:

```
  SELECT last_name, count(*)
    FROM customer
GROUP BY last_name
ORDER BY last_name;
```

Its needs can be satisfied entirely with the values contained in an index on `customer.last_name`. The output of `SET EXPLAIN` confirms that only the index is needed to complete the query:

```
Estimated Cost: 80
Estimated # of Rows Returned: 10
1) informix.customers: INDEX PATH
    (1) Index Keys: last_name  (Key-Only)
```

The single index suffices to supply the data and to enable the `GROUP BY`, the `ORDER BY`, and the `COUNT` operations.

Bi-Directional Indexes

Bi-directional indexes are introduced in OnLine-DSA version 7.2. With them, OnLine can traverse an index in either direction. Whether a single column index is created in ascending or descending order is irrelevant. Indexes are still created ascending by default. Composite indexes can also be accessed from either direction but are reversed at the column level when they contain column-specific direction instructions. For example, consider the following index:

```
create index ix_cust3 on customers (last_name asc, first_name asc, cust_no desc);
```

Access from the opposite direction acts as if the rows were sorted in the reverse order on every column. For the preceding index, reading it in the opposite direction is the same as reading the following index:

```
create index ix_cust4 on customers (last_name desc, first_name desc, cust_no asc);
```

Horizontal Index Traversal

Informix index pages can be traversed in two ways. The one used for index-based standard lookups starts at the root node and follows the traditional root to branch to leaf pattern. But there is another way. In the page header of every index leaf node and branch node page are horizontal links to sibling index pages. They are pointers to the adjacent left and right pages.

When Informix does a sequential index scan, such as a non-discriminatory key-only select from a composite index, the index nodes are traversed in sequential index order, left to right, at the leaf node level only. Data pages are never read, nor are the root or branch nodes accessed. This efficient means of navigating indexes is not tunable but is just one of the ways Informix optimizes its index structure.

Logging

In all Informix versions prior to XPS, database logging is not required. However, without it, explicit transactions cannot be performed; that is, rollbacks are not available. For most operations, business constraints make this unacceptable. There are exceptions, such as turning off logging for bulk database loads, but, in general, logging overhead must be incurred. Often, the only choice is how to minimize the overhead.

Databases with logging can be created either buffered or unbuffered. Buffered logging routes transactions through a buffer pool and writes the buffer to disk only when the logical log buffer fills. Although unbufferred logging transactions also pass through the logical log buffer, with them the entire buffer is written after any transaction is completed. Because of the frequent writes, unbuffered logging provides greater data integrity in case of a system failure.

CAUTION

With buffered logging, transactions in memory can be lost if the system crashes.

Nonetheless, the I/O savings afforded by buffered logging are almost always worth the small risk of data loss. This is especially true in active OLTP systems in which logical log writes are often the greatest source of disk activity.

NOTE

All databases share logical logs and the logical log buffer. If one database is unbuffered, it will cause flushing of the entire log buffer whenever a transaction within it is committed. This action can negate the advantage of buffered logging for all other databases in the instance.

Using Non-Logging Tables

Non-logging databases are no longer supported in INFORMIX-OnLine XPS. Rather, within a database that has logging, new table types exist for specific operations that need not incur the overhead of logging. For example, when you load raw data from an external source into a table for initial scrubbing, logging is often superfluous, because you can usually perform the load again should the initial attempt fail. Table 23.1 summarizes the table types available with OnLine XPS.

Table 23.1. OnLine XPS table types.

Table Type	*Duration*	*Logged*	*Writes Allowed*	*Indexes Allowed*	*Restorable from Archive*
`SCRATCH`	temporary	no	yes	no	no
`TEMP`	temporary	yes	yes	yes	no
`RAW`	permanent	no	yes	no	no
`STATIC`	permanent	no	no	yes	no
`OPERATIONAL`	permanent	yes	yes	yes	no
`STANDARD`	permanent	yes	yes	yes	yes

A common tactic is to use a `RAW` table to load data from an external source and then alter it to `STATIC` after the operation is finished. As an added bonus, whereas all temporary tables can be read with light scans because they are private, `STATIC` tables can always be read with light scans because they are *read-only.*

Locking

Locking in Informix is available at the following decreasing levels of granularity, or scope:

- Database
- Table
- Page
- Row

For a complete discussion of locking, refer to Chapter 15, "Managing Data with Locking." Generally, the demands of increased concurrency in a multi-user application force locking to be assigned at the smallest granularity. Unfortunately, this constraint also invokes the greatest overhead. Although the number of locks is tunable, they are finite resources.

TIP

Lock at the highest granularity possible. Generating, holding, and checking for a lock all take time. You should make every effort to reduce the number of locks by increasing their granularity.

Certainly for bulk off-hour operations, you should consider the `LOCK DATABASE` *`databasename`* `EXCLUSIVE` command. Finally, be cautious about creating large tables with row-level locking; with it, mass inserts or deletes to a table can quickly exhaust the available locks. Even with tables that have page level locking, using `LOCK TABLE` *`tablename`* `IN EXCLUSIVE MODE` whenever possible is best.

Isolation Levels

The isolation level dictates the degree to which any reads you perform affect and are affected by other concurrent users. The different levels place increasingly stringent requirements on what changes other processes can make to rows you are examining and to what degree you can read data currently being modified by other processes. Isolation levels are meaningful only for reads, not for data manipulation statements.

In decreasing order of permissiveness, the isolation levels available in OnLine are as follow:

- Dirty Read
- Committed Read
- Cursor Stability
- Repeatable Read

Dirty Read is the most efficient and simplest isolation level. Effectively, it does not honor any locks placed by other processes, nor does it place any. Regardless of whether data on disk is committed or uncommitted, a Dirty Read scan will copy the data. The danger is that a program using Dirty Read isolation might read a row that is later uncommitted. Therefore, be sure you account for this possibility, or read only from static tables when this isolation level is set.

TIP

For greatest efficiency, use the Dirty Read isolation level whenever possible.

The Committed Read isolation level ensures that only rows committed in the database are read. As it reads each row, OnLine checks for the presence of an update lock. If one exists, it ignores the row. Because OnLine places no locks, the Committed Read isolation level is almost as efficient as the Dirty Read isolation level.

Cursor Stability causes the database to place a lock on the current row as it reads the row. This lock ensures that the row will not change while the current process is using it. When the server reads and locks the next row, it releases the previous lock. The placement of locks suggests that processes with this isolation level will incur additional overhead as they read data.

With Repeatable Read, processes lock every row that has been read in the current transaction. This mode guarantees that reading the same rows later would find the same data. As a result, Repeatable Read processes can generate many locks and hold them for a long time.

CAUTION

Be careful when you use the Repeatable Read isolation level. The number of locks generated could exceed the maximum available.

Data Types

Two key performance principles apply when you're selecting a data type: minimize space and reduce conversions. Smaller data types save disk space, create tidier indexes, fit better into shared memory, and allow faster joins. For example, never use an `INTEGER` when a `SMALLINT` will do. Unless you need the added range (an `INTEGER` can store from –2,147,483,647 to 2,147,483,647, whereas the limits for a `SMALLINT` are –32,767 and 32,767) use the 2-byte `SMALLINT` rather than the 4-byte `INTEGER`. In a similar fashion, minimize the precision of `DECIMAL`, `MONEY`, and `DATETIME` data types. Their storage requirements are directly related to their precision.

In addition, use data types most appropriate for the operations being performed on them. For example, do not store numeric values in a `CHAR` field if they are to be used for calculations. Such type mismatches cause the database to perform a conversion for every operation.

Small Join Keys

When Informix joins two tables, it performs the operation in memory as much as it is able. The smaller the keys, the less likely a join operation is to overflow to disk. Operations in memory are fast; disk operations are slow. Creating a small join key might mean replacing large composite keys with alternatives, often serial keys. It is common that the natural keys in a table offer no concise join candidate. For example, consider the following table:

```
CREATE TABLE transactions (
cust_no      INTEGER,
trans_type   CHAR(6),
trans_time   DATETIME YEAR TO FRACTION,
trans_amount MONEY(12,2),
PRIMARY KEY (cust_no, trans_type, trans_time));
```

Imagine that business rules demand that it often be joined to the following:

```
CREATE TABLE trans_audits (
cust_no       INTEGER,
trans_type    CHAR(6),
trans_time    DATETIME YEAR TO FRACTION,
auditor_no    INTEGER,
audit_date    DATE,
FOREIGN KEY (cust_no, trans_type, trans_time) REFERENCES transactions);
```

If these tables are large, joins will be slow. The transaction table is an excellent candidate for an artificial key whose sole purpose is to make joins of this sort more efficient. Such a scheme would look like the following:

```
CREATE TABLE transactions (
trans_no      SERIAL PRIMARY KEY,
cust_no       INTEGER,
trans_type    CHAR(6),
trans_time    DATETIME YEAR TO FRACTION,
trans_amount MONEY(12,2));
CREATE TABLE trans_audits (
trans_no      INTEGER REFERENCES transactions,
auditor_no    INTEGER,
audit_date    DATE);
```

At the cost of making the transactions table a little larger and forcing the maintenance of an added key, the joins are more efficient, and the `trans_audit` table is considerably smaller.

Blobs

Blobs can be stored in a table's tblspace with the rest of its data or in a custom blobspace. Blobspaces comprise blobpages, which can be defined to be multiple pages.

TIP

Place large blobs in blobspaces, and define the blobpages large enough to store the average blob.

With blobpages large enough, most blobs will be stored contiguously. Blobs stored in blobspaces also bypass the logical log and buffer cache; blobs stored in tblspaces do not. Another hazard of storing blobs in tblspaces is that they could flood the cache buffers and force out other, more useful pages.

Constraints

One of the most insidious means of sapping performance is to allow bad data to infiltrate your database. Disk space is wasted. Application code becomes convoluted as it tries to accommodate data that should not be there. Special processes must be run to correct or cull the invalid data. These violations should be prevented, not repaired. Using Informix's constraints to enforce integrity upon your database is almost always worthwhile. Constraints are mostly enabled via indexes, and indexes can have high costs. But the existence of costs should not preclude implementing a good idea.

In the real world, performance is almost never considered in a vacuum. Usually, you are faced with trade-offs: Indexing to improve query speed uses extra disk space; adding more cache buffers increases the paging frequency; an efficient but tricky piece of application code requires a greater maintenance effort. The principle applies here as well: Using constraints to enforce integrity carries with it significant overhead. Do it anyway.

Table 23.2 shows how key elements critical to a sound data model can be enforced with constructs available in Informix.

Table 23.2. Using constraints to enforce integrity.

Relational Object	*Enforcement Mechanism*

Primary Key	`PRIMARY KEY CONSTRAINT`
	`UNIQUE CONSTRAINT`
	`NOT NULL CONSTRAINT`

Domain	data types
	`CHECK CONSTRAINT`
	`DEFAULT` values
	`NOT NULL CONSTRAINT`

Foreign Key	`FOREIGN KEY CONSTRAINT`, including `ON DELETE CASCADE` triggers and stored procedures

For more information on enforcing primary key and foreign key constraints, refer to Chapter 17, "Managing Data Integrity with Constraints."

Denormalization

For every rule, you'll find exceptions. On occasion, conforming to absolute relational strictures imposes too great a performance cost. At such times, well considered denormalization can perhaps provide a performance gain significant enough to justify the effort. A fully normalized model has no redundant data or derived data. The examples in this section suggest times when introducing redundancy or derived data might be of value.

Maintain Aggregates Tables

A stock-in-trade of data warehouse applications, aggregate tables often store intermediate levels of derived data. Perhaps a retail DSS application reports frequently on historical trends of sales for each product by store and by day. Yet the base data available in the normalized database is at the transaction level, where thousands of individual rows must be aggregated to reach what to the DSS application is an atomic value. Furthermore, although historical transaction data is static, queries often summarize transactions months or years old.

Such an environment calls for creating an aggregate table like the following:

```
CREATE TABLE daily_trans (
product_no  INTEGER,
store_no    INTEGER,
trans_date  DATE,
sales_total MONEY(16, 2));
```

New aggregates can be summed nightly from base `transaction` data and added to the aggregate. In addition to creating efficient queries at the granularity of one `daily_trans` row, this table can be used as the starting point for other queries. From it, calculating sales by month or daily sales by product across all stores would be simple matters.

Maintain Aggregate Columns

Storing a denormalized aggregate value within a table is often reasonable, especially if it is referenced often and requires a join or aggregate function (or both) to build. For example, an orders table might commonly store an `order_total` value, even though it could be calculated as follows:

```
SELECT SUM(order_details.line_total)
  FROM orders, order_details
 WHERE orders.order_no = order_details.order_no;
```

Application code, or perhaps a trigger and a stored procedure, must be created to keep the `order_total` value current. In the same fashion for the following example, `customers.last_order_date` might be worth maintaining rather than always recalculating:

```
SELECT MAX(orders.order_date)
  FROM customers, orders
 WHERE customers.cust_no = orders.cust_no;
```

In these cases, you must monitor your application closely. You have to weigh whether the extra complexity and overhead are justified by any performance improvements.

Split Wide Tables

Wide tables are those with many columns, especially those with several large columns. Long character strings often contribute greatly to a table's width. Few of the long rows from a wide table can fit on any given page; consequently, disk I/O for such a table can be inefficient. One tactic to consider is to split the table into components that have a one-to-one relationship with each other. Perhaps all the attributes that are rarely selected can be segregated to a table of their own. Possibly a very few columns that are used for critical selects can be isolated in their own table. Large strings could be expelled to a companion table. Any number of methods could be considered for creating complementary tables; you have to consider individually whether the performance gain justifies the added complexity.

Tuning Your Informix Operations

You can improve the overall operation of your environment by balancing system resources effectively. For example, as much as possible, only run resource-intensive processes when the system is least frequently used, generally at night. Candidates for off-hour processing include calculating aggregates and running complex reports. Also during the off-hours, perform the background operations that keep your system healthy, such as archiving and updating statistics.

Update Statistics

To optimize SQL statements effectively, Informix relies on data it stores internally. It uses the `sysindexes`, `systables`, `syscolumns`, `sysconstraints`, `sysfragments`, and `sysdistrib` tables to store data on each table. It tracks such values as the number of rows, number of data pages, and depth of indexes. It stores high and low values for each column and, on demand, can generate actual data distributions as well. It recognizes which indexes exist and how selective they are. It knows where data is stored on disk and how it is apportioned. With this data, it can optimize your SQL statements to construct the most efficient query plan and reduce execution time.

Informix can perform these jobs well only when the internal statistics are up-to-date. But they often are not—these values are not maintained in real-time. In fact, most of the critical values are updated only when you run the `UPDATE STATISTICS` statement. Therefore, you must do so on a regular basis.

Whenever you run `UPDATE STATISTICS`, you specify the objects on which it should act: specific columns, specific tables, all tables, all tables and procedures, specific procedures, or all procedures.

NOTE

If you execute `UPDATE STATISTICS` without specifying `FOR TABLE`, execution plans for stored procedures are also re-optimized.

In addition, you can specify how much information is examined to generate the statistics. In `LOW` mode, `UPDATE STATISTICS` constructs table and index information. `UPDATE STATISTICS MEDIUM` and `HIGH` also construct this data but, by scanning data pages, add data distributions.

UPDATE STATISTICS LOW

With the default UPDATE STATISTICS mode (LOW), the minimum information about the specified object is gathered. This information includes table, row, and page counts along with index and column statistics for any columns specified. This data is sufficient for many purposes and takes little time to generate. The following statements show examples of these operations:

```
UPDATE STATISTICS LOW FOR TABLE customers (cust_no);
UPDATE STATISTICS LOW FOR TABLE customers;
UPDATE STATISTICS LOW;
```

You can even use the UPDATE STATISTICS statement on a temporary table. Also, with the DROP DISTRIBUTIONS clause, you can drop previously generated data distribution statistics:

```
UPDATE STATISTICS LOW FOR TABLE customers DROP DISTRIBUTIONS;
```

Distributions are values that have been generated by a previous execution of UPDATE STATISTICS MEDIUM or UPDATE STATISTICS HIGH. If you do not specify the DROP DISTRIBUTIONS clause, any data distribution information that already exists will remain intact.

UPDATE STATISTICS MEDIUM

The MEDIUM and HIGH modes of UPDATE STATISTICS duplicate the effort of UPDATE STATISTICS LOW, but they also create data distributions. With MEDIUM, data is only sampled; with HIGH, all data rows are read. These data distributions are stored in the sysdistrib table. Informix creates distributions by ordering the data it scans and allocating the values into bins of approximately equal size. By recording the extreme values in each bin, it can recognize the selectivity of filters that might later be applied against these columns. Thus, Informix can recognize when the data values are skewed or highly duplicated, for example. You can alter the sampling rate and the number of bins by adjusting the CONFIDENCE and RESOLUTION parameters. For example, the following statement generates 25 bins (100/RESOLUTION) and samples enough data to give the same results as UPDATE STATISTICS HIGH approximately 98 percent of the time:

```
UPDATE STATISTICS MEDIUM FOR TABLE customers (cust_no) RESOLUTION 4 CONFIDENCE 98;
```

UPDATE STATISTICS HIGH

When you specify UPDATE STATISTICS HIGH, Informix reads every row of data to generate exact distributions. This process can take a long time. Normally, HIGH and MEDIUM gather index and table information, as well as distributions. If you have already gathered index information, you can avoid recalculating it by adding the DISTRIBUTIONS ONLY clause:

```
UPDATE STATISTICS LOW FOR TABLE customers;
UPDATE STATISTICS HIGH FOR TABLE customers (cust_no) DISTRIBUTIONS ONLY;
```

With the DISTRIBUTIONS ONLY clause, UPDATE STATISTICS MEDIUM and HIGH generate only table and distribution data.

Comprehensive UPDATE STATISTICS Plan

Your goal should be to balance the performance overhead of creating statistics inefficiently or too often with the need for regular recalculations of these values. The following plan strikes a good balance between execution speed and completeness:

1. Run the `UPDATE STATISTICS MEDIUM` command for the whole database. It will generate index, table, and distribution data for every table and will re-optimize all stored procedures.
2. Run the `UPDATE STATISTICS HIGH` command with `DISTRIBUTIONS ONLY` for all columns that head an index. This accuracy will give the optimizer the best data about an index's selectivity.
3. Run the `UPDATE STATISTICS LOW` command for all remaining columns that are part of composite indexes.

If your database is moderately dynamic, consider activating such an `UPDATE STATISTICS` script periodically, even nightly, via `cron`, the UNIX automated job scheduler. Finally, remember to use `UPDATE STATISTICS` specifically whenever a table undergoes major alterations.

Parallel Data Query

OnLine-DSA offers the administrator methods of apportioning the limited shared memory resources among simultaneous DSS queries. Primary among these parameters is `MAX_PDQPRIORITY`, a number that represents the total fraction of PDQ resources available to any one DSS query. For a complete description of the PDQ management tools available to the administrator, refer to Chapter 19, "Parallel Database Query."

Archiving

If you use ON-Archive, you can exercise very specific control over the dbspaces archived. By carefully allocating like entities to similar dbspaces, you can create an efficient archive schedule. One tactic is to avoid archiving index-only dbspaces. Generally, indexes can be reconstructed as needed from the base data. In addition, arrange a schedule that archives active dbspaces more frequently than less dynamic ones. By giving some thought to the nature of individual dbspaces, you can design an archive strategy that balances a quick recovery with a minimal archiving time.

Bulk Loads

When you need to load large amounts of data into a table, consider ways to reduce the overhead. Any of the following procedures could improve performance or, at the least, minimize the use of limited system resources such as locks:

- Drop indexes to save shuffling of the B+ tree index structure as it attempts to stay balanced.

- Lock the table in exclusive mode to conserve locks.
- Turn off logging for the database to avoid writing each insert to the logical logs and perhaps creating a dangerous long transaction.

Be sure to restore the database or table to its original state after the load is finished.

In-Place ALTER TABLE

Starting with OnLine version 7.2, `ALTER TABLE` statements no longer necessarily rebuild a table when executed. If a column is added to the end of the current column list, then an in-place `ALTER TABLE` operation will be performed. With this mechanism, the table is rewritten over time. Inserts of new rows are written with the updated format, but an existing row is rewritten only when it is updated. As a result, a small amount of additional overhead is required to perform this conversion. Although the in-place `ALTER TABLE` is generally efficient, you might find it useful to explicitly force the table to be rebuilt when you issue the `ALTER TABLE` statement. Including the `BEFORE` clause in the `ALTER TABLE` statement ensures this action will occur. By forcing an immediate rebuild, you can avoid the ongoing update overhead.

Tuning Your Informix Application

Application programs generally contain numerous components: procedural statements intermingled with various embedded SQL commands. Foremost in tuning an application is identifying the element that is slow. Often, users do this work for you. A query that previously was fast is suddenly slow, or a report takes too long to run. When you start trying to isolate the specific bottleneck, recognize that almost never is it anything other than a database operation.

TIP

If an Informix-based application program is slow, the culprit is an SQL statement.

When an application is generally slow, you need to peer inside it as it runs to identify the bottleneck. Two monitoring tools are especially useful to help you with this job. The first is `onstat -g sql`:

```
onstat -g sql sesid -r interval
```

With the preceding command, you can take a series of snapshots of the SQL statement currently being run for a given session. Generally, a single statement will emerge as the one that needs attention.

The second important tool is `xtree`. Normally, `xtree` is invoked as a component of the performance monitoring tool `onperf`. With `xtree`, you can examine the exact execution path of a query in progress and track its joins, sorts, and scans.

Given that most application performance tuning will address making queries more efficient, understanding how Informix analyzes and executes them is important.

The Cost-Based Optimizer

Informix employs a cost-based optimizer. This means that the database engine calculates all the paths—the *query plans*—that can fulfill a query. A query plan includes the following:

- Table evaluation order
- Join methods
- Index usage
- Temporary table creation
- Parallel data access
- Number of threads required

The engine then assigns a cost to each query plan and chooses the plan with the lowest cost. The cost assignment depends on several factors, enumerated in the next section, but chief of which is accurate data distribution statistics. Statistics on data distributions are not maintained in real-time; in fact, they are updated only when you execute `UPDATE STATISTICS`. It is critical that statistics be updated in a timely fashion, especially after major insert or delete operations.

Query Plan Selection

To calculate the cost of a query plan, the optimizer considers as much of the following data as is available (certain of these values are not stored for SE):

- How many rows are in the table
- The distribution of the values of the data
- The number of data pages and index pages with values
- The number of B+ tree levels in the index
- The second-largest and second-smallest values for an indexed column
- The presence of indexes, whether they are clustered, their order, and the fields that comprise them
- Whether a column is forced via a constraint to be unique
- Whether the data or indexes are fragmented across multiple disks
- Any optimizer hints: the current optimization level and the value of `OPTCOMPIND`

Of these factors, the first five are updated only with the `UPDATE STATISTICS` statement. Based on the query expression, the optimizer anticipates the number of I/O requests mandated by each type of access, the processor work necessary to evaluate the filter expressions, and the effort required to aggregate or order the data.

Understanding Query Plans

The SQL statement `SET EXPLAIN ON` tells Informix to record the query plans it selects in a file named `sqexplain.out`. The directive stays in effect for the duration of the current session, or until you countermand it via `SET EXPLAIN OFF`. Because the `sqexplain.out` file continually grows as new query plans are appended to it, you should generally toggle `SET EXPLAIN ON` only long enough to tune a query and then turn it off again. Additionally, a small amount of overhead is required to record the query plans.

Some sample excerpts from `sqexplain.out` follow, with line-by-line explanations.

```
Estimated Cost: 80234
```

The cost is in arbitrary disk access units and is generally useful only to compare alternative plans for the same query. A lower cost for different access methods for the same query is usually an accurate prediction that the actual query will be faster.

```
Estimated # of Rows Returned: 26123
```

When the data distributions are accurate, this estimated number can be very close to the actual number of rows that eventually satisfy the query.

```
Temporary Files Required For: Group By
```

Temporary files are not intrinsically bad, but if Informix must keep re-creating the same one to handle a common query, it could be a signal that you should create an index on the `GROUP BY` columns. Notice that not all `GROUP BY` operations can be handled with an index. For example, if a `GROUP BY` clause includes columns from more than one table or includes derived data, no index can be used.

```
1) informix.orders: SEQUENTIAL SCAN
2) informix.customers: INDEX PATH
    (1) Index Keys: cust_no
        Lower Index Filter: informix.customers.cust_no = informix.orders.cust_no
```

In the preceding example, the optimizer chooses to examine the `orders` table first via a sequential scan. Then it joins `orders` rows to `customers` rows using the index on `customers.cust_no`.

`SET EXPLAIN` can reveal myriad variations of query plans. You should examine the output from several queries to familiarize yourself with the various components of `sqexplain.out`. When you're tuning specific queries, spending your time examining query plans is critical. Look for sequential scans late in the process. If the table being scanned is large, a late sequential scan is probably a sign of trouble and might merit an index. Look for any failure to use indexes that should be used; look for data scans when key-only reads make sense; look for high relative costs; look for unreasonable index choices.

Experience here counts. Part of that experience must include understanding the join methods available to the database engine.

Join Methods

When Informix must join tables, it can choose any of three algorithms. All joins are two-table joins; multi-table joins are resolved by joining initial resultant sets to subsequent tables in turn. The optimizer chooses which join method to use based on costs, except when you override this decision by setting `OPTCOMPIND`.

- Nested Loop Join: When the join columns on both tables are indexed, this method is usually the most efficient. The first table is scanned in any order. The join columns are matched via the indexes to form a resultant row. A row from the second table is then looked up via the index. Occasionally, Informix will construct a dynamic index on the second table to enable this join. These joins are often the most efficient for OLTP applications.
- Sort Merge Join: After filters are applied, the database engine scans both tables in the order of the join filter. Both tables might need to be sorted first. If an index exists on the join column, no sort is necessary. This method is usually chosen when either or both join columns do not have an index. After the tables are sorted, joining is a simple matter of merging the sorted values.
- Hash Join: Available starting in version 7, the hash merge join first scans one table and puts its hashed key values in a hash table. The second table is then scanned once, and its join values are looked up in the hash table. Hash joins are often faster than sort merge joins because no sort is required. Even though creating the hash table requires some overhead, with most DSS applications in which the tables involved are very large, this method is usually preferred.

NOTE

The hash table is created in the virtual portion of shared memory. Any values that cannot fit will be written to disk. Be sure to set `DBSPACETEMP` to point to enough temporary space to accommodate any overflow.

Influencing the Optimizer

Much of how you can influence the optimizer depends on your constructing queries that are easily satisfied. Nonetheless, you can set two specific parameters to influence the OnLine optimizer directly.

For version 7, you can set the `OPTCOMPIND` (OPTimizer COMPare INDex methods) parameter to influence the join method OnLine chooses. You can override the `onconfig` default of `2` by setting it as an environmental variable. `OPTCOMPIND` is used only when OnLine is considering the order of joining two tables in a join pair to each other: Should it join table A to B, or should it join table B to A? And, when it makes the decision, is it free to consider a dynamic-index nested loop join as one of the options? The choices for `OPTCOMPIND` are as follow:

- `0`—Only consider the index paths. Prefer nested loop joins to the other two methods. This method forces the optimizer to behave as in earlier releases.
- `1`—If the isolation level is Repeatable Read, act as if `OPTCOMPIND` were `0`. Otherwise, act as if `OPTCOMPIND` were `2`. The danger with the Repeatable Read isolation level is that table scans, such as those performed with sort merge and hash joins, could lock all records in the table.
- `2`—Use costs to determine the join methods. Do not give preference to nested loop joins over table scans.

These options are admittedly obscure. If you choose to tune this parameter, first try the following tip.

> **TIP**
>
> For OLTP applications, set `OPTCOMPIND` to `0`. For DSS applications, set `OPTCOMPIND` to `1`.

`OPTCOMPIND` is not used with INFORMIX-XPS. XPS always chooses the join method based solely on cost.

You can explicitly set the optimization level with `SET OPTIMIZATION LOW`. The default, and only other choice for `SET OPTIMIZATION`, is `HIGH`. Normally, the cost-based optimizer examines every possible query path and applies a cost to each. With `SET OPTIMIZATION LOW`, OnLine eliminates some of the less likely paths early in the optimization process, and as a result saves some time in this step. Usually, the optimization time for a stand-alone query is insignificant, but on complex joins (five tables or more), it can be noticeable. Generally, the best result you can expect is that the optimizer will choose the same path it would have taken with `SET OPTIMIZATION HIGH` but will find it quicker.

Optimizing SQL

Identifying which process is slow is half the tuning battle. Understanding how Informix optimizes and performs the queries is the other half. With those facts in hand, tuning individual queries is generally a matter of persuading Informix to operate as efficiently as it can. The following suggestions offer some specific ways of doing that.

UPDATE STATISTICS

By now, this refrain should be familiar. If Informix seems to be constructing an unreasonable query plan, perhaps the internal statistics are out of date. Run the `UPDATE STATISTICS` command.

Eliminate Fragments

With OnLine-DSA, tables and indexes can be fragmented across multiple disks. One way to accomplish this horizontal partitioning is to create the table or index with a `FRAGMENT BY EXPRESSION` scheme. Consider this example:

```
CREATE TABLE orders (
order_no    SERIAL,
order_total MONEY (8,2))
FRAGMENT BY EXPRESSION
order_no >=     0 AND order_no <  5000 IN dbspace1,
order_no >=  5000 AND order_no < 10000 IN dbspace2,
order_no >= 10000                      IN dbspace3;
```

A query such as

```
SELECT SUM(order_total)
  FROM orders
 WHERE order_no BETWEEN 6487 AND 7212;
```

can be satisfied wholly with the data in `dbspace2`. The optimizer recognizes this and spawns a scan thread only for that fragment. The savings in disk access when fragment elimination occurs can be considerable. Additionally, contention between users can be significantly reduced as they compete less for individual disks. For a complete explanation of this topic, refer to Chapter 20.

Change the Indexing

Be guided by the optimizer. If it suggests an auto-index, add a permanent one. If it continues to create a temporary table, try to construct an index to replace it. If a very wide table is scanned often for only a few values, consider creating an artificial index solely to enable key-only reads. If a sequential scan is occurring late in the query plan, look for ways that an index can alter it, perhaps by indexing a column on that table that is used for a filter or a join. Indexes allow you to experiment without a large investment. Take advantage of this fact and experiment.

Use Explicit Temp Tables

Sometimes a complex query takes a tortuous path to completion. By examining the query path, you might be able to recognize how a mandated intermediate step would be of value. You can often create a temporary table to guarantee that certain intermediate steps occur.

When you use explicit temporary tables in this way, create them using `WITH NO LOG` to avoid any possibility of logging. Indexing temporary tables and running `UPDATE STATISTICS` on them are also legal. Examine whether either of the these operations might be worthwhile.

Select Minimal Data

Keep your communication traffic small. Internal program stacks, fetch buffers, and cache buffers all operate more efficiently when less data is sent. Therefore, select only the data that you need. Especially, do not select an aggregate or add an `ORDER BY` clause when one is not needed.

Avoid Non-Initial Substring Searches

Indexes work left to right from the beginning of a character string. If the initial value is not supplied in a filter, an index cannot be used. For example, no index can be used for any of the following selection criteria:

```
WHERE last_name MATCHES "*WHITE"
WHERE last_name[2,5] = "MITH"
WHERE last_name LIKE "%SON%"
```

Rewrite Correlated Subqueries

A *subquery* is a query nested inside the `WHERE` clause of another query. A *correlated subquery* is one in which the evaluation of the inner query depends on a value in the outer query. Here is an example:

```
SELECT cust_no
  FROM customers
 WHERE cust_no IN (SELECT cust_no
                     FROM orders
                    WHERE order_date > customers.last_order_date);
```

This subquery is correlated because it depends on `customers.last_order_date`, a value from the outer query. Because it is correlated, the subquery must execute once for each unique value from the outer `SELECT`. This process can take a long time. Occasionally, correlated subqueries can be rewritten to use a join. For example, the preceding query is identical to this one:

```
SELECT c.cust_no
  FROM customers s, orders o
 WHERE c.cust_no = o.cust_no
   AND o.order_date > c.last_order_date;
```

Usually, the join is faster. In fact, INFORMIX-XPS can do this job for you on occasion. Part of its optimization includes restructuring subqueries to use joins when possible.

Sacrificing a Goat (or Overriding the Optimizer)

Wave the computer over your head three times in a clockwise direction. If that fails, and you are desperate, you might try these arcane and equally disreputable incantations. The Informix optimizer has continually improved over the years, but it is still not foolproof. Sometimes, when the query plan it has constructed is simply not the one you know it should be, you can try underhanded ways to influence it. Be aware, though, that some of the techniques in this section work only in older versions of Informix, and recent versions of the optimizer might even negate your trick (such as stripping out duplicate filters) before constructing a query plan.

CAUTION

Trying these techniques will get you laughed at. And they probably won't work.

Rearrange Table Order

Put the smallest tables first. The order of table evaluation in constructing a query plan is critical. Exponential differences in performance can result if the tables are scanned in the wrong order, and sometimes the optimizer is unable to differentiate between otherwise equal paths. As a last resort, the optimizer looks at the order in which the tables are listed in the FROM clause to determine the order of evaluation.

Complete a Commutative Expression

Completing a commutative expression means explicitly stating all permutations of equivalent expressions. Consider the following statement:

```
SELECT c.cust_no, o.order_status
  FROM customers c, orders o
 WHERE c.cust_no = o.cust_no
   AND o.cust_no < 100;
```

The optimizer might select an index on orders.cust_no and evaluate that table first. Perhaps you recognize that selecting the customers table first should result in a speedier query. You could include the following line with the preceding query to give the optimizer more choices:

```
AND c.cust_no < 100
```

The optimizer might change its query plan, using the following statement:

```
SELECT r.*
  FROM customers c, orders o, remarks r
 WHERE c.cust_no = o.cust_no
   AND o.cust_no = r.cust_no;
```

Older versions of the optimizer would not consider that all customer numbers are equal. By stating it explicitly, as follows, you offer the optimizer more ways to satisfy the query:

```
AND c.cust_no = r.cust_no
```

Duplicate an Important Filter

Without duplicating the filter in the following query, the optimizer first suggests a query plan with a sequential scan. Indexes exist on `orders.cust_no`, `customers.cust_no`, and `customers.last_name`. The output from `sqexplain.out` follows the query.

```
SELECT o.order_no
  FROM customers c, orders o
 WHERE c.cust_no = o.cust_no
   AND c.last_name MATCHES "JON*";

1) informix.o: SEQUENTIAL SCAN
2) informix.c: INDEX PATH
    Filters: informix.c.last_name MATCHES 'JON*'
    (1) Index Keys: cust_no
        Lower Index Filter: informix.c.cust_no = informix.o.cust_no
```

One trick is to duplicate the filter on `last_name` to tell the optimizer how *important* it is. In this case, it responds by suggesting two indexed reads:

```
SELECT o.order_no
  FROM customers c, orders o
 WHERE c.cust_no = o.cust_no
   AND c.last_name MATCHES "JON*"
   AND c.last_name MATCHES "JON*";

1) informix.c: INDEX PATH
    Filters: informix.c.last_name MATCHES 'JON*'
    (1) Index Keys: last_name
        Lower Index Filter: informix.c.last_name MATCHES 'JON*'
2) informix.o: INDEX PATH
    (1) Index Keys: cust_no
        Lower Index Filter: informix.o.cust_no = informix.c.cust_no
```

You have no guarantee that the second method will actually execute faster, but at least you will have the opportunity to find out.

Add an Insignificant Filter

For the following query, Informix uses the index on `cust_no` instead of `order_no` and creates a temporary table for the sort:

```
   SELECT *
     FROM orders
    WHERE cust_no > 12
ORDER BY order_no;
```

In this instance, perhaps you decide that the index on `cust_no` is not very discriminatory and should be ignored so that the index on `order_no` can be used for a more efficient sort. Adding the following filter does not change the data returned because every `order_no` is greater than 0:

```
AND order_no > 0
```

However, adding this filter might force the optimizer to select the index you prefer.

Avoid Difficult Conjunctions

Some versions of the optimizer cannot use an index for certain conjunction expressions. At such times, using a UNION clause, instead of OR, to combine results is more efficient. For example, if you have an index on customers.cust_no and on customers.last_name, the following UNION-based expression can be faster than the OR-based one:

```
SELECT last_name, first_name
  FROM customers
 WHERE cust_no = 53 OR last_name = "JONES";

SELECT last_name, first_name
  FROM customers
 WHERE cust_no = 53
 UNION
SELECT last_name, first_name
  FROM customers
 WHERE last_name = "JONES";
```

In the preceding examples, the optimizer might choose to use each index once for the UNION-based query but neither index for the OR-based expression.

Optimizing Application Code

Especially in OLTP systems, the performance of application code is crucial. DSS environments often run more "naked" queries and reports, where the specific queries are apparent. With languages such as ESQL/C and INFORMIX-4GL that can have embedded SQL statements, it is often unclear which statement is slow and, furthermore, how to make it faster. When you're examining a piece of slow code, assume first that an SQL statement is the bottleneck. The performance differences of non-SQL operations are generally overshadowed. Although a linked list might be microseconds slower than an array, for example, SQL operations take milliseconds, at least. Spend your time where it is most fruitful: Examine the SQL.

Identify the Culprit

One way to study the query plans of embedded SQL commands is to include an option that invokes SET EXPLAIN ON as a runtime directive. Within the code, check for the existence of an environmental variable that can be toggled by the user. For example, consider this INFORMIX-4GL code:

```
IF (fgl_getenv("EXPLAIN_MODE") = "ON") THEN
   SET EXPLAIN ON
END IF
```

By placing code such as this at the beginning of your 4GL MAIN routine, you can enable SET EXPLAIN exactly when you need it.

Extract Queries

Queries buried deep within complex application code can be difficult to optimize. It is often beneficial to extract the query and examine it in isolation. With DBaccess, you can give a troublesome query special treatment, using `SET EXPLAIN ON` to examine the query plan. Performing many iterations of modifying a query with DBaccess is much easier than it is when the statement is embedded within many layers of application code.

Prepare SQL Statements

When an SQL statement gets executed on-the-fly, as through DBaccess, the database engine does the following:

1. Checks the syntax
2. Validates the user's permissions
3. Optimizes the statement
4. Executes the statement

These actions require reading a number of system tables and incur considerable overhead when performed often. For very simple statements, steps 1 through 3 can take longer than step 4. Yet for an application, only step 4, executing the statement, is needed for each iteration. The `PREPARE` statement allows the database to parse, validate, and assemble a query plan for a given statement only once. After it does so, it creates an internal statement identifier that you can use as a handle to execute the statement repeatedly.

TIP

Use `PREPARE` to create efficient handles for commonly used SQL statements.

Often used to construct dynamic SQL statements at runtime, the `PREPARE` statement can significantly help performance as well. The first place to look for good candidates to use with `PREPARE` is inside loops. Consider the following theoretical fragment of INFORMIX-4GL code:

```
DECLARE good_cust_cursor CURSOR FOR
 SELECT cust_no
   FROM customers
  WHERE acct_balance <= 0

FOREACH good_cust_cursor INTO good_cust_no
    UPDATE customer
       SET credit_rating = 100
     WHERE cust_no = good_cust_no
END FOREACH
```

For this example, ignore that the operation could be performed with a single SQL statement. Instead, notice that the UPDATE statement, with its concomitant overhead, is executed once for each "good" customer. Compare the preceding to this next example:

```
PREPARE update_cust FROM
"UPDATE customer SET credit_rating = 100 WHERE cust_no = ?"

FOREACH good_cust_cursor INTO good_cust_no
    EXECUTE update_cust USING good_cust_no
END FOREACH
```

Note the use of a placeholder ("?") to allow the substitution of different values each time it is executed. Because the UPDATE statement does not need to be reevaluated for each execution, this method is more efficient than the first.

Most SQL statements can be prepared. Aside from optimizing individual SQL statements, preparing commonly called SQL statements such as those in loops or in library functions will generally provide the biggest performance gain.

UPDATE WHERE CURRENT OF

In the preceding example, you already know which customer row is being updated; it is likely in memory. Yet when the UPDATE statement executes, the database server must reselect the customer row. To update (or delete) a row you have already selected, use the UPDATE WHERE CURRENT OF statement. This way, the server avoids the extra lookup. To do so, you must first declare the cursor FOR UPDATE, as follows:

```
DECLARE good_cust_cursor CURSOR FOR
 SELECT cust_no
   FROM customers
  WHERE acct_balance <= 0
FOR UPDATE OF credit_rating

PREPARE update_cust FROM
"UPDATE customer SET credit_rating = 100 WHERE CURRENT OF good_cust_cursor"

FOREACH good_cust_cursor INTO good_cust_no
    EXECUTE update_cust
END FOREACH
```

A cursor of this type, prepared only once and repeatedly executed, is exceedingly efficient.

Use Insert Cursors

Normally, as inserts occur, they are written to disk; an insert cursor is a mechanism that instead allows these writes to be buffered in memory. This insert buffer is written to disk only when it fills, when you issue the FLUSH statement, or when you commit a transaction. As a result, communication traffic is minimized, and disk usage is consolidated. For bulk insert operations, creating and using an insert cursor is essential for best performance.

Minimize Scroll Cursors

A scroll cursor is a convenient applications code construction that allows you to operate flexibly on an active set. With it, you can move back or forward in the active set to any relative or absolute row. However, Informix uses an implicit temporary table to enable this action. If you do not need so much flexibility in positioning, avoid using a scroll cursor.

Custom ESQL/C Functions

Informix has created a set of ESQL/C library functions optimized for each installed platform. These functions can be noticeably faster than their C library counterparts. If your applications code performs these operations numerous times, the performance gain from using the Informix flavor is probably worth the effort of including them. Table 23.3 shows several of these ESQL/C functions and their C library complements.

Table 23.3. INFORMIX-ESQL/C library functions.

Informix	*C*	*Description*
`stcat()`	`strcat()`	Concatenate two null-terminated strings
`stcmpr()`	`strcmp()`	Compare two null-terminated strings
`stcopy()`	`strcpy()`	Copy one null-terminated string to another
`stleng()`	`strlen()`	Count the bytes in a null-terminated string
`bycmpr()`	`memcmp()`	Compare two sets of bytes for a given length
`bycopy()`	`memcpy()`	Copy a fixed number of bytes from one location to another
`byfill()`	`memset()`	Fill a variable with a fixed number of a single character
`rdownshift()`	`tolower()`	Convert all letters in a null-terminated string to lowercase
`rupshift()`	`toupper()`	Convert all letters in a null-terminated string to uppercase
`rstod()`	`atof()`	Convert a null-terminated string to a double
`rstoi()`	`atoi()`	Convert a null-terminated string to an integer
`rstol()`	`atol()`	Convert a null-terminated string to a long

These library functions are automatically included by the ESQL preprocessor.

Compile Efficiently

After you build and debug INFORMIX-4GL or ESQL/C code, you should make the executables as efficient as possible. Include the `-O` directive in both ESQL/C and 4GL compile instructions to enable compile-time optimization. To reduce the size of the executable, add the `-nln` option to avoid storing line numbers for embedded SQL. Finally, strip the executable, removing its symbol table, to reduce the size of the final executable program.

Pass Minimal Data to Functions

Within applications code, especially INFORMIX-4GL, avoid sending unneeded values to a function. INFORMIX-4GL allows the simple definition of a record with the `DEFINE RECORD LIKE` *`tablename`*`.*` syntax. It is convenient, but inefficient, to pass the entire record to a function when, often, most of the values are unnecessary. To pass data between functions, INFORMIX-4GL passes each value onto and off an internal stack. This data shuffling causes unnecessary overhead if done to excess. Only pass the values you need.

Stored Procedures and Triggers

Stored procedures are sequences of SQL statements and program logic that are stored in the database. When they are created, they are parsed, checked for validity, and optimized. Later, they can execute more quickly because these steps do not need to be repeated. However, stored procedures are no panacea. They garner their own overhead because they must be selected from the database, and they must be converted to executable format. Nonetheless, stored procedures that comprise more than one SQL statement are usually faster than the equivalent dynamic SQL statements. Another stored procedure benefit is that they reduce messaging traffic. If network traffic is a bottleneck, stored procedures can be especially worthwhile. For more information on these topics, refer to Chapter 14, "Managing Data with Stored Procedures and Triggers."

Summary

The task of tuning your Informix environment will fill the time allotted, and more. The demanding part of the job is to recognize what improvements are reasonable to implement and to stop when the returns no longer justify the cost. After you know what enhancements can be expected, you need to educate your user community and set their expectations accordingly. Tuning your Informix environment does not have to be a never-ending process.

CHAPTER 24

Anticipating Future Growth

by Ron M. Flannery

IN THIS CHAPTER

This chapter presents strategies to help you plan for the inevitable changing needs of the design and implementation of a database application. This information includes everything from project planning to hardware to the database engine. I will discuss how to prepare for these needs before you implement.

Thinking in terms of the future is extremely important. Creating a database to meet the needs of the future is an ongoing process. It is a way of thinking that helps drive all the decisions that are made for an application. In this chapter, I will help you develop a mindset to aid in this process. If you are a chief information officer (CIO), manager, designer, programmer, or contractor, this chapter will help prepare you for the future.

In this chapter, I will describe a complete methodology for ensuring the success of your application. I begin by presenting a complete philosophy of project implementation. Applying these strategies will help make the rest of the process work. After that, I discuss the actual database design process, with a particular emphasis on Informix products. I then describe different considerations for database engine, operating system, hardware, network, and Internet. Included are checklists to help you cover all the bases. Finally, I give specific examples and tie all the information together.

Today and Tomorrow

You've got a great database design, and you know everything there is to know about administering databases. Your team spent many long hours, and now you're ready to go live. Good job! But how will the database look in three months, six months, or a year? Has the design taken into consideration changing user, management, and business needs? What about the computers and the network?

The first point to keep in mind is to always think ahead. Everything might seem to fit together now, but that could easily change, and much faster than you can imagine. Keeping the future needs of the system in perspective now can greatly reduce implementation time later. You must consider the future in every design decision. Technology, tools, and user needs change so fast that your original solution could be obsolete before you even deliver it. So, let me just emphasize this:

> *Always think ahead!*

Data warehouses are excellent examples of the importance of proper planning. They tend to be very large, enterprise-wide projects with sky-high budgets. They often have an impact on hundreds or thousands of users. Determining the needs of all users can be almost impossible. Without proper planning, the costs and time required for data warehouse projects often well exceed initial estimates. This cost overrun can become very difficult to explain to a CIO, especially if you're the one doing the explaining.

Planning ahead is the cornerstone of data warehouse development and should be the cornerstone of every database project. I will now present some principles to help you incorporate planning for the future into every project with which you are involved.

> **NOTE**
>
> In the context of this chapter, the following terms are used somewhat interchangeably: *application, project, implementation,* and *database*.
>
> For your needs, they all mean basically the same thing: creating a database application. This application has no particular size. It can be anywhere from 1 user to 10,000 users, from 50 kilobytes to 50 terabytes. Nor is there any particular *type* of application. The principles can apply to an OLTP system, a Web system, or whatever you want. The important point is that the principles can help you be prepared for the future in any project that your company performs.

Project Roles

Database implementations can impact many different levels of an organization. In turn, many different roles exist within these implementations. This arrangement can vary, depending on the size of the project, corporation, and so on. The following list describes some of the many persons who can have an impact on database projects:

- End users and data entry clerks
- CIO, president, CEO, and other high-level decision-makers
- Directors
- Managers
- Project and team leaders
- Technical writers
- Database designers
- Programmers
- Quality assurance workers and testers
- Consultants

This list is meant to give you an idea of how many people can actually be involved when implementing a database project. If you can keep this information in perspective, taking into account the future needs of the database is much easier.

Consider how all these different levels of an organization relate to planning a project. If planning is kept within the scope of any one of these groups, the needs of the whole corporation might not be met. During the development of your application, be sure to review this list and consider the needs of everyone.

Using the guidelines in the following sections can help you keep everything in perspective, regardless of your role and the size of the project. Remember that no matter which role you have in the project, you have a part in its success.

Planning Checklist

The process of designing and implementing a new database application isn't easy. The larger the application and the larger the corporation, the harder the design tasks. Considering the needs of one, a dozen, or hundreds of users can be quite a daunting task. No matter how many times you've done it, complications that were impossible to forecast often exist. Don't worry: Discovering complications is part of implementing a new system. Proper planning and preparation can make the process as simple and painless as possible.

This section is not meant to be a project management guide; it is meant to help you develop a mindset that you can use throughout the whole process. This section can help you always consider the future needs of your database application. No matter what role you have in the implementation, these guidelines apply to you. Applying these principles the whole way through the process (for example, database design) can help ensure that the application will meet everyone's needs.

Let's see, have I said this before?

Always think ahead!

In the planning stage, the scope, cost, resources, and timeline for the project are determined—or at least estimated. Considering the future needs is crucial in successful planning and implementation. During the planning stage, many later problems can be avoided.

Checklist 24.1 summarizes many principles that you should always keep in mind during implementation of a project. I will refer to this checklist throughout the chapter. You can use these principles as an overall guide to help meet the needs of the future. This list is by no means complete. In fact, I have included two blank lines for you to add your own principles.

Checklist 24.1. A list of project planning principles.

___ Always think ahead!

___ Use experience—your experience and others' experience.

___ Believe in organization: Be organized from the beginning, and don't keep saying, "We'll create that plan later."

___ Never stop planning.

___ Consider everyone's opinion—user's and management's.

___ Use idea buckets and brainstorming.

___ Capture the ideas.

___ Make meetings work.

___ Be a team: Work with each other, not against each other.

___ Don't panic: Don't get overwhelmed, and keep everything in perspective.

___ Avoid constant firefighting: Follow your plan and take time to readjust it.

___ Admit mistakes in planning: This way, you can save a great deal of time and money later. Avoid the surprise factor!

___ Ensure an open communication process.

___ Adapt to new technology and solutions: Keep up with the incredible rate of change, and be sure to add new solutions as they become available.

___ Provide management justification: This rule is important—and necessary.

___ Costs of improper planning can be enormous.

___

___

In the following sections, I give an overview of each of these principles and how each one can help you implement your project successfully now and into the future.

Always Think Ahead!

Here I go again with the "think ahead" thing! I can't say enough about this basic principle. It means seeing the forest for the trees. Thinking outside your realm. Seeing the big picture. Developing this mentality and remembering it at all times will greatly increase the chances for a successful project implementation. Make sure that all the members of your project are also in tune with this principle.

Use Experience

Experience is a great teacher. Be sure to use your own experience: *Learn from the past!* If every project you've worked on for this company missed budget or due dates, consider what happened on those projects. Use your past experiences to help make this project a success. Don't be shy about calling on all appropriate colleagues to understand their experiences. Listen to the voices of experience and use that information to build a successful implementation.

Technical experience is also very important. You'll often find a trade-off between using current internal employees and hiring new employees or contractors with specialized skills. Making sure that the cost of using current employees in a new role will not have a great impact on the project, especially where specialized experience is needed, is very important. See the later sections on database design, hardware, and networks for examples.

Believe in Organization

Be organized from the beginning, and don't keep saying, "We'll create that plan later." Set up the overall structure and methodology of the project right at the beginning and stick to it (unless it has problems). Use whatever project planning tools work for your organization. Set up responsible resources for the project, and make sure that their roles are clearly defined. After the initial project setup is organized, make sure that it remains organized.

Never Stop Planning

Planning continues through the life of the project, up to and including implementation. In fact, it continues as long as the project lives. Planning must be an ongoing part of any project. After you create an initial design, do not consider it the final plan. Thinking of everything is impossible. Be open to changing the plan as needed as the project moves forward.

Consider Everyone's Opinion

A successful project will make people happy at all levels of an organization. Therefore, everyone the project affects must be considered during the "planning" (remember the definition of planning). To do so, team members must be sure to meet the proper users and understand all their needs.

Use Idea Buckets and Brainstorming

One of the frustrating aspects of a project can be taking advantage of the many ideas and organizing them. In fact, capturing all necessary ideas is *crucial*. One method of doing so is to create an "idea bucket." An idea bucket is just a dumping of ideas into one place. It can be a spreadsheet, a small database, or a simple text file. It does not have to be organized at first: You can do that later.

Brainstorming sessions work hand-in-hand with idea buckets. A brainstorming session is a collective dumping of ideas, thoughts, needs, and plans by many people. Having these sessions is a good way to get many ideas out on the table at once. You can then place the ideas directly into the idea bucket. Brainstorming sessions should be conducted with all levels of people in a project (users, management, and so on).

Here is a sample brainstorming session on determining how to create an information tracking system in a small company:

> "Let's put it in Microsoft Access! We can keep it on my computer!"
>
> "But then no one else can use it."
>
> "We can use the Windows 95 networking option."
>
> "What if you're not here, and no one has your password?"
>
> "Your computer will always have to be on."
>
> "What about Windows NT?"
>
> "We don't have that."
>
> "I hear it's cheap, and maybe we can use Informix Workgroup Server."
>
> "Oh yeah, we can use NT for our printers and e-mail, too!"
>
> "Don't forget about UNIX! We can get an SCO OpenServer for about the same price, and it does the same things."

And on and on. The point is, if enough people put their minds to the job, they can create many new ideas.

NOTE

You might be wondering at this point what a brainstorming session has to do with future planning of a database application. A lot! By having such sessions, you can get a lot of ideas out into the open long before they become problems. If these sessions are not used, the ideas might not be revealed until much later in the process. Remember that a major aspect of future planning is making sure that all the necessary ideas are on the table and incorporated into the plans.

Capture the Ideas

After you have a brainstorming session, you can use the following methodology to incorporate the ideas into a project plan:

1. Set up a meeting with project design and planning teams. (See the next section for meeting tips.)
2. Discuss how the project is organized and how brainstorming results can be used.
3. Go through brainstorming ideas one at a time:
    a. Is the idea necessary? If not, delete it and move on to the next item.
    b. To which section of the project does it apply?
    c. What is its priority?
    d. If follow-up is required, schedule a time to meet with the right people.
    e. Move the item to whatever project planning methodology is being used. Assign resources and so on.
    f. Remove the item from the brainstorming list.

Make Meetings Work

Meetings are an inevitable part of any successful project. That's okay because everyone loves meetings. Okay, maybe not everyone. In fact, maybe hardly anybody! But why not? If you let me go out on a limb, I'd say a possible reason for the overall dislike for meetings is that they tend to not be productive. Here are some guidelines on how to make meetings more productive to the project and its overall goals:

- Invite only people who need to be there.
- Create an agenda with time limits and responsible parties. At the beginning of the agenda, clearly state the purpose of the meeting. Allow for an open discussion at the end of the meeting, but not for too long.
- Send out a notice of the meeting in time to make sure that all parties are aware of it.
- Start the meeting right on time. Starting a meeting late tends to breed overall inefficiency.
- Appoint a meeting leader (probably the agenda author), and make sure that everyone is aware that this person is in charge.
- Stay with the agenda as much as possible. Digressions are another meeting killer.
- If a new topic comes up, save it for the "open discussion" section of the meeting.

Be a Team

For the project to be successful, people on all levels need to remember that the end result is a successful project. Sure, the "team" concept is much overused, so avoiding use of the "team" word might be best. However, people need to be aware that to complete a project, they have to cooperate with others and allow for proper future planning.

Don't Panic

If things start getting out of hand, simply stick to the process that was set up from the beginning. For this reason, the philosophy in Checklist 24.1 is very important. If you need more meetings, have them. If you need to change the design, change it. If you need to get new approval, get it. Panicking when things start to go astray only adds to stress and threatens the proper implementation of the project.

Avoid Constant Firefighting

Avoiding constant firefighting generally ties in with a number of the preceding sections. If the project is laid out in an organized fashion, you will have little need to do firefighting; changes will be part of the plan. And as I stated in the "Don't Panic" section, if something goes wrong, do what it takes to fix the problem. Keep an organized state of mind with respect to the whole project.

Admit Mistakes in Planning

Any flaws uncovered by the preceding—or any—methodology must be immediately addressed. People tend not to admit that they have made a mistake, and it ultimately is very costly, both in time and money. Ask your boss if he or she would rather know about a problem now or find out about it at the last minute. Keeping the mentality that a project is constantly evolving helps make admitting mistakes much easier. If the whole team understands the mentality and principles outlined here, they will understand that changes happen and that the changes simply need to be plugged in and fixed.

Ensure an Open Communication Process

One of the key aspects in developing a new application is getting the right information. Getting the right information is contingent in large part on proper communication. It is a fact of life that users, managers, and programmers tend to talk different languages. Programmers and developers tend to be more technical and sometimes have trouble getting the necessary information from users and managers. Properly "translating" when developing the design is important. Bring a translator if you want! Be sure to verify what you're communicating. A common way to do so is to follow this axiom:

> *Say what you're going to say. Say it. Say what you said.*

Also, be sure to acknowledge what you heard by restating it to the person.

Adapt to New Technology and Solutions

In today's world, everything is evolving at an incredible pace. "Everything" includes specific software and hardware solutions, and project needs in general. During the life of a medium- or large-sized project, portions of the project will almost certainly have better solutions. Make sure that resources are available to keep up with these solutions and plug them back into the whole development process.

WARNING

Although being able to always have the "latest and greatest" is nice, it is not always practical—or necessary. Be sure to take into consideration the timing and needs of the project. Decide whether you really do need this cool new computer or software package right now. On the other hand, you also must be sure that you are prepared for the future.

Provide Management Justification

Someone has to pay for the project. Generally speaking, there must be management buy-in to support current and future spending. Following the principles outlined here will create an efficient means of determining a proper direction and adjusting for changes and the future. If managers understand this need, the support will be much easier to obtain. They must understand how fast things evolve and that a change now can save a great deal in the future.

Summary: The Costs of Improper Planning

Let me reiterate that the cost of not planning for the future can be great. Be sure to always take into account what will be needed a year or five years from now. Looking ahead can often be the most difficult aspect of design. Decide how these things can be incorporated into your system. Be sure that the design selected allows for the future growth of the system, be it in software, hardware, or people. Follow an organized and well-balanced approach, considering the needs of others.

Projects can always succeed; sometimes you just need to help them a little.

Question Checklist

Checklist 24.2 shows examples of many questions you can ask users, managers, and others involved in the project. If nothing else, this checklist will help you start to think about issues to keep in mind during planning and into the future. Because the questions can cross over between various types of users (for example, managers and end users), they are not categorized in any particular order.

Checklist 24.2. Planning question checklist.

- ___ Do you have an existing way to track this data? If so, provide details.
- ___ How fast does the current data grow? Do you think this speed will increase or decrease?
- ___ What are some of the projected changes in the overall company applications, networks, and databases? Do they fit in with the new application?
- ___ How fast is the company growing? Do you anticipate that these changes will affect the new system?
- ___ Which other parts of the company use this data? What are their needs?
- ___ Does the current system have problems that need to be corrected in the new system?
- ___ Where will the users be located? Will they be in the same office, across the country, or worldwide?
- ___ Do you have an Internet connection? If so, provide details.
- ___ What is the current setup of your network (Internet, Ethernet, and so on)?
- ___ Who are the other users of the system? How can I contact them?
- ___ What types of people use the system (experience level, and so on)?
- ___ What software do you currently own? Include databases, PC packages, and so on.
- ___ What hardware do you currently own? Include computers, PCs, and so on.
- ___ What is the budget for the new system?
- ___ Who needs to approve the system?
- ___ Which resources are available for the project?
- ___ What is the skill level of your existing employees?
- ___ Will you be using contractors?
- ___ Is the current system hard to use? How could it be made easier?
- ___ How do you picture the "perfect solution"?
- ___ What is the current organizational structure?
- ___ Which project management tool do you use (for example, Microsoft Project)?
- ___ Do you currently use a project management methodology?
- ___ Will this project realistically be a big part of the future of the company?
- ___ Does a prepackaged software package meet these needs? Maybe one that would need just minor modification?
- ___ How willing to change are the users of the system?
- ___ What types of deadlines does the system have?

The Pieces: Technology

Now that you've learned about general project planning, you can get to the nitty-gritty: the technology! In the following sections, I explain how to structure your application properly to meet the future needs of the project. I discuss the following:

- Database design
- Database engines and versions
- Physical design
- Operating systems
- Hardware
- Networks
- Internet

NOTE

Remember that the project principles in Checklist 24.1 can help you move toward the right decisions in all parts of the planning process, including hardware and software. All the preceding pieces need to work together to create a successful long-term implementation. Keep the future in mind and have fun!

Database Design

Now you're ready to design the database. To finalize the database design, you can use many of the basic principles discussed in this chapter. Consider the needs of the application, and remember to solicit information from all necessary users and management. Make sure that you truly consider all the future needs of the application. Ensure that experienced database designers are used when possible. Spend a lot of time designing, honing, and getting approval for the design. Work at all levels of the chain (users, managers, developers, and designers).

NOTE

As you learn later in this chapter, a relationship exists among database design, database engines, hardware, networks, and the Internet. They all tend to drive each other. However, the database design is a necessary part of any implementation, so I have separated it from the process (see Figure 24.1). In some cases, the database design will be more driven by the database engine, but I believe it should be separate.

Figure 24.1 illustrates how the many parts of a database implementation drive each other.

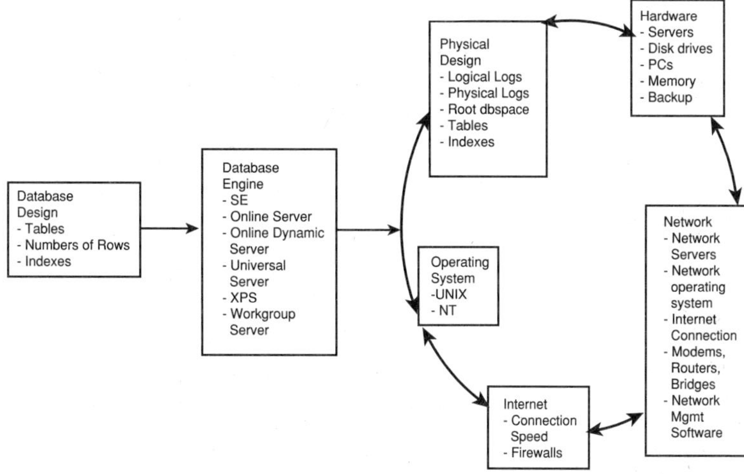

FIGURE 24.1.
Database implementation flow.

A lot of time must be taken to design the database properly. Improper planning can start a chain reaction of changes. Consider some of the possible events that can occur if the database is not designed properly:

- Redesigning some or all of the database. New project plans need to be made, people resources need to be maintained, the budget needs to be approved, and so on.
- Getting different hardware. Upgrading hardware to meet new needs of the system might be necessary. Upgrading can include a whole new computer, disk drives, network upgrades, and more.
- Rewriting programs. Programs need to be changed to meet new database table and column definitions.
- Time loss. Any big changes mean more time before the application will be available.
- Profit and loss. At this stage, the higher levels of management might become a bit unhappy. The increased costs and possible loss of profit from time delays can make for a very bad situation.

All in all, the best way to avoid these problems is to *take the time to do the job right the first time!* The following sections discuss the different aspects of proper database design: table, index, and physical design.

Table Design

The design of the tables is the core of the whole system. If the table design is wrong, then everything else fails—or at least doesn't function as well as it can. Take the time up front to make sure you have covered all the bases in your table designs.

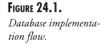

Following are some overall pointers to help make sure table design is properly handled. Note that the project and communication process outlined in Checklist 24.1 will inherently help satisfy many of these needs.

- Discuss initial needs with users and managers.
- Create preliminary design of tables and discuss with the appropriate people.
- Create a data dictionary or graphical representation. Many software packages do this job.
- Work through several data scenarios with the design.
- Make any necessary modifications and go through the process again.

In the following sections, I describe the different aspects of table design.

Column Selection and Naming

Obviously, a table is made up of columns, which represent the data in the database. But they have to be the correct columns. As I've said time and time again, doing the job right the first time is very important, and table column selection is no exception. Not adding columns or adding incorrect columns can cause major headaches after the database is online. Spend as much time as possible making sure that you get the columns right the first time.

TIP

If a column is used in two different tables, which is frequently the case in a relational database (for joined tables), there are two schools of thought: Name the column with a piece of the table name (for example, `billing_cust_code` in the `Billing` table and `cust_code` in the `Customer` table), or keep the column name the same in each table. I highly recommend the latter: Keep the column name the same. This naming method greatly simplifies the understanding of the database. You'll always know what `cust_code` means. Also, you can make database changes much more easily (because you'll know where all the `cust_code` fields are found).

Normalization

Table design always includes at least some level of normalization. Normalization of a table involves designing the table in a way that removes redundant data. There are different levels of normalization: first, second, and third normal form.

Here is an example. A customer has an address that is stored in the `Customer` table in the database. A bill is generated, and its data is placed in the `Bill` table. When a bill is sent to the customer, the address is read directly from the `Customer` table; it does not need to be repeated in the `Bill` table.

Different types of databases require different degrees of normalization. OLTP databases should be as normalized as possible. Data warehouses tend not to be as normalized. Object-oriented (OO) databases are different beasts altogether: Table design is based on a hierarchical structure, which is outside the scope of this text (and doesn't apply to the current Informix database). Object-relational database management systems (ORDBMS) such as Informix Universal Server are generally more relational in nature than OO databases and must give consideration to proper normalization techniques.

Table 24.1 lists some different types of databases and how much normalization should be applied to each.

Table 24.1. Database normalization considerations.

Type of Application	*Level of Normalization*	*Comments*
OLTP/Data Entry	High	High normalization results in less hard drive storage. Because data is usually entered by users, it should be less redundant. This level of normalization helps prevent user data entry errors because users do not have to repeat entries (such as company or employee name and address information). Use efficient indexing to join OLTP tables.
DSS/Data Warehouse	Medium to Low	Data is often loaded by batch processes, not manually. Less normalization means that data is repeated in these tables, allowing fewer joins and quicker lookups. Joins are done based on linking a central detail ("fact") table (often with redundant data) to several lookup ("dimension") tables. This is known as a star schema.
OLTP/DSS	High to Low	Use object-relational database management systems (ORDBMS) to handle a mix of different types, including multimedia and relational.
Multimedia	Low	Use an object-oriented database for pure media management. Because ORDBMS gives object as well as relational capabilities, using it would be best.

Experience is important in choosing a design to meet the future needs of an application. Someone used to working in a mainframe environment, for example, might not be as familiar with the proper normalization techniques. Databases might repeat data, as in a mainframe-type flat file. The proper techniques must be applied to the database for your application. Getting the proper resources, whether consultants or employees, is of utmost importance in proper database design.

Numbers of Rows

The number of rows is probably one of the most common underestimates in system design. Determining the initial numbers of rows in the tables might be fairly easy, but how accurately can you determine how many rows these tables will have a year from now?

Understand that the number of rows in tables will affect how the database is physically designed (see the "Physical Design" section). It helps to determine how much disk space is needed, which indexes are practical, how the data is partitioned, and more. Improperly estimating this information can greatly add to the costs of the project as more hardware is needed.

TIP

Projecting the number of rows in database tables requires serious interaction with users. This number is often one of the issues that the users (and designers!) can grossly underestimate. You must always take a close look at the application, past growth, and future growth projections as well as what the users tell you.

Your corporation might not be able to afford the hardware for the database needs a year from now. Nonetheless, be sure to give your company an accurate idea of what will be needed further down the road. Understanding the future application needs now is much better than having to adjust to them after the system is online. Again, *avoid the surprise factor*!

Indexes

After determining *all* the table designs, you're ready to create the indexes. Indexes are created to increase the speed of database lookups and ensure database integrity. Improperly designed indexes can make or break an application. They are an integral part of design. If you've ever heard "this screen always takes so long to run," chances are, the problem has something to do with an index.

You can use several different index tuning strategies. The strategies are often very specific to the Informix product you're using. As much as anything, index planning is a case in which you should read the dreaded manuals.

WARNING

Besides being careful not to create too few indexes, be sure not to create too *many*! As I stated in the "Normalization" section, data warehouses have different index considerations. For example, trying to over-index a data warehouse can greatly slow query times if queries will be selecting too much data out of one table. Techniques such as fragmentation can greatly reduce the query times in a data warehouse.

For normalized relational databases, you can easily create too many indexes. Redundant indexes (for example, indexes that use columns with too few unique values or use the same "head" columns) not only take more disk space, but also confuse the Informix optimizer, slowing queries. Too many indexes can also greatly increase the time it takes to insert and delete data (because indexes need to be rearranged to accommodate the data). If an index column is often updated, performance can also be affected.

A crucial part of a good index design is creating *primary key* or *unique indexes* on the tables. They help ensure data integrity and provide for overall better programming of the application. Even if your table "will never have duplicates," make sure you put a unique index on the table to enforce it. Find out now what the unique indexes are, and make sure they are part of the initial design.

Making the Design Pretty

You can visualize and document the database design in many good ways. Doing so helps the designers and the users of the system, and can help point out possible flaws. The following are some of the methods:

- E/R diagram: An efficient method to build and maintain a table design is through an E/R design tool (for example, ERwin or S-Designer). This diagram helps chart the tables and put them in a graphical form. It better illustrates the tables both for designers and users and can help identify any necessary changes. Figure 24.2 is an example of an E/R diagram generated from ERwin. Note how easily you can see the relationship between the tables.
- Data dictionary: A data dictionary describes the tables and their attributes. It includes column sizes, indexes, and text descriptions of their attributes. Some software packages can greatly simplify this process. You can use it in conjunction with the E/R diagram. In fact, many E/R diagram tools can generate a corresponding data dictionary. Table 24.2 shows an example of a data dictionary. The description of each table in this data dictionary contains table name, description, join fields, and detail for each column. This example is simple; data dictionaries can be much more detailed and/or user-friendly.

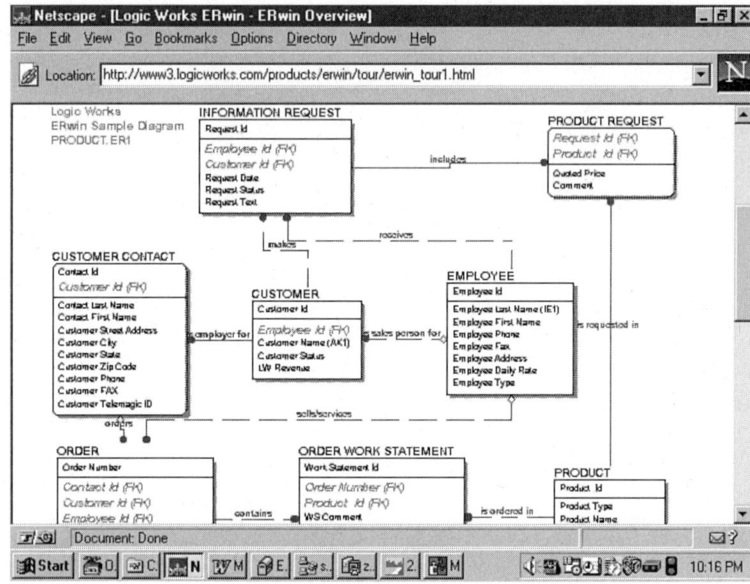

FIGURE 24.2.
An example of an ERwin E/R diagram.

For the data dictionary in Table 24.2, the following information applies:

Table Name:	Customer.
Description:	This table supplies information about each customer. It is used by many other tables in the database.
Join Fields:	The table is usually joined by `cust_nbr`.

Table 24.2. An example of a data dictionary.

Column Name	*Column Type*	*Description*
`cust_nbr`	serial	Number assigned by system; uniquely identifies each customer
`last_name`	character(30)	Last name
`first_name`	character(25)	First name
`address1`	character(30)	First address line
`address2`	character(30)	Second address line
`city`	character(30)	Customer city
`state`	character(10)	State, province, or other
`postal_code`	character(10)	Zip or postal code
`phone`	character(15)	Phone number

Verifying the Design

After you create the designs of the tables, make sure to work through some scenarios. Here are some ways to do so:

- Show users and other analysts E/R diagrams, data dictionaries, and other documentation.
- Work through all the user business processes, and make sure the tables will meet user needs.
- Create queries that the users would do.
- Go through as many iterations as possible until you get it right; don't "get back to it later."
- Write sample programs if you need to.

The information in the database design phase is of utmost importance to the implementation of the project. After the design is finalized, many decisions are made for the rest of the project. Make sure that the information is as accurate as possible, for now and a year from now. Again, the time you spend now can save incalculable time and money later.

Do what it takes and do it now.

Current and Future Products

As everyone knows, technology is changing at a blinding rate of speed. How many times have you heard the complaint, "I just bought my computer six months ago, and now I can get a computer that's twice as powerful for the same money!" or "I'm just waiting for the new features to come out and the prices to come down before I buy." There is no single right time to buy software or hardware. Life must go on, and so must applications.

Be as aware as possible of the upcoming hardware and software products for your application. Plan to upgrade and move into them. Build applications with the future needs in mind: Make sure they can grow into the needs of applications instead of being completely upgraded. And most importantly, be sure your choices can *grow into the future.*

On the flip side of the coin, if the company currently owns a product (hardware or software), determine whether the new application instead merits upgrading of current software. Consider the upgrade costs associated with the current license of the product: Some upgrades are free or very low cost for current owners of products. Also, if you have a high level of familiarity with a product, the cost and time savings can be great. Remember the future, though. Don't lock yourself into an obsolete product just for the sake of not changing.

If this application is simply replacing a database on an existing system (that is, you already own the software), you must consider the necessity of changing database engines. Why upgrade if you don't have to? For example, suppose you're replacing a database running on Standard

Engine. If it is in a small office with limited technical resources, upgrading to another Informix version might not be necessary.

Budget

The budget allocated to the project might prohibit some of the remaining choices. Just be sure to have all your design "ducks in a row" before you actually try to estimate how much hardware is needed. If the database absolutely needs to have certain pieces, making a case for it business-wise is much easier if you have the proper documentation.

Putting the Pieces Together

In the following sections, I describe considerations for the database engine, operating system, hardware, and network. Note that these decisions tend to somewhat drive each other. Many of these choices are made based on the size and design of the database. Figure 24.1 illustrates this process.

Database Engines and Versions

You often hear recommendations to select the database engine before the hardware, operating system, and other physical pieces of the system. Why? Because the database is often (not always) the driving force of the application. After you understand the needs of the database, you can choose the proper Informix database engine. You can then choose the rest of the hardware and software needs based on the needs of this engine. This situation might not *always* be the case, but it is a good general assumption.

When choosing the database engine, you must take into account the future growth and needs of the application. The engine you choose must be able to grow as your application grows. It should also keep on top of the necessary technology. Because you will, of course, be using an Informix database, I will structure this discussion around specific Informix products.

To assess properly which database engine to use, consider the following:

- Size of the database: Use the size of tables and indexes determined following the logic in the "Table Design" section. As described in the Informix product overview in Table 24.1, the size of the database helps determine which product is most appropriate.
- Database administration skills: In this area, training, hiring, or contracting certainly is essential.
- Tuning: How much performance tuning will likely be done to the database?
- Future support: What are Informix's future plans for this engine?
- Types of queries: Queries returning millions of rows joining several tables require a more high-end solution.
- Types of solutions: Is it OLTP, data warehouse, and so on? (See Checklist 24.2 for more information.)

While you have this information in mind, look at Table 24.3, which summarizes current Informix engines. The chapters in Part II of this book give a detailed description of each of these products. Note that the order of the products is the approximate order in which they were released.

Table 24.3. Informix database engine summary.

Informix Database Engine	*Comments*
Standard Engine	1.0–5.*x* ■ Good for lower-end databases. ■ If you already own it, it might meet your needs. ■ Very little database administration needed. ■ Uses UNIX file system, which is not as efficient for larger tables but is simpler for smaller (fewer than 1,000,000 rows) tables. Much depends on the number and size of indexes. ■ Easily backed up with UNIX utilities.
OnLine Server	5.*x* ■ Good for medium to large databases. ■ Allows users to distribute the database across multiple disks and file systems. ■ Can use raw disk space, resulting in increased performance. ■ Allows a great deal of tuning and administration through the `tb` utilities. ■ Requires more database administrator support.
OnLine Dynamic Server	6.*x*–7.*x* ■ Can handle very large databases. ■ Exploits parallel processing capabilities of UNIX and NT, greatly increasing speed. ■ Adds more tuning options and complexity to those introduced in OnLine Server. ■ Has many more administrative and backup utilities than OnLine Server. (The `on` commands replace `tb` commands.) ■ Requires more database administration than OnLine Server.

continues

Table 24.3. continued

Informix Database Engine	*Comments*
Universal Server	■ Contains all features of OnLine Dynamic Server, with the addition of nonstandard data types (for example, video and audio). ■ Provides a wide variety of vendor-created DataBlades, which allow powerful manipulation of all types of data. ■ Has very powerful Web site development capabilities. ■ Contains all administrative utilities in OnLine Dynamic Server—and more. ■ Could require more training to exploit object-oriented capabilities.
XPS	■ Designed for very high-end database applications such as data warehouses. ■ Allows distributing the data over several computer "nodes" (massively parallel processing). ■ Contains all features of OnLine Dynamic Server and more. ■ Contains SQL extensions that are optimized for data warehouse queries, as well as other powerful SQL extensions. ■ Requires more database administration than OnLine Dynamic Server.
Workgroup Server	■ Easy to install and administer; everything is GUI-based. ■ Designed for small to mid-sized applications. ■ Supported on NT and UNIX.

TIP

Go to the Informix Web site at `www.informix.com` to get all the latest information and specifications on all Informix products.

Physical Design

The physical design of a database is crucial: It determines how the database is to be stored on disk. This design can include some of the following database configuration parameters:

- Logical logs
- Physical logs
- Root dbspace
- Tables
- Indexes
- Extent sizes

These parameters vary depending on the version of Informix being used. Generally speaking, the larger and more complex the database, the more physical design should be incorporated. See the "Database Engines and Versions" section for specific information.

The physical design is the place where all the table and index designs and row counts come into play. For every row in an indexed table, the following index overhead for *each* index exists:

(*index size* + *overhead*) * *number of rows*

For example, if your index is 10 bytes long, and you have 10,000,000 rows in your database, the index is 100,000,000 bytes. But that's just for the data portion of the index. The overhead (approximately 4 bytes) must be added for each row. Overhead can consist of more bytes in later versions of Informix. Informix is an efficient database for indexing, but disk space can add up in a hurry.

After the size for the indexes, you need to account for the data. You can generally calculate it with this equation:

(*row size* + *overhead*) * *number of rows*

Use the information gathered from the preceding equation to help determine disk space requirements. Again, be sure to *consider the future needs* of the database.

WARNING

The preceding calculations do not determine *where* the data is to be stored, just the number of kilobytes. Physical design really comes into play here. In larger databases, you increase performance by "striping" tables and indexes across different hard drives and physical devices. In versions 7.x and greater, you can also "fragment" the tables. This part of the physical design is crucial. Because it is engine-specific, I highly recommend you carefully read those sections in your Informix manuals.

The physical design can also include distributing the database across a network. It can become very complex, depending on the application. Physical design is something that can be very hard to change in the future. For example, it might require adding or changing specific computer setups, disk arrays, and more. Be prepared up front!

Operating System

Generally speaking, your choices in an operating system to support an Informix product are UNIX and NT. Versions of Informix for Windows are also available, but they are generally single-user applications. The operating system choice should be based on these factors:

- Availability of the database engine on the platform
- Speed and performance needs of the database
- User familiarity
- Ease of use
- Future support of the operating system

While you have that information in mind, I provide in the following sections some high-level overviews of the operating system choices and how they might fit into your future plans.

UNIX

UNIX was the only choice in operating system platform for Informix databases until recently. In fact, Informix was originally written for UNIX (Information+UNIX = Informix). The programs in the database engine were optimized for UNIX. Only recently did NT come onto the scene.

One of the main reasons to use UNIX over NT is that it is a well-developed operating system. It has been around for almost 30 years. With the rapid growth of computing applications, hardware vendors have been very supportive of UNIX releases and optimizations and certainly will only get more competitive.

Comparing NT and UNIX systems can create some great debates. Perhaps more than anything else, the choice of operating system can be a real source of loyalty—and bias. Many UNIX pundits are just now beginning to accept NT as an option. By the same token, Microsoft loyalists might be giving UNIX more credit for its power. Nonetheless, a UNIX versus NT debate can become quite intense.

Here are some of the advantages of using UNIX as the operating system for your Informix database:

- Longevity: UNIX has been around for a long time and is well developed.
- Tuning: UNIX allows a high level of tuning.

- Parallel processing: Although NT claims to be a parallel processing system, it is still behind the power of UNIX, particularly on the high end.
- Scalability: UNIX can scale to the high end very well. It can scale to many CPUs as well as cluster a number of computers. NT currently is much more limited in this area.
- Portability: UNIX systems are very open, allowing you to move applications to different UNIX platforms fairly easily. Microsoft products tend to be more proprietary.

Looking into the future, the UNIX market and its processing power are growing fast. The advent of 64-bit operating systems allows for incredible processing speed that will be very hard to rival by NT.

NT

NT is a very new entry in the Informix product market. The first Informix database engine for NT (Workgroup Server) became available in mid-1996. Because of the incredible growth rate of NT (some say its sales will soon outpace UNIX on the server end), Informix needed to be in the NT sector of the market.

NT currently offers the most threat to UNIX in smaller or departmental applications. However, Microsoft is working hard to change that to include all sizes of database applications. Because Microsoft is working closely with Intel and other chipmakers, database processing power on NT could give UNIX a run for the money (some say it does now) on the high end as well. For these reasons, Informix provides strong products in the NT market.

You might read claims that NT just isn't ready to compete at the enterprise level yet. You should read as many *independent* comparisons as possible. The intention of this book is not to judge or evaluate. You should, however, consider the fact that NT is very new in the database market.

Because this chapter concerns future planning, you should note that Microsoft has long-term plans for NT: It is their operating system of the future. Object-oriented and 64-bit versions are in development. And Microsoft's future is something that must at least be considered in corporate planning.

Currently, OnLine Dynamic Server and Workgroup Server are the only Informix database engines available for NT. Universal Server support is coming soon. The NT versions of these engines are much easier to administer because of GUI interfaces, though Informix is beginning to ship an enterprise-wide GUI interface for all its databases.

The advantages of using NT as the operating system of choice include the following:

- Price: NT competes well with UNIX from a price/performance aspect.
- Ease-of-use: With almost everything being GUI-driven, configuring and administering NT can be much easier than configuring and administering UNIX.

- Availability of applications: Many Windows 3.11 and 95 applications can be run on NT.
- Integration: NT applications can integrate well with other Microsoft desktop products.

Hardware

As I discussed previously, the hardware you use is in large part driven by other portions of the application (for example, database engine). Hardware includes all computers and related devices. This can go all the way to the desktop (user) level. It includes the following:

- Servers, where the database runs (which can include a number of networked servers, depending on the application)
- Disk drives and arrays
- User desktops
- Memory
- Backup devices

Hardware can be the most frustrating aspect of future development if you let it. Consider the speed at which new processors are being released by Intel and others. Here are some pointers on how to buy hardware that will help meet your future needs:

- Verify that the hardware vendor provides an easy upgrade path.
- Consider the vendor's reputation in this and other markets.
- Evaluate how the hardware will handle the initial needs of your system. If it *just* handles your needs, consider spending a little more money to handle more of the future needs of the system.

Again, be sure to consult the proper hardware specialists when making hardware decisions. Often, hardware decisions are much more complicated than you can imagine. Be sure to plan and select carefully, and make sure the hardware is compatible with the rest of the picture. Again, your choices all go back to the individual needs of the system: You must consider the interoperability of all the parts.

Network

The network is what allows your applications to communicate. The network portion of the application includes the following:

- Network servers and operating systems (for example, Novell and NT)
- Physical cabling
- Internet connection

- Modems, routers, and bridges
- Network management software

I won't go into a detailed description of these elements in this chapter. Networks are also a specialized field that must be handled by experienced people, at least as much as the other parts of the project.

A poor network setup can create responses such as, "I spent all this money and look at the response time I get!" "I hate the new computer," "The system is too slow," and "You're fired!" In other words, other pieces of the system—the application or database—can actually get blamed for a poor or inadequate network configuration.

Be sure to determine these factors:

- Number of users
- Number and size of queries (if your users will be creating many queries that return large query sets to their desktops, add more bandwidth)
- Integration with current networks
- Structure of applications (Are they "client-centric" or "server-centric"?)
- Networking costs
- Communication among different corporate offices

Many network decisions can influence application design decisions, and vice versa. For example, if a corporation decides to create Java applications that run on the server, it might want to supply end users with network computing devices or diskless workstations. This setup takes much of the processing off the user desktops but puts much more of a burden on the network. Be sure you consider all these bandwidth needs.

Internet

With the advent of the Internet and World Wide Web, many decisions must focus on how to use the Internet with the application you're developing. It is estimated that most—if not all—companies will have Internet connections by 1999. Certainly, this fact does not mean that you *have* to create your application for the Internet, but chances are that your company will be connected.

Generally speaking, unless your company needs to share data across multiple locations or with the outside world, you don't need an Internet connection for an application. Because such a connection is becoming so much easier to implement, however, more and more applications will benefit from it. See Chapter 42, "Serving Data on the WWW," for more information on how to create Web-enabled applications. You need to address a number of additional considerations (for example, security) when creating an Internet or intranet application.

Examples

In the following sections, I provide some examples to help illustrate the complex preparation process.

Example 24.1: Small System

The application to be designed will be used in an office of 10 people. The company is not expected to grow much, and the application should remain somewhat stable. This example is about as easy as it can get. But don't worry, complications can still exist. Here are some examples:

- Don't take the simplicity of the system for granted. Treat it the same as you would any large application.
- Be sure to talk to all the users and remember the future!
- After an application is created, users discover its power and tend to want more features.

Now, cut through the many stages of the design process and look at what type of configuration you might expect:

- **Database Design:** Meet with all users of the system, go through their needs, and create the proper design document. This part is different from any implementation only in size of application and user base.
- **Database Engine:** Informix Workgroup Server, or OnLine Server if some database expertise is available in-house or via contract. Base this choice on how much bigger the application and data needs are expected to get.
- **Physical Design:** Depends on the database engine. In an application like this, though, the physical design should be fairly straightforward.
- **Operating System:** Depends on the company's experience level on the operating system and availability of the database engine on the operating system. For example, if users have strong NT or UNIX experience, use one or the other, but make sure that the database engine is supported.
- **Hardware:** An application of this size will likely not need a lot of hardware (for example, disk drives), and there is a good chance it will all be contained on the same computer as the database.
- **Network:** You likely can use an existing network. It will probably need to support TCP/IP.
- **Internet:** Unless there is a real need for Internet connectivity (for example, users travel often), chances are that the Internet will not be needed. It would not be worth the expense of creating a firewall and paying for the connection. If remote access is needed, set up dial-in lines.

Example 24.2: Medium to Large System

This application will serve a nationwide company. It will be an OLTP system with reporting capabilities. It will be an intranet, an application that uses Internet technologies (for example, TCP/IP). The amount of data entry will be somewhat large, perhaps 5,000 entries a day.

Here are some of the considerations for this type of application:

- **Database Design:** Meet with many users of the system, go through their needs, and create the proper design document. This part is different from any implementation only in size of application and user base.
- **Database Engine:** It will likely be OnLine Dynamic Server (ODS) version 7.*x*. Because it is a robust product and this is a larger company, ODS would likely be the best choice.
- **Physical Design:** Because this application will be fairly large, it will include many more pieces than Example 24.1. For example, the database administrator might opt to use several different hard drives for the tables, dbspaces, and physical and logical logs. In versions 7.*x* and greater, the tables could be fragmented.
- **Operating System:** This application would almost certainly need to be on a UNIX server. Not only can UNIX servers scale better than NT servers, but the Informix products are much more developed on UNIX.
- **Hardware:** As I mentioned in the preceding sections, this system will require a decent amount of hardware. It will likely require at least one server with multiple disk drives. Depending on the amount and setup of data, the database might span multiple database servers. It will also need to include any special needs of the physical design.
- **Network:** For nationwide applications like this one, you must make many considerations network-wise. The offices will need to be connected somehow, probably through the Internet or high-speed dedicated lines. In addition, the internal networks will need to handle the added traffic.
- **Internet:** For an application that is nationwide, the Internet is fast becoming a more viable option. Many security standards and products are being created. An Internet connection will add to the need for this additional security but can also save the high costs of dedicated lines. The response time on the Internet, however, might be a big consideration for an OLTP system.

As you can see, applications come in many different types. The number of factors involved can be immense. But the whole system is manageable. You should lay out all the pieces of the system (as in this chapter) to help map out a path. Be sure to follow many of the overall project implementation guidelines in Checklist 24.1, and life will be much easier.

Summary

A great deal of work goes into creating a computing application, no matter what kind of application it is. Developing a database for your company's current needs is hard, and developing what you will need in a year or more is even harder. In this chapter, I gave you guidelines on how to think in terms of now *and* the future. As companies and technologies move forward, planning for the future will become more difficult, but if everyone on a project follows a few simple guidelines, the future will fall into place.

CHAPTER 25

The INFORMIX-Enterprise Gateway Manager

by Robert Donat

IN THIS CHAPTER

The Enterprise Gateway Manager is an important product for Informix database applications that need to access data from other databases. It allows simple, transparent access to third-party data sources, and it greatly reduces the complexity of such applications. The Enterprise Gateway Manager has many different uses and is a helpful tool in most development and production environments that do not exclusively rely on Informix products. Many application development products benefit from the Enterprise Gateway Manager, and if the main thrust of a database environment is toward Informix, this product is invaluable.

What Is the Enterprise Gateway Manager?

The INFORMIX-Enterprise Gateway Manager is a relatively new product from Informix, which provides OnLine instances the communication necessary to query and update non-Informix data sources. It acts as a bridge to databases such as Sybase and Oracle, as well as to mainframe VSAM, IMS, and DB2 data through third-party middleware applications such as CrossAccess. Any level-two compliant UNIX ODBC driver can be used with the Enterprise Gateway Manager to provide both read and write access to a number of data sources.

These data sources appear to Informix clients as if they were actually INFORMIX-OnLine instances. The communication and data conversion is transparent to the client, and the client needs to know only the Gateway Manager service and data source names in order to use this data (when authorized to do so). When the Enterprise Gateway Manager has been set up and client authorization mappings have been created, direct or distributed queries are handled in the same way they are with any one or more Informix data sources.

What Are the Uses for the Enterprise Gateway Manager?

The Enterprise Gateway Manager is a very important piece of the Informix product line, and it allows tremendous flexibility in the way applications are developed and used. Three types of uses are immediately apparent: cross-platform application development, database or data migration, and data warehousing.

Cross-Platform Application Development

If a business requires an application to have access to data in more than one type of database, there are a few ways to approach the implementation. One way is to use the client application itself to coordinate the data access at the client level. This means loading more than one set of low-level database communications libraries and perhaps several ODBC drivers, depending on the application. Another way to approach this situation would be to replicate the data from one type of server to the other on a weekly, nightly, or continual basis. A third, and much better, solution is to use a product such as the Enterprise Gateway Manager.

With the first approach, a client application—perhaps a Visual Basic front end—must be used to obtain data from more than one data source such as Informix, Sybase, and Oracle. At the minimum, a communications library for each of the three databases and, possibly, an ODBC driver for each database must be installed on the client PC. When cross-platform joins are performed, they are done on the client machine, which is most likely a single-processor PC with limited memory and storage space. Large data operations cannot be performed in a timely manner, if at all, when this scenario is present. The drawbacks of this approach are serious. The application must manage several different low-level database communications libraries or multiple ODBC data sources and configurations. In addition, it will be an application that is intensive in terms of memory, storage, and network activity, which must coordinate and join data from all the necessary database sources.

The second approach, where one database replicates all of the disparate data for the application, solves several of the problems of the first, but it also introduces new problems. Rather than multiple connections and data sources to maintain for the application, there is only one. Joins and data processing can now take place on the database server, where they receive the benefits of more memory, processing power, and storage capacity. Also, network traffic is kept to a minimum, because only the result set must be transmitted to the client application, instead of every row from every source from which a result set is obtained. The drawback of this method is the development effort that is necessary to synchronize data from several sources on one server. Typically, this would be done as a batch process, which would unload data from one source on an hourly or more appropriate basis. This data, in ASCII form, would then be loaded into the central target database. Depending on the needs of the application, hourly, nightly, or weekly synchs could be appropriate. Perhaps data must be up to the second, though, in which case complicated programs will be necessary to synch data on demand. If there is a large amount of data, and only a small but indeterminable subset is updated regularly, the data unload, transport, and subsequent load become more overhead than is desired.

The best approach for an application that needs to use multiple data sources from different database types is to use a product such as the Enterprise Gateway Manager. The client is required to connect to only one data source, because all data is available through the Enterprise Gateway Manager service. Processing and joins still take place on the Enterprise Gateway Manager database server where they belong, and no regular batch processing is necessary in order to ensure that data is current. Data will be as fresh as the most recent update. Although table joins can take place across a network rather than on the same database server, the network speeds between servers are usually much greater than on a typical PC—and this situation is no different from having two different INFORMIX-OnLine instances that reside on separate UNIX servers. The only downside to this approach is the slower data manipulation speeds that result due to the ODBC connection, which is slower than a native connection.

Clearly, in most situations where multiple databases are used for an application, using the Enterprise Gateway Manager is the best approach, and it gives the application developer the least amount of time spent managing connections and batch processes.

Database and Application Migration

When an application and its database are ported from a non-Informix database to an OnLine instance, the Enterprise Gateway Manager can help bypass several hurdles. Usually, applications such as these are moved from one database or front end to another because of unmanageable data or business rules growth, or a change in corporate standards.

The first and most obvious benefit of the Enterprise Gateway Manager is the ease of data migration. Instead of unloading and reloading all of the data from ASCII files, you can accomplish this much more quickly and easily using the Enterprise Gateway Manager directly. Another benefit becomes apparent if an application is upgraded or rewritten during the process of porting the database. In cases like this, the Enterprise Gateway Manager can help to facilitate the eventual move.

If application data currently resides in a non-Informix database but will be ported to Informix eventually, the application must also eventually be changed to point toward a completely different database type. The Enterprise Gateway Manager can be used to service the current data needs without requiring the rewrite of the communications type when the port is completed, so that you don't have to develop against the current non-Informix database directly. For example, if a Sybase database will soon be ported to an Informix database, but an application must be developed and used prior to the port of the database, the Enterprise Gateway Manager can be used. The application can be written to point toward the INFORMIX-Enterprise Gateway Manager, instead of the actual Sybase database. The data is available to the application immediately. And when the database is ported, rather than change the application dramatically from a Sybase back end to an Informix back end, only a change in the Enterprise Gateway Manager data source is required. No further change is necessary for the client application, and significant development time is cut from the application port.

Data Warehousing

Data warehouses are now a large part of many corporations' immediate plans. However, because legacy systems and many different Relational Database Systems are in use at most companies, centralizing all of the data becomes a large problem. The INFORMIX-Enterprise Gateway Manager is a perfect tool to use to populate a data warehouse with Informix data, or to populate an Informix data warehouse with outside data. In fact, although it is not the best use for the INFORMIX-Enterprise Gateway Manager, it can be used to populate a non-Informix warehouse with non-Informix data. An example is selecting from a Sybase instance and inserting into an Oracle instance if no other convenient way exists to exchange data between the two.

The use of the Enterprise Gateway Manager for a data warehouse depends entirely on the company's needs and environment. The Enterprise Gateway Manager can be used for summarizing and archiving time-sensitive mainframe data into an Informix history file if the more expensive mainframe DASD storage is unavailable. It can also be used for populating a large Oracle instance with Informix detail information at the end of each month before it is summarized and purged from the smaller Informix instance. Whatever the corporate warehousing needs, if they involve Informix at some level, the Enterprise Gateway Manager is an appropriate tool.

Products Supported by the Enterprise Gateway Manager

Because the Enterprise Gateway Manager is essentially an INFORMIX-OnLine instance, it supports all the same products that Informix typically supports. The versions that are currently supported are as follows:

- 7.10 and higher INFORMIX-OnLine Dynamic Server and OnLine Optical
- 5.05 INFORMIX-OnLine database server
- 7.10 and 5.05 INFORMIX-ESQL/C and COBOL for UNIX
- 6.10 and 4.13 INFORMIX-4GL for UNIX

Also, through the standard Informix connectivity products, most clients such as NewEra, PowerBuilder, SQLWindows, and Visual Basic are able to make use of the Enterprise Gateway Manager's functionality. You should read the release notes file that comes with the Enterprise Gateway Manager (`EGMREL_7.x`) to determine any specifics for your platform.

Enterprise Gateway Manager Installation and Configuration

The Enterprise Gateway Manager is installed in the same manner as all other Informix products, and it is usually one of the last products that should be installed on a new installation. If the Sybase and Oracle Informix ODBC drivers are used, they should be installed after installing the Enterprise Gateway Manager itself. As with any other installation, some planning and custom configuration will be required.

Requirements and Planning

A few requirements are necessary in order to install and use the INFORMIX-Enterprise Gateway Manager. One or more ODBC drivers must be obtained, either from Informix or from another vendor. For each data source that is used with the Enterprise Gateway Manager, that data source's communications libraries must be obtained and available on the same server. It is best to map out the first few data sources, which will be used to help visualize and document your installation before it takes place. This also helps to standardize your installation and naming conventions.

Additional ODBC Drivers

When the INFORMIX-Enterprise Gateway Manager ships, it comes with only an Informix ODBC driver. This driver does not allow any additional Informix connectivity beyond what is inherent to an OnLine instance. Therefore, you probably won't need to use the Enterprise Gateway Manager unless another ODBC driver is obtained. The only benefit that the Enterprise Gateway Manager provides by itself is the capability to logically group networked databases together so that they look like separate databases on the same server.

Communications Libraries

Because other database drivers are probably needed, those native database libraries must exist on the same machine as the Enterprise Gateway Manager. It is not necessary for a full-blown Sybase or Oracle instance to exist on the same server as the Enterprise Gateway Manager, but their respective communications libraries must exist in the library path in order to allow connectivity. These can usually be obtained in the `lib` directory, which exists under a typical Sybase or Oracle installation. If you are unsure which libraries must exist for communications to take place, the third party documentation or Informix technical support might help.

Planning of Anticipated Data Sources

If you intend to install more than a few data sources, you might want to fully document the server types, server names, and database names to which you want to connect. This helps you to determine exactly what your expectations are prior to the configuration. A data source naming standard should be established, because you will need to adequately derive the actual data source type, server name, and database name from each Enterprise Gateway Manager data source. If only Oracle and Sybase will be used, perhaps a convention such as `s_dev_pubs` would be adequate to indicate a Sybase connection to the pubs database on the development server.

Installation of the Enterprise Gateway Manager

When the Enterprise Gateway Manager is installed, it is expanded from its UNIX tar format like any other Informix product and installed as root with the `./installegm` command line. You should read the release notes for the Enterprise Gateway Manager, as well as for the Sybase and Oracle drivers that come from Informix if they are also installed. Each of the add-on ODBC drivers must be installed as well, with its own `./installxxx` script as root. The platform-specific libraries must be linked to `/usr/lib` or some appropriate area of your server, where they can be found during runtime. At some point during the installation, you must create a new entry in `/etc/services` to be used for your Enterprise Gateway Manager network connections. This can be simply `egm` or any appropriate entry that conforms to your naming conventions. That service must then be mapped in the `$INFORMIXDIR/etc/sqlhosts` file to a new Informix gateway instance. After the files have been copied and properly licensed during installation, the data sources must then be defined and configured in order to use the Enterprise Gateway Manager.

ODBC File Configuration

After installation, a file called `.odbc.ini` is created in the `$INFORMIXDIR/egm/odbc` directory. If you want to keep this file as your default ODBC configuration file, the environmental variable `ODBCINI` must be set to this file in order to start and use the Enterprise Gateway Manager properly. The only Enterprise Gateway Manager configuration file is the `.odbc.ini` file. Be aware when you look for it that it is a hidden file, because it starts with a period. Therefore, you must use `ls -a` in order to see it. The `.odbc.ini`, or `$ODBCINI`, file contains the details of your Enterprise Gateway Manager setup and connectivity options.

It contains three main sections. The first section, `[ODBC Data Sources]`, lists the names of each mapped data source, as well as the type of driver that is used. The second section has an entry for each of the line items in the first section. The driver library that is used is specified here, as well as a description, the server, and database names. Depending on the type of driver, certain fields may vary and will be noted in the accompanying documentation. The last section of the `.odbc.ini` file is the `[ODBC]` section, which has information on trace levels, trace files, and the installation directory. A sample `.odbc.ini` file is shown in Listing 25.1.

Listing 25.1. The Enterprise Gateway Manager `.odbc.ini` file.

```
[ODBC Data Sources]
sams_stores=Informix Driver
s_dev_pubs=Sybase Driver
SFVSAM=Cross Access Criver

[jerry_stores]
Driver=/usr/informix/egm/odbc/lib/libifmx07.so.1
Description=stores database on sams server
Database=stores@sams

[s_dev_pubs]
Driver=/usr/informix/egm/odbc/lib/libsybs10.so.1
Description=pubs database on sybase development server
Server=SYS10DEV
Database=pubs2

[SFVSAM]
Driver=/usr/informix/cxa/libdrvr.so
Description=VSAM gateway

[ODBC]
Trace=0
TraceFile=odbctrace.out
InstallDir=/usr/informix/egm/odbc
```

Bringing the Enterprise Gateway Manager Online

After the Enterprise Gateway Manager has been installed and configured, it can be brought online. The command line necessary to do this is

```
egmd instancename -s egm -l /usr/informix/egm/egm.log
```

The `instancename` refers to the name of the online connection that was specified in the `sqlhosts` file, and the service name that was placed in both `/etc/services` and `sqlhosts` is specified after the `-s` flag. When the Enterprise Gateway Manager daemon is running, you can then map users and test connections with the `egmdba` utility.

The egmdba Utility

The `egmdba` utility is used to administer and test connections that are specified in the `.odbc.ini` file. It is also used to install platform-specific UNIX users, which are mapped to data source logins. Additionally, the system catalogs, which Informix uses for each data source, can be managed and updated through the `egmdba` utility.

User Mappings in the egmdba Utility

The way Informix authenticates itself to sources such as Sybase or Oracle is by mapping a corresponding user and password to each UNIX user. Because both Sybase and Oracle use a third-level security scheme, an Informix user must be a valid UNIX user and map to a valid Sybase or Oracle user as well. The `egmdba` allows users to create mappings between their UNIX logins and third-party database IDs for different data sources. The main screen and its options are shown in Figure 25.1.

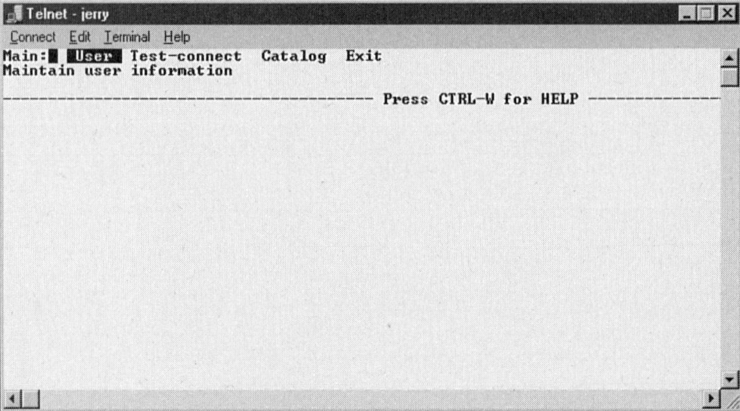

FIGURE 25.1.
The main `egmdba` *screen.*

First, you choose the User menu, and under the Add-one menu you enter a valid UNIX name. If the user `informix` uses this program, any name can be specified. If a user other than `informix` uses the program, only the current user login can be specified. You specify a data source from the `$ODBCINI` file and enter a corresponding user and password that will be used to log into the data source. This can be seen in Figure 25.2.

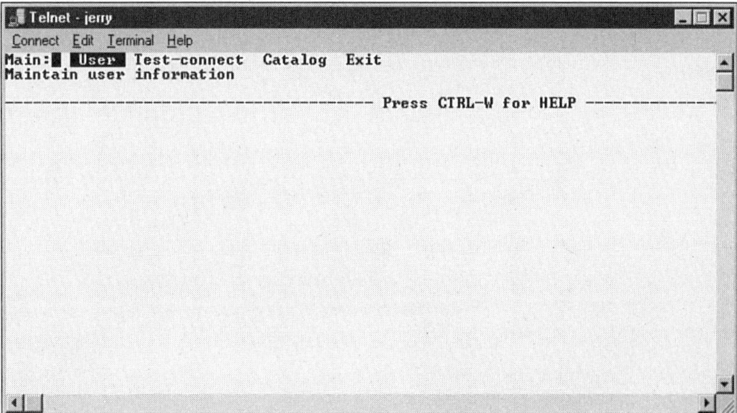

FIGURE 25.2.
The egmdba *user administration screen.*

Test Connections with the egmdba Utility

After the correct user mappings have been entered, a test connection can be made. This is done by choosing Test-connect and entering the appropriate data source name and Enterprise Gateway Manager name, as shown in Figure 25.3.

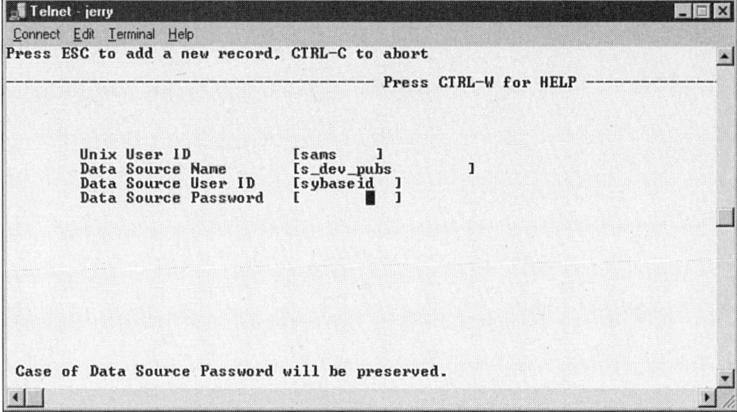

FIGURE 25.3.
The egmdba *test connect screen.*

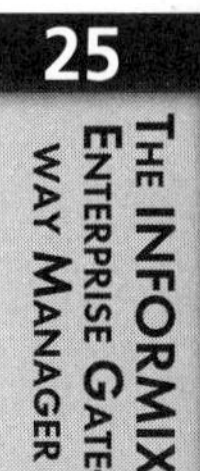

When you've made a connection, the test can be run against any table in the database that is in use. An owner and table name are specified, and if the test is successful, the number of rows in that table is shown. The results from a successful test are shown in Figure 25.4. If there are problems with the connection, the corresponding error code should be investigated in the Enterprise Gateway Manager documentation.

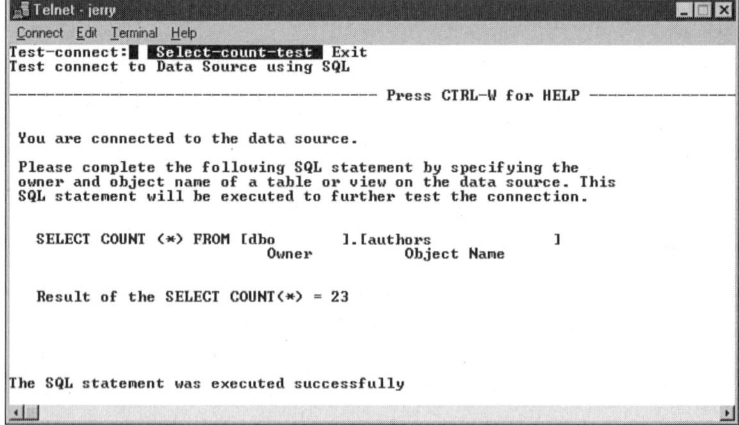

FIGURE 25.4. *A successful connectivity test to the Sybase pubs database.*

Installing the System Catalogs with the egmdba Utility

The Enterprise Gateway Manager relies on its own set of system tables, which reside on each data source. These tables help Informix to achieve some of its functionality and performance. Although it is not necessary to install and populate these tables, it is recommended, especially if you encounter any difficulty with your data sources. The main catalog menu is shown in Figure 25.5.

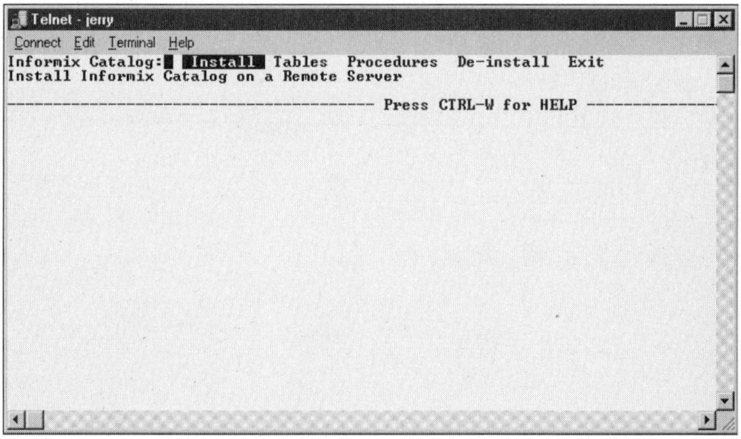

FIGURE 25.5. *The* egmdba *main catalog menu.*

Telnet - jerry
Connect Edit Terminal Help
Informix Catalog: Install Tables Procedures De-install Exit
Install Informix Catalog on a Remote Server
Press CTRL-W for HELP

This screen allows you to install and uninstall the catalogs, and to refresh their data with new table and stored procedure data. This must be done when changes occur to the data source objects in order to make them known to the INFORMIX-Enterprise Gateway Manager. In order to install the catalog, choose the Install option and provide a data source and Enterprise Gateway Manager name. When the connection is made, you are offered a choice of catalogs. When connecting to a Sybase or Oracle data source, you should install the respective catalog. When the data source is an Informix or other ODBC-connected source, the generic catalog should be installed. This choice is shown in Figure 25.6.

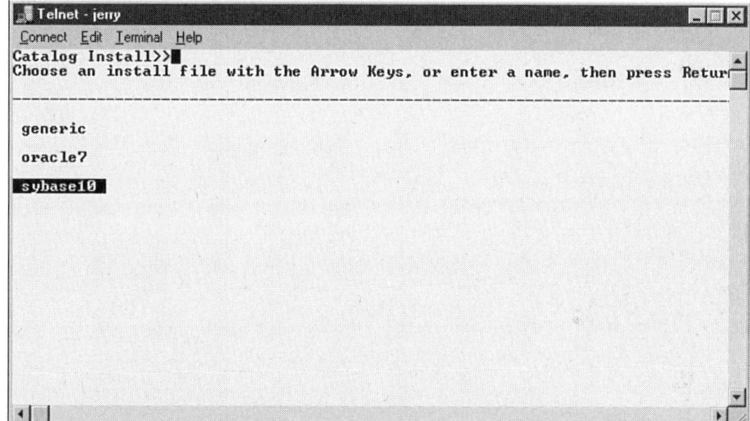

FIGURE 25.6.
Catalog installation choices.

> **TIP**
>
> On the remote database, you need to provide a user named `informix`. This user must have the ability to read system tables and create new tables, and must exist before you can install the catalogs.

After the catalog has been installed, you are done with the installation and can now begin work on your application. Remember that the catalogs must be refreshed periodically if changes are made that affect the database objects.

Summary

The Enterprise Gateway Manager is a tremendous help to cross data source development. When you use its capability to both read and write to Sybase and Oracle databases, as well as to ODBC-mapped VSAM, IMS, and DB2 mainframe data sources, the development effort required for new applications is greatly lessened. Although the INFORMIX-Enterprise Gateway Manager is still a relatively new product, it will certainly become a frequently used and valuable tool for many sophisticated database developers in the future.

CHAPTER

Problem Handling

by Jan Richardson

IN THIS CHAPTER

This chapter focuses on methods of handling and resolving problems in an operational environment. Effective problem handling and resolution employ a step-by-step process. The first topic addresses the most basic step in the process, dealing with pressure. The successful handling of problems requires the successful handling of pressure. Under pressure, the programmer, database administrator (DBA), or system administrator must determine the cause of the problem, remedy the problem, and then recover the normal operational environment. These topics comprise the remainder of the chapter.

The second topic describes methods and tools for determining the source of the problem. Confining the problem so that its impact can be limited is the third topic. Next, I address effective utilization of the Informix technical support hotline. This information is followed by a discussion of various approaches for correcting system problems. For the final topic, I discuss capitalizing on successful experiences.

In this chapter, I focus on system-level problems rather than on debugging actual programs. For more information on debugging programs, refer to the documentation for the tools you're using for your applications development.

Dealing with the Pressure

In compiling this chapter, I contacted several Informix engineers and asked, "If you could tell your customers something about approaching problem resolution, what would you tell them?" The most common response was some version of "Calm down and think." So what creates an atmosphere in which normally intelligent, competent professionals lose their good senses and methodical habits, becoming stressed-out candidates for the burnout ward?

A critical problem generally has high visibility within an organization. Users and managers want an immediate response, a guaranteed fix, and the "responsible" agent. The responsible agent is to be "fixed," regardless of whether it is hardware, software, or a human. Lost computer time costs the organization too much to allow weak links. In today's technological environment, these costs are real. They include financial realities such as lost productivity, increased costs, and ultimately lost profits. The financial health of an organization quickly affects the bottom line for staff—that is, job security and paychecks. With these issues weighing on the individual attempting to resolve a problem, the pressure for swift recovery and non-recurrence is often excessive. This pressure can cause a normally intelligent, competent professional to lose his or her good senses and methodical habits.

Because problem handling and its associated pressures are an integral part of the DBA's or system administrator's position, individuals in these positions must learn to manage their responses to the pressure. Nonproductive management of pressure can result in ulcers, irritability, reduced productivity, and burnout. None of these consequences of employment are desirable. Effective handling of pressure can result in self-confidence, job satisfaction, job enjoyment, and promotion. These consequences of employment are all desirable. You should know that you can take some simple steps to help improve your pressure-handling skills.

Prepare and Be Confident

Nothing assists you in handling pressure more than the confidence afforded by preparation. This preparation can be gained as the result of training or experience. Training can be formal classroom training, on-the-job training, or self-study. Informix offers several classes to learn the basics of its database engines and tools products. These classes form a sound foundation on which to base your preparation. They provide you with a fact-based grounding in standard, routine operations of the products. When you have a good understanding of what should happen, you can learn to sense problems before they explode and thus anticipate their possible consequences. By being able to anticipate possible fallout from a problem, you can avoid surprises that generate additional problems and added stress.

On-the-job training can occur in two ways: with a mentor or on your own. In the optimal situation, a mentor walks you through the steps to resolve situations. In this situation, you learn to resolve the problem with a safety net. Your individual exposure is limited by having another person with more experience to rely on for guidance. You learn from the experience, and your confidence grows with limited risk. You're in a position to learn the questions and thought processes used to analyze the situation from an individual who has already been through the process.

The on-your-own scenario can be risky, frightening, and dangerous. The dangers associated with making errors on your own are significant enough for me to recommend this method be used only in an emergency or with a relatively minor problem. If a mentor is not available, and the problem is serious, contact the Informix technical support line and let the tech support staff be your mentors. You can find a more detailed discussion of the Informix technical support line later in this chapter.

Self-study is a tremendous preparation tool. You can find articles and books on problem resolution, performance tuning, and debugging in numerous publications. The newsgroups on the Internet can provide information on problems others have encountered and how those problems were solved. The newsgroup `comp.databases.informix` is a good place to begin your reading. Be careful when reading this newsgroup, though. The information contained in the postings is not necessarily accurate, often contains gossip, and should always be tested before it is applied to your system. Remember, the Internet is only a tool, not an official source.

A user group can also be an excellent source of information for self-study. Attending user group meetings affords you the chance to ask questions of your peers and any Informix representatives present. Additionally, the training and discussion sessions provided by most user groups are excellent vehicles to expand your skill set.

Lock the Door and Screen Your Calls

This advice to lock the door and screen your calls sounds flippant, but the most distracting experience I have ever encountered in attempting to resolve a major crisis is having the boss constantly asking, "Is it fixed yet?" or worse, sitting in my cubicle acting important while I try to troubleshoot. During these stressed-out times, I have actually considered keeping a baseball bat in my cubicle. The bottom line is this: To ensure that the job is done correctly, you must limit interruptions. Do whatever you can to isolate yourself so that your concentration is not broken. You must keep focused so that you can think through the consequences of each of your actions.

To avoid irritating your peers or your boss, try putting a message on your voice mail with the status of the situation; then turn down or turn off the ringer. If people need to leave messages, they can, and you can return their calls according to your schedule. You can use a similar approach by posting a notice on your door or outside your cubicle with the status and a polite request that you not be disturbed unless another emergency occurs. Your peers have probably been in a similar situation at some point in their careers and will appreciate your need to concentrate. The boss is concerned about the status and expected clearing time; if the notices or voice mail provide sufficient information, his or her requirements will be fulfilled. If you are still interrupted, and you do not have a private office, look for a private location away from your office, perhaps in your company's data center. Being in a familiar environment with your reference material is always best, but being able to concentrate is more important, even if that means relocation.

Breathe Deeply and Control Stress

The first sign I notice that the pressure and stress are affecting me is getting tight shoulders. If I ignore this signal, I begin to grow grouchy; then my back begins to ache, followed rapidly by a headache, nervousness, and an inability to concentrate effectively. As a result, the more the pressure affects me, the less I am capable of quickly resolving the problem while avoiding cascading issues. Accepting this fact took me several years because I always felt I worked best under pressure. What I didn't realize is that there is a point at which pressure becomes counterproductive. This pivot point is different for everyone. I think that we all need pressure of some level, and we therefore do work best under pressure, but with too much pressure, productivity decreases.

You can find hundreds of workshops and books teaching methodologies for handling pressure and stress. What works for one person might not work for another, so you have to learn the tools that work best for you. Some of the techniques I have learned over the years to release some of the tension are very simple. I've included some of the best here:

- Bow your head; then roll your head slowly in a circle. Try to make your head roll to the farthest point in each direction and go slow.
- Roll your shoulders in circles and arch your back.
- Stand up and stretch. Pace slowly in your office or cubicle while stretching out your muscles.
- Take five slow, deep breaths. Count slowly to five while inhaling, hold for a count of three, exhale slowly for a count of five, and then hold for a count of three. This way, you can get oxygen to your brain.

You can perform these simple techniques in your work area. Don't be fooled by their deceptive simplicity. Their true power comes from their simplicity and portability. You can use these techniques anywhere at any time to assist in controlling your response to pressure or stress.

Determining the Source of the Problem

Armed with the ability to control the pressure, you must sort through the confusion to determine the actual source of a problem. This task is daunting. I can't possibly cover even a fraction of the possible scenarios faced in the day-to-day operations of a database. Any attempt to accomplish this task would be incomplete, inaccurate, and futile. Therefore, in this section, I try to help you identify the places to look in researching the problem. You can find many sources of information on how the Informix engine is performing.

Informix SQL Error Messages

Informix provides several types of error messages. The SQL error messages are received when an SQL statement is executed. The application submitting the SQL statement to the engine receives the message back from the Informix engine or INET. The messages are returned in a structure that must be analyzed by the application. Most applications pass the content of the error back to the user. A good application also logs unknown error messages to an application log file so that they can be analyzed further. An unknown error message requires further investigation into its cause. A simple duplicate index or record not found might not warrant an entry in the application log file.

Each of these messages has the format of a numeric identifier and a text string. The numeric identifiers are in logical groupings such as

- Operating system errors
- DBaccess
- Connectivity
- SQL

Therefore, all the positive number error messages refer to configuration and startup errors, all errors from –1 to –79 refer to operating system errors, and so on.

Error messages generally stay the same from release to release, with the exception that new messages are added with each release and often each dot release of the Informix products. The Informix manual *Informix Error Messages* for your release of the engine is the only accurate documentation for these messages. The text explanations associated with these error messages give some insights as to the possible causes of the problems. If the error message indicates that you should notify Informix technical support of the problem, you should follow this advice and notify the support staff. They might be the only people with access to the utilities required to fix the error.

Although Informix has made concerted efforts to make the descriptions of these error messages informative, they are often inadequate to resolve the problem. My favorite error message is `-32766 Unknown error message` *`number`*. The *`number`* is unknown to the Informix error message subroutines. In my experience, if the environment variables are set correctly and no other symptoms occur, these errors must be referred to the Informix staff so that they can use the `grep` command on the source code and find the cause of the error. If other symptoms occur, you can use other investigative tools to research the problem.

Log Files

Interpreting the entries found in the Informix log files can be critical to identifying the cause of a problem. When the Informix daemon is started, a log file is specified. Informix logs periodic messages to this file. These messages are both routine and exceptional. They can be important in determining the cause of a problem as well as in evaluating recovery capabilities. You can see a sample log file in Figure 26.1.

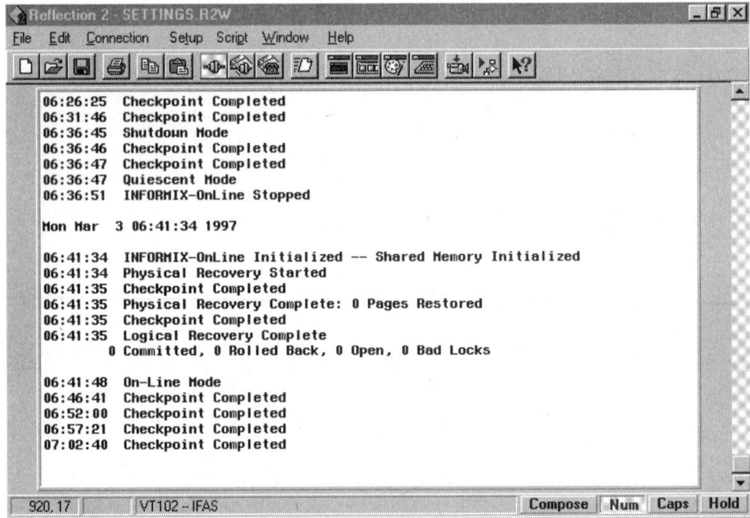

FIGURE 26.1.
A normal Informix log file during a system shutdown and startup for an Informix 5 engine.

The log file shown in this figure is from an Informix 5 engine. It illustrates several types of log entries. Each time the Informix engine issues a checkpoint, the activity is noted in the engine log file. The entry marked `06:36:45` begins a shutdown of the Informix engine. Any errors encountered in the shutdown are added to the log. The message marked `06:36:51` indicates that the engine was successfully stopped. When the engine is started, the first entry in the log indicates the date and time, as noted in the sample. This information is followed by all messages generated during engine startup. Figure 26.1 illustrates a normal, successful shutdown and startup of an Informix 5 engine.

Other normal operational messages that can be monitored through the engine log files include logical log and archive activity. These messages assist in recovery of the database by indicating when the last log file was backed up. This information is useful if the engine aborts and log files that have not been backed up are lost. This way, you can notify the user community as to how much processing will have to be re-created after operations are restored. Information about the most recent archive can also be important when you're recovering a database. Figures 26.2. and 26.3 show some examples of normal operational messages.

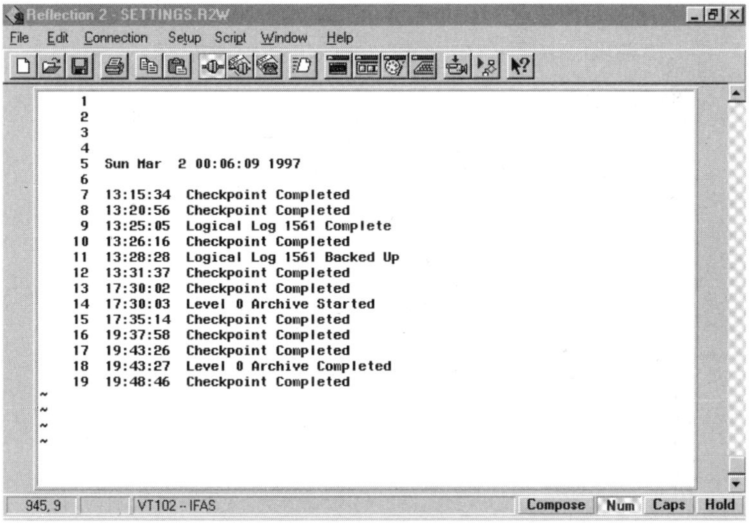
Reflection 2 - SETTINGS.R2W
File Edit Connection Setup Script Window Help
1
2
3
4
5 Sun Mar 2 00:06:09 1997
6
7 13:15:34 Checkpoint Completed
8 13:20:56 Checkpoint Completed
9 13:25:05 Logical Log 1561 Complete
10 13:26:16 Checkpoint Completed
11 13:28:28 Logical Log 1561 Backed Up
12 13:31:37 Checkpoint Completed
13 17:30:02 Checkpoint Completed
14 17:30:03 Level 0 Archive Started
15 17:35:14 Checkpoint Completed
16 19:37:58 Checkpoint Completed
17 19:43:26 Checkpoint Completed
18 19:43:27 Level 0 Archive Completed
19 19:48:46 Checkpoint Completed
945, 9
VT102 -- IFAS
Compose
Num
Caps
Hold

FIGURE 26.2.
A normal Informix log file during routine activity for an Informix 5 engine.

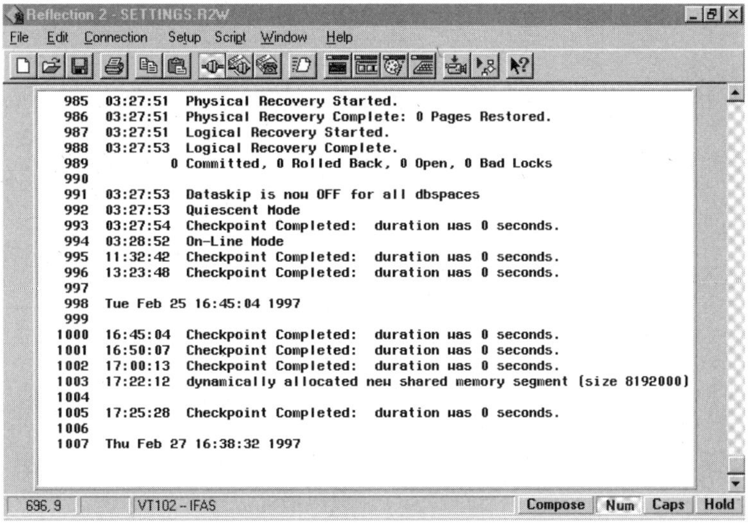
Reflection 2 - SETTINGS.R2W
File Edit Connection Setup Script Window Help
985 03:27:51 Physical Recovery Started.
986 03:27:51 Physical Recovery Complete: 0 Pages Restored.
987 03:27:51 Logical Recovery Started.
988 03:27:53 Logical Recovery Complete.
989 0 Committed, 0 Rolled Back, 0 Open, 0 Bad Locks
990
991 03:27:53 Dataskip is now OFF for all dbspaces
992 03:27:53 Quiescent Mode
993 03:27:54 Checkpoint Completed: duration was 0 seconds.
994 03:28:52 On-Line Mode
995 11:32:42 Checkpoint Completed: duration was 0 seconds.
996 13:23:48 Checkpoint Completed: duration was 0 seconds.
997
998 Tue Feb 25 16:45:04 1997
999
1000 16:45:04 Checkpoint Completed: duration was 0 seconds.
1001 16:50:07 Checkpoint Completed: duration was 0 seconds.
1002 17:00:13 Checkpoint Completed: duration was 0 seconds.
1003 17:22:12 dynamically allocated new shared memory segment (size 8192000)
1004
1005 17:25:28 Checkpoint Completed: duration was 0 seconds.
1006
1007 Thu Feb 27 16:38:32 1997
696, 9
VT102 -- IFAS
Compose
Num
Caps
Hold

FIGURE 26.3.
A normal log file for an Informix 7.2 engine.

Knowing what entries to expect in a normal log file enables you to identify abnormal messages quickly. You can now review an abnormal log file and search for clues as to the cause of the problem. You might find clues as entries in the log file, as shown in Figure 26.4, or as omissions to the log file, as you can see in Figure 26.5.

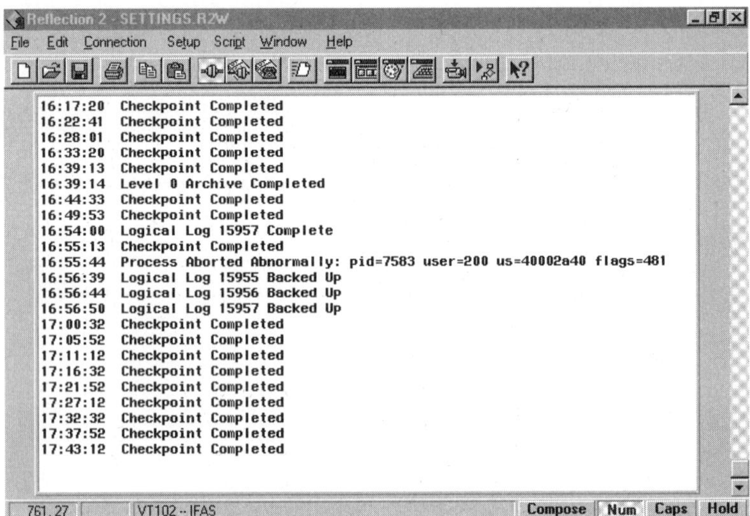

FIGURE 26.4.
An aborted process message on an Informix 5 engine.

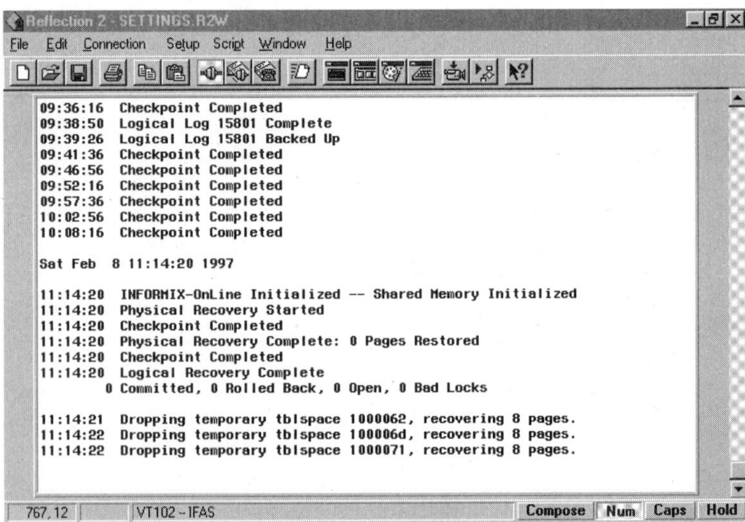

FIGURE 26.5.
A sample log file for an Informix 5 engine.

The `process aborted abnormal` message can be caused by many factors, but it is an indication that a problem occurred. If this message correlates to problems with the engine, it might be an appropriate place to begin your research. The *process id number* (pid) can be useful if the process is still active in the system and can therefore be identified and traced. The user number is also useful in tracking down the process originator. After you locate the offending process or user, you can begin more detailed analysis to isolate the actual cause of the incident.

Compare Figure 26.5 with Figure 26.1. In this log, the engine stops without the proper shutdown sequence messages. This problem indicates that something happened outside the normal Informix processing to stop the engine—for example, an operating system command to kill the daemon. You now have a direction to begin your investigation. You are also immediately alerted to the fact that you will have database recovery issues when the engine is restarted. The Informix engine will attempt to recover itself and note the recovery messages, but data can still be lost.

Log file messages are just one source of information that you can use in researching the cause of a database problem. These samples are merely an indication of a few of the messages that you can find in a log file. Log files are important and significant sources of information. They are usually the first place to begin an investigation. Utilizing the log files, you can quickly rule in or out many possible causes of system problems. If no abnormal messages appear, there's a good chance the culprit is either an application program or the operating system. If error messages appear, you can use them as the starting points to track down the cause of the problem.

INET and Isolating the Location of the Problem

Isolating whether the problem is with the application, network, or database engine is probably the most challenging task faced in problem resolution. Whether this task is done in a network environment or not, much of the logic is the same. Therefore, for this discussion, I will assume that you have the additional complicating factor of network connections. If your environment does not involve this level of complication, you can still follow this logic by simply eliminating the steps and questions that do not apply to your environment.

INET is used to access databases on machines other than the one to which the user is currently attached. This example is best illustrated using the client/server architecture. In a client/server environment in which INET is used to access the databases, problem identification can be more complicated. The problem can have three possible locations: the client, the network, and the servers. Each of these locations has a complete set of possible causes for the problem. Therefore, the first step is to isolate the location of the problem. To identify the location of the problem, you must be able to isolate the pieces of the client/server world.

The possible sources for the problem include the following:

- The client application
- The client-to-Informix communications
- The network
- The application server in a three-tier environment
- The server in which the database engine is running

To isolate the problem to a specific location, you must test each step in the process. A sample procedure in a two-tier client/server environment could resemble the following:

1. Does the application work correctly on the client? Chances are, it doesn't; otherwise, you wouldn't need to follow this problem-resolution pathway. Therefore, proceed to step 2.
2. Can INET on the client access the database using some other application? This question can be tested using any query tool that uses INET. If no such tools exist, use the Informix ISQL tool. One PC tool from Informix allows you to enter queries from the PC in a manner similar to the ISQL server-based query tool. Try a query to the database; if it works, the problem is probably in the application. If it doesn't work, proceed to step 3.
3. Try to ping the server from the PC. If you can ping the server using your PC TCP/IP tools, then check your INET installation procedures. INET might be installed incorrectly. If INET is installed correctly, proceed to step 4. If you cannot ping the server, you might have a problem on the network. Also check the Informix network/services log file on the server. It should have an entry for each attempted network login and the status of the attempt.
4. At this point, you know that you cannot query the database, and you can communicate across the network. Use the ISQL tool to attempt a query against the database. If the query fails, try a query against another database on the same machine. If both fail, begin an investigation on the status of the database engine. If the second query succeeds, begin an investigation into the status of the database used in the first query.

These steps, shown in Figure 26.6, assist in isolating a starting point for the problem resolution. They are not fail-proof and should be used with that knowledge, but they are good locators for a starting point.

FIGURE 26.6.
A troubleshooting schematic for Informix problems.

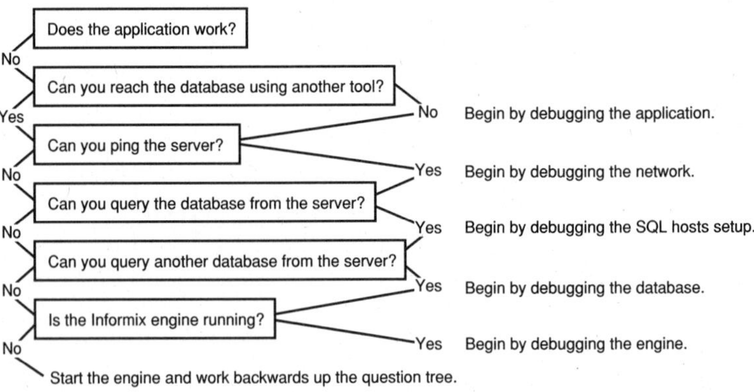

Engine Utilities

Some of the Informix engine utilities can be invaluable for identifying problems on a system. They include `tbstat/onstat`, `tbcheck/oncheck`, and `tbmonitor/onmonitor`. Each of these utilities is covered in more depth elsewhere in this book, but this discussion addresses their use in helping to identify problems on the database.

The naming conventions for these utilities indicate the release of the engine that the product supports. If the utility name starts with `tb`, it supports release 5 and earlier; if it starts with `on`, it supports release 7 and greater. On both versions, you can get an online summary of the options by typing `utilityname --`. This command gives you a brief list of the options for the utility. Some of the options between the utilities overlap, but each utility presents the information in a slightly different format. Sometimes the difference in the presentation makes the difference in identifying a potential problem.

`tbstat/onstat` provides a wealth of statistical information about the current status of the Informix engine. The specific options vary depending on the release of the engine running. You can use this information to find the cause of both system hangs and performance problems. The following list indicates some of the information available:

- Buffer statistics and statuses
- tblspaces and chunk details
- dbspaces details
- Read and write statistics
- Lock statistics and statuses
- Physical and logical log information
- Queue information
- User information
- Profile information

`tbcheck/oncheck` also provides several options. You can use it to fix or repair as well as to analyze the database. You must use extreme care, however, when running this utility to prevent accidental updating of the database. The primary purpose of `tbcheck/oncheck` is to look at disk structures for problems. These structures include the following:

- Blobspaces
- Chunks and extents
- Data rows
- Indexes
- Pages

The utility can review any of these structures to determine if any errors or inconsistencies exist. Inconsistencies can point to database problems. For example, a broken index tree could result in invalid queries or performance problems. Because this utility scans the actual physical device, it can also assist you in locating physical problems with a disk drive.

`tbmonitor/onmonitor` provides information in a menu rather than in a report format. It provides a quick view into the following items:

- Key database statuses
- Database engine setup parameters
- dbspace status
- The current operating mode of the engine

In addition to learning status information, you can also use `tbmonitor/onmonitor` to change various engine settings, archive a database, force a checkpoint, and start or stop the database engine. In problem resolution, `tbmonitor/onmonitor` is most effective in reviewing engine parameters, checking space issues, checking the logical logs, and checking the engine status.

Engine Parameters

Often Informix error messages refer to issues that involve engine tuning parameters such as semaphores or engine locks. To troubleshoot these issues, you need to refer to your system parameters and the Informix database administration manuals for your release of the Informix engine. Carefully review the error message; some messages point you to a particular engine parameter. Check the setting for your system, and then refer to the detailed description in the manual for that setting.

These problems are probably the most technically challenging to resolve. Because having the same problem occur repeatedly is rare, do not hesitate to call Informix technical support if you do not understand the cause of the error. Many of the engine parameters interact with each other, and the results can be difficult to trace.

Database Issues

Database issues are often the cause of system problems. Deadlocks, queries, space, extents, and so on, all contribute to system performance issues. When a problem has been isolated to a database issue, you must determine whether only certain queries or programs are affected or whether the entire database is affected.

If only certain queries or programs are affected, review the affected processes. Look for common tables, indexes, tblspaces, or dbspaces. If you find some commonalities, look at the statistics for those areas. If the commonality is tblspaces or dbspaces, check to see whether you have sufficient space in the areas. Also check to determine whether you have a hardware problem. If you have common tables or indexes, use `tbcheck/oncheck` to determine whether the tables or indexes have damage. If no cause is apparent, take the queries in question and run `set explain`. You also might need to run `update statistics` or check the lock mechanisms setting for the table.

If the problem affects the entire database, using the Informix utilities is the best method of beginning an investigation. Check for space issues; then check the integrity of the table data and indexes. This step-by-step process is slow. There are no easy answers for a general database problem. Finding answers often becomes a process of elimination. Be methodical and document each item checked to ensure that you're not duplicating efforts.

A Sample Resolution Process

You receive a call that a client machine is hung and can't process. How do you begin to investigate the problem? Following is a step-by-step account of a problem-resolution effort for a common situation—long transactions.

1. Check another client to determine whether the problem is isolated to one user. For this example, it is not. If the clients are on different sections of the network, the problem is probably not INET or the network.
2. Log in to the server and access the database through ISQL. In this case, you cannot run a query.
3. Transaction logging is active. Run `tbmonitor` and check the logical logs. If they are full, back them up or change the tape as appropriate. In this case, they are full, but you can't seem to force them to tape.
4. A check of the users indicates one user is holding all the locks. A quick check of the log file supports this conclusion.
5. You contact the user and find that she is doing a massive update without transaction processing and has generated a long transaction situation.
6. The process is canceled, and you discuss with the user how to prevent long transactions in your environment.

Confining a Problem

When a problem occurs on the database that impairs only the database, you might have to confine the impact of the problem. Some of the methods of accomplishing this task are limiting new users to the system, asking users to sign off the system, forcing users off the system, or disabling batch jobs. In two primary situations, confining the problem becomes necessary: first, when the problem cause is unknown, but there is significant chance of additional activity furthering the problem; and second, when the problem cause is known, but a resolution might take some time and furthering processing might exacerbate the problem.

In deciding to limit processing, you must consider several issues. Database integrity is the key issue. You must be knowledgeable enough in the cause of the problem to be able to assess the impact of additional processing on the integrity of the database. If additional processing holds the potential for compromising database integrity, your decision must be to limit processing. If you're operating under Informix 7 and dataskip is active, additional processing might cause data integrity issues by reading only partial databases.

The simplest method of limiting processing is to shut down the database. You can do so by using either `tbmonitor/onmonitor` or `tbmode/onmode`. Shutting down the database prevents any users from doing any additional work on the database. Your ability to shut down bits and pieces of engine access depends on your release of the engine and your application programs. If you can shut down segments of the application, your users' access to the system is only impaired rather than prevented.

Using the "Hotline"

Professionals do not avail themselves of the support services Informix provides to all users for two common reasons: pride and fear. Neither reason is especially productive in the business world. The Informix technical support line is organized to route your call to a group of individuals skilled in the knowledge area for which you're seeking assistance. If you have contracted with Informix for maintenance on your products, the bottom line is this: "You paid for it, so use it!"

Before you call, you need to know certain information. You need to know your serial numbers. Always have your engine serial number and exact release number. To obtain the engine serial number, enter the following command:

```
isql -v
```

The response provides your release number and serial number. A similar command works for 4GL:

```
i4ql -v
```

You should also have ready any additional information needed to pass to the engineer answering your call. This information can include sample SQL statements, database schema, `tbstat` or `tbcheck` output files, error messages, or configuration file listings. The more information you have ready for the engineer, the quicker the problem will be resolved. Also know whether a modem or other network connection is available so that the engineer can access your system. Have the number or network access information, a user ID, and password available.

Armed with this information, you are ready to call the Informix technical support services. You will be greeted by an automatic call direction system that lists a number of options. Don't panic. If you don't catch the correct option the first time, you can repeat your options. Always remember to listen to the options because they change periodically. If you select a wrong option, you can always hang up and dial back; the number is toll free. If you're unsure of what option to select—some problems may be difficult to isolate as engine, SQL, INET, and so on—select the option you think might be correct. The customer service representative will help direct your call if it needs to go to another section. You can always play dumb and say, "I don't know if I have the right option. Would you mind assisting me?" This tactic works great. It makes the customer service representative feel important and challenges him or her to assist you even more courteously.

Always remember that the customer service representatives and engineers are on the other end of a phone line. They cannot bite, and barking is just a great deal of hot air. You can also be assured that you can never have a stupid question. You are the customer, and your questions are always valid. Informix would rather have you call with questions than be dissatisfied with their products.

WARNING

When you call the technical support line, you should observe certain protocols. A 911 option is available for a system down. Do not abuse this option! This tool is very important for individuals who have production systems down and need to restore them as soon as possible. Down means dead, non-functional. It does not mean a single query is not working or slow. In determining whether a system is a candidate for 911 services, always make sure that the problem is the engine, not the network or the application.

When you talk to a customer services representative, you will be given a case number. This number will track your case from open to close, through all hands that are involved. This number is important; write it down. If you need to call back for more information, have the case number available, and the system will automatically contact the engineer currently assigned to the case. If you need documentation on the case, you can request a report from Informix for the ticket number.

The engineers are assigned times to be on the phone and times to be researching problems. If you're calling the support line on an existing, nonemergency problem, be patient with the engineer if he or she cannot take your call immediately. He or she might be assigned to the support line at the current time. Leave a message; the engineer will return the call. If the engineer has not returned the call in a reasonable time frame—say, 24 to 48 hours—call back and speak with a customer services representative. The representative will make sure that someone returns your call.

If you need to escalate a call because you do not feel that your problem is being resolved effectively, merely ask a customer services representative to transfer you to the supervisor for the engineer. Explain the situation to the supervisor. After a problem is escalated, management will track the ticket and ensure that the problem is resolved as efficiently as possible.

Fixes

The next step in the problem-resolution process is to fix the identified problem. There are levels of severity in fixing the problem. Always try the gentlest method first. The stronger the tool used to correct the problem, the more likely you'll have further ramifications from the problem resolution.

The Good

The "good" fixes are the gentlest methods to be used in resolving problems. They provide a clean solution—that is, one with the least chance for database corruption. These fixes are preferred over all other resolution methods.

If an application program is in error, fix the program. Correct the code and place the new module in production. You also need to assess what damage might have already been done to the integrity of the database. If data issues result from the error, use programs or `isql` commands to correct the database. After you correct the data and have the new module in place, the problem is resolved.

If the problem involves changing Informix engine parameters, it is doubtful that the data integrity has been affected. Begin by asking all users to exit the system. When the users are off, shut down the engine completely; take it offline. You can do so by using `tbmonitor/onmonitor` or `tbmode/onmode`. Make the changes to the database parameters. If the changes require UNIX kernel parameter changes, you have to make the changes following the instructions for kernel changes in your operating system. Then make any changes required to the Informix engine parameters in the Informix configuration files. If kernel changes are required, reboot your system after making the changes. If only engine parameter changes are required, bring Informix back online. Your system problems should be resolved.

You also might have to make changes to the network parameters for the Informix system, such as the hosts file. You might not be required to start and stop the Informix engine in order for these parameters to become active. The necessity of restarting the engine depends on the parameter changed. For example, the engine does not need to be restarted to add a new client on the network. If all changes are on a client, you do not need to do anything to the server. If the changes are on the server, consult your Informix release manuals to determine whether you need to stop and restart your Informix engine.

If you have to kill an Informix process because of an endless loop or other problem, use `tbmonitor` or `tbstat -u` to get the process id (pid) of the offending process. Use `tbmode` to kill the command as follows:

```
tbmode -z pid
```

This approach is the only guaranteed safe method of killing an Informix process. However, it does not always work. If it does not work, you have to go to the operating system to kill the process. This dangerous process is addressed in the next section.

You can use one of two methods to shut down the Informix engine. Always try the `graceful` option first. This method will wait for users to finish before shutting down. If you cannot wait or if you have hanging processes, use the `immediate` option. `Immediate` tells you who is still on the system and asks whether you still want to continue. If you do, this command attempts to shut down all users and then the engine. After the engine is quiescent, take it offline. If an immediate shutdown request hangs, go to the next discussion on the "bad" fixes. If it succeeds, go to the operating system and make sure that you have no orphan processes associated with the engine. If you do, attempt to kill these processes with this operating system command:

```
kill pid
```

If this approach does not work, you have to use a more destructive `kill` method, as discussed in the next section.

Now you know a few of the good or gentle methods of resolving problems. If they don't work, continue reading.

The Bad

The "bad" fixes are serious methods used in resolving problems. You should use them only if a good method fails. These methods can have serious repercussions for your database and system. They can corrupt files and databases. Be extremely careful in employing these methods.

You might encounter difficulty in killing processes using `tbmode`. You might also encounter difficulties shutting down the Informix engine because of the inability to kill processes. If an immediate shutdown fails or hangs, you must resort to killing the processes through the operating system.

Killing operating system processes generally requires the use of the `kill` command. The options on the `kill` command vary from system to system. To use the `kill` command, you must know the process id. (I discussed finding the process id number previously in this chapter.) Informix processes often spawn subordinate processes. Killing one process in the chain can leave dangling or orphaned processes. It is important that you follow the process id hierarchy to determine the highest level parent in the process chain. To identify the chain, use the `ps` operating system command. Be sure to use the option that identifies parent process ids.

After you identify the chain, you can try to kill the process. Identify the parent process, and use the `kill` command option that tries to kill all subordinate processes. Monitor the progress of the `kill` command, checking the `ps` output listing for the subordinate and parent processes. If the processes don't appear to be dying, try to kill the subordinate processes one by one. If they can't be killed using the subordinate process option, try using `kill -9` *`pid`*. It is a last resort to kill a process.

If you cannot get the processes to die using the `kill` command, attempt to shut down the database engine as I describe in the preceding section. If you cannot perform an immediate shutdown of the Informix engine, you might have to kill the Informix process. Doing so brings the system down hard. When you restart the system, it will have to attempt to recover. Be sure to run `tbcheck/oncheck` utilities to verify the database before allowing users back on the system. The engine usually recovers successfully without intervention, but be prepared for possible problems. To kill the Informix engine, use the `ps` command to identify the correct process id number for your version of the engine. Attempt a kill using the option to kill all subordinate processes. If this approach fails, you can try to use `kill -9 pid`.

At this point, you still have a few other options to bring down the system. If you cannot kill the Informix process from the operating system, you are down to the final options—the "ugly" fixes.

The Ugly

You've tried everything else to fix the problem, and the system is still hung. The "ugly" fixes are the last-resort options. You stand an excellent chance of having fallout problems, but you have no other choices.

Your first option is to shut down the server. Do not use the regular shutdown process, because you have probably altered it to perform a shutdown of the Informix engine. Because you have already attempted to accomplish this and failed, you want to just shut down the engine. If you are successful, the operating system will shut down in a normal fashion; however, Informix will be killed in mid-process. You must be prepared to handle recovery issues when you try to restart the engine. Be sure to run the `tbcheck/oncheck` utilities to verify the database before allowing users back on the system.

If the system is hung to the point that you cannot shut down the operating system, the absolute final step is the power switch. This fix has the potential for corrupting not only database files, but also operating system files. Be prepared for a difficult restart because, in addition to the `tbcheck/oncheck` utilities, file system checks should be run on all operating system file systems before any user is allowed on the system.

If you employ either of these two options, be sure you document what causes the problem and what fixes the problem before restarting the system. These serious problems need to be resolved immediately. Both of these options are akin to playing Russian roulette with your computer systems. You might get by a few times without serious repercussions, but you will eventually get caught.

Recovering the Production Environment

After a problem is resolved, the final step is to restore and ensure the integrity of the production environment. This step is the test of your system's archive and backup strategies. Recovery can be simple or complicated. The problem and its signature determine the severity of the recovery process.

If the problem resolution required changes only to the engine parameters or required you to install a new program, you have no recovery issues to address. If, however, the problem resolution affected the database in either data integrity or database integrity, recovery might be necessary.

When you restart the engine, it always checks its status and attempts to correct any errors it finds. It does not check data integrity, indexes, or data blocks in the database. The applications personnel are the only people who can determine whether an applications problem affected data integrity. If the integrity has been compromised, these people need to create scripts or programs that will correct any errors and run these scripts against the database prior to allowing users on the system. If the errors cannot be corrected programatically, restoring the database to a level prior to the applications errors that caused the problem might be necessary. These solutions are unique to every outage. Your guidelines must be whether the data can be scrubbed with a script or program.

If database integrity is compromised, using `tbcheck/oncheck` is the best method of attempting to recover. If `tbcheck/oncheck` cannot fix the problem, you need to do further processing. If the integrity problems involve indexes only, you can drop and re-create the indexes. If data is compromised, you might have to restore the database from a previous archive. If a restoral is required, forward recovery with the database logs might be possible. You can be guaranteed to have access only to the logs that have been backed up. If recovery from these logs does not reintroduce a problem, you might lose less data. If the problem was an applications program error, however, recovering from the logs might not be advisable, because it will carry data integrity errors forward.

The prime factors in a successful restoral are to understand the nature of the problem and to be careful not to duplicate the problem. You must think through each step of the recovery and ask yourself exactly what impact this step will have on the database. Taking thoughtful, logical steps is the only way to ensure a problem-free restoral.

Success

After you have the system restored and operating, it is important that problem-resolution success activities take place. These activities are as important as solving the problem. The first activity that you should engage in is taking a deep breath and congratulating yourself and your team. The system is restored; with luck, no data was lost, and the pressure is gone. Then look back, analyze the situation, and learn from what happened. You can learn a great deal from problems and mistakes.

One of the most detrimental activities performed after a problem has been resolved is finger-pointing. Don't fall into this trap. Finger-pointing creates a negative atmosphere and can generate a fear of progress. Progress often involves risks. Risks must be calculated and taken intelligently, but taking risks is part of the job. You must understand what happened and prevent it from recurring, but that job does not require finger-pointing. Always keep the post-problem assessment positive.

Positive assessment involves the entire team. A thorough understanding of the cause of the problem should be disseminated to all team members. This information will assist in preventing a recurrence and promotes learning within the team. Next, review the steps required to prevent such a problem in the future. As a team, analyze the response to the problem: Was recovery effective or was data lost? What new steps or training are required to prevent a recurrence? Engaging in such a team activity minimizes individual self-consciousness without negating individual responsibility. Everyone learns from every other member of the team. Each member of the team learns that everyone makes mistakes; the response to the mistakes identifies the true professionals.

Avoiding Downtime: Preventing Future Occurrences

System availability is the key performance index used to measure the effectiveness of a system. The costs of system downtime to an organization can be profound. Therefore, minimizing downtime is important. Several routine tasks can assist in identifying problems before they reach the production environment or can identify production problems before they become critical. Here are some of these steps:

- Review all system logs on a daily basis.
- Schedule periodic system statistics to run. Store these statistics to watch for trends.
- Check all e-mail to user Informix daily.
- Implement a test system and enforce system testing before implementing system changes in production.
- Require walk-throughs on all system changes. Have all programmers, systems administrators, and database administrators present.
- Provide proper and complete training for staff professionals.
- Make sure that all manuals are readily available to staff and encourage their use.

These tasks are all designed to be preemptive of problems. The best solution for problem resolution is avoidance. It is better to be proud of a job done right than to be proud of fixing the job on something that should not have been broken in the first place.

Summary

Problems cannot be avoided. The true test is how quickly and professionally the problems are handled. Quick assessment of the problem assists in isolating the cause. After a general cause can be identified, a more detailed problem-identification process can be employed. After the problem is identified, corrective action can be taken.

Problem resolution involves differing severities. It is important that extreme actions are taken only with full knowledge of their potential fallout. After the problem is corrected, the database recovery activities are equally important to the problem resolution. Thought and care are required to ensure that database integrity and data integrity are maintained and that minimal user data entry and processing are lost.

After the problem is resolved and the database is again operational, the post-problem assessment is as important as the problem-resolution process. During the post-assessment phase, learning can be shared with other team members, ensuring that the problem does not happen again. This time is also important for brainstorming to identify new procedures and methods required to support what was learned from this problem. With effective assessment, follow-through, and preventive planning, problems can be minimized.

IV
PART

IN THIS PART

Informix Database Development

CHAPTER 27

Informix Development Introduction

by Mark D. Stock

IN THIS CHAPTER

This chapter gives a brief introduction to relational database design. It looks at database design concepts and terminology, entity relationship diagrams and their uses, normalization of the design, and the conversion from logical design to the physical design or database.

Database Design Concepts and Terminology

Any database management system relies on a good database design. Get the design wrong, and the system never fully attains the required goals or is difficult to maintain. To fulfill the requirements of the system and therefore the users, database design relies on good data modeling. The data model is a logical representation of the required data. The data model is used to visualize, organize, and plan the database design. It also serves as a communication tool between end users and database designers.

A simple approach to data modeling is the entity relationship data model. This involves developing an entity relationship diagram (ERD). A database designer must have a comprehensive and in-depth understanding of the business, which includes identifying the various pieces of data that are required to run the business. These are uncovered during the user interview, or joint analysis and design (JAD) sessions. This is when users describe their business activities and the relationships between the various pieces of data. These can then be represented in an ERD.

Classes of Objects

The elements required to construct an ERD are often referred to as objects. There are three classes of object: entities, relationships, and attributes.

Entities

The first step in relational data modeling is to identify the entities. An entity is a major data object that is of significant interest to the user. An entity can represent something real, tangible, or abstract. Entities are usually nouns in the form of a person, place, thing, or event of informational interest.

Entities are uncovered during the JAD sessions. This is when users describe their business activities. Any information items the users reference during such sessions are recorded. A list of entities can then be accumulated. The key to successful design is to identify all entities required by the business.

Example entities in an ordering system might be identified as those shown in Figure 27.1.

At this time, it is also useful to identify entity instances. An entity instance is a particular occurrence or individual instance of an entity. If customer is identified as an entity, then a specific customer is an occurrence of that entity, or an *entity instance.* Identifying entity instances helps the designer understand the use of the entity and how it fits into the overall design. They also assure the user that the designer is speaking the same language.

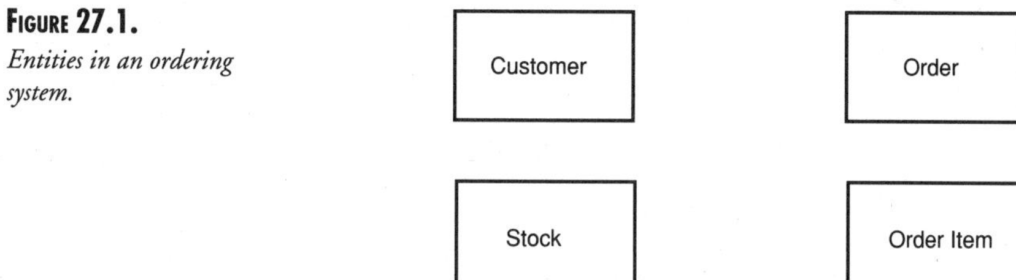

FIGURE 27.1.
Entities in an ordering system.

Relationships

After the entities are defined, the next step is to identify the relationships between the entities. A relationship is an association or join between two entities representing real world associations. A relationship can usually be described by a verb or preposition connecting two entities. The most important aspect of the relational database design process is identifying and understanding the entities and relationships.

The relationships identified in Figure 27.2 are examples that may be found in the ordering system. A simple verb or preposition is placed between the entities identifying the relationship. The simple verb or preposition located on the left describes the relationship from left to right. The simple verb or preposition located on the right describes the relationship from right to left.

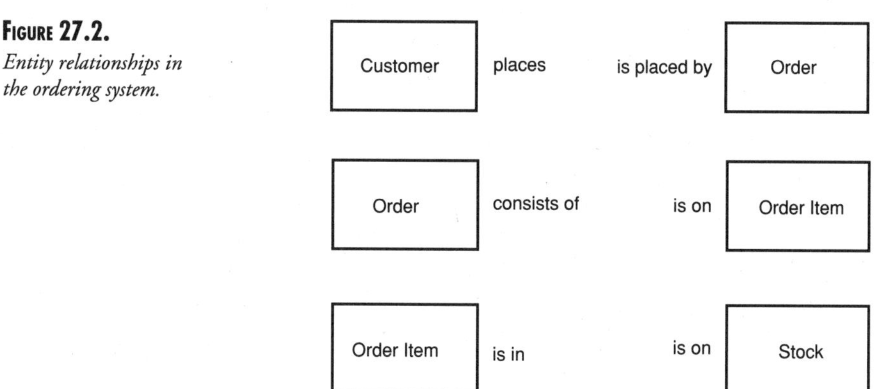

FIGURE 27.2.
Entity relationships in the ordering system.

You need to examine the relationship both ways to determine the correct connectivity. Connectivity is discussed in the following pages. It does not matter which entity is placed on the left or right. This physical arrangement is not significant once an ERD is constructed from the entities.

A relationship between entities is described in terms of connectivity, cardinality, and existence. The most common representation is the connectivity between entities. Connectivity, cardinality, and existence help define the business rules. The entity relationship approach to data modeling allows you to represent connectivity, cardinality, and existence diagrammatically.

Connectivity

Connectivity describes the number of entity instances based on the business rules. There are three types of connectivity:

- One-to-one (1:1)
- One-to-many (1:N)
- Many-to-many (M:N)

The most common connectivity is one-to-many. Try to represent all relationships as one-to-many.

The business rules ultimately define and determine the design of your ERD. You need to determine whether exceptions are accommodated in the final ERD. A useful tip to help identify the connectivity type is to think of the connectivity in terms of entity instances.

The connectivity of the entities for the order system is shown in Figure 27.3 from left to right. One customer places many orders. One order consists of many order items. One order item can be in stock many times.

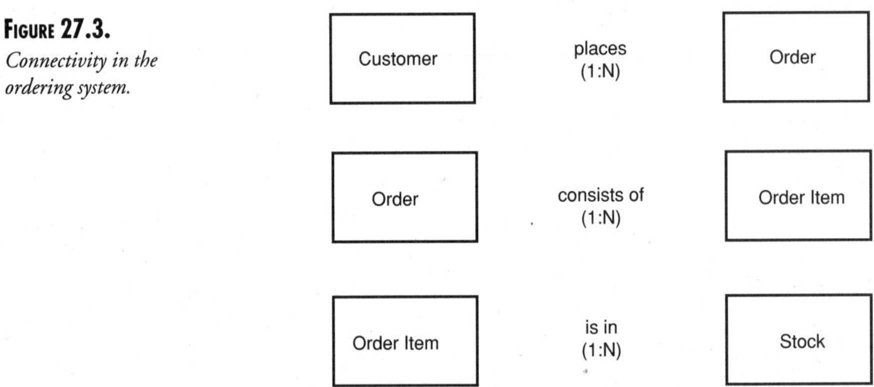

FIGURE 27.3.
Connectivity in the ordering system.

You need to examine the relationship in reverse (from right to left) to determine the correct connectivity and uncover any many-to-many relationships. Resolving many-to-many relationships is discussed in the following pages.

The connectivity of the entities examined in reverse is shown in Figure 27.4. One order is placed by one customer. One order item is on one order. One stock item may be on many order items.

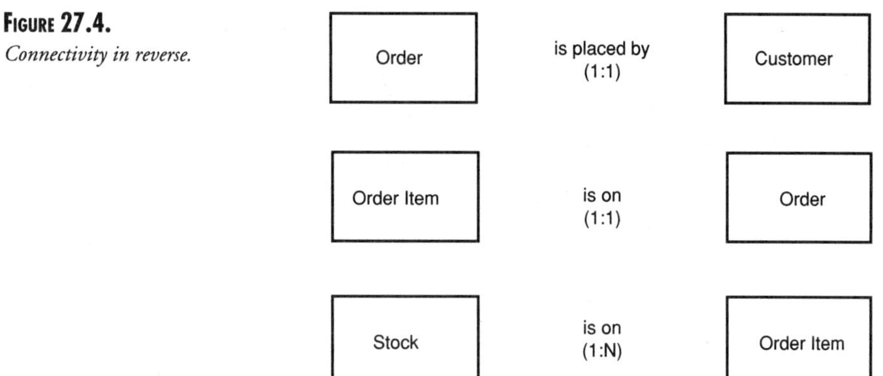

FIGURE 27.4.
Connectivity in reverse.

Now examine the relationships both ways. By combining the relationships, you can determine the correct connectivity. The rules for combining the different connectivity types are as follows:

- Two one-to-one (1:1) = one-to-one (1:1)
- Two one-to-many (1:N) = many-to-many (M:N)
- One one-to-one (1:1) and one one-to-many (1:N) = one-to-many (1:N)

By combining the relationships, the correct connectivity for the ordering system entities are

- Customer to order 1:N and order to customer 1:1 = 1:N
- Order to order item 1:N and order item to order 1:1 = 1:N
- Order item to stock 1:N and stock to order item 1:N = M:N

The order-item-to-stock relationship is many-to-many. Resolving many-to-many relationships is discussed in the following pages. The other relationships are one-to-many.

Cardinality

Cardinality defines any constraints on the expected or maximum number of entity instances. There might be a cardinality constraint between an order and an order item entity. An order can be restricted to a maximum of 20 items. Instead of indicating the connectivity as (1:N), it is shown as (1:20). It is important to identify any cardinality constraints in the database design. The constraints must be considered in the application design. The ERD becomes a valuable reference for application developers.

Existence Dependency

Existence dependency describes whether the existence of an entity in a relationship is optional or mandatory. Sometimes, the existence of both entities in a relationship is required in order for the relationship to exist.

You must decide the connectivity of each entity in a relationship and determine if it is mandatory or optional. The entity relationship data model allows you to indicate the existence dependency diagramatically. This is an important consideration when designing the physical database and developing applications.

Attributes

An attribute is a fact or piece of information describing an entity. You cannot further decompose an attribute without losing the original meaning. For example, a general ledger account number might be represented as 210-1891-0520. If the general ledger number actually represents a cost center number, a department number, and an account number, it can be broken down into three separate attributes. An order number might be represented as 100542, but it cannot be further decomposed without losing its original meaning.

Attributes are generally uncovered during JAD sessions. If you identified the entities, you can simply ask the users what information they need to know about the entity. You also find that reports, forms, and other documents are excellent sources of the required attributes.

Types

Attributes are generally classified into two types—identifiers and descriptors. An identifier is also known as a key and is an attribute that specifies a unique characteristic of a particular entity. An identifier attribute of the entity customer might be a company registration number. A company registration number always uniquely identifies a company.

A descriptor is an attribute that specifies a non-unique characteristic of a particular entity instance. A descriptor attribute of the entity customer might be the last name. A last name does not always uniquely identify a customer if two customers have the same last name. Sample attributes for the ordering system are shown in Figure 27.5.

Derived Data

Derived data are usually values that are calculated from other attributes. It is generally not recommended to store derived data in a relational database because it can impact both performance and data integrity. It is recommended that the data be obtained through calculations performed in the application or in stored procedures, rather than from values stored in the database.

In the ordering system, the order total is derived data, as shown in Figure 27.6. Whenever the unit price or quantity is changed on an order item, the order total also changes.

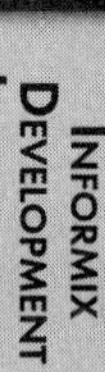

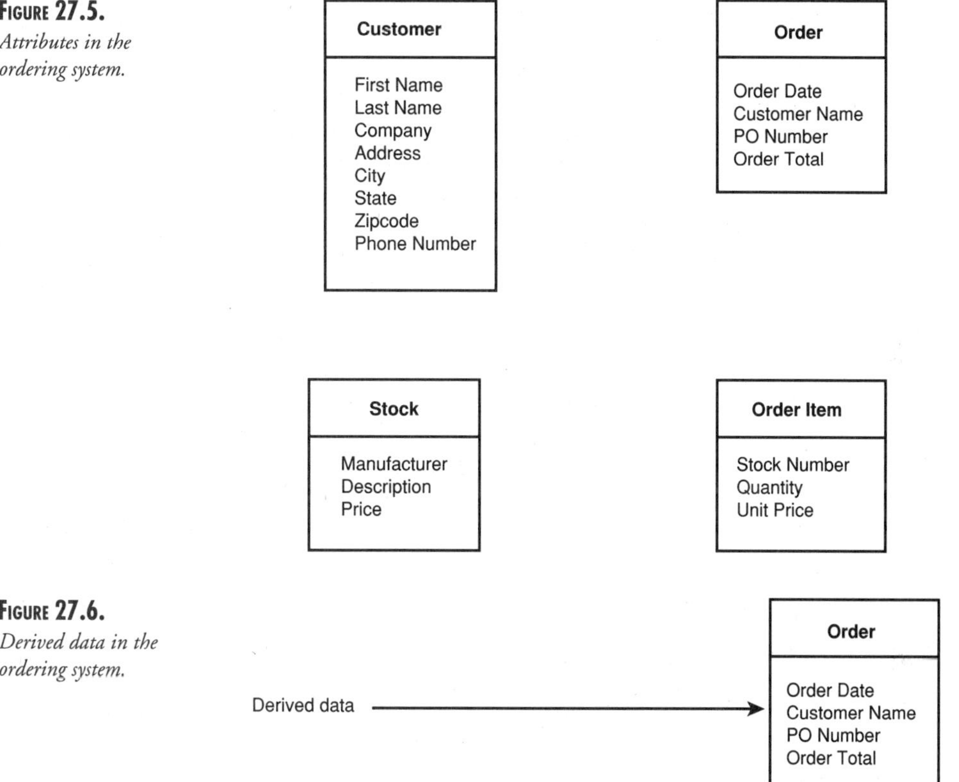

FIGURE 27.5.
Attributes in the ordering system.

FIGURE 27.6.
Derived data in the ordering system.

Domain

A domain describes the constraints on the values of attributes. You must examine each attribute and identify any domain characteristics. Domain characteristics may be a set of valid values or identification of similar groupings or characteristics.

Usually, the set of valid values can be represented by codes. Such codes are often used to represent more meaningful data. These domains in many cases result in the creation of a new entity, often referred to as a lookup table.

A sample domain is state codes. This is represented by a state entity with state code and description as attributes. The use of codes generally reduces storage requirements and can reduce data entry key strokes.

The valid list of states and the valid list of manufacturers as shown in Figure 27.7 could be considered valid domains in the ordering system. Initially, all possible domains should be documented as possible code tables. When finalized, these can be added to the data model.

The decision to create a new entity is normally based on the number of unique values in the domain. Creating a new entity for a small number of values might not be necessary. However, creating a new entity for what is initially identified as a small set of values adds flexibility to the design by enabling the list of values to grow without requiring changes to the design at a later stage.

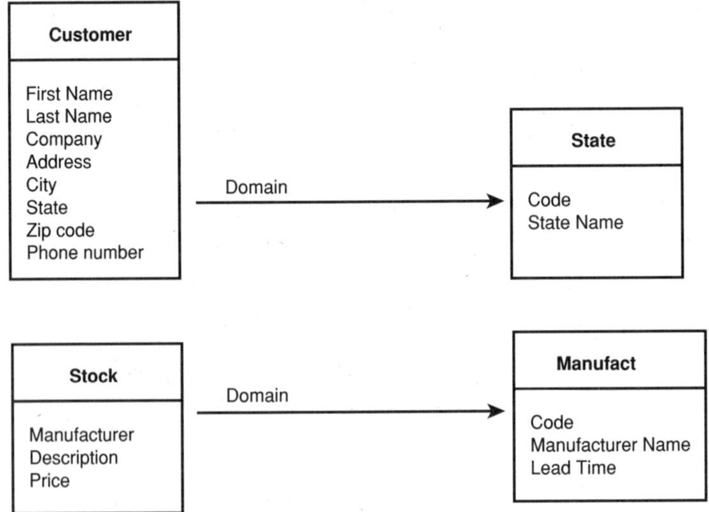

FIGURE 27.7. *Domains in the ordering system.*

Entity Relationship Diagrams

Entity relationship diagrams (ERDs) are a valuable tool to model the information needs of a business. They are used to model entity relationships identified during JAD sessions. ERDs are an excellent source of documentation for users, application developers, and database administrators. Ultimately, they are used to create the physical database schema.

Styles

There are several different styles of ERD. The entity-relationship approach has undergone many changes over the years to support extensions for more complex models.

Many styles in use today combine a mixture of several original styles. They provide for a diagrammatic syntax that is easy to understand.

I use one of the more commonly used styles. An entity is represented by a squared box. The entity name is placed inside the box in singular, lowercase form. A relationship is depicted by a single solid line drawn between two entities.

A dotted line drawn between two entities indicates that the existence of the relationship is optional. In most cases, the business rules of the enterprise determine the relationship's existence. If a relationship is optional, it is important to denote that on the diagram.

The use of crows feet at either end of a relationship implies a one-to-many relationship. A relationship depicted by a single line with no crows feet implies a one-to-one relationship. This is illustrated in Figure 27.8.

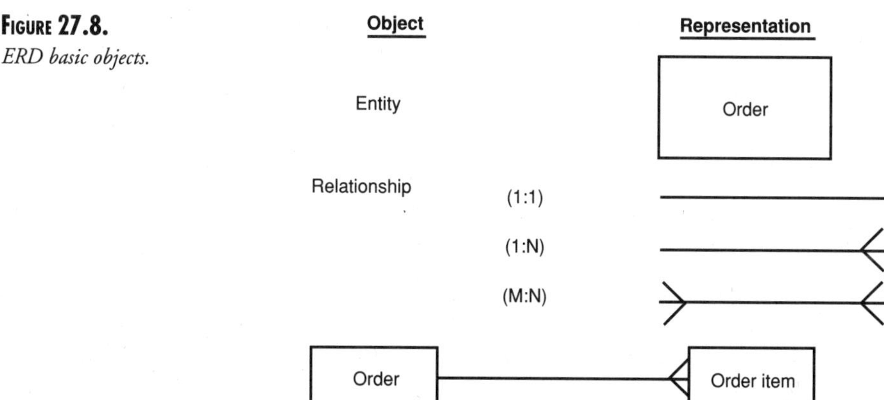

FIGURE 27.8.
ERD basic objects.

The ERD for the ordering system is shown in Figure 27.9.

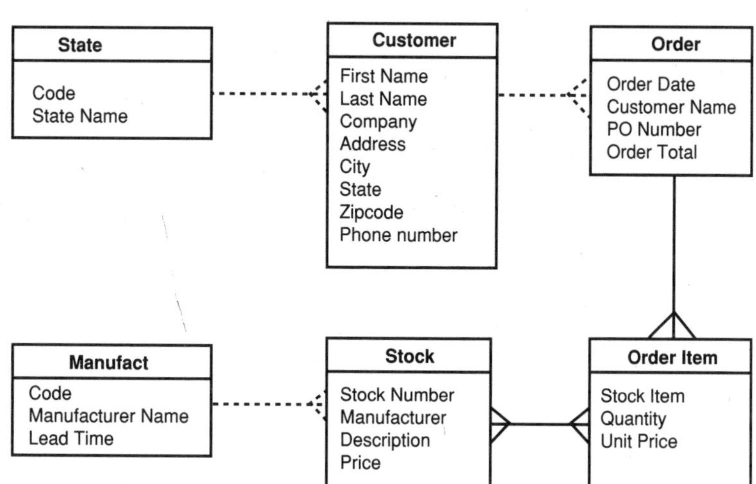

FIGURE 27.9.
The ordering system ERD.

Several different styles of ERD can be used in a data model. Select and standardize on the style you find most useful for your requirements. You can even add some of your own extensions to the syntax to aid your development efforts. Some alternative styles are shown in Figure 27.10.

FIGURE 27.10.
ERD alternative objects.

Connectivity	Alternative Styles		
1:1			1 1
1:N			1 N
M:N			M N
Mandatory			1 1
Optional			1 N

Resolving One-to-One Relationships

One-to-one relationships are very rare. Probably 90 percent of relationships are one-to-many. When a one-to-one relationship is detected, one entity is usually just a set of attributes that can be merged with the other entity.

In Figure 27.11, the entity order could be expanded to incorporate the attributes of the entity shipping information. This results in the one-to-many relationship depicted in Figure 27.12.

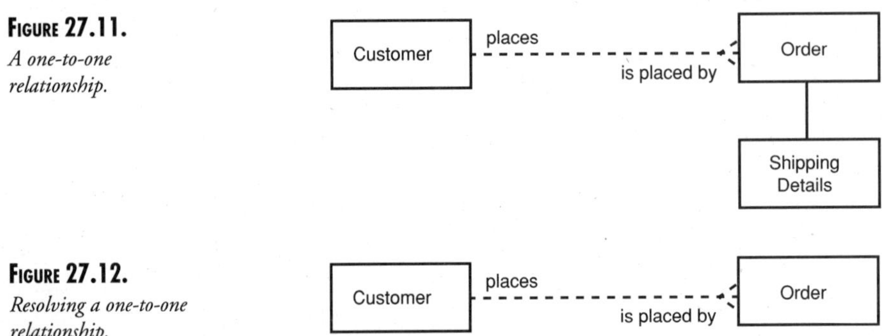

FIGURE 27.11.
A one-to-one relationship.

FIGURE 27.12.
Resolving a one-to-one relationship.

Resolving Many-to-Many Relationships

One of the strengths of ERDs is that they allow you to detect and resolve many-to-many relationships.

The key to resolving many-to-many relationships is to separate the two entities and create two one-to-many relationships with a third intersect entity. This reduces complexity and confusion in both the design and the application development process.

The first ERD for the ordering system contained a many-to-many relationship between the order item and stock entities. An order item is in stock many times and a stock item can be ordered many times.

To resolve the many-to-many relationship, you can separate the two entities and create two one-to-many relationships with a third intersect entity. This new entity intersect entity is shown in Figure 27.13.

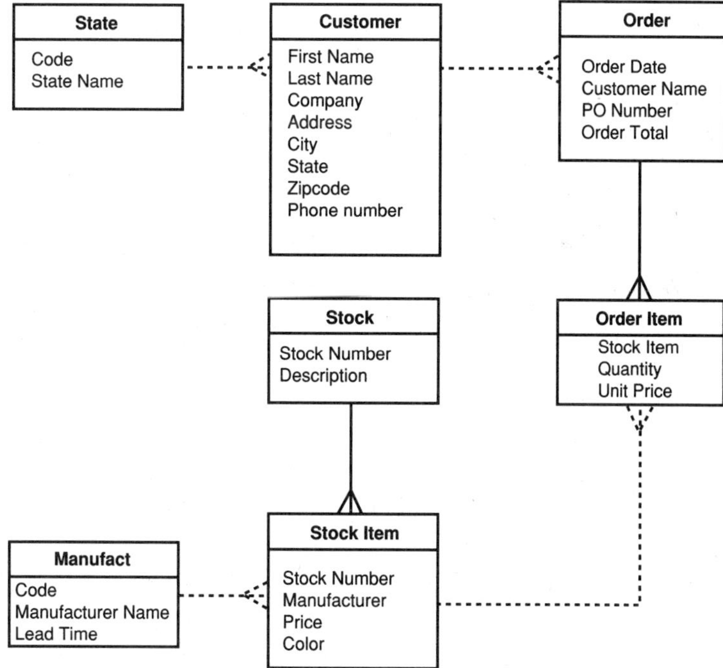

FIGURE 27.13.
Resolving many-to-many relationships in the ordering system.

The many-to-many relationship that existed between the order item and the stock entities was resolved by creating an intersect entity, stock item, and two one-to-many relationships. The new stock entity contains static (non-changing) information about a stock item. The stock item name does not change regardless of the number of those items in stock.

The stock item entity is the intersect entity and contains detailed information about each item in stock. Regardless of whether there are one or more items in stock, the stock item entity contains information about the particular item: the manufacturer, the price, and the color.

The stock entity can have many stock items, and a stock item can be listed on many order items.

Entity Instance

Figure 27.14 shows a diagram representing an entity instance in the ordering system. It is very useful to diagram an entity instance representing the attributes. The entity instance diagram can help verify the model that represents the data requirements. It can verify the relationships between entities.

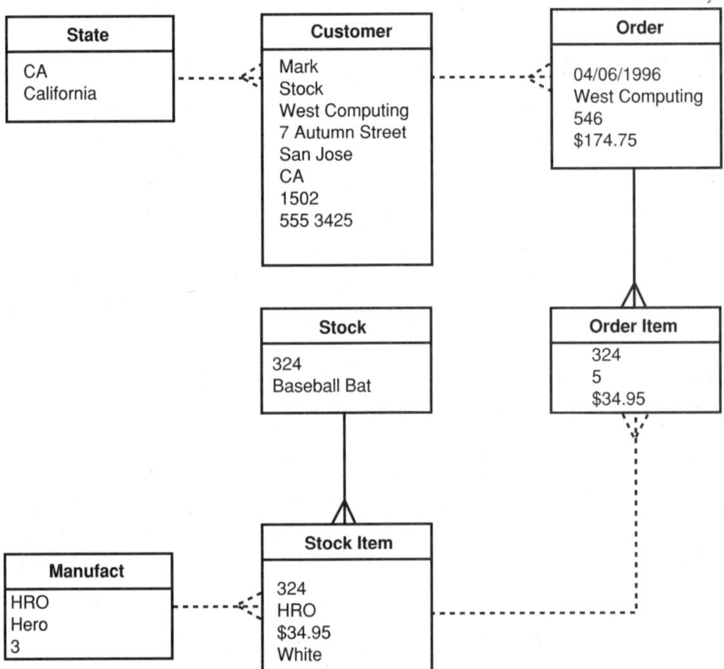

FIGURE 27.14.
Entity instance for the ordering system.

Primary Key

All entities should have exactly one primary key. The primary key must be an attribute or combination of attributes that uniquely identifies an entity instance. Identifier attributes are generally used for primary keys because they meet the unique constraint requirements. A primary key must exist for all entity instances. A unique constraint is enforced for every primary key.

You can enforce primary key rules through the database definition when the table is created. These concepts are covered later in the book.

Special Primary Keys

If you cannot identify an attribute that adheres to the unique constraint requirement, you should consider the use of a special primary key.

A composite key is a key using two or more attributes. Using composite keys increases uniqueness.

You can use a system-generated key to guarantee uniqueness. You can add a new attribute with a serial data type. The unique value assigned to the attribute is automatically generated by the database engine.

Primary Key Rules

Each primary key must adhere to the following rules:

- Unique
- Not null
- Cannot be updated
- Does not influence row or column order
- Does not influence row access

NOTE

It is not recommended to use long character strings for performance reasons.

The primary keys for the ordering system entities are shown in Figure 27.15. A primary key should be a numeric data type (integer, smallint, or serial) or short character codes (char). It is not recommended to use long character strings or composite keys that consist of several long character strings for performance reasons.

The order, order item, stock, and stock item entities did not have attributes that meet the qualifications for a primary key. A system-generated key was added for each entity. A new attribute with a serial data type was added to each entity.

The customer entity possessed an identifier attribute—the customer name. However, it is not recommended to use long character strings as a primary key. A system-generated key was added to the customer entity.

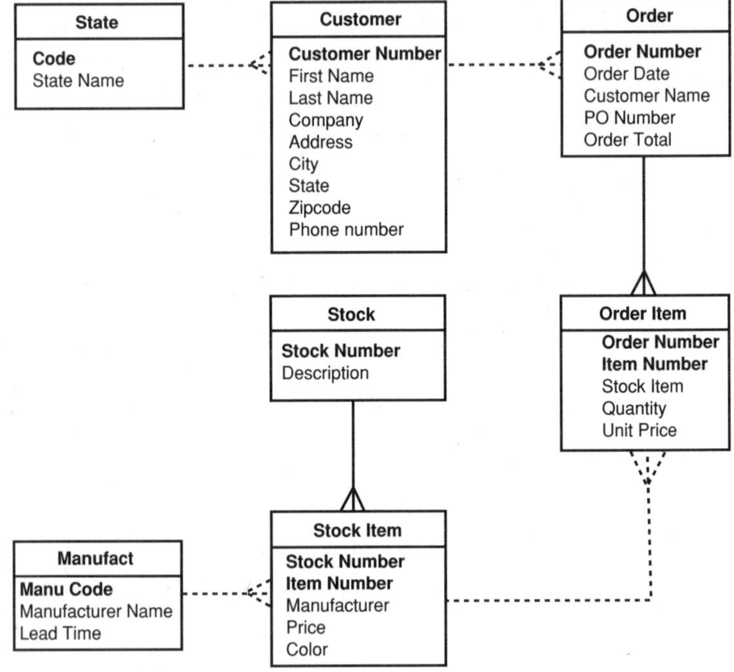

FIGURE 27.15.
Primary keys for the ordering system. (Primary keys are shown in bold.)

Foreign Key

A foreign key is used to establish the relationship between entities. A foreign key must reference an existing primary key in the associated entity. There may be multiple foreign keys in an entity if the entity is related to multiple entities.

Foreign keys can be null, although this is not recommended to enforce referential constraints. Foreign keys can contain duplicates and can be changed.

You can enforce the primary key and foreign key association through the database definition using the `CREATE TABLE` statement. This concept is covered later in the book. The foreign keys for the ordering system are shown in Figure 27.16.

> **NOTE**
>
> In one-to-many relationships, the many entity usually contains the foreign keys.

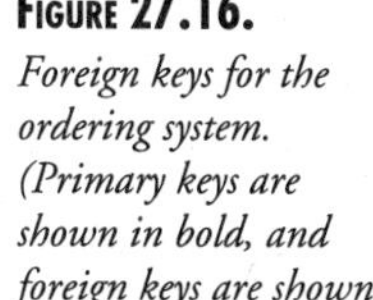

FIGURE 27.16.
Foreign keys for the ordering system. (Primary keys are shown in bold, and foreign keys are shown in italic.)

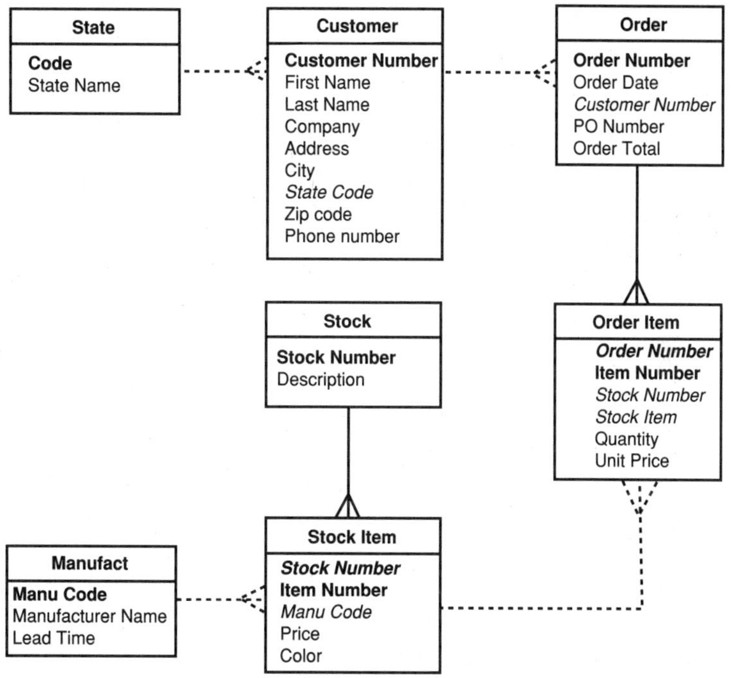

Special Relationships

Three special types of relationships require consideration when designing the data model.

Complex

A complex relationship is an association among three or more entities. It requires all three (or more) entities to be present for the relationship to exist. To resolve all complex relationships, reclassify them as an entity, related through binary relationships to each of the original entities.

Complex relationships are difficult to evaluate and define. They are difficult to diagram and sometimes impossible to translate directly into a database schema.

An example of a complex relationship is depicted in Figure 27.17. This shows the sale of a cell phone by a salesperson to a customer. In order for the relationship to exist, all three entities must be represented.

The complex relationship can be simplified by defining a new entity called Sale. As shown in Figure 27.18, Sale is related through simple relationships to each of the original entities: Salesperson, Cell Phone, and Customer.

FIGURE 27.17.
Complex relationship.

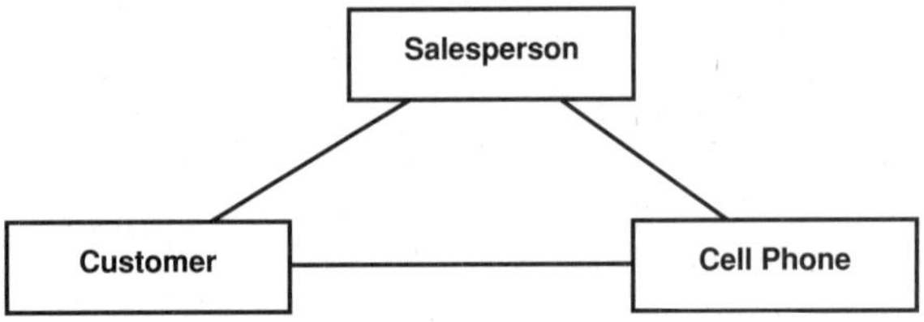

FIGURE 27.18.
Resolving complex relationships.

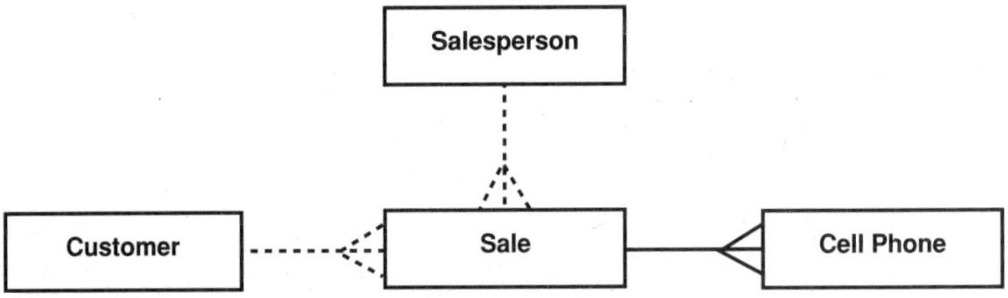

Recursive

A recursive relationship is an association between occurrences of the same entity type. An entity can be related to itself. This type of relationship is also known as a self-referencing or looped association.

Recursive relationships do not occur frequently but are very powerful for defining organization structures and bill-of-materials (BOM) requirements. Examples include

- An employee manages many employees
- A part is composed of many parts

You should be very careful to identify these related entities as the same actual entity. As shown in Figure 27.19, the sample entities supervisor and employee are identified during the JAD sessions.

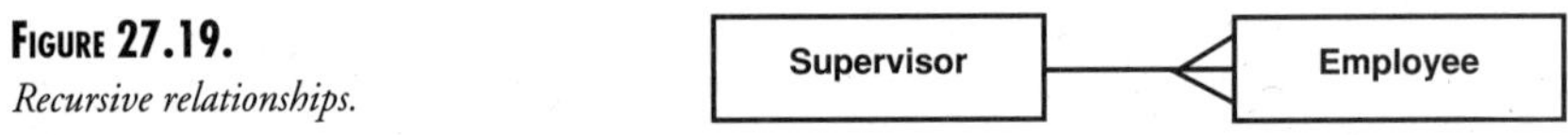

FIGURE 27.19.
Recursive relationships.

With a little more information about the usage of these entities, this initial design can be reduced to a single entity with a self-join as shown in Figure 27.20.

FIGURE 27.20.
Resolving recursive relationships.

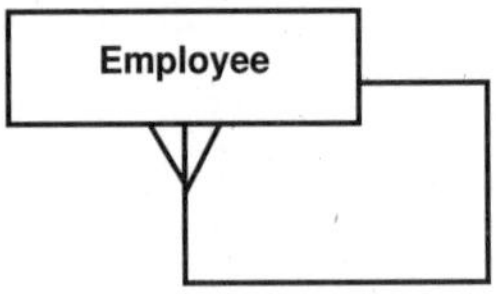

Redundant

Redundant relationships are usually two or more relationships that are used to represent the same concepts. You should analyze redundant relationships very carefully and eliminate them from your data model.

Two or more relationships between the same two entities are acceptable as long as the two relationships have different meanings.

There are several reasons for eliminating redundant relationships:

- Redundant relationships add complexity.
- Redundant relationships result in unnormalized relations when transforming into a relational database schema.
- Redundant relationships might lead to incorrect placement of attributes.
- Application developers and analysts might interpret redundant relationships as non-redundant and not take both entities into consideration in data manipulation operations.

The example in Figure 27.21 assumes that the postal address and physical address entities contain the same attributes. The postal address entity and physical address entity represent the same entity participating in different relationships with the company.

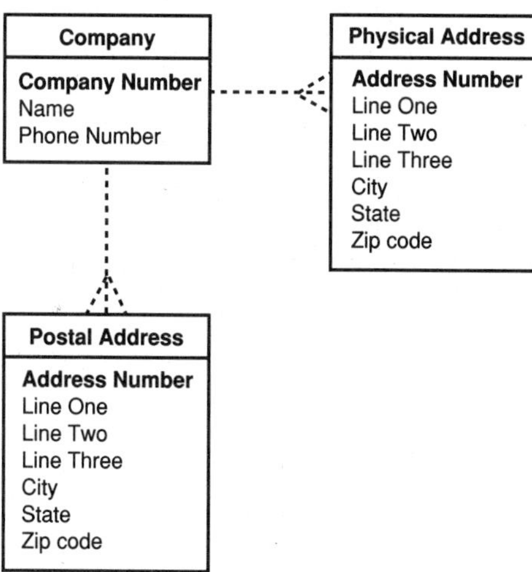

FIGURE 27.21.
Redundant relationships.

A new entity, company address, was added to the model, and the address and company entities are related to it through two simple relationships. These new relationships are shown in Figure 27.22.

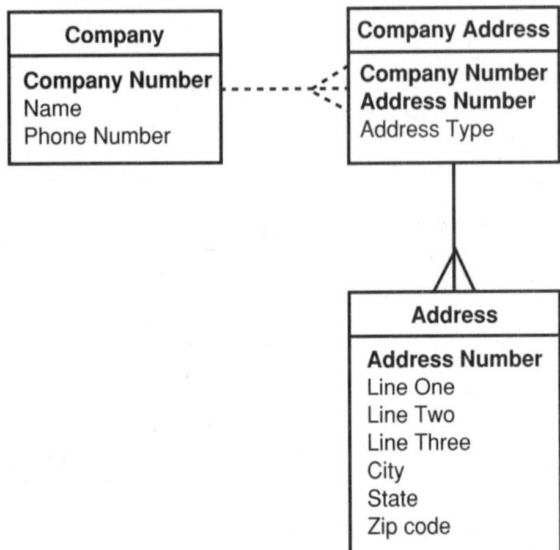

FIGURE 27.22.
Resolving redundant relationships.

Normalization

Normalization is a formal approach to applying a set of rules used in associating attributes with entities. The set of rules is designed to help the designer convert the logical entities into a conceptual model for the database design.

During normalization, the structure of the logical model that may translate into undesirable properties in the physical model is examined and resolved.

The normalization process is used to ensure that the conceptual model of the database will work. An unnormalized model can be implemented, but it will present problems in application development and data manipulation operations.

Benefits

A normalized model is more flexible and better able to meet a wide range of end-user application requirements with minimal structural change. New applications are less likely to force a database design change.

Normalization reduces redundant data, minimizing the amount of disk storage required to store the data and making it easier to maintain accurate and consistent data.

A simple and logical design can result in increased programmer productivity. Normalization reduces the maintenance costs for an application because changes to the application are easier.

The benefits gained from normalization can be summarized as follows:

- Greater flexibility
- Ensures attributes are placed in proper tables

- Reduces data redundancy
- Increases programmer productivity
- Decreases application maintenance costs
- Maximizes stability of the data model

Although there are benefits, do not over-normalize. A normalized data model might not meet all design objectives. You can use selective denormalization in some areas of the data model to increase performance.

Rules

Normalization includes several rules for converting the logical design to a more effective physical design. These rules are referred to as the normal forms.

There are several normal forms used to organize data. The first three forms—first normal form (1NF), second normal form (2NF), and third normal form (3NF)—are the most commonly used.

Each normal form constrains the data to be more organized than the previous form. For this reason, each normal form must be achieved in turn before the next normal form can be applied.

First Normal Form

An entity relationship is in first normal form if there are no repeating groups (domains). Each entity must have a fixed number of single-valued attributes.

Figure 27.23 shows an order entity that is not in first normal form because it contains attributes that repeat. The item and quantity information appears up to five times, depending on the number of items in an order.

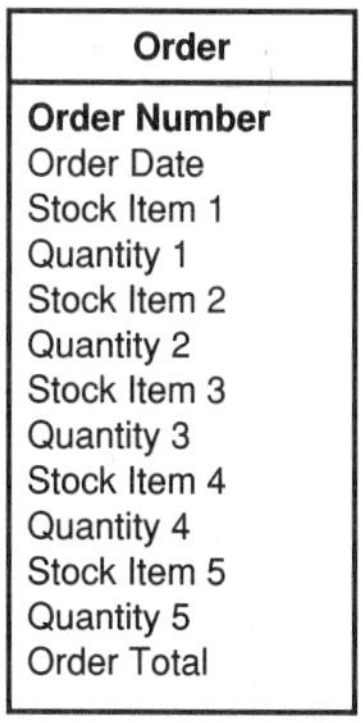

FIGURE 27.23.
Before first normal form.

Order
Order Number
Order Date
Stock Item 1
Quantity 1
Stock Item 2
Quantity 2
Stock Item 3
Quantity 3
Stock Item 4
Quantity 4
Stock Item 5
Quantity 5
Order Total

In this example, the maximum number of items that can be ordered is five. If a customer wants to order 10 items, the database structure cannot accommodate it and must be changed. A table that is not in first normal form is less flexible and can also waste disk storage space. If a customer orders only one item, this design still stores five items, regardless.

Finally, a table not in first normal form makes data searches more difficult. Finding orders that contain a particular item in this example requires a search on all five repeats of the item attribute.

To put this order entity into first normal form, separate the entity into two. The first entity removes the repeating groups. The second entity has a single copy of the attribute group, together with a new primary key and a foreign key reference to the first entity. This leaves you with the example shown in Figure 27.24.

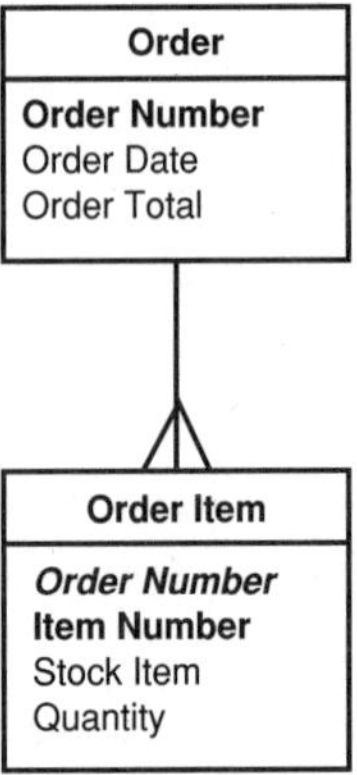

FIGURE 27.24.
After first normal form.

Notice that the restriction on the number of order items was removed. Only items that are ordered now use disk storage space. Also, searching for a particular item on order requires a search on only one attribute.

Second Normal Form

An entity relationship is in second normal form if it is in first normal form and all its attributes depend on the whole primary key. Remember that the primary key is a minimal set of attributes that uniquely identify an entity instance. Second normal form requires that every attribute must be fully functionally dependent on the primary key. Functional dependence means there is a link between the values in the different attributes.

Figure 27.25 shows that the attributes stock item and quantity depend on order number and item number, which form the primary key. The order date attribute, however, depends on the order number only, which forms only part of the primary key. This means the value of order date can be determined for a particular row if the value of order number is known, regardless of the value of item number.

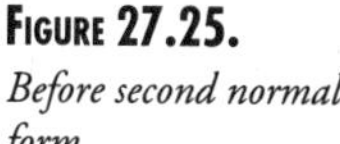

FIGURE 27.25.
Before second normal form.

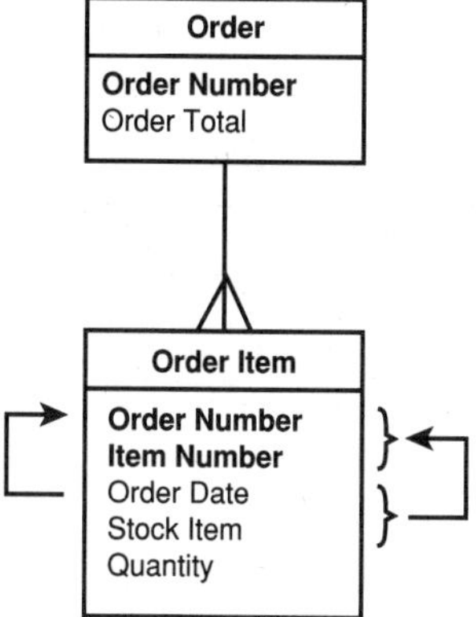

To convert the order item entity to second normal form, you need to remove the order date attribute, as shown in Figure 27.26. The appropriate table to place this attribute is the order table because the primary key for this entity is order number alone and order date depends on only order number. If the value of paid date is changed now, it must be changed in only one place, regardless of how many items are ordered.

FIGURE 27.26.
After second normal form.

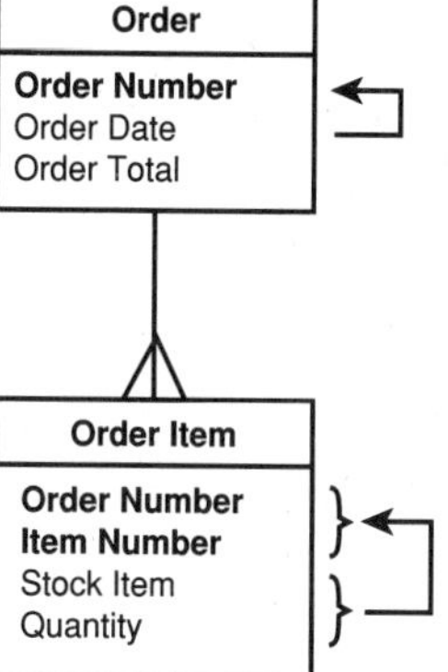

Third Normal Form

An entity relationship is in third normal form if it is in second normal form and all its attributes depend on the whole primary key and nothing but the primary key. This eliminates attributes that not only depend on the whole primary key but also on other non-key attributes, which in turn depend on the whole primary key. This is known as transitive (indirect) dependence.

An example of transitive dependence is shown in Figure 27.27. In this example, unit price is not only dependent on the primary key but on stock number and manu code as well. This leads to the following problems:

- A unit price cannot be entered unless the stock item is ordered.
- A unit price is lost if all orders containing the stock item are deleted.
- Unit price information is redundant because the same stock item has a unit price entered whenever it is ordered.
- If the unit price for a stock item changes, each order on which the item appears must be updated.

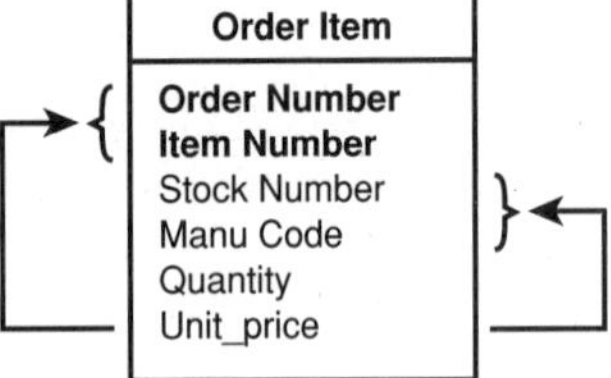

FIGURE 27.27.
Before third normal form.

To convert the order entity to third normal form, the unit price attribute must be moved to another entity. A new entity was created called Stock, as shown in Figure 27.28.

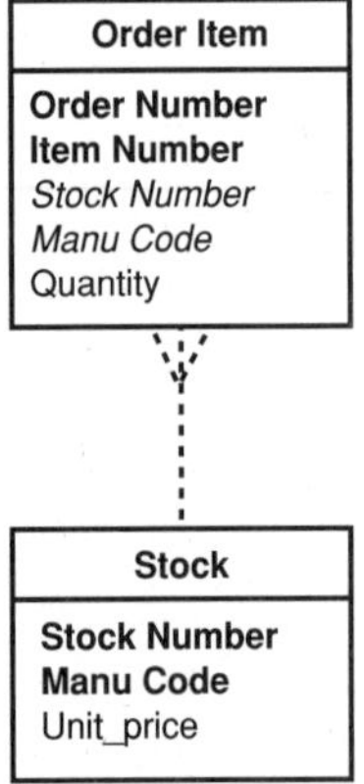

FIGURE 27.28.
After third normal form.

Because unit price is also dependent on stock number and manu code, these are copied from the order entity to form the primary key for the new Stock entity.

This new design has the following advantages:

- The unit price can be entered for any stock item, even if there are no orders for it.
- If all orders containing a particular stock item are deleted, the unit price is not lost.

- If the unit price changes, it must be changed in only one place.
- There is no redundancy because unit price exists once per stock item, thus reducing disk storage requirements.

NOTE

The way to remember the first three normal forms is to remember the saying, "The key, the whole key, and nothing but the key."

Applying these concepts to the ordering system gives the design shown in Figure 27.29. Notice that the contact details were identified as a repeating group, even though only one set was stored. You must be careful to identify such groups, even though they may appear as a group of one. The JAD sessions should identify the requirements, and if only one contact is ever required, then this normalization might not be necessary. Of course, adding this flexibility at the design stage does no harm.

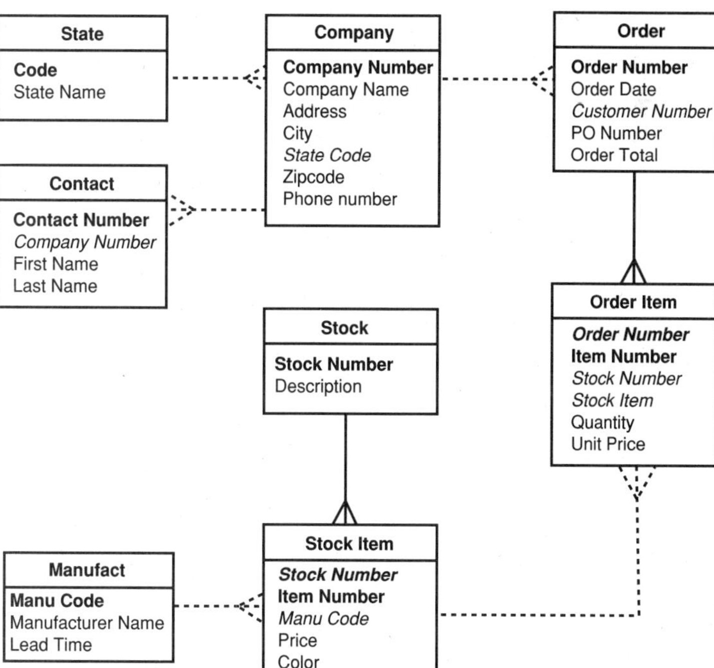

FIGURE 27.29.
The ordering system in third normal form. (Primary keys are shown in bold, and foreign keys are shown in italic.)

Logical to Physical Design

The logical data model should usually be a platform-independent design. This means that you should be able to use the design on any hardware platform with any operating system. You should be able to implement it with any relational database management system (RDBMS) and application development tools.

When considering the physical design, as its name suggests, you need to consider the physical aspects of implementing the design. You need to consider the terminology used by Informix, the different data types available, the various design concepts available, and how they are implemented.

Logical Versus Physical Terminology

Table 27.1 illustrates the use of logical versus physical terminology in relational database design.

Table 27.1. Logical versus physical terminology.

Logical	*Physical*
ER data model	Database schema
Entities	Tables
Attributes	Columns
Relationships	Primary and foreign keys
Entity instance	Row

A schema is the physical definition for the tables in the database. A table is a two-dimensional representation of columns and rows.

When converting relational data models to the Structured Query Language (SQL), you use the following constructs:

- Attribute name
- Data type
- Null values
- Primary keys
- Foreign keys
- Unique (non-duplicating)

When defining attribute names, it is a good practice to establish naming conventions. Generally, you should use unique and meaningful names. Avoid using synonyms (different names with the same meaning) and homonyms (same name with different meanings).

Assigning Data Types

You must assign a data type to each attribute. The data type indicates the kind of information you intend to store in that attribute. The general data types to consider are listed in Table 27.2.

Table 27.2. General data types.

Data Type	*Description*
Character	Any combination of letters, numbers, or symbols
Numeric	Numbers only
System assigned	Sequential numbers assigned by the system
Date	Calendar dates
Money	Currency amount
Date-time	Calendar dates with time of day
Interval	Intervals of time
Variable length	Variable-length character values
Binary large object (BLOB)	Large text or binary-based information

When selecting appropriate data types, you need to consider the data types available with Informix. These general data types relate to the Informix data types as detailed in Table 27.3.

Table 27.3. Informix data types.

General Data Type	*Informix Data Type*
Character	`char`
Numeric	`integer, smallint, float, smallfloat, decimal`
System assigned	`serial`
Date	`date`
Money	`money`
Date-time	`datetime`
Interval	`interval`
	OnLine Database Engine Only
Variable length	`varchar`
Binary large object (BLOB)	`text, byte`

Informix treats a null as having a special meaning. A null value assignment specifies a missing or unknown value. You can define whether an attribute can accept null values or whether an attribute requires a value to be entered.

A null value is not the same as a blank or zero. If a user enters a blank space or zero in a field, SQL interprets it as a blank space or zero.

You can specify a unique constraint for an attribute. A unique constraint ensures a unique value for every attribute. If you define an attribute to enforce a unique constraint, you are prevented from entering the same information in multiple rows of a column.

NOTE

You can use the serial data type to establish a unique constraint for an attribute. A serial data type is generally used to generate system-assigned primary keys and is assigned to an identifier attribute to establish a unique constraint.

When identifying not null and unique constraints, you should select a naming convention to represent these on your ERD. The naming convention used in Figure 27.30 is as follows:

- NN indicates a not null constraint.
- U indicates a unique constraint.

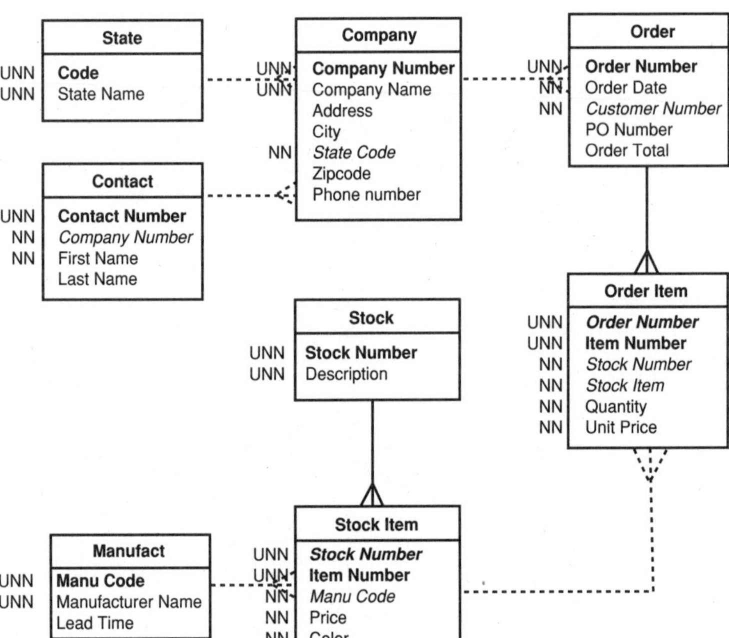

FIGURE 27.30.
Identifying constraints. (Unique constraints are labeled with U, and not null constraints are labeled with NN.)

Assigning Variable-Length Data Types

You should note that variable-length data types (`varchar`, `text`, and `byte`) are only available with the OnLine database engine. These data types should be selected carefully. Although you can use the `varchar` data type to save storage space, the use of the blob data types generally require large storage areas that can store up to 2GB in a single column.

Indexes

The primary purpose of an index is to improve performance for data retrieval. However, you can use indexes to ensure the uniqueness of attributes. By creating an index on a column with the `UNIQUE` keyword, you place a unique constraint on every value entered for the column.

A foreign key usually has an index, and a primary key always has a unique index.

Remember that composite keys increase uniqueness in a table. A composite index is an index created on more than one column.

Referential and Entity Integrity

Referential integrity is the concept of enforcing the relationships between tables. Integrity is defined as the accuracy or correctness of the data in the database. Entity integrity is enforced by creating a primary key that uniquely identifies each row in the table. Referential integrity is enforced by creating a foreign key that references the primary key of the related table.

By creating primary and foreign keys, you can enforce master-detail (parent-child) relationships. When you use referential constraints in this way, the database engine enforces the following rules:

- All values within a primary key must be unique. An attempt to insert a duplicate value into a primary key fails.
- If a user attempts to delete a primary key and there are corresponding foreign keys, the delete fails.
- If a user attempts to update a primary key and there are foreign keys corresponding to the original values of the primary key, the update fails.
- There are no restrictions associated with deleting foreign keys.
- If a user attempts to update a foreign key and there is no primary key corresponding to the new, non-null value of the foreign key, the update fails.
- When a user attempts to insert a row into a child table, if all foreign keys are non-null and there are no corresponding primary keys, the insert fails.

NOTE

To enforce mandatory referential integrity, you should allow no nulls in the primary and foreign key columns.

Summary

Successful database development relies on a good understanding of the business. To ensure an accurate database design, use data modeling. Identify all the entities required by the business and their relationships, and use this information to design the ERD. By using data modeling techniques, the ERD can be expanded to not only cater to the existing requirements, but allow some flexibility for future growth.

Use normalization rules to convert the logical entities into a conceptual model for the database design. The normalization process is used to ensure that the conceptual model of the database will work. You can implement an unnormalized model, but it will present problems in application development and data manipulation operations.

When you are converting the logical design to the physical design, or database schema, consider the Informix data types available. Also use referential and entity integrity to enforce relationships at the database level.

A good database design not only ensures that the requirements of the system are fulfilled, but that the system is easy to maintain and enhance. A successful system relies on a good database design.

CHAPTER

INFORMIX-SQL

by John McNally

IN THIS CHAPTER

This chapter covers INFORMIX-SQL, which is a data access language used to communicate with the database manager. INFORMIX-SQL, INFORMIX-DBaccess, INFORMIX-4GL, and INFORMIX-NewEra are all Informix products that use SQL. Also, INFORMIX-ESQL/C and INFORMIX-ESQL/COBOL are used for SQL Application Programming Interfaces (APIs). These APIs allow programmers to place SQL commands within their C or COBOL coded programs.

In addition, this chapter discusses the following topics:

- What is SQL?
- The history of SQL
- Uses of SQL

SQL is an industry-standard query language product developed by the IBM Corporation. Informix uses an enhanced version of this.

What Is SQL?

The name *SQL* stands for *Structured Query Language.* It is a data access language used for communicating with a database manager. The free-form, English-like simplified language is used for any number of relational database management systems (RDBMS).

SQL is a complete database language with statements that do the following:

- Initial creation of the database
- Creation of physical objects
- Creation of logical objects (views)
- Provide authorizations/grants and privileges
- Data Manipulation and retrieval from the database
- Management and/or use of databases

SQL makes the decision on how to get your data from the database. You specify the requirements, and SQL completes the process. This is also known as *non-navigational data processing.* SQL statements can be executed directly against the database or embedded in one of many programming languages.

SQL has many processing capabilities, which are as follows:

- Data Definition Language (DDL)
- Data Manipulation Language (DML)
- Cursor manipulation
- Dynamic management
- Data access

- Data integrity
- Query optimization information
- Stored procedures
- Auxiliary statements
- Client/server connection

One main feature of SQL is that statements can be processed interactively, which means that an SQL statement is processed when it is submitted to the database server. Unlike most programming languages, SQL does not have to be compiled into an executable program to run. Using an interface or other program, SQL commands can be executed while the system is operating. The following lists describe each of the processing statements.

The following *data definition statements* allow creation of the database and the data structures for the system:

```
ALTER FRAGMENT
ALTER INDEX
ALTER TABLE
CLOSE DATABASE
CREATE DATABASE
CREATE INDEX
CREATE PROCEDURE
CREATE PROCEDURE FROM
CREATE ROLE
CREATE SCHEMA
CREATE SYNONYM
CREATE TABLE
CREATE TRIGGER
CREATE VIEW
DATABASE
DROP DATABASE
DROP INDEX
DROP PROCEDURE
DROP SYNONYM
DROP TABLE
DROP TRIGGER
DROP VIEW
RENAME COLUMN
RENAME DATABASE
RENAME TABLE
```

The following *data manipulation statements* allow you to add, delete, modify, and query data in the database:

```
DELETE
INSERT
```

```
LOAD
SELECT
UNLOAD
UPDATE
```

Cursors are used to deal with a group of specific data rows. As each row is processed, the cursor keeps track of where you are in the group. The following *cursor manipulation statements* are used while working with cursors:

```
CLOSE
DECLARE
FETCH
FLUSH
FREE
OPEN
PUT
```

Dynamic management statements are used to manage resources at runtime. Dynamic management SQL statements are used at a program's runtime and are built with variables needed at this specific run. Whereas most SQL statements are static and never-changing, dynamic statements can change at each run. Just as an interactively run SQL can be changed by the user, a dynamic SQL statement can be changed by the program within which it is embedded. Here are the dynamic management statements:

```
ALLOCATE DESCRIPTOR
DEALLOCATE DESCRIPTOR
DESCRIBE
EXECUTE
EXECUTE IMMEDIATE
FREE
GET DESCRIPTOR
PREPARE
SET DESCRIPTOR
```

The following *data access statements* are used to determine the access of the data. Such access is used in case of permissions and data security.

```
GRANT
LOCK TABLE
REVOKE
SET ISOLATION
SET LOCK MODE
SET ROLE
SET SESSION AUTHORIZATION
SET TRANSACTION
UNLOCK TABLE
```

The following *data integrity statements* are used to ensure the data's integrity. These statements ensure that the data is safe and is tracked in multiple places:

```
BEGIN WORK
CHECK TABLE
COMMIT WORK
CREATE AUDIT
DROP AUDIT
RECOVER TABLE
REPAIR TABLE
ROLLBACK WORK
ROLL FORWARD DATABASE
SET CONSTRAINTS
SET LOG
START DATABASE
```

The following *query optimization information statements* are used to gather information on the query in execution. These are great to use when trying to investigate why a certain SQL statement runs a very long time and how to improve it.

```
SET EXPLAIN
SET OPTIMIZATION
SET PDQ PRIORITY
SET STATISTICS
```


The following *stored procedure statements* are used to execute and debug stored procedures. A stored procedure is a group of SQL statements that resides in the database server. Rather than submit the entire group of statements from a program or submit them interactively, just submit the command to run the stored procedure.

```
EXECUTE PROCEDURE
SET DEBUG FILE TO
```

The following *auxiliary statements* are supplemental statements that are part of SQL but are not grouped with any of the prior processing categories:

```
INFO
OUTPUT
GET DIAGNOSTICS
WHENEVER
```

The following *client/server connection statements* are used to establish application connection for a specific environment and/or database:

```
CONNECT
DISCONNECT
SET CONNECTION
```

SQL statements are used to perform all direct functions on the database. The statements and keywords used will lead to the database operations being performed. SQL commands consist of command verbs, optional clauses, keywords, and parameter operands. The use of these in SQL syntax permits exact specification of the data requests. The language allows single and double byte characters to be used in identifiers and variables. SQL has many types of commands; some are for handling the data, and some are for controlling administrative matters. Chapters 29 through 32 explain these commands in greater detail and tell you how and when to use them.

In relational database systems such as Informix, the data is organized and stored in tables or entities, which are just a collection of columns and rows. Figure 28.1 shows an example of a database table. Rows are the horizontal parts of the table or are otherwise referred to as *instances.* Columns are the vertical parts of the table, which are also known as *attributes.* Tables, rows, and columns are a way of organizing the data and giving you an understanding of a relational model.

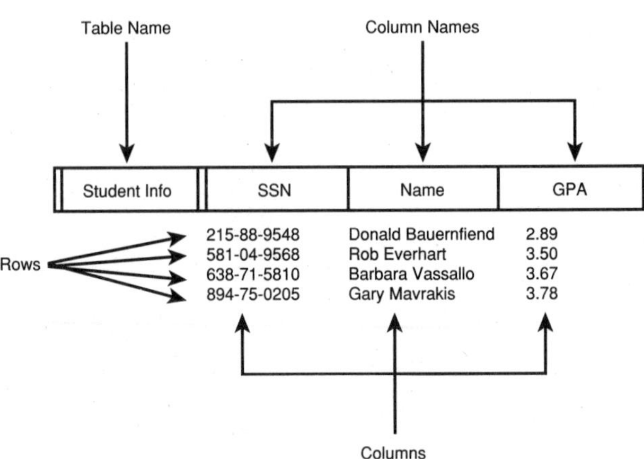

FIGURE 28.1.
A relational database table.

The process of organizing data brings you to the definition or values that can be stored in the columns of a table. Table 28.1 shows the data types that are supported by Informix.

Table 28.1. Data types supported by Informix.

Data Type	*Definition*
`BYTE`	Stores binary data
`CHAR`	Stores letters, numbers, and special characters
`DATE`	Stores calendar date
`DATETIME`	Stores calendar date with the time of day
`DECIMAL`	Stores decimal numbers with digits of numeric precision
`DOUBLE PRECISION`	Stores double-precision floating numbers

Data Type	Definition
FLOAT	Stores double-precision floating numbers
INTEGER	Stores numbers ranging from -2,147,483,648 to 2,147,483,647
INTERVAL	Stores span of time
MONEY	Stores currency amount
NUMERIC	Stores decimal numbers with digits of numeric precision
NCHAR	Stores a native string of letters, numbers, and special characters
NVARCHAR	Stores native character strings of varying length
SERIAL	Stores sequential integers
SMALLFLOAT	Stores single-precision floating numbers
SMALLINT	Stores numbers ranging from -32,767 to +32,767
TEXT	Stores text data
VARCHAR	Stores character strings of varying length

A significant feature of SQL is that it can be used by two different interfaces. SQL is both an interactive query language and a database programming language. This means that any SQL statement that can be entered at a terminal can also be embedded in a program.

Finally, SQL processing is also known as a *set level* language, which means your updates will change records and return the results. You simply state what you want without specifying a procedure, and the system automatically completes the process.

SQL is the communicating device to the relational database management system. You will find SQL to be a simplified and straightforward process for accessing data. When you are familiar with the language, fairly sophisticated data processing can be done. The following list logically summarizes the SQL language:

- Simple, flexible database access language
- Standard relational language
- English-like query language
- Supports many relational products, such as these:

    DB2
    SQL/DS
    QMF
    Oracle
    Informix
    Sybase

Focus

REXX

XDB

As you will see, relational database systems have two aspects. First, all information is represented by data values, and second, the system supports a high-level language. SQL is the high-level language.

History

SQL was initially developed by D.D. Chamberlain and others at IBM in San Jose, California, in the late 1970s. The language was originally known as *SEQUEL* (Structured English Query Language) and was implemented and tested under the name of *System R*. Many relational database management system products have evolved from the System R technology. SQL is commonly pronounced *sequel* today. And, just to confuse matters, others pronounce it by spelling out *S-Q-L*.

Since the birth of SQL, many vendors have created their own SQL-oriented database products. The American National Standards Institute (ANSI) and the International Organization for Standardization (ISO) have stated SQL standards. These standards are similar to the standards of the IBM SQL language, which is the official interface to relational systems. Since then, many vendors have created an enhanced SQL language to use with their relational products. This allows a SQL command created with the standard to run on any system, as long as one vendor's enhanced command is not used on another vendor's system.

At the start of the relational database system project, many goals were established. The goals were as follows:

- Provide different types of database uses
- Support a rapidly changing database environment
- Provide a high-level non-navigational user interface
- Provide maximum user productivity
- Provide means of database recovery
- Provide flexible means of defined data
- Provide a high level of database performance

The SQL interface was created with goals of being simple, powerful, and data-independent. The SQL language was simple enough that users with minimal prior experience could learn it without difficulty. At the same time, the language was very powerful in functionality.

In the early stages, suggestions were made to make improvements to SQL, while developing applications. Users requested simple syntax, capabilities for searching partial character strings, dynamic SQL, and outer table joins. The SQL language has progressed tremendously since these initial development days.

The user can issue statements from an online terminal interface or from other programming languages. The user does not need to know where things are physically stored or what access paths are available. SQL statements do not require the user to know anything about the access path for data retrieval. This means that an SQL statement can be made without the user knowing which columns have indices or how much data will be retrieved. However, keep in mind that for better performance from your database, knowing the access paths and indexes will help to keep processing efficient.

During the initial System R project, many phases and goals were set. The first phase was to execute high-level SQL statements from a PL/I program. The SQL statements contained basic queries and updates to the database. From this testing, a decision was made that a system catalog was needed. The catalog would consist of tables that describe the structure of the database. The catalog would automatically be updated as changes to the database were made. Along with making processing more efficient, the following additional objectives were important:

- Minimize the number of rows retrieved
- Perform measurements of I/O
- Improve CPU time usage and lower I/O count
- Determine the importance of "join" processing
- Manage complex and then simple queries

Much time was spent on how to optimize SQL processing. Starting with complex queries and then working back to simple queries, the following functions were established:

Function	*Description*
Optimizer	A component of the database that makes the decision of how the query should be performed
Views	A synthetic table
Authorization	Control of privileges by the central administration
Recovery	Safeguarding the database
Locking	Providing isolation levels

It has been proven that System R and SQL could be applied to a relational database system in a production environment. Since the time of the original implementation, many improvements have been made, including an enhanced Optimizer and a Distributed Database System. All of the enhancements and improvements placed in SQL are available in Informix database systems.

Uses of SQL

The SQL language has many uses. The most important use is the `SELECT` statement. The `SELECT` statement allows you to look at data from a relational database, whereas `INSERT`, `UPDATE`, and `DELETE` allow you to manipulate data in the database. When you combine the `SELECT` statement with a manipulating statement, SQL allows you to change specific data.

The SQL Query

The SELECT statement by itself can retrieve data from the database, and this action is commonly referred to as a query. When a SELECT is used with the INSERT statement, additional data can be added to the database, similar to how data can be updated on the database using SELECT with the UPDATE statement.

The five SELECT statement clauses are as follows:

- SELECT
- FROM
- WHERE
- ORDER BY
- INTO TEMP

When doing a simple query, only the SELECT and FROM clauses are necessary. When a WHERE, ORDER BY, or INTO TEMP are added, specific requests are made in the query.

Before you can select on the database, you must have connect privileges given to you by the administrator. Otherwise, the query will always fail, regardless of whether or not it is correctly formed.

You can select data from one table and complete the following functions:

- Select specific rows or all rows from the table.
- Select specific columns or all columns from the table.
- Order the data selected (on two or more columns).
- Perform functions on the retrieved data.

As previously stated, to form a basic SELECT statement, you need only the SELECT and FROM clauses. The following is a sample of selecting all rows from a table:

```
SELECT * FROM  table1
```

The * in the SELECT statement is a wildcard, which stands for all the columns in the specified table.

To specify certain columns from a table, the statement should be as follows:

```
SELECT column1, column2, column3 FROM table1
```

While retrieving data from a specific table, you can have the system sort the results by adding an ORDER BY to the SELECT statement. In the SELECT statement, you must list the columns that you want to be sorted. An additional option is to have the data returned in ascending or descending order. Here's how it looks:

```
SELECT  column1, column2, column3
    FROM table1
    ORDER BY column2
SELECT * FROM table1
    ORDER BY column1 DESC
```

You can sort multiple columns from your table. The statement is set up by selecting specific columns and then listing the order in which you want the data to be returned, like this:

```
SELECT column1, column2, column3
    FROM table1
    ORDER BY  column2, column3
```

The `WHERE` clause of a statement allows you to specify exactly which rows you would like to see. When using the `WHERE` clause, you can use many operators or keywords:

Keywords	
BETWEEN	
LIKE	
MATCHES	

Operators	
<	less than
>	greater than
<=	less than or equal to
>=	greater than or equal to
!=	not equal to

You can use one of the preceding keywords or operators to create a comparison in the query. Here is an example:

```
SELECT column1, column2, column3
    FROM table1
    WHERE column1 = valueA
```

To identify a table from which you want data, you place the table name after the `FROM` clause. To identify the column names, you place them in the `SELECT` clause. To code any conditions in the query, you use the `WHERE` clause.

NOTE

Be aware that if no conditions are stated, all rows will be selected.

This has covered the basic simple `SELECT` statements. A query can go from simplistic to very complex. Some of the functions in the more advanced `SELECT` statements are using `GROUP BY` or

HAVING, creating Self Joins, creating Outer Joins, and creating Multiple-Table Joins. Subqueries in a SELECT statement can be used along with set operations such as UNION, difference, and intersection.

In Chapters 29 through 32, greater detail is given to complex queries and additional SQL functions. The following list gives summaries of additional functions that a query can perform:

- DISTINCT or UNIQUE keywords can be used to eliminate duplicates.
- Use operators AND, OR, or NOT for additional search criteria.
- Search for Null values by using the IS NULL or IS NOT NULL keywords.
- Use aggregate functions such as AVG, COUNT, MAX, MIN, and SUM in the SELECT.
- Use time functions in the SELECT (such as DATE, YEAR, CURRENT).
- Join two or more tables.
- Select data into a temporary table.

Modifying SQL Statements

Modifying data is also a function that SQL is used for. In Chapters 29 through 32, greater detail is given to SQL statements that modify data. The following statements modify data:

- DELETE
- INSERT
- UPDATE

The DELETE statement can remove one or many rows from a table. After a DELETE statement has been executed and the transaction has been committed, the deleted rows cannot be recovered. The DELETE statement specifies a table name and a WHERE clause to specify the delete criteria. If the DELETE statement does not contain a WHERE clause, all rows in the table will be deleted.

The INSERT statement adds one or many new rows to a table. The values must be supplied and have an exact correspondence to the table you are inserting into.

The UPDATE statement is used to change the existing data from one or many columns of a table. The UPDATE statement can use the WHERE clause to determine exactly which rows should be modified.

Privilege SQL Statements

One major use for SQL is for managing *database privileges.* There are two levels of privileges: database level and table level. For a more in-depth look at privileges and security, refer to Chapter 16, "Privileges and Security Issues."

Here are the database-level privileges:

- CONNECT enables you to open a database and run queries, as well as create and index temporary tables.
- RESOURCE enables you to create tables.
- DBA allows CONNECT and RESOURCE privileges, along with additional grant privileges.

Here are the table-level privileges:

- SELECT enables you to select rows from a table.
- DELETE enables you to delete rows.
- INSERT enables you to insert rows.
- UPDATE enables you to update specific rows.

Referential Integrity SQL Statements

SQL is also used for setting up the referential integrity on a database. *Referential integrity* is the relationship between tables. For a more in-depth look at referential integrity, refer to Chapter 17, "Managing Data Integrity with Constraints."

Each table must have a primary key. When the primary key is used in other tables, not as the primary key but as a reference point back to the table that uses that value as the primary key, it is called the *foreign key.*

The foreign key is what is used to establish the relationship between the two tables. The tables form a hierarchy, and this can cause cascading changes within the tables. Primary and foreign keys are defined by using the REFERENCES clause on the CREATE TABLE and ALTER TABLE statements. INFORMIX-OnLine does not allow the referential integrity to be violated; this means that if a change (such as a deletion) takes place in the child table before the change is made in the parent table, an error occurs.

NOTE

When using Informix, Transaction Logging must be on in order for a cascade delete to work.

Embedded SQL Statements

SQL can also be used with almost any programming language. Here are the options that are available when programming with SQL:

- SQL in SQL APIs
- SQL in Application Language

- Static SQL
- Dynamic SQL

When using an SQL API, the SQL is embedded in the source code, which then goes through a program that converts the SQL statements into procedure calls and data structures. The source code then goes through a compiler and creates an executable program. For the Application Language, using embedded SQL enables you to have the SQL as part of its natural statement set.

Static SQL statements are the most common and simple way of including SQL statements in your program. The statements are included as part of the source code.

Dynamic SQL statements are not part of the source code. These SQL statements are composed from user input and then passed to the database for execution. The program creates a character string from the input and puts it to memory prior to the pass to the database server. Whenever information is passed from the program to the database server, information and/or results must be returned. A data area known as SQLCA (SQL Communications Area) is where all information about the statements comes from.

SQL statements can be written into any program just like any ordinary statement. Static statements are used in the source program, whereas dynamic statements take input and use the database servers for execution.

Summary

In summary, SQL is used as the communicating device to the relational database management system. SQL is a simplified and straightforward process for accessing data. SQL statements and keywords are used to perform all direct functions on the database.

Many uses of the SQL language were covered in this chapter. The `SELECT` statement allows you to look at data from a relational database, and `INSERT`, `UPDATE`, and `DELETE` allow you to manipulate data in the database.

In addition, SQL statements can be written into any program. Static statements are used in the source program, whereas dynamic statements take the SQL as input and use the database server for execution.

All SQL functionality explained in this chapter is supported by all Informix database servers.

Creating a Database Using SQL

by John McNally

IN THIS CHAPTER

This chapter reviews the fundamentals of database design and determines the factors of designing the database from a physical standpoint. I start by reviewing what an entity-relationship (ER) data model is, how it can be used, and which data objects—such as entities, relationships, and attributes—must be defined.

There are many ways to approach the design of a database, but this chapter reviews the basic three-step design. This process consists of the following steps:

1. Name the entities.
2. Define the relationships.
3. List the attributes.

INFORMIX-SQL is the primary tool, along with DBaccess, which is used for creating and testing your database design. Refer to Chapter 32, "SQL Tools," for additional information on DBaccess.

In addition, this chapter discusses

- Determining the database layout
- Size requirements
- Creating tables
- Altering tables
- Creating indexes
- Altering indexes
- Privileges
- Data integrity

Determining the Database Layout

The database layout is the most important part of an information system. Just as you don't want to build a house without a blueprint, creating a database without a predesigned layout could be disastrous. The more design and thought put into a database, the better the database will be in the long run.

You should gather information about the user's requirements, data objects, and data definitions before creating a database layout and definitely before creating the database in Informix.

Creating a Data Model

The first step you take when determining the database layout is to build a data model that defines how the data is to be stored. For most relational databases, you create an entity-relationship (ER) diagram or model. For more information about relational databases, see Chapter 27, "Informix Development Introduction," which goes into more detail on how to use the relational database model when you create a database system.

The steps to create this model are as follows:

1. Identify and define the data objects (entities, relationships, and attributes).
2. Diagram your objects and relationships.
3. Translate your objects into relational constructs (such as tables).
4. Resolve your data model.
5. Perform the normalization process.

First, define your entities and the relationships between them. An entity is something that can be distinctively identified. An example of an entity is a specific person, place, or thing. The relationship is the association between the entities, which is described as connectivity, cardinality, or dependency.

Connectivity is the occurrence of an entity, meaning the relationship to other entities is either one-to-one, one-to-many, or many-to-many. The cardinality term places a constraint on the number of times an entity can have an association in a relationship. The entity dependency describes whether the relationship is mandatory or optional.

After you identify your entities, you can proceed with identifying the attributes. Attributes are all the descriptive features of the entity. When defining the attributes, you must specify the constraints (such as valid values or characters) or any other features about the entity.

After you complete the process of defining your entities and the relationship of the database, the next step is to display the process you designed. Graphically displaying or diagramming your entities and relationships gives you a complete layout of the process. Figure 29.1 shows an example of an ER diagram.

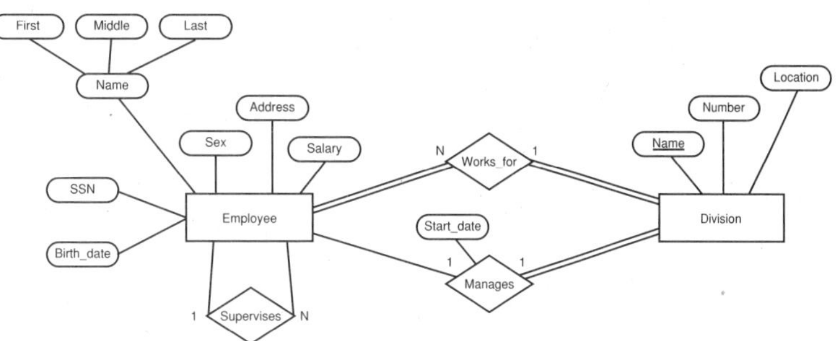

FIGURE 29.1.
An example of an ER diagram.

There are many purposes for diagramming your data objects:

- Organizes information, allowing you to work smarter
- Documents for the future and gives people new to the project a basic understanding of what is going on
- Identifies entities and relationships
- Determines the logical design to be used for the physical layout

After your diagram is complete, the next step is to translate the data objects (entities and attributes) into relational constructs. You translate all the data objects that are defined into tables, columns, and rows. Each entity is represented as a table, and each row represents an occurrence of that entity.

A table is an object that holds data relating to a single entity. Table design includes the following:

- Each table is uniquely named within the database.
- Each table has one or more columns.
- Each column is uniquely named within the table.
- Each column contains one data type.
- Each table can contain zero or more rows of data.

The tables contain two types of columns: keys or descriptors. A key column uniquely defines a specific row of a table, whereas a descriptor column specifies non-uniqueness in a particular row.

When you create tables, you define primary and foreign keys. The primary key consists of one or more columns that make each row unique. Each table must have a primary key. The foreign key is one or more columns in one table that match the columns of the primary key of another table. The purpose of a foreign key is to create a relationship between two tables so you can join tables.

The next step in your data model is to resolve your relationships. The most common types of relationships are one-to-many (1:m) and many-to-many (m:n). In some instances, a one-to-one relationship may exist between tables. In order to resolve the more complex relationships, you must analyze the relational business rules, and in some instances, you might need to add additional entities.

The final step in building your data model is normalization. The three forms of normalization are

- First normal form: A table defined with no repeating columns.
- Second normal form: A table that is in first normal form and contains columns dependent on the primary key.
- Third normal form: A table that is in second normal form and contains columns that are dependent on the primary key along with descriptive columns.

When you finish normalization, you should have a complete data model for your database design with minimal data redundancy. If the process is correctly designed at the first, later performance problems should not occur.

Implementing a Data Model

Next, I review the procedures for implementing your data model. After the data model is complete, it must be implemented. The two steps in the implementation process are

1. Define the domain for every column.
2. Use SQL to create the actual data model into a new or existing database.

The domain is defined for each column. This means that restrictions are put on the valid values for that particular column. There are three ways to specify constraints: data types, default values, and check constraints.

The data type constraint allows you to choose a data type for the column and allows storage of data only of that specific type. (Refer to Chapter 28, "INFORMIX-SQL," for additional information on data types.) Data type is important because it sets the rules for the type of data that can be stored, and it can specify the amount of disk space that is utilized. Default values are values that can be inserted into a column of a table when the specific values are not indicated.

Check constraints check the requirements on a value before any updating or inserting is done to a specific column. If a constraint is defined and a value is not valid, the database server returns an SQL error code.

Creating a Database

A database is the object that holds all the parts of your data model together. The parts include the tables, views, and indexes. You must create the database before anything else can be created.

You create a database by running the `CREATE DATABASE` SQL statement. The database usually resides in one dbspace as specified in the statement, but if no dbspace name is specified, the database is created in the root dbspace by default. In your create statement, you can also specify what type of logging you want for the database.

To build a database, you must follow these steps:

1. Type the words `CREATE DATABASE`.
2. Provide the database name.

The following statement creates a database in the root dbspace:

```
CREATE DATABASE database1
```

The following two steps are enough to create the database:

1. Designate the dbspace where the database is to reside by using the `IN` clause.

   The following statement creates a database in a specific dbspace:

   ```
   CREATE DATABASE database1 IN dbspace1
   ```

2. Specify the logging for the database.

   INFORMIX-OnLine offers four types of transaction logging. They are

   None

   Unbuffered

Buffered

ANSI-Compliant

The database administrator can turn the transaction logging on and off at any time. Sometimes when you perform maintenance or large inserts, you might choose to turn logging off. Note that only the servers from INFORMIX-OnLine allow for logging to be turned on and off.

The following statements specify the type of logging on the database at creation time:

```
CREATE DATABASE database1 WITH NO LOG
CREATE DATABASE database1 WITH LOG
CREATE DATABASE database1 IN dbspace1 WITH BUFFERED LOG
CREATE DATABASE database1 IN dbspace1 WITH LOG MODE ANSI
```

Note that you can add transaction logging to a no-log database by using the `START DATABASE` statement. When you complete your `CREATE DATABASE` statement, that becomes your current and selected database. Each database name must be unique within your INFORMIX-OnLine system or instance. Additional statements you can use with the database include `DATABASE`, `START DATABASE`, `CLOSE DATABASE`, and `DROP DATABASE`.

You use the `DATABASE` statement to open the database, whereas the `START DATABASE` statement is used for specifying the log type or starting the transaction processing. You use the `CLOSE DATABASE` statement to close the current database, and the `DROP DATABASE` statement deletes the entire database including all data, indexes, and system catalog information.

You can perform all the preceding database functions with the Informix DBaccess tool. The tool is primarily used for accessing and manipulating data from a relational database. Refer to Chapter 32 for information on the DBaccess tool.

You can create a database by entering statements interactively, or you can write statements into a file to execute automatically. A utility called DBSCHEMA generates SQL statements from the contents of your database and allows you to generate a duplicate database. You use this type of utility when you want to create a testing or full volume database that matches your existing production database. The DBSCHEMA utility creates the SQL for the entire database including tables, indexes, and granted privileges.

I covered the process of how you determine your database layout. As a review of this process, the following list shows the steps you must complete and where to focus next:

1. Create a data model.
2. Perform the normalization process.
3. Use SQL to create the database.
4. Denormalize if necessary.
5. Start on table and index creation.

Next, you focus on the sizing requirements and how volumes can determine the functioning of your database.

Size Requirements

When you create tables and the data volumes and users are minimal, the database is easy to manage. As the tables grow larger and more users are concurrent, you begin the process of how to measure and manage the growing OnLine system.

Data management is a large part of a successful OnLine environment. The following is a list of functions involved in data management:

- Organization of the database on disk space
- Proper use of disk space
- Data access

INFORMIX-OnLine has its own procedures for managing the data on disk. When working with INFORMIX-OnLine, you deal directly with disk storage. At the time of table creation, you determine how much disk space is reserved. The data is stored in disk pages. The disk pages are managed by the initial extent size and next extent size. When you first create the table, the initial extent size is reserved; when the initial extent is full, OnLine adds the next extent. The default for the initial and next extent size is eight pages.

There are many ways you relate to disk storage. The following section briefly describes the different types of space.

Chunks

A chunk is a unit of disk or actual physical space that is used by Informix in the OnLine system. A chunk can be either a raw device or a cooked file. When you structure your OnLine system, you define your chunks using the following parameters: pathname, offset, and size.

The pathname is the name of the raw device or cooked file that is used to create the chunk. A raw device is the complete disk space or a portion of it that is managed totally by Informix. The operating system has no control of that space and is not allowed to use it. All reads and writes to that space are performed by Informix. An example of the pathname for a raw device is `/dev/rdsk`. Cooked space is managed and maintained by the operating system. All reads and writes must go through UNIX in a cook scenario. A cooked file is a file that Informix uses to store information, but that is managed by UNIX. An example of the pathname for a cooked file is `/usr/informix/cooked/file1`.

The offset parameter is the beginning point on the device that is used in your chunk. This is specified in kilobytes.

The size parameter is the amount of space, also specified in kilobytes, that is used in the device for the chunk you create. The amount of space specified in the size parameter starts at the point where the offset was set.

Note that when you use a cooked device for chunks, you should use an offset of zero.

Pages

Pages are the basic unit of I/O that OnLine uses. There are data pages and index pages, but you cannot store both data and indexes on the same page.

Extents

When you create a table, you allocate disk space in a unit called *extents.* An extent is the amount of space in kilobytes that is allocated for a table to grow into. After an extent is allocated, no other process or table can use that space. Each table has two extent sizes associated with it. First is the `EXTENT SIZE` parameter, which is the first extent of disk space that is allocated at the time the table is created. Second is the `NEXT SIZE` parameter, which is the subsequent disk space extent added to the table. You can alter the `NEXT SIZE` parameter with the `ALTER TABLE` statement.

The minimum size that an extent can be is four pages (8KB), and it must be in even multiples of the page size of the current system. Also, when the table reaches 64 extents, the system doubles the next extent size for each new extent from that point forward. Every time the amount of extents passes a multiple of 64, the size is doubled again. Informix automatically does this to limit the amount of extents allocated. But remember, it is always best to keep the number of extents to a minimum. Reorganize the table by unloading all the rows, deleting the table, re-creating the table, and then reloading the rows. The key to this procedure is to set the extent size on the re-created table equal to the size of all the original extents added together.

INFORMIX-OnLine also has a unit called a tablespace. When the extents for one given table are logically grouped, this is known as a tablespace. A tablespace can contain one or more extents.

dbspaces

A dbspace is a collection of chunks that are used for storing tables and databases. When a dbspace is created, it must have at least one chunk, also known as the primary chunk. A dbspace can consist of many chunks. After initial creation, you can add additional chunks to the dbspace.

At the time you create your tables and databases, you can specify what dbspace you want them to be placed in. If a dbspace comprises many chunks, you cannot specify what chunk your tables are created on.

When the dbspace is created, space is automatically allocated to store system information. An example of what is stored in this space is information to help track what data is in the particular dbspace.

One table in shared memory is called the dbspaces table. This table is created by the OnLine system to keep track of all the dbspaces that are created. The dbspaces table has an entry for each dbspace created.

Blobspaces

Blobspaces, like dbspaces, are also collections of chunks, but they are used to store blob (binary large object) data types. A blob data type holds items such as images, sounds, or text files. A blobspace can hold blob data from one or more tables, but no additional indexes or rows are stored. When you create your blobspace, you need to specify the size of the blobpage, and pages throughout the blobspace must be the same size. The blobpage is the unit of storage for the blob data types stored in the blobspace.

The reason for storing large blob data types in blobspaces is to achieve more efficient processing. The blob values are not buffered in the buffer cache and are not written to the logical logs on disk. The process keeps the before and after values on disk until you back up the logical log file.

The dbspaces shared memory table, mentioned in the last section, contains entries for blobspaces as well as standard dbspaces.

Root Dbspace

When creating an INFORMIX-OnLine system, you must have a root dbspace. The primary chunk for the root dbspace is used to store the `sysmaster` database (INFORMIX-OnLine Dynamic Server) and the physical and logical logs. The default root name specified is `rootdbs`. The root dbspace is the area where all the system information is located. This is a critical part of the OnLine environment.

It has always been recommended that you do not create tables in the root dbspace.

When you configure your OnLine system, you must calculate what is stored in the root dbspace so that you have enough space allotted. The following list outlines the components in the root dbspace:

- Physical log
- Logical logs
- OnLine system information
- Temporary tables (internal)

The root dbspace contains more system information than any other dbspace. The first 12 pages of the primary chunk in the root dbspace are automatically allocated for the OnLine system information. Some of the data stored in the 12 reserve pages is as follows:

- dbspace pages
- Primary chunk pages
- Mirror chunk pages
- Checkpoint pages
- Archive pages

Size Requirement Considerations

When looking at size requirements for your OnLine system, there are many things to take into consideration. First, you must look at your data model and decide the most appropriate physical layout of the database. At this time, the data volume and data processing information comes into play. You decide what type of architecture should be implemented for your system.

The placement of data on disk components (raw devices) is a large part of the architecture, along with your shared memory components. The shared memory plays a large part when you cache data from disk.

If you configure an OnLine production environment, the best solution is to set up a configuration worksheet to help size your OnLine environment. You can break down the worksheet into the following groups to help set values for the new environment:

- Root dbspace configuration:
  - Physical log
  - Logical logs
  - Root dbspace size
  - Temporary table disk space
  - Reserve pages
- Additional disk space:
  - Primary chunks
  - Mirror chunks
  - Buffers
  - Cleaners

This should give you at least a high-level overview of what you need to configure to come up with the appropriate size requirements for your system.

Creating Tables

When creating a table, you must use the `CREATE TABLE` statement. You must define several things such as the table name, which is unique within the database, and the column names, which are unique within the table. Every column must have an associated data type, and a column constraint is optional. You use the `CREATE TABLE` statement to define the initial and next extents plus the locking method for the table.

Temporary table names must be different from existing tables within the current database. You do not need uniquely defined temporary tables that might already exist and are being used by other users.

The CREATE TABLE statement is used to create all tables defined in the data model. When you create the table, you define the columns and supply the following information:

- Column name
- Data type for each column
- Primary key constraint on one or more columns and the UNIQUE constraints for not allowing duplicates
- Foreign key constraints for one or more columns
- Not Null constraint
- Default value constraint
- Check constraint
- FRAGMENT BY option
- Extent option
- Lock mode option
- Logging option

This section reviews all the preceding options for the CREATE TABLE statement. Keep in mind that putting constraints on columns of a table helps to establish the data integrity of the table. For an in-depth look at constraints, refer to Chapter 17, "Managing Data Integrity with Constraints."

Constraint Limitations

You have a few limitations on constraints when creating a table. You cannot define more than 16 columns for a unique primary key. Also, the length of all the columns cannot exceed 255 bytes.

When defining constraints on the column level, you are limited to defining only one. When defining constraints on the table level, they can apply to single or multiple columns.

Dropping and Adding Constraints

After you create your table using the CREATE TABLE statement, you must use the ALTER TABLE statement to add or drop a constraint. Later in this chapter, the "Altering Tables" section takes a more detailed look at the ALTER TABLE statement.

Defining a Unique Column

You define a unique constraint on a column or columns of a table to ensure that only unique data is inserted into the table. You cannot insert any duplicate values as long as the unique constraint is defined.

Defining a Primary and Foreign Key

The primary key is a single column or a group of columns that create a unique value for each row of the table. Every table can have only one primary key, and it cannot contain a column that is defined as unique. Note that a primary key cannot be defined as BYTE or TEXT.

The foreign key establishes the relationship or dependencies of tables. The foreign key references the primary or unique key of another table; each column defined in the foreign key must exist in the primary or unique key it references. Note that a foreign key cannot be defined as BYTE or TEXT.

Defining Check Constraints

You can define check constraints at the column or table level. At the column level, if a row is to be inserted or updated and the conditions on a specific column are not met, an error is returned. With a constraint defined on the table level, each column must meet the conditions defined.

Table Storage

A table storage option on the CREATE TABLE statement allows you to specify where the table of a certain database is to be stored. The clause used in the statement is IN dbspace. This option is for INFORMIX-OnLine, and the specified dbspace must already exist in your system. If a dbspace is not specified, then the table is created in the space where the current database resides.

The purpose of using the IN dbspace clause is to enable you to control where the tables are created. For example, if you create two tables and you want them to be placed on different disk areas, you specify different dbspaces in the create statement.

Extent Option

When you create a table, you can specify in your statement the size of the first extent and next extent you want to be defined for that table. The EXTENT SIZE and NEXT SIZE options have a default of 8KB (or four pages).

Lock Mode Option

When you create a table, you can specify the lock mode of page-level or row-level locking. Page-level locking is the default if nothing is specified, and this allows you to lock an entire page of rows. Row-level locking allows concurrent processing at a row level, but the number of locks could escalate when many rows at a time are locked. Row-level locking does give you the highest level of concurrency, but the configuration must be set up to avoid reaching the maximum number of locks.

Temporary Tables

Temporary tables last for the time that your application program is processing or until your database is closed. A temporary table cannot have referential constraints placed on any defined columns nor can any column of the table be referenced from another table. If the user has connect privileges on the database, he can create a temporary table and build indexes on that temporary table.

When creating your tables, the only elements that are necessary are a unique table name within the database and unique column names within each table.

The following code segments show examples of `CREATE TABLE` statements:

```
CREATE TABLE department
            (deptno        char(3)          not null,
             deptname     char(20)        not null,
             mgrgrp          char(10),
           location     char(15),
             primary key     (deptno)
            );

CREATE TABLE department
        (deptno         char(3)          not null,
             deptname     char(20)        not null,
             mgrgrp          char(10),
           location     char(15),
             primary key     (deptno,deptname)
     )
     in dbspace1  extent size 24 next size 12;

CREATE TABLE project
        (projno         char(8)        not null,
         projname         char(20)        not null,
         department     char(20),
         prjstart         date,
         prjend         date,
         vendor         varchar(50,10)
    )
    lock mode row;

CREATE TABLE  accounts
        (acctno         INTEGER,
         acct_type    INTEGER,
        subven        varchar(50,20)
REFERENCES project (vendor),
        );

CREATE TEMP TABLE dba
        (lname         char(20),
         fname         char(20),
         manager    char(20))
    WITH NO LOG;
```

Creating Views

You use the CREATE VIEW statement to create a new view with its definition based upon a current table or another view of the database.

A view is also known as a synthetic table. You can query or update the view as if it is a table. You must remember that in actuality, the table data is a view of what is stored in the real table. Refer to Chapter 16, "Privileges and Security Issues," for an in-depth look at views.

Views are created for many purposes:

- Restrict users to specific rows or columns of tables.
- Control the insert and update data of the table.
- Avoid redundancy of data.

A view acts just like any other table and consists of all rows and columns that are a result of the select statement used at creation time. The data attributes for each column are derived from the original table. The user must have the select privilege on the table in order to create the view.

The statement used to create the view is stored in the Informix sysviews table. Each time the view is referenced by a statement, the server performs the SELECT.

You can name each column at the time you do your CREATE VIEW statement, but if no column names are specified, the names from the referenced tables are used. Keep in mind that naming columns follows an all-or-none rule. If you are not going to name all the columns of the view, you don't name any. Also, if some columns have duplicate names, you must label each column name in the view statement.

You can use a view in all SQL statements that deal with data viewing and manipulation, such as SELECT, INSERT, DELETE, or UPDATE. A view cannot be used in database layout SQL statements such as the following:

- Alter Index
- Create Index
- Drop Index
- Alter Table
- Create Table
- Drop Table
- Lock Table
- Rename Table
- Unlock Table

There are additional restrictions when using views. Because a view is not a real table, you cannot create an index , and the INTO TEMP, UNION, and ORDER BY functions cannot be processed. A view is based on one or more tables, so it should always reflect the most current changes of the tables.

You can perform updates and inserts on a view with certain restrictions. First, you can update a view only if the columns are not derived from the select statement that creates the view. An insert follows the same rules, and the view must be modifiable for any function to complete.

The privileges on a view are checked at the time the CREATE VIEW statement is processed. The authorization is checked from the table from which you want to create your view. When a table is created, the grant to public is automatic, but that is not the case with a view. If the view is modifiable, the database server grants delete, insert, and update privileges.

The following code shows examples of two CREATE VIEW statements:

```
CREATE VIEW  dept_view AS
    SELECT * FROM  department where deptno = ABC
CREATE VIEW  proj_view AS
    SELECT projno, projname FROM project
```

A view is a way to control the data that users can access. The authorization can control who can modify the data and restrict users from accessing confidential data.

Altering Tables

You use the ALTER TABLE statement to make modifications to an existing table. The following list outlines uses for the statement:

- Add columns.
- Drop columns.
- Modify data constraints on a column.
- Add data constraints to a column.
- Drop constraints on a column.
- Modify the NEXT SIZE parameter.
- Modify the LOCK MODE of table.

The next few pages review all these options for the ALTER TABLE statement.

ADD Clause

You use the ADD clause for the ALTER TABLE statement to add a column to an existing table. You can add the column to the end of the table by default, or you can state a BEFORE clause and the column name before which you want the new column placed.

When you add a column, the NOT NULL option is not allowed. Also, if the table being altered contains data, you cannot define the new column as a primary or unique key.

DROP Clause

You use the DROP clause for the ALTER TABLE statement to drop an existing column of a table. You state the DROP keyword with the name of the column to be dropped. Keep in mind that when a column is dropped, all constraints associated with that column are also dropped. The following summarizes the constraints dropped:

- Referential constraints
- Check constraints
- Single column constraints
- Primary or unique key constraints
- Multiple column constraints

When a column is dropped, the structure of associated tables can also be altered. This is especially true when the primary key or referential constraints are altered.

MODIFY Clause

You use the MODIFY clause for the ALTER TABLE statement to change the data type of an existing column, change the length of a column, or change the value to allow or not allow nulls. When the data type is changed in an existing column, the data in the table is automatically converted to the new data type.

When a column is modified, all previous values and attributes are also dropped. In the MODIFY clause, you must list all attributes again if you want to retain what was previously defined before the statement. As with the DROP clause, all single column and referential constraints are dropped.

ADD CONSTRAINT Clause

You use the ADD CONSTRAINT clause for the ALTER TABLE statement to add a constraint to a new or existing column. When a unique constraint is defined, the column must contain only unique values. A unique name is also used for each constraint; if you do not specify one, the database server gives you one by default. All constraint information is stored in the system catalog table SYSCONSTRAINTS.

DROP CONSTRAINT Clause

You use the DROP CONSTRAINT clause of the ALTER TABLE statement to drop an existing constraint. The statement uses the DROP CONSTRAINT keywords with the constraint name. If you do not know the constraint name, you can query the SYSCONSTRAINTS system catalog table.

If you drop a constraint that has a foreign key relation, the referential constraint is also dropped.

MODIFY NEXT SIZE Clause

You use the `MODIFY NEXT SIZE` clause of the `ALTER TABLE` statement to change the size of the next extent. When a table is created, the `EXTENT SIZE` and `NEXT SIZE` are included in the statement. This clause allows you to modify only the `NEXT SIZE` value.

LOCK MODE Clause

You use the `LOCK MODE` clause of the `ALTER TABLE` statement to change the locking mode of an existing table. The default at the time of the initial table creation is page-level locking.

The following code contains examples of `ALTER TABLE` statements:

```
ALTER TABLE department
    ADD  (deptcode      char(10)    NOT NULL
               BEFORE mgrgrp) ;
ALTER TABLE department
    DROP CONSTRAINT  mgr_con ;
ALTER TABLE  project
    MODIFY   (department    SMALLINT    NOT NULL) ;
ALTER TABLE project LOCK MODE (ROW) ;
```

With the `ALTER TABLE` statement, you can use more than one of the described clauses in a single statement. Also when altering a table with an associated view, be aware that the view may become invalid.

Creating Indexes

When creating an index, you must use the `CREATE INDEX` statement. You can create an index on one or more columns of the same table. At the time of the index creation, the database server puts an exclusive lock on the entire table until the index build is complete. With the create statement, you define an index name that is unique for that table.

You have some options with the `CREATE INDEX` statement. First is the `UNIQUE` option. The unique option prevents duplicates from being inserted into the table. Next is the `CLUSTER` option. The cluster option orders the table by the design of the index. You are allowed only one `CLUSTER` index on a physical table.

NOTE

The `CREATE INDEX` statement has additional keywords:

- You use the `DISTINCT` keyword exactly as you use the `UNIQUE` keyword. This option does not allow duplicates in the table.
- The `ASC` keyword keeps the index in ascending order. `ASC` is the default if not specified in the create statement.
- The `DESC` keyword keeps the index in descending order.

The following code shows examples of the CREATE INDEX statement:

```
CREATE  UNIQUE INDEX  dep_ix1 ON department (deptno) ;
CREATE  CLUSTER INDEX c_dep_ix1 ON department (deptno) ;
CREATE INDEX proj_ix1 ON project (projno DESC) ;
```

Altering Indexes

When altering an index, you must use the ALTER INDEX statement. There are only two reasons to use the statement; one is to change the CLUSTER option of an existing index, and one is to reorder the data by the existing index. For the alter statement to work, the index must have been previously created with the CREATE INDEX statement and you must have the proper permissions to perform the ALTER INDEX statement.

The TO CLUSTER option allows you to add clustering to an existing index. This forces all existing data rows to reorder to comply with the indexed order. Any new inserts to the table are placed in the clustered order. Inserts require more processing overhead, but a clustered index provides the fastest queries. This does not work if there is already an existing clustered index on the same table.

The TO NOT CLUSTER option drops the cluster option of the index. When this is done, the table is not affected. Any new inserts are placed randomly. Searches require a little more effort, but using this option is still faster than a non-indexed table.

The following code shows two examples of the ALTER INDEX statement:

```
ALTER INDEX dept_ix1 TO NOT CLUSTER ;
ALTER INDEX proj_ix1 TO CLUSTER ;
```

NOTE

Only one clustered index is allowed per physical table. You must drop an existing clustered index if you want to add a new clustered index.

Privileges

A privilege is the authorization given for a database or table. You can control authorizations by granting and revoking privileges to users. As stated, the two groups for privileges are for the database and for individual tables. For more information on privileges, refer to Chapter 16.

You use the GRANT statement to specify the privileges given on tables and views. In the granting process, there is a grantor and a user. The grantor is the user who gives the privileges to another user. A user is the receiver of the granted privileges.

Note that you can grant privileges to individual users or to PUBLIC. PUBLIC grants privileges to users who currently use the tables or to users who will use them in the future. When privileges are granted, they remain until the original grantor REVOKEs them.

Database-Level Privileges

There are three types of privileges on the database:

- Connect
- Resource
- Database administrator

The lowest level of database privileges is connect. The connect privilege allows the users to query and modify tables. This privilege allows the following operations:

- SELECT, INSERT, UPDATE, and DELETE
- Create views
- Create temporary tables
- Execute stored procedures

NOTE

The user must have the appropriate table-level privileges, and if you do not have the connect privilege, you cannot access the database.

The resource privilege has the same authorization as the connect privilege, but additionally, it allows access and modification to permanent tables, indexes, and stored procedures. The database administrator privileges are the highest level of database authorization. When you create the database, you automatically become the administrator. Every database has an owner, and with this privilege, you can create objects that are owned by others.

Some of the functions that the database administrator privilege allows include

- DROP DATABASE and START DATABASE
- Alter extent size
- Drop or alter any object
- Create objects owned by other users
- Grant database privileges

Table-Level Privileges

There are seven table-level privileges. If you are the owner of the table (the person who created the table), you have control of the table and receive all seven privileges. Note that the DBA, even if he or she isn't the owner, also has all privileges on the table.

The following list contains a brief description of each of the seven privileges:

SELECT	Privilege to name any column of a table in a SELECT statement
UPDATE	Privilege to name any column in an UPDATE statement
INSERT	Privilege to insert rows into a table
DELETE	Privilege to delete rows from a table
ALTER	Privilege to add or delete columns, add or delete table-level constraints, and modify column data types
INDEX	Privilege to create indexes (permanent) on a table
REFERENCES	Privilege to reference columns in referential constraints

To grant a user all the preceding privileges, you use the ALL keyword in your GRANT statement. Note that for creating permanent indexes or incorporating referential constraints on your tables, you must have the resource privilege.

When a table is created, the database server automatically grants all privileges to PUBLIC. In most instances, you then REVOKE all from PUBLIC and grant the table-level privileges you want. An additional option or keyword is WITH GRANT OPTION. When a user is granted privileges with this keyword, he is also given the authorization to grant those same privileges to additional users.

Stored Procedures

Stored procedures, like tables, have privileges granted to PUBLIC when they are created. The EXECUTE ON option allows you to grant users the capability to run a defined stored procedure. For more information on stored procedures, refer to Chapter 14, "Managing Data with Stored Procedures and Triggers."

Views

When you create a view, as the owner, you must grant all privileges to the users. Like the table privileges, the view does not give an automatic grant to PUBLIC. To create a view, you must have at least select privilege on the tables being used. For more information on views, refer to Chapter 16.

If you want to see what privileges were granted for a table, you can select the information from the SYSTABAUTH system catalog table.

The following code shows examples of privileges granted:

```
GRANT CONNECT ON database1 to PUBLIC;
GRANT SELECT ON department TO user1;
REVOKE ALL ON department FROM PUBLIC;
GRANT EXECUTE ON procedure_1 TO user1;
```

Integrity

When designing your database, try to define tables with minimum data redundancy. After entities are defined, begin to develop their relationships. Your primary goal is to create an efficient database with data integrity playing a large part of the process. For more information, refer to Chapter 17, which is dedicated to data integrity.

Three types of data integrity are incorporated into the database design:

- Entity
- Semantic
- Referential

Entity Integrity

Every entity in a model represents a table. When the table is created, you must have a primary key. The primary key of the table is the column or columns whose values are different for every row of the table or are unique. This is called the entity integrity constraint.

Semantic Integrity

Semantic integrity is used to ensure that each time data is entered into the table, the values match what was defined for that column. Semantic integrity uses the following constraints to ensure the values are all within the correct domain:

Data type	Defines the values allowed to be stored in the column
Default value	The default value that can be stored when no value was inserted
Check constraint	Conditions on the data that is inserted into the table

Referential Integrity

Referential integrity is the relationship that is built between tables. This process works when the primary key of one table is found as the key of another table. This is known as the foreign key. The foreign key actually establishes the relationship or dependencies between the two tables.

You define the relationships using the `CREATE TABLE` and `ALTER TABLE` statements. When the constraint is created, an exclusive lock is held on the referenced table until the statement is complete.

Summary

This chapter discussed the fundamentals of database design starting with the three-step process of naming entities, defining relationships, and listing attributes. These steps are all part of defining a data model. When the logical model is complete, you start to define your data objects into tables, columns, and rows.

The reasons for diagramming your data objects include providing documentation, organizing information, identifying entities and relationships, and creating a logical design layout. The process of determining your database is based on the data model that was defined. You use SQL to create your database, tables, and additional objects from your data model. This chapter also covered the following functions to implement the data model:

- Creating tables
- Altering tables
- Creating indexes
- Altering indexes
- Data integrity and privileges

CHAPTER

Data Management Using SQL

by John McNally

IN THIS CHAPTER

This chapter discusses data management using the Structured Query Language (SQL). SQL is the data access language used to communicate with the database manager. You use SQL's data manipulation statements to view and store rows in a table, as well as modify and delete these rows. Here are the statements you use:

- `SELECT`
- `INSERT`
- `UPDATE`
- `DELETE`

The `SELECT` statement is the definitive command found in SQL. Not only does it allow you to see anything within the database, but it also helps the next three commands to be more precise. You use the `INSERT` statement to store rows in a table. The statement can add a row to an empty table or a table that already has populated data. You use the `UPDATE` statement if you want to change any of the existing rows in a table. You use the `DELETE` statement to delete one or more rows in a table. This chapter reviews the execution of each statement.

Informix uses an enhanced version of the industry standard query language product. Putting SQL statements into a program allows you to query a database as well as make modifications to existing rows.

The following list outlines the types of data management functions that are discussed in this chapter:

- Querying
- Inserting
- Updating
- Deleting

Querying Data

Using the `SELECT` statement is the primary way to query your database. It is the most important SQL statement and can be the most complex. The `SELECT` statement does not modify data in the database; you use it only to query the data. You can select from a database table, a view, or the system catalog tables.

You can use the `SELECT` statement in the following ways:

- Retrieve data from a database.
- Create new rows with the `INSERT` statement.
- Update data with the `UPDATE` statement.

There are five SELECT statement clauses, even though only two clauses—SELECT and FROM—are required. You must use the clauses in the following order:

- SELECT
- FROM
- WHERE
- ORDER BY
- INTO TEMP

Two additional clauses for more advanced queries are GROUP BY and HAVING.

To select from a database, you must have the CONNECT privilege to the database and the SELECT privilege for any tables to be accessed.

You can run a query on a single table of a database to retrieve all or specific columns or rows and order the data in different ways. If you specify an asterisk (*) in your select statement, all the columns are returned in their defined order. You can specify which columns you want by including the list of column names immediately after the SELECT keyword in the statement. The order in which the columns are selected is the order in which they are returned by default.

You can eliminate duplicate rows from being returned by using the DISTINCT keyword in your SELECT statement. You can also use the UNIQUE keyword for the same purpose.

The following code shows an example of syntax:

```
SELECT * FROM table1
       SELECT column1, column2, column3 FROM table1
```

You use the WHERE clause of the SELECT statement for two specific purposes:

- Specify the criteria for searching specific rows.
- Create join conditions with multiple tables.

You can use many keywords and operators to define your search criteria:

Keywords	*Results in*
BETWEEN	Range of values
IN	Subset of values
LIKE	Variable text search
MATCHES	Variable text search
IS NULL	Search for NULL strings
IS NOT NULL	Search for non-NULL strings
AND/OR/NOT	Logical operators used to connect two or more conditions

Relational Operators	*Description*
=	Equals
!= or <>	Does not equal
>	Greater than
>=	Greater than or equal to
<	Less than
<=	Less than or equal to

Arithmetic Operators	*Description*
+	Addition
-	Subtraction
*	Multiplication
/	Division

In addition to using the LIKE and MATCHES keywords, you can use a wildcard for variable text search strings.

Use with LIKE	*Description*
%	Evaluates to 0 or more characters
_	Evaluates to a single character
\	Specifies a literal for the next character

Use with MATCHES	*Description*
*	Evaluates to 0 or more characters
?	Evaluates to a single character
[ ]	Specifies valid values for a single character or a range of values
\	Specifies a literal for the next character

You can instruct the system to sort the selected data in a specific order by using the ORDER BY clause on the SELECT statement. By default, data that is retrieved is sorted in ascending order. You can add the DESC keyword to your SELECT statement to sort the data in descending order. The ORDER BY column must be in the select list. Columns that are frequently used with the ORDER BY clause should be indexed for best performance of the query.

With the SELECT statement, you can use a display label to replace the default header on derived data columns. The display label must start with a letter and can be a combination of letters and numbers up to 18 characters in length.

You can use additional functions with the `SELECT` statement. You use aggregate functions to summarize groups of selected rows in a table:

`COUNT`	Counts the number of rows that are a result of the `SELECT` statement
`SUM`	Sums the value of a given numeric column
`AVG`	Arithmetic means of a given numeric column
`MAX`	Maximum value of a given column
`MIN`	Minimum value of a given column

You can use the `COUNT`, `SUM`, and `AVG` functions in combination with the `DISTINCT` clause in the `SELECT` statement.

The next set of functions is the time functions:

`DAY`	Integer that represents the day
`MONTH`	Integer that represents the month
`WEEKDAY`	Integer that represents the day of the week (values `0` through `6`, where `0` represents Sunday)
`YEAR`	Four-digit integer that represents the year
`MDY`	Returns the date in *mm/dd/yyyy* format
`DATE`	Returns a date value
`EXTEND`	Adjusts the precision of the `DATE` or `DATETIME` value
`CURRENT`	Returns a date/time value that represents the current date and time

In addition to the aggregate and time functions, you can also use the following functions:

`LENGTH`	Returns the length of a character column
`USER`	Returns the login account name of the current user
`TODAY`	Returns the system data
`SITENAME`	Returns the server name for the INFORMIX-OnLine system (defined in the `onconfig` file where the current database resides)
`HEX`	Returns the hexadecimal encoding of an expression
`ROUND`	Returns the rounded value of an expression
`TRUNC`	Returns the truncated value of an expression

As mentioned earlier in this chapter, additional functionality for the `SELECT` statement is found in the `GROUP BY` and `HAVING` clauses. The `GROUP BY` clause produces a single row for each group of rows that have the same value in a given column. The data is sorted into groups and then compressed into a single row for end results.

A GROUP BY clause does not order the result data. If you include an ORDER BY statement in the select after the GROUP BY clause, the rows are sorted in the specified order.

The HAVING clause provides a filter for the grouped-by results. This works in conjunction with the GROUP BY clause to apply conditions on the groups after they are formed. You do not need to use a HAVING clause with a GROUP BY clause, but in most cases they appear in the query together. For more information on the GROUP BY and HAVING clauses, refer to Chapter 31, "Advanced SQL."

Multiple Table SELECT Statements

You can select data from two or more tables by using the SELECT statement with the FROM and WHERE clauses. The SELECT clause lists the columns from each table that you want, the FROM clause lists the tables you are selecting from, and the WHERE clause lists the matching columns in order to join the tables.

A simple join gets the information from two or more tables with a basis of one column for each table. A composite join is a join between two or more tables with two or more columns in each table used for the relationship. The following is an example of a simple join to get customer information from two tables:

```
SELECT * FROM customer_table, address_table
     WHERE customer_table.cust_num = address_table.cust_num;
```

Inserting Data

The SQL INSERT statement allows a user to enter a row or rows of values into a table. The INSERT statement has two functions: The first is creating one single new row by supplying the column values and the second is creating a group of new rows with values derived from another table.

Single Row Inserts

Adding a single row is the simplest form of the INSERT statement. The statement creates one new row in a table from a list of defined column values. You use a VALUES clause in the statement, and the values to be inserted must have a one-to-one equivalence with the columns of the table.

The following code shows an example of the syntax:

```
INSERT INTO table1
          VALUES (123, "ABC")
```

If you do not want to specify every column of the table where you insert a row, you can list the column names after the table name and then supply the values for the columns you list.

The VALUES clause accepts only constant values. You can use the following values:

- Literal numbers, date and time values, and interval values
- Strings of characters (quoted)
- NULL for null values
- TODAY for today's date
- CURRENT for the current date and time
- USER for the user's name
- DBSERVERNAME for the database server name

When inserting a value into a column, you might find that restrictions were placed on the column. For example, some columns might not allow null values or duplicate values. Also, a column restriction can specify the exact values that are allowed to be inserted.

One column in a table can be defined as a SERIAL data type. The database server generates values for a serial column. When you specify 0 as the value, the database server generates the next value in the sequence. Serial columns do not allow you to insert NULL values.

When performing inserts, the database server makes conversions if necessary. For example, when you insert a number or date into a character column, the server converts the values to character strings. The database server can also convert between numeric and character data types.

Multiple Row Inserts

For the more enhanced INSERT statements, you can replace the VALUES clause with a SELECT statement. This option allows you to insert multiple rows of data with only one statement. Using the SELECT clause in the INSERT statement has the following restrictions:

- You cannot use the INTO clause.
- You cannot use the INTO TEMP clause.
- You cannot use the ORDER BY clause.
- You cannot use the same table in the INTO clause of the INSERT statement and the FROM clause of the SELECT statement.

When inserting multiple rows, you have a risk of including invalid data, so the database server terminates the statement if it reaches an invalid value.

INSERT Statement Within a Program

You can embed an INSERT statement in a program just as if you were performing any simple SQL statement. An additional feature allows you to use host variables in expressions for both the VALUES and WHERE clauses.

INSERT Within a Cursor

You can use the insert cursor to place multiple rows into a table. You use the PUT and FLUSH statements to efficiently insert the rows. You create the cursor by declaring a CURSOR FOR and INSERT statement, not a SELECT statement. When you define this type of cursor, you cannot use it for fetching data—only for inserting data.

When the insert cursor is opened, a buffer is created in memory to store a block of rows that were received from the program. They are passed to the database server when the buffer is full, and the server inserts the rows into the table. This type of processing decreases the amount of communication between the program and the database server. The insert buffer is already defined at 2KB.

The following steps show what happens when an insert buffer is flushed:

- Determine that the buffer is full.
- The FLUSH statement is executed.
- The COMMIT WORK statement is executed.
- The CLOSE statement is executed (closes the cursor).
- The OPEN statement is executed (closes the cursor and reopens the cursor).

Inserting and Transactions

When you insert a row into a database without using transactions, you cannot automatically recover the data if the insert fails, and some of the processing may have already completed.

If you insert a row into a database with transactions and the insert fails, the database server automatically rolls back any modifications that were made. Also, if you include a ROLLBACK WORK statement with the insert, the modifications are rolled back if they are not successful.

When using transactions, the row being inserted remains locked until the work is committed. If you perform a large number of inserts, you might reach the limit of locks allowed. You can avoid reaching the limit by locking the entire page of the table prior to inserting the new rows.

Inserting with a View

You can insert rows into a view as long as the view is modifiable and you have the privilege to do so. An insert is allowed as long as there are no derived columns. When inserting, you must provide values for all the columns or the database server fails the attempted insert. When a view has no derived columns, the insert function works exactly as it does on a table.

A view can have restrictions that affect the insertion of rows. For example, when creating a view, you can use a WITH CHECK OPTION on the statement, which forces the database server to check that all rows meet the criteria defined in the statement (set by the WHERE clause).

Insert Using Stored Procedures

Rows of data that are a result of a procedure call into a table can be inserted into another table. When using this procedure, you must make sure all values match the values or data types of the columns in the table you indicate.

Updating Data

You use the SQL UPDATE statement to change the values of one or more rows of a table. The two forms of the UPDATE statement are uniform value updates and select value updates.

To update data in a table, you must be the owner of the table or have the UPDATE privilege for that table. If you update rows in a database without transactions and the update fails, your database can be in a state with a half-processed update, and it is not rolled back. If your database has transactions, you do the update with the ROLLBACK WORK statement, which automatically rolls back any modifications if the statement fails or does not completely finish processing.

When an update is processed, the database server acquires an update lock for the rows you are updating. Update locks allow other users to read the row but do not allow them to update or delete it. Just before the row is updated, the server places the shared update lock to an exclusive lock, which prevents all users from reading or modifying the row until the lock is released.

Keep in mind that for updates done on rows with data integrity enforced, you must make the changes within the constraints of the defined column.

The UPDATE statement can end in a WHERE clause, which determines what rows are affected. If you do not include a WHERE clause, then all rows of the table are modified. The WHERE clause consists of standard search criteria.

Uniform Value Updates

Updating with uniform values happens when you use the SET keyword to add a value for a column. The value is uniformly added to every row unless you state a WHERE clause to be more specific on your UPDATE statement:

```
UPDATE table1
            SET field1 = ABC
```

The SET clause identifies each column to be changed and specifies the value that is used in making the change. You can have any amount of single-column-to-single-expression functions in an UPDATE statement.

You can use the NULL keyword as a column value with the UPDATE statement.

Selected Value Updates

Updating with selected values happens when you take a list of columns and set them to a list of values. This method is basically the same as the first form of updates, but it assigns bulk values to existing columns:

```
UPDATE table1
            SET (field1, field2, field3) = ('ABC', 'DEF', 'GHI')
```

UPDATE Statement Within a Program

You can embed the UPDATE statement in a program just as you set up the statement for any other data-modifying SQL update.

Updating Within a Cursor

An update cursor allows you to update the current row or the most recently fetched row. The reason you use the keyword UPDATE in the cursor is to let the database server know that the program can update any row that it fetches. When you use the UPDATE keyword in the cursor, the database server puts a higher level of locking on the fetched rows, as compared to fetching a row with a cursor without the UPDATE keyword.

Updating with a View

You can update data through a view (a single table view only) if you have update privilege on that particular view. To do this, the SELECT statement can only select from one table and it cannot use any of the following functions:

- The DISTINCT keyword
- The GROUP BY clause
- A virtual column
- An aggregate value

When updating a table through a view, make sure you are aware of the view's definition. For example, a view might contain duplicate rows where the table used in the SELECT statement to create the view has only unique rows. You can also use data integrity constraints to control the updates in the underlying table when the update values are not as defined in the SELECT statement for the view.

Deleting Data

The SQL DELETE statement removes one or more rows from a table. If you use transaction processing, you cannot recover the deleted rows after the statement is committed. Also, when you delete a row, the row is locked for the duration of the transaction. If a large number of rows are deleted, keep in mind that all rows are locked. You can lock the entire table prior to deleting if you know you are processing a lot of rows.

Using transaction logging while preparing for the DELETE statement can be very beneficial. If you reach any kind of error during your statement, you can have a ROLLBACK WORK clause that lets the database server put the database back to its original state prior to the DELETE process before the work is committed. The advantage of using transaction processing is that, regardless of what happens during your process, the database is left in the original state if the statement cannot be completely processed correctly.

When you delete data from a table, you must know the structure and constraints of the database. If you delete rows from a table that has a dependent table, you must make sure the values from the dependent table are also deleted. This process can be controlled with the ON DELETE CASCADE constraint. This option, which is stated on the CREATE TABLE or ALTER TABLE statement, causes deletes from a parent table to be also processed on the child table.

First, you start by reviewing the statement for deleting all rows from a table. When a DELETE statement is created, you specify the table name and, in most cases, a WHERE clause. If the WHERE clause is not on the statement, all rows are automatically deleted from the table.

If you are using INFORMIX-SQL or Informix DBaccess when you use the DELETE statement without a WHERE clause, you are asked to confirm that you do want to delete all rows in the existing table. Please note that if you use the DELETE clause in a program, you are not asked for confirmation, and the DELETE processes automatically. The following example deletes all rows from the specified table, which is table1:

```
DELETE FROM table1
```

The general syntax for a DELETE statement is simple, but you must be careful that you accurately delete the rows that you want. The DELETE keyword identifies the operation you are to perform. The FROM clause is next followed by the table name. The WHERE clause identifies the rows to be deleted. The search conditions are the same as those in the SELECT and UPDATE statements; they can be used to identify many rows, and therefore an accurate deletion process takes place. The following example now deletes only the rows from table1 that have a balance of zero:

```
DELETE FROM table1
    WHERE balance = 0;
```

You can uniquely specify a value in your DELETE statement with the WHERE clause to guarantee that only the data meeting the criteria is deleted. This delete is based on the unique constraints on the column of the table. You can also perform a delete on non-unique or non-indexed columns, which might delete many rows from the table.

When you plan to delete rows from a table and you are not sure what the results will be, it is suggested that you first run the query using the SELECT statement prior to the DELETE so that you at least have an approximation of the end results.

DELETE Statement Within a Program

A program deletes rows from a table by executing the DELETE statement. The statement can refer to specific rows or single a row out by using the WHERE clause. You can delete a single row by using the last fetched row through a cursor.

The same rules apply in a program when table dependency occurs and you delete rows.

You can embed the DELETE statement in a program using INFORMIX-ESQL/C. The statement always works directly on the selected database. You can also execute a statement dynamically, and it works directly against the database to delete the specified rows.

Deleting Within a Cursor

You can use a DELETE statement through a cursor to delete the last fetched row. A program can also scan through a table and delete specific rows. Note that without transaction logging on the database, the recovery process is not a simple one.

To delete from a table, a user must have the delete privilege on the table. The user may have connect database privileges, which allow a DELETE statement to run, but he also needs the table-level privilege.

Deleting with a View

You can use a modifiable view with the DELETE statement as if it is a table. The database server handles the process of deleting the associated row of the underlying table.

To modify the data of a database, specific privileges must be granted to specific tables. For example, the insert, delete, and update privileges are granted by the table owner. This allows you a way to control the modification of your data.

You can use the DELETE statement to remove one or more rows of a table. You can use the UPDATE statement to modify the contents of existing rows. You can use the INSERT statement to add a single row or a block of rows to a table.

If data integrity constraints are on the database, the rules are applied when modifying the data.

Summary

This chapter discussed how SQL can be the language used to communicate with the database manager. You can use SQL statements such as SELECT, INSERT, DELETE, and UPDATE to manipulate the data within the database.

The INSERT statement allows a user to enter a row or rows of values into a table. There are single row inserts and multiple row inserts. The UPDATE statement changes the values of one or more rows of a table. The two forms of UPDATE are uniform value updates and select value updates.

The DELETE statement removes one or more rows from a table. The SELECT statement used by itself allows access to any amount of information stored within the database. Combining the SELECT with the INSERT, UPDATE, or DELETE statements provides a means to perform more specific data manipulations.

With each of the SQL statements, you can use many additional keywords and operators for more explicit processing. Your statement can also range from a simple insert to a mass delete of data. It is always recommended that you run a SELECT prior to processing an INSERT, UPDATE, or DELETE so that you can be aware of the impact of the changes prior to actually running the SQL statement.

CHAPTER

Advanced SQL

by John McNally

IN THIS CHAPTER

This chapter discusses the management and use of advanced Structured Query Language (SQL). SQL is used to communicate with the database manager. SQL also has a large effect on the performance of the database. The preceding chapter discussed basic SELECT statements, and this chapter describes more complex queries and data manipulation.

Advanced SQL consists of complex database queries. This includes table joins and extensive subqueries within a SELECT statement. As your SQL commands become complex, the need to optimize them will arise.

This chapter discusses

- Advanced queries
- Optimizing queries

Advanced Queries

You can use additional syntax with the SELECT statement for advanced or more powerful SQL. The first two functions are GROUP BY and HAVING, which are used with the SELECT statement.

GROUP BY Clause

The GROUP BY clause produces a single row of results for each group of rows (or set) having the same values in a given column. The data is sorted into groups, and then all the rows of like values are grouped into a single row. You cannot group BYTE or TEXT columns because you must be able to sort, and that is not a normal function for these data attributes.

You can use the GROUP BY clause with aggregate functions to produce summarized information. A good time to use GROUP BY is when a query is needed to get a total of all the employees in each department of a company.

The GROUP BY clause does not automatically order by the end result data. You can include an ORDER BY statement within your query to sort the data being returned.

The following examples show SELECT statements with the GROUP BY clause:

```
SELECT column1
    FROM table1
    GROUP BY column1;

SELECT column1,  column2, max(column3), min(column4)
    FROM table1
    GROUP BY column1, column2;

SELECT column1, avg(column2)
    FROM table1
    WHERE column1 = 'ABC'
    GROUP BY column1;

SELECT dept_name, COUNT (*)_
    FROM employee_table
    GROUP BY dept_name;
```

HAVING Clause

You can use the HAVING clause in addition to the GROUP BY clause to add conditions to groups after they are formed. You do not have to use the HAVING clause with the GROUP BY clause, but you do use them together in most cases. The HAVING clause provides a filter for the GROUP BY results. However, HAVING does not sort the output; ORDER BY does that for you.

The HAVING condition must reflect a group-level value, something that is common to all rows in the group. In most cases, it is necessary to specify a column function in the HAVING clause. It is also possible to specify the name of a grouping column with a condition that all rows must meet.

For example, using the same query used in the GROUP BY section, you might want to produce a list of all the departments that are understaffed. To produce this list, add a HAVING clause to check for departments that have fewer than five employees.

The following examples show SELECT statements with the HAVING clause:

```
SELECT column1, column2
    FROM table1
    GROUP BY column1, column2
    HAVING column2 > 0;

SELECT column1, avg(column2)
    FROM table1
    GROUP BY column1
    HAVING avg(column2) <
       (SELECT avg(column2)
          FROM table1);

SELECT dept_name, COUNT (*)_
    FROM employee_table
    GROUP BY dept_name
    HAVING COUNT (*) < 5;
```

Note that if you have a HAVING clause without a GROUP BY clause, the HAVING condition applies to all rows that satisfy the search condition. This means that all rows that are satisfied by the search conditions are returned in one single group.

Simple Joins

Sometimes you want data from more than one table. To retrieve the data from two or more tables, you must enter additional information in your SELECT statement. The following list outlines the step-by-step process for creating your statement:

1. In the SELECT statement, list all the columns you want from each of the tables.
2. In the FROM clause, list all the tables you are selecting from.
3. In the WHERE clause, list all the columns to be matched from each table in order to join the tables.

The following sample code shows a simple join:

```
SELECT *
    FROM table1, table2
    WHERE table1.column1 = table2.column2;

SELECT enrolledstudents.ssn, studentname,  major, gradepoints.currentaverage
    FROM enrolledstudents,  gradepoints
    WHERE enrolledstudents.ssn = gradepoints.ssn;
```

When joining large tables, the best performance can be achieved when the user really understands the meaning of the data, the relationship between the tables, and whether the columns used in the join are indexed. If the columns used in the join are indexed, the query is more efficient.

The two types of simple joins are equi-joins and natural joins. An equi-join is a join based on matching values of the WHERE clause in the SELECT statement, which uses the = operator. A natural join is the same as the equi-join with the duplicate columns eliminated. The previous example, using the enrolledstudents and gradepoints tables, is an example of a natural join because ssn is displayed only once. The following example is the same query without any columns specified, but all columns from each table will be shown due to the *. This query displays ssn twice—once from enrolledstudents and the other from gradepoints, even though the ssn value is the same.

```
SELECT *
        FROM enrolledstudents,  gradepoints
        WHERE enrolledstudents.ssn = gradepoints.ssn;
```

Joins using three or more tables with columns associated between them are considered multiple table joins. You can perform multiple table joins as long as there is a connection between the tables on one or more columns. If there is no connection but multiple tables are used, you have just a basic query, such as `SELECT * FROM table1, table2, table2`. A multiple table join can be an equi-join or a natural join.

The following code shows an example of a multiple table join using the same student table example. Now the query is extended to include a description of each student's major.

```
SELECT enrolledstudents.ssn, studentname,  major, majortable.desc,
➥gradepoints.currentaverage
        FROM enrolledstudents,  gradepoints, majortable
        WHERE enrolledstudents.ssn = gradepoints.ssn
              AND enrolledstudents.major = majortable.major;
```

Self-Joins

A self-join occurs when you join a table to itself. You can use a self-join if you want to compare values in a column to other values of the same column. When doing a self-join, you list the same table twice in the FROM clause assigning it an alias. The alias is then used in the SELECT and WHERE clause. You can join a table to itself more than once, depending on the resources available. The self-join is a very powerful join, but in large tables it sometimes performs slowly, depending on your index strategy. Complicated self-joins might perform better if you use a temporary table to store half the query, and then use the original and the temporary table to perform the main part of the query.

The following sample shows a self-join. Assume that the current average of each student is within the enrolledstudents table and not in a separate table as shown in the previous example. This example pairs higher-average students with lower-average students within the same major:

```
SELECT  x.studentname, x.major, x.currentaverage.
        y.studentname, y.major, y.currentaverage
        FROM enrolledstudents x,  enrolledstudents y
        WHERE x.major = y.major
        AND x.currentaverage > y.currentaverage
        ORDER BY x. major, x.currentaverage;
```

Outer-Joins

An outer-join is different from a simple join. In a simple join, the tables are treated equally; in an outer-join, the joining tables establish a subordinate role to a distinct table or set of tables. Unlike the simple join, where only matching data is displayed as output, outer-joins use one table to drive the query against other tables. Think of a simple join as saying, "show me what these tables (or table) have in common." An outer-join can be thought of as saying, "out of these tables, show me everything about a specific table and any related information from these other tables (or table)."

To specify the servant tables, use the `OUTER` keyword as part of the `FROM` statement, like this:

```
FROM dominant-table OUTER servant-table
```

All of the other keywords and statements of the `SELECT` statement are the same as for any other `SELECT` statement.

There are four types of outer-joins. The first type of outer-join involves two tables, with the first table being the dominant table and the second being the servant. The query goes through every row of the dominant table and displays its information. Any match with the servant table is also displayed. For example, using the same student query, you might want to display a report on every student enrolled and their major's full description. But some students might not have chosen a major yet. In this example, the enrolledstudents table will be the dominant table and the majortable will be the subservient table. The results of this query will provide all students in the enrolledstudents table and any students with majors will have a description included.

```
SELECT enrolledstudents.ssn, studentname,  major, majortable.desc
        FROM enrolledstudents,  OUTER majortable
        WHERE enrolledstudents.major = majortable.major;
```

Also known as a *nested simple join*, the second type of outer-join uses a third table, with the second and third tables being joined and being the servants of the first table. The dominant table is still completely used, but now only matches from the joined servers are applied.

For example, reverse the previous example in which student information, average, and major are displayed. Make the average table the dominant table so that all students and their averages will be used. Make enrolledstudents the servants, and make majortable the servers. Assume that you want to display student information only if the student has a major; therefore, the join will be on the major field between the two tables.

```
SELECT  x.ssn x.currentaverage, y.studentname, y.major, z.majordesc
        FROM gradepoints x OUTER (enrolledstudents y,  majortable z)
        WHERE x.ssn = y.ssn
           AND y.major = z.major
        ORDER BY x.ssn;
```

The third type of outer-join, known as a *nested outer-join*, performs an outer-join on an outer-join. In this case, a dominant and server comparison is performed, and then the results of the comparison become the servant to another table. This way, using the last example, you can make the enrolledstudents table the dominant table to the major table. Therefore, all enrolledstudents with or without majors will be used as the servants of gradepoints.

```
SELECT  x.ssn x.currentaverage, y.studentname, y.major, z.majordesc
        FROM gradepoints x OUTER (enrolledstudents y, OUTER  majortable z)
        WHERE x.ssn = y.ssn
           AND y.major = z.major
        ORDER BY x.ssn;
```

The final type of outer-join uses a dominant table that is over two separate servant tables. In this case, you don't have to join the two tables and use that combination as a servant. For example, make the enrolledstudents table the dominant table, with gradepoints and majortable as servants. The results will list all enrolledstudents, and any student with a gradepoint average or major will have that information included in the results.

```
SELECT  x.ssn x.currentaverage, y.studentname, y.major, z.majordesc
        FROM enrolledstudents x, OUTER gradepoints y, OUTER  majorytable z
        WHERE x.ssn = y.ssn
           AND x.major = z.major
        ORDER BY x.ssn;
```

SELECT Statements Using Subqueries

A subquery is a SELECT statement that is embedded within another SELECT statement (or INSERT, DELETE, or UPDATE statement). Each subquery must include a SELECT and FROM clause, which is inside parentheses and notifies the database server that this SELECT is to be completed first.

The two types of subqueries are correlated and uncorrelated. A subquery is correlated when the end product of the SELECT depends on the value produced by the outer SELECT statement. This type of query must be executed for each value of the outer select. The uncorrelated subquery is executed only once.

Many keywords introduce a subquery in the WHERE clause of a SELECT statement:

- ALL
- ANY

- IN
- EXISTS

The ALL keyword determines whether a comparison is true for all the values returned in the subquery.

The ANY keyword determines whether a comparison is true for at least one of the values returned in the subquery.

The IN keyword is a true value when it matches one or more values in the subquery.

The EXISTS keyword is a qualifier that is used when the outer SELECT in a subquery finds an appropriate row.

The following code shows some examples using subqueries:

```
SELECT column1, column2, column3
    FROM table1
    WHERE column2 < ALL
       (SELECT column2 FROM table1
           WHERE column1 = 123);

SELECT column1, column2, column3
    FROM table1
    WHERE column2 IN
     (SELECT  columna from table2
         WHERE columna IN (1, 2, 3));

SELECT majordesc
    FROM majortable
    WHERE major = ANY
       (SELECT major FROM enrolledstudents
          WHERE average > 3.5);
```

Set Operations

You can use three set operations to manipulate data: union, intersection, and difference.

The UNION keyword combines two queries into one combined query. You use the UNION keyword between two SELECT statements. The function selects all the result rows from both queries, removes all the duplicates, and returns the completed results. In order for a UNION to be successful, each data item in the union must be of the same data type and, when appropriate, the same size. For example, a union can't be made between a character string of 10 and a character string of 30. This applies only to data type definition; the data can be smaller, as long as it is defined as 10 characters, even though only 5 characters are actually stored in that field.

You can use the UNION ALL keyword to make sure that all duplicate values remain in the end results.

The following code shows the syntax:

```
SELECT column1
    FROM table1
```

```
UNION
SELECT column1
    FROM table2;
```

Continuing with the student theme, suppose that a college keeps tables of student averages by semester, and a report is needed to see which students hold a B or higher average for both the spring and fall semesters. Here's an example:

```
   SELECT ssn
     FROM gradepoints
     WHERE semester = "F97"
     AND average > 3.5
UNION
SELECT ssn
     FROM gradepoints
     WHERE semester = "S98"
     AND average > 3.5;
```

When two sets of rows from two tables produce an additional table containing only the rows that were found in both tables, this is considered an *intersection.* Two different SQL keywords can be used to produce an intersection—`EXISTS` and `IN`. Both keywords produce the same results.

```
SELECT column1, column2,
    FROM  table1
    WHERE EXISTS
        (SELECT *
          FROM table2
          WHERE table1.column1 = table2.column1);
```

When two sets of rows from two tables produce a table containing the rows that are in the first set but not in the second set, that table is said to contain the *difference.* Difference is considered to be the opposite of intersection. You can use the `NOT EXISTS` or `NOT IN` keywords to produce the difference of two sets. The syntax is as follows:

```
SELECT column1, column2, column3
    FROM table1
    WHERE column2 NOT IN
        (SELECT column2 from table2);
```

You can use advanced queries to retrieve data from a relational database. You can use additional clauses with the `SELECT` statement along with extensions of the simple join process.

Optimization

The most important part of querying data is writing the SQL queries for optimum performance. The key is to access your data in the most efficient way. Two ways to optimize your queries are to read fewer rows and avoid sorts.

Query Optimizer

The optimizer is part of the database server that decides how a query should be processed. It makes the decision about the most efficient way to access a table.

The following short list outlines functions used for querying your data that should be considered carefully for optimization:

Table joins	Two or more tables connected by one or more common columns
Subqueries	`SELECT` statement used within a `WHERE` clause
`ORDER BY`	Orders selected data
`GROUP BY`	Groups the selected table data into sets
`UNION`	Combines two queries into a single combined query
`DISTINCT`	Eliminates duplicate rows from the results of the query

SQL statements are divided into many categories. The query optimization information statements I discuss include the following:

- `SET EXPLAIN`
- `SET OPTIMIZATION`
- `UPDATE STATISTICS`

SET EXPLAIN

The `SET EXPLAIN` statement occurs when a query is initialized or when a cursor is opened. To use the explain function, you issue a `SET EXPLAIN ON` statement. This puts all the procedures and queries with their paths chosen by the optimizer into a file in the directory named `sqexplain.out`.

The output file contains the query, the execution plan chosen by the database optimizer, and an estimate of the amount of work that is done to process the query. The following list shows the output from the `SET EXPLAIN` statement:

- Estimated number of rows returned
- Estimated cost
- Order in which the tables are accessed
- Type of access method the optimizer chooses for each table
- List of columns used for filtering

When the optimizer reads each table, it chooses a method. The following list outlines a possible access path:

Sequential scan	Sequentially reads rows
Index scan	Scans indexes
Autoindex path	Creates a temporary index at execution time
Merge join	Uses a sort merge join; includes filters
Sort scan	Sort is processed on table scan prior to join

The following code shows the syntax for the SET EXPLAIN statement:

```
Set EXPLAIN ON;
         SELECT field1, field2, field5 from table1;

                                 ---------
         SELECT field1, field2, field3 form table1;
        Estimated Cost:  3
        Estimated # of Rows Returned:   50
        1)  owner1.table1:  SEQUENTIAL SCAN
```

SET OPTIMIZATION

The SET OPTIMIZATION statement specifies a high-level or low-level optimization of the database server. The statement can be executed at any time but applies only to the current database. The default is SET OPTIMIZATION HIGH when not specified.

Running either optimization level slows down your Informix server's performance. The optimization process in the Informix server looks at every SQL statement as it is being processed. A low setting of the optimizer saves processing overhead because it looks at only the shortest processing scenarios for the SQL statement being optimized, especially when dealing with joins. But using the low setting does not guarantee that the best solution will be found. The high setting causes the most overhead and runs the longest time when processing each SQL statement, but it will find the best possible solution.

The following code shows the syntax for the SET OPTIMIZATION statement:

```
SET OPTIMIZATION LOW;
```

UPDATE STATISTICS

The UPDATE STATISTICS statement updates the data in the system catalog tables that are used for optimization strategies. The optimizer uses the system data to determine the most efficient way to retrieve the requested data. The database server does not automatically update this data, so UPDATE STATISTICS is a necessary function.

The UPDATE STATISTICS process can run for an entire database, a single table, or a procedure. If you do not include a table or procedure name in your statement, the procedure is done for the entire database by default.

You should update the statistics when an extensive amount of modifications are done on the table or tables that are used in database procedures. You always want the optimizer to have the most recent statistics on your database tables.

The following code shows the syntax for the UPDATE STATISTICS statement:

```
UPDATE STATISTICS;
        UPDATE STATISTICS FOR table1;
        UPDATE STATISTICS FOR PROCEDURE procedure1;
```

When querying your database, it is important that you know the definitions of all the tables, views, and indexes. The data model can be helpful at this point. When the queries are created, it is important to know the indexes built on the tables and the types of data that are stored in each of the tables. Knowing this type of information can make the query optimization more efficient.

After testing a query with the `SET EXPLAIN` statement, you can choose to look again at the query and decide whether there is a simpler way to process the query. The following list outlines possible solutions when looking at your query plan:

- Simplify sorts by using indexed columns.
- Avoid sequential access on large tables.
- Use composite indexes.
- Avoid correlated subqueries.
- Maintain indexes. (Run `tbcheck` and drop and re-create indexes after extensive updating.)
- Avoid regular expressions (`LIKE`).

In most cases, the optimizer does not use an index when determining the best solution. Because of this, having the optimizer on when running takes more time for SQL processing to complete. Remember to turn off optimizing when it is not needed.

Temporary Tables

Using temporary tables can sometimes speed up queries. They can simplify work that the optimizer has to do. The temporary tables are read sequentially, but the amount of data in the table is less than in the primary tables. In addition, no sorts are necessary because when the temporary table is created, the data is in the desired order.

The main things to keep in mind when querying your tables is to find out the fastest, most efficient way to access the tables. Make sure that the database server avoids the following:

- Avoid reading more pages from disk.
- Avoid reading sequentially.
- Avoid sorts, or if not possible, sort on fewer rows.

Summary

This chapter discussed how you can query and manipulate data in a database using more advanced and complex queries. Advanced queries use additional syntax with the `SELECT` statement. Two examples used the `GROUP BY` and `HAVING` clauses. The SQL language also allows you to use the join functions, which select data from multiple tables within one query. I reviewed simple joins, self-joins, and outer-joins.

In addition, I reviewed how you use subqueries. A subquery is a `SELECT` statement embedded within another `SELECT`, `DELETE`, `INSERT`, or `UPDATE` statement. I also defined keywords that introduce a subquery in the `WHERE` clause of a `SELECT` statement.

Finally, I discussed how the optimizer works when executing your query. The optimizer can only be successful if the necessary information is supplied. The optimizer estimates the most efficient way to access the tables of the current query.

CHAPTER

SQL Tools

by Jan Richardson

IN THIS CHAPTER

This chapter reviews the DBaccess and ISQL utilities provided by Informix Software. In this chapter, I discuss how to use these utilities in the day-to-day work environment. The chapter addresses how to use each utility, what options are available with the utility, and when the utility is the right tool for the job.

Because all Informix installations have access to the `stores` database, all the examples in this chapter utilize this database. Wherever possible, the examples noted are alterations to program examples provided with the Informix system. This way, you can easily enter the code for testing on your own system.

Using DBaccess and ISQL

DBaccess and ISQL use the standard Informix menu types and keystrokes. To enter the DBaccess tool, type `dbaccess` on the command line. If you know the database name you want to access, you can specify it on the command line by typing `dbaccess` *`databasename`*. To enter the ISQL tool, type `isql` on the command line. You can also specify a database name when entering ISQL in the same manner as you do with DBaccess. The rest of the examples in this section use DBaccess; note that movement in ISQL uses the same keystrokes. Figure 32.1 shows the DBaccess main menu. The menu options are listed across the top of the screen.

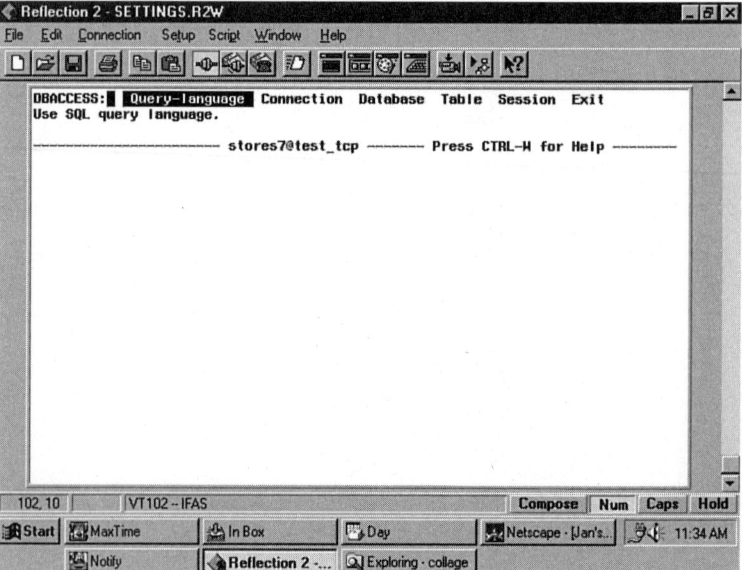

FIGURE 32.1.
The main DBaccess menu.

To select between options in DBaccess, you can press the spacebar or the right and left arrow keys to move sequentially through the options. Figure 32.2 shows the effect of pressing the spacebar once. After you select the correct option, press the Enter key. You also can type the capital letter for the option you want; the main menu for that option is then displayed. For example, pressing the T key displays the Table menu. This basic method of menu movement is used in both DBaccess and ISQL.

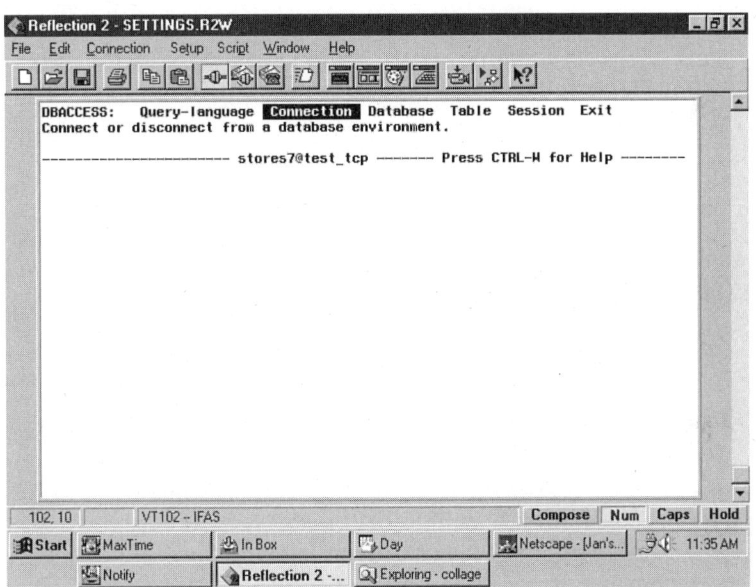

FIGURE 32.2.
Moving between options on the DBaccess main menu.

When you enter DBaccess, your first task is to select a primary database. After you select a database, you can access other databases by fully qualifying their database names and table names. To fully qualify a database or table name, type `database@servername.tablename`. You don't need to fully qualify table names in the primary database. You can select a primary database on the command line when entering DBaccess. If you do not, you can select the Database option and then select a database. If you select an option that requires a database and none has been selected, you have to select a database before proceeding any further.

When you're offered a list of files, tables, or databases to select from, you can move through the list by using the arrow keys. All four arrow keys operate. If more than one screen of options is available, use the arrow keys. A sample selection screen is shown in Figure 32.3.

If you select an option you do not want, and no Exit option is displayed, you can back out of the option by pressing Ctrl+C. You then return to the previously displayed menu. You also can access the online help during a DBaccess or ISQL session by pressing Ctrl+W.

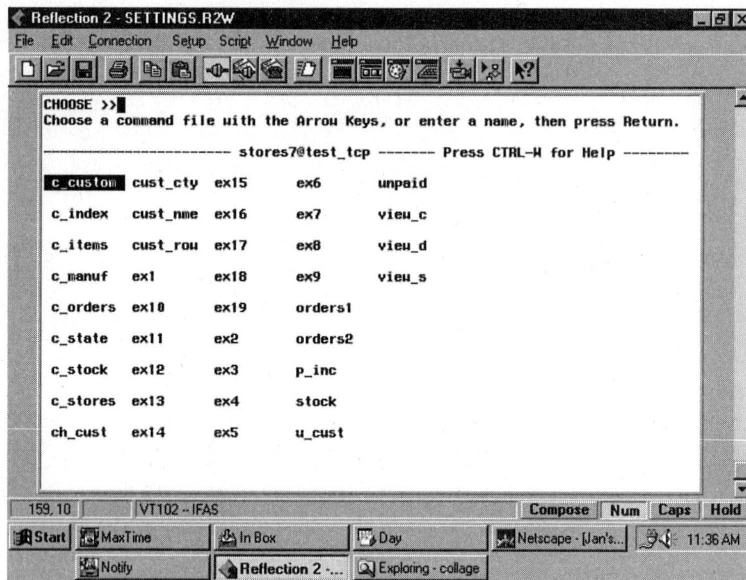

FIGURE 32.3.
A sample option selection screen in DBaccess.

DBaccess

DBaccess is a tool designed to enable you to access and manipulate the structure of the database as well as the data within the database. It provides menu-driven access to basic database functionality. DBaccess supports a query option to allow you to issue SQL commands against the data in the database tables. It also supports altering tables through a menu-driven environment. DBaccess supports most actions that can be performed against a database table, including `create`, `drop`, `alter`, and `fragment`. DBaccess can also be used to gather information about a table including the current table size, active constraints, current triggers, indexes, and existing security privileges.

The specific functions supported depend on the release of the engine you're operating. The options also vary depending on the type of engine running. The INFORMIX-SE engine and the OnLine engine have different capabilities and, therefore, different options within the DBaccess tool.

The environment variables set for your engine are active within DBaccess. You don't need to set special variables for use with the tools; however, you might want to alter your environment when using DBaccess. If you alter your environment variables for use with DBaccess, remember that you might need to reset them to their original state when you exit the tool.

For more information on DBaccess and its specific capabilities with your engine, consult the Informix *DBaccess User Manual* for your database engine.

When Is DBaccess the Right Tool Set?

DBaccess is the right tool set for many database administrator (DBA) activities, including database maintenance and table maintenance. By using the menu options, you can easily perform these tasks. DBaccess automatically formats complicated SQL statements such as `alter table`. It displays most statistics for a database table without requiring the DBA to remember the correct options for the `tbstat/onstat` command. In general, the purpose of the DBaccess tool is to make the syntax of table and database maintenance less complicated.

DBaccess also allows you to create tables and databases rapidly. It provides a screen interface so that you can enter the information for a new table. You no longer end up frustrated while looking for a misplaced comma. The DBaccess process is performed step by step, allowing the table to be created by selecting various options from a list. The main errors that occur while you're creating a table using DBaccess are spelling mistakes in the column names—and even they can be corrected rapidly if you use the same screen interface.

You also can use DBaccess to test SQL statements rapidly. These statements can be tests for an application or SQL statement to review data on the database. The results of the query can be quickly obtained and reviewed. Often, using `set explain` from within a program is difficult. Using DBaccess, you can set up `set explain` quickly to test the query plan for a statement in a single execution manner.

DBaccess is not the appropriate tool if your goal is to create a report output from a query or a data entry screen. It does not have formatting or screen-painting capabilities.

Query Language

The first option on the DBaccess main menu is Query language, as you saw in Figure 32.1. The main Query language menu is shown in Figure 32.4.

You can find this same Query language tool in the ISQL tools. The following options are on this menu:

- *New* allows you to enter a new query by using a rudimentary text editor.
- *Run* submits the query currently visible on the screen to the engine for execution.
- *Modify* allows you to modify the query currently visible on the screen by using a rudimentary text editor.
- *Use-editor* allows you to specify a text editor to be used in creating and editing SQL statements.
- *Output* allows you to send the results of the query to an output device, a file, or another program.
- *Save* allows you to save the query currently visible on the screen to an operating system file.

- *Info* allows you to select a table and display information about that table.
- *Drop* allows you to delete an operating system file storing a query previously saved using the Save option.
- *Exit* returns you to the main DBaccess menu.

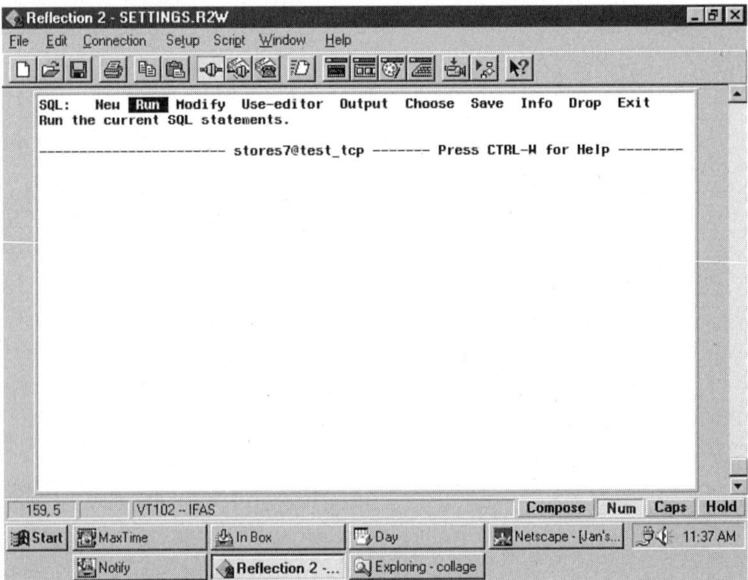

FIGURE 32.4.
The main Query language menu in DBaccess.

Practical uses for the Query language option abound. It is probably the most frequently used option of either DBaccess or ISQL. The following sections cover some practical examples of using the Query language menu option.

Example 1

An applications programmer needs to test an SQL query and determine whether it returns the expected results without running an entire program. She types the query into the Query language screen. The query is executed, and the results are reviewed on the screen. The programmer can modify the query as many times as necessary, until the results are accurate. The query can be saved in an operating system file. The programmer can later access this file while she's editing the program and copy it directly into the source code.

Example 2

A user doesn't think a report is correct. The programmer can quickly enter SQL commands into the Query language screen and check the data to determine whether the report is accurate. If it is not, the programmer can save the queries used in operating system files and compare them to the logic in the program to determine what caused the discrepancy. The output of the Query language queries can be saved to an operating system file using the Output option for comparison to the printed report.

Example 3

A DBA needs to update statistics on a database or table. He can type the SQL command into the Query language screen and execute it. The DBA knows when the command is completed because the screen is locked until the process is complete.

Example 4

A DBA needs to administer database security options. She types the appropriate `grant` commands into the Query language screen, and she can run the commands against the database.

Example 5

The results of a simple SQL query are sufficient to meet the request of a user for a report. The application programmer can run the SQL query statement and output the results to a file. This file can serve as the report.

Example 6

While the programmer is testing an SQL query against the database, an SQL error is encountered, indicating an incorrect column name. The programmer can quickly jump to the Info option and get the correct name for the column. Upon his return to the Query language screen, the query in question is still on the screen, so he can modify it for the correct column name. The query then can be reexecuted.

The preceding are just a few examples of using the Query language option of DBaccess to assist the programmers or DBAs with their jobs. If you take the query capabilities even further, you can write small programs and run them entirely from the Query language screen. Listing 32.1 shows a small insert and correction program created and run in Query language.

Listing 32.1. A sample database correction program using Query language.

```
insert into customer
    values (0, "Jan", "Richdson", "Merry World", "1470 S. Bank",
            null, "Mississippi", "MO", "99876", "800-555-1234");

select *
    from customer
    where
         state = "MO";
```

continues

Listing 32.1. continued

```
update customer
    set lname = "Richardson"
    where
         lname = "Richdson";

select *
    from customer
    where
         state = "MO";
```

Query language executes each of the SQL statements in turn.

CAUTION

Query language displays a message after each SQL statement, identifying the results of the SQL statement. For example, a message might read `1 row inserted`. In the case of multiple SQL statements, such as Listing 32.1, because the SQL statements execute immediately following each other, the final return statement is the only one visible upon completion. In this example, you see no update or insert messages; the only message visible is `1 row selected`.

WARNING

The usefulness of this tool in analyzing and correcting database data issues cannot be overstated. When you're using this tool, however, be aware that you're bypassing safeguards built into an application, such as audit control, data integrity, and data edits. Unless these items are constraints or triggers defined to the database, data corruption can result from using the Query language tool. Any changes you make using this tool, therefore, must be carefully thought-out and executed.

Connection

The connection option of the main DBaccess menu is useful in connecting to alternative database engines or servers. When you choose Connect, a list of valid connections or servers is displayed. Simply select the connection you want. You are allowed to enter a user ID and password for verification purposes. After successful validation of user ID and password, you are connected. You can then access the databases valid to that connection as if they were on the same machine and database server as when you initially entered DBaccess.

This capability allows DBAs to do remote database administration. It also enables you to run an SQL statement on multiple machines without requiring a direct login to the new machine or database engine. This capability saves time. If your company has only a single server, but both test and production database instances, you can use this connection to access both environments without separate logins.

> **NOTE**
>
> This powerful option can also cause difficulties. You must be constantly vigilant about what database and server you are connected to. DBaccess assists in this task by displaying the connected database at all times, as shown in Figure 32.5.

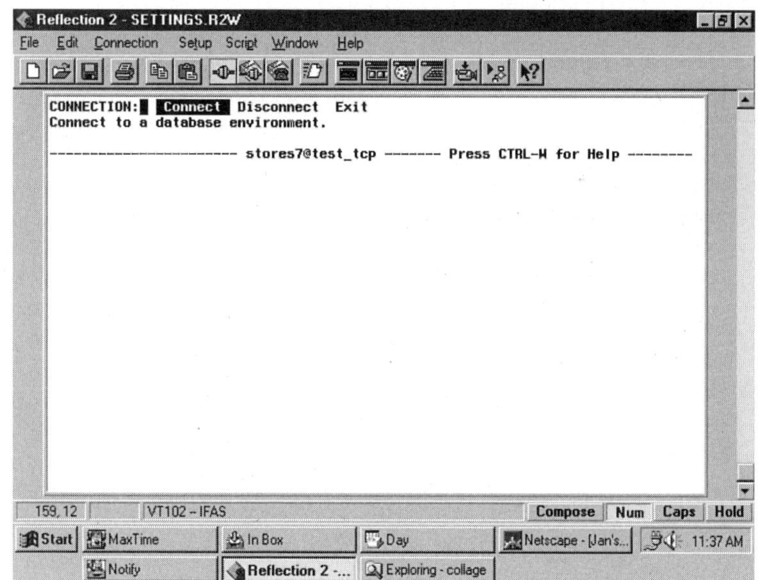

FIGURE 32.5.
Identifying the active database and Informix instance.

Database

The Database option of DBaccess is primarily used by DBAs. Here are the primary uses of this command:

- It prevents DBAs from needing to remember the details of the `create database` command.
- It displays rudimentary statistics about a database.
- It allows DBAs to view stored procedures.

Creating a database by using DBaccess has two advantages. You don't need to remember the exact syntax of the `create database` statement, and the system prompts you for the dbspace. It is all too common to create a database and forget to specify a dbspace. As a result, the database goes in the root database space. This location for a database is not advisable. The Create option of Database always prompts for the dbspace.

The ability to view stored procedures is valuable. You can analyze the stored procedure without having to remember the exact SQL syntax to retrieve the procedure from the database. If a copy of the procedure is required, you can use cut and paste or command-line options of DBaccess to place the stored procedure code in an operating system file.

Table

Undoubtedly, the second most important option of DBaccess is the Table option. Both DBAs and programmers will find constant use for this option. Whether it is to look up a table and column name or perform complex database maintenance, this option has capabilities to perform the needed work. The various options of the Table selection under Informix 7 include the following options, which have a hierarchy indicated by the letters and numbers preceding the elements:

- A. Create
  - 1. Add
  - 2. Modify
  - 3. Drop
  - 4. Table Options
    - a. Storage
    - c. Extent Size
    - d. Next Size
    - e. Lock Mode
  - 5. Constraints
    - a. Primary
    - b. Foreign
    - c. Check
    - d. Unique
    - e. Defaults
- B. Alter
  - 1. Add
  - 2. Modify
  - 3. Drop

4. Table Options
   a. Storage
   b. Extent Size
   c. Next Size
   d. Lock Mode
   e. Rowids
5. Constraints
   a. Primary
   b. Foreign
   c. Check
   d. Unique
   e. Defaults

C. Info
1. Column
2. Indexes
3. Privileges
4. Reference
5. Status
6. Constraints
   a. Reference
   b. Primary
   c. Check
   d. Unique
   e. Defaults
7. Triggers
8. Table
9. Fragments

D. Drop

This list covers almost everything usually needed for a table. With the expanded capabilities of DSA in the Informix arena, table maintenance has become a task requiring a higher level of skill. Writing the syntax of an SQL statement to create a table can be as complicated as writing an entire program. By using DBaccess, you can create and alter tables without the daunting task of writing a syntactically correct SQL statement.

The Info option of DBaccess is read-only, and creating a new table using DBaccess usually doesn't affect others on the system. Most of the potential complications of DBaccess occur with the Alter table option. If you use DBaccess to modify a table, you are prompted to build a new table or discard changes before you exit the Alter table section. If you choose to build a new table, the system immediately tries to modify the table in question based on the changes you made during the Alter table work session. Selecting the *build a new table* option can pose several difficulties.

If you're modifying a table definition, the system actually executes an Alter table command for the table selected. This command immediately modifies the table in the database. If programs are run against this data, the programs could be affected by the table change. Potentially, SQL errors can appear or erroneous results can occur if the table change is not coordinated correctly with program modification.

If the table being modified is allocated to a production system, and users currently have locks in the table, the modification might not succeed. Most modifications require a lock on the table being modified. If the modification does not succeed, an error message appears, and you are taken back to the Alter table session. You can then coordinate with the individuals who have the table locks to attempt to get control of the table, or you can cancel out of the Alter table session by choosing Exit and then Discard changes.

If a large amount of data appears in the table, and transaction logging is active, choosing to build a new table can fail for many reasons. You can have insufficient work space to create the new table schema and copy the data into the new table, or violations of triggers or constraints can also occur within the database. The most serious problem is the long transaction. If you have a great deal of data, enough to fill the allocated logical logs for the system, the alteration will fail. If this happens, the only way to alter the table is to stop transaction processing prior to altering the table. I strongly recommend that you do not perform this procedure on a live database in production while users are continuing normal operations. Turning off the transaction processing stops all logging during that period, and the system might be unable to recover completely in the event of a database or system problem.

As with any system change, all changes to tables should be thoroughly considered and analyzed for their impact on both the database and the applications that access the database. For example, adding a new column to or dropping an existing column from a table might seem harmless; however, if an application program utilizes `select * from` *`tablename`*, the `select` statement will probably fail because of a column and variable mismatch. This failure will happen if the receiving variables or array are not set up to match the new table definition.

Modifying an existing table column can also have unforeseen results. For example, changing the length of a column can generate system issues. If the column is shortened, DBaccess issues a warning message that data may be truncated. Lost data cannot be recovered unless it has been backed up. Lengthening a field can cause truncation at runtime in applications. If you lengthen a field to 25, and a screen or report displays only 20 characters, bad conclusions or decisions can be the result.

Therefore, although DBaccess makes the job of creating and altering tables significantly easier than directly typing standard SQL statements, you must use DBaccess with the same caution and care required of all system utilities. The danger is that because the changes are more easily accomplished, they might be less thoroughly thought-out. You must take care to ensure that these problems do not happen.

Session

The Session command displays information about the Informix session you're currently connected to. Sample output is shown in Figure 32.6. This information can be valuable if you're supporting a multihost or server environment in which different system environments are supported by the different hosts or servers. This information helps you keep straight what the settings are in the current environment.

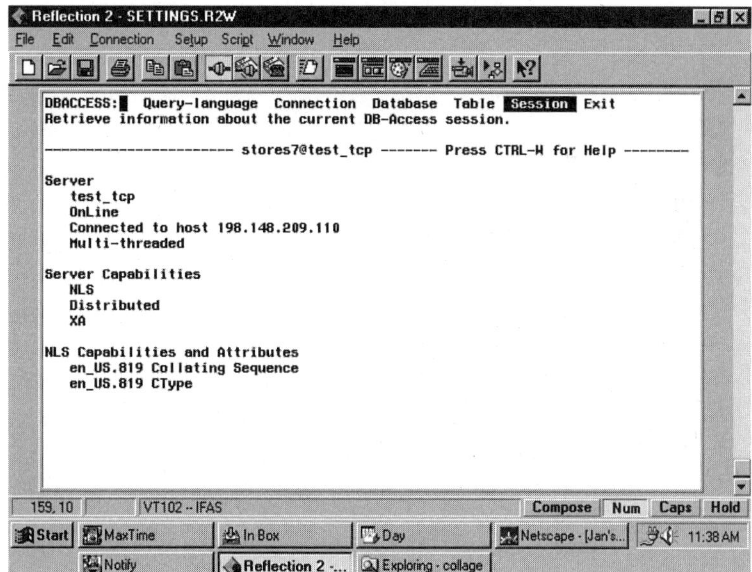

FIGURE 32.6.
The results of an Informix 7 DBaccess Session command.

ISQL

INFORMIX-SQL, commonly known as ISQL, is a set of tools provided by Informix Software to support developers. ISQL has a long history with Informix. These tools were provided with Informix software products before the corporation was named Informix. Prior to the advent of INFORMIX-4GL, they were the only fourth-generation tools available through Informix.

In today's technological environment, these tools might seem crude and rudimentary. They are. However, they still perform useful functions. When Report, SQL, Form, or the User Menu will do the job, they are quick to use and efficient to run. The main ISQL menu is shown in Figure 32.7.

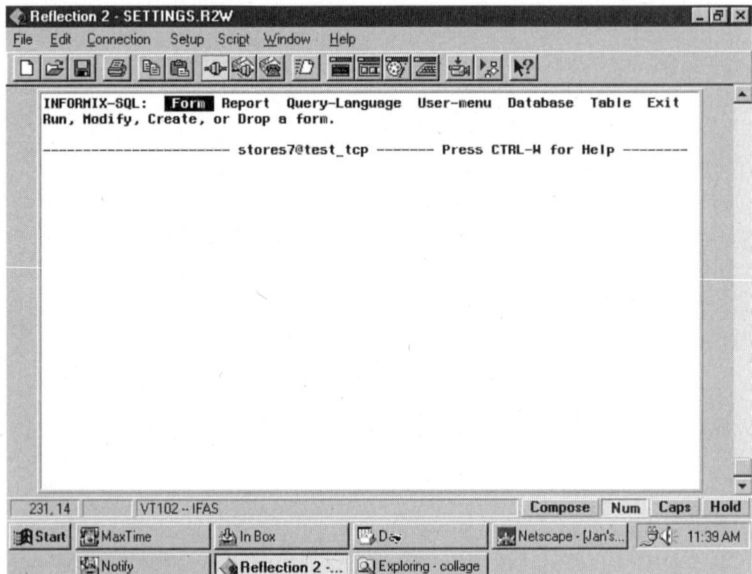

Figure 32.7.
The main ISQL menu.

When Is ISQL the Right Tool Set?

ISQL is a set of tools, and each tool has its unique purpose. In general, ISQL is the right set of tools when you need a quick prototype or a simple application.

The Report option invokes the ACE report generator. ACE is excellent for generating quick reports. It supports SQL `select` statements, including the creation of temporary tables. Some very complex SQL select logic is supported with ACE. It also contains good report formatting capabilities with built-in control break logic for totals and subtotals. It does have some limited logic capabilities, including temporary variables. I discuss these elements in more detail later in this chapter.

The Form option creates Perform screens. Perform is a screen-generation utility. The entry screens created by Perform can facilitate data validation, enable intelligent cursor movement, and process multiple table relationships. Perform screens are, however, limited in their capabilities to accomplish these tasks. They are excellent for quick data maintenance screens for data entry tables such as state abbreviations. They are also effective if the application requires no major logic supporting the data entry process. If extensive logic is necessary, Perform has limitations. These limitations are discussed in more detail later in this chapter.

The User-menu option creates quick, hierarchically based menu structures. They are reasonably flexible and often sufficient for the menuing needs of a system. However, the presentation of the menus is not customizable. Therefore, menus can present visual issues to the look and feel of an application. For example, if the screen standard has the date and time always displayed on line 23 in column 1, this standard can't be adhered to using menus created with this utility.

ISQL is the right tool when you want to execute an SQL query from the operating system. To execute a query from the command line, type

```
isql databasename -qc c_querycommandfile
```

When you specify your query command file, you must name it `file.sql`. Do not type the `.sql` extension on the line; it is added by the system.

Form

The Form option displays a subordinate menu where Perform screens can be created and edited. The Perform utility generates data entry screens. They are most effectively utilized when the screen uses only fields from one table or where a definite master-detail relationship exists between the multiple tables in a screen.

You can generate a simple Perform screen by choosing Generate from the menu and selecting a table from the subsequent screen. Form will automatically create a default data entry screen. In the `stores` database is a table named `call_type`. Listing 32.2 shows a generic generated form for the `call_type` table.

Listing 32.2. A generic form for the `call_type` table.

```
database stores7@test_tcp
screen size 24 by 80
{
call_code           [a]
code_descr          [f000                          ]
}
end
tables
call_type
attributes
a = call_type.call_code;
f000 = call_type.code_descr;
end
```

The first line of Listing 32.2 specifies the database and server instance. Any table included in this screen is assumed to be included in this database unless explicitly stated otherwise. The second line specifies the screen size. This information is important because the compile of the screen code will use this information to determine how to process error message and multipage screens.

The opening brace ({) begins the screen description; it is ended by the closing brace (}). Everything between these two symbols describes how the screen will appear to the user. Everything will appear exactly as typed, except the items included in brackets ([]). These items represent entry fields. The word in the [] points to the attributes section of the code and is the field name for the database or screen field that will be displayed in this position. The user will see the brackets, but not the field name inside the brackets. In this example, the flow of the cursor on the screen is guided by the sequence of the fields. This flow can be modified by using special keywords. The end marks the end of the screen definition. If this were a multipage screen, the screens would be separated by

```
}
screen
{
```

where the closing brace (}) ends the first screen and the opening brace ({) begins the next screen.

The tables section of the perform definition identifies all tables used in the screen. If the author is not the owner, you should specify *owner.tablename*. You can alias your tables in this section by using the syntax *alias = owner.tablename*. This syntax is extremely useful in cutting the number of keystrokes required to complete the attributes section. For example, if the owner and tablename are informix.cust_upd_yr, and they are aliased as cuy, you need to type only cuy.*columnname* when accessing a column in the cust_upd_yr table rather than type informix.cut_upd_yr.*columnname*.

The attributes section of the perform definition can be complex. Perform does not have the flexibility of INFORMIX-4GL or the newer client/server development tools, but it can do some editing. In this example, no editing is done. You simply map the field identified as a to the database field call_type.call_code and the field identified as f000 to call_type.code_descr. This way, you identify which database field is displayed on the screen and which screen field is placed in a certain location on the database.

To make this default screen format appear more polished, you, as the programmer, can select the Modify option from the Form menu. ISQL displays a list of forms to edit. You can select the form matching the name you specified when creating the default form in the preceding step. Here, the code for the form you selected is placed into your editor's buffer. You can then change the spacing, field title, form title, and so on to make the screen appear according to the standards of your development team. You can also alter the code for readability. Listing 32.3 shows a few simple changes made to the previously generated screen code. Figure 32.8 shows how the modified form will appear on the screen.

Listing 32.3. A modified generated entry screen.

```
database stores7@test_tcp
screen size 24 by 80

{
```

```
                        CALL TYPE CODES

  Call Code:          [a]
  Code Description:   [f000                           ]
}
end

tables
call_type

attributes
a = call_type.call_code;
f000 = call_type.code_descr;

end
```


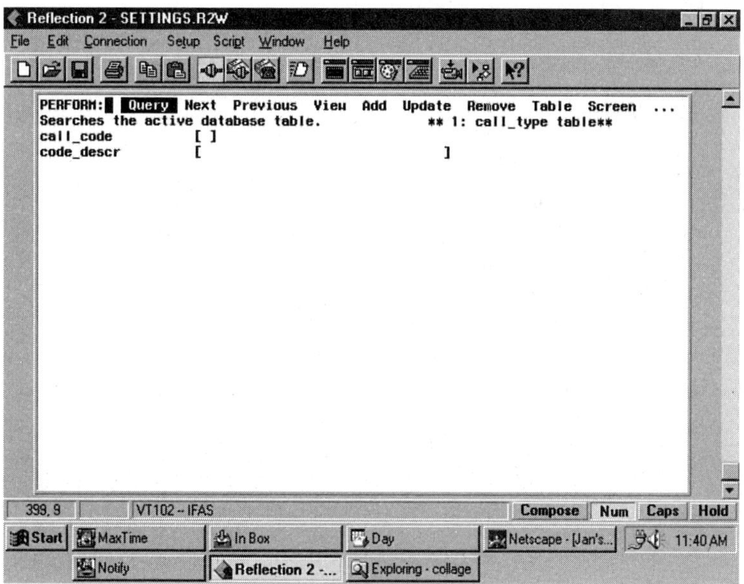

FIGURE 32.8.
A Perform screen created using the Form menu.

Additional features can be added to this screen. Using the built-in functions, you can add field edits to your screens. Here's a simple edit example:

```
a = call_type.call_code, include = ("A","B","C",1 to 9, "D" to "Q"),
    comments = "The valid entries are A - Q and 1 - 9".;
```

This code changes the screen performance by adding both edits and an informational message to explain the reason an edit failed. The `include` option gives a list of valid values to be included for the screen. Because no lowercase values are included in the list, they are not valid in the entry field. You can add the `upshift` keyword to change any entered lowercase letters into uppercase letters. The `comments` keyword specifies the message to be displayed if the edits on this field fail. The default location for the message to be displayed is the last line of the screen.

Several keyword options can be included in a field description. They are reviewed in detail in the Informix Software manuals for your system. Some of the capabilities include the following:

- Specifying a table to use in validating an entry using a verify join
- Automatically populating another field based on an entered field using a lookup
- Specifying color for a field
- Specifying field default values
- Automatically downshifting or upshifting a field's values
- Formatting fields to appear in a certain manner without storing format characters in the database
- Restricting viewing or entry on a field using invisible or `noentry/noupdate`
- Requiring an entry in a field
- Zero-filling a field
- Allowing a field to wrap its words automatically

The last section of the Perform screen is the instruction section. The composite section is used most commonly when you have more than one table or when control blocks are to be defined.

Two issues can affect screens involving more than one table; they must be addressed in the instruction section. If you have more than one table, you might want to define a composite join to ensure uniqueness. For example, to ensure uniqueness, you might need to set up a composite to uniquely identify a line in an order that would include both the order number and the item number. You must define such a composite so that it can be used elsewhere in the screen definition. You might also need to define a master/detail relationship between tables. Such a definition is required if Perform is to process a one-to-many relationship between tables.

Control blocks allow more control over the screen processing. The valid control blocks are `before`, `after`, `on beginning`, and `on ending`. You can use these blocks to define activities to be done when a certain event occurs such as `before editadd of` *`table.column`*. Although they're not a complete language, these control blocks do allow minimal `if-then-else` processing. Note that a control block is performed only if the event occurs. As a result, some code might be ignored in a screen. For example, if a user stops entering data after the fourth field and presses Esc to process the screen, `editadd`, `editupdate`, or `remove` on fields later than the fourth field will not be executed. The only additional control block that is executed after the Esc is the `on ending` block. This information is important when you're designing the screen. The `before` and `after` blocks are executed only if the entry fields they are associated with are touched.

Although Perform screens can be functional and, with careful formatting and attribute control, visually acceptable, the utility is probably not robust enough for major applications development. It should be viewed as a simple, quick method of creating uncomplicated data entry and query screens.

Report

The Report menu takes you into a submenu that allows you to generate, edit, compile, and run ACE reports. The ACE report writer quickly formats simple reports. You can enter a sequence of SQL statements that generate a final sorted output. This single output thread is used as the input to the report formatting section of the report. Complex selection logic can be supported if it can be accommodated using multiple `select` statements and temporary tables to generate a final single output stream.

ACE does not support table updating. If the application requires the ability to update tables, ACE is not the appropriate tool. ACE can do the selection and create an output file that can be used as input to an update procedure, but updating within an ACE report is not supported.

ACE does not support extensive logic. Although ACE does support `if-then-else` constructs, its ability to do extensive logic handling is limited. ACE has a built-in limit of SQL variables. It also has a tendency to fail on deeply nested `if` statements. I recommend limiting complex nesting to five or six levels when using ACE. This way, you can perform some advanced logic but limit that logic in extent.

ACE has a built-in totaling mechanism for control breaks. These control breaks must be specified in the `order by` clause of the final SQL statement. Complex totaling can be cumbersome in ACE. If totaling must be done on fields outside the control breaks, you must use defined variables. The built-in limit can restrict the flexibility and quantity of such totals.

You can generate a simple report program using the menus. Select Generate and then give the report a name. Next, select the table for which you are reporting. The system automatically generates a routine report that prints all lines in the table. Listing 32.4 shows such a sample generated report.

Listing 32.4. A generated default ACE report.

```
database stores7@test_tcp end

select
        catalog_num,
        stock_num,
        manu_code,
        cat_descr,
        cat_picture,
        cat_advert
from catalog end

format every row end
```

To run this report, choose Report|Run; then select the report name you used in generating the report. See Figure 32.9 for a sample run of the report. This report continues to print on the screen until it is complete. If you have more data than will appear onscreen, the generated report allows the data to scroll off the screen.

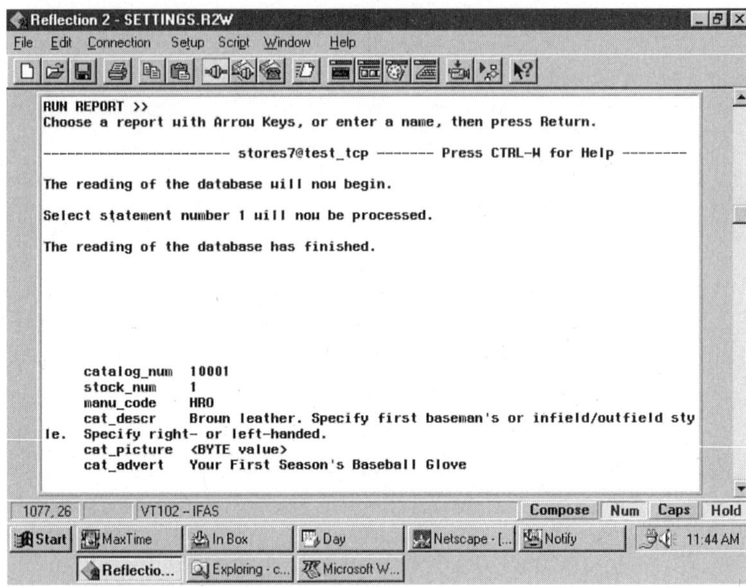

FIGURE 32.9.
A sample run of a generated ACE report.

To make this report more usable, choose Forms|Modify. The following are quick modifications you can make to the report to make it more usable:

- Prompt for input to limit the amount of data reported.
- Send the report to an operating system file rather than to the screen.
- Change the output format of the report to read across the page.

The new code for these quick modifications is shown in Listing 32.5.

Listing 32.5. A modified ACE report.

```
database stores7@test_tcp end

define
    variable begin_num integer
    variable end_num integer
end

input
    prompt for begin_num using "Enter beginning catalog number:    "
    prompt for end_num using "Enter ending catalog number:    "
end

output
    left margin 0
    right margin 132
    report to "catalog.out"
end
```

```
select
        catalog_num,
        stock_num,
        manu_code,
        cat_descr,
        cat_picture,
        cat_advert
from catalog end

format

    first page header
    print column 10, "===================================================",
       "========================================="
    print column 10, "                  Daily Catalog Report"
    print column 10, "===================================================",
       "========================================="
    skip 1 line
    print column 10, "FROM:  ", begin_num,
          column 43, "RUN DATE:  ",  today using "mm/dd/yy"
    print column 10, "  TO:  ", end_num,
          column 43, "RUN TIME:  ", time
    skip 1 line
    print column 2, "Cat Num",
    column 15, "Stock Num",
    column 35, "Man. Code",
    column 55, "Description"
    skip 1 line

on every row
    print column 1, catalog_num, column 15, stock_num,
          column 38, Manu_code, Column 55, cat_descr wordwrap

end
```

This report has been modified to accept input from the user running the report. Notice that the `input` statements utilize both a prompting string and a variable. The variable must be defined to the ACE report. When the report is run, the program prompts the user, as shown in Figure 32.10. The prompts appear one at a time and must be answered before the processing continues. ACE has no recovery capability. If the user answers the prompt incorrectly, the program either runs or returns an error. Figure 32.11 shows the messages returned to the user as the report runs. The message gives the user the name of the file where the report is stored. If two people run the report at the same time, they will overwrite each other's reports. ACE does not allow the user to specify the report output file; consequently, it writes to the same filename on each run. Figure 32.12 shows the output from an ACE report.

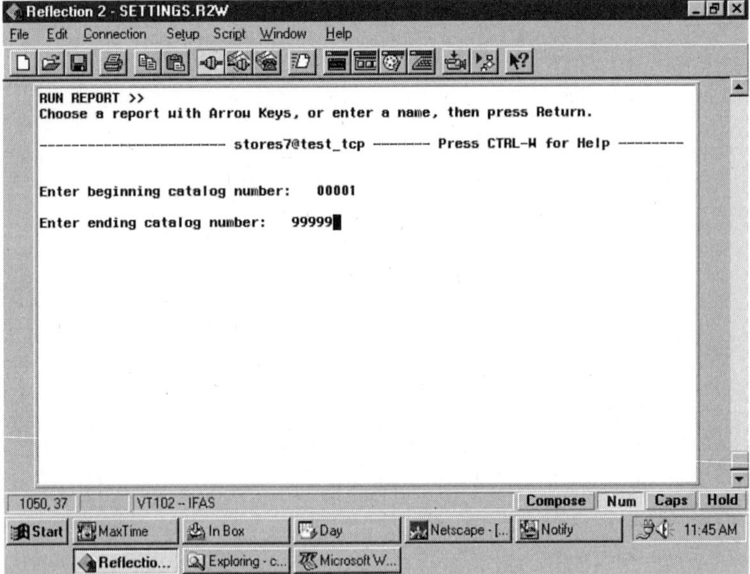

FIGURE 32.10.
A sample ACE report run with prompts.

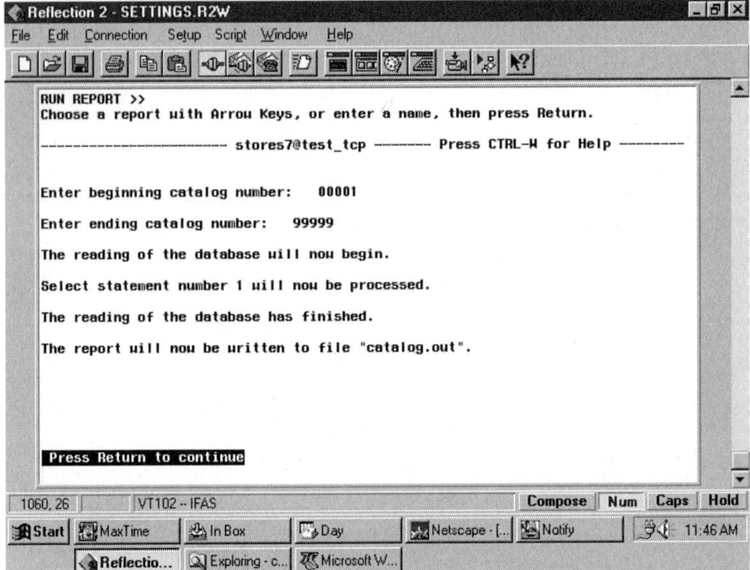

FIGURE 32.11.
Sample runtime ACE report messages.

FIGURE 32.12.
A sample report created using the ACE report writer.

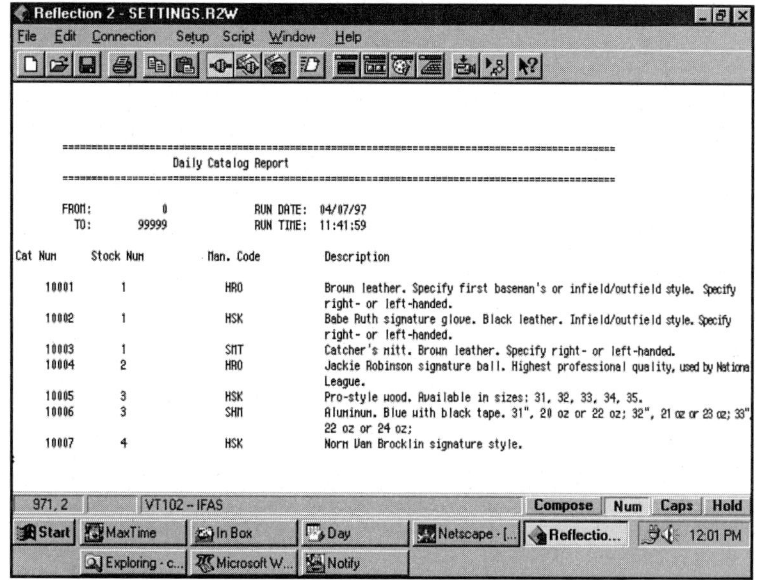

The ACE report language offers additional facilities and sophistication. Within ACE, the following control blocks can be utilized:

- After Group Of
- Before Group Of
- First Page Header
- On Every Row
- On Last Row
- Page Header
- Page Trailer

These blocks combine to support most simple report requirements. In addition to the control blocks, ACE supports many formatting options, aggregates, and structures. The most important structures are `while`, `for`, and `if-then-else`. Also important are aggregate functions. Here are some of them:

- `Count`
- `Total`
- `Percent`
- `Average`
- `Minimum`
- `Maximum`
- `Total`

Each of these aggregates is available on a group or report level. ACE has powerful formatting options that provide a great deal of flexibility in determining the look of the printed output.

ACE comes with no interactive debugging capabilities. To debug using ACE, you must print variables and fields at special places in the code. Then you must run the report. Your debugging statements are printed intermixed at the appropriate times with your output report. Review these messages to debug the program.

ACE is a powerful tool for quick reports that do not require extensive logic. Used appropriately, they can speed development time. ACE does have limitations, though. Most problems or dissatisfaction occurs when ACE is used to create complex logic reports. These types of reports are best created with another tool.

User-menu

By using the User-menu, you can quickly create a hierarchically based menu system. To utilize the tool, your menuing design must be entirely based on a master menu/detail menu relationship. Each entry on the main menu can be one of the following types:

- F: Run a form
- M: Call another menu
- P: Execute another program or operating system command
- Q: Execute an ISQL query or other command file
- R: Run a report
- S: Execute a script menu

Figure 32.13 shows the User-menu entry or modify screen. This screen has two separate sections separated by a dashed line.

To toggle back and forth between the sections of the screen, press M for Master or D for Detail.

The menus are stored in the database. You should have the menu structure designed before entering the menu items. To begin entering the information, select the lowest level menu and give it a name. This menu does not call any other subordinate menus.

Press M for Master, and then press A for Add. Type the name of the menu and the title you want the user to see on the screen. The title can be long and descriptive; the name is limited in length. The name is used only within by the menuing system to track relationships between menus. Next, press the Esc key.

You have added your first menu. Next, add the individual items for the menu. It is best if they already exist or if you at least know the exact names the called programs, reports, procedures, and so on will have. You can always modify the menus, but planning ahead is best. To begin entering the menu selections, press D for Detail. The cursor then moves to the bottom half of the screen on Selection Number. Press A for Add. Then type the selection number and selection type. Next, enter the selection text as you want it to appear to the user. The final entry is the exact command string as it should be executed from the operating system.

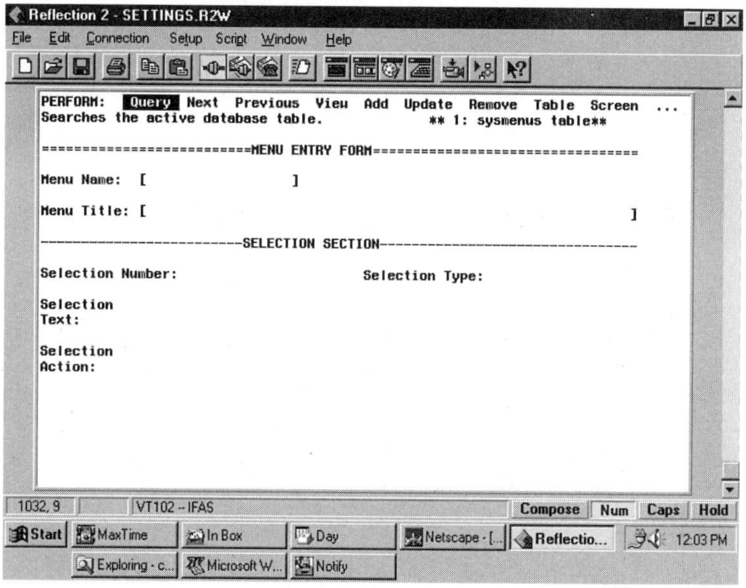

FIGURE 32.13.
The main User-menu entry/modification screen.

```
PERFORM:  Query  Next  Previous  View  Add  Update  Remove  Table  Screen  ...
Searches the active database table.              ** 1: sysmenus table**

=========================MENU ENTRY FORM================================

Menu Name:  [                      ]

Menu Title: [                                                        ]

-------------------------SELECTION SECTION------------------------------

Selection Number:                          Selection Type:

Selection
Text:

Selection
Action:
```


TIP

If your command string is too long, place it inside a shell script and call the shell script.

Continue to enter your menu one item at a time. To test the current structure at any time, exit from the entry modification screen and choose Run. Your menu is then displayed onscreen. You can test your work immediately.

There is an inconsistency between the Perform screen and the User-menuing system. The User- menuing system presents a standard menu interface, as shown in Figure 32.14, whereas Perform screens present their options along the top of the screen. This difference can cause confusion, especially if the options along the top of the screen also call subordinate screens. I suggest that you keep menus consistent if they are employed in your system. This means that the options in the Perform screens or 4GL programs should be kept as options affecting only the displayed screen. This way, you can keep all menus consistent and all screen options consistent.

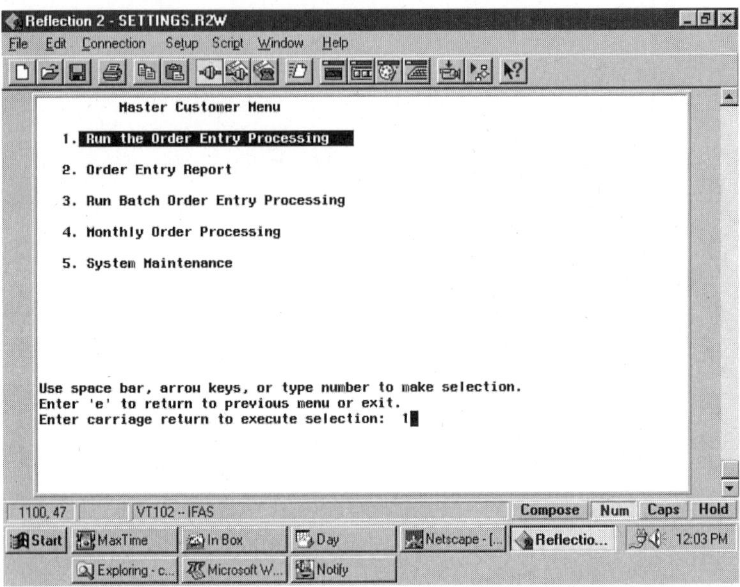

FIGURE 32.14.
A sample User Menu.

The User-menu option is a great tool for creating menus quickly. Its flexibility in calling any type of operating system program enhances its ability to support any type of application developed in the UNIX environment.

Summary

Informix Software provides some basic tools with its systems that can assist programmers and database administrators quite effectively in their jobs. These tools are not a substitute for full application development tools, but they can assist and augment routine and simple tasks.

DBaccess is a powerful tool for developers and database administrators. For the developers, DBaccess provides a quick, efficient interface to test SQL statements and obtain information about the tables and databases on the system. For database administrators, DBaccess can save hours of frustration in writing `add` and `alter table` statements manually.

ISQL provides application developers with rudimentary tools to do quick applications. The tools do not support complex logic constructs, but they do a great job on simple, straightforward data entry or query applications.

Using the User Menu is a quick, effective way to develop a menu system for any type of UNIX-based application where text-based menus are acceptable. The entries are stored in a database, making them easy to maintain.

CHAPTER 33

Understanding the Informix Optimizer

by Gavin Nour

IN THIS CHAPTER

This chapter explains the role of the Informix optimizer (including how to read the output from `SET EXPLAIN`) and offers some tips to help improve SQL performance.

The best tool to use for optimizing a query or for the quality-assurance process is the SQL command `SET EXPLAIN ON`.

You should remember first that although you can optimize the queries, proper database design plays a major part in the query performance, and often, redesigning tables and implementing an effective indexing strategy solves many problems. This chapter focuses on the `SET EXPLAIN ON` option and explains how this command can help you optimize queries. First you have to understand the Informix optimizer.

Understanding the Informix Optimizer

This section explains what the Informix optimizer is and gives some insight into how the optimizer makes its decisions when executing a query.

What Is the Optimizer?

The optimizer is the part of the Informix engine that anticipates the best route to take before running a given query. Because there are often many paths that can be taken to get to the data, some paths take much longer than others. This is especially true when many tables are involved in a join. Developers usually develop the query and then leave the task of finding the best route to the optimizer and assume that the engine will use the best method available. Unfortunately, because the optimizer does a good job most of the time, we tend to forget that the engine does not always make the right decision. Sometimes, we know more than the engine does and can see a better way of doing things. The output from `SET EXPLAIN ON` explains how the optimizer chose to access the data. With this information available, you might discover that the optimizer chose a path that is time consuming, and you can take steps to restructure the query. Sometimes, a small alteration influences the optimizer to take an alternative route. Other times, you realize that you can add an index to improve performance, or you might just find that it is fine the way it is, but you need to add more temporary space to cater for a sort.

How Does the Optimizer Make Its Decision?

The answer to this question is very complex. The main aim of the optimizer is to reduce I/O by limiting the amount of data to search in order to obtain the requested data in the most efficient way. The optimizer makes its decisions based on information in the system catalogues. This information consists of

- The number of rows in each table used in the query (`systables.nrows`).
- How many pages are used for data and how many pages are used for indexes (`systables.npused`).

- Whether columns values are unique (`sysconstraints`).
- What indexes exist (`sysindexes`).
- Whether the indexes are ascending or descending (`sysindexes`). (No longer required in version 7 databases.)
- Whether the data is in the same order as the index—that is, clustered (`sysindexes.clust`).
- How many levels are in an index (`sysindexes.levels`).
- What the second largest and second lowest values are for each column. This gives the optimizer a rough idea of the range of values (`syscolumns.colmin` and `colmax`). Version 7 can obtain more detail about the distribution of data (`sysdistrib`).

Using all this information, the optimizer determines all possible routes and then weighs each method with an estimated cost. The cost is based on several considerations including disk access, CPU resources required, and network access. In the process, the optimizer determines in what order to join tables, whether to perform sequential scans, whether it should create temporary tables, and whether it can use an index for the select list, for the filter, for the sort, or for a group by. After the optimizer selects a plan that it believes is the most cost effective, it passes the query for processing, and if `SET EXPLAIN ON` is in effect, the chosen method is recorded in a file.

To illustrate how important it is for the optimizer to have the right information available, you can look at a very simple query and a decision that must be made by the optimizer to perform a join.

Suppose you have two tables, one with 500,000 rows (`tab2`) and the other with 200 rows (`tab1`), both with a unique index on the joining column. A simple select to find related rows from the two tables is

```
SELECT * FROM tab1, tab2
WHERE tab1.col1=tab2.col2
```

If the optimizer chooses to select from the smaller table first and then join to the second using the index, this would result in 1,000 disk reads. (Assume there is one row per page and it takes three index reads and one data read per row in `tab2`—that is, 200 for `tab1` + 200×4 for `tab2`.)

Suppose the optimizer did not have accurate information available about the number of rows and the number of unique values and chose to select from `tab2` first. This results in two million reads! (Assume it takes just two index reads and one data read per row in `tab1`—that is, 500,000 + 500,000×3.)

Of course, if the optimizer has even less accurate information, doesn't know about an index, and uses a sequential scan for each row returned from `tab1`, the database would have to perform around one billion reads (200×500,000)!

You can see from this example using a very simple query that the wrong information and the wrong decision can have dramatic effects on performance, such as 1,000 reads versus 1,000,000,000 reads. If many tables are involved along with more filter conditions in the WHERE clause, the decision process becomes much more complex and the importance of accurate statistics is magnified.

How Accurate Are Your Statistics?

It is very important to remember that the information in the system catalogues used by the optimizer is only updated when the UPDATE STATISTICS command is executed. The optimizer is only as good as the information it is provided, so, rule number one is to execute UPDATE STATISTICS as regularly as possible. You should execute UPDATE STATISTICS more often for very dynamic tables than for tables that rarely change. If the system catalogue information is out of date, the optimizer might make the wrong decision and severe performance problems could be experienced when the query is executed. It is surprising to see how many sites fail to update the system catalogue information.

You can execute UPDATE STATISTICS for the whole database, for individual tables, for columns in a table, and for stored procedures.

Instead of relying on memory, consider automating the execution of UPDATE STATISTICS (using the guidelines later in this chapter) every night via a cron command. Be careful when you run the UPDATE STATISTICS command while other applications are running because the system tables are momentarily locked when the catalogues are updated. This can result in other processes receiving errors. Do not update unnecessarily, because the UPDATE STATISTICS command can take a long time for large tables. For example, updating statistics on large static tables every night is obviously an overkill when the statistics written back to the system tables are going to be as they were before. Similarly, if a table is rarely updated, consider updating the statistics for that table less frequently than the suggested nightly automation.

When Does the Engine Perform the Optimization?

The optimization occurs whenever an SQL statement is prepared, providing there are no host variables. If there are host variables, the optimizer does not have all the information required until the variables are passed (when the cursor is opened), and in this case, the optimization occurs on the OPEN statement. With standard SQL (that is, not prepared), the query is optimized whenever it is executed. If an SQL statement is used repeatedly within a program, it is best to PREPARE the SQL statement to improve performance. This way, the SQL is only optimized once within a program instead of every time it is used (unless specifically requested to re-optimize by using the re-optimization keyword). With stored procedures, the SQL is optimized when the procedure is created or when UPDATE STATISTICS is executed for that stored procedure.

Suddenly Slow?

Even after running UPDATE STATISTICS regularly in production, you may notice one day that a query that previously took 10 minutes suddenly takes one hour. This change can be the result of the optimizer choosing a new path based on new information in the system catalogues. This may mean the query needs restructuring to influence the optimizer to make a better decision. Because of this circumstance, you should have the capability to use SET EXPLAIN ON for any program in production instead of being forced to recompile the program to find out the query plan. Consider building a simple function into all programs that enables you to either pass a parameter or set an environment variable to turn SET EXPLAIN ON.

Development Versus Production

Remember, not only can the statistics used by the optimizer change, but also, if you test a query in development on a small database, the statistics may be quite different from what is in production. A query might appear to perform well in development, but once it is in production, the optimizer might choose (rightly or wrongly) to take a totally different route. The only way to get around this problem in the quality assurance process is to run the query against a test database that is a similar size to the production database with the same data. Alternatively (providing the database schemas are the same), one might consider manually updating some of the columns in the system catalogue tables after running UPDATE STATISTICS on the test database so the optimizer makes the same decisions. However, this is definitely not recommended and Informix might not support you if corruption results.

Controlling the Optimizer

The optimizer can be influenced by using the SET OPTIMIZATION command or by altering the default setting of OPTCOMPIND, which are both described in the following sections.

Optimization Level

Versions 5.*x* and later have the capability to influence how much information the engine attempts to obtain. You can do this by using the command SET OPTIMIZATION HIGH or LOW. HIGH (which is the default) causes the engine to examine all access paths, and LOW causes the engine to eliminate less likely options at an earlier stage in order to improve optimization time. LOW can be useful if many tables are used in a join (five or more) because the optimization time can hinder performance. The downside to using OPTIMIZATION LOW is that an access path may be eliminated too early when in fact it could be the most suitable option.

OPTCOMPIND

Version 7 provides a little more control over the optimizer. Previous versions assumed that if an index existed, it was the most cost-efficient access path. Now, you can specify that you want the optimizer to compare the cost of an index read versus the cost of a table scan so that the most cost-efficient path is chosen. You specify this by setting `OPTCOMPIND=2` (default). You can still emulate the functionality of previous versions by setting `OPTCOMPIND=0`. Setting `OPTCOMPIND=1` instructs the optimizer to work as it does when set to `2` unless `REPEATABLE READ` is set, in which case it works like it does when set to `0`. This option exists because a sequential scan with repeatable read effectively places a shared lock on the whole table (as it scans all rows) during the read. This situation is usually undesirable!

Obtaining Data Distribution for the Optimizer

Beginning with version 6, Informix introduced data distribution analysis and storage to help the optimizer make more informed decisions. Data distribution analysis gives the optimizer a better understanding of the values contained in a column, such as how many unique values are in each area of the table. This information is provided by sampling the data in a column and storing information about sections of the table in various bins. This information can be extremely valuable to the optimizer when dealing with large tables. To generate distribution for a column, you use the `UPDATE STATISTICS` command. The amount of data sampled is controlled by the keywords `MEDIUM` and `HIGH`—for example, `UPDATE STATISTICS HIGH FOR` *`table(column)`*. `MEDIUM` merely samples the data and is very quick, whereas `HIGH` evaluates all the rows in the table and is therefore slower but more accurate. `LOW` is like using previous versions of `UPDATE STATISTICS` and does not obtain any distribution data at all. You can influence the distribution analysis further by using the keyword `RESOLUTION` and by specifying a resolution value (number of bins) and a confidence value (level of sampling). Refer to the manual for more information on using these parameters.

An UPDATE STATISTICS Strategy for OnLine DSA Version 7

The recommended `UPDATE STATISTICS` strategy for Informix DSA version 7 is to perform the following steps (in the same order):

1. Run `UPDATE STATISTICS MEDIUM` on all tables using `DISTRIBUTIONS ONLY` without listing columns and using the default `RESOLUTION` parameters. If you use a version before 7.10.UD1, it is better to actually list the columns that do not head an index for better performance.
2. Run `UPDATE STATISTICS HIGH` for all columns that head an index or the columns that are definitely part of a query. Execute a separate command for each column.
3. Run `UPDATE STATISTICS LOW` for all other columns in composite indexes.

Step one is very fast because it only samples data but still gathers useful distribution information. You use this step first to obtain information about all the columns that are not in an index. From 7.10.UD1, it is not worth specifying each column due to the speed of `MEDIUM`. Step two is to get as much distribution information as possible for all columns that are important for query performance (such as joining columns). Because the index can be used by `UPDATE`

STATISTICS (in version 7), the statistics can be gathered relatively quickly, but note that you should specify only one column at a time with HIGH so that it can make use of an index. In the final step, the remaining columns in all the indexes that are not at the beginning of the index can be referenced in the one statement (per table) using the LOW parameter.

Do not re-run UPDATE STATISTICS for large static tables.

Please see the enclosed CD-ROM, which contains a program provided by Select Software Solutions that will automate the generation of an UPDATE STATISTICS command file using the preceding recommended guidelines.

When the UPDATE STATISTICS steps are complete, you can view any data distribution profiles by using the -hd option with dbschema—for example, dbschema -d *databasename* -hd *tablename*.

TIP

The preceding dbschema command is a very useful method to help you determine a good fragmentation strategy.

Examining the Optimizer's Choice

When you are comfortable knowing that you supplied the optimizer with enough information, you can see what query plan the Informix optimizer chose. To do this, use SET EXPLAIN ON within the query or within the NewEra, 4GL, or ESQL program. When this is set, the optimizer writes output for all queries (for the same process) to a file called sqexplain.out in the current directory. (Usually, the filename and location depend on the operating system and whether the query is executed on a remote host.) When the query is submitted, it is at the point of no return. The only way to examine the optimizer output without completing the query is to hit the interrupt key just after the query starts (after the status line in DBaccess reads explain set).

The following code shows a typical SET EXPLAIN output:

```
QUERY:
------
select cust_id, order.* from orders, customers
where order_date > "01/12/1995" AND order_date < "01/01/1996"
AND customers.cust_id = orders.cust_id order by order_date DESC

Estimated Cost: 10

Estimated # of Rows Returned: 200

Temporary Files Required For: Order By

1) informix.orders: INDEX PATH
```

```
(1) Index keys: order_date
    Lower Index Filter: informix.orders.order_date > "01/12/1995"
    Upper Index Filter: informix.orders.order_date < "01/01/1996"

2) informix.customers: INDEX PATH

(1) Index keys: cust_id (Key-Only)
    Lower Index Filter: informix.customers.cust_id = informix.orders.cust_id
```

Understanding the SET EXPLAIN Output

This section discusses each line of the preceding code in detail. Each code line is shown in bold, with a detailed explanation following it.

`Query:{LOW}`

This section of the output shows the actual query that was optimized. `LOW` is displayed if `SET OPTIMIZATION` is set to `LOW`. Note that `sqexplain.out` is appended to if the file already exists.

`Estimated Cost:`

This value is simply a number the optimizer assigned to the chosen access method. The value is not meaningful except to the optimizer because it bears no relationship to real time. It cannot be compared to the estimated cost of other queries and is best ignored. You can use it, however, to compare changes made for the same query (such as an index change).

`Estimated # of Rows Returned:`

This is the optimizer's estimate based on information in the system catalogue tables. Remember that the catalogue information is fairly limited (especially before version 7), so this value is often inaccurate (more so if the query involves a join). In OnLine DSA version 7, you can obtain distribution information for the data, which helps the optimizer estimate the number of rows more accurately.

`Temporary Files Required For: Order By ¦ Group By`

When this is displayed, there is a `GROUP BY` or an `ORDER BY` statement in the query, and the optimizer determined that there is no corresponding index available to obtain the data in the required order. A temporary file will be created to order the result set. This file could be very large (depending on the size of tables), so check available disk space and be aware of the effect this sort could have on performance. You cannot use indexes when the columns to be sorted come from more than one table. Note that in version 7, the optimizer can choose to traverse an index in the direction of the `ORDER BY` regardless of whether the `INDEX` is in the same order as the `ORDER BY`. Before version 7, the capability of the optimizer to use the index for an `ORDER BY` depended on whether the `ASCENDING` and `DESCENDING` values on the index and the `ORDER BY` matched.

```
1) owner.table: INDEX PATH (Key-Only)
```

This is the table that the optimizer chose to read first (indicated by the 1). Subsequent table accesses (for a nested loop join, for example) are displayed further down in the explain output and are indicated by a higher number. For each row returned at this level, the engine will query the tables at a lower level. INDEX PATH indicates an index will be used to access this table.

The (Key-Only) notation (with OnLine only) indicates that only the index will be read and the actual data value (row) will not be read from this table. Key-only access is generally very efficient (before version DSA 7.2) due to the smaller size of the index compared to the row. Not only is the read for the data row eliminated, but also more index key values are likely to fit on the one page, which in turn reduces I/O. This type of access is achieved only if no columns are selected from the same table. Avoid using SELECT * if possible and select only the required columns. Note that with OnLine DSA 7.2, key-only reads are in fact slower in most cases due to the read-ahead capabilities.

```
(1)Indexkeys: column_name
Lower Index Filter: owner.table.column > x
Upper Index Filter: owner.table.column < y
```

column_name is the name of the column to be used in the INDEX PATH read.

Lower Index Filter shows the first key value (x) where the index read will begin.

Upper Index Filter shows the key value (y) where the index read will stop.

```
1) owner.table: SEQUENTIAL SCAN (Serial, fragments: ALL)
```

In the preceding case, all rows will be read from this table using a sequential scan.

The section in parentheses relates to version 7. If Parallel is displayed instead of Serial, the engine will perform a parallel scan. (This behavior is influenced by the PDQPRIORITY setting.) The ALL notation indicates that all fragments must be scanned because the optimizer cannot eliminate fragments after examining the WHERE predicates. NONE indicates the opposite; that is, the optimizer eliminated all fragments and therefore none must be examined. A number (or list of numbers) indicates that the engine will examine only the fragments listed. (Numbers are relative to the order in the sysfragments table.)

Pay special attention if the sequential scan is performed at a lower level in the query plan (indicated by a higher number) because this could mean the whole table is scanned for each row returned in a previous step. Often, this is one of the warning bells when optimizing or performing quality assurance on a query. Sequential scans are not so bad when they are for small tables or when they are in the first step of a query plan, providing that the engine does not have to scan a large table to retrieve a fraction of the table.

```
AUTOINDEX PATH: owner.table.column
```

This statement is used more in version 4. To avoid sequential access, a temporary index is built on the `owner.table.column` to perform a join. You see this statement if an index does not exist on the join column, and it is generally an indication that you need a permanent index.

```
SORT SCAN: owner.table.column
```

This statement is used in combination with a sequential scan when no index is available on the join column. The `owner.table.column` will be sorted for later use with a join.

```
MERGE JOIN
Merge Filters: owner.table.column = owner.table.column
```

A merge join is used to join the results of the two previous selections sets, which were prepared for a join. After the join columns are obtained in the appropriate order (possibly via a `SORT SCAN` if an index does not exist), the server sequentially reads both result sets and merges them before accessing the rows. A merge join is considered faster than a nested loop join in many cases.

```
DYNAMIC HASH JOIN (Build Outer)
   Dynamic Hash Filters: owner.tab1.col = owner.tab2.column ...
```

In version 7 only, a hash join is used to join the two preceding tables in the explain output. The `Build Outer` notation tells you which table is used first. The filter shows how the tables will be joined. When some complex queries cannot use an index, the hash join takes over. A hash join is also used instead of a sort-merge join and is considered more efficient. Whereas a sort-merge join sorts both tables, a hash join typically sorts only one. Hash joins are favored with large amounts of data, especially for parallel database queries (PDQ) with fragmentation. Rows are placed in a hash table after using an internal hash algorithm. The cost of a hash join can be lower than using an index, especially when more than around 15 percent of data from a large table must be scanned. When the data is not clustered (in a different order to the index), the cost of traversing the index in addition to retrieving the actual rows (in a different order) is quite high compared to a table scan with a hash join. `OPTCOMPIND=2` (which is the default) causes the optimizer to consider hash joins instead of an index. Note that `OPTCOMPIND` should be set to `1` when `REPEATABLE READ` is used (and arguably should be the default).

SQL Query Quality Assurance and Optimization

The following paragraphs cover tips, warnings, some things to check, and some things to avoid.

Avoid sequential scans on a large table if it is not in the first position of the query plan because the whole table scan is repeated for every row in the preceding table. This can severely affect performance. This not only affects the query in action but can also impact other tasks by changing the recently used pages in shared memory (as it keeps reading the whole table into shared memory). This increases disk I/O all around as other processes are forced to read from disk. Consider adding an index if the query cannot be restructured and performance is slow.

Avoid potentially large temporary sort files. They can consume all available CPU resources, increase disk I/O, and consume all available disk space. Consider adding an index on the columns being sorted. A hint: If the optimizer is not using an existing index for the `ORDER BY`, this may be because the column being ordered is not in the `WHERE` clause. In this case, you can influence the optimizer to use the index instead of creating a temporary file by adding a "dummy" `WHERE` condition on the `ORDER BY` column (such as `AND order_num>=0`). Before version 7, the index had to be in the same order as the `ORDER BY`. When sort files are used, check the `$PSORT_DBTEMP` and `$DBSPACETEMP` settings because these can help significantly to improve performance by enabling the engine to use more than one disk for the sort file.

Some more complex correlated subqueries might need to be rewritten by joining one of the permanent tables to a temporary table. Subqueries that make reference (in the `WHERE` clause) to a selected column in the main query can severely affect performance. This causes the subquery to execute repeatedly for each main table row. Be very cautious when using statements such as `EXISTS` with large tables because logical logs can fill very quickly in the process. Temporary table space is allocated and logged for each row in the main table (even if no rows are returned in the final select). The worst effect of this is filling the logs and restoring from an archive. You should rewrite correlated subqueries to use a join wherever possible. Some more complex rewrites may involve joining to a temporary table.

`OR` statements on different columns can prevent the optimizer from using an existing index. If an index does exist and the optimizer chooses a sequential scan in the query plan, consider using a `UNION` statement (one for each `OR` condition) to provide the opportunity for the optimizer to use the index.

If the query is slow even when an `INDEX PATH` is chosen on all levels of the query plan, do not assume the optimizer made the right decision. Check the query plan to see if the tables are filtered in the right order. The aim is usually to eliminate as many rows as possible in the early stages of the query, but unfortunately, the optimizer does not always have enough information to do this correctly (especially in versions before 6). Using `UPDATE STATISTICS HIGH` in version 6 and above gives the optimizer more information about the data distribution so that the right tables are eliminated first. Also note that the `INDEX` reads are not necessarily the best. For example, a sequential scan of a table can be faster than an index scan if the data pages must be retrieved and the pages are not in the same physical order.

Converting data types and comparing character columns is very expensive (for example, `tab.character_col=tab2.integer_col`). If possible, consider changing the column types to numeric. Remember that if the join columns are character types, the columns must be compared byte-by-byte for each row. Although version 7 handles conversions better, the cost of the conversion overhead is still not considered by the optimizer.

Look out for the WHERE predicates that might not be able to use indexes. These include OR, LIKE, or MATCHES with a wildcard at the beginning (such as MATCHES "*NOUR"), functions (such as MONTH, DAY, and LENGTH), negative expressions (such as != "NOUR"), and non-initial substring searches (such as postcode[4,5]>10).

Except for very old versions of the engine, the order of tables in a SELECT list or the order of elements in the WHERE clause do not have an effect; however, in some cases when the optimizer believes the cost is the same for two different paths, the order of the statements in the WHERE clause may have an effect. Some tricks have been suggested in the past (such as repeating predicates in the WHERE clause) to force the optimizer to use a particular index, but this is no longer recommended and does not work with future versions. (In version 7, the optimizer query re-write feature eliminates duplicates in the WHERE clause.)

Avoid long transactions in logged databases. You probably know by now that long transactions threaten to destroy your databases by filling the logical logs. Warning bells should ring with the following statements: LOAD statements, INSERT INTO *xx* SELECT *yy* FROM *zz*, and UPDATE or DELETE statements spanning many rows. Consider locking the table in exclusive mode to avoid excessive lock usage (hindering performance and, even worse, running out of locks).

Check the placement of WHERE conditions with joining columns to see if all combinations of the WHERE predicate are included. For example, the WHERE predicate, tab1.x=tab2.x and tab1.x >1000, would probably cause the optimizer to use the index on tab1.x, but the index on tab2.x might be much more appropriate. Adding the condition and tab2.x > 1000 gives the optimizer more choices to evaluate. Another example is tab1.x=tab2.x AND tab2.x=tab3.x. The optimizer in version 5 does not consider joining tab1 directly to tab3, so adding tab1.x=tab3.x again provides more choices. Note that the optimizer in OnLine DSA V7 rewrites queries so that all possible combinations are examined and these suggestions are not applicable.

Select only the columns required; this reduces the communication between the front end and back end and reduces I/O. Avoid the temptation to use SELECT * (all columns) when it is not required.

Use temporary tables when a subset of data is reselected with different WHERE predicates. An example is a SELECT with the WHERE clause:

```
orderdate> "01/12/1995" and x=1
```

This might be followed by a SELECT with a WHERE clause:

```
orderdate> "01/12/1995" and x=2
```

In this case, if the table is very large, you could improve performance by first selecting all rows WHERE orderdate>"01/12/1995" into a temporary table and then performing subsequent selects on the temporary table.

Use temporary tables to influence the optimizer to take the route that you know is best. You can do this by first selecting the rows you want from a large table into a temporary table and then joining the temporary table to the rest of the tables. The optimizer might use a different query plan, knowing that the temporary table is much smaller than the original large table.

Consider creating indexes on temporary tables—an option that is often overlooked just because the table is temporary.

When using temporary tables for subsequent selects with `ORDER BY`s, create the temporary table using an `ORDER BY`. An example is `SELECT` *x* `FROM` *y* `ORDER BY` *x* `INTO TEMP` *temp_tab*. This syntax is not available in earlier versions of the engine (before 4.1).

Consider running `UPDATE STATISTICS` (within the application) for large temporary tables. This option is often overlooked just because the table is temporary.

Use the `WITH NO LOG` statement when explicitly creating temporary tables; this helps performance by eliminating the overhead of writing to the logical logs. This also avoids the possibility of creating a long transaction with a large temporary table. In version 7, you can create temporary tables in a special dbspace that is not logged. Use this feature whenever possible.

Time commands with the UNIX `time` or `timex` command, or use the following before and after the query being tested or optimized:

```
SELECT CURRENT FROM systables WHERE tabid=1
```

When testing or timing queries, remember that the second time the query is executed, it is much more likely to be faster because the pages read the first time are probably still in memory. Be aware that this may distort the test results. Use `tbstat -p` to monitor disk and buffer usage. When timing queries, consider restarting the instance between tests in order to re-initialize shared memory.

The subject of Parallel Database Queries and fragmentation is a whole new book in its own right. It is important to fragment the data in a way that makes it easy for the optimizer to determine which fragments are active. Making the `WHERE` predicates clear enough to enable the optimizer to eliminate fragments reduces I/O and enables parallelism.

Summary

The Informix cost-based optimizer does an excellent job with what it is supposed to do—that is, shielding you from the task of thinking about the best way to retrieve your data. For this reason, you might often take it for granted. Just imagine if you had to make the same complex decisions the optimizer does every time you want to access your data. Nevertheless, it is important that you understand the optimizer and the consequences of the decisions it makes. More importantly, you need to provide the optimizer with the information it needs to perform its job effectively.

Informix is constantly refining the optimizer and finding new ways to improve performance. Some of the comments made in this chapter may not apply to future releases.

Part V

Application Development

IN THIS PART

Application Development Introduction

by John McNally

IN THIS CHAPTER

This chapter provides

- A description of the types of applications that use Informix database management systems (DBMS)
- A breakdown of batch and OLTP processing
- A definition of client/server architecture and how it relates batch and OLTP processes to the Informix DBMS
- A description of tools available to build applications to access Informix DBMSs

Building an Application That Accesses an Informix Database

The Informix DBMS is not a system created to satisfy the requirements of a small application. The needs of a small application include the following:

- DBMS running on a desktop computer
- Application running on the same desktop computer
- Serving a single database user

Although an Informix DBMS can satisfy these requirements, it is a waste to use it in this manner. The latest Informix DBMS, Parallel Server, was designed to satisfy the needs of an entire business. These needs include

- Running on an open system (UNIX or Windows NT)
- Managing multiple databases of varying size
- Managing different databases in multiple locations
- Managing different parts of a database in different locations
- Handling multiple users and performing different tasks against the database

The last item, handling multiple users who perform different tasks, is managed by the application. An application can be one of two types: batch or OLTP.

A batch application is a process that performs non-user involved work. For example, a company receives a daily file of names and addresses. A batch process reads this file, changes the format and layout of the data, and then stores this rearranged data into the database's tables. Whether the daily file contains 10 records or 10 million is not important; the process to store the file's information does not require user intervention. As shown in Figure 34.1, a batch process performs many tasks within a single transaction. This means that a batch process does not commit each task's data to the database until all its work is complete.

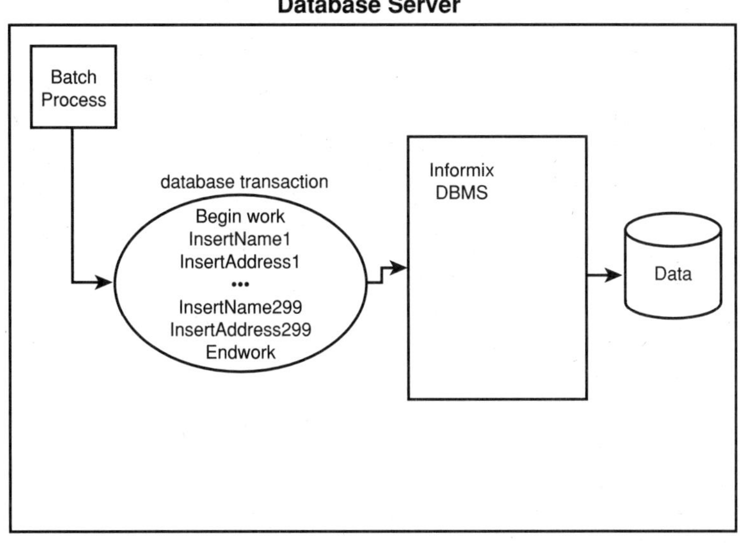

FIGURE 34.1.
A batch process accessing an Informix DBMS.

The other type of application is OLTP, or online transaction processing. An OLTP process performs small tasks, usually one task per transaction. For example, instead of receiving a file containing names and addresses once a day, an application is available for users to type that information into a computer. After each name and address combination is entered, it is stored in the database. As shown in Figure 34.2, each name and address combination is stored by a single transaction containing only the one insert task.

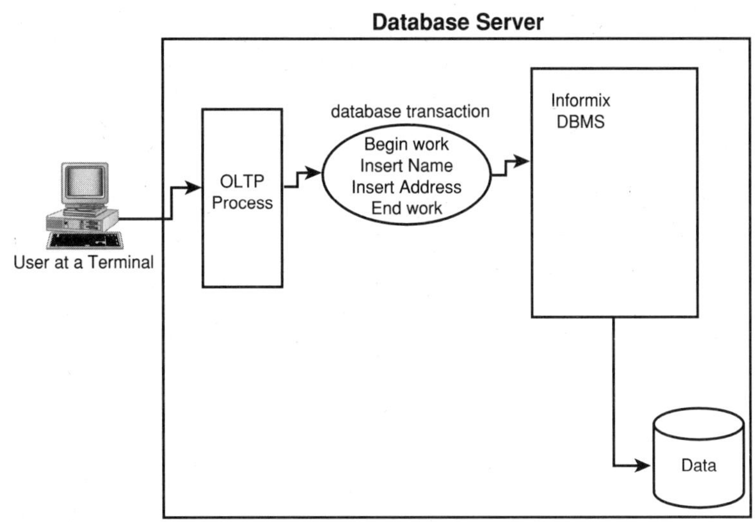

FIGURE 34.2.
An OLTP process accessing an Informix DBMS.

An OLTP system and a client/server system can be confusing. A client/server system is where the application programs, known as clients, must run as processes separate from the programs that maintain and store the data, called servers. A client process does not necessarily have to be running on a different machine from the server. It just has to be a different process. The client/server relationship is possible only because the clients must communicate with the server to access the data.

Because Informix DBMS is a server, any application accessing that server is considered a client. An example of a non-client/server database system is one in which the program maintaining the database also controls the user's access to that data, such as Microsoft Access. To Informix DBMSs, all processes accessing the database, even if they perform OLTP or batch processing, are considered clients. To clear some of the confusion, it is best to refer to an application by the type of transaction it performs. The long multi-task single transaction is referred to as a batch application or batch client, whereas the small single task per transaction is referred to as an OLTP application or OLTP client.

In the business world, as shown in Figure 34.3, very few DBMSs are set up to deal with only one type of client—batch or OLTP. The stored data is useful for many areas of the business, and each of these business areas requires certain ways to use that data. This requirement determines the types and multitude of clients needed. Usually, the system has multiple OLTP clients that perform many different tasks. On that very same system are multiple batch clients that also perform many different tasks. These batch and OLTP clients may or may not access the database server at the same time. Administrators usually like to separate OLTP and batch processing at different times of the day to configure the system for the best throughput possible. Throughput is the time it takes to perform a specific database task, such as adding an address.

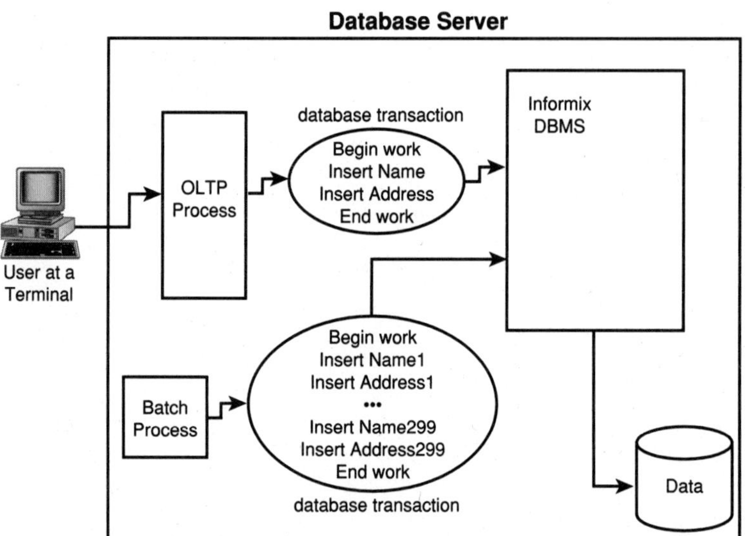

FIGURE 34.3.
Multiple OLTP and batch processes accessing an Informix DBMS.

Throughput can also determine how OLTP clients are designed and developed. Businesses with hundreds of OLTP clients might not want each of these clients to access the database server at the same time. For example, an application is needed to manage customer information. The database contains the customer's name, address, and phone number. The client process must have the capability to view, add, change, or remove a customer, which is a select, insert, update, or delete database-related task. The design of the client depends on several factors:

- The amount of data per task or transaction
- The maximum expected size of the database
- The amount of client processes
- The processing speed and capacity of the network, client, and server hardware and operating systems

In this example, the amount of data per task is very small, 50 bytes or less, and should suffice for a customer's name, address, and phone number. For the database's size, an average size is less than a gigabyte. The information needed and the database layouts determine the overall size. Informix DBMSs can manage data and databases over a terabyte, if needed. The amount of client processes also depends on the business' needs. A company that sells a single product, one distinct computer game, might have one or two people to enter addresses for catalog mailings. On the other hand, a company that sells an entire line of business and entertainment software might have hundreds of people entering addresses. Expected amounts of client work combined with the processing capacity of the hardware and operating system for the clients and the server determine the scalability of the system.

A system dealing with small-sized data transactions on an average-sized database, running a few clients that actually do the data entry, running on an average-powered machine, probably designs the clients as shown in Figure 34.4. This is an example of the most basic client/server configuration, where the client process runs on the same machine as the DBMS, using the same operating system and CPUs.

You can develop clients to perform different tasks. For example, you can develop two clients that are used along with the original customer information OLTP client. You can use this new OLTP process to track customer loyalty. Used by management, this new process determines, at any time, the amount of customers added, deleted, or returned. The other new process can be a batch client that produces mailing labels. If activity and data size remain average to low, then all three clients can run on the same machine, as shown in Figure 34.5. When the clients and the server run on the same machine, you have a single-tier architecture.

When the single machine is unable to handle the processing required of it, the scalability of the clients and the server become important. You might want to build applications to run on remote machines that connect to the DBMS through a communications protocol such as TCP/IP. In this way, the processing needed for the application is done on the remote machine's CPU and operating system. As shown in Figure 34.6, the machine running the DBMS is dedicated to the DBMS and batch processing. All OLTP applications are run on either of the other servers running applications that handle multiple users or on stand-alone workstations or PCs that handle single users. This situation is known as a two-tier architecture.

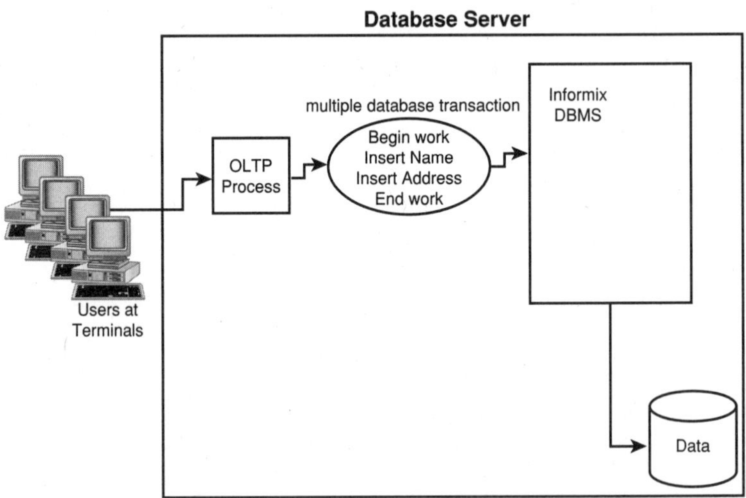

FIGURE 34.4.
Multiple OLTP running on the same machine as the Informix DBMS.

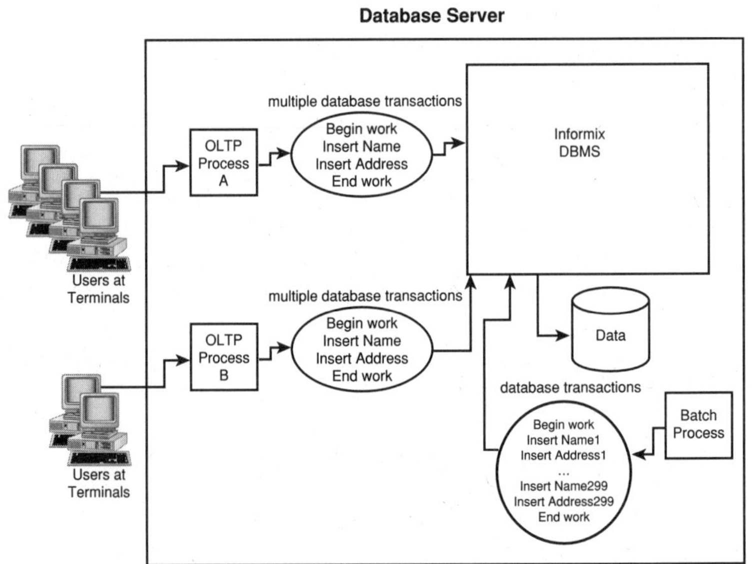

FIGURE 34.5.
Multiple and different OLTP clients and a batch client running on the same machine as the Informix DBMS.

If that is not enough to handle the expected workload of OLTP users, you can use other techniques to spread out the CPU workload. Figure 34.7 shows a system that is configured in a three-tier architecture.

FIGURE 34.6.
A two-tier configuration where multiple and different OLTP clients and batch clients access the same Informix DBMS.

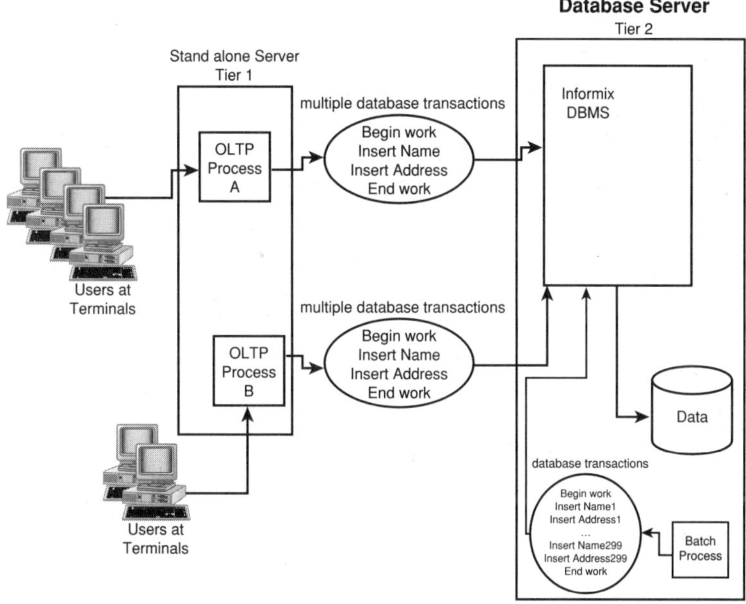

FIGURE 34.7.
A three-tier configuration where multiple and different OLTP clients and batch clients access the same Informix DBMS.

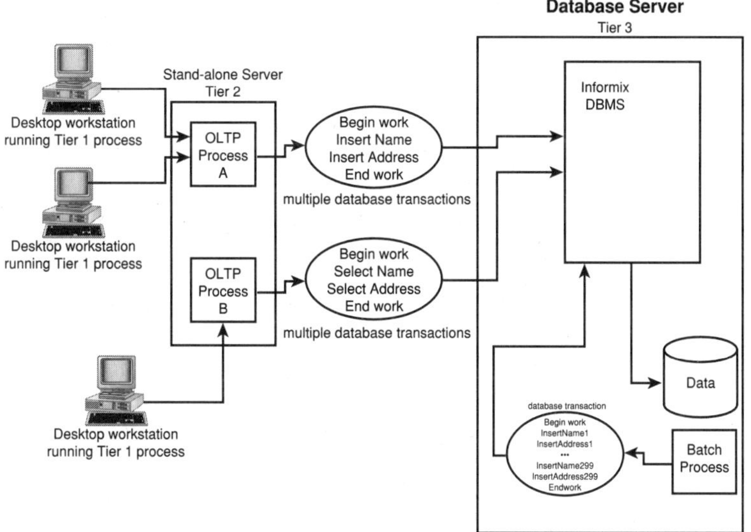

Think of each tier in this architecture as one step to achieve a goal, with each step requiring some work to be performed. Client applications run on stand-alone work stations, where all the data is collected and used. When that client needs to store or retrieve data from the database, it communicates with a server that is running a process waiting for database requests. That middle process then arranges the request into the format required of the Informix DBMS's database layout. This middle process creates OLTP transactions and sends them to the machine running the DBMS. That machine uses its CPUs to run the DBMS and process the transactions, processing in parallel as much as possible. The DBMS sends the results to the middle server process, which can process the results some more and then send the results back to the client.

For example, the client process wants all the information on a specific customer. It sends a request for "all information on Customer X" to the middle server. The middle server knows that "all information" means name, address, and phone numbers. The middle process creates three transactions, one for each task: retrieve X's name, retrieve X's address, and retrieve X's phone number. All three transactions are sent to the DBMS at the same time. The DBMS processes all three in parallel and sends the results back to the middle server as each task is completed. The middle sever takes the three individual results, combines them into one result, and sends it back to the client.

Another way to spread out the processing across multiple machines is to have a distributed database or even distributed database servers. The first has a single DBMS that manages databases stored on different disk devices, as shown in Figure 34.8. This spreads out the I/O activity required of each database to specific disk devices.

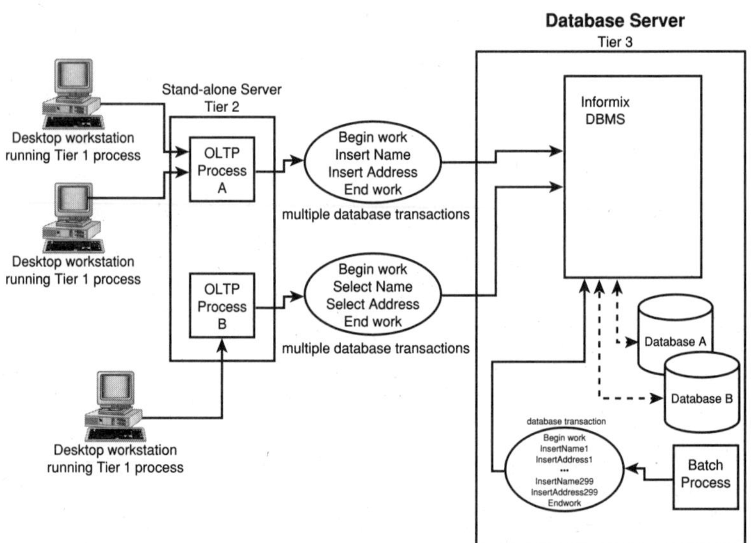

FIGURE 34.8.
A distributed database configuration using the same Informix DBMS.

The second method is to have multiple DBMSs on different machines, as shown in Figure 34.9. That way, each DBMS is able to process more on its machine's CPU. These two situations dictate how an application interacts with the databases and where it gets its data, but any of the application situations mentioned previously work on either of these distributed options or on a non-distributed option.

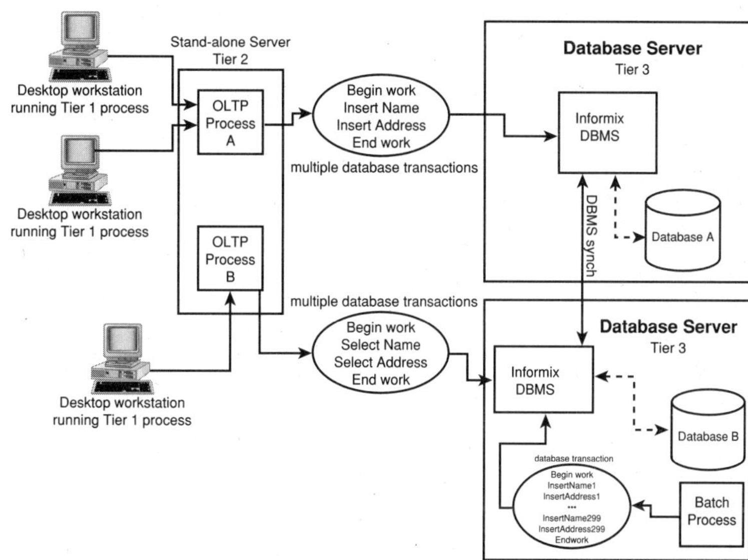

FIGURE 34.9.
A distributed Informix DBMS.

When developing applications to work with an Informix DBMS, it is best to determine the workload required. Any of the situations previously discussed work with an Informix DBMS and can be combined in many different ways. For example, a single DBMS with a distributed database can have local OLTP and batch clients as well as two-tiered and three-tiered clients. Always develop systems that are scalable to the needs of the business. A well-built application can start out small and expand easily over the years.

Not only is it a good idea to put some thought into the type of client application that is built, but also it may be wise to use one of the accepted methodologies for application design.

Many different methodologies are available, so choose the one that best fits the size of the application, business needs, available development resources, and time frame. Upon completion of the client design and architecture, you must decide what tool to use to actually develop the application.

Tools for Application Development

Informix and other vendors provide many tools to develop applications that access an Informix DBMS. Choosing a development tool depends on the business's needs, the size of the application to build, the available development resources, and the time frames and knowledge base of developers.

Tools to choose from include

- Embedded SQL
- INFORMIX-4GL

- INFORMIX-NewEra
- Open Database Connectivity (ODBC) Tools
- Prebuilt applications

Embedded SQL

Embedded SQL is the process of embedding SQL statements among other statements in many different programming languages and producing the same results as stand-alone SQL.

The four embedded SQL products offered by Informix are

- INFORMIX-ESQL/C
- INFORMIX-ESQL/COBOL
- INFORMIX-ESQL/Ada
- INFORMIX-ESQL/FORTRAN

The ESQL products allow a programmer to use SQL for accessing and manipulating databases from a third-generation language; they are INFORMIX-SQL application program interfaces. In addition, I discuss

- What is ESQL?
- Uses of ESQL

What Is ESQL?

ESQL is the Informix Corporation abbreviation for embedded SQL. Embedded SQL is the SQL statements that are embedded in the program. You can write the SQL statements into the programs just as if they were a normal statement of the programming language.

Informix created an ESQL product for the following languages: C, COBOL, FORTRAN, and Ada. These products work as application programming interfaces (APIs). The following list shows the step-by-step processing procedures that the Informix APIs follow:

1. You start with an ESQL source program containing embedded SQL.
2. The ESQL preprocessor is a program that locates the embedded SQL statements within your source program and converts them into procedures.
3. The new source program contains the converted procedures.
4. The source program runs through the language compiler.
5. After going through the language compiler, the source program is an executable program after it links with the API procedures.
6. The SQL API is a library containing application programming interface procedures.

After these processing steps are complete, the database server follows through with the SQL statements. SQL API products allow you to embed SQL statements into the host languages. SQL statements can be used two ways: static embedding or dynamic SQL.

Static embedding is the use of SQL statements as part of the source code, whereas dynamic SQL is statements that are not part of the source code but are SQL statements composed of a string of characters constructed at the time of execution. Dynamic SQL can create SQL statements from the user input. After the input is received, the program creates and stores the SQL statements. Next, it prepares a statement and has the database server review it prior to execution. Note that a select statement that produces a single-row response will process, but if multiple rows of data are to be returned, the server will return an error code.

ESQL enables you to use statements that return one row of data or no data at all. If a statement will return more than one row of data, a cursor is used. A cursor is a data structure that processes the current query. The following list provides a brief description of how a cursor is used to process your SQL statements:

1. `DECLARE` the cursor.
2. `OPEN` the cursor.
3. `FETCH` the data.
4. `CLOSE` the cursor.

The `DECLARE` statement specifies a cursor name and allocates storage for the associated select statement. The `OPEN` cursor statement opens the cursor and starts the processing by passing the select statement to the database server. The `FETCH` statement retrieves the output data. The `CLOSE` statement closes the cursor after the last row is fetched. All of these statements—`DECLARE`, `OPEN`, `FETCH`, and `CLOSE`—are used as part of the program.

A statement returning single rows of data or no data can be handled like standard statements of the language. Statements returning more than one row of data are used with a cursor. Static SQL statements can be used directly in the program and dynamic SQL statements can be created at execution time.

The following code shows SQL statements embedded in a COBOL program:

```
EXEC SQL
         DELETE FROM  table1
          WHERE field1 =  fld-1
END-EXEC.
```

The following code shows SQL statements embedded in an Ada program:

```
EXEC SQL
        DELETE FROM table1
         WHERE field1 = $fld1;
```

The following code shows SQL statements embedded in a FORTRAN program:

```
EXEC SQL
        DELETE FROM table1
         WHERE field1 = :fld1
```

Uses of ESQL

The main use for embedded SQL (ESQL) is to allow SQL statements to be written into programs as if they were the normal statements for that programming language. A preprocessor translates the SQL statements into data structures for the specific source programming language.

You can put SQL statements into programs written in other languages and the program executes and retrieves data from the database.

The use of the `DELETE`, `INSERT`, and `UPDATE` SQL statements within your program modifies the data in the database. The program can also create a cursor for updating, inserting, or deleting rows of data. Remember that your program should be set up to return errors while this type of processing is in the program.

The two additional uses for embedded SQL are

- Embedding data definition statements
- Embedding grant and revoke privileges

Data definition statements are used to create a database and define the structure. This type of processing is usually not part of the program because a database is created only once but updates are done many times. The selection of the database can be embedded as part of the program's SQL code.

Granting and revoking privileges can also be embedded in your program. Grant and revoke statements either give access or revoke access to a database or specific tables. This allows you to control who can perform specific functions on your database. Because the grant and revoke statements are performed so often, it is simpler to embed the authorizations in a program.

Informix's Fourth-Generation Language

A fourth-generation language or 4GL is a simple-to-use, easy-to-learn programming language. To develop with a 4GL, the developer does not have to be an expert programmer. INFORMIX-4GL is a complete application development tool. When building applications through INFORMIX-4GL, the developer can automatically create an executable or code that can be incorporated into other C or COBOL programs.

INFORMIX-4GL was designed for database users to actually build their own applications without learning how to be programmers. Using INFORMIX-4GL may be a viable solution to meet a business's needs. Chapters 35 through 38, "Introduction to 4GL," "4GL Coding," "4GL Development," and "Advanced 4GL Development," provide the insight on how to use INFORMIX-4GL for building applications.

Informix's NewEra

An even easier way to build applications to use an Informix DBMS is through Informix's NewEra. NewEra is a graphical user interface or GUI, which is a front door into INFORMIX-4GL. To build an application, all the coding is replaced by drag and drop and point and click. INFORMIX-NewEra is a great tool to use for rapid application development, especially in environments where applications are thrown away and redeveloped. Chapters 39 through 41, "Introduction to NewEra," "NewEra Language," and "The NewEra Development System," provide a complete explanation of creating applications using INFORMIX-NewEra.

Open Database Connectivity

ODBC, or Open Database Connectivity, is a Microsoft standard interface for generic database access. An application programming interface (API), ODBC is a set of database calls that can be used within application programs to access any database system. ODBC doesn't care what type of database server is being used, as long as that database server being accessed is ODBC-compliant. Any program written with ODBC calls should be able to work with all of these database systems: Informix, Sybase, Oracle, Access, and FoxPro.

Besides being ODBC ready, Informix provides three tools to make the development of ODBC applications easier. Each of these tools uses ODBC to perform its specific tasks. The three tools are

- INFORMIX-CLI
- INFORMIX-DCE/NET
- INFORMIX-Enterprise Gateway Manager

INFORMIX-CLI is another layer of calls around ODBC that allows SQL to be dynamically run. Usually, SQL contained within application code must be compiled with the code and be part of the application's executable. With CLI, which stands for *call level interface*, SQL does not have to be preprocessed, but can be interactively submitted to Informix at any time.

INFORMIX-DCE/NET, which stands for *distributed computing environment/network*, allows ODBC-based clients, which can usually access local Informix database servers, the ability to access remotely distributed Informix database servers.

INFORMIX-Enterprise Gateway Manager is very much like DCE/NET except it uses ODBC to allow Informix-based clients the ability to access other database servers such as Oracle or Sybase systems.

Purchase

Sometimes, the application a company needs is built by some other company. With ODBC, more applications, even though they were written for Oracle or Sybase systems, can now be easily ported and used with an Informix database. Usually, a consulting firm creates a system for one company and then sells it to other companies, making minor changes to meet the buying companies' special processing and database layouts. This is a big decision to make with cost as the primary factor. Weigh the pros and cons carefully. Just like buying a used car, you also purchase the problems. When buying a prebuilt application, you get the bugs with it.

Summary

Having a DBMS on a computer system provides applications that are responsible for data processing only, not data management. With a DBMS, there is one central process that manages data and serves that data when requested. This allows the application developer to concentrate on building efficient data processing programs.

When building an application, determining the type of process to build depends on the requirements of the new application. Building a batch or OLTP process that accesses data within a database is possible with an Informix DBMS. Informix DBMSs also allow for different types of application architectures, such as local or remotely run clients.

Not only does the Informix server allow for different types of clients, but it also provides tools to build these client applications. Informix provides tools to embed SQL within programs written in C and COBOL. There are also Informix tools that build programs using 4GL or GUI screens.

CHAPTER

Introduction to 4GL

by José Fortuny

IN THIS CHAPTER

This chapter is the first of a series of four chapters that introduce the INFORMIX-4GL character-based development environment. This chapter is an overview of the features of the 4GL development products of Informix and presents the basic language constructs as well as the programmer's development and debugging environments. Chapter 36, "4GL Coding," deals in detail with the components of the INFORMIX-4GL language, paying particular attention to the specialized programming statements that Informix provides for dealing with the database and the screen display of database-bound information. Chapter 37, "4GL Development," begins the discussion of issues of unique importance for the software developer in 4GL: screens and reports. Database application developers write programs to take input from the user who fills in the contents of a screen display. Later, the data collected in the database is used to create reports to be displayed to the screen, printed in a document, or transmitted electronically. Chapter 38, "Advanced 4GL Development," continues the discussion of screens and reports initiated in Chapter 37 and provides you with more complex screen designs and report layouts. Chapter 38 also includes a discussion of error handling in INFORMIX-4GL and covers other, more advanced, miscellaneous topics.

If you think of INFORMIX-4GL in terms of a language, Chapter 35 reviews its overall framework and richness. Chapter 36 provides you with its basic vocabulary. Chapter 37 introduces the basic grammar of the language, and Chapter 38 discusses its advanced grammar.

What It Is and the Environment in Which It Works

INFORMIX-4GL is a fourth-generation programming language that caters effectively to the development of database applications with a character-based interface. INFORMIX-4GL operates primarily on UNIX platforms, although there is also a PC-based version.

As a language, INFORMIX-4GL provides all the standard constructs of third-generation languages: variable assignments, looping, testing, and flow of control, as well as a rich collection of data types and programming statements for managing the interactions of a user with an Informix database engine. In addition to the standard data types that you find in most languages, such as integer and character, INFORMIX-4GL allows you to define two exceptionally powerful data structures: the record and the array. The record data type is a collection of members in which each member can have any valid Informix data type (either a simple data type, another record, or an array). The array is a data structure of up to three dimensions of values of the same data type; the values in an array can be any simple Informix data type or records (an array of arrays is not allowed). The combination of a record data type and an array of record data types is, as you see later, a most useful data structure in representing and dealing with one-to-many relationships.

INFORMIX-4GL enables you to process database records one at a time, and some of your programs might have a record-oriented structure in which you interact with the database one record at a time. Because INFORMIX-4GL was designed to interface with any of the Informix relational database engines, it supports direct SQL statements within the code. This provides the developer the capability to request, in a single statement, that the database engine process an active data set, a collection of rows that satisfy a common set of criteria.

Because it was originally designed to operate in UNIX environments, INFORMIX-4GL integrates well in such an environment. Like any other program, an INFORMIX-4GL program can receive options and arguments from the command line when invoked and can return exit codes to the environment upon termination. In addition, an INFORMIX-4GL program can read the values of environment variables and behave appropriately based on the values.

TIP

Suppose you define a UNIX environment variable that identifies the database to use—for example, `DBNAME=testdb`—and your program is designed to read and use this environment variable or is designed to receive an argument from the command line when invoked. When you finish developing and testing your code, no further changes to the code are required to place it into production. The software accesses whatever database you set in the environment (`DBNAME=proddb`) or pass to the program as an argument.

INFORMIX-4GL, as a product, comes equipped with the facilities required for assisting application developers to design, code, and test software systems:

- A menu-driven development environment: the Developer's Environment.
- Command-line development facilities.
- An interactive debugger (available only with the Rapid Development System).

Compiled or Rapid Development System

INFORMIX-4GL development licenses are available in two different versions: a compiled version, distributed under the name INFORMIX-4GL, and an interpreted version, named INFORMIX-4GL Rapid Development System (RDS). To match the two development versions, Informix delivers runtime licenses for both products.

If you develop using INFORMIX-4GL, you produce an executable program file that runs in the UNIX environment in which it is compiled. If you develop using INFORMIX-4GL RDS, you produce a p-code file that is portable across machines and UNIX environments; the runtime INFORMIX-4GL RDS can receive and execute a p-code file created in another system that uses a development license of the same version. The rationale for delivering compiled executables is speed; loading the compiled executable is faster than loading the interpreted runner and p-code program. After the products are loaded into memory, speed of execution does not favor decisively one product over the other.

The programs written in both flavors of the development product are identical, and many developers use the INFORMIX-4GL RDS environment to develop and debug code and, when the software is ready, recompile the source with the INFORMIX-4GL product and produce an executable file for distribution.

NOTE

There is actually a minor difference in the behavior of the compiled and the interpreted versions of the language: The interpreted version initializes variables automatically, but the compiled version does not. In any case, the program should be in control of initializing variables appropriately, and the difference in versions should otherwise not be noticeable.

CAUTION

If you develop in RDS and distribute compiled executables, do test the compiled version as thoroughly as you did the interpreted version. Compiled and interpreted identical versions of the product can have different bugs, and they often do.

Debugging programs in INFORMIX-4GL RDS is a much easier task than in INFORMIX-4GL. The former comes equipped with a debugger, whereas the latter does not.

The Process of Creating Programs

Whether you use the compiled or the interpreted environments, the process of developing and delivering software is essentially the same in both cases:

1. Design your program.
2. Create an ASCII file for each screen form in your program.
3. Compile each form and correct syntactical errors detected by the compiler.
4. Create an ASCII file for each source code module in your program.
5. Compile each module and correct syntactical errors detected by the compiler.
6. Define and compile the complete program.
7. Test, debug, and correct both syntax and logic.

You can accomplish these tasks within the UNIX shell, using editors to create the ASCII files required and commands to compile and link the modules into a program, but it is easier to accomplish them within the Programmer's Environment, a menu-driven development environment provided by Informix. The Programmer's Environment actually guides you through the process of creating and editing the required ASCII files using the editor of your choice and compiling and linking the final program. If you work with the RDS product, the Programmer's Environment also offers you debugging options.

The Files Required and the Files Produced

The directory that stores your program contains a mixture of files: source files for forms and modules, compiled forms, object files or p-code for compiled modules, and executables. All or some of these files can be present in the system at any one time. In addition, while you are working in the development environment, the system creates backup files of the code you are editing. To distinguish between files, Informix uses different suffixes that identify the nature and contents of each file. Table 35.1 outlines the list of possible file suffixes.

Table 35.1. File contents and identifying suffixes.

Suffix	*Contents*
`per`	Form source code
`4gl`	Module source code
`err`	Error file for both forms and modules; contains source, errors, and warnings
`frm`	Compiled screen form
`4go`	Interpreted module p-code
`o`	Compiled module object
`4gi`	Interpreted program p-code (concatenated `.4go` files)
`4ge`	Compiled program
`c`	C code source equivalent to 4GL source
`ec`	Intermediate C source file
`erc`	Object error; contains source and errors
`pbr`	Form source code backup (Programmer's Environment)
`fbm`	Form object backup (Programmer's Environment)
`4bl`	Module source code backup (Programmer's Environment)
`4bo`	Object backup (Programmer's Environment)
`4be`	Program backup (Programmer's Environment)
`4db`	Debugger initialization file

A typical directory listing containing a small application program is likely to look like the image in Figure 35.1. Note that, at the moment the listing was taken, the module `main.4gl` was open for editing; the corresponding backup files are displayed in the listing.

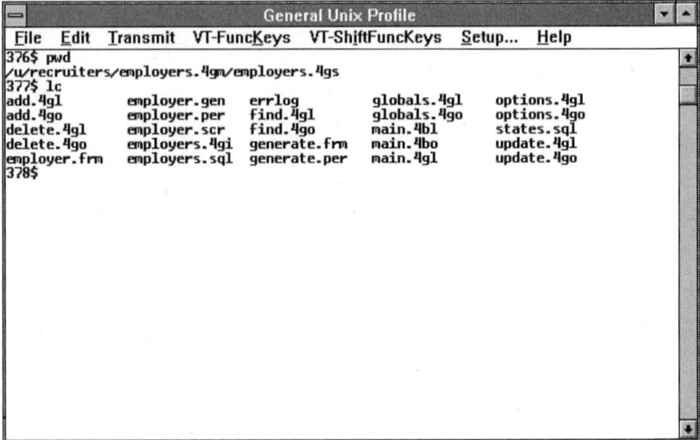

FIGURE 35.1.
A listing of a typical program directory.

The Development Environment

Informix provides two interfaces for developing applications: a menu-driven environment, named the Programmer's Environment, and a command-line environment.

The Menu-Driven Environment (Programmer's Environment)

The Programmer's Environment is a menu-driven application development system that caters to the entire process of creating programs. It facilitates the process by guiding the developer through the steps required, from creating the ASCII files that contain forms and source code modules, through the compilation and generation of objects, to the final assembly of an executable program.

To invoke the Programmer's Environment, use the command `i4gl` if you use the compiled version of the software or `r4gl` if you use the Rapid Development System.

The Programmer's Environment uses ring menus at every level. You can access the various options of each ring menu by either typing the capital letter that identifies the option or by moving the cursor with the space bar or the arrow keys and pressing the Enter or Return key when the desired option is highlighted.

The main menu of the Programmer's Environment is displayed in Figure 35.2.

The options in the main menu functionally group the various tasks that are performed on each component of a completed application program. You are provided with a submenu to create and edit source code modules (Module), create and edit screen forms (Form), and assemble modules into a complete program (Program), and if you installed INFORMIX-SQL on your system, you can access its main menu (Query-language). All menus and submenus in the Programmer's Environment offer an Exit option to navigate through the menus or to terminate the development session.

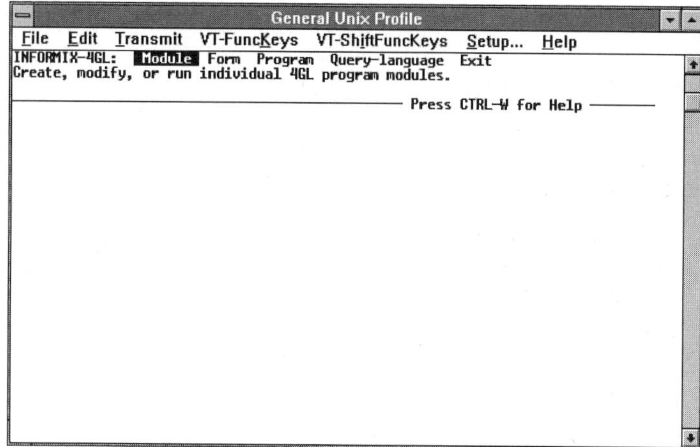

FIGURE 35.2.
The Programmer's Environment main menu.

The Module submenu of the Programmer's Environment shows a slight difference between the compiled and the RDS versions of INFORMIX-4GL. Figure 35.3 shows the submenu for the RDS version.

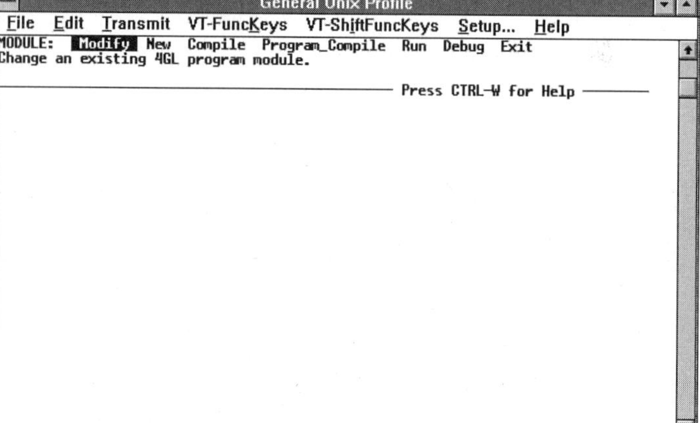

FIGURE 35.3.
The Module submenu in the RDS version of the Programmer's Environment.

The options in the Module submenu allow you to create (New) or edit (Modify) a source code module; when you make either of those selections, the system opens a window with the editor you chose by setting the environment variable `DBEDIT` and loads the file to modify if appropriate. Usually, the default editor is vi, but you can reset that variable to emacs (`DBEDIT=emacs`), for instance. Make sure the editor you select to create source code module files actually creates ASCII files that are free from formatting and printing embedded controls. Other options in the Module submenu allow you to create an object code file (Compile) for the source code module that you select, assemble the executable file for the program you select (Program Compile), and execute the program located in the working directory (Run). If you have the RDS version of the product, you can also start the Debugger with the compiled program in the current directory (Debug). The Debugger is not available with the compiled version of the product.

After New or Modify, when you exit the edit session of your source code module, INFORMIX-4GL presents you with a submenu that offers you choices of actions to execute on your edited file. This Modify Module submenu is displayed in Figure 35.4.

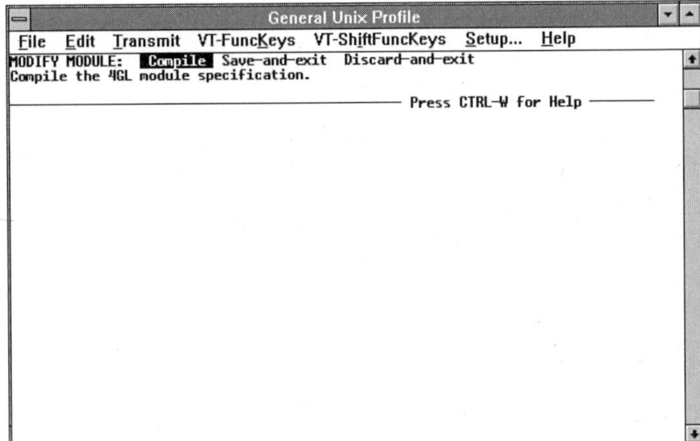

FIGURE 35.4.
The Modify Module submenu.

From the Modify Module submenu, you can create an object file (Compile), save the code (Save and Exit), or do away with your modifications (Discard and Exit).

If you choose Compile, you see the submenu displayed in Figure 35.5.

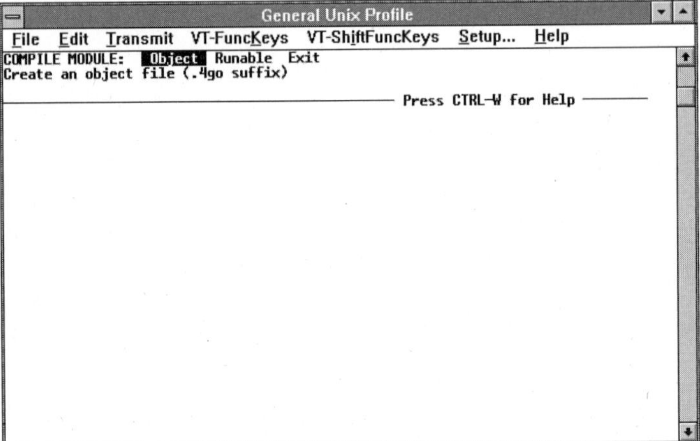

FIGURE 35.5.
The Compile (1) Module submenu.

If your application has multiple source code modules to assemble into the finished executable, you choose the option to create an object file (Object) for the current module. If your program has only one source code module, the one about to be compiled, and there are no other library objects to be linked into the program, then you choose to make both the object code file and the executable file (Runable) at the same time.

If the compiler finds no errors in your code, it quietly places you back in the Modify Module submenu with the Save-and-Exit option highlighted so that you can press Return and accept it, saving the modified source code you just compiled. If the compiler encounters errors in your source code module, it presents you with the Compile (2) submenu, displayed in Figure 35.6.

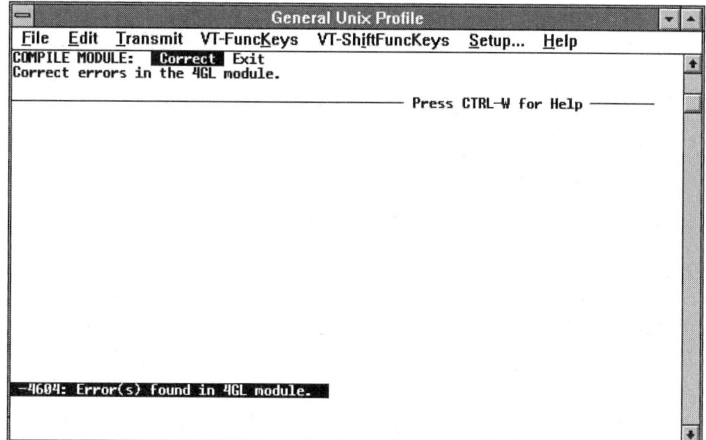

FIGURE 35.6.
The Compile (2) Module submenu.

The most sensible option at this point is to fix the errors found (Correct), which places you back in editing mode. This time, however, the edit file contains both your original code as well as embedded error messages. These error messages highlight the compiler's sense of where the error occurred (indicated by the up caret on the line immediately below the error) and what the error was (with an error number so that you can refer to the *Informix Error Messages* manual for an idea of how to solve the problem, and a brief error description, which, for the most part, should be enough to correct the error). Figure 35.7 shows a sample error message.

When correcting errors in the module error file, you do not have to do anything about the error messages that the compiler embedded in the file. The compiler removes them as you exit the edit session, and they are no longer there when you save the contents of the file.

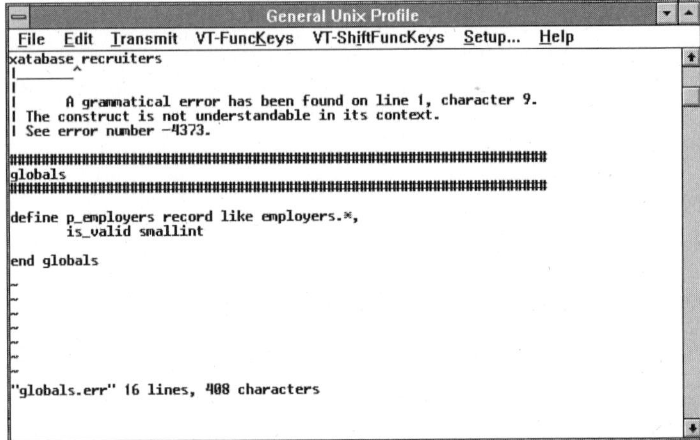

FIGURE 35.7.
A sample `module.err` *file.*

> **TIP**
>
> Most of the time, INFORMIX-4GL is accurate at assessing where an error in a source code module occurred. With statements that require a termination clause that is missing, such as `if...end if`, `while...end while`, `case...end case`, and so on, it does not know where the end of the statement should have been and lists those errors at the end of the file. Errors of this kind can mask the location of other errors. If you are presented with an error within your program that makes no sense to you, check the end of the error file for possible statement block terminators that are missing before you start correcting otherwise perfect statements.

Figure 35.8 shows the Form submenu of the Programmer's Environment.

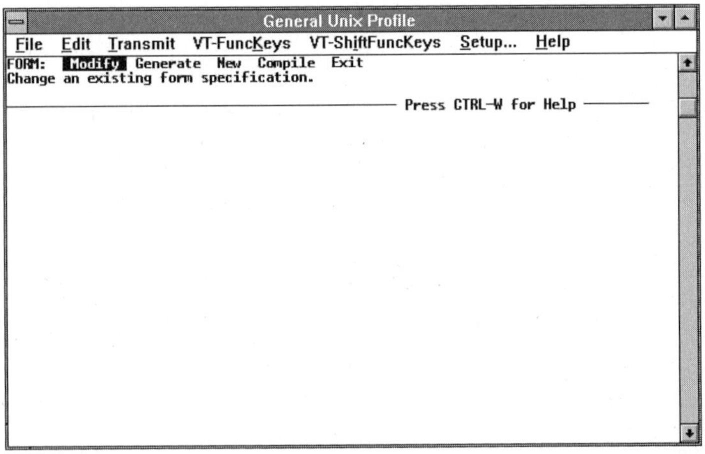

FIGURE 35.8.
The Programmer's Environment Form submenu.

```
General Unix Profile
File  Edit  Transmit  VT-FuncKeys  VT-ShiftFuncKeys  Setup...  Help
FORM:  Modify  Generate  New  Compile  Exit
Change an existing form specification.
------------------------------------------------- Press CTRL-W for Help --------
```

The options in the Form submenu allow you to create (New) or edit (Modify) a form source file; when you make either of those selections, the system opens a window with the editor you chose by setting the environment variable `DBEDIT` and loads the file to modify if appropriate. Other options of the Form submenu allow you to create a compiled form file (Compile) for a form that you select or create a skeleton form that includes all the columns from the tables you select (Generate).

After New or Modify, when you exit the edit session of your form source module, INFORMIX-4GL presents you with a submenu that offers you choices of actions to execute on the edited file. This Modify Form submenu is very similar to the Modify Module submenu displayed in Figure 35.4. In fact, all the submenus described for modules apply equally to forms; the Compile Form module is similar to the Compile (2) Module displayed in Figure 35.6, and error messages found in the form error file look the same as those displayed in Figure 35.7, except that the pipe symbol (¦) is replaced by the pound sign (#).

The Program submenu of the Programmer's Environment is somewhat different between versions of INFORMIX-4GL. Figure 35.9 shows the submenu for the RDS version.

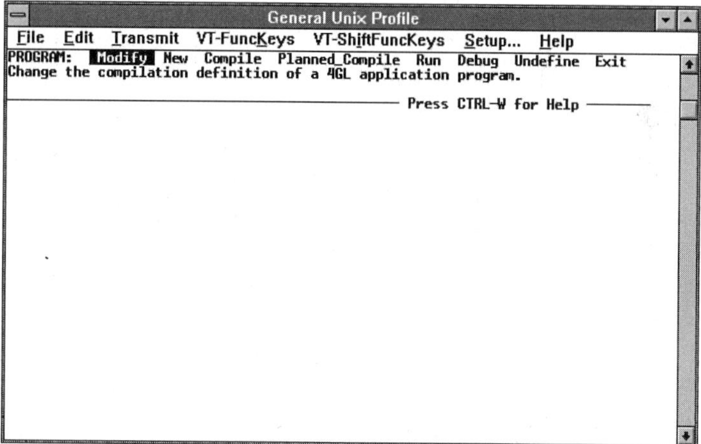

FIGURE 35.9.
The Program submenu for the RDS version of the Programmer's Environment.

The options in the Program submenu allow you to create (New) or alter (Modify) program definitions—that is, define the component source code modules and objects that make up the completed program. Other options in the Program submenu allow you to assemble an executable file for the program you select (Compile) and execute the program located in the working directory (Run) or just list the tasks required to create an executable for the program you select (Planned Compile) without actually compiling and linking the objects. You can also remove the definition of a Program from the database (Drop in the compiled version or Undefine in the RDS version). If you have the RDS version of the product, you can also start the Debugger with the compiled program in the current directory (Debug).

NOTE

INFORMIX-4GL keeps program definitions in a database named `syspgm4gl`. If your system runs multiple database engine instances, make sure that your environment is set up properly to access the instance of the database engine that stores `syspgm4gl`. When INFORMIX-4GL cannot find the `syspgm4gl` database, it asks you whether it is permissible to create it.

The New Program or Modify Program submenus show a slight difference between the compiled and the RDS versions of INFORMIX-4GL. Figure 35.10 shows the submenu for the RDS.

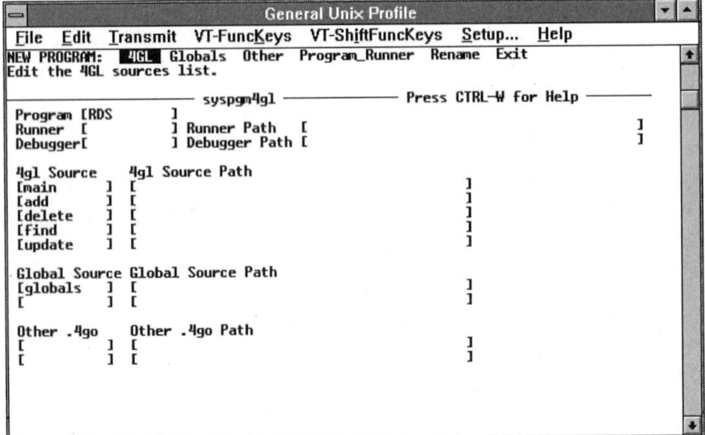
```
NEW PROGRAM:  4GL  Globals  Other  Program_Runner  Rename  Exit
Edit the 4GL sources list.

---------------- syspgm4gl ---------------- Press CTRL-W for Help ----------
Program [RDS          ]
Runner  [             ] Runner Path   [                                    ]
Debugger[             ] Debugger Path [                                    ]

4gl Source    4gl Source Path
[main      ]  [                          ]
[add       ]  [                          ]
[delete    ]  [                          ]
[find      ]  [                          ]
[update    ]  [                          ]

Global Source Global Source Path
[globals   ]  [                          ]
[          ]  [                          ]

Other .4go    Other .4go Path
[          ]  [                          ]
[          ]  [                          ]
```

FIGURE 35.10.
The New/Modify Program submenu for the RDS version.

The name of the program appears in the Program field and can be altered (Rename). In the RDS version of the software, you can change the name of the RDS runner, which displays in the Runner field and is used to execute the p-code (Program Runner). (By default, it is `fglgo` but can be relinked to incorporate other objects, usually `.o` files, instead of those provided by Informix.) There is no Runner in the compiled version of the software because you link executables for the environment. In the RDS version of the software, you can also change the name of the RDS debugger, which displays in the Debugger field and is used to debug the p-code (Program Debugger). (By default, it is `fgldb` but can be relinked to incorporate other objects, usually `.o` files, instead of those provided by Informix.) You use the remaining options (4GL, Globals, and Other in the RDS version of the software; 4GL, Other Source, Libraries and Compile Options in the compiled version) to modify the appropriate entries in the multiline sections of the screen form.

The Global Source and Globals Source Path section identifies the source code modules that contain the definitions of the global variables in this program and the location of those files. This section appears exclusively in the RDS version of the software. The 4gl Source and 4gl

Source Path section identifies the modules that are to be included in the Program and linked into the p-code or executable as well as the location of those files. The Other `.4go` and Other `.4go` Path section allows you to link into the p-code of the Program module objects stored elsewhere (usually in libraries).

In the compiled version of the software, the Other Source/Ext and Other Source Path allow you to link into the Program executable module sources (extension `.c`) or objects (extension `.o`) stored elsewhere. Finally, you can include and link into the program existing libraries (Libraries), and the compiler will automatically include the `-l` prefix. The Compile Options entries will be passed to the compiler as typed.

The Command-Line Environment

In the command-line environment, the application developer creates first the ASCII files that define the forms (`.per` files) and source code modules (`.4gl` files) that make up a program. Usually, these files are created using an editor if the designer develops the source code modules from scratch. These files can also be created using an application generator that assists the developer in automating some of the repetitive tasks in developing database applications.

TIP

All commands provided by Informix to invoke a product respond to the argument `-v` by displaying the version of the product and its serial number. These values are always required when you communicate with Informix technical support for reporting and resolving problems.

Compiling Forms

When the source files for screen forms are available, they are compiled using the `form4gl` command. The structure of this command is identical whether you use the compiled version or the RDS version of INFORMIX-4GL. The command is invoked as follows:

```
form4gl { [-l <screen lines of display (default = 24)>]
          [-c <display columns >]
          [-v]
          [-q] } <file name>.per
```

The options in this command are defined as follows:

- `-l` indicates the lines available on the terminal screen for displaying the form.
- `-c` indicates the columns available on the terminal screen for displaying the form.
- `-v` makes the compiler verify that the allocated display space for fields matches the definitions of the fields.
- `-q` makes the compiler operate in silent mode; no messages are sent to the terminal screen unless there are errors in compilation.

> **NOTE**
>
> To distinguish options and arguments that are required in a command line or in a statement from those that are optional, I have enclosed the optional arguments in square brackets (`[]`), whereas the required arguments are not enclosed in brackets. I have used curly brackets (`{}`) to denote a grouping of items, and pointed brackets (<>) to illustrate that the contents are to be filled in as appropriate.

An alternative form of the `form4gl` command is used to generate default forms:

```
form4gl -d
```

Invoked in this manner, INFORMIX-4GL prompts the developer for the required information: database to use, tables to include in the form, and name for the form. When it is done, the system generates the corresponding `.per` and `.frm` files.

Compiling Source Code Modules

The commands to compile `.4gl` files are different in the two versions of INFORMIX-4GL. In the RDS version, the command `fglpc` used to create object files (`.4go` files) is

```
fglpc { [-ansi]
        [-a]
        [-anyerr]
        [-p <pathname>] } <.4gl source code module> ...
```

The options in this command are defined as follows:

- `-ansi` makes the compiler check all SQL statements for ANSI compliance.
- `-a` makes the compiler check array bounds at runtime. (Use only for debugging, because of its overhead.)
- `-anyerr` makes the runner set the status variable after evaluating expressions (overriding the `WHENEVER ERROR` statement in the code).
- `-p` stores objects in the directory specified in `<pathname>`.

You can compile multiple `.4go` source code module files by including them in the list, or you can use standard UNIX wildcards to specify the `.4gl` files to compile. If the compilation is successful, the corresponding `.4go` files appear in the directory. Otherwise, the appropriate `.err` files are placed in the current directory (or in the directory indicated by the `-p` argument) and the developer receives a warning on the terminal screen.

To collect all the object modules and concatenate them into a p-code executable file (`.4gi`), use the UNIX command `cat` as follows:

```
cat <file name>.4go>  ...    <program name>.4gi
```

In the compiled version of the software, the object files are created by using the command `c4gl` as follows:

```
c4gl { [-ansi]
       [-a]
       [-e]
       [-anyerr]
       [-args]
       [-o <program nam>.4ge] } <.4gl source code module> ...
                                 <.ec files> ...
                                 <.c files> ...
                                 <.o files> ...
                                 <library>
```

The options in this command are defined as follows:

- `-ansi` makes the compiler check all SQL statements for ANSI compliance.
- `-a` makes the compiler check array bounds at runtime. (Use only for debugging because of its overhead.)
- `-e` makes the compiler perform only preprocessing steps; no compilation is performed.
- `-anyerr` makes the runner set the status variable after evaluating expressions (overriding the `WHENEVER ERROR` statement in the code).
- `-args` are other arguments that you want to use with the C compiler.
- `-o <program name>.4ge` is the name you want to give the executable. (By default, it is `a.out`.)
- `<.4gl source code module>` is a list of source code module files to compile and link into the program executable.
- `<.ec files>` is a list of ESQL/C files to compile and link into the program executable.
- `<.c files>` is a list of C language source code files to compile and link into the program executable.
- `<.o files>` is a list of object code files to link into the program executable.
- `<library>` is the name of the library to use in resolving function names that are not part of INFORMIX-4GL or ESQL/C.

Executing Programs

To execute programs in the RDS version of the software, use the command `fglgo` as follows:

```
fglgo { [-a]
        [-anyerr] }  <program name>.4gi  <program arguments>
```

The options in this command are defined as follows:

- `-a` makes the runner check array bounds at runtime.
- `-anyerr` makes the runner set the status variable after evaluating expressions (overriding the `WHENEVER ERROR` statement in the code).

- <program name>.4gi is the name of the p-code program to execute.
- <program arguments> are command-line options and arguments that your program was designed to receive at runtime.

To execute programs in the compiled version of the software, invoke it with the following syntax:

```
<program name>.4ge  <program arguments>
```

The options in this command are defined as follows:

- <program name>.4ge is the name of the executable file.
- <program arguments> are command-line options and arguments that your program was designed to receive at runtime.

The Debugger

The Debugger is available only with the RDS version of INFORMIX-4GL. You can invoke the Debugger within the Programmer's Environment or from the command-line as follows:

```
fgldb { [-I <pathname>, ... ]
        [-f <initfile>] }  <program name>.4gi
```

The options in this command are defined as follows:

- -l <pathname> uses the directories specified in the <pathname> entries to locate 4GL source code modules.
- -f <initfile> uses the file <initfile> as the initialization file for the debugger and sets parameters for the debugging session.
- <program name>.4gi is the name of the p-code program to execute.

When it is invoked, the Debugger starts as displayed in Figure 35.11.

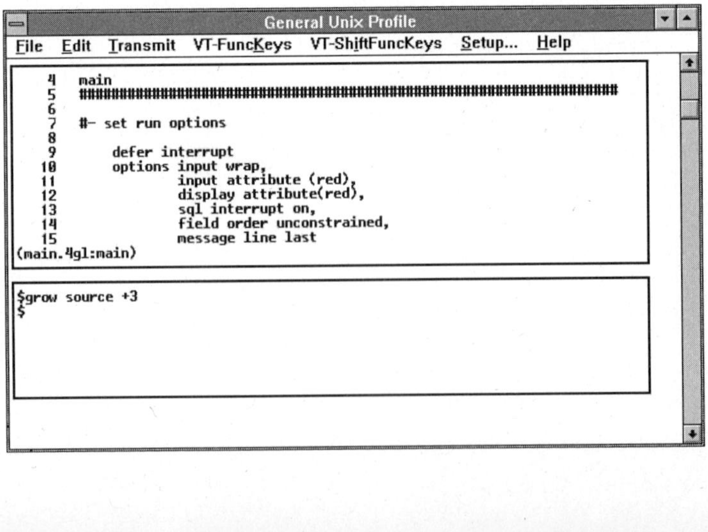

```
General Unix Profile
File  Edit  Transmit  VT-FuncKeys  VT-ShiftFuncKeys  Setup...  Help

   main
   ##########################################################

   #- set run options

       defer interrupt
       options input wrap,
               input attribute (red),
               display attribute(red),
               sql interrupt on,
               field order unconstrained,
               message line last
(main.4gl:main)

$grow source +3
$
```

FIGURE 35.11.
The interactive Debugger screen with command and source windows.

The Debugger uses two screens to interact with the developer. An application screen is a window that displays the running application. A debugger screen has two windows: a source window that displays the listing of the source code module currently under review (this window is displayed at the top of Figure 35.11) and a command window (at the bottom of Figure 35.11), which allows the developer to issue commands to the Debugger for various purposes. In Figure 35.11, the developer issued the command `grow source +3`. Chapter 38 presents a more complete discussion of the Debugger.

Basic Language Features

The INFORMIX-4GL language was introduced in 1986, and it is a fourth-generation language that is particularly suited to creating relational database applications. The language includes standard SQL statements for accessing a relational database and operating on tables and 4GL statements that operate on program variables stored in memory. Statements in INFORMIX-4GL are case-insensitive except when included within quotation marks as part of a string. Programs in INFORMIX-4GL are completely free form; that is, the compiler ignores extra blank, tab, or newline characters. You can use these characters to make programs more readable.

You can freely include comments in an INFORMIX-4GL program. Comments on a single line are coded with the `#` (pound sign) in front of the comment string or with `--` (two hyphens) in front of the comment string; anything from the `#` or `--` to the end of the line is treated as a comment. (Note that these comments needn't start at the beginning of a line; they can begin at the end of a statement.) Comments that occupy more than one line of text are enclosed between curly braces. The left brace (`{`) initiates a comment that can span multiple lines of text and is terminated by the right brace (`}`).

User Interaction: Windows, Forms, and Menus

The major methods that INFORMIX-4GL provides for interacting with users on a terminal screen are windows, forms, and menus. INFORMIX-4GL also provides other minor methods for interacting with a user sitting at a terminal screen: prompts, messages, and errors.

Windows

A window is a named rectangular area on the terminal screen. Windows can be opened and closed. A list of open windows is kept by INFORMIX-4GL in the window stack. Of all the open windows, the one that was last opened becomes the current window and is placed on top of all others on the terminal screen. After you close the current window, INFORMIX-4GL removes it from the terminal screen and from the top of the windows stack and reinstates as the current window the one that was opened just prior. You can programmatically switch the current window to another open window, and INFORMIX-4GL moves the window you choose to the top of the stack and displays it on top of all other open windows visible on the terminal screen.

All activity in your application occurs in the current window, and it is a good practice to frame your windows with a border to make the separation between windows clear, particularly when multiple windows are open and visible on the terminal screen. Figure 35.12 shows a screen with multiple windows.

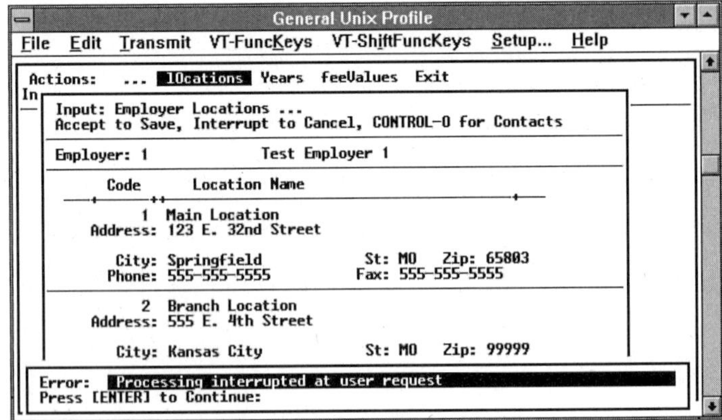

FIGURE 35.12.
Application with multiple windows open.

Figure 35.12 shows four windows open and visible on the terminal screen. (More windows could be open but completely hidden under other windows.) To frame each window, a border was defined as an attribute of the window. Note that the error window is the current window; Figure 35.12 shows the cursor on this window. At this point in the application, the user can only input information in the current window; pressing the Enter (Return) key continues processing.

Figure 35.12 illustrates the various components that a window can contain: forms, menus, and prompts. The error window at the bottom of Figure 35.12 contains a prompt. The visible input window (Location Contacts) contains a form. The largest window, at the bottom of all windows and partially hidden by the input windows, contains a menu labeled Actions, which is visible at the top of Figure 35.12.

Forms

A form is a collection of labels and input fields in which the user can input or edit information that is stored in memory on program variables. Forms are the standard means of entering information into the database. Figure 35.13 shows a screen form labeled Input: Employer Locations.

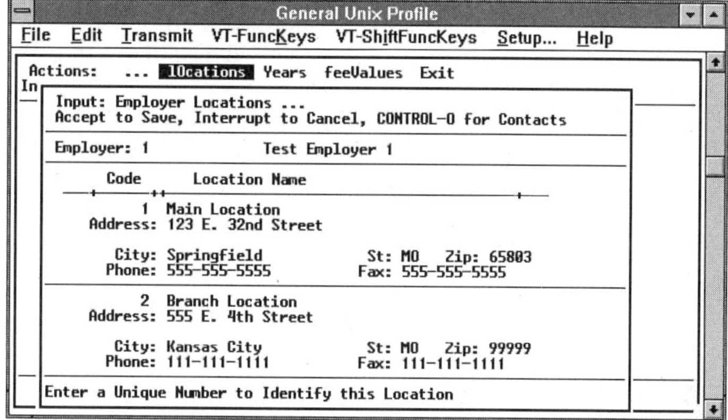

FIGURE 35.13.
A screen form with multiple rows.

Figure 35.13 has labels, such as Code and Location Name, that appear above the input fields they represent, and other labels, such as Address, City, St(ate), Phone, and Fax, that appear to the left of the input fields they represent.

Forms can facilitate input of multiple records into a single table. (Figure 35.13 allows the user to enter multiple locations for an employer.) Forms can also provide inputs of a single record into a single table in the database. (Figure 35.14 allows the user to define new employers into the system, one employer or record at a time.) They can also allow the user to enter records in multiple tables at the same time. (Chapter 38 presents an example of this technique.)

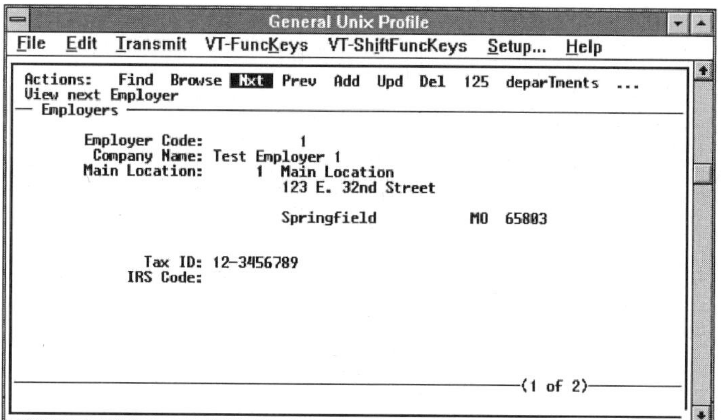

FIGURE 35.14.
Menu and screen form.

Menus

Menus provide users with a list of actions that, once selected, perform the task represented by the choice. Figure 35.14 shows an example of a menu in INFORMIX-4GL. The menu in Figure 35.14 is named Actions.

INFORMIX-4GL uses ring menus to display options. Ring menus use two lines to display the menu options. The first line, called the menu line, displays the title of the menu (Actions in Figure 35.14) and the options. The second line, named the menu help line, displays a more verbose description of the menu option highlighted. (Nxt is the option highlighted in Figure 35.14.) If the list of available options exceeds the screen space to display them, INFORMIX-4GL displays an ellipsis (...) at the end of the line to indicate that more options are available.

To select an option from the menu, the user can move to the desired option by using either the arrow keys or the space bar and pressing Enter (or Return), at which time, the program executes the code associated with the selected choice.

Users can also select and execute an option from the menu by typing the first letter of the option. If multiple options start with the same letter (such as Del and deparTments in Figure 35.14) and the user presses the letter d, INFORMIX-4GL cannot decide which is the desired option and it displays a submenu with the options under contention in the menu help line and keeps changing the options in this menu with every user keystroke until there is a single option left. This option is then executed. In Figure 35.14, the user must type three characters to break the tie between the Del and deparTments options. A common practice in managing menu choices is to key each menu option on a different character and display that character capitalized. Then the user types in the capital letter associated with the desired option and the option is executed immediately. (Figure 35.14 illustrates this; pressing the letter t, capitalized in the option deparTments, the user expects to immediately execute the code for that option.)

In addition to visible options, there can be two other types of options in a menu. Hidden options are menu options that are disabled programmatically and cannot be executed while hidden but can be redisplayed when they become active again. Invisible options are options that are never displayed in the menu but are executed if the user presses the key that activates them.

TIP

Many INFORMIX-4GL programs use an invisible option that allows the user to execute a UNIX command and then return control to the application. Typically, the bang (!) is the key that triggers this behavior to match its counterpart in other UNIX commands. It is a good practice to include this hidden option in your program.

Programming Blocks

An application usually consists of a collection of source code module files. Within each source code module file, there can be one or many program blocks. A program block is a collection of statements that are designed as a unit. The three types of program blocks in an INFORMIX-4GL program are the `MAIN`, `FUNCTION`, and `REPORT` program blocks. There must be only one `MAIN` block in any program, and the statements it includes must be terminated by the `END MAIN` keywords. There can be many `FUNCTION` or `REPORT` blocks, and for that reason, these are named and terminated: `FUNCTION <function name> ... END FUNCTION` or `REPORT <report name> ... END REPORT`.

INFORMIX-4GL supports structured programming techniques, and it behooves you to make extensive use of functions to encapsulate discrete, well-defined, single-purpose tasks with a clearly defined set of arguments and return values. These can then be reused in other applications that require the same functionality.

Within a program block, you can include INFORMIX-4GL statements, some of which define statement blocks themselves and also require a termination clause. An example of this type of statement is the `CASE` statement, which offers multiple branching capabilities. The statement block starts with the keyword `CASE` and ends with the keywords `END CASE`. Anything in between is part of the statement block.

CAUTION

Make sure you terminate the statement blocks! The compiler becomes thoroughly confused if statement blocks are not terminated properly, and it might list a large number of errors that are due to that omission and not to the syntax of the statements deemed in error.

Standard Language Constructs

The INFORMIX-4GL command set includes all the standard statements that you expect of any programming language: definitions and declarations, flow of control, compiler directives, and storage management. The statements in the following lists are described in detail in Chapters 36 and 37. Some of them are ignored altogether (for instance, `GOTO` and `LABEL`) because they promote sloppy programming practices.

Definitions and Declarations

```
DEFINE
FUNCTION
MAIN
REPORT
```

Flow of Control

CALL

CASE

CONTINUE

END

EXIT

FINISH REPORT

FOR

FOREACH

GOTO

IF

LABEL

OUTPUT TO REPORT

RETURN

RUN

START REPORT

WHILE

4GL Compiler Directives

DATABASE

DEFER

GLOBALS

WHENEVER

Storage Management

INITIALIZE

LET

LOCATE

VALIDATE

Screen I/O Language Constructs

The INFORMIX-4GL command set includes a collection of statements designed to facilitate screen and keyboard interactions. Note that all user's interactions occur between the computer's memory and the screen or between the keyboard and the computer's memory. The commands in the following list make those exchanges possible. The screen I/O language constructs listed here are described in detail in Chapters 36 through 38:

```
CLEAR
CLOSE FORM
CLOSE WINDOW
CONSTRUCT
CURRENT WINDOW
DISPLAY
DISPLAY ARRAY
DISPLAY FORM
ERROR
INPUT
INPUT ARRAY
MENU
MESSAGE
OPEN FORM
OPEN WINDOW
OPTIONS
PROMPT
SCROLL
SLEEP
```

Database-Related Language Constructs

The INFORMIX-4GL command set includes all the SQL statements for data definition, data manipulation, cursor management, dynamic management, query optimization, data access, and data integrity. These statements were covered in the SQL sections of this book (Chapters 26 through 29). The statements are used in the context of INFORMIX-4GL programming in the three chapters following this one (Chapters 36 through 38).

Error-Handling Language Constructs

INFORMIX-4GL uses a global variable `status` and a global record `SQLCA` (SQL communication area) to detect, record, and handle all exceptions in processing.

The global variable `status` indicates errors from SQL statements and interactive statements. The global record `SQLCA` contains extensive information about the actions carried out by the database engine and the errors and warnings encountered in executing SQL statements and only SQL statements.

The SQLCA record is defined as follows:

```
DEFINE sqlca RECORD
    sqlcode integer,
    sqlerrm char(71),
    sqlerrp char(8),
    sqlerrd array[6] of integer,
    sqlwarn char(8)
END RECORD
```

The values contained in the SQLCA record are as follows:

sqlca.sqlcode	0 for a successful execution of the SQL statement.
NOTFOUND(100)	For a successful SQL execution that returns no rows or runs out of rows.
Negative number	Error number after an unsuccessful SQL execution. The variable status is set to sqlca.sqlcode.
sqlca.sqlerrm	Not used.
sqlca.sqlerrp	Not used.
sqlca.sqlerrd[1]	Not used.
sqlca.sqlerrd[2]	The serial value of the record inserted or the ISAM error code.
sqlca.sqlerrd[3]	Number of rows processed by the SQL statement.
sqlca.sqlerrd[4]	Estimated CPU cost for the query.
sqlca.sqlerrd[5]	Offset of the error into the SQL statement.
sqlca.sqlerrd[6]	The rowid of the last row selected.
sqlca.sqlwarn[1]	Blank if there are no other warnings; W if one of the other array elements is set.
sqlca.sqlwarn[2]	W if a value was truncated to fit into a char variable or for a DATABASE statement, if this is a database with transactions.
sqlca.sqlwarn[3]	W if an aggregate function encountered a NULL when evaluating or for a DATABASE statement, if this database is ANSI-compliant.
sqlca.sqlwarn[4]	W if the number of items in the select list is not the same as the number of variables in the into clause or for a DATABASE statement, if this is an INFORMIX-OnLine database.
sqlca.sqlwarn[5]	W if float-to-decimal conversion is used.

`sqlca.sqlwarn[6]`	`W` if the `DBANSIWARN` variable is set and the last statement executed is not ANSI-compliant.
`sqlca.sqlwarn[7]`	Not used.
`sqlca.sqlwarn[8]`	Not used.

Summary

This chapter has given you a broad perspective of the facilities that INFORMIX-4GL provides for creating robust character-based applications. The next three chapters will take you through an increasingly rich exploration of the use and application of the language features introduced in this chapter. Enjoy the journey.

4GL Coding

by José Fortuny

IN THIS CHAPTER

This chapter deals in detail with the components of the INFORMIX-4GL language and their use, paying particular attention to the specialized programming statements that INFORMIX-4GL provides for dealing with the database and the screen display of database-bound information.

From this point, you deal with a sample application for a fictitious company that specializes in recruiting long-haul truck drivers. This chapter uses two tables from this company's database, named recruiters, to illustrate the basic principles of INFORMIX-4GL program development. These tables are employers and states.

The database schema can be extracted from the database by using the utility `dbschema`, which is provided with all Informix products. This is only one of a group of utilities provided by Informix for the purpose of migrating data between databases or engines. This utility creates an ASCII file that can be used to re-create the table with the same structure it had originally. The `dbschema` command is used as follows:

```
dbschema {[-t <tabname>]
          [-s <user>]
          [-p <user>]
          -d <dbname>
          [-ss]
          [<filename>]}
```

The options in this command are defined as follows:

> `-t` *<tabname>* is the name of the table to extract or the word `<all>` to generate the schema for all tables in the database.
>
> `-s` *<user>* generates `create synonym` statements for *<user>* or `<all>` for all users.
>
> `-p` *<user>* generates `grant` statements to grant permissions to *<user>* or `<all>` for all users.
>
> `-d` *<dbname>* indicates the name of the database used to extract the schema files.
>
> `-ss` generates server-specific syntax.
>
> *<filename>* is the name of the ASCII file that receives the SQL statements generated. (It is a good practice to name this file `.SQL` so that you can deal with it as you do any other SQL script.)

NOTE

To distinguish options and arguments that are required in a command line or in a statement from those that are optional, I have enclosed the optional arguments in square brackets ([ ]), whereas the required arguments are not enclosed in brackets. I have used curly brackets ({}) to denote a grouping of items, and pointed brackets (<>) to illustrate that the contents are to be filled in as appropriate.

The database schema for these tables is displayed in Listing 36.1.

Listing 36.1. Schema of employers and states tables.

```
{ TABLE "jose".employers row size = 179 number of columns = 16 index size = 78 }
create table "jose".employers
  (
    empl_code serial not null constraint "jose".n103_18,
    employer char(35) not null constraint "jose".n103_19,
    add_line1 char(35),
    add_line2 char(35),
    city char(18),
    state char(2),
    zip char(5),
    phone char(10),
    trl_len char(2),
    freight char(10),
    area char(15),
    nbr_trks char(4),
    authority char(1),
    leased char(1),
    dac char(1),
    authorized char(1),
    primary key (empl_code) constraint "jose".pk_employers
  );
revoke all on "jose".employers from "public";
create index "jose".ix100_2 on "jose".employers (employer);
create index "jose".ix100_16 on "jose".employers (authorized);

{ TABLE "jose".states row size = 17 number of columns = 2 index size = 9 }
create table "jose".states
  (
    state char(2) not null constraint "jose".n101_4,
    state_name char(15) not null constraint "jose".n101_5,
    primary key (state) constraint "jose".pk_states
  );
revoke all on "jose".states from "public";
```

The schema for these tables shows all permissions revoked from `"public"`. The database administrator must grant connect permissions to the database and table permissions to the appropriate users before these tables are accessible to users.

What Should an INFORMIX-4GL Program Do?

Generally, an INFORMIX-4GL program should have a discrete, focused purpose and encompass only the tasks that are directly related either to the tables being processed or to the functional business process that the software serves. Try to apply to INFORMIX-4GL programs the same principles of normalization that you apply to relational databases. In the same way you don't create a single table to represent all aspects of your enterprise, you design the scope of your programs to facilitate the execution of a single business process. The larger the scope of your program, the larger the executables the compiler generates. Larger executables are slower to load into memory and usually more cumbersome for the user to navigate. An application in this scenario becomes a collection of limited, focused purpose programs, glued together by some form of menu system.

NOTE

It was once common practice to develop an application by first developing an INFORMIX-4GL program that provided only a cascading menu system. When the user selected a specific task from any of the submenus of this program, the program executed a call to run the selected task in a subshell, while the menu program went dormant waiting for its child to be completed. Current Informix database engines count both programs as separate users because both hold connections to the database engine. Keep this user count in mind when determining your user licenses, or perhaps use a different menu management strategy for your application.

In this chapter, you develop software to query and input data into the employers table. The fictitious company that recruits long-haul drivers needs software to support multiple business endeavors: managing potential employers, receiving applications from prospective drivers, and verifying employment histories of prospective drivers. Your application should strive to mimic the nature of your business and support each business function with separate programs. One program collects the functionality to support all tasks related to managing potential employers, and another program collects all functionality to receive applications from prospective drivers. This is not to say that the programs are completely isolated islands; the program that manages potential employers is likely to offer a peek at the prospective drivers that an employer hired but is unlikely to provide facilities for receiving new driver applications.

Basic Program Design

If you embrace the concepts that each program in your application should have a narrow, defined focus and that programs should be structured and modular so component reuse is facilitated, then it becomes important to organize the various programs, forms, and components of your application in such a way that sharing those components is simple. In this section, I suggest a directory structure that provides an adequate infrastructure in support of these principles.

Directory Structure

A possible organization of the UNIX directory structure to support these criteria for developing applications is as follows (with the indentation indicating hierarchy):

```
Application Directory
  Module Directory    Module Directory    System Library
    Program Directory     Program Directory    Module Library    Module Screens
      Module File #1         Module File #2        Module File #n
```

At the root of the tree is the application directory. This directory collects all the organized components that make up the application. Directly under the application directory, you find the module directories. A module directory contains a logical grouping of program directories and libraries, which contain programs that cooperate to perform various tasks of a business function. In the fictional company, the application directory could be named corporate accounting. The module directories could be accounts receivable, operations, general ledger, recruiting, and so on. The system library, located at this level in the hierarchy, contains components: source code module files and objects and form source files and objects that are used by all modules. For instance, the company-wide logo that is displayed whenever a specific program is loaded is an example of a component located here. Within the recruiting module, you might find a program directory named employers (the example developed in this chapter) that collects all the functionality that is needed to manage prospective employers. You might also have another program directory named drivers that collects all the information about the truck drivers and provides the required functionality to manage them: taking applications, verifying employment records, verifying driving records, and so on.

In a directory structure like this, executable files (`*.4gi` or `*.4ge`) reside in the program directories. Source and compiled screen forms (`*.per` and `*.frm`) reside also in program directories but may be found in module screens directories and perhaps even in the system library. Source code modules (`*.4gl`) and object modules (`*.4go` or `*.o`) are located in the program directories, module libraries, and the system library. Each program directory also contains the error log file for the program it defines. Defining a program in any of the program directories requires that you identify the local globals file and local source code modules and you include other objects that are located in `../<module library>` or in `../../<system library>`.

Executing a program in any program directory requires that your `DBPATH` variable point to the directory where the executables are (usually the current directory), as well as to directories that contain forms that are called by the program. The definition of `DBPATH`, in this directory structure, becomes `DBPATH=$DBPATH:.:../`*`<module screens>`*`:../../`*`<system library>`*.

Libraries

In this context, libraries are defined as repositories of functions or reports that perform a specific task. These functions receive a collection of arguments and return a collection of values without interacting with the calling program in any way other than through arguments and returned values.

Libraries tend to be organized along the same criteria used to organize module directories. There are multiple library directories, both at the module and system levels, that collect similar types of objects. A library of error management routines collects all error detection, error display, and reporting mechanisms, as well as adequate responses depending on the severity of the runtime errors encountered. There may also be a library of common database delivery functions that collects source code modules that are defined to receive a key for a table and return some descriptive value from that table. (For example, upon receiving an employee code, it returns a string that concatenates the first name, middle initial, and last name of an employee with appropriate spacing.) There may also be a library of conversion functions that perform numeric-to-string conversions and vice versa while rounding or truncating the numeric values to the desired number of decimal places. There may also be a library of string-manipulation functions that collect functions that find substrings within a string or center or right justify a string.

Common Forms and Modules

In the context of a programming language that is designed to deal with database information, common forms and modules are defined as repositories of functions that perform a task that requires user and database interaction through query or input within a form or prompt. These functions respond to the user's action by returning a collection of values to the calling program. Common forms and modules tend to be organized within libraries along the same criteria used to organize module directories.

Many business applications require that you provide users with pop-up, zoom, or drill-down facilities to fill in values during data entry that have to exist in a parameter table. For instance, in the fictitious company, while entering the code for a state in an employer address, you want to make sure that the spelling of the state is correct and force the value entered to be validated against a table of valid state codes. If the user does not remember the state code or if he fails to provide a correct state code, you want to provide a pop-up window that allows the user to view the valid state codes and select the appropriate value, which is then returned to the calling program. The screen forms and source code modules for this type of zooming operation is used throughout an application and become prime candidates for a common library.

Accounting applications usually require the user to provide an account, or a pair of accounts, for recording or posting a business transaction. A pop-up window for providing the suggested defaults and allowing the user to alter the defaults is also a typical example of a screen form and its processing source code that are candidates for placement in a common access library.

Skeleton of an INFORMIX-4GL Program

The basic skeleton for an INFORMIX-4GL program consists of the following program blocks (placed in a single source code module file or in multiple source code module files):

```
[database <dbname>] --Required if the program interacts with a database

[globals] --Only one globals definition per program

 <global variable definition>
 end globals ]
```

```
[globals "<file containing globals definitions>"]
 --Many global declarations per program

main --One, and only one, is required in a program

  <local variable definitions>
  <4GL statements>
  <function calls>
  <database interactions>
end main

[function <function name> (<parameters>) --A program may have many functions

    <local variable definitions>
    <4GL statements>
    <function calls>
    <database interactions>
    [return <return variables>]
 end function]

[report <report name> (<parameters>) --A program may have many reports

    <local variable definitions>
    <4GL statements>
    <report statements>
    <function calls>

end report]
```

Each of these program blocks is defined in more detail in the following sections, except for reports, which are covered in Chapter 37, "4GL Development."

Database

The `database` statement has the following syntax:

```
[database <dbname> [exclusive]]
```

The options in this command are defined as follows:

> `<dbname>` is a database name on your database server.
>
> `[exclusive]` opens the connection to the database in exclusive mode if there are no open connections and prevents any other user from connecting to the database.

The `database` statement performs two functions. While developing the program, it provides the compiler with a database to use when you define variables by reference to database tables and columns. On execution, it opens a connection to a specific database `<dbname>` and closes the connection to the database that was open prior to its execution.

The database name `<dbname>` used in this statement is a reference to a database in the database server (`dbservername`) that is referenced by your environment (`INFORMIXSERVER` setting). You may specify a different server and establish a connection to a remote database by using the following notation `<dbname>@<dbservername>` or `'//<dbservername>/<dbname>'` for the OnLine engine or `'//<dbservername>/<pathname>/<dbname>'` or `'/<pathname>/<dbname>@<dbservername>'` for the SE engine.

Examples of the `database` statement are

```
database recruiters
database recruiters@on_fort_tcp
```

Globals

The `globals` program block has two forms. The first version declares and defines the program variables that have global scope throughout the program. The second version identifies a file that contains global definitions to be used in the source code module that includes the statement.

The syntax for the first version of the statement is

```
[globals
   <global variable definition>
 end globals ]
```

It is useful to isolate the `globals` definitions in a source code module file that can then be referenced by the second version of the statement. It is convenient to include the `database` statement in the globals source code module so that it is inherited by the source code modules that use the second version of the `globals` statement.

The syntax for the second version of the statement is

```
[globals "<file containing globals definitions>"]
```

An example of the `globals.4gl` file used for the fictitious company is provided in Listing 36.2.

Listing 36.2. `globals.4gl` for the fictitious company.

```
database recruiters
##################################################################
globals
##################################################################
define p_employers record like employers.*,
       is_valid smallint
end globals
```

The keywords `globals` and `end globals` encapsulate the `globals` program block. Within a `globals` program block, you include global variable definitions. Variable scope is discussed further in the section "Variables Definition, Initialization, and Scope," later in this chapter.

Main

The `main` program block is required in a program. A program must have only one `main` program block. This is the starting point in the execution of an INFORMIX-4GL program:

```
main
  <local variable definitions>
  <4GL statements>
  <function calls>
  <database interactions>
end main
```

The keywords main and end main encapsulate the main program block. Within the main program block, you can include local variable definitions, function calls, and any other valid 4GL statement. The main program block is usually kept very small and often limited to managing the flow of control for the application.

An example of a main program block is

```
main
    call InitEnv()
    call FlowOfControl()
end main
```

This sample program first calls a function called InitEnv and then calls the function FlowOfControl. The program then terminates when it reaches end main unless it was terminated programmatically before reaching the end main statement.

Function

A function can be called within the main program block or within another function or report program block. The syntax for the call to a function, if the function returns more than one value, must be as follows:

```
call <function name> (<parameters>) [returning <return variables>]
```

The options are as follows:

> *<function name>* identifies the function called.
>
> <parameters> is a list of values or variables passed to the function as arguments.
>
> *<return variables>* is a list of program variables that are loaded with the values returned by the function to the calling program.

If a function returns a single value, the call statement can be used to invoke it, but the function can also be invoked within another command-line argument without using the keyword call.

For example, the function MakeName is defined to receive three arguments—first name, middle initial, and last name—and return a concatenated string with the structure *<Last Name>, <First Name> <Middle Initial>*. The function could be invoked as follows:

```
call MakeName(p_employee.fname, p_employee.mi, p_employee.lname)
            returning p_full_name
```

Because it returns a single value, the MakeName function could be invoked as part of a statement involving other components, as follows:

```
let p_print_name = "Employee: ", MakeName(p_employee.fname, p_employee.mi,
   p_employee.lname) clipped, " (", p_employee.emp_no, ")"
```

This statement concatenates the string "Employee: ", the string returned by the MakeName function, removing trailing blanks (clipped), and it follows this with the string " (", followed by the employee code, followed by the string ")".

A function definition has the following syntax:

```
[function <function name> (<parameters>)
    <local variable definitions>
    <4GL statements>
    <function calls>
    <database interactions>
    [return <return variables>]
 end function]
```

The options in this definition are covered in detail later in this chapter. As an example, I define the function MakeName:

```
function MakeName (fn, mi, ln)
    define fn, mi, ln char(80),
           full_name char(256)
    let full_name = ln clipped, ", ", fn clipped, " ", mi
    return full_name
end function
```

The order of the arguments in the calling clause and in the function definition is important because the first argument in the calling statement is passed to the first parameter in the function. This function returns a single value and therefore can be called in the two forms described. Functions that return multiple values can be invoked only by means of the call statement.

TIP

The function program block is reentrant, thereby allowing recursive programming; a function can call itself. INFORMIX-4GL manages the stack on your behalf.

Report

The report program block defines the format of a report. A report must be started (initialized) before it receives output and must be finished after all output is sent to the report. To manage a report, you must use the following logical sequence of statements:

```
start report <report name> [to {[<file name>]
                                [printer]
                                [pipe <program name>]}
```

The options in this command are defined as follows:

<report name> is the specific report to initialize.

to is the destination of the report and supersedes the destination defined in the report program block.

<file name> sends the output of the report to a file.

printer sends the output of the report to the default printer or the printer specified by your LPDEST settings.

pipe <program name> sends the output of the report to be processed by the program <program name>.

To continue with the example for function MakeName, you can initialize a report that prints the name stored in variable p_print_name and sends its output to the command pg:

```
start report PrintName to pipe "pg"
```

After the report is initialized with the statement start report, the program sends records to the report formatter within some form of a loop using the output to statement as follows:

```
output to report <report name> (<parameters>)
```

The options in this command are defined as follows:

<report name> is the specific report to send the record to.

<parameters> is the list of variables or constants to be sent to the report formatter.

Within a loop, you invoke the output to report statement as follows:

```
let p_print_name = "Employee: ", MakeName(p_employee.fname, p_employee.mi,
    p_employee.lname) clipped, " (", p_employee.emp_no, ")"
output to report PrintName (p_print_name)
```

The order of the arguments in the output to report and in the report definition is important because the first parameter in the output to report statement is passed to the first parameter in the report.

Finally, after all records are sent to the report, the report must be terminated with the finish report statement as follows:

```
finish report <report name>
```

The options in this command are defined as follows:

<report name> is the specific report to finish.

After looping through all the employee records in the fictitious company that you want to print, you issue a finish report statement as follows:

```
finish report PrintName
```

A report definition has the following syntax:

```
[report <report name> (<parameters>)
    <local variable definitions>
    <4GL statements>
    <report statements>
    <function calls>
  end report]
```

The options in this definition are covered in detail in Chapter 37. As an example, I define the report `PrintName` with the simplest possible syntax in a report:

```
report PrintName (p_name)
    define p_name char(256)
    format every row
end report
```

Data Types, Operators, and Functions

Most of the data types available in INFORMIX-4GL are part of the basic set of data types that Informix engines support. The basic data types that Informix provides with its database engines were introduced in Chapter 30, "Data Management Using SQL." A summary of those basic data types is included in Table 36.1 for easy reference.

Table 36.1. Basic Informix data types by engine.

Type and Structure	*SE*	*OnLine*
`char (n)`	Y	Y
`character (n)`	Y	Y
`dec (precision, scale)`	Y	Y
`decimal (precision, scale)`	Y	Y
`double precision (float precision)`	Y	Y
`float (float precision)`	Y	Y
`int`	Y	Y
`integer`	Y	Y
`money (precision, scale)`	Y	Y
`numeric (precision, scale)`	Y	Y
`real`	Y	Y
`serial (starting number)`	Y	Y
`smallfloat`	Y	Y
`smallint`	Y	Y
`date`	Y	Y

Type and Structure	*SE*	*OnLine*
`datetime <largest> to <smallest> <fraction precision>`	Y	Y
`interval <largest> to <smallest> <fraction precision>`	Y	Y
`byte in <tablespace or blobspace>`	N	Y
`text in <tablespace or blobspace>`	N	Y
`varchar (<maximum length>, <reserve length>)`	N	Y

INFORMIX-4GL offers two additional data types that are unique to 4GL. The declaration and definition of all data types is covered in detail in the next section. These additional INFORMIX-4GL–only data types are listed here to complete the list of available data types in INFORMIX-4GL:

```
record {[like <tabname>.*]
        [[<varname> like <tabname>.<colname>, ...]
        [<varname> <datatype>, ...]]}
end record
array "[" <integer count> [, <integer count> [ , <integer count> ] ] "]"
      of <non-array datatype>
```

See the next section for the definitions and examples of these two types of variables.

Variables Definition, Initialization, and Scope

Variables of all types are declared and their data type is identified in the `define` statement as follows:

```
define <varname> <datatype> , ...
```

It is appropriate to apply to INFORMIX-4GL programs the same variable-naming conventions that are applicable in other programming environments at your organization. In lieu of any other naming conventions, a very simple naming arrangement uses a `p_` prefix to identify program variables, an `s_` prefix to define screen records in forms, perhaps a `pa_` prefix to identify program arrays, and an `sa_` prefix to define screen records in forms. A more comprehensive naming set is shown in Table 36.2.

Table 36.2. Variable naming standards.

Variable Name	*Used for*
`g_<varname>`	Global variables
`p_<varname>`	Non-record program variables
`r_<varname>`	Record program variables
`a_<varname>`	Array program variables

continues

Table 36.2. continued

Variable Name	*Used for*
`ra_<varname>`	Array of record variables
`s_<record>`	Screen record in form definitions
`sa_<record>`	Screen array of records in form definitions

No matter what your naming standards are, adherence to the standards greatly simplifies both development and maintenance tasks.

Examples of variable definitions have already appeared earlier in this chapter. Here are some more examples, particularly for record and array data types:

```
define p_print_name char(256),
       is_valid smallint,
       p_emp_count, p_counter integer
```

This declaration makes `p_print_name` a character string of a fixed 256–byte length. The `is_valid` variable, defined as a small integer, does not follow the naming conventions illustrated earlier, but in the environment, it is always used as a Boolean test, so it has also become a standard. The variables `p_emp_count` and `p_counter` are both defined as integers.

Variables can also match the data types of the columns in database tables that they represent. The `like` keyword is used to match the declaration to a column data type as follows. (Please refer to the schema files for the fictitious company example, listed at the beginning of this chapter.)

```
define p_empl_code  integer,
       p_employer like employers.employer,
       p_state like states.state
```

The `p_empl_code` variable is defined as an integer to match the `serial` data type that the column `employers.empl_code` has. `p_employer` inherits the data type and attributes of the `employers.employer` column, and `p_state` inherits from `states.state`. Because there is no reference to a database engine, INFORMIX-4GL attempts to find these variables in the database managed by the server defined by the `INFORMIXSERVER` setting unless the `database` statement in your program specifically points to a remote database. To specifically define a variable from a remote database, while most of your variables are defined by the database in the `database` statement, use the same notation illustrated when defining the `database` block:

```
define p_remote_empl_code like test@on_fort_tcp:employers.empl_code
```

`test@on_fort_tcp` uses the notation `<database>@<dbservername>`, and `employers` is the name of the table sought. `p_remote_empl_code` refers to column `employers.empl_code` in the database `test` in database server `on_fort_tcp`.

A record variable is a data structure that collects multiple members that can be addressed collectively or individually. One of the frequent uses of a record variable is to match an entire table definition in the database to a program variable in memory. This definition looks like

```
define p_employers record like employers.*,
       p_states like states.*
```

The record variable `p_employers` has as many members as there are columns in the employers table. You can address members in a record singly or in groups as follows: `p_employers.city` refers to the element `city` of the record `p_employers` and is often used in this form for testing, assigning, entering, or printing. `p_employers.employer` through `phone` refers to all members included between the `employer` and `phone` in the same sequence as they are defined in the database table and is often used in entering or when fetching records from the database. `p_employers.*` refers to all members of the record and is often used to enter or to retrieve records from the table.

You can also make up records for program-specific purposes and define their members individually as follows:

```
define p_address record
    empl_code like employers.emp_code,
    state like employers.state,
    state_long_name like states.state_name,
    employee_count integer,
    regional_airport char(25)
  end record
```

This record inherits data types from two tables for part of its members and uses basic data types for others.

A variable of type `array` is defined as follows:

```
define pa_calendar array [12] of date,
       pa_employers array [500] of record like employers.*
```

The `pa_calendar` is an array of up to 12 dates, but the array `pa_employers` may contain up to 500 elements, each of which has a record data structure that matches that of the table employers. To refer to a specific entry in an array, you indicate the position of the member in the array (the first member is identified by `1`) as in `pa_employers[100].empl_code`, which refers to the `empl_code` value of the 100th element of the array `pa_employers`.

To initialize variables, INFORMIX-4GL uses the statement `initialize` and at times the assignment statement `let` (which is covered later). The syntax for `initialize` is

```
initialize <varname> to null
```

An example is

```
initialize p_employers.* to null
initialize p_states.state_code to null
initialize is_valid to null
```

You can define variables in three places in an INFORMIX-4GL program: in globals, outside of any program block, or inside a program block (main, function, or report). The scope of a variable is determined by the position of the `define` statement that declares it. Variables declared in the globals program block are available and visible throughout an entire program; their values can be altered anywhere and are preserved when the flow of control moves from program block to program block. Variables declared inside a program block, as in a `function` program block, are available and visible only within that program block. Variables defined outside all program blocks within a source code module are global to all functions and reports (and main) also defined in that source code module. When the name of a local variable is the same as the name of a global variable, the value of the local variable is used in preference over the value of the global variable within the local function. In general, when name conflicts occur, the most local variable wins.

Data Types and Implicit Conversions

INFORMIX-4GL supports assignments of variables of different data types and attempts to convert them implicitly as best it can. If it fails, it issues an error message.

Conversion between numeric data types is successful if the destination can actually store the value it receives. For instance, assigning an integer to a smallint fails if the magnitude of the integer exceeds 32,767, the value of the largest smallint. Numeric conversion always occurs within an arithmetic expression because INFORMIX-4GL performs all arithmetic with decimal data types of differing precision and scale.

Conversion between numeric data types and character data types is also possible in both directions. A numeric data type can be assigned to a character data type, and as long as the character string is large enough, the conversion functions. When the character variable is not large enough to receive the numeric value, truncation occurs and the `SQLCA` record reports that action. Assigning a character data type to a numeric data type is acceptable as long as the characters are numbers or proper punctuation, such as a comma, period, or plus or minus sign.

Conversion between character data types of different size may result in truncation if the destination character variable is smaller than the original.

Dates are stored as integer values in INFORMIX-4GL and can be assigned to an integer variable without problems. The reverse assignment from integer to date is also possible. Dates start at 1/1/1900 (integer value 1 represents 1/1/1900; an uninitialized date variable is displayed as 12/31/1899). Values smaller than 1 yield dates earlier than 1/1/1900. Dates can also be converted to character, and as long as a character variable contains a valid date format, it converts properly to a date.

The most difficult conversions are from date or character to datetime and interval variables. A date variable can be converted to a datetime variable, but if the precision of the datetime is smaller than day, Informix fills the time units smaller than day with zeroes. A better method to convert date variables to datetime variables is to use the `extend` operator and manage the conversion in your own terms. A character variable can be converted to a datetime as long as the format within the string matches the expectations of the datetime for the precision in its definition. The character variable requires a format like `yyyy-mm-dd hh:mm:ss.fffff` with a space between the date and the time or the appropriate portion of this format that matches the precision of the datetime variable. Converting character variables to interval variables requires the same formatting as the conversion between character and datetime variables.

Operators

INFORMIX-4GL supports operators that are also valid in SQL, such as those shown in Table 36.3.

Table 36.3. SQL operators supported in INFORMIX-4GL.

Operator	*Functional Description*
	Mathematical Operators
`+`	Unary plus and addition
`-`	Unary minus and subtraction
`*`	Multiplication
`/`	Division
	Relational Operators
`<`	Less than
`<=`	Less than or equal to
`>`	Greater than
`>=`	Greater than or equal to
`=`	Equal
`<>`	Not equal
`!=`	Not equal
`[not] between`	Inclusive range
	Boolean Operators
`not`	Unary
`and`	Conditional and
`or`	Conditional or
	String Operators
`||`	Concatenation
`matches`	Pattern matching
`like`	Pattern matching

continues

Table 36.3. continued

Operator	Functional Description
	Set Operators
`[not] in`	Value contained (or not) in list
`[not] exists`	True if at least one row is returned by subquery
`all`	True if all values returned by subquery are true
`any`	True if any values returned by subquery are true
`some`	True if some values returned by subquery are true
	Null Operators
`is [not] null`	True if the argument is not null

In addition, INFORMIX-4GL also supports some operators that are not available in SQL. These are listed in Table 36.4.

Table 36.4. Additional INFORMIX-4GL operators.

Operator	Functional Description
`**`	Exponentiation
`mod`	Modulus (division remainder)
`,`	Concatenate strings
`clipped`	Clip trailing blanks from a string
`using`	Format data for display or report purposes

For example, the following statements result in the variable `p_result` receiving the value `8`:

```
let p_value1 = 2
let p_value2 = 3
let p_result = p_value1 ** p_value2
```

In the following code, the variable `p_result` receives the value `3`:

```
let p_value1 = 17
let p_value2 = 20
let p_result = p_value2 mod p_value1
```

In the following code, the character variable `p_result` receives the value `"John Doe"`:

```
let p_string1 = "John          "
let p_string2 = "Doe           "
let p_result = p_string1 clipped, " ", p_string2
```

Formatting with the `using` operator allows you to display dates and numbers in the format you specify. For date values, the `using` clause uses the strings identified in Table 36.5.

Table 36.5. Date formatting with `using`.

String	*Results in a Display of*
`dd`	Day of the month from 1 to 31
`ddd`	Day of the week: Sun, Mon, ...
`mm`	Month of the year from 1 to 12
`mmm`	Abbreviation of the month: Jan, Feb, ...
`yy`	Two-digit year
`yyyy`	Four-digit year

For example, to place the string `Tue, Apr 15, 1997` in the character variable `p_result`, you use a date variable `p_date` with the appropriate value, as in the following code:

```
let p_date = "4/15/97"
let p_result = p_date using "ddd, mmm dd, yyyy"
```

`using` is used extensively in reporting and display statements. To format numbers, the `using` clause uses the strings identified in Table 36.6.

Table 36.6. Number formatting with `using`.

String	*Results in a Display of*
`#`	Number or blank
`&`	Number or zero
`*`	Number or asterisk
`<`	Left justify and remove trailing blanks
`,`	Display a comma if there is a number to the left
`.`	Display a period
`-`	Display a minus if the value is negative
`+`	Display a plus or a minus for the value
`()`	Display parentheses around a negative value
`$`	Display the dollar sign

For example, the value `-12345.6789` is displayed as `($12345.68)` using the string `"(((((($&.&&)"`. More examples of the formatting that can be achieved with `using` appear in Chapter 37.

General-Purpose Library Functions

INFORMIX-4GL provides functions that can be called from C programs, but those are not covered here. The functions that can be called within a 4GL program are listed in bold below, followed by a brief description of their functionality.

`arg_val ( <integer expression> )`

Returns the argument in position `<integer expression>` from the command line. The argument in position zero is the program name itself. The value in `<integer expression>` must be between `0` and `num_args()`, the count of arguments.

`arr_count ()`

Returns the number of records entered into a program array.

`arr_curr ()`

Returns the number of the program array row that the cursor is on when entering or displaying arrays.

`ascii ( <integer number> )`

Converts the `<integer number>` argument into its corresponding ASCII character.

`<character variable or text string> clipped`

Removes trailing blanks from a character variable.

`current [ <larger datetime value> to <smaller datetime value> ]`

Returns the system date and time in the precision defined by its arguments.

`date`

Returns a string with the system date, by default, in the following format: weekday, month, day, year. This default format can be changed with the `using` clause.

```
date ( <character date expression> ¦
       <character datetime expression> ¦
       <integer expression>)
```

Converts the argument into a date value.

`day ( <date expression> )`

Extracts the day of the month from a date contained in `<date expression>` and returns it as an integer value.

`downshift ( <character string> ¦ <character variable> )`

Returns a string with all uppercase characters in its argument replaced by lowercase characters.

```
err_get ( <integer expression> )
```

Returns a character string that contains the description for the error message in the argument <integer expression>.

```
err_print ( <integer expression> )
```

Displays in the error line the description for the error message in the argument <integer expression>.

```
err_quit ( <integer expression> )
```

Displays in the error line the description for the error message in the argument <integer expression> and terminates the program.

```
errorlog ( <character string> ¦ <character variable> )
```

Places the contents of its argument in the error log file for this program.

```
extend ( <date expression> ¦
         <datetime expression>  [ ,
         <larger datetime value> to
         <smaller datetime value> ] )
```

Returns a datetime expression equivalent to the date or datetime argument with the precision specified.

```
fgl_getenv ( <character string> ¦ <character variable> )
```

Returns a character string with the contents of the environment variable in its argument.

```
fgl_keyval ( <special key character string> )
```

Returns the integer value of the key specified in its argument. It is used in connection with fgl_lastkey().

```
fgl_lastkey ()
```

Returns the integer value of the last key the user pressed.

```
field_touched (  { <name of a screen form field> }  [ ,... ] ) ¦
                   <name of a screen record>.*¦
                   <name of a screen array>.* )
```

Returns True if any of the fields on a screen have been altered; otherwise, it returns False. The function filters out keystrokes that do not alter the contents of the fields visited.

```
get_fldbuf (  { <name of a screen form field> } [ ,... ] ¦
                <name of a screen record>.* ¦
                <name of a screen array>.* )
```

Returns a string with the contents of the specified arguments.

```
infield (  { <name of a screen form field> } [ ,... ] ¦
             <name of a screen record>.*¦
             <name of a screen array>.* )
```

Returns `True` if the cursor is currently on the field indicated by the argument.

```
length ( <character string> ¦ <character variable> )
```

Returns the number of characters in the argument.

```
mdy ( <month number>, <day number>, <year number> )
```

Returns a date value created with the integer arguments.

```
month ( <date expression> )
```

Extracts the month from a date contained in `<date expression>` and returns it as an integer value.

```
num_args ()
```

Returns the number of command-line arguments used when invoking the program.

```
scr_line ()
```

Returns the number of the screen array row that the cursor is on when entering or displaying arrays.

```
set_count ( <integer expression> )
```

Specifies that `<integer expression>` is the number of rows that have been loaded into a program array.

```
showhelp ( <help number> )
```

Displays a message in the help line whose contents are those of the item `<help number>` in the current help file.

```
startlog ( <error log file name> ¦ <error log file pathname> )
```

Opens (and creates if necessary) an error log file named in its argument.

```
time
```

Returns a character string with the current reading of the system clock.

```
today
```

Returns a date value with the current system date.

```
<numeric expression> units <datetime unit>
```

Returns an interval data type with the value of `<numeric expression>` converted to the unit of measure represented in `<datetime unit>`.

upshift (*<character string>* ¦ *<character variable>*)

Returns a string with all lowercase characters in its argument replaced by uppercase characters.

{ *<numeric expression>* ¦ *<date expression>* } using "*<format string>*"

Formats the numeric or date expression as specified by the *<format string>*. Refer to Tables 36.5 and 36.6.

weekday (*<date expression>* ¦ *<datetime expression>*)

Returns a number that indicates the day of the week for its argument. Sunday is represented by 0, Monday by 1, and so on.

year (*<date expression>*)

Extracts the year from a date contained in *<date expression>* and returns it as an integer value.

The next section provides examples of the use of some of the functions described here. Further examples appear in the next two chapters.

Basic Programming Statements

INFORMIX-4GL basic statements are presented in this section classified under various logical groupings. Later in this chapter and the next, I introduce other, more specialized statements that handle the functionality provided by the user interface.

Assignment

The assignment of a value to a variable is handled by the `let` statement with the following syntax:

```
let <varname> = <expression>
```

Some examples of assignments are

```
let is_valid = true
let p_string = "Hello world!"
let p_date = today + 7
let p_weekday = weekday(today)
```

Display to Screen

To display a program variable to a specific location of the screen that is not related to fields in a form, you use the `display` statement with an `at` clause with the following syntax:

```
display <varname> [ , ... ]
        [ at <row>, <column>
        [ attribute ( <attribute> [ , ... ] ) ] ]
```

The at clause places the displayed value in the location specified relative to the current window. If the at clause is omitted, INFORMIX-4GL switches the display to line mode and displays successive statements on consecutive lines. The attributes that can be used in displays, prompts, and inputs are discussed in the section titled "Option Setting for the Overall Program."

Some examples of the use of display are

```
display p_string at 1,1 attribute (red, blink)
display p_date using "Today's date is: mm/dd/yyyy" at 2,1 attribute (reverse)
```

Prompts, Errors, and Messages

Prompts, errors, and messages are three forms of interactions that INFORMIX-4GL uses to relate to a user outside a screen form.

To elicit a response from a user without using a form, you can use the prompt statement with the following syntax:

```
prompt { <varname> ¦ <string> } [ ,... ]
       [ attribute ( <attribute> [ ,... ] ) ]
       for [ char ] <varname>
       [ help <help number> ]
       [ attribute ( <attribute> [ ,... ] ) ]
       [ on key ( <key> [ ,... ] )
            <4GL program statements> }
end prompt
```

There are two segments in the prompt statement: the question and the response. Each may have separate attributes. In addition, the prompt statement can turn into a statement block if you provide for logical checks to be performed in response to the on key clause, triggered when the user presses certain keys.

Examples of the prompt statement and statement block are

```
prompt "Are you ready to continue? (y/n): " attribute (yellow)
       for char p_answer attribute (reverse)
prompt "Enter the employer to process: " attribute (yellow)
        for p_empl_code attribute (white)
    on key interrupt
        call process_exit()
end prompt
```

When the program needs to advise the user that she made an error, INFORMIX-4GL provides the error statement to produce a beep on the terminal and display a message in the error line of the display, by default in reverse video. The error line is cleared from the screen as soon as the user presses a key. The syntax of the error statement is

```
error { <varname> ¦ <string> } [ ,... ]
      [ attribute ( <attribute> [ ,... ] ) ]
```

Examples of the `error` statement are as follows:

```
let error_line = "State ", p_employers.state,
                 " is not valid; try again"
error error_line attribute(red)
```

When the program needs to advise the user that some action took place or provide some information that confirms performed activity, you can use the `message` statement with the following syntax:

```
message { <varname> ¦ <string> } [ ,... ]
        [ attribute ( <attribute> [ ,... ] ) ]
```

The `message` statement is an `error` without a beep that displays in the message line of the screen.

Examples of the `message` statement are

```
let msg_line =  "You shouldn't do that!"
```

and

```
message msg_line
message "Searching ... Please wait ... " attribute (blink, green)
```

Prompts, messages, and errors display by default in the allocated prompt line, message line, and error line. The location of these lines can be changed using the `options` statement. If you want to display these types of messages elsewhere in the form, you can use a `function` program block to manage the display any way you want. For instance, Listing 36.3 provides a sample of a simple `function` to handle the display of errors.

Listing 36.3. A function to manage displays of errors.

```
#########################################################################
function error_display(my_error_line)
#########################################################################
# This function receives a local error message to display in a box
#
define my_error_line char(80),
       answer char(1)

    open window errwin at 22,2 with 2 rows, 78 columns attribute(border,white)
    display "Error: " at 1,1
    display " ", my_error_line clipped, " " at 1,10 attribute(reverse)
    prompt "Press Return to Continue: " for answer
    close window errwin

return

end function
```

Delays

To hold the execution of a program for a certain number of seconds, use the `sleep` statement as follows:

```
sleep <seconds>
```

Testing and Looping

INFORMIX-4GL offers two types of conditional tests (`if` and `case` statements) and two types of standard loops (`for` and `while` loops). (INFORMIX-4GL also offers the combination `goto` and `label` to manage flow of control, but its discussion is omitted.) These operate like their counterparts in other programming languages.

The `if` and `case` statement blocks are the standard conditional two-way or multiple branching blocks. The syntax of these statements is as follows:

```
if <Boolean expression>
then
  <4GL statements>
else
  <4GL statements>
end if

case [ ( <expression> ) ]
when <expression>
    { <4GL statements> | exit case } [ ,... ]
[ ... ]
[ otherwise
    { <4GL statements> | exit case } [ ,... ] ]
end case
```

The syntax for the unconditional `for` loop is as follows:

```
for <integer variable> = <beginning integer expression>
to <ending integer expression>
     [ step <integer increment> ]
  { <4GL statements> |
     continue for |
     exit for }
end for
```

The `for` statement block is executed starting at the value `<beginning integer expression>` as long as the `<integer variable>` is less than or equal to the `<ending integer expression>`. Each iteration through the loop increases the `<integer variable>` by the amount specified in the `step <integer increment>` clause. The statements `continue for` and `exit for` within the body of the statement block provide for further flow of control; if the `continue for` statement is reached, the program returns to the `for` statement, bypassing all statements after the `continue for`. If the `exit for` statement is reached, control flows to the statement following the `end for` statement.

The syntax for the conditional while loop is as follows:

```
while <Boolean expression>
  { <4GL statements> ¦
     continue while ¦
     exit while }
end while
```

The while statement block is executed as long as the <Boolean expression> evaluates to True. The statements continue while and exit while within the body of the statement block provide for further flow of control; if the continue while statement is reached, the program returns to the while statement, bypassing all statements after the continue while. If the exit while statement is reached, control flows to the statement following the end while statement.

System Variables

The INFORMIX-4GL programming language provides two system-wide variables to detect termination conditions within a program. The int_flag variable is set to true if the user presses the interrupt key—by default, the Delete key. The quit_flag variable is set to true if the user presses the quit key—by default, Ctrl+\. The interrupt key can be redefined in the options statement.

In addition to the system variables discussed, INFORMIX-4GL also offers three system-wide constants: false with an integer value of zero, true with an integer value of one, and notfound with a value of 100. You can use these values in regular expressions.

Error Handling

By default, INFORMIX-4GL terminates a program's execution when it encounters an error and displays a message to the terminal screen but does not record the reasons for this termination anywhere. This is the lowest common denominator for handling errors in INFORMIX-4GL.

One step up from doing nothing is error logging. If the developer implements error logging, an error still terminates the program's execution, but the cause of the error and the source code module location where the program aborted is recorded in the error log file. Each error in the error log file is recorded in four lines: the date and time of the run that caused the error, the location of the error, and the error code and description of the error. Here is a sample error log file:

```
Date: 10/23/1996    Time: 10:19:10
Program error at "update.4gl", line number 11.
SQL statement error number -201.
A syntax error has occurred.
```

A higher level of error management is also provided. Using the whenever error statement, the program is not terminated when an error occurs but rather transfers control to a developer-provided error-handling routine.

Error management is covered in detail in Chapter 38.

Basic INFORMIX-4GL User Interface

The most common method by which an INFORMIX-4GL program interacts with a user is through the use of menus and forms. A developer can control the way the overall program behaves in this interaction by setting options and providing adequate help. The design and development of forms is postponed until the next section. Here you deal with options, menus, and help.

Option Setting for the Overall Program

It is important in any development project that the settings used for interacting with users through screens, menus, and submenus be standardized and reflect your preferences regarding the interface. The `options` statement allows you to define the look and feel of the application. You can use the `options` statement more than once in a program and effectively change the look and feel of different sections of the program. The definition of the `options` statement is as follows, and the standard default values for each option are included between parentheses in the definition as well:

```
options { comment line <window line number (last - 1)>
          error line <window line number (last)>
          form line <window line number (first + 2)>
          message line <window line number (first + 1)>
          menu line <window line number (first )>
          prompt line <window line number (first)>
          accept key <key name (escape )>
          delete key <key name (F2)>
          help key <key name (Control-w )>
          insert key <key name (F1)>
          next key <key name (F3)>
          previous key <key name (F4)>
          help file <help file name>
          display attribute (  <attribute (normal )> [ ,... ] )
          input attribute ( <attribute (normal )> [ ,... ] )
          input { wrap ¦ no wrap (no wrap )}
          field order { constrained ¦ unconstrained (constrained )}
          SQL interrupt { on ¦ off (off )}
```

All options that indicate a line are referencing the position of the line from the top of the container window. If you look at the defaults, you notice that the menu (two lines) appears at the very top of the window; the form starts immediately below the menu. The comment and message lines share the same space, the prompt line is at the very top, and the error line is at the very bottom of the window.

The accept key terminates interaction with the screen input or display and accepts the inputs. The first four function keys are used in managing arrays in a display: Insert allows the user to insert a line above the cursor; delete allows the user to delete the line where the cursor resides; next and previous navigate through an array one screen at a time, forward and back.

Attributes that can be used in display and input are of three kinds: color, appearance, and special effects. Available colors are black, blue, cyan, green, magenta, red, white, and yellow; these are automatically mapped to bold, normal, or dim on monochrome screens. Appearance attributes are normal, bold, dim, and invisible. Special effects are blink, reverse, and underline. These attributes can be used in combination.

The option `input` defines the behavior of the `input` statement when the user reaches the last field in a form. If it is `wrap`, the cursor moves to the first field in the form when the user presses enter; if it is `no wrap`, pressing enter after the last field in the form is equivalent to pressing the accept key, forcing input to be terminated.

The option `field order` defines the behavior of arrow keys during screen interactions. If it is `constrained`, the cursor always moves in the order in which the fields have been defined by the programmer, the down arrow takes the user to the next field, and the up arrow takes the user to the previous field. If it is `unconstrained`, the arrows take the user to the fields that logically are directly on the path of the selected arrow key: The up arrow key moves the cursor to the field that is above the current field, and the down arrow key moves the cursor to the field just below.

The option `SQL interrupt` allows the user to terminate the execution of an SQL query prematurely if `on` or not if `off`. This is a very useful option whose default is counterintuitive. You normally want this option turned on.

You can find an example of the `option` statement later in this chapter, in Listing 36.6.

Menus

Menus are at the core of the INFORMIX-4GL user interface and are used to provide the user with a mechanism for selecting actions to perform. You could view them similar to the way you view a `case` statement block—multibranching selections driven by the user choices. The style of INFORMIX-4GL menus created using the `menu` statement block is the ring menu style.

Ring menus use two lines to display the menu options. The first line, called the menu line, displays the title of the menu and the options. The second line, named the menu help line, displays a more verbose description of the menu option. If the list of available options exceeds the screen space to display them, INFORMIX-4GL displays an ellipsis (...) at the end of the line to indicate that there are more available options. Actually, an ellipsis on either side of the menu indicates that there are more options to be displayed in the direction the ellipsis points.

To select an option from the menu, the user can move the cursor over to the desired option by using either the arrow keys or the spacebar and pressing Enter (or Return), at which time the program executes the code associated with the selected choice.

Users can also select and execute an option from the menu by typing the first letter of the option. If multiple options start with the same letter, INFORMIX-4GL can't decide which is the desired option, and it displays a submenu with the options under contention in the menu help line and keeps changing the options in this menu with every user keystroke until a single option remains. This option is then executed. A common practice in managing menu choices is to key each menu option on a different character and display that character capitalized. Then the user types in the capital letter associated with the desired option and the option is executed immediately.

In addition to visible options, two other types of options can be in a menu. Hidden options are menu options that are disabled programmatically and cannot be executed while hidden, but they can be redisplayed and then become active again. Invisible options are options that will never be displayed in the menu but will be executed if the user presses the key that activates them.

The syntax for the menu statement block is as follows:

```
menu <menu name>
         { [before menu] ¦
           command { [ key ( <command key> [ ,... ] ) ]
                     [ <command name> ]
                     [ "<description>" ]
                     [ help <help number> ]
         }

              { [hide option { all ¦ <command name> [ ,... ]] ¦
                [show option { all ¦ <command name> [ ,... ]] ¦
                [next option <command name>] ¦
                [continue menu] ¦
                [exit menu] }

end menu
```

A menu statement block can have two types of clauses. The before menu clause is used to execute a collection of statements while the menu is activated and before the user can make any selections. The command clause is used to define the menu options that the user can select. Within either of these two clauses, there can be four subclauses. The hide option clause is used to deactivate menu options and render them inaccessible and invisible. The show option is the opposite of the hide option clause. The next option directs INFORMIX-4GL to highlight the option indicated upon exit from the current menu option. The continue menu option stops processing the statements in the current subclause and transfers control back to the menu statement for the user to make another selection. Finally, the exit menu option transfers control to the statement immediately after the menu control block ends (after the end menu statement).

A menu can contain invisible options, which are defined by using a command clause that has a key but no name. These options are always available to a user, as long as the user knows the keys that trigger the invisible option.

An example of a menu showing most of these options is provided in the section titled "Menu Options and Menu Definition," later in this chapter.

Help

INFORMIX-4GL uses customizable help files to provide context-sensitive help for an application. In addition, I have already discussed the use of the menu help line to provide a more descriptive, one-line message about a menu option. Screen forms also provide a method for displaying a one-line message regarding the contents of the field that the cursor is on. Help files provide the most comprehensive method by far for providing help.

Beyond the three forms of help delivery indicated, you could devise a complete help subsystem that stores help messages in database tables and triggers the appropriate selections from those tables when the user requests it.

In this section, I cover the principles used in designing help files. A help file is an ASCII file that mixes help messages (lines that start with a character other than the period or a pound sign), comment lines (lines that start with a pound sign), and control lines (lines that begin with a period and are followed by a number). The basic structure of a help file is as follows:

```
.<help number>
<help message>
[ ... ]
```

Here is an example:

```
# Help message on menu selection Exit
.1
Pressing E, Q or X will exit the current menu
# Help on Printer Selection
.2
Use this option to select a printer.  A pop-up window will appear that lists ...
```

The help files created must be compiled using `mkmessage`, whose syntax is as follows:

```
mkmessage <ASCII help file> <executable help file>
```

The `<executable help file>` that the program will use is declared in the `options` statement block in your application.

Help in your application can be invoked by using the clause `help` in statements that allow it, like this:

```
help <help number>
```

This will display the message associated with `<help number>` when the user presses the Help key, which is also declared in the `options` statement block. Help can also be displayed, at the programmer's discretion, by calling the function `showhelp` at any time, like this:

```
showhelp (<help number>)
```

Processing Inputs to a Single Table One Record at a Time

This section contains an annotated collection of source code modules and a screen form source file that have been designed to carry you from the beginning of the development process to the production of a complete data entry and query program.

The steps in developing this application are carried out in basically the same order that you would use to develop any INFORMIX-4GL program. The steps follow this sequence: First, you develop the form source file and compile it; later, you develop the program. You start the program by defining the window that will frame the application and developing the options and menu for managing the interactions with the form defined. You then develop, one after another, the functions that support the menu options. You start with the Find command and introduce Query-By-Example, cursors, and the `construct` statement; after the data is retrieved, the `display` statement shows records on the form. Along with the retrieval of records from the database, you develop the mechanism for navigating through the records (with menu options Next and Previous). Afterward, I introduce the `input` statement in support of the Add and Update menu commands. Finally, the Delete menu option allows you to develop a submenu to confirm the action.

The purpose of this example is to allow you to see the various statements in action. It has been designed with training in mind. It is not intended to be robust enough for production use; in fact, in many places you are told what is wrong with the software design, and you are given alternative courses of action to implement as enhancements to the example.

The software presented here allows a user to input information into the employers table and uses an interface composed of a menu and a form, as shown in Figure 36.1. Developing software to handle all basic interactions within this interface is the goal in this section.

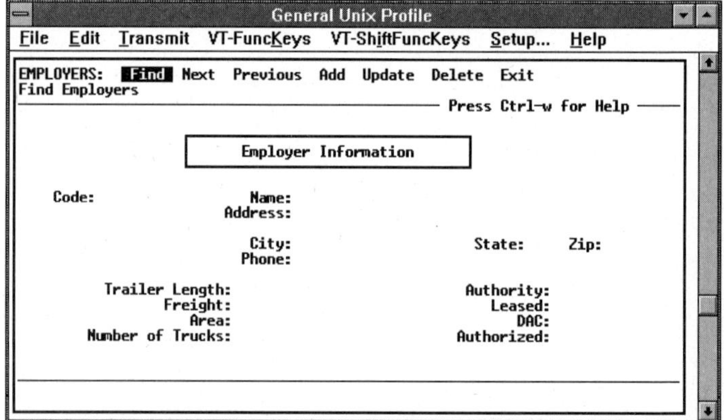

FIGURE 36.1.
The application interface.

Interactions between the user and the database are normally carried out through screens (or screen forms). The user queries the database by making selections on a screen and inputs or updates data in a database table through changes in a screen.

A screen form is displayed within a window. The first two lines of the window are normally devoted to displaying a menu associated with the screen form. A screen form consists of labels and fields. Information input on screen fields or retrieved from the database is stored in program variables; thus, there is always an interaction between the user and the computer's memory, or between the disk storage and the computer's memory, in order for the ultimate exchange between the user and the database to take place.

Defining Effective Screens

Here are some ideas to consider when you are laying out the screen forms for your application:

- Use window borders to delineate the screen and distinguish it from the rest of the desktop.
- Use the largest possible area of terminal screen that you can spare to define the form. Lay the screen out clearly. Do not crowd too much information into a single screen; use multiple screens to collect all the information required even if you're dealing with a single table.
- Place the menu at the top of the window and visually separate it from the form. I use a dashed line in this example.
- Place a title in the form in a visible and always consistent position, toward the top of the form. The title should make sense to the user. (A better placement for the title than the one in this example, which wastes a lot of space, is on the dashed line that divides the menu from the form—the third line in the window, toward the left, and in red or bold.) Form titles should always be consistently placed on the same spot.
- Wherever possible, try to use whole words as screen field labels. The labels should use names that are part of the everyday vocabulary of the users. If more description is needed, use the comment line associated with each form field. Minimize the use of abbreviations, and use only abbreviations that are commonplace.
- Align the fields and field labels in your screen form so that they form easily distinguishable sections that collect common information. If the form has multiple sections, provide a visible separation between the sections by using either a blank line or a dashed line.
- Place a dashed line that spans the whole width of the window two lines up from the bottom border of the window. Display messages, errors, and other useful information on the line between the dashed line and the bottom border of the window.
- If the form contains a one-to-many relationship, place the *one* part of the relationship at the top of the form and the *many* rows at the bottom of the form. Labels for the *one*

part of the relationship appear to the left of the fields; labels for the *many* part of the relationship appear at the top of the fields.

- Arrange fields on the screen logically from top to bottom and left to right. For the *one* part of a relationship, place the fields in a column; for the *many* part of the relationship, place the fields of information in rows (like a table). Do not confuse users by displaying fields in one order and have the users input data in a different order.

Screen File Coding: Automatic Generation and Further Editing

Screen forms are defined in an ASCII file that is created using the following syntax:

```
database { <dbname> ¦ formonly }  [ without null input ]

screen [ size <lines>  [ by <columns> ] ]
 "{" [ "<field label>" ] ¦
     [\g <graphics characters: -¦pqbd> \g ] ¦
     "[" <field tag> "]"
 "}"
end

tables
{ <tabname> ¦ <table alias> = <tabname> }
end

attributes
<field tag> = { <tabname>.<colname> ¦ formonly.<field name> }
                 [ <field attribute>  [, ... ] ] ;
end

instructions
  [ delimiters "<start><end>" ]
  [ screen record <record name> [ "[" <array size> "]" ]
           ( {  <tabname>.* ¦
                <tabname>.<colname> through <tabname>.<colname> ¦
                <tabname>.<colname> , <tabname>.<colname>, ... }
            )
end
```

Several sections make up a form. You must have one database section and one attributes section; you could have multiple screen sections, at most one tables section, and at most one instructions section.

The `database` section specifies the name of the database to work with, unless you use the keyword `formonly`, in which case the fields on the screen cannot be defined by reference to columns in database tables. If you specify `without null input`, the system requires that you do not leave any fields of information null on the screen, and it fills the empty fields with a default of blank or zero.

The `screen` section of the form definition lays out the form and optionally declares its size. Within this section, you include labels, fields, and graphics characters. The fields are enclosed between square brackets (`[]`) and are given a tag to associate the field on the form with a column and a collection of attributes. A graphics character string on the screen starts and ends with the sequence `\g`. To form the character to display, use the following characters:

- `-` creates a horizontal line.
- `|` creates a vertical line.
- `p` makes the upper left corner.
- `q` makes the upper right corner.
- `b` makes the lower left corner.
- `d` makes the bottom right corner.

The `tables` section of the form definition identifies the database tables that are used in this screen. If you declare a `database formonly`, you do not need to include the `tables` section in your screen form file.

The `attributes` section relates the field tags on the `screen` section with either database table columns or `formonly` columns and with other attributes. The `attributes` section of a screen form can utilize the attributes that are described briefly under the following bold headings.

`autonext`

When the end of the field is reached, automatically place the cursor in the next field.

`color = <color attribute> [ where <conditional expression> ]`

Display contents of the field in `<color attribute>` color when the condition in the `where` clause is true. `<color attribute>` can be `blink`, `underline`, `reverse`, `left`, `white`, `yellow`, `magenta`, `red`, `cyan`, `green`, `blue`, or `black`.

`comments = "<comment>"`

Display this message when the cursor enters the field.

`default = <default value>`

Insert this `<default value>` in the field on input.

`display like <tabname>.<colname>`

Display the contents of the field using the display attributes defined for the column identified in `<tabname>.<colname>`.

`downshift`

Convert all characters input to lowercase.

`format = "<format string>"`

Format date or numeric field as follows: Date values are formatted using the same rules that were specified in Table 36.5. To format numbers, use the pound sign and a period. Pound signs indicate a position for a digit, and the period indicates the position of the decimal point.

```
include = ( { <value> ¦ <value> to <value> }  [ , ... ] )
```

Only accept values included in the list as input.

```
noentry
```

Do not allow data entry on this field.

```
picture = "<format string>"
```

Format strings as indicated by the `<format string>` mask. The mask can use the following characters: `#` for numeric values, `A` for character values, `X` for any printable character, and `<other>` for characters that will appear as is.

```
required
```

You must enter a value in this field.

```
reverse
```

Display field contents in reverse video.

```
type { <data type>  [ not null ] ¦ like [ <tabname>.]<colname> }
```

Assign the data type indicated by `<data type>`, or use the data type `like <tabname>.<Colname>` for this `formonly` field.

```
upshift
```

Convert all characters input to uppercase.

```
validate like <tabname>.<colname>
```

Use the validation rules defined for `<tabname>.<colname>` to check the data input in this field.

```
verify
```

After input, make the user input the contents of this field a second time.

```
wordwrap [ compress ]
```

In a multiline field, make the system wrap long words to the next line. The `compress` clause prevents extra blanks required for proper display to be included in the program variables that are associated with the fields.

Screen File Coding: The Instructions Section

The `instructions` section of the form definition file allows you to redefine the field delimiters, which are square brackets by default. It also allows you to declare and define screen records with the `screen record` clause. Screen records are defined collections of fields on the screen that can be referred to as a unit.

To initiate the process of laying out your form, you can use the Forms: Generate option of INFORMIX-4GL to get a starting screen that includes all columns of table employers. The resulting form generated by INFORMIX-4GL looks like the one in Listing 36.4.

Listing 36.4. The generated form.

```
database recruiters
screen size 24 by 80
{
empl_code           [f000       ]
employer            [f001                              ]
add_line1           [f002                              ]
add_line2           [f003                              ]
city                [f004              ]
state               [a0]
zip                 [f005 ]
phone               [f006       ]
trl_len             [a1]
freight             [f007       ]
area                [f008           ]
nbr_trks            [f009]
authority           [a]
leased              [b]
dac                 [c]
authorized          [d]
}
end
tables
employers
attributes
f000 = employers.empl_code;
f001 = employers.employer;
f002 = employers.add_line1;
f003 = employers.add_line2;
f004 = employers.city;
a0 = employers.state;
f005 = employers.zip;
f006 = employers.phone;
a1 = employers.trl_len;
f007 = employers.freight;
f008 = employers.area;
f009 = employers.nbr_trks;
a = employers.authority;
b = employers.leased;
c = employers.dac;
d = employers.authorized;
end
```

This generated form includes all columns in the table (or tables you have selected), and it labels each column with the column name. Using vi, or your editor of choice, Listing 36.5 displays the form layout that matches Figure 36.1.

Listing 36.5. The edited form.

```
DATABASE recruiters
SCREEN
{
------------------------------------------------- Press Ctrl-w for Help ----
                   \gp-------------------------------q\g
                   \g¦\g      Employer Information      \g¦\g
                   \gb-------------------------------d\g

 Code:[f000      ]     Name:[f001                              ]
                    Address:[f002                              ]
                            [f003                              ]
                       City:[f004              ] State:[a0] Zip: [f005 ]
                      Phone:[f006      ]

       Trailer Length:[a1]                        Authority:[a]
              Freight:[f007      ]                   Leased:[b]
                 Area:[f008          ]                  DAC:[c]
     Number of Trucks:[f009]                     Authorized:[d]


----------------------------------------------------------------------------
}
END
TABLES
    employers
ATTRIBUTES
f000 = employers.empl_code, reverse, noentry;
f001 = employers.employer, required, upshift,
          comments = "Enter the Employer Business Name";
f002 = employers.add_line1,
          comments = "Enter the First Line of the Address";
f003 = employers.add_line2,
          comments = "Enter the Second Line of the Address";
f004 = employers.city, upshift, required,
          comments = "Enter the City for this Address";
a0 = employers.state, required, upshift,
        comments = "Enter the State for this Address";
f005 = employers.zip, required, picture = "#####",
          comments = "Enter the Zip Code for this Address";
f006 = employers.phone;
a1 = employers.trl_len;
f007 = employers.freight;
f008 = employers.area;
f009 = employers.nbr_trks;
a = employers.authority;
b = employers.leased;
c = employers.dac;
d = employers.authorized;
END
INSTRUCTIONS
```

```
   delimiters "  "
   screen record s_employers(employers.empl_code,
                             employers.employer,
                             employers.add_line1,
                             employers.add_line2,
                             employers.city,
                             employers.state,
                             employers.zip,
                             employers.phone,
                             employers.trl_len,
                             employers.freight,
                             employers.area,
                             employers.nbr_trks,
                             employers.authority,
                             employers.leased,
                             employers.dac,
                             employers.authorized)
END
```

This form design illustrates the use of graphics characters in the screen section of the form. Graphics are used to furnish a title for the form. It also illustrates the use of the `required` keyword, the `upshift` and `downshift` keywords, and the `reverse`, `noentry`, `comments`, and `picture` keywords. The `instructions` section illustrates the use of the `delimiters` clause, which in this instance removes the visible delimiters by making them blank and defines a `screen record`.

To manage the use of forms in a program, INFORMIX-4GL provides the following three statements:

```
open form <form name> from "<filename>"
```

This statement names the form `<form name>` and opens it with the contents of file `"<filename>"`, which must match a compiled form file. Note that this statement does not display the form; it merely opens it and places it in the stack. From now on, refer to this form as `<form name>` in the program. To display the form, use the following statement:

```
display form <form name> [ attribute ( <attribute> [ , ... ] ) ]
```

In this statement, `<attribute>` can be `reverse`, `blink underline`, `normal`, `bold`, `dim`, `invisible`, `white`, `yellow`, `magenta`, `red`, `cyan`, `green`, `blue`, or `black`. The form is displayed within a container window, and if attributes are not provided, the form inherits the attributes of the container window or, if those are missing, the attributes defined as overall program options. The `close form` statement closes the form, and its syntax is as follows:

```
close form <form name>
```

The use of forms is exemplified in Listing 36.6 in the next section.

Window Management

Windows are the standard containers for forms in INFORMIX-4GL programs, and the following four statements in the language are used to manage them:

```
open window <window name> at <row>, <column>
        with {  <rows> rows, <columns> columns ¦
                form "<form file>" }
       [ attribute ( <window attribute> [ , ... ] ) ]
```

This statement names a window, opens it, positions it in row `<row>` and column `<column>`, and displays it. The number of rows and columns for the display are either defined in the `with` clause directly (`<rows> rows, <columns> columns`) or are inherited from the `form "<form file>"` clause, which, if used, not only opens and displays the window large enough to contain the form, but also opens and displays the form in `<form file>`. The attributes in `<window attribute>` can be of three kinds: The general window layout can be `border`, `reverse`, `normal`, `bold`, `dim`, or `invisible`. The color can be `white`, `yellow`, `magenta`, `red`, `cyan`, `green`, `blue`, or `black`. The location of contained objects can be `prompt line <line number>`, `message line <line number>`, `form line <line number>`, or `comment line <line number>`. If attributes are not provided, the window inherits the attributes defined as overall program options.

To activate a window that is not currently active but has already been opened, you use this command:

```
current window <window name>
```

This statement places the window at the top of the window stack. All interactions between the user and the program can occur only in the current window.

The following command, `clear`, performs the function that its name implies and can act upon the whole screen, a named window, or the fields of a form individually or collectively. Its syntax is as follows:

```
clear { screen ¦ window <window name> ¦ form [ <form field name> [ , ... ] ] }
```

When you are finished using a window, the `close window` statement removes it from view and from the stack. The statement is used as follows:

```
close window <window name>
```

Note the use of these statements in `main.4gl` in Listing 36.6. For the definition of the tables involved, refer to Listing 36.1. Global definitions are collected in Listing 36.2.

Listing 36.6. `main.4gl`.

```
globals "globals.4gl"

#####################################################################
main
#####################################################################
```

```
#- set run options

    defer interrupt
    options input wrap,
        input attribute (red),
        display attribute(red),
        sql interrupt on,
        field order unconstrained,
        message line last

#- capture errors to file errlog in current directory

    call startlog("errlog")

#- initialize global variables

    call init_vars()

#- open the main window and display employer form

    open window w_top at 2,2 with 22 rows, 78 columns
     attribute(border)
    open form f_employers from "employer"
    display form f_employers

#- display the menu and wait for user action

    menu "EMPLOYERS"
    command key ("!")
        call sh_unix()
    command "Find" "Find Employers"
        call find_it()
        next option "Next"
    command "Next" "View next Employer"
        call next_row()
    command "Previous" "View previous Employer"
        call previous_row()
    command "Add" "Add Employers"
        call add_it()
    command "Update" "Update Employers"
        call update_it()
    command "Delete" "Delete Employers"
        call delete_it()
        next option "Find"
    command key(Q,E,X) "Exit" "Exit the menu and the Program"
        exit menu
    end menu

#- clean up and leave

    close form f_employers
    close window w_top
    exit program

end main

###################################################################
function init_vars()
```

continues

Listing 36.6. continued

```
####################################################################

    initialize p_employers.* to null
    let is_valid = false

end function
```

Menu Options and Menu Definition

In Listing 36.6, the `menu` statement encapsulates all activity associated with each menu choice within a subroutine call. This is typical in many INFORMIX-4GL programs, which use `main` as the flow of control block.

Listing 36.6 does not use the `before menu` block or the `hide menu` and `show menu` statements. If you want to manage the menu options dynamically, you hide all options in the `before menu` clause, and use `show menu` to display the Find, Add, and Exit options. After a successful Find, the `show menu` command could be used to activate the Next, Previous, Update, and Delete options. After a successful Add, the `show menu` command could be used to activate the Update and Delete options.

First Encounter with Cursors

The Find menu option in this trucking firm application (shown earlier in Figure 36.1) probably will return multiple rows from the employers table. When a query has the potential to return more than a single row from a table, you must manage the result set by means of a cursor. The cursor allows you to access each row in the result set individually, rather than as a block, by pointing to a row in the result set. Because, by nature, SQL is designed to process a set of rows as a unit, cursors allow you to bridge the set-oriented nature of SQL with the programmatic need to process rows one at a time. Think of a cursor as a pointer to a row in the result set that a query has returned.

Because cursors are related to queries, this is a good time to introduce the sequence of events that a program must follow to retrieve data from the database, display it on a screen form, and eventually modify it. The steps are as follows:

1. Query-By-Example builds the `where` clause of the query with the `construct` statement.
2. Build the complete SQL statement, using the `where` clause from step 1, normally with the `let` and the `concatenate` operators and the `clipped` keyword.
3. Preprocess the SQL statement prior to execution with the `prepare` statement.
4. If the SQL statement is supported by the engine but not by your version of 4GL, run the statement using the `execute` command.
5. If the query can return more than a single row from the database, `declare` a cursor to retrieve the rows sequentially.

6. Now you can start retrieving rows in one of two scenarios: First, you can explicitly open the cursor and fetch the records until you are done, and then close the cursor and free the system resources the cursor took. Or, second, you can initiate a foreach loop that automatically performs all of the functions required for the retrieval.
7. When the data resides in program variables or program arrays, use display to format it and display it on the screen form; use display array if the display shows many rows simultaneously; or use output to report to send it to a report.
8. To modify the data displayed on the screen or to add new information, use input to edit and validate the data, or use input array if your screen displays many rows for editing at any one time.

The various statements in the preceding list are described in detail here and illustrated further with an example in the next section.

The Query-By-Example workhorse is the construct statement block. The syntax for the construct statement can have four main forms, each of which can use a variety of clauses. The main forms of the construct statement are listed first, followed by the clauses that the construct statement block can contain:

```
{ construct by name <where string> on <tabname>.* ¦
  construct <where string> on <tabname>.<colname> [ , ... ]
            from <field name> [ , ... ] ¦
  construct <where string> on <tabname>.<colname> [ , ... ]
            from <screen record>.* ¦
  construct <where string> on <tabname>.<colname> [ , ... ]
            from <screen record>.<colname [ , ... ]
} attribute ( <attribute> [ , ... ] )
   { before construct
          { <4GL statements> }
     after construct
         { <4GL statements> }
     before field <field name>
         { <4GL statements> }
     after field <field name>
         { <4GL statements> }
     on key <special key>
         { <4GL statements> }
     next field { next ¦ previous ¦ <field name> }
     continue construct
     exit construct
    }
end construct
```

The construct statement builds a character variable, <where string>, that contains the where clause that the user creates dynamically by entering criteria in the various fields of the screen form. The clauses of the construct statement are the same as those of the input statement and will be discussed in detail in relation to the input statement. Here's an example of the construct statement:

```
construct by name where_clause on employers.*
```

The by name clause requires that the fields in the form and the columns of the table use the same names for the same purpose, because it performs the pairing implicitly. Alternatively, you can specify the matching of table columns and form fields as follows:

```
construct where_clause on employers.empl_code,
                          employers.employer,
                          employers.add_line1,
                          employers.add_line2,
                          employers.city,
                          employers.state,
                          employers.zip,
                          employers.phone,
                          employers.trl_len,
                          employers.freight,
                          employers.area,
                          employers.nbr_trks,
                          employers.authority,
                          employers.leased,
                          employers.dac,
                          employers.authorized
           from s_employers.*
```

You can limit the screen fields that the construct statement will use (and the cursor will visit) and, at the same time, limit the fields that the user can use in a query as follows:

```
construct where_clause on employers.state, employers.lease
          from s_employers.state, s_employers.lease
```

After building the <where clause> of the select statement that will be used to query the database, you proceed to build the complete SQL statement by using the concatenation operator as follows:

```
let sql_stmt = "select * from employers where ",
               where_clause clipped, " ",
               "order by empl_code"
```

The prepare statement is used to parse and validate a dynamic SQL statement. Its syntax is as follows:

```
prepare <statement id> from { <SQL string> ¦ <char variable> }
```

<statement id> is an identifier for the statement to be used in the declare to follow. The prepare statement can operate on either a quoted string (<SQL string>) or on a character variable. An example that continues in the footsteps of the previous example is

```
prepare statement_1 from sql_stmt
```

Another example of a prepare statement is

```
prepare statement_2 from
       "select * from employers where state = ? order by empl_code"
```

This prepare statement shows the use of placeholders (?) that will be provided a value when the cursor is opened.

After the statement has been prepared, you declare a cursor with the following syntax:

```
declare <cursor name> [ scroll ] cursor [ with hold ] for
    { <select statement> [ for update [ of <colname> [ , ... ] ] ]  ¦
      < insert statement>  ¦
      <statement id>  }
```

The cursor is given the name `<cursor name>`, and it can be declared for a `<select statement>`, for an `<insert statement>`, or for a preprocessed `<statement id>`. If rows will be retrieved only sequentially, you can use a regular cursor, but if you want to navigate back and forth within the result set, you need to use the `scroll` clause to declare a scroll cursor. By default, after you open a cursor in INFORMIX-4GL, the system closes the cursor every time it completes a transaction. The `with hold` clause keeps the cursor open after ending a transaction. If you intend to update the current row, use the `for update` clause. Here are examples of a `declare` cursor statement:

```
declare c_employers scroll cursor with hold for statement_1
declare c_employers2 scroll cursor with hold for statement_2
        for update of freight
declare c_employers cursor for select * from employers order by empl_code
```

Now that the cursor is declared, you need to activate its result set by using the `open` statement, like this:

```
open <cursor name> [ using <program var> [ , ... ] ]
```

When the program invokes this statement, the server receives the SQL it represents for the first time. The server performs error checking, sets the SQLCA variable, and stops short of delivering the first row of the result set. If the `select` statement that was prepared contained placeholders (question marks) for replacement by program variables at execution time, the `using` clause delivers these variables to the `open` statement. Here are examples of both forms of `open` statements:

```
open c_employers

let p_state = "MO"

open c_employers2 using p_state
```

Now that the cursor is open, you can start retrieving records and placing them in program variables. The `fetch` statement serves this purpose, and its syntax is as follows:

```
fetch   { next ¦ previous ¦ prior ¦ first ¦
          last ¦ current ¦
          relative <relative row number> ¦
          absolute <absolute row number>
        } <cursor name> [ into <program var> ]
```

A sequential cursor (one declared without the scroll clause) can perform only a `fetch next`, but a scroll cursor can use any of the positioning clauses indicated earlier. (The next and previous clauses are used in the example in Listing 36.7.) The record retrieved by the `fetch` is placed in program variables listed in the `into <program var>` clause. Here's an example of this statement:

```
fetch first c_employers into p_employers.*
```

After you are finished using the cursor, you need to close it and free the resources it holds. The `close` statement uses the following syntax:

```
close <cursor name>
```

The `free` statement uses the following syntax:

```
free { <cursor name> ¦ <statement id> }
```

An alternative to the `open`, `fetch`, and `close` combination is the `foreach` statement, which performs all these functions on your behalf. The `foreach` statement is widely used in reports or when loading static arrays, and it is discussed in that context in Chapter 37.

To display the data placed in program variables to the form on the screen, you use the `display` statement as follows:

```
display { by name <var name> [ , ... ] }
                   [ attribute ( <attribute> [ , ... ] ) ] ¦
          <constant> [ , ... ] ¦
          <varname> [ , ... ]
[ { to { <form field name> [ , ... ]                       } ¦
         <screen record>["["<row number>"]"].*
    at <row>, <column> }
         [ attribute ( <attribute> [ , ... ] ) ]
]
```

The `display` statement is used to display program variables onto screen fields. You can also display a `<constant>` to a screen field. If the program variables and the screen fields use the same names, you can use the `by name` clause; otherwise, you have to match the program variable and the screen field to display it with the `to` clause. The `at <row>, <column>` clause was covered earlier in this chapter.

Here are some examples of the `display` statement:

```
display by name p_employers.*

display p_employers.* to s_employers.*
```

To modify the program variables on the screen form and ultimately the database rows, you use the `input` statement. This statement is discussed in the section titled "Adding, Deleting, and Updating Records." Take some time to look at the `find.4gl` module in Listing 36.7, which covers the entire process described here in function `find_it()`.

Finding Records and Displaying Records

The Find menu option in Figure 36.1 is designed to allow the user to create a query dynamically. After the user chooses the Find option, the cursor drops down to the form and allows the user to specify the criteria desired for any of the displayed screen fields. This process allows the user to create a Query-By-Example. A collection of characters is available to build the Query-By-Example. These special characters are listed in Table 36.8.

Table 36.8. The Query-By-Example special characters.

Character	*Purpose*
=	Equal to (if followed by nothing will look for null values)
>	Greater than
>=	Greater than or equal to
<	Less than
<=	Less than or equal to
<>	Not equal to
!=	Not equal to
:	Between
..	Between datetimes or intervals
*	Match zero or more of any character
?	Match a single character
¦	Or
[]	Create an include list; used with other operators
^	Not in the list within the brackets when in first position

An example of some of these operators is provided in Figure 36.2.

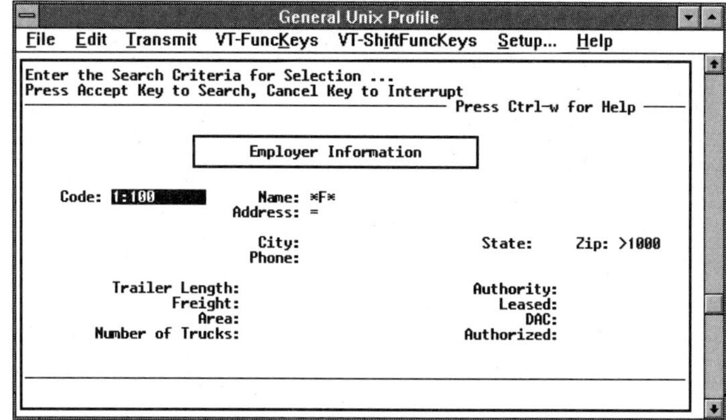

FIGURE 36.2.
Query-By-Example.

In Figure 36.2, note that the query requests that the Code (`empl_code`) ranges between 1 and 100 (`1:100`), that the name has the letter F anywhere within it (`*F*`), that the first line of the address is null (`=`), and that the Zip code is greater than 1000 (`>1000`). The user expects that the menu options Next and Previous will allow navigation through the record set that the query has returned. Listing 36.7 displays the code used in processing the various functions required to retrieve and navigate through a set of records and display these records on the screen.

After the user types in the selections on the form and presses the Accept Key, the program processes the Query-By-Example, declares the cursor, opens it, fetches the first record, and displays it. The option Next is highlighted in the menu, and the software awaits user action. (Instead of automatically placing the highlight in the Next option after a Find, a better approach would be to test whether the find returned any rows and, if it did, suggest Next as the next menu option; otherwise, suggest Find or Add as the next menu option.)

Listing 36.7. The `find.4gl` module.

```
globals "globals.4gl"

################################################################
function find_it()
################################################################
# Gather search criteria, find the first employer and display it
################################################################

    define where_clause char(512),
           sql_stmt char(1024)

#- clear form on the screen and initialize variables

    clear form
    let int_flag = false
#    call close_cursor_emp()
    initialize p_employers.* to null

#- replace menu with instructions for query-by-example

    display "" at 1,1
    display "" at 2,1
    display "Enter the Search Criteria for Selection ..." at 1,1
            attribute(green)
    display "Press Accept Key to Search, Cancel Key to Interrupt"
            at 2,1 attribute(yellow)

#- construct the query statement dynamically: the where_clause
#- variable will contain the query string based on the criteria
#- for selection that the user inputs

    construct where_clause on employers.empl_code,
                              employers.employer,
                              employers.add_line1,
                              employers.add_line2,
                              employers.city,
                              employers.state,
```

```
                                employers.zip,
                                employers.phone,
                                employers.trl_len,
                                employers.freight,
                                employers.area,
                                employers.nbr_trks,
                                employers.authority,
                                employers.leased,
                                employers.dac,
                                employers.authorized
    from s_employers.*

#- if the user interrupted, cancel the query request and return to
#- the calling program after advising the user

    if int_flag
    then
        message " Search Cancelled at User Request "
        let int_flag = false
        return
    end if

#- proceed with the query: replace query-by-example instructions
#- by flashing message indicating search for records is proceeding

    display "" at 1,1
    display "" at 2,1
    display "Searching ..." at 1,1 attribute(green, blink)

#- construct the complete SQL statement to query the database:
#- include the select clause, the from clause, the dynamically
#- created where clause and an order by clause.  Concatenate
#- those clauses into the program variable sql_stmt

    let sql_stmt = "select * from employers where ",
                   where_clause clipped, " ",
                   "order by empl_code"

#- prepare the SQL statement for execution, declare a cursor that
#- will represent the active set of rows returned by the engine
#- and activate the cursor by opening it

    prepare statement_1 from sql_stmt
    declare c_employers scroll cursor with hold for statement_1
    open c_employers

#- if the open has succeeded, retrieve the first row in the active
#- data set, place it in the program variable p_employers and
#- display this variable; otherwise handle the failure with an
#- error message that is descriptive of the type of failure

    if status = 0
    then
        fetch first c_employers into p_employers.*
        if status = 0
        then
            display p_employers.* to s_employers.*
        else
```

continues

Listing 36.7. continued

```
            if status = notfound
            then
                message "No employers satisfy search criteria"
            else
                error " Could not get employers information; ",
                      "status ", status using "-<<<<<<<<<<"
            end if
        end if
    else
        error " Could not access employers information "
    end if

end function


#####################################################################
function next_row()
#####################################################################
# fetch and display the next row
#####################################################################

#- to display the next row, one must already be displayed

    if p_employers.empl_code is null
    then
        error " Must find first "
        return
    end if

#- retrieve the next row in the active set, place it in the program
#- variable p_employers and display this variable; otherwise handle
#- the failure with an error message that is descriptive of the
#- type of failure

    fetch next c_employers into p_employers.*
    if status = 0
    then
        display p_employers.* to s_employers.*
    else
        if status = notfound
        then
            message "Reached the end of the list"
        else
            error " Could not retrieve next employer "
        end if
    end if

    return

end function

#####################################################################
function previous_row()
#####################################################################
# fetch and display the previous row
#####################################################################
```

```
#- to display the previous row, one must already be displayed

    if p_employers.empl_code is null
    then
        error " Must find first "
        return
    end if

#- retrieve the previous row in the active set, place it in the
#- program variable p_employers and display this variable;
#- otherwise handle the failure with an error message that is
#- descriptive of the type of failure

    fetch previous c_employers into p_employers.*
    if status = 0
    then
        display p_employers.* to s_employers.*
    else
        if status = notfound
        then
            message "At the beginning of the list"
        else
            error " Could not retrieve previous employer "
        end if
    end if

    return

end function
```

Adding, Updating, and Deleting Records

When the user sees the contents of a record on the screen, the Update menu choice allows the user to change the contents of that record and store the updated information in the database. The Add menu choice allows the user to input a new record and store it in the database. Both use the `input` statement with the following syntax:

```
input { by name <program var> [ , ... ]  [ without defaults ]
        from { <form field name>  }  [ , ... ] ¦
                 <screen record>.*
               [ attribute ( <attribute> [ , ... ] ) ) ]
    before input
        { any 4GL statement }
    before field <form field name>
        { any 4GL statement }
    after field <form field name>
        { any 4GL statement }
    after input
        { any 4GL statement }
    on key ( <special key> )
        { any 4GL statement }
   next field { next ¦ previous ¦ <form field name> }
   continue input
   exit input
end input
```

The `input` statement block permits the user to input or change data in the screen fields of the form it is associated with. The options of this statement are as follows:

- `by name` clause implicitly binds the screen fields to equally named program variables.
- `<program var>` lists the program variables to input. (Normally a record variable is used.)
- `without defaults` keeps the system from filling the screen fields with default values, and instead it uses the current values of the `<program var>` variables.
- `from` binds the `<program var>` to either a `<form field name>` or a `<screen record>`. This is used instead of the `by name` clause.
- `before input` causes INFORMIX-4GL to execute the statements in this clause before allowing the user to input data onto the form.
- `before field <form field name>` causes INFORMIX-4GL to execute the statements in this clause as the cursor enters `<form field name>` and before allowing the user to input data on the field.
- `after field <form field name>` causes INFORMIX-4GL to execute the statements in this clause as the cursor is about to leave `<form field name>`.
- `after input` causes INFORMIX-4GL to execute the statements in this clause when the user presses any of the keys that terminate input (Accept, Interrupt, or Quit) but before input is actually terminated.
- `on key ( <special key> )` causes INFORMIX-4GL to execute the statements in this clause when the user presses a `<special key>` that the system recognizes.
- `next field { next ¦ previous ¦ <form field name> }` moves the screen cursor to the appropriate selection.
- `continue input` skips all statements in the current control block.
- `exit input` terminates input and transfers control to the statement immediately following the `end input` clause.

Here is an example of the `input` statement:

```
input p_employers without default from s_employers.* attribute(red)
before input
    if p_employers.empl_code is null
    then
        message "Beginning Input of a New Employer"
    else
        message "Altering Employer definition"
    end if
after input
    call validate_input() returning error_flag, field_name
    if error_flag
    then
        next field field_name
    end if
end input
```

More examples of the `input` statement are found in Listings 36.8 and 36.9, which illustrate the `after field` and `before field` clauses. Examples are also found in Chapters 37 and 38.

Although the sample code uses separate functions to add and update records so that the `input` statement can be illustrated in two of its forms, normally only one module would be designed to manage both add and update tasks with the same code. The Delete menu choice allows the user to remove the current record from the database after the user is asked to reconfirm the delete choice.

The contents of the `add.4gl` file appear in Listing 36.8. The contents of the `update.4gl` file appear in Listing 36.9. The `delete.4gl` file is contained in Listing 36.10. Please spend some time looking over the code in these three listings.

Listing 36.8. The add.4gl file.

```
globals "globals.4gl"

##################################################################
function add_it()
##################################################################
# input row, validate and store
##################################################################

#- clear all fields in the form and initialize the variables
#- to input

    clear form
    let int_flag = false
    initialize p_employers.* to null

#- replace the menu with directives for the input

    display "" at 1,1
    display "" at 2,1
    display "Add a New Employer ..." at 1,1 attribute(green)
    display "Press Accept Key to Search, Cancel Key to Interrupt"
            at 2,1 attribute(yellow)

#- input the values for the employer, i.e., take keyboard input and
#- store it in memory in record variable p_employers

    input by name p_employers.*

#- perform tasks before the user is allowed to input a value in a
#- screen field

        before field add_line2

            if p_employers.add_line1 is null
            then
                next field next
                continue input                -- this statement was
                                        -- redundant but was
                                        -- included for
```

continues

Listing 36.8. continued

```
                                                -- illustration
            end if

#- perform validations after the user has input a value in a
#- screen field

        after field state

            call valid_state(p_employers.state) returning is_valid

            if not is_valid
            then
                error " Not a valid State code; try again "
                next field state
            end if

    end input

#- for this example, ignore multiuser issues and transaction
#- management issues

#- input has terminated: if the user interrupted, tell the user,
#- otherwise insert the employers record and tell the user whether
#- the insert worked and, if it did, retrieve and display the
#- serial value assigned by the engine

    if int_flag
    then
        let int_flag = false
        error " Insert interrupted at user request "
    else
        let p_employers.empl_code = 0        -- Serial value: if set to
                                             -- zero, engine will assign
        insert into employers values (p_employers.*)
        if status = 0
        then
            let p_employers.empl_code = SQLCA.sqlerrd[2]
            display by name p_employers.empl_code
            message "Employer added"
        else
            error " Could not insert employer; status ", status, " "
        end if
    end if

    return

end function
```

Listing 36.9. The update.4gl file.

```
globals "globals.4gl"

###################################################################
function update_it()
```

```
#################################################################
# update row, validate and store
#################################################################

    define p_old_employers record like employers.*

#- before updating a record, make sure one is already selected

    if p_employers.empl_code is null
    then
        error " Must find first "
        return
    end if

#- set the record variable p_old_employers to the current value of
#- p_employers; if the user cancels out, you will be able to reset
#- the old values to the screen

    let p_old_employers.* = p_employers.*
    let int_flag = false

#- replace the menu with directives for the input

    display "" at 1,1
    display "" at 2,1
    display "Update Employer ..." at 1,1 attribute(green)
    display "Press Accept Key to Search, Cancel Key to Interrupt"
            at 2,1 attribute(yellow)

#- input the values for the employer, i.e., take keyboard input and
#- store it in memory in record variable p_employers

    input by name p_employers.* without defaults

#- perform validations after the user has input a value in a
#- screen field

        after field state

            call valid_state(p_employers.state) returning is_valid

            if not is_valid
            then
                error " Not a valid State code; try again "
                next field state
            end if

    end input

#- for this example, ignore multiuser issues and transaction
#- management issues

#- input has terminated: if the user interrupted, tell the user,
#- reset the values of p_employers to the original values and
#- display them to the form; otherwise update the employers record
#- and tell the user whether the update worked

    if int_flag
```

continues

Listing 36.9. continued

```
    then
        let int_flag = false
        error " Update interrupted at user request "
        let p_employers.* = p_old_employers.*
        display by name p_employers.*
    else
        update employers
        set (employers.employer, employers.add_line1,
             employers.add_line2,
             employers.city, employers.state, employers.zip,
             employers.phone, employers.trl_len,
             employers.freight, employers.area,
             employers.nbr_trks, employers.authority,
             employers.leased, employers.dac,
             employers.authorized)
        = (p_employers.employer through p_employers.authorized)
        where empl_code = p_employers.empl_code
        if status = 0
        then
            message "Employer updated"
        else
            error " Could not insert employer; status ",
                  status using "-<<<<<<<<<<", " "
        end if
    end if

    return

end function
```

Listing 36.10. The delete.4gl file.

```
globals "globals.4gl"

###################################################################
function delete_it()
###################################################################
# prompt for confirmation and then act accordingly
###################################################################

    let int_flag = false

#- test that the user selected a record to be deleted; if no
#- records are displayed on the screen, error out

    if p_employers.empl_code is null
    then
        error " Must find first "
        return
    end if

#- display a new menu to confirm the deletion

    menu "Delete?"
```

```
        command "No" "Do not delete this employer"
            message "Deletion of employer cancelled"
            exit menu
        command "Yes" "Delete this employer"
            delete from employers
            where empl_code = p_employers.empl_code
            if status = 0
            then
                message "Employer deleted" attribute(reverse)
                clear form
                initialize p_employers.* to null
            else
                error " Could not delete employer "
            end if
            exit menu
        end menu

    return

end function
```

Note that the function `delete_it()` illustrates a generic mechanism for providing the user with one more chance to change his mind before actually deleting the record from the database. This mechanism develops a submenu for a menu option.

Useful Hidden Menu Options

The menu in Listing 36.6 starts with these command lines:

```
command key ("!")
    call sh_unix()
```

The user will not see a reference to the menu option triggered by the character `!` on the menu line, but if the user presses the key `!`, the system triggers a call to the function `sh_unix()` in Listing 36.11. Listing 36.11 contains functions that are candidates for placement in a library. Many programs are likely to use the `sh_unix()` function, and you will also need to validate the `State` that a user inputs through the use of the `valid_state()` function.

Listing 36.11. The `options.4gl` file.

```
globals "globals.4gl"

##################################################################
function sh_unix()
##################################################################
# Prompt for command and execute it
##################################################################

    define unix_command char(80)

#- open UNIX prompt window and issue prompt showing a !
```

continues

Listing 36.11. continued

```
    open window w_unix at 23,2 with 1 rows, 78 columns
         attribute(border, white)
    prompt "! " for unix_command

#- no matter what the answer to the prompt, close the
#- UNIX prompt window

    close window w_unix

#- if the user issued an interrupt, reset the interrupt flag,
#- otherwise execute the command

    if int_flag
    then
        let int_flag = false
    else
        run unix_command
    end if

#- we're done, leave

    return

end function

##################################################################
function valid_state(p_state)
##################################################################

    define p_state like employers.state,
           state_count smallint

#- count the number of states that match the argument received

    select count(*) into state_count
    from states
    where state = p_state

#- for this example, we ignore errors in reading the states table
#- if the count of states returned by the query is 1, the state
#- exists and we return true, otherwise we return false to the
#- calling function

    if state_count = 1
    then
        return true
    else
        return false
    end if

end function
```

The combination of Listings 36.2 and 36.6 through 36.11 makes up the complete program to run this application. Defining the modules `main.4gl`, `add.4gl`, `update.4gl`, `delete.4gl`, and `options.4gl`, as well as the `globals` in `globals.4gl` in a Program makes INFORMIX-4GL produce an executable that allows inputs into the employers table. Listing 36.2 contains the form file that the program needs in order to operate.

Summary

This chapter has provided you with the basic concepts and constructs of the INFORMIX-4GL language. In particular, you have been introduced to the main program blocks that make up an INFORMIX-4GL application. In addition, you have learned the data types, operators, functions, and statements that can be used to create an INFORMIX-4GL program. The example developed in this chapter has illustrated the concepts covered and has provided you with the framework for building a simple INFORMIX-4GL application in which you input data into a single table in the database. The following two chapters build upon and expand the concepts covered here.

4GL Development

by José Fortuny

IN THIS CHAPTER

This chapter expands on the concept of screen forms that was introduced in Chapter 36, "4GL Coding," and introduces reports for the first time.

The Standard Components of Database Applications

Screens and reports are the two major tools that any database application developer relies upon to interact with the database. This chapter discusses the standard, most common screen types in use and the most typical report layouts. I explore some examples of screens and reports and extend the reach of both to more complex inputs and reports in the next chapter.

Screens and Screen Forms: A Primer

Forms are the basic method that a database application uses to collect and manage information. Forms are the electronic counterpart of the paper documents that your business uses to collect information. An order entry application in your computer is likely to use a form that looks like its paper equivalent in your business; a customer data entry form might look like your typical Rolodex card with more room to include other items. Successful forms are those that feel comfortable to your company's employees and, at the same time, facilitate and simplify their work. General guidelines for designing forms were outlined in Chapter 36, but your best guide in designing effective forms is to listen and pay attention to the comments that the users of your electronic documents make about how they feel.

You typically find several screen form layouts in database applications in business:

- The header-only style represents one record of one table on the screen.
- The detail-only style displays a list of many records from a table.
- The header/detail style, sometimes called master/slave, represents a one-to-many relationship, in which the screen displays one record of the header table and zero or many records for the detail table.

Samples of these types of screen forms follow.

Figure 37.1 displays an employer record from a fictitious trucking company. The design, coding, and usage of this form are discussed in the next section.

In business database applications, the header-only style of form has two main uses. The most obvious use is a data capture for information to be stored in the database; the second main use is to prompt the user for information that is required by a program but is not stored by the database. Figure 37.1 represents an example of the former; the screen was designed to collect and manage information that is stored in the employers table in the recruiters database. If a table in the database contains so much information that it doesn't fit on a single screen form, the program collects the required information by displaying various forms in sequence but still uses the header-only layout for each form. On occasion, if the database designer breaks a one-to-one relationship into two separate tables (normalization indicates that these tables should be stored in a single table, but efficiency might dictate otherwise), the screen might still collect information for both tables in one form and the program might perform separate inserts, deletes, and updates to the two tables involved.

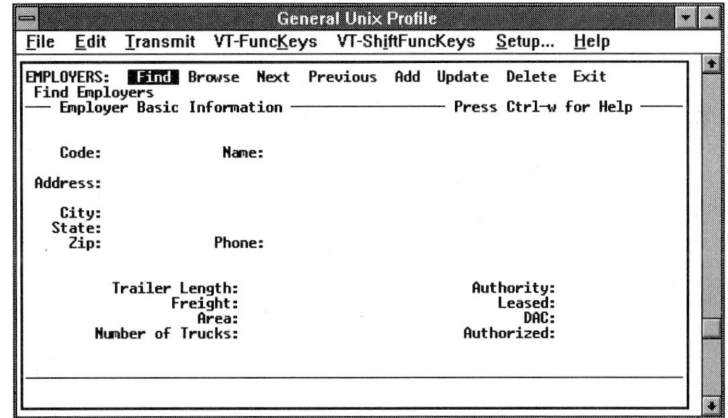

FIGURE 37.1.
Header-only screen form.

Figure 37.2 displays a list of employers from a fictitious trucking company. The design, coding, and usage of this form are introduced in the section titled "Multiple Row, Single Table Displays: Browsers and Zooms," later in this chapter.

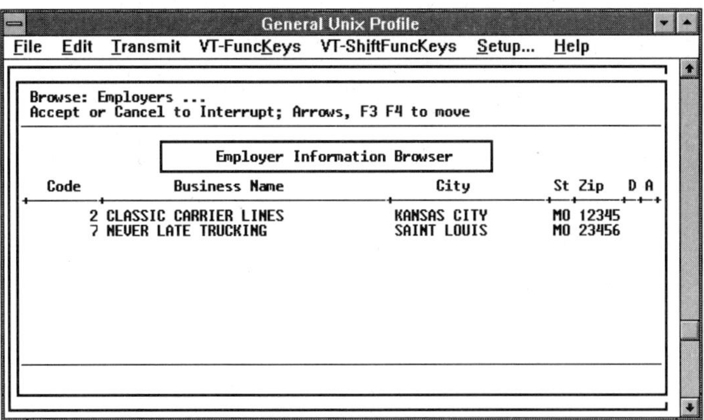

FIGURE 37.2.
Detail-only screen form.

In business database applications, the detail-only style of screen form has three main uses. The most obvious use is as a data-capture mechanism for information to be stored in the database, particularly when all the information required to fill one database record can fit in a single row of the multi-row display. The second use of this type of form is exemplified by Figure 37.2, which displays a browser for employers. A browser is a scrollable list of all or some of the columns of database tables. The third use for this type of form is to display a pop-up list of values that the user can choose. Forms that allow the user to make a selection and display the results in a list are sometimes called zoom forms. Zoom forms, which allow the user to cursor over the row desired, accept the user's selection and return some values to the calling program.

Figure 37.3 displays a driver's work history. The top portion of the form identifies the basic information for a driver and represents the "one" portion of the one-to-many relationship. The bottom portion of the form, the work history section, displays the jobs that this driver has held and represents the "many" part of the one-to-many relationship. An example of this type of input is presented in Chapter 38, "Advanced 4GL Development."

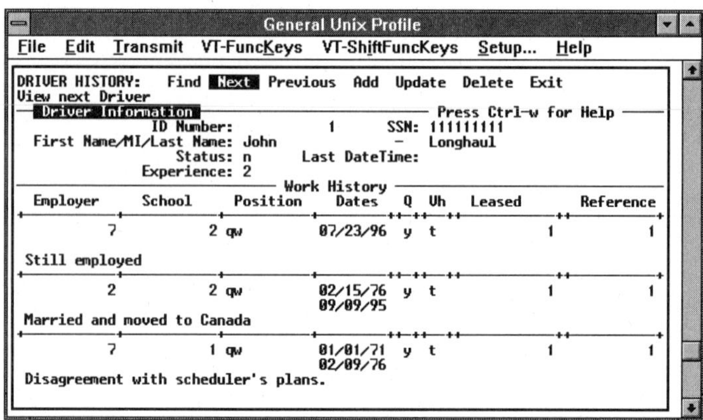

FIGURE 37.3.
Header/detail screen form.

Single Row, Single Table Management: Inputs

The contents of this section are based on the example introduced in the "Processing Inputs to a Single Table One Record at a Time" section of Chapter 36. The code presented here advances the programming effort closer toward production-caliber code, although it still doesn't meet that target. Some of the enhancements that were recommended for implementation in Chapter 36 are implemented here, and both a browse and a zoom are implemented and discussed fully in the next section. You should review the differences between the code included here and the code in the "Processing Inputs to a Single Table One Record at a Time" section of Chapter 36. After each source code module, I discuss the most salient differences between the two versions, and the comments included in the listings themselves also emphasize the contrasts.

Listing 37.1 displays the contents of the modified screen form employers.

Listing 37.1. The `employers.per` screen form.

```
DATABASE recruiters
SCREEN
{
-----------------------------------------------------------------
➥----------


    Code:[f000       ] Name:[f001                              ]

 Address:[f002                              ]
         [f003                              ]
    City:[f004              ]
   State:[a0] [sn                  ]
     Zip:[f005 ]      Phone:[f006      ]


          Trailer Length:[a1]                         Authority:[a]
                 Freight:[f007      ]                    Leased:[b]
                    Area:[f008           ]                  DAC:[c]
        Number of Trucks:[f009]                      Authorized:[d]


-----------------------------------------------------------------
➥----------
}
END
TABLES
    employers
    states
ATTRIBUTES
f000 = employers.empl_code, reverse, noentry;
f001 = employers.employer, required, upshift,
       comments = "Enter the Employer Business Name";
f002 = employers.add_line1,
       comments = "Enter the First Line of the Address";
f003 = employers.add_line2,
       comments = "Enter the Second Line of the Address";
f004 = employers.city, upshift, required,
       comments = "Enter the City for this Address";
a0 = employers.state, required, upshift,
     comments = "Enter the State for this Address";
sn = formonly.state_name type like states.state_name, noentry,
     color = cyan;
f005 = employers.zip, required, picture = "#####",
       comments = "Enter the Zip Code for this Address";
f006 = employers.phone;
a1 = employers.trl_len;
f007 = employers.freight;
f008 = employers.area;
f009 = employers.nbr_trks;
a = employers.authority;
b = employers.leased;
c = employers.dac;
d = employers.authorized;
END
INSTRUCTIONS
```

continues

Listing 37.1. continued

```
  delimiters " "
  screen record s_employers(employers.empl_code,
                            employers.employer,
                            employers.add_line1,
                            employers.add_line2,
                            employers.city,
                            employers.state,
                            employers.zip,
                            employers.phone,
                            employers.trl_len,
                            employers.freight,
                            employers.area,
                            employers.nbr_trks,
                            employers.authority,
                            employers.leased,
                            employers.dac,
                            employers.authorized)
  screen record s_other(formonly.state_name)
END
```

The layout of the screen form is somewhat different from what it was in the "Screen File Coding" section of Chapter 36. The main difference between the two instances of this form design is the inclusion, in this form, of a `formonly` field `state_name` that displays the name of the state selected by the user for the employer's address. This `formonly` field was included in a new screen record `s_other`, which collects all such display-only fields.

The contents of `globals.4gl` are displayed in Listing 37.2.

Listing 37.2. The `globals.4gl` source code module file.

```
database recruiters

###################################################################
globals
###################################################################

define p_employers record like employers.*,
       p_old_employers record like employers.*,
       p_display record
           state_name like states.state_name
       end record,
       p_old_display record
           state_name like states.state_name
       end record,
       is_valid smallint,
       where_clause char(512),
       sql_stmt char(1024),
       error_msg char(70),
       u_employer smallint,
       go_to_field, p_dbname char(18),
       curr_row, total_rows integer

end globals
```

In this version of `globals.4gl`, a number of program variables that were local to functions are now global. I included `p_old` versions of the program variables used for input fields and display fields. The `where_clause` and `sql_stmt` variables can be shared between different functions, particularly between `find.4gl` and `browse.4gl`, and the remainder of the globals were incorporated to provide some added functionality.

Listing 37.3 provides the contents of `main.4gl`.

Listing 37.3. The `main.4gl` source code module file.

```
globals "globals.4gl"

#################################################################
main
#################################################################

#- define local variables

    define ret_code char(10)

#- set run options

    defer interrupt
    options input wrap,
            input attribute (red),
            display attribute(red),
            sql interrupt on,
            field order unconstrained,
            message line last,
            prompt line last

#- capture errors to file errlog in current directory

    call startlog("errlog")

#- open the main window

    open window w_top at 2,2 with 22 rows, 77 columns
         attribute(border)

#- verify database to use on this run: get the command line
#- parameter that follows -d; if provided, close the database
#- and open the new database

    call get_arg_pair("-d") returning p_dbname
    if p_dbname is null
    then
        let p_dbname = "recruiters"
        let error_msg = "No database selected; using recruiters"
        call error_display (error_msg)
    else
        close database
        database p_dbname
        if status <> 0
        then
```

continues

Listing 37.3. continued

```
            exit program
        end if
    end if

#- initialize global variables

    call init_vars()

#- open and display employer form

    open form f_employers from "employer"
    display form f_employers
    display " Employer Basic Information " at 3,4 attribute(red)

#- display the menu and wait for user action

    menu "EMPLOYERS"
        command key ("!")
            call sh_unix()
        command "Find" " Find Employers"
            call find_it()
            if p_employers.empl_code is not null
            then
                next option "Next"
            else
                next option "Find"
            end if
        command "Browse" " Display Employers in a Browse List"
            call browse()
        command "Next" " View next Employer"
            call next_row() returning ret_code
            case
            when ret_code = "last"
                next option "Previous"
            when ret_code = "findfirst"
                next option "Find"
            end case
        command "Previous" " View previous Employer"
            call previous_row() returning ret_code
            case
            when ret_code = "first"
                next option "Next"
            when ret_code = "findfirst"
                next option "Find"
            end case
        command "Add" " Add Employers"
            call add_it("A") returning ret_code
            if ret_code = "accept"
            then
                call insert_them("A")
            end if
        command "Update" " Update Employers"
            call add_it("U") returning ret_code
            if ret_code = "findfirst"
            then
                next option "Find"
            end if
```

```
            if ret_code = "accept"
            then
                call insert_them("U")
            end if
        command "Delete" " Delete Employers"
            call delete_it() returning ret_code
            if ret_code = "deleted"
            then
                next option "Find"
            end if
        command key(Q,E,X) "Exit" " Exit the menu and the Program"
            exit menu
    end menu

#- clean up and leave

    close form f_employers
    close window w_top
    exit program

end main

##################################################################
function init_vars()
##################################################################

    initialize p_employers.* to null
    initialize p_old_employers.* to null
    initialize p_display.* to null
    let is_valid = false
    initialize where_clause to null
    initialize sql_stmt to null
    initialize error_msg to null
    let u_employer = false
    initialize p_dbname to null
    initialize go_to_field to null
    let curr_row = 0
    let total_rows = 0

end function
```


The first difference between the `main.4gl` here and the one in Chapter 36 is the introduction of a call to the function `get_arg_pair` to allow the code to receive the database name as an argument through the command line and to use the default database recruiters if it's omitted. The function `get_arg_pair`, an obvious candidate for the system library, is included in the `options.4gl` source code module file, displayed later in this section. The next major change is provided by the menu, which is responsive to the return codes of the functions that the menu options call. For example, navigating with the Next and Previous menu commands detects whether you invoked the command without a selection and, if so, places the highlight on the Find command option. If the user reaches the end of the list, the code switches the next option appropriately. Lastly, note that the Add and Update options invoke the same function `add_it`, and the input and database interactions are separated. `add_it` deals with the screen input and `insert_them` handles the database interaction.

The add.4gl source code module file is displayed in Listing 37.4.

Listing 37.4. The add.4gl source code module file.

```
globals "globals.4gl"

#####################################################################
function add_it(p_mode)
#####################################################################
# input row, validate and store
#####################################################################

#- define local variables

    define p_mode char(1),
           ret_code char(10)

    let int_flag = false
    let u_employer = false

#- before updating a record, make sure one is already selected

    if p_mode = "U" and p_employers.empl_code is null
    then
        let error_msg = " Must find first "
        call error_display(error_msg)
        return "findfirst"
    end if

#- prepare the p_old_employers record and replace menu
#- with directives for input

    display "" at 1,1
    display "" at 2,1
    display "--------------------" at 21, 60 attribute(white)

case

#- when adding a new employer record

when p_mode = "A"

#- clear all fields in the form and initialize the variables
#- in the input clause (or on display) to null

    clear form
    initialize p_employers.* to null
    initialize p_old_employers.* to null
    initialize p_old_display.* to null
    display "Add a New Employer ..." at 1,1 attribute(green)

#- when updating the current employer record

when p_mode = "U"

#- set the p_old variables to the current values of the p_
#- variables.
```

```
#- If the user interrupts, we'll restore the p_old values

    let p_old_employers.* = p_employers.*
    let p_old_display.* = p_display.*
    display "Updating Employer ..." at 1,1 attribute(green)
end case

display "Press Accept Key to Search, Cancel Key to Interrupt"
        at 2,1 attribute(yellow)


#- input the values for the employer, i.e., take keyboard input and
#- store it in memory in record variable p_employers; the without
#- defaults clause preserves the p_employers current values

    input by name p_employers.* without defaults attribute(red)

#- perform validations after the user has input a value in a
#- screen field

        before field state
            display "(Zoom)" at 3,66 attribute(red)

        on key (control-z)
            case
                when infield (state)
                    call zoom ("state")
                otherwise
                    error "No zoom available for this field"
            end case

        after field state
            display "------" at 3,66 attribute(white)
            call valid_state(p_employers.state)
                 returning is_valid, p_display.state_name
            if not is_valid
            then
                let error_msg = "Not a valid State code; try again"
                call error_display(error_msg)
                next field state
            else
                display by name p_display.state_name
            end if

        on key (accept)

            display "------" at 3,66 attribute(white)
            call check_employers(p_mode)
                 returning is_valid, go_to_field
            if is_valid
            then
                let ret_code = "accept"
                let u_employer = true
                exit input
            else
                case
                    when go_to_field = "employer"
                        next field employer
```

continues

Listing 37.4. continued

```
                    when go_to_field = "add_line1"
                        next field add_line1
                    when go_to_field = "city"
                        next field city
                end case
            end if

        on key (interrupt)

            display "------" at 3,66 attribute(white)
            let ret_code = "interrupt"
            let u_employer = false
            exit input

    end input

#- for this example, ignore multiuser issues and transaction
#- management issues

#- input has terminated: if the user interrupted, tell the user,
#- otherwise insert the employers record and tell the user whether
#- the insert worked and, if it did, retrieve and display the
#- serial value assigned by the engine

    if int_flag
    then
        let int_flag = false
        let error_msg = " Insert interrupted at user request "
        call error_display(error_msg)
        let p_employers.* = p_old_employers.*
        display by name p_employers.*
        let p_display.* = p_old_display.*
        display by name p_display.*
    else
        let u_employer = true
    end if

    return ret_code

end function

###################################################################
function insert_them(p_mode)
###################################################################

#- define local variables

    define p_mode char(1),
           ret_code char(10)

    let int_flag = false

    if u_employer
    then
        case
        when p_mode = "A"
            let p_employers.empl_code = 0
```

```
            insert into employers values (p_employers.*)
            if status = 0
            then
                let p_employers.empl_code = sqlca.sqlerrd[2]
                display by name p_employers.empl_code
                message "Employer added"
            else
                let error_msg =
                    " Could not insert employer; status ",
                    status using "-<<<<<<<<<<"
                call error_display(error_msg)
            end if
        when p_mode = "U"
            update employers
            set (employer, add_line1, add_line2, city, state, zip,
                 phone, trl_len, freight, area, nbr_trks,
                 authority, leased, dac, authorized)
            = (p_employers.employer thru p_employers.authorized)
            where empl_code = p_employers.empl_code
            if status = 0
            then
                message "Employer updated"
            else
                let error_msg =
                    " Could not update employer; status ",
                    status using "-<<<<<<<<<<"
                call error_display(error_msg)
            end if
        otherwise
            let error_msg = " Mode ", p_mode, " is invalid; ",
                    "no action taken"
            call error_display(error_msg)
        end case
    end if

    return

end function

###################################################################
function check_employers(p_mode)
###################################################################
define p_mode char(1)

#- This is the place to make final validations before the input
#- statement block ends and the data input by the user is accepted
#- as good enough to be stored.

#- The following are just a sample of validations that you might
#- include here.  Generally, you would perform single field
#- validations in an after field clause, more than here (though
#- these are the examples included).  After inputting all records
#- validations tend to evaluate the overall information in the
#- screen form and the relationship between different field
#- values (data consistency).

if p_employers.employer is null or p_employers.employer = " "
then
```

continues

Listing 37.4. continued

```
    return false, "employer"
end if

if p_employers.add_line1 is null or p_employers.add_line1 = " "
then
    return false, "add_line1"
end if

if p_employers.city is null or p_employers.city = " "
then
    return false, "city"
end if

return true, ""

end function
```

Note that the add_it function receives a flag, p_mode, that determines whether this call deals with a new record or an existing one and acts accordingly when initializing program variables and displaying the directives for input. Note also that the input statement uses the clause without defaults, which tells the system not to initialize the input variables with the default values defined in the form. In the input statement block, notice the processing around the state field: The before field clause displays the string "(Zoom)" on the line that separates the input directives from the form itself. This is to indicate to the user that there is a pop-up window that he can invoke from the state field. The on key (control-z) statement block actually manages the pop-up calls that are possible in this application. If the user presses Ctrl+Z while the cursor is in the state field (infield), then the flow of control jumps to the function zoom, which invokes the right pop-up window. The after field clause, as well as the on key (accept) and on key (interrupt) clauses, cover the string "(Zoom)" on the screen. Note that the function add_it only sets the flag u_employer upon exit: It is set to true if the user exits input wishing to update the employer record and false if the user exits input with an interrupt. Notice that an interrupt causes the system to restore the p_ variables to the values they had before the user changed them: p_old_.

The function insert_them also responds to the flag p_mode it receives that indicates whether this is a new record or an update of an existing record.

The function check_employers was included more as a concept than as actual working code. When the user presses the Accept key during input, this function is called to verify and validate the fields the user input. Actually, the software performs validations field-by-field as the user inputs information, but this is the last opportunity to evaluate the consistency of the relationships of fields to one another before accepting the data for storage. You can place this type of validation in the after input statement block if the on key (accept) statement block is not used.

Note that this version of the software does not contain an `update.4gl` source code module file because this work was included in the `add.4gl` file. This makes maintenance of the code easier because there is only one place where you have to contend with the input and update of the data (only one `input` statement).

The code for the `find.4gl` source code module appears in Listing 37.5.

Listing 37.5. The `find.4gl` source code module file.

```
globals "globals.4gl"

####################################################################
function prep_cursor()
####################################################################

#- prepare the SQL statement for execution, declare a cursor that
#- will represent the active set of rows returned by the engine
#- and activate the cursor by opening it

    prepare statement_1 from sql_stmt
    declare c_employers scroll cursor with hold for statement_1
    open c_employers

end function

####################################################################
function count_them()
####################################################################

    define sql_count char(512)

    let sql_count = "select count(*) from employers where ",
                    where_clause clipped
    prepare statement_count from sql_count
    declare c_count cursor for statement_count
    open c_count
    fetch c_count into total_rows
    close c_count
    free c_count

    return

end function

####################################################################
function find_it()
####################################################################
# Gather search criteria, find the first employer and display it
####################################################################

#- clear form on the screen and initialize variables

    clear form
    let int_flag = false
    let curr_row = 0
    let total_rows = 0
```

continues

Listing 37.5. continued

```
    initialize p_employers.* to null
    display "--------------------" at 21,60 attribute(white)

#- replace menu with instructions for query-by-example

    display "" at 1,1
    display "" at 2,1
    display "Enter the Search Criteria for Selection ..." at 1,1
            attribute(green)
    display "Press Accept Key to Search, Cancel Key to Interrupt"
            at 2,1 attribute(yellow)

#- construct the query statement dynamically: the where_clause
#- variable will contain the query string based on the criteria
#- for selection that the user inputs

    construct by name where_clause on employers.*

#- if the user interrupted, cancel the query request and return to
#- the calling program after advising the user

    if int_flag
    then
        message " Search Cancelled at User Request "
        let int_flag = false
        return
    end if

#- proceed with the query: replace query-by-example instructions
#- by flashing message indicating search for records is proceeding

    display "" at 1,1
    display "" at 2,1
    display "Searching ..." at 1,1 attribute(green, blink)

#- construct the complete SQL statement to query the database:
#- include the select clause, the from clause, the dynamically
#- created where clause and order by clause.  Concatenate
#- those clauses into the program variable sql_stmt

    let sql_stmt = "select * from employers where ",
                   where_clause clipped, " ",
                   "order by empl_code"

#- count the records that match the query and prepare the cursor
#- and open it (this is now done in prep_cursor())

    call count_them()
    call prep_cursor()

#- if the open has succeeded, retrieve the first row in the active
#- data set, place it in the program variable p_employers and
#- display this variable; otherwise handle the failure with an
#- error message that is descriptive of the type of failure

    if status = 0
    then
```

```
        fetch first c_employers into p_employers.*
        if status = 0
        then
            let curr_row = 1
            display by name p_employers.*
            call valid_state(p_employers.state)
                 returning is_valid, p_display.state_name
            display by name p_display.*
            call records (21,60, curr_row, total_rows)
        else
            if status = notfound
            then
                clear form
                message "No employers satisfy search criteria"
            else
                let error_msg = " Could not get employers ",
                    "information; ",
                    "status ", status using "-<<<<<<<<<<"
                call error_display(error_msg)
            end if
        end if
    else
        let error_msg = " Could not access employers ",
            "information; ",
            "status ", status using "-<<<<<<<<<<"
        call error_display(error_msg)
    end if

end function


###################################################################
function next_row()
###################################################################
# fetch and display the next row
###################################################################

#- to display the next row, one must already be displayed

    if p_employers.empl_code is null
    then
        let error_msg = " Must find first "
        call error_display(error_msg)
        return "findfirst"
    end if

#- retrieve the next row in the active set, place it in the program
#- variable p_employers and display this variable; otherwise handle
#- the failure with an error message that is descriptive of the
#- type of failure

    fetch next c_employers into p_employers.*
    if status = 0
    then
        let curr_row = curr_row + 1
        display by name p_employers.*
        call valid_state(p_employers.state)
             returning is_valid, p_display.state_name
```

continues

Listing 37.5. continued

```
        display by name p_display.*
        call records (21,60, curr_row, total_rows)
        return "found"
    else
        if status = notfound
        then
            message "Reached the end of the list"
            return "last"
        else
            let error_msg = " Could not retrieve next employer; ",
                "status ", status using "-<<<<<<<<<<"
            call error_display(error_msg)
            return "error"
        end if
    end if

    return "ok"

end function

###################################################################
function previous_row()
###################################################################
# fetch and display the previous row
###################################################################

#- to display the previous row, one must already be displayed

    if p_employers.empl_code is null
    then
        let error_msg = " Must find first "
        call error_display(error_msg)
        return "findfirst"
    end if

#- retrieve the previous row in the active set, place it in the
#- program variable p_employers and display this variable;
#- otherwise handle the failure with an error message that is
#- descriptive of the type of failure

    fetch previous c_employers into p_employers.*
    if status = 0
    then
        let curr_row = curr_row - 1
        display by name p_employers.*
        call valid_state(p_employers.state)
             returning is_valid, p_display.state_name
        display by name p_display.*
        call records (21,60, curr_row, total_rows)
        return "found"
    else
        if status = notfound
        then
            message "At the beginning of the list"
            return "first"
        else
            let error_msg = " Could not retrieve previous ",
```

```
                "employer; ",
                "status ", status using "-<<<<<<<<<<"
            call error_display(error_msg)
            return "error"
        end if
    end if

    return "ok"

end function
```


A number of changes were made between this version of the software and the version in Chapter 36. First, the preparation of the cursor was encapsulated in the function `prep_cursor`. Following the same logic, you could, and should, encapsulate the user's query by example and separate it from the process of retrieving records from the database. This is left as an exercise. If you look at function `prep_cursor`, you notice that if you call the cursor by a generic name, rather than `c_employers`, you can utilize this code unchanged in any program that requires preparing, declaring, and opening a cursor (just about any database program you can imagine).

This version of the code is also designed to provide the user with a running tally of the records the query returned and the position of the record displayed on the screen with regard to the list returned. The function `count_them` uses the `where_clause` that the user defined with query by example to actually count the records returned by the query that retrieves the data. Now you see the reason for making the program variables associated with the query global, although you see an alternative to this definition of scope later in this section. The function `records` actually displays the current record count and the total count of records on the screen. This function is actually defined in the `options.4gl` source code module file because it is yet another candidate for a library. Note that the function `records` was defined with four arguments: the row and column to display the information, the current row's relative position in the list, and the total row counts, which allows you to place this information anywhere on the current window.

Note that the other functions in `find.4gl`—`next_row` and `previous_row`—must be modified in the same manner.

The `delete.4gl` source code module appears in Listing 37.6.

Listing 37.6. The `delete.4gl` source code module file.

```
globals "globals.4gl"

#################################################################
function delete_it()
#################################################################
# prompt for confirmation and then act accordingly
#################################################################

#- define local variables
```

continues

Listing 37.6. continued

```
    define del_flag char(10)

    let int_flag = false

#- test that the user selected a record to be deleted; if no
#- records are displayed on the screen, error out

    if p_employers.empl_code is null
    then
        let error_msg = " Must find first "
        call error_display(error_msg)
        return "findfirst"
    end if

#- display a new menu to confirm the deletion

    menu "Delete?"
        command "No" "Do not delete this employer"
            message "Deletion of employer cancelled"
            let del_flag = "interrupt"
            exit menu
        command "Yes" "Delete this employer"
            delete from employers
            where empl_code = p_employers.empl_code
            if status = 0
            then
                message "Employer deleted" attribute(reverse)
                clear form
                initialize p_employers.* to null
                initialize p_display.* to null
                display "-------------------"
                        at 21, 60 attribute(white)
                let del_flag = "deleted"
            else
                let error_msg = " Could not delete employer; ",
                                "status ", status
                                using "-<<<<<<<<<"
                call error_display(error_msg)
                let del_flag = "problem"
            end if
            exit menu
        end menu

    if int_flag
    then
        let int_flag = false
        return "interrupt"
    else
        return del_flag
    end if

end function
```

This code differs from that in Chapter 36 in the use of the return code. It is used only to place the highlight in the Find menu option within `main.4gl` but could also be used to automatically re-create the list of currently active records. In this source code module file, like in all the others in this version of the software, I replaced the `error` statement of INFORMIX-4GL with my own method for displaying errors through the use of the function `error_display`, described later in `options.4gl`.

The source code module file `options.4gl` is shown in Listing 37.7.

Listing 37.7. The `options.4gl` source code module file.

```
globals "globals.4gl"

####################################################################
function sh_unix()
####################################################################
# Prompt for command and execute it
####################################################################

    define unix_command char(80)

#- open UNIX prompt window and issue prompt showing a !

    open window w_unix at 23,2 with 1 rows, 78 columns
         attribute(border, white)
    prompt "! " for unix_command

#- no matter what the answer to the prompt, close the
#- UNIX prompt window

    close window w_unix

#- if the user issued an interrupt, reset the interrupt flag,
#- otherwise execute the command

    if int_flag
    then
        let int_flag = false
    else
        run unix_command
    end if

#- we're done, leave

    return

end function

####################################################################
function valid_state(p_state)
####################################################################

    define p_states record like states.*,
           p_state like employers.state
```

continues

Listing 37.7. continued

```
#- find the state that matches the argument received

    declare c_states cursor for
    select * into p_states.*
    from states
    where state = p_state

    open c_states
    fetch c_states

#- for this example, we ignore errors in reading the states table

    if status = 0
    then
        return true, p_states.state_name
    else
        return false, ""
    end if

end function

##################################################################
function records(p_row, p_column, this_row, total_rows)
##################################################################
define this_row, total_rows integer,
       i, p_length, p_row, p_column smallint,
       p_string char(20)

#- build the displayable information into p_string

     let p_string = "(", this_row using "<<<<<<<<<<", " of ",
                    total_rows using "<<<<<<<<<<", ")"

#- stuff the remaining characters up to 20 with dashes

     let p_length = length(p_string) + 1
     for i = p_length to 20
         let p_string = p_string clipped, "-"
     end for

#- display the 20 character string in row p_row, column p_column

    display p_string at p_row, p_column attribute(white)

    return

end function

##################################################################
function get_arg_pair(arg)
##################################################################

#- this function parses the command line in search of argument
#- 'arg' and, when found, returns the argument following it;
#- otherwise, it returns a null argument

    define
```

```
        arg char(20),
        arg_value char(512),
        n smallint,
        number_of_args smallint
#
    let arg_value = null
    let number_of_args = num_args() - 1
#
    for n = 1 to number_of_args
        if arg_val(n) = arg
        then
            let arg_value = arg_val(n + 1)
            exit for
        end if
    end for
    return arg_value

end function

##################################################################
function error_display(err_msg)
##################################################################

    define err_msg char(70), answer char(1)

    open window win_err at 22,3 with 2 rows, 76 columns
                        attribute(border,white)

        display "Error: " at 1,2 attribute(red)
        let err_msg = " ", err_msg clipped, " ", ascii 7
        display err_msg at 1,10 attribute(reverse)

        prompt " Press [ENTER] to Continue: " for char answer

    close window win_err

 return

end function
```

I placed in `options.4gl` all the functions that are candidates for inclusion in a library. Although the file contains a `globals` declaration, it is only there to bind the database to the program variables in the function `valid_states`, and it could be replaced by the `database recruiters` statement. All other functions included in `options.4gl` do not require database binding. Pay special attention to the function `get_arg_pair` for the use of the `num_args` and `arg_val` functions, which are part of the INFORMIX-4GL set that allows your program to receive parameters or arguments from the command line.

The program requires two more source code module files, `browse.4gl` and `zoom.4gl`, but these illustrate new concepts that I introduce in the next section, so they are listed there.

Multiple Row, Single Table Displays: Browsers and Zooms

Many times, you need to display information retrieved from the database in the form of a list that displays many rows at the same time, and you need to provide the user with the capability to scroll through the list and perhaps select one row from the list to drop its information back in the calling function. Zooms and browsers perform these functions.

A zoom is a window containing a form that allows the user to perform a query by example, scroll through the list of retrieved rows, select one row to return the key value (and perhaps other columns) to the calling program, and drop that information in the program variable that matches the screen field where the user opened the zoom screen. A browser is a window containing a form that allows the user to scroll through the list of rows that satisfy the query that selected the records to retrieve in the main (top) window of the application.

The first step in developing a browser or a zoom is to build the form that displays the rows. Basically, the process is the same as that for developing the form to display a single row from a table, but you need to develop a screen record array to reflect the number of rows that are displayed in a screen of data. The two newly introduced forms now follow: Listing 37.8 contains `browser.per` and Listing 37.9 displays `z_state.per`.

Listing 37.8. The `browser.per` form source file.

```
DATABASE recruiters
SCREEN
{
-------------------------------------------------------------------
➥----------
                \gp-------------------------------------q\g
                \g¦\g      Employer Information Browser     \g¦\g
                \gb-------------------------------------d\g
   Code           Business Name                     City          St
➥ Zip   D A
+---------+--------------------------------+------------------+--+
➥----+-+-+
[f000     ¦f001                             ¦f004              ¦a0¦
➥f005 ¦c¦d]
[f000     ¦f001                             ¦f004              ¦a0¦
➥f005 ¦c¦d]
[f000     ¦f001                             ¦f004              ¦a0¦
➥f005 ¦c¦d]
[f000     ¦f001                             ¦f004              ¦a0¦
➥f005 ¦c¦d]
[f000     ¦f001                             ¦f004              ¦a0¦
➥f005 ¦c¦d]
[f000     ¦f001                             ¦f004              ¦a0¦
➥f005 ¦c¦d]
[f000     ¦f001                             ¦f004              ¦a0¦
➥f005 ¦c¦d]
[f000     ¦f001                             ¦f004              ¦a0¦
➥f005 ¦c¦d]
[f000     ¦f001                             ¦f004              ¦a0¦
➥f005 ¦c¦d]
```

```
[f000    |f001                                  |f004             |a0|
➥f005 |c|d]
-----------------------------------------------------------------------
➥----------
}
END
TABLES
    employers
ATTRIBUTES
f000 = employers.empl_code;
f001 = employers.employer;
f004 = employers.city;
a0 = employers.state;
f005 = employers.zip;
c = employers.dac;
d = employers.authorized;
END
INSTRUCTIONS
  delimiters " "
  screen record s_browse[10](employers.empl_code,
                             employers.employer,
                             employers.city,
                             employers.state,
                             employers.zip,
                             employers.dac,
                             employers.authorized)
END
```


Here are two important items to note:

- When you design a screen, the square brackets ([ ]) represent the boundaries that contain screen fields. When you display the information within the application, each square bracket takes one space on the screen. If screen space is at a premium, you can use the pipe symbol (|) to delimit adjacent screen fields (it replaces the closing bracket from the first screen field and the opening bracket from the second screen field), thus leaving only one space to separate screen fields.
- To display (or input information) from a multi-record form, you need to define a screen record array that differs from the screen records introduced earlier only in the designation of how many records are to be displayed on the screen following the screen record name.

Otherwise, screens for browsers and zooms can use the same features discussed in Chapter 36 for all screens.

Listing 37.9. The `z_state.per` form source file.

```
DATABASE recruiters
```

```
SCREEN
{
---------------------------------------
```

continues

Listing 37.9. continued

```
          \gp-----------q\g
          \g¦\g    States   \g¦\g
          \gb-----------d\g
      Id.          State
-----+---+---+--------------------+-----
     [a0 ]   [f000                ]
     [a0 ]   [f000                ]
     [a0 ]   [f000                ]
     [a0 ]   [f000                ]
     [a0 ]   [f000                ]
     [a0 ]   [f000                ]
     [a0 ]   [f000                ]
     [a0 ]   [f000                ]
     [a0 ]   [f000                ]
     [a0 ]   [f000                ]
----------------------------------------
}
END

TABLES
states

ATTRIBUTES
a0 = states.state, upshift;
f000 = states.state_name;

INSTRUCTIONS
  delimiters "  "
  screen record s_states[10] (states.state, states.state_name)
END
```

To process the browse display, you only need to add another menu option for this purpose (see Listing 37.3) and collect and display the browse information into the screen array defined in the form.

Before you display the code that you developed for processing the browser, I introduce the `display array` statement and the `foreach` loops that the code uses to display the array and retrieve the data from the database.

NOTE

To distinguish options and arguments that are required in a command line or in a statement from those that are optional, I have enclosed the optional arguments in square brackets (`[]`), and the required arguments are not enclosed in brackets. I use curly brackets (`{}`) to denote a grouping of items, and I use pointed brackets (<>) to illustrate that the contents are to be filled in as appropriate.

To display the data placed in program array variables to the form on the screen, you use the `display array` statement as follows:

```
display array <array name> to <screen array>.*
 [ attribute ( <attribute> [ , ... ] ) ]
    { [ on key (key) [ , ... ]
            <4GL statements>
             exit display
      end display }
```

The options in this statement are

<array name> is the name of a program array.

<screen array> is the name of a screen array defined in the form that displays the information.

`(key)` is one of the special keys that INFORMIX-4GL can recognize.

Listing 37.10 contains an example of the use of the `display array` in the code for the `browse.4gl` source code module. An additional example appears in Listing 37.11.

To retrieve records sequentially from the database, an alternative to the `open`, `fetch`, and `close` approach, discussed in various places earlier, you can use the `foreach` statement block, which performs those functions on your behalf. Its syntax is

```
foreach <cursor name> [ into <program var> [ , ... ] ]
    {  <4GL statements> ¦
       continue foreach ¦
       exit foreach }
end foreach
```

The options in this statement are

<cursor name> is the name of a cursor that is declared in the program.

<program var> is a list of program variables or arrays that receive the information retrieved.

`continue foreach` skips execution of the statements following in the `foreach` statement block and proceeds to retrieve the next record.

`exit foreach` sends control of the program to the statement just following the `end foreach` clause.

`end foreach` delimits the `foreach` statement block.

Listing 37.10 contains an example of the use of the `foreach` statement in the code for the `browse.4gl` source code module. Additional examples appear in Listing 37.11.

After reviewing the component parts that you use in managing this display, review the overall programming logic for this process. For now, you only display information to a screen array.

This information is stored in memory in a program array. The process of loading the array and displaying it is as follows:

1. Open the browse window with the appropriate browse form.
2. Display information on how to navigate through the window or a navigation menu. (This is particularly useful if the array is large and you provide a method for jumping to a certain row.)
3. Load the program array with data from the tables using a cursor and some form of looping (probably a `foreach` loop because this operation is sequential in nature).
4. Set the array count.
5. Close and free the browse cursor.
6. Display the array.
7. Upon user exit, close the window.

The code for managing the browser is displayed in Listing 37.10.

Listing 37.10. The browse.4gl source code module file.

```
globals "globals.4gl"

define max_rows, row_count smallint

####################################################################
function browse()
####################################################################
# display array of employers in a list
####################################################################

define p_browse array[250] of record empl_code like employers.empl_code,
                                     employer like employers.employer,
                                     city like employers.city,
                                     state like employers.state,
                                     zip like employers.zip,
                                     dac like employers.dac,
                                     authorized like employers.authorized
       end record

if p_employers.empl_code is null
then
    let error_msg = " Must find first "
    call error_display (error_msg)
    return
end if

let max_rows = 250

#- open window with form and display guidelines for use

open window w_browse at 3,3 with form "browse" attribute(border, white)
display " Browse: Employers ... " at 1,1 attribute(red)
display " Accept or Cancel to Interrupt; Arrows, F3 F4 to move "
```

```
        at 2,1 attribute(yellow)

#- create a browse cursor to select the columns that fit in the
#- browse form

    let sql_stmt = "select empl_code, employer, city, state, zip, ",
                   "dac, authorized ",
                   "from employers where ",
                   where_clause clipped, " ",
                   "order by employer"
    prepare query_browse from sql_stmt
    declare c_browse cursor for query_browse

#- reinstate the sql_statement for the main cursor

    let sql_stmt = "select * from employers where ",
                   where_clause clipped, " ",
                   "order by empl_code"

#- fill in the array
    let row_count = 0
    foreach c_browse into p_browse[row_count + 1].*
        let row_count = row_count + 1
        if row_count >= max_rows
        then
            error " Employer List exceeds the limits of the display "
            exit foreach
        end if
    end foreach
    call set_count(row_count)
    close c_browse
    free c_browse

#- display the array

    display array p_browse to s_browse.*
    on key (accept)
        exit display
    on key (interrupt)
        let int_flag = false
        exit display
    end display

close window w_browse
return

end function
```

After the user decides to press Ctrl+Z to open the zoom window, the zoom function determines which specific window and processing is required to deliver the information to the calling screen field. The coding for the zoom function appears in `zooms.4gl`. Note that the zoom function behaves as a switching mechanism; it receives a name and directs the flow of the program to the right function.

The processing of the zoom functionality is, in general, as follows:

1. Open the zoom window with the appropriate zoom form.
2. Display information on how to prepare the query by example.
3. Construct a query by example on the first row of the screen array (or construct by name).
4. Load the program array with data from the table using a cursor and some form of looping (probably a `foreach` loop because this operation is sequential in nature).
5. Set the array count.
6. Close and free the zoom cursor.
7. Display the array and information on how to navigate the array and how to select a row to return to the calling program the value of the appropriate key column.
8. Upon user exit, close the window.
9. Return null if the user interrupts the zoom selection of the values of the key column in the row where the cursor was when the user accepted the zoom selection.

The `zooms.4gl` file is contained in Listing 37.11.

Listing 37.11. The `zooms.4gl` source code module file.

```
globals "globals.4gl"

define sel_criteria char(512),
       sel_stmt char(1024),
       i, max_rows, row_count, row_selected smallint

###################################################################
function zoom(field_id)
###################################################################

define field_id char(18),
       p_old_state like employers.state

case
    when field_id = "state"
        let p_old_state = p_employers.state
        call z_state() returning p_employers.state
        if p_employers.state is null
        then
            let p_employers.state = p_old_state
        end if
        display by name p_employers.state

end case

return

end function

###################################################################
```

```
function z_state()
#####################################################################
# query, display and collect key pressed; return row or not
#####################################################################
define p_state array[60] of record
                state like states.state,
                state_name like states.state_name
       end record

let max_rows = 60

#- open window with form and display header

open window w_state at 3,3 with form "z_state"
     attribute(border, white)
display " Zoom: States ... " at 1,1 attribute(red)
display " Accept to Search, Cancel to Interrupt "
        at 2,1 attribute(yellow)

#- construct the query and create the cursor

construct by name sel_criteria
       on states.state, states.state_name
    on key (interrupt)
        exit construct
    end construct
    if int_flag
    then
        let int_flag = false
        let error_msg = " No Criteria Identified for Selection "
        call error_display(error_msg)
        close window w_state
        let p_state[1].state = null
        return p_state[1].state
    else
        let sel_stmt = "select state, state_name from states ",
                       "where ", sel_criteria clipped, " ",
                       "order by state"
        display "" at 1,1
        display "" at 2,1
        display "Searching ... " at 1,1 attribute(green)
    end if
    prepare query1 from sel_stmt
    declare c_state cursor for query1

#- fill in the array

    let row_count = 0
    foreach c_state into p_state[row_count + 1].*
        let row_count = row_count + 1
        if row_count >= max_rows
        then
            let error_msg = " States exceed the limits of the ",
                            "display "
            call error_display(error_msg)
            exit foreach
        end if
    end foreach
```

continues

Listing 37.11. continued

```
    call set_count(row_count)
    close c_state
    free c_state

# display the array and receive selection
    display " Zoom: States ... Arrows, F3, F4 to move"
            at 1,1 attribute(red)
    display " Accept to Select, Cancel to Interrupt "
            at 2,1 attribute(yellow)
    display array p_state to s_states.*
    on key (interrupt)
        exit display
    end display
    if int_flag
    then
        let int_flag = false
        let error_msg = " No State Selected "
        call error_display(error_msg)
        close window w_state
        let p_state[1].state = null
        return p_state[1].state
    else
        let row_selected = arr_curr()
        close window w_state
        return p_state[row_selected].state
    end if
end function
```

Note that while the `zoom` function must be local to the program at hand, the `z_state` function and corresponding form can become part of the libraries for your entire application because they are fully encapsulated. The form that displays states and the processing of the query and eventual return of a state to the calling function are common throughout the system, no matter what the calling function requires this information for. The zoom function, on the other hand, must be local to the current program because it must deal with the display of the returned value in the current program.

Also note that both the `browse.4gl` and `zooms.4gl` source code modules use `define` statements that are outside any program block, thereby making the defined variables available in scope to all the functions within the source code module file.

Reports

Whether the software needs to produce invoices or deliver information for financial analysis or sales statistics, reporting turns data into usable information. This section introduces reports and report design and develops a complete example for use either as an independent program or as another menu option for the example in the "Screens and Screen Forms: A Primer" section, earlier in this chapter. The example presented here follows the standard basic structure for a database report. The next chapter introduces more report types and layouts that deviate from the standard and require special handling.

Report Design: A Primer

Unlike screen forms, which present themselves in three major layouts, report layouts show a lot more variety. Reports in INFORMIX-4GL are a vehicle for both displaying information in some form, such as screen, paper, and electronic transfer, and for posting and batch processing data. Within the group of reports that display information, you can distill some report layouts that you commonly find in business applications:

- Sequential, one-dimensional lists of similar content report rows, with breaks provided by logical row groupings. An example of this report is an invoice that lists, line after line, the items included in the sale and provides a total section and a customer information and mailing section at the header of the report. The lines of the report can also be separated in blocks that represent items in different categories or different departments and subtotals by category or department.
- Sequential listings of blocks of dissimilar report rows and reports with multiple content sections. An example of this type of report is a sales analysis report that displays multiple views of sales for each group. An example is a report that displays, by company division, sales, inventory movements, returns and pilferage, and commissions.
- Two-dimensional, matrix-like reports. These are very common to display some activities against a timeline; the timeline is usually displayed horizontally across the report, one column for each month, while the activity, such as sales by division, is displayed vertically, with one division in each row, producing a spreadsheet-like display.

The Report Driver and the Report Formatter

A report in INFORMIX-4GL usually consists of two distinct sections:

- The report driver gathers and manipulates data required by the report and passes the organized data to the formatter.
- The report formatter (`report` program block) displays the data in the proper layout and within the proper groupings.

The report driver is a regular INFORMIX-4GL function and is stored in a separate source code module from the report formatter. If the report is not very extensive, the report driver source code module contains `main` and whatever other functions are required to collect and prepare the output data. Within the body of the report driver functions are statements to start and finish the report and statements to pass data to the report:

```
start report <report name> [ to {<file name> ¦ pipe <program> ¦ printer }
finish report <report name>

output to report <report name> (<parameter list>)
```

These statements were already discussed at some length in the "Skeleton of an INFORMIX-4GL Program: Report" section of Chapter 36. The report formatter structure is discussed in detail in the next section.

Report Sections

The report formatter contains various sections, whose structure and syntax are as follows:

```
report <report name> ( <parameters> )

    <parameter definitions>
    <local variable definitions>

    output
        top margin 3
        left margin 5
        right margin 132
        bottom margin 3
        page length 66
        report to screen

    order [ external ] by <variable> [, <variable>, ... ]

    format
        <control blocks>
            <format statements>

end report
```

The first section of the report consists of definitions for the variables passed to the report formatter by the `output to report` statement of the report driver and any other variable definitions for local variables that are required to display the data in the report.

The second section of the report, the `output` section, defines the overall page layout of the report and the default report destination, which can be overridden by the `start report` statement in the report driver. The numbers included in each clause indicate the defaults that INFORMIX-4GL uses if the clause is omitted.

The third section of the report, the `order by` clause, dictates how to sort the records in the report and controls the sequence of execution of the various control blocks in the report. If the `external` keyword is included, the report formatter assumes that the records it receives are already sorted properly by the report driver. It is usually more efficient to order the records as they are collected by the report driver than to hold them for sorting until the report formatter receives all the records to be displayed.

The fourth section of the report, the `format` section, defines the layout of the display for each control block.

The INFORMIX-4GL reporting system is based on the concept of processing each row of output as it is received in the report formatter and completing the production of the report with a single pass through the data. This processing holds true if the data was sorted in the report driver or there are no aggregates in the report formatter; otherwise, INFORMIX-4GL holds the data it needs (all output records passed for sorting or group block output records for aggregate calculations) and processes it within a second pass. Special reports that do not follow these conventions must be organized somewhat differently.

Control Blocks

Control blocks structure the report layout within its various sections. Every report statement in the `format` section must be executed within a control block. Table 37.1 lists the available control blocks.

Table 37.1. INFORMIX-4GL report control blocks.

Control Block	*Executed When*
`first page header`	Before the first record received is processed.
`page header`	Before processing the first record displayed on each page (or from page two onward if there is a `first page header` control block).
`before group of <variable>`	Before processing the first record of a group for a `<variable>` in the `order by` clause. If there are ties in processing `before group` blocks, precedence in processing is dictated by dominance of the `<variable>` in the sort list. Higher order variables in the `order by` clause have their `before group` statement block execute before lower order variables.
`on every row`	For each record received by the report formatter.
`after group of <variable>`	After processing the last record of a group for a `<variable>` in the `order by` clause. If there are ties in processing `after group` blocks, precedence in processing is dictated by dominance of the `<variable>` in the sort list. Lower order variables in the `order by` clause have their `after group` statement block execute before higher order variables.
`page trailer`	After processing the last record displayed on each page.
`on last row`	After processing the last record of the report.

Any valid INFORMIX-4GL statement can be executed within a control block, but reports cannot embed SQL statements within them. (These must be executed by the report driver.) In addition, Table 37.2 lists statements that are exclusive to INFORMIX-4GL reports.

Table 37.2. INFORMIX-4GL report statements in control blocks.

Statement	Purpose and Functionality
print [<expression> [, ...] [;]]	Prints <expression> in the report; many <expression> items can be concatenated with the , operator. Every print statement is fully contained within a report line except when the ; operator terminates the print statement to indicate that the next print statement should continue the current print line.
skip { <number of lines> ¦ to top of page }	Inserts <number of lines> blank lines in the report or starts a new page (to top of page) of the report.
need <number> lines	Either there are <number> lines still left on this page, in which case the report continues printing on this page, or there aren't, in which case the report continues printing on a new page.
pause ["<string>"]	Used only when the report is displayed on the screen, it is used to pause the display and show <string> on the screen.
print file "<filename>"	Inserts the contents of file <filename> in the report.

Within a print statement, an INFORMIX-4GL report can use the special operators listed in Table 37.3.

Table 37.3. Print statements operators.

Operator	Purpose and Functionality
ASCII <value>	Returns the ASCII character represented by the number <value>.
column <number>	Starts printing whatever follows this operator in column <number> from the left margin of the page. If the current position on the line is already greater than <number>, this operator is ignored.

Operator	Purpose and Functionality
lineno	Returns the value of the line number the report is currently printing.
pageno	Returns the value of the page number the report is currently printing.
<number> space[s]	Inserts as many blanks spaces as dictated by <number> in the print line.
<character string> wordwrap [right margin <number>]	Wraps the contents of <character string> onto multiple printed lines and uses the temporary right margin indicated by <number> or the actual page right margin if the clause is omitted.

Grand Totals and Subtotals

Within a report block that signals the end of a group, you can use the following aggregate report functions:

```
[ group ]  { count (*) ¦ percent (*) ¦ { sum } ( <expression> ) }
                                     ¦   avg
                                     ¦   min
                                     ¦   max
[ where <where clause> ]
```

Examples of these aggregates are included in the report code in the next section.

Formatting the Display

Using the example of the fictitious trucking firm, you are going to produce a report that displays the employers' basic information ordered by state and alphabetically by employer name within each state. After each state, you display the count of employers contained within the state, and at the end of the report, you display the count of all the employers listed. Also at the end of the report, you display the count of employers whose phone is missing (null) and not missing. The report driver for this example is included in Listing 37.12, and the report formatter is included in Listing 37.13.

Listing 37.12. The driver.4gl source code file.

```
database recruiters

#################################################################
main
#################################################################

#- define variables to collect data from the database
```

continues

Listing 37.12. continued

```
    define p_states record like states.*,
           p_employers record like employers.*

#- declare the cursor to collect data; at this point we're
#- including all employer records in the report but, if we
#- wanted to limit the query to user selected parameters,
#- this would be the place to prompt the user for those
#- parameters

    declare c_data cursor for
    select states.*, employers.*
    from states, employers
    where states.state = employers.state
    order by states.state, employers.employer

#- initialize the report

    start report rpt_employers to printer

#- fetch the data and loop until exhausted

    foreach c_data into p_states.*, p_employers.*

#- send data to the report formatter

        output to report rpt_employers (p_states.*, p_employers.*)

    end foreach

#- finish the report and flush the buffers

    finish report rpt_employers

#- we're done, quit

    exit program

end main
```

Note that instead of defining the report driver within a separate program, you could have replaced a `function` for `main` and made this report another menu option in the application discussed in the "Screens and Screen Forms: A Primer" section, earlier in this chapter. If that were the case, you could replace the static cursor declaration with a dynamic cursor declaration that uses the same *`where_clause`* that the `find.4gl` source code module constructed.

Listing 37.13. The `report.4gl` source code file.

```
database recruiters

################################################################
report rpt_employers (rpt_states, rpt_employers)
################################################################
```

```
#- define report arguments and local variables

define rpt_states record like states.*,
       rpt_employers record like employers.*,
       i, j smallint

#- output section

output

    left margin 0
    right margin 80
    top margin 1
    bottom margin 3
    page length 66
    report to "report.out"

#- order by section

order external by rpt_states.state, rpt_employers.employer

#- format section

format

page header

    print column  1, "Listing of Employers by State",
          column 70, "Page ", pageno using "<<<"
    print column  1, "Run on ", today using "mm-dd-yyyy"
    skip 2 lines
    print column  5, "Code",
          column 20, "Employer",
          column 50, "City",
          column 69, "Phone Number"
    print column  1, "+--------+ +-----------------",
                     "-------------+ +------------",
                     "--+ +-----------+"

page trailer

    print column  1, "-----------------------------",
                     "-------------------------------",
                     "-----------------"
    skip 1 line
    print column 70, "Page ", pageno using "<<<"

before group of rpt_states.state

    skip to top of page
    skip 2 lines

#- center the name of the state within the 24 column box we're
#- building

    let i = length(rpt_states.state_name)
    let j = ( (24 - i) / 2 ) + 1
    print column  1, "********** ", rpt_states.state clipped,
```

continues

Listing 37.13. continued

```
                        " **********"
    print column  1, "* ",
          column  j, rpt_states.state_name clipped,
          column 23, " *"
    print column  1, "************************"

    skip 1 line

on every row

#- if the phone number is null, do not print it at all; otherwise
#- format the phone number by placing () around the area code and
#- the - in its proper place using substrings of the phone
#- column

    if rpt_employers.phone is null
    then
        print column  2, rpt_employers.empl_code using "#########",
              column 13, rpt_employers.employer clipped,
              column 48, rpt_employers.city clipped
    else
        print column  2, rpt_employers.empl_code using "#########",
              column 13, rpt_employers.employer clipped,
              column 48, rpt_employers.city clipped,
              column 66, "(", rpt_employers.phone[1,3], ") ",
                         rpt_employers.phone[4,6], "-",
                         rpt_employers.phone[7,10]
    end if

after group of rpt_states.state

    skip 2 lines
    print column  1, "Tally of employers in ",
                     rpt_states.state_name clipped, " (",
                     rpt_states.state clipped, ") is ",
                     group count(*) using "<<<"

on last row

    need 8 lines
    skip 2 lines
    print column  1, "Employers without Phone Numbers: ",
                     count(*) where rpt_employers.phone is null
                     using "#####"
    print column  1, "Employers with Phone Numbers:    ",
                     count(*) where rpt_employers.phone is not null
                     using "#####"
    print column  1, "Employers in this report:        ",
                     count(*) using "#####"
    skip 2 lines
    print column  1, "***** End of Report *****"

end report
```

Summary

This chapter formalized the description of the most common building blocks of an INFORMIX-4GL application: screens and reports (particularly the latter). It expanded the code provided in Chapter 36 that deals with Input Management and provided you with new source code versions to compare and contrast with those in Chapter 36. The code is not yet of production caliber, but it is moving in that direction. After the next chapter, you should be able to revise it and convert it to a robust application.

Advanced 4GL Development

by José Fortuny

IN THIS CHAPTER

This chapter closes the series of four chapters devoted to INFORMIX-4GL programming. I continue to develop the example that I have been using: the fictitious trucking company. In this chapter, I expand inputs to the case of header/detail data entry environments, one very common way to manage the inputs for the one-to-many relationships. To accomplish this, you need to add another table to the database. This table, named depots, will store information about the various locations each employer operates from; for each employer, there will be zero or many depots. The schema for this table appears in Listing 38.1.

Listing 38.1. Schema of depots table.

```
{ TABLE "jose".depots row size = 148 number of columns = 9 index size = 88 }
create table "jose".depots
  (
    empl_code integer not null constraint "jose".n105_25,
    depot_code serial not null constraint "jose".n105_26,
    depot char(35) not null constraint "jose".n105_27,
    add_line1 char(35),
    add_line2 char(35),
    city char(18) not null constraint "jose".n105_28,
    state char(2) not null constraint "jose".n105_29,
    zip char(5) not null constraint "jose".n105_30,
    phone char(10) not null constraint "jose".n105_31,
    primary key (depot_code) constraint "jose".pk_depot
  );
revoke all on "jose".depots from "public";

create index "jose".ix_depots_1 on "jose".depots (empl_code,depot);

alter table "jose".depots add constraint (foreign key (empl_code)
    references "jose".employers  constraint "jose".fk_depot_1);
```

In this chapter, in addition to header/detail inputs, you also learn about a number of issues that can't be classified as specifically as I have classified the subject matter so far but that, nonetheless, merit consideration. The chapter covers advanced reporting issues, such as managing multiple reports within a single program, and developing nonstandard report layouts. In the previous three chapters, you have used the basic INFORMIX-4GL error management and error reporting tools; this chapter introduces an alternative methodology for error management, in which your program actually controls the way in which it wants to deal with errors. I also introduce the salient features of the INFORMIX-4GL debugger and issues dealing with the relationships of your program database to other databases and to the UNIX environment around it.

Screen Inputs

Chapter 36, "4GL Coding," introduced inputs to a single table using a header-only form. Chapter 37, "4GL Development," introduced displays of data coming from multiple tables onto a header-only form, and it also introduced the management of multiline, detail-only forms that listed multiple records from a single table. In particular, you looked at browsers that just display records from a table and zooms that perform three duties: They allow the user to perform a query by example to make a selection from the table; then they display the list of records returned from the query (as browsers do); and, finally, the user can make a selection of one of the records returned, and the selected record, or portions of it, is returned to the calling program. I review zooms a bit further in this section and the concepts underlying query by example before introducing the header/detail inputs. The only input type not covered is that of inputs to a detail-only screen, but such inputs are just a subset of the header/detail input and can be derived easily from it.

Multiple Row, Single Table Displays and Selections: Pop-Up Window Selections

The concept of zooms was introduced in Chapter 37. This section further analyzes the programming of zooms. Listing 38.2 contains the file `zooms.4gl`, which allows the user to zoom over the tables of states.

Listing 38.2. The `zooms.4gl` file.

```
globals "globals.4gl"

define sel_criteria char(512),
       sel_stmt char(1024),
       i, max_rows, row_count, row_selected smallint

#################################################################
function z_state()
#################################################################
# query, display and collect key pressed; return row or not
#################################################################
define p_state array[60] of record
                state like states.state,
                state_name like states.state_name
       end record

whenever error continue
let max_rows = 60

#- open window with form and display header

open window w_state at 3,3 with form "z_state"
     attribute(border, white)
display " Zoom: States ... " at 1,1 attribute(red)
display " Accept to Search, Cancel to Interrupt "
        at 2,1 attribute(yellow)

#- construct the query and create the cursor

construct by name sel_criteria
       on states.state, states.state_name
```

continues

Listing 38.2. continued

```
    on key (interrupt)
        exit construct
    end construct
    if int_flag
    then
        let int_flag = false
        let error_msg = " No Criteria Identified for Selection "
        call error_display(error_msg)
        close window w_state
        let p_state[1].state = null
        return p_state[1].state
    else
        let sel_stmt = "select state, state_name from states ",
                       "where ", sel_criteria clipped, " ",
                       "order by state"
        display "" at 1,1
        display "" at 2,1
        display "Searching ... " at 1,1 attribute(green)
    end if
    prepare query1 from sel_stmt
    declare c_state cursor for query1

#- fill in the array

    let row_count = 0
    foreach c_state into p_state[row_count + 1].*
        let row_count = row_count + 1
        if row_count >= max_rows
        then
            let error_msg = " States exceed the limits of the ",
                            "display "
            call error_display(error_msg)
            exit foreach
        end if
    end foreach
    call set_count(row_count)
    close c_state
    free c_state

# display the array and receive selection
    display " Zoom: States ... Arrows, F3, F4 to move"
            at 1,1 attribute(red)
    display " Accept to Select, Cancel to Interrupt "
            at 2,1 attribute(yellow)
    display array p_state to s_states.*
    on key (interrupt)
        exit display
    end display
    if int_flag
    then
        let int_flag = false
        let error_msg = " No State Selected "
        call error_display(error_msg)
        close window w_state
        let p_state[1].state = null
```

```
        return p_state[1].state
    else
        let row_selected = arr_curr()
        close window w_state
        return p_state[row_selected].state
    end if
end function

###################################################################
function zoom(field_id)
###################################################################

define field_id char(18),
       p_old_state like employers.state

case
    when field_id = "state"
        let p_old_state = p_employers.state
        call z_state() returning p_employers.state
        if p_employers.state is null
        then
            let p_employers.state = p_old_state
        end if
        display by name p_employers.state

end case

return

end function
```

Please note that the first 25 lines of the program (just up to the construct section) initialize the display and provide the user with directives on how to proceed. The next 25 lines of code first perform a query by example in the `construct` block, and either terminate the zoom if the user cancels out or construct and declare the cursor that will perform the retrieval of records from the database. Note that the function uses the first two lines of the display to keep the user abreast of progress. Following the construct, the array is filled with a standard `foreach` loop, and the records loaded onto the array are specified with the `set_count` function. After the array is loaded, you place the user in the `display` block. If the user cancels out, you return a null state; otherwise, when the user accepts the row where the cursor is resting, you return the state identified in that row:

```
let row_selected = arr_curr()
return p_state[row_selected].state
```

The function `arr_curr` is used to return the number (`row_selected`) of the program record that is currently displayed in the screen array. That number is then used to retrieve and return the state to the calling function.

The general processing of the zoom function was discussed at length in the "Multiple Row, Single Table Displays: Browsers" section of Chapter 37, and it is summarized again in the following steps:

1. Open the zoom window with the appropriate zoom form.
2. Display information on how to prepare the query by example.
3. Construct a query by example on the first row of the screen array (alternatively, construct by name).
4. Load the program array with data from the table by using a cursor and some form of looping (probably a `foreach` loop, because this operation is sequential in nature).
5. Set the array count.
6. Close and free the zoom cursor.
7. Display the array and information on how to navigate the array, and how to select a row to return to the calling program the value of the appropriate key column.
8. Upon user exit, close the window.
9. Return null if the user interrupted the zoom selection or the values of the key column in the row where the cursor was when the user accepted the zoom selection.

Cursors Revisited and a Further Look at Query by Example

In all the examples covered so far—and even in the example discussed in the "Master/Detail Relationships: Single Row Master Table and Multiple Row Detail Table Inputs" section later in this chapter—the `construct` statement has been used with columns of a single table. At this point, I want to introduce the new version of the `employers.per` form that will be used in that upcoming section and develop `construct` statements to illustrate more complex query by example setups.

When considering the form in Figure 38.1, you might conceive two types of queries. In one, the user is allowed to make selections only on employer information and not on employer depot information (that is, a query on the header portion of the form only). For instance, find all employers whose headquarters office is located in Arkansas. Alternatively, you might want to let your users make queries on the detail portion of the form: for instance, `find all employers that have a depot located in Iowa`. Let's examine the meaning of both queries in the context of the form that will display the results.

If the query is on the header-only portion of the screen, your `construct` statement will deal with the columns of table `employers` only and, when the first employer is retrieved, your program will proceed to retrieve all depots for this employer. The `construct` statement you are likely to use is `construct by name where_clause on employers.*`, and the results you expect to see are all the depots for each employer, as you scroll through the list of employers. In Figure 38.1, you see the depots of CLASSIC CARRIER LINES, which is the first employer selected in a list of three retrieved (1 of 3).

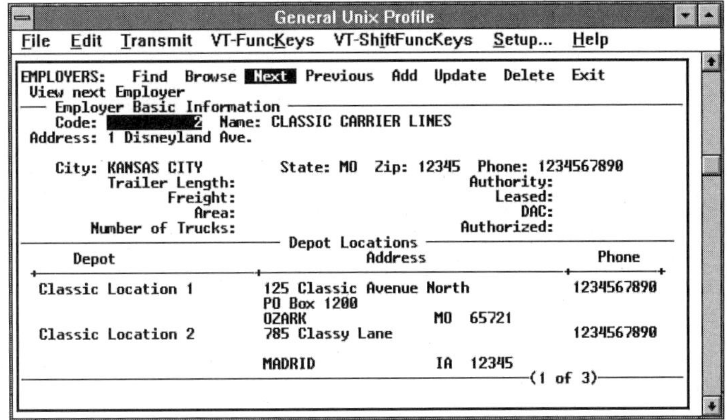

FIGURE 38.1.
The employer header/detail input form.

If, on the other hand, you want to query both the header and the detail, you might find users trying to define the following query: `show me all depots in the state of Iowa...`, and they might expect to see only depots in Iowa listed on the screen. That is not what this screen is designed for. Rather, it is designed to display all depots for an employer. It represents the employer-to-depot relationship; it can't deal with the depot portion of the relationship alone. (For that you could create a detail-only listing for depots by state.) Thus, when the users query for Iowa in the detail, the query they are really firing off is

```
show me all employers that have a depot in Iowa and, for those employers
that do, show me all their depots, whether in Iowa or not
```

The construct statement you might use in this case is `construct by name where_clause on employers.*, depots.*`, assuming that you allow them to query on all the fields on the screen. (Note that although all the depot columns are displayed on the screen, the `construct` statement doesn't really know, or care, and it still constructs the `where_clause` variable properly.) With that `where_clause`, the `sql_stmt` you would build is

```
let sql_stmt = "select * from employers where ",
               "employers.empl_code = depots.empl_code and ",
               where_clause clipped,
               "order by employers.empl_code"
```

You define the relationship between the two tables in the `where` clause (`employers.empl_code = depots.empl_code`), and you select only the employer's information that satisfies the query the user created in `where_clause`. After you have retrieved the header (`employers`) rows, you will find all the detail (`depots`) rows that belong to that employer and display them along with the employer information.

Multiple Table Displays

Typically, displays from multiple tables come in one of two flavors: header/detail screens, which will be discussed further in the next section, and descriptions of coded information in any type of screen form. In Chapter 37, Listing 37.1 displays a header-only form (the previous version of `employers.per`) that displays the long name of the state following the state two-letter code.

One of two methods is normally used to retrieve information from multiple tables simultaneously: Either a query is defined that contains columns from the various tables, or two queries are performed in sequence. The first query retrieves the information from the primary table, and the second query uses the information retrieved to select the required information from the second table, and so on. The latter was the strategy followed in Listing 37.5 (in Chapter 37), whose relevant portion is displayed here:

```
fetch first c_employers into p_employers.*
        if status = 0
        then
            let curr_row = 1
            display by name p_employers.*
            call valid_state(p_employers.state)
                 returning is_valid, p_display.state_name
            display by name p_display.*
            call records (21,60, curr_row, total_rows)
```

First, you retrieve information from table employers and, after you have the state code, you use the function `valid_state` to retrieve the `state_name`. The only rationale for doing this is that you already had the function `valid_state` defined and could actually reuse it.

The alternative would have been to redefine the `sql_stmt` clause from

```
let sql_stmt = "select * from employers where ",
               where_clause clipped, " ",
               "order by empl_code"
```

to the following:

```
let sql_stmt = "select employers.*, states.state_name from employers, states ",
               "where employers.state = states.state and ",
               where_clause clipped, " ",
               "order by empl_code"
```

The database engine would have retrieved the records in one pass.

Master/Detail Relationships: Single Row Master Table and Multiple Row Detail Table Inputs

To input information into the screen form in Figure 38.1, you first need to define the form source file. Listing 38.3 contains the `employer.per` source form file that matches the display in Figure 38.1.

Listing 38.3. The `employer.per` source form file.

```
DATABASE recruiters
SCREEN
{
------------------------------------------------------------------
```

```
➥----------
    Code:[f000       ] Name:[f001                            ]
 Address:[f002                        ]
         [f003                        ]
    City:[f004              ] State:[a0] Zip:[f005 ] Phone:
➥[f006     ]
          Trailer Length:[a1]                      Authority:[a]
                 Freight:[f007      ]                 Leased:[b]
                    Area:[f008          ]                DAC:[c]
        Number of Trucks:[f009]                   Authorized:[d]
------------------------------ Depot Locations -----------------
➥----------
      Depot                              Address
➥Phone
 +----------------------+-------------------------------+--
➥--------+
 [d1                     ¦d2                             ¦d7
➥         ]
                         [d3                             ]
                         [d4                ][d5][d6    ]
 [d1                     ¦d2                             ¦d7
➥         ]
                         [d3                             ]
                         [d4                ][d5][d6    ]
-------------------------------------------------------------------
➥----------
}
END
TABLES
    employers
    depots
    states
ATTRIBUTES
f000 = employers.empl_code, reverse, noentry;
f001 = employers.employer, required, upshift,
       comments = "Enter the Employer Business Name";
f002 = employers.add_line1,
       comments = "Enter the First Line of the Address";
f003 = employers.add_line2,
       comments = "Enter the Second Line of the Address";
f004 = employers.city, upshift, required,
       comments = "Enter the City for this Address";
a0 = employers.state, required, upshift,
     comments = "Enter the State for this Address";
f005 = employers.zip, required, picture = "#####",
       comments = "Enter the Zip Code for this Address";
f006 = employers.phone;
a1 = employers.trl_len;
f007 = employers.freight;
f008 = employers.area;
f009 = employers.nbr_trks;
a = employers.authority;
b = employers.leased;
c = employers.dac;
d = employers.authorized;
d1 = depots.depot, comments = "Enter the Name of This Location";
```

continues

Listing 38.3. continued

```
d2 = depots.add_line1,
     comments = "Enter the First Line of the Address";
d3 = depots.add_line2,
     comments = "Enter the Second Line of the Address";
d4 = depots.city, upshift, required,
     comments = "Enter the City for this Address";
d5 = depots.state, required, upshift,
     comments = "Enter the State for this Address";
d6 = depots.zip, required, picture = "#####",
     comments = "Enter the Zip Code for this Address";
d7 = depots.phone;
END
INSTRUCTIONS
  delimiters " "
  screen record s_employers(employers.empl_code,
                            employers.employer,
                            employers.add_line1,
                            employers.add_line2,
                            employers.city,
                            employers.state,
                            employers.zip,
                            employers.phone,
                            employers.trl_len,
                            employers.freight,
                            employers.area,
                            employers.nbr_trks,
                            employers.authority,
                            employers.leased,
                            employers.dac,
                            employers.authorized)
  screen record s_depots[2](depots.depot,
                            depots.add_line1,
                            depots.add_line2,
                            depots.city,
                            depots.state,
                            depots.zip,
                            depots.phone)
END
```

Other than its layout, the main feature to emphasize (which is not covered earlier) is the definition of a screen record array `s_depots` with two rows of display.

To construct the program, use the same source code modules used in Chapter 37, which are `add.4gl`, `browse.4gl`, `delete.4gl`, `find.4gl`, `globals.4gl`, `main.4gl`, `options.4gl`, and `zooms.4gl`. The only source code modules that differ between the two versions are `add.4gl`, `delete.4gl`, `find.4gl`, and `globals.4gl`. (`main.4gl` differs only in the initialization of variables.) The source code modules that differ will be listed in this section and the differences discussed. The most significant differences between these source code modules and their previous counterparts are found in `add.4gl`, discussed last in this section.

The `globals.4gl` source code module is displayed in Listing 38.4.

Listing 38.4. The `globals.4gl` source code module.

```
database recruiters

###################################################################
globals
###################################################################

define p_employers record like employers.*,
       p_old_employers record like employers.*,
       p_depots array[100] of record
           depot like depots.depot,
           add_line1 like depots.add_line1,
           add_line2 like depots.add_line2,
           city like depots.city,
           state like depots.state,
           zip like depots.zip,
           phone like depots.phone
       end record,
       p_depots_nv array[100] of record
           empl_code like depots.empl_code,
           depot_code like depots.depot_code
       end record,
       p_old_depots array[100] of record
           depot like depots.depot,
           add_line1 like depots.add_line1,
           add_line2 like depots.add_line2,
           city like depots.city,
           state like depots.state,
           zip like depots.zip,
           phone like depots.phone
       end record,
       p_old_depots_nv array[100] of record
           empl_code like depots.empl_code,
           depot_code like depots.depot_code
       end record,
       is_valid smallint,
       where_clause char(512),
       sql_stmt char(1024),
       error_msg char(70),
       u_employer smallint,
       go_to_field, p_dbname char(18),
       curr_row, total_rows, p_cur, s_cur, counted_rows,
           detail_rows integer

end globals
```

This version of `globals.4gl` contains definitions for the new variables required to input the detail, `p_depots`, as well as to manage the columns from table `depots` that are not displayed in the screen form, `p_depots_nv`, and their `p_old` versions. Note that these variables have been defined as arrays of 100 records. In addition, two more counters—`detail_rows`, used to define the maximum number of rows in the detail array (100), and `counted_rows`, used as a counter for the actual rows loaded—are used to manage the input and display of the newly introduced arrays.

The `find.4gl` source code module is displayed in Listing 38.5.

Listing 38.5. The `find.4gl` source code module.

```
globals "globals.4gl"

###################################################################
function prep_cursor()
###################################################################

#- prepare the SQL statement for execution, declare a cursor that
#- will represent the active set of rows returned by the engine
#- and activate the cursor by opening it

    whenever error continue
    prepare statement_1 from sql_stmt
    declare c_employers scroll cursor with hold for statement_1
    open c_employers

end function

###################################################################
function count_them()
###################################################################

    define sql_count char(512)

    let sql_count = "select count(*) from employers where ",
                    where_clause clipped
    prepare statement_count from sql_count
    declare c_count cursor for statement_count
    open c_count
    fetch c_count into total_rows
    close c_count
    free c_count

    return

end function

###################################################################
function find_it()
###################################################################
# Gather search criteria, find the first employer and display it
###################################################################

#- clear form on the screen and initialize variables

    clear form
    let int_flag = false
    let curr_row = 0
    let total_rows = 0
```

```
    initialize p_employers.* to null
    display "--------------------" at 21,60 attribute(white)

#- replace menu with instructions for query by example

    display "" at 1,1
    display "" at 2,1
    display "Enter the Search Criteria for Selection ..." at 1,1
            attribute(green)
    display "Press Accept Key to Search, Cancel Key to Interrupt"
            at 2,1 attribute(yellow)

#- construct the query statement dynamically: the where_clause
#- variable will contain the query string based on the criteria
#- for selection that the user inputs

    construct by name where_clause on employers.*

#- if the user interrupted, cancel the query request and return to
#- the calling program after advising the user

    if int_flag
    then
        message " Search Cancelled at User Request "
        let int_flag = false
        return
    end if

#- proceed with the query: replace query by example instructions
#- by flashing message indicating search for records is proceeding

    display "" at 1,1
    display "" at 2,1
    display "Searching ..." at 1,1 attribute(green, blink)

#- construct the complete SQL statement to query the database:
#- include the select clause, the from clause, the dynamically
#- created where clause and order by clause.  Concatenate
#- those clauses into the program variable sql_stmt

    let sql_stmt = "select * from employers where ",
                   where_clause clipped, " ",
                   "order by empl_code"

#- count the records that match the query and prepare the cursor
#- and open it (this is now done in prep_cursor())

    call count_them()
    call prep_cursor()

#- if the open has succeeded, retrieve the first row in the active
#- data set, place it in the program variable p_employers and
```


continues

Listing 38.5. continued

```
#- display this variable; otherwise handle the failure with an
#- error message that is descriptive of the type of failure

    if status = 0
    then
        fetch first c_employers into p_employers.*
        if status = 0
        then
            let curr_row = 1
            display by name p_employers.*
            call find_detail(p_employers.empl_code, "D")
            call records (21,60, curr_row, total_rows)
        else
            if status = notfound
            then
                clear form
                message "No employers satisfy search criteria"
            else
                let error_msg = " Could not get employers ",
                    "information; ",
                    "status ", status using "-<<<<<<<<<<"

              call error_display(error_msg)
            end if
        end if
    else
        let error_msg = " Could not access employers ",
            "information; ",
            "status ", status using "-<<<<<<<<<<"
        call error_display(error_msg)
    end if

end function


##################################################################
function next_row()
##################################################################
# fetch and display the next row
##################################################################

#- to display the next row, one must already be displayed

    if p_employers.empl_code is null
    then
        let error_msg = " Must find first "
        call error_display(error_msg)
        return "findfirst"
    end if

#- retrieve the next row in the active set, place it in the program
#- variable p_employers and display this variable; otherwise handle
#- the failure with an error message that is descriptive of the
#- type of failure

    fetch next c_employers into p_employers.*
    if status = 0
```

```
    then
        let curr_row = curr_row + 1
        display by name p_employers.*
        call find_detail(p_employers.empl_code, "D")
        call records (21,60, curr_row, total_rows)
        return "found"
    else
        if status = notfound
        then
            message "Reached the end of the list"
            return "last"
        else
            let error_msg = " Could not retrieve next employer; ",
                "status ", status using "-<<<<<<<<<<"
            call error_display(error_msg)
            return "error"
        end if
    end if

    return "ok"

end function

##################################################################
function previous_row()
##################################################################
# fetch and display the previous row
##################################################################

#- to display the previous row, one must already be displayed

    if p_employers.empl_code is null
    then
        let error_msg = " Must find first "
        call error_display(error_msg)
        return "findfirst"
    end if

#- retrieve the previous row in the active set, place it in the
#- program variable p_employers and display this variable;
#- otherwise handle the failure with an error message that is
#- descriptive of the type of failure

    fetch previous c_employers into p_employers.*
    if status = 0
    then
        let curr_row = curr_row - 1
        display by name p_employers.*
        call find_detail(p_employers.empl_code, "D")
        call records (21,60, curr_row, total_rows)
        return "found"
    else
        if status = notfound
        then
            message "At the beginning of the list"
            return "first"
```


continues

Listing 38.5. continued

```
        else
            let error_msg = " Could not retrieve previous ",
                "employer; ",
                "status ", status using "-<<<<<<<<<<"
            call error_display(error_msg)
            return "error"
        end if
    end if

    return "ok"

end function

##################################################################
function find_detail(p_employer, p_mode)
##################################################################
# get detail and display the array
##################################################################
define p_mode char(1),
       p_employer like employers.empl_code,
       depot_stmt char(1024),
       i smallint

#- initialize detail array clearing it from any previous values

let int_flag = false
for i = 1 to detail_rows
  initialize p_depots[i].* to null
  initialize p_depots_nv[i].* to null
end for

#- prepare the cursor to select based on empl_code and
#- load the detail array

let depot_stmt = "select * from depots where empl_code = ",
                  p_employer,
                " order by empl_code, depot"
prepare depot_stmt from depot_stmt
declare c_depots scroll cursor with hold for depot_stmt

let i = 0

#- note that we're loading both the part of the depot row that is
#- displayed on the detail screen as well as the portion that is
#- not displayed (p_depots_nv)

foreach c_depots into p_depots_nv[i + 1].*, p_depots[i + 1].*
    let i = i + 1
    if i > detail_rows
    then
        let error_msg = " List Exceeds the limits of the display "
        call error_display(error_msg)
        let i = detail_rows
        exit foreach
```

```
    end if
end foreach

#- set the count of rows in the array

let counted_rows = i
call set_count(i)

close c_depots
free c_depots

case
    when p_mode = "D"

#- display the first screenful of the detail

        for i = 1 to 2
            display p_depots[i].depot,
                    p_depots[i].add_line1,
                    p_depots[i].add_line2,
                    p_depots[i].city,
                    p_depots[i].state,
                    p_depots[i].zip,
                    p_depots[i].phone
                 to s_depots[i].depot,
                    s_depots[i].add_line1,
                    s_depots[i].add_line2,
                    s_depots[i].city,
                    s_depots[i].state,
                    s_depots[i].zip,
                    s_depots[i].phone
        end for
    otherwise
        let error_msg = " Display not specified "
        call error_display(error_msg)
end case

end function
```


The main difference between this version of `find.4gl` and the previous version in Chapter 37 is due to the need to manage the detail rows. After an employer record is fetched, you proceed to call the function `find_detail`, which defines its own cursor, loads the arrays `p_depots` and `p_depots_nv` using a `foreach` clause, and then displays the first screen full of detail rows (the first two rows). The structure of the function `find_detail` is very similar to the structure of a zoom, but in the case of the detail, the cursor is defined statically based on the key values provided by the header (`employers`).

An addition to this `find.4gl` source code module, which has not been introduced in this example but rather left as a simple exercise, is the display of the count of rows retrieved in the detail array. Note that the `records` function displays the position of the employers record in the list of employers retrieved and the count of such employers. It could be easily modified to display also the count of rows (counted_rows) that represent the depots for the employer on the screen.

Note also that the construct statement you have used to define the main cursor that retrieves employers is based solely on the employers table. Some discussion on this subject was presented in the "Cursors Revisited and a Further Look at Query by Example" section, earlier in this chapter. Additionally, when you have a header/detail relationship displayed on the screen and you perform a query by example that includes the detail, the cost of retrieving rows increases dramatically while the records returned are only those of the header. It pays to experiment before providing a query by example that includes the detail.

The delete.4gl source code module is displayed in Listing 38.6.

Listing 38.6. The delete.4gl source code module.

```
globals "globals.4gl"

#################################################################
function delete_it()
#################################################################
# prompt for confirmation and then act accordingly
#################################################################

#- define local variables
    define del_flag char(10),
           i smallint

    whenever error continue
    let int_flag = false

#- test that the user selected a record to be deleted; if no
#- records are displayed on the screen, error out

    if p_employers.empl_code is null
    then
        let error_msg = " Must find first "
        call error_display(error_msg)
        return "findfirst"
    end if

#- display a new menu to confirm the deletion

    menu "Delete?"
        command "No" "Do not delete this employer"
            message "Deletion of employer cancelled"
            let del_flag = "interrupt"
            exit menu
        command "Yes" "Delete this employer"

#- whether you have set up referential integrity through the
#- DB engine or not, you should delete first the detail
#- records before deleting the header record

            delete from depots where empl_code =
                                         p_employers.empl_code
```

```
            if status = 0
            then

#- when the delete of the detail record has succeeded, then delete
#- the header record

                delete from employers
                where empl_code = p_employers.empl_code
                if status = 0
                then
                    message "Employer deleted" attribute(reverse)
                    clear form
                    initialize p_employers.* to null
                    for i = 1 to detail_rows
                        initialize p_depots[i].* to null
                        initialize p_depots_nv[i].* to null
                    end for
                    display "-------------------"
                            at 21, 60 attribute(white)
                    let del_flag = "deleted"
                else
                    let error_msg = " Could not delete employer; ",
                                    "status ", status
                                    using "-<<<<<<<<<"
                    call error_display(error_msg)
                    let del_flag = "problem"
                end if
                exit menu
            else
                let error_msg = " Could not delete depots; ",
                                "status ", status
                                using "-<<<<<<<<<"
                call error_display(error_msg)
                let del_flag = "problem"
            end if
        end menu

    if int_flag
    then
        let int_flag = false
        return "interrupt"
    else
        return del_flag
    end if

end function
```

When dealing with a header/detail relationship, and whether or not the database tables are handled with referential integrity managed by the database engine, you must process the deletion of the depots (`detail`) before you process the deletion of the employer (`header`) to avoid generating orphaned records. If referential integrity is enforced by the database engine, that order of deletions will be required.

Before you learn about the code for the `add.4gl` source code module, I should introduce the `input array` statement that the code uses to manage input to the detail array:

```
input array <program array variable> [without defaults]
from <screen record array>.*
     [help <number>] [ attribute ( <attribute> [ , ... ] ) ]
 [ { before {input, row, insert, delete}
        { any 4GL statement }
    before field <form field name>
        { any 4GL statement }
    after field <form field name>
        { any 4GL statement }
    after {input, row, insert, delete}
        { any 4GL statement }
    on key ( <special key> )
        { any 4GL statement }
   next field { next ¦ previous ¦ <form field name> }
   continue input
   exit input} ]
end input
```

`<program array variable>` lists the program array variable to input (normally an array of records is used).

`without defaults` keeps the system from filling the screen fields with default values and instead uses the current values of the `<program array variable>` variables.

`from` binds the `<program array variable>` to a `<screen record array>`.

`before input` is executed before allowing the user to input data onto the form.

`before row` is executed the moment the cursor enters a row.

`before insert` is executed when the user is about to enter records onto a blank row (first of the array, if the Insert key is pressed, or the next blank row at the end of the rows currently filled).

`before delete` is executed after the user presses the Delete key but before actually deleting the row.

`before field <form field name>` is executed as the cursor enters `<form field name>` and before allowing the user to input data on the field.

`after field <form field name>` is executed as the cursor is about to leave `<form field name>`.

`after input` is executed when the user presses any of the keys that terminate input (Accept, Interrupt, or Quit) but before input is actually terminated.

`after row` is executed the moment the cursor leaves a row.

`after insert` is executed after the user has inserted a record on a blank row.

`after delete` is executed after the user presses the Delete key.

`on key ( <special key> )` is executed when the user presses a `<special key>` that the system recognizes.

next field { next ¦ previous ¦ <form field name> } moves the screen cursor to the appropriate selection within the current screen array row.

continue input skips all statements in the current control block.

exit input terminates input and transfers control to the statement immediately following the end input clause.

In executing clauses within the input array statement block, INFORMIX-4GL follows this sequence:

1. before input
2. before row
3. before insert, before delete
4. before field
5. on key
6. after field
7. after insert, after delete
8. after row
9. after input

The add.4gl source code module is displayed in Listing 38.7.

Listing 38.7. The add.4gl source code module.

```
globals "globals.4gl"

#####################################################################
function add_it(p_mode)
#####################################################################
# start input in the header and allow the user to jump to the
# detail section by pressing the tab key
#####################################################################

#- define local variables

define p_mode char(1),
       ret_code char(10),
       i smallint

#- before updating a record, make sure one is already selected

    whenever error continue
    if p_mode = "U" and p_employers.empl_code is null
    then
        let error_msg = " Must find first "
        call error_display(error_msg)
```

continues

Listing 38.7. continued

```
        return "findfirst"
    end if

#- initialize variables appropriately and display input directives

#- prepare the p_old_employers record and replace menu
#- with directives for input

    display "" at 1,1
    display "" at 2,1
    display "-------------------" at 21, 60 attribute(white)

case

#- when adding a new employer record

when p_mode = "A"

#- clear all fields in the form and initialize the variables in
#- the input clause to null; we need to do both header and detail

    clear form
    initialize p_employers.* to null
    initialize p_old_employers.* to null
    for i = 1 to detail_rows
        initialize p_depots[i].* to null
        initialize p_depots_nv[i].* to null
    end for
    display "Add a New Employer ..." at 1,1 attribute(green)

#- when updating the current employer record

when p_mode = "U"

#- set the p_old variables to the current values of the p
#- variables.
#- If the user interrupts, we'll restore the p_old values

    let p_old_employers.* = p_employers.*
    for i = 1 to detail_rows
        let p_old_depots[i].* = p_depots[i].*
        let p_old_depots_nv[i].* = p_depots_nv[i].*
    end for
    display "Updating Employer ..." at 1,1 attribute(green)
end case

display "Press Accept to Store, Cancel to Interrupt, ",
        "Tab to change Section, F3 & F4 or Arrows"
        at 2,1 attribute(yellow)

#- overall input while loop; to allow the user the ability to jump
#- from the header to the detail input, we set up a nested while
```

```
#- loop that has no conditions for termination unless one of the
#- while loops contained within it exits the outer while

while true

#- header while loop; when you exit with a tab, it will continue
#- execution within the outer loop; when you interrupt or accept
#- it will return control to the calling function

    while true
        call add_header(p_mode) returning ret_code
        case
            when ret_code = "tab"
                exit while
            when ret_code = "interrupt"
                let int_flag = false
                let error_msg =
                    " Insert interrupted at user request "
                call error_display(error_msg)
                return ret_code
            when ret_code = "accept"
                call insert_them(p_mode) returning ret_code
                return ret_code
        end case
    end while

#- detail while loop; when you exit with a tab, it will continue
#- execution within the outer loop; when you interrupt or accept
#- it will return control to the calling function

    while true
        call add_detail(p_mode) returning ret_code
        case
            when ret_code = "tab"
                exit while
            when ret_code = "interrupt"
                let int_flag = false
                let error_msg =
                    " Insert interrupted at user request "
                call error_display(error_msg)
                return ret_code
            when ret_code = "accept"
                call insert_them(p_mode) returning ret_code
                return ret_code
        end case
    end while

end while

end function


###################################################################
function add_header(p_mode)
###################################################################
```

continues

Listing 38.7. continued

```
# input row, validate and store
####################################################################

#- define local variables

    define p_mode char(1),
           ret_code char(10),
           junk char(10),         -- Placeholder for the state name
                                  -- which we don't display anymore
           i smallint

    let int_flag = false
    let u_employer = false

#- input the values for the employer, i.e., take keyboard input and
#- store it in memory in record variable p_employers; the without
#- defaults clause preserves the p_employers current values

    input by name p_employers.* without defaults attribute(red)

#- perform validations after the user has input a value in a
#- screen field

        before field state
            display "(Zoom)" at 3,66 attribute(red)

        on key (control-z)
            case
                when infield (state)
                    call zoom ("state")
                otherwise
                    error "No zoom available for this field"
            end case

        after field state
            display "------" at 3,66 attribute(white)
            call valid_state(p_employers.state)
                 returning is_valid, junk
            if not is_valid
            then
                let error_msg = "Not a valid State code; try again"
                call error_display(error_msg)
                next field state
            else
            end if

        on key (accept)

            display "------" at 3,66 attribute(white)
            call check_employers(p_mode)
                 returning is_valid, go_to_field
            if is_valid
            then
                let ret_code = "accept"
                exit input
            else
```

```
            case
                when go_to_field = "employer"
                    next field employer
                when go_to_field = "add_line1"
                    next field add_line1
                when go_to_field = "city"
                    next field city
            end case
        end if

    on key (interrupt)

        display "------" at 3,66 attribute(white)
        let ret_code = "interrupt"
        exit input

#- when the user presses tha tab key, we want to exit input and go
#- edit the detail records

    on key (tab)
        display "------" at 3,66 attribute(white)
        call check_employers(p_mode)
             returning is_valid, go_to_field
        if is_valid
        then
            let ret_code = "tab"
            exit input
        else
            case
                when go_to_field = "employer"
                    next field employer
                when go_to_field = "add_line1"
                    next field add_line1
                when go_to_field = "city"
                    next field city
            end case
        end if

    end input

#- for this example, ignore multiuser issues and transaction
#- management issues

#- input has terminated: if the user interrupted, tell the user,
#- otherwise, return the return code set at the appropriate on key
#- clause to continue processing

    if int_flag
    then
        let int_flag = false
        let u_employer = false
        let p_employers.* = p_old_employers.*
        display by name p_employers.*
        for i = 1 to detail_rows
```

continues

Listing 38.7. continued

```
            let p_depots[i].* = p_old_depots[i].*
            let p_depots_nv[i].* = p_old_depots_nv[i].*
        end for

#- display the first screenful of the detail

        for i = 1 to 2
            display p_depots[i].depot,
                    p_depots[i].add_line1,
                    p_depots[i].add_line2,
                    p_depots[i].city,
                    p_depots[i].state,
                    p_depots[i].zip,
                    p_depots[i].phone
                 to s_depots[i].depot,
                    s_depots[i].add_line1,
                    s_depots[i].add_line2,
                    s_depots[i].city,
                    s_depots[i].state,
                    s_depots[i].zip,
                    s_depots[i].phone
        end for
    else
        let u_employer = true
    end if

    return ret_code

end function

####################################################################
function add_detail(p_mode)
####################################################################
# input multiple rows in detail, validate and store
# tab key is used to jump between the header and the detail
####################################################################

#- define local variables

define p_mode char(1),
       ret_code char(10),
       i smallint

#- input the values for the depots, i.e., take keyboard input and
#- store it in memory in record array p_depots; the without
#- defaults clause preserves the p_depots current values.
#- in an input array, Informix 4GL manages the array you are
#- inputting to automatically: if you insert a row, it will open
#- up the space and shift records in the array appropriately; but,
#- since we're keeping a parallel array of columns from table
#- depots which are not displayed in the array, we must manage
```

```
#- programatically the array p_depots_nv:  notice the code when
#- inserts and deletes occur.

input array p_depots without defaults
from s_depots.* attribute(red)

    before row

#- keep track of the current array row and screen row the cursor
#- is now on

        let p_cur = arr_curr()
        let s_cur = scr_line()

    before insert

#- shift the p_depots_nv array up, from the current row to the end;
#- it is more convenient to start at the end and come down to the
#- current entry (note the use of the step -1 clause of the for
#- loop

        for i = detail_rows to p_cur step -1
            if p_depots_nv[i].depot_code is null
            then
                continue for
            else
                let p_depots_nv[i+1].* = p_depots_nv[i].*
                let p_old_depots_nv[i+1].* = p_old_depots_nv[i].*
            end if
        end for
        initialize p_depots_nv[p_cur].* to null
        initialize p_old_depots_nv[p_cur].* to null

    after insert

        let p_depots_nv[p_cur].empl_code = p_employers.empl_code
        let p_depots_nv[p_cur].depot_code = 0

    before delete

#- delete the current row from the database if it is not a new row

        if p_depots_nv[p_cur].depot_code is not null and
           p_depots_nv[p_cur].depot_code <> 0
        then
            delete from depots where depot_code =
                        p_depots_nv[p_cur].depot_code
            if status <> 0
            then
                let error_msg = " Couldn't delete this row; ",
                                "status ",
                                status using "-<<<<<<<<<<"
                call error_display (error_msg)
                let ret_code = "interrupt"
```

continues

Listing 38.7. continued

```
                let int_flag = true
                exit input
            end if
        end if

#- shift the p_depots_nv array down, from the current row to the
#- end; since we're deleting the current row, we must close the gap
#- in the p_depots_nv array from the current row onwards.  Informix
#- 4GL will automatically do this for the array in the input array
#- clause

        for i = p_cur to (detail_rows - 1)
            let p_depots_nv[i].empl_code =
                    p_depots_nv[i+1].empl_code
            let p_depots_nv[i].depot_code =
                    p_depots_nv[i+1].depot_code
        end for
        initialize p_depots_nv[detail_rows].* to null
        initialize p_old_depots_nv[detail_rows].* to null

#- when the user presses the tab key, we want to exit input and go
#- edit the header records

    on key (tab)
        call check_detail(p_mode) returning is_valid
        if is_valid
        then
            let ret_code = "tab"
            let p_depots_nv[p_cur].empl_code =
                    p_employers.empl_code
            if p_depots_nv[p_cur].depot_code is null
            then
                let p_depots_nv[p_cur].depot_code = 0
            end if
            exit input
        else
            next field depot
        end if

    on key (accept)
        call check_detail(p_mode) returning is_valid
        if is_valid
        then
            let ret_code = "accept"
            let p_depots_nv[p_cur].empl_code =
                    p_employers.empl_code
    if p_depots_nv[p_cur].depot_code is null
    then
                let p_depots_nv[p_cur].depot_code = 0
    end if
            exit input
        else
            next field depot
        end if

    on key (interrupt)
        for i = 1 to detail_rows
```

```
            let p_depots[i].* = p_old_depots[i].*
            let p_depots_nv[i].* = p_old_depots_nv[i].*
        end for
        let ret_code = "interrupt"
        exit input

end input

#- count the actual rows in the array; note that if the cursor is
#- on an empty row of the array, that row too is going to be
#- counted: you need to deal with this fact in storing records in
#- the database

let counted_rows = arr_count()


    if int_flag
    then
        let int_flag = false
        let u_employer = false
        let p_employers.* = p_old_employers.*
        display by name p_employers.*
        for i = 1 to detail_rows
            let p_depots[i].* = p_old_depots[i].*
            let p_depots_nv[i].* = p_old_depots_nv[i].*
        end for

#- display the first screenful of the detail

        for i = 1 to 2
            display p_depots[i].depot,
                    p_depots[i].add_line1,
                    p_depots[i].add_line2,
                    p_depots[i].city,
                    p_depots[i].state,
                    p_depots[i].zip,
                    p_depots[i].phone
                 to s_depots[i].depot,
                    s_depots[i].add_line1,
                    s_depots[i].add_line2,
                    s_depots[i].city,
                    s_depots[i].state,
                    s_depots[i].zip,
                    s_depots[i].phone
        end for
    else
        let u_employer = true
    end if

    return ret_code

end function

###################################################################
function insert_them(p_mode)
```

continues

Listing 38.7. continued

```
#######################################################################

#- define local variables

    define p_mode char(1),
           ret_code char(10),
           i smallint

    let int_flag = false
    let ret_code = "ok"

    if u_employer
    then
        case
        when p_mode = "A"
            let p_employers.empl_code = 0
            insert into employers values (p_employers.*)
            if status = 0
            then
                let p_employers.empl_code = sqlca.sqlerrd[2]
                display by name p_employers.empl_code
                for i = 1 to counted_rows
                    insert into depots
                    values (p_employers.empl_code, 0,
                            p_depots[i].depot through
                            p_depots[i].phone)
                    if status <> 0
                    then
                        let error_msg = " Couldn't insert depot; ",
                                        "status ",
                                        status using "-<<<<<<<<<<"
                        call error_display(error_msg)
                        let ret_code = "failinsert"
                        exit for
                    end if
                end for
                if ret_code = "ok"
                then
                    message "Employer added"
                end if
            else
                let error_msg =
                    " Could not insert employer; status ",
                    status using "-<<<<<<<<<<"
                call error_display(error_msg)
            end if

        when p_mode = "U"
            update employers set employers.* = p_employers.*
            where empl_code = p_employers.empl_code
            if status = 0
            then
                for i = 1 to counted_rows

#- even if we counted the last row as valid, if it does not have a
#- 'depot' name, we will ignore it; the input array clause 'after
```

```
#- field depot' should guarantee that the depot name is not left
#- empty if you want to store the record

                    if p_depots[i].depot is null
                    then
                        let ret_code = "ok"
                        exit for
                    end if

#- the clue to distinguish between inserts and updates used here is
#- whether the depot_code in the parallel array p_depots_nv is null
#- (or zero), which means it wasn't retrieved with a Find, but
#- rather it is a new record to be inserted.

                    if p_depots_nv[i].depot_code is null
                    or p_depots_nv[i].depot_code = 0
                    then
                        insert into depots
                        values (p_employers.empl_code, 0,
                                p_depots[i].depot through
                                p_depots[i].phone)
                        if status <> 0
                        then
                            let error_msg = " Couldn't insert ",
                                            "depot; status ",
                                            status
                                            using "-<<<<<<<<<<"
                            call error_display(error_msg)
                            let ret_code = "failinsert"
                            exit for
                        end if
                    else
                        update depots set
                        (empl_code, depot, add_line1, add_line2,
                         city, state, zip, phone) =
                           (p_employers.empl_code,
                         p_depots[i].depot,
                         p_depots[i].add_line1,
                         p_depots[i].add_line2,
                         p_depots[i].city,
                         p_depots[i].state,
                         p_depots[i].zip,
                         p_depots[i].phone)
                        where empl_code = p_employers.empl_code and
                              depot_code =
                                  p_depots_nv[i].depot_code
                        if status <> 0
                        then
                            let error_msg = " Couldn't update ",
                                            "depot; status ",
                                            status
                                            using "-<<<<<<<<<<"
                            call error_display(error_msg)
                            let ret_code = "failupdate"
                            exit for
                        end if
                    end if
                end for
```


continues

Listing 38.7. continued

```
                if ret_code = "ok"
                then
                    message "Employer updated"
                end if
            else
                let error_msg = " Could not update employer; ",
                                "status ",
                                status using "-<<<<<<<<<<"
                call error_display(error_msg)
            end if
        otherwise
            let error_msg = " Mode ", p_mode, " is invalid; ",
                    "no action taken"
            call error_display(error_msg)
        end case
    end if

    return "ok"

end function

###################################################################
function check_employers(p_mode)
###################################################################
define p_mode char(1)

#- This is the place to make final validations before the input
#- statement block ends and the data input by the user is accepted
#- as good enough to be stored.

#- The following are just a sample of validations that you might
#- include here.  Generally, you would perform single field
#- validations in an after field clause, more than here (though
#- these are the examples included).  After inputting all records
#- validations tend to evaluate the overall information in the
#- screen form and the relationship between different field
#- values (data consistency).

if p_employers.employer is null or p_employers.employer = " "
then
    return false, "employer"
end if

if p_employers.add_line1 is null or p_employers.add_line1 = " "
then
    return false, "add_line1"
end if

if p_employers.city is null or p_employers.city = " "
then
    return false, "city"
end if

return true, ""

end function

###################################################################
```

```
function check_detail(p_mode)
#######################################################################
define p_mode char(1)

#- this is just a stub function; appropriate validations should
#- be added to verify the detail input

return true

end function
```

The add.4gl source code module is fully commented; please review it carefully. A number of features worth highlighting are discussed next.

The menu in main.4gl calls the function add_it, which consists essentially of two sections: an initialization section that sets the values of the program variables and arrays involved in input, and a looping section that manages jointly the input for both the header and the detail. The overall structure of the looping section is as follows:

```
while true  #- overall loop

    while true  #- header processing loop
        {header processing statements}
    end while

    while true  #- detail processing loop
        {detail processing statements}
    end while

end while
```


INFORMIX-4GL manages the input to the header in an input statement block and the input to the detail in a separate input array statement block. To allow the user to jump from one to the other, this example has selected the Tab key. After the user presses the Tab key in either the header or the detail processing loops, an exit while occurs, and the user is then sent to the other processing loop. Only when the user presses the Accept or Interrupt keys in either processing loop is control returned to the calling function—in this case, main. Note how the code for the on key (tab) section of the input and input array statement blocks interacts with the while loops by returning a ret_code of "tab".

In the detail section, the input array statement block deals with all but two columns of the depots table. The columns displayed in the array are input through the p_depots array of records variable; the variables that are not input are managed by a parallel array named p_depots_nv.

The input array statement block illustrates the use of a variety of input blocks: the before row block to identify the current program array row and current screen array row, and the before insert so that the program can expand the p_depots_nv array. INFORMIX-4GL manages the array identified in the input array clause—in this case, p_depots—automatically on your behalf, but it is up to you to manage the parallel array p_depots_nv. The before insert clause gives you an example of how to perform that task. The after insert block is used by the program to initialize the parallel program array variables for the current row. (You are in insert mode, so it sets the `empl_code` to the value in the header and the `depot_code` to zero because this is a serial column, and you want the database engine to assign a value to it.) The `before delete` clause allows you to manage the database interactions and the closure of the gap in the parallel array `p_depots_nv`. The `on key` sections perform the same tasks they did in the previous version of the software.

Note that the function `insert_them` now includes a section to manage the detail rows. Often, when you are dealing with a header/detail input, the program deletes all the rows of the detail table from the database and performs an insert of the rows in the detail program array. That practice is acceptable when the table dealt with in the `input array` block does not contain a serial column. If it does, it would not be a good practice to renumber the primary key of those records every time you edit anything in any record. Thus, this version of the software uses a combination of inserts and updates to manage the detail table depots. If a record has a null or zero value in `p_depots_nv[i].depot_code`, it must be a new record; otherwise, the `foreach` operation in `find.4gl` would have returned the proper, non-zero, serial value for that column. New records are inserted into the database, and existing records are updated. Note that this method of management for the detail records requires that you delete records of the depots table in the `before delete` clause; if you were using the method of deleting all rows of the table and reinserting the filled rows of the program array, you would not have to bother about managing deletes of depot records as you go along.

Reports

Reports are commonly used to perform multiple duties in INFORMIX-4GL. For example, a report can be run with an edit argument at one time and later with a posting argument—the former to be used for printing an edit report, and the latter to update the database. In addition, reports are required to print in different locations, to display to a screen, or, sometimes, to store data in an ASCII file. These reporting features are covered in this section.

Managing Multiple Report Destinations in a Single Report

If you want your report to be managed differently depending on your needs at the time, it is common to include in your reporting program menu a choice for Report destination separate from the Find menu choice. The Find menu choice allows the user to set the criteria for reporting, and the Report destination menu choice allows the user to select the proper destination, which is then used in the `start report <report name> to <destination variable>` statement to direct the report to the right location.

Producing Multiple Reports within a Single Program Module

A common practice in reporting programs, particularly those that also do postings (database updates), is to report on the database interactions separately from the primary report output.

In other cases, the same data can be used to simultaneously produce a variety of reports. It is possible to accomplish these tasks within a single reporting program run by using the `start report` statement multiple times within the report driver and by using the appropriate `output to report` commands to send the appropriate data to each of the reports initialized. Normally, the primary report receives the data sorted by the report driver, and the other reports have to run a two-pass sequence to sort the data within the report formatter. Do not forget to use `finish report` for each of the reports you initialized.

Multiple Section Reports

To produce a multiple section report—one in which multiple views of the data, each formatted differently, are intermingled—requires that you modify the basic structures for both the report driver and the report formatter, as follows:

1. In the report driver, declare a cursor for the table (or tables) that are common throughout the report (and all of its sections).
2. Start the report and begin the `foreach` loop that retrieves data for the cursor defined in the preceding step.
3. For each row returned, declare a new cursor for each type of statement that needs to be printed.
4. Process each of these new cursors in order and pass to the report the cursor type along with the information you want to print. Close and free the cursors as appropriate.
5. In the report formatter, select what to print based on the cursor type passed along with the data. Normally, a `before group of <cursor type>` section will print the required headings.
6. Finish the report, and then close and free your main cursor.

Nonstandard Report Layouts

To produce a Matrix Report, one in which the output records received by the report formatter must be printed across columns rather than row by row, requires that you artificially flag the output records so that you can print the output in a group block statement (`after group of` or `on last row`).

In the case of our fictitious company example, suppose that you want to produce a report that prints the number of employers in each of four sections of the country (Eastern, Central, Mountain, and Pacific) in a row with one column for each section of the country. You would gather the records in the report and pass each record to the formatter. The formatter would process only an `on last row` control block, in which a group count with a `where` clause by section of the country would be used to fill a single `print` statement with four values spaced out across the single row.

Similar concepts would apply to a two-dimensional table in which you have each employer listed in a row showing the same four columns as before, which count the number of depots each employer has in each section of the country. In this case, your report driver would define a cursor ordered by employer and pass each record to the formatter. The formatter would process an `after group of employer` control block, in which a group count with a `where` clause by section of the country would be used to fill a single `print` statement with four values for this employer spaced out across the single row.

Error Management

Errors in INFORMIX-4GL programs crop up at various stages. Syntactical errors in screen forms and source code modules are trapped and reported by the compiler. The only exception to this rule is for prepared statements that are not interpreted by the compiler but are passed to the engine for validation and execution at runtime. Errors that occur at runtime are SQL errors or program execution 4GL errors. In your sample programs, you have already been addressing some of the error management features that INFORMIX-4GL offers. This section formalizes their use and introduces new error management features.

Trapping Errors

By default, when INFORMIX-4GL encounters a fatal error during execution, it halts execution of the program and returns control to the command line. In this exit process, it reports the error number and description, as well as the line of the program that failed to the terminal screen where the user may or may not have time to review it.

To alter this behavior, use the `whenever error` statement. This statement tends to be used as a wrapper for the sections of code that you want to handle in a way other than the default. The `whenever error` statement is a compiler directive rather than a command in INFORMIX-4GL. It operates in the source code module where it is defined, and only from the point at which it is defined. Its behavior continues until either the source code module ends or the compiler encounters another `whenever error` statement. These are the reasons for using it as a wrapper for the sections of code you want to handle your own way. The syntax for this command is as follows:

```
whenever { [ any ]  error
                    sqlerror
                    warning
                    sqlwarning
                    not found
                 }
     { call <error handling function>
       continue
       stop
     }
```

The any clause in the whenever error command strengthens the behavior of the detection: whenever error traps database and screen interaction errors; whenever any error traps those errors and, in addition, errors in the execution of any 4GL expression.

Typical examples of this command are

```
whenever error call error_handler
whenever not found continue
```

The whenever error call error_handler clause is typically used at the top of every source code module, so that you can manage the error trapping within a central function named error_handler; whenever not found continue is placed before a select statement so that you can handle the return of no rows locally. (Note that this select statement must be followed by another whenever error call error_handler command to reinstate the error-trapping behavior.)

Generic Error Management

In the examples, you have used two of the error management tools that INFORMIX-4GL provides. You have used the status variable to detect SQL errors and not found conditions, and you have also used the startlog function to record in an ASCII file the runtime errors encountered.

In addition, you have displayed SQL errors within an error window that forces the user to take notice before the program terminates. Actually, for these to work, you need to include a whenever error continue command at the top of each of the source code modules in the program. (These statements have been included in the listings in this chapter for the first time.) Otherwise, an error will still terminate the program without ever reaching the call to the error_display function. Try the program with and without the whenever error clause and verify the behavior described.

To go beyond what you have already done, you would define your own function to manage errors trapped during execution. If, instead of the clause whenever error continue in your source code modules, you use the whenever error call error_handler, INFORMIX-4GL will call the function error_handler whenever it encounters an error and, upon entry into that function, the values of status and SQLCA will still reflect the engine's recorded parameters for the statement that caused the error.

The function error_handler could simply use the errorlog, err_print, or err_quit functions, or it could use the status and SQLCA variables to add some logic to the program's execution.

Using the SQLCA Record and Its Components

Consider the following section of code for a generic error handling function:

```
function error_handler()
define em char(70),
          p_sqlcode integer

whenever error stop

let p_sqlcode = SQLCA.sqlcode
let int_flag = false

case (p_sqlcode)
    when 0
        exit case
    when notfound
        call error_display(" Row Not Found ")
    when -206
        call error_display(" Table doesn't exist; exiting program ")
        exit program
    when -242
        call error_display(" Table locked by another user; bailing out ")
        exit program

    ...

    otherwise
        let em = "Error: ", p_sqlcode using "-<<<<<<<<<<",
                       "; can't decide what to do.  Ask for help!"
        call error_display(em)
        exit program
end case
```

The components of the SQLCA record were discussed at length in the "Error Handling Language Constructs" section of Chapter 35, "Introduction to 4GL." Any of its featured values can be stored in a local variable and then used to decide what to do.

The 4GL Debugger

The Interactive Debugger was first introduced in Chapter 35. Programmer control is provided through the Command window of the Debugger screen in which you can issue commands to the Debugger to perform a variety of tasks discussed in the following sections.

The debugger can be invoked from the command line or from the developer's environment. In either case, the application developer can customize the way in which he or she interacts with the debugger in various ways.

From outside of the debugger, the programmer can set the UNIX environment variable DBSRC. DBSRC is defined in the same manner as PATH or DBPATH, as a concatenated series of directories delimited by colons. When set, the debugger will have access to source code modules in the directories specified by DBSRC. In addition, if the debugger is invoked from the command line, the `-I` option provides for defining a search path for source code modules in the same manner as the DBSRC variable is defined.

The Debugging Environment

From inside of the Debugger, the developer can customize the display parameters, source code file search path, aliases, breakpoints, traces, and so on, and can store those settings in a `*.4gb` file that can then be retrieved in the next session. Unless the developer provides a name for this file, the file will be stored with the name of the program and the extension `.4db`. To save the debugging environment for the next session, use the command

```
write [ break ] [ trace ] [ display ] [ aliases ] [  >> "<filename>" ]
```

To retrieve the environment the next time around, use the command

```
read "<filename>"
```

`<filename>` is the name of the `.4db` file that will contain debugging setup directives. This file is an ASCII file and can be edited manually. If omitted, the name of the program followed by the extension `.4db` is used to store the debugging environment, and this command will automatically be loaded in the next debugging session. A sample `*.4db` file is shown in Listing 38.8.

Listing 38.8. The `employers.4db` debugging environment file.

```
alias f1 = help
alias f2 = step
alias f3 = step into
alias f4 = continue
alias f5 = run
alias f6 = list break trace
alias f7 = list
alias f8 = dump
alias f9 = exit
grow source 4
use =  .,/u/eb/src/lib.4gm/common.4gs,/u/eb/src/lib.4gm/zooms.4gs
turn on autotoggle
turn off sourcetrace
turn on displaystops
turn on exitsource
turn off printdelay
timedelay source 1
timedelay command 0
list display
```

This listing reflects the `grow source +4` command you used in Chapter 35, as well as the DBSRC settings in the `use` command. The basic function keys have not been modified, and the `alias` commands represent their default behavior. To start the debugging session, press the F5 function key. If you had defined breaks, defined traces, and then used `write`, the `.4db` file would reflect all of the settings that were active at the time it was saved.

To use the debugger, the developer issues a run command, and the software switches to the Application Screen and begins execution. When the developer wants to interrupt execution and switch back to the Debugger screen, he presses the Interrupt key. From the Debugger screen, after interrupting the program, the developer can view the contents of the Application Screen by pressing Ctrl+T (and can switch back with another Ctrl+T).

The basic navigation and display functionality provided by the function keys can also be achieved by using the following commands:

```
run
```

```
continue [ { interrupt ¦ quit } ]
```

If the developer wants to test the behavior of the program in response to an Interrupt or a Quit, instead of using the F4 function key, he uses the continue interrupt or continue quit command, and the program receives the signal and proceeds accordingly. Otherwise, because Interrupt is trapped to transfer the view to the Debugging screen, testing its behavior would be impossible.

```
step
```

```
list [ break ] [ trace ] [display]
```

The preceding code displays a list of active breaks, traces, or display parameters.

Often, you will want to see the source code in a specific module or function. As you start the debugger, main will be displayed on the Source window of the Debugger screen. To display the contents of another source code module or the contents of a specific function, and to place the cursor in the Source window of the Debugging screen, you use the view command:

```
view  {  <module: .4gl>  ¦  <function name>  }
```

In the case of modules, you do not need to specify the .4gl extension. In this way, you can view any function that is in the defined search path. The command view without arguments will move the cursor to the Source window. Both the Source window and the Command window have a scrollable display. You can use vi-like scrolling commands to move forward and back through the two windows: Ctrl+F, Ctrl+D, Ctrl+B, and Ctrl+U.

Displaying the Contents of Program Variables and Arrays

To view the contents of program variables and arrays, use the following commands:

```
print  <varname>
```

This command displays the contents of <varname> in the Command window. The variable <varname> can be an array, but you need to limit the display to the row you want to see by indexing it in the same way you do in the program; otherwise, the entire array will be displayed.

```
print <expression> [ >> "<filename>" ]
```

```
dump  [ { globals ¦ all } ] [ >> "<filename>" ]
```

The two preceding commands have the capability to print an `<expression>` or the contents of the currently active variables to the Command window or to a file `<filename>`.

Breaks

To stop execution of the program at predetermined points within the code, you use `break` in one of its various forms.

The following version stops execution at line `<line number>` of the module that is displayed in the Source window:

```
break <line number>
```

The following version stops execution at line `<line number>` of the module displayed in the Source window if `<condition>` is true, and then executes `<command>`:

```
break <line number> [ if <condition> [ "{" <command> "}" ] ]
```

The following version stops execution at line `<line number>` of the function identified by `<function>`:

```
break <function>[.<line number>]
```

The following version stops execution whenever `<varname>` changes value:

```
break <varname>
```

The following version stops execution whenever `<varname>` changes value if `<condition>` is true, and then executes `<command>`:

```
break <varname> [ if <condition> [ "{" <command> "}" ] ]
```

The following version permanently removes the breakpoint identified by number `<break number>`:

```
nobreak <break number>
```

The following version allows breakpoints and traces to be temporarily disabled and then re-enabled:

```
enable { <break number> ¦ <trace number> ¦ all }
disable { <break number> ¦ <trace number> ¦ all }
```

Traces

Sometimes you want to know when a certain code line is executed, when a function is invoked (and the value of the parameters passed), or when the value of a variable is changed. To accomplish this, use the `trace` command:

```
trace <line number>
trace <function>[.<line number>]
trace <varname>
trace functions
```

Other Features

There are more commands in the Interactive debugger than those covered here, but the preceding commands are the workhorses of your work. You have already seen some of these miscellaneous commands, such as `grow` and `alias`, used earlier.

Miscellaneous Topics

By the time you reach this point, it might seem that there is nothing more for INFORMIX-4GL to offer you. I can guarantee that you have missed some features that will be important to you at one point or another. Some of those features that are used often or just on occasion are discussed here.

Multiple Database Capable Programs

The sample program has already illustrated one method of using the same program with different databases: Pass the database to use as an argument in the command line that invokes the program. You could indeed provide a hidden menu option that would perform the same task. It is important to plan your application in this way so that, at least, you can use the same code for both testing and production, and you can use either database at will.

Dealing with Multiple Databases in a Single Program

Your program might have to deal with tables of different databases at the same time. For example, your local store updates its inventory and the central warehouse inventory at the same time, or just places an order to the central warehouse if the item is not found locally. To use multiple databases in a single program, all you have to do is declare variables by defining the complete access to the remote database and use its tables in the same manner. For example, to declare a record with the structure of a table in a remote database named `<remote database>` that is handled by the server `<remote server>`, use the following notation:

```
define p_remote record like <remote database>@<remote server>:<table name>.*
```

You could declare cursors in a similar manner:

```
declare c_cursor cursor for
"select * from <remote database>@<remote server>:<table name> ...
```

Indeed, you could perform any database operation, particularly joins, between tables in different databases within the same or different database servers. You might just need to discuss your needs with your database administrator to make sure that your server and the remote server are properly set up to network and share data.

The Interaction Between the UNIX Environment and a 4GL Program

A number of parameters that are required and/or useful for the adequate operation of INFORMIX-4GL are set through the UNIX environment. For the development environment to work, you must set at least the following variables: `INFORMIXDIR`, `PATH`, `INFORMIXTERM`, `TERM`, and either `INFORMIXSERVER` and `SQLEXEC` for an SE database or `INFORMIXSERVER` and `ONCONFIG` for an OnLine database (versions 6 and higher). In addition to these required environment variables, it is useful to set some defaults for the printer to direct output to, for your favorite editor, for the source code module path for the debugger, and so on. Because the definition of these variables is normally initiated through the system-wide profile or through the user profile, I recommend that you discuss your needs with both the UNIX system administrator and the Database Administrator.

In addition to the INFORMIX-4GL interaction with the environment, your program can also interact with the UNIX environment. You have already seen how you can pass arguments to the program through the command line, and I also discussed the use of the function `fgl_getenv` to retrieve the value of environment variables within your program. Your program can also return an exit code through the `exit program` statement. This is particularly useful if you call one INFORMIX-4GL program from within another. If the called program returns an exit code, the caller can determine what course of action to follow.

Using SQL Within the 4GL Program

The example that has been developed in these four chapters on INFORMIX-4GL has made use of the two modes that you can utilize to make your program use SQL statements: either directly by embedding the statement in your code, or through the use of cursors (`prepare`, `declare` and either `execute` or `foreach`, or `open` and `fetch`).

If you use SQL directly in your code, the statement must not be a `select` statement; or, if it is, the statement must return a single row at most. Otherwise, an error will occur.

Using C Functions in the 4GL Program

If you need to include C functions within your 4GL code, you need to link them into your executable if you use the compiled version of INFORMIX-4GL; or you will have to create a customized RDS runner and debugger if you are using the Rapid Development System.

Transaction Management and Staleness Alerts

Although I have not made a big deal of this, rest assured that INFORMIX-4GL was designed with transaction management in mind. The reason I have not made a big point of it is that it is very simple to implement programmatically. To initiate a transaction, use the `begin work` statement; follow it by the collection of SQL statements that must be handled within the transaction as a unit; and end it with either a `commit work` or `rollback work` statement.

If you consider the sample programs, both the `delete.4gl` and `add.4gl` source code modules are candidates for using transaction management. You want to make sure that you either delete both the depots and the employer records as a whole or delete none at all, or that you update all the records for depots of an employer and the employer record as a unit or don't update any. Thus, you wrap the section of code that performs the update or the delete with the `begin work` and `commit work` clauses.

Both `add.4gl` and `delete.4gl` are also candidates for providing alerts for staleness. Consider the user that triggered a `Find` and decided to go for coffee while the computer retrieved the records, not knowing this database engine was much faster than what he was used to. By the time he returns to `Update` a record, another user might have changed that record, but the version displayed on the screen is the old version prior to changing. The record is indeed stale. To remedy this and to lock the record, it is normal practice that, when the user chooses an action that could result in database alterations (update or delete), you define a new, more restrictive cursor that deals exclusively with the records to update (a single employer and its depots) and that you declare it with the `for update` clause, so that the engine will lock it on your behalf within a transaction. If the record is locked, you know that another user is updating it; if it is not found, you know that another user deleted it; if it is available, you lock it. After locking it, when you display its current contents on the screen, you can also alert the user as to whether the previous version (by now perhaps stored in the `p_old` variables) was different from the newly retrieved version.

Summary

This chapter introduced you to the input of one-to-many relationships and showed you how to manage the database interactions with multiple tables simultaneously. It also showed you how to develop reports with complex structures. Those subjects cover the greatest complexities that you are likely to encounter in developing business applications with INFORMIX-4GL.

In addition, this chapter introduced you to the debugger and collected some odds and ends that did not fit precisely under the previous headings.

You are now equipped to convert the code included in the last four chapters to production caliber or to develop such code on your own. Enjoy the practice!

CHAPTER 39

Introduction to NewEra

by Gordon Gielis

IN THIS CHAPTER

This chapter provides an overview of the NewEra development system. I identify the major features of the development system so that you can make a more informed judgment about whether NewEra is the product for your project.

What Is NewEra?

INFORMIX-NewEra is a simple, graphical, object-oriented software development system designed for development of enterprise-wide, database-centric applications.

In developing the NewEra system, Informix has clearly focused on the corporate, enterprise-wide database application paralleling the rising popularity of Informix database products in the corporate marketplace. NewEra is well suited to cope with the rapidly rising size and complexity of corporate databases. NewEra possesses a rich set of database access options from industry-standard ODBC to high-performance embedded SQL. One of the great strengths of NewEra is its flexibility: NewEra supports visual RAD, structured or object-oriented development approaches, or a mixture of all three.

The major features of NewEra are

- Extensive database access capabilities
- Rapid development of graphical user interfaces
- Enterprise-wide development
- Flexible language
- Support for large-scale project management

The major features of NewEra are covered in more detail throughout the rest of this chapter.

Database Access

NewEra is an application development system from a major relational database vendor, so it comes as no surprise to learn that it has a very rich set of database access features.

Many client/server tools have limited database support mainly provided via the Open Database Connectivity standard. Although ODBC provides a much needed industry standard, it is too restrictive for many mission-critical applications. The amount and complexity of data being stored in corporate databases is increasing dramatically. NewEra provides high-performance solutions to very large database access problems, and it fully supports the ODBC standard.

NewEra provides database access that

- Supports the ODBC standard
- Allows simultaneous connection to multiple databases
- Supports embedded SQL

- Distributes processing
- Includes database-aware grids
- Supports binary large objects
- Includes a fully featured Windows database

The NewEra development system provides a Microsoft ODBC interface to ODBC drivers. This allows NewEra applications to connect to any database with an ODBC standard driver. The ODBC interface is implemented as a collection of object-oriented class libraries.

Application programmers are increasingly required to access data spread across the enterprise in a number of disparate databases. NewEra supports simultaneous connection to multiple databases.

The NewEra language allows Structured Query Language statements to be embedded directly into the language. Embedded SQL can take advantage of all of the features of the Informix database. Typically, it takes less effort to develop applications in embedded SQL than with ODBC.

Database access and processing can be distributed across multiple database servers using NewEra's application partitioning capabilities. The programmer can structure the application so that processing occurs on the database server. This can vastly reduce network traffic. In high-performance applications, the programmer can take advantage of ESQL/C routines executing on the database server.

NewEra comes with a database-aware grid, called a *supertable*, with extensive database access and update capabilities. Using a supertable, the programmer can construct fully functional database applications with almost no coding. Supertables can take advantage of the Informix database's capability to store formatting and presentation rules in the database, considerably increasing productivity.

Informix was one of the first major database vendors to support binary large objects. The NewEra language implements a number of object-oriented class libraries to assist in the management of blob data types. NewEra has implemented both a `Byte` data type and a `Text` data type.

The NewEra development system comes standard with an Informix version 6 database for Windows. The version 6 database is a fully featured database supporting stored procedures, triggers, and transaction logging. Users can store local or sensitive data on the client PC while maintaining data integrity. Programmers are able to develop applications on stand-alone or notebook PCs and distribute to client/server without any code changes.

GUI Development

Development of graphical user interfaces is made easy with NewEra. Windows are constructed visually with a variety of prebuilt graphical objects. The major features of NewEra as a GUI development tool are as follows:

- A visual Window Painter
- Reuse of graphical objects
- Visual class library
- Business graphics library
- Microsoft Windows and Motif support

Central to the use of NewEra for GUI development is the Window Painter tool. The Window Painter allows the programmer to "paint" event-driven windows visually using the mouse to place the visual object. NewEra provides an assortment of GUI components including buttons, list boxes, grids, and text fields. Each visual component can detect the occurrence of an event, such as a mouse click from the user, and the NewEra Window Painter supports this by allowing you to attach procedures to handle these events. The Window Painter allows new window classes to be created or allows the current window to inherit the properties of previously developed window classes.

Visual objects can be reused through object inheritance or through the use of reusable object files. Reusable object files allow you to set a standard look and feel for use throughout your project. Inheritance of Window properties from base class windows reduces development time, improves consistency, and reduces errors.

The NewEra system comes with an extensive visual class library. The visual class library comes complete with the following visual objects for use in developing windows:

- Buttons
- Radio buttons
- List boxes
- Combo list boxes
- Text fields
- Frames
- Menus
- Picture buttons
- Database-aware supertable (grid) and fields

Because it's a database-centric development system, the supertable objects come with a rich set of features to assist in developing database access windows. Supertables support optimistic or pessimistic locking, support master-detail relationships to more than one level, and detect that changes have been made to the current data set by other users (sometimes called "dirty data"). Supertables also come with an optional set of buttons that initiate all of the common database activities such as query-by-forms, deletion, and insertion. By using supertables, you are able to develop database applications directly from the Window Painter with little coding.

Additionally, a number of graphical objects are available from third-party vendors, including calendar, status, database-aware list boxes, and tab controls.

Also included standard with NewEra is the Business Graphics Class library. This contains visual classes that make it easy to develop charts and graphs. The class supports many graph and chart types that can be manipulated programmatically. Furthermore, the charts can be bound to a database-aware grid, minimizing the amount of coding required.

Windows developed under NewEra can be deployed under Microsoft Windows or Motif environments with no changes except for recompilation.

Enterprise-Wide Development

NewEra is a development system targeted for a large enterprise-wide system. The sophisticated code reuse capabilities of NewEra yield maximum benefit in a planned system with a coherent architecture. Enterprise-wide developments also need to support heterogeneous environments in client operating systems, database management systems, and user interface presentation systems. NewEra enables enterprise-wide developments with these features:

- Support for both GUI and character-based presentation
- Scalable performance
- Both MS Windows and Motif runtime environments
- Access of databases from other vendors

Enterprises are not restricted to the administration offices. Many locations in the enterprise are not suitable for deployment of a GUI system. Enterprises might need to deploy computer interfaces to the point-of-sale, factory floor, hand-held stocktake units, or truck fleets, to name a few. It is not always suitable or even possible to deploy the typical GUI interface into these locations. The architect of the enterprise system is faced with the problem of developing separate applications for deployment to these locations. Often these "other" applications need to be developed in another programming system, which increases the logistical problem. Ideally, the development system used for most of the enterprises will support deployment into these, usually character-based interface, environments. This maximizes code reuse. The NewEra development system supports a character-based interface that allows deployment on character-based devices such as VT100 terminals and hand-held data capture units.

Scalable performance is another major concern of the large enterprise. Network bottlenecks are the main cause of poor performance for large enterprise applications. NewEra supports application partitioning that allows parts of the application to be executed on dedicated servers. The application server can be located near or on the database server, minimizing network bottlenecks. This feature, together with the high-performance database access, can greatly reduce the resource usage of applications.

Flexible Language

The NewEra language allows the programmer a number of approaches to the project of application development. The programmer can choose an object-oriented, structured, or mixed method of development. The choice depends upon the application requirements, the size of the project, and requirements for extension and reuse of the project.

The NewEra language has these major features:

- Simple-to-use English-like 4GL syntax
- High-performance execution
- Object-oriented capabilities
- Capability to extend with third-party libraries
- Strong data typing

The NewEra language is a simple language. The developers of the language have consciously tried to keep the number of language constructs to a minimum, to use self-explanatory English-like syntax wherever possible, and to eliminate some of the constructs that frequently cause errors in object-oriented programming.

A major source of errors when programming with some languages such as C occurs because of the misuse of pointers. NewEra does not support pointers. NewEra replaces the pointer with the reference variable. A reference variable refers to an object and can be thought of as a "strongly typed" pointer to the object. The reference variable refers only to a particular class (or its ancestors) of the object. The major difference between a reference variable and a C-style pointer is that a NewEra reference variable cannot be treated as an integer. You cannot cast a reference variable into an integer or perform pointer arithmetic on reference variables, and you cannot access memory locations directly through reference variables. This brings considerable improvements in code reliability.

Memory management is a source of many errors in languages where the programmer is required to handle it manually. Memory management in NewEra is automatic; memory is allocated by the language when an object is created and is automatically deallocated by the language when the object is no longer used.

NewEra can be used as an interpreted language, like Java, or a high-performance compiled language. Compiling source code modules with an interpreted language is typically quicker than machine code compilation, so NewEra is frequently used in interpreted mode during development that is then machine code compiled for deployment.

NewEra has all the capabilities central to the object-oriented technique. Inheritance, polymorphism, and encapsulation are all supported. The programmer is able to think of the application as a collection of cooperating objects rather than in terms of algorithms and data storage structures. Each object can be responsible for all of its actions and states. Object orientation allows the programmer to more clearly visualize the problem space, increasing productivity and reducing the learning curve for new programmers.

You can extend the facilities of NewEra through the inclusion of class libraries developed by a third-party or through the inclusion of functions written in a foreign language (such as C++). This allows NewEra to be used to solve exotic problems such as process control and document imaging.

Strong data typing at compile time minimizes errors and enforces a much more consistent development style. Strong data typing prevents the programmer from accidentally casting a variable into an incompatible variable. Class members must be explicitly declared, allowing the compiler to do type declaration.

Support for Large-Scale Project Management

Large projects have different management requirements than small projects. Typically, a large project will consist of a number of independent but cooperating programming teams. To be effective, the repository for the project meta-data has to be located on a central server accessible to all programmers. NewEra assists in the management of large projects by providing the following:

- Tools to manage multiprogram projects
- Integration with version control software
- Library development
- Supporting dynamic link libraries
- An interactive visual debugger
- Graphical report writing
- Easy migration of existing INFORMIX-4GL code
- Platform-independent online help system
- Support for internationalization and NLS

The main project management tool provided by NewEra is the Application Builder. The Application Builder allows you to create one or more projects, each project consisting of one or more programs. The Application Builder is also the repository where the module dependency of each program is defined. The Application Builder is thus a visual replacement for the make file. Project and program definitions are all stored centrally in an Informix database. The Application Builder integrates with widely used source code control software such as PVCS.

The Application Builder allows the programmer to manage the creation of project libraries. The programmer can create static or dynamic link libraries and include those libraries in the dependencies of other programs. This allows the project management to more easily divide the project into a group of small teams. Libraries can be exported throughout the project or even to external customers with total source code security.

The application can be deployed as a collection of dynamic link libraries. This allows for the project manager to ease the logistics of deploying the project's executables as well as reducing the overall size of the project's executables. Upgrades and enhancements can be confined to a small number of dynamic link libraries, reducing the burden of upgrades.

The NewEra interactive debugger assists maintenance programs to debug applications. By using the interactive debugger, the programmer can set break points, determine the value of variables, and visually monitor the operation of the program.

Typically, the development of reports consumes a significant portion of the project resources. The NewEra development system includes the Informix ViewPoint report writer, which allows you to visually develop reports. The ViewPoint system is more than just a report writer, because it allows the developer to create "database objects" that are meaningful to an end user. A large relational database is commonly highly normalized. Normalized databases are good for data integrity but are very often unintelligible to end users. The ViewPoint system allows the developer to overcome this problem by creating superviews that correlate to business objects the end user can understand. A superview is a sophisticated view on the database that can incorporate rules beyond the capability of normal database views.

NewEra is compatible with most of the INFORMIX-4GL language, with the exception of some screen interface statements. In fact, many INFORMIX-4GL functions and applications can be used with minimal or no code changes. NewEra includes utilities that can convert some INFORMIX-4GL screen files (`*.per`) into NewEra windows complete with supertables. This can be invaluable when converting an existing INFORMIX-4GL project to NewEra, because much of the business logic, including reports, can be migrated. INFORMIX-4GL programmers can be quickly cross-trained to the NewEra language.

Today's applications demand online help, and NewEra provides a platform-independent help display system. The programmer can bind a help topic in the help file to any of the visual objects in the application. NewEra also supports the Microsoft Windows help system.

The NewEra development system provides class libraries and techniques to assist with internationalization of your project. Translation strings can be stored in the database or in operating system files. The class libraries are compatible with the Natural Language Syntax of the Informix database server.

Summary

This chapter covered the capabilities of the NewEra development system and the types of development projects to which NewEra is best suited.

NewEra is perfect for enterprise-wide, database-centric applications. Using NewEra, you can perform the following tasks:

- Develop interface windows
- Interactively debug applications
- Distribute application logic across multiple servers
- Deploy your application to Microsoft Windows clients, Motif clients, or character-based terminals
- Easily control build dependencies on large projects

CHAPTER 40

NewEra Language

by Gordon Gielis

IN THIS CHAPTER

The goal in this chapter is to investigate the features of the NewEra language and gain an appreciation of how you, the programmer, can best use these features to develop applications. NewEra is well equipped to support both structured programming and object-oriented approaches to project development and, with NewEra's rich set of database capabilities, is an ideal choice for commercial database projects.

NewEra is backward-compatible with most of the INFORMIX-4GL language, with the exception of the screen I/O statements.

Language Basics

This section covers procedural language syntax and structure. Most programming languages allow programmers to declare and assign values to variables and to divide a program into named sections. NewEra has inherited the language syntax of the highly successful INFORMIX-4GL.

Simple Data Types

Simple data types represent discrete items of data. Like most languages, NewEra supports the standard data types such as integers and character strings. Through the Data Class Library (DCL), NewEra also offers an assortment of object classes that provide equivalent functionality to most of the simple data types. Although DCL objects are not strictly simple data types, you can use them in place of simple data types. DCL objects obey the rules of object declaration and usage. I describe objects and classes later in this section. Table 40.1 lists the NewEra simple data types and their DCL equivalents.

Table 40.1. Simple data types.

Type	*DCL Equivalent*	*Data Represented*
`SMALLINT` `BOOLEAN`	`ixSmallInt`	Whole numbers between –32,767 and +32,767 inclusive.
`INTEGER` `INT`	`ixInteger`	Whole numbers between –2,147,483,647 and +2,147,483,647 inclusive.
`SMALLFLOAT` `REAL`	`ixSmallFloat`	A floating-point binary number with the precision of a C float.

`FLOAT`
`DOUBLE`
`PRECISION`
	`ixFloat`	A floating-point binary number with the precision of a C double.

`DECIMAL(p,s)`
`DEC`
`NUMERIC`
	`ixDecimal`	A fixed-point decimal number with precision of *p* and scale of *s*.

Type	*DCL Equivalent*	*Data Represented*
MONEY(*p*,*s*)	ixMoney	A currency amount with precision of *p* and scale of *s*.
DATE	ixDate	A calendar date.
DATETIME	ixDateTime	A point in time with a maximum precision of YYYY-MM-DD HH:MM:SS.FFFFF. A contiguous subset of this precision is permissible; for example, you can specify month to hour.
INTERVAL	ixIntervalDF ixIntervalYM	An interval of time. Intervals can be specified with two maximum precision ranges, either from years to months, or days to fractions of a second. A contiguous subset of either precision range is permissible; for example, you can specify hour to second.
CHARACTER(*n*) CHAR(*n*)	ixString	A character string of fixed length *n* up to a maximum of 32,767 characters.
VARCHAR(*n*)	ixString	A character string of variable length to a maximum of *n* characters.
CHAR(*) VARCHAR(*)	ixString	A character string of unspecified length.
TEXT	ixText	A character string of any length.
BYTE	ixByte	A type of binary large object that is a string of data.

Each variable in a NewEra program must be declared. Variables can be assigned an initial value when they are declared. You declare variables by using the NewEra VARIABLE statement. The following example declares a variable called p_counter, of type INTEGER, and assigns an initial value of 20:

```
VARIABLE  p_counter INTEGER = 20
```

You also can state the data type of a variable by reference to a database column. The following example shows how to declare a variable p_var with the same type as the column sams_column of table sams_table in the database called sams_database of the server named sams_server:

```
VARIABLE p_var LIKE sams_database@sams_server:sams_table.sams_column
```

The server and database identification is not required when a default database has been declared as discussed in the "Database Access" section later in this chapter. The advantage of this feature is that it requires recompilation of the program only to keep the program variable data type synchronized with the data type in the database.

User-Defined Data Types

The NewEra language includes three types of user-defined data types: records, arrays, and user-defined classes.

Records allow you to group a collection of other variables and treat the collection as a single unit, as shown in Listing 40.1. The record can consist of variables of differing types including object references. The individual items in the record are referred to as *members* of the record.

Listing 40.1. Declaring records.

```
VARIABLE  sams_record RECORD
             part_1 INTEGER,
             part_2 CHAR(*)
                      END RECORD
VARIABLE  sams_database_record RECORD LIKE sams_table.*
```

Individual variables within the record can be referenced using *dot* notation. For example, `sams_record.part_1` refers to the integer in the record declared in Listing 40.1.

Arrays are ordered collections of homogeneous data types. The individual variables in the array are called *elements*. Each element of an array can be referenced by its position in the array starting at position 1. You also can declare arrays with multiple dimensions. The elements of an array can also be record and object data types. The following example declares an array of 10 elements, each of data type `INTEGER`:

```
VARIABLE sams_array[10] ARRAY OF INTEGER
```

The expression `sams_array[1]` references the first element of the array `sams_array`, whereas `sams_array[10]` references the last, or tenth element. The following example declares an array of 625 (5 * 5 * 5 * 5) elements, each of data type `sams_database_record`:

```
VARIABLE sams_new_array[5,5,5,5] ARRAY OF RECORD sams_database_record.*
```

The expression `sams_new_array[1,1,1,1]` references the first element—in this case, a record of `sams_database_record` type—in the array.

The memory used by a program for both arrays and records is allocated when the array or record is declared. The memory usage of both arrays and records is therefore fixed while the array or record is in scope. Arrays can have up to 32,767 elements for each dimension.

Using user-defined classes, you can define objects that can provide all the facility of both records and arrays. In fact, the user-defined classes may well have records or arrays, or both, as part of their internal structure. You examine classes and objects in greater detail later in this chapter.

Program Blocks

Programs can be divided into logical units called *program blocks.* The program blocks supported by NewEra are `FUNCTION`, `HANDLER`, `REPORT`, and `MAIN`. The start of a program block is identified by the appropriate keyword, and the end is identified by the same keyword preceded by the `END` keyword.

In the `MAIN` program block, your program begins execution. Each program has only one `MAIN` program block. The following example shows a `MAIN` program block:

```
MAIN
    DISPLAY "Hello world"
END MAIN
```

Scope of Reference

In the preceding section, I discussed the data types available to you with NewEra and the methods by which variables are declared. The other important issue to consider when declaring a variable is the timing of variable declaration. The time at which the variable is declared determines the *scope of reference* of the variable and the timing of memory allocation for that variable.

NewEra supports three *scopes of reference* for variables of simple data types: local, global, and module. A variable declared within a function, handler function, or report has local scope of reference within that program block (functions, handlers, and reports are discussed later in this chapter). Variables declared outside any function, handler function, or report have module scope of reference within that module. In a program that consists of more than one source code module, variables with module scope of reference in one module have no scope of reference within other modules. You can declare a variable with global scope of reference by using the keyword `GLOBAL` when declaring the variable. Declaring a variable with global scope of reference in more than one source code module allows that one variable to be shared between modules. In a program that consists of only one source code module, there is no difference between module and global scope of reference.

The scope of reference controls the timing of any memory allocation NewEra must make for the variable. Variables of global and module scope of reference have memory allocated for them when the program first starts. Variables of local scope have memory allocated only when the function in which they are declared is executed. After execution of the function ceases, memory for variables of local scope of reference is deallocated.

Variables that represent an object data type are subject to the same scope of resolution rules as other variables; however, the memory allocation rules are different and are discussed in detail in later sections.

Assignment, Expressions, and Comparisons

NewEra supports automatic type coercion of compatible data types. For example, you can assign an integer to a decimal or an integer to a character successfully. Of course, if you try to assign a character to an integer, an error will result.

NewEra supports assignment of values to variables using the = operator, as shown here:

```
LET sams_counter = 1
LET my_pay_packet = ( number_hours  /  rate_per_hour ) *
➥                    ( ( 1 - tax_rate ) / 100 )
```

This example sets the value of `sams_counter` to `1` and calculates the value of `my_pay_packet`, respectively.

The three examples shown in the following code block result in the same value being assigned to `my_character`. The third example illustrates the use of the concatenation operator `||`.

```
LET my_character =  "now is the time for all good persons"
LET my_character =  "now is the "  , "time for all good persons"
LET my_character =  "now is the "  || "time for all good persons"
```

Variables can also be assigned value by the return of a call to a function, as shown here:

```
CALL my_function() RETURNING my_variable
LET my_variable = my_function()
```

The preceding statements are equivalent. I discuss functions in more detail later in this chapter.

Variables also can be assigned value by an SQL operation, as in the following example:

```
SELECT my_column
    INTO  my_variable
    FROM my_table
```

This example selects data from the `my_column` column in the `my_table` table and assigns it to the variable `my_variable`.

Record type variables can be assigned one to the other, as shown in Listing 40.2, if each of the members of the records is compatible for type conversion.

Listing 40.2. Assignment of records.

```
VARIABLE
    record_one RECORD
        item1 INTEGER,
        item2 INTEGER,
        item3 CHAR(10)
               END RECORD,
    record_two RECORD
        item4 INTEGER,
        item5 INTEGER,
        item6 INTEGER
               END RECORD
```

```
LET record_one.* = record_two.*                                    O.K.
LET record_one.item1 THRU item2 = record_two.item4 THRU item5      O.K.
LET record_two.item6 = record_one.item3                            FAIL
```

The third assignment in Listing 40.2 will fail because it attempts to assign the value of a member of data type `character` to a member of data type `integer`.

Variables of an object data type can be assigned using the `=` operator; however, the operation is fundamentally different in nature when applied to object data types. I discuss object assignment in detail in a later section.

The values of variables must be compared, and NewEra supports a range of relational and Boolean operators for this purpose. Relational and Boolean operators evaluate to an integer value of `1` or `0` corresponding to `TRUE` and `FALSE`, respectively. `TRUE` and `FALSE` have been declared as constants.

NewEra supports the keyword `NULL`, which is used to indicate an indeterminate or unknown value. Comparisons involving variables with a `NULL` value always evaluate to `FALSE`, with the exceptions of the `IS NULL` and `IS NOT NULL` operators. Table 40.2 lists the relational and Boolean operators supported by NewEra.

Table 40.2. Comparison operators for simple data types.

Operator	*Function*
`=`	Evaluates to `TRUE` if the values of the operands are equivalent.
`==`	Equivalent to the `=` operator.
`<`	Evaluates to `TRUE` if the left operand is less than the right operand.
`<=`	Evaluates to `TRUE` if the left operand is less than or equal to the right operand.
`>`	Evaluates to `TRUE` if the left operand is greater than the right operand.
`>=`	Evaluates to `TRUE` if the left operand is greater than or equal to the right operand.
`<>`	Evaluates to `TRUE` if the left operand is not equivalent to the right operand.
`NOT`	Logical inverse.
`AND`	Logical intersection.
`OR`	Logical union.

continues

Table 40.2. continued

Operator	*Function*
`MATCHES`	Allows pattern matching using the `?` and `*` wildcards. The `?` wildcard eliminates one position from the comparison. The `*` wildcard eliminates an unspecified number of positions from the comparison. Evaluates to `TRUE` if the pattern matches with the appropriate eliminations made.
`NOT MATCHES`	Logical inverse of `MATCHES`.
`BETWEEN` *`<lower>`* `AND` *`<upper>`*	Evaluates to `TRUE` if the value falls between *`<lower>`* and *`<upper>`* inclusive.
`IS NULL`	Evaluates to `TRUE` if the value is null.
`IS NOT NULL`	Evaluates to `FALSE` if the value is null.

Flow Control

Flow control statements allow you to control the order of execution of statements in a program. NewEra supports the flow control statements shown in Table 40.3.

Table 40.3. Flow control statements.

Statement	*Purpose*

`IF` *`(expression)`* `THEN`
`statement_one`
`ELSE`
`statement_two`
`END IF`
	The `IF` statement is used to make decisions. If the *`(expression)`* evaluates to `TRUE`, then the *`statement_one`* will be executed; otherwise, *`statement_two`* will be executed. The `ELSE` statement is optional.

`CASE`
`WHEN` *`(expression_one)`*
`statement_one`
`WHEN` *`(expresson_two)`*
`....`
	The `CASE` statement is used to make decisions. Each expression is evaluated in order, and if it evaluates to `TRUE`, it is executed. Control then passes to after the `END CASE` statement.

`OTHERWISE`
`statement_two`
`END CASE`
	The `OTHERWISE` statement is optional and is executed only if all the preceding expressions evaluate to `FALSE`. You can break out of a `CASE` statement at any time by using an `EXIT CASE` statement.

`WHILE` *`(expression)`* *`statement_one`* *`statement_two`*	The `WHILE` statement is an iteration control statement that allows an unspecified number of iterations.

Statement	*Purpose*

`CONTINUE WHILE`
`statement_three`
`EXIT WHILE`
`END WHILE`
	The `WHILE` statement evaluates `(expression)` and, if `TRUE`, the statements are executed. The `WHILE` statement continues to execute until `(expression)` evaluates to `FALSE`. The `CONTINUE WHILE` statement allows the `WHILE` statement to be repeated without executing the statements after the `CONTINUE WHILE`. The `EXIT WHILE` statement causes control to be passed to after the `END WHILE` statement.

`FOR counter = start`
`TO end`
`STEP number`
`statement_one`
`CONTINUE FOR`
`statement_two`
`EXIT FOR`
`END FOR`
	The `FOR` statement is an iteration control statement that allows for a specified number of iterations. The `FOR` statement initially assigns the value of `start` to `counter` and then executes the enclosed statements. On subsequent iterations `counter` is incremented by the value of `number` and if `END FOR` is less than or equal to `end`, the enclosed statements are executed. If `counter` exceeds `end`, then control passes to after the `END FOR` statement. The `EXIT FOR` and `CONTINUE FOR` statements operate in the same way as the `EXIT WHILE` and `CONTINUE WHILE` statements described previously.

`GOTO label_name` `LABEL : label_name`	You also can cause control to jump to a location specified in the `LABEL` using the `GOTO` statement. Only locations within the same module are permitted.

Functions

Using functions, you can subdivide programs into more logical and manageable units. The use of functions is crucial to the implementation of structured programming techniques. Most languages allow the use of functions (sometimes called *methods* or *procedures*); however, a language that claims to support structured programming techniques should make the use of functions both easy and robust.

Features such as named arguments and default values for arguments increase the ease of use of functions. Formal prototyping of a function allows the compiler to check the validity of any calls made to a function, thereby increasing the robustness of the program. Named function calls are permitted only for formally declared functions.

NewEra supports the function features mentioned here. An example of a function prototype is shown in Listing 40.3.

Listing 40.3. Function prototype.

```
EXTERNAL FUNCTION GetAccountBalance
                    (
                    CustomerNumber  INTEGER,
                    AccountType  CHAR(8) :   "STANDARD"
                    )
 RETURNING MONEY(16,2)
```

This example declares a function called `GetAccountBalance()`. The function has been declared as an external function. The `external` keyword indicates that the source code for the function is in another module. The compiler does not complain if you include a call to this function without declaring it as in the example, but in doing so, you are forgoing allowing the compiler to check the arguments and return signature of the call to the function. This approach is obviously so undesirable as to suggest that it would be wise to include as a standard in any project that all functions used in a module are formally declared. NewEra makes this easy with the `INCLUDE` statement discussed later in this chapter.

NewEra allows you to declare a default value for a function argument. If you do not provide this argument, the compiler substitutes the default value into the function call at compile time.

The function in Listing 40.3 has been declared to accept two arguments: an integer called `CustomerNumber` and a character string called `AccountType`. The arguments become local variables within the source code for the function (in this case, in another module). The function can be called by explicitly naming the arguments in the function call or by calling the function with the arguments in the correct order, as Listing 40.4 illustrates. (The example assumes that the function has been formally declared with a prototype.)

Listing 40.4. Function calls.

```
VARIABLE AccountBalance MONEY(16,2)
VARIABLE BadDateTime DATETIME YEAR TO SECOND
CALL GetAccountBalance(100, "STANDARD") RETURNING AccountBalance
CALL GetAccountBalance(CustomerNumber : 100, AccountType : "STANDARD")
    RETURNING AccountBalance
CALL GetAccountBalance(AccountType : "STANDARD", CustomerNumber : 100)
    RETURNING AccountBalance
CALL GetAccountBalance(100) RETURNING AccountBalance
CALL GetAccountBalance("STANDARD", 100) RETURNING AccountBalance  FAIL
CALL GetAccountBalance(100,  "STANDARD") RETURNING BadDateTime    FAIL
```

In Listing 40.4, the first four calls are correct. In call number one, the position of each of the variables correlates to the correct argument in the function. The second call makes this explicit by naming the arguments. The third call demonstrates one of the strengths of formal prototyping in that you are relieved from calling the function with the arguments in the correct order. The fourth call is successful because the compiler knows to substitute a default of `"STANDARD"` for the second argument. The fifth and sixth calls fail to compile because the compiler checks the prototype of `GetAccountBalance` and detects that the program is trying to assign incompatible variables. If you do not declare the prototype, the compiler will not detect this defect.

TIP

A project of any significant size involves the development of several functions that can be extensively reused throughout the project. I highly recommend that the project managers devote some time to setting naming and usage standards for functions in a project.

Functions can also be included as part of the definition of an object. This aspect of functions is explained in the discussion of objects later in this chapter.

INCLUDE Statement

Prototyping of functions imposes some administrative overheads upon you, the programmer. Most commercial applications consist of several source code modules, increasing this administrative overhead dramatically. To alleviate this burden, NewEra provides you with the `INCLUDE` compiler directive. The `INCLUDE` directive allows you to name a file to be included in the source file at the line of the `INCLUDE` statement. In effect, the source code file becomes one large source code module combining the original file and the included file. You don't have access to this larger expanded file because it is passed directly to the next phase of compilation. The `INCLUDE` statement will import the included file regardless of content. It does not have to be a function declaration statement; however, the expanded file has to be syntactically correct to pass through the remaining steps of compilation.

When the compiler encounters an `INCLUDE` statement, it first looks for the file in the current directory and then in the directories named in the include directories' pathway. The include directories can be specified in the Application Builder, the Source Compiler, or as a command-line option to either of the compilers. See the appropriate section for details. Include files usually have a file type extension of `4gh`—for example, `filename.4gh`.

TIP

The `INCLUDE` statement thus allows programmers and system architects to control the declaration of functions, variables, or even a collection of program statements to be centralized into a small number of standard files. This capability is particularly useful for standardizing issues such as error handling. The compiler looks in the include directories in the order they are specified, so care needs to be taken with naming conventions and include directory locations in the project standards. Time spent developing a consistent use of include files will yield significant efficiency gains, even on small projects.

Constants

The CONSTANT statement allows you to declare a name for a static or constant value, as in this example:

```
CONSTANT
   Pi   FLOAT  = 3.1415926,
   DevelopersName = "MY_NAME"
```

The compiler substitutes the stipulated value for every occurrence of the constant in the program. In this example, note that the second constant does not have a data type declared. The NewEra compiler assumes a data type compatible with the stipulated value. In this example, the constant DevelopersName is declared a character data type by the compiler. A compilation error occurs if you attempt to assign a new value to a constant.

TIP

Constants are commonly used to make a source code module more readable, more easily modified, and more reliable by reducing typing errors. Constants can be declared within an include file that can be used to propagate the constant throughout the project. Project managers should identify any constants applicable to either the problem space of the project or the coding standards adopted and publish these constants as an include file early in the project development cycle.

Built-In Functions

A *built-in function* is a function provided by the core NewEra language to perform commonly used routines or functions. NewEra also provides an extensive number of functions through the various class libraries that come standard; these functions are covered in more detail in later sections. Table 40.4 lists the most important built-in functions.

Table 40.4. Built-in functions.

Function Name	*Use*
ARG_VAL(*n*)	Returns the *n*th placed argument passed to the program.
DOWNSHIFT(*char*)	Downshifts all characters in a string.
ERR_GET(*n*)	Returns the Informix error text for error *n*.
ERRORLOG(*char*)	Writes string *char* to the previously defined error file.
FGL_GETENV(*char*)	Retrieves the value of the environment *char* from the operating system.

Function Name	*Use*
`FGL_KEYVAL(char)`	Returns the ASCII number for the key pressed by the user. Includes such keys as Backspace, Tab, and Return.
`LENGTH(char)`	Determines the number of characters in string `char` after trimming trailing spaces.
`MESSAGEBOX`	Displays a user dialog box with various user options.
`NUM_ARGS()`	Returns the number of arguments passed to the program.
`PACKROW()`	"Packs" a record of simple data types into an `ixRow` object.
`PROMPTBOX()`	Displays a dialog window prompting the user to enter a string.
`SHOWHELP(n)`	Invokes the help display system displaying item `n`.
`SQLEXIT()`	Terminates the connection of an application to an Informix server.
`STARTLOG(char)`	Starts the error logging facility to error file `char`.
`UNPACKROW`	"Unpacks" an `ixRow` object into a record of simple data types.
`UPSHIFT(char)`	Upshifts all characters in the character string `char`.
`TODAY`	Returns today's date.
`MDY()`	Converts a numeric month, day, and year to a date.
`CURRENT`	Returns the date and time of day from the system clock.
`DAY(date)`	Returns an integer representing the day of the week for any given date.
`MONTH(date)`	Returns an integer representing the month of the year for any given date.
`YEAR(date)`	Returns an integer representing the year for any given date.
`TIME`	Returns the current time of day from the system clock.
`WEEKDAY(date)`	Returns an integer representing the day of the week for `date`.

NewEra also provides aggregate functions `AVG()`, `COUNT(*)`, `MAX()`, `MIN()`, `PERCENT(*)`, and `SUM()`. These can be used only in `REPORT` program blocks.

NewEra as an Object-Oriented Language

What makes a language object oriented? Many languages, particularly those designed for development of graphical user interfaces, use objects such as graphical widgets. Are these languages object oriented? With an heroic programming effort and a rigorous adherence to project standards, making a 3GL, such as C, behave like an object-oriented language would be possible.

However, most programmers would accept that C is not an object-oriented language. Stroustrup, the designer of the C++ language, says this:

> If the term "object-oriented language" means anything, it must mean a language that has mechanisms that support the object-oriented style of programming well. There is an important distinction here. A language is said to support a technique if it provides facilities that make it convenient (reasonably easy, safe, and efficient) to use that style.

First, I should define the object-orientation technique. Object-oriented programming is a technique that implements solutions as a collection of independent but cooperating objects. An *object* is a unique instance of a complex data type. An object has behavior characteristics specified by its class. Further, object-oriented programming allows objects of new classes to be created that inherit some or all of the behavior characteristics of objects of another class.

Important elements of the preceding definition are *object, instance, class,* and *inherit.* In my opinion, all these important elements must be supported by a language for that language to be object oriented. A language that uses objects but does not allow inheritance of object characteristics is not object oriented but merely object based.

In the following chapter, you will learn that NewEra provides facilities that make it easy, safe, and efficient to use objects, classes, and inheritance, and that NewEra is a fully featured object-oriented programming language.

Objects

An *object* is a software construct that associates data structures with the operations permissible with that data structure. Objects present a defined interface that controls the permission of external processes to read or manipulate the object's data structure or invoke the object's operations.

The process of associating data with operations is called *encapsulation* and is one of the most exciting features of object-oriented programming. It is important to realize that the *public interface* displayed by the object cannot reveal any of the internal data structure or operations.

Classes

You can think of a *class* as a template or declaration for an object. A class defines the structure and behavior of an object (that is, the data structure and the associated operations, or functions, of an object). Booch describes a class like this: "A class is a set of objects that share a common structure and a common behavior." The data structure and associated operations of the class are called the *members* of the class.

Objects and Classes with NewEra

In this section, you begin to examine how to use objects and classes with NewEra. Figure 40.1 illustrates a simple module structure of a NewEra program that uses objects and classes.

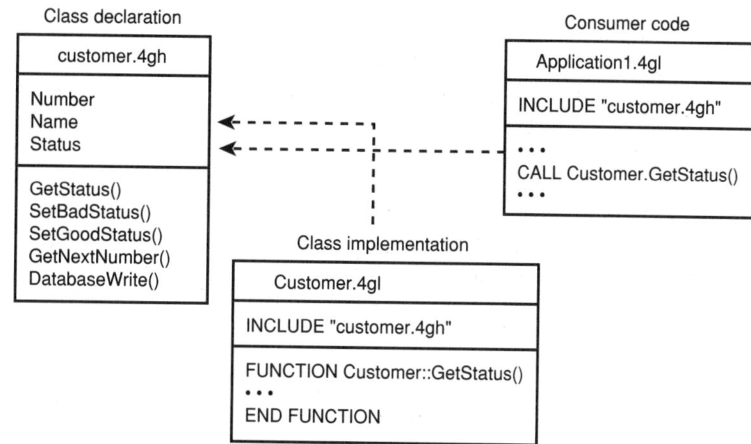

FIGURE 40.1.
Module structure.

You can follow these basic steps to use objects and classes in NewEra:

1. Design a class and declare it by using the `CLASS` statement. Usually, you declare the class in a separate source module with a file type extension of `.4gh`. This file is called the Class declaration file in Figure 40.1.
2. Develop the code that implements the class. This module contains the code that implements the internal workings of the objects of the class. This file is called the Class implementation file in Figure 40.1.
3. Develop the application that uses the object. The application need only concern itself with the *public interface* presented by the object. These files are called Consumer code files in Figure 40.1.

Both the class implementation and consumer code modules use the `INCLUDE` compiler directive to reference the class definition. Before I discuss the details of each of these steps, you should consider two important similarities that objects and simple data types share. Both types of variables need to have their data type (or class) declared before being used, and both objects and simple data types cannot be referenced by a program outside their scope of reference.

Class Declaration

NewEra requires that every object variable have a declared class. The structure of the class must be declared, traditionally in a class definition file as in Figure 40.1, so that the compiler can check the use of the object within the implementation or consumer code. A class declaration is achieved by the NewEra `CLASS` statement. The `CLASS` statement only declares the class; it does not create any objects, does not allocate any memory, and contains no executable statements. The class declaration contains only instructions used by the compiler. You should examine the `CLASS` statement in detail because it is at the core of object-oriented programming and design. Listing 40.5 declares a class called `Customer`.

Listing 40.5. Class declaration.

```
01     CLASS Customer
02
03         FUNCTION Customer
04                   (
05                   aNumber  INTEGER,
06                   aName CHAR(32) : NULL
07                   )
08
09         CONSTANT
10             Good SMALLINT = 0,
11             Bad SMALLINT = 1
12
13         VARIABLE
14             Number  INTEGER,
15             Name CHAR(32),
16             Status SMALLINT
17
18         SHARED VARIABLE
19             NumberOfObjects  INTEGER
20
21         FUNCTION GetStatus() RETURNING SMALLINT
22         FUNCTION SetBadStatus() RETURNING VOID
23         FUNCTION SetGoodStatus() RETURNING VOID
24         SHARED FUNCTION GetNextNumber() RETURNING INTEGER
25
26         EVENT DatabaseWrite(Mode SMALLINT) RETURNING BOOLEAN
27
28     END CLASS
```

With the exception of `EVENT` and `SHARED` keywords, most of the statements that form the class declaration in Listing 40.5 are familiar to you from structured programming techniques. This use should not surprise you, because object-oriented techniques are an extension of the information-hiding and modular-decomposition techniques already recognized as good structured programming. In this sense, the transition to object-oriented techniques is an evolutionary, not revolutionary, change. Next, I discuss each element of the class declaration in detail.

The Constructor Function

The statement on line 03 of the class definition in Listing 40.5 is a `FUNCTION` statement declaring a function called `Customer`. Note that the function has the same name as the class and that the function does not have a return signature. This special function called the *constructor* must be present in every class definition. This function is called when consumer code creates a new object of this class. Creating a new object of a class is called *instantiation* because it produces a new *instance* of an object of that class. Remember that the class declaration is only declaring the prototype of any functions in the class, not the actual function itself that is in the implementation file. Creation and destruction of objects within the consumer code module are discussed in detail in a later section.

Member Constants

Line 09 of Listing 40.5 declares a member constant. A member constant behaves just like a normal constant with the compiler substituting the declared value of the constant at compile time. A member constant of a class has module scope of reference and is referenced using the class name and the module scope resolution operator. Consider the following example from a consumer code module:

```
INCLUDE "customer.4gh"
VARIABLE p_local SMALLINT
LET p_local = Customer::Good
```

This code fragment assumes that the `Customer` class is declared in a file called `customer.4gh`. The variable `p_local` is assigned the value of `0`, which is the value of the class constant.

Member Variables

Line 13 of Listing 40.5 declares three variables: `Number` as an `integer`, `Name` as a `char(32)`, and `Status` as a `small integer`. The example uses only a simple data type, but the variables can be of any data type, including other classes such as the DCL classes discussed earlier. The statement on this line declares the internal data structure of the class. These variables are called the *member variables* of the class.

Member variables can be either *normal*, as are the member variables on line 13, or *shared*, as in line 18. The `SHARED` statement modifies the scope of resolution of the member variable. A normal member variable forms part of the data structure of the object. One variable is located in memory for each object instantiated. A shared member variable, on the other hand, is shared among all instances of objects of the class. Only one variable is located in memory for all objects of the class. Operations on a shared member variable by one object affect the value of the member variable for all objects.

Normal member variables of a class can be referenced using dot notation; for example, implementation code can reference the `Status` member variable of an object of class `Customer` as `Customer.Status`. This method is similar to the way in which the members of a record are accessed.

Shared member variables do not belong to any particular object, but instead they belong to the class as a whole. The syntax to reference a shared member variable is similar to that used to reference member constants. The `NumberOfObjects` member variable of the class `Customer` would be referenced as `Customer::NumberOfObjects`, as shown here:

```
INCLUDE "customer.4gh"
VARIABLE NumberOfObjects INTEGER
LET NumberOfObjects = Customer::NumberOfObjects
```

In this example, note that resolving the class scope of the shared member variable allows you to use two variables of the same name without conflict.

Member Functions

The statement on line 21 of Listing 40.5 declares a function called `GetStatus()`. This statement declares one of the operations permissible for objects of this class. These functions are called the *member functions* of the class.

You can call a normal member function by using the dot notation similar to the way a normal member variable is referenced, as shown in Listing 40.6.

Listing 40.6. Calling a member function.

```
INCLUDE "customer.4gh"
VARIABLE CustomerStatus SMALLINT
LET CustomerStatus = OurCustomer.GetStatus()
IF CustomerStatus = Customer::Good THEN
    --- a good customer
END IF
```

You can modify the scope of member functions in the same way you do with member variables by using the `SHARED` statement. In Listing 40.5, line 24 is a member function declared as a shared member function. Thus, the function `GetNextNumber()` belongs to the class rather than to objects of the class. Shared member functions are called by resolving their scope to their class, like this:

```
INCLUDE "customer.4gh"
VARIABLE NextCustomerNumber INTEGER
LET NextCustomerNumber = Customer::GetNextNumber()
```

As the name suggests, you can use shared member functions for any functions that are specific to the class rather than objects of the class.

Defining Events for a Class

Line 26 of Listing 40.5 illustrates the declaration of an event called `DatabaseWrite()` for the `Customer` class. The declaration of an event is similar to the declaration of a normal member function. Events can accept arguments and have return signatures.

Events behave very much like normal member functions. Events cannot be declared as shared. I discuss events more fully in a later section.

Access Control for Class Members

I said earlier that objects declare a *public interface* and control access to the objects' member variables and member functions. Part of the goal of object-oriented programming is *information hiding*, reducing the complexity of the solution to a collection of cooperating objects. The internal workings of each object are not relevant to the solution, only the external behavior of the object. Information hiding is achieved by *access control.*

NewEra supports three levels of access for member variables and member functions: public, protected, and private. Access control statements modify the `VARIABLE` or `FUNCTION` statement. The following example declares the function `GetStatus()` as a protected function:

```
PROTECTED FUNCTION GetStatus() RETURNING SMALLINT
```

Public access allows any consumer code to reference the class member. Consumer code, therefore, can evaluate or assign value to public member variables, and that consumer code can call a public member function. The operations shown in the following example are legal from consumer code:

```
CALL Customer.GetStatus() RETURNING CustomerStatus
IF Customer.Status = 0 THEN
     --- good customer
END IF
```

Protected access allows the member variables or functions to be referenced only from the implementation code of the class or a class derived from the class. I will show you how to derive a class in the "Inheritance" section. Essentially, declaring a class member as protected prevents consumer code from operating on or referencing that class member directly. Consumer code is forced to perform operations with the object only through the class members declared as `PUBLIC`. Thus, the public class members form the public interface of the object. The power and security that this capability gives the software developer is quite remarkable.

With private access, the member variables or functions of a class can be referenced only from the implementation code of the class. Private members cannot be referenced from the implementation code of derived classes. Private access allows you to create "black box" objects that cannot have the internal operation changed. Other programmers can create new classes by inheritance and modify some of the behavior of the class, but essential internal elements can remain inaccessible. I discuss more details about private access in the "Inheritance" section of this chapter.

The access control statements are in addition to the scope modifier statements; for example, you can declare a private shared member.

Class Implementation

In the preceding section, you declared the `Customer` class. The next step is to develop the class implementation code. The class implementation code actually instantiates new objects and performs the operations you have declared in the various member functions.

Listing 40.7 illustrates the class implementation code for the `Customer` class.

Listing 40.7. Class implementation.

```
01  INCLUDE "customer.4gh"    #   the class declaration (for the compiler)
02
03  VARIABLE NumberOfObjects  INTEGER #   shared variables "instantiated"
04
05  FUNCTION Customer::Customer    # the implementation of the constructor
06                      (
07                      aNumber INTEGER,
08                      aName CHAR(32)
09                      )
10
11      LET SELF.Number = aNumber
12      LET SELF.Name = aName
13
14  END FUNCTION
15
16  FUNCTION Customer::GetStatus() RETURNING SMALLINT
17     RETURN SELF.Status
18  END FUNCTION
19
20  FUNCTION Customer::SetBadStatus() RETURNING VOID
21     LET SELF.Status = Customer::Bad
22  END FUNCTON
23
24  FUNCTION Customer::SetGoodStatus() RETURNING VOID
25     LET SELF.Status = Customer::Good
26  END FUNCTION
27
28  FUNCTION Customer::GetNextNumber() RETURNING INTEGER
29     VARIABLE NextNumber ixInteger
30      . . . do something - maybe SQL from database to set value of NextNumber
31     RETURN NextNumber
32  END FUNCTION
```

Line 03 of Listing 40.7 illustrates the way in which shared member variables are *initialized.* As you might recall, shared member variables are created only once for each class.

Lines 05 through 14 define the constructor function. The main purpose of the constructor in this example is to initialize the internal data structure. You are not limited to data initialization; however, the constructor can perform almost any valid NewEra statement including database access statements. In the example, the member variables `Number` and `Name` are simple data types, and they are initialized by assigning the constructor arguments to them. Alternatively, the constructor can instantiate other objects (that is, call the other objects' constructor function) as part of its internal data structure.

An interesting feature is the use of the `SELF` qualifier to reference the object itself. Line 11 illustrates the way in which implementation code can refer to the object itself. This qualification is not strictly necessary, because the compiler would have been able to resolve the correct variable; however, it makes the code clearer.

The definition of the member functions starts on line 16. The member functions look very much like normal functions, except that the function name is qualified by the class name. The shared member function `GetNextNumber()` is defined on line 28. With the exception of the `SHARED` keyword, it is not noticeably different from any of the other member functions.

Using Objects and Classes in Consumer Code

In the two preceding sections, you declared the `Customer` class and defined the implementation code for the class. Now you can get to the business end of the project and see how you can use this simple class in some consumer code (that is, an application).

Listing 40.8 shows some consumer code that uses the `Customer` class.

Listing 40.8. Sample consumer code.

```
01   INCLUDE "customer.4gh"
02
03   MAIN                       #    the entry point for the program
04
05   VARIABLE OurCustomer Customer # declare a variable named OurCustomer
06                                 # of class Customer
07   VARIABLE NewNumber INTEGER    # a program variable to hold the next number
08
09   LET NewNumber = Customer::GetNextNumber()  # gets the next customer
10                                              # number
11   LET OurCustomer = NEW Customer
12                          (
13                          aNumber : NewNumber  # customer number
14                          )
15
16 CALL OurCustomer.SetGoodStatus() # we set the status of the customer
17
18
19 END MAIN
```

You have now created the first simple application. Listing 40.8 illustrates the use of the `MAIN` statement on line 03; this statement indicates where program execution begins.

Variables Must Have Data Types

Each variable, including an object variable, is required to have a data type (or class). Line 05 of Listing 40.8 declares a variable named `OurCustomer` of class (data type) `Customer`. The compiler knows about the permitted public interface of this class because you have included the declaration of the class with the `INCLUDE` statement on line 01. You also declare an integer called `NewNumber`.

Object Instantiation

An object is instantiated with the `NEW` statement combined with calling the constructor function as illustrated in line 11 of Listing 40.8. Note that the constructor function has been called with just the `aNumber` argument. The `aName` argument has been declared with a default value, and therefore a value is not required (although in Listing 40.8, the member variable `Name` will be assigned the default value of `NULL`).

When an object is instantiated, NewEra creates two memory structures: the object and a reference variable. Figure 40.2 illustrates this concept.

FIGURE 40.2.
Object instantiation.

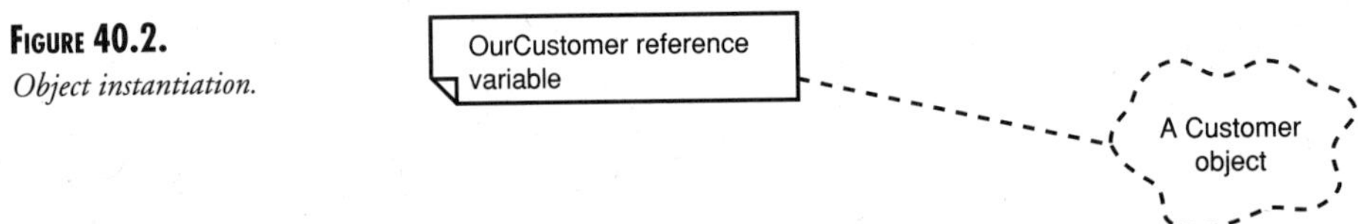

The reference variable is the variable `OurCustomer` in the example. It is called a *reference variable* because this variable is the only way of accessing or referencing the object itself. You see in a later section that an object can have more than one reference variable. If you omit line 11 of Listing 40.8, the subsequent statement on line 16 (where a member function of the object is called) fails because the object at that point does not exist. (In fact, the program would not compile because the compiler would detect that the object has not been created.) This is the major difference between declaring variables of simple data types and reference variables. After the statement on line 07, the integer variable `NewNumber` is available to be used throughout the program. In contrast, the reference variable `OurCustomer` is available only after it has been declared and instantiated (line 05 and line 11).

Now change the example as shown in Listing 40.9 to illustrate more clearly the difference between declaring and instantiating reference variables.

Listing 40.9. Declaring and instantiating reference variables.

```
INCLUDE "customer.4gh"

MAIN                           #    the entry point for the program

VARIABLE   Counter  INTEGER    # a looping variable
VARIABLE   CustomerArray  ARRAY[5] OF Customer   # an array of five
                                                 # customers
FOR Counter = 1 TO 5        #    loop through all the elements of the array
   LET CustomerArray[Counter] = NEW Customer
                                    (
                                    aNumber : Counter #  use looping variable
                                    )                 #  as customer number
END FOR
END MAIN
```

In this example, you are populating an array with five elements, each of which is a variable of class `Customer`. The statement on line 09 creates a new `Customer` variable for each iteration of the `FOR` loop. At the end of the `FOR` loop, you have five quite separate *instances* of a `Customer` reference variable in the array, each of which "points" to a separate `Customer` object. Each of those `Customer` objects can be manipulated independently of any of the other `Customer` objects.

Class Inheritance

One of the essential features of an object-oriented language is the ability to create new classes that inherit some or all of the properties of an existing class. This feature is called *inheritance.* Inheritance allows you to modify and extend the capability of applications easily by incrementally improving the facilities offered by the applications' classes. New application features can be built on a solid known foundation of the existing application. Appropriately designed access control can minimize or even prohibit subsequent development from altering the internal operations of the existing classes.

The best way to demonstrate this facility is by example. You can create a new class based on the `Customer` class previously introduced. In this example, create a class of `Customer` members who are students. You call this new class `StudentCustomer`. The `StudentCustomer` class is a subclass of the `Customer` class. The class declaration statement is shown in Listing 40.10.

Listing 40.10. Inheritance.

```
01  INCLUDE "customer.4gh"
02
03  CLASS StudentCustomer DERIVED FROM Customer
04
05      FUNCTION StudentCustomer
06               (
07               aNumber INTEGER,
08               aName CHAR(32),
09               aStudentNumber INTEGER
10               aCampus CHAR(32)
11               )
12      PROTECTED VARIABLE
13          StudentNumber INTEGER,
14          Campus CHAR(32)
15
16      PUBLIC FUNCTION GetStudentNumber() RETURNING INTEGER
17      PUBLIC FUNCTION GetCampus() RETURNING CHAR(32)
18      PUBLIC FUNCTION SetBadStatus() RETURNING VOID
19  END CLASS
```

The compiler needs to know the declaration of the `Customer` class so that it can properly declare the `StudentCustomer` class members. You therefore include the declaration of the `Customer` class with the `INCLUDE` compiler directive on line 01.

The `StudentCustomer` class is declared on line 03 with the statement `DERIVED FROM` qualifying the class that `StudentCustomer` derives from. The `StudentCustomer` class inherits all the features of the `Customer` class.

The constructor of the `StudentCustomer` class is declared in lines 05 to 11. Note that the prototype of the constructor has changed from that of the `Customer` class.

Lines 12 to 14 declare two member variables: `StudentNumber` and `Campus`. These two new member variables are unique to the `StudentCustomer` class. `StudentCustomer`, however, has five member variables; the `StudentCustomer` class inherits the three member variables of the `Customer` class in addition to the two new member variables declared here. New member variables cannot have the same name as inherited member variables because the member variables will have the same scope within the new class.

Lines 16 and 17 declare two new member functions: `GetStudentNumber()` and `GetCampus()`. These member functions are in addition to the member functions inherited from the `Customer` class.

I said that inheritance allows the programmer to alter the behavior of the new class from that of the old class. The example illustrates how you can change the behavior of member functions. Line 18 declares a member function called `SetBadStatus()`; this is not a new member function because this member function was declared in the `Customer` class. By including another declaration in the `StudentCustomer` class, you are informing the compiler that you intend to alter the behavior of the member function in the new class. This method is called *overriding* the member function. The prototype of the overridden function must not be changed. Unlike the other member functions you inherit from the `Customer` class, you need to define a new implementation for the overridden member function.

To complete the inherited class, you need to define the class implementation code, as shown in Listing 40.11.

Listing 40.11. Implementation of subclass.

```
INCLUDE "studcust.4gh"  # include class declaration for the StudentCustomer

FUNCTION StudentCustomer::StudentCustomer        #    constructor
                                (
                                aNumber INTEGER,
                                aName CHAR(32),
                                aStudentNumber INTEGER,
                                aCampus CHAR(32)
                                ) : Customer
                                    (
                                    aNumber : aNumber,
                                    aName : aName
                                    )
    LET SELF.StudentNumber = aStudentNumber
    LET SELF.Campus = aCampus
END FUNCTION

FUNCTION StudentCustomer::GetStudentNumber() RETURNING INTEGER
```

```
19      RETURN SELF.StudentNumber
20   END FUNCTION
21   FUNCTION StudentCustomer::GetCampus() RETURNING CHAR(32)
22      RETURN SELF.Campus
23   END FUNCTION
24   FUNCTION StudentCustomer::SetBadStatus() RETURNING VOID
25      VARIABLE MailCommand CHAR(*)
26      #   send an e-mail to the student liaison officer (example command only)
27      LET MailCommand = "mail liaison_officer" || SELF.Name
28      RUN MailCommand
29
30      CALL Customer::SetBadStatus()
31   END FUNCTION
```

The constructor of the `StudentCustomer` class calls the constructor of the `Customer` class on line 09. Listing 40.11 also illustrates how you can override a function. Lines 24 to 31 define the function `SetBadStatus()`, which was also defined in the `Customer` class. When the member function `SetBadStatus()` is called for an object of `StudentCustomer` class, this code is executed. However, you can still call the `SetBadStatus()` member function of the `Customer` class, as demonstrated on line 30 (although you do not need to do so). This way, you can either completely override the operation of the member function or add additional steps to the existing function.

Inheritance is obviously a very powerful feature; it is used extensively by the NewEra language itself to provide the Standard Class Libraries discussed in the next chapter. If you do not derive a class from a specific class, NewEra derives the class from a class called `ixObject`. The declaration of this "root" object is well documented in the NewEra language reference, and members of this object provide many useful features that I discuss further in the "Object Assignment" section of this chapter. In other words, you also can define the class declaration of the `Customer` class as in the following example:

```
CLASS  Customer  DERIVED FROM ixObject
```

You can inherit new classes from inherited classes to as many levels as is appropriate for the project under development. Each class extends or modifies the behavior of the class it is derived from. The chain of inheritances is called the *class hierarchy*. Figure 40.3 illustrates a simple class hierarchy involving the `Customer` and `StudentCustomer` classes and their descendants.

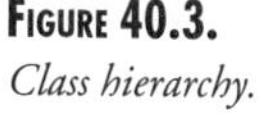

FIGURE 40.3.
Class hierarchy.

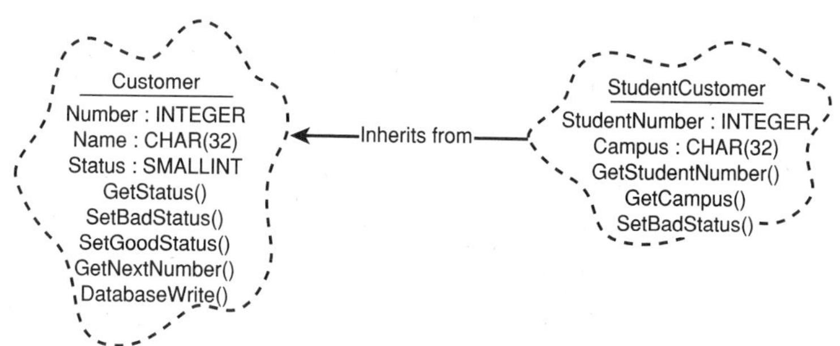

The NewEra language, in common with other high-level object-oriented languages such as Java, does not support multiple inheritance. Multiple inheritance occurs when a class is derived directly from more than one class. This limitation eliminates some problems that arise through namespace conflicts. I discuss class hierarchy design further in a later section.

More on Events

I briefly touched on events earlier in this chapter; now I will describe events in more detail. You noted in the `Class` declaration section that the prototype of an event is similar to the prototype of a member function. In fact, events are sometimes called *reference functions.* The event is implemented (or handled) by a special function called a *handler.* Except for the fact that it uses the `HANDLER` statement instead of the `FUNCTION` statement, a handler is syntactically identical to a function. Why have events and handlers then? A handler can be assigned (or bound) to handle an event at runtime. This behavior is commonly called *dynamic* or *late-binding.* In contrast, the implementation code for a function is bound to the member function at compile time.

Dynamic binding allows consumer or implementation code to change the handler that handles a call to a member event during program execution. Classes that demonstrate multiple behavior are said to be demonstrating *polymorphic* behavior. If no handler has been assigned to an event, calls to that member event are effectively ignored.

In the following example, you make the `Customer` class change its behavior dynamically. The consumer code should be able to make the `Customer` object write the values of its member variables into a table called `cust_table` or to e-mail the details to another user. You use the event mechanism to set up this example.

First, you need to define the implementation code that will perform each of the different types of write. Then add the code shown in Listing 40.12 to the class implementation file of the `Customer` class (`customer.4gl`).

Listing 40.12. Handler implementation.

```
HANDLER Customer::DoDatabaseWrite() RETURNING BOOLEAN
   INSERT INTO cust_table_one (Number, Name)
   VALUES(SELF.Number, SELF.Name)
   RETURN TRUE
END HANDLER

HANDLER Customer::DoEmailWrite() RETURNING BOOLEAN
   VARIABLE MailCommand CHAR(*)
   #  send an e-mail to another user; note simplified for clarity
   LET MailCommand = "mail other_user " || SELF.Number || " " || SELF.Name
   RUN MailCommand
   RETURN TRUE
END HANDLER
```

You have defined the implementation code for the handlers, which, as you can see, are very similar to function definitions. Note that the handlers must have the same prototype as the event declaration.

Now look at the example of consumer code shown in Listing 40.13 that uses the event mechanism.

Listing 40.13. Dynamic use of handlers.

```
IF p_database_write THEN
    HANDLE OurCustomer.DatabaseWrite WITH Customer::DoDatabaseWrite
ELSE
    HANDLE OurCustomer.DatabaseWrite WITH Customer::DoEmailWrite
END IF
CALL  OurCustomer.DatabaseWrite RETURNING p_database_write
```

In Listing 40.13, you see how you can dynamically bind different handlers to the event `DatabaseWrite`. If the program variable `p_database_write` is `TRUE (1)`, the event `DatabaseWrite` is handled with `Customer::DoDatabaseWrite`. If `p_database_write` is `FALSE`, the event `DatabaseWrite` is handled with `Customer::DoEmailWrite`.

In a simple example such as this one, you could have just as easily solved the problem using a member function called `DatabaseWrite` accepting an argument that would control whether the information was written to the database or e-mailed. However, consider what would happen if you wanted to introduce a third option—perhaps a write to a printer instead of the database. If you had chosen a member function, you would have had to recode the member function, potentially introducing errors into what was a fully debugged program. With the event mechanism, you merely have to define the handler for the write to the printer and dynamically bind that handler to the event when required. A further benefit is that the developer of the original handlers does not have to release the source code for them. The existing class implementation need not be disturbed. As the size of the project increases, the complexity of providing polymorphic behavior using traditional functions and control flow statements imposes an unmanageable burden on the project.

So far, you have used the `CALL` statement to execute an event. A `CALL` statement is a synchronous execution of the event. An event executed in this manner behaves exactly like a member function. Events can be executed asynchronously by using the `POST` statement. Posted events are not executed immediately; instead, the event is placed in the NewEra event queue, and the handler for the event is executed the next time NewEra is waiting for user input. The consumer code that posted the event continues to execute the statements after the `POST` statement. Using the `Customer` class example, you can post the event `DatabaseWrite()` as shown here:

```
POST OurCustomer.DatabaseWrite()
```

Note that the POST statement does not expect any return data from the event, even though the event was declared to return a Boolean. NewEra ignores any return from posted events that, because the event handler has not yet executed, would be meaningless in any case. Posting an event is useful in performing tasks that are not on the "critical path" of program execution and can be deferred until the program is idle.

Object Assignment

You can assign simple data type variables to each other by using the = operator. How do you assign values to objects?

Before considering this issue, remember that when an object is instantiated in NewEra, a reference variable and the object are created. The reference variable points to the memory location of the object. (In this sense, it is similar to the pointers used in C++.) The important point to remember is that the variable and the object do in fact occupy two different memory locations. Subject to certain rules, NewEra allows the reference variable to be operated on independently of the object itself. NewEra does not allow you to manipulate the objects independently of the reference variables. You can manipulate the values contained within the member variables of the object only by using the member function or events of the object.

Confused? Consider an example using objects of class `ixString`. An `ixString` is a class that is provided by the Data Class Library. You first met the `ixString` when I discussed simple data types. It is an object that you can use to replace simple character strings. The `ixString` is widely used in all NewEra applications. In the following example, you declare and instantiate three `ixStrings`:

```
VARIABLE  FirstString ixString = NEW ixString("AAAAAA")
VARIABLE  SecondString ixString = NEW ixString("BBBBBB")
VARIABLE  ThirdString ixString = NEW ixString("CCCCCC")
```

Figure 40.4 illustrates the reference variables and objects created by the preceding statements.

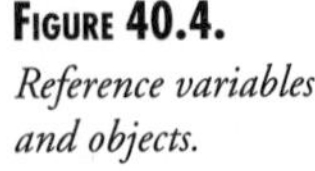

FIGURE 40.4.
Reference variables and objects.

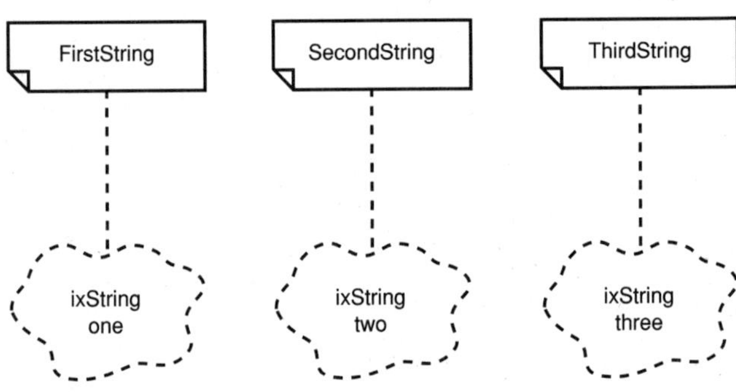

Now you can assign the reference variable `SecondString` to the reference variable `FirstString`, as shown in the following example:

```
LET FirstString = SecondString
```

Figure 40.5 illustrates the relationship between the reference variables and the objects after the assignment statement shown in the preceding example.

FIGURE 40.5.
Memory structure after assignment.

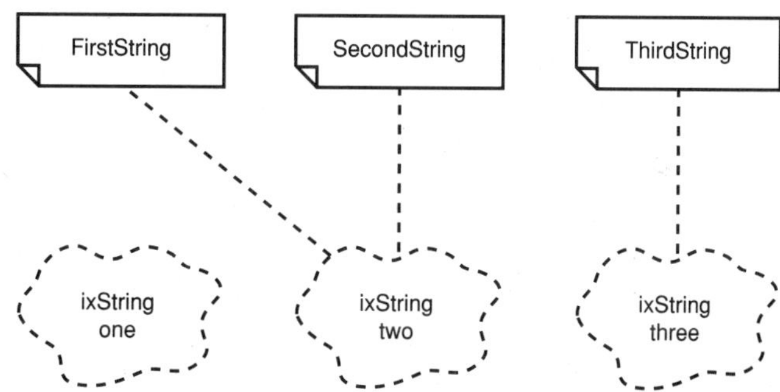

As you can see, the object marked `ixString one` now has no reference variables referring to it at all, but the object marked `ixString two` is referenced by both the `FirstString` and the `SecondString` reference variables. The `ixString one` object is effectively lost; it cannot be re-referenced, and therefore you cannot perform operations on it. The `ixString one` object will have its memory deallocated when NewEra performs garbage collection. (See the "Object Destruction" section later in this chapter.)

How can you change the value of the objects themselves? If the designer of the class declared the member variables as `PUBLIC`, and the member variables are simple data types, you can manipulate the member variables directly using dot (`.`) notation. However, most designers specify member variables as `PROTECTED` to prevent uncontrolled manipulation. In this case, to change the value of the objects, you must use member functions declared for that purpose. If the designer of the class has not declared any member functions to change the value, you simply cannot change the values. The `ixString` class has been declared with a public member function `setValueStr()`, which allows you to change the value of the `ixString` object. To change the value of object `"ixString two"` to `"XXXX"`, you enter the following changes:

```
CALL FirstString.setValueStr("XXXX")
OR;
CALL SecondString.setValueStr("XXXX")
```

Because both reference variables in the preceding example refer to the same object, both statements have the same effect.

You have seen how you can use the = operator to copy one reference variable to another. NewEra allows you to copy one object to another with the `COPY` operator.

There is more to copying objects than to copying reference variables, however. Recall from the discussion of member variables that a member variable can be *normal*, meaning a simple data type or a member variable can be a reference variable. When you copy an object with a reference member variable, the reference member variable in the new object is assigned the same value as the reference variable in the old object. This means that the reference member variable in the new object *points to* or refers to the same underlying object as the old object.

To demonstrate this behavior, in the following example you derive a new class called `IntegerString` that inherits from the `ixString` class but adds a reference member variable of class `ixInteger`. An `ixInteger` class is another DCL class that provides integer-like properties. The class declaration of an `IntegerString` class is shown in Listing 40.14.

Listing 40.14. A class with reference member variables.

```
CLASS IntegerString DERIVED FROM ixString
    FUNCTION IntegerString
                (
                aStringValue CHAR(*),
                aIntegerValue INTEGER
                )
    PROTECTED VARIABLE IntegerValue ixInteger

    PUBLIC FUNCTION getIntegerValue() RETURNING INTEGER
    PUBLIC FUNCTION setIntegerValue(aInteger INTEGER) RETURNING VOID
END CLASS
```

The member variable `IntegerValue` is a reference member variable referring to an object of class `ixInteger`.

Now you can instantiate two reference variables of class `IntegerString` using the `NEW` statement, as shown here:

```
LET VariableOne = NEW IntegerString(aStringValue : "ONE", aIntegerValue : 1)
LET VariableTwo = NEW IntegerString(aStringValue : "TWO", aIntegerValue : 2)
```

The object structure shown in Figure 40.6 will result. The figure shows the two variables together with the `ixInteger` reference member variables.

The constructor of the `IntegerString` objects (which you have not shown) instantiates the `IntegerValue` reference member variables for each of the `IntegerString` objects.

Now examine what happens if you copy one of these variables to the other using the `COPY` statement, as in the following example:

```
LET VariableOne = COPY VariableTwo
```

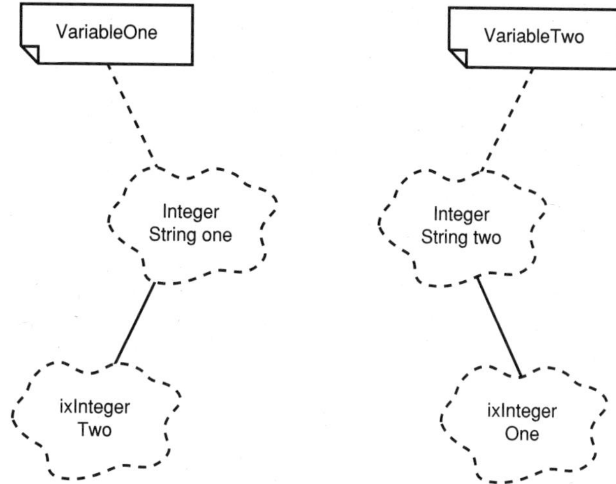

FIGURE 40.6.
Memory structure.

The object structure shown in Figure 40.7 will result. The normal member variables are copied in the sense that new memory storage is allocated for them, but the reference member variables are only assigned one to the other.

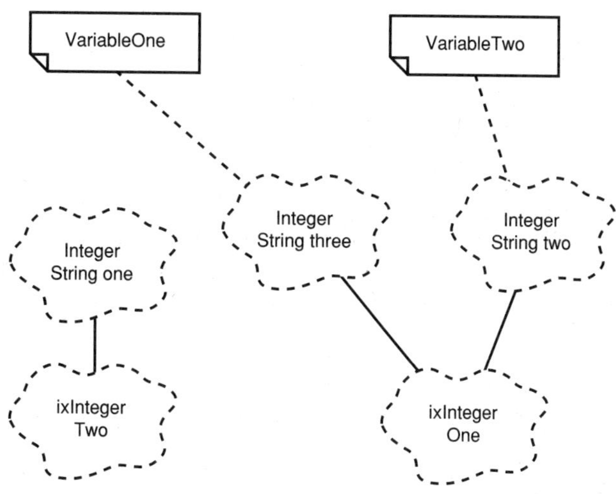

FIGURE 40.7.
Objects after a shallow COPY.

Copying a reference variable to another reference variable without copying the underlying object is called *shallow* copying. This is the default behavior of NewEra objects. The designer of the class can change this behavior if required. You can specify two other types of copying for the reference member variables: *null* and *deep*. You do so in the class declaration. For example, you can specify deep copying for the `IntegerValue` reference variable in the example class, as shown in Listing 40.15.

Listing 40.15. Declaration of DEEP COPY.

```
CLASS IntegerString DERIVED FROM ixString
    FUNCTION IntegerString
                (
                aStringValue CHAR(*),
                aIntegerValue INTEGER DEEP COPY
                             )
    PROTECTED VARIABLE IntegerValue ixInteger

    PUBLIC FUNCTION getIntegerValue() RETURNING INTEGER
    PUBLIC FUNCTION setIntegerValue() RETURNING VOID
END CLASS
```

If you instantiate and copy the objects as shown here, it would result in the object structure shown in Figure 40.8.

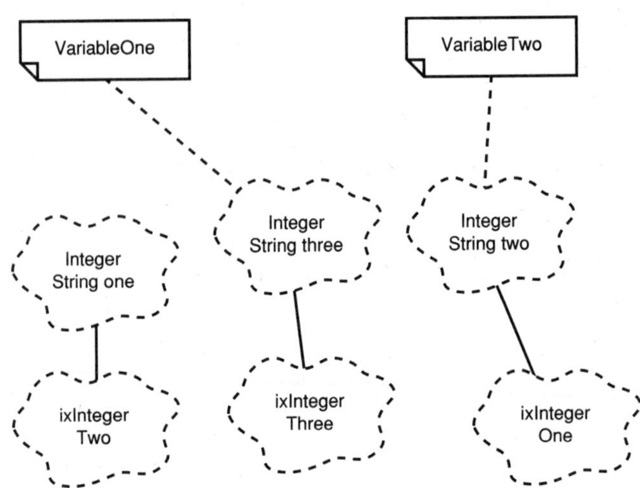

FIGURE 40.8. *Objects after a* DEEP COPY.

If you had specified NULL COPY, this object structure would have resulted in the structure shown in Figure 40.9.

Object Evaluation

You know that objects are accessed only through their reference variables. Objects themselves are complex data types that can contain members that themselves are reference variables. How then do you compare objects?

First, consider the operators that compare reference variables, as shown in Table 40.5.

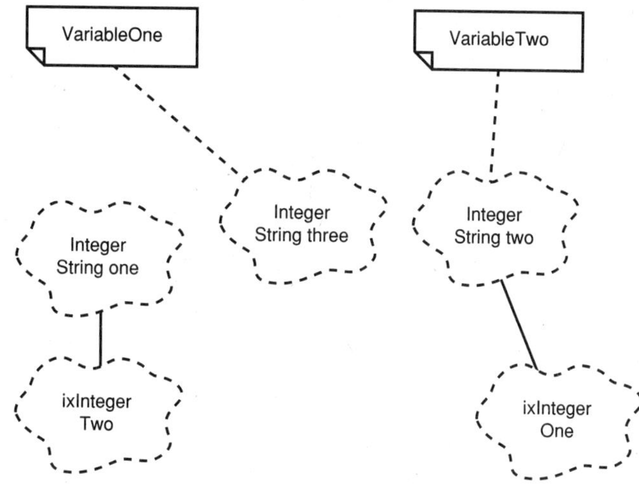

FIGURE 40.9.
Objects after a `NULL COPY`.

Table 40.5. Reference variable comparison operators.

Operator	*Use*
= or ==	Returns `TRUE` when two reference variables refer to the same object; returns `FALSE` otherwise.
!= or <>	Returns `TRUE` when two reference variables do not refer to the same object; returns `FALSE` otherwise.
`IS NULL`	Returns `TRUE` if the reference variable is null. In this case, the reference variable has been declared, but the reference variable (and therefore the object) has not been instantiated. Returns `FALSE` otherwise.
`IS NOT NULL`	Returns `TRUE` if the reference variable is not null.

The operators in Table 40.5 do not compare the values held in the member variables of the object. It is not possible to compare the values held in the member variables of the objects unless the designer of the class has provided a member function specifically for this purpose. Remembering this point is important when designing your own classes.

TIP

If the consumer code in your project needs to compare the values held in the member variables of the objects you declare, you need to provide a member function specifically for this purpose.

I mentioned that all NewEra classes ultimately derive from a base class called `ixObject`. The `ixObject` class has a member function called `isEqualTo`. This member function does a byte comparison of the member variables of each of the objects and returns `TRUE` if the two objects contain the same values. Some of the standard classes that are provided with NewEra, particularly the visual objects, cannot support a byte comparison, so this member function is *overridden* to trigger a runtime error. (See the "Error Handling" section.) Consequently, this member function might not work for all your user-defined classes. Check the class library reference for each of the member variables you propose in your class. You can override the `isEqualTo()` member function yourself to provide a customized comparison. You use the `isEqualTo()` member function, like this:

```
IF  ObjectOne.isEqualTo(ObjectTwo) THEN
     #  values are equal
ELSE
    #  values are different
END IF
```

The values contained in an object's member variables are not the only way the object can be evaluated. Specifically, you might want to determine the following information about an object:

- The class of the object
- The derivation of the object
- The data type, precision, and scale of a member variable of the object

To determine the class of an object, you use the member function `getClass()`. The `getClass()` member function is another member function that all objects inherit from the `ixObject` class. The `getClass()` member function returns a lowercase character string containing the class name. For example, `getClass()` returns `ixstring` for an object of the `ixString` class.

Sometimes you might want to know if a particular object is of a class derived from another class. The `ixObject` class has a shared member function called `isClassDerivedFromClass()`, which can be used to determine derivation, as shown in Listing 40.16.

Listing 40.16. Determining class derivation.

```
IF ixObject::isClassDerivedFromClass(Object1.getClass(), Object2.getClass()) THEN
      #   Object1 is derived from Object2
ELSE
      #   Object1 is not derived from Object2
END IF
```

Objects are often used to hold simple data type information such as integers and character strings. As you have seen, NewEra provides the Data Class Library to provide such functionality. The classes in the Data Class Library are derived from a class called `ixValue`, which in turn is derived from the `ixTypeInfo` class (as well as the `ixObject` class higher in the hierarchy). The ixTypeInfo class provides a member function, getTypeCode(), that returns an integer value. The integer values returned by getTypeCode() correspond to constants declared in the ixTypeInfo class. You can use the getTypeCode() member function in the manner shown in Listing 40.17.

Listing 40.17. Use of getTypeCode().

```
CASE Object.getTypeCode()
WHEN ixTypeCode::SQLMoney
      #  Object is of  SQL money type
WHEN ixTypeCode::SQLInteger
WHEN ixTypeCode::SQLChar
```

Obviously, the ixTypeInfo member variables are only available to objects that have the ixTypeInfo class somewhere in their class hierarchy. The ixTypeInfo class also provides the getPrecision(), getScale(), and getLength() member functions that allow you to examine the precision, scale, and length of the data type. For example, you might want to know the number of the fractional positions (scale) of a decimal data type.

Object Destruction

You have seen how you can create a new object. How then are objects destroyed when they are no longer required? For every object that is created, NewEra records the number of reference variables that refer to the object. Periodically, NewEra examines all the objects to find any that are no longer referenced (that is, the number of times the object is referenced is zero). If an object is no longer used, NewEra automatically scavenges the memory that the object uses. This process is commonly called *automatic garbage collection.* You are relieved of the task of manually deallocating the memory for objects. Memory deallocation is a source of many programmer errors in languages such as C++ where it is a manual task.

When a reference variable loses scope of reference permanently, NewEra decreases the number of references for its object. If the number of references is zero, the memory for the object is deallocated.

In certain circumstances, you might want to hasten the process of memory deallocation by assigning the reference variables for an object with the value of NULL. This approach is particularly useful for memory hungry objects such as those that contain byte or text member variables.

Objects and Functions

A reference variable can be passed as an argument to a function. If a normal variable is passed to a function, the argument becomes a local variable inside the function. This process is commonly referred to as *call by value.* However, when a reference variable is passed to a function, the reference variable still points to the same object. (That is, the function does not make a copy of the object as discussed previously in the "Object Assignment" section.) Any operations that are performed on the object persist after the function has ceased execution. This process is commonly referred to as *call by reference.*

Calling by reference is useful in many operations. For example, in INFORMIX-4GL, you cannot pass an array to a function as an argument. In NewEra, however, you can declare a class that contains an array as a member variable and pass a reference variable for an object of this class to the function. The individual elements of the array are then accessible (depending on the access control rules of the class) within the function.

When a reference variable is passed to a function, the class of the reference variable is checked against the prototype of the function. The class must be either the class named in the function prototype or a class derived from the class named in the function prototype. Inside the function, the reference variable behaves as if it references an object of the class named in the function prototype. Consider the example shown in Listing 40.18 using the `IntegerString` class you declared previously. Remember that the `IntegerString` class has a member function called `setIntegerValue()`.

Listing 40.18. Use of functions with objects.

```
01  MAIN
02
03  VARIABLE  aChar   CHAR(*)
04  VARIABLE  AnIntegerString IntegerString = NEW IntegerString
05                                                (
06                                                aStringValue : "A",
07                                                aIntegerValue : 1
08                                                )
09  .  .  .
10  CALL ExampleFunction( AnIxString : AnIntegerString) RETURNING AnIntegerString
11
12  CALL AnIntegerString.getValueStr() RETURNING aChar
13  .  .  .
14  END MAIN
15
16  FUNCTION ExampleFunction( AnIxString ixString) RETURNING ixString
17      CALL AnIxString.setValueStr("B")
18      CALL AnIxString.setIntegerValue(2)         #   bad will fail compile
17  END FUNCTION
```

Listing 40.18 calls a function named `ExampleFunction` on line 10. The prototype of this function declares that it should be passed an `ixString`. However, you passed the function a reference variable to the user-defined class `IntegerString`. An object can be treated as if it is an object of one of its base classes. Because the object has inherited from this base class, it can use all the member functions and variables of that base class. However, inside the function, the object can be treated only as an object of class `ixString`. If you attempt to access a member that belongs to the derived class `IntegerString`, the compiler reports an error.

This feature of inherited classes is powerful. You can treat them as objects of the base class or objects of their actual class depending on your goals. For example, you can be assured that libraries defined to work with particular classes will also work with any classes derived from those classes.

Functions that return a reference variable allow a shorthand notation that can reduce errors and increase clarity. The `ExampleFunction` discussed in Listing 40.18 returns an `ixString` reference variable. If you want to access the value of the `ixString` that is returned by this function, you can use the notation shown in Listing 40.19.

Listing 40.19. Function call notation.

```
VARIABLE StringOne ixString = NEW ixString("A")
VARIABLE StringTwo ixString
VARIABLE aChar CHAR(*)
CALL ExampleFunction(AnIxString : StringOne) RETURNING StringTwo
CALL StringTwo.getValueStr() RETURNING aChar
```

The variable `aChar` has the value you are seeking.

Alternatively, you can use the following notation:

```
VARIABLE StringOne ixString = NEW ixString("A")
VARIABLE aChar CHAR(*)
CALL ExampleFunction(AnIxString : StringOne).getValueStr() RETURNING aChar
```

Again, the `aChar` variable has the value you seek. NewEra evaluates the call to the function `ExampleFunction(AnIxString : StringOne)` and determines that it returns a reference variable to an `ixString` object. It knows this from the prototype of the function. NewEra then calls the `getValueStr()` member function for the referenced `ixString` object.

Asserting the Class of an Object with Casting

In the preceding section, you learned that an object reference can be treated as an object of its declared class or an object of any class it is derived from. You frequently have an object reference of a declared class that you know really refers to an object of a class derived from the declared class. Object references like this are often obtained as the return signatures of library functions.

Using the `CAST` operator, you can assert the actual class of the object rather than the declared class.

Consider the following scenario: In the Visual Class Library that comes standard with NewEra, you can find a number of visual object classes such as buttons and text boxes. You use these visual objects to create graphical user interfaces. Each visual object is placed within a window. It is often useful for a visual object to access its window, so each object in the Visual Class Library has a member function called `getWindow()`. The `getWindow()` function returns a reference to an `ixWindow` class object. (`ixWindow` is the NewEra window class.) In most sophisticated applications, creating a number of user-defined classes derived from the `ixWindow` class is common. The user-defined classes can display a company logo or standard menu, for example.

In the following example, you declare a window class called `OurWindow` that derives from `ixWindow`. The `OurWindow` class has a member function called `DisplayLogo()`. A button object called `OurButton` placed in this window gets a reference to the window by calling its `getWindow()` member function. However, the prototype of the `getWindow()` member function declares the class of the reference variable it returns as an `ixWindow` class. If you enter the statement shown in the following example, the compiler evaluates `OurButton.getWindow()` and determines that it returns a reference variable to an object of class `ixWindow`:

```
CALL OurButton.getWindow().DisplayLogo()
```

The problem is that the `ixWindow` class does not have a member function called `DisplayLogo()`. The compiler then returns an error. The casting operator overcomes this problem by allowing you to recast the object reference temporarily to a derived class. You use the `CAST` operator as shown here:

```
CALL (OurButton.getWindow() CAST OurWindow).DisplayLogo()
```

Here, the compiler is instructed to assert the class of `OurButton.getWindow()` to the `OurWindow` class, thus allowing you to use the `DisplayLogo()` member function.

The following are some important points about casting:

- The `CAST` operation does not change the declared class of the reference variable permanently. If you want to call the `DisplayLogo()` member function again, you have to perform another `CAST` operation.
- The `CAST` operation does not create memory structures that are not available. You cannot change the object to a derived class with a `CAST` operation. Remembering the `Customer` and `StudentCustomer` classes, if an object is created as a `Customer` class object, then a `CAST` does not turn it into a `StudentCustomer`. If you cast a `Customer` object into a `StudentCustomer` class and try to use the `getCampus()` member function, you receive an error because the memory structure that supports the `getCampus()` member function does not exist! Casting asserts only the true class of the object.
- The `CAST` operation is safe to use. If you attempt an invalid `CAST` operation, the cast returns a `NULL` reference. If you cast a `StudentCustomer` as an `IntegerString`, the cast returns a `NULL` error, not a runtime error. (However, if you attempt to access a member of a `NULL` reference variable, you receive the ubiquitous `-1392` error.) Testing for `NULL` after each cast using the `isNull()` member function (inherited from `ixObject`) would be wise.

Object Lists

NewEra provides facilities to manage lists of objects with the `ixVector` class. The `ixVector` class is one of the really neat features of the NewEra language; it combines and surpasses the features of linked lists and arrays.

An `ixVector` is a one-dimensional, dynamic vector of object references. Figure 40.10 illustrates the concept.

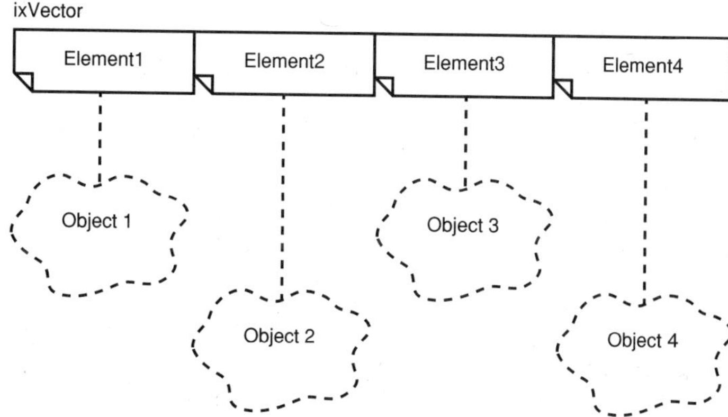

FIGURE 40.10.
`ixVector`.

An `ixVector` is declared and instantiated as follows:

```
VARIABLE OurList ixVector = NEW ixVector()
```

Informix has implemented the `ixVector` as a class, allowing you to create your own classes inheriting some or all of the behavior of the `ixVector`. For example, you can implement a class that accepts only reference variables for `Customer` class objects.

The standard `ixVector` class provides member functions to help manage the list. The functions shown in Table 40.6 are the most important.

Table 40.6. Important member functions of `ixVector`.

Member Function	*Purpose*
`getCount()`	Returns the number of positions in the `ixVector` occupied by items (reference variable).
`getSize()`	Returns the total number of available positions in the `ixVector`. Not all positions need be occupied.
`Insert(`*`pos, elem`*`)`	Inserts a reference variable for *`elem`* at the position specified by *`pos`*. All positions greater than this are shuffled up one position.

continues

Table 40.6. continued

Member Function	*Purpose*
`Delete(pos)`	Deletes the reference variable at the position specified by `pos`. All positions greater than this are shuffled down one position.
`DeleteAll()`	Deletes all the reference variables in the `ixVector`.
`Get(pos)`	Returns the reference variable at the position specified by `pos`. (Note that in this case, the `CAST` operator is often used to assert the declared class of the reference variable.)
`set(pos, elem)`	Assigns the reference variable at `pos` to `elem`.

The `ixVector` can provide multidimensional array-like behavior. The reference variables managed by the `ixVector` can be reference variables pointing to other `ixVectors`. Therefore, you can easily create an array of `ixVectors` to manage a custom object structure. The array structure does not have to be regular and can assume a schema as shown in Figure 40.11.

FIGURE 40.11.
Irregular `ixVector` *array.*

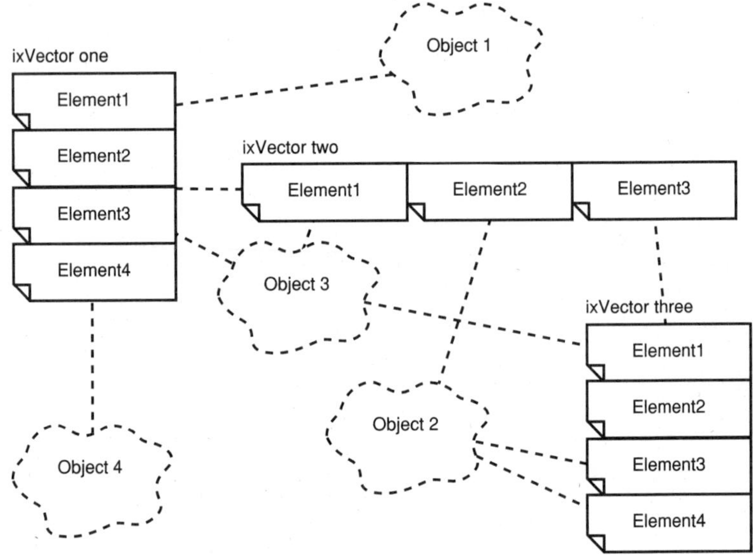

The `ixVector` manages memory dynamically, unlike an array, and can be passed by reference to functions.

NewEra provides two more list management classes that are derived from the `ixVector`: the `ixRow` and the `ixRowArray` class. The `ixRow` is a list of reference variables whose class has been derived from the `ixValue` class. Recall that the `ixValue` class of objects contains SQL data types only. The `ixRow` is used predominantly for database access. The `ixRowArray` class implements an array of `ixRow` objects. I discuss both of these classes in more detail in the "Database Access" section.

Class Hierarchy and Associations

NewEra provides three types of *object associations* with which you can develop your class hierarchy:

- Inheritance
- Using
- Containment

I have discussed Inheritance associations, so now you can look at the other association types.

In a Using association, one object uses the public interface of another object. When designing your class hierarchy, you must develop a procedure for *mapping* the calls to an objects' members by other objects. Doing so is particularly important if you're allocating responsibility for developing the classes among separate programming teams.

In the Containment association, a class uses another class as a member. You saw this association with the `IntegerString` example. You can use Containment associations to declare classes that combine the behaviors of two or more classes. Consider the example shown in Figure 40.12.

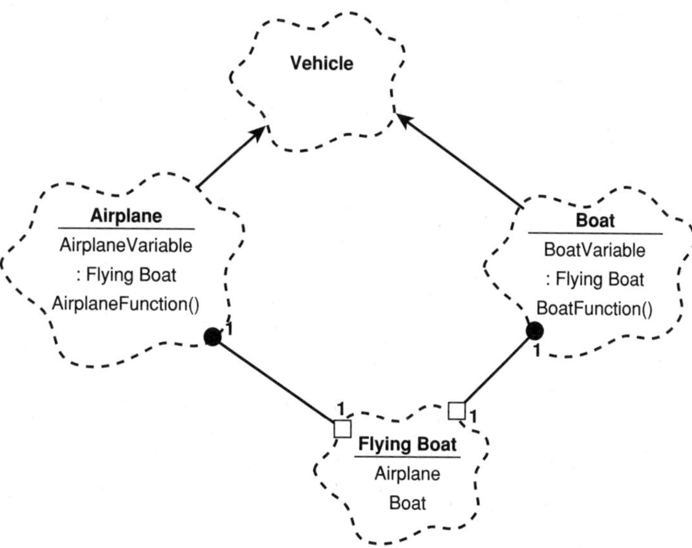

FIGURE 40.12.
Containment.

In this example, you see two declared classes, `boat` and `airplane`, which inherit from the ancestor called `vehicle`. Each of these classes has been given custom class members specific to its nature. What if you discover (maybe some time later) that you also have a hybrid object called a `flying boat` that has the behaviors of both the `boat` and `airplane` classes? You could inherit directly from the `vehicle` class, but then you would have to re-include the members from both the `boat` class and the `airplane` class. As well as being a lot of work, this approach introduces the possibility of inconsistencies between the old members and the re-included members.

A possible way around this dilemma is to declare one or both of the `boat` and `airplane` classes as members of the new class. These classes should be referenced in the constructor of the `flying boat` class if required. You might want to make these member variables protected, so you need to provide a public interface to access them. Listing 40.20 shows this pseudo-code.

Listing 40.20. Containment.

```
INCLUDE "boat.4gh"
INCLUDE "airplane.4gh"

CLASS FlyingBoat

   FUNCTION FlyingBoat
            (
            aBoat  Boat,
            aAirplane  Airplane
            )

   PROTECTED VARIABLE aBoat  Boat
   PROTECTED VARIABLE aAirplane  Airplane

   PUBLIC FUNCTION GetBoat() RETURNING Boat
   PUBLIC FUNCTION GetAirplane() RETURNING Airplane

END CLASS
```

This compound class can then demonstrate the behavior of both the `boat` and `airplane` classes. To access a `boat` member, you call the `GetBoat()` member function and then the required `boat` member. For example, you would use `CALL MyFlyingBoat.GetBoat().ABoatMemberFunction()` (assuming the `ABoatMemberFunction()` has been declared `PUBLIC`). This sort of arrangement is good for imitating multiple inheritance hierarchies.

Implicit Application Object

NewEra provides an implicit application object defined by the class `ixApp`. The `ixApp` class contains shared member functions that provide application and system-level functions. For example, the `ixApp` class provides the shared member function `ixApp::setCursor()`, which sets the appearance of the screen cursor. All the members of the `ixApp` class are shared, so you don't need to instantiate an `ixApp` object.

Error Handling

NewEra provides a number of mechanisms to handle errors. Three main classes of errors and warnings with NewEra are categorized as follows:

- NewEra code errors are caused by the incorrect execution of some code.
- SQL database errors occur because of some problem with the database engine or the SQL statement sent to the database for execution.
- Object errors occur when a problem occurs with the execution or use of an object member.

The NewEra language supports a `GLOBAL` variable called `STATUS` that is set to the return status of the last operation.

NewEra Code Error

NewEra code errors are either fatal or non-fatal. A fatal error cannot be ignored and always causes termination of your program (meaning that a fatal error cannot be *trapped*). An example of a fatal error is `-1319: The NewEra program has run out of run-time data memory space.` NewEra usually displays a message dialog window advising you of a fatal error.

Non-fatal errors (and warnings) can be further divided into four groups: SQL, Screen I/O, Validation, and Expression. I deal with SQL errors in the next section.

Screen and I/O errors and warnings occur when NewEra attempts to access a system resource, such as an operating system file, and is not successful.

Validation errors and warnings could occur when the program tries to assert the type of a variable against the data type stored in the `syscolval` table of an Informix database. This table allows you to include discrete values for a database column. In the following example, the codes for the U.S. states are included in the `syscolval` table entry for `state.state_code`. To pass the `VALIDATE` statement on line 03, the value of `p_state_code` must be one of the state codes.

```
01  VARIABLE p_state_code LIKE state.state_code
02
03  VALIDATE p_state_code LIKE state.state_code
```

Expression errors and warnings might occur when an expression used in the program violates a language rule. A good example is a situation in which a program attempts to divide by zero.

The WHENEVER Directive

NewEra allows you to deal with code errors with the `WHENEVER` compiler directive. The `WHENEVER` directive must occur within a program block. The `WHENEVER` directive is followed by two keywords; the first indicates the runtime condition you're trapping and the action to take. The `WHENEVER` directive has the syntax shown in the following example:

```
WHENEVER <run-time condition> <action>
```

Table 40.7 summarizes the options for runtime conditions.

Table 40.7. WHENEVER runtime conditions.

Directive	*Runtime Condition*	*Purpose*
`WHENEVER`	`ERROR`	Traps any errors except Expression errors.
	`ANY ERROR`	Traps all errors including Expression errors.
	`WARNING`	Traps all warnings.

Using the `WHENEVER` directive, you also can specify an action to take if the program encounters the specified runtime condition. The actions shown in Table 40.8 are supported.

Table 40.8. WHENEVER action options.

Option	*Use*
`CONTINUE`	The program is to continue operation.
`STOP`	The program is to terminate upon error.
`CALL` *`function()`*	The program should call *`function()`* when an error is encountered.
`GOTO` *`label`*	The program should go to the label named *`label`*.

Error Logging

NewEra also supports logging of errors with the `ERRORLOG()` built-in function. The `ERRORLOG()` function writes the error message to an operating system file. The date and time of the error are also written. To use the `ERRORLOG()` function, you must have already specified the operating system file. You do so with the `STARTLOG(`*`filename`*`)` function. `STARTLOG()` creates the file if it does not already exist. Obviously, `STARTLOG()` requires that you have operating system permission to write to the file specified.

Warnings are not automatically logged.

SQL Errors

Embedded SQL errors are handled with the `WHENEVER` directive in a similar fashion to NewEra code errors. You can specify other runtime conditions reflecting the different nature of SQL operations. Table 40.9 lists the SQL runtime conditions you can trap.

Table 40.9. SQL WHENEVER runtime conditions.

Runtime Condition	*Use*
`NOT FOUND`	Used to trap an SQL operation that does not find any rows in the database or a cursor that has reached the last row.
`SQLERROR`	Used to trap SQL errors that have occurred in the database.
`SQLWARNING`	Used to trap warnings issued from the database.

When you're using ODBC, errors are trapped automatically by the ODBC interface classes. The ODBC interface classes provide member functions that allow you to determine the nature of the error or warning.

NewEra also supports the SQLCA global record. The SQLCA stores information about the status of the last SQL operation. You can have only one SQLCA global record. If you're using ODBC, the SQLCA record applies to the implicit connection. NewEra also supplies an object-based equivalent called the `ixSQLCA` class. See the section on this class later in the chapter for details.

For database operations, the `SQLCA.SQLCODE` member is equivalent to the `STATUS` global variable.

TIP

Always using the `SQLCA.SQLCODE` member to check database operations rather than the `STATUS` is a good practice because it is a more consistent approach.

Object Errors

The standard member functions of an object from the Informix Standard Classes are external to the NewEra language. The member functions can be written in C++ or even assembler language. Therefore, you can use NewEra error handling for errors within these member functions. NewEra provides an event-based solution for handling runtime errors from these member functions.

An error within a standard member function of the Informix Standard Classes calls an event named `rtError()`. This event has a default handler function called `ixApp::uponRtError()`. The `ixApp::uponRtError()` calls `ixApp::showRtError()`, which displays a dialog window with error information. You can provide an alternative handler for this event to perform additional tasks such as logging the error message to an operating system file.

If you declare a custom class and implement the member functions in NewEra, you can still use the error-handling facilities discussed previously.

TIP

In a large client/server environment, consider locating the error log file on a shared network hard disk or partitioning the error-logging object onto a central server. This way, you can monitor only one error file instead of one on each PC. Of course, you still will need to handle the occasional network error.

Database Access

The NewEra language is database-centric, providing a rich set of facilities for database access. The choice of database access technique is dictated by the size of and flexibility required of the application.

NewEra provides the Connectivity Class Library, which provides an object-oriented, vendor-independent mechanism for accessing databases. The Connectivity Class Library has two versions: CCL/Informix and CCL/ODBC. The two versions are very similar, with the exception that CCL/ODBC extends the functionality provided in CCL/Informix to enable you to examine meta-data about the database. Using the Connectivity Class Library, you can connect to one or more databases simultaneously.

The Connectivity Class Library consists of three classes: the `ixSQLCA` class, the `ixSQLConnect` class, and the `ixSQLStmt` class.

The `ixSQLCA` class declares an object that provides the same facilities as the SQLCA record discussed in the preceding section. You can examine the value of members of this object to determine the status of any database operations. You can create an `ixSQLCA` object for each database connection.

Objects of class `ixSQLConnect` provide members that allow you to connect to and disconnect from databases. Objects of class `ixSQLConnect` also allow you to manage transactions, isolation options, and cancellation options.

Objects of the `ixSQLStmt` class provide members that allow you to manage SQL statements and cursors. You can prepare and execute SQL statements, declare named cursors, and execute most Database Definition statements.

Embedded SQL

NewEra allows you to embed SQL commands directly into the language. You can use the `SELECT`, `UPDATE`, `DELETE`, `INSERT`, and `EXECUTE` commands to manipulate the database directly from your application. NewEra also supports embedded Database Definition Language statements such as `CREATE TABLE`.

Embedded SQL is undoubtedly the easiest database access method. It is also very familiar to INFORMIX-4GL programmers. Unfortunately, you cannot access ODBC data sources using embedded SQL.

NewEra's embedded SQL also supports scroll cursors.

The Database Connection Object: `ixSQLConnect`

Objects of the `ixSQLConnect` class provide capabilities that allow you to connect to databases, set database options, and manage transactions. The CCL/ODBC version also allows you to obtain table and column information from the database (meta-data). The `ixSQLConnect` class declaration includes several constants corresponding to data types and occurrences in the ODBC standard.

Connecting to a Database

You create an `ixSQLConnect` object in the usual way for an object, as you see in the following example:

```
INCLUDE "ixconno.4gh"
VARIABLE MyConnection ixSQLConnect
LET MyConnection = NEW ixSQLConnect()
```

The connection object is created in the preceding example, but it has not yet been connected to a database. To do so, you must call the `connect()` member function. The code fragment in Listing 40.21 shows a call to the connect member function.

Listing 40.21. Database connect.

```
CALL MyConnection.connect
                  (
                  SourceName : "MY_DATABASE",
                  UserId : "MY_NAME",
                  authorization : "PASSWORD"
                  )
IF MyConnection.getODBCErrorCode() != ixSQLConnect::SQL_Success THEN
      #   an error connecting
END IF
```


Here, the `SourceName` indicates the ODBC data source that you want to connect to. (ODBC data sources are usually databases but not always.) You must establish the data source by using the ODBC manager (in the ODBC Manager for Microsoft Windows) or an Informix database connection available through I-Net. The `UserId` and `authorization` parameters are optional and are required only if the data source requires them.

The `connect()` member function has no return. You check for errors by calling the `getODBCErrorCode()` member function to check for errors. Line 07 of Listing 40.21 demonstrates how you check for connection errors.

Connecting to an ODBC data source is sometimes a little more complicated than in the preceding example. The ODBC standard caters to many different types of databases. Some of these databases have different connection requirements. The ODBC driver manager allows you to interrogate the data sources available and the connection requirements for each of these drivers. The `ixSQLConnect` class supports this capability with two member functions: `browseConnect()` and `driverConnect()`.

The syntax of the `browseConnect()` member function is `browseConnect(connStrIn CHAR(*)) RETURNING CHAR(*)`. The `connStrIn` element must contain the data source name in the ODBC format `DSN=`*`data source name`*. The function loads the ODBC driver for this data source (previously set by the ODBC manager) and interrogates the driver for the information it requires. `BrowseConnect()` returns a string that contains login attributes. For example, it might return `DB=MY_DATABASE; UID=?; PWD=*?`. The question mark indicates that the attribute has an unknown value; an asterisk followed by a question mark indicates an optional unknown value. Most of the ODBC driver developers have used similar labels for login attributes. The `browseConnect()` member function allows you to create a customized login dialog window for a data source.

The syntax of the `driverConnect()` member function is

```
driverConnect(window ixWindow, connStrIn CHAR(*),
➥driverCompletion INTEGER) RETURNING CHAR(*)
```

Using this function, you can request a connection to a data source. If the `connStrIn` string does not contain sufficient information for the ODBC driver manager to make the data source connection, the ODBC driver manager displays a dialog window to request the missing login attribute. The `driverCompletion` parameter controls the manner in which the ODBC driver manager operates the login window.

Implicit Connection

When a NewEra program begins execution, NewEra automatically creates an `ixSQLConnect` object. This process is called the *implicit connection.* The `ixSQLConnect` class has a shared member function called `getImplicitConnection()` that returns a reference to this connection. The implicit connection is only instantiated automatically; you must still attempt to connect it to a data source.

Setting Database Options

NewEra allows you to control the behavior of any of the database connections you have made. You control the behavior by setting database options through the `setConnectOption()` member function of the connection. The prototype of this member is

```
setConnectOption(option SMALLINT, param ixValue) RETURNING VOID
```

You call this member function, passing it an option number and an `ixValue` containing a valid value for the option. The eight options shown in Table 40.10 are supported.

Table 40.10. ODBC connection options.

Option	*Use*

`SQL_Access_Mode`	Allows you to make the database connection either `READ/WRITE` or `READ ONLY`. The valid values are defined by two class constants:
	`ixSQLConnect::SQL_Mode_Read_Write`
	`ixSQLConnect::SQL_Mode_Read_Only`

`SQL_Autocommit`	Allows you to specify that database operations performed on this connection automatically commit. Valid values are 1 = On 2 = Off (default)

`SQL_Txn_Isolation`	Specifies the isolation level you want for this database connection. Valid values are
	`ixSQLConnect::SQL_Txn_Uncommitted`
	`ixSQLConnect::SQL_Txn_Committed`
	`ixSQLConnect::SQL_Txn_Repeatable_Read`
	`ixSQLConnect::SQL_Serializable`
	`ixSQLConnect::SQL_Versioning`

`SQL_Login_Timeout`	Specifies the number of seconds you will allow for a login request to succeed. The default is 15. A value of zero indicates an indefinite wait.
`SQL_Opt_Trace`	ODBC allows you to write certain trace information to a log file. Valid values are 1 = On 2 = Off (default)
`SQL_Opt_Tracefile`	The log file for an ODBC trace. Defaults to `sql.log`.
`SQL_Translate_DLL`	Specifies the name of the DLL that contains character translation functions.
`SQL_Translate_Option`	Specifies the current translation option. Valid values are determined by the developer of the translation DLL.

You set a database option after you instantiate a connection object and successfully connect the object to a data source. You can change database options at any time during your program. The `ixSQLConnect` class provides a member function, `getConnectOption()`, that allows you to determine the currently selected options for a database connection.

Transaction Management

In the "Setting Database Options" section of this chapter, you learned how to set some default transaction- and isolation-level behaviors. The `ixSQLConnect` class also enables you to manage explicit transactions. Transactions are managed with the `transact()` member function. The prototype of this member function is

```
transact(mode SMALLINT : ixSQLConnect::SQL_Commit) RETURNING VOID
```

The `mode` can be one of two values: `ixSQLConnect::SQL_Commit` or `ixSQLConnect::SQL_Rollback`, which commit and roll back the transaction, respectively. You don't need to explicitly declare the beginning of a transaction because a transaction is declared after each call to `transact()`, as shown in Listing 40.22.

Listing 40.22. A connection example.

```
VARIABLE  MyConnection ixSQLConnect = NEW ixSQLConnect()
VARIABLE MyStatement ixSQLStmt

CALL MyConnection.connect("my_database")
LET MyStatement = NEW ixSQLStmt(MyConnection)    #  see next section
                                  # for ixSQLStmt discussion
CALL MyStatement.execDirect("DELETE FROM my_table")

IF MyStatement.getODBCErrorCode() < ixSQLConnect::SQL_Success THEN
    CALL MyConnection.transact(mode : ixSQLConnect::SQL_Rollback
ELSE
    CALL MyConnection.transact(mode : ixSQLConnect::SQL_Commit)
END IF

 #  we are automatically back in a transaction
```

WARNING

Do not issue `BEGIN WORK`, `COMMIT WORK`, or `ROLLBACK WORK` statements using the `execute()` or `execDirect()` member functions of `ixSQLStmt`. If you're explicitly managing transactions, you must use `transact()`.

Disconnecting from a Data Source

You can disconnect from a data source by using the `disconnect()` member function. This function does not destroy the `ixSQLConnect` object; this object is subject to the normal referencing rules of objects. Any `ixSQLStmt` objects you have created using this connection will become invalid (because they no longer have a database connection).

WARNING

Disconnecting from a data source rolls back any pending transactions.

Canceling an SQL Operation

Using the CCL/Informix version, you can cancel SQL operations. You can also set cancellation options so that all SQL operations that exceed a predefined time limit are canceled. A modal dialog window is displayed when an SQL operation is canceled, and you can control the text displayed in this window. The member functions involved are `cancel()`, `getAutoCancel()`, `getCancelMode()`, `getCancelText()`, `getCancelTimeout()`, `isCancelAllowed()`, `setAutoCancel()`, `setCancelMode()`, `setCancelText()`, and `setCancelTimeout()`.

TIP

Always set a maximum time limit on an SQL operation. You can declare a class of connection objects that have the project default time-out set by their constructor.

Meta-data

Using the CCL/ODBC, you can interrogate the data source to determine the names of tables and names and data types of columns. The `ixSQLConnect` class offers a number of member functions for this purpose. Table 40.11 summarizes the major meta-data functions and their uses.

Table 40.11. Meta-data functions.

Member Function	*Use*
`tables`	Allows you to determine the names of all the tables in the data source. You can search for tables by table name, table owner, and table type. The function supports character string matching. This function returns an `ixSQLStmt` object that is already prepared and executed. This `ixSQLStmt` object allows you to fetch rows of data describing the tables (see the "`Using ixSQLStmt`" section for specific details on fetching data rows).

continues

Table 40.11. continued

Member Function	*Use*
`columns`	Allows you to determine the name and data type of columns in the data source. You can search for columns similar to the way you search for tables. Similarly, this function returns an `ixSQLStmt` object that you can use to fetch the column information.
`getTypeInfo`	Allows you to determine the data type information supported by the data source. You pass an argument to this function specifying the ODBC data type of interest. Class constants have been declared for the ODBC data types. This function returns an `ixSQLStmt` object that allows you to fetch the information.
`getInfo`	Along with `getTypeInfo`, provides information about the `getFunctions` ODBC facilities supported by the ODBC driver.

Error Detection

The `ixSQLConnect` class provides the `SQLError()` member function that returns error and warning information about the last database operation. You pass to the `SQLError()` function the `ixSQLStmt` object that performed the last operation. `SQLError()` returns the ODBC `SQLState`, the native error code from the database server, and the native error message from the database server.

The SQL Statement Object: `ixSQLStmt`

Using the `ixSQLStmt` class, you can perform database operations. Objects of the `ixSQLStmt` class are used to replace embedded SQL commands. Remember that they are objects and subject to the same declaration, instantiation, and scope rules as other objects.

Using `ixSQLStmt`

The constructor of the `ixSQLStmt` class has the following prototype: `ixSQLStmt(conn : ixSQLConnect : NULL)`. You cannot use an `ixSQLStmt` object without a valid connection. However, the constructor of the `ixSQLStmt` allows a `NULL` value. This device merely accesses the `SQLError()` member function of the `ixSQLConnect` object. (Recall that the `SQLError()` member function requires an `ixSQLStmt` object.)

Listing 40.23 demonstrates the instantiation and use of an `ixSQLStmt` object.

Listing 40.23. `ixSQLStmt` example.

```
INCLUDE SYSTEM "ixstring.4gh"
INCLUDE SYSTEM "ixstmto.4gh"        #   declaration file ixSQLstmt
INCLUDE SYSTEM "ixconno.4gh"        #   declaration file ixSQLConnect
INCLUDE SYSTEM "ixrow.4gh"          #    declaration file ixRow
INCLUDE SYSTEM "ixrowar.4gh"        #    declaration file ixRowArray

VARIABLE stmtSelect ixSQLStmt = NEW ixSQLStmt(conn :
➥ixSQLConnect::getImplicitConnection())
VARIABLE rwData ixRow
VARIABLE rárData ixRowArray
VARIABLE SQLState, NativeMessage CHAR(*)
VARIABLE Counter INTEGER = 0
VARIABLE ErrorCode INTEGER

CALL stmtSelect.Prepare(stmt : "SELECT * FROM my_table WHERE my_col = ? ")
IF stmtSelect.getODBCErrorCode() != ixSQLStmt::SQL_Success THEN
       --   an error occurred preparing the statement
END IF

LET rwData = stmtSelect.allocateRow()
➥#  instantiates ixRow with correct number of
                                             #   values
LET rarData = NEW ixRowArray(rowSchema : rwData)
➥# creates an ixRowArray with rows like the
                                                          #   ixRow

CALL STMTselect.setParam(n : 1, val : NEW ixString("MY_MATCHING_VALUE"))

CALL stmtSelect.execute()
IF stmtSelect.getODBCErrorCode() != ixSQLStmt::SQL_Success THEN
       --   an error occurred executing the statement
       CALL ixSQLConnect::getImplicitConnection().SQLError(stmtSelect)
       RETURNING SQLState, ErrorCode, NativeMessage
END IF

WHILE Counter < 100
➥#   we shall have a maximum of 100 rows fetched
    CALL stmtSelect.fetchInto(oldRow : rwData)
    IF stmtSelect.getODBCErrorCode() != ixSQLStmt::SQL_Success THEN
        EXIT WHILE
    ELSE
        LET Counter = Counter + 1
        IF rarData.insertRow(theRow : COPY rwData) = 0 THEN
            -- error inserting into row array
        END IF
    END IF
END WHILE
```

Listing 40.23 instantiates an `ixSQLStmt` object and then executes an SQL `SELECT` statement. The `ixSQLStmt` object fetches data into an `ixRow`, which you then use to create an `ixRowArray`.

I touched on ixRows and ixRowArrays in the section on ixVectors. An ixRow is a class that inherits from the ixVector class. The ixRow accepts only ixValue references. (An ixValue object equates to SQL data types.) The ixRowArray is a class derived from the ixVector class, which accepts only references to ixRow objects. All the ixRows in an ixRowArray must have the same rowSchema. The ixRowArray is therefore similar to a standard two-dimensional array of SQL data types. (The ixRowArray has a number of other facilities that make it very useful.)

Listing 40.23, therefore, uses an ixSQLStmt to fetch data and populate an ixRowArray.

Lines 00 to 04 declare the classes to be used in the example. The ixSQLStmt object is instantiated on line 06. Note that you're using the implicit connection in this example. Lines 06 to 11 declare the variables to be used, including the ixRow and ixRowArray.

In line 13, you call the member function prepare(). This function accepts a CHAR(*), which is the SQL operation you want to execute. You prepare an SQL statement with a placeholder denoted by the question mark. The SQL statement is checked for validity against the database. It is possible that you have made an error in the SQL. Therefore, you must check whether the prepare statement was successful. You do so by calling the getODBCErrorCode() member function. This member function returns a smallint for which valid constants have been declared in the ixSQLStmt class. Table 40.12 lists the return values.

Table 40.12. ODBC error codes.

SQL_Success	The database operation executed successfully.
SQL_Success_With_Info	The database operation executed successfully but with information.
SQL_No_Data_Found	No data matches the WHERE criteria entered.
SQL_Error	The database operation failed.
SQL_Invalid_Handle	The operation failed because of an internal ODBC error.
SQL_Still_Executing	An asynchronous operation is still executing.
SQL_Need_Data	The driver requires parameter data values.

On line 18, you call the allocateRow() member function that instantiates an ixRow object with the correct number and type of ixValue objects to receive the result of the SQL operation. On line 20, you instantiate an ixRowArray object. The constructor of the ixRowArray accepts an ixRow, and this *schema* is used for all ixRows in the ixRowArray.

Line 23 illustrates how you set parameter values for any placeholders. In the example, you substitute the string "MY_MATCHING_VALUE" for the "?" in the SQL statement. The SQL statement would then read

```
"SELECT * FROM my_table WHERE my_col = "MY_MATCHING_VALUE""
```

You can reset the parameters and reuse the `ixSQLStmt` object without preparing the SQL statement again (as in line 13) if required.

Line 25 executes the SQL statement. If your SQL statement does not return any data, all you need to do is check the status of the database operation. However, this example fetches some data, and you begin to do this on line 33 by calling the `fetchInto()` function. Because you anticipate multiple rows, you place the `fetch` into a `WHILE` loop that fetches data into an `ixRow` and then inserts the `ixRow` into the `ixRowArray` (line 38). The `ixSQLStmt` class provides both the `fetch()` and `fetchInto()` member functions. The `fetch()` function instantiates a new `ixRow` object each time it is called, whereas `fetchInto()` updates the values in the nominated `ixRow`. If you're expecting multiple rows of data, `fetchInto()` is faster.

Line 28 illustrates the use of the `SQLError()` function (of the connection object) to retrieve error information from the database server.

That's all there is to using the `ixSQLStmt` class! As you can see, there is a fair bit more to this operation than to the equivalent operation in embedded SQL. That's the price you have to pay to achieve multi-database access. This process is not quite as bad as it might seem, however. Note that most of the variables in Listing 40.23 are reference variables and, therefore, can be passed by reference into and out of a function. A single function in your application can handle the execution and error checking for all SQL operations.

TIP

Develop a `SHARED` application function that executes all the SQL statements. Error checking (and logging) can get quite involved and could become tedious if not modularized.

Parameters for Prepared Statements

You have seen how you can set parameters using `setParam()`. You can also use the `setParams()` function. The prototype is

```
setParams(rowParams ixRow) RETURNING VOID
```

This function is slightly more efficient but, importantly, allows you to set all the parameters in a generic fashion (meaning that one function can set a multiple number of parameters).

Database Cursors

The `ixSQLStmt` class supports named cursors. You can set a name for an `ixSQLStmt` object by calling the `setCursorName()` member function. The prototype is

```
setCursorName(name CHAR(*)) RETURNING VOID
```

You can determine the cursor name of an `ixSQLStmt` using the `getCursorName()` member function. NewEra assigns a default cursor name. You must call `setCursorName()` prior to `prepare()` or `execDirect()`.

Named cursors are particularly useful when you're using a `FOR UPDATE` statement in your SQL. They allow you to issue an update SQL statement utilizing the `WHERE CURRENT OF` *`cursor_name`* syntax.

The SQL Communication Area: ixSQLCA

You do not call the constructor of the `ixSQLCA` object directly; the constructor is called by the `getSQLCA()` member function of the `ixSQLConnect` class. An `ixSQLCA` object is meaningless unless it is associated with a database connection (`ixSQLConnect`).

The `ixSQLCA` has the members shown in Table 40.13.

Table 40.13. ixSQLCA members.

Members	*Use*
SQLAWARN	The `SQLAWARN` member variable is an eight-place character string. Normally, all characters are blank. However, after certain database operations, some of the characters can be set to `"W"` (for warning). If any of the characters are set to `"W"`, the first character, `SQLAWARN[1]`, is set to `"W"`. So you can test for this first. `SQLAWARN[2]` is set if a database with transactions is opened or a data value is truncated to fit a character. `SQLAWARN[3]` is set if an ANSI-compliant database is opened or a `NULL` is encountered in an SQL statement. `SQLAWARN[4]` is set if an INFORMIX-OnLine database is opened or the number of data values in an SQL select is not the same as the number of `INTO` variables. `SQLAWARN[5]` is set if a float-to-decimal conversion occurs. `SQLAWARN[6]` is set when an extension to the ANSI/ISO standard is executed, and the `DBANSIWARN` environment variable is set. `SQLAWARN[7]` and `SQLAWARN[8]` are not used.
SQLCODE	An integer that records the status code of the last SQL operation. A value of zero indicates a successful operation. A value of `100(NOTFOUND)` indicates that a `SELECT` operation found no rows. A negative value indicates a failure.

Members	Use
SQLERRD	An array of six integers. SQLERRD[1] is not used. SQLERRD[2] is set to the last ISAM error code or serial number generated by the SQL operation. SQLERRD[3] is the number of rows processed. SQLERRD[4] is the estimated CPU cost for the query. SQLERRD[5] is the offset of the error into the SQL statement. SQLERRD[6] is the ROWID of the last row.
SQLERRM	Not used.
SQLERRP	Not used.

The implicit connection object is automatically assigned the global record SQLCA (not an `ixSQLCA` object). You can create an `ixSQLCA` object for the implicit connection if required.

If you have previously created an `ixSQLCA` object for a connection, it is not automatically updated after a database operation. After a database operation, you need to create an `ixSQLCA` object by calling `getSQLCA()` for the `ixSQLConnect` object that you want to test.

Stored Procedures

Stored procedures are executed like any other SQL statements using either embedded SQL statements or `ixSQLStmt` objects. Stored procedures are important to the client/server application. Most client/server applications make extensive use of stored procedures to minimize network traffic.

TIP

Informix stored procedures support named parameters, and I recommend that all stored procedures be used with them.

Summary

This chapter covered the basic syntax of the NewEra language. You learned about NewEra as a procedural language and as an object-oriented language. You saw that NewEra supports both procedural and object-oriented styles of development.

Finally, because NewEra is a database-centric language, you learned about the facilities NewEra provides for database access.

CHAPTER 41

The NewEra Development System

by Gordon Gielis

IN THIS CHAPTER

This chapter describes the development tools you can use to implement the features of the NewEra language (which were discussed in the preceding chapter).

The NewEra development system consists of the following seven tools:

- *Window Painter:* A graphical tool that enables you to develop event-driven windows. You can use the Window Painter to place visual components, such as buttons and text fields, in the window. You also can attach code procedures to handle any of the supported window events. You can use the Window Painter to create new classes of windows to extend the properties of an existing window to meet specific requirements.
- *Application Builder:* A project-management tool that provides a visual interface to a project's dependency structure. You can use this tool to control the module structure of a project and to define `INCLUDE` directories, compilation types, and the libraries to include in the project.
- *Source Compiler:* Controls the compilation of source modules. Source can be compiled into C code object files or Informix p-code object files. The Source Compiler also controls any special instructions you need to pass to the Informix compiler or to the C compiler.
- *Interactive Debugger:* A tool you can use to visually check the execution of your program. You can use the Interactive Debugger to step through your code one line at a time, set break points, and examine the value of variables in your program.
- *SuperView Editor:* Defines SuperViews in an Informix database. A *SuperView* is a mechanism used to simplify the complexities of a highly normalized database. What the user understands as a single business object might be contained in a number of tables. The user might understand the customer business object to have attributes such as the name, phone number, and address, for example. If the attributes were all stored in the one table, this would not present a great problem; however, a normalized database might store these attributes in a number of tables. The user then would need to understand the relational concept of joins to be able to extract the customer information. Obviously, this method is undesirable and subject to error. By using SuperViews, you can create views into the database that denormalize the database for the user (and other programmers). SuperViews are more than just database views, though, because they allow formatting information and some business rules to be incorporated into their definition.
- *Application Launcher:* Provides a convenient method for invoking your programs. Controls any runtime arguments that need to be sent to your program, such as the resource files or *dynamic link libraries* (DLLs) required.
- *Help Compiler:* A command-line tool that compiles a text Help file into a format suitable to be presented by the NewEra Help browser. The NewEra Help browser is a platform-independent Help system. NewEra also supports Microsoft Help files for Microsoft Windows applications.

Window Development with NewEra

Most NewEra projects require the development of graphical user interfaces. This section explores the tools that NewEra provides to develop graphical interfaces. The following topics are covered:

- The general characteristics of windows interfaces
- The NewEra Window Painter, which allows you to visually construct your window
- Relating the code generated by the Window Painter to the NewEra object implementation method
- Visual database access objects provided by NewEra
- Standard visual components provided by NewEra

Window Basics

Window development with NewEra is centered around an object-oriented window class called the `ixWindow` class. All windows you develop in NewEra are derived from `ixWindow`. It is important to remember that NewEra is a cross-platform system, so although windows under Motif and windows under MS-Windows share much in common, differences exist in the way some visual objects are presented and activated. Figure 41.1 shows a basic `ixWindow` class, and Table 41.1 lists the significant components of this window class.

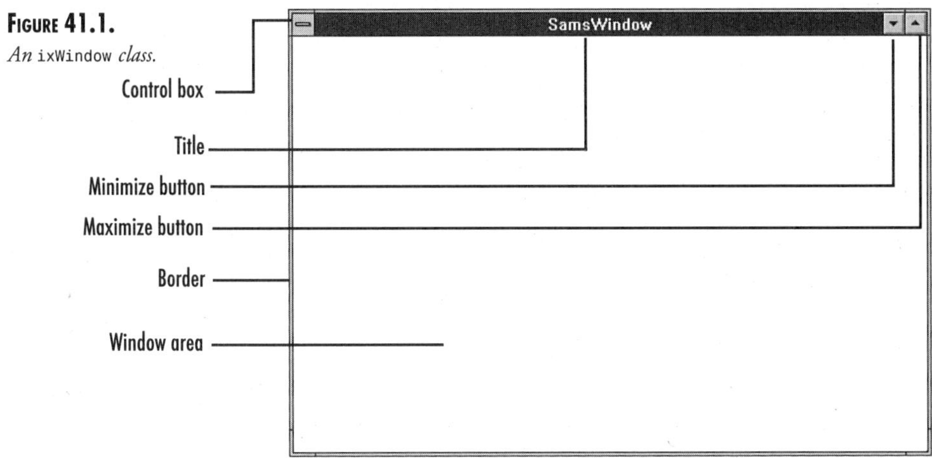

FIGURE 41.1.
An `ixWindow` *class.*

Table 41.1. Basic window items.

Component	*Function*
Title	Describes the window to the user—for example, `SamsWindow`
Control box	Controls the minimizing and maximizing of the window
Maximize button	Increases the window to its maximum size
Minimize button	Decreases the window size to an icon onscreen
Border	Contains the window; borders come in various thicknesses
Window area	The area of the window in which the visual controls are placed

A major difference between GUI windows and the windows provided by procedural languages, such as INFORMIX-4GL, is that the GUI window is event-driven. This means that the window responds to user-initiated events such as a mouse click, and the window has only limited control over the order of user-initiated events. A GUI window, for example, cannot control where the user next clicks the mouse cursor in the window. Contrast this with the INFORMIX-4GL window, in which the programmer has total control over the position of the cursor. It is the duty of the programmer to ensure that all necessary user-initiated events are responded to correctly. This has obvious consequences for the structure of the window program; the program no longer can call functions in a strictly sequential fashion and control at all times the position of the user in the program. Window programs achieve this change in the flow of control by using the message loop. Listing 41.1 shows the declaration and instantiation of a window under NewEra.

Listing 41.1. A message loop.

```
1  MAIN
2      LET SamsWindow = NEW ixWindow()
3      CALL SamsWindow.open()
4      RETURN
5  END MAIN
```

The `MAIN...END MAIN` program block constitutes the message loop. Conceptually, the program loops through this program block by entering the event-driven window `SamsWindow` and waiting for user-initiated events. After it receives an event, the program re-enters the message loop and passes the event back to `SamsWindow`, which then responds to the event. The macro `RETURN` on line 4 tells the compiler that this `MAIN` program block should behave as a message loop. NewEra does not redeclare and instantiate the window on every iteration. (I use the word *conceptually* here because this is a simplification of the process. This is a good example of how NewEra makes window programming easy. Compare the code in Listing 41.1 with the message-loop code in a Visual C++ program, and you will appreciate the simplicity of NewEra.)

Windows come in four types under NewEra:

- *Modal dialog box:* A dialog box is a box that is initiated from another window and displays information to or requests input from the user. A dialog box is said to be *contained* by the other window. A modal dialog box is a dialog box that traps focus; users must deal with this box and cannot go back to the original window until they close the modal dialog box.
- *Non-modal dialog box:* This dialog box enables users to return to the previous window without having to first close the non-modal dialog box.
- *Top window:* This is a window that does not have a containing window. Top windows, therefore, are modeless.
- *Main top window:* This is a top window that closes all other windows and quits the application when it is closed.

A NewEra window is an object of an `ixWindow` class (or a class inherited from `ixWindow`). You can treat NewEra window classes like other object classes. You can inherit a new class from an existing class, add new member variables and functions, and override existing member functions. You can build business rules and data structures into the window class. You will see in the next section how the Window Painter makes these tasks easy.

The `ixWindow` class is the *container* of all other visual objects. When you paint a visual object onto an `ixWindow`, that object becomes a `PUBLIC` member variable of the `ixWindow`. Table 41.2 lists the important member functions that come with the `ixWindow` class.

Table 41.2. ixWindow member functions.

Member Function	*Use*
`close`	Closes the window. The window no longer is available for use.
`getWindow`	Returns a reference variable to the window. The reference variable is of type `ixWindow`, and you might need to `CAST` it to the class of your window to access custom members.
`hide`	Makes the window invisible to the user. You cannot hide modal dialog boxes.
`ixWindow (constructor)`	NewEra enables you to extend the constructor to provide custom behavior. Typically, you might want to perform some security validations, such as checking to make sure that the user has permission to use this window.

continues

Table 41.2. continued

Member Function	*Use*
`minimize`	Reduces the display of the window to an icon onscreen.
`open`	Opens the window.
`restore`	Restores a minimized window to its former size on the user's screen.
`setTitle`	Sets the text displayed in the title of the window.
`show`	Makes the window visible to the user.
`start`	An event called from `open`. Typically, you can use the handler for this event to perform initialization tasks, such as populating a listbox with database values.

The NewEra Window Painter

You use the Window Painter to develop windows, dialog boxes, and their attached menus. (See Figure 41.2.) You can use the Window Painter to visually place objects, such as buttons and listboxes, on your window. You can set properties for the visual objects you are using, and you can attach code procedures to the event handlers of those objects.

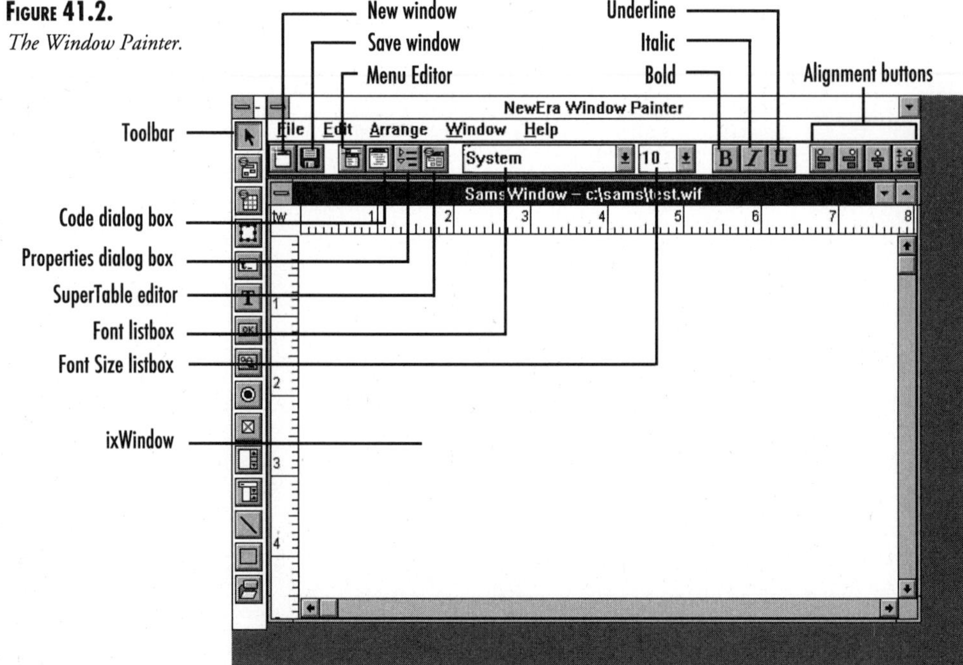

FIGURE 41.2.
The Window Painter.

You also can use the Window Painter to declare new window classes to extend the behavior of existing window classes through inheritance.

When you save your work, the Window Painter generates a *Windows Intermediate File* (WIF), a 4GH class declaration file, and a 4GL implementation code file for the window you have painted. You should not edit the WIF file directly, because it is overwritten each time you save your work in the Window Painter.

Table 41.3 lists the options on the Window Painter menu.

Table 41.3. The Window Painter menu options.

Menu	*Option*	*Function*
File	New	Creates a new `ixWindow`.
	Open	Opens an existing `ixWindow`.
	Close	Closes a current `ixWindow`.
	Save, Save As	Saves the current `ixWindow` into a file with the existing name or a new name.
	Revert to Saved	Retrieves last saved version.
	Print Setup	Enables you to choose printing options such as paper size and page orientations.
	Print	Prints an image of the `ixWindow`.
	Exit	Closes the Window Painter.
Edit	Undo, Redo	Undoes/redoes the last operation.
	Cut, Copy, Paste	Enables you to perform standard Clipboard operations.
	Delete/Clear	Deletes the currently selected visual object.
	Select All	Selects all the visual objects.
	Export ROF	Exports the currently selected visual object as a *reusable object file* (ROF).
	Import ROF	Imports a previously exported ROF.
	SuperTable	Invokes the SuperTable Editor.
	Menu	Invokes the Menu Editor.

continues

Table 41.3. continued

Menu	*Option*	*Function*
Arrange	Align Objects	Invokes the Alignment dialog box for the selected visual objects.
	Bring to Front	Enables you to paint visual objects over the top of other visual objects. If you select a visual object that lies under another and then use this option, the lower object is displayed on top.
	Send to Back	The reverse of the Bring to Front option. If you select a visual object that lies over another object and then use this option, the lower object is displayed on top.
	Lock Object	Locks the selected visual object and prevents the object from being moved inadvertently.
	Unlock Object	Enables you to move an object that was previously locked.
Window	Show Properties	Invokes the Properties dialog box for the selected visual object.
	Show Code	Invokes the Code window for the selected visual object.
	Show Tool Palette	Shows/hides the tool palette.
	Show Command Bar	Shows/hides the command bar.
	Preferences	Invokes the Preferences dialog box so that you can set system options.
	Rulers & Grids	Invokes the Rulers & Grids dialog box.
	Refresh ROF	Updates all the ROFs in `ixWindow` to the latest version.
	Arrange Windows	Enables you to specify tiled, stacked, side-by-side, or cascaded display.
Help		Invokes the standard window Help options.

You can access some of the Window Painter menu options by using the toolbar. Figure 41.3 shows the toolbar in a horizontal configuration and includes callouts to the associated dialog boxes.

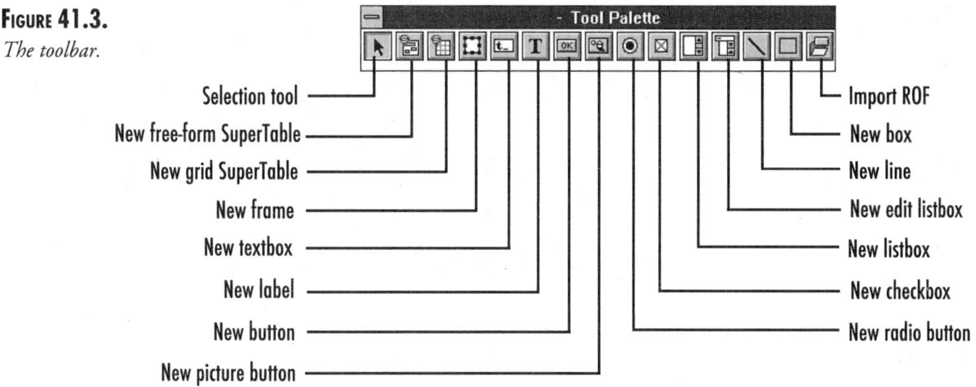

FIGURE 41.3.
The toolbar.

The Properties Dialog Box

You use the Properties dialog box to set the properties of visual objects. You access the Properties dialog box by selecting the visual object (in this case, the window) and clicking the Properties button on the toolbar, choosing Window|Show Properties, or pressing Shift+F2.

The properties correspond to some of the `PUBLIC` member variables of the visual object. Figure 41.4 shows the Properties dialog box for the sample `SamsWindow` window.

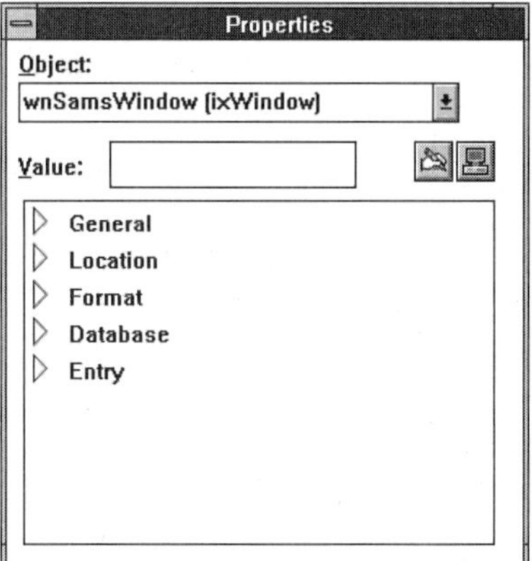

FIGURE 41.4.
The Properties dialog box.

The Properties dialog box for `ixWindow` has five sections. Each of these sections has a group of properties for the window. Remember that the properties equate to some of the member variables of the window class. The Properties sections are as follows:

- *General:* Contains properties of the `ixWindow`, such as the `Name` and `Class` of the `ixWindow`. This section is described in detail in Table 41.4.
- *Location:* Contains the `Top`, `Left`, `Width`, and `Height` properties, which control the location and size of the window.

- *Format:* Contains properties that control how the window is displayed—for example, the background color of the window.
- *Database:* Indicates the database to which the window is connected. The window does not need a database; however, if you want to include SuperTables that refer to a particular database, this is the section in which to specify the database.
- *Entry:* Specifies whether the window can receive data entry.

Figure 41.5 shows the Properties dialog box with the General section expanded.

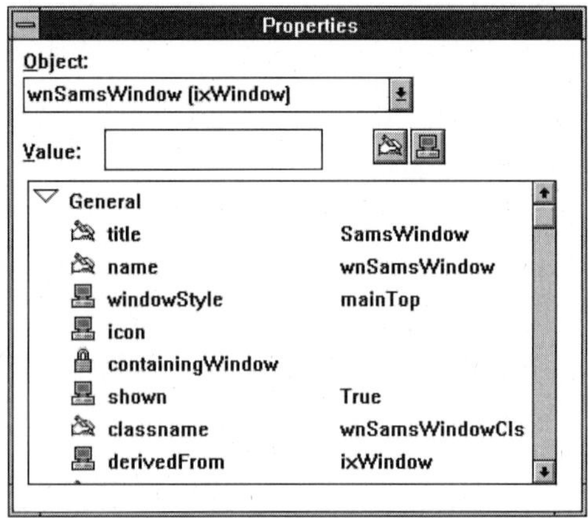

FIGURE 41.5.
The General section of the Properties dialog box.

As you can see, the General section contains quite a few properties. These properties are listed in Table 41.4.

Table 41.4. The `ixWindow` General properties.

Property	*Use*
`title`	Controls the text displayed in the title of the window. Note the Pen-in-Hand icon. This indicates that you have changed this property from the system default.
`name`	Specifies the name of the window. Used when instantiating a new window.
`windowStyle`	Specifies the type of window. The sample window is a `mainTop` window. Note the PC icon, which indicates that this is the system default for this property.
`icon`	Specifies the file containing the icon displayed when the user minimizes this window.

Property	*Use*
`containingWindow`	Specifies the window from which this window is initiated. This window is a `mainTop` window and, therefore, is not initiated from any other window. Note the lock on this property, which tells you that you cannot change this property. Remember that modal dialog boxes are initiated from other windows.
`shown`	Specifies `TRUE` for a visible window and `FALSE` for a hidden window.
`classname`	Specifies the name of the class of this window. You can create a new class of window by using the Window Painter. This is where you specify the name of the new class.
`derivedFrom`	You can inherit the behavior of another class for your new class. In this chapter's example, this window is the `wnSamsWindowCls` class, which inherits from `ixWindow`. You could inherit from another class, however, that you declared previously. In this way, you could create base windows for your project with standard functions.
`theStartUp`	Specifies `TRUE` if this is the first window to be displayed by your application; specifies `FALSE` if it is not. If `TRUE`, NewEra generates a `MAIN` program block similar to the earlier sample block.
`helpFile`	Specifies the file containing the online Help for this window.
`helpNum`	Specifies the number of the Help item in the Help file related to this window.
`topicName`	Specifies the topic within the Help file for this window.
`direction`, `menuDirection`, and `titleReadingOrder`	Determine the behavior of the keyboard, menus, and titles. These properties help support the internationalization of your software.

Changing a property is merely a matter of double-clicking the property and then changing the value in the textbox near the top of the Properties dialog box. If only a small number of permitted values exists, the textbox is replaced with a listbox.

The Code Window

Code usually must be attached to the event handlers of an event-driven window. The Window Painter enables you to do this by using the Code window, as shown in Figure 41.6. You access the Code window by double-clicking the visual object, clicking the Code button on the toolbar, choosing Window|Show Code, or pressing F2.

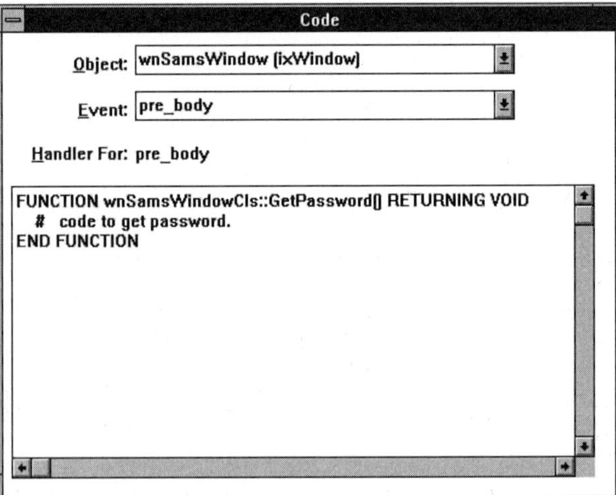

FIGURE 41.6.
The Code window.

You can enter code for each of the events for the selected visual object in the Code window. Different visual objects have different events; for example, a button has an `ACTIVATE` event that `ixWindow` does not. The code you enter in the Code window becomes the `HANDLER` code for the event selected. You do not need to type the `HANDLER` and `END HANDLER` statements, because NewEra writes those for you.

Using the Code window is different for `ixWindow` objects than for other visual objects. Because `ixWindow` is the base for all GUI development, the Code window enables you to enter statements that extend the class of the window under development. These extensions are not handlers for events but are accessible through the Code window for ease of use. Figure 41.6 shows the `pre_body` section of the `wnSamsWindow` `ixWindow`. You will examine the code sections for `ixWindow` in some detail. Table 41.5 lists the most important Code window sections for `ixWindow`.

Table 41.5. Code sections for `ixWindow`.

Event	*Use*
`class_extension`	Code entered here extends the class declaration of the window. You could declare a `PUBLIC` function called `checkPassword()`, for example, that would be called to check a password. The Window Painter generates a class

Event	*Use*
	declaration file exactly as you would if you were declaring a custom class yourself. Any members declared here are included in that definition file.
`click`	An event initiated when the user clicks the mouse in the window. Code entered here is executed in response to that event.
`constructor_extension`	Code entered here extends the constructor. This code is executed immediately after the constructor is executed (when the window is instantiated).
`finish`	This code is executed after the window is closed. The `close` event calls the `finish` event.
`pre_body`	This is where you can enter the implementation code for the window. If your window does not declare any new member functions, you are not required to enter anything here. If you have declared member functions in the `class_extension` sections, this is where you can enter the implementation code for these member functions.
`pre_header`	This is where you declare the dependencies for this window. If your window is going to reference custom classes, you need to include the declaration of their class types (just as you would for any class declaration). Standard visual classes, such as `ixButton` and `ixListBox`, that you can paint on your window using the Window Painter are handled by the Window Painter; you do not need to declare them here. Typically, this section has a series of `INCLUDE` compiler directives referencing the declaration files of the custom classes.
`start`	This event is initiated when the window is opened. You could include code here, for example, to populate listboxes from the database.

TIP

Entering code into the `pre_body` section of the Code window can become unmanageable if the code becomes very large. Consider locating the implementation code that usually is located in the `pre_body` section in a separate source code module. You then must include this module in the project definition by using the Application Builder.

The Code window for visual objects other than `ixWindow` enables you to enter the code to be executed for the event selected. Figure 41.7 shows the Code window used to enter the `ACTIVATE` event-handler code for the `ixButton bnCancel`.

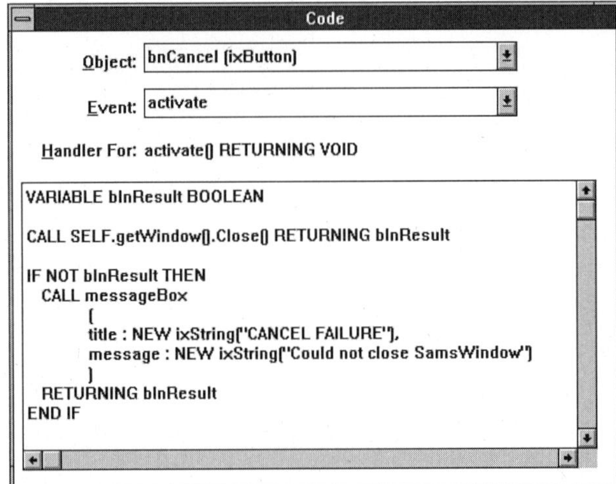

FIGURE 41.7.
The Code window for an `ixButton`.

This handler calls the `close()` member function of `wnSamsWindow`. It demonstrates the use of the `getWindow()` member function of the `bnCancel ixButton` to return a reference variable (pointer) to `wnSamsWindow`.

The Menu Editor

Most, if not all, windows require a menu. You can use the NewEra Menu Editor to design a menu for your window. You can access the Menu Editor by clicking the Menu Editor button on the toolbar, choosing Edit|Menu, or pressing Ctrl+M. Figure 41.8 shows the Menu Editor used to develop the menu for `wnSamsWindow`.

You can use the Menu Editor to create menus and nested submenus. You can attach code to handle the `ACTIVATE` event for each menu item. Menu items can be enabled or disabled, checked or unchecked. You also can define accelerator keys for each submenu item.

When you inherit from a window class that has a menu defined, the new window class has the menu from the ancestor class. If you define new menu items for the new window class, the new options appear to the right of the menu options from the ancestor class.

Code Generated by the Window Painter

The Window Painter generates the class declaration file (`*.4gh`) and the class implementation file (`*.4gl`) for the window you have painted.

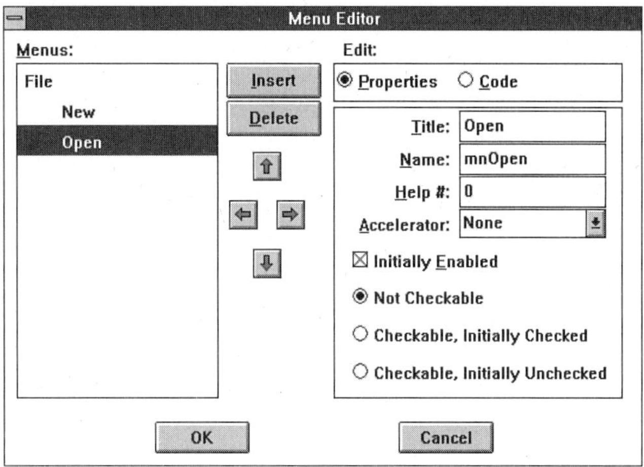

FIGURE 41.8.
The Menu Editor.

The Class Declaration File

Listing 41.2 shows the class declaration file generated by the Window Painter for `wnSamsWindowCls`.

Listing 41.2. The class declaration generated by the Window Painter.

```
INCLUDE SYSTEM "ixrow.4gh"
INCLUDE SYSTEM "ixwindow.4gh"
INCLUDE SYSTEM "ixbutton.4gh"
INCLUDE SYSTEM "ixlstbox.4gh"

INCLUDE SYSTEM "ix4gl.4gh"      #    for the messageBox function
INCLUDE "myapp.4gh"     #   includes the class MyApp used in the
➥constructor

CLASS wnSamsWindowCls DERIVED FROM ixWindow
  FUNCTION wnSamsWindowCls(
      geometry ixGeometry : NEW ixGeometry(
          top : 0,
          left : 0,
          height : 6225,
                  width : 8160
      ),
      appearance ixAppearance : NULL,
          topicName CHAR(*) : NULL,
      containingWindow ixWindow : NULL,
          icon CHAR(*) : NULL,
      windowStyle SMALLINT : ixWindow::mainTop,
      enabled BOOLEAN : TRUE,
          title CHAR(*) : "SamsWindow",
      helpFile CHAR(*) : NULL,
      name CHAR(*) : "wnSamsWindow",
      helpNum INTEGER : 0,
```

continues

Listing 41.2. continued

```
27          shown BOOLEAN : TRUE,
28          source BOOLEAN : TRUE
29      )
30   PUBLIC VARIABLE
31     mnFile ixMenu,
32     bnCancel ixButton,
33     bnOk ixButton,
34     lbOptions ixListBox
35
36   PUBLIC FUNCTION GetPassword() RETURNING VOID
37
38   END CLASS -- wnSamsWindowCls
```

As you can see in Listing 41.2, `wnSamsWindowCls` is a class derived from the `ixWindow` class to which you have added some custom members. It is an object class and can be treated in much the same way as any object class, as discussed in the preceding chapter.

Lines 1 through 4 declare some `INCLUDE` files. These files are included by the Window Painter when you paint the visual objects on your window.

Lines 6 and 7 declare some `INCLUDE` files as well. These files were included by you in the `pre_header` section of the Code window. In this way, you can access members of these classes.

Line 9 begins the constructor declaration. The name of the class, `wnSamsWindowCls`, was defined in the Window Painter Properties dialog box. Most of the properties of `wnSamsWindowCls`—for example, `windowStyle`—are defined in the Properties dialog box (or by sizing the window with the mouse).

Line 30 shows how the visual objects you painted with the Window Painter become a `PUBLIC` member variable of the `wnSamsWindowCls` class. In this example, you painted four visual objects: one `ixMenu`, two `ixButtons`, and an `ixListBox`. You assigned names to those visual objects by using the Properties dialog box for each object. Those names become the names of the member variables.

In the `class_extension` section of the Window Painter, you declared a `PUBLIC` member function called `GetPassword()`. This member function is shown on line 36.

The Implementation File

The Window Painter generates the class implementation file (`*.4gl`), as shown in Listing 41.3.

Listing 41.3. Class implementation generated by the Window Painter.

```
INCLUDE "test.4gh"

FORWARD wnSamsWindowCls

FUNCTION wnSamsWindowCls::GetPassword() RETURNING VOID
```

```
  #  code to get password.
END FUNCTION

HANDLER wnSamsWindowCls::wnSamsWindow_start() RETURNING VOID
  #   Some start logic
END HANDLER -- wnSamsWindowCls::wnSamsWindow_start

HANDLER ixButton::wnSamsWindow_bnCancel_activate() RETURNING VOID
  VARIABLE blnResult BOOLEAN

  CALL SELF.getWindow().close() RETURNING blnResult

  IF NOT blnResult THEN
    CALL messageBox
        (
        title : NEW ixString("CANCEL FAILURE"),
        message : NEW ixString("Could not close SamsWindow")
        )
   RETURNING blnResult
  END IF
END HANDLER -- ixButton::wnSamsWindow_bnCancel_activate

FUNCTION wnSamsWindowCls::wnSamsWindowCls(
                                        geometry ixGeometry,
                                        appearance ixAppearance,
                                        topicName CHAR(*),
                                        containingWindow ixWindow,
                                        icon CHAR(*),
                                        windowStyle SMALLINT,
                                        enabled BOOLEAN,
                                        title CHAR(*),
                                        helpFile CHAR(*),
                                        name CHAR(*),
                                        helpNum INTEGER,
                                        shown BOOLEAN,
                                        source BOOLEAN
                                        )
                                        : ixWindow(
                                          containingWindow : containingWindow,

                                          name : name,
                                          enabled : enabled,
                                          shown : shown,
                                          helpNum : helpNum,
                                          geometry : geometry,
                                          appearance : appearance,
                                          helpFile : helpFile,
                                          title : title,
                                          icon : icon,
                                          windowStyle : windowStyle,
                                          topicName : topicName,
                                          source : source
                                          )

      VARIABLE itemList ixVector
      VARIABLE includeTable ixRow
```

continues

Listing 41.3. continued

```
VARIABLE result INTEGER
LET result = 0

HANDLE start WITH wnSamsWindowCls::wnSamsWindow_start
-- Begin ixButton bnCancel
LET bnCancel = NEW ixButton(
                           geometry : NEW ixGeometry(
                                                    top : 1620,
                                                    left : 5730,
                                                    height : 495,
                                                    width : 1590
                                                    ),
                           appearance : NULL,
                           tabIndex : NULL,
                           tabEnabled : TRUE,
                           enabled : TRUE,
                           title : "Cancel",
                           theDefault : FALSE,
                           name : "bnCancel",
                           helpNum : 0,
                           shown : TRUE,
                           container : SELF
                           )
HANDLE bnCancel.activate WITH
➥ixButton::wnSamsWindow_bnCancel_activate
-- End ixButton bnCancel
-- Begin ixButton bnOk
   LET bnOk = NEW ixButton(
                           geometry : NEW ixGeometry(
                                                    top : 840,
                                                    left : 5730,
                                                    height : 495,
                                                    width : 1590
                                                    ),
                           appearance : NULL,
                           tabIndex : NULL,
                           tabEnabled : TRUE,
                           enabled : TRUE,
                           title : "OK",
                           theDefault : FALSE,
                           name : "bnOk",
                           helpNum : 0,
                           shown : TRUE,
                           container : SELF
                           )
-- End ixButton bnOk
-- Begin ixListBox lbOptions
LET itemList = NEW ixVector()
LET result = itemList.insert(NEW ixString("ListItem1"))
LET result = itemList.insert(NEW ixString("ListItem2"))
LET result = itemList.insert(NEW ixString("ListItem3"))
LET lbOptions = NEW ixListBox(
                           geometry : NEW ixGeometry(
                                                    top : 990,
                                                    left : 585,
                                                    height : 1740,
                                                    width : 2505
                                                    ),
```

```
118                                         appearance : NULL,
119                                         tabIndex : NULL,
120                                         tabEnabled : TRUE,
121                                         enabled : TRUE,
122                                         sorted : TRUE,
123                                         itemList : itemList,
124                                         style : ixListBox::singleSelect,
125                                         name : "lbOptions",
126                                         helpNum : 0,
127                                         shown : TRUE,
128                                         container : SELF
129                                         )
130          -- End ixListBox lbOptions
131          -- Begin ixMenu mnFile
132          LET mnFile = NEW ixMenu(
133                                   appearance : NULL,
134                                   enabled : TRUE,
135                                   accelerator : NULL,
136                                   title : "File",
137                                   checkState : ixMenu::notACheck,
138                                   name : "mnFile",
139                                   helpNum : 0,
140                                   parentMenu : SELF.getMenuBar()
141                                   )
142          -- End ixMenu mnFile
143          CALL  MyApp::SecurityCheck()
144     END FUNCTION -- wnSamsWindowCls::wnSamsWindowCls
```

This file defines the implementation code for the `wnSamsWindowCls` constructor and the implementation code for any custom member functions.

Line 1 includes the class declaration file `test.4gh`. The compiler uses the declaration file to check the prototype and access permissions for any custom members. Line 3 illustrates the use of the `FORWARD` *`class_name`* statement. This keyword instructs the compiler that the declaration of the class *`class_name`* will follow. It is not needed in this example, because the `wnSamsWindowCls` class was declared by the `INCLUDE "test.4gh"` statement.

Lines 5 through 7 define the custom member function `GetPassword()` that was declared as a member of `wnSamsWindowCls`. This is the code you entered into the `pre_body` section of the Code window for `wnSamsWindow`.

Lines 9 through 11 show the code you entered in the Code window for the `start` event of `wnSamsWindow`. Note that the Window Painter automatically provided the `HANDLER` and `END HANDLER` definition. All you have to provide is the implementation code. Similarly, lines 16 through 26 show the code you entered for the `ACTIVATE` event of the `bnCancel` `ixButton`. You call the `close()` member function of the containing window for the `bnCancel` `ixButton`. You get a reference to the containing window by calling the `getWindow()` member function of `bnCancel`.

Lines 28 through 132 define the constructor for wnSamsWindowCls. Like all derived classes, the constructor calls the constructor for its ancestor class—in this case, ixWindow. The ixWindow constructor is called on lines 43 through 57.

Lines 59 through 62 declare some variables: itemList, includeTable, and result. These variables are used by the ixListBox class and are declared automatically by the Window Painter whenever you paint an ixListBox.

Line 64 shows how you bind the start event with the wnSamsWindowCls::wnSamsWindowCls handler. This is done automatically whenever you enter some code into the start section of the Code window. For any event, if the Window Painter detects that you have entered code into an event handler, it automatically binds the event to the event handler. If you do not enter any code, no handler is generated and no binding takes place.

Lines 65 through 105 show how the member variables bnOk and bnCancel are instantiated. Each of these members is instantiated like any other object with the NEW statement and a call to the appropriate constructor function.

Lines 106 through 130 show the instantiation of the lbOptions member variable. This variable is an ixListBox. In the Properties dialog box of this visual object, you can specify the initial items in the list (ListItem1, ListItem2, and ListItem3, for example). The ixVector named itemList is populated with ixStrings with each of these values. The itemList ixVector then is passed as one of the parameters to the constructor of the ixListBox. The ixListBox constructor inserts the values into its list.

NOTE

The ixListBox class provides member functions to insert and delete items from its list. Listing 41.3 shows how you can accomplish this as part of the ixListBox constructor, however.

Lines 131 through 142 show the instantiation of the mnFile ixMenu.

Finally, on line 143, the constructor executes any statements included in the constructor_extension section of the Code window. In this example, the SecurityCheck() member function is called. This function is a member of the MyApp class, which was included on line 7 of the class declaration file. (The implementation of this function is in the implementation file of the MyApp class.)

SuperViews

SuperViews enable you, as a developer, to hide the complexities of the database from the user. You can aggregate data from more than one table into one view. You can rename columns and tables to be more user-friendly. You also can specify data ranges and presentation formats.

SuperViews can be used by SuperTables (see the next section) and by the ViewPoint-Pro report writing tool. In NewEra 2.20, SuperViews are created by using the ViewPoint-Pro system. Future versions of NewEra will incorporate the SuperView Editor directly into the Window Painter.

Figure 41.9 shows the SuperView Editor used to create a SuperView that combines two tables associated in a one-to-one relationship. The SuperView name is `SamsSuperView`. Additionally, you can define the sort order of the SuperView.

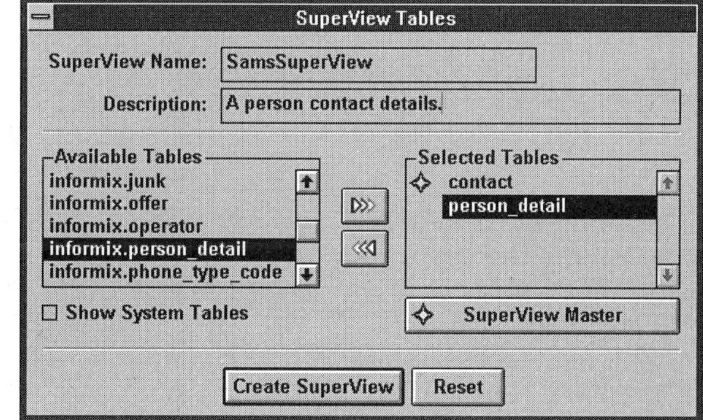

FIGURE 41.9.
The SuperView Editor.

SuperTables

The SuperTable is a data-aware visual object that provides sophisticated database manipulation and query capabilities. SuperTables come in two types: *free-form* SuperTables and *grid-form* SuperTables. A free-form SuperTable presents a simple form to the user, whereas a grid-form SuperTable presents a scrolling grid.

Two or more SuperTables can be made to coordinate their database activities to support master-detail table manipulations. SuperTables are object-oriented classes and can be manipulated programmatically like any other object variable. You also can declare your own classes derived from SuperTables to provide customized behaviors.

SuperTables come with a collection of buttons that are precoded to perform standard database operations, such as updating and deleting. SuperTables do not need to be displayed; you can use invisible SuperTables to drive reports and perform database manipulations.

SuperTables prepare statements for the SQL operations you require. These SQL statements then are executed by `ixSQLStmt` objects. These SQL statements can be manipulated programmatically.

SuperTables are objects of the `ixSuperTable` or `ixMDSuperTable` class. The `ixMDSuperTable` class inherits from the `ixSuperTable` class and adds master-detail support. A SuperTable usually relates to a table, database view, or SuperView.

A SuperTable is also a *visual container* (inheriting from the `ixVisualContainer` class), so it can contain other visual objects. SuperTables almost always contain SuperFields. A *SuperField* is a visual object of class `ixSuperField` or `ixMDSuperField`. The SuperField enables users to enter data or query strings. The SuperField usually relates to a column in a table or SuperView, although manual SuperFields are allowed. SuperTables are divided logically into a number of cells. In a free-form SuperTable, a SuperField represents a cell in the SuperTable. In a grid-form SuperTable, a SuperField represents a column of cells in the SuperTable. Each cell maintains a change state; the SuperField knows whether it has been changed, created, or flagged for deletion by the user.

The SuperTable maintains a collection of `ixRow` objects that represent the data or query rows of the SuperTable. When the user requests that the SuperTable save the database operations the user has requested, the SuperTable examines this collection and prepares the appropriate SQL operations for each row. In a grid-form SuperTable, for example, the user can add some new rows and then delete some old rows. The SuperTable stores these changes internally in `ixRows` (in an `ixRowArray`) until the user asks the SuperTable to save itself.

SuperTable Properties, Functions, and Events

Like most classes, SuperTables and SuperFields have member variables (properties), member functions, and events. Tables 41.6 through 41.11 list the most important properties, functions, and events. SuperTables have a large number of functions and events. The way in which these functions and events are used depends on the database operation being requested. A complete discussion of these members is beyond the scope of this book; I thoroughly recommend that you spend some time investigating these members in the NewEra documentation.

Table 41.6. SuperTable properties.

Property	*Use*
`deleteStmt`	An `ixSQLStmt` object. This object encapsulates the `DELETE` SQL to be used by the SuperTable.
`insertStmt`	An `ixSQLStmt` object. This object encapsulates the `INSERT` SQL to be used by the SuperTable.
`lockStmt`	An `ixSQLStmt` object. This object encapsulates the SQL to be used by the SuperTable to lock a database row.
`maxRows`	Specifies the maximum number of rows you want a `SELECT` operation to fetch from the database.
`selectFilterPart`	Specifies the `WHERE` clause of your SQL.
`selectFromPart`	Indicates the database table that the SuperTable accesses. You can specify more than one table.
`selectJoinPart`	Specifies the `join` clause between the tables.

Property	*Use*
`selectOrderByPart`	Specifies the `order by` clause of your SQL.
`selectStmt`	An `ixSQLStmt` object. This object encapsulates the `SELECT` SQL to be used by the SuperTable.
`updateStmt`	An `ixSQLStmt` object. This object encapsulates the `UPDATE` SQL to be used by the SuperTable.

Many member functions are required to provide the sophisticated behavior of the SuperTable. Table 41.7 summarizes some of the more important SuperTable functions.

Table 41.7. SuperTable functions.

Function	*Use*
`acceptRow`	Checks the validity of the data in each of the SuperFields (cells).
`addDetailSuperTable`	Links another SuperTable to this SuperTable as a detail table.
`apply`	Causes the SuperTable to attempt to update, insert, or delete each of the modified rows. `apply()` calls `acceptRow()` and then `applyRowSQL()`.
`applyMasters`	Causes the master SuperTable to apply itself. Because the foreign keys in a detail SuperTable are based on the primary keys of the master SuperTable, the master SuperTable must be applied before the detail SuperTable.
`buildDeleteStr`, `buildInsertStr`, `buildLockStr`, `buildSelectStr`, `buildUpdateStr`	Build the various SQL statements. These functions generally call lower-level functions that provide the various components of the SQL. For example, `buildInsertStr()` calls `getUpdateTable()` to obtain the name of the table for `INSERT`.
`BuildFilterPart`	Builds the `WHERE` part of your `SELECT` statement. SuperTables enable users to enter wildcard matching. This function translates those wildcards into SQL syntax.
`doSQLDelete`, `doSQLFetch`	One or more of these functions are called by the `doSQLUpdate apply ()` and `retrieve()` functions, depending on the `doSQLInsert` operations requested by the user.
`getCellBuffer`	Returns the editing buffer of the current cell (SuperField).

continues

Table 41.7. continued

Function	*Use*
`getChangeFlag`	Returns a flag to indicate whether a particular row in the SuperTable has been changed, deleted, or newly created.
`getNumStoredRows`	Returns the number of rows fetched by the SuperTable.
`getSuperField`	SuperFields are contained within the SuperTable, but they are not members of the SuperTable. SuperFields, like all visual objects, are members of `ixWindow`. To reference a SuperField from a SuperTable, you use `getSuperField()`.
`retrieve`	Causes the SuperTable to fetch data from the database. The `retrieve()` function can rebuild the SQL statement from user input or accept a programmatically specified SQL.
`revert`	Voids any changes made by the user to the data prior to an `apply()`.
`setCellValue`	Sets the value of the current cell.

A lot of the functions described in this chapter are called by the handler for various SuperTable events. SuperTables are designed this way to enable you to easily modify their behavior. Table 41.8 lists some of the more important events.

Table 41.8. SuperTable events.

Event	*Use*
`afterApply`, `beforeApply`	Called before and after each row is applied to the database.
`AfterRow`, `beforeRow`	Called before and after each row becomes the row with the current cell.
`maxRowsExceeded`	Called when the number of rows fetched exceeds the value of the `maxRows` member variable. You can provide a handler to this event that enables the user to continue or cancel.
`SQLDelete`, `SQLFetch`, `SQLInsert`, `SQLUpdate`, `staleData`	Call the appropriate function. When a SuperTable applies changes to a row in the database, it compares the row currently in the database with the row it originally fetched from the database (not applicable to `INSERT` operations). If there is a difference, it indicates that another process has changed the database row since it was fetched. This change probably was by another user. You can develop a handler for this event to prevent overwriting the other users' changes.

An `ixSuperField` is a visual object that combines display characteristics, such as background color and font, with system catalog information from the associated database column. SuperFields always are contained by a SuperTable.

SuperFields also can be used independently of a database column, in which case you need to specify the data characteristics manually. Manual SuperFields enable you to display aggregate fields—for example, the total of a column in a grid SuperTable.

Table 41.9. SuperField properties.

Property	*Use*
`includeTable`	Lists valid values for the SuperField.
`required`	Indicates that the SuperField requires a value when in data-entry mode.
`useIncludes`	Indicates that the SuperField requires a value from the `includeTable`.
`verify`	Forces users to enter input twice when in data-entry mode.

Table 41.10. SuperField functions.

Function	*Use*
`focus`	Sets keyboard focus to the SuperField.
`getSQLRole`	Returns the SQL role of the SuperField. Valid values are `updateRole`, `noUpdateRole`, `expressionRole`, and `noRole`. The SQL role determines whether the SuperField takes part in the creation of SQL statements.
`getText`	Gets the displayed text of the SuperField.
`setText`	Sets the displayed text of the SuperField.

Table 41.11. SuperField events.

Event	*Use*
`afterCell`, `beforeCell`	Called before and after the `Cell` becomes the current cell.
`cellKeyPress`	Called after the user presses a key. Enables you to intercept the user's keystrokes.

continues

Table 41.11. continued

Event	*Use*
`conversionFailed`	Indicates that the user entered an inappropriate value (entered a character into an integer SuperField, for example).
`includeFailed`	Indicates that the value entered by the user is not in the `include` table.
`requiredFailed`	Indicates that the user should have entered a value.
`userValidateData`	Called after the cell ceases to be the current cell. The handler for this event is where you would place code to check the values entered by the user against your business rules.
`verifyFailed`	Indicates that the user failed to enter the same value twice.

Developing with SuperTables

SuperTables are visual objects painted onto a window by using the SuperTable Editor of the Window Painter. SuperTables can be used independently of SuperViews. A SuperTable can be associated directly with database tables or with a SuperView.

You can access the SuperTable Editor by clicking the SuperTable Editor button on the toolbar, choosing Edit|SuperTable, or pressing Ctrl+T. Figure 41.10 shows the SuperTable Editor.

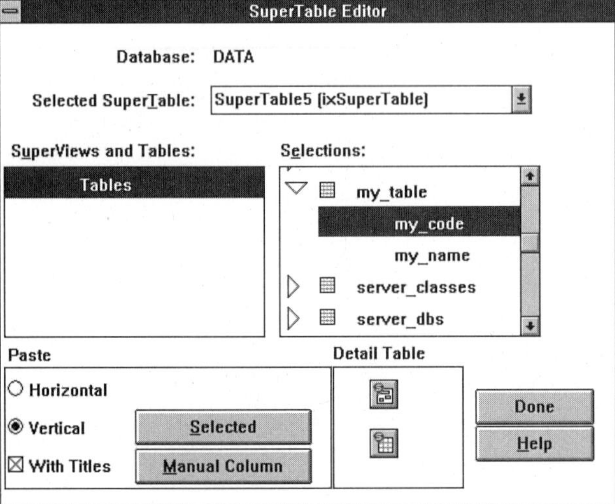

FIGURE 41.10.
The SuperTable Editor.

Painting a SuperTable is easy. Just follow these steps:

1. Ensure that the `ixWindow` database property is set to the database to which you want to connect.
2. Click the SuperTable button on the toolbar for the type of SuperTable you want.
3. Draw the area on the window to be occupied by the SuperTable. The SuperTable Editor appears.
4. Select the table (or SuperView), the columns, and any SuperTable buttons you want. The columns you select are automatically assigned the data type of the column in the database you have selected. You can click the Select button to include the columns and buttons you have chosen.
5. Click the Done button to exit the SuperTable Editor.
6. Position the SuperFields with the mouse, change properties, and add handler code for various events.

The SuperTable being created in Figure 41.10 is a single table. SuperTables also support master-detail relationships.

Master-Detail SuperTables

NewEra automatically creates master and detail SuperTables based on master-detail SuperViews. Use the SuperView Editor in ViewPoint-Pro to create a master-detail SuperView. Select this SuperView and the required columns in the SuperTable Editor, and NewEra creates the appropriate SuperTables. Figure 41.11 shows a master-detail SuperTable.

FIGURE 41.11.
A master-detail SuperTable.

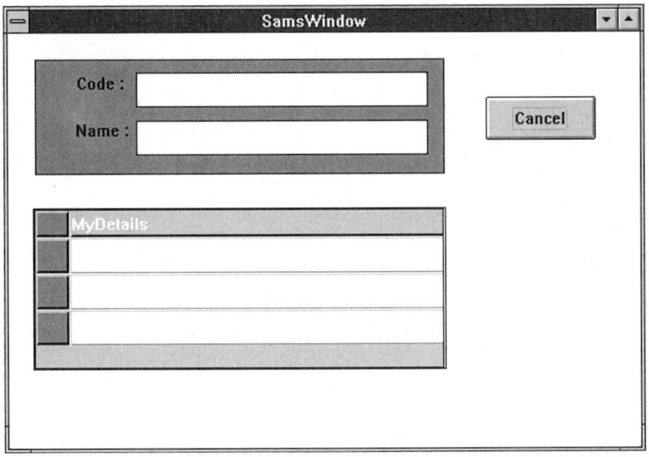

TIP

Remember that SuperFields and SuperTables are objects and, therefore, are addressed through reference variables. A reference variable can be passed into a generic function or passed to a member function of another `ixWindow`. In this way, your program easily can reference SuperFields and SuperTables in another window.

Visual Objects

So far, you have looked at the NewEra window, SuperTables, and SuperViews. NewEra also provides a number of standard visual objects. All the visual objects provided by NewEra are object-oriented classes that enable you to modify and extend their behavior quite easily. Like other objects, visual objects need to be instantiated by calling their constructor function. The NewEra Window Painter automatically generates this code for visual objects you have painted. You can instantiate a visual object programmatically, however. Listing 41.4 shows the constructor function for an `ixButton` visual object.

Listing 41.4. `ixButton` instantiation.

```
-- Begin ixButton bnSamsButton
LET bnSamsButton = NEW ixButton(
                                 geometry : NEW ixGeometry(
                                                          top : 885,
                                                          left : 810,
                                                          height : 705,
                                                          width : 1605
                                                          ),
                                 appearance : NULL,
                                 enabled : TRUE,
                                 title : "Button",
                                 tabIndex : NULL,
                                 tabEnabled : TRUE,
                                 theDefault : FALSE,
                                 name : "bnSamsButton",
                                 helpNum : 0,
                                 shown : TRUE,
                                 container : SELF  # the name of the
➥containing object
                                 )
-- End ixButton bnSamsButton
```

Listing 41.4 illustrates some of the common features of NewEra visual objects. NewEra controls the initial size of a visual object (height, width, top, and left) by passing an `ixGeometry` variable to the constructor of the visual object. The `ixGeometry` variable is itself an object. The container parameter indicates the name of the visual container for the button (for example, the `ixWindow` if the `ixButton` is painted directly onto the Window).

The visual objects—ixFrame, ixSuperTable, and, of course, ixWindow—can act as visual containers for other visual objects. In other words, you can place a visual object into one of these visual objects, and it will be displayed on top. Any visual object that can act as a container must be derived from the abstract ixVisualContainer class.

You can paint visual objects onto a window by using the Window Painter; you also can create visual objects programmatically.

The following visual objects are supplied by NewEra:

ixBox

ixButton

ixCheckBox

ixEditListBox

ixFrame

ixLabel

ixLine

ixListBox

ixPictureButton

ixRadioButton

ixTextBox

ixBox

The ixBox class provides a way of drawing rectangular boxes on your window. Typically, this allows a grouping of visual objects. The ixBox cannot act as a visual container (even though it might look as though it does).

ixButton

The ixButton class provides a GUI button. A button can display a title. You activate a NewEra button by clicking it or pressing the space bar.

ixCheckBox

The ixCheckBox displays as a toggle. It has a state: checked or unchecked. The ixCheckBox appears as a checkmark in a small box, a dot in a round object, or an inversion of a three-dimensional button's shadow, depending on the GUI platform.

The ixCheckBox usually has a text label to the right that describes the purpose of the object.

ixEditListBox

The `ixEditListBox` is similar to the `ixListBox`, except that users can type in a value that is not in the list. This capability enables you to provide a standard set of values in the list, while still giving users the flexibility they need to enter other values.

ixFrame

The `ixFrame` is a visual container that can contain other visual objects. The `ixFrame` can have a visible border. An `ixFrame` can be visible or hidden. You can use an `ixFrame` to provide tab- and wizard-style windows. The Application Framework Class Library contains classes derived from the `ixFrame` that provide special capabilities, such as 3D effects.

> **TIP**
>
> The `ixFrame` provides an easy way to handle a group of visual objects as a collection. In a complicated window, you might want to show or hide different groups of visual objects as the user performs tasks. I find it useful to create an `ixFrame` with nearly every window I develop. Typically, simple windows evolve into complicated windows. Containing all the visual objects in an `ixFrame` makes it easy to add an `ixFrame` with another group of visual objects.

ixLabel

The `ixLabel` class enables you to place static text on your window. The text displayed by the `ixLabel` can be changed programmatically. The `ixLabel` wraps text but does not automatically resize the label to fit; you must do this programmatically.

ixLine

The `ixLine` enables you to draw lines on your window (or within another visual container).

ixListBox

The listbox displays a vertical list of items. Listboxes can be drop-down boxes or fixed-size boxes. You can declare a listbox as *single select*, where the user can select only one item from the list, or *multiselect*, where the user can select one or more items from the list.

ixPictureButton

The `ixPictureButton` is similar to the `ixButton`, except that it displays bitmap pictures instead of title text. You generally need to supply three versions of the bitmap picture: an up version, a down or pressed version, and a disabled version.

WARNING

Differences in the platform and the resolution used might cause problems, so you might need to develop bitmap pictures for each environment. You will need to dynamically load the correct bitmaps.

ixRadioButton

The `ixRadioButton` is similar to the `ixCheckBox`, because it is a toggle. The difference is that only one `ixRadioButton` in any visual container can be selected at a time. If the user selects one `ixRadioButton`, all other `ixRadioButtons` in the visual container automatically are unselected. The appearance of the `ixRadioButton` varies between platforms.

ixTextBox

The `ixTextBox` is a visual object that enables users to enter characters. The `ixTextBox` supports the standard Cut and Paste operations for the platform used.

The `ixTextBox` also operates in both single-line and multiline mode. In single-line mode, characters are accepted up to the `maxChars` member variable. In multiline mode, `ixTextBox` draws a vertical scrollbar to the right. You can embed Tab (Ctrl+I) or newline characters (`\n\r` under Microsoft Windows and `\n` under Motif).

Reusable Object Files

Reusable object files (ROFs) enable you to create a library of visual objects for reuse throughout your project. A ROF can consist of one or more visual objects. To create a ROF, you first paint the visual objects onto a window. You then select the visual objects with the mouse and choose Edit|Export ROF from the Window Painter. A File dialog box appears so that you can save the ROF to an operating system file (and the file is given the extension `.rof`).

To include a ROF in a window, choose Edit|Import ROF and then select the ROF file; the visual objects then are painted onto your form. If you change the ROF, you must refresh the imported ROF by choosing Window|Refresh ROF from the Window Painter.

TIP

If your window contains a large number of controls or accesses the database, it might draw slowly when it first opens. It sometimes is useful to declare the window as not shown when painting it in the Window Painter and then to call the `Show()` member function after instantiating and opening the window in your application. The time taken is usually the same, but the process looks better.

The Application Builder

A project consists of one or more programs. Each program consists of one or more source code modules. Additionally, each program may require linking to static or dynamic libraries.

The Application Builder helps you manage projects and the programs contained in them. The Application Builder stores all this information in an Informix database. This database can reside on a server accessible to all members of the development team.

The Application Builder provides the visual interface shown in Figure 41.12. The project in this figure consists of two programs, imaginatively called `prog_1` and `prog_2`.

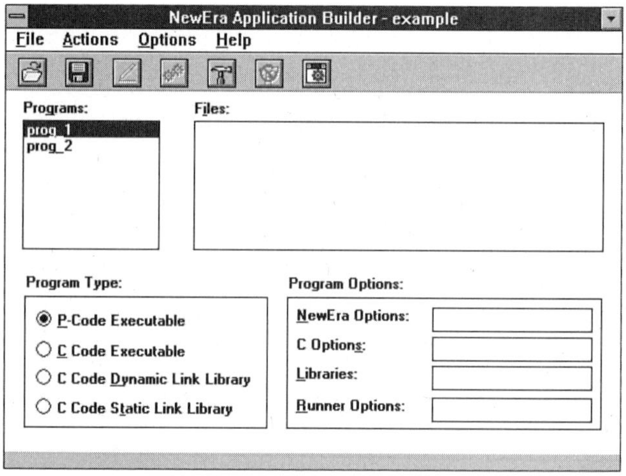

FIGURE 41.12.
The Application Builder.

Creating a Project

You can create a project by pressing Ctrl+N or choosing File|New Project. The Application Builder then displays a dialog box similar to the one shown in Figure 41.13. Here, you specify the name and the working directory of the project.

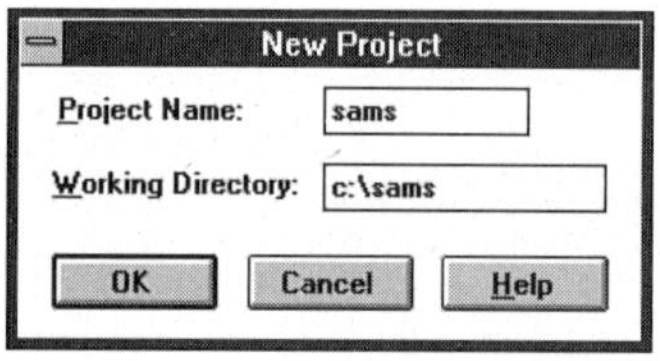

FIGURE 41.13.
The New Project dialog box.

The Application Builder saves this initial definition of the project to the `syspgm4gl` database. The server on which the `syspgm4gl` database is located is dictated by the I-Net settings (see your installation guide) and can be on the local PC or a central server.

Creating a Program and Project Maintenance

When you create a project, a default program is created with the same name as the project. In this chapter, I have created a project called `Sams` that now contains a program called `Sams`. You can rename this program if required, or you can create new programs. Just choose the Project Maintenance option by pressing Ctrl+J or choosing File|Project Maintenance. The Project Maintenance dialog box appears, as shown in Figure 41.14.

FIGURE 41.14.
The Project Maintenance dialog box.

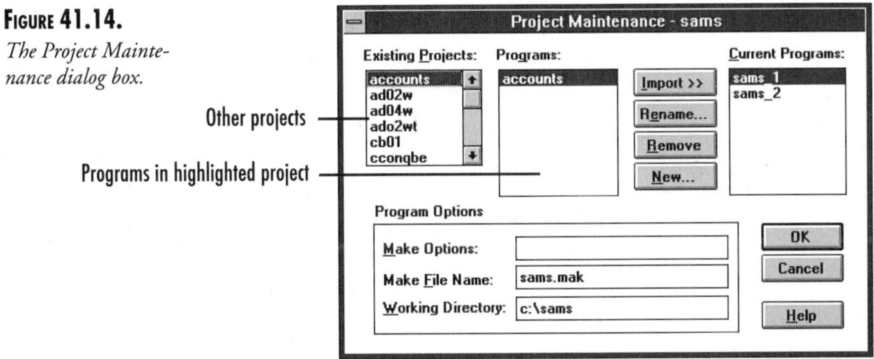

You can use the Project Maintenance dialog box to easily control the programs in your project. You can perform the following tasks:

- Import a program from another project. The Existing Projects and Programs sections show you all the other projects and programs in the `syspgm4gl` database.
- Rename a program in your project to another name.
- Remove a program from your project.
- Create a program in your project.

The programs currently in your project are listed in the Current Programs listbox.

In the Program Options section of the Project Maintenance dialog box, you can specify makefile options and the current working directory. The makefile is written to the project's working directory.

Program Maintenance

Each program in the `Sams` project consists of one or more modules—usually, but not always, of source code. You can use the Program Maintenance dialog box to specify the source code modules that make up each program. (See Figure 41.15.)

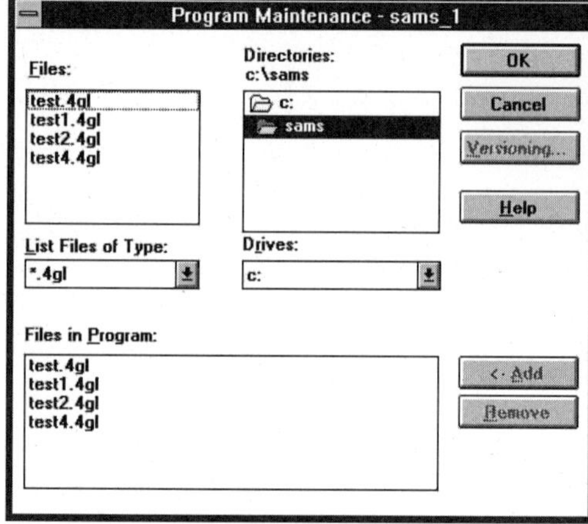

FIGURE 41.15. *The Program Maintenance dialog box.*

You can use the Program Maintenance dialog box to add and remove modules from the definition of the program. The available modules are listed in the Files listbox. This listbox not only displays NewEra source code modules (`*.4gl`) but also C source, object files, resource files, and libraries. You also can browse to other directories and drives to include modules.

You can define the module dependency of the program by highlighting the module and then clicking the Add or Remove buttons. The modules on which the program is dependent are listed in the Files in Program section. After you define the program, click OK to save the definition; you then are returned to the main Application Builder window. You must repeat this procedure for every program in your project. If you imported a program from another project, you might not need to change the module dependency of the program.

Finally, you need to declare the type of the program. You do this from the main Application Builder window. Figure 41.16 shows the `Sams` project, which consists of two programs: `sams_1` and `sams_2`. Note that the `sams_1` program consists of four source code modules. For each program in the project, you need to declare the type of the program and any program options; you do this in the Program Type and Program Options sections.

Program Types

Four program types exist:

- *p-code executable:* Produces an interpreted executable program that must be executed by using the INFORMIX-NewEra pseudocode runner. The file extension for this type is `*.4gl`. This is the type of program required for the Interactive Debugger.
- *C code executable:* Produces an executable program. The file extension for this type is `*.exe`.

- *C code dynamic link library:* Creates a DLL. DLLs can be shared between runtime applications. Many developers of components or class libraries distribute their products as one or more DLLs.
- *C code static link library:* Creates a static library. Static libraries are linked to other programs.

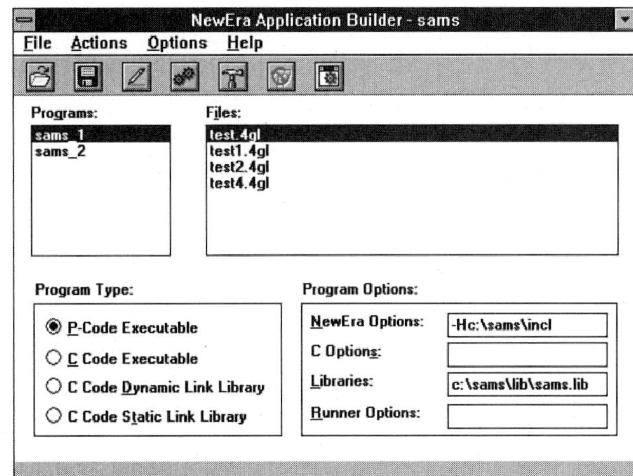

FIGURE 41.16.
Program types.

Program Options

You use the Program Options section to declare options to pass to the NewEra compiler and to the C compiler (if any). The Application Builder enables you to set these options and passes them to the appropriate compiler when you request a build. (See "The Source Compiler," later in this chapter, for details of these options.)

You can declare the location of any libraries you want to link to the program. In the Runner Options field, you declare any arguments to be passed to the NewEra pseudocode runner.

Generating a Makefile

You set the dependencies of the project and its constituent programs so that the Application Builder can generate a makefile. A *makefile* is a file that contains compilation instructions for the make utility. The make utility is invoked with a target name as an argument. The target name is one of your programs with the appropriate extension. In the `Sams` example, the first target of the project is `sams_1.4gi`.

The makefile contains a series of rules on how to create the target. It also contains the modules on which the target depends. In the `Sams` example, the target `sams_1.4gi` depends on the source code modules `test.4gl`, `test1.4gl`, `test2.4gl`, and `test4.4gl`. The make utility checks the date and time of modification of each of these files. If the module has been altered since the last time the target was built, the make utility invokes the appropriate build rule (usually, recompiling the module).

The objective of the makefile is to automatically include the latest modifications to the program. In a complex project, this would be very error-prone if it was a manual task—particularly if there were a number of programmers.

The Application Builder generates the makefile for you if you choose Actions|Generate Makefile. The Application Builder also regenerates the makefile when you change the project definition by using the Program Maintenance or Project Maintenance dialog box.

WARNING

If your project has source code stored on a network server, ensure that the system clock on the server is synchronized with the clock on your PC (and every other programmer's PC). Otherwise, the timestamp on the files could cause incorrect builds.

Building a Project

You can build a project with the Application Builder by pressing Shift+F8, choosing Actions|Build Project, or clicking the Build button on the toolbar. The Application Builder then invokes the make utility. For a large project, a build can take a long time, so the Application Builder enables you to selectively build each program within the project. You also can compile each module separately. All these options are located on the Action menu.

The Application Builder produces a log of the build that you can review by choosing Action|Review Build. If a build is unsuccessful, you can use this log to determine the error. Usually, the error is caused by a syntax error in one of the source code modules, but it also could be caused by a linking error.

You can cancel a build in progress by pressing Alt+F9, choosing Action|Cancel Build, or clicking the Cancel Build button on the toolbar.

Options

You can use the Application Builder to create templates for projects and programs. The program template declares a default program type and default NewEra and C compiler options. You also can specify project preferences by using the Preferences dialog box. Figure 41.17 shows the Application Builder options.

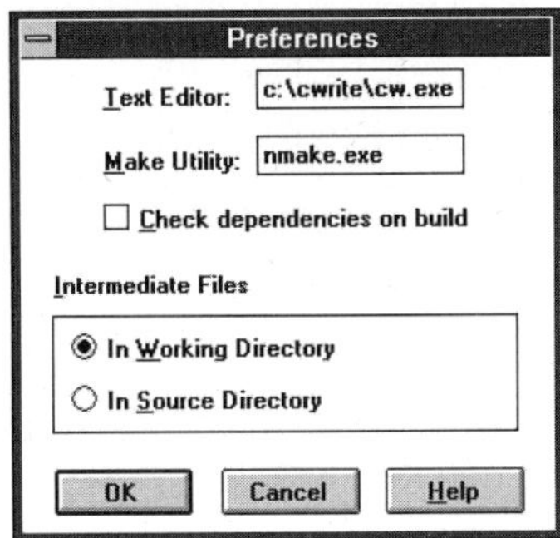

FIGURE 41.17.
The Application Builder options.

You use the Application Builder dialog box to specify a text editor for source code files and a make utility. You can specify the directory where intermediate files, such as `*.4go` and `*.obj`, are created.

Generally, the Application Builder does not recheck dependencies on every build. Dependency checking usually is performed only after you have altered the project definition with the Program or Project Maintenance dialog box or after you have generated a makefile. You can alter project dependencies by editing a source code module and including an `INCLUDE` statement to another source code or declaration module. Ideally, the Application Builder would check dependencies on every build; unfortunately, for a large project, dependency checking is very time consuming.

TIP

Set a project standard to periodically have the Application Builder check the dependencies of the project—especially if a number of programmers are working on the project.

The Source Compiler

NewEra provides a visual interface to the two compilers (pseudocode and C code) that come standard with NewEra. The Source Compiler is a tool that enables you to compile a source code module directly without recompiling the entire program or project. (See Figure 41.18.) The Source Compiler generally is used by programmers in the early stages of development.

You can use the Source Compiler to compile your code into pseudocode or a C object file. You can specify any arguments for the NewEra compiler and the C compiler. Table 41.12 lists some of the most important Source Compiler options.

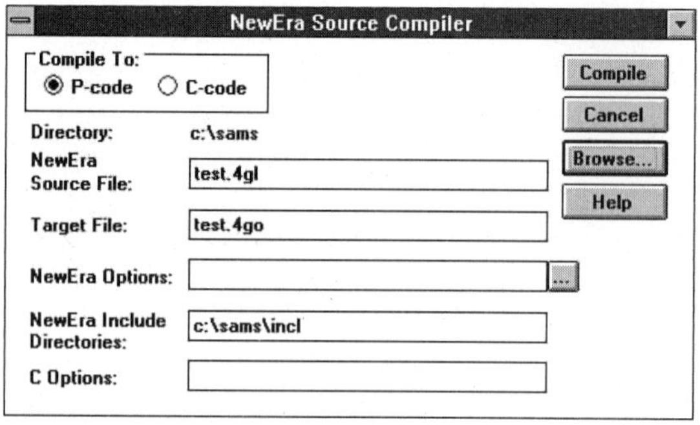

FIGURE 41.18.
The Source Compiler.

Table 41.12. Source Compiler options.

MS-Windows	*Motif*	*Use*
`-H`	`-H`	Searches path for `INCLUDE` files
`-A`	`-a`	Performs array bounds checking
`-ANYERR`	`-anyerr`	Sets global variable `STATUS` after expressions
`-ANSI`	`-ansi`	Checks SQL statements for ANSI compliance
`-DCURSOR`	`-dcursor`	Uses dynamic cursors
`-GLOBAL`	`-global`	Uses global cursors
`-SCURSOR`	`-scursor`	Uses static cursors
`-Z`	`-z`	Allows a variable number of arguments to informal functions

You also can invoke each of the compilers from the command line.

The Interactive Debugger

The NewEra Interactive Debugger enables you to visually inspect the operation of your program. You can use the Interactive Debugger to perform these tasks:

- Set breakpoints in your code.
- Ignore breakpoints.
- Examine the value of variables.
- Step into or over functions.
- View the status of operations, including SQL operations.

You must compile your program into pseudocode to use the Interactive Debugger. You cannot examine step-through C code or NewEra built-in functions.

When you start the Interactive Debugger, you see the dialog box shown in Figure 41.19.

FIGURE 41.19.
The Interactive Debugger.

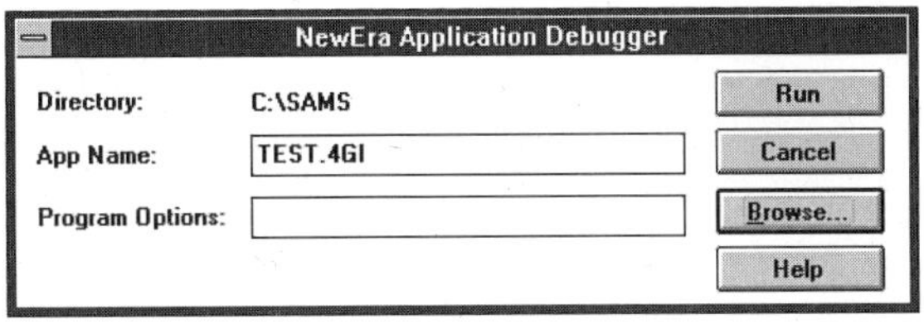

This dialog box enables you to select the program you want to debug. You can type the program name into the App Name field, or you can search for the program by using the Browse option. Pseudocode programs have a file extension of `*.4go` or `*.4gi`.

You use the Program Options field to specify options to be passed to your program. You can indicate DLLs to load with the `-u <dll_name>` option, any resource files with the `-res <resource_file>` option, and any other arguments you need.

After you choose the program and click the Run button, you see the window shown in Figure 41.20.

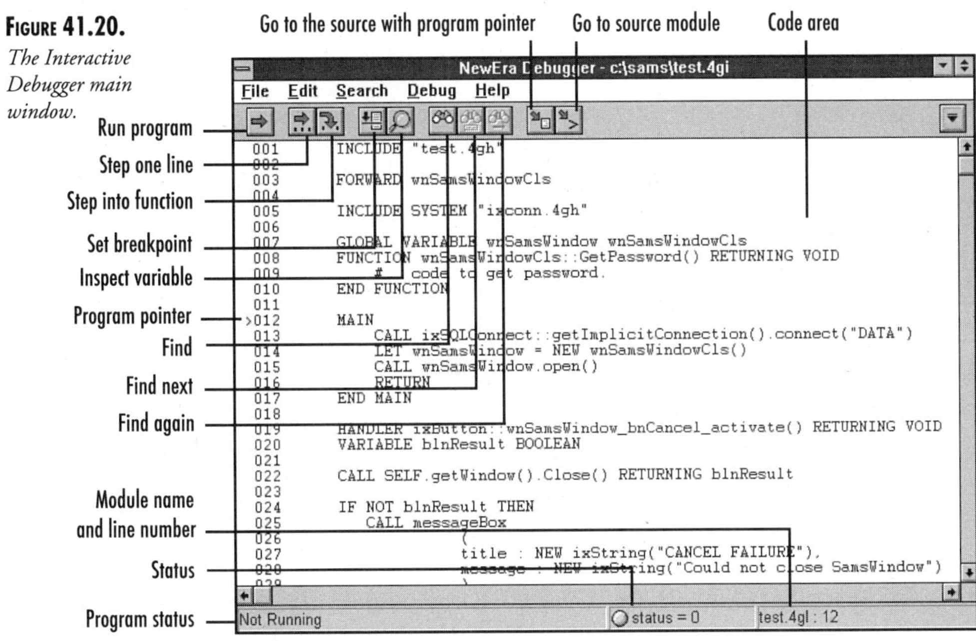

FIGURE 41.20.
The Interactive Debugger main window.

This is the Interactive Debugger main window. It offers options to set breakpoints, remove breakpoints, step through the code one line at a time, inspect the value of variables, and continue the execution of the program without stopping.

Executing the Program

You can execute the program by pressing F3, choosing Debug|Run, or clicking the Run button on the toolbar. The program executes until the next breakpoint or until a statement returns an error status.

The currently executing line of the program is indicated by the program pointer, which is a greater than (>) symbol to the left of the source code in the source code area.

Stepping Through Code One Line at a Time

Often, you will want to step through the code one line at a time. You can do this by pressing F5, choosing Debug|Step, or clicking the Step button on the toolbar.

Stepping into a Function

When your code calls a function, the Interactive Debugger does not automatically step into the function. You need to instruct the Interactive Debugger to do this by pressing F6, choosing Debug|Step In, or clicking the Step In button on the toolbar.

If you previously set a breakpoint in the function, execution stops at that breakpoint, and the source code of the function is displayed in the source code area.

You can step into only functions that have been compiled to pseudocode and for which you have a source. You cannot step into functions contained within DLLs, custom runner functions, or NewEra built-in functions. If a source code module has an `INCLUDE` file that contains executable statements (not just a `CLASS` definition, for example), you can step into the included file just as you can a function.

Locating Source Code

The Interactive Debugger looks in the current working directory for source code files. If it does not find the source code files, it looks in the directories specified by the `DBSRC` environment variable. If the source code files are not found, the Interactive Debugger displays a dialog box with a message that it could not find the source code file. You can use this dialog box to specify a particular source code file for the Interactive Debugger to use.

Breakpoints

A *breakpoint* is a line in the source code module at which you want execution to stop or break. You set a breakpoint by placing the cursor on the required line and pressing Ctrl+B, choosing Debug|Break On Line, or clicking the Breakpoint button on the toolbar. When a breakpoint is set, a B is displayed at the left of the source code line in the source code area.

When execution of the program reaches the line of the breakpoint, the program stops execution, and the source module with the breakpoint is displayed in the source code area.

You can remove a breakpoint by placing the cursor on the source code line that contains the breakpoint and pressing Ctrl+B, choosing Debug|Break On Line, or clicking the Breakpoint button on the toolbar. The B no longer appears at the left of the source code line. You also can remove all breakpoints by pressing Ctrl+R or choosing Debug|Remove All Breakpoints.

By default, the Interactive Debugger breaks on all SQL errors. You can stop this action by toggling the Debug|Stop On SQL Errors option. Similarly, you can toggle the Interactive Debugger to stop or not stop on all SQL warnings.

Choosing a Source Code Module

Most programs consist of a number of source code modules. The Interactive Debugger enables you to select one of these modules by pressing Ctrl+M, choosing Search|Go To Source, or clicking the Go To Source button on the toolbar. A dialog box with all the source code modules appears. You then can select the required module. The source of this module is displayed in the source code area.

You can return to the source code module that contains the program pointer by pressing Alt+S+G, choosing Search|Go To Program Pointer, or clicking the Go To Program Pointer button on the toolbar.

Inspecting Variables

You can examine the value of most simple data types by highlighting the variable and pressing Ctrl+I, choosing Debug|Inspect Variable, or pressing the Inspect Variable button on the toolbar. The Variable Inspector dialog box appears, as shown in Figure 41.21.

You can display only the value of variables that are in scope. If the source code module contains more than one function, for example, and you select a local variable from a function other than the inspected function (the currently executing function), you receive an error.

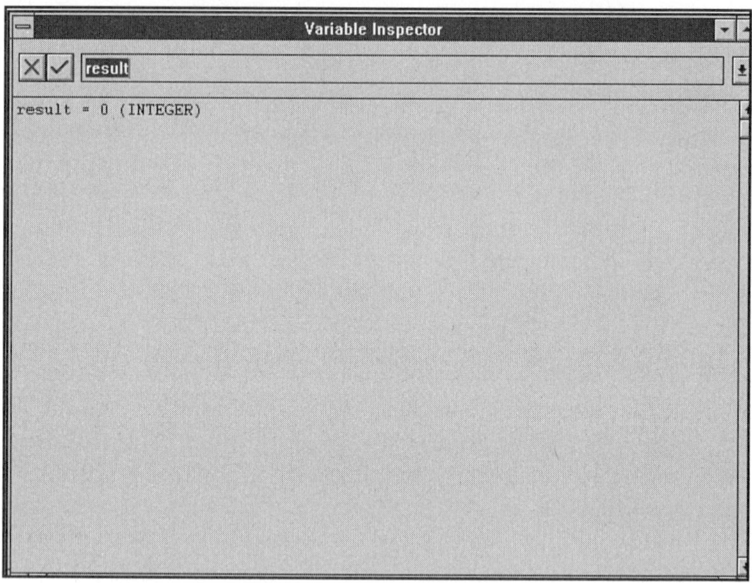

FIGURE 41.21.
The Variable Inspector dialog box.

If the variable you selected is a reference variable, the variable inspector details the members of the inspected variable, as shown in Figure 41.22.

FIGURE 41.22.
Inspecting a reference variable.

```
Variable Inspector
Window1

Window1 = window1 OF TYPE Class window1
        helpnum (inherited from Class ixvisualobject),
        name (inherited from Class ixvisualobject),
        __appearance (inherited from Class ixvisualobject),
        __availflag (inherited from Class ixvisualobject),
        __container (inherited from Class ixvisualobject),
        __enabled (inherited from Class ixvisualobject),
        __geometry (inherited from Class ixvisualobject),
        __ipixelheight (inherited from Class ixvisualobject),
        __ipixelleft (inherited from Class ixvisualobject),
        __ipixeltop (inherited from Class ixvisualobject),
        __ipixelwidth (inherited from Class ixvisualobject),
        __shown (inherited from Class ixvisualobject),
        __vctobj (inherited from Class ixvisualobject),
        __visible (inherited from Class ixvisualobject),
        __fullyenabled (inherited from Class ixvisualobject),
        __readingorder (inherited from Class ixvisualobject),
        __keyboardlanguage (inherited from Class ixvisualobject),
        helpfile (inherited from Class ixvisualcontainer),
        __containedobjs (inherited from Class ixvisualcontainer),
        __focusedobj (inherited from Class ixvisualcontainer),
        __direction (inherited from Class ixvisualcontainer),
        arg_val (inherited from Class ixwindow),
        arg_val (inherited from Class ixwindow),
        arg_val (inherited from Class ixwindow),
        arg_val (inherited from Class ixwindow),
        arg_val (inherited from Class ixwindow),
        arg_val (inherited from Class ixwindow),
        arg_val (inherited from Class ixwindow),
```

If the inspected variable is a record, the Variable Inspector displays the nature of the members of the record. You can select the members of the record individually.

Searching Through Source Code

At times, you will need to search through source code modules looking for a particular statement or variable. The Interactive Debugger enables you to do this by pressing Ctrl+F, choosing Search|Find, or clicking the Find button on the toolbar. A dialog box appears in which you can enter the search string. You can specify a search that is not case-sensitive.

After you enter a search string, you can find the next occurrence of that string by pressing Ctrl+G, choosing Search|Find Again, or clicking the Find Again button on the toolbar.

Project Development

The Interactive Debugger is particularly useful when application coding begins to help examine program logic. It is again very useful when trying to correct subtle data-related bugs. Because the debugger works only with pseudocode, this capability has implications for the way in which projects are developed.

Generally, it is more efficient to develop the program in pseudocode initially and then to compile to C code for testing. Not only can you use the Interactive Debugger during development, but pseudocode generally compiles faster than C code.

After the program deploys, it often is very useful to be able to step through the program to find bugs caused by unexpected or missing data.

TIP

If possible, it is handy to have a pseudocode version of the final application. This makes maintenance debugging more efficient.

The Application Launcher

You use the Application Launcher to execute your programs. (See Figure 41.23.) The Application Launcher is a tool for the programmer; typically, deployed applications are started from an icon in the Window Manager (or the Program Manager in Microsoft Windows). You can use the Application Launcher to specify a runtime argument to be passed to your program.

FIGURE 41.23.
The Application Launcher.

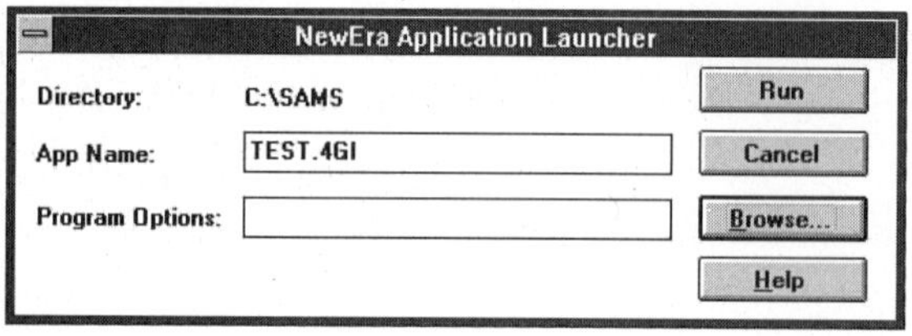

The Help Compiler

NewEra provides a platform-independent Help system and supports the Microsoft Help system.

You declare the Help system you are using by setting the value of the `helpStyle` member variable of the `ixApp` application object. Each visual container has two member variables—`helpFile` and `helpNum`—that enable you to specify the help to be displayed for that object. Each visual object has a member variable, `helpNum`, that specifies the Help number for this object.

You display the Help item by calling the `displayHelp()` member function of the visual object. Depending on the Help style selected, the Help item is displayed by using the NewEra Help Viewer or the System Help Viewer. `DisplayHelp()` uses the Help number for the visual object and the `helpFile` for the visual object's container to find the appropriate Help item. If the visual object does not have a Help number, `displayHelp()` uses the `helpNum` of the container. If the container does not have a Help number, `displayHelp()` uses the application's Help number.

The Help Compiler compiles a text file into a file suitable for use by the NewEra Help Viewer. (See Figure 41.24.) Preparation of System Help files (such as Microsoft Help) are system-dependent. You can embed compiler directives into the text file and conditionally compile the Help file. This capability enables you to create platform- (or version-) dependent help by using one source file.

FIGURE 41.24.
The Help Compiler.

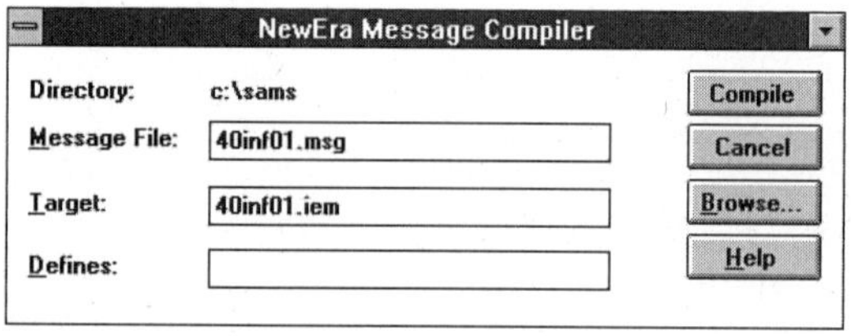

Reports

Reports are a significant task in almost every project. You can develop reports in one of three ways:

- Generating character-based reports developed with the NewEra language
- Using the ViewPoint-Pro report writing tool
- Using third-party report writing tools

The NewEra language inherits all the report writing capabilities of the INFORMIX-4GL. You can use the `REPORT` function of NewEra to format and output reports to files or printers. The `REPORT` function only directly supports ASCII character reports. If you want to include graphics, you need to embed the appropriate commands into the report file. This style of report is ideal for producing large, character-based reports.

The NewEra development system comes with the ViewPoint-Pro product. ViewPoint-Pro enables you (or your users) to visually develop reports. You easily can draw graphics and embed images. ViewPoint-Pro reports are based on SuperViews and Query objects that ViewPoint enables you to define. NewEra integrates with the ViewPoint system to enable you to generate reports. The ViewPoint-Pro system also enables you to define data query and input forms. These forms again are based on SuperViews, including master-detail SuperViews.

NewEra is an extensible system; you can use class libraries from tool vendors to provide you with report writing capabilities. The widely used Crystal Reports product provides NewEra-compatible class libraries.

Application Partitioning

Application partitioning probably is the best feature of the NewEra development system. Application partitioning enables you to distribute processing to a number of servers. Your application can access resources on the most appropriate server. It makes sense to locate a database-intensive application as close to the database (in a network sense) as possible. Not only does this reduce network traffic, but it can reduce database contention significantly, which is important for OLTP.

Application partitioning services are provided by three classes from the Application Server Class Library: `ixASRequestMgr`, `ixASRequestor`, and `ixASResponder`.

Application partitioning is simple in implementation but requires deep thought when designing the class hierarchy. Two main differences exist when designing a normal class hierarchy versus a class hierarchy that uses application partitioning:

- The partitioned classes (`Requestor` and `Responder`) must be directly derived from the `ixASRequestor` or `ixASResponder` classes. This fact has obvious implications for the nature of the class hierarchy.
- The interface across the network between the `Requestor` and `Responder` objects can pass only a subset of simple data types. You cannot pass an object across the network interface—for example, an `ixString`. Objects are accessed only via their reference variables; programs cannot access memory locations on remote computers. The interface presented by application partitioning closely parallels that provided by OLE Automation servers.

NewEra 3.0 provides a Partition Class Wizard that generates a `Responder` and `Requestor` class from one of your classes. This major improvement removes most of the drudgery of application partitioning.

TIP

Depending on the degree to which you want to partition your application, you might consider developing interface classes. An *interface class* manages the interface in that part of your application running on the server. This capability enables you to develop your application with a normal, object-oriented class hierarchy that inherits from as many classes as appropriate and uses reference members in the class `PUBLIC` interfaces.

The interface classes would call the member functions of the applications' objects and translate the function signatures into simple data types so that they could be passed across the partition (network).

OLE Objects

OLE objects will be supported by NewEra 3.0+. OLE objects are black-box components written to the Common Object Model standard. Many third-party vendors offer OLE components. OLE objects can provide many services, from document management to data capture.

The most common use of OLE components probably is to improve the appearance of your window. A complete list of available OLE objects is beyond the scope of this book, but the following are some of the important visual objects you can provide via OLE:

- Outlines (used in the File Manager under Microsoft Windows)
- Tab controls

- Grids and spreadsheets
- Floating toolbars

OLE Automation Servers

An *OLE Automation server* is an OLE object that can request services from other applications. NewEra enables you to create your own OLE Automation servers that can request services from partitioned NewEra applications. Because OLE objects are developed according to the COM standard, any OLE-compliant application can use the NewEra OLE Automation server. This feature enables you to provide services from your NewEra application to a diverse assortment of client tools. User interfaces written in Visual Basic, or office tools such as Word and Excel, can access services from your NewEra application through the inclusion of your OLE Automation server.

The Partition Class Wizard enables you to choose between creating a normal ASCL partition (see "Application Partitioning," earlier in this chapter) and an OLE Automation server. The wizard then generates the C++ code necessary to create the OLE server. The COM standard allows only particular data types; however, the Partition Class Wizard handles the translation between the NewEra data types and the data types required by the COM standard. The interface you define is restricted to using only simple data types. (Blobs are not permitted.)

OLE Automation servers enable you to construct genuine, enterprise-wide database solutions. You can develop flexible, object-oriented applications executing on dedicated servers and distribute application services to almost every desktop tool in a controlled manner.

Summary

This chapter presented the NewEra Development System, focusing on the tools NewEra provides to develop applications. You learned about the relationship between the tools, particularly the Window Painter and the NewEra language syntax discussed in Chapter 40, "NewEra Language."

Finally, the chapter presented an overview of application partitioning and OLE automation—two important technologies that will become increasingly important to the software development strategies of large enterprises.

CHAPTER 42

Serving Data on the WWW

by Ron M. Flannery

IN THIS CHAPTER

There is just no way to avoid hearing about the Internet and how it will be the solution to everyone's business and personal needs. The World Wide Web—which I will hereafter call the *Web* or *WWW*—exploded onto the scene in an incredibly short period of time and helped create this love for the Internet. This chapter gives you an understanding of what's behind Web applications and how you can make them interact with Informix databases.

The methodologies involved in creating Web applications are changing. Web application development is moving toward a very open, object-oriented approach. This chapter describes new and existing methodologies, as well as how Informix is changing with the Web.

This chapter begins with histories of the Internet and Web and describes how they evolved into what they are today. You'll then examine some of the specific pieces that make Web applications work, including TCP/IP, DNS, browsers, Web servers, HTTP, and HTML. After that, you'll look at an analysis of some of the new standards driving the Web: CORBA, IIOP, and DCOM. Then you'll get into the specifics of creating Web-enabled database applications by using the following:

- CGI—using Perl, INFORMIX-4GL, and ESQL/C
- Java
- JavaScript
- ActiveX
- Third-party tools

The chapter concludes with a discussion of the future of Informix Web-enabled applications: the *Informix Universal Web Architecture* (IUWA). Informix has created this architecture to meet the open standards of the Web. This chapter helps you prepare for the future of Informix and the Web.

Internet and World Wide Web History

The Internet and the World Wide Web have pretty much become one and the same as far as most people are concerned. But they are different. Here is a brief history of both.

Internet

Back in the late 1950s, the *Advanced Research Projects Agency* (ARPA) was created within the United States Department of Defense (DoD). This agency was created to help establish the United States as the leader in technology and science. In 1969, ARPANET was created as an experiment in networking remote computers. A handful of computers were connected successfully. The experiment actually was performed to help enable communications between military sites in case of nuclear attack!

The communications protocols on the Internet place the responsibility of communication between the *computers*, not the network. The network is not considered reliable. Thus, if a portion of the network were interrupted, communications theoretically could continue between computers; the communication would just need to follow a different path.

As people began to see the power of such a system, the Internet became more and more developed. More universities and government agencies were connected, and more people heard about it. In the early 1980s, TCP and IP were established formally as standards by which computers could communicate. Then the Internet exploded and started moving toward where it is today.

NOTE

Many great references on the history of the Internet and World Wide Web are available. This text is not meant to give a detailed history. If you are interested in more information, it is freely available on the Internet and World Wide Web and through many great books.

So what makes the Internet work? It is basically a global network of networks connected through telephone lines, high-speed network cables, and about anything else imaginable. But it still is designed to provide the "reliable communication" standard established way back in 1969. Figure 42.1 shows a high-level overview of the Internet.

FIGURE 42.1.
An overview of the Internet.

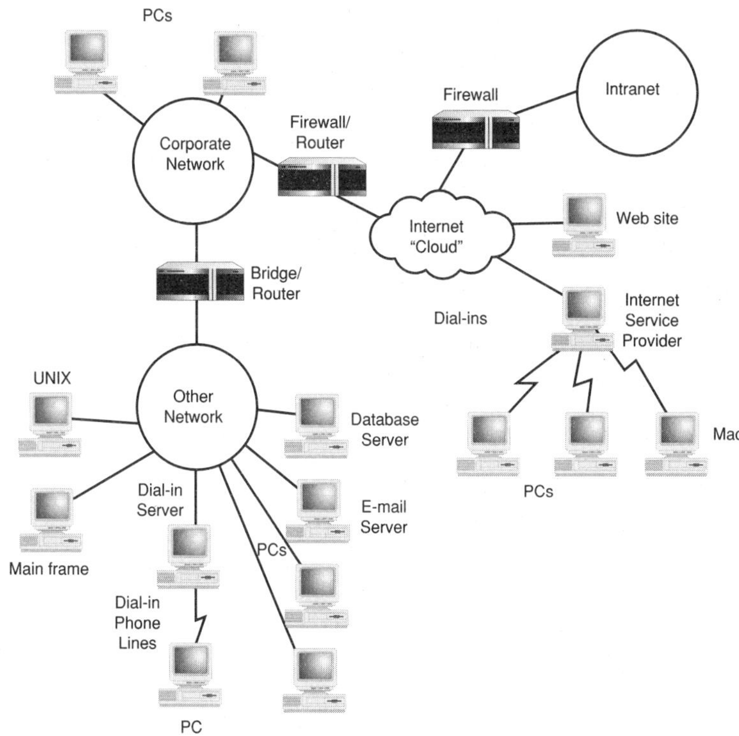

As the Internet grew, it became more and more connected to other networks and soon began to grow at an incredible rate. It still didn't enable a lot of business communication and advertising. Many people knew about the Internet but didn't understand it, feared it, or thought it was too much trouble. Enter the World Wide Web.

The World Wide Web Yesterday

The Internet was based mostly on command-line interfaces such as Telnet, Gopher, and FTP. As powerful as these interfaces are, they still aren't the most user-friendly ways to do things.

In 1990, the first Web browser was developed at the European Laboratory for Particle Physics (CERN). The browser was designed as a way to efficiently transport ideas and information. The browser read hypertext as its means for displaying information.

Hypertext is what is behind Web pages. It is based on the concept of linking to other information when it is desired. The language created to implement hypertext is the *Hypertext Markup Language* (HTML). The links to other documents are *hyperlinks.* The original Web browsers allowed simple interaction based on these hyperlinks. By using hyperlinks, the CERN researchers were able to easily cross-reference documents needed in their research.

In 1993, a group from the *National Center for Supercomputing Applications* (NCSA) developed Mosaic. Mosaic ran on many types of computers, which made it available to many more people. This multiplatform capability, in fact, gives the Web much of its power today. Mosaic also added the capability to process images, videos, and sound.

After that, Netscape created Navigator, and the Web began its incredible ascent. Many companies began making browsers, and the Web basically exploded. In 1996, Microsoft jumped on the bandwagon, essentially bringing Web browsing to any user's desktop for free.

A major strength of using the Web is the capability of browsers to make information easily available. Users do not need to be familiar with what some people consider cryptic utilities (FTP, for example); they just need to know how to use their browsers. Not only that, but browsers added the capability to embed pictures, sounds, and more. These capabilities are what really caused the Web to explode.

The World Wide Web Today

The rest is history… I probably don't need to describe the presence of the Web in today's world. It is everywhere. On commercials. On business cards. On brochures. People and companies use Web pages for everything from personal Web pages to full-blown, multimillion-dollar Web catalog applications.

In today's business world, the Web has become the world's biggest marketing tool. It is fairly simple to create a Web site available for the whole world to see. If people want to find out about your company, they no longer have to call a phone number and navigate through a maze of people and menus, and they don't need to read marketing pamphlets. They just need to go to your company's Web site, where all the information on your company is freely available. It is so easy.

The Web has become a big part of our everyday lives. It will continue to grow at an incredible rate. A major portion of this growth will be for business-related applications—not only for marketing companies, but also for increasing company communications (intranets, for example). That's where Informix comes into the picture, and that's why I'm writing this chapter.

One Interface for Applications: The Browser

You should remember a very important concept when looking at Web applications: Applications that use a browser as a front-end do not have to run on the Internet!

I need to make a very important clarification. This chapter will describe how to build applications that can be used with a Web browser front-end. This does not mean that the application has to use the World Wide Web. The Web pages to which you are connecting can be on your hard drive, the network in your office, a *wide area network* (WAN) that uses phone lines, or the World Wide Web. The common thread is the Web browser. For this reason, you can refer to the applications you develop as *browser-enabled applications* rather than *Web applications.* Both descriptions are used interchangeably in this chapter.

Because of the flexibility of internetworking and other standards, you can build an application that runs on one interface: the Web browser. The back-end application can be connected via anything that supports the proper protocols; Figure 42.2 illustrates this concept.

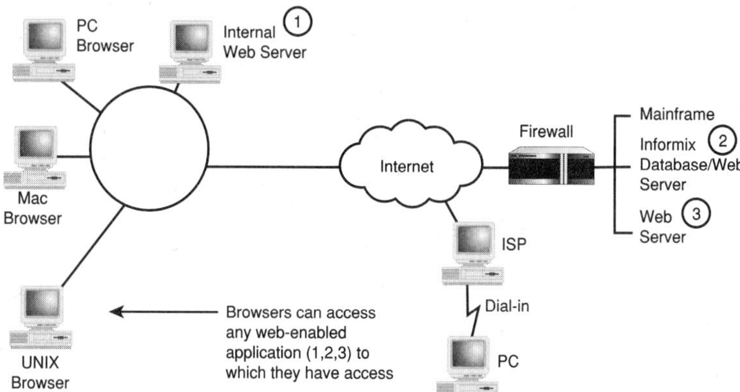

FIGURE 42.2.
The browser as one interface.

Think about how easy the capability to build an application that runs on one interface makes application development and deployment. Any computer with the proper Web browser can run a browser-enabled application. This capability eliminates the need to develop different interfaces for each different operating system in your company; the browser companies do that for you. Less training is necessary, fewer installation problems occur, and no separate support staff is needed for each application. The flexibility and cost savings can be enormous.

The Basics: What Makes Browser-Enabled Technologies Work

The Web still is much like a "black box" to many people, and that really is all it *needs* to be to many of its users. To fully understand how to create browser-enabled applications, though, you need to get under the covers a little and understand some of the basics.

OSI Reference Model

The Open Systems Interconnect (OSI) Reference Model is a common reference for describing network communications. It is made up of seven layers. The model defines communications protocols within and between each of the layers. Using these layers, end-to-end network connections can be made. For example, when you initiate a connection to a Web site, the OSI reference model defines how the data is exchanged between your computer and the target computer. When describing Internet communications, the OSI Reference Model is generally split into the following four layers:

- Application Layer: Applications and processes that you directly access (Web browsers, for example).
- Host-to-Host Transport (TCP) Layer: Ensures that the message is properly transported between computers.
- Internet (IP) Layer: Handles the routing of data.
- Network Access Layer: Defines transportation on the physical networks.

All layers of the model are used in Internet communications, but the portions of the OSI Reference Model that you will hear the most about are TCP and IP.

TCP/IP

The basic means of electronically transporting data on the Internet is by using the *Transmission Control Protocol/Internet Protocol* (TCP/IP). TCP and IP work on two different layers of the OSI Reference Model (Transport and Internet). Together, these protocols allow reliable transmissions between different types of computers. TCP/IP ensures that data packets arrive at their destinations (if at all possible), even if the packets need to be re-sent. This capability is the glue that supports reliable communications over the Internet and any other TCP/IP network.

Think about it: When you send an e-mail message to someone, do you think it always gets there the first time? The path it takes and the amount of times it is sent often vary.

TCP/IP is defined for many computing platforms (UNIX, for example). Any computer that "talks" TCP/IP can communicate with any other computer. TCP/IP opens the door to company-wide and worldwide communications. Standards are very important in allowing computers to communicate.

Internet Protocols

The Internet was built on many different services (or protocols)—the most important is TCP/IP. As mentioned, TCP and IP work on two different layers of the OSI Reference Model. These layers are used to transport data. Another layer, known as the Application layer, includes protocols that use TCP/IP as their transport mechanisms. Some of these protocols follow:

- File Transfer Protocol (FTP)
- Network News Transfer Protocol (NNTP)
- Simple Mail Transfer Protocol (SMTP)
- Remote Login (Telnet)
- Gopher
- Domain Name Service (DNS)
- Hypertext Transfer Protocol (HTTP)
- Internet Inter-ORB Protocol (IIOP)

These and other protocols help facilitate different types of communications by setting standards. In fact, the Internet moved happily along for about 20 years or so simply by using many of these protocols. They enabled worldwide communications and were fairly easy to use. Not only do these protocols have their own standard commands (FTP, for example), but they can be used as part of a *Uniform Resource Locator* (URL) in a browser (`ftp://ftp.microsoft.com`, for example).

Domain Name Service (DNS)

DNS is the lookup mechanism for TCP/IP communications. It is software that can reside on a local network server or on the Internet. It translates the IP address (`1.1.1.1`, for example) or domain name (`www.microsoft.com`, for example) so that your computer can determine how to find the requested server. DNS does this by maintaining host tables, which it coordinates through other DNS servers.

Hypertext Transfer Protocol (HTTP)

When Web browsers first became available, they too needed a standard way to communicate, so the *Hypertext Transfer Protocol* (HTTP) was created.

Of course, you know about HTTP from your Web browsing. Basically, it is just another protocol that enables any Web browser to connect to a Web server. HTTP is the standard protocol used between a browser and a Web server. (There are other ways to handle browser-to-server communications. See "Objects: Another New Web Paradigm," later in this chapter.)

Web browsers generally use HTTP to communicate with their target destination but do allow other protocols (FTP, for example). The protocol for the browser's current connection is defined in the URL. Here is the format of a URL; the `[..]` notation indicates optional information:

```
protocol://server[/pathname][:port][url_query_string]
```

Table 42.1 explains the elements of the URL.

Table 42.1. Anatomy of a URL.

Element	*Specifies*
protocol	The protocol to use. Each browser inherently handles http. Browsers use different methods to handle other protocols, such as FTP and Telnet. Most browsers support other common protocols but enable you to use an external application (Telnet, for example).
server	The server that contains the Web page. This server is found using DNS and can exist on any network to which you are attached (Internet, LAN, WAN, and so on). Note that, with some URLs (files, for example), the server can be a path to your local hard drive.
pathname	The pathname of the Web page on the server. Usually, the pathname is an HTML file or an executable program that dynamically processes your requests. If *pathname* is a directory, browsers look for `index.htm`, `index.html`, and `default.asp` by default.
port	The well-known port on which to connect. *Port* is a TCP/IP concept that defines a unique port number for each type of communication. The port for HTTP is 80, for example. Usually, you will not need to supply the *port* parameter, but it is here for reference. You also can create user-defined ports to enable applications.
url_query_string	A string of characters used as input to the Web page. You often see this string after submitting a Web page. Query strings are discussed in the "`Get` and `Post` Methods and the `url_query_string`" section, later in this chapter.

The Browser

As you learned earlier in this chapter, one of the most powerful aspects of creating a Web-enabled application is having one front-end: the browser.

Web browsers communicate with Web servers by using HTTP. HTTP is a two-way communication ending with the Web server returning an HTML-formatted page back to the browser. The browser then simply processes and displays the page. The browser also must be able to process different extended tags, such as those specifying Java, JavaScript, and others. It also must download images, sounds, and other things. That's all there is to it.

The current most popular Web browsers are Netscape Navigator and Microsoft Internet Explorer. Navigator is credited with being the browser that got the world excited about the Web. Explorer is a late entry by Microsoft in its effort to embrace the Internet.

Both browsers are very powerful and are changing at an incredible rate. Not long ago, many browsers were available, but the rate at which Navigator and Internet Explorer have developed has made it almost impossible for other browsers to keep up. Internet Explorer is free and now is bundled with Office 97. Navigator is not free, but it is being offered with a bundle of products by Netscape (Communicator). The competition between the two browsers is intense, which is great for the rest of the market; this competition makes the browsers better and better.

Another class of browsers consists of character-based browsers. One of the more popular text-based browsers is Lynx. Lynx is freely available on the Internet. The advantage of text-based browsers is that they save the download time associated with images and other extensions. On the downside, they don't support many of the tags that can make your applications more powerful.

Both Netscape and Microsoft create HTML extensions, which make the language more powerful. It is amazing how much has been added in the last year alone. To remain competitive, both browsers have had to incorporate each other's extensions. Generally, the browsers can process *most* of the same operations, although lag periods sometimes exist.

TIP

Be sure not to overuse proprietary extensions created by Netscape or Microsoft unless you are sure that all your users have the necessary browser. Both browsers eventually support the same tags, but you need to consider which versions are available to your users. One of the most powerful aspects of browser-enabled applications is that any computer with the proper browser can run them. This certainly is not to say that you shouldn't use the HTML extensions! They can be very powerful and save a great deal of time. Just be careful.

In the context of this chapter, then, the browser is the front-end to the applications you create. You will learn to write browser-enabled applications that can be accessed with just about any current browser. The applications can communicate with databases such as Informix.

The Web Server

A Web server is the software that processes Web communications. It uses HTTP to translate requests from a browser into useful information. The server provides all the services needed to support Web-enabled applications. Any time you access a Web page using HTTP, your browser initially talks to a Web server. Figure 42.3 shows a diagram of where a Web server fits into Web applications.

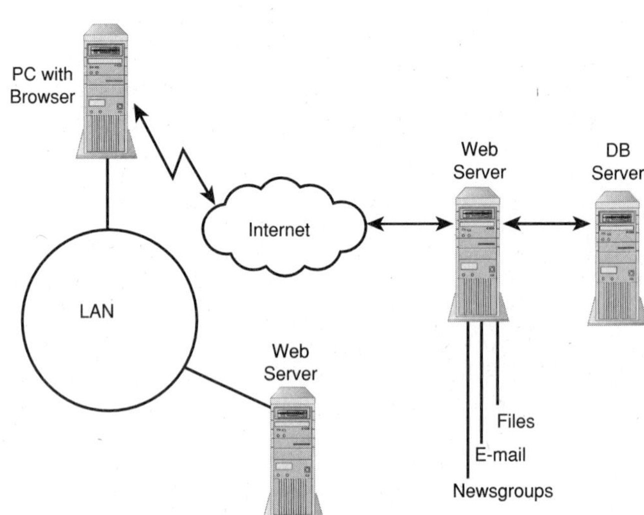

FIGURE 42.3.
A Web server managing communications.

The following are some of the tasks a Web server enables you to perform:

- Processing HTTP requests from a browser
- Managing files used in Web applications
- Providing security
- Providing encryption

Here are some of the more popular Web servers:

- CERN (free)
- NCSA (free)
- Apache (free)
- Netscape FastTrack (comes integrated with Informix workgroup servers)
- Netscape Enterprise server
- O'Reilly
- Microsoft Internet Information Server (IIS)
- Jigsaw (written in Java and free)

The functionality of these servers varies quite a bit. The CERN and NCSA servers are free and have been around for a long time. The Apache server—a more recent free Web server—has been classified as the most common server on the Web. Microsoft's IIS is bundled with its NT 4.0 operating system, which makes it an attractive option. Netscape's servers often are considered more open to standards. The Jigsaw Web server—one of the most common—is free and very open to evolving standards, because it is written completely in Java. As you should with anything else on the Internet, it is best to do some research and evaluate the strengths and weaknesses of the products and how they fit your needs.

It is important to note that the Netscape and Microsoft servers provide NSAPI and ISAPI, respectively. These are *application program interfaces* (APIs) that enable software vendors and developers to communicate directly with the server. This capability creates more efficient applications.

Objects: Another New Web Paradigm

As the age of Web computing evolves, so does the way we develop applications. In this section, you'll be introduced to objects and how they relate to the Web. Objects are becoming an integral part of Web-oriented computer applications. This section discusses some of the new ways of communicating via the Web: Common Object Request Broker Architecture (CORBA) and Distributed Component Object Model (DCOM).

The concept of object-oriented programming has been around for some time. In a nutshell, *object-oriented programming* deals with reusing things. Objects are based on other objects and inherit their properties. They can communicate with each other via well-defined methods. In the open world of the Internet and the World Wide Web, such communications are *essential.* CORBA and DCOM provide TCP/IP busses that define how different objects on a network communicate without really knowing about each others' underlying program structures.

The two distinct methods of providing these object communications today are CORBA and DCOM. CORBA is the product of the *Object Management Group* (OMG), which is a group of hundreds of companies hoping to develop open standards; DCOM is the product of Microsoft.

NOTE

CORBA/DCOM is probably the biggest example to date of "Microsoft versus everyone else." CORBA was developed as an open standard by almost all the major hardware and software vendors. DCOM often is considered Microsoft's way of trying to retain control of the data-processing world. Many people believe that the computing industry really wants to move toward open standards, whereas Microsoft continues to try to do things its way.

continues

continued

To Microsoft's credit, it has developed a strong DCOM following and has demonstrated that DCOM is a viable standard for network and Internet communications. And this standard certainly enables the legion of Microsoft-aware developers (Visual Basic and Visual C++, for example) to easily adapt to DCOM. CORBA, on the other hand, is very much dedicated to *all* computing platforms. Be sure to take your target environment and future needs into account when deciding how to implement your application.

At the core of these two methodologies is the concept of objects being able to communicate with each other, regardless of the language in which they are written. Objects communicate with each other via standard interfaces that define the properties of the object. *Interface definition languages* (IDLs) can be used to invoke other objects. It also is very important to note that the objects do not have to be on the same computer or network; they can be anywhere. Think about how this fits in with the goal of the World Wide Web: worldwide, open communications.

The CORBA and DCOM architectures enable objects to find out about each other, including the methods they support and the objects they provide. Each object must be able to provide information about its properties and can dynamically obtain information about other objects available to it.

The CORBA standard now includes *Internet Inter-ORB Protocol* (IIOP). IIOP is basically TCP/IP with CORBA-controlling communications. IIOP enables CORBA for the Internet. In fact, quite a few people are predicting that IIOP will replace HTTP, considering IIOP's power and open operability.

So what does all of this mean to you and your Web programming? It means a lot, and it probably will have a major impact on how you work with applications in the future. Think about how easy life would be if applications didn't really need to know the details of other applications; they just spoke the same "language." They could find out about each other dynamically. This capability is really at the core of the computing world of the future. If you don't know about this methodology now, you will.

Informix is very supportive of these open standards. The Informix Universal Web Architecture is supportive of both CORBA and DCOM. (For more information, see "The Next Generation: Informix Universal Web Architecture," later in this chapter.)

Again, coverage on everything about every Web development technique is beyond the scope of this book. This chapter gives you a high-level overview of the direction of Web-enabled computing. You easily can find detailed references on any of these methodologies via the Web or books. The future direction of Web computing is very exciting, and this chapter will try to help you "ride the right wave." Here are some URLs that will provide you with all the information you'll need:

For CORBA and IIOP:

```
http://www.omg.org
http://www.w3.org/pub/WWW/
http://www.netscape.com
```

For DCOM:

```
http://www.microsoft.com
```


A Web Application Overview

Now it's time to plug in the pieces that have been described and to explain how a Web-enabled application works.

Types of Web Applications: Internet, Intranet, Extranet

Table 42.2 provides an overview of three of the most common types of Web applications. The Web development methodologies described in this chapter are excellent ways to create all these applications.

Table 42.2. Common types of Web applications.

Type of Web Application	*Description*
Public/Internet	Generally, this is the type of application that links customers to a company via the World Wide Web (a Web site, for example). This type of application is provided to help market the company and sell its products.
Intranet	An intranet is created to enable internal communications within a company, whether it is in one building or across the world. Providing electronic communications (e-mail and document management, for example) within a company can result in enormous cost savings. To enable its communications, an intranet uses networks and possibly the Internet.
Extranet	An extranet is a kind of hybrid between a public application and an intranet. Companies can allow customers to access limited portions of their intranet—generally, to get information on products and services.

HTML

HyperText Markup Language (HTML) is the language used by the Web. Any page accessed by the familiar `http://` is written in HTML; it is the language used in HTTP communications. You will need to write the Web pages you create for database applications in HTML.

HTML is the language of hypertext. As mentioned earlier, hypertext enables you to include hyperlinks, which can embed graphics, sounds, links to other Web pages, programs (Java and others), and various specialized formatting commands (boldface, for example) within a Web page.

A very important thing to remember is that HTML is just ASCII text; you don't need a word processing program. HTML is ASCII text with a few hypertext commands in it. Many HTML authoring tools also are available that help simplify Web page creation.

HTML is based on tags. *Tags* are markers within the text of the Web page that have special meaning. A tag begins with `<TAGNAME>` and usually ends with `</TAGNAME>`. When a browser encounters a tag, it knows that it will begin the processing associated with that tag. Tags also can be embedded within other tags. HTML ignores tags that it doesn't know about. Remember that the browser makers—particularly, Microsoft and Netscape—add their own HTML extensions, so a particular extension won't always be handled by your current browser.

Listing 42.1 shows the bare-bones format of a Web page.

Listing 42.1. The basic format of a Web page.

```
<HTML>
<HEAD>
<TITLE>Title to a Simple Web Page</TITLE>
</HEAD>
<BODY>
<H1>Basic Web Page</H1>
This simple Web page shows you the basics of HTML and how to use it.
It helps you build on HTML so that you can use it to access Informix databases.
</BODY>
</HTML>
```

Figure 42.4 shows what Listing 42.1 looks like when displayed on a browser.

The simple example in Listing 42.1 displays the four required tags in an HTML document:

`HTML`	This must be the first thing in an HTML document. It tells the browser that this is indeed an HTML document.
`HEAD` and `BODY`	Every HTML document is divided into a title and body. These tags tell the browser which is which.
`TITLE`	This is the title that appears at the top of your Web browser when you are looking at the Web page.

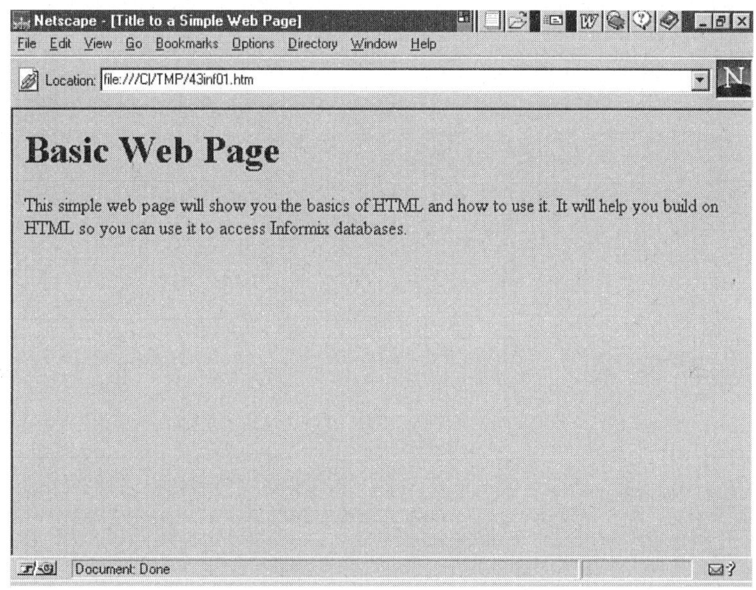

FIGURE 42.4.
A basic Web page.

Simple enough? Okay, let's jump right to the good stuff. The example used here is an e-mail list for Sams Publishing and includes last name, first name, e-mail address, occupation, and mailing list. Listing 42.2 shows the HTML behind the page.

> **NOTE**
>
> If you are not familiar with HTML, you can just focus on the *basics* at this point. The goal of this chapter is not to make you an expert at HTML; many detailed references exist on that subject. This example demonstrates how to use values entered from the screen. Don't be concerned with the formatting details. As a programmer, the only values you really need to understand in the form in Listing 42.2 are `FORM ACTION`, `NAME`, `OPTION`, and `VALUE`.

Listing 42.2. HTML for the sample application.

```
<HTML>
<HEAD>
<TITLE>Sams E-Mail list</TITLE>
</HEAD>
<BODY>
<H1>Sams E-Mail List</H1>
<FORM ACTION="URL_to_your_program">
<P>To become a part of our exciting new E-Mail list, enter the fields
➥ below and click the "Submit" button below.</P>
<TABLE COLS=2 BORDER=0>
```

continues

Listing 42.2. continued

```
<TR><TD ALIGN=right>Last Name:</TD>
    <TD COLSPAN=5><INPUT TYPE=text NAME="last_name" SIZE=40></TD></TR>
<TR><TD ALIGN=right>First Name:</TD>
    <TD COLSPAN=5><INPUT TYPE=text NAME="first_name" SIZE=40></TD></TR>
<TR><TD ALIGN=right>E-Mail:</TD>
    <TD COLSPAN=5><INPUT TYPE=text NAME="email" SIZE=40></TD></TR>
<TR><TD ALIGN=right>Occupation:</TD>
    <TD><SELECT NAME="occupation"><OPTION>Programmer
<OPTION>Consultant<OPTION>Manager<OPTION>Writer<OPTION>
Owner/CEO<OPTION>Student<OPTION>Other</SELECT></TD></TR>
</TABLE>
<P>
Select Mailing List:
<INPUT TYPE="RADIO" NAME="which_list" VALUE="weekly">Weekly
<INPUT TYPE="RADIO" NAME="which_list" VALUE="monthly">Monthly<BR>
<BR>
<INPUT TYPE="submit" VALUE="Submit"><INPUT TYPE="reset"></FORM>
</BODY>
</HTML>
```

Figure 42.5 shows what Listing 42.2 looks like when displayed on a browser.

FIGURE 42.5.
The Web page for the e-mail list.

How's that? Now it's starting to get fun! The following tags are used in Listing 42.2:

- *TABLE:* Tells the browser that the text until the `</TABLE>` tag should be formatted as a table. For the purpose of this example, `TABLE` simply lines up the text-entry fields on the form, making them more presentable on-screen. The `ALIGN`, `SIZE`, `TR`, and `TD` tags describe the formatting of the individual fields (`Last Name`, for example).
- *INPUT TYPE=TEXT...:* Creates a text field for data entry by the user (`First Name`, for example).
- *SELECT...:* Creates a drop-down list of items for the user to select.
- *INPUT TYPE=RADIO:* Creates radio buttons, which allow only one button to be selected at a time.

You will need to understand the following tags in order to create applications:

- *FORM ACTION="URL.." and INPUT TYPE="submit"...:* Specify that clicking the Submit button directs the browser to `URL_to_your_program`, which is generally an executable program of some type.
- *NAME:* The name of the variable that will be used in your program. This name is assigned and passed to your program via the `url_query_string` portion of the URL, which helps you determine the value of the items entered on-screen. If you are using a Perl program for the value `URL_to_your_program`, for example, the Perl program needs to parse the `url_query_string` variables.
- *OPTION and VALUE:* For the radio button display, `OPTION` describes the actual value that will be assigned to the `NAME` field. `VALUE` does the same for a drop-down list. If the user selects Programmer for Occupation, for example, the value of the `Occupation` variable is `Programmer`.

Get and Post Methods and the url_query_string

You've almost certainly seen something like

```
?last_name=your_last_name&first_name=your_firstname
```

appended to the end (`url_query_string`) of a URL. These are the name/value pairs. The question mark (`?`) separates the rest of the URL with the `url_query_string`, the ampersand (`&`) indicates a new name/value pair, and the equal sign (=) indicates the value for a `NAME` field on a form. Also, a plus sign (+) indicates a space. These values are used by Web applications to do their processing. For example, the `url_query_string` in Listing 42.2 could be something like this:

```
?first_name=Ed&last_name=Smith&email=esmith@abcdef.com&occupation=
➥Writer&which_list=monthly
```

After you click the Submit button, the Web server automatically creates this string and then sends it back to your CGI program (`URL_to_your_program`, in this example). This string is known as *URI-encoded data.* Data can be sent to a CGI application by one of two methods: `Get` or `Post`. Each method handles the `url_query_string` a little differently. Here is a brief summary of each method:

- *`Get`:* The `Get` method places the values of the `FORM` into an operating system environment variable called `QUERY_STRING`. The `Get` method is the default method for the `<FORM>` tag. In this case, after you click the Submit button, the browser appends the `url_query_string` to the URL that runs your CGI program. This string is separated from the rest of the URL by the question mark (`?`) character. `Get` has its advantages, but it has its disadvantages as well. The length of an input buffer (in this case, the value of `QUERY_STRING`) might have a size limit on the operating system, for example. `Post` is considered a better method.
- *`Post`:* The `Post` method uses the standard input (`stdin` on UNIX) of the operating system to send its data. The main advantage of this method is that all the user's query data is sent on standard input; it isn't confined by the limitations of `Post`, and it generally is more efficient. There is no limit on the amount of data that can be sent via the `Post` method.

Web Pages On-the-Fly

Take another look at Listing 42.2. That HTML code displays the Web page in Figure 42.5. If you are familiar with programming languages, ask yourself this question: Can I create a program to print that HTML code?

Of course you can! This is how Web page development is done. The program driving the application simply creates HTML code to communicate with the Web browser. The HTML created in Listing 42.2 just as easily could have been created by a program. This capability is called creating Web pages *on-the-fly* or creating *dynamic* Web pages. A Web page on-the-fly is simply a Web page created by some application program. These programs read values passed by the browser as input and then format and send the appropriate HTML back to the browser.

The HTML in Listing 42.2 theoretically could be created by someone typing the HTML directly into an editor. Because that isn't really practical in an online application, though, Web applications were developed. A program processes what the user inputs on the Web page, formats a new page, and sends it back. With that in mind, take a look at how dynamic, on-the-fly Web pages are created.

Interaction Between Browsers and Servers

A browser-enabled application works as shown in Figure 42.6. The steps involved are as follows:

1. Type a URL in the browser and press Enter. To get to Netscape's products page, for example, enter the URL `http://www.netscape.com/comprod/index.html`. To connect to *any* URL, of course, you need to have established the proper network or Internet connection.
2. The DNS on your network or the Internet helps you find the URL. Remember that the URL consists of the protocol (`http`), server (`www.netscape.com`), and pathname (`/comprod/index.html`). If any part of the URL is not found, you see the dreaded `Server not found` error message.
3. The browser sends a command to the server to get the Web page (`Contacting host` in Netscape) and waits for the reply (`Host contacted. Waiting for reply.`).
4. This is when a custom Web application can come into the picture. If the URL represents a program, it processes the page on-the-fly and formats a new page. If the URL is simply another HTML page, that page is used. In either case, the Web server sends the HTML-formatted page to the browser.
5. The browser parses the HTML page, following this process:
   - The browser processes any HTML commands that it knows about; it ignores any unknown HTML tags.
   - Some HTML commands require the browser to download something more from the Web server. The `<IMG..>` tag, for example, inserts an image. If one of these tags exist, the Web site is contacted by the browser and is asked to send the image.
   - If one of the commands specifies that a Java, ActiveX, or other component is involved, it is downloaded and executed by the browser.
   - If some type of HTML-embedded scripting language exists (JavaScript or ActiveScript, for example), it is run by the browser.
   - After all these steps are complete, the browser and Web server acknowledge each other (`Document: done` in Netscape).

In fact, this browser process more or less describes the interaction of any Web application. In a simple Web application, if no user input is required, the pages sent back to the user are simply HTML files. If that is all your application needs, life can be much simpler. If not, read on.

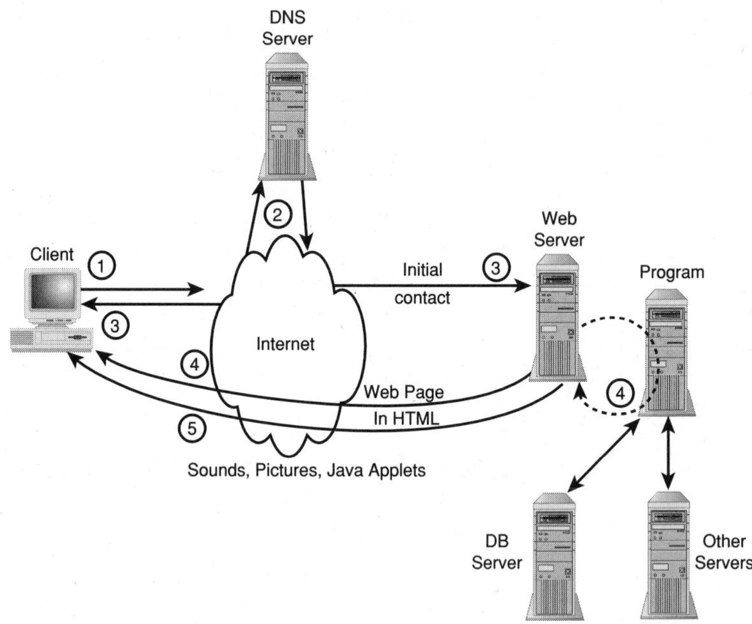

FIGURE 42.6.
Interaction between a Web browser and an application.

Adding an Application to a Web Site

An interactive Web application enables intelligent communications between the browser and the application. The application is created on-the-fly, based on the data the user supplies. This occurs in step 4 in the preceding section. Instead of sending back a simple Web page, the program does some custom processing and sends back a new page.

Creating an interactive Web site requires some type of software intervention. This intervention can be via custom-written software or third-party products. The rest of this chapter discusses the current ways to create an interactive Web site. Again, the basis of an interactive Web application is simple: The user enters data in a browser, the browser sends it to the Web server, the Web server sends it to the application, and the application processes it and sends back a new Web page. The data sent back can be obtained from the following:

- A normal system file (a flat file with user names, for example)
- A database, such as Informix
- The program itself (it can dynamically generate the data for a Web page without accessing a database)

The paradigm presented in Figure 42.6 now can be extended to include the software layer.

This architecture is very much like the proverbial black box; the user sends a request to a Web page, and it comes back as a new, usable Web page. This section examines what is inside the black box. With the incredible rate of change in Web-enabled applications, the black box can consist of various items. Informix has greatly simplified this process with the *Informix Universal Web Connect (IUWC)*, but for now, this section focuses on performing this process with existing applications that are not IUWC-enabled. The IUWC is described in detail later in this chapter.

Connection States

One of the important considerations of a Web-enabled application is the state of the connection. The *state* describes the communication between the browser and the application. The types of connections are stateless and stateful.

Stateless Connections

HTTP is a connectionless protocol or *stateless* connection. This means that when a browser sends a Web page, it connects to the Web server, gets the page it wants, and then says goodbye. If the user then selects something else on the Web page, it is as though this is the first time she accessed the page; the Web server has no record of who she was or what she last did.

A stateless connection is sufficient in many cases. If your application is a read-only application with only queries and static HTML files, there is no need to maintain the state. A customer might want to search for all widgets your company produces, for example. The search simply returns information; it does not need to maintain a connection. As Web applications are evolving, though, the need to maintain state is becoming more important.

Stateful Connections

A *stateful* connection maintains an open communication between browser and Web server. The Web server remembers the user and what he or she did last. Generally speaking, this applies only to Web applications with a back-end database. Stateful connections are important for the following reasons:

- They preserve the user's place in an active data set.
- They enable users to lock rows for update.
- They provide greater efficiency. The browser does not need to reestablish the connection to the database for each new action; the connection remains open.

One good example of the need for stateful connections is an OLTP application. Users query rows they will be updating. It is important that they maintain a shared lock on the row. A stateful connection can provide this maintenance. If the proper locking mechanism is used, other users will not be able to update the row. After the user updates the row and clicks the Submit button, the open database connection already has access to the row and updates it. Even in this situation, it might be best to implement some type of time-out strategy; if the user disconnects or doesn't do anything for a certain amount of time, free the row for updating.

WARNING

The methods for maintaining stateful connections are very new. A lot of hype exists, and a lot of companies claim that they fully implement stateful connections. With stateful connections–and just about any Web technology–be sure to look under the covers and make absolutely sure that they will work in your environment.

Efficiency is an important consideration in a stateful environment. Reattaching to a database—even in a read-only environment—can create high overhead. If the connection already is established, it greatly improves performance. If not, the Web server needs to reestablish the connection and run the proper system processes and programs.

The stateful environment generally is implemented via ports. A *port* is a TCP/IP concept that defines a communications channel. A process establishes a port number that is used by the process. A port can be used in various ways. Many well-known ports are predefined (FTP, for example), and user-defined ports can be used to establish communications.

You can establish a stateful connection in several ways; generally, the first two methods are the most reliable:

- *TP Monitor or CORBA:* A TP Monitor runs on the server and efficiently manages connections. It also helps balance transaction loads. CORBA can perform these tasks inherently and might replace TP Monitors in the not-so-distant future.
- *Vendor software:* Many vendors supply software that enables stateful connections. Informix Universal Web Connect (IUWC) and Prolific's JAMWEB are two such packages.
- *Cookies:* A Netcape cookie (also supported in Microsoft) can be used to track user activity. The cookie is exchanged between the Web server and the browser and provides users with a unique identifier. Programs need to track cookies in order to be effective.
- *Custom programming:* You can use programming methods to establish and maintain a connection. You can do this fairly easily in Java.

It is important to consider the state required for your application and to program your application accordingly. The IUWC is a particularly efficient way of doing this; it works very closely with Informix databases and provides all the hooks you need. If the IUWC is not available, you need to consider the other methods.

CGI: The Good Old-Fashioned Way

Common Gateway Interface (CGI) is a fairly straightforward way to create Web-enabled applications. Refer to Figure 42.6; the process in step 4 can be CGI. CGI is a protocol that forks operating system processes on a Web server. These processes can be any program that is executable on the Web server, including these:

- Perl
- Shell scripts (`sh`, `ksh`, `bash`, and `csh`, for example)
- TCL
- C, C++, and so on
- INFORMIX-4GL

The Web browser (user) sends data to the Web server, which in turn sends the data to the CGI program named in `FORM ACTION`. The data can be sent via the `Get` or `Post` method. The program parses the `url_query_string` using the method. Refer to Listing 42.2 for examples. After the program parses the data, it can access a database if necessary and pass the results back to the Web browser. Sound easy? It is. In fact, CGI applications are an excellent alternative for creating simple Web applications. CGI applications also can create powerful Web applications, but with a cost (discussed in the next paragraph). CGI applications don't require any additional software—other than the language—and can be programmed to handle a variety of needs.

Of course, CGI does not address the issues of state and performance. Because the CGI process is invoked by the Web server, it must reconnect with the database for each request. This necessity not only hurts performance but makes it very difficult to maintain state. If state and performance are issues, they can be addressed by the means described in "Stateful Connections," earlier in this chapter. Sometimes, it might be easiest, however, to use a method other than CGI or to use IUWC to create your applications.

Perl

The Perl language was created by Larry Wall and is freely available on the Internet. It is a very powerful language that is similar to a hybrid of C, Shell scripts, `awk`, `sed`, and other UNIX commands. Perl can run on UNIX and DOS/Windows platforms. Because of its flexibility, Perl is very popular for Web applications. You can find a great deal of information on Perl at its official Web site at

```
http://www.perl.com/perl/index.html
```

TIP

A Perl library is available for Informix at

```
http://iamwww.unibe.ch/~scg/FreeDB/FreeDB.60.html
```

The Perl/C-ISAM library is located at

```
http://iamwww.unibe.ch/~scg/FreeDB/FreeDB.54.html
```

This includes all libraries necessary to connect to an Informix database through Perl scripts.

Now take a look at a sample CGI application using Perl. This sample goes back to the sample application presented in Listing 42.2. Change the HTML line

```
<FORM ACTION="URL_to_your_program">
```

to

```
<FORM ACTION="/cgi-bin/maillist.pl">
```

Now, after the user fills in the information and clicks the Submit button, the operating system runs the program `maillist.pl`, which is shown in Listing 42.3. This program is an example of interfacing with a flat file on the Web server. This program creates a delimited file with the fields the user entered on-screen. To see how to perform database access, take a look at the Perl libraries in the previous Tip box, or see Listing 42.4 for an INFORMIX-4GL example.

Listing 42.3. A sample Perl CGI program.

```
#!/usr/local/bin/perl
require 'my-lib.pl';
&ParseQueryString(*in);
print "Content-type: text/html\n\n";
open(datafile,">>/data/email_list.dat");
print datafile "$in{'first_name'}\¦";
print datafile "$in{'last_name'}\¦";
print datafile "$in{'email'}\¦";
print datafile "$in{'occupation'}\¦";
print datafile "$in{'which_list'}\¦";
close(datafile);
print "<HTML>\n";
print "<HEAD><TITLE>Survey Complete</TITLE></HEAD>\n";
print "<BODY>\n";
print "<CENTER><H1>Thank you!</H1>\n";
print "<P>Your request has been processed.
Watch for your first E-Mail soon!</P></CENTER>\n";
print "</BODY>\n";
print "</HTML>\n";
....
```

After the user clicks the Submit button on the form, the browser places the values into the `url_query_string` and sends the string to the Web server, which passes it to the Perl program via the `Get` method. The function `ParseQueryString` parses the name/value pairs and places them into the appropriate Perl variables. (Note that `ParseQueryString` must be in `my-lib.pl`. Numerous HTML `url_query_string` parsers exist on the Web.) The line `print datafile "$in..` prints the variables to the file. The `print "<HTML>"` block prints a thank-you page on-the-fly and sends it back to the browser.

It's not pretty, but it works! Seriously, though, Perl is a very good language for implementing CGI applications. It has a great deal of power and flexibility and provides database hooks. Again, you *can* manage state in other ways.

This is a simple example of how to use CGI. You can develop full-blown Web sites by extending this architecture. You can create a similar form to query an Informix database and process data accordingly, for example. Because Perl is a programming language, it basically can be programmed to do anything.

Many examples of this type of CGI application exist on the Web. This chapter is not intended to give you the nitty-gritty details; it provides a high-level overview and explains the concepts. Many other references are available that focus more on this area, including *Teach Yourself CGI Programming with Perl in a Week*, published by Sams.net.

INFORMIX-4GL, C, and Other Languages

Remember that you can use *any* executable program as a CGI program. Your program just must be able to read and process values sent by the Web server. Languages that can be compiled, such as C and INFORMIX-4GL, therefore can greatly simplify Web application development.

C has more functionality than Perl, but it requires more programming knowledge and a C compiler. Although writing in C tends to be more complicated than writing in Perl, it might be worth the effort. Many Web application tools (including Informix) provide a rich variety of API libraries for C programming. This greatly enhances what can be done.

INFORMIX-4GL and NewEra are very easy to use and can perhaps be easier to implement than C.

Informix provides Webkits to allow CGI programs to be created in ESQL/C, 4GL, and NewEra. The Webkits, which you can download from Informix's Web site, provide many of the hooks you will need to interact with a Web application. The Webkits enable you to create a program and use it as a CGI process to talk to your database. The program processes the variables and prints the new Web page; it then sends the data to the Web server, which sends the page back to the Web browser.

You can find the Webkits at

`http://www.informix.com/informix/products/dlprod/Webkits/docentry.htm`

The Webkits are free to registered users of Informix products.

The example in Listing 42.4 shows how to use some of the functions in the 4GL Webkit. An ESQL/C program would be very much the same, except it would use C conventions. For this example, assume that someone is using the HTML form created by Listing 42.2. The user enters a first name, last name, e-mail address, occupation, and choice of mailing list. In the form, the value `URL_to_your_program` is replaced by the pathname to a compiled version of the 4GL program shown in Listing 42.4. In this case, the e-mail list from the example is stored in the `email_list` table.

Listing 42.4. A sample 4GL CGI program.

```
database mailing_list
main
   whenever error call html_error_msg()
....
    call init()
    callget_and_insert_values()
end main
...
function init()
# perform initialization functions
# icgi_start initializes the structure that helps get values
# of environment variables and HTML form fields
    if (icgi_start() == 0 ) then
         call html_error_msg("")
end if
#  .. perform other initialization functions ... see documentation
#     for complete details..
end function    # init()
function get_and_insert_values()
# this function will read values that the user entered from the Web page,
# insert them into the email_list table, and then create a new HTML page
# that thanks the user.
# define input rec.. email_list table
define    p_email_list    record like email_list.*
# icgi_getvalue will return values of fields that the user
# entered on the HTML form.
# the following statements populate the p_email_list RECORD
    let p_email_list.first_name = icgi_getvalue("first_name")
    let p_email_list.last_name = icgi_getvalue("last_name")
    let p_email_list.email = icgi_getvalue("email")
    let p_email_list.occupation = icgi_getvalue("occupation")
    let p_survey.which_list = icgi_getvalue("which_list")
# check if user exists and do other error checking...
    select COUNT(*) into user_count
    from email_list
   where last_name = p_email_list.last_name
      and first_name = p_email_list.first_name
      and email = p_email_list.email
    if user_count > 0 THEN
        call html_error_msg("E-Mail record already exists!")
    end if
# insert the rows into your E-Mail table
    insert into email_list values (p_email_list.*)
    IF sqlca.sqlcode != 0 then
        let err_msg = err_get(sqlca.sqlcode)
        call html_error_msg(err_msg)
    end if
# Now display a thank you page for the user
    call icgi_print_text("<HTML><HEAD>")
    call icgi_print_text("<TITLE>Survey Complete</TITLE>")
    call icgi_print_text("</HEAD><BODY>")
    call icgi_print_text("<H1>Thank you!</H1>")
    call icgi_print_text
➥("Your request has been processed.  Watch for your first E-Mail soon!")
    call icgi_print_text("</BODY></HTML>")
    ....
```

```
end function    # get_and_insert_values
function html_error_msg(msg)
# this function will format and display an error message
define msg char(80)
    if msg is null then
      let msg = "Unknown error."
    end if
    call icgi_print_text("<HTML><HEAD>")
    call icgi_print_text("<TITLE>Survey Error</TITLE>")
    call icgi_print_text("</HEAD><BODY>")
    call icgi_print_text("<H1>Error Occurred!</H1>")
    call icgi_print_text(msg)
    call icgi_print_text("</BODY></HTML>")
end function   # html_error_msg
```


If no errors occur, this program creates an HTML page that produces the output shown in Figure 42.7. If an error occurs, the `function html_error_msg()` is called, and a similar HTML form is displayed, except that it contains the error message.

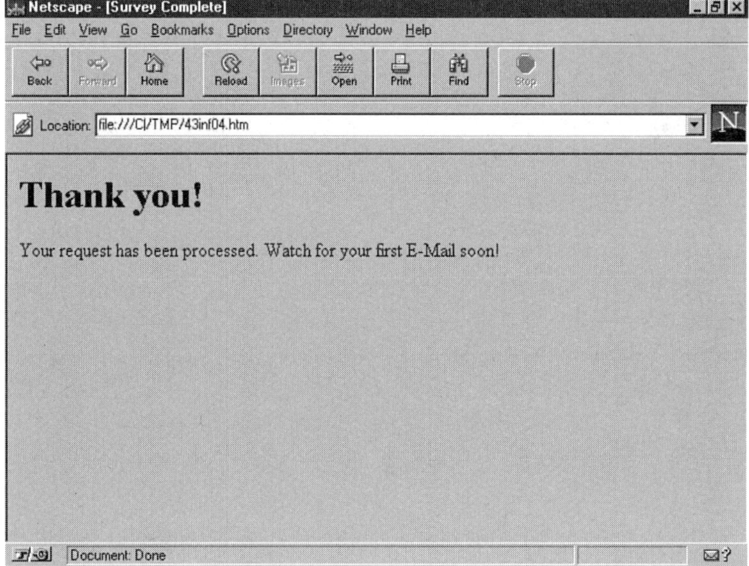

FIGURE 42.7.
A page dynamically generated by 4GL Webkit.

The method used in this example is very similar to that used in other CGI programs. The program uses its CGI method to read the values, process them, interact with the database, and return a new page to the user. For this sample, try to think of ways you can add more to the Web page returned to the user. You probably would print a link back to the home Web site or calculate a date when the user will next receive an e-mail message from the mailing list. This is how Web pages can be turned into interactive applications.

CGI Summary

The procedures used to create CGI programs are fairly straightforward. If you are familiar with a language and you have some type of CGI support for it, it might be a good way to implement your Web site. Just be sure to consider the strengths and weaknesses of CGI.

Java

Java is a programming language that enables object-oriented, platform-independent communications. Any computer that supports Java can run a Java program. This is exactly what the Web is about: open communications with computers around the world. Java is an excellent solution for writing Web applications, because it was built from the ground up with the concept *write once, run anywhere* in mind.

Java is developing a very widespread acceptance. A good number of software and hardware vendors are very supportive of this open aspect of Java. Java is considered an excellent threat to the Microsoft behemoth; it enables you to create platform-independent programs in a powerful, object-oriented language. Microsoft responded with ActiveX, which is discussed later in this chapter in the "ActiveX" section.

One of the big selling points of Java is its security features. Through a variety of methods, Java protects the local computer from malicious programs. Any Java program (applet) downloaded to a user's computer must go through a battery of security checks before it can be executed. In addition, programs are prevented from accessing the user's hard drive and other system resources.

You can use Java to create two types of executables—applets and applications:

- *Applets:* Applets are Java programs that can run on any Java virtual machine (a browser, for example). When a Web browser encounters an `<APPLET>` tag, it first verifies that the applet meets Java's security requirements and then downloads the applet. Java then can execute the applet in one of two ways: through an interpreter that runs the byte codes directly or after using a *just-in-time* (JIT) compiler. One of the main shortcomings of Java is that it is inherently slower than compiled programs. The applets have to be interpreted, because they can run on any computer with a Java virtual machine. JIT compilers translate the byte codes into native code, which greatly increases execution time.
- *Applications:* Java also can create stand-alone applications that typically run on any computer with a Java virtual machine. One advantage of applications is that they run on the server and don't need to be downloaded across the network or Internet. This method, in turn, saves an extra browser-to-server connection. Figures 42.8 and 42.9 illustrate how Java applets and applications work.

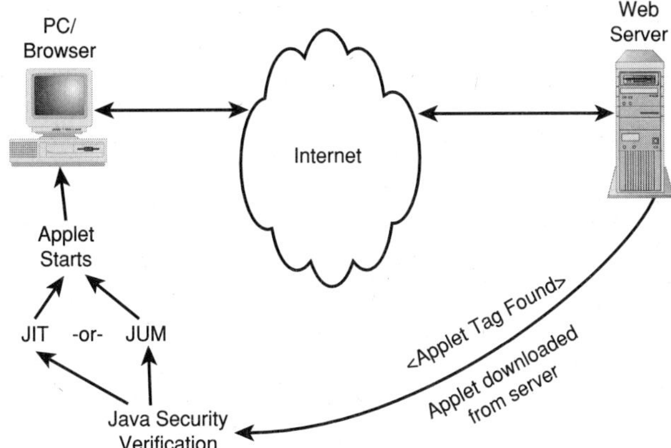

FIGURE 42.8.
Executing Java applets.

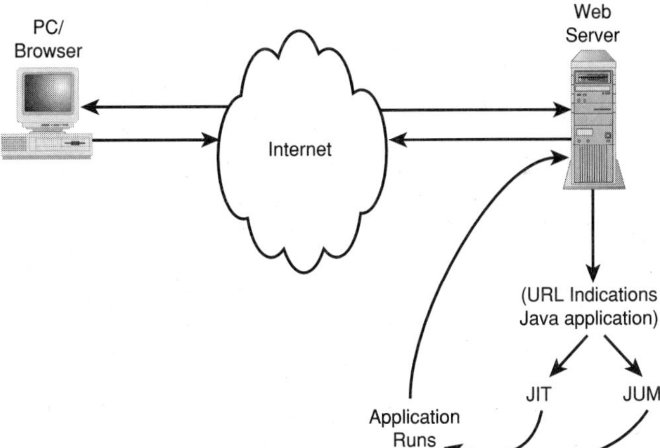

FIGURE 42.9.
Executing Java applications.

The Java libraries are a set of packages. In Java, a *package* is something that groups different classes that have various specific functions. The *Abstract Windowing Toolkit* (AWT) package, for example, includes classes that help create the user interface. Some of the classes in the AWT follow:

- *Event:* Describes some type of GUI event
- *Frame:* Allows creation of an application window
- *Graphics:* Defines methods for imaging, line drawing, and other graphics

Within individual Java classes are methods, which basically make things happen within that class. The graphics class has a method called `drawPolygon` (guess what that does?), for example. Likewise, every other class in Java provides similar functionality. It is easy to see the true object-oriented nature of each class.

TIP

Java was built with the Internet and World Wide Web very much in mind. It is very easy to get information on Java, including white papers, sample programs, and tutorials. Two good starting places are `www.javasoft.com` and `www.gamelan.com`. These two sites not only have very comprehensive information and examples, but they also provide links to an enormous number of sites.

Java also is very supportive of CORBA and IIOP. (See "Objects: Another New Web Paradigm," earlier in this chapter.) This support enables you to communicate with other IIOP-compliant objects on your hard drive, local network, or the Internet. Java talks to objects written in other languages, and vice versa.

JDBC

Java can communicate with databases such as Informix by using the *Java Database Connection* (JDBC) API, which is a set of Java classes. Informix was one of the developers of the JDBC specification. JDBC is a lot like ODBC, which enables programs to communicate with various back-end databases. JDBC has added many new hooks that just weren't considered when ODBC was created, though. JDBC enables you to use the power of Java to create fully interactive, Web-enabled database applications. Many people consider JDBC to be a much improved and more open version of ODBC. JDBC is available in version 1.1 of the *Java Development Kit* (JDK).

A number of JDBC drivers are in various stages of availability. JDBC provides a JDBC-ODBC bridge that enables you to use existing ODBC drivers when no JDBC driver is available. Because Informix was involved with creating the JDBC specification, JDBC drivers are available for Informix. Companies that provide JDBC drivers include Visigenic, Intersolv, OpenLink, and I-Kinetics. Check the Web to find out about the availability of JDBC drivers.

Informix and Java

Informix is embracing Java and Internet standards head-on. This is evidenced by its Universal Web Architecture, Data Director for Java, and Universal Tools strategy. (See the section "The Next Generation: Informix Universal Web Architecture," later in this chapter.) For now, though, you can use Java and JDBC to connect to databases that aren't IUWC-enabled.

As you probably can see, many companies (Sun, Netscape, and Informix, for example) are supporting a worldwide, open computing environment. This will change the way databases are created, applications are written, and business is conducted.

JavaScript

JavaScript is a scripting language created by the king of open Web standards: Netscape. It is a language somewhat similar to Java in its syntax and object orientation. JavaScript does have one big difference when compared to Java: JavaScript is a scripting language that is functional *only* as part of an HTML-formatted Web page. Also, JavaScript requires no special tools, whereas Java is a full-fledged language that requires a development tool (JDK) and a compiler. You develop and then test JavaScript by running it in a Web browser.

The two ways to create JavaScript are client-side and server-side:

- *Client-side (browser):* Client-side JavaScript is embedded as part of an HTML Web page. It is specified by a tag starting with `<SCRIPT LANGUAGE="JavaScript">` and ending with `</SCRIPT>`. Everything in the middle is the actual JavaScript code. You can use client-side Java very effectively to perform operations that save an extra interaction with the Web server. Client-side JavaScript provides many functions that are provided in Java, but it involves less overhead than downloading a Java applet. (It's already in the HTML that makes up the Web page.) These client-side functions include confirmation windows, forms, warning messages, drop-down menus, and arrays.

  Another very important use for JavaScript is performing client-side, data-entry validation. A data-entry form that accepts user input, for example, might need to verify different values on-screen. Instead of having the user submit the form, send it to the Web server, and wait for a reply, the validation is performed on the client side *before* sending the form to the Web server.

  Here is a brief example of some JavaScript code that verifies that the salary entered on the form is greater than 1,000 and less than 100,000:

  ```
  if ((obj.salary < 1000) || (obj.salary > 100000))
       alert("Invalid Salary: Must be between 1000 and 100000")
  ```

- *Server-side:* Server-side JavaScript is stored as part of an HTML page between the `<SERVER>` and `</SERVER>` tags. This type of JavaScript typically is used to perform database operations such as inserts and updates. This JavaScript is executed on the database server, which moves the processing to the server and eliminates an extra browser-server connection. Informix and Netscape provide native connections to Informix databases through JavaScript on a Netscape server. For example, Netscape LiveWire products at

  `http://www.netscape.com/comprod/products/tools/livewire_datasheet.html`

  provide native Informix connections and the capability to create JavaScript database applications. In fact, many third-party Web development products create applications that use JavaScript.

Netscape supplies the AppFoundary as part of its SuiteSpot package. AppFoundary also is available for free at www.netscape.com and includes code samples of real-world JavaScript applications.

JavaScript has many advantages but also some shortcomings. It isn't as robust a language as Java, for example. Also, all the JavaScript program code easily can be viewed by looking at the HTML code behind a Web page; this capability brings up obvious security concerns, although it can be prevented by creating server-side applications. Nonetheless, JavaScript has its advantages, it definitely has its applications, and you don't need to be a programmer to use it.

ActiveX

Not known for letting others steal its thunder, Microsoft developed its own Internet strategy. Internet Explorer was developed to place Microsoft back on the desktop as the browser. In fact, Microsoft's whole Office 97 was created as an Internet-aware desktop. ActiveX is the technology Microsoft created to enable distributed applications such as those on the Web.

ActiveX is basically an extension of Microsoft's OLE2 technology. In a nutshell, ActiveX enables objects to communicate with each other as though they were all right on the user's PC. ActiveX now uses DCOM as its transport mechanism. (See the section "Objects: Another New Web Paradigm," earlier in this chapter.) An object is used as a proxy to make any other object appear to be local, whether it is on the user's hard drive, local network, or the Internet. These objects are referred to as *controls*. ActiveX controls can be written in any language that can create them. Figure 42.10 shows how ActiveX controls interact.

FIGURE 42.10.
ActiveX controls.

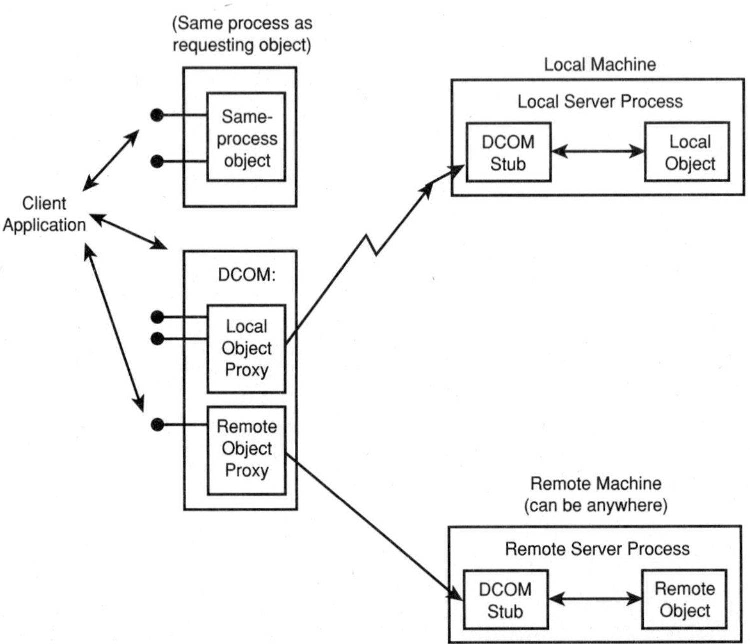

ActiveX objects currently are supported only on Microsoft platforms such as Windows 95 and NT. This limited support is both an advantage and a disadvantage. It definitely can provide quicker execution time in most cases; ActiveX controls are compiled programs for their native (Microsoft) platforms. The open nature of the Internet is somewhat defeated, though. In its defense, Microsoft—through third parties—is developing ActiveX capabilities for UNIX and other platforms.

One other diversion from open Internet standards is Microsoft's insistence on using COM and DCOM. COM and DCOM also are very proprietary and different from CORBA. The APIs are different and provide good connectivity on Microsoft-enabled products but again digress from commonly accepted Web standards. This fact might change soon; methods might be available that allow DCOM and CORBA to communicate.

Security is a big concern with ActiveX. If the user allows a control to download, it can virtually take control of the PC. Microsoft currently handles this by *digitally signing* ActiveX controls. This mechanism simply tells the browser that this control has not been changed since it was last registered; it does not guarantee that it won't do anything destructive. This might not be an issue on company networks, but it definitely is a consideration for Web applications. Watch `www.microsoft.com` for changes in how ActiveX handles security.

Something that definitely works in Microsoft's favor is the large number of developers that can create ActiveX controls using programming languages they already know, such as Visual C++ and Visual Basic. In addition, a great number of vendors (Powersoft Powerbuilder, for example) have added the capability to generate ActiveX controls right from their products. So ActiveX is definitely a viable alternative to creating Web-enabled applications.

The speed of execution is another advantage of using ActiveX. Because controls are compiled into native object code, their execution time can be much faster than Java. This issue has been addressed somewhat with Java JIT compilers, but it is still a consideration.

ActiveX controls can use ODBC and native methods to interact with Informix databases. After users are connected to the proper database-enabled control, database communications can occur.

Major software vendors are allowing ActiveX controls to be created directly from their products (Borland Delphi, for example). These controls then would allow access to various databases across the network or Internet. This capability definitely shows that ActiveX works and is making its mark in the software community. Just like everything else discussed in this chapter, though, all factors must be considered before deciding on a development method.

Third-Party Tools

Many third-party tools are available that empower the creation of Web-enabled database applications. There are many advantages to using these tools:

- They offer you simple ways to create controls, such as buttons and data-entry fields.

- They give you a one-step process to generate a basic form that can be customized.
- They enable you to create a form simply by using drag-and-drop procedures.
- They eliminate the need to "start at ground zero."

Available tools can create applications in many ways. Applications can be CGI (JavaScript and Perl, for example), Java, and proprietary HTML (processed by the product on the Web server). Here is a list of some of these tools:

- Borland IntraBuilder
- Allaire Cold Fusion
- Prolifics JAM and JAM/Web
- Netscape LiveWire Pro (includes Informix Workgroup Server)

Here are some tools that enable Java development:

- Informix Data Director for Java
- Microsoft J++
- Symantec Visual Café (Symantec is now partnered with Informix)
- NetDynamics

A common feature is a screen painter that enables you to drag and drop data fields and controls (OK buttons, for example) onto screens. After you create a form, it has all the basic code to get users up and running. Generally, you will need to perform modifications, but your form certainly can provide a good start.

Many of these tools include a server component that runs right on the Web server. The server can manage state and more efficient connections. Also, for products that provide HTML extensions (Informix Web DataBlade and Web Connect, for example), the server component interprets the page, adding functionality.

The Next Generation: Informix Universal Web Architecture (IUWA)

Informix always has stayed on the leading edge of technology, which helps explain its phenomenal growth rate and acceptance in the industry. The IUWA is the latest example of Informix staying on top of technology. Informix recognizes the importance of Web-enabled technologies to the future of data processing and is building it into each of its products.

The IUWA allows much easier creation of Web applications for Informix databases. IUWA can work with all the methods described earlier—CGI, Java, JavaScript, ActiveX, and third-party tools. IUWA adds a wrapper that allows easy deployment of browser-enabled applications based on open standards. The architecture includes the following elements, some of which are described in the following sections:

- *Informix Universal Web Connect:* The glue that enables IUWA to create Web applications based on open standards. Web Connect allows for the necessary connectivity between all the pieces and enables various Web technologies. This includes push technology, which allows *pushing* of data to the user's desktop without the user actively having to get the data.
- *Java support:* Enables developers to use Java on the client, middleware, or server level.
- *Data Director:* Allows developers to use Visual Café and other tools to create Java- and ActiveX-enabled applications for Informix databases.
- *Informix Web DataBlade:* Enables users to easily create dynamic Web applications and Web pages on-the-fly.
- *Partner support:* Many third-party developers are using the IUWA API to build hooks into their Web development products.
- *Web solution specialists:* Consulting organizations that help deliver custom Web applications to customers.
- *Electronic commerce:* Informix is partnering with many companies that offer electronic commerce, providing solutions using IUWA and DataBlades.

You can use IUWA with the complete line of Informix DSA-enabled products: Universal Server, OnLine Dynamic Server, OnLine Workgroup Server, OnLine Workstation, and XPS. Any one of these database servers can be very much Web-enabled by using IUWA. IUWA can work with Java/IIOP and ActiveX components.

It is important to note how Informix is embracing the workgroup world, which generally covers the small- to mid-sized applications. OnLine Workgroup Server and OnLine Workstation are two excellent solutions for this type of environment. Both are based on the Dynamic Scalable Architecture that is the basis for most Informix servers, but they are not as complex as OnLine Dynamic Server. These products are powerful yet easy to administer, and they come Web-enabled. Informix is providing these products for both UNIX and NT environments. Of course, OnLine Dynamic Server also is available for these platforms.

Informix has developed a strong relationship with Netscape. This includes the bundling of Netscape servers and development products (FastTrack Server and LiveWire Pro, for example) with workgroup products—and vice versa. This relationship is important because Netscape—as much as anyone—supports the open nature of Web-enabled applications.

Intelligent Web Applications

The main focus of IUWA is the creation of intelligent Web applications. Basically, this means products that have interactive Web applications as their core. Some intelligent Web applications follow:

- *Easily managed Web site content:* Because most or all of the Web site (HTML files, for example) is actually in the database, it is easy to add to or change.
- *Custom content:* The content of Web sites can be tailored to the users. After a user enters a Web site, he or she can enter some basic information. After that, the Web site can track the user's preferences and tailor content accordingly.
- *Broadcast and subscribe:* Broadcast or push technology is the capability to send up-to-date information on products. If users subscribe to a service (catalog pricing, for example), the Web site can e-mail changes to them.
- *Intelligent query:* Users can query Web applications based on content such as pictures and documents. A query can include elements such as demographics and color. The Web site will be able to parse the query and provide the appropriate content.

Informix Universal Web Connect

The *Informix Universal Web Connect* (IUWC) is a framework that makes it easy to build database-enabled Web applications. It handles many basic Web application issues, such as state, scalability (adding many users), and open standards. IUWC enables just about any type of Web application (Java and CGI, for example) to interact with the database. Figure 42.11 shows IUWC communicating with an INFORMIX-Universal Server database.

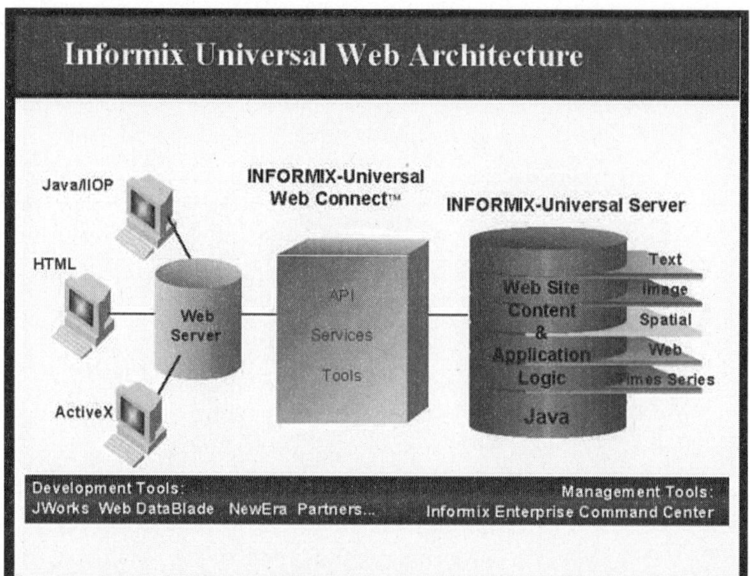

FIGURE 42.11.
The Informix Universal Web Connect.

The IUWC provides a type of middleware that enables Web pages to be stored in the database and exploded into HTML when needed. Every time a Web page is extracted from the database, all dynamic portions of the Web page are read and interpreted by IUWC. Everything on a Web site can be stored in an Informix database, including Web pages, pictures, and Java applets.

Much of the IUWC's architecture is derived from INFORMIX-Universal Server (formerly Illustra) and its DataBlade modules. Informix is working toward an all–Universal Server environment in the future, and the IUWC provides an easy upgrade path.

Here are some of the key features of the IUWC:

- *Maintaining state:* As described earlier, a major consideration is maintaining *state*, meaning a connection to the database. In an interactive, online application, the database state must be maintained for elements such as cursors. This capability is built into the IUWC.
- *Web servers:* The IUWC works with any HTTP-based Web server, including Microsoft, CERN, and Netscape. Programs are vendor-independent, enabling them to be transferred easily to other Web servers.
- *Web driver:* The Web driver will pull HTML pages, images, and other information out of the database, exploding them into a full-blown Web page. This is much like the Web DataBlade.

The Web driver is a process that runs on the server. It exists in shared memory and can communicate with a Web server by using *native Netscape API* (NSAPI), *native Microsoft API* (ISAPI), or CGI. Of course, NSAPI and ISAPI provide quicker response time.

The Web driver is called like a CGI program. The URL points to Webdriver, which is the executable portion of IUWC. A `url_query_string` can be placed at the end of the URL (`www.informix.com/cgi-bin/Webdrive?MIVal=main`, for example). It is typical to see `?MIVal=main` or some such thing on the Informix Web site. Any string starting with `MIVal` tells Webdriver to look for a Web page in the database; in this case, it is the page with `main` as its unique key. Figure 42.12 demonstrates this process.

As mentioned, these Web pages are stored in the database. The Web page in this example is created in HTML and can include tags that begin with `<?MI`. When submitted to the Web driver, all tags beginning with `<?MI` are exploded and executed in the database, returning a formatted HTML page to the server. When included as part of a Web page, for example, the `<?MISQL` tag in Listing 42.5 performs an insert into the database by using the values the user entered on the form (`$FIRST_NAME`, for example):

Listing 42.5. Using Webdriver to perform an insert into the database.

```
<?MISQL SQL=
    "insert into email_list
        (first_name,last_name,email,occupation,which_list)
        values ('$FIRST_NAME','$LAST_NAME',
       '$EMAIL','$OCCUPATION','$WHICH_LIST'); ">
<?/MISQL>
```

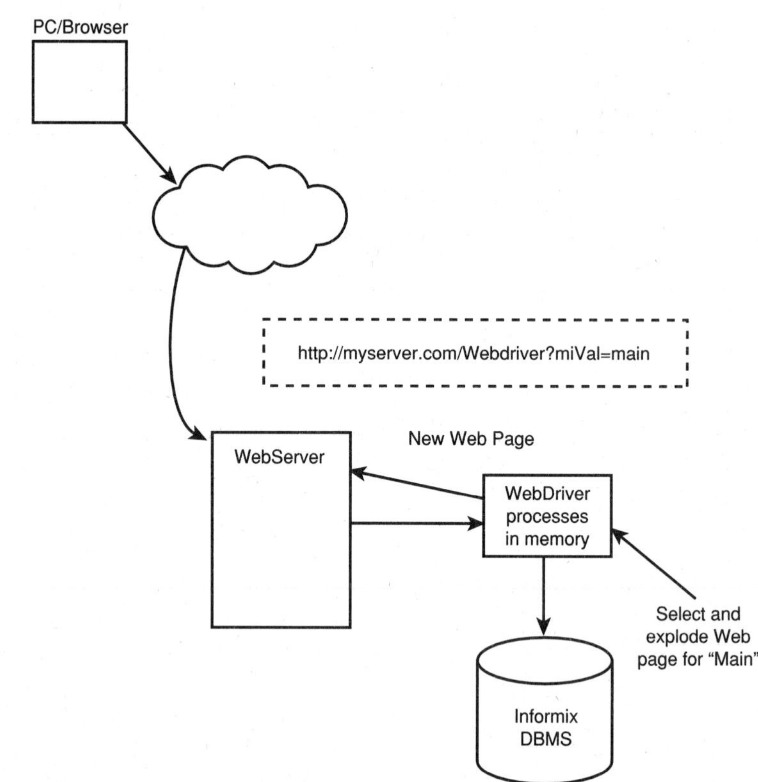

FIGURE 42.12.
The steps involved in using the Web driver.

Note that the code between the `<?MISQL>` and `</MISQL>` tags is what is executed. The Web driver looks for these special tags and executes them. Listing 42.6 shows a `select` statement. This statement also can be embedded in the Web page and create a nicely formatted HTML table by using the HTML `<TR>` and `<TD>` tags. An embedded `select` statement is used in Listing 42.6.

Listing 42.6. Using Webdriver for `select`.

```
<?MISQL SQL=
    "select first_name,last_name,email
➥ from email_list order by last_name,first_name;" >
<?/MISQL>
```

Java Support

The IUWC is very supportive of Java. In fact, it enables you to create Web logic in Java and to execute it on the Web browser, a middle layer, or the Web server. This capability supports easy programming of Web sites based on Java. The IUWC also has built-in support for CORBA standards.

Universal Tools Strategy and Data Director

The Informix Universal Tools Strategy makes it fast and easy to develop applications for Informix's database servers. Data Director is a drag-and-drop Web development environment. Using Universal Tools Strategy in conjunction with Data Director allows using various third-party tools to create Web-enabled applications. These tools can use Java, ActiveX, and other methodologies to create applications, which greatly enhances application development.

Universal Server and the Web DataBlade

The *INFORMIX-Universal Server* (IUS) is the object-relational database management system (ORDBMS) that is one of the major keys to Informix's future direction; it is covered in detail in Chapter 8, "INFORMIX-Universal Server." IUS is a combination of an object-oriented database and a relational database. An ORDBMS enables you to use a mixture of data types in the same database. These data types can be standard relational data, videos, pictures, audio, Java, and Web pages. The IUWC uses many of the same concepts as IUS. Eventually, all of Informix's database will be Universal Server–enabled.

The Web DataBlade is Universal Server's key to creating Web applications. DataBlade runs only on Universal Server and supports embedded HTML tags that can be parsed to create custom Web pages. DataBlade is very much like the Web driver and the architecture shown in Figure 42.12.

Partner Support

Because IUWA is an open architecture, any software vendor can create hooks into it via the API interfaces. This is done through C programs. Many application development vendors, including HAHT Software, Bluestone, and NetDynamics, provide integration with IUWC, enabling you to write Informix applications using their products.

NOTE

Writing a chapter on Web applications definitely supports the cliché about trying to hit a moving target. The Web—and the ways of using it—is changing at breakneck speed. Informix changes with the Web. To keep up with the latest enhancements to the IUWA, keep an eye on `www.informix.com`. The following URLs specifically discuss Universal Tools and Data Director:

`http://www.informix.com/informix/products/tools/comptool/ddjava.htm`

`http://www.informix.com/informix/products/tools/index.htm`

The Universal Web Architecture is a big part of Informix's plans for the future. It helps simplify the creation of dynamic Web applications. Also, Informix Universal Web Connect is very efficient at managing the database connection between the Web driver and the Web server. It helps fit your application's development into emerging, open standards.

Summary

This chapter presented many of the ever-changing ways to develop browser-enabled applications. Remember that a *browser-enabled* application simply is an application that uses a browser as a front-end; it doesn't have to be on the Internet. In this chapter, you learned ways to use many popular technologies to implement Web applications. These ways work now and will continue to work in the future. You then examined the new Informix Universal Web Architecture, which helps pull all the other technologies together.

Objects are becoming a very big part of the future of technology. They enable applications to communicate with each other. Objects on the Web are enabled through CORBA and DCOM. The data-processing world is becoming very open to industry-wide standards, and CORBA and DCOM are two examples.

The Web and its related technologies are ever changing. It is almost impossible to keep up with them. But they are now a part of life in the data-processing world, and it is important to understand their power. Data processing is a very exciting field, and one thing is certain: There is never a dull moment. I encourage you to keep moving forward with Informix and technology, and use the best technologies to create your applications, now and in the future.

IN THIS PART

Data Modeling

Model-Driven Development for the Informix RDBMS

by Jim Prajesh

IN THIS CHAPTER

This chapter discusses the need for modeling and then outlines the most important concepts in modeling and how modeling relates to building a database application. I also look at how these models can be implemented in Informix RDBMS and provide various tricks (theoretically accurate, of course) I picked up over the years of training people and implementing model-based solutions. Even advanced modelers will find the concepts in this chapter useful. Due to the fact that in most cases, people have limited time to become efficient in modeling, I developed some techniques that teach people all the aspects of modeling in a short time. To achieve this, instead of teaching people how to build models, I describe how to tell whether a model is a good one. When you know this, you can build models using the most convenient approaches. I discuss the structures that you need to build good models and how to implement these concepts in INFORMIX-OnLine. A list of possible approaches to collect data for building models is provided at the end of this chapter. I have not covered concepts directly related to information modeling, such as procedures, triggers, physical constructs such as dbspaces, table fragmentation expression, and so on.

Although there are many types of models, this chapter focuses on information modeling, which is sometimes referred to as data modeling or structural modeling. The next two chapters build on the concepts described in this chapter. I made each section independent and modular so that it is easy for you to refer to each section without reading the whole chapter.

All the examples (including the diagrams and the code listings) in this chapter were created with the SILVERRUN Relational Data Modeler (SR-RDM) tool version 2.4.4. This tool is developed and supported by SILVERRUN Technologies, Inc. A trial version of this tool is provided on the CD-ROM that comes with this book.

Why Model?

Models are a way to describe and document any system—whether it is a car, a building, your applications, systems, databases, and so on—before it is actually built. There are many ways of representing models. The most accurate models are mathematical equations, and the most ambiguous models are textual or verbal definitions (which is why legal documents are so long and use terms nobody understands). I use something in between by utilizing graphical models of the database applications. This approach is a good compromise between the two extreme types of models. You don't need to be a mathematician to decipher the models or try to guess what the designer was actually trying to say in long, drawn-out memos. In my case, a model is to a database what an architect's blueprint is to a building. Although most of us wouldn't even think of building a house without having a professional draw the plans, many managers don't seem to care if a model of an application is created. I do blame management for not insisting on models for every application built, purchased, or modified. This is one of the primary reasons why most organizations don't have any idea about what information they have or provide support for new or changing business needs. Those of us who took business courses were told that an organization has four types of assets—money, people, technology, and information. Modeling as discussed in this chapter helps you focus on the information asset. It helps you track what information your organization has, does not have, will need, and so on.

Uses for a Model

Because an information model is an abstract representation of your data, you can use it primarily for four purposes:

- As a blueprint for designing, validating, and implementing new applications: Building models for your applications helps you conceptualize the design and eliminate most, if not all, functional bugs. It is easier for peers and users to validate models as opposed to your SQL script. Building models also allows for validation of concepts before the model is implemented as an application, thus minimizing functional problems later on.
- As a reference model when purchasing packages: This is a very important reason for building models. When I ask managers why they don't build models, on plenty of occasions they tell me that they don't need them because they usually purchase packages. It is in this situation that you absolutely must have models. The two high-level steps require you to first build a model of what your organization currently uses and needs in the package, and this, of course, assumes that you gather the requirements of all the potential users of the package. You then compare your model to the model of the application and see if the package supports your needs. This exercise also tells you how much customization of the package, if any, is required. After the most appropriate package is selected, the models help you migrate the data from your existing system to the new package. I also find that this approach is a lot more objective than determining whether a package supports your needs based on the sales presentation or the type of restaurant the salesperson takes you to for lunch. I know your salesperson might not try to cover the deficiencies in the package with a fancy multimedia presentation, but you are still better off with a more scientific approach.
- For migrating between databases: Assuming you use a CASE tool (which you should) when you want to migrate between DBMSs or between different versions of the same DBMS, you should reverse-engineer the old application to create an "as is" model, make appropriate changes, and then use the new model to generate code for the new DBMS. A lot of the syntax conversion is usually handled by the CASE tool. One of the main reasons that people switch to a new DBMS is because the current DBMS might not have the technology to handle the needs of the organization any more. For example, if a DBMS does not provide record-level locking (in this day and age, there are mainstream databases that do not have record-level locking) and you are not able to support your users because of this, it might be time to switch. Also, you might want to take advantage of some new features in a new release of your existing DBMS. For

example, Informix version 5 did not support declarative referential integrity specification, and INFORMIX-OnLine version 7 does. It is a lot easier to reverse an Informix 5 database into a CASE tool, assign referential integrity rules, take advantage of new data types, and generate INFORMIX-OnLine 7 compliant DDL than to manually apply these changes. As an additional bonus, in the process, your database gets documented. Because these models are technology-independent (except for the physical constructs such as dbspaces, table fragmentation rules, and so on), these models last forever. In most organizations that use model-driven development, switching to new databases or to new technology is pretty painless.

- As an inventory of your information asset: This inventory can let the organization know whether the information needed to perform a certain function (such as a new marketing campaign) is available. This can also form the basis of building specific types of applications such as data warehouses and data marts ("star" schemas).

Notations

Before I discuss the modeling concepts, let's begin with a brief discussion of the various notations used in modeling. In the models you examine, I use pictorial representations of physical concepts. The type of graphical representation used is generally referred to as the notation. Although many experienced modelers would tell you that the notation used does not really matter, I beg to differ. Because the models are used by people new to modeling and nontechnical people, the notation should be simple enough for people to understand but comprehensive enough to represent a wide variety of business rules. The notation should avoid using cryptic symbols whenever possible. Keeping these factors in mind, I chose a notation based on the methodology called Datarun.

I clarify my point with a comparison between Information Engineering (a popular notation as defined by Clive Finkelstein) and Datarun. I'll define three business rules and compare the representations using Information Engineering and Datarun notations:

- You need to keep track of the following properties for a television series: the series number, the series name, the season, and the name of the current producer.
- You also need to keep track of the episodes for the series and keep track of the series number and the date planned to air.
- A series must have at least one episode but can have a maximum of 22 episodes.

As you can see in Figure 43.1, the Information Engineering notation tells you the series must have at least one but can have many episodes. It is not clear from the diagram what properties each one of the entities has. The business rule specifying that a series can have a maximum of 22 episodes cannot be specified in the diagram. In the Datarun notation in Figure 43.2, the properties of the entities and the business rule are explicitly specified. Because it is the properties of an entity that can hold values, it is very important to see them. Also, specific business rules can be shown. I have also found that people new to modeling and nontechnical people find the Datarun notation easier to read and understand. Please remember that both notations represent the same business concepts; the difference is in the amount of information shown and the amount of information that you must specify in textual descriptions.

FIGURE 43.1.
A representation of the rules in Information Engineering notation.

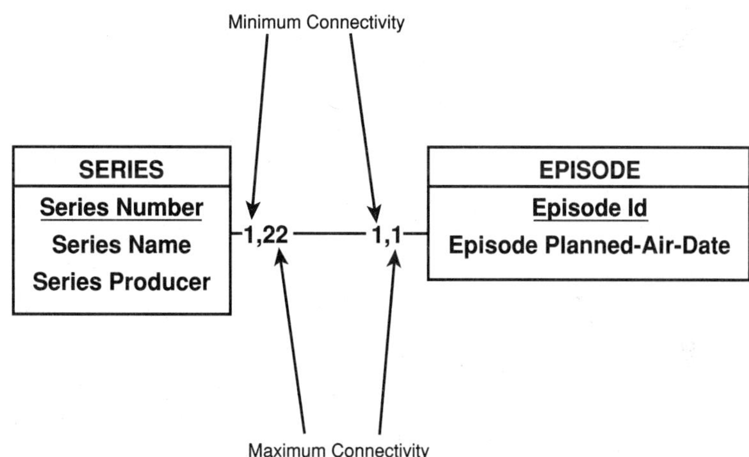

FIGURE 43.2.
A representation of rules using Datarun notation.

The Various Models

The rest of the chapter deals with certain rules that you must follow to ensure that your relational information model (RIM) is of good quality. It is best to stick to these rules when you initially build the models. If for some reason (usually performance reasons) you want to violate these rules, you can do it for your physical implementation. This way, your model is stable. Some methodologies separate these two types of models; the ideal model that obeys the rules of modeling is sometimes referred to as the logical model, and the model that is optimized for physical implementation is called the physical model. I believe that in most cases while using a database such as INFORMIX-OnLine, it is not necessary to have two separate models with different structures. Because of the high performance of the database engine, the need to denormalize is minimized. There are other reasons to have separate logical and physical models. One good reason is when you must have multiple physical implementations of the same information in multiple sites in your organization. In this case, the physical model could contain information such as dbspaces and table fragmentation rules for each site, but the logical structure is the same.

Additionally, most methodologies also propose the need for a high-level business data model, sometimes referred to as a *conceptual data model* or an *entity relationship model.* In this case, you end up with three levels of models: conceptual, logical, and physical. This schema is usually referred to as the three-schema architecture. You can use the models in this chapter as logical and physical models but not conceptual models.

Primary Concepts in a Relational Information Model

At the semantic level, the information models for relational databases such as INFORMIX-OnLine are referred to as relational information models. Primarily, four basic concepts make up the relational information model (RIM). Some of the names are similar to what you already know from your DBMS experience:

- Table
- Column
- Primary keys and Alternate keys
- Connector

Additional concepts are used to implement the models in INFORMIX-OnLine. Concepts such as foreign keys are used to implement connectors. Additionally, rules govern the basic concepts. For example, the rule that tells you what values are allowed for a column is known as the domain, and rules governing the connectors are known as referential integrity constraints. I examine these additional concepts in the section "Implementing Models in INFORMIX-OnLine," later in this chapter.

Table and Column

Syntactically, the concept of a table is the same as the table in any SQL DBMS. Essentially, it is used to define a group of columns. In RIM, a table has some specific rules that must be met before it can be defined as a table. As in all modeling, some of these rules are semantic whereas others are syntactic. In RIM, for a table to be correct, it must meet the following conditions:

- Relevancy
- Uniformity
- Identifiability
- Single-valued columns

Relevancy

The relevancy rule essentially asks whether this table or concept is necessary for the organization. Another way of putting it is to ask whether the organization is willing to spend money to keep track of this table. At this stage in modeling, it is not very expensive to put it in. You should also consider what information you want to track.

Uniformity

Uniformity is an often-ignored but important rule. This rule states that all the attributes should be applicable to all instances of the concept represented by the table.

For example, in Figure 43.3, not all columns are applicable for all employees. This is a violation of this rule.

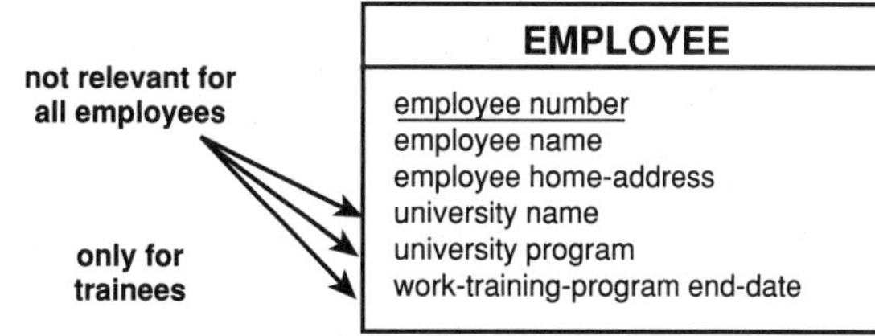

FIGURE 43.3.
A table in which all attributes are not applicable for all instances.

It is easy to fix the situation where all attributes are not applicable by splitting the columns that belong to trainees into another table, as shown in Figure 43.4.

FIGURE 43.4.
The results of decomposing a table.

EMPLOYEE
employee number
employee name
employee home-address

TRAINEE
employee number
university name
university program
work-training-program end-date

In Figure 43.4, it is very clear which columns are applicable to all employees and which columns are applicable to trainees. Clarity is one of the goals in RIM. There has to be a connector between the two tables. Depending on the business rule, the type of connector might be different. I discuss the options in the "Connectors" section of this chapter.

Identifiability

A table can have any number of rows. The identifiability rule states that there must be a way to tell the rows of a table apart. You use a column or a group of columns to make the instances unique. This column or group of columns forms the primary key of the table. In addition to the fact that the primary key has to be unique, the columns of the primary key cannot have null values. This makes sense because if they have null values, you cannot tell them apart. In Datarun notation (and most other notations), the columns composing the primary key are underlined.

In Figure 43.5, the columns author first-name, author last-name, and author initials together make up the primary key.

FIGURE 43.5.
Specification of primary key.

AUTHOR

author first-name
author last-name
author initials
author address
author telephone

Sometimes, there might be more than one way of identifying an instance of a table. In that case, one of the column groups becomes the primary key, and the others become alternate keys. Alternate keys are denoted by numbers in carats, as shown in Figure 43.6.

FIGURE 43.6.
An example of columns used as alternate keys.

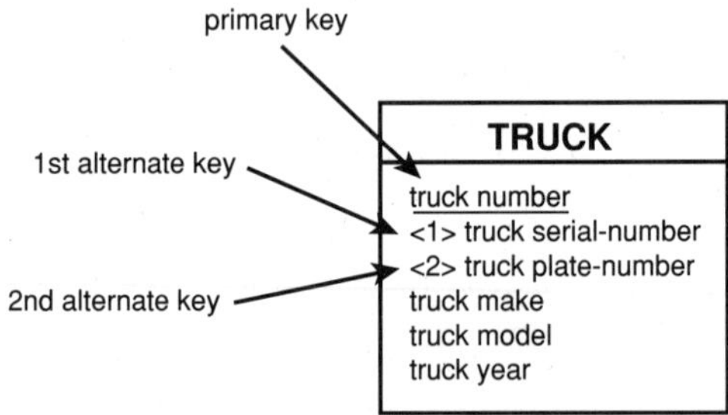

Additionally, you might use a column in multiple key combinations at the same time. In the example in Figure 43.7, the employee last name is part of the first alternate key combination (along with employee phone) and part of the second alternate key combination (along with employee birthday).

FIGURE 43.7.
A column participating in multiple key combinations.

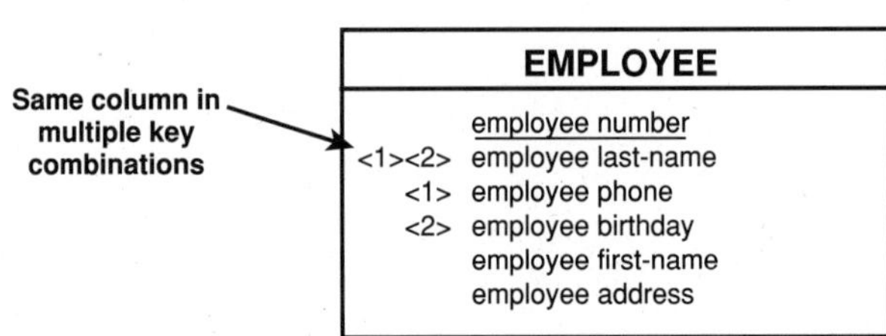

It makes sense to pick primary keys that don't change. As you see later, I use the primary keys to create links with other tables (foreign keys). You are a lot better off if you don't have to re-establish the foreign keys. This is the reason that a lot of organizations ask their developers to use meaningless codes as primary keys. Because they don't have any meaning, there is no reason for them to change. These meaningless codes are sometimes referred to as surrogate keys. Databases such as INFORMIX-OnLine make it easy to use surrogate keys with specific data types such as serial to help create serial numbers for your primary keys.

Connectors

Connectors are used to represent relationships between tables. In RIM, all relationships are binary. This means that at one time, only two tables can be related. Because there can only be two tables related, a line is a convenient way to represent connectors. Additionally, the RIM supports only what is usually referred to as one-to-many connectors (one-to-one connectors are a subset of one-to-many). This implies that all your other relationships must be reduced to one-to-many. You will see how to represent various situations that you might encounter.

One-to-Many Binary Connector

One-to-many binary connectors are the most common connectors. These are called one-to-many because the maximum connector on one end is N (for many), and the maximum connector on the other end is 1. The following two examples are considered one-to-many, even though the minimum connectivities are different. An example of a one-to-many connector is shown in Figure 43.8.

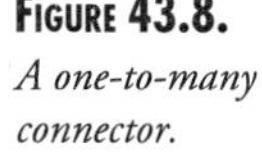

A one-to-many connector.

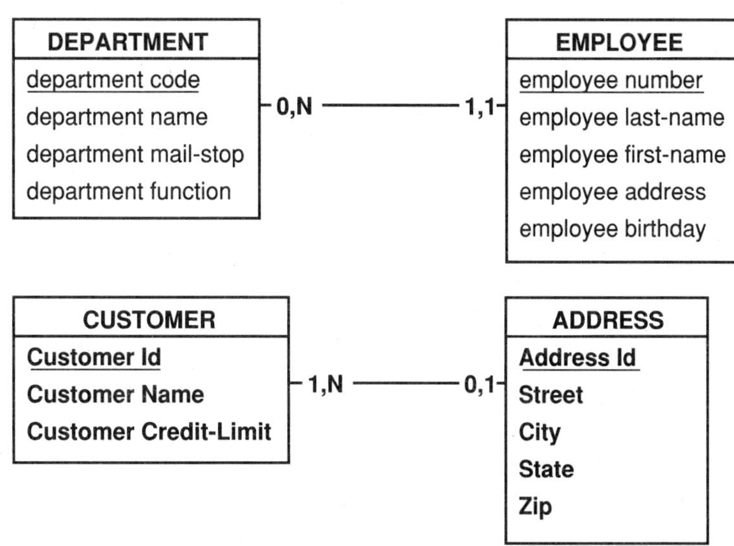

One-to-One Binary Connector

In the example in Figure 43.9, the maximum connectivities on both directions are 1—hence the name *one-to-one connector.*

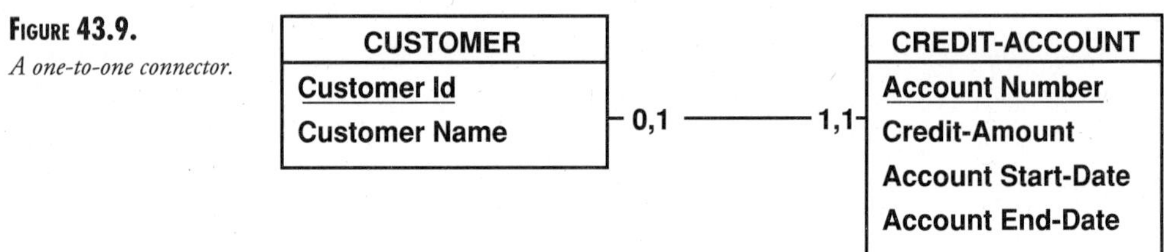

FIGURE 43.9.
A one-to-one connector.

This example depicts the fact that not all customers have credit accounts, and if they do, they can have only one credit account. You can examine other variations of one-to-one connectors in the "Columns in One-to-Many Relationship Tables" section, later in this chapter.

One-to-Many Recursive Connector

At times, a table might be related to itself. The one-to-many recursive connector structure is used to represent hierarchical structures such as organizational charts and family trees.

Figure 43.10 indicates that an employee does not have to have a supervisor (for employees at the top of the organizational chart) but can have at most one supervisor. The recursive connector indicates that the supervisor is also an employee. An employee might supervise no employees (for employees at the bottom of the organizational chart or, as one of my clients calls us, individual contributors). This structure works only for hierarchical organizations. For matrix structures and other organizational structures, you need a different structure for the data model.

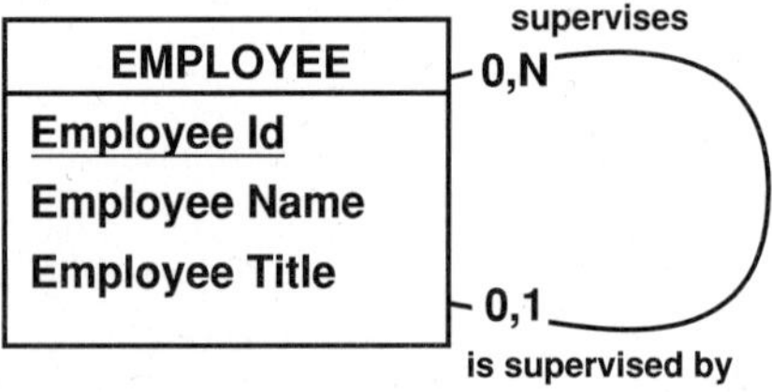

FIGURE 43.10.
A recursive connector.

Key Dependency

Before you proceed to the more complex relationships, you need to understand the concept of key dependency. In all the examples of tables you have seen so far, all the tables had their own primary keys. Sometimes, a table does not have its own key, and other times, a table's key is not enough for uniqueness. In these situations, you use key dependencies. For example, in Figure 43.11, you can say that line number is not unique (because every order has a line number 1).

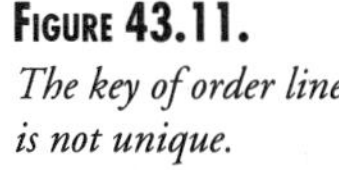

FIGURE 43.11.
The key of order line is not unique.

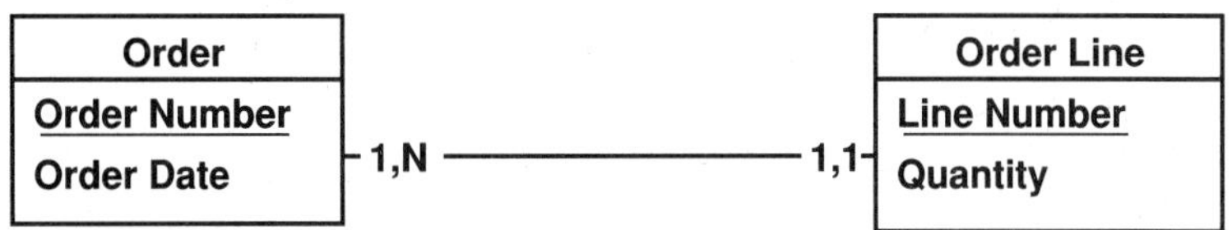

Within the context of an order, the line number is unique. In other words, if the primary key of order line is the combination of the primary key of order (order number) and the primary key of order line (line number), then the key is unique. In the notation, the way you specify that a table is dependent on another table is by underlining the `1,1` connectivity. You use underlines because that is the same symbol you use to denote a primary key. Essentially, Figure 43.12 is specifying that the order line gets its key from the order table.

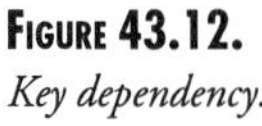

FIGURE 43.12.
Key dependency.

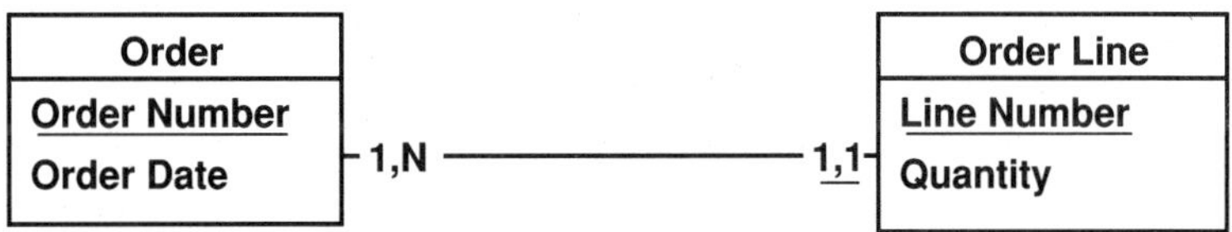

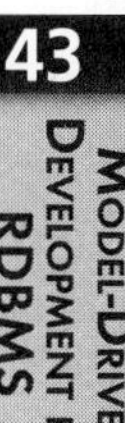

In the notation, you should not type in the order number column in the order line table. In RIM, columns are local to a table. It is obvious in Figure 43.13 that the two columns called Name in the tables represent totally different facts.

FIGURE 43.13.
An example of "same" columns.

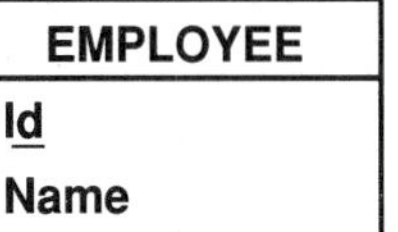

One Name column represents the employee's name and the other represents the vendor's name. The fact that they are in different boxes (tables) makes it easy for most people to understand this. Extending the same logic to the example in Figure 43.11, if you type an order number into the order line table, it is not the same order number as the one from the order table. Of course, after you generate foreign keys for order line, you have order number as part of the primary key as well as the foreign key.

You have seen how to depict tables that get their keys from other tables. You are ready to go on to more complex relationships.

Many-to-Many Relationship

A many-to-many relationship occurs when the maximum connectivity for both tables linked by the connector is N. If you want to represent the fact that a customer can own many bank accounts and a bank account can be owned by many customers (joint accounts), you cannot model it as shown in Figure 43.14.

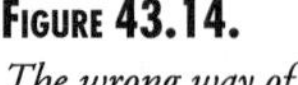

FIGURE 43.14.
The wrong way of representing many-to-many relationships in RIM.

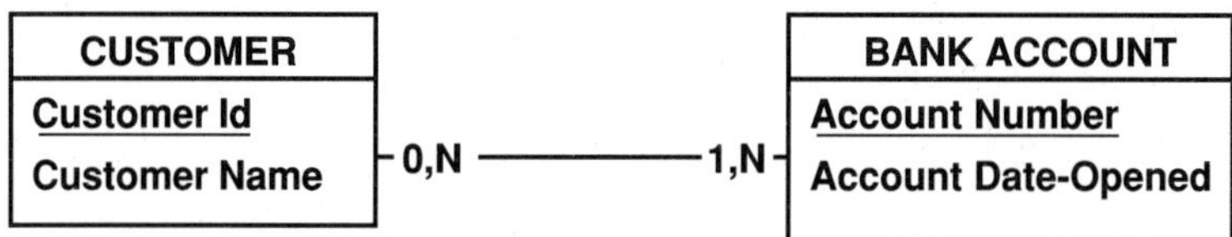

This structure cannot be implemented in relational databases. The only type of connectors that can be implemented in a relational database are ones with one-to-many connectivities. Remember that one-to-one connectivities are a subset of one-to-many connectivities. The reason for this limitation is obvious when you get to the section on foreign keys. The bottom line is that many-to-many connectivities must be reduced to one-to-many connectivities so that you can implement the models in a relational DBMS.

The way you should depict the model in Figure 43.14 is to change the many-to-many connectivities to two one-to-many connectors and represent them as shown in Figure 43.15.

FIGURE 43.15.
Representing many-to-many relationships.

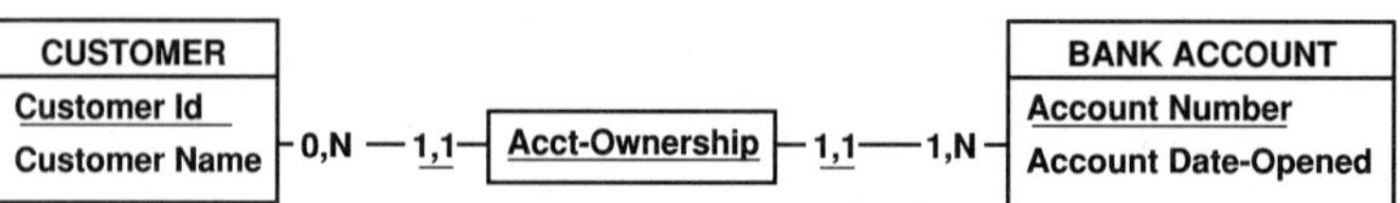

What you do is "reduce" the many-to-many connectivity to two one-to-many connectors. You can now implement this structure without any problem. The new table introduced as a result of trying to resolve the many-to-many relationship is referred to as a *relationship table.* It is also sometimes called an *intersection table.* A relationship table does not have its own keys. As denoted by the key dependency, the key of the relationship table is a combination of customer ID (the primary key of customer) and account number (the primary key of account). This is usually the case in many-to-many relationships. A relationship table does not have its own keys but inherits the keys from the tables it is related to.

Ternary Relationship

You can use the concept of relationship tables to reduce ternary (or three-way) relationships, too. Suppose you want to specify that an employee can be involved in zero or many projects and zero or many activities. A project must have at least one employee and one activity but can have many employees and many activities. An activity can have zero or many employees and can be used for zero or many projects. You can use a relationship table and specify it as shown in Figure 43.16.

The same concept can be extended to four-way relationships and n-way or n-nary relationships.

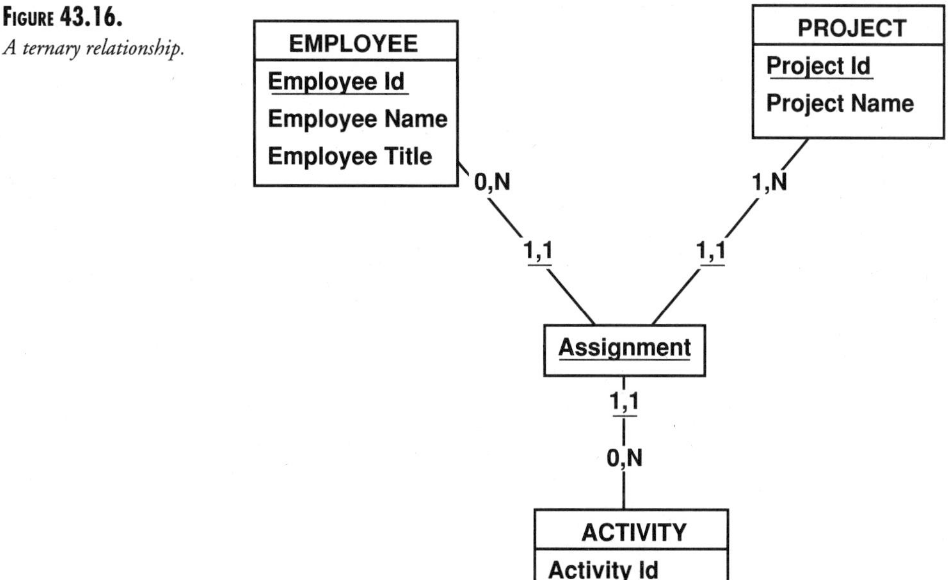

FIGURE 43.16.
A ternary relationship.

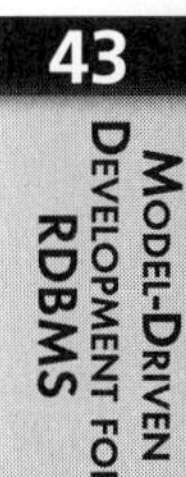

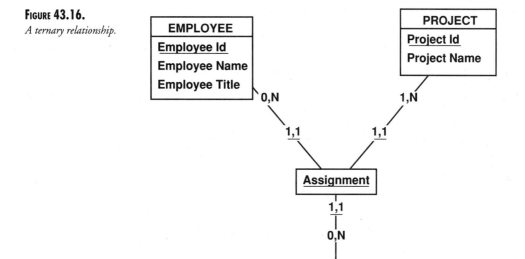

Columns in Many-to-Many Relationship Tables

Sometimes, there are columns whose values are defined by information in more than one table. In Figure 43.15, if you assume that different customers can own different percentages of the account, you need a column called percent owned in the model. You cannot put this new column into the customer table because a customer can own many accounts. You cannot put this into the account table because an account can be owned by many customers. The most appropriate table in which to include this column is the relationship table Acct-Ownership. In summary, the columns that go into the relationship table are columns that are dependent on all the tables connected to the relationship table. In Figure 43.17, the column percent owned is put into the relationship table.

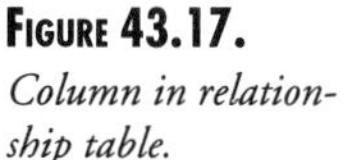

FIGURE 43.17.
Column in relationship table.

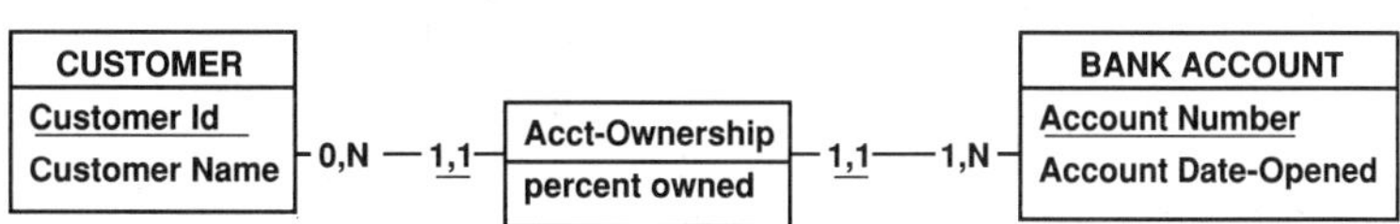

For the ternary relationship shown in Figure 43.16, if you want to keep track of the number of hours an employee spent on a project doing a particular activity, you can add a column called number of hours in the relationship table assignment. Figure 43.18 illustrates this.

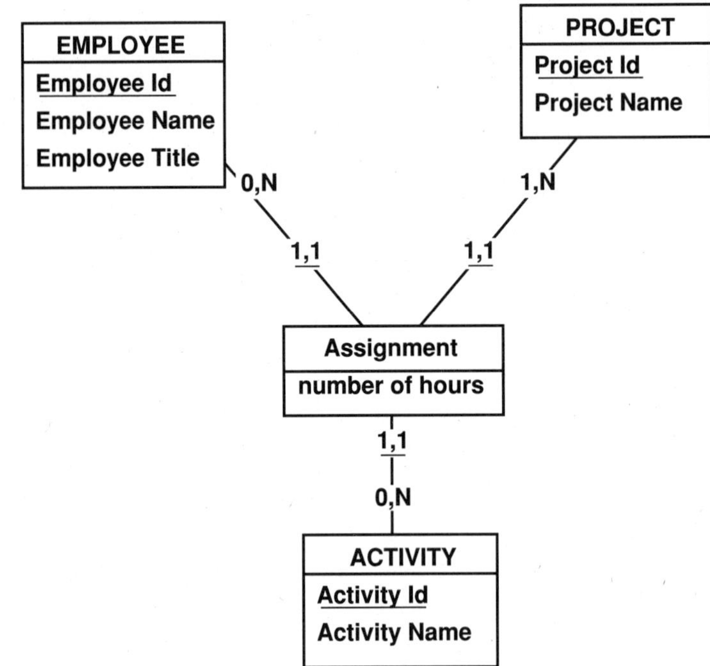

FIGURE 43.18.
A column in the ternary relationship.

The key point to remember when using columns in relationship tables is to make sure that the column is dependent to all the tables linked to the relationship table.

Columns in One-to-Many Relationship Tables

Sometimes, it is necessary to use relationship tables in one-to-many connectivities. This is usually best when you have a minimum connectivity of 0 on both ends of the connector. For example, a business rule states that an employee might be involved in, at most, one project but need not be involved in any project. Also, a project could have no employees assigned (before the project is initiated) but could have many employees assigned. You want to keep track of two columns—date assigned to project and date done with project. Remember that these dates are valid only for employees assigned to project. You cannot put them into the employee table because of the uniformity rule. You also cannot put them into the project table because a project can have multiple employees assigned. Figure 43.19 illustrates the correct way of modeling this.

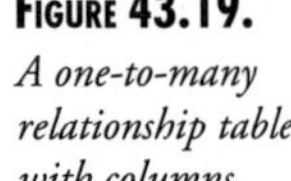

FIGURE 43.19.
A one-to-many relationship table with columns.

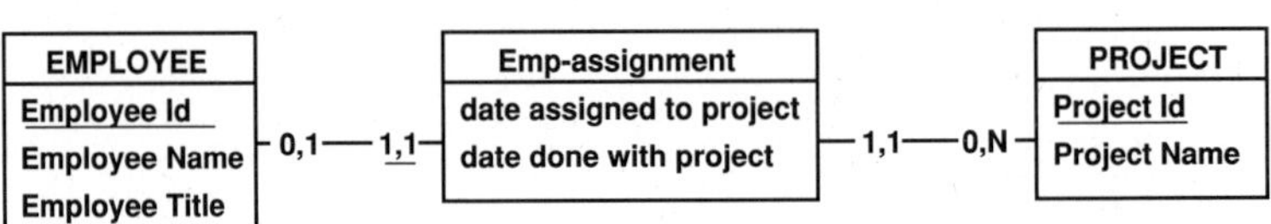

As you can see from Figure 43.19, it is very clear what columns are applicable to all employees and what columns are applicable to employees assigned to a project. In other words, it is obvious which columns are applicable if the relationship happens.

I have seen several cases where experienced modelers put the columns that I have in the relationship table into the employee table. There are a couple of problems with this. One is the clarity of the model. In the model, it is not clear which columns apply to all employees and which ones apply to just employees involved in a project. The other issue is that every application accessing the data must be aware of the fact that these two columns do not apply to all employees but only to employees assigned to a project. If 20 applications access this database (which is possible with data warehouse applications), every one of these applications must be aware that the two columns are not applicable for every instance of the table.

Also note that in Figure 43.19, the relationship table is dependent on only the employee table for its key. Because an employee can be involved in at most one project (I wish this were true in my company), the employee ID is enough to make the key of Emp-assignment unique. If the rules are different and you say that an employee can be involved in many projects, the key of the relationship table is key-dependent on both tables.

Many-to-Many Recursive Relationship

The next sample relationship is very similar to the many-to-many relationship you saw in Figure 43.15, Figure 43.17, and Figure 43.18, but the relationship is recursive. This can define any type of multidimensional structures such as matrix organizations, bill of materials structures, project team compositions, and so on. Suppose you want to define a table of products that can be used to make other products. If you want to track how many units of each product are used to manufacture other products, you can use a structure similar to the one defined in Figure 43.20.

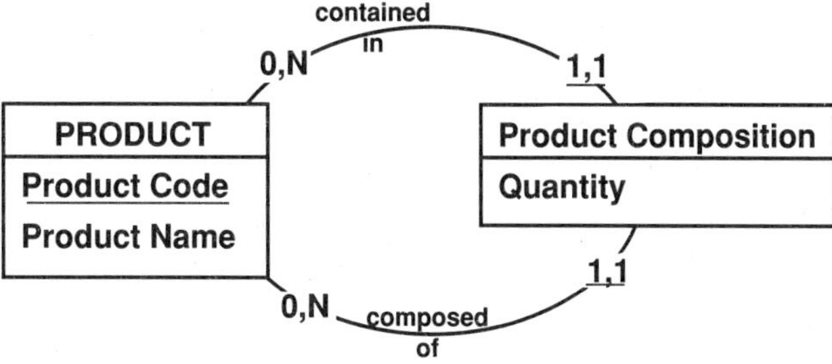

FIGURE 43.20.
A many-to-many recursive relationship.

A similar structure can model "matrix" organizations and other complex structures. These structures are extremely flexible for keeping track of various combinations and permutations of relationships.

You can add a lot more flexibility to these recursive relationships by creating another table that keeps track of relationship types—for example, if you want to track all types of relationships among employees. The relationship might be a reporting relationship, a project member relationship, a sibling relationship, the fact that an employee changed his name, a spousal relationship, and so on. Adding a time factor to the key structure also helps you keep track of changes in relationships over time. Figure 43.21 gives you a structure that helps with these requirements.

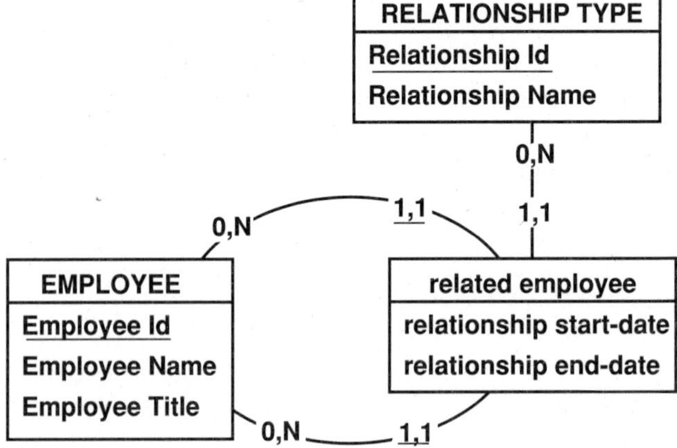

FIGURE 43.21.
The structure to support any type of relationship between employees.

This structure supports any type of relationship between employees. If you need to track a type of relationship that does not currently exist in the organization, all you need to do is add another row in the relationship table. You do not have to change the structure of your model, which implies that you do not have to alter the structure of your database.

If you want to track the relationships among employees over time, you have to make the relationship start-date column part of the key.

Subtypes (Specialization)

The concept of subtypes has become very popular in information modeling. Subtypes are used when you have some columns that are common to all instances of a table and other columns that are applicable only under certain situations. Another reason to use subtypes might be to keep track of various states of a table. I start with the most classical of subtype structures and then examine some variations. I discuss a couple of issues. The tables involved are usually referred to as subtypes or supertypes. The type of relationship is referred to as specialization or generalization, depending on which direction you are going. When you create subtypes from the columns of the supertype table, it is usually referred to as *specialization.* If you create the supertype table by picking the common columns from a group of tables, the process is called *generalization.* Either way, you end up with a special type of relationship that you use a little triangle to represent. (See Figure 43.22.) The triangle indicates that the relationship between the involved tables is a supertype/subtype relationship. The supertype is also referred to as the generic table because it contains the common columns. The subtypes are referred to as specialized tables because they contain the specific columns applicable for each specialization. It is important to understand the connectivities associated with specialization.

If you want to keep track of employees and certain employees have some specific columns that are not applicable to all employees, a subtype/supertype structure is the most appropriate.

Figure 43.22 indicates that all employees have an employee ID, employee name, and employee title. It also indicates that a manager has two specific columns—budget and sales quota—that are applicable only to managers. For consultants, you are interested in keeping track of the rate, unit for rate, and tax ID. You do not have specific attributes for a regular employee.

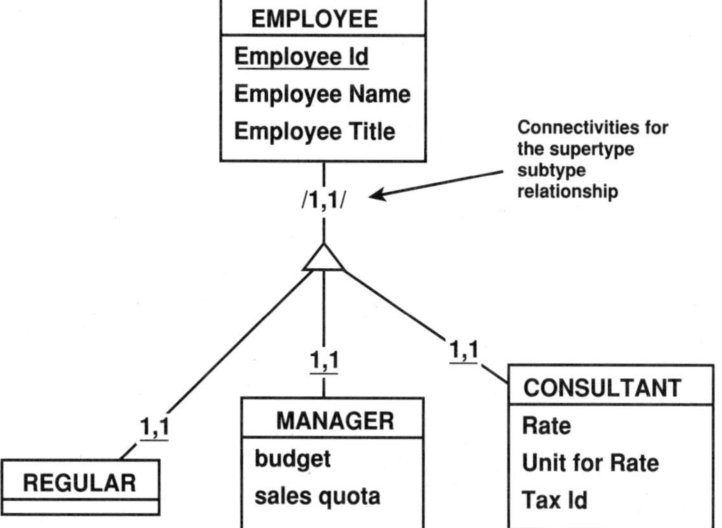

FIGURE 43.22.
An example of a subtype structure.

A note on the specialization connectivities: You put them in slashes just to graphically differentiate these connectivities from other connectivities. In Figure 43.22, the minimum connectivity of 1 indicates that all employees are a regular employee, a manager, or a consultant. The maximum connectivity of 1 indicates that an employee can be only one of the three options.

A regular employee does not have any additional columns. In this case, it does not make sense to keep an empty table in the model. If you remove the empty entity, you must update the connectivities of the specialization to be optional. Figure 43.23 is the new model.

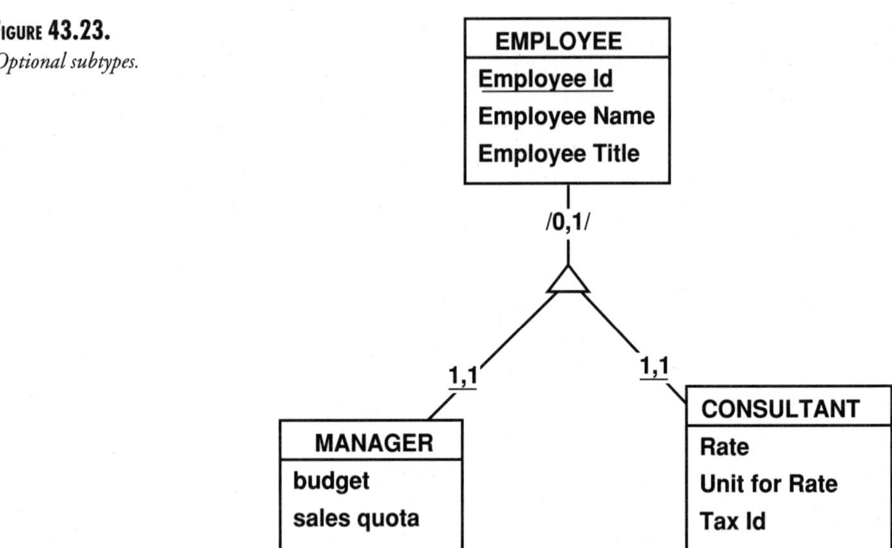

FIGURE 43.23.
Optional subtypes.

The minimum connectivity of 0 for the supertype/subtype relationship implies that an employee need not be a manager or a consultant. The maximum connectivity of 1 specifies that you can either be a manager or a consultant but not both.

Change the rules once more and say that an employee can be a manager and a consultant at the same time. Again, all you have to do is change the connectivities to reflect the new rules. Figure 43.24 shows the result of the change.

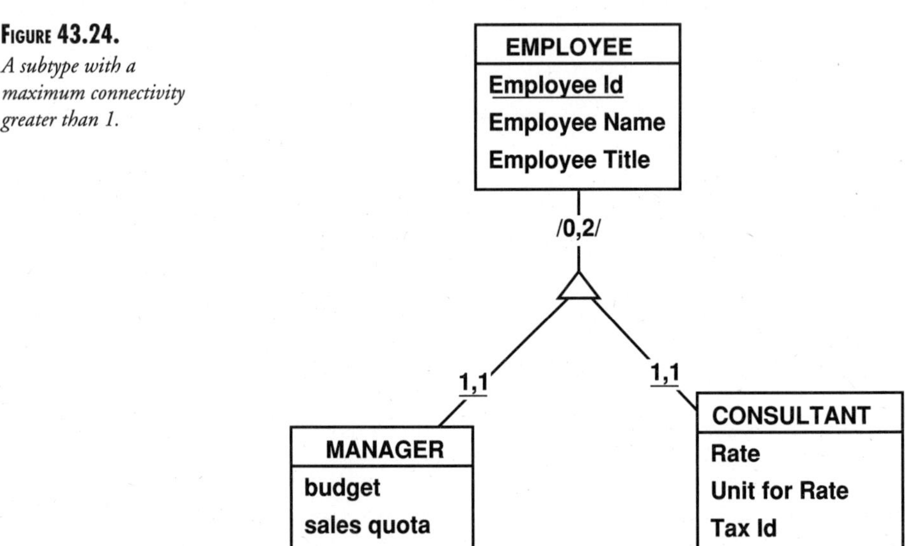

FIGURE 43.24.
A subtype with a maximum connectivity greater than 1.

The ease with which you can change the business rules is also a testimonial to the notation I chose. In most notations, you cannot depict these variations in rules for subtypes.

Conditional Connectors (Mutually Exclusive Connector)

At times, you need a mutually exclusive connector. This is used when you have a choice of using connectors with more than one table, but you have some restrictions on how a table can be connected to the other. For example, if an order can be placed by a customer or an employee but not both at the same time, this qualifies as a mutually exclusive connector. Again, you use the connectivities to clarify the rules.

Figure 43.25 indicates that an order must belong to an employee or customer (minimum connectivity is 1) and the order can belong to either a customer or an employee (the maximum connectivity for the conditional is 1). To differentiate the conditional connectivities from the others, you put them in brackets. If the maximum connectivity for the connector is 1, the relationship is said to be *mutually exclusive.* If the maximum connectivity is more than one, the relationship is *mutually inclusive.* Because this notation can be used to support both mutually inclusive and exclusive relationships, you cannot call the relationship mutually exclusive. An example of a conditional connector is shown in Figure 43.25.

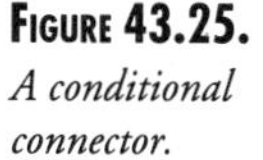

FIGURE 43.25.
A conditional connector.

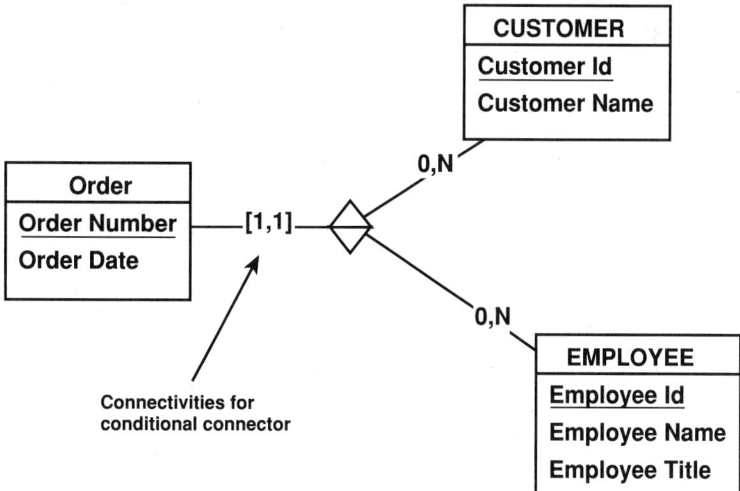

Two Common Problems

Before I discuss the things you need to do to implement these models in INFORMIX-OnLine, I want to discuss two concepts I have seen a lot of my clients struggle with.

Multiple Connectors Between the Same Tables

It is possible to have multiple business relationships between the same table. In that case, you need multiple connectors between the same tables. As an example, suppose you want to document the fact that a department can have many employees. Assuming that department heads are also employees, keeping track of the department head warrants another connector between the two tables involved. Figure 43.26 illustrates this.

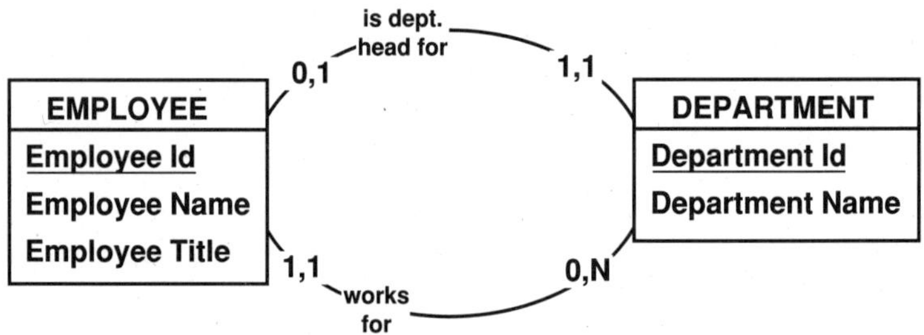

FIGURE 43.26. *Multiple connectors between the same tables.*

In Figure 43.26, the connectivities are different for each connector. Sometimes this is not the case. For an order, if you want to keep track of the salesperson (who is an employee), the shipper (who is an employee), and the person who authorized the order, then you need three connectors between the same set of tables, as shown in Figure 43.27.

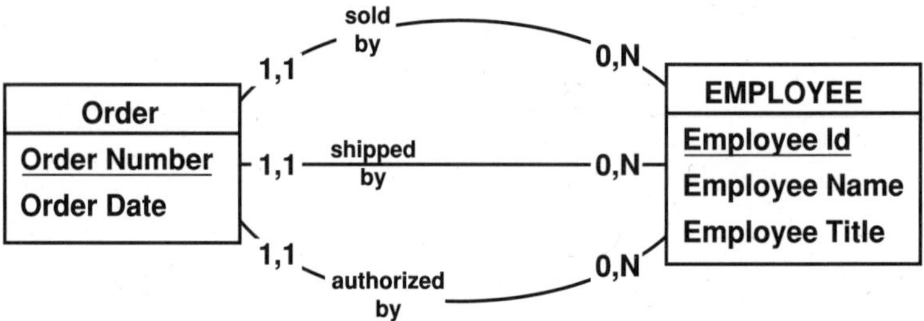

FIGURE 43.27. *Another example of multiple connectors between the same tables.*

In this case, the connectivities are the same between the tables, so it is very important to label the connectors.

Modeling Reality

While modeling, it is important to remember that the only way you get quality models that are stable is by making sure you model reality or facts. This is not as easy as it sounds. Most database systems I encounter use different tables for storing information about customers and vendors. When a customer is also a vendor, such as when I teach a class at the bank where I have my accounts, I end up repeating the same information such as name, address, phone, and so on. This is not necessary if the information was modeled and implemented correctly. Suppose that in the model I am represented as a person with columns such as name, address, phone, and so on and stored only once. Then, I have a role as a customer and another role as a vendor. I do not have to repeat the personal information for every role I take. Reality-based modeling is not hard to pick up, but you have to change the way you think about things around you. In most cases, our thinking comes from an application perspective probably because that is how our deadlines are based. When you look at things from an application perspective, you have a skewed view of things. Take things outside of the application context and you are on your way to building good models. This is one instance where taking things out of context helps. Do not confuse the view I am asking you to take with the scope of the models. In most cases, the scope of the model might be for the project but your view is global. In other words, you are concerned about the tables needed for the project, but you model them with an organizational perspective.

Implementing Models in INFORMIX-OnLine

The hard part is building the models using the concepts discussed previously. When the semantic part is done, you have to follow a few steps to implement the model in INFORMIX-OnLine. The following steps are usually automated by most CASE tools. The order of these tasks is not important:

- Create physical names for tables and columns.
- Create domains and data types for columns.
- Specify foreign keys.
- Create indexes if necessary.
- Add referential integrity constraints.
- Create triggers and procedures if needed.
- Add physical constructs such as dbspaces for tables and indexes, fragmentation clause for tables and indexes, extent size for tables, lock mode, and so on.
- Generate the DDL.

For the purposes of this chapter, I discuss the concepts of physical names, domains and data types, foreign keys, and some DDL that can be generated. For the purposes of this chapter, I do not discuss specifying referential integrity (other than foreign keys), triggers, procedures, and the physical constructs.

Create and Generate Physical Names

Syntactically physical names should obey the length limitations of the RDBMS and use only legal characters (no spaces). Additionally, most organizations have some standard abbreviations that are used in constructing the physical names. For example, the organization might have a list of abbreviations such as those provided in Table 43.1.

Table 43.1. Abbreviation list.

Word	*Abbreviation*
Customer	Cust
Number	Num
Organization	Org
Employee	Emp
Department	Dept
Address	Addr
Account	Acct

A column in the model that is named account number has a physical name of `acct_num`.

Specify Domains and Data Types for Columns

In this step, you specify the length, precision, null or not null status, default value, and list of values or range of values for all columns. These can be specified as domains, which are reusable across the organization. After you specify the domains, you can specify the data types to be used with the domains. After you specify the domains, data types, and physical names, your employee table might look like the one in Figure 43.28.

FIGURE 43.28.
A table with physical names, domains, and data types.

EMP				
emp_id	Id	SERIAL		NOT NULL
emp_name	Name	CHAR	(40)	NULL
emp_title	Name	CHAR	(40)	NULL

Listing 43.1 contains the corresponding DDL code generated.

Listing 43.1. DDL generated.

```
CREATE TABLE EMP
  (
    emp_id              SERIAL NOT NULL,
    emp_name            CHAR(40),
    emp_title           CHAR(40),

    PRIMARY KEY (emp_id)
      CONSTRAINT emp_pri
  );
```

Specifying Foreign Keys

One way of looking at a foreign key is as a physical implementation of the connector. In the database, the way you specify that a table is connected to another is by using a foreign key. In the model, you specify that a table is connected to another by using a connector. When you have the graphical connectors, you can generate foreign keys based on the connectivities. Figure 43.29 shows a model fragment without a foreign key.

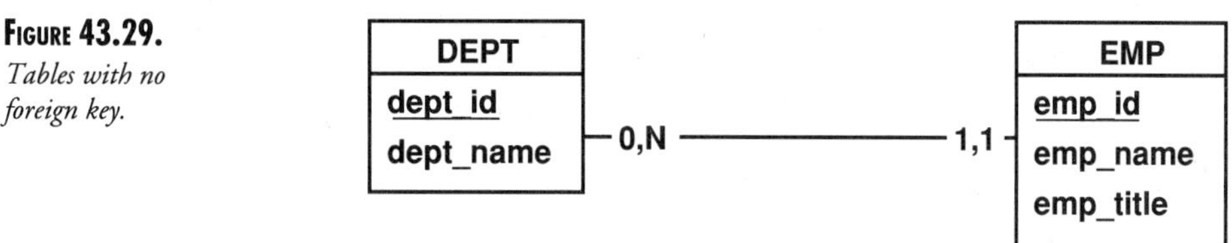

FIGURE 43.29.
Tables with no foreign key.

Figure 43.30 shows the model with a foreign key generated.

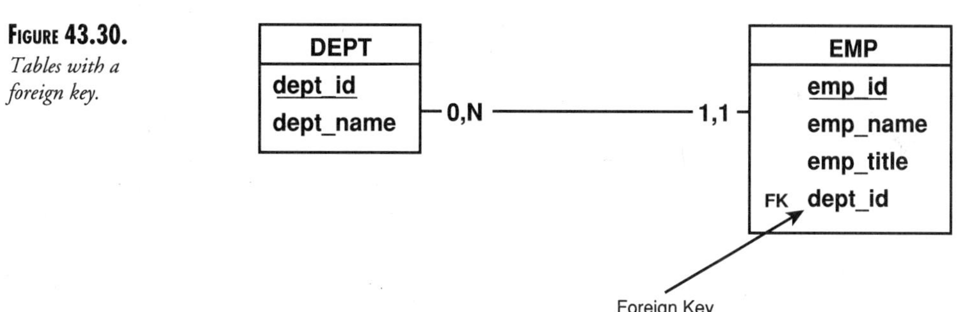

FIGURE 43.30.
Tables with a foreign key.

To graphically differentiate the foreign keys from other columns, you use a prefix of FK. I now illustrate the fact that the foreign key implements the functionality of the connectivity. The minimum connectivity of 1 for the EMP (employee) table says that an employee must belong to a department. This is implemented by making the foreign key `dept_id` not null. The maximum connectivity of 1 is implemented by the fact that you have one column. The maximum connectivity of N from the DEPT (department) table is implemented by making the foreign key `dept_id` not unique.

Listing 43.2 shows the code fragment generated for the two tables and the foreign key shown in Figure 43.30.

Listing 43.2. DDL generated for foreign key.

```
-----------------------------------------------------------
--CREATE TABLE DEPT
-----------------------------------------------------------

CREATE TABLE DEPT
  (
    dept_id              SERIAL NOT NULL,
    dept_name            CHAR(40),

    PRIMARY KEY (dept_id)
      CONSTRAINT pri_dept
  );


-----------------------------------------------------------
--CREATE TABLE EMP
-----------------------------------------------------------

CREATE TABLE EMP
  (
    emp_id               SERIAL NOT NULL,
    emp_name             CHAR(40),
    emp_title            CHAR(40),
    dept_id              INTEGER NOT NULL,

    PRIMARY KEY (emp_id)
      CONSTRAINT emp_pri
  );


--*********************************************************
--    FOREIGN KEY CONSTRAINT STATEMENTS
--*********************************************************


-----------------------------------------------------------
--ADD FOREIGN KEY CONSTRAINT works_for
--ON TABLE EMP
-----------------------------------------------------------

ALTER TABLE EMP
  ADD CONSTRAINT
  (
    FOREIGN KEY (dept_id)
      REFERENCES DEPT
        CONSTRAINT works_for
  );
```

Foreign Keys for Many-to-Many Relationships

When you create foreign keys for many-to-many relationships, the foreign key is also the primary key for the relationship table. Figure 43.31 shows a graphical representation.

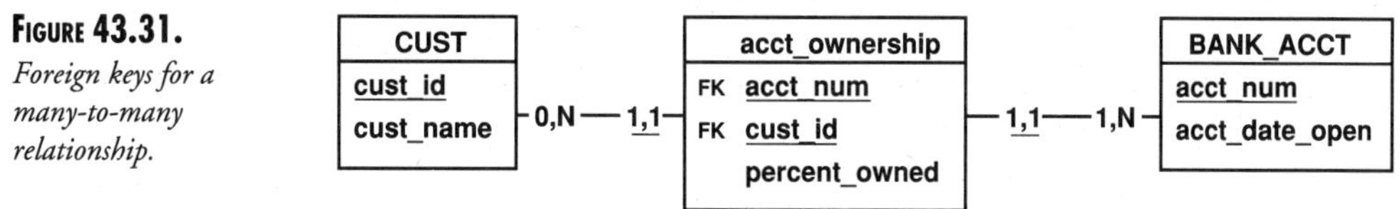

FIGURE 43.31.
Foreign keys for a many-to-many relationship.

Listing 43.3 shows the code fragment generated from the model in Figure 43.31.

Listing 43.3. DDL generated for many-to-many relationship.

```
-------------------------------------------------------------
--CREATE TABLE acct_ownership
-------------------------------------------------------------

CREATE TABLE acct_ownership
  (
    acct_num                INT NOT NULL,
    cust_id                 INT NOT NULL,
    percent_owned           FLOAT(3),

    PRIMARY KEY (acct_num, cust_id)
      CONSTRAINT pri_acct_own
  );


-------------------------------------------------------------
--CREATE TABLE BANK_ACCT
-------------------------------------------------------------

CREATE TABLE BANK_ACCT
  (
    acct_num                SERIAL NOT NULL,
    acct_date_open          DATE,

    PRIMARY KEY (acct_num)
      CONSTRAINT pri_acct
  );


-------------------------------------------------------------
--CREATE TABLE CUST
-------------------------------------------------------------

CREATE TABLE CUST
  (
    cust_id                 SERIAL NOT NULL,
    cust_name               CHAR(40),

    PRIMARY KEY (cust_id)
      CONSTRAINT pri_cust
  );
```

continues

Listing 43.3. continued

```
--*************************************************************
--    FOREIGN KEY CONSTRAINT STATEMENTS
--*************************************************************


-------------------------------------------------------------
--ADD FOREIGN KEY CONSTRAINT foreign_cust
--ON TABLE acct_ownership
-------------------------------------------------------------

ALTER TABLE acct_ownership
  ADD CONSTRAINT
  (
    FOREIGN KEY (cust_id)
      REFERENCES CUST
        CONSTRAINT foreign_cust
  );


-------------------------------------------------------------
--ADD FOREIGN KEY CONSTRAINT for_bank_acct
--ON TABLE acct_ownership
-------------------------------------------------------------

ALTER TABLE acct_ownership
  ADD CONSTRAINT
  (
    FOREIGN KEY (acct_num)
      REFERENCES BANK_ACCT
        CONSTRAINT for_bank_acct
  );
```

Similar rules apply for ternary relationships. Figure 43.32 shows a ternary relationship with foreign keys.

Foreign Keys for Subtypes

To implement subtypes, you need to add a type discriminator column. Additionally, you can use the primary key of the supertype as the primary key of the subtypes. The combination of the type discriminator columns and the foreign key allows you to implement this concept in any RDBMS. A representation of subtypes is shown in Figure 43.33.

The type discriminator indicates whether the employee is a manager, a consultant, or a regular employee. If the employee is a manager, you access the manager table, and because you use the same primary key as the employee table, you can use the key to look up the information for the appropriate manager.

FIGURE 43.32.
A ternary relationship with foreign keys.

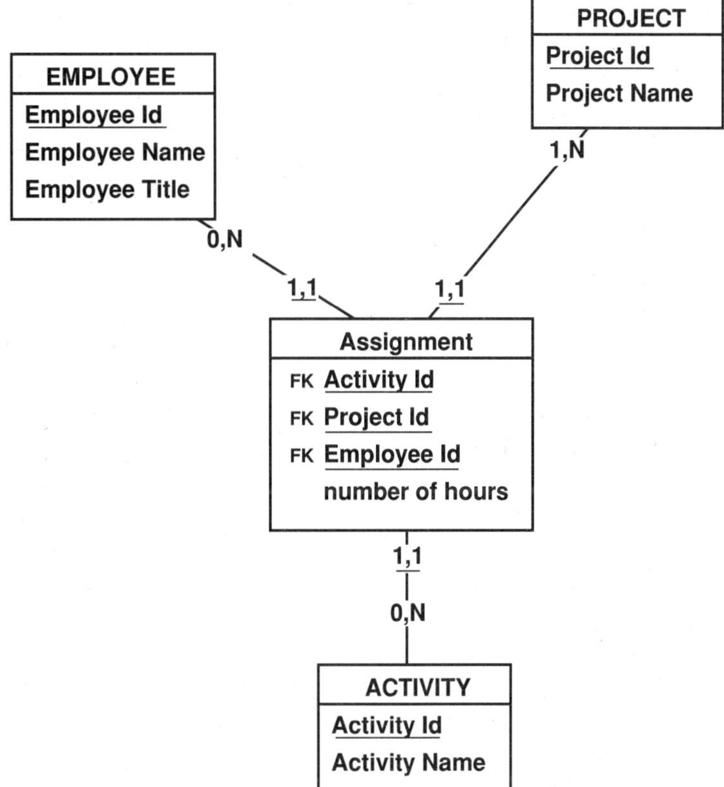

In cases when the maximum connectivity for the subtype relationship is more than one, it is easier to use more than one type discriminator to support all possible permutations of the subtypes. Figure 43.34 illustrates this.

According to the connectivities, an employee can be a manager, a consultant, both, or neither; using the two discriminator columns with boolean values satisfies all the possible conditions.

Foreign Keys for Conditional Connectors

To implement conditional connectors, you use another technique with foreign keys. Figure 43.35 illustrates the example you used earlier with foreign keys generated by SILVERRUN-RDM.

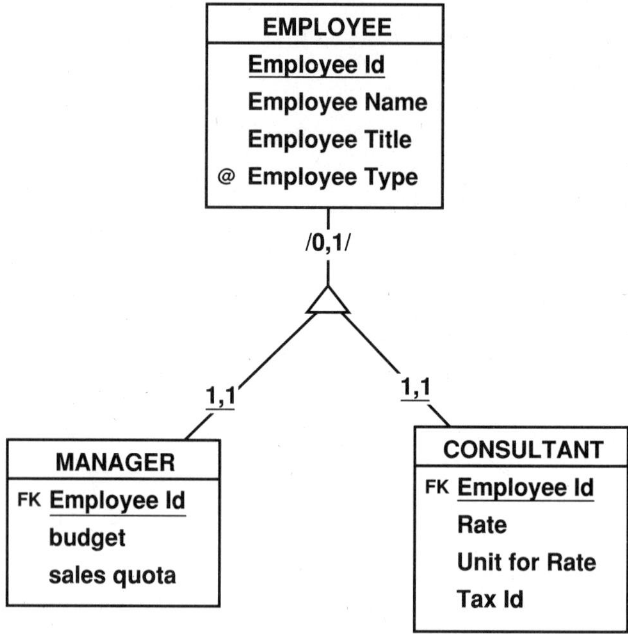

FIGURE 43.33. *Subtypes with foreign keys.*

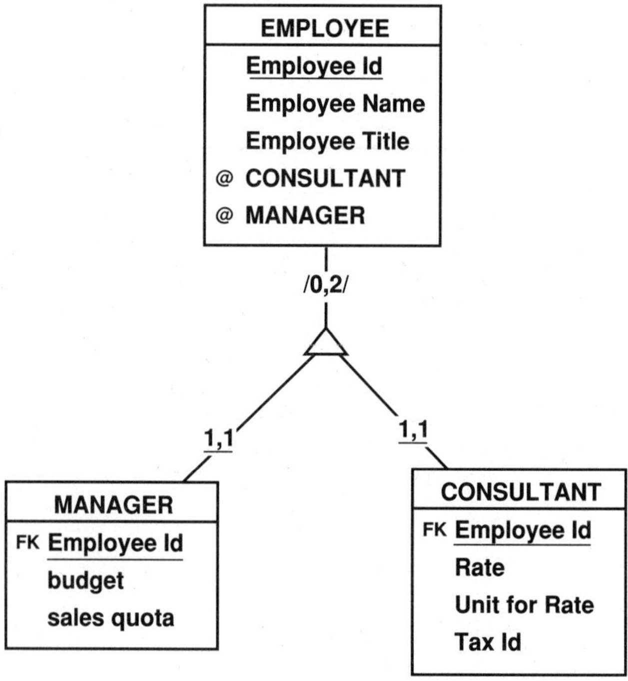

FIGURE 43.34. *Foreign keys for subtypes with maximum connectivity greater than 1.*

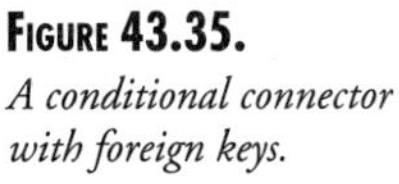

FIGURE 43.35.
A conditional connector with foreign keys.

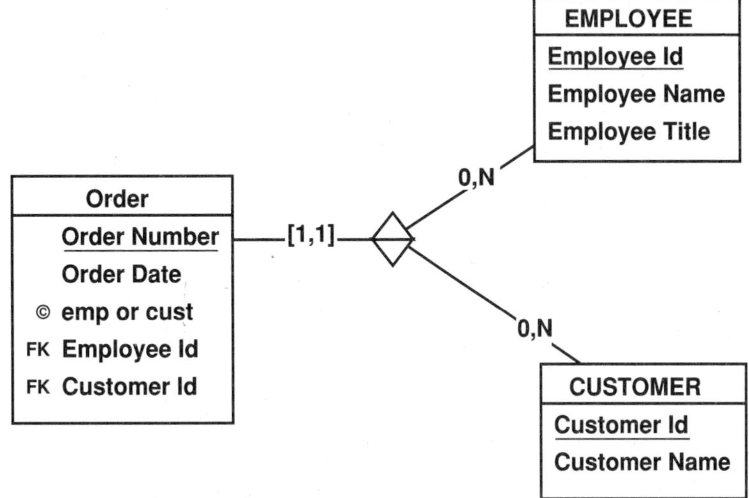

In this case, you use the choice discriminator column emp or cust to indicate whether the order is for an employee or the customer. If the choice discriminator indicates that the order is for a customer, the foreign key `Order.Customer Id` indicates which customer the order belongs to. If the choice discriminator indicates that the order is for an employee, the foreign key `Order.Employee Id` indicates which employee the order belongs to. Because this is a mutually exclusive connector, one of the foreign keys has a null value. This can be enforced easily with a constraint on the choice discriminator column.

Summary

This chapter discussed the major constructs in information modeling, which include tables, columns, primary keys, foreign keys and alternate keys, connectors, subtypes, and conditional connectors. I provided some sound techniques for putting together models using these concepts. If the model is a good one, implementing, maintaining, and enhancing your databases is easy. Although I did not discuss the theories behind these concepts, the techniques were tried and proven over the years at various organizations around the world. I am sure they will help you and your organization. Extensions to these concepts are sometimes referred to as extended relational modeling, which I did not discuss in this chapter.

CHAPTER 44

Designing and Implementing SuperViews for INFORMIX-NewEra

by Jim Prajesh

IN THIS CHAPTER

This chapter discusses the concepts behind designing SuperViews and also shows how to create and implement SuperViews using the SILVERRUN Relational Data Modeler (RDM) CASE tool. Because this is the only graphical SuperView designer that supports graphical design and generation and validation of both INFORMIX-OnLine and SuperViews, I used this tool to demonstrate the concepts involved with SuperViews. This chapter also builds on the concepts introduced in Chapter 43, "Model-Driven Development for the Informix RDBMS."

A View of a SuperView

A SuperView is a database-aware layer that provides an efficient online link between the client layer (forms, reports, and queries) and the database. This layer is needed to build enterprise-scale applications for various reasons. The information needed to build a form or a report might not be the same as the information stored in the database. For example, a form usually requires a subset of the information stored in the table. Additionally, the information needed for the form might come from multiple databases. A separate layer allows you to integrate data from multiple sources into a form, report, or query. To clarify the content of the client objects, you might need to use descriptive labels, lookup values, and so on. This can also be done at the SuperView level. You might need to create a different set of non-key joins for the form. It does not make sense to keep all these non-key connectors at the database level. From a maintenance perspective, it is best to keep only the primary key and foreign key joins at the database level and define other types of connectors at the SuperView level. Additionally, you might need to keep track of some extended attributes for displaying input. For these practical reasons, it makes sense to have this layer to build screen-based applications. Functionally, the SuperView provides the middle layer in a three-tier client/server application. Figure 44.1 provides a simplistic approach to looking at SuperViews and their usefulness in screen-based applications.

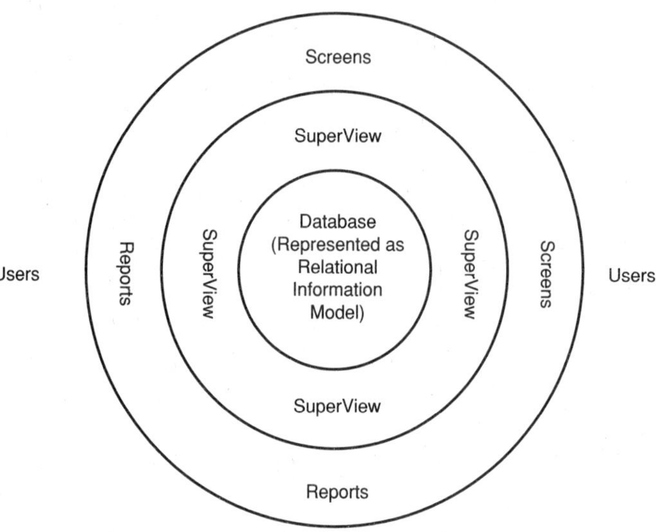

FIGURE 44.1.
A SuperView's role in application development.

Approaches to Building SuperViews

Based on the discussion in the previous paragraph, it should be obvious that a SuperView is a denormalized view of the database. You can also consider screens and reports as denormalized views of the database. You can take two approaches to come up with SuperViews and databases:

- View integration
- Database driven

One approach is to build the SuperViews (based on user needs) and then normalize the views and create the database structure. This is the approach in which a consultant visits all the users and spends months collecting each one of the user's views. When you have all the views, you then figure out what the users intend to do with the views, normalize the views, and create the database structure. This approach is sometimes referred to as *view integration.* A lot of the RAD-based (rapid application development) methodologies use this concept. Although RAD-based approaches might seem faster, primarily because you see screens first and therefore have the impression that something is delivered, the quality of the systems and the underlying database is usually compromised. You don't have a stable database structure and usually have to change the database structure every time a new user requests a new screen or a new report.

Although it might seem faster when you develop the first prototype or application, in the long run, you pay for this in database maintenance because of two reasons. One reason for the maintenance is that the data structure in the database might not be complete, and you have to modify the structure with new screens or SuperViews. Another reason is that organizations that use view integration to build databases tend to have many more tables than are necessary. The tables are built from an application perspective and do not support applications other than the ones they were designed for. When they need new functionality, most developers just add the tables they need when an existing table might suffice; either they did not know that an existing table could be used or they did not want the hassle of modifying the table structure and then modifying all the applications that use that table.

For example, I once found 65 tables in a human resources system used to maintain information about employees, but if they had designed the database correctly, they would have needed only 15 or 17 tables. Imagine the unnecessary amount of resources an organization spends in terms of people, money, time, hardware, and software because nobody bothers to come up with an integrated design. I only mentioned one small subject area within a system. Rapid does not necessarily mean quality and longevity, and a cleaner approach does not mean slow. Of course, you don't see any screens in the first two days of the project, but there is a lot more to a system than screens. The primary reason that rapid prototyping approaches fail is that when you build views, you look at the data from one person's or one application's perspective and not from an organizational perspective.

In the database-driven approach, you first model the database structure using the concepts and techniques described in Chapter 43. When you have that model, you can select the tables and connectors needed for a SuperView and separate them into a work area (referred to as *subschema* in SILVERRUN-RDM). You then modify the structure to remove columns you don't need and add other information such as labels. Because the database model is built with an organizational perspective, adding new SuperViews should not affect any changes in the database structure. This approach is also faster, and you end up with better systems.

Using SILVERRUN for Designing, Creating, and Implementing SuperViews

Although NewEra provides ViewPoint Pro as a tool to build SuperViews, I found SILVERRUN-RDM (SR-RDM) a lot easier and more flexible for complex systems. Here are some of the reasons for using SILVERRUN instead of ViewPoint Pro:

- SR-RDM provides a graphical representation of the database and the SuperView. This is a user-friendly way of defining SuperViews and also saves a lot of typing, which is especially useful for bad typists such as myself and most of my colleagues.
- SR-RDM provides a special work mode for INFORMIX-NewEra. When you select this work mode, the tool changes the menu structures and menu content with NewEra-specific information. This makes it easy for those of us familiar with NewEra concepts and cuts down on the learning curve tremendously.
- In SR-RDM, it is not necessary to redefine the relationships that already exist at the database level. If you build SuperViews directly in ViewPoint Pro, you end up redefining all the relationships again. In SR-RDM, you add only information you absolutely need at the SuperView level. If you did not design the database in SR-RDM, you can easily reverse-engineer an existing database, automatically bringing the existing relationships into SR-RDM. This is still a lot faster than creating them manually for each SuperView.
- The information about SuperView is represented in a concise format and is easy to understand, even for nontechnical folks. This makes it easy to validate the screen or report content before actually building it.
- When you design SuperViews, SR-RDM is not connected to NewEra dynamically. This makes the design phase faster and allows you to be more creative. After you are done with the design, you can connect to the database and create the SuperViews automatically.

- SR-RDM validates the SuperViews to make sure that they run against the specified database while respecting all the referential integrity rules. This synchronization is difficult to achieve in ViewPoint Pro.

Building and Implementing SuperViews Using SR-RDM

This section discusses the steps needed to design and implement SuperViews. The hardest part is coming up with the good model for the database layer. You can use the concepts described in Chapter 43; then, creating and implementing SuperViews is pretty close to trivial:

1. Have the database structure defined in SR-RDM.
2. Define the database-extended attributes.
3. Create non-key relationships, reorder columns, and add table or column comments if necessary.
4. Create SuperViews by selecting necessary tables.
5. Add SuperView-specific information such as specifying master tables, specifying SuperView-specific relationships, denormalizing columns, hiding columns not needed, and assigning SuperView-level extended attributes.
6. Verify SuperViews.
7. Transfer SuperViews from SR-RDM to Informix.

Defining the Database Structure

There are many ways you can design the database structure in SR-RDM. In this section, I discuss two of them. One way is to type the tables and columns into the tool. If you use an existing database to build NewEra applications, you should reverse-engineer the database into SR-RDM using the reverse-engineering facility that comes with SILVERRUN. If you create the model yourself, you should work in the RDM mode. Figure 44.2 shows the possible modes you could choose. For more help in creating tables, columns, connectors, and so on, refer to the documentation that is part of the help files installed with the version of SR-RDM included on the CD-ROM accompanying this book. Note that although SR-RDM allows for a number of various notations, I used the notation discussed in Chapter 43.

Assuming that you built the generic data model, you can now switch to the NewEra work mode to put NewEra-specific information into the model. After you switch the work mode, the tools palette and some of the menu options change. As you enter only the New Era-specific information, note that the palette is much smaller when in NewEra mode. Notice the changes in Figure 44.3.

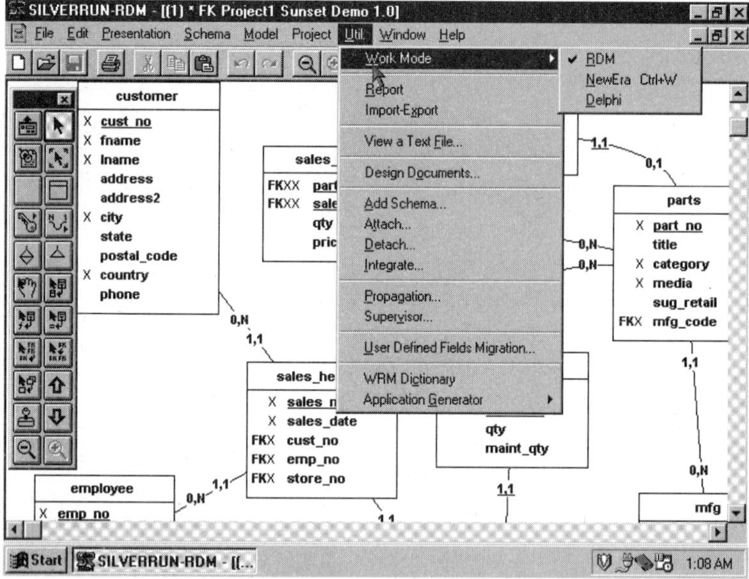

FIGURE 44.2.
Different work modes in SR-RDM.

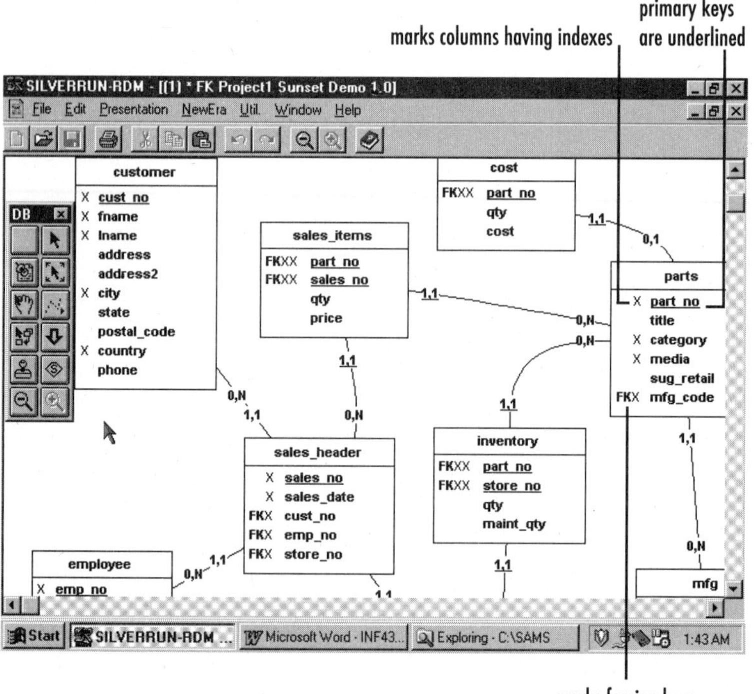

FIGURE 44.3.
After switching to NewEra mode in SR-RDM.

Please note that this level is the database level. This is evident by the DB on the tools palette. Figure 44.4 provides a summary of the tools in the tools palette for NewEra.

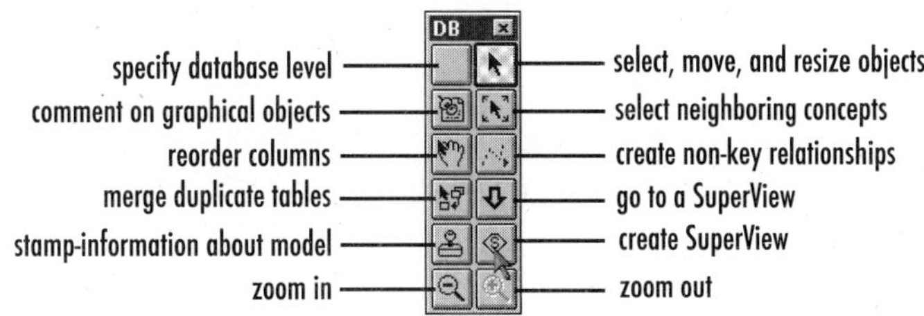

FIGURE 44.4.
Details of the tools palette.

After you switch to the NewEra mode, you can then add the NewEra-specific information. You can do this by double-clicking a table or connector or accessing the NewEra menu option. When you access the NewEra menu options, you notice that in Figure 44.5, certain options are grayed out. These options are available only at the SuperView level.

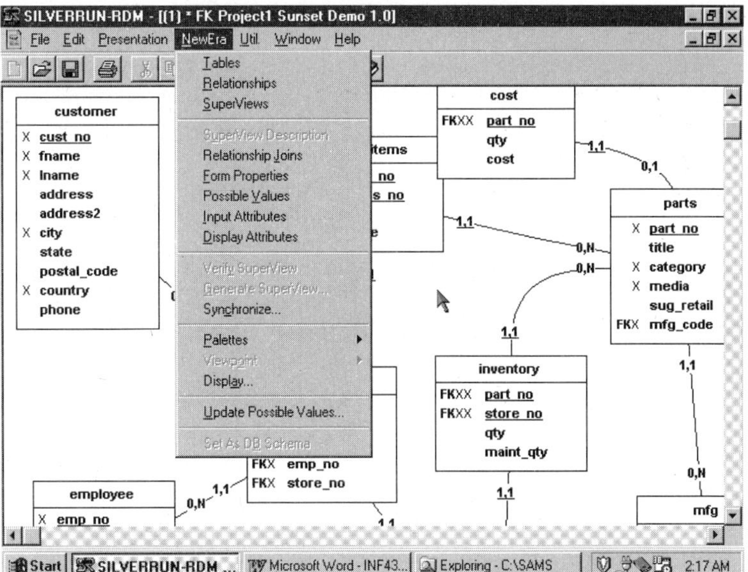

FIGURE 44.5.
Details of the NewEra menu.

Putting in the Extended Attributes

Now you are ready to enter the NewEra-specific attributes. These are primarily NewEra aliases for tables, columns, and connectors (which are now called relationships), form properties, input and display attributes, and possible values for a column.

Table Aliases

At the table level, you can assign a corresponding NewEra alias for a table. By default in SR-RDM, the NewEra alias is the same as the name of the table in the database. Of course, you can change it by typing a new name. The screen for entering table aliases is shown in Figure 44.6.

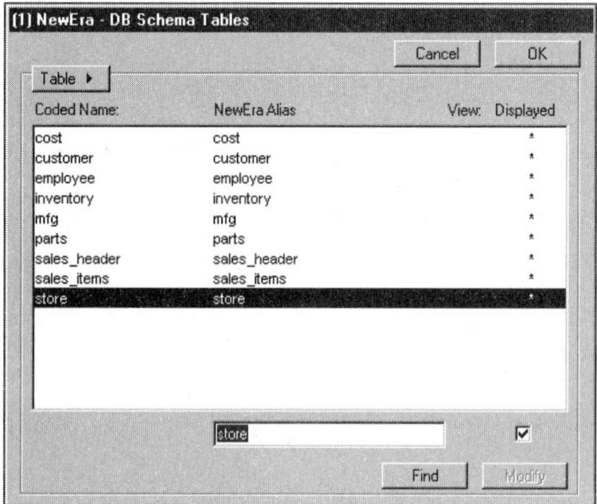

FIGURE 44.6.
The screen for entering table aliases.

Column Aliases, Labels, and Titles

To enter the aliases, labels, and titles for columns, select the NewEra|Form Properties menu option. You get a list of the columns in your database schema, such as the one shown in Figure 44.7.

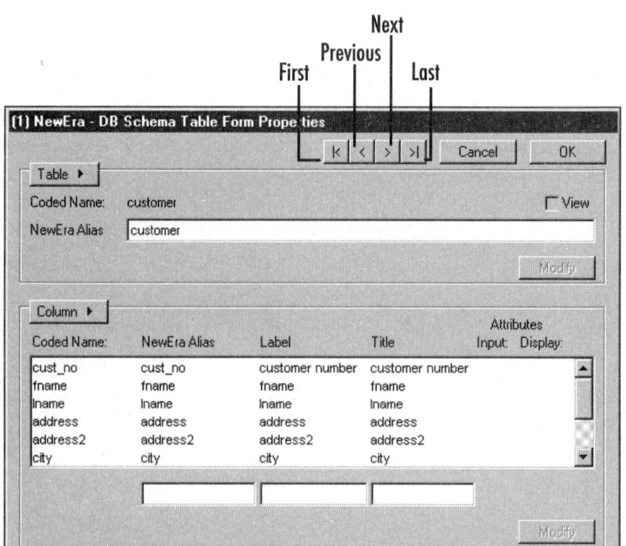

FIGURE 44.7.
The screen for entering column aliases, labels, and titles.

Notice that SR-RDM provides the default values for these concepts. You need to type in only the ones you want to change. To change the descriptors for the column, select the columns, enter the appropriate information, and click the Modify button.

Default Display Rules

Specify the display rules for the columns if necessary. Specifying the display rules at this level gives you the default rules for the SuperView level. Select a column from the screen in Figure 44.8, and from the drop-down menu, pick default display attributes.

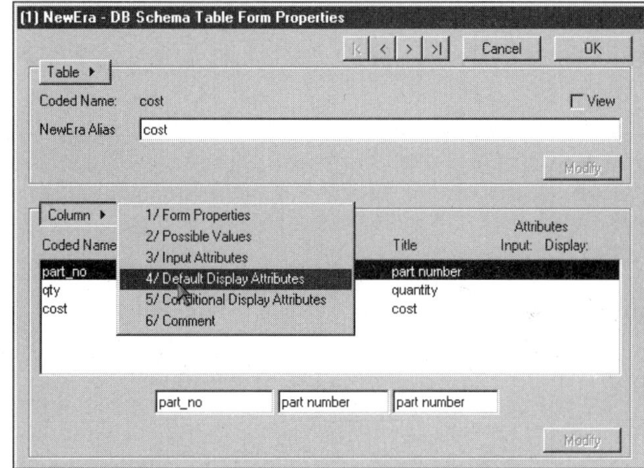

FIGURE 44.8.
The screen for accessing the default display rules for columns.

After you select this, you can enter the default display options. These options are also carried over to the SuperView level and can be overridden either by certain conditions or at the SuperView level. Figure 44.9 shows the options available for the default display properties.

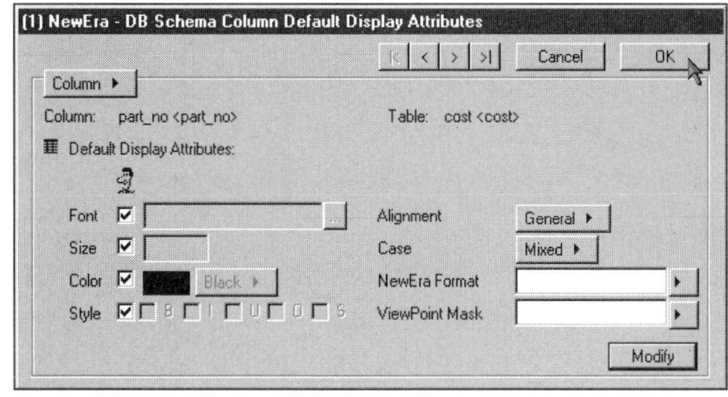

FIGURE 44.9.
The screen for entering the default display rules for columns.

To enter your preference for the various options, uncheck the boxes and put in the various values for font, color, format, size, and so on. If the checkbox is checked, the default preferences in ViewPoint Pro are used.

Conditional Display Rules

For each column in the database level, you might want to specify some value-based display options, called *conditional display rules.* For example, you might want to specify that if the customer is from NY state, the color should be set to red. Figure 44.10 shows you how to specify this in SR-RDM.

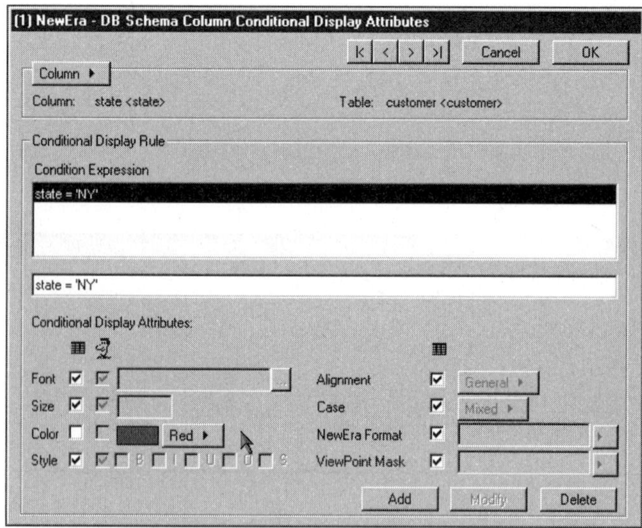

FIGURE 44.10.
Conditional display rules for columns.

These rules are useful to visually distinguish certain columns for various reasons. For example, you might need to charge sales tax for NY residents only. Using a different color might make it easy for the data entry person to remember this.

Input Attributes and Possible Values for Columns

Input attributes and possible values can also be kept as NewEra-specific attributes so that all SuperViews can use the same rules for columns. You can enter them into SR-RDM and reuse them at the SuperView level. Figure 44.11 shows the panel to enter the input attributes.

Define Global Non-Key Relationships

If you believe that non-key relationships will be used, you can specify them at the database level. This way, you do not have to specify the same rule for each SuperView. For example, if you never want to look at parts whose price is less than the cost (I am not saying this rule makes sense), you might want to specify this as a rule at the database level using non-key relationships. In SR-RDM, a primary key and foreign key relationship is denoted by a solid line and a non-key relationship is denoted by a dotted line. Figure 44.12 shows an example of a non-key relationship.

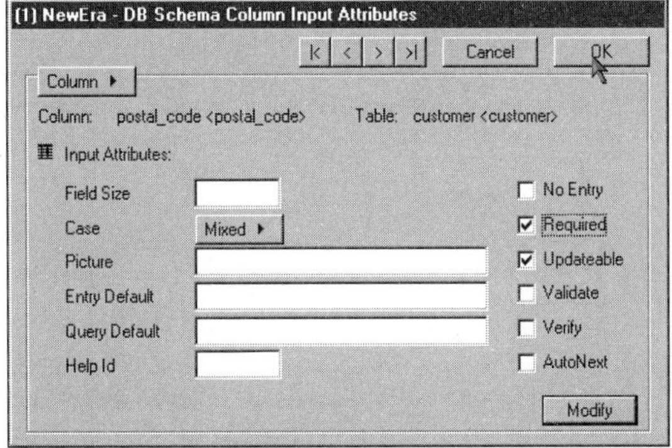

FIGURE 44.11.
Input attributes for columns.

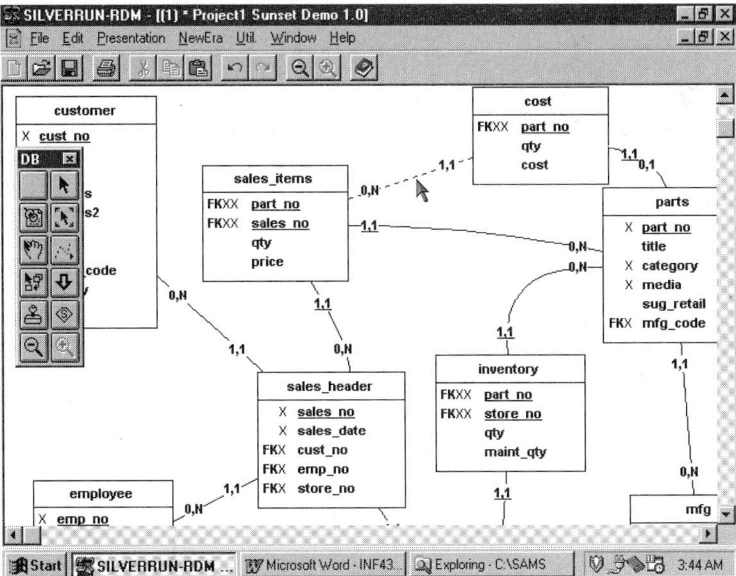

FIGURE 44.12.
Non-key relationships are indicated with dotted lines.

You can then specify the rules for the non-key relationships by double-clicking the connector. After you do that, you see the screen shown in Figure 44.13 where you can specify the join conditions.

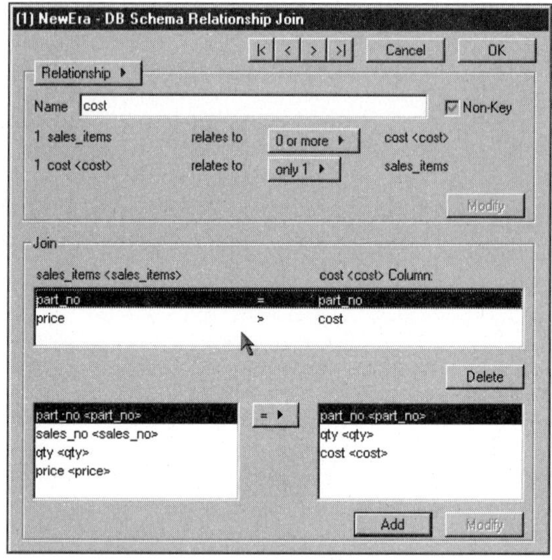

FIGURE 44.13.
Specify the non-key relationship conditions.

Transfer Extended Attributes from and to Informix

After you enter all the default properties you might need for the SuperView, you can then transfer these rules to the Informix database so that these attributes appear in ViewPoint Pro. Similarly, if the database already has extended attributes, you can just reverse them into your model. You need the ODBC drivers for Informix to make the connection so that you can forward or reverse the extended attributes. To get to the connection screen shown in Figure 44.14, select NewEra|Synchronize.

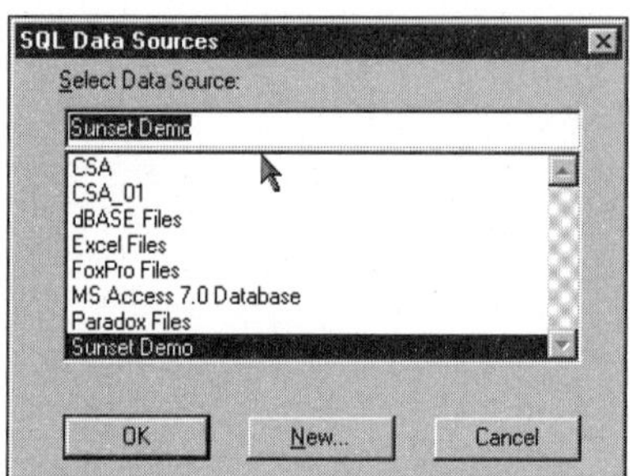

FIGURE 44.14.
Connecting to the database and transferring extended attributes from and to SR-RDM.

Defining the SuperView Structure

In this section, you see how to create SuperViews in SR-RDM, how to enter SuperView-specific information, and how to update the database to transfer the SuperViews to the database so that you can paint screens and reports based on the SuperViews.

Creating a SuperView

To create a SuperView, you first must select all the tables and connectors you use in the SuperView. You can use a special tool to select an object and its neighboring elements. This tool and the result of the selection are shown in Figure 44.15.

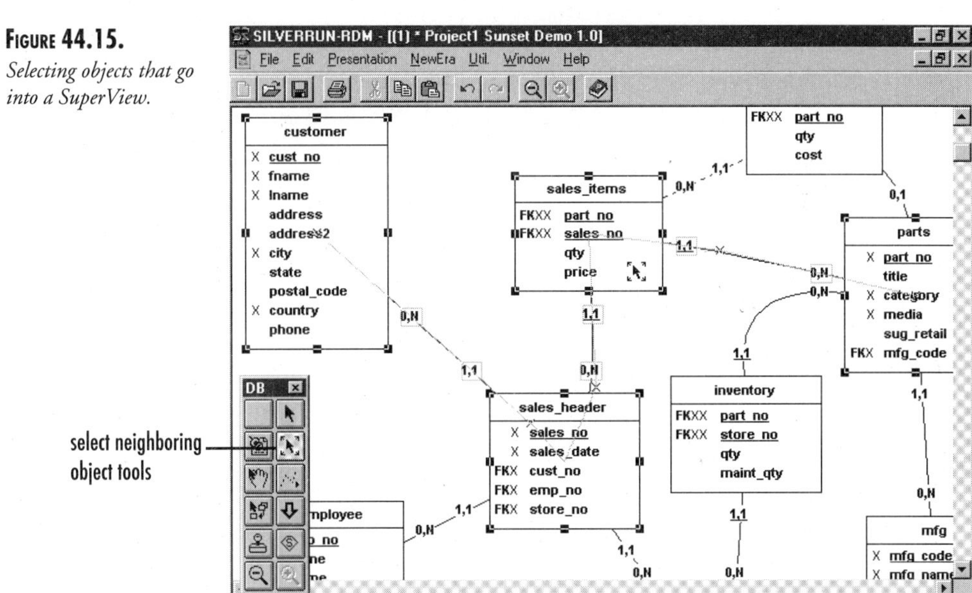

FIGURE 44.15.
Selecting objects that go into a SuperView.

Then you click the Create SuperView icon. SR-RDM prompts you for the name of the SuperView. You can provide a name for the SuperView, and you have a schema with just the objects you selected for the SuperView. See Figure 44.16 for the result of creating a graphical SuperView.

Note that the tools palette changed, and there are tools you might need at the SuperView level. Figure 44.17 gives you a summary of the tools palette for the SuperView level.

Adding Details to a SuperView

You are now ready to add some SuperView-specific information. Some of the information is similar to the information at the database level. You might need to specify similar information at this level if it is different from the database level. For example, suppose that for most cases, you want the input format for currency to have two places after the decimal points, but in one case, you want five places after the decimal point. You should specify the column with two places after the decimal point at the database level and override it for one SuperView that needs a higher level of precision.

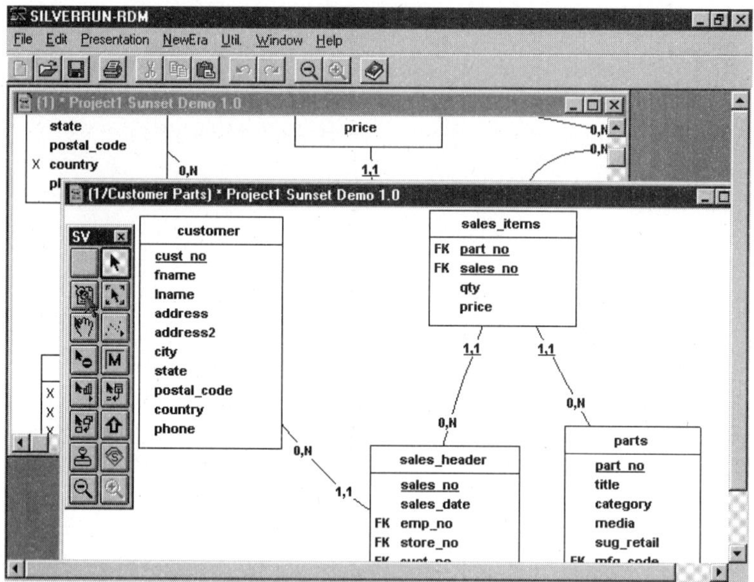

FIGURE 44.16.
A graphical representation of a SuperView.

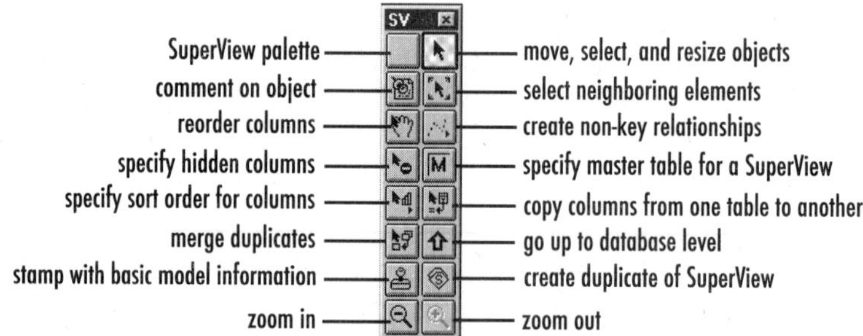

FIGURE 44.17.
The SuperView tools palette.

Specifying the Master Table in a SuperView

When you first create a SuperView, no master table is selected. You have to manually specify the master table and SR-RDM figures out the children table levels automatically. You choose the master table by using the Master Table tool and clicking the master table. After you do this, SR-RDM puts an M next to the name of the table to graphically denote which table is the master as well as the different levels. Figure 44.18 shows the results after picking the master table.

The master table and the tables with the levels L1 through L*n* are considered anchor tables. Tables numbered N1 through N*n* are considered neighbor tables.

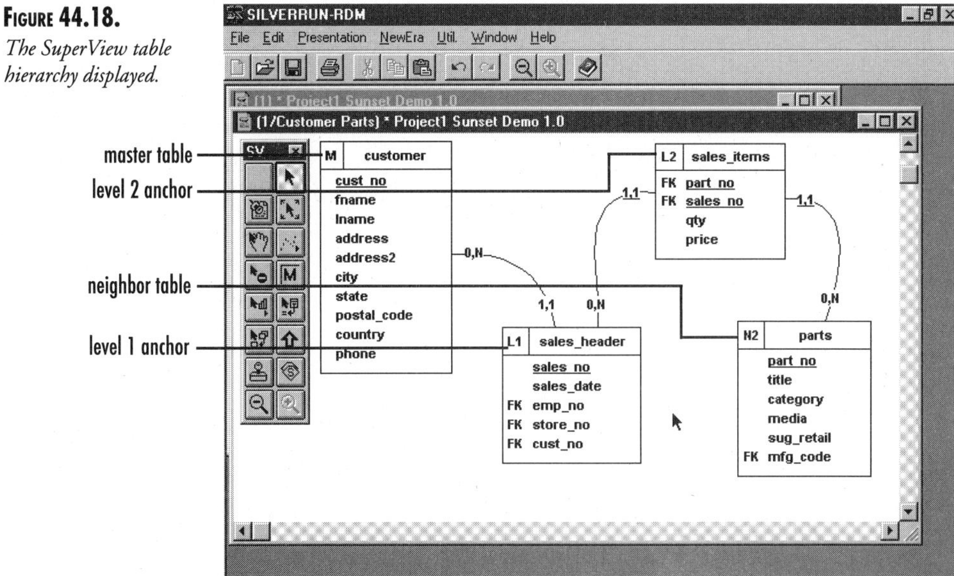

FIGURE 44.18.
The SuperView table hierarchy displayed.

Specifying Hidden Columns and Sort Order for a Column

In a SuperView, you need not use all the columns in a table. In SR-RDM you can hide a column at the SuperView level. When a column is hidden, it is not available to the screen painter. Using the Hide column tool, you just click the columns you want to hide. Figure 44.19 shows the graphical representation of columns not used in the screen.

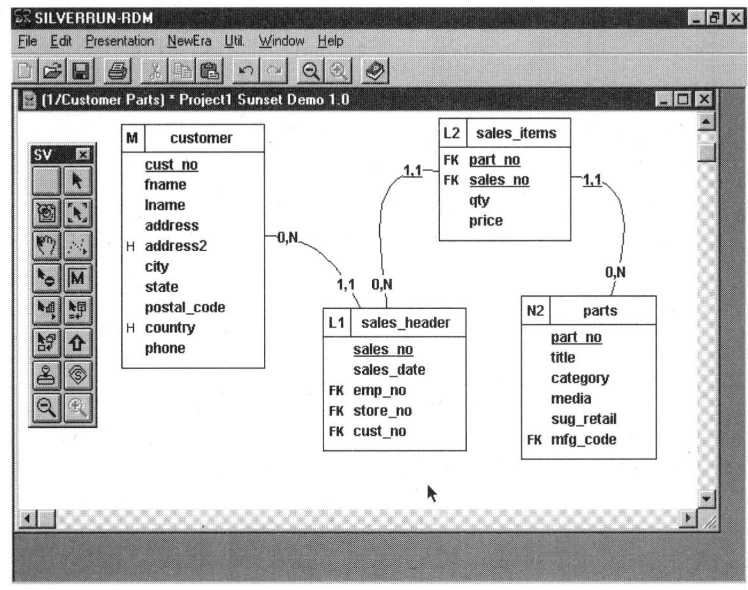

FIGURE 44.19.
The customer table has the `address2` *and* `country` *columns hidden (denoted by a prefix H).*

You can also delete a column from the SuperView. Deleting a column in the SuperView is irreversible. If a column is deleted and you want it back, you have to bring the whole table into the SuperView and specify the column rules again. If you want to unhide a column, all you need to do is click the column with the same tool.

To specify the sort order for columns, use the Sort Columns tool. The default sort order is ascending. To change it to descending, click the right mouse button on the icon, pick the descending icon, and tag the columns in the order you want. Figure 44.20 shows that in the customer table, `lname` and `fname` are sorted by ascending order.

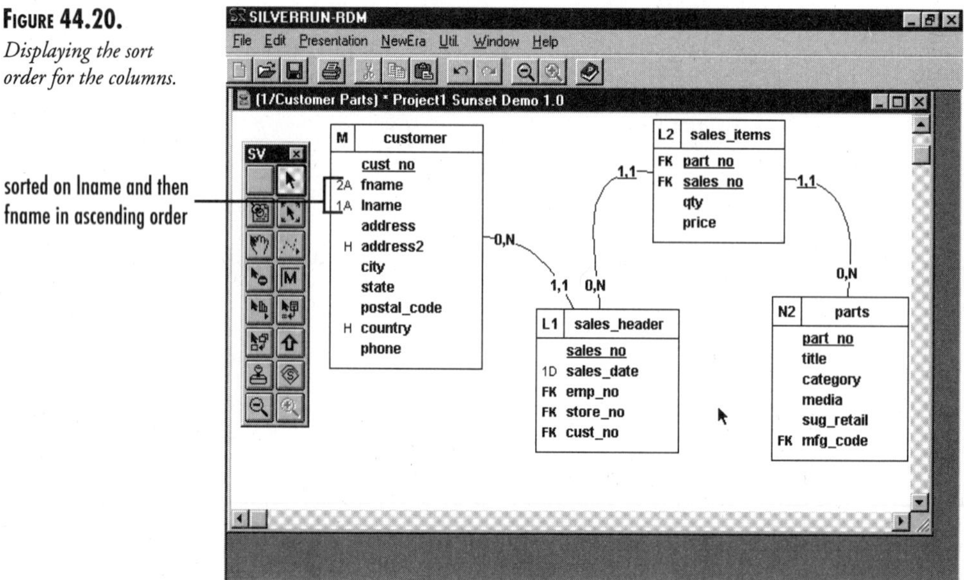

FIGURE 44.20.
Displaying the sort order for the columns.

In Figure 44.20, you see that in the customer table, the sort order is `lname` and then `fname` by the numbers. The suffix of A indicates that it is an ascending sort. In the sales header table, the sort for `sales_date` is descending.

Copying Columns from Neighbor Tables into Anchor Tables

The only columns available for screens and reports from a SuperView are the columns in the anchor tables. If you want columns from the neighbor tables, you must copy the desired columns into the anchor tables using the Derive by Copy tool. Figure 44.21 shows the tool and the fact that the sales_items table has two columns from the parts table.

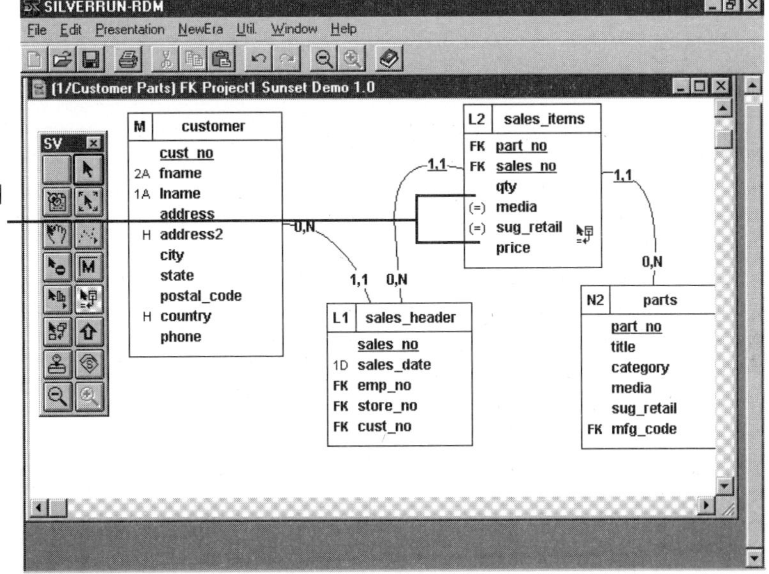

FIGURE 44.21.
Copied columns from neighbor tables into anchor tables.

Specifying Other Rules at the SuperView Level

Other rules such as display attributes, input attributes, possible values, conditional display rules, labels, titles, and NewEra aliases can be specified or overridden exactly the way you did it at the database level. Refer to the "Putting in the Extended Attributes" section, earlier in the chapter, for this information.

Verifying and Generating the SuperView

I highly recommend that you verify the SuperView to make sure that you will not have problems when you implement it. SR-RDM has a menu option that performs this task for you. If there are errors, a log file is generated. You can then view or print this file.

Duplicating SuperViews

Sometimes, you might have multiple SuperViews that use the same tables and connectors but might have some small differences. These differences might be the columns that are hidden, a different sort order, or other minor differences. In these situations, it might be easier to make a copy of an existing SuperView and then make the minor changes as opposed to creating a SuperView from the beginning. To do this, while you are in the SuperView you want duplicated, just click the Duplicate SuperView icon. SR-RDM asks you for the name of a new SuperView and then copies the existing SuperView as a new one.

Deleting SuperViews

To delete a SuperView, you must go to the database level, select NewEra|SuperViews, and delete the one you do not want. Figure 44.22 shows the screen to do this.

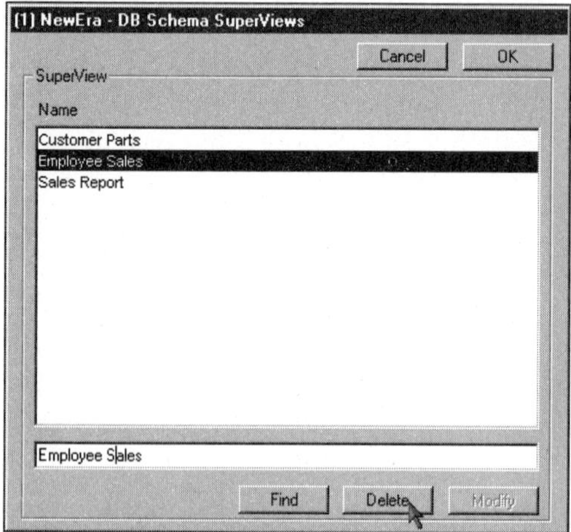

FIGURE 44.22.
Deleting SuperViews from SR-RDM.

Updating SuperViews in the Informix Database

When you are satisfied with the design of the SuperView, it is time to implement the SuperView in Informix. Again, you use an ODBC connection to connect to the database. When you are connected to the database, you have the option of generating selected SuperViews in the Informix database. This interface also provides a list of the existing SuperViews, which can then be reverse-engineered into SR-RDM. You can also delete SuperViews from Informix using the screen in Figure 44.23.

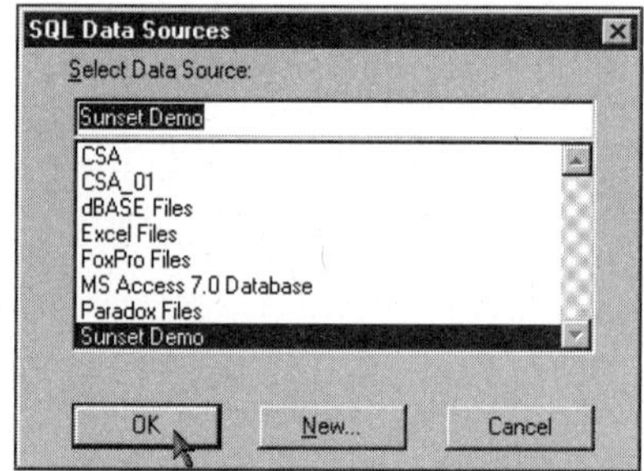

FIGURE 44.23.
Implementing SuperViews from SR-RDM.

Summary

This chapter discussed the need for and the uses of SuperViews in Informix database management systems. Although the concept of the SuperView is powerful, it is not very easy to create one manually. Using SR-RDM makes it easy to create SuperViews and update the database. This way, when you are ready to build the interfaces, you already have the SuperViews on which you can build the screens and reports. All in all, the SR-RDM tool provides an efficient way for designing and implementing SuperViews.

CHAPTER 45

Modeling Types for INFORMIX-Universal Server

by Jim Prajesh

IN THIS CHAPTER

What Is INFORMIX-Universal Server?

In this chapter, I briefly discuss the major concepts you need to understand to build models and generate code for INFORMIX-Universal Server. The INFORMIX-Universal Server (from now on referred to as IUS) is the first of what is expected to be the "next wave" of data storage and retrieval technology. The database technology used is usually called Object Relational Databases. As you will see in the following sections (assuming you continue to read on), this technology enables you to use concepts that you are already familiar with in relational technology and additionally has support for certain concepts from object-oriented techniques. The SQL committee, ANSI, and ISO will include these concepts in the standard currently called SQL3. As was the case with SQL-92, vendors will come out with databases using the new "standard" before the standard is officially published.

Because I discuss some concepts used in object orientation in this chapter, I use a notation called Unified Modeling Language (UML) for the diagrams. This notation is becoming the de facto standard for modeling object-oriented concepts and is initially being defined by the Rational Corporation. I used the SILVERRUN tool to create the diagrams used in this chapter.

Advantages of INFORMIX-Universal Server

In INFORMIX-Universal Server, you can still use the concepts that you use in standard relational technology. This capability is a big advantage because it implies that you do not have to rebuild your existing systems. Because backward compatibility with existing systems and support for building new systems with the older technology will be maintained, the cost of taking advantage of the Object Relational technology in terms of retraining employees can be spread out over time, implying that all your staff need not go to weeks of classes because you upgraded your database. Additionally, the cost (including time) of migrating to the new technology can be tied into new systems being built as opposed to the costs of going back and rebuilding old systems just to take advantage of the new technology. Of course, using this new technology also implies that systems built using the new technology can coexist with new systems.

To take full advantage of the new capabilities of the technology, you will have to understand some new concepts and how they can be implemented. One of the important advantages in INFORMIX-Universal Server is the support for extensible data types. Extensible data types along with user-definable functions for the new data types simplify your database definitions. Another important advantage is the support for DataBlades. DataBlade modules allow you to reuse sets of extended data types. Therefore, organizations can easily reuse these types while building new systems and also purchase predefined industry data types or create project-specific extended data types and use them, thus saving the cost and trouble of creating their own extensions to the basic data types. If your organization needs to store and retrieve movies, for example, you need special data types to support multimedia information. If a DataBlade vendor already has these types, you can just purchase them. Although purchasing and plugging in industry-specific data types and associated functions will become commonplace, at the time of this writing Informix is the only major database vendor that has this technology available.

A number of vendors are already providing DataBlade modules for specialized purposes such as the following:

- Statistical functions that come with predefined functions for financial risk management, returns on various types of financial instruments, and so on
- Text access and retrieval with functions to make rapid retrieval and storage of text data easier
- 2D and 3D spatial functions that can be used for various purposes, including Geographical Information Systems (GIS) and seismology
- Web-specific types and functions providing support for dynamically creating, updating, and retrieving Web content such as HTML and Java applets
- Image storage and retrieval for managing multimedia information in industries such as desktop publishing, digital studios, and multimedia production facilities
- Audio information storage, analysis, and retrieval of sound for industries such as the music and television industry
- Modules with customized data types and functions for time series analysis such as performance of the stock market over time
- Various modules for managing lists, including merge and purge functionality to help maintain mailing and other lists

Because the DataBlade modules not only provide data types but also come with necessary functions, the complexity of your application will be reduced greatly. Most modules are also optimized for performance.

Concepts and Modeling for Universal Server

Chapter 43, "Model-Driven Development for the Informix RDBMS," describes modeling for INFORMIX-OnLine/SE Relational Database Management systems. In that chapter, you learned about modeling occurrences of business concepts. One of the problems with that approach is the lack of support for reuse. For example, you want to define an Employee table. If another table has the same properties as the Employee table, however, you still have to re-create the new table even though you have already defined a similar table. In some cases, you can use the `LIKE` clause, but it is not an efficient mechanism.

In the Object Relational world, you can define a data type called "employee type" that has the necessary attributes of an employee, and then you can reuse this extended data type for defining tables that have similar properties of an employee. Functions related to the new data type can also be defined. Of course, the extended data types can also be used to define the data types of columns. Essentially, you're switching from modeling organizational entities to organizational types. Also, existing types can be extended to create new types. So while you're building applications using this new technology, you are always looking to reuse and extend existing types. Extending existing types is obviously easier than creating new ones. In this chapter, you will look at the various types of data types supported in INFORMIX-Universal Server and how to model them. You will also look at how to specify tables using the new data types.

You need to understand and model certain specific definitions. You can create the following different types of data types in the INFORMIX-Universal Server:

- Built-in data types: These types are equivalent to the data types relational database management system (DBMS). They are types such as `CHARACTER`, `INTEGER`, `FLOAT`, and so on.
- Row types: A row type is composed of a set of fields, each of which can be of *any* data type (including opaque types), not only of built-in or other row types.
- Opaque types: These extended data types are defined in an external language such as C and registered in the IUS system catalog and can be used whenever this type is needed. Support functions for this type have to be created (at least for now) using the C language and created outside the database.
- Collection data types: You can define three types of collections: sets, lists, and multisets.

Figure 45.1 shows the hierarchy of types supported in IUS; I used the UML notation to create this figure. The arrow with the open arrowhead tells you that the object at the tail of the arrow is a subtype of the object to which the arrowhead is attached. Note that all the user-defined types can be created from other user-defined types. You might find some restrictions on how certain user-defined types can be used to define other types.

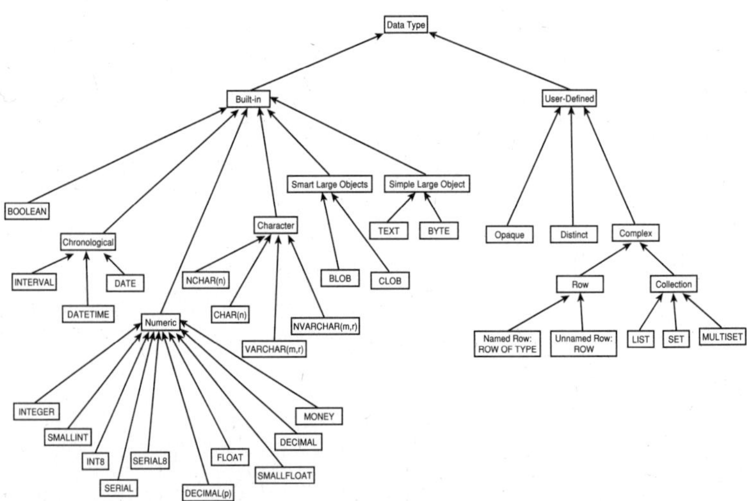

FIGURE 45.1.
Type hierarchy in INFORMIX-Universal Server.

Figure 45.1 describes the topology of types supported by IUS. The actual types are the ones listed in the leaf nodes. The other nodes are semantical categories.

Most CASE tools supporting IUS can reverse-engineer existing libraries of types, so you will have them available for creating new types, modifying existing types, and assigning tables and columns to the new types created.

Built-In Types

Built-in types are provided by the databases. They are also sometimes called *simple* types. Examples of this type are `CHARACTER`, `INTEGER`, `NUMERIC`, `SERIAL`, and so on. You cannot modify these types. They give you a basic set of types to start from. The operations that can be performed on these types are also fixed. These data types can be modeled as objects with a specific flag telling you that they are built-in types. You can use these types for creating row types. It is conceivable that you might want to add functions to the built-in types. Figure 45.2 shows one way of specifying built-in types as objects.

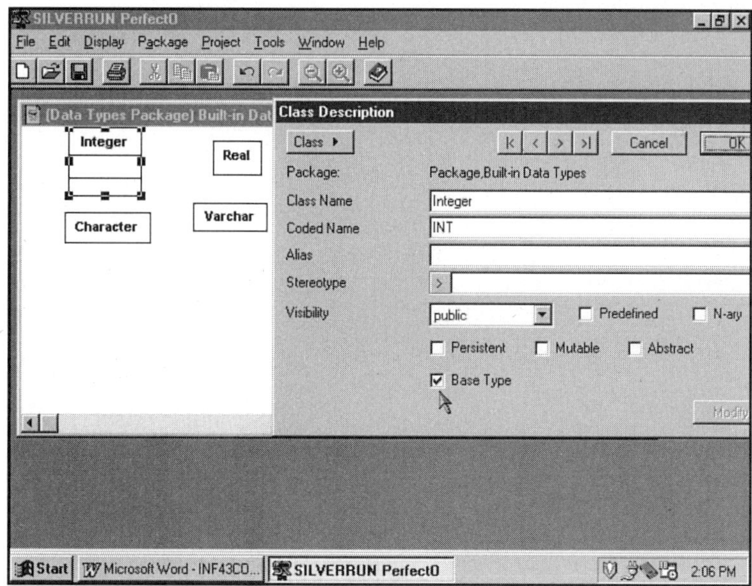

FIGURE 45.2.
A graphical representation of built-in types.

Functions

IUS, which allows you to specify functions and procedures, differentiates between the two. Functions return one or more values, whereas procedures don't. Functions can be stored in the database when created using Stored Procedure Language (SPL), or they can be stored external to the database. External functions are usually written in the C language. Among other things, functions can be used to specify the rules associated with the extended data types discussed in the following sections. Functions are not explicitly attached to the types like you do methods (operations or services) in object-oriented systems. However, using the SILVERRUN tool, the functions can be dynamically linked to extended types by the parameters these functions use. I discuss this subject further in the sections on the various types.

Row Types

Row types are stored within the database. They can be created using built-in types or other row types. They also can be created as subtypes of other row types. You can use a row type to define either a row or a table. Figure 45.3 shows a graphical representation of a row data type that uses a combination of built-in types and other row types.

Person Name Type	
Preferred Salutation	: Salutation
First name	: Character
Surname	: Character
Middle Initial	: Character

FIGURE 45.3.
An example of a row type created using other types.

In Figure 45.3, you can see that a row type can be created using built-in types as well as other row types. This capability saves you a lot of time in defining new types. You have to specify only how the new type is different from the old type.

You can create other row types as subtypes of other row types because subtypes inherit the properties (including functions) of the supertypes. For this reason, you can easily create specialized, predefined types for specific purposes without re-creating the whole type. For the new row type created as a subtype, you just have to add the new properties and the types associated with the new properties. Figure 45.4 shows a row type created as a subtype of another row type.

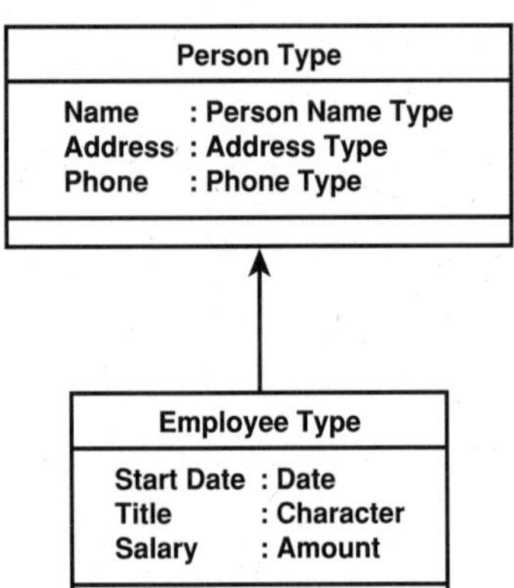

FIGURE 45.4.
A row type inheriting from another row type.

In Figure 45.4, the employee type is a subtype of a person. In the employee type definition, therefore, you need only add the properties specific to the employee that are not in the definition of person.

Of course, you might have many levels of inheritance, as shown in Figure 45.5.

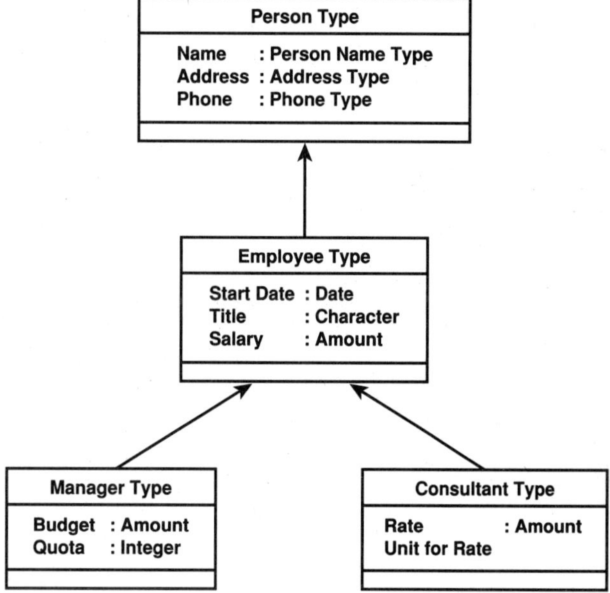

FIGURE 45.5.
Subtype hierarchy for row types.

A row type can theoretically be inherited from multiple supertypes. This capability is called *multiple inheritance.* Multiple inheritance is not supported in the current version of INFORMIX-Universal Server; it will, however, be supported in a future version of IUS.

After you design the row types, you have to create the types in IUS. A minimal syntax for specifying the row types is shown in Listing 45.1.

Listing 45.1. Creating row types.

```
CREATE ROW TYPE manager type
(
budget amount
quota integer
)
UNDER employee type
```

Functions for Row Types

Row types can have functions associated with them. These functions define the rules specific to the type. You can specify the functions using SPL. In this case, they are stored in the database, or they can be specified as "external." For external functions, the actual code is not stored in the database. A reference and the path to the function are stored in the database.

A function can be used by multiple types if needed. Assuming functions are designed for reusability, you get a lot more flexibility than if functions were local to a type. Figure 45.6 shows the representation of functions for the types.

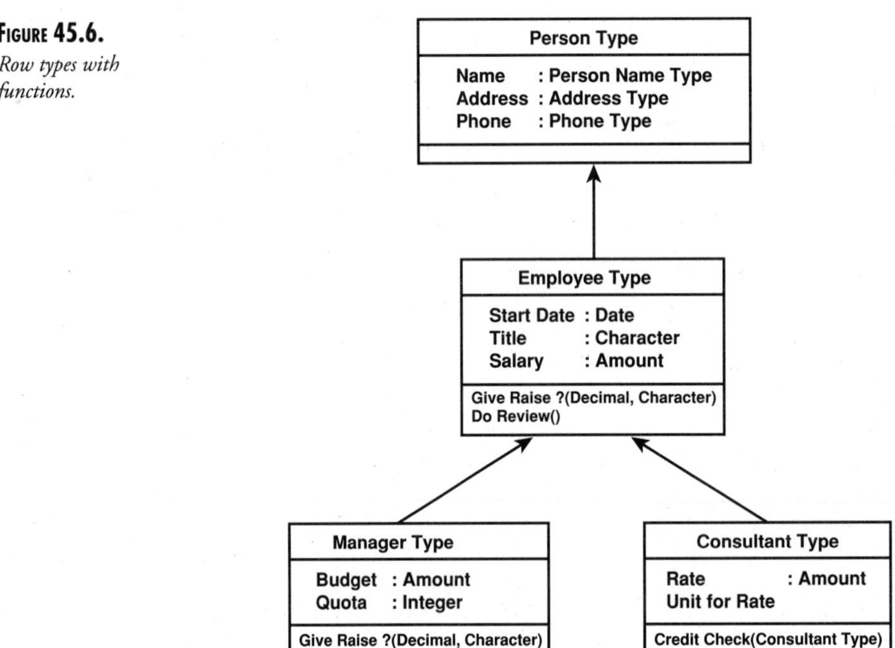

FIGURE 45.6.
Row types with functions.

Note that in Figure 45.6 some functions are specified for more than one type. In this case, the function at the *leaf* (lowest) level is the one that is executed.

Opaque Types

Opaque types are defined outside the DBMS, but a list of the types and the reference to the paths are kept in the database. Only the parameters and the path where the function is stored are kept in the database. The data type is not visible to the database, hence the name *opaque*. The functions used with opaque types have to be written in the C language. This function is registered in the database using the `CREATE FUNCTION` statement, but during execution, the executable stored outside the database is executed.

Collections

Any type can be defined as a collection. IUS has three types of collections.

- Set: This collection is an unordered group of values that are distinct.
- Multiset: This collection is an unordered group of values that can have duplicates in the values.
- List: This collection is an ordered set of values.

The syntax for defining a row or a row type is shown in Figure 45.7.

FIGURE 45.7.
Type definition with collections.

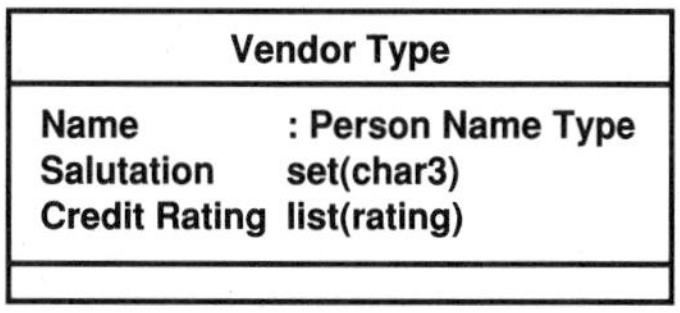

Vendor Type	
Name	: Person Name Type
Salutation	set(char3)
Credit Rating	list(rating)

Creating Tables in INFORMIX-Universal Server

You can create two types of tables in IUS:

- Typed tables are tables that are defined by a row data type.
- Untyped tables are created the same way you create tables in INFORMIX-OnLine or INFORMIX-SE. All the columns have to be defined explicitly, and the built-in data types are used to define the characteristics of the columns.

I don't discuss creating untyped tables in this section, but it's nice to know that you can still use the techniques you're already familiar with if you need to. These techniques are discussed in Chapter 43.

Defining Typed Tables

After you define an extended data type, you can define a table name and assign it to a row type. This process makes defining a table extremely simple. Because the functions are also defined in the extended data type, you do not have to redefine them for every table created using the extended data type. Currently in IUS, one of the limitations is that the typed tables cannot have any additional columns defined. Listing 45.2 shows the syntax for specifying a typed table. Note that I have used a "logical" name to help you relate to the preceding examples, but in actuality, you have to use a syntactically correct name.

Listing 45.2. Creating a typed table.

```
CREATE TABLE person OF TYPE person type;
```

As you can see, the amount of work needed to create a table is minimal. Most of the work is done in designing the types. But the types can be designed once and reused with little or no modifications. If you want to create an employee table, for example, the syntax would be as shown in Listing 45.3

Listing 45.3. Creating an employee table.

```
CREATE TABLE employee OF TYPE employee type;
```

Now, if you want the database to maintain a supertype-subtype relationship between the tables, you have to change the syntax slightly to specify the relationships between the tables, as shown in Listing 45.4.

Listing 45.4. Specifying a supertype-subtype hierarchy.

```
CREATE TABLE employee OF TYPE employee type
UNDER person;
```

Of course, the supertype table has to exist. You also can add extensions to the syntax, such as specifications for fragmentation expression and check constraints. These syntax rules are not covered in this chapter.

Defining Tables with Row Types

In this section, I briefly discuss the use of a row type to define columns. This capability gives you some flexibility in using the types because you can add additional columns to the table that is defined using relational technology. This capability also allows you to modify existing tables to have typed rows first and then eventually to have typed tables. Listing 45.5 gives an example of using row types for columns.

Listing 45.5. Using row types for columns.

```
CREATE TABLE vendor
(
vendor_name  VARCHAR(30)
vendor-address  address type
vendor status  CHAR(1)
)
```

The example in Listing 45.5 uses the address type for the definition of a row. In reality, this row might contain more than one column if the row type is a composite row type.

Summary

Having the ability to create types or plug in predefined types gives your organization much needed flexibility in keeping track of your information. Allowing for typed tables enables organizations to reuse designs created by various people (internal or external to the organization). The next issue will be keeping track of the types that were created. A good modeling tool will help you keep track of the types you or anybody else has previously defined and documented. A combination of a good modeling tool, people with good design background, and INFORMIX-Universal Server will provide your organization with a flexible way of managing your information assets, no matter what format your information is in.

Part VII

IN THIS PART

Appendixes

APPENDIX A

Finding Help

by Kerry Sainsbury

IN THIS APPENDIX

There are times when you've been working with an Informix problem all day, and nothing seems to be going right. Your database is crawling and your programs keep giving some strange error code that you just can't understand. People are demanding action, and they're demanding it now.

This appendix provides you with sources of Informix information that can help you out if you're in a genuine crisis or, preferably, keep you so well informed that you'll be able to preempt any problems before they arise at your site.

Electronic Help

Often the most up-to-date information can be found electronically via the World Wide Web or Internet newsgroups. This information is generally provided by real-world users of Informix products, so you tend to get honest responses to questions, rather than precooked marketing presentations.

Informix Answers OnLine

Informix Answers OnLine is Informix's official online technical support area, which is broken down into sections dedicated to Support, Publications, and Training. Because it is run by the technical support people, you'll find most of the information here to be genuinely useful (or at least interesting).

You can find Informix Answers OnLine at the following address:

```
http://www.informix.com/answers/
```

NOTE

All of the useful information provided within Informix Answers OnLine (IOL) is free to Informix users with a current support contract. IOL is also available on compact disc. Contact your local Informix representative for more information.

Product Alerts

Alerts are serious bugs that you urgently need to know about. Fortunately, these are few and far between, and they are usually so obscure that you wonder how anybody ever found them in the first place. Still, it's nice to know that Informix is honest enough to tell people about them, rather than bury its head in the sand and hope the problems go away.

Product Defects

Informix provides a search engine designed to help you identify Informix bugs. If you're having a strange problem that you can't explain, it can be very comforting to discover that it's a known bug. Often, you can use a workaround to avoid the bug, or you'll find a note indicating which version of the product the bug has been fixed in—so that, if possible, you can upgrade to that release.

Product Life-Cycle

If you ever have a question about Informix's plans for your tool of choice (for example, is INFORMIX-4GL a dead language?), this is the company's official word on the subject. Informix places each product in a category representing Informix's level of support, and it puts a date at which it will descend to the next level of disinterest.

Porting Information

Occasionally, you read about the latest version of an Informix product, and you get excited about the new features that will be available in that release. This is the time to turn to the Porting Information section of Informix Answers OnLine to find out when the version will become available on your hardware.

> **TIP**
>
> Like most things in the computer industry, you're usually better off not being among the first to get a new major release of a product. It's often better to let other people, on the "bleeding edge," find the bugs for you.

Other Documentation

Also available within Informix Answers OnLine is a variety of additional documentation in the form of release notes and information specific to particular hardware platforms. This can be invaluable when you're in the process of considering whether to upgrade, and the people inside Informix's marketing department aren't able to supply the technical detail you need.

Internet News

The prime electronic source for Informix-related information is definitely the Internet newsgroup (or, more properly, the Usenet newsgroup) `comp.databases.informix`.

This newsgroup harbors hundreds of experienced Informix professionals prepared to help one another solve Informix problems and discuss Informix in general.

It's here where people discuss topics such as "Is it better to use INFORMIX-OnLine mirroring, HP-UX mirroring, or Hardware mirroring?" (It's also where people ask "What's mirroring?") This is a very friendly newsgroup, with plenty of people prepared to help newcomers to Informix.

Point your Web browser to `news://comp.databases.informix`.

Informix E-Mail List

If you don't have access to newsgroups, you'll be pleased to know that all the information that appears in `comp.databases.informix` is also available via an e-mail mailing list, which is run by Walt Hultgren.

In order to subscribe, send an e-mail to `informix-list-request@rmy.emory.edu`, and include your contact information. This e-mail will be handled by a real person, so there are no special instructions that you need to include. Just be courteous!

NOTE

This list generates approximately 1,100 to 1,200 messages a month, so if you're in the habit of taking long vacations, be prepared for some information overload when you get back.

The Fourgen Mailing List

A mailing list is dedicated to helping people use the INFORMIX-4GL–based CASE tool Fourgen.

NOTE

This product was also sold directly by Informix under the name Informix-FORMS for a time.

To subscribe to the mailing list, send an e-mail to `4gen-list-request@garpac.com`, with the command `subscribe` *`<your email address here>`* in the body of the message.

After you have subscribed, you can post to the list by sending an e-mail to `4gen-list@garpac.com`.

If you send a message to the list, you are automatically subscribed.

This list is maintained by Clay Irving (at the addresses `clay@panix.com` and `http://www.panix.com/~clay`).

International Informix User Group

The International Informix User Group (IIUG) is an organization that attempts to be a "one-stop shop" for individual Informix users and Informix User Groups. In addition to technical information, the group can also put you in touch with your local user group, or provide you with a kit to help you establish one in your area.

NOTE

In addition to help, the IIUG provides a direct channel to the Informix Head Office for issues users feel are important. The group procures training and conference discounts for members and generally does what it can to make Informix users and user groups happy. Currently, membership in the IIUG is free.

Among other things, IIUG's Web site, at `http://www.iiug.org`, includes the items covered in the following sections.

Free Software

The IIUG provides a home to the largest collection of Informix-related software on the Internet. INFORMIX-4GL code generators, database utilities, 4GL menu routines, and more are all available to Informix users.

Technical Documents

A comprehensive collection of technical articles related to Informix products is available at the IIUG. Many of the articles that appear here go on to be featured in magazines or books, so this is a great way to stay ahead of your colleagues. Conversely, if you've got some information you want to share with the world, this is the place to put it.

Search Engine for `comp.databases.informix`

The IIUG archives all postings that are sent through the `comp.databases.informix` newsgroup, and it makes available an engine capable of keyword searches through those messages. Often, you're not the first person to encounter a particular problem, so a search here can find the answer instantly—which is better than having to repeat the question on `comp.databases.informix` and wait for a reply.

More Web Sites

The IIUG isn't the only Web site with Informix-related material. The better ones are listed in this section.

`www.access.digex.net/~waiug/`

The Washington Area User Group is a well-established group and has one of the best collections of articles to be found anywhere.

`www.dataspace.com.au`

This Australian site contains a good collection of articles, including some related to Informix's competitors, which can make for interesting reading.

`www.mindspring.com/~tschaefe`

Tim Schaefer's site is home for his collection of 4GL utilities, which includes code generators and tools to assist in the use of "troff" to generate high-quality reports with 4GL. These are all available without charge.

A new feature is a monthly Informix e-zine that shows great promise.

`www.ece.vill.edu/~dave/Free`

Dave Snyder's site is another home for Informix utilities, including a product that can create an entire 4GL maintenance program for a given table and a handy little tool called "vie," which greatly increases your productivity when editing 4GL error files.

`www.rl.is/~john/pow4gl.html`

This is the home of Power-4GL, a library of INFORMIX-4GL routines designed to make your coding quicker, easier, and more productive. Although this is a commercial product, a Power-4GL-Lite is available for free, and it includes full source code.

`www.inquiry.com/techtips/info_pro/`

This is the home of "Ask the Informix Expert." At the time of writing, this is a very new service, and it's unclear how many people know that it exists. However, it's a great idea as long as it can keep up with the potential demand.

The people answering the questions are genuinely "Informix Experts," so it should be a good source of quality answers. The service is free.

Printed Help

If you're electronically challenged, or if you like the idea of pulverizing trees, then a number of printed publications are available that should help satisfy your needs.

Books

A growing number of Informix books (including this one) are available in your local bookstore. Most of these books are well-written and worth investigating. Here is a short list:

- *Informix Performance Tuning, 2/E.* Elizabeth Suto. Informix Press. ISBN: 0-13-239237-2.
- *INFORMIX-OnLine Performance Tuning.* Elizabeth Suto. Informix Press. ISBN: 0-13-124322-5.
- *Programming Informix SQL/4GL: A Step-By-Step Approach.* Cathy Kipp. Informix Press. ISBN: 0-13-149394-9.

- *Informix Database Administrator's Survival Guide.* Joe Lumbley. Informix Press. ISBN: 0-13-124314-4.
- *Advanced INFORMIX-4GL Programming.* Art Taylor. Informix Press. ISBN: 0-13-301318-9.
- *Optimizing Informix Applications.* Robert D. Schneider. Informix Press. ISBN: 0-13-149238-1.
- *Informix Stored Procedure Programming.* Michael L. Gonzales. Informix Press. ISBN: 0-13-206723-4.
- *INFORMIX-NewEra: A Guide for Application Developers.* Art Taylor and Tony Lacy-Thompson. Informix Press. ISBN: 0-13-209248-4.
- *Using INFORMIX-SQL, Second Edition.* Jonathan Leffler. ISBN: 0-201-56509-9.
- *Informix Client/Server Application Development.* Paul R. Allen, Joseph J. Bambara, and Richard J. Bambara. McGraw-Hill. ISBN: 0-07-913056-9.

Periodicals

In addition to the mainstream periodicals, such as *DBMS Magazine* or *Database Programming & Design*, there are also some Informix-specific publications (most of which are published by Informix itself).

Informix Systems Journal (ISJ)

ISJ is an independent magazine that tends to be published somewhat irregularly. The content is generally good, however, and the magazine's current policy of free subscriptions is certainly attractive.

For more information, contact the editor, Tom Bondur, via e-mail at `73311.3553@compuserve.com`, or at the following address:

Informix Systems Journal
40087 Mission Boulevard, Suite 167
Fremont, CA 94539-3680
phone: 800-943-9300

TechNotes

This is Informix's official vehicle for technical articles. Content is provided not only by Informix employees, but also by general members of the Informix community. The quality of articles is variable, ranging from excellent technical detail to blatant marketing propaganda—with more recent issues leaning toward the latter.

TechNotes is available for free to users maintaining INFORMIX-OpenLine and "Regency" support agreements. Contact your local Informix office for more information.

TIP

If you're surprised that you've never heard of this magazine, and you know that you have a support agreement, check whether the magazine is being sent to the person in your organization who ordered Informix. It is quite common to find somebody in your administration department with a great pile of *TechNotes* on a shelf collecting dust.

The Informix Solutions Guide

This publication, which is also available at Informix's Web site and on CD-ROM, is a guide to providers of products that in some way complement Informix's tools and databases. This includes CASE tools, code generators, programs to translate from 4GL to NewEra, consultancy companies, complete INFORMIX-4GL Manufacturing packages, and a myriad of other products. If you're looking for a quick fix, you might be able to find it here.

Other Informix Publications

Informix produces two other periodicals, *Customer Service Times* and *Informix Times*, which provide general Informix information in a glossy newsletter style. Contact your local Informix office to see whether these are available in your area; in most places, a subscription is available at no charge.

Help You Can Talk To!

Occasionally, reading books and Web sites just isn't enough. To express a problem clearly, sometimes you need to speak to real people. Talking to real people is pleasant in other ways, too.

TechSupport

The least entertaining but most useful people to tell your problems to are the people who are paid by Informix to help you. The Informix TechSupport people have access to an awesome amount of accumulated knowledge, as well as access to the people who actually write the database engines and programming languages we use. If your database explodes in a ball of flames, these are the guys and gals you can rely on to dial in and get you going again as soon as possible.

Training

Although there is no alternative to experience and to reading the Informix manuals, a good way to get a jump-start on a new product is to attend an Informix training course. Some third-party companies also run Informix training courses, which can be as good or better than the official Informix ones. Talk to other Informix users in your community to learn whether any such classes are available to you.

TIP

Sometimes, it can be a good idea to attend a training course *before* you decide whether you want to use a product. You can often learn a great deal more with a bit of hands-on experience and quiet interrogation of your trainer than you learn by just reading a product's sales literature.

Local User Groups

Local User Groups usually meet every few months, and they generally try to provide members with useful information that is somehow connected to Informix. This might be somebody giving a demonstration of their latest product, an explanation of how the Informix Optimizer works, or a case study of how a user implemented a data warehouse at his site.

User Groups vary widely in their facilities. Some charge membership dues, provide regular newsletters, organize training classes, and hold miniature conferences. Others are less structured.

One of the major benefits of any user group is simply getting together with like-minded professionals in your area and talking with them. It's a great way to stay up-to-date with local events, and it's a good way to meet interesting people.

A listing of current User Groups appears in Table A.1. If none of the groups looks local to you, contact Informix's User Group Liaison (`usergrp@informix.com`) for more help. They can always send out their information pack to help you set up your own group.

Table A.1. Informix User Groups around the world.

Location	*Contact*	*Phone*	*E-mail*
Australia Canberra	Dominic Lancaster	6.243.6590	`dlancaster@das.gov.au`
Australia NSW	Gavin Nour	0419.803.113	`nourg@acslink.net.au`
Australia Victoria	Tony Moore	3.98.94.2500	`agm@labsys.com.au`
Australia Perth	Peter Fillery	9.351.7685	`fillery@BA1.curtin.edu.au`
Belgium/Luxembourg	Dominique Wilms	2.255.0909	`dw@maxon.be`
Canada, Ontario	Shawn Dagg	613.782.2237	`sdagg@bradson.com`
Denmark	Thomas Keller	4.289.4999	`keller@uniware.dk`
Germany	Bernd Langer	525.113.5824	`100042.2455@compuserve.com`

continues

Table A.1. continued

Location	Contact	Phone	E-mail
Great Britain	Malcolm Weallans	181.421.1227	PBarnett@CIX.Compulink.co.UK
Italy	Ivan Zoratti	26.604.8423	asitaly@mbox.vol.it
The Netherlands	Mr Steins-Bisschop	73.692.1692	j.steins.bisschop@spc.nl
Norway	Nils Myklebust	2.205.3156	Nils.Myklebust@ ➥ccmail.telemax.no
Philippines	Jonash Santa Ana	2.811.5470	
Sweden	Bjorn Gustavsson	13.145.200	bjorn@kloster.se
Switzerland	Felix Schenker	62.834.1500	
U.A.E.	Nitasha Kohli	659.9848	Infodsh@emirates.net.ae
West Indies	Simone De Sousa	636.2878	sds@opus-networx.com
USA Arizona	Bob Baskett	602.244.4796	rzbj40@email.sps.mot.com
USA CA, North	Federico Hubbard	408.366.9745	fred@infosoft.com
USA CA, South	Sandee Gilbert	310.320.4300	dgc@ix.netcom.com
USA Colorado	Cathy Kipp	970.226.0240	ckipp@verinet.com
USA FL, South	Bruce Hard	407.750.5238	bocadbsi@ugn.com
USA Georgia	Walt Hultgren	404.727.0648	walt@rmy.emory.edu
USA Illinois	Maria Lupetin	708.390.6660	102216.2713@CompuServe.com
USA Indiana	Frank Catrine	513.985.6004	frankc@collegeview.com
USA Kansas	Orv Einsiedel	913.345.6370	orv@igate.sprint.com
USA Kentucky	Frank Catrine	513.985.6004	frankc@collegeview.com
USA Michigan	Ron Flannery	313.464.3700	rflannery@zenacomp.com
USA Minnesota	John Hite	612.333.3164	
USA Missouri	Jan Richardson	314.838.8527	jr4676@strydr.com
USA Nebraska	Kevin Graham	402.491.2658	Kevin_Graham@firstdata.com
USA New England	Stuart Litel	617.527.4551	slitel@netcom.com
USA New Jersey	Ronald Wanat	908.469.4070	ronw@summitdata.com
USA New York	Steve Husiak	212.753.3920	husiak@informix.com
USA North Carolina	Tim Howerton	910.625.9198	timh@summitdata.com
USA Ohio	Frank Catrine	513.985.6004	frankc@collegeview.com
USA Oregon	Rick Crecson	503.639.0816	PNIUG@meridiangroup.com
USA PA, Philadelphia	Laurence Sigmond	215.848.8889	larry@logsys.com
USA PA, West	Joseph Wynn	412.562.0900	wynn@aii.edu
USA TX, Austin	Christine Schramm	512.795.6213	christine_schramm@bmc.com
USA TX, North	Leo Liu	214.985.6384	leo@pagenet.com

Location	Contact	Phone	E-mail
USA Utah	Carlton Doe	801.572.6165	dbaresrc@xmission.com
USA Washington	John Waltersi	206.635.0709	john.walters@asix.com
USA Washington D.C.	Lester Knutsen	703.256.0267	lester@access.digex.net
USA Wisconsin	Sally Koskinam	612.449.6632	sallyk@informix.com

The latest user group information can be found at

`http://www.informix.com/informix/corpinfo/usrgrups/usrgrups.htm`

User Conferences

Every year Informix holds the Informix World-Wide User Conference in the United States. This event runs for three or four days, and it includes a great deal of Informix information targeted at everybody from your company's directors to the technical staff on the front line. Sessions run for about 45 minutes, in one of three broad themes (which are outlined in the following sections).

The conference also features a trade show, housing exhibits from companies with products that complement Informix's products. Being able to talk to these companies directly and get some hands-on experience with their products is far more efficient than pondering glossy brochures and magazine articles.

Similar, but smaller, events also run irregularly outside the U.S.

Theme One: The Future

Informix talks about where it is going and what its plans are for the next year or two. There are discussions on the latest technologies and how they fit into Informix's future. It's all quite good stuff, designed to let you know that Informix is aware of current trends and hasn't gone to sleep just yet.

Theme Two: Case Studies

Informix clients get on stage and talk about their experiences with a tool or technique. Subjects might include "Converting from 4GL to NewEra," "How we implemented a Data Warehouse," or "Making Informix talk to Borland's Delphi."

These sessions can be immensely useful because the people giving the presentations have actually done the job. Therefore, they can talk about the subject at a practical level rather than a conceptual one.

Theme Three: Technical Information

These sessions provide the real technical “meat” for developers and DBAs. Information on database tuning, how to generate Web pages using 4GL, and NewEra coding techniques would appear here. These are almost like miniature training courses, and they are usually well worth the effort of attending.

Summary

You can find plenty of help out there when you need it. The best free help is probably the `comp.databases.informix` newsgroup or the International Informix User Group’s home page at `www.iiug.org`.

Don’t forget to keep up-to-date with Informix itself, either directly via its publications or through your local user group. And if you can get to one of Informix’s World-Wide User Conferences, you’ll run into more help than you can shake a stick at. Good luck!

I

INDEX

Symbols

B

D

G

J

K

L

M

O

P

Q

T

U

W

X - Y - Z

Teach Yourself Database Programming with Visual Basic 5 in 21 Days, Second Edition

—Michael Amundsen & Curtis Smith

Visual Basic, the 32-bit programming language from Microsoft, is used by programmers to create Windows and Windows 95 applications. It also can be used to program applications for the Web. This book shows programmers how to design, develop, and deploy Visual Basic applications for the World Wide Web. The lessons are presented in a daily format, with each week focusing on a different area of database development. This book is written by a Microsoft Certified Visual Basic Professional. The book's CD-ROM includes sample code and third-party utilities.

$45.00 USA/$63.95 CDN *New–Casual–Accomplished*
0-672-31018-X *1,000 pages*

Teach Yourself Active Web Database Programming in 21 Days

—Dina Fleet, et al.

Based on the best-selling *Teach Yourself* series, this must-have tutorial uses a day-by-day approach and real-world examples to teach readers the ins and outs of Visual Basic programming with databases for the Web. This book shows how to use Visual Basic to create powerful content on the Web. It explores data-aware controls, database connectivity with Visual Basic, and HTML scripting.

$39.99 USA/$56.95 CDN *New–Casual*
1-57521-139-4 *700 pages*

Teach Yourself Database Programming with JDBC in 21 Days

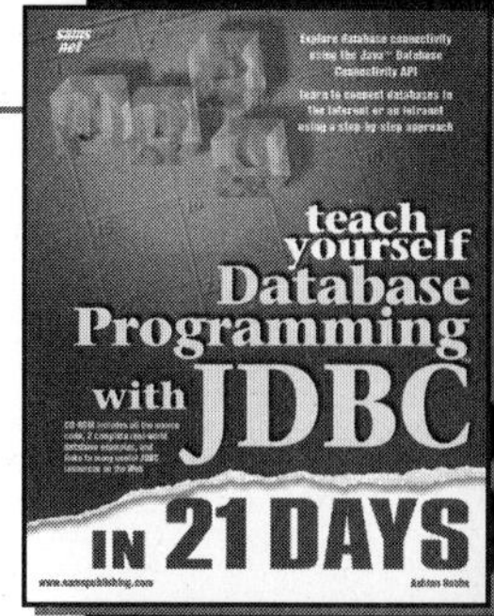

—Ashton Hobbs

Linking both corporate and home databases to the Web is critical for a Web site to be successful. And Sun's JDBC API allows users to do just that! Using a step-by-step, conversational approach, users will learn how to develop JDBC components to create complete database applications for Web connection. This book explores database basics, JDBC interfaces, database connectivity and transactions, and more. The book's CD-ROM is packed with all the source code from the book, two complete real-world database examples, and a Web page linking to several useful JDBC resources.

$39.99 USA/$56.95 CDN *New–Casual–Accomplished*
1-57521-123-8 *600 pp.*

Teach Yourself Database Programming with Visual J++ in 21 Days

—John Fronckowiak & Gordon McMillan, et al.

Using an easy-to-follow step-by-step format, this complete resource takes users beyond the basic product information and guides them through database integration and interface development. This book highlights new technologies, including JavaBeans, JDBC, DAO Object Library, RDO Object Library, ActiveX, and COM. The book's CD-ROM is loaded with scripting and author source code.

$39.99 USA/$56.95 CDN *New–Casual–Accomplished*
1-57521-262-5 *750 pages*

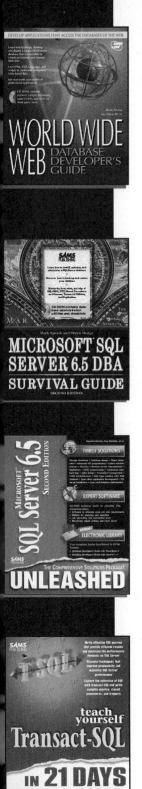

Book ISBN 0-672-30650-6

Technical Support:

If you need assistance with the information in this book or with a CD/Disk accompanying the book, please access the Knowledge Base on our Web site at **http://www.superlibrary.com/general/support**. Our most Frequently Asked Questions are answered there. If you do not find the answer to your questions on our Web site, you may contact Macmillan Technical Support **(317) 581-3833** or e-mail us at **support@mcp.com**.

What's on the Disc

The companion CD-ROM contains all of the authors' source code and samples from the book and many third-party software products.

Windows NT Installation Instructions

1. Insert the CD-ROM disc into your CD-ROM drive.
2. From File Manager or Program Manager, choose Run from the File menu.
3. Type `<drive>\SETUP.EXE`, where `<drive>` corresponds to the drive letter of your CD-ROM, and press Enter. For example, if your CD-ROM is drive D:, type `D:\SETUP.EXE` and press Enter.
4. Installation creates a program group named "Informix Unleashed." This group contains icons to browse the CD-ROM.

Windows 95 Installation Instructions

1. Insert the CD-ROM disc into your CD-ROM drive.
2. From the Windows 95 desktop, double-click on the My Computer icon.
3. Double-click on the icon representing your CD-ROM drive.
4. Double-click on the icon titled `SETUP.EXE` to run the installation program.
5. Installation creates a program group named "Informix Unleashed." This group contains icons to browse the CD-ROM.

NOTE

If Windows 95 is installed on your computer and you have the AutoPlay feature enabled, the `SETUP.EXE` program starts automatically whenever you insert the disc into your CD-ROM drive.